Freedom from Fear

The Oxford History of the United States

C. Vann Woodward, *General Editor*

Volume III

ROBERT MIDDLEKAUFF

THE GLORIOUS CAUSE

The American Revolution, 1763–1789

Volume VI

JAMES MCPHERSON

BATTLE CRY OF FREEDOM

The Civil War Era

Volume IX

DAVID M. KENNEDY

FREEDOM FROM FEAR

The American People in Depression and War, 1929–1945

Volume X

JAMES T. PATTERSON

GRAND EXPECTATIONS

The United States, 1945–1974

FREEDOM FROM FEAR

The American People in
Depression and War,
1929–1945

DAVID M. KENNEDY

New York   Oxford
OXFORD UNIVERSITY PRESS
1999

Oxford University Press

Oxford   New York
Athens   Auckland   Bangkok   Bogotá   Buenos Aires   Calcutta
Cape Town   Chennai   Dar es Salaam   Delhi   Florence   Hong Kong   Istanbul
Karachi   Kuala Lumpur   Madrid   Melbourne   Mexico City   Mumbai
Nairobi   Paris   São Paulo   Singapore   Taipei   Tokyo   Toronto   Warsaw

and associated companies in
Berlin   Ibadan

Published by Oxford University Press, Inc.
198 Madison Avenue, New York, New York 10016

Oxford is a registered trademark of Oxford University Press

Library of Congress Cataloging-in-Publication Data
Kennedy, David M.
Freedom from fear : the American people in depression and war, 1929–1945
/ David M. Kennedy.
p.   cm. — (The Oxford history of the United States: v. 9)
Includes bibliographical references and index.
ISBN 0-19-503834-7
1. United States — History — 1929–1933.
2. United States — History — 1933–1945.
I. Title.   II. Series.
E173.094   vol. 9   [E801]   973 s — dc21   [973.91]   98-49580

1 3 5 7 9 8 6 4 2

Printed in the United States of America
on acid-free paper

This book is for Ben, Bess, and Tom
qui laetificant vitam meam.

Contents

Maps   ix

Acknowledgments   xi

Editor's Introduction   xiii

Abbreviated Titles Used in Citations   xvii

Prologue: November 11, 1918   1

1. The American People on the Eve of the Great Depression   10

2. Panic   43

3. The Ordeal of Herbert Hoover   70

4. Interregnum   104

5. The Hundred Days   131

6. The Ordeal of the American People   160

7. Chasing the Phantom of Recovery   190

8. The Rumble of Discontent   218

9. A Season for Reform   249

10. Strike!   288

vii

11. The Ordeal of Franklin Roosevelt   323

12. What the New Deal Did   363

13. The Gathering Storm   381

14. The Agony of Neutrality   426

15. To the Brink   465

16. War in the Pacific   516

17. Unready Ally, Uneasy Alliance   565

18. The War of Machines   615

19. The Struggle for a Second Front   669

20. The Battle for Northwest Europe   709

21. The Cauldron of the Home Front   746

22. Endgame   798

Epilogue: The World the War Made   852

Bibliographical Essay   859

Index   877

Illustrations appear following pages 332 and 652.

Maps

The Undeclared Naval War in the Atlantic, 1941   489
Pearl Harbor, December 7, 1941   521
The Southwest Pacific, 1941–1942   528
Midway, June 4, 1942   540
Guadalcanal and the Solomons, 1942–1945   550
The Battle of the Atlantic, December 1941–July 1942   567
The Battle of the Atlantic, August 1942–May 1943   567
North Africa, November 1942–May 1943   582
The Sicilian Campaign, July 10–August 17, 1943   593
The Italian Campaign, 1943–1945   597
The Air War in Europe, 1942–1943: Major U.S. Attacks   607
The China-Burma-India Theater, 1942–1945   672
D-Day and the Battle for Northwest Europe, 1944   719
The Battle of the Bulge, Dec. 1944–Jan. 1945   740
The Southwest and Central Pacific Campaigns, 1943–1945   815
The Battle of Leyte Gulf, Oct. 23–25, 1944, and the
    Philippine Campaign   823
Iwo Jima, Feb.–March, 1945   830
Okinawa, April 1–June 22, 1945   831
The Final Assault on Japan, 1945   846
World War II: European Theater   872
World War II: Pacific Theater   874

Acknowledgments

In writing this book I have drawn on a rich body of scholarship and imposed on the kindness of a great many colleagues, friends, and kin. I want to say a special word of appreciation for the pioneering work on the New Deal era by a remarkable generation of scholars, including John Morton Blum, James MacGregor Burns, Kenneth S. Davis, Frank Freidel, William E. Leuchtenburg, and Arthur M. Schlesinger Jr. Though I sometimes disagree with their emphases and evaluations, they laid the foundation on which all subsequent study of that period has built, including my own. I also learned much about World War II from the veterans with whom I traveled to battlefields in Italy, the Solomon Islands, and Normandy. For their service to their country, and for their generosity to me, I thank them.

Several research assistants have given me invaluable help: Leslie Berlin, Elizabeth Kopelman Borgwardt, Mark Brilliant, Kyle Graham, Tom Jackson, Sean Malloy, John McGreevy, and Jonathan Schoenwald. Their contributions and the comments of participants in Stanford's faculty–graduate student American History Workshop have greatly improved this book.

Stanford University granted me two research leaves, one spent at the Center for Advanced Study in the Behavioral Sciences, the other at the Stanford Humanities Center, both partly financed by the National Endowment for the Humanities, which greatly facilitated my research and writing. The Harmsworth Family, the Faculty of Modern History, and the Provost and Fellows of Queen's College, Oxford, provided material support and stimulating collegiality during a year I spent as the Harmsworth Professor of American History at Oxford University. A seminar I co-taught there with John Rowett of Brasenose College proved particularly helpful in shaping my thinking about the New Deal.

I am especially indebted to Jack Beatty of the *Atlantic Monthly*, James T. Patterson of Brown University, and James J. Sheehan of Stanford University, each of whom read the entire manuscript, rescued me from innumerable errors and infelicities, and challenged me to think harder and write more clearly. Co-teaching a course on World War II with my Stanford colleague Jim Sheehan has contributed substantially to my work on this project, not least because of his example of deeply thoughtful scholarship and inspired teaching. I also want to thank others who acceded to my requests to comment on various parts of the manuscript: Barton J. Bernstein, Lizabeth Cohen, Paul David, Peter Duus, James Kloppenberg, Karen Sawislak, and Gavin Wright. Henry Archer rescued me from countless mistakes.

Sheldon Meyer at Oxford University Press first asked me to undertake this book, and his wisdom and counsel, not to mention patience, cheer, and good company, have sustained me over the years of work on it, as have the invariably thoughtful commentaries of the general editor of the Oxford History of the United States, C. Vann Woodward. Joellyn Ausanka, India Cooper, and Susan Day provided the excellent editorial support for which Oxford Press is justly renowned.

My wife, Judy, read the entire manuscript, endured life as a writer's widow, and provided unflagging support. Our three children, Ben, Bess, and Tom, grew up with this book, and to them I lovingly dedicate it, with the hope that this history may prove useful to their voyage, and their generation's, into the future.

Stanford, California   David M. Kennedy
July 4, 1998

Editor's Introduction

The brief period from 1929 to 1945 is unique in American history for its complexities of change and violence of contrasts. People who lived through the years of the Great Depression, the New Deal, and the Second World War—only half the years normally assigned to one generation—experienced more bewildering changes than had several generations of their predecessors. These changes included a transition from economic and social paralysis to unprecedented outbursts of national energy, the emergence from wretched years of poverty to unparalleled levels of prosperity, and the repudiation of a century-and-a-half of isolation as America entered World War II.

Events of this magnitude and global significance make extraordinary demands upon the historian. Fortunately, David M. Kennedy is richly endowed with the talents and skills required by his challenging task—plus gifts as a writer. He is not the kind of historian who dwells upon abstract "forces." His emphasis is upon *people*—not only leaders but followers and opponents as well as victims and beneficiaries. Readers of *Freedom from Fear* will encounter vivid portraits not only of American statesmen and commanders, but of their foreign counterparts as well. Their decisions, errors, blunders, and such measures of luck as shaped the course of history are given due attention, but not to the neglect of the people who suffered or endured the results.

It was the people who suffered in the Great Depression that receive David Kennedy's primary attention, and more of them did suffer, and more deeply, and longer, than has been generally assumed. Southern white sharecroppers, for example, averaged an annual cash income of $350, black sharecroppers $294. At wages of $1 a day miners subsisted on a diet suggesting that of domestic animals. Emaciated children who never tasted milk wandered the streets, some shoeless in winter, too poorly clad to go to school. Milch cows dried up for lack of feed, and starving horses dropped in their harnesses. More surprising than the people's despair was their prevailing submissiveness. Their creed of individualism may account for much of this: If success and prosperity were due to merit and striving, failure and poverty must be due to the lack of them. Much more common than rebellion among Americans of those years was a sense of shame and a loss of self-respect. Year after year of depression went by with little or no sign of the recovery promised by politicians.

Franklin D. Roosevelt and his New Deal have been both credited with recovery from the depression and blamed for the failure of recovery. David Kennedy refuses to settle for either simplification. He traces the complex interplay between continuing economic stagnation and Roosevelt's remarkable programs of social and economic reform, new ones almost every year until 1938. Granting the inconsistencies, contradictions, and failures of the New Deal, Kennedy nevertheless summarizes its "leitmotif" in a single word: security. Its programs extended security not only to vulnerable individuals, races, and classes but to capitalists and consumers, bankers and homeowners, workers and employers, as much security and freedom from fear as democratic government might provide. F.D.R. set out, he once declared, "to make a country in which no one is left out." Without resort to revolution or abandonment of the Constitution, the New Deal constructed an institutional framework for such a society as its main heritage. What it did *not* do was to end the Great Depression and restore prosperity. That proved in the end to be the incidental and ironic work of a terrible war.

It was a war — really two wars — that the will of the people as expressed repeatedly by congressional majorities wanted no part in. As for the quarrelsome Europeans, let them settle their differences themselves this time, as American intervention had failed to do in the previous war. And as for the Japanese, let the vast Pacific Ocean serve as our shield. Appeals and threats from both sides of the globe seemed only to increase the zeal of American isolationists and the stubborn resistance to intervention. What military preparation the country made (and it started virtually from scratch) must be limited to the protection of national rights and property. Increasingly, however, the survival of Britain, and then of the Soviet Union, came to be seen as crucial to America's own survival. After years of agonizing neutrality, war eventually came to America with the Japanese attack on Pearl Harbor.

In the half of his book that deals with the war, its coming and its conduct, Kennedy exhibits remarkable talents in discussing diplomacy, especially relations with Churchill and Stalin. He also shows unusual skills in analyzing and depicting modern warfare in two hemispheres, including naval war and air combat. Readers are not spared accounts of the most gruesome and brutal atrocities, especially in the savage Pacific War. Without neglecting any essentials of military history, including the greatest naval battle ever fought and the development and use of the most powerful weapon ever made, *Freedom from Fear* also gives us a superb account of what the war did to the hundreds of millions of noncombatants on the homefront. Their lives were as much revolutionized as the lives of those in uniform. Women replaced or joined men in the work force; blacks gained jobs and skills; southerners moved north, easterners moved west. The whole population was profoundly shaken up and the American way of life deeply changed.

This volume of the Oxford series covers an incomparable period of American history, a period of extraordinary challenges and demands upon the historian, demands that David Kennedy has met surpassingly well.

C. Vann Woodward

Abbreviated Titles Used in Citations

C&R	Warren F. Kimball, ed., *Churchill and Roosevelt: The Complete Correspondence*, 3 vols. (Princeton: Princeton University Press, 1984)
Cantril	Hadley Cantril, ed., *Public Opinion, 1935–1946* (Princeton: Princeton University Press, 1951)
Churchill	Winston S. Churchill, *The Second World War*, 6 vols. (Boston: Houghton Mifflin, 1948–53)
Craven and Cate	Wesley Frank Craven and James Lee Cate, *The Army Air Forces in World War II*, 6 vols. (Chicago: University of Chicago Press, 1953)
Dallek	Robert Dallek, *Franklin D. Roosevelt and American Foreign Policy, 1932–1945* (New York: Oxford University Press, 1979)
Davis	Kenneth S. Davis, *FDR*, 4 vols. (New York: Random House, 1985–93)
FRUS	*Foreign Relations of the United States* (Washington: USGPO, various years)
HSUS	*Historical Statistics of the United States*, 2 vols. (Washington: USGPO, 1975)
Ickes Diary	Harold L. Ickes, *The Secret Diary of Harold L. Ickes*, 3 vols. (New York: Simon and Schuster, 1953–54)

L&G, *Challenge* William L. Langer and S. Everett Gleason, *The Challenge to Isolation, 1937–1940* (New York: Harper and Brothers, 1952)

L&G, *Undeclared* William L. Langer and S. Everett Gleason, *The Undeclared War, 1940–1941* (New York: Harper and Brothers, 1953)

Leuchtenburg William E. Leuchtenburg, *Franklin D. Roosevelt and the New Deal* (New York: Harper and Row, 1963)

Morgenthau Diary John Morton Blum, *Roosevelt and Morgenthau* (Boston: Houghton Mifflin, 1972)

Morison Samuel Eliot Morison, *The Two-Ocean War* (Boston: Little, Brown, 1963)

PDDE Alfred D. Chandler Jr. et al., eds., *The Papers of Dwight David Eisenhower*, 19 vols. (Baltimore: Johns Hopkins Press, 1970–   )

PPA *The Public Papers and Addresses of Franklin D. Roosevelt*, 13 vols. (New York: Random House and Harper and Brothers, 1938–50)

Schlesinger Arthur M. Schlesinger Jr., *The Age of Roosevelt*, 3 vols. (Boston: Houghton Mifflin, 1956–60)

Spector Ronald H. Spector, *Eagle Against the Sun: The American War with Japan* (New York: Free Press, 1985)

Stimson Diary Diary of Henry L. Stimson, microfilm, Green Library, Stanford University (original in Sterling Library, Yale University)

Freedom from Fear

Prologue: November 11, 1918

...and a knell rang in the ears of the victors, even in their hour of triumph.

—Winston Churchill, 1927

The Great War ended on November 11, 1918. It had lasted 1,563 days, claimed the lives of some ten million soldiers, wounded twenty million others, and devoured more than $300 billion of the world's treasure. It destroyed empires and dethroned dynasties—the Hohenzollerns in Germany, the Hapsburgs in Austria, the Romanovs in Russia. In the war's final hours, new regimes were aborning in Vienna, Warsaw, Budapest, Prague, and Dublin, while revolutionaries huzzahed through the streets of Berlin and Petersburg.

A strange stillness settled over the fighting fronts, a grim herald of two decades of tense armistice in the twentieth century's Thirty-Year War.

News of the war's end reached Lance Corporal Adolf Hitler in a military hospital in the town of Pasewalk, near Stettin in Pomerania. A twice-decorated message runner with the Sixteenth Bavarian Reserve Infantry Regiment, Hitler had huddled through the night of October 13 on a hillside in Flanders while the British rained gas grenades on the German trenches. Through the darkness the gas hissed from the canisters toward the German lines. By morning Hitler's eyes were "red-hot coals," and he was blind. Clutching his last report of the war, he groped his way to the rear and was put aboard a train for the east.[1]

Now, four weeks later, on November 10, a sobbing hospital chaplain informed Hitler and his recuperating comrades that a revolution had dethroned the kaiser. The civilian leaders of the new German republic

1. Adolf Hitler, *Mein Kampf* (New York: Stackpole Sons, 1939), 200–201.

1

had sued for peace, even while the German army was still intact in the field. For the good soldier Hitler this was "the greatest infamy of this century." Still half blind, he stumbled back to his cot, buried his head in his pillow, and wept. "So it had all been in vain," he grieved. "In vain all the sacrifices and starvation, in vain the hunger and thirst often of months without end . . . in vain the death of two millions." Revolution and surrender, Hitler concluded, were the work of depraved Marxist and Jewish criminals. Their infamy must be avenged. Tossing on his cot, he conjured legions of his slain comrades arising from their graves to restore the Fatherland. His destiny would be to lead them. "The flush of indignation and shame burned in my cheek," he wrote, and "in the next few days I became conscious of my own fate. . . . I resolved to become a politician."[2]

While Hitler's mind spun with ghoulish fantasies in Pomerania, Winston Churchill, minister of munitions in Britain's War Cabinet, stood musing at the window of his makeshift office in the Hotel Metropole in London. He stared up Northumberland Avenue toward Trafalagar Square, awaiting the first chime of Big Ben at 11:00 A.M., Greenwich Mean Time, which would signal the war's official conclusion. "Our country had emerged from the ordeal alive and safe," he reflected, "its vast possessions intact . . . its institutions unshaken." How different was the fate of Germany, "shivered suddenly into a thousand individually disintegrating fragments. . . . Such a spectacle appalls mankind; and a knell rang in the ears of the victors, even in their hour of triumph."

And then at last, "suddenly the first stroke of the chime." Through the pane Churchill spotted the slight figure of a lone girl dart from a hotel doorway into the street. As all the bells of London began to clash, the pavement around her filled with shouting, screaming, triumphant Britons. The scene was exhilarating, but Churchill remained pensive. "Safety, freedom, peace, home, the dear one back at the fireside — all after fifty-two months of gaunt distortion. After fifty-two months of making burdens grievous to be borne and binding them on men's backs, at last, all at once, suddenly and everywhere the burdens were cast down. At least," Churchill brooded, "so for the moment it seemed."[3]

Nearly two thousand miles to the east, Josef Stalin, people's commissar for nationalities, also brooded. He scanned the patchy news reports

2. Hitler, *Mein Kampf*, 203.
3. Winston Churchill, *The World Crisis, 1916–1918* (New York: Charles Scribner's Sons, 1927), 2:273–75.

from the west for confirming proof that the war's chaotic end signaled the predicted death of capitalism in the collapsing belligerent countries. Awaiting the moment of world revolution, he meantime fought savagely to protect the revolution in Russia, imperiled in its very infancy by civil war and foreign intervention. Commissar Stalin's special assignment was the defense of the southern front, centered on the Volga River city of Tsaritsyn—later Stalingrad, still later Volgograd—gateway to the Caucasus and its precious supplies of grain. There he dealt with suspected counterrevolutionaries in the summer and fall of 1918 with the calculating terror that was to become his hallmark. On a large black barge anchored in midriver, he nightly ordered the shooting of dozens of prisoners, whose bodies were then tossed into the current. "Death solves all problems," Stalin said. "No man, no problem." Returning to Moscow in November, he gloated at the execution of Roman Malinovsky, the informer who had betrayed him to the czar's Ohkrana in 1913, resulting in Stalin's banishment to Siberia. There, alone and embittered for four years, he had plotted his way to power and retribution.[4]

Franklin Delano Roosevelt spent those same four years savoring a measure of power as assistant secretary of the navy, in Washington, D.C. On the morning of November 11, 1918, Roosevelt awoke in Washington to a riotous din of honking automobile horns, pealing bells, piping whistles, and shouting people. "The feeling of relief and thankfulness," his wife, Eleanor, remembered, "was beyond description."[5]

Yet for Franklin Roosevelt the end of the war also came as something of a disappointment. Impetuous, romantic, ambitious, he had been compelled to serve out the war bound to his desk as a civilian administrator. His magical political name, his familial Rooseveltian vigor, his handsome, youthful presence, his apparent ubiquity, his volleys of crisply phrased memos had all earned him a reputation as one of the most able and charismatic of Washington's wartime personalities. But it was not enough. Like his kinetic cousin Theodore, he longed for the fray, yearned to emulate his legendary "Uncle Ted," who had resigned the

4. H. Montgomery Hyde, *Stalin: The History of a Dictator* (New York: Farrar, Straus and Giroux, 1971), 156–64. A somewhat less lurid, but not inconsistent, account of Stalin's role in Tsaritsyn is given in Robert C. Tucker, *Stalin as Revolutionary, 1879–1929* (New York: Norton, 1973), 190ff. See also Dmitri Volkogonov, *Stalin: Triumph and Tragedy* (London: Weidenfeld and Nicolson, 1991), 40; and Robert Conquest, *Stalin: Breaker of Nations* (New York: Viking, 1991), 79.
5. Eleanor Roosevelt, *This Is My Story* (New York: Garden City, 1939), 272.

very position that Franklin now held to take up arms in the Spanish-American War.

Neither Franklin Roosevelt nor the world had yet absorbed the dreadful lessons of the Great War, and in his martial yearnings the youthful assistant secretary had something in common with both Hitler and Churchill. Hitler, the sulking and penurious Viennese art student, had abandoned his native Austria and fled to Munich to join the German army in 1914. In his military regiment he found the warmth of comradeship that had eluded him in the aching vacuity of his civilian life. The outbreak of war, he wrote, "seemed like deliverance from the angry feelings of my youth."[6] Churchill owed both his manhood and his fame to his soldierly exploits in India and in the Boer War. In 1914, while a cabinet minister, he had dashed across the Channel to take personal charge of the defense of Antwerp. Having "tasted blood," Prime Minister Herbert Asquith wryly noted, Churchill was "beginning like a tiger to raven for more and begs that . . . he may be . . . put in some kind of military command." He soon got his wish. In January 1916, a middle-aged man accustomed to brandy and silks, Lieutenant Colonel Churchill led an infantry battalion of the Sixth Royal Scots Fusiliers up to their rough billets in the front near Ypres—facing the Germans across the same hellish landscape into which Adolf Hitler's Sixteenth Bavarian Reserve Infantry Regiment was repeatedly sent.[7]

Roosevelt knew no such satisfactions. Late on the night of October 31, 1918, he called at the White House to ask President Woodrow Wilson for a naval commission. "Too late," Wilson replied; he had already received the first armistice proposals from the newly forming German government, and the war would be over very soon.[8]

Roosevelt had to content himself with an official inspection trip to the front in the summer of 1918. It was this journey that underlay the claim he made nearly twenty years later: "I have known war." On July 31 a British destroyer put him ashore at Dunkirk, not forty miles from the spot where Hitler was to be gassed some ten weeks afterward. Impatient and reckless, Roosevelt plunged about the battlefields and courted such danger as he could find. In Belleau Wood, where Amer-

6. Hitler, *Mein Kampf*, 163.
7. William Manchester, *The Last Lion: Winston Spencer Churchill: Visions of Glory, 1874–1932* (Boston: Little, Brown, 1983), 477–651.
8. Frank Freidel, *Franklin D. Roosevelt: The Apprenticeship* (Boston: Little, Brown, 1952), 370. See also Davis 1:548 and Geoffrey C. Ward, *A First-Class Temperament* (New York: Harper and Row, 1989), 417.

ican troops had helped to stop the final German advance just weeks earlier, he threaded his way around water-filled shell holes and past countless rude graves, marked only by whittled wooden crosses or bayoneted rifles stuck in the earth. At Mareuil en Dole he jerked the lanyards to fire artillery shells at a German rail junction some twelve miles distant. At Verdun he donned helmet and gas mask and clambered underground into the fetid labyrinth of Fort Douamont. He heard the muffled thudding of German artillery shells bursting on the earthworks above. On August 7, after a whirlwind battleground tour of less than a week, Roosevelt departed the front. In September he returned to the haven of the United States, where he remained at the time of the armistice on November 11. Like the vast majority of his countrymen, he had not truly known war. "He was fascinated rather than repelled," a biographer concludes, "thrilled by the patriotism and heroism of the American Allied troops, and oppressed by a sense of guilt and deprivation because he was not sharing their vicissitudes."[9]

FOUR MEN IN NOVEMBER 1918: Each of them molded by the Great War, each fated to lead a nation, each nation destined to be convulsed by the war's aftermath and eventual resumption. All four men coveted power, and all would hugely possess it. The two victors had already drunk at the well of power and now thirsted for even greater drafts. Stalin struggled to close his hand over power amidst the chaos of revolution. Hitler lusted for power sufficient to avenge his nation's humiliating defeat. The wheel of time would eventually carry all four of these men into one of history's darkest circles. Indeed, history had already thrown them into sometimes eery proximity, physical as well as metaphorical.[10] Churchill and Roosevelt had both passed within a day's march of the trenches where Lance Corporal Hitler scurried with his

9. Freidel, *Apprenticeship*, 358–61. As Freidel observes elsewhere, at this stage of his life the young Roosevelt was "impatient and far from reflective." In 1936, an older and more seasoned Roosevelt would famously recollect his time at the front by observing that "I have seen war. . . . I have seen blood running from the wounded. I have seen men coughing out their gassed lungs. . . . I have seen the agony of mothers and wives. I hate war." (Freidel, 287, 356); *PPA* (1937), 289.

10. Each of these men, too, would know his own kind of imprisonment. Stalin had already chewed the salt bread of exile in the frozen reaches of Siberia. Hitler, arrested after the failed Beer Hall Putsch in Munich in 1923, was to spend nine months in the Fortress of Landsberg, dictating *Mein Kampf* (My Struggle) to Rudolph Hess. Churchill was to feel the oppressive confinement, for him, of being

dispatches. All three, like moths to the flame, felt drawn by the thrilling allure of soldiering and battle. The Briton and the American actually met at a dinner at Gray's Inn in London on July 9, 1918, though neither made much impression on the other at the time.[11]

Stalin, born in the Caucasus on the frontier between Europe and Asia, dreamt of a new Red empire that would arise from the ashes of the Romanovs' Russia and spread far beyond its old imperial boundaries — just as Hitler, born on the frontier that separated Germany from Austria, nursed his febrile dream of fusing all the Germanic peoples of the toppling Hohenzollern and Hapsburg regimes into a vast, new, racially pure Teutonic *Reich*. The clash of those dreams would one day be the world's nightmare.

BUT IN NOVEMBER 1918, the fighting momentarily ended, humankind could still for a fleeting season dream the dreams of hope. Much of that hope was invested in the person of the American president, Woodrow Wilson. "What a place the President held in the hearts and hopes of the world!" when he boarded the *George Washington* for the Paris Peace Conference on December 4, 1918, exclaimed the British economist John Maynard Keynes. Buoyant and eager, Roosevelt followed his chief to Paris aboard the same ship a month later. But there, hovering on the periphery of the peace negotiations, he witnessed the remorseless demolition of the liberal settlement that Wilson had championed.

It was the young Keynes who most famously chronicled the hope-smothering defects of the treaty that was signed on June 28, 1919, in the Hall of Mirrors at the Palace of Versailles. Wilson had envisioned a liberal peace, a peace without victory, a peace that would magnanimously restore Germany to its rightful place in an open world of free trade and democracy. In that world commerce would be unshackled from political constraint, politics would be based on the principle of self-determination, and order would be maintained by a new international body, the League of Nations. But what emerged from the ordeal of the Paris peace negotiations was a document that mocked those ideals.

---

deprived of political office in 1922 and 1923, when he began to write *The World Crisis*, his history of the Great War. Roosevelt would be partly imprisoned in his immobile body after suffering an attack of poliomyelitis in 1921.

11. Roosevelt failed to record the meeting in his detailed diary, and Churchill apparently forgot the episode entirely. Freidel, *Apprenticeship*, 354.

The Versailles Treaty, Keynes wrote in his embittered and astute tract of 1919, *The Economic Consequences of the Peace*, contained three lethal flaws. It transferred important coal, iron, and steel properties from Germany to France and prohibited their utilization by German industry. "Thus the Treaty strikes at organization," Keynes declared, "and by the destruction of organization impairs yet further the reduced wealth of the whole community." The treaty further stripped Germany of her overseas colonies, foreign investments, and merchant marine and restricted her control of her own waterways and tariffs. Most economically punishing of all, the victorious powers then imposed on this drastically weakened Germany a colossal bill for some $33 billion in reparations payments. Adding insult to injury, the treaty's Article 231—the notorious "guilt clause"—forced the Germans to acknowledge sole responsibility for the outbreak of the war.[12]

The treaty, Keynes concluded, insanely perpetuated in peacetime the economic disruptions of the war itself. To the military catastrophe of the fighting was now added the economic burden of a vengeful peace. Germany, struggling to become a republic, bore most of the fearful tonnage. But all nations, victors and vanquished alike, were bowed beneath its crushing ballast in the interwar decades.

Keynes was not the only observer to sense mortal liabilities in the legacy from Versailles. A young statesman who had come to Paris from a distant corner of the planet, twenty-seven-year-old Prince Fumimaro Konoye of Japan, also found grounds for complaint. Konoye warned his countrymen in a celebrated article to "reject the Anglo-American–centered peace." Why should Japan, he asked, accept a settlement that refused to acknowledge the principle of racial equality? That refused to honor Japan's rightful claims in China? That perpetuated in the name of high idealism a world order that relegated small, resource-poor Japan to second-class status? Like Germany, Konoye argued, Japan had "no resort but to destroy the status quo for the sake of self-preservation." Two decades later, Premier Konoye would link Japan's fate to that of Nazi Germany and Fascist Italy in the Tripartite Pact—an aggressive bid to destroy the status quo in Europe and Asia alike, not merely for the sake of self-preservation but for the sake of imperial expansion.[13]

12. John Maynard Keynes, *The Economic Consequences of the Peace* (New York: Harcourt, Brace and Howe, 1920), 100–101, 152.
13. Yoshitake Oka, *Konoe Fumimaro: A Political Biography* (Tokyo: University of Tokyo Press, 1983), 13.

The Versailles Treaty thus sowed the wind that would eventually lash the world with gale fury. Woodrow Wilson's adviser, Colonel Edward House, reflected as he watched the German representatives scratch their signatures on the parchment in the Hall of Mirrors that "it was not unlike what was done in olden times, when the conqueror dragged the conquered at his chariot wheels." The Berlin *Vorwärts* urged its readers: "Do not lose hope. The resurrection day comes."[14]

Adolf Hitler aimed to be the agent of that resurrection. Returning to Munich in 1919, he plunged into the furtive, turbulent world of political organizing among the discontented army veterans who shared his resentment of their army's betrayal by civilian leaders in 1918. By 1920 he had helped to organize the National-sozialistische Deutsche Arbeiterpartei—the Nazi Party, with its distinctive *Hakenkreuz*, or swastika, symbol. By 1921 he was its undisputed leader, and its brown-shirted toughs, the Sturmabteilungen (SA), stood ready to enforce his will. He played like a virtuoso the swelling chords of German resentment, and the Nazis advanced as Germany's democratic experiment retreated. The Weimar Republic, saddled from birth with the ignominy of defeat and the harsh economic and psychological weight of the Versailles settlement, staggered and reeled through the 1920s. When it defaulted on reparations payments in 1922, France occupied the Ruhr, Germany's industrial heartland, touching off a fantastic spiral of hyperinflation that rendered the German *Mark* virtually worthless. Hitler seized the occasion to attempt a coup in Munich—the failed "Beer Hall Putsch" that earned him a jail sentence in the fortress at Landsberg. Released in late 1924, he again focused his demonic energy on building the Nazi Party, including now an elite personal bodyguard, the black-shirted Schutz Staffeln (SS). By 1928 the party claimed more than a hundred thousand members and polled 810,000 votes in the Reichstag elections.[15]

Then came the world economic crisis that began in 1929, and with it Hitler's great opportunity. As German unemployment mounted to three million persons in 1930, Nazi Party membership doubled. When Germans went to the polls in September 1930, the Nazi vote vaulted to 6.4 million. Hitler now commanded the second-largest party in the Reichstag, with 107 seats. Two years later the Nazis won an additional

14. Both remarks quoted in Thomas A. Bailey, *Woodrow Wilson and the Lost Peace* (New York: Macmillan, 1944), 302–30.
15. The account of Hitler's rise to power is drawn from Alan Bullock, *Hitler: A Study in Tyranny* (New York: Harper and Row, 1962) and from Joachim Fest, *Hitler* (New York: Harcourt Brace Jovanovich, 1974).

113 seats, and Hitler demanded that he be given the chancellorship. On January 30, 1933, he got it. Five weeks later, Franklin D. Roosevelt was inaugurated as president of the United States.

Time takes strange turnings. As former lance corporal Hitler and former assistant secretary Roosevelt now stepped to the center stage of history, another figure whom the Great War had summoned to that stage prepared to leave it: Herbert Hoover, the great humanitarian who had organized food relief for occupied Belgium in 1914 and fed much of the world in the tumultuous months that followed the armistice. He was "the only man," said John Maynard Keynes, "who emerged from the ordeal of Paris with an enhanced reputation." Keynes believed that if Hoover's realism, his "knowledge, magnanimity, and disinterestedness," had found wider play in the councils of Paris, the world would have had "the Good Peace."[16]

But there would be no good peace, only a precarious truce followed by a decade of depression and then an even greater war. When the global economic hurricane of the 1930s stripped power from Hoover and conferred it on Hitler and Roosevelt, Hoover knew the source of the storm: "[T]he primary cause of the Great Depression," reads the first sentence of his *Memoirs*, "was the war of 1914–1918."[17]

16. Keynes, *Economic Consequences of the Peace,* 247.
17. Herbert Hoover, *The Memoirs of Herbert Hoover: The Great Depression, 1929–1941* (New York: Macmillan, 1952), 2.

1

The American People
on the Eve of the Great Depression

We in America today are nearer to the final triumph over poverty than ever before in the history of any land.
— Herbert Hoover, August 11, 1928

Like an earthquake, the stock market crash of October 1929 cracked startlingly across the United States, the herald of a crisis that was to shake the American way of life to its foundations. The events of the ensuing decade opened a fissure across the landscape of American history no less gaping than that opened by the volley on Lexington Common in April 1775 or by the bombardment of Sumter on another April four score and six years later.

The ratcheting ticker machines in the autumn of 1929 did not merely record avalanching stock prices. In time they came also to symbolize the end of an era. The roaring industrial expansion that had boomed since the Civil War hushed to a near standstill for half a generation. The tumult of crisis and reform in the ten depression years massively enlarged and forever transformed the scanty Jeffersonian government over which Herbert Hoover had been elected to preside in 1928. And even before the battle against the Great Depression was won, the American people had to shoulder arms in another even more fearsome struggle that wreathed the planet in destruction and revolutionized America's global role.

None of this impending drama could have been foreseen by the tweedy group of social scientists who gathered at the White House for dinner with President Hoover on the warm, early autumn evening of September 26, 1929. The Crash, still four weeks away, was unimagined and almost unimaginable. Nearly three decades of barely punctuated economic growth, capped by seven years of unprecedented prosperity, gave to the mood in the room, as in the entire country, an air of masterful confidence in the future. The president personified the national temper. Attired as always in starched high collar and immaculate business suit, he greeted his guests with stiff, double-breasted dignity. He exuded the laconic assurance of a highly successful executive. He was arguably the most respected man in America, a man, said the novelist Sherwood Anderson, who had "never known failure."[1] A wave of popular acclamation had lifted him to the White House just six months earlier, after a famously distinguished career as a mining engineer, international businessman, relief and food administrator in the Great War of 1914–18, and exceptionally influential secretary of commerce in the Republican administrations of Warren G. Harding and Calvin Coolidge.

Hoover was no mossback conservative in the Harding-Coolidge mold, and the men gathered in the White House dining room knew it. "[T]he time when the employer could ride roughshod over his labor is disappearing with the doctrine of 'laissez-faire' on which it is founded," he had written as early as 1909.[2] Long sympathetic to the progressive wing of his party, Hoover as secretary of commerce had not only supported the cause of labor but also urged closer business-government cooperation, established government control over the new technology of radio, and proposed a multibillion-dollar federal public works fund as a tool to offset downswings in the business cycle. As president, he meant to be no passive custodian. He dreamt the progressive generation's dream of actively managing social change through informed, though scrupulously limited, government action. "A new era and new forces have come into our economic life and our setting among nations of the world," he said in accepting the Republican presidential nomination in 1928. "These forces demand of us constant study and effort if prosperity, peace, and contentment shall be maintained."[3]

Organizing that study was the dinner meeting's agenda. The little assemblage around the president's dining table symbolized, in a sense, the core progressive faith in knowledge as the servant of power. Hoover intended to possess knowledge, and with it to rule responsibly. After

1. Joan Hoff Wilson, *Herbert Hoover: Forgotten Progressive* (Boston: Little, Brown, 1975), 121.
2. Herbert Hoover, *Principles of Mining* (New York: McGraw-Hill, 1909), 167–68.
3. Herbert Hoover, *The Memoirs of Herbert Hoover: The Cabinet and the Presidency, 1920–1933* (New York: Macmillan, 1952), 195.

methodically interrogating each of his guests over the coffee cups as the table was cleared, Hoover explained his ambitious project. He meant to recruit the best brains in the country, he said, to compile a body of data and analysis about American society that would be more comprehensive, more searching, and more useful than anything ever before attempted. Their findings, he went on, would serve as "a basis for the formulation of large national policies looking to the next phase in the nation's development."[4]

The following month's upheavals in the financial markets, and their aftershocks, rendered ironic Hoover's confident anticipation of "the next phase in the nation's development." Underscoring the irony, Hoover eventually disowned the study he so confidently commissioned on that Indian summer evening. In the four years between its conception and its publication—the four years of Herbert Hoover's presidency—the world changed forever. Among the casualties of that violent mutation was Hoover's research project and the hope of an orderly command of the future that it represented—not to mention his own reputation. A massive dreadnought of scholarship, its pages barnacled with footnotes, it was launched at last in 1933 onto a Sargasso Sea of presidential and public indifference.

Useless to Hoover in 1933, the scholars' work has nevertheless provided historians ever since with an incomparably rich source of information about the pre-Depression period. Entitled *Recent Social Trends*, it ran to some fifteen hundred pages densely packed with data about all aspects of American life. It ranged from an inventory of mineral resources to analyses of crime and punishment, the arts, health and medical practice, the status of women, blacks, and ethnic minorities, the changing characteristics of the labor force, the impact of new technologies on productivity and leisure, and the roles of federal, state, and local governments. From its turgid prose and endless tables emerged a vivid portrait of a people in the throes of sweeping social, economic, and political change, even before they were engulfed by the still more wrenching changes of the Depression era.

President Hoover's charge to the assembled scholars at that hopeful supper registered his commitment to what Walter Lippmann in 1914

4. President's Research Committee on Social Trends, *Recent Social Trends in the United States* (Westport, Conn.: Greenwood, 1970), 1: xi; French Strother, memorandum of June 26, 1934, E. H. Hunt Collection, box 23, "Memoranda," Hoover Institution Archives, Stanford, Calif. See also Barry Karl, "Presidential Planning and Social Science Research: Mr. Hoover's Experts," *Perspectives in American History* 3:347–409.

had called mastery, not drift, in the nation's affairs and to government as the instrument of that mastery.[5] Hoover's dinner-table speech to the social scientists also accurately reflected their shared sense — indeed the sense of most Americans in pre-Crash 1929 — that they dwelt in a land and time of special promise. "A new era," Hoover called it, one that was witnessing breathtaking transformations in traditional ways of life and that demanded commensurate transformations in the institutions and techniques of government.

This sense of living through a novel historical moment pervaded commentaries on American society in the 1920s. Even the sober academic authors of *Recent Social Trends* marveled at the social and economic forces that "have hurried us dizzily away from the days of the frontier into a whirl of modernisms which almost passes belief."[6] The same sense of astonishment suffused the pages of the decade's most famous sociological inquiry, Robert and Helen Merrell Lynd's *Middletown*, drawn from an exhaustive examination of Muncie, Indiana, in 1925. Measuring from the baseline of 1890, the Lynds found dramatic alterations in every conceivable aspect of the Middletowners' lives. "[W]e today," they concluded, "are probably living in one of the eras of greatest rapidity of change in the history of human institutions."[7]

The list of changes in the generation since the close of the nineteenth century seemed endlessly amazing. *Recent Social Trends* began with a brief recital of some of the "epoch-making events" that had filled the first third of the twentieth century: the Great War, mass immigration, race riots, rapid urbanization, the rise of giant industrial combines like U.S. Steel, Ford, and General Motors, new technologies like electrical power, automobiles, radios, and motion pictures, novel social experiments like Prohibition, daring campaigns for birth control, a new frankness about sex, women's suffrage, the advent of mass-market advertising and consumer financing. "These," the researchers declared, "are but a few of the many happenings which have marked one of the most eventful periods of our history."[8]

THE SHEER SCALE of America in the 1920s was impressive, and its variety was downright astonishing. The nation's population had nearly

5. Walter Lippmann, *Drift and Mastery* (New York: Mitchell Kennerley, 1914).
6. *Recent Social Trends* 1:xii.
7. Robert S. Lynd and Helen Merrell Lynd, *Middletown: A Study in Modern American Culture* (New York: Harcourt, Brace and World, 1929), 5.
8. *Recent Social Trends* 1:xi.

doubled since 1890, when it had numbered just sixty-three million souls. At least a third of the increase was due to a huge surge of immigrants. Most of them had journeyed to America from the religiously and culturally exotic regions of southern and eastern Europe. Through the great hall in the immigrant receiving center on New York's Ellis Island, opened in 1892, streamed in the next three decades almost four million Italian Catholics; half a million Orthodox Greeks; half a million Catholic Hungarians; nearly a million and a half Catholic Poles; more than two million Jews, largely from Russian-controlled Poland, Ukraine, and Lithuania; half a million Slovaks, mostly Catholic; millions of other eastern Slavs from Byelorussia, Ruthenia, and Russia, mostly Orthodox; more millions of southern Slavs, a mix of Catholic, Orthodox, Muslim, and Jew, from Rumania, Croatia, Serbia, Bulgaria, and Montenegro. The waves of arrivals after the turn of the century were so enormous that of the 123 million Americans recorded in the census of 1930, one in ten was foreign born, and an additional 20 percent had at least one parent born abroad.[9]

Immigrants settled in all regions, though only scantily in the South and heavily in the sprawling industrial zone of the Northeast. To an overwhelming degree they were drawn not to the land but to the factories and tenements of the big cities. They turned urban America into a kind of polyglot archipelago in the predominantly Anglo-Protestant American sea. Almost a third of Chicago's 2.7 million residents in the 1920s were foreign born; more than a million were Catholic, and another 125,000 were Jews. New Yorkers spoke some thirty-seven different languages, and only one in six worshiped in a Protestant church.[10]

Everywhere immigrant communities banded together in ethnic enclaves, where they strove, not always consistently, both to preserve their old-world cultural patrimony and to become American. They were strangers in a strange land, awkwardly suspended between the world they had left behind and a world where they were not yet fully at home. They naturally looked to one another for reassurance and strength. The Jewish ghettoes and Little Italys and Little Polands that took root in American cities became worlds unto themselves. Immigrants read newspapers and listened to radio broadcasts in their native languages. They

9. Thomas J. Archdeacon, *Becoming American: An Ethnic History* (New York: Free Press, 1983), 112–42.
10. Harvey Green, *The Uncertainty of Everyday Life* (New York: HarperCollins, 1992), 5.

shopped at stores, patronized banks, and dealt with insurance companies that catered exclusively to their particular ethnic group. They chanted their prayers in synagogues or, if they were Catholic, often in "national" churches where sermons were preached in the old-world tongue. They educated their children in parish schools and buried their dead with the help of ethnic funeral societies. They joined fraternal organizations to keep alive the old traditions and paid their dues to mutual aid societies that would help when hard times came.

Times were often hard. Huddled on the margins of American life, immigrants made do with what work they could find, typically low-skill jobs in heavy industry, the garment trades, or construction. Isolated by language, religion, livelihood, and neighborhood, they had precious little ability to speak to one another and scant political voice in the larger society. So precarious were their lives that many of them gave up altogether and went back home. Nearly a third of the Poles, Slovaks, and Croatians returned to Europe; almost half the Italians; more than half the Greeks, Russians, Rumanians, and Bulgarians.[11] Old-stock Americans continued to think of the foreigners who remained in their midst as alien and threatening. Many immigrants wondered if the fabled promise of American life was a vagrant and perhaps impossible dream.

The flood of newcomers, vividly different from earlier migrants in faiths, tongues, and habits, aroused powerful anxieties about the capacity of American society to accommodate them. Some of that anxiety found virulent expression in a revived Ku Klux Klan, reborn in all its Reconstruction-era paraphernalia at Stone Mountain, Georgia, in 1915. Klan nightriders now rode cars, not horses, and they directed their venom as much at immigrant Jews and Catholics as at blacks. But the new Klan no less than the old represented a peculiarly American response to cultural upheaval. By the early 1920s the Klan claimed some five million members, and for a time it dominated the politics of Indiana and Oregon. The nativist sentiment that the Klan helped to nurture found statutory expression in 1924, when Congress choked the immigrant stream to a trickle, closing the era of virtually unlimited entry to the United States. The ethnic neighborhoods that had mushroomed in the preceding generation would grow no more through further inflows from abroad. America's many ethnic communities now began to stabilize. Millions of immigrants awaited the day when they might become American at last.

11. Archdeacon, *Becoming American*, 118–19, 139.

From peasant plots in the basins of the Volga and Vistula, from rough pastures high in the Carpathians and Apennines, as well as from the cotton South and the midwestern corn belt, new Americans as well as old flowed to the throbbing industrial centers in the northeastern quadrant of the United States. The region of settlement defined as the "frontier" had officially closed in 1890. By 1920, for the first time in the nation's history, a majority of Americans were city dwellers. In the following decade, some six million more American farmers quit the land and moved to the city.

Yet the urbanization of early twentieth-century America can be exaggerated. More than one in five working Americans still toiled on the land in the 1920s. Forty-four percent of the population was still counted as rural in 1930. Well over half the states of the Union remained preponderantly rural in population, economy, political representation, and ways of life.

In many respects, those country ways of life remained untouched by modernity. The fifty million Americans who dwelt in what F. Scott Fitzgerald called "that vast obscurity beyond the city" still moved between birth and death to the ancient rhythms of sun and season. More than forty-five million of them had no indoor plumbing in 1930, and almost none had electricity. They relieved themselves in chamber pots and outdoor latrines, cooked and heated with wood stoves, and lit their smoky houses with oil lamps. In the roadless Ozark mountains, future Arkansas governor Orval Faubus's mother could not do the family laundry until she had first boiled the guts of a freshly butchered hog to make lye soap. In the isolated Texas Hill Country, future president Lyndon Johnson's mother grew stoop-shouldered lugging buckets of water from well to kitchen. As it had for most of mankind for all of human memory, sunset routinely settled a cloak of darkness and silence over that immense domain where the fields of the republic rolled on under the night. Another Texas Hill Country woman remembered from her girlhood the scary after-dark trips to the outhouse: "I had a horrible choice of either sitting in the dark and not knowing what was crawling on me or bringing a lantern and attracting moths, mosquitoes, nighthawks and bats."[12]

The widening gap between country and city life had helped to fuel the Populist agitation of the late nineteenth century and had prompted

12. Robert A. Caro, *The Years of Lyndon Johnson: The Path to Power* (New York: Knopf, 1982), 513.

Theodore Roosevelt to appoint a Commission on Country Life in 1908. By the 1920s a stubborn agricultural depression, the product of war and technological change, badly exacerbated the problems of the countryside. When the guns of August 1914 announced the outbreak of fighting in Europe, American farmers had scrambled to supply the world's disrupted markets with foodstuffs. They put marginal lands under the plow, and they increased yields from all acreage with more intensive cultivation, aided especially by the advent of the gasoline-engine tractor. The number of motorized farm vehicles quintupled in the war years, to some eighty-five thousand. With the return of peace this trend accelerated. By the end of the 1920s nearly a million farmers chugged along their furrows mounted atop self-propelled tractors. And as tractor-power substituted for horse- and mule-power, some nine million work animals were destroyed, releasing an additional thirty million acres of pastureland for the planting of wheat or cotton or for the grazing of dairy animals.[13]

After the armistice of November 1918, however, world agricultural production returned to its familiar prewar patterns. American farmers found themselves with huge surpluses on their hands. Prices plummeted. Cotton slumped from a wartime high of thirty-five cents per pound to sixteen cents in 1920. Corn sank from $1.50 per bushel to fifty-two cents. Wool slid from nearly sixty cents per pound to less than twenty cents. Although prices improved somewhat after 1921, they did not fully recover until war resumed in 1939. Farmers suffocated under their own mountainous surpluses and under the weight of the debts they had assumed to expand and to mechanize. Foreclosures increased, and more and more freeholders became tenants. The depopulation of the countryside proceeded ever more rapidly.

Congress tried repeatedly to find a remedy for the ills of farmers in the 1920s. As the agricultural depression persisted through the decade, the federal government assumed regulatory control over commodity markets and eventually established a modestly funded federal agency to provide financing for agricultural cooperatives. Congress twice passed, and President Coolidge twice vetoed, the McNary-Haugen Bill. It proposed that the federal government should become the buyer of last resort of surplus farm products, which it should then dispose of—or "dump"—in overseas markets.

Herbert Hoover needed no comprehensive study to know that the farm issue was urgent. Virtually his first act as president, even before he

13. *HSUS*, 469; *Recent Social Trends* 1:105.

commissioned his wide-ranging examination of recent social trends, was to convene a special congressional session to resolve the farm crisis. It produced the Agricultural Marketing Act of 1929, which created several government-sponsored "stabilization corporations" authorized to buy surpluses and hold them off the market in order to maintain price levels. But as the agricultural depression of the 1920s merged with the general depression of the 1930s, the corporations quickly exhausted both their storage capacity and their funds. The misery of rural America knew no relief. As the decade of the Great Depression opened, the already reeling farmers would be its hardest-hit victims.

THE SOUTH IN THE 1920s was the nation's most rural region. Not a single southern state met the superintendent of the census's modest definition of "urban" in 1920—having a majority of its population in cities of twenty-five hundred or more souls. From the Potomac to the Gulf the land looked little different than it had at the end of Reconstruction in the 1870s. Inhabiting a region of scarce capital and abundant labor, southerners planted and picked their traditional crops of cotton, tobacco, rice, or sugarcane with mules and muscle, just as their ancestors had done for generations. And like their forebears, they bled not only against the blade of chronic agricultural depression but also against the uniquely American thorn of race.[14]

The Great War had drawn some half a million blacks out of the rural South and into the factories of the North. With the throttling of immigration in 1924, northern industry needed to find new sources of fresh labor. Southern blacks (as well as some half a million Mexicans, who were exempted from the new immigration quotas) seized the opportunity. By the end of the 1920s another million African-Americans had left the old slave states to take up employment in the Northeast and upper Midwest (only about a hundred thousand blacks dwelt west of the Rockies). There they found jobs in metalworking shops, automobile factories, and packing houses. The political implications of this migration were vividly illustrated in 1928 when Chicago alderman Oscar De Priest, a Republican loyal to the party of the Great Emancipator, became the first black elected to Congress since Reconstruction and the first ever from a northern district.

Yet as late as 1930 more than four out of five American blacks still

14. Jack Temple Kirby, *Rural Worlds Lost: The American South, 1920–1960* (Baton Rouge: Louisiana State University Press, 1987), 49.

lived in the South. There they tortuously made their daily way through what the historian C. Vann Woodward has called an "anthropological museum of Southern folkways," which history knows as the Jim Crow system. Despite its antiquated and grotesquely burdensome character, that system was deeply entrenched in southern life. Indeed, as Woodward notes, it "reached its perfection in the 1930s."[15]

Jim Crow meant, above all, that blacks could not vote. They had been almost universally disfranchised throughout the South in the post-Reconstruction decades. In the eleven states of the former Confederacy, fewer than 5 percent of eligible African-Americans were registered to vote as late as 1940.[16] Jim Crow also meant social and economic segregation. Blacks sat in separate waiting rooms in railroad and bus stations, drank from separate drinking fountains, worshiped in separate churches, and attended strictly segregated and abysmally inferior schools. The South's few industrial jobs were largely barred to them. Southern blacks thus constituted an extreme case of rural poverty in a region that was itself a special case of economic backwardness and isolation from modern life. Hoover's social scientists discovered that infant mortality rates for blacks were nearly double those for whites in 1930 (10 percent and 6 percent respectively) and that blacks had an average life expectancy fifteen years shorter than whites (forty-five years compared with sixty). African-Americans in the South were bound as fast to the land by debt, ignorance, and intimidation as they had been by slavery itself. As for the white folk of the South, declared the eminent southern historian Ulrich B. Phillips in 1928, they shared "a common resolve indomitably maintained—that it shall be and remain a white man's country."[17]

To AMERICANS who were white and lived in the city, blacks were nearly invisible and the complaints of the farmers seemed a distant annoyance, the mewlings of laughably untutored hayseeds as modernity passed them by. Urban sophisticates snickered with approval when H. L. Mencken lampooned the South as the "Sahara of the Bozart." They nodded knowingly when Sinclair Lewis, in books like *Main Street* (1920) and *Babbitt* (1922), satirized the same midwestern small towns

15. C. Vann Woodward, *Thinking Back: The Perils of Writing History* (Baton Rouge: Louisiana State University Press, 1986), 87.

16. Nancy J. Weiss, *Farewell to the Party of Lincoln: Black Politics in the Age of FDR* (Princeton: Princeton University Press, 1983), 21.

17. *Recent Social Trends* 1:584; Ulrich B. Phillips, "The Central Theme of Southern History," *American Historical Review* 34 (1928):31.

from which many of them had fled to the metropolis. They clucked appreciatively when Lewis unmasked the tawdry hypocrisy of rural America's fundamentalist faiths in *Elmer Gantry* (1927). They smirked at the biblical literalism of the "yokels" who swarmed out of the east Tennessee hills in 1925 to gape at the trial of John T. Scopes, indicted for violating Tennessee law by teaching Darwinian evolution to high school students. They smiled with satisfaction when street-smart Chicago attorney Clarence Darrow humiliated rural America's historic paladin, William Jennings Bryan, in the course of that trial.

Bryan's mortification symbolized for many the eclipse of rural fundamentalism and the triumphant ascendancy of the metropolis as the fount and arbiter of modern American values. New national magazines, like *Time*, first published in 1923, Mencken's *American Mercury* in 1924, and the *New Yorker*, whose first issue appeared in 1925, catered to the "caviar sophisticates" and testified to the new cultural power of the great urban centers. Urban America was confident that the city—like Darrow's and Carl Sandburg's Chicago, "stormy, husky, brawling . . . proud to be Hog Butcher, Tool Maker, Stacker of Wheat, Player with Railroads and Freight Handler to the Nation"—was the big-shouldered master to whom rural America must pay tribute.

But to thoughtful observers and policymakers the contrast between country and city life was a matter for neither laughter nor poetry. They worried obsessively about "balance" between rural and urban America, which *Recent Social Trends* called "the central problem" of the economy. Politicians sought interminably for ways to solve it.[18]

The economic disparities between the agricultural and industrial sectors were gaping. Both areas of the economy had grown since the turn of the century, but the urban-based manufacturing sector had expanded far more robustly. While American farmers brought about 50 percent more product to market in 1930 than they had in 1900, manufacturing output had doubled and redoubled again over the same period, to four times its earlier level. Factory workers had achieved remarkable productivity improvements of nearly 50 percent, thanks largely to more efficient means of industrial organization and to the revolutionary introduction of electrically driven machinery on the shop floor. Fully 70 percent of American industry was powered by electricity in 1929, much of it from generating plants fueled by oil from newly developed fields in Texas, Oklahoma, and California. By 1925 a completely assembled Model T

18. *Recent Social Trends* 1:xxxi.

Ford rolled off the continuously moving assembly line at Henry Ford's Highland Park plant every ten seconds. Just a dozen years earlier it had taken fourteen hours to put together a single car.[19]

Shrinking export markets, along with the dampening of American population growth after the closure of immigration, spelled stable or even declining demand for American agricultural products. Yet the capacity of Americans to buy ever more industrial goods seemed limitless, as the automobile revolution vividly illustrated. Essentially a cottage industry when the century opened, automobile manufacturing accounted for 10 percent of the nation's income two decades later and employed some four million workers. The motorcar in 1900 had been the plaything of the rich, who purchased some four thousand vehicles. By 1929 ordinary Americans were driving more than twenty-six million motor vehicles, one for every five people in the country. They bought nearly five million vehicles in that year alone, and they paid far less for them than they had a generation earlier.

In a stunning demonstration of the fruitful marriage of innovative technologies to mass markets, the effective price of an automobile fell steeply from the century's opening onward. A car that cost the average worker the equivalent of nearly two years' wages before the First World War could be purchased for about three months' earnings by the late 1920s. This low-price, high-volume marketing strategy was among the miracles of mass production — or "Fordism," as it was sometimes called in honor of its most famous pioneer. Largely an American invention, the technique of mass-producing standardized products was in a sense an American inevitability, as, in its time, would be the revolution in consumer electronics: a means to tap the economic potential of a democratic society whose wealth was nearly as widely diffused as its formal political power.

Yet even this fabulously successful strategy had limits. Mass production made mass consumption a necessity. But as Hoover's investigators discovered, the increasing wealth of the 1920s flowed disproportionately to the owners of capital. Workers' incomes were rising, but not at a rate that kept pace with the nation's growing industrial output. Without broadly distributed purchasing power, the engines of mass production would have no outlet and would eventually fall idle. The automobile industry, where Fordism had begun, was among the first to sense the

19. William E. Leuchtenburg, *The Perils of Prosperity* (Chicago: University of Chicago Press, 1958), 179.

force of this logic. A spokesman for General Motors Corporation acknowledged in 1926 that

> while the industry has been subject to an unusually rapid rate of expansion in the past, the volume has now reached such large proportions that it seems altogether unlikely that tremendous annual increases will continue. The expectation is rather for a healthy growth, in line with the increase in population and wealth of the country, and the development of the export market.[20]

Here was among the first recognitions that even a youthful industry like automobile manufacturing might rapidly grow to "maturity." The carmakers had apparently saturated available domestic markets. The introduction of consumer credit, or "installment buying," pioneered at General Motors in 1919 with the creation of the General Motors Acceptance Corporation, constituted one attempt to stretch those markets still further by relieving buyers of the need to pay full cash for cars at the moment of sale. The explosive growth of advertising, an infant industry before the 1920s, provided further sign of the fear that the limits of "natural" demand were being reached. General Motors alone annually spent some $20 million on advertising in the 1920s in an effort to nurture consumer desires that transcended consumer needs. Together, credit and advertising sustained automobile sales for a time, but without new foreign outlets or a significant redistribution of domestic purchasing power—especially to the impoverished rural half of the country—the boundaries of consumer demand were apparently being approached.

Yet in the pulsing industrial cities, virtually all Americans dramatically improved their standards of living over the course of the post–World War I decade. While farmers' living standards eroded through the 1920s, real wages for industrial workers rose by nearly 25 percent. By 1928 average per capita income among nonagricultural employees had reached four times the average level of farmers' incomes. For urban workers, prosperity was wondrous and real. They had more money than ever before, and they enjoyed an amazing variety of new products on which to spend it: not only automobiles but also canned foods, washing machines, refrigerators, synthetic fabrics, telephones, motion pictures

20. Albert Bradley, "Setting Up a Forecasting Program," *Annual Convention Series*, American Management Association, no. 41 (March 1926), quoted in Alfred D. Chandler Jr., *Giant Enterprise: Ford, General Motors, and the Automobile Industry* (New York: Harcourt, Brace and World, 1964), 132.

(with sound after 1927), and — along with the automobile the most revolutionary of the new technologies — radios. In the unelectrified countryside, of course, many of these modern conveniences were nowhere
to be found.

THE AUTHORS OF *Recent Social Trends* found that thirty-eight
million male and ten million female workers produced and distributed
this abundance of goods in 1930. Agricultural laborers had constituted
the largest category of employment as recently as 1910, but by 1920 the
number of workers in manufacturing and mechanical industries eclipsed
the number in farming. The workweek of the typical nonfarm employee
had shortened since the turn of the century, but the regimen of virtually
continuous labor long familiar on the farm had been imported onto the
factory floor in the earliest days of industrialization and had only slowly
relaxed. Not until 1923 did United States Steel Corporation grudgingly
abandon the twelve-hour day, its grinding human damage made worse
by the periodic "turnover" of the night and day gangs, when the men
were required to stand a continuous twenty-four-hour shift. Most industrial workers in 1930 put in forty-eight hours a week. The two-day "weekend" was not yet a fixture of American life, and paid vacations for workers were almost unknown. "Retirement," too, was still an elusive fantasy
for the average American worker, whose days of toil extended virtually
to the end of the life cycle.[21]
The very forces that increased productivity and benefited consumers
also carried some implications that deeply troubled Hoover's experts.
The most serious issue, they explained, stemmed from "the widespread
introduction of machinery [which] is having the general effect of replacing skilled with semi-skilled and unskilled labor and is thus reducing
the status of the trained and skilled worker, if, in fact, it is not tending
to eliminate him entirely from many industries." Machine power presented a paradox. It offered employment to large numbers of the unskilled, which was why millions of European peasants and American
farmers migrated to the cities in search of industrial jobs and the chance
for a better life. At the same time, it commodified labor and volatilized
it, robbing workers of craft pride and, most important, of job security.
What was more, the longer-term effect of increased mechanization
might be the disappearance of some jobs altogether. The irregularity of
employment patterns in the technologically innovative mass-production
industries was especially worrisome. Somewhat surprisingly, given the

21. *Recent Social Trends* 2:829, 1:277.

decade's reputation, the annual rate of unemployment in those sectors exceeded 10 percent at the height of "Coolidge prosperity" from 1923 to 1928. Few features of the emerging industrial economy were more potentially troublesome.[22]

The Lynds' study of Muncie detailed the complex personal and social implications of those employment patterns. The principal factor that distinguished the "working class" from the "business class," they found, was insecurity of employment with its consequent disturbance in the rhythms of life. The business class, they noted, "are virtually never subject to interruptions of this kind," while among the working class "the 'shut-down' or 'lay-off' is a recurrent phenomenon." Indeed, they suggested that interruption in employment, even more than occupational category or income, was the chief defining characteristic for membership in the social group they called "working class." Those members of the community who enjoyed a measure of job security were not, virtually by definition, "the workers." They had careers, not jobs. Their very conception of time was different, as were their life chances. They planned with confidence for their futures and for their children's futures. They took annual vacations. They aspired to a better way of life. They also built and sustained the elaborate network of organizations—the Rotary Club, the PTA, the Chamber of Commerce, the Women's Club, and, not least, the political parties—that bound the community together and gave it organic life. From much of that activity the workers were excluded, less by active discrimination than by the simple but cruel forces of circumstance.[23]

Workers without job security lived in what the Lynds called "a world in which neither present nor future appears to hold . . . much prospect" of job advancement or social mobility. They worked feverishly when times were good, when the mills were roaring and the forges hot, in order to lay something away against the inevitable moment when times would turn bad, when the factory gates would swing shut and the furnaces be banked. The unpredictable perturbations in their lives constantly disrupted relations among family members and left little oppor-

22. Reliable government statistics on unemployment were not compiled in the 1920s. *Recent Social Trends* 2:806–8 cites Paul Douglas' estimates that unemployment ran at about 9 percent from 1923 to 1926. Considerably higher estimates, ranging from 10 percent to 13 percent between 1924 and 1929, are cited in Irving Bernstein, *The Lean Years: A History of the American Worker, 1920–1933* (Boston: Houghton Mifflin, 1960), 59.
23. Lynd and Lynd, *Middletown*, 55–56.

tunity for social or civic involvement, or even for trade union organization. This precarious, disconnected, socially thin, pervasively insecure way of life was the lot of millions of Americans in the 1920s. They had a periodic taste of prosperity but precious little power over their conditions of work or the trajectories of their lives.[24]

Few employers, no state, and surely not the federal government provided any form of insurance to cushion the blows of unemployment. As late as 1929 the American Federation of Labor (AFL) remained in agreement with employers in adamantly opposing government unemployment insurance, already an established practice in many European countries. Samuel Gompers, the AFL's longtime leader who died in 1924, had repeatedly denounced unemployment insurance as a "socialist" idea and therefore inadmissable in the United States. His successors perpetuated that philosophy right down to the eve of the Great Depression. The rigidity of the AFL's leadership, combined with the hostility of most employers and the general prosperity of the decade, remorselessly thinned the ranks of organized labor. Trade union membership steadily declined from its wartime high of some five million to less than three and a half million by 1929.

The AFL itself deserved some of the blame for this shrinkage. Embittered by a long history of government interventions on the side of management, Gompers preached the philosophy of "voluntarism." In his view, labor should shun government assistance and depend only on its own resources to wring concessions from employers. Unfortunately, those resources were painfully meager. Their value, in fact, was diminishing, as unskilled workers relentlessly displaced the skilled craftsmen whose craft-based guilds composed the AFL. Unskilled laborers were heavily concentrated in the behemoth mass-production industries like steel and automobiles that increasingly dominated the American economy. The health of the union movement depended on organizing them according to the principles of "industrial unionism," which gathered all the workers in an industry into a single union. But that strategy clashed headlong with the elitist and exclusionary organizational doctrines of the AFL, which grouped workers according to skills — as machinists, carpenters, or sheet-metal workers, for example.

Fancying themselves as labor's aristocracy, craft unionists ignored the problems of their unskilled co-workers. Ethnic rivalries exacerbated the troubles in the house of labor. Skilled workers tended to be old-stock,

24. Lynd and Lynd, Middletown, 80.

native-born white Americans, while the unskilled were mostly recent urban immigrants from the hinterlands of Europe and rural America. The AFL, in thus insulating itself from the men and women who were fast becoming the majority of industrial workers, handed management a potent antilabor weapon. Management knew how to use it. U.S. Steel cynically exploited the ethnic divisions that were the bane of American unionism when the AFL in 1919 hesitantly abandoned its traditionally elitist attitudes and led a strike to organize an industrial union in steel. The corporation sent agents into the steel districts around Chicago and Pittsburgh to spawn animosity between native and immigrant workers. They excited the strikers' darkest anxieties by recruiting some thirty thousand southern blacks, hungry to possess previously forbidden jobs, to cross the picket lines. On these rocks of racial and ethnic distrust, the great steel strike of 1919 foundered miserably. Following its catastrophic failure, the American Federation of Labor retreated to its historic exclusiveness and largely left unskilled workers to fend for themselves.

Manipulating ethnic and racial fears was only one among the several tools that management used to suppress workers' organizations. The most fearsome of those tools was the "yellow-dog" contract, which bound individual workers, as a condition of employment, never to join a union. Employers also relied upon friendly judges to issue injunctions prohibiting strikes, picketing, the payment of strike benefits, and even communication between organizers and workers. "[T]he marriage of the labor injunction with the yellow-dog contract," says labor historian Irving Bernstein, "was a peril to the survival of trade unionism in the United States. The Supreme Court had officiated at the wedding in 1917 in the case of *Hitchman Coal & Coke Co. v. Mitchell.*" The Hitchman doctrine made yellow-dog contracts enforceable at law. In effect, it rendered illegal almost any effort to organize a union without the employer's consent. Employers seized on this legal instrument with a vengeance in the 1920s. Fully half of the labor injunctions recorded in the half century after 1880 were issued in that single decade. This judicial animosity spawned frustration and outrage among workers. "The growing bitterness of organized labor toward the federal courts," declared conservative Pennsylvania senator George Wharton Pepper in 1924, threatened "revolutionary" results. Congress at last provided some relief in the Norris–La Guardia Anti-Injunction Act of 1932, which forbade federal courts from issuing injunctions to enforce yellow-dog contracts. But even as he signed the bill, Herbert Hoover instructed his attorney general to declare that its provisions "are of such a controversial nature that they . . . can only be set at rest by judicial decision." Pepper's warning about labor's restiveness thus resounded loudly into the Depression decade. In 1937 it would shake the very pillars of the Supreme Court.[25]

The organized labor movement was also being killed by kindness. The precepts of "welfare capitalism" found increasing favor with personnel managers who adopted the industrial management techniques promulgated earlier in the century by Frederick Winslow Taylor. Some corporations, typically large and antiunion, sought simultaneously to win the loyalty of their workers and to defang union organizers. They set up "company unions" and offered stock bonuses and profit-sharing plans, as well as life insurance, recreational facilities, and even old-age pensions. It was among the precepts of welfare capitalism, however, that control of all these programs remained tightly in the hands of their corporate sponsor, who could modify or terminate them at will. When the Crash came, the transient generosity of employers was starkly revealed as a shabby substitute for the genuine power of collective bargaining that only an independent union could wield — or for the entitled benefits that only the federal government could confer.

THE TEN MILLION WOMEN who worked for wages in 1929 were concentrated in a small handful of occupations including teaching, clerical work, domestic service, and the garment trades. As the service sector of the economy had expanded, so had women's presence in the labor force. Women made up about 18 percent of all workers in 1900 and 22 percent in 1930, when about one of every four women was gainfully employed. The typical woman worker was single and under the age of twenty-five. Once she married, as almost every woman did, typically before the age of twenty-two, she was unlikely to work again for wages, particularly while she had children at home. Only one mother in ten worked outside the household, and the numbers of older women workers, with or without children, were few. Even in this late phase of the industrial era, the traditional division of family labor that the industrial revolution had introduced a century earlier — a husband working for wages outside the home, and a wife working without wages within it — still held powerful sway in American culture.[26]

25. Bernstein, *Lean Years*, 196, 201, 414. For the full text of the *Hitchman* decision, see 245 U.S. 229 (1917).
26. *Recent Social Trends* 1:277. See also Alice Kessler-Harris, *Out to Work: A History of Wage-Earning Women in the United States* (New York: Oxford University Press, 1982), esp. chap. 8.

Yet traditional definitions of the family, and of women's place within it, were weakening. Married women might remain a distinct minority of all women workers, but their numbers were increasing at a rate nearly triple the rate of growth in female employment as a whole. Here, well before the century's midpoint, the dynamic changes in women's employment patterns that would transform the very fabric of family life by the century's end were already visible, however faintly.[27]

Other evidences of changes in women's status were more immediately apparent. The legendary "flapper" made her debut in the postwar decade, signaling with studied theatrical flourishes a new ethos of feminine freedom and sexual parity. The Nineteenth Amendment, enacted just in time for the 1920 presidential election, gave women at least formal political equality. The Equal Rights Amendment, first proposed by Alice Paul of the National Women's Party in 1923, sought to guarantee full social and economic participation to women. An organized movement for the promotion of birth control, founded by Margaret Sanger in 1921 as the American Birth Control League, heralded a growing feminine focus on reproductive control and erotic liberation. Countless women, especially if they were urban, white, and affluent, now used the new technologies of spermicidal jelly and the Mensinga-type diaphragm, both first manufactured in quantity in the United States in the 1920s, to limit the size of their families. This development worried the authors of *Recent Social Trends*, who feared that the old-stock, white, urban middle class would be demographically swamped by the proliferation of the rural and immigrant poor, as well as blacks.

Many of these developments unsettled the guardians of traditional values, but others they found pleasing. The exploitation of child labor, a practice that had outraged critics from Charles Dickens in Victorian England to Jane Addams in early twentieth-century America, had slowly receded as rising wages enabled a single wage-earner to support a family. While almost one in five ten- to-fifteen-year-olds was employed in 1890, fewer than one in twenty was in 1930, though the Supreme Court repeatedly struck down federal efforts to legislate a total ban on child labor.[28]

27. *Recent Social Trends* 1:666. See also Kessler-Harris, *Out to Work*, 229.
28. *Recent Social Trends* 1:271ff. The Keating-Owen Child Labor Act of 1916 had been invalidated by the Supreme Court in 1918 in the case of *Hammer v. Dagenhart* (247 U.S. 251), on the grounds that the act illegitimately relied on the commerce power to regulate local labor conditions. Four years later the Court threw out a second child labor act on similar grounds, in *Bailey v. Drexel Furniture* (259 U.S. (20).

Fewer children working meant more children in school. The authors of *Recent Social Trends* saw grounds for celebration in their finding that in the 1920s, for the first time, a near majority of high school–age students remained in school — constituting an eightfold increase in high school enrollments since 1900. This, they concluded, was "evidence of the most successful single effort which government in the United States has ever put forth."[29]

THE EDUCATIONAL SUCCESSES of the decade were as costly as they were dramatic. Virtually all of that cost was borne by the states, as were most of the expenditures for improved roads on which to drive all those new automobiles. As a consequence, the indebtedness of the states increased sharply in the 1920s, in many cases rising to formal ceilings defined by legislation or to practical ceilings imposed by the credit markets. State and local taxes also rose steeply, far outpacing the rate of growth of personal income. By 1929 government at all levels collected in taxes a share of the national income twice as large as in 1914. Americans were devoting a growing share of their wealth not just to private consumption but to collective purposes — and many of them resented it. Though the 15 percent of the value of gross national product that went to taxes in 1929 looked puny by later standards, it represented a historically unprecedented tax bite and was beginning to provoke a political backlash. The rising cry for "balanced budgets" and for restraints on government spending arose not only from the musty vaults of fiscal orthodoxy but at least as loudly from the throats of citizens whose tax bills had doubled in little more than a decade.[30]

The federal government had also vastly increased its tax levies, though most of that new revenue went not to pay for new social infrastructure like education and roads but to service the debt incurred while fighting the World War. To a later generation the debt created by the war might seem trifling, but to contemporaries it was enormous — some $24 billion, or ten times the indebtedness generated by the Civil War. Interest payments on the national debt rose from an insignificant level of about $25 million annually before 1914 to the largest single government expendi-

---

These cases symbolized the social and economic conservatism on the Court that so outraged reformers from Theodore Roosevelt to Franklin Roosevelt, whose frustration finally erupted in the notorious "Court-packing" proposal of 1937 (see Chapter 11).

29. *Recent Social Trends* 1:xlvii.
30. *Recent Social Trends* 2:1333–39.

ture in the 1920s: nearly a billion dollars a year, or a third of the federal budget.

Together with expenditures for veterans' benefits, another obligation that mushroomed because of the war, interest payments composed more than half the federal budget through the postwar decade. Expenses for a modest army of some 139,000 men and a navy of about 96,000 sailors accounted for virtually all the remainder. Beyond these items, all of them related to national security, the federal government spent and did little. Calvin Coolidge thus spoke with small exaggeration when he said: "If the Federal Government should go out of existence, the common run of people would not detect the difference in the affairs of their daily life for a considerable length of time." So negligible was the role of the federal government in their lives that a majority of citizens did not even bother to vote in presidential elections. For the first time since the emergence of mass-based democratic politics in the age of Andrew Jackson, electoral participation rates fell below 50 percent in the election of 1920; they sank still further in 1924. Some observers attributed this precipitous drop-off to the recent enfranchisement of women, who were largely unfamiliar with the ballot and perhaps justifiably indifferent to a national political apparatus that was in turn indifferent to their particular political interests. Others pointed to the apparent political apathy of immigrants, many of whom had not yet made a permanent commitment to remaining in the United States. But women and immigrants may have only been special cases of a general unconcern in American culture for the federal government, which remained a distant, dim, and motionless body in the political firmament.[31]

Since the election of William McKinley in 1896, with the singular interruption of Woodrow Wilson's presidency from 1913 to 1921, the federal government had been securely in the hands of the Republican Party. Grover Cleveland, president from 1885 to 1889 and again from 1893 to 1897, was the only other Democrat besides Wilson to have occupied the White House since before the Civil War. For generations after Appomattox, the Democrats had retained much of the character of a purely regional party, with the "solid South" their only sure electoral base. They struggled to win presidential elections, with only fitful success, by adding to this core of support what votes they could muster from immigrant communities in northeastern cities like Boston and New York. Occasionally, too, they could count on support in the "But-

31. Coolidge quoted in Schlesinger 1:57.

ternut" regions of the Illinois-Indiana-Ohio tier of states populated largely by white migrants from the Old South and still very much southern in temperament and political preference.

Democrats, strong in the cotton region, generally agreed on a low-tariff policy but on little else. Hard-money "Bourbon" Democrats in the Grover Cleveland mold clashed with inflationists whose perennial champion was William Jennings Bryan, "Boy Orator of the Platte," the "Great Commoner" whose affected rusticity symbolized the economic and cultural gulf that separated Main Street from Wall Street. Self-made men like James Michael Curley of Boston or Al Smith and Robert Wagner of New York, champions of labor who had scrambled up out of immigrant ghettoes like Roxbury or Hell's Kitchen, sat uneasily in party councils with cotton-South barons like Mississippi's Senator Pat Harrison or rural Texans like John Nance Garner, men who saw in cheap, nonunion labor their region's major economic resource. Cerebral reformers like Harvard law professor Felix Frankfurter barely coexisted in the same party with antic populist demagogues like Louisiana's Huey Long. Cultural differences, too, cleaved the party along the lines that separated Catholics and Jews from old-stock Protestants, divided anti-Prohibition "wets" from fundamentalist "drys," and distanced urban immigrants from rural Klansmen. These conflicting forces had locked in such irreconcilable conflict at the Democrats' presidential nominating convention of 1924 in New York that only after 103 ballots did the weary and sweltering delegates settle on a compromise ticket. It had corporation lawyer John W. Davis at its head and Nebraska governor Charles W. Bryan, brother of the Great Commoner, in the vice-presidential slot. Davis's crushing defeat by Calvin Coolidge seemed to confirm the suspicions of many pundits that the roiling, fractionated mob known as the Democratic Party could never be fashioned into a coherent instrument of governance. "I don't belong to an organized political party," quipped America's favorite humorist, Will Rogers. "I'm a Democrat."

Hoover's decisive victory over Al Smith in 1928 clinched the point. Smith was not merely defeated. He was humiliated, the victim of an electoral mortification that may have contributed to his later political transmutation from working-class hero to embittered foe of the New Deal. Following a campaign notoriously marred by religious bigotry against the Catholic Smith, Hoover swept to one of the most decisive victories in the history of American presidential elections. He even cracked the solid South, winning five former Confederate states. Smith took Massachusetts, Rhode Island, and the tier of six "black belt" states—South Carolina, Georgia, Alabama, Mississippi, Arkansas, and Louisiana—that held to their traditional Democratic allegiance. That was all. The remainder of the country thunderously rejected a candidate who was not only Catholic but a "wet" foe of Prohibition as well as a rasping symbol of the urban, immigrant culture that America was still not ready to recognize as its own. Democrats took what comfort they could from the fact that Smith cobbled together a majority of votes in the dozen biggest cities—foreshadowing the urban-based coalition that the New Deal would fully forge in the next decade.[32]

The Republican Party, then as always, was more economically and ethnically homogenous than the Democratic Party, but it too, in the manner of mass-based, "catch-all" American parties, contained its own conflicting elements. Under Theodore Roosevelt's leadership in the century's first decade, the Republicans had bid for a brief season to recapture their birthright claim to be the party of reform. But TR had shepherded his progressive followers out of the Republican fold and into the third-party "Bull Moose" schism of 1912. He thereby ensured the election of Wilson and contributed as well to the consolidation of conservative rule in the GOP. Some former Bull Moosers, like Chicago reformer and future New Deal secretary of the interior Harold Ickes, became Democrats in all but name; others, like Nebraska's Senator George Norris, were relegated to an impotent minority in party councils during the triumphal conservative ascendancy of the 1920s.

The progressives of Theodore Roosevelt's day were a varied lot, and some of their disagreements would reverberate, often loudly, right through the New Deal. But they shared a commitment, as Walter Lippmann had said, to substitute mastery for drift, or, as Hoover might have put it, social planning for laissez-faire: a commitment, in short, to use government as an agency of human welfare. Progressives of all persuasions believed that government must somehow superintend the phenomenal economic and social power that modern industrialism was concen-

32. Samuel Lubell, *The Future of American Politics* (New York: Harper and Row, 1952), first made the argument that "before the Roosevelt Revolution there was an Al Smith Revolution," one that began the process of gathering into a durable electoral majority the urban ethnic voters who sustained the New Deal and the Democratic Party well into the post–World War II period. That view has been sharply challenged by Allan J. Lichtman, *Prejudice and the Old Politics* (Chapel Hill: University of North Carolina Press, 1979), which concludes that Smith's urban majorities were paper thin and that it was not, therefore, the events of the 1920s but the catastrophe of the Depression that truly realigned American political behavior.

trating into fewer and fewer hands. No longer could the public interest simply be assumed to flow naturally from the competition of myriad private interests. Active governmental guidance was required.

The conservative Republicans who recaptured the Congress in 1918 and the White House in 1920 had small use for any form of government activism. The Republican administrations of the 1920s abandoned or reversed many progressive policies and eviscerated most others. Harding's attorney general, Harry M. Daugherty, extinguished a railroad workers' strike in 1922 by successfully petitioning a federal judge for the most stifling antilabor injunction ever issued. In the same year, Congress reverted to traditional Republican protectionism, as the Fordney-McCumber Tariff raised import duties to the forbidding levels that obtained before the World War. Coolidge appointed to the chairmanship of the Federal Trade Commission in 1925 a man who believed the commission was "an instrument of oppression and disturbance and injury," a statement that only slightly exaggerated conservative opinion about all regulatory agencies. Both the Harding and Coolidge administrations resisted progressive proposals for federal development of hydroelectric generating stations on the Tennessee River, notably at Muscle Shoals, Alabama. And Harding's minions displayed their rapacious regard for the nation's environmental endowment in the Teapot Dome and Elk Hills scandals, when they tried to lease the U.S. Navy's oil reserves in Wyoming and California to private interests with which they were associated.[33]

No one better represented the hoary precepts of laissez-faire that were now reenshrined in policy than the unfortunate Harding's phlegmatic successor, Calvin Coolidge. "Mr. Coolidge was a real conservative, probably the equal of Benjamin Harrison," said Herbert Hoover, who was frequently at odds with his chief. "He was a fundamentalist in religion, in the economic and social order, and in fishing," added Hoover, who had a fly fisherman's disdain for Coolidge's artless reliance on worms. Famously mum, Coolidge occasionally emitted pithy slogans that summarized conservative Republican orthodoxy. "The chief business of the American people is business," he legendarily pronounced in 1925. He declared only somewhat more expansively on another occasion that "the man who builds a factory builds a temple; the man who works there worships there."[34]

33. William E. Humphrey quoted in Schlesinger 1:65.
34. Hoover, *Memoirs: The Cabinet and the Presidency*, 56; Coolidge quoted in Schlesinger 1:57.

Coolidge's epigrams faithfully reflected the principles of frugality and laissez-faire that informed federal policies in the 1920s. The few, frail organs of the positive state spawned by the prewar progressives withered from inanition. Coolidge personally quashed Herbert Hoover's ambitious plans for federally financed river-control projects, especially in the parched West, because he deemed them too expensive. On similar grounds, he vetoed proposals for farm relief and for accelerated "bonus" payments to veterans of the World War. He resisted all efforts to restructure the $10 billion in Allied war debts owed to the U.S. Treasury. ("They hired the money, didn't they?" he declared in another pellet of policy summary.) Content with "Coolidge prosperity," he napped peacefully and often. He played pranks on the White House servants. He stayed silent. ("If you don't say anything, you won't be called on to repeat it," he reportedly said.) He believed, Hoover later recounted, that nine out of ten troubles "will run into the ditch before they reach you" and could therefore be safely ignored. "The trouble with this philosophy," Hoover commented, "was that when the tenth trouble reached him he was wholly unprepared, and it had by that time acquired such momentum that it spelled disaster. The outstanding instance was the rising boom and orgy of mad speculation which began in 1927, in respect to which he rejected or sidestepped all our anxious urgings and warnings to take action." For his part, Coolidge said of Hoover in 1928: "That man has offered me unsolicited advice for six years, all of it bad."[35]

Fortune smiled on the recumbent Coolidge until he made his somnambulatory exit from the White House in early 1929. (A wit allegedly greeted the news that Coolidge was dead in 1933 by asking: "How can you tell?") "In the domestic field there is tranquility and contentment," he serenely informed the Congress in his last State of the Union message on December 4, 1928. The country should "regard the present with satisfaction and anticipate the future with optimism."[36]

PROSPERITY LASTED long enough for Coolidge to sound plausible in 1928. But deep down in the bowels of the economy, small but fateful contractions had already set in. The agonies of agriculture had long been apparent. Now other sectors began to feel similar pain. Automobile manufacturing slowed its prodigious rate of growth as early as

35. Hoover, *Memoirs: The Cabinet and the Presidency*, 56; Wilson, *Herbert Hoover*, 122.
36. Quoted in John Kenneth Galbraith, *The Great Crash* (Boston: Houghton Mifflin, 1955), 6.

1925. Residential construction turned down in the same year. A boom in Florida real estate drowned in a devastating hurricane in September 1926. Bank clearings in Miami sank from over a billion dollars in 1925 to $143 million in 1928, a chilling adumbration of the financial clotting that would soon choke the entire banking system. Business inventories began to pile up in 1928, nearly quadrupling in value to some $2 billion by midsummer of 1929.[37]

Most ominous of all was what Hoover bluntly labeled the "orgy of mad speculation" that beset the stock market beginning in 1927. Theory has it that the bond and equity markets reflect and even anticipate the underlying realities of making and marketing goods and services, but by 1928 the American stock markets had slipped the bonds of surly reality. They catapulted into a phantasmagorical realm where the laws of rational economic behavior went unpromulgated and prices had no discernible relation to values. While business activity steadily subsided, stock prices levitated giddily. By the end of 1928, John Kenneth Galbraith later wrote, "the market began to rise, not by slow, steady steps, but by great vaulting leaps." Radio Corporation's stock, symbolic of the promise of new technologies that helped to feed the speculative frenzy, gyrated upward in ten-and twenty-point jumps. By the summer of 1929, Frederick Lewis Allen recorded, even as unsold inventories accumulated in warehouses, stock prices "soared . . . into the blue and cloudless empyrean."[38]

Money to fuel the skyrocketing stock market flowed from countless spigots. It flowed so copiously, according to Galbraith, that "it seemed as though Wall Street were by way of devouring all the money of the entire world." Some of the money flowed directly from the pocketbooks of individual investors, though their resources were generally meager and their numbers surprisingly few. More money poured from big corporations. Their healthy profits in the 1920s endowed them with lavish cash reserves, a good share of which they began to divert from productive investment in plant and machinery to stock market speculation. Still more money came from the banking system. It, too, was flush with funds that found fewer and fewer traditional outlets. By 1929 commercial bankers were in the unusual position of loaning more money for stock market and real estate investments than for commercial ventures. The Federal Reserve Board flooded the banks with more liquidity in 1927 by

37. Frederick Lewis Allen, *Only Yesterday*, (New York: Harper and Brothers, 1931), 282.
38. Galbraith, *Great Crash*, 17; Allen, *Only Yesterday*, 309.

lowering its rediscount rate to 3.5 percent and undertaking heavy purchases of government securities.[39]

This easy-money policy was due largely to the influence of Benjamin Strong, the stern and influential governor of the New York Federal Reserve Bank. Strong's policy was meant to support the imprudent decision Chancellor of the Exchequer Winston Churchill had made in 1925 to return Britain to the prewar gold standard at the old exchange rate of $4.86 to the pound. That unrealistically high rate crimped British exports, boomed imports, and threatened to drain the Bank of England of its gold reserves. Strong reasoned, not incorrectly, that lower interest rates and cheaper money in America would stanch the hemorrhage of gold from London to New York, thus stabilizing an international financial system that was still precariously recovering from the strains of the World War. The same policies, of course, facilitated vast speculative borrowing in the United States. It was that disastrous consequence that prompted Herbert Hoover's contemptuous description of Strong as "a mental annex to Europe"—a remark that also hinted at Hoover's conception of where the blame for the ensuing depression should be laid.

Significantly, much of the money lent by banks for stock purchases went not directly into stocks but into brokers' call loans. Call loans enabled purchasers to buy stocks on margin, leveraging a cash payment (sometimes as little as 10 percent, but more typically 45 or 50 percent, of the stock's price) with a loan secured by the value of the stock purchased. The lender could theoretically "call" for repayment if the stock price dropped by an amount equal to its collateral value. Though some of the larger brokerage houses shunned the call-loan device, most made profligate use of it. The practice became so popular that brokers at the height of the boom could charge prodigious interest rates on their stock-secured loans to customers. Thanks to the Federal Reserve System's low rediscount rate, member banks could and did borrow federal funds at 3.5 percent and relend them in the call market for 10 percent and more. When the demand for call loans overwhelmed even the abundantly liquid resources of the banking system, corporations stepped in. They accounted for roughly half the call-loan monies in 1929. Standard Oil

39. Galbraith, *Great Crash*, 73. The composition of banks' loan portfolios had changed significantly in the 1920s. In 1913 commercial banks placed 53 percent of their loans in commercial ventures, 33 percent in securities, and 14 percent in real estate. By 1929 those figures were respectively 45, 38, and 17 percent. Susan Estabrook Kennedy, *The Banking Crisis of 1933* (Lexington: University Press of Kentucky, 1973), 13.

of New Jersey was then loaning some $69 million a day; Electric Bond and Share, over $100 million.[40]

All of this extravagantly available credit did not in itself cause the boom, just as fuel alone does not make a fire. Combustion in the financial world, no less than in the physical, requires not only fuel but also oxygen and ignition. No observer has succeeded in pinpointing the spark that set off the roaring conflagration that swept and eventually consumed the securities markets in 1928 and 1929. Clearly, however, its sustaining oxygen was a matter not only of recondite market mechanisms and traders' technicalities but also of simple atmospherics — specifically, the mood of speculative expectation that hung feverishly in the air and induced fantasies of effortless wealth that surpassed the dreams of avarice.

Much blame has been leveled at a feckless Federal Reserve System for failing to tighten credit as the speculative fires spread, but while it is arguable that the easy-money policies of 1927 helped to kindle the blaze, the fact is that by late 1928 it had probably burned beyond controlling by orthodox financial measures. The Federal Reserve Board justifiably hesitated to raise its rediscount rate for fear of penalizing non-speculative business borrowers. When it did impose a 6 percent rediscount rate in the late summer of 1929, call loans were commanding interest of close to 20 percent — a spread that the Fed could not have bridged without catastrophic damage to legitimate borrowers. Similarly, the board had early exhausted its already meager ability to soak up funds through open-market sales of government securities. By the end of 1928, the system's inventory of such securities barely exceeded $200 million — a pittance compared to the nearly $8 billion in call loans then outstanding. By ordinary measures, in fact, credit was tight after 1928. Mere money was not at the root of the evil soon to befall Wall Street; men were — men, and women, whose lust for the fast buck had loosed all restraints of financial prudence or even common sense.

The first rumbles of distress were heard in September 1929, when stock prices broke unexpectedly, though they swiftly recovered. Then on Wednesday, October 23, came an avalanche of liquidation. A huge volume of more than six million shares changed hands, wiping out some $4 billion in paper values. Confusion spread as the telegraphic ticker that flashed transactions to traders across the country fell nearly two hours behind.

40. Galbraith, *Great Crash*, 36.

In this atmosphere of anxiety and uncertainty, the market opened on "Black Thursday," October 24, with a landslide of sell orders. A record-shattering 12,894,650 shares were traded. By noon, losses had reached some $9 billion. The ticker ran four hours late. Yet when it clacked off the day's last transaction at 7:08 in the evening, it appeared that a small recovery in prices had contained the session's losses to about a third of the previous day's.

If Thursday was black, what could be said of the following Tuesday, October 29, when 16,410,000 shares were bought and sold—a record that stood for thirty-nine years? "Black Tuesday" pulled down a cloak of gloom over Wall Street. Traders abandoned all hope that the frightful shake-out could somehow be averted. For two more ghastly weeks stock prices continued to plummet freely down the same celestial voids through which they had recently and so wondrously ascended. The stark truth was now revealed that leverage worked two ways. The multiplication of values that buying on margin made possible in a rising market worked with impartial and fearful symmetry when values were on the way down. Slippage of even a few points in a stock's price compelled margin loans to be called. The borrower then had to put up more cash or accept forced sale of the security. Millions of such sales occurring simultaneously blew the floor out from under many stocks. The mercilessly downward slide went on for three weeks after Black Tuesday. By mid-November some $26 billion, roughly a third of the value of stocks recorded in September, had evaporated.[41]

Much mythology surrounds these dramatic events in the autumn of 1929. Perhaps the most imperishable misconception portrays the Crash as the cause of the Great Depression that persisted through the decade of the 1930s. This scenario owes its durability, no doubt, to its intuitive plausibility and to its convenient fit with the canons of narrative, which require historical accounts to have recognizable beginnings, middles, and ends and to explain events in terms of identifiable origins, development, and resolution. These conventions are comforting; they render understandable and thus tolerable even the most terrifying human experiences. The storyteller and the shaman sometimes feed the same psychic needs.

41. Colorful accounts of the stock market crash of 1929 can be found in Allen's *Only Yesterday* and Galbraith's *Great Crash*. Somewhat more reliable are Robert Sobel's *The Great Bull Market: Wall Street in the 1920s* (New York: Norton, 1968) and *Panic on Wall Street* (New York: Macmillan, 1968).

The disagreeable truth, however, is that the most responsible students of the events of 1929 have been unable to demonstrate an appreciable cause-and-effect linkage between the Crash and the Depression. None assigns to the stock market collapse exclusive responsibility for what followed; most deny it primacy among the many and tangled causes of the decade-long economic slump; some assert that it played virtually no role whatsoever. One authority states flatly and summarily that "no causal relationship between the events of late October 1929 and the Great Depression has ever been shown through the use of empirical evidence."[42]

Certainly contemporaries took this view of the matter in the immediate aftermath of the Crash, as 1929 gave way to 1930. They could scarcely do otherwise, since in point of fact there was as yet no evident depression, "Great" or otherwise, to be explained. Some writers later made much sport of Herbert Hoover for pronouncing on October 25, 1929, that "the fundamental business of the country, that is, production and distribution of commodities, is on a sound and prosperous basis."[43] Yet in retrospect that statement appears reasonably and responsibly accurate. To be sure, a business slowdown was detectable by midsummer 1929, but as yet there was little reason to consider it anything more than a normal dip in the business cycle.

What was clearly abnormal was the explosive near doubling of stock prices since 1928. Hoover had long warned against speculative excesses and could now credibly regard the Crash as the long-predicted correction, one that would at last purge the economic system of unhealthy toxins. In this view he had abundant company, much of it distinguished. John Maynard Keynes opined from England that Black Thursday had been a healthy development that would redirect funds from speculative to productive uses. The respected New York Times financial writer Alexander Dana Noyes called the Crash "a reaction from an orgy of reckless speculation" and echoed Hoover's appraisal by adding that "no such excesses had been practiced by trade and industry." The American Eco-

---

42. Sobel, Great Bull Market, 147. Other recent scholars are not quite this categorical but substantially share Sobel's conclusion. See, for example, Peter Temin, Did Monetary Forces Cause the Great Depression? (New York: Norton, 1976), esp. 69–83; and Michael A. Bernstein, The Great Depression: Delayed Recovery and Economic Change in America, 1929–1939 (Cambridge: Cambridge University Press, 1987), esp. 4–7.

43. Notably Schlesinger in The Crisis of the Old Order (Schlesinger 1) and Galbraith in The Great Crash.

nomic Association in December 1929 predicted recovery by June 1930. Early in 1930 the *New York Times* obliquely indicated contemporary assessment of the significance of the Crash when it declared that the most important news story of 1929 had been Admiral Byrd's expedition to the South Pole.[44]

The behavior of the financial markets themselves confirmed these sentiments in the weeks following the Crash. By April 1930 stock prices had regained some 20 percent of their losses of the previous autumn. The *New York Times* average of industrial stocks then stood about where it had at the beginning of 1929, which was approximately double the level of 1926. Unlike previous panics on Wall Street, this one had thus far seen the failure of no major company or bank. As the last moments of 1929 slipped away, the great crash could be plausibly understood as an outsized but probably freakish event. For many individual stockholders, the Crash had assuredly constituted a calamity, but the calamity was not a depression. Not yet.

Another of the fables that has endured from that turbulent autumn — thanks largely to the immense popularity of Frederick Lewis Allen's nostalgic essay of 1931, *Only Yesterday* — portrays legions of slap-happy small stockholders, drunk with the dreams of the delirious decade, suddenly wiped out by the Crash and cast en masse into the gloom of depression.[45] This familiar picture, too, is grossly distorted. Allen probably relied on an estimate by the New York Stock Exchange in 1929 that some twenty million Americans owned stocks. That figure was later shown to be wildly exaggerated. The chief actuary of the Treasury De-

44. Sobel, *Great Bull Market*, 136–37, 145–46; David Burner, *Herbert Hoover: A Public Life* (New York: Knopf, 1979), 250. Noyes, it is true, prudently added: "We do not yet know whether this present episode is or is not an old-time 'major crisis.'"

45. Galbraith cites Allen's description of a chauffeur, a window cleaner, a valet, a nurse, and a cattleman who all played the market. Even so august an authority as Paul Samuelson, citing Allen, declares: "In the United States during the fabulous stock-market boom of the 'roaring twenties,' housewives, Pullman porters, college students between classes—all bought and sold stocks." See Galbraith, *Great Crash*, 82, and Paul Samuelson, *Economics: An Introductory Analysis*, 5th ed. (New York: McGraw-Hill, 1961), 143–44. Peter Temin also blames Allen in part for giving powerful impetus to the myth of the Crash as the principal cause of the Depression: "The stock-market crash was for [Allen] the dividing point between unbounded optimism and equally uncontainable pessimism. . . . In Allen's mind . . . the stock-market crash became the symbol of the vast discrepancy between the 1920s and the 1930s. . . . [But] the symbol and the reality must be carefully distinguished." Temin, *Did Monetary Forces*, 75–76.

partment calculated that only about three million Americans — less than 2.5 percent of the population — owned securities in 1928, and brokerage firms reported a substantially lower number of 1,548,707 customers in 1929.[46]

So, legend to the contrary, the average American — a description that in this case encompasses at least 97.5 percent of the population — owned no stock in 1929. Even indirect ownership of stock must have been minimal, in this age before the creation of pension funds gave millions of workers a financial stake in capitalism. Accordingly, the Crash in itself had little direct or immediate economic effect on the typical American. The Depression, however, would be another story.

As 1930 OPENED, the investigators compiling *Recent Social Trends* were just beginning their researches. Taking their presidential mission seriously, they were much interested in that typical American.[47] His age, they determined, was twenty-six. (He would have been a male, this hypothetically abstracted individual, as men continued to outnumber women in the United States until 1950, when the effects of declining immigration, heavily male, and rising maternal survival rates made women for the first time a numerical majority in the American population.) He had been born during the first term of Theodore Roosevelt's presidency, in the midst of the progressive reform ferment. His birth occurred about the time that Japan launched a surprise attack on the Russian fleet at Port Arthur, China — an attack that led to war, Russian defeat, and the first Russian revolution (in 1905) and that heralded Japan's ambition to play the great-power game.

About a million immigrants — virtually none of them Japanese, thanks to a distasteful "gentlemen's agreement" by which the Japanese government grudgingly agreed to limit its export of people — entered the United States in every year of his early childhood. He had reached the age of ten when World War I broke out in 1914, and he had just become a teenager — a term, indeed a concept, not yet in wide use — when President Woodrow Wilson took the United States into the war. By the time the fighting ended, in 1918, he had left the eighth grade and completed his formal schooling. (He would have completed it some three years earlier if he had been black.)

46. Sobel, *Great Bull Market*, 73–74; Galbraith, *Great Crash*, 83.
47. The discussion that follows is mainly based on *Recent Social Trends*, passim, and on HSUS. It takes as its point of departure for defining the life cycle of the "typical" American of 1930 the datum that the median age in that year was 26.5.

He was too young to have seen battle, but he soon concluded that the whole business of sending American troops to Europe was a useless, colossal blunder and an inexcusable departure from the venerable American doctrine of isolation. The spectacle of wretched Europeans going bankrupt in Germany, knuckling under to a fascist dictator in Italy, welcoming Bolsheviks — Bolsheviks! — in Russia, and then, to top it off, refusing to pay their war debts to the United States confirmed the wisdom of traditional isolationism, so far as he was concerned.

Raised in the country without flush toilets or electric lighting, as the 1920s opened he moved to the city, to an apartment miraculously plumbed and wired. In the streets he encountered the abundant and exotic offspring of all those immigrants who had arrived when he was a baby. Together they entered the new era when their country was transiting, bumpily, without blueprints or forethought, from an agricultural to an industrial economy, from values of simple rural frugality to values of flamboyant urban consumerism, and, however much the idea was resisted, from provincial isolationism to inevitable international involvement.

Jobs were plentiful for the moment and paid good wages. With hard work he was making a little more than a hundred dollars a month. He had been laid off several times in the preceding years but had built a small cushion of savings at his bank to tide him over when unemployment hit again, as he knew it must. The stock market had just crashed, but it seemed to be recovering, and in any case he owned no stocks — for that matter, neither did anybody he knew. Evenings he "radioed." Weekends he went to the movies, better now that they had sound. Sometimes he broke the law and lifted a glass. On his one day a week off, he took a drive in the car that he was buying on the installment plan.

He was living better than his parents had ever dreamed of living. He was young and vigorous; times were good, and the future promised to be still better. He had just cast his first presidential vote, in 1928, for Herbert Hoover, the most competent man in America, maybe in the world. In that same year he married a girl three years younger than he. She gave up her job to have their first baby. They started to think of buying a house, perhaps in one of the new suburbs. Life was just beginning.

And their world was about to come apart.

2

Panic

You know, the only trouble with capitalism is capitalists; they're too damn greedy.

—Herbert Hoover to Mark Sullivan

When Herbert Hoover was inaugurated on March 4, 1929, wrote journalist Anne O'Hare McCormick, "[w]e were in a mood for magic. . . . [T]he whole country was a vast, expectant gallery, its eyes focused on Washington. We had summoned a great engineer to solve our problems for us; now we sat back comfortably and confidently to watch the problems being solved. The modern technical mind was for the first time at the head of a government. . . . Almost with the air of giving genius its chance, we waited for the performance to begin."[1] The wait was not long, as Hoover promptly summoned Congress into special session to deal with the stubborn depression in agriculture.

Convening on April 15, the representatives quickly learned that the new president would not tolerate any revival of McNary-Haugen proposals for export subsidies. Instead, Hoover demanded "the creation of a great instrumentality clothed with sufficient authority and resources to . . . transfer the agricultural question from the field of politics into the realm of economics."[2] Awed by Hoover's aura of command, Congress swiftly obliged. "The President is so immensely popular over the country," said one senator, "that the Republicans here are on their knees and the Democrats have their hats off."[3] On June 15 the president signed

1. Anne O'Hare McCormick, "A Year of the Hoover Method," *New York Times*, March 2, 1930, sec. 5, 1.
2. Quoted in Harris Gaylord Warren, *Herbert Hoover and the Great Depression* (New York: Oxford University Press, 1959), 169.
3. South Dakota Republican senator Peter Norbeck to G. J. Moen, April 20, 1929, quoted in Jordan A. Schwarz, *The Interregnum of Despair: Hoover, Congress, and the Depression* (Urbana: University of Illinois Press, 1970), 6.

the Agricultural Marketing Act, creating the Federal Farm Board, with capital of $500 million, to promote agricultural cooperatives and stabilization corporations. The cooperatives were to sustain orderly markets in various commodities—cotton, wool, and pecans, for example—by facilitating voluntary agreements among producers. If the co-ops failed to bring order to their respective markets, the stabilization corporations would stand ready to buy unmanageable surpluses. When the members of the Farm Board gathered at the White House on July 15, a triumphant Hoover rightly informed them that they had been invested with "responsibility, authority and resources such as have never before been conferred by our government in assistance to any industry."[4]

The great performance seemed well begun, and not without a touch of magic. In just sixty days the Great Engineer had wrung from Congress a bold remedy for the agricultural depression that had persisted for nearly a decade. What was more, the remedy bore the unmistakable signs of Hoover's own distinctive political genius. It embodied the principle of government-stimulated voluntary cooperation that lay at the heart of his social thought, even while it provided for direct government intervention in the private economy if voluntarism proved inadequate.

To a degree uncommon among presidents, Hoover was a reflective man of scholarly bent, even something of a political philosopher. Ironically, the very care with which he had crafted his guiding principles, and the firmness of his commitment to them, would in time count among his major liabilities as a leader. So would his habits of solitude, formed early in life and reinforced by cruel experience.

Hoover had been born into a Quaker family in West Branch, Iowa, in 1874. His father died when Herbert was six; his mother, just over three years later. The shy orphan child was shunted among Quaker relatives and friends, first in Iowa, and then all the way to Newberg, Oregon, where at the age of fifteen he was sent to live with an uncle who was a schoolmaster and a stern disciplinarian. All his life he bore the imprint of his rural, Quaker origins. He dressed plainly, spoke simply, faced the world with a serenely impassive demeanor, and listened gravely to the voice of his conscience. The early loss of his parents and his upbringing among near strangers forged the growing boy's natural

---

4. By the time the Farm Board was fully functional, the deepening global depression had so dampened agricultural prices that even the unprecedented sums appropriated in June 1929 were woefully insufficient to stem the downward slide. The board went out of existence in 1933, after having lost some $371 million in the futile effort to prop up prices. Schwarz, *Interregnum of Despair*, 172, 176.

aloofness into the mature man's studiously glacial reserve. By the time he arrived in Oregon, Hoover had already established his reputation as a withdrawn but conscientious loner, "the quietest, the most efficient, and the most industrious boy" she had ever met, said an Oregon acquaintance.[5]

After graduating with a degree in geology in Stanford University's "pioneer class" in 1895, Hoover worked briefly as a day laborer in the nearly spent Sierra mining fields. Then in 1897 he accepted a job with Bewick, Moreing, a London-based international mining concern that sent the intense young engineer to Australia to scout for gold. He soon found it and quickly thereafter helped to develop new technologies for more efficiently extracting gold from ore. His employers were well pleased. When Hoover returned from an another assignment to China in 1900 with the deed to a vast new coalfield, Bewick, Moreing made him a partner. For the next fourteen years Hoover traveled the world, developing and supervising mining operations in Australia, Asia, Africa, and Latin America. In 1909 he published *Principles of Mining*, a manual for engineers and managers that advocated collective bargaining, the eight-hour day, and serious attention to mine safety. The book became a standard text in mining schools and helped spread Hoover's reputation as an unusually progressive, enlightened businessman. In 1914, at the age of forty, having amassed a fortune estimated at some $4 million, he retired from active business. His Quaker conscience prodded him toward good works. So did his wife, Lou Henry Hoover, a fellow Stanford geology graduate he had married in 1899. She was a formidable woman who was his lifelong shield against the intrusive world, the organizer of punctiliously correct dinner parties at which Hoover took refuge behind a mask of decorum and formality.

When the Great War broke out, Hoover volunteered to organize international relief efforts for Belgium, then suffering under German occupation. His success at "feeding the starving Belgians" earned him an international reputation as a great humanitarian. Hoover returned to the United States in 1917 to serve as food administrator in Woodrow Wilson's wartime government. At war's end he accompanied Wilson to Paris as the president's personal adviser and as economic director of the Supreme Economic Council, chairman of the Inter-Allied Food Council, and chairman of the European Coal Council. As much as any one man

5. Joan Hoff Wilson, *Herbert Hoover: Forgotten Progressive* (Boston: Little, Brown, 1975), 10.

could, he got the credit for reorganizing the war-shattered European economy. He caused mines to be reopened, rivers to be cleared, bridges and roads rebuilt, food and medicine delivered. By the time the signatories penned their names on the treaty at Versailles, Hoover was a celebrated figure, an object of admiration tinged with awe. The reforming jurist Louis Brandeis thought him "the biggest figure injected into Washington life by the war." Hoover's "high public spirit, extraordinary intelligence, knowledge, sympathy, youth, and a rare perception of what is really worth-while for the country," enthused Brandeis, "would, with his organizing ability and power of inspiring loyalty, do wonderful things in the presidency." Assistant Secretary of the Navy Franklin D. Roosevelt proclaimed Hoover "certainly a wonder and I wish we could make him President of the United States. There could not be a better one."[6] Hoover's party affiliation was unknown at the war's end, and progressives of both parties courted him. But before long he declared himself a Republican, campaigned for Warren G. Harding, and was rewarded with appointment as secretary of commerce, a post he held for eight years.

Hoover's many years overseas had bred in him an acute interest in his own country's distinguishing cultural traits, and in 1922 he gathered his thoughts on this subject into a little book, *American Individualism*. A reviewer in the *New York Times* placed it "among the few great formulations of American political theory."[7] That praise may have been exaggerated—the product, perhaps, of the reader's wonder that a modern secretary of commerce could even hold his own in the intellectual precincts of Hamilton, Madison, and Jay—but *American Individualism* was by any measure an unusually thoughtful reflection on the American condition. It also provided an instructive guide to the ideas that informed Hoover's behavior as president.

"Individualism" was, after all, a concept that had been invented to describe a social development considered unique to American society. Alexis de Tocqueville had first given the term currency a century earlier in *Democracy in America*, in which he declared that "individualism is of democratic origin." It was different from mere selfishness, and in many ways more dangerous because more isolating. Selfishness, said Tocqueville, "leads a man to connect everything with himself, and to prefer himself to everything in the world," but individualism was still

6. Schlesinger 1:80–82.
7. Quoted in Wilson, *Herbert Hoover*, 55.

more pernicious, because it "disposes each member of the community to sever himself from the mass of his fellows, and to draw apart."[8]

Hoover argued, in effect, that Tocqueville had it all wrong; that *American* individualism was in its essence neither selfish nor solipsistic. Rather, it embraced regard for others and attachment to the community as a whole. In Hoover's lexicon, the word that captured the essence of American individualism was *service*. "The ideal of service," Hoover wrote in *American Individualism*, was a "great spiritual force poured out by our people as never before in the history of the world." It was a uniquely American ideal, and one that happily rendered unnecessary in America the repugnant growth of formal state power that afflicted other nations.[9]

Hoover revived, in a sense, the vision of a spontaneously mutualistic society inhabited by virtuous, public-spirited citizens that had inspired the republican theorists of the American Revolutionary era. No doubt his thinking was also influenced by his Quaker upbringing, with its gentle but firm emphasis on the values of consensus and reciprocity. From whatever source, Hoover gave voice to an individualism that was not simply the "rugged" and solitary sort that caricaturists somewhat unfairly put into his mouth (though he did in fact utter the phrase). His ideal individualism was, rather, communal and cooperative, arising from a faith in the better self of each citizen. The chief role of government was to articulate and orchestrate the aspirations of these better selves and to provide the information as well as the means for them to come together. Government might indeed step in where voluntarism had manifestly failed, but only after a fair trial. It was decidedly not the government's role arbitrarily and peremptorily to substitute coercive bureaucracy for voluntary cooperation. That way lay tyranny and the corruption of America's unique political soul.

Hoover could believe without difficulty that this vision was as practical as it was idealistic. He had made it work, after all, in the administration of Belgian relief and as food administrator during the war, when he self-consciously rejected the coercive techniques of the European belligerents and relied instead on massive educational and propaganda campaigns to spur production and limit domestic consumption of food

8. Alexis de Tocqueville, *Democracy in America* (New York: New American Library, 1956), 192–93.
9. Herbert Hoover, *American Individualism* (Garden City, N.Y.: Doubleday, Page, 1923), 28–29.

crops. He had made it work again in the sharp recession of 1921, when he had taken the unprecedented initiative of organizing the President's Conference on Unemployment. The conference publicized the plight of the nation's nearly five million unemployed workers, goading management to take corrective measures. It called for the routine collection of reliable statistical data on unemployment, so as to provide an informed basis for future federal policy. It envisioned combating future episodes of unemployment with countercyclical spending on public works. No previous administration had moved so purposefully and so creatively in the face of an economic downturn. Hoover had definitively made the point that government should not stand by idly when confronted with economic difficulty. Two years later, Hoover successfully shamed the steel industry into abandoning the man-killing twelve-hour day, again without resorting to formal legislation. Throughout the decade of the 1920s, he had promoted trade associations with the purpose of stabilizing prices, protecting employment, and rationalizing production in various industrial sectors, all through enlightened, voluntary cooperation among businessmen, with government's encouragement.

Now Hoover had the power and the pulpit of the presidency, and he meant to use the office vigorously. He had every reason to be satisfied, even exultant, over his performance in the special session of Congress that produced the Agricultural Marketing Act. He had given the country an impressive demonstration of his campaign declaration that "government must be a constructive force."[10] He intended to resurrect the reform spirit of the progressive era, buried by the war and by Harding-Coolidge conservatism. "Little had been done by the Federal government in the fields of reform or progress during the fourteen years before my time," he later reflected. "[B]y 1929 many things were already fourteen years overdue. I . . . had high hopes that I might lead in performing the task." He specified some of the reforms he had in mind: "We want to see a nation built of home owners and farm owners. We want to see their savings protected. We want to see them in steady jobs. We want to see more and more of them insured against death and accident, unemployment and old age. We want them all secure."[11]

10. Quoted in Albert U. Romasco, *The Poverty of Abundance: Hoover, the Nation, the Depression* (New York: Oxford University Press, 1965), 16.
11. Herbert Hoover, *The Memoirs of Herbert Hoover: The Cabinet and the Presidency, 1920–1933* (New York: Macmillan, 1952), 223; Arthur M. Schlesinger Jr., ed. *His-*

But Hoover's moment of exaltation was pitifully brief, and not just because of the financial crash that overtook him in the autumn of 1929. He
had masterfully shepherded the Agricultural Marketing Act through Congress, but he proved far less able to control another issue that was also unleashed in the special session: revision of the tariff. The Fordney-
McCumber Tariff Act of 1922 had already pegged most import levies at
forbiddingly high levels, yet the Republican platform in 1928 (as well as the
Democratic) called for still higher duties.[12] Hoover went along with his
party's plan for tariff revision because he wanted two things: higher duties
on certain agricultural imports, as part of his program to aid farmers, and a
strengthened Tariff Commission, with power to adjust import duties by 50
percent. This "flexible tariff," said Hoover, would "get the tariff out of Congressional logrolling" and thus be a large step toward reducing "excessive
and privileged protection." As for tariffs on manufactured goods, they
should be revised upward only where "there has been a substantial slack-
ening of activity in an industry during the past few years, and a consequent
decrease of employment due to insurmountable competition."[13]

Unfortunately, this last provision, however reasonably intended, was
an invitation to what progressive Republican senator George W. Norris
called "protection run perfectly mad."[14] Hoover showed himself utterly
unable to control the tariff legislation, and Congress proceeded to pass
the Hawley-Smoot Tariff of 1930, raising import duties to their highest

tory of American Presidential Elections, 1789–1968 (New York: Chelsea House,
1971), 3:2708–9.

12. Some writers, notably Jude Wanninski, have contended that the weakening of the
stock market in the fall of 1929 can be attributed to traders' fears about the prospect
of higher tariffs as the legislation made its way through Congress in the summer of
1929. Other writers even blame the historically high Hawley-Smoot Tariff of 1930
for causing the Depression itself. But both these charges, especially the latter, ignore
the fact that the Fordney-McCumber rates, as one historian puts it, were "already
. . . high enough to cause a depression if a tariff can have such a result." Warren,
Herbert Hoover and the Great Depression, 84. Both the Fordney-McCumber and
the Hawley-Smoot tariffs are better regarded as symptoms, not causes, of economic
distress in 1921 and 1929, respectively, and as continuing expressions of the protectionist pressures that were built into the very structure of congressional tariff-
making. It was his desire to remedy this structural defect that led Hoover to swallow
the Hawley-Smoot bill, since it provided him with a mechanism, in the form of a
reinvigorated Tariff Commission, by which he might circumvent Congress in administering the tariff law and eventually lowering rates.

13. Hoover, Memoirs: The Cabinet and the Presidency, 292–93.

14. Warren, Herbert Hoover, 90.

level in American history. In the end, Hoover swallowed Hawley-Smoot because of its provisions for flexibility, but in fact the tariff bill represented both an economic and a political catastrophe.

Economically, the Hawley-Smoot Tariff signaled the world that as the depression lowered the United States was moving toward the same autarkic, beggar-thy-neighbor, protectionist policies with which other nations were already dangerously flirting. Many observers warned of the perils of this position. One thousand economists signed a petition urging Hoover to veto the bill. Thomas Lamont, a partner in J. P. Morgan and Company and usually an influential economic adviser to Hoover, recalled that "I almost went down on my knees to beg Herbert Hoover to veto the asinine Hawley-Smoot Tariff. That Act intensified nationalism all over the world."[15]

Hoover himself appreciated these arguments but possessed neither the political power to stop the congressional steamroller nor the political will to veto the final legislation. He eventually signed the tariff into law in June 1930, prompting Walter Lippmann to complain that the president had "surrendered everything for nothing. He gave up the leadership of his party. He let his personal authority be flouted. He accepted a wretched and mischievous product of stupidity and greed." In this direct confrontation with a contrary-minded Congress, Hoover had failed the first great test of his capacity for political leadership. Now even supporters like Lippmann, who had praised Hoover in 1928 as "a reformer who is probably more vividly conscious of the defects of American capitalism than any man in public life today," began to doubt him. "He has the peculiarly modern, in fact, the contemporary American, faith in the power of the human mind and will, acting through organization, to accomplish results," Lippmann wrote, but "the unreasonableness of mankind is not accounted for in Mr. Hoover's philosophy. . . . In the realm of reason he is an unusually bold man; in the realm of unreason he is, for a statesman, an exceptionally thin-skinned and easily bewildered man. . . . He can face with equanimity almost any of the difficulties of statesmanship except the open conflict of wills. . . . The political art deals with matters peculiar to politics, with a complex of material circumstances, of historic deposit, of human passion, for which the problems of business or engineering as such do not provide an analogy." Ominously, the Great Engineer was showing himself to be a peculiarly artless politician.[16]

15. David Burner, *Herbert Hoover: A Public Life* (New York: Knopf, 1979), 298.
16. Lippmann quoted in Ronald Steel, *Walter Lippmann and the American Century* (Boston: Little, Brown, 1980), 287–88. See also Lippmann, "The Peculiar Weakness of Mr. Hoover," *Harper's* 161 (June 1930):1.

LIPPMANN'S ASSESSMENT was characteristically cogent and, as events were to prove, prescient. But at this point Lippmann was almost alone in his doubts. The implications of Hoover's failure on the tariff and of what that failure suggested about the president's political ineptitude were only faintly visible in the first weeks of 1930. Most commentators were much more impressed, even dazzled, by the vigorous response that Hoover had made to the stock market crash of October 1929. No previous president, wrote Anne O'Hare McCormick, "would have been so well prepared as Hoover to deal with the emergency when the bright bubble broke. He had a concrete program ready; he gave the effect of having thoroughly anticipated the debacle and mapped out the shortest road to recovery." The liberal economists William T. Foster and Waddill Catchings declared: "For the first time in our history, a President of the United States is taking aggressive leadership in guiding private business through a crisis." The *New York Times* said: "The President's course in this troublous time has been all that could be desired. No one in his place could have done more; very few of his predecessors could have done as much."[17]

Orthodox economic theory held that business downturns were inevitable parts of the business cycle. Depressions, said Oklahoma's Democratic senator Thomas P. Gore, were "an economic disease. You might just as well try to prevent the human race from having a disease as to prevent economic grief of this sort."[18] Orthodox political theory accordingly prescribed that government should refrain from interfering with the natural course of recovery in the economic organism. Conspicuous among what Hoover called the "leave it alone liquidationists" was Treasury Secretary Andrew Mellon. "Mr. Mellon had only one formula," Hoover later wrote. "Liquidate labor, liquidate stocks, liquidate the farmers, liquidate real estate," Mellon preached to the president. "It will purge the rottenness out of the system. High costs of living and high living will come down. People will work harder, lead a more moral life."[19] Mellon was a prime exemplar of those rigidly conventional devotees of laissez-faire whom William T. Foster impishly described as the "lazy fairies." Liberal journalist Stuart Chase also made

17. McCormick, "Year of the Hoover Method"; Foster and Catchings quoted in Romasco, *Poverty of Abundance*, 36; *New York Times*, December 1, 1929, sec. 3, 4.
18. Quoted in Schlesinger 1:226.
19. Herbert Hoover, *The Memoirs of Herbert Hoover: The Great Depression, 1929–1941* (New York: Macmillan, 1952), 30.

sport of their intellectual orthodoxy: "[T]he great advantage of allowing nature to take her course," wrote Chase, "is that it obviates thought. . . . There is no need to take concrete action. Just sit and watch with folded hands."[20]

Hoover would have none of it. Despite Mellon's towering prestige and the imposing weight of the conventional wisdom that he represented, Hoover believed "that we should use the powers of government to cushion the situation. . . . [T]he prime needs were to prevent bank panics such as had marked the earlier slumps, to mitigate the privation among the unemployed and the farmers which would certainly ensue. . . . [W]e determined that the Federal government should use all of its powers."[21]

The president was not pushed into this forward position in 1929 by pressure from capital. All to the contrary, wrote Hoover, "for some time after the crash" businessmen refused to believe "that the danger was any more than that of run-of-the-mill, temporary slumps such as had occurred at three-to seven-year intervals in the past." But Hoover sensed that something far more poisonous was brewing, and though he realized that "no president before had ever believed there was a governmental responsibility in such cases," he resolved to act, swiftly and dramatically.[22] Here was the promise, at least, of innovative, imaginative leadership.

Hoover's overriding intention was to prevent the shock waves from the stock market collapse from blasting through the economy as a whole. His fundamental premises were that the basic productive facilities of the country remained healthy and intact and that government, if it moved smartly, was fully capable of insulating them from the psychological and financial explosion reverberating in the canyons of Wall Street. Offering rhetorical reassurance to bolster the confidence of nervous investors, employers, and consumers was a conspicuous part of this strategy, but it was by no means the whole of it.

"The great task of the next few months," the progressive-minded *Nation* proclaimed in November 1929, "is the restoration of confidence — confidence in the fundamental strength of the financial structure notwithstanding the strain that has been put upon it, confidence in the essential soundness of legitimate industry and trade."[23] Hoover agreed,

20. Foster quoted in Schlesinger 1:187; Chase quoted in Romasco, *Poverty of Abundance*, 25.
21. Hoover, *Memoirs: The Great Depression*, 31.
22. Hoover, *Memoirs: The Great Depression*, 29–30.
23. *Nation*, November 27, 1929, 614.

but he also knew "that words are not of any great importance in times of economic disturbance. It is action that counts."[24] Accordingly, he summoned to the White House, beginning on November 19, 1929, leaders of the nation's banking system, railroads, manufacturing industries, and public utilities. For nearly two weeks they emerged from daily sessions with the nation's chief executive emitting ritual pronouncements of confidence in the basic soundness of the economy and of their optimistic outlook for the future. These words were comforting. But as the country was about to learn, the business leaders did more than talk. They also responded to the president's call for "action."

On December 5, 1929, Hoover reviewed the results of his November meetings before an audience of some four hundred "key men" from all corners of the business world. The occasion itself was cause for remark. "The very fact that you gentlemen come together for these broad purposes represents an advance in the whole conception of the relationship of business to public welfare," Hoover told them. "This is a far cry from the arbitrary and dog-eat-dog attitude of the business world of some thirty or forty years ago. . . . A great responsibility and a great opportunity rest upon the business and economic organization of the country."[25] He was pleased to report, Hoover continued, that his conferences of the preceding fortnight had already produced tangible results in three significant areas. The Federal Reserve System, he announced, had eased credit by open-market purchases and by lowering its discount rate to member banks. The Fed was also refusing discounts to banks that made stock market call loans. Taken together, these measures ensured the availability of investment capital for legitimate business needs.

Further, the industrialists he had summoned to the White House had agreed to maintain wage rates. This was a major concession, and a novel one. The reflex of management in all previous recessions had been to slash paychecks. Now employers acceded to Hoover's request that "the first shock must fall on profits and not on wages."[26] Holding the line on wages, according to Hoover, would not only preserve the dignity and well-being of individual workers. It would also sustain purchasing power in the economy as a whole and thus arrest the downswing by bolstering consumption—a point of economic theory later credited to the Keynes-

24. Hoover quoted in Herbert Stein, *The Fiscal Revolution in America*, (Chicago: University of Chicago Press, 1969), 16.

25. Hoover, *Memoirs: The Great Depression*, 44–45.

26. Notes of Hoover's meeting with industrial leaders on November 21, 1929, quoted in Hoover, *Memoirs: The Great Depression*, 44.

ian revolution but actually quite commonplace among economic analysts in the 1920s and well understood by Hoover.

The actions of the Federal Reserve System and the agreement on wages, together with the Federal Farm Board's support of agricultural prices, were designed to brake the deflationary spiral before it could gather momentum. The final measure that Hoover announced on December 5 was potentially the most important component of his antidepression program. It looked not merely to stabilization but to revitalization of the economy by stimulating construction work. At his urging, Hoover explained, railway and public utilities executives had agreed to expand their building and maintenance programs. He had, in addition, wired the governors of each state and the mayors of major cities suggesting that "road, street, public building and other construction of this type could be speeded up and adjusted in such fashion as to further employment." Within a few months, Hoover would add the resources of the federal government to this effort by requesting from Congress a supplemental appropriation of some $140 million for new public buildings.[27]

It became fashionable in later years to dismiss these various measures as tragicomic evidence of Hoover's quaint, ideologically hidebound belief that responsibility for economic recovery lay with private business and state and local governments and that the federal government had only a modest, hortatory role to play in combating the depression. Some writers have especially mocked Hoover's conferences with business leaders in November 1929 as "no-business meetings" that had merely a ceremonial, incantatory function.[28] Their limited, do-nothing agenda, so the argument runs, confirms Hoover's fatal reluctance to depart in any significant measure from the obsolescent dogmas of laissez-faire.

To be sure, Hoover himself fastidiously gave the conventional assurances to his business audience on December 5 that his program was "not a dictation or interference by the government with business.

27. Romasco, *Poverty of Abundance*, 29. Almost every governor responded with pledges of cooperation. New York's Franklin D. Roosevelt added a cautionary note that exemplified the pervasive fiscal orthodoxy of the day: "expect to recommend to legislature . . . much needed construction work program . . . limited only by estimated receipts from revenues without increasing taxes." William Starr Myers and Walter H. Newton, *The Hoover Administration: A Documented Narrative* (New York: Charles Scribner's Sons, 1936), 29.

28. See John Kenneth Galbraith, *The Great Crash* (Boston: Houghton Mifflin, 1954), 145, and Schlesinger 1:165.

It is a request from the government that you co-operate in prudent measures to solve a national problem."[29] The *New Republic* observed at the time that "the historical role of Mr. Hoover is apparently to try the experiment of seeing what business can do when given the steering wheel. Mr. Hoover insists that there should be a steering wheel," the magazine conceded, "but he will also let business do the driving."[30] That indictment has echoed for decades in the history books, where Hoover has been embalmed as a specimen of the "old order" of unbridled laissez-faire capitalism. "No American," concluded Arthur M. Schlesinger Jr., "could have provided a fairer test of the capacity of the business community to govern a great and multifarious nation than Herbert Hoover."[31]

But Hoover's reliance on private business and on state and local governments for fiscal stimulus in late 1929, notes economist Herbert Stein, "is better understood if the relatively small size of the federal government at the beginning of the Depression is appreciated."[32] Federal expenditures in 1929 accounted for about 3 percent of gross national product (GNP). By the century's closing decade, by way of comparison, the federal budget represented more than 20 percent of GNP. State and local government expenditures were about five times larger than the federal budget in 1929; by century's end, those figures would be nearly equal.[33]

To that consideration it might be added that the structure, as well as the size, of the federal government severely limited the scope of its fiscal action, whatever the ideology of its chief executive. The Federal Reserve Board, for example, was legally independent of the executive branch. It could not be counted upon to help finance a large federal deficit even if the president had inexplicably chosen to profane all the canons of economic writ and request one.

When Hoover determined "that the Federal government should use all of its powers," therefore, he was professing a radical conviction, one that heralded a coming revolution in attitudes about the government's proper economic role. But he was not, by the very nature of things in the world of 1929, reaching at that historical moment for a truly powerful instrument. In the last analysis, Hoover's earliest responses to the

29. Hoover, *Memoirs: The Great Depression*, 45.
30. *New Republic*, December 11, 1929, 56.
31. Schlesinger 1:88.
32. Stein, *Fiscal Revolution in America*, 14.
33. *HSUS* 228, 230, 1104.

economic crisis revealed as much about the boundaries of available intelligence and inherited institutions in Depression-era America as they did about the alleged narrowness of his beliefs. Those boundaries were destined to circumscribe not only Hoover's struggle against the Great Depression but Franklin D. Roosevelt's as well.

Ignorance befogs all human affairs, and it enshrouded policymakers in the months after the Wall Street debacle of 1929. The future, as ever, remained veiled and inscrutable. No one—including Hoover, whose anxieties were keener than most—suspected that the country was teetering at the brink of an economic abyss out of whose depths it would take more than ten years to climb. As for the past, little in the lived or remembered experience of Americans provided useful analogies for understanding their situation in 1929. Andrew Mellon, for example, took his chief point of reference for assessing that situation to be the depression of the 1870s, which began when Mellon was eighteen years old. Mellon badgered Hoover tediously with grave lectures about that dimly remembered decade. Hoover's own memories of the depression of the 1890s could not have been powerfully instructive; he had graduated from college in the midst of it and set out almost immediately to make his fortune. Both of those downturns had in any case lasted less than five years. They were also long ago and far away. They had virtually happened in another country, a country still overwhelmingly rural and agricultural, many of whose inhabitants participated but marginally in the market economy and felt its distant gyrations only as faint seismic shrugs.

The more recent recession of 1921 served as the most accessible model for interpreting the events of 1929. It had been severe but brief. Unemployment was estimated to have peaked at about 11.9 percent of the work force. That was considered a historical apogee, and Commerce Secretary Hoover's decisive intervention in convening the President's Conference on Unemployment had shown that the business cycle could be shaped, and its downswing truncated, by purposeful leadership. Thus in 1929, notes Stein, "America was not prepared to visualize a decade in which unemployment never fell below 14 per cent."[34] And as the events of the gray decade that followed were to show, no politician's art, neither Hoover's nor Roosevelt's, proved capable of significantly bending upward the stubbornly bottoming curve of the economy.

Policymakers were not only unprepared to visualize the decade that lay ahead of them; they were almost equally unable to see what was

34. Stein, *Fiscal Revolution in America*, 15.

going on around them in late 1929 and through much of 1930. Despite the call of the President's Conference on Unemployment in 1921 for better information on the status of the work force, reliable data on unemployment simply did not exist. Only in April 1930 did census takers for the first time attempt a systematic measurement of unemployment. Even a year later, in mid-1931, lawmakers were still guessing, on the basis of anecdotes, impressions, and fragmentary reports, at the numbers of the unemployed.[35]

In the crucial area of construction work, long recognized as a potentially powerful countercyclical tool, the states dramatically outspent the federal government. Federal construction expenditures were scarcely $200 million in 1929. The states paid out ten times that much, nearly $2 billion, mostly for highways. Federal outlays for construction, excepting the years of World War II, would not reach that level until the 1950s. Still more dramatic was the comparison with private industry, which spent some $9 billion on construction projects in 1929.[36]

Under these circumstances, it was not simply ideological timidity but practical realism that led Hoover to search for a countercyclical instrument not in the federal budget but in the undertakings of private business and of the states. There, not in Washington, D.C., were the financial resources and the shelf of backlogged projects, their time-consuming engineering work already completed, that might be swiftly brought into play. Though Hoover was increasingly challenged by proponents of allegedly "vast" federal public works projects that envisioned spending up to $5 billion over a year or two, Stein rightly asserts that "these suggestions could not be taken seriously. The federal government could simply not raise its construction expenditures quickly by one or two billion dollars a year, for instance, and have any structures to show for it. Federal construction expenditures were only $210 million in 1930—a small base on which to erect a program of several billion dollars. . . . It is significant that the New Deal did not succeed until 1939 in raising the annual amount of public construction by $1.5 billion over the 1930 rate, in 1930 prices." Given the constraints under which he labored, in short, Hoover made impressively aggressive countercyclical use of fiscal policy. Measured against either past or future performance, his accom-

35. See, for example, the remarks of Senator Borah in the New York Times, March 12, 1931, 21.
36. HSUS, 1123, 1127. For a general discussion of this matter, see Romasco, Poverty of Abundance, chap. 4; Stein, Fiscal Revolution in America, chap. 1; and Joan Wilson, Herbert Hoover: Forgotten Progressive, chap. 5.

plishment was remarkable. He nearly doubled federal public works expenditures in three years. Thanks to his prodding, the net stimulating effect of federal, state, and local fiscal policy was larger in 1931 than in any subsequent year of the decade.[37]

By the spring of 1930 many observers were cautiously optimistic. Hoover himself, in a statement that would later haunt him, proclaimed to the U. S. Chamber of Commerce on May 1, 1930: "I am convinced we have passed the worst and with continued effort we shall rapidly recover."[38] The following month he told a delegation from the National Catholic Welfare Conference that their pleas for further expansion of federal public works programs were "sixty days too late. The depression is over."[39]

Given available information, and given the scale against which the events of late 1929 and early 1930 could then be measured, these statements were not as outrageous as they appeared in retrospect. The wish for recovery might have been father to the thought, but circumstances lent the idea a measure of plausibility. The stock market had by April 1930 recouped about one-fifth of its slippage from the speculative peak of the preceding autumn. Some rural banks had begun to crack, but the banking system as a whole had thus far displayed surprising resilience in the immediate wake of the crash; deposits in operating Federal Reserve member banks actually increased through October of 1930.[40] The still sketchy reports on unemployment were worrisome but not unduly alarming. Major employers were apparently abiding by their pledge to maintain wage standards, and private industry as well as local and state governments had publicly acceded to Hoover's request to accelerate construction projects.

But the reality, still only obscurely visible in the meager statistical data that the government could then muster, was that the economy was continuing its mystifying downward slide. By the end of 1930 business failures had reached a record 26,355. Gross national product had slumped 12.6 percent from its 1929 level. In durable goods industries especially, production was down sharply: as much as 38 per cent in some steel mills, and

37. Stein, *Fiscal Revolution in America*, 23–24. The calculation of net fiscal stimulus is provided by E. Cary Brown, "Fiscal Policy in the Thirties: A Reappraisal," *American Economic Review* 46 (December, 1956) 857.
38. Hoover, *Memoirs: The Great Depression*, 58.
39. Schlesinger 1:231.
40. Milton Friedman and Anna Jacobson Schwartz, *A Monetary History of the United States, 1867–1960* (Princeton: Princeton University Press, 1963), 308–9. See also Lester Chandler, *America's Greatest Depression* (New York: Harper and Row, 1970), 80.

about the same throughout the key industry of automobile manufacturing, with its huge employment rolls. Despite public assurances, private business was in fact decreasing expenditures for construction; indeed, in the face of softening demand it had already cut back construction in 1929 from its 1928 peak, and it cut still further in 1930.[41] The exact number of laid-off workers remained conjectural; later studies estimated that some four million laborers were unemployed in 1930.

Yet most Americans in 1930 saw these developments less clearly than did later analysts and evaluated what they could see against the backdrop of their most recent experience with an economic recession in 1921. Then GNP had plummeted almost 24 percent in a single year, twice the decline of 1930. Unemployment was somewhat larger in absolute terms in 1921 than in 1930 (4.9 million versus 4.3 million) and significantly larger in percentage terms (11.9 percent versus 8.9 percent). Americans could justly feel in 1930 that they were not—yet—passing through as severe a crisis as the one they had endured less than a decade earlier. This perception of the gravity of the crisis, joined with the recurrent belief that its momentum had been arrested and the corner turned, as had happened so swiftly in 1921, inhibited Hoover from taking any more aggressive antidepression fiscal action in 1930.[42] Nor was he yet coming under any significant pressure to do more. He stood securely in mid-1930 as the leader of the fight against the depression, and he seemed to be winning—or at least not losing. Hoover, predicted the powerful Democratic financier and economic sage Bernard Baruch in May 1930, would be "fortunate enough, before the next election, to have a rising tide and then he will be pictured as the great master mind who led the country out of its economic misery."[43]

BY THE END OF 1930, however, the tide of Hoover's fortune had begun to ebb relentlessly. Congressional elections in November elimi-

---

41. See the slightly differing estimates of reductions in private construction expenditures in Stein, *Fiscal Revolution in America*, 22, and Romasco, *Poverty of Abundance*, 57–58. Both authors arrive at totals over $2 billion, or at least 20 percent below 1929 levels.

42. See Stein, *Fiscal Revolution in America*, 25–26, for further development of this idea. The events of 1930 were overshadowed in seriousness not only by those of 1921. In retrospect, neither 1930 nor even 1931 would look all that bad. All but one subsequent year (1937) of the entire decade of the 1930s saw greater unemployment than the 1931 level of eight million.

43. Schwarz, *Interregnum of Despair*, 15.

nated Republican majorities in both houses. Reflecting the still imperfect national focus on the severity of the economic crisis, many races turned more on the issue of Prohibition than on the depression, and though Republican losses were not overwhelming, especially by midterm election standards, they were bad enough to greatly complicate Hoover's political life. The GOP lost eight seats in the Senate, which would now be composed of forty-eight Republicans, forty-seven Democrats, and one Farmer-Labor member. This gave the Republicans a nominal plurality, but in Hoover's judgment "actually we had no more than 40 real Republicans, as Senators Borah, Norris, Cutting, and others of the left wing were against us." (The "left wing," in Hoover's view, consisted of those politicians who were calling for irresponsibly large budget deficits and direct federal aid to the unemployed.) Discouraged by the election results, a still politically innocent Hoover made the astounding suggestion that the Democrats be allowed to organize the Senate "and thereby convert their sabotage into responsibility."[44] Senate Republicans, of course, jealous of their chairmanships and other privileges of majority status, instantly rejected this proposal. The Senate remained in Republican hands, though just barely.

The situation in the House was worse. On election day in November 1930, Republicans and Democrats broke exactly even, winning 217 seats each, with the balance of power briefly held by a single Farmer-Labor congressman. Under the electoral laws then in force, the new Seventy-second Congress was at last seated only some thirteen months later, in December 1931. By that time thirteen elected representatives had died, a majority of them Republicans. Democrats thus held a slender majority, and they proceeded to organize the House for the first time in twelve years. As speaker, they elected Representative John Nance Garner of Texas.

The sixty-two-year-old Garner represented a sprawling congressional

---

44. Hoover, *Memoirs: The Great Depression*, 101. While it is true that Republicans lost control of the House and nearly lost the Senate in the elections of 1930, close study of the election must qualify any reading of the results as a repudiation of Hoover's— and the Republican Party's—handling of the depression. Republicans remained easily the majority party in the country as a whole, winning some 54.1 percent of the votes cast for major-party candidates in the 1930 congressional elections. They handily dominated in all regions outside the South, and in three key states—Pennsylvania, Michigan, and Massachusetts—they actually increased their 1928 share of popular votes cast for congressional candidates. See Schwarz, *Interregnum of Despair*, 19.

district in the parched Nueces River country in southwest Texas. He was an ill-educated, self-made sagebrush squire who delighted in tending to the sheep, cattle, and mohair goats that roamed his dusty estates. The first speaker from Texas, he dreamed that he might also become the first Texan to live in the White House. With his icy blue eyes and stubbly white hair framing a frequently unshaven face, his stocky body draped in a rumpled gray suit, his feet encased in big, blunt-toed shoes, he presented a colorful figure to the amused Washington press corps, who took to dubbing him "Mustang Jack" or "Cactus Jack." Hoover deemed him "a man of real statesmanship when he took off his political pistols" but also a partisan infighter of reptilian cunning. (Garner had once proposed dividing Texas into four states—whose eight senators would presumably all be Democrats.) First elected to the House in 1902, Garner had risen steadily through the rigid hierarchy of the congressional seniority system. He had ingratiated himself with his colleagues, especially rural southern and western representatives, many of whom still affected frock coats and string ties, by saying and doing little. His taciturnity led some to think of him as a kind of Texas Coolidge—a perception reinforced by statements like Garner's 1931 declaration that "the great trouble today is that we have too many laws." Like Coolidge, too— indeed, like virtually every credible public figure of the time—Garner regarded a balanced budget as the rock on which all government financial policy rested. Garner would now be the most influential figure in the Seventy-second Congress, the "Depression Congress" with which Hoover would have to deal as the depression deepened drastically in 1931 and 1932. He had it in his power to save or to break Hoover's political neck.[45]

"I thought my party had a better program for national recovery than Mr. Hoover and his party," Garner later wrote. But if the Democratic speaker had a program, Hoover retorted, "he never disclosed it. . . . His main program of public welfare was to put the Republicans out." In fact, Garner and many, perhaps most, congressional Democrats stood at this time somewhere to Hoover's political right. This was especially true of the Democratic leadership, overwhelmingly southern in origin and agrarian in outlook, including Garner in the House and Joseph T. Robinson of Arkansas, the Democratic leader in the Senate. Incredibly enough, the national chairman of the Democratic Party was a former

45. *Time*, December 7, 1931, 10; Schlesinger 1:227–29; Hoover, *Memoirs: The Great Depression*, 101–2.

Republican, the archconservative industrialist John J. Raskob, an economic reactionary and notorious wet. His paramount cause was the repeal of Prohibition, a goal to which he aspired primarily because the restoration of tax revenues from the sale of liquor would dampen the need for a progressive income tax. As for Speaker Garner, virtually his first antidepression initiative in the new Seventy-second Congress was to support a frankly regressive national sales tax as a budget-balancing measure.

As the depression thickened in 1931 and 1932, the main purpose of Garner, Robinson, and Raskob was to obstruct the president and prepare to reap the political reward in the upcoming presidential election. Democrats, said a North Carolina Democratic senator, should avoid "committing our party to a definite program. The issue in the [1932] election is Hoover. Why take any step calculated to divert attention from that issue?" Only the Democratic Party's "failure to function," said Tennessee's Cordell Hull, "can save the Republican party and its Hoover administration from overwhelming defeat in 1932." Another observer commented in 1931 that the Democrats were "more hopeful than bold[.] . . . [E]vents seemed to be going their way; they had no wish to incur premature responsibility."[46] But they did wish—and they had the ability—to make Hoover's life miserable. Raskob at the National Committee hired Charles Michelson, a seasoned publicist with a well-earned reputation for mischief, to ensure that the humiliation of Hoover would be executed with professional expertise. Michelson methodically proceeded to hang the responsibility for the gathering depression around Hoover's neck like a leper's bell. "It was Michelson's job," said Garner, "to whittle Hoover down to our size." As for himself, Garner boasted, "I fought President Hoover with everything I had, under Marquis of Queensberry, London prize ring and catch-as-catch-can rules."[47]

On Hoover's political left in the Congress stood a loose assortment of progressive and former Bull Moose Republicans like Nebraska's George Norris, New York's Fiorello La Guardia, Idaho's William Borah, Wisconsin's Robert M. La Follette Jr., and New Mexico's Bronson Cutting, along with a smattering of maverick Democrats like Montana's Burton Wheeler, Colorado's Edward Costigan, and New York's Robert Wagner. Hoover had some natural sympathies for this group's outlook. Like many of them, he had voted the Bull Moose ticket in 1912. But his measured,

46. Schwarz, *Interregnum of Despair*, 62, 180, 59.
47. Burner, *Herbert Hoover*, 314; Hoover, *Memoirs: The Great Depression*, 101n.

prudent management style and his greater degree of caution about governmental activism, especially in the area of unemployment relief, frequently set him at odds with the progressives.

Norris in particular was a perpetual thorn in Hoover's flesh. Melancholic and ascetic, clad in black suit and string tie, gray-haired and plain-spoken, Norris had the air of a conscience-ridden country parson. He was approaching his fourth decade of service in Congress. First elected to the House, like Garner, in 1902 and then to the Senate in 1912, he had metamorphosed from an orthodox McKinley Republican into a ferociously independent progressive. In April 1917, for example, he had cast one of six votes in the Senate against American entry into the European War. In 1928 he refused to endorse Hoover as the Republican presidential nominee, feeding a bitter enmity between the two men.

The issue that most divided them was hydroelectric power, and their skirmish lines had been drawn long before the onset of the depression. Hoover had consistently favored conservation and reclamation projects, including the unprecedentedly ambitious Hoover Dam on the Colorado River. But he flatly and unremittingly opposed Norris's pet proposal for federal operation of the waterpower facilities constructed during World War I on the Tennessee River at Muscle Shoals, Alabama. Hoover explained this apparent contradiction by drawing a distinction between "socialist" hydroelectric plants like Muscle Shoals, which would directly compete with private power companies, and facilities that only produced power "as a by-product of dams for the multiple purpose of irrigation, flood control and improvement of navigation."[48] Norris, not without cause, railed against this reasoning as hairsplitting sophistry, another example of Hoover's maddening tendency to subordinate real human needs to his obsessive desire for ideological consistency. Norris, in contrast, remembered the inky black nights of his frugal rural childhood and saw in government hydroelectric projects the means to shed light over the darkened countryside. He dreamed of harnessing the power of all the streams in America that flowed from the mountaintops to the sea.

The rustic Nebraskan's dogged fidelity to the cause of publicly owned and operated hydroelectric plants took on the trappings of a crusade in the 1920s. Muscle Shoals became a powerfully symbolic issue. Under its banner Norris mustered a small but dedicated troop of progressives who shared his dream of an inexpensively electrified America. They also

48. Hoover, *Memoirs: The Great Depression*, 325.

shared his revulsion at the financial prestidigitation of electric utility magnates, notoriously typified by Chicago's Samuel Insull. As Insull's byzantine corporate manipulations came to light in the wake of the Crash, Insull himself was about to become a potent symbol of the shattered business idols of the 1920s.

Calvin Coolidge had vetoed a bill embodying Norris's Tennessee River plan in 1928. Nearly seventy years old in 1930, Norris morosely reflected that "the end cannot be very many years in advance. I think I have, to a great extent, run my race."[49] Before the grave closed over him, he was determined to see his crusade for Muscle Shoals succeed. Herbert Hoover was to veto another Muscle Shoals bill of Norris's in 1931. Norris grimly held on until a more friendly administration might appear.

Norris and a few of his like-minded associates in Congress called for a Progressive Conference to convene in Washington in March 1931. The date fell shortly after the adjournment of the Seventy-first Congress and some nine months before the new Seventy-second Congress was scheduled to assemble—a decidedly dead season for meeting what the conference planners called "the imperative need of formulating a constructive legislative program."[50] In two days of deliberations on March 11 and 12 at Washington's Carleton Hotel, some three dozen progressives inconclusively discussed the electrical power industry, agriculture, the tariff, representative government, and unemployment. The curious timing of the meeting, its diffuse agenda, and its meager results all served as another reminder of just how ill-focused and uncertain the perception of the depression's gravity remained, even among self-styled progressives. At this late date in March 1931, nearly a year and a half after the stock market crash, they still had no coherent analysis of what was happening and no agreed plan of action. And the sparse attendance at the Progressive Conference—New York governor Franklin D. Roosevelt declined an invitation, though he sent a sympathetic message emphasizing his agricultural and hydroelectric policies, endearing him to Norris—illustrated the continuing political weightlessness of organized alternatives to Hoover's leadership in the antidepression battle. Hoover may have lost control of the Congress, but he did not as yet face a distinct, organized opposition.

After the adjournment of the lame-duck session of the Seventy-first Congress in March 1931, Congress would not assemble again until De-

49. Schlesinger 1:123.
50. Quoted in Romasco, *Poverty of Abundance*, 218.

cember 1931 unless the president summoned it into special session —
something that Hoover, with his memories of the tariff debacle in the
last special session and with the prospect of a Democratic House and
an uncontrollable Senate in the new Congress, understandably declined
to do. The hugger-mugger of partisan politics continued to offend him.
He remained a manager, not a politician. Perhaps the long adjournment
of Congress even struck him as an opportunity to take charge of the
antidepression battle without being pestered by nattering, grandstanding
legislators. The virulence of Democratic antagonism, a sorely beset Hoover complained in his *Memoirs,* "no man could measure or conciliate."[51]
These anxieties over a runaway legislature reinforced Hoover's already
deep commitment to fight the economic crisis not with statutes but with
presidentially orchestrated voluntary cooperation. Nineteen thirty-one
thus marked a long season of solitary presidential combat against the
massing forces of the nation's greatest economic disaster.

IT ALSO MARKED a savage quickening of those forces. Down to
the last weeks of 1930, Americans could still plausibly assume that they
were caught up in yet another of the routine business-cycle downswings
that periodically afflicted their traditionally boom-and-bust economy.
Their situation was painful but not unfamiliar, and their president was
in any case taking unprecedentedly vigorous corrective actions. Then,
in the closing weeks of the year, an epidemic of failures flashed through
the banking system, auguring the economy's slide into dark and alien
depths.

"Our banking system was the weakest link in our whole economic
system," Hoover believed, "the element most sensitive to fear ... the
worst part of the dismal tragedy with which I had to deal."[52] American
banks were rotten even in good times. They failed at a rate of well over
five hundred per year throughout the 1920s. Nineteen twenty-nine saw
659 bank suspensions, a figure easily within the normal range for the
decade. Nineteen thirty witnessed about the same number of collapses
through October. Then, with a sickening swiftness, six hundred banks
closed their doors in the last sixty days of the year, bringing the annual
total to 1,352.

Underlying the weakness of the American banking system was the
sheer number of banks and the muddled structure that held them to-

51. Hoover, *Memoirs: The Great Depression,* 84.
52. Hoover, *Memoirs: The Great Depression,* 21, 84.

gether—or failed to. A lingering legacy of Andrew Jackson's long-ago war on central banking, the freewheeling American financial system had grown haphazardly for a century and counted some twenty-five thousand banks in 1929, operating under fifty-two different regulatory regimes. Many institutions were pitifully undercapitalized. Carter Glass, father of the Federal Reserve System launched in 1913, denounced them as no more than "pawn shops," often run by "little corner grocery-men calling themselves bankers—and all they know is how to shave a note."[53] Branch banking, by which well-capitalized metropolitan institutions filled the banking needs of small, outlying communities, might have provided stability to the banking system. But branch banking was the historical target of populist attacks on the diabolical "Money Power" and therefore was virtually unknown in the United States, in contrast to almost all other comparably developed nations; only 751 American banks operated branches in 1930. The overwhelming majority of American banks were, for all practical purposes, solitary (in banking jargon, "unitary") institutions that could look only to their own resources in the event of a panic. About a third of all banks were members of the Federal Reserve System, which theoretically could provide some succor at a time of difficulty, but as events were to show, the Fed proved fatefully inadequate at the crucial moment.[54]

Through this ramshackle financial structure in late 1930 fear licked like fire through a house of cards. Precisely what kindled the blaze is not clear, but disaster first flared in November 1930 at Louisville's National Bank of Kentucky, then spread virulently to groups of affiliated banks in neighboring Indiana, Illinois, Missouri, and eventually Iowa, Arkansas, and North Carolina. Mobs of shouting depositors shouldered up to tellers' windows to withdraw their savings. The banks, in turn, scrambled to preserve their liquidity in the face of these accelerating withdrawals by calling in loans and selling assets. As the beleaguered banks desperately sought cash by throwing their bond and real estate portfolios onto the market—a market already depressed by the Crash of 1929—they further drove down the value of assets in otherwise sound institutions, putting the entire banking system at peril. This vicious cy-

53. Glass quoted in Schwarz, *Interregnum of Despair*, 218, and in Caroline Bird, *The Invisible Scar* (New York: McKay, 1966) 97–98.
54. Data taken from Friedman and Schwartz, *Monetary History of the United States*, chap. 7, and Susan Estabrook Kennedy, *The Banking Crisis of 1933* (Lexington: University Press of Kentucky, 1973), chap. 1. Canada, where branch banking was the norm, saw no bank failures in this period.

cle—a classic liquidity crisis magnified to monstrous scale in the inordinately plural and disorganized world of American banking—soon
threatened to become a roaring tornado that would rip the financial
heart out of the economy.

At first the fever of panic afflicted only the chronically anemic rural
banks. But on December 11, 1930, it struck close to the central nervous
system of American capitalism when New York City's Bank of United
States closed its doors. The Bank of United States, known colloquially
as the "Pantspressers' Bank," was owned and operated by Jews and held
the deposits of thousands of Jewish immigrants, many of them employed
in the garment trades. Some observers then and later attributed its downfall to the deliberate refusal of the old-line Wall Street financial houses,
especially the militantly gentile House of Morgan, to heed the Federal
Reserve System's call to come to its rescue.[55]

The suspension of the Bank of United States represented the largest
commercial bank failure in American history up to that time. It held
the savings of some four hundred thousand persons, totaling nearly $286
million, but the damage done by its closing could not be calculated in
cold ciphers. The locking of its doors provided a grotesque example of
the manner in which psychological perception counted as heavily as the
accountants' computations in shaking confidence in the banking system.
The bank's very name misled many people at home and abroad into
regarding it as some kind of official institution, amplifying the fearful
effects of its collapse. More important, the failure of the Federal Reserve
System to organize a rescue operation, as one upstate New York banker
put it, "had shaken confidence in the Federal Reserve System more than
any other occurrence in recent years."[56] With that confidence broken,
banks rushed still more frantically to protect themselves, with little heed
to the health of the banking system overall.

The banking panic of late 1930 was frightful, but what did it portend?
Was it an end or a beginning? Was it only the banking system that was
sick, or were American banks merely the most visible victims of a worldwide deflationary cycle? Some observers regarded the banking panic at
the end of 1930 as the last awful spasm of the economic illness that had
begun a year earlier. The difficulties of the midwestern banks could be
attributed to the continuing agricultural depression; the collapse of the

55. See Ron Chernow, *The House of Morgan* (New York: Atlantic Monthly Press, 1990),
    323–24.
56. Quoted in Friedman and Schwartz, *Monetary History of the United States*, 357.

Bank of United States could be understood as a delayed consequence of the Crash of 1929. (Its securities affiliate had speculated in dubious stocks, and two of its owners were later jailed.) Indeed, in the first quarter of 1931 the rate of bank failures slowed dramatically, and many indices of economic activity turned upward. Industrial production rose. So did payrolls and personal income. Many Americans, including Herbert Hoover, permitted themselves the guarded hope that the financial convulsions of late 1930 might have marked the beginning of the end. Some later observers have concurred. "All in all," two leading students of the Depression conclude, "the figures for the first four or five months of 1931, if examined without reference to what actually followed, have many of the earmarks of the bottom of a cycle and the beginning of a revival."[57] But "what actually followed" showed that this apparent bottom was only a way station to still deeper depression. The banking panic of late 1930 was eventually seen to have opened the trapdoor to a still more ghastly disaster to come.

What the banks needed in this critical hour was liquidity: money with which to meet the demands of depositors. But perversely, the effort of individual banks to maintain liquidity contracted the money supply, tightened credit, and inexorably clotted the system as a whole. In Utah, banker Marriner Eccles managed to keep his institution open through an agonizing day of massive withdrawals by depositors only by instructing his tellers to work in slow motion, deliberately counting out sums in small-denomination bills to the noisy throngs of customers who crowded onto his banking floor, clamoring for their cash. Thereafter, said Eccles, "we had to adopt a rough and distasteful credit and collection policy. Living with oneself was not a pleasant experience under those circumstances."

Reflecting on his predicament, Eccles "began to wonder whether the conduct of bankers like myself in depression times was a wise one. Were we not all contributing our bit to the worsening of matters by the mere act of trying to keep liquid under the economic pressures of deflation? By forcing the liquidation of loans and securities to meet the demands of depositors, were we not helping to drive prices down and thereby making it increasingly difficult for our debtors to pay back what they had borrowed from us? By our policies of credit stringency in a time of drastic deflation, were we not throwing a double loop around the throat

---

57. Friedman and Schwartz, *Monetary History of the United States*, 313.

of an economy that was already gasping for breath? In a time of deflation, would not the rational policy be one of monetary ease?"[58]

That would indeed have been the rational policy. It was, in fact, the policy Hoover had promoted in the weeks immediately following the Crash. But now, in the fateful second half of 1931, a peculiar constellation of factors blocked its effective implementation. Ironically, the very existence of the Federal Reserve System seemed to relieve the big private banks like the House of Morgan from playing the liquefying role they had assumed in earlier panics, such as 1907. At the Federal Reserve System itself, a vacuum of leadership left by the death in 1928 of Benjamin Strong, governor of the New York Federal Reserve Bank and long the Fed's dominant personality, wrought near paralysis after the failed effort to prop up the Bank of United States at the end of 1930. Above all, as events were soon to demonstrate, developments beyond the confines of the United States fatally confounded the system's efforts to cope with the banking crisis.

Down to early 1931, the American depression seemed largely to be the product of American causes. A decade of stagnation in agriculture, flattening sales in the automobile and housing markets, the piratical abuses on Wall Street, the hair-raising evaporation of asset values in the Crash, the woes of the anarchic banking system—these were surely problems enough. Still, they were domestic problems, and no American better understood them than Herbert Hoover, nor was any leader better prepared to take up arms against them. But now Europe was about to add some dreadful, back-breaking weight to Hoover's already staggering burden. In short order, what was still in 1931 called the depression was about to become the unprecedented calamity know to history as the Great Depression.

58. Marriner S. Eccles, *Beckoning Frontiers* (New York: Knopf, 1951), 70–71.

3

The Ordeal of Herbert Hoover

Hoover will be known as the greatest innocent bystander in history . . .
a brave man fighting valiantly, futilely, to the end.
                                            —William Allen White, 1932

As early as December 1930 Hoover claimed that "the major forces of the depression now lie outside of the United States." His statement may at that moment have been overly self-protective and premature, but events soon gave the president's words the chill ring of prophecy, as shock waves from the collapsing international economic system smote the United States with lethal wallop. Until early 1931, midway through his presidency, Hoover had been aggressive and self-confident, a front-line fighter taking vigorous offensive against the economic crises. Now international events remorselessly pushed him back onto the defensive. His overriding goals became damage control and even national economic self-preservation. In late 1931 he starkly announced: "We are now faced with the problem, not of saving Germany or Britain, but of saving ourselves."[1]

From the spring of 1931 onward, this became Hoover's constant theme: that the calamity's deepest sources originated beyond American shores. From this time, too, it began to be clear that this depression was not just another cyclic valley but a historic watershed, something vastly greater in scale and more portentous in its implications than anything that had gone before. An unprecedented event, it must have extraordinary causes. Hoover found them in the most momentous episode of the century. It was now that he began to elaborate the thesis with which he

---

1. Herbert Hoover, *The Memoirs of Herbert Hoover: The Great Depression, 1929–1941* (New York: Macmillan, 1952) 59, 90.

began his *Memoirs*: "In the large sense the primary cause of the Great Depression was the war of 1914–1918."[2]

In the spring of 1931, Hoover explained, "just as we had begun to entertain well founded hopes that we were on our way out of the depression, our latent fears of Europe were realized in a gigantic explosion which shook the foundations of the world's economic, political, and social structure. At last the malign forces arising from economic consequences of the war, the Versailles Treaty, the postwar military alliances with their double prewar armament, their frantic public works programs to meet unemployment, their unbalanced budgets and the inflations, all tore their systems asunder."[3]

History lends much credibility to this view. The war had indeed set the stage for disaster, not least by hobbling the Germany economy with reparations payments, thus weakening the European economy as a whole and, not incidentally, paving the path for Adolf Hitler's rise to power. The malign forces to which Hoover referred stalked onto this stage in September 1930, when the Nazi Party exploited festering resentments over reparations and the deeply depressed state of the German economy to score ominous gains in parliamentary elections. This sharp Nazi advance ignited a serpentine chain reaction whose detonations eventually rocked even the remotest reaches of the American heartland. Americans, Hoover later drily noted, "were to learn about the economic interdependence of nations through a poignant experience which knocked at every cottage door."[4]

Seeking to rob Hitler of his main electoral appeal by bolstering the German economy, German chancellor Heinrich Bruning proposed in March 1931 a German customs union with Austria. The French government, darkly suspicious, regarded Bruning's proposal as a first step toward the Weimar Republic's annexation of Austria—something that the defeated Germans and Austrians had wanted to accomplish in 1919

2. Hoover, *Memoirs: The Great Depression*, 2.
3. Hoover, *Memoirs: The Great Depression*, 61.
4. Hoover, *Memoirs: The Great Depression*, 80. The economic historian Peter Temin has recently lent support to Hoover's analysis of the causes of the Depression. "The origins of the Great Depression lie largely in the disruptions of the First World War," Temin writes in *Lessons from the Great Depression* (Cambridge: MIT Press, 1989), 1. Yet it remains the case that economists are if anything less confident than they once were that they have identified the precise causes of the Depression. A singular event, the Depression has thus far resisted comprehensive explanation by analysts applying supposedly universal theories of economic behavior.

but that the Versailles Treaty explicitly prohibited. The prospect that France might begin squeezing Austrian banks as a way of frustrating Bruning's design touched off a banking panic in Vienna. By May depositors were rioting outside the largest Austrian bank, Louis Rothschild's Kreditanstalt, and the bank shut its doors. The trouble then spread to Germany. Panic swelled, and many German banks closed, followed by more closures in neighboring countries.

Underlying and complicating this alarming chain of events was the tangled issue of international debts and reparations payments stemming from the war of 1914–18. One obvious way to relieve the pressure on the beleaguered Germans and Austrians was to break the chain by repudiating or suspending those obligations. The United States might lead the way by forgiving or rescheduling the $10 billion it was owed by the Allies, chiefly Britain and France, as a result of loans made from the U.S. Treasury during and immediately after the war. Morgan partner Thomas P. Lamont telephoned Hoover on June 5, 1931, to suggest just that. Hoover was already exploring the idea on his own, but he reminded Lamont of its political explosiveness. "Sitting in New York, as you do," Hoover lectured, "you have no idea what the sentiment of the country at large is on these inter-governmental debts."[5]

Lamont had rasped a knotted political nerve, its ganglia embedded in the Versailles peace settlement of 1919, and its endings raw and sensitive in the America of 1931. At Versailles the victors had forced defeated Germany to acknowledge sole guilt for the war and as a consequence to pay some $33 billion in reparations. The Germans had groaned under that debt burden through the 1920s. They had twice renegotiated its terms, securing an extended schedule of payment in the Dawes Plan of 1924 and winning further rescheduling, as well as a reduction in the overall amount owed, in the Young Plan of 1929.

Though the United States made only nominal claims for reparations from Germany, both Charles G. Dawes and Owen D. Young were Americans. They owed their eponymous roles in the debt negotiations to the fact that their country had emerged from the World War in the unaccustomed position of a leading international creditor. The U.S. Treasury had loaned money to the Allied governments in wartime, and private American bankers had loaned significant sums to Germany in the 1920s. The Germans relied on the continuing infusion of private American loans to make reparations payments to the British and the

5. Ron Chernow, *The House of Morgan* (New York: Atlantic Monthly 1990), 325.

French, who in turn applied those sums to their own bills at the American treasury.

This surreal financial merry-go-round was inherently unstable. It had been rudely shoved out of balance when the stock market crash of late 1929 dried up the well of American credit, knocking a crucial link out of the circuit of international cash flows. In this sense it could be argued that the American crash had helped to initiate the global depression, but Hoover's point still stands that the shock of the Crash fell on a global financial system already distorted and vulnerable because of the war.

For their part, the Allies had more than once offered to relax their demands on Germany, but only if their own obligations to the United States could be forgiven. The French Chamber of Deputies in 1929 made a dramatic point of this idea when it explicitly resolved to cover its payments to the United States with the proceeds of German reparations. That gesture outraged Americans.

The tightfisted Republican administrations of the 1920s had refused to admit any connection between German reparations and the debts owed by the Allied governments to the U.S. Treasury. All efforts to scale back those intergovernmental debts were widely regarded in the United States as ploys to shift the burden of the war's cost from Europeans to Americans. As disillusionment spread in the postwar decade about the futility and error of Woodrow Wilson's departure from isolationist principles in 1917, Americans were in no mood to consider absorbing a greater share of the war's cost. Popular feeling on this issue was further aroused by the attitude of Wall Street, which favored war-debt cancellation not least of all because forgiving the governmental loans would render its own private loans more secure. On Main Street, especially in the post-Crash atmosphere, this kind of thinking, so obviously willing to sacrifice taxpayers' dollars to the cause of securing the bankers', was anathema. Iron-toothed insistence on full payment of the Allied war debts thus became not only a financial issue but a political and a psychological issue as well, a totem of disgust with corrupt Europe, of regret at having intervened in the European war, and of provincial America's determination not to be suckered by silky international financiers.

THIS WAS THE SENTIMENT —penny-pinching, isolationist, anti–European, anti–Wall Street, and hotly felt—about which Hoover reminded Lamont over the telephone on June 5. To understand its depth and temperature is to appreciate the political courage of Hoover's proposal on June 20, 1931, that all nations observe a one-year moratorium on "all payments on intergovernmental debts, reparations and relief debts, both principal and interest."[6] Though Congress eventually ratified this proposal, Hoover was savagely attacked for bringing it forward. One Republican congressman denounced him as an "Oriental potentate drunk with power . . . an agent of Germany." Somewhat inconsistently, California Republican senator Hiram Johnson, already mistrustful of what he took to be Hoover's dangerous internationalism, took to calling him "the Englishman in the White House." Hoover's old nemesis George Norris expressed the anxiety of many when he said that "I cannot help but be suspicious that [the one-year moratorium] is a fore-runner for the cancellation of the balance . . . due us from foreign governments."[7] (Norris's suspicion was eventually confirmed, nourishing even more robust isolationist sentiment later in the decade.)

The moratorium on intergovernmental debt payments was intended to provide the reeling German bankers with a needed respite. Hoover followed it with a "standstill" agreement whereby private banks also pledged themselves not to present their German paper for payment. Taken together, these measures were aimed at calming the German eye of the global financial hurricane, thus sparing the American financial system from its fury. These were positive and forceful initiatives, but as Hoover later lamented, they provided "only a momentary breathing spell, for the larger forces [of the crisis] had now begun to gnaw like wolves into the financial vitals of Britain."[8] Despite his efforts, said Hoo-

6. Hoover, *Memoirs: The Great Depression*, 70.
7. Other voices praised Hoover and even saw political advantage for him in this forthright, statesmanlike move. The *Nation*, usually unfriendly to the president, called the moratorium "President Hoover's Great Action . . . the most far-reaching and the most praiseworthy step taken by an American President since the treaty of peace." One newspaper opined that the moratorium rendered Hoover "a marvelously rehabilitated candidate" for 1932. Another concluded that his action made "the picture of a cowering, dismayed and bewildered Hoover which the extremists have been so busily painting seem more or less ridiculous." Jordan Schwarz, *The Interregnum of Despair* (Urbana: University of Illinois Press, 1970), 85, 47, 82, 79.

The French balked at Hoover's proposal but eventually acquiesced, though French premier Laval, visiting Washington in October, secured Hoover's agreement that at the moratorium's expiration and before the next reparation payment fell due the twin questions of debts owed the United States and reparations due from Germany might be comprehensively discussed. These matters were now implicitly linked by the inclusive terms of Hoover's initiative, though the American government still officially denied any connection. Fatefully, the date scheduled for the first postmoratorium debt payment, and hence the target date for resolution of this vexatious issue, fell on December 15, 1932—five weeks *after* the quadrennial American presidential election.
8. Hoover, *Memoirs: The Great Depression*, 80.

ver, in a metallurgical figure of speech that befitted his mining background, "apprehension began to run like mercury through the financial world."[9]

But the metal that mattered in 1931 was not mercury. It was gold. Most countries still adhered to the gold standard, and with few exceptions most economists and statesmen reverenced gold with a mystical devotion that resembled religious faith. Gold underlay the most sacred token of national sovereignty: money. It guaranteed the value of money; more to the point, it guaranteed the value of a nation's currency beyond its own frontiers. Gold was therefore considered indispensable to the international trade and financial system. Nations issued their currencies in amounts fixed by the ratio of money in circulation to gold reserves. In theory, incoming gold was supposed to expand the monetary base, increase the amount of money in circulation, and thereby inflate prices and lower interest rates. Outflowing gold supposedly had the inverse effect: shrinking the monetary base, contracting the money supply, deflating prices, and raising interest rates. According to the rules of the gold-standard game, a country losing gold was expected to deflate its economy—to lower prices so as to stimulate exports, and to raise interest rates so as to reverse the outflow of capital. Indeed, these effects were assumed to happen virtually automatically. In actual practice, the gold-standard system was less systematic, less rule-bound, and more asymmetrical than the theory allowed. Nor did it necessarily work automatically. Countries losing gold were indeed under strong pressure to tighten credit or risk defaulting on their exchange-rate commitments. The latter option was thought to be prohibitively costly; events soon proved it was not. And creditor countries were under no like obligation to inflate when gold flowed in. They could simply "sterilize" surplus gold and carry on as before, leaving gold-losing countries to fend for themselves.

By tying the world's economy together, the gold standard theoretically ensured that economic fluctuations in one country would be transmitted to others. It was in fact that very transmission that was supposed to dampen erratic movements and keep the global system in equilibrium. In fair economic weather, the gold standard was thought to operate more or less mechanically as a kind of benign hydraulic pump that kept prices and interest rates stable, or fluctuating only within narrow bands, throughout the world trading system.

In the foul economic weather of 1931, however, huge surges emanat-

9. Hoover, *Memoirs: The Great Depression*, 63.

ing from the national economic crises in Austria and Germany threatened to swamp other countries, and the international plumbing broke
down. What Hoover called "refugee gold" and "flight capital" began to
course wildly to and fro through the conduits of the gold-standard pumping system. Hoover likened the panicky and lurching movements of gold
and credit, "constantly driven by fear hither and yon over the world," to
"a loose cannon on the deck of the world in a tempest-tossed sea."[10]

Nations with already depressed economies proved to have little stomach for suffering further deflation through the loss of gold. To protect
themselves, they raised tariff barriers and slapped controls on the export
of capital. Almost all of them eventually jettisoned the gold standard
itself. Frightened and battered, reefed and battened, virtually every ship
of state thus set cowering and solitary course for safe haven. When the
storm at last abated, it left the world forever transformed. The pre-1931
gold standard, which had been the Ark of the Covenant of the international economic order for more than a century, would never again be
fully restored to the tabernacle of global commerce.

Britain took the fateful step on September 21, 1931. Drained of gold
by jumpy European creditors and politically unwilling to take the deflationary steps to bid gold back to English shores, Britain defaulted on
further gold payments to foreigners.[11] More than two dozen other countries quickly followed suit. John Maynard Keynes, already tinkering with
heretical theories about "managed currency," rejoiced at "the breaking
of our gold fetters."[12] But most observers, including Hoover, regarded
the British abandonment of the gold standard as an unmitigated catastrophe. In an apt metaphor, Hoover likened the British situation to that
of a failing bank, faced with depositors' demands but unable to turn its
assets into cash, and thus forced to bar its doors. The difference was that
Britain was not a piddling country bank but a central pillar of the global
financial structure. When it suspended payments, world commerce shivered to a stop.

---

10. Hoover, *Memoirs: The Great Depression,* p. 67.
11. At the Royal Navy base at Invergordon, Scotland, a strike—sometimes described as
    a mutiny—over proposed pay cuts convinced the British government of the political
    impossibility of imposing the kind of austerity program that would have been re-
    quired to stay on the gold standard.
12. Chernow, *House of Morgan,* 331. As early as 1923 former U.S. Treasury official and
    Morgan partner Russell Leffingwell had warned that "Keynes . . . is flirting with
    strange gods and proposing to abandon the gold standard forever and to substitute
    a 'managed' currency [.] . . . [I]t is better to have some standard than to turn our
    affairs over to the wisdom of publicist-economists for management" (271).

The moratorium, the standstill agreement, and the British departure from gold meant that a vast volume of the world's financial assets — anything that constituted a claim on Austrian, German, or British banks, or those of any of the other countries that repudiated gold — were now frozen. The United States had already helped to clog the arteries of world trade by erecting high tariff barriers and by constricting its capital outflows after the Wall Street crash. Now, as the world's financial life-blood congealed, the international economy slowed to an arctic stillness. Germany would soon declare policies of national self-sufficiency. Britain in the Ottawa Agreements of 1932 effectively created a closed trading bloc — the so-called Imperial Preference System — sealing off the British empire from the commerce of other nations. The volume of global business shrank from some $36 billion of traffic in 1929 to about $12 billion by 1932.

The blow to American foreign trade was a harmful consequence of Britain's departure from gold, but hardly a fatal one. The United States at this time simply did not depend on foreign trade to the degree that other nations did, a fact to which the high protective tariffs of 1922 and 1930 testified.

More directly hurtful was the punishment that the German panic and the British abandonment of gold inflicted on the already crippled American financial system, still shuddering from the rash of bank failures in the final weeks of 1930. American banks held on the asset side of their ledgers some $1.5 billion in German and Austrian obligations, which were for the moment effectively worthless. Worse, the psychology of fear was rapidly overflowing international frontiers, running dark and swift from central Europe to Britain. It now washed over the United States. Foreign investors began withdrawing gold and capital from the American banking system. Domestic depositors, once bitten, twice shy, renewed with a vengeance their runs on banks, precipitating a liquidity crisis that dwarfed the panic in the final weeks of 1930. That earlier crisis thus served both as rehearsal and foundation for the full-blown catastrophe that hit in 1931. Five hundred twenty-two banks failed in the single month following Britain's farewell to gold. By year's end, 2,294 American banks had suspended operations, nearly twice as many as in 1930 and an all-time American record.[13]

American banks now bled profusely from two wounds: one inflicted

13. A larger number of banks suspended in 1933, but the figures for that year are not comparable because of the peculiar circumstance of the national "banking holiday" declared in March. *HSUS*, 1038, n. 8.

by domestic runs on deposits and the other by foreign withdrawals of capital. Unfortunately, the rules of the gold-standard game, as Hoover and most American bankers understood them, dictated that the latter problem take precedence over the former. In theory, American central banking authorities should now undertake deflationary measures; in practice, they did. This forced deflation in the context of an already deflated economy was the perverse logic of the gold standard against which Keynes was railing. To stanch the outflow of gold, the Federal Reserve System raised its rediscount rate, as gold-standard doctrine dictated that it should. In fact, the Fed moved with unprecedented muscularity, bumping the rate by a full percentage point in just one week's time. What the banking system as a whole needed, however, was not tighter money but easier money, as Marriner Eccles and other bankers knew, so that it might meet the demands of panicky depositors.

The starkly deflationary discipline of the gold standard now stood nakedly revealed to Americans as it had to Britons just weeks earlier. Britain had slipped that discipline by breaking loose from gold, freeing it to advance down a path toward at least a modest economic recovery in 1932. Within a year and a half, Franklin Roosevelt would do the same for the United States, creating a wholly new context for the exercise of monetary and fiscal policy. For the moment, however, Hoover chose to struggle within the gold standard's severely constraining framework. Why?

The answer is to be found in a legacy of perception and understanding of economic theory that would give way only grudgingly in the generation following Hoover's presidency. The world down to his time, for a century or more, had known only brief and painful interruptions of the gold-standard regime. It was widely assumed that there was simply no other workable basis on which currencies could be rendered reliable and on which the international economy could function. Without the link to gold, the value of a nation's money was deemed to be arbitrary and unpredictable. Its currency became "soft," perhaps unconvertible, and transactions across its national frontiers were turned into risky gambling ventures. The abandonment of gold, as Hoover put it, meant that "no merchant could know what he might receive in payment by the time his goods were delivered."[14] John Maynard Keynes had been trying for nearly a decade by 1931 to develop a theory of national and international monetary management that would not depend on gold. But even Keynes's ideas at this stage were not fully developed (his great work,

14. Hoover, *Memoirs: The Great Depression*, 66.

The General Theory of Employment, Interest, and Money, would not appear until 1936), and on this point at this time he commanded the barest of audiences among both economists and statesmen.

HOOVER THUS CONFRONTED an altogether more severe and complicated crisis in late 1931 than he had just a year earlier. In the face of this new circumstance, he resorted to a new tactic: an aggressive effort to balance the federal budget by raising taxes. This policy was sharply criticized by later economists who were to learn from Keynes's *General Theory* that the cure for depressions was not fiscal balance but deliberate deficit spending. In fact, the notion that government deficits might offset downturns in the business cycle had been current in academic and policymaking circles throughout the 1920s, and Hoover himself was conversant with this line of thinking. In May of 1931, Secretary of State Henry Stimson recorded in his diary that Hoover argued strenuously against the budget balancers in his own cabinet. "The President likened it to war times," according to Stimson. "He said in war times no one dreamed of balancing the budget. Fortunately we can borrow."[15]

After the British departure from gold and renewed runs on banks in the last half of 1931, however, Hoover changed his mind and asked for a sizeable tax increase. He drafted and submitted to Congress a bill that became the Revenue Act of 1932. He faced, to be sure, prospective deficits that, like so much else in this era, went wildly beyond all known precedent. The 1932 federal budget would end up $2.7 billion in the red—by far the largest peacetime deficit in American history to that time, and a figure that represented almost 60 percent of federal expenditures. No New Deal deficit would be proportionately larger. Ironically enough, Franklin D. Roosevelt was soon to make the federal budget deficit a centerpiece of his attack on Hoover in the presidential election campaign of 1932.

But neither reflex fiscal orthodoxy nor even the staggering size of the budget numbers fully accounts for Hoover's decision in late 1931 to ask Congress for a tax increase. At least as important as those considerations were the state of Hoover's thinking at this point about the depression's causes, character, and cure and the peculiar constellation of circumstances in which he found himself. In Hoover's mind, the depression—or the Great Depression, as it might now be legitimately called—originated in the collapse of the European banking and credit structures,

15. Schwarz, *Interregnum of Despair*, 112–13.

disfigured as they were by the stresses of the World War. As Hoover saw things, the force of that collapse transmitted itself to the United States through the mechanism of the gold standard, and its impact threatened to inundate the already chaotic and floundering American banking system. Strict adherence to the gold-standard rules dictated further deflation for the United States, but outright deflation was intolerable to Hoover. His overriding goal was to pump life-giving liquidity into the American credit system, desiccated as it was by domestic runs, foreign withdrawals, and the Federal Reserve System's tight-money policies to protect the gold standard. By liquefying the system, he would make money available for business borrowing, thus promoting general economic activity and recovery. Through a complex reasoning process, one that comprehended psychological factors as well as strictly economic ones, Hoover convinced himself that a tax hike would stabilize the banking system and thus generate the desired liquidity.

Hoover's critics then and later insisted that this indirect or "trickledown" approach was insufficient—that only a direct stimulus to the economy by large government expenditures for relief and public works would have the necessary tonic effect. An exchange between Hoover's secretary of the treasury, Ogden Mills, and New York Democratic senator Robert Wagner during hearings on an unemployment relief bill in 1932 nicely captured the differences in economic philosophies. "I want to break the ice by lending to industry so that somebody will begin to spend some money," said Mills. "I'm trying to put men to work and you won't cooperate," charged Wagner.[16]

Even Keynes at this time offered encouragement for Hoover's approach. Appearing in May 1931 at a conference on unemployment at the University of Chicago, he said: "I think the argument for public works in this country is much weaker than it is in Great Britain. . . . I think in this country . . . the means of getting back to a state of equilibrium should be concentrated on the rate of interest" — in other words, on easing credit by shoring up the banking system. Only later would Keynes develop at length the argument he briefly adumbrated in his 1930 volume, A *Treatise on Money*: that in some cases "it is not sufficient for the Central Authority to stand ready to lend . . . it must also stand ready to borrow. In other words, the Government must itself promote a programme of domestic investment."[17]

16. Schwarz, *Interregnum of Despair*, 167.
17. Herbert Stein, *The Fiscal Revolution in America* (Chicago: University of Chicago Press, 1969), 146, 140.

It is in this context of the state of economic knowledge and the particular circumstances in the United States and the world in late 1931 that Hoover's request for a tax increase must be understood. A government's budget was universally regarded as both symbol and substance of a nation's commitment to maintain the value of its currency. Balancing the budget, therefore, by reassuring foreign creditors, should dampen their withdrawals of gold. More concretely, raising revenues by taxation, as distinguished from borrowing, would take the government out of competition with private borrowers in the already squeezed credit markets, thus helping to keep interest rates low. Keeping interest rates low, in turn, would not only facilitate business borrowing but would preserve the value of bonds still held in the banks' badly weakened portfolios, thus easing pressures for further liquidation of bank assets. The request for higher taxes, in short, as Herbert Stein has explained, "was a kind of bond support program, to be carried out with tax receipts rather than with newly created money. It must be understood in the light of the unwillingness, or inability, of the Federal Reserve to support bonds by creating more new money in the fall of 1931. . . . The important point is that the decision to raise taxes was made in a condition of rising interest rates, falling bond prices, increasing bank suspensions, and a large gold outflow. A more relaxed attitude toward balancing the budget [such as Hoover had adopted just six months earlier] did not appear in government policy until the Roosevelt administration when all of these conditions were radically changed."[18]

The Revenue Act of 1932 made its way through Congress with only nominal opposition. A controversial proposal for a national sales tax was eventually deleted, but the final legislation raised taxes across the board and brought a half million new taxpayers (for a total of about 1.9 million) into the federal revenue net by reducing low-income exemptions. The act envisioned doubling federal tax receipts and set the essential features of the tax structure for the remainder of the decade. All subsequent efforts to revise the tax code in the 1930s, in fact, were aimed at increasing tax yields still further. On the question of the sanctity of a balanced budget, in short, Hoover stood safely within a broad consensus that endured until World War II, when, not incidentally, the federal tax system was expanded even more dramatically. Speaker Garner grudgingly withdrew his support for the sales tax feature, but he told his colleagues in the House: "I would levy any tax, sales or any other kind, in order to . . . balance the budget. . . . The country at this time is in a

18. Stein, *Fiscal Revolution in America*, 32, 35.

condition where the worst taxes you could possibly levy would be better than no taxes at all." He then histrionically requested all members who believed with him in a balanced budget to arise from their seats. Not a single representative remained seated.[19]

HOOVER'S COMMITMENT to the maintenance of the gold standard represented the purest, most conventional economic orthodoxy. But while his devotion to a balanced budget had the same appearance of orthodoxy, it actually owed more to the peculiar circumstances of the moment than to uncritical faith in the received fiscal wisdom. In his ongoing effort to liquefy the credit system Hoover would soon show himself capable of the most pragmatic, far-reaching economic hetero-doxy. The effort would test all his powers of creativity and command and would in the end carry him and the country into uncharted eco-nomic and political territory. From this phase of the crisis dates the onset of a period of experimentation and institutional innovation that would continue into the New Deal.

Hoover took the first steps into that new territory on the Sunday eve-ning of October 4, 1931, when he quietly slipped out of the White House to join a group of bankers he had summoned to meet him at Treasury Secretary Mellon's elegant home on Massachusetts Avenue. In a tense conversation that extended into the small hours of the morning, he urged that the stronger private banks create a $500 million credit pool to assist weaker institutions. Out of these talks emerged the Na-tional Credit Association. It was a private bankers' pool, and as such it testified to Hoover's continuing preference for nongovernmental, vol-untaristic approaches. But the circumstances of its birth and brief life also testified to the growing recognition, even in the highest circles of capitalism long thought to be mortally opposed to governmental intru-sion, and indeed in Hoover's own mind, of the irrelevance of the vol-untaristic approach.

The bankers gathered under Mellon's glittering chandeliers on Oc-tober 4 acceded to Hoover's request, but, he later wrote, "they constantly reverted to a proposal that the government do it. . . . I returned to the White House after midnight more depressed than ever before." After only a few weeks of activity, and after dispensing a paltry $10 million in loans, wrote Hoover, "the bankers' National Credit Association be-came ultraconservative, then fearful, and finally died. . . . Its members—

19. Schwarz, *Interregnum of Despair*, 124–25.

and the business world—threw up their hands and asked for governmental action."[20]

At this moment Hoover stood on the shore of a political and ideological Rubicon. He had gingerly waded into it more than two years earlier with the creation of federally funded agricultural stabilization corporations. Now he plunged in deeply. Desperate to save the banking system, disappointed at the timidity of private capital, and faced with the business community's own demand for "governmental action," he proposed a series of measures that amounted to a repudiation of his own voluntaristic principles. Sometimes lumped together as Hoover's "second program" against the Depression (to distinguish them from the voluntary wage and private construction agreements of late 1929), these measures would eventually help to revolutionize the American financial world. They would also lay the groundwork for a broader restructuring of government's role in many other sectors of American life, a restructuring known as the New Deal.

The entire national credit apparatus was under siege. The president's understanding of economic theory instructed him that what it needed was money. The Federal Reserve System, committed to protecting the nation's gold stock by lifting interest rates, was an uncooperative partner in this effort. Thus Hoover, with the grudging acquiescence of Congress, moved to reform the system and to create wholly new instrumentalities to bolster the sagging credit structure.

Among the first of his initiatives was the Glass-Steagall Act of February 1932, which markedly broadened the definition of acceptable collateral for Federal Reserve System loans and for the issuance of Federal Reserve notes. These actions allowed the system to release large amounts of gold from its reserve holdings and still significantly expand the monetary base.

Hoover also proposed in November 1931 that Congress provide for home-mortgage holders a rediscounting service similar to that which the Federal Reserve System offered to banking and commercial interests. Mortgage paper could not be presented for discounting at the Federal Reserve, but Hoover asked that it be made eligible as security for loans at up to twelve new Home Loan Banks. Like the Glass-Steagall Act, this legislation was designed to thaw millions of dollars in frozen assets. To

20. Hoover, *Memoirs: The Great Depression*, 86, 97. See also Albert U. Romasco, *The Poverty of Abundance: Hoover, the Nation, the Depression* (New York: Oxford University Press, 1965), 87–96.

Hoover's bitter regret, Congress weakened his bill by setting higher collateral requirements than he wanted and delayed final passage of the Federal Home Loan Bank Act until July 1932. In the meantime, thousands of families lost their homes. "All this seems dull economics," Hoover noted, "but the poignant American drama revolving around the loss of the old homestead had a million repetitions straight from life, not because of the designing villain but because of a fault in our financial system."[21]

By far the most radical, innovative, and ultimately consequential initiative in Hoover's "second program" was the creation in January 1932 of the Reconstruction Finance Corporation (RFC). The failure of the short-lived National Credit Association had shown the inadequacy of private measures to shore up the buckling banks. The bankers themselves wanted federal action. Swallowing his dearest principles, Hoover now gave it to them. Patterned on the War Finance Corporation that had been created to fund the construction of military plants in 1918, the RFC was an instrument for making taxpayers' dollars directly available to private financial institutions. Congress capitalized the new agency at $500 million and authorized it to borrow up to $1.5 billion more. The RFC was to use these sums to provide emergency loans to banks, building-and-loan societies, railroads, and agricultural stabilization corporations.

Business Week called the RFC "the most powerful offensive force [against the Depression] that governmental and business imagination has, so far, been able to command." Even critics of Hoover like the *New Republic* conceded that "there has been nothing quite like it." Its swift creation and sweeping mandate left Senator Norris "dazed. . . . I have been called a socialist, a bolshevik, a communist, and a lot of other terms of a similar nature," said Norris, "but in the wildest flights of my imagination I never thought of such a thing as putting the Government into business as far as this bill would put it in."[22]

However grudgingly, Hoover had now unmistakably compromised his belief in voluntarism and embraced direct government action. "Mr. Hoover," commented Columbia University economist Rexford Tugwell, "who has always described himself as one who believes 'that government is best which governs least,' is now in process of pushing the government into the banking business. At the very least his program may be de-

21. Hoover, *Memoirs: The Great Depression*, 111.
22. Romasco, *Poverty of Abundance*, 189; Schwarz, *Interregnum of Despair*, 92.

scribed as 'bank relief.' These weeks and months of depression are rapidly and inevitably weaving governmental controls into the American economy. . . . [O]ut of such a development," concluded Tugwell, who would soon become a major architect of the New Deal, "one may imagine what pictures of government in business one pleases; none of them would conform to Mr. Hoover's expressed horror of governmental interference."[23]

Tugwell astutely recognized that the creation of the RFC constituted a historical pivot. The turning was not uncontroversial. New York's Fiorello La Guardia denounced the RFC as "a millionaire's dole." But soon he and other progressives discerned, as Tugwell had, the fateful precedent that the creation of the RFC had established. If Hoover could be made to support federal relief for the banks, why not federal relief for the unemployed? By agreeing to the bankers' demands for the RFC — "bank relief," as Tugwell had called it — the president had implicitly legitimated the claims of other sectors for federal assistance. Hoover had given up the ground of high principle. He now stood ideologically shorn before a storm of demands for unemployment relief.

IT WAS NOW the third winter of the Depression. In the long-blighted countryside, unmarketable crops rotted in fields and unsellable livestock died on the hoof, as the Federal Farm Board's stabilization corporations exhausted their price-support funds. In towns and cities across the country, haggard men in shabby overcoats, collars turned up against the chill wind, newspapers plugging the holes in their shoes, lined up glumly for handouts at soup kitchens. Tens of thousands of displaced workers took to the roads, thumbs up, hitching west, huddled in boxcars, heading south, drifting north, east, wherever the highways and the railroads led, wherever there might be a job. Those who stayed put hunkered down, took in their jobless relatives, kited the grocery bills

23. Rexford G. Tugwell, "Flaws in the Hoover Economic Plan," *Current History*, January 1932, 531. Tugwell later conceded that "practically the whole New Deal was extrapolated from programs that Hoover started. . . . When it was all over I once made a list of New Deal ventures begun during Hoover's years as secretary of commerce and then as president. I had to concluded that his policies were substantially correct. The New Deal owed much to what he had begun. . . . Hoover had wanted — and had said clearly enough that he wanted — nearly all the changes now brought under the New Deal label." Tugwell quoted in Joan Hoff Wilson, *Herbert Hoover: Forgotten Progressive* (Boston, Little, Brown, 1975), 158; see also Tugwell, *Roosevelt's Revolution: The First Year, a Personal Perspective* (New York: Macmillan, 1977), xiii–xiv; and Tugwell, *The Brains Trust* (New York: Viking, 1968), xxii.

at the corner store, patched their old clothes, darned and redarned their socks, tried to shore up some fragments of hope against the ruins of their dreams.

The Depression struck with especially harsh fury in the ethnic communities so shallowly rooted in American soil. The frail institutions so painstakingly erected by the first immigrant generation simply fell apart. Banks serving immigrant neighborhoods were among the first to close their doors when the round of panics began. In Chicago, the Binga State Bank, which served the black community, folded in 1930; it was soon followed by the First Italian State Bank, the Slovak Papanek-Kovac State Bank, the Czech Novak and Stieskal State Bank, the Lithuanian Universal State Bank, the Jewish Noel State Bank, and "Smulski's Bank," where many Poles had deposited their meager savings. The mutual benefit and fraternal insurance societies and the religious welfare organizations with which immigrants had tried to defend themselves against the abundant uncertainties of everyday life collapsed under the weight of the demands now put upon them. Chicago's Jewish Charities in 1932 struggled to support some fifty thousand jobless Jews. Unemployed men skulked at home while their wives and children scrounged what work they could find. Traditional patterns of family authority and status eroded. A Polish woman told a social worker in Chicago that because she had been working for four years while her husband was jobless, "I am the boss in the family for I have full charge in running this house. You know, who make the money he is the boss." "One of the most common things," one Chicagoan later reflected about his Depression-era childhood, "was this feeling of your father's failure. That somehow he hadn't beaten the rap."[24]

No one starved, Hoover claimed, but in New York City school officials reported some twenty thousand malnourished children in 1932, while apples fell to the ground in Oregon orchards for want of buyers. This spectacle of dire want in the midst of wasting plenty bred perplexity and anger. Hillocks of unsold wheat shadowed the prairies, while in Seattle, Chicago, New York, and dozens of other cities men and women nightly scratched through dank alleys, grubbing for scraps of food in garbage cans.

No issue plagued Hoover more painfully, or caused him more political and personal hurt, than the plight of the unemployed. By early 1932

24. Lizabeth Cohen, *Making a New Deal: Industrial Workers in Chicago, 1919–1939* (Cambridge: Cambridge University Press, 1990), 248.

well over ten million persons were out of work, nearly 20 percent of the labor force. In big cities like Chicago and Detroit that were home to hard-hit capital goods industries like steelmaking and automobile manufacturing, the unemployment rate approached 50 percent. Chicago authorities counted 624,000 unemployed persons in their city at the end of 1931. In Detroit, General Motors laid off 100,000 workers out of its 1929 total of some 260,000 employees. All told, 223,000 jobless workers idled in the streets of the nation's automobile capital by the winter of 1931–32. Black workers, traditionally the last hired and the first fired, suffered especially. In Chicago blacks made up 4 percent of the population but 16 percent of the unemployed; in the Pittsburgh steel districts they were 8 percent of the population but accounted for almost 40 percent of the unemployed.[25]

Many workers who remained on the payroll went on shorter hours. Perhaps one-third of all employed persons were working part-time, so that in the aggregate almost 50 percent of the nation's human workpower was going unutilized. Those lucky enough still to hold some kind of job also found themselves working for smaller paychecks. U.S. Steel cut wages by 10 percent in September 1931, the first major employer to break the 1929 agreement with Hoover about maintaining wage rates. Its action was swiftly followed by General Motors and other major corporations employing some 1.7 million workers. Unemployment now loomed not as a transient difficulty but as a deep, intractable problem that showed no sign of abating. The feeling spread that the nation had turned a historical corner, to find itself facing an endless future of pervasive, structural unemployment. "The real problem in America," one prominent Democrat said in 1932, "is not to feed ourselves for one more winter, it is to find what we are going to do with ten or twelve million people who are permanently displaced."[26]

The country had never before known unemployment of these magnitudes or of this duration. It had in place no mechanism with which to combat mass destitution on this scale. Private unemployment insurance plans, sponsored by employers and unions, including a pioneering program at General Electric, covered fewer than two hundred thousand workers as the Depression began, less than 1 percent of the private-sector

25. Romasco, *Poverty of Abundance*, 155, 167; figures on black unemployment are from Lester Chandler, *America's Greatest Depression* (New York: Harper and Row, 1970), 40.
26. Schwarz, *Interregnum of Despair*, 160.

work force. Relief for the poor had traditionally been the responsibility of state and local governments and private charities, but their combined resources were no match for the enormous national calamity they now confronted. Many states that tried to raise more money for relief by increasing taxes faced revolts from angry and hard-pressed citizens. Almost all state and local governments had by 1932 exhausted their legal or market-dictated borrowing capacity. Pennsylvania, for example, was constitutionally prohibited from incurring a debt of more than $1 million, as well as from levying a graduated income tax.

Hoover characteristically tried to stimulate local government and charitable assistance to the unemployed with two voluntary committees, the President's Emergency Committee for Employment, chaired by Arthur Woods from its inception in October 1930 to its demise in April 1931, and its successor, the President's Organization on Unemployment Relief, headed by Walter S. Gifford, the president of American Telephone and Telegraph and chairman of the Charity Organization Society of New York City. By certain measures, these bodies achieved commendable results. Municipal government payments for relief in New York City, for example, rose from $9 million in 1930 to $58 million in 1932. New Yorkers' private charitable giving increased from $4.5 million in 1930 to $21 million in 1932. But though those figures testified to the compassion of City Hall and the perhaps surprisingly soft hearts of individual New Yorkers, they were pathetically inadequate. Combined public and private relief expenditures of $79 million in New York City for the entire year of 1932 amounted to less than one month's loss of wages for the eight hundred thousand New Yorkers out of work. In Chicago, lost wages from unemployment were estimated at $2 million per day in late 1931; relief expenditures totaled $100,000 per day.[27]

In the face of this breakdown of the traditional relief apparatus, the cry for direct federal assistance grew ever more insistent. "We can no longer depend on passing the hat, and rattling the tin cup," the famed Kansas editor William Allen White wrote to his senator in Washington. "We have gone to the bottom of the barrel." Others sounded even more alarming notes. Chicago mayor Anton Cermak gruffly informed a House committee that the federal government could either send relief to Chicago or it would have to send troops. "[I]f something is not done and starvation is going to continue," a labor leader warned a Senate com-

27. Romasco, *Poverty of Abundance*, 153–55.

mittee, "the doors of revolt in this country are going to be thrown open."[28]

These cries of impending revolution were largely empty rhetorical posturings. True, some Communists and others on the far left thought they heard the knell of capitalism and cried for action in the streets. But what struck most observers, and mystified them, was the eery docility of the American people, their stoic passivity as the depression grindstone rolled over them. There might be some nervous stirring on Capitol Hill in the winter of 1931–32, Anne O'Hare McCormick wrote, but "beyond the Potomac there is silence . . . a vacuum; no life-giving breath of popular enthusiasm or popular indignation, no current of that famous energy that propels the American dynamo. . . . Is America growing old? Have we . . . slumped into that sad maturity which submits to events?" Like Mr. Micawber, she concluded, "we are all waiting for something to turn up."[29]

The historian Gerald W. Johnson explored the popular mood at greater length in early 1932. "In the mind of the average American," he wrote, "1931 was the year of the Great Depression, for it was in the past 12 months that it really affected us who are just ordinary people, not international bankers, not financiers of any sort, not great executives, and not derelicts who are chronically on the verge of unemployment in all years." Americans were beginning to be scared, Johnson conceded, but

> we are by no means in despair. . . . [W]e do not believe for a moment that the hard times are going to continue for the next 6 years. Nineteen thirty-one was a hard year, but it saw no bayonets, heard no firing in the streets, afforded no hint of the dissolution of our institutions. . . . The revolutionists have gained no following worth mentioning in this country. There has been a great outcry against the Reds, and some persons confess to be very much frightened by them; but the sober truth is that their American campaign has fallen flatter than their campaign in any other country. To date the capitalist system seems to be as firmly entrenched in America as the Republic itself. . . . Under the most terrific strain to which it has been subjected since Gettysburg, the Republic stands unshaken.[30]

28. Schwarz, *Interregnum of Despair*, 160–61; Schlesinger 1:176.
29. Schwarz, *Interregnum of Despair*, 74.
30. Gerald W. Johnson, "The Average American and the Depression," *Current History*, February 1932, 671–75.

This odd apathy would persist and would continue to puzzle contemporaries and historians alike. Even Franklin Roosevelt found the submissiveness of the American people baffling. "There had never been a time, the Civil War alone excepted," Tugwell remembered Roosevelt saying, "when our institutions had been in such jeopardy. Repeatedly he spoke of this, saying that it was enormously puzzling to him that the ordeal of the past three years had been endured so peaceably."[31]

Then in 1932 this passivity modestly receded, giving way to a demand for federal action on at least one front—relief for the unemployed. Even this demand was qualified and halting and only gradually came to define a significant difference between the two major political parties.

The issue was older than the Depression, going back at least to Senator Robert Wagner's introduction of his "Three Bills" in 1927, calling for better statistical information on unemployment, countercyclical public works, and reforms in the United States Employment Service, a job placement bureau created during the World War. Hoover endorsed the first two of the Three Bills but rejected the third on technically niggling states'-rights grounds. When Wagner in 1930 introduced a Senate bill for federal unemployment insurance, Hoover opposed it on deeper philosophical grounds of antipathy to the bureaucratic state and fear of creating a welfare-dependent class. The president had, in fact, himself called for insurance against industrial death and accidents, as well as unemployment and old-age insurance, but he had in mind encouraging private plans, not creating new government programs.

In New York State, meanwhile, Governor Franklin Roosevelt had in 1930 publicly endorsed government-sponsored unemployment insurance and old-age pensions. In 1931 Roosevelt had secured the enactment of the New York Temporary Emergency Relief Administration, originally authorized for just seven months and funded at $20 million. Its very name and brief projected tenure bespoke the continuing anxieties in American culture, as well as in Roosevelt's own mind, about the danger of creating a permanent welfare class dependent on a government "dole." Yet Roosevelt also forthrightly declared that relief "must be extended by Government, not as a matter of charity, but as a matter of social duty; the State accepts the task cheerfully because it believes

---

31. Tugwell, *Brains Trust*, 295.

that it will help restore that close relationship with its people which is necessary to preserve our democratic form of government."[32]

Here was an attitude toward government—to call it a philosophy would be too much—that defined a distinct difference from Hoover, who stewed in anxieties about the dole and endlessly lashed the Congress and the country with lectures about preserving the nation's moral fiber, not to mention the integrity of the federal budget, by avoiding direct federal payments for unemployment relief. No issue more heavily burdened Hoover in the presidential election year of 1932. The Great Humanitarian who had fed the starving Belgians in 1914, the Great Engineer so hopefully elevated to the presidency in 1928, now appeared as the Great Scrooge, a corrupted ideologue who could swallow government relief for the banks but priggishly scrupled over government provisions for the unemployed. Declaiming against budget deficits and the dangers of the dole, Hoover vetoed the Garner-Wagner relief bill on July 11, though he did in the end reluctantly accede to a compromise, the Relief and Reconstruction Act, which he signed on July 21. It authorized the RFC to finance up to $1.5 billion in "self-liquidating" public works and to loan up to $300 million to the states for relief purposes. California's Senator Hiram Johnson thought Hoover's acquiescence in this legislation constituted a "remarkable somersault" from his previous opposition to all such measures.[33]

HOOVER'S SOMERSAULT came too late to bring him political credit. Cartoonists now routinely caricatured him as a dour, heartless skinflint whose rigid adherence to obsolete doctrines caused men and women to go jobless and hungry. At the Democratic National Committee, Charles Michelson's propaganda machine went into high gear, missing no chance to label the crisis the "Hoover Depression." Folk usage added its own epithets. Tarpaper-and-cardboard hobo shantytowns became "Hoovervilles." Pulled-out empty trouser pockets were "Hoover flags." Hoover grew increasingly isolated, both politically and personally. A joke circulated that when the president asked for a nickel to make a telephone call to a friend, an aide flipped him a dime and said, "Here, call them both." A newspaperman noted how the Depression trans-

32. Schlesinger 1:392.
33. Hiram Johnson to "My Dear Boys," May 14, 1932, in *The Diary Letters of Hiram Johnson* (New York: Garland, 1983), 5:n.p.

formed Hoover both physically and psychologically, mussing his customarily fastidious appearance, sapping his confidence, and eliciting a bitterness alien to his Quaker upbringing: "He didn't look to me like the Hoover I had been seeing. His hair was rumpled. He was almost crouching behind his desk, and he burst out at me with a volley of angry words . . . against the politicians and the foreign governments . . . in language that he must have learned in a mining camp."[34]

The expulsion of the "Bonus Army" from Washington in late July 1932 proved especially politically damaging to Hoover. Thousands of unemployed veterans of the World War American Expeditionary Force converged on Washington in the spring and summer of 1932. Styling themselves the Bonus Expeditionary Force, they lobbied Congress for early cash payment of the war service "bonus" due them in 1945. When the Senate refused to pass the bonus bill, many disappointed veterans returned to their homes, but several thousand remained, and when District of Columbia police tried on July 28 to evict them from buildings they had occupied on Pennsylvania Avenue, an ugly riot erupted. Two bonus marchers were shot dead. The district authorities thereupon appealed to Hoover for help, and he called in federal troops. Late in the afternoon, a detachment of mounted cavalrymen, sabers drawn, accompanied by six tanks and a column of infantry with fixed bayonets, cleared the buildings. The commanding officer, General Douglas MacArthur, then exceeded his orders, which were to secure the buildings and contain the marchers at their campsite on Anacostia Flats on the outskirts of the district. Instead, MacArthur's troops proceeded to Anacostia and drove the marchers out of the camp with tear gas. The soldiers then put their tumbledown shacks to the torch.

The spectacle of the United States Army routing unarmed citizens with tanks and firebrands outraged many Americans. The Bonus Army episode came to symbolize Hoover's supposed insensitivity to the plight of the unemployed. In fact the worst violence, resulting in two deaths, had come at the hands of the district police, not the federal troops, and the blame for the torching of Anacostia Flats was MacArthur's, not Hoover's. But Hoover chose to ignore MacArthur's insubordination and assumed full responsibility for the army's actions.

"The Battle of Anacostia Flats," coming just seventeen days after Hoover's unpopular veto of the Garner-Wagner relief bill, marked the lowest ebb of Hoover's political fortunes. He had been nominated for a second

34. Wilson, *Herbert Hoover*, 162.

presidential term by a dispirited Republican convention in June, but the honor was worth little. He was already a beaten man. He had grappled with the wildly swooning economy and been brought down by it. He had been broken not by "the Great Depression" but by a concatenation of crises that only cumulatively and only by sometime in 1931 deserved the perverse appellation of "Great." By the end of 1931 he had in fact taken off his ideological gloves and done bare-knuckle combat with the crisis — the "battle on a thousand fronts," he later called it. But it was too little too late, especially and woefully so in the politically crucial area of relief. He had been overwhelmed by events too large and swift even for his capacious and agile mind to grasp. He had lost. No one doubted that his defeat would be ratified by the voters in November.

Nor was the Depression the only crisis whose resolution eluded Hoover's once-vaunted genius. In faraway Asia, an explosion on the night of September 18, 1931, damaged a Japanese-controlled railroad in China's northern province of Manchuria. In a response so swift that it suggested the work of agents provocateurs, Japanese military forces overran the province. In February 1932 Japan installed a puppet government in Manchuria, which it officially recognized as the new state of Manchukuo, a prelude to an ambitious scheme to colonize the area with millions of Japanese settlers.

Those moves climaxed decades of Japanese machinations against China and foreshadowed a wider conflict to come. The incident also foretold the timid course of American diplomacy in the Depression decade and revealed the debilitating effects of American aloofness from the League of Nations. When Hoover refused to participate in an international boycott of Japan, the league could do little more than pass a resolution censuring Tokyo's action. That feeble effort to drive Japan out of Manchuria eventually resulted only in driving Japan out of the league, further weakening an already feeble instrument for maintaining international peace. Though Secretary of State Henry L. Stimson counseled a stiffer American response, a cautious Hoover stopped short of economic sanctions that might provoke Japan. Most of his countrymen had no quarrel with the president's restraint. "The American people don't give a hoot in a rain barrel who controls North China," said the *Philadelphia Record*.[35] Washington contented itself with proclaiming the ironically named Stimson Doctrine (it might more properly have been

---

35. Thomas A. Bailey, A *Diplomatic History of the American People*, 10th ed. (Englewoood Cliffs, N.J.: Prentice-Hall, 1980), 699.

called the Hoover Doctrine), by which the United States refused to recognize Manchukuo as an independent state — but refused as well to back nonrecognition with either economic or military muscle. Faced with outright aggression, the Americans seemed capable of no more than this timid parchment protest. Japan drew the appropriate conclusions: it had little to fear either from the league or from Depression-plagued America. It could pursue its expansionist schemes with impunity. On the wind-scoured plains of Manchuria, Japan thus set the match in 1931 to the long fuse that would detonate the attack on Pearl Harbor just ten years later.

To White House visitors, the president by this time seemed prematurely aged. He kept up a punishing regimen of rising at six and working without interruption until nearly midnight. His clothes were disheveled, his hair rumpled, eyes bloodshot, complexion ashen. He grew increasingly testy and brittle. "How I wish I could cheer up the poor old President," wrote the venerable Stimson, Hoover's senior by seven years.[36] Never temperamentally suited to the pelting and abuse of the political arena, a man naturally diffident and inordinately self-protective, Hoover was painfully bruised by blows from both the left and the right. As early as 1919 he had conceded that "I do not . . . have the mental attitude or the politician's manner . . . and above all I am too sensitive to political mud."[37] By the fall of 1932 he had lost all stomach for political campaigning. He took to the hustings only in October and seemed to campaign more for vindication in the historical record than for affection in the hearts of voters. Just four years earlier he had won one of the most lopsided victories in the history of presidential elections. Now he took an even worse drubbing than he had given to Al Smith. On November 8, 1932, Hoover won just six states. The Great Engineer, so recently the most revered American, was the most loathed and scorned figure in the country. All eyes now looked to his successor, Franklin D. Roosevelt.

HOOVER BROUGHT a corporate executive's sensibility to the White House. Roosevelt brought a politician's. Hoover as president frequently dazzled visitors with his detailed knowledge and expert understanding of American business. "His was a mathematical brain," said his admiring secretary, Theodore Joslin. "Let banking officials, for instance, come into his office and he would rattle off the number of banks in the

36. Schwarz, *Interregnum of Despair*, 51n.
37. Wilson, *Herbert Hoover: Forgotten Progressive*, 77.

country, list their liabilities and assets, describe the trend of fiscal affairs, and go into the liquidity, or lack of it, of individual institutions, all from memory."[38] Roosevelt, in contrast, impressed his visitors by asking them to draw a line across a map of the United States. He would then name, in order, every county through which the line passed, adding anecdotes about each locality's political particularities.[39] Where Hoover had a Quaker's reserve about the perquisites of the presidency, Roosevelt savored them with gusto. By 1932 Hoover wore the mantle of office like a hair shirt that he could not wait to doff. Roosevelt confided to a journalist his conviction that "no man ever willingly gives up public life— no man who has ever tasted it."[40] Almost preternaturally self-confident, he had no intimidating image of the presidential office to live up to, it was said, since his untroubled conception of the presidency consisted quite simply of the thought of himself in it.

Hoover's first elected office was the presidency. Roosevelt had been a professional politician all his life. He had spent years charting his course for the White House. To a remarkable degree, he had followed the career path blazed by his cousin Theodore Roosevelt—through the New York legislature and the office of assistant secretary of the navy to the governor's chair in Albany. In 1920 he had been the vice-presidential candidate on the losing Democratic ticket.

The following year, while vacationing at his family's summer estate on Campobello Island, in the Canadian province of New Brunswick, he had been stricken with poliomyelitis. He was thirty-nine years of age. He would never again be able to stand without heavy steel braces on his legs. Through grueling effort and sheer will power, he eventually trained himself to "walk" a few steps, an odd shuffle in which, leaning on the strong arm of a companion, he threw one hip, then the other, to move his steel-cased legs forward. His disability was no secret, but he took care to conceal its extent. He never allowed himself to be photographed in his wheelchair or being carried.

Roosevelt's long struggle with illness transformed him in spirit as well as body. Athletic and slim in his youth, he was now necessarily sedentary, and his upper body thickened. He developed, in the manner of many paraplegics, a wrestler's torso and big, beefy arms. His biceps, he

38. Theodore G. Joslin, *Hoover off the Record* (Garden City, N.Y.: Doubleday, Doran, 1934), 17.
39. William Manchester, *The Glory and the Dream* (Boston: Little, Brown, 1974), 50.
40. Davis 2:64.

delighted in telling visitors, were bigger than those of the celebrated prizefighter Jack Dempsey. Like many disabled persons, too, he developed a talent for denial, a kind of forcefully willed optimism that refused to dwell on life's difficulties. Sometimes this talent abetted his penchant for duplicity, as in the continuing love affair he carried on with Lucy Mercer, even after he told his wife in 1918 that the relationship was ended. At other times it endowed him with an aura of radiant indomitability, lending conviction and authority to what in other men's mouths might have been banal platitudes, such as "all we have to fear is fear itself." Many of Roosevelt's acquaintances also believed that his grim companionship with paralysis gave to this shallow, supercilious youth the precious gift of a purposeful manhood.

Roosevelt's illness also gave him, paradoxically enough, political opportunity. By keeping him abed and convalescing for years, it made him the sole Democrat with a national reputation who was unscarred by his party's lacerating internecine battles and crushing electoral losses in the 1920s. He even turned the forced idleness of his convalescence into positive advantage. Working from a small office at the family home in Hyde Park, New York, he used the time to carry on a vast correspondence, much of it cranked out over his forged signature from what amounted to a letter-writing factory run by his shrewd and faithful operative, a crater-eyed, gnarled, wheezing homunculus named Louis McHenry Howe. Eleanor Roosevelt, meanwhile, became his public surrogate, traveling in her husband's stead and speaking on his behalf.

No less than for Franklin, his illness also proved a turning point for Eleanor. She was no stranger to grief. Her mother had died when Eleanor was barely eight years old. Within two more years, her younger brother and her father also passed away. Her surviving brother, like their father, was a chronic alcoholic, as were several of her uncles. Against the menace of their boozy, nocturnal forays the young Eleanor's bedroom door was triple-locked. After 1918 the dull ache of her husband's betrayal never left her. Her suffering deepened immeasurably in 1921 when the marriage she had agreed to preserve, despite Franklin's infidelity, was further strained by his affliction with polio. Yet despite these abundant travails, little in her life until this time had distinguished her from the smug and goosy crowd of wealthy socialites into which she was born. On her honeymoon in Europe in 1905, she had been utterly unable to answer a simple question about the structure of American government. She had taken little interest in the debate over women's suffrage that came to a climax in 1920 with the passage of the Nineteenth Amendment. She had lived complacently in an upper-crust ambience of grand houses, sumptuous entertainments, and foreign travel. Her attitudes were thoroughly conventional, her correspondence studded with examples of what a biographer calls "flip, class-bound arrogance and egregious racism."[41]

With the onset of Franklin's illness, however, Eleanor shucked off the chrysalis of the conventional society matron and emerged as an independent woman and a public figure. She got a job, as a teacher at the Todhunter School in New York. She made speeches and wrote magazine articles. She championed women's rights and spoke out against racial segregation in the South. She chaired the women's platform committee at the Democratic national convention in 1924. And all the while she worked tirelessly to keep her stricken husband's political career alive.

The Democratic Party remained badly divided in the 1920s between its urban-northeastern-wet-Catholic wing and its rural-southern-western-dry-Protestant wing. Neither faction could command a winning majority in the electorate at large, but each possessed enough power to frustrate the aspirations of the other and thus block the party from gaining a presidential victory. The denial of the nomination to William Gibbs McAdoo in 1924 demonstrated the intraparty veto power of the urban wing; the desertion of the Catholic New Yorker, Al Smith, by many southern Democrats in 1928 underscored the electoral veto power of the rural wing. The successive Democratic electoral disasters of 1920, 1924, and 1928 graphically illustrated the Democrats' weaknesses and emphasized the necessity of somehow reconciling their two wings if they were ever to win the presidency.

Roosevelt was a master reconciler. As governor, he had taken the working-class, New York City ethnic voters led by the sachems of Tammany Hall and welded them into a winning combination with the conservative, antiurban agrarian voters of upstate New York, to whom anything associated with the Tammany machine had historically been anathema. Throughout the decade of the 1920s, he had applied the same techniques on a national scale. During the years of his convalescence from polio, he had frequently sojourned at a hydrotherapy center in Warm Springs, Georgia, using it as a kind of embassy from which to conduct a diplomatic mission of reconciliation to the southern wing of his party.

41. Blanche Wiesen Cook, *Eleanor Roosevelt: A Life*, vol. 1, 1884–1933 (New York: Viking, 1992), 171.

Roosevelt believed that even a united Democratic Party could probably not win a presidential election as long as Republican prosperity lasted. He told fellow Democrats that their party's eventual success must wait "until the Republicans had led us into a serious period of depression and unemployment," a revealing indication of his sense of the relationship between economic crisis and political opportunity.[42] Through most of the 1920s, he did not foresee such an opportunity opening in the near future. His plan was to rebuild his broken body, then run for governor of New York in 1932 and perhaps the presidency in 1936. But in 1928 Al Smith persuaded him to make a bid for the New York governorship, and he won handsomely, even while Smith went down to humiliating defeat. That singular victory in a Republican year, and his massive reelection majority in 1930, positioned Roosevelt as the frontrunner for the Democratic nomination in 1932. The Depression, sooner and larger than anything Roosevelt or any one else had anticipated, now made that nomination a coveted prize.

AL SMITH, STILL STINGING from his defeat in 1928 and sensing that this was surely a Democratic year, sought to be nominated a second time. John Nance Garner also commanded considerable support. But it was Roosevelt who grasped the great prize on the fourth ballot at the Democratic national convention at Chicago on the evening of July 1, 1932. The rural, southern element in the party took comfort from Garner's selection as his vice-presidential running mate. In an unprecedented gesture, Roosevelt flew to Chicago to accept the nomination in person. "Let it also be symbolic that in so doing I broke traditions," he declared to the cheering delegates. "Let it be from now on the task of our Party to break foolish traditions." There followed a familiar litany of alleged Republican misdemeanors and invocations of past Democratic heroes. The speech meandered through somewhat inconsistent proposals for cutting government spending and providing unemployment relief, for regulation of securities markets and of agricultural production, for the repeal of Prohibition, lower tariffs, and reforestation projects. And then the simple phrase that would give a name to an era: "I pledge you, I pledge myself, to a new deal for the American people."[43]

42. Frank Freidel, *Franklin Roosevelt: The Ordeal* (Boston: Little, Brown, 1954), 183.
43. See accounts of the nomination and acceptance speech in Schlesinger 1, chaps. 27 and 28; Davis 2, esp. chap. 10; and James MacGregor Burns, *Roosevelt: The Lion and the Fox* (New York: Harcourt, Brace, 1956), chaps. 7 and 8.

Conservative Democrats were aghast. Some delegates, notably those pledged to Roosevelt's old mentor and patron, Al Smith, petulantly refused to give Roosevelt the customary honor of a unanimous nomination. Smith, said H. L. Mencken, now nurtured a "fierce hatred of Roosevelt, the cuckoo who had seized his nest." Reactionary party chairman John J. Raskob regarded the Roosevelt supporters as "a crowd of radicals, whom I do not regard as Democrats." (This was strange stuff from someone who had until recently himself been a Republican.) "When one thinks of the Democratic Party being headed by such radicals as Roosevelt, Huey Long, [William Randolph] Hearst, [William Gibbs] McAdoo, and Senators [Burton] Wheeler and [Clarence] Dill," Raskob continued, "as against the fine, conservative talent in the Party as represented by such men as [Jouett Shouse], Governor Byrd, Governor Smith, Carter Glass, John W. Davis, Governor Cox, Pierre S. DuPont, Governor Ely and others too numerous to mention, it takes all one's courage and faith to not lose hope completely."[44]

What worried the Democratic old guard? In what might the "New Deal" consist? Roosevelt's prior political career offered only a few clues. He had long championed low tariffs and assistance to agriculture, but these were both familiar staples of Democratic policy. More innovative was his advocacy of public hydroelectric power projects and his passionate, even romantic, interest in conservation—positions that endeared him to many western progressives, including progressive Republicans like George Norris. Since 1930 he had embraced government-financed unemployment and old-age insurance, which brought him the warm support of urban Democrats like Robert Wagner.

Beneath these few specific policies lay a conception of government that contained elements of the patrician's condescending sense of noblesse oblige but also marked Roosevelt in the context of the 1920s and early 1930s as a progressive politician. "What is the state?" he asked in his message requesting unemployment relief from the New York legislature in August 1931. "It is the duly constituted representative of an organized society of human beings—created by them for their mutual protection and well being. The state or the government is but the machinery through which such mutual aid and protection is achieved. . . . Our government is not the master but the creature of the people. The

44. Arthur M. Schlesinger Jr., *History of American Presidential Elections, 1789–1968* (New York: Chelsea House, 1971), 3:2729; Schwarz, *Interregnum of Despair*, 191–92.

duty of the state towards the citizens is the duty of the servant to its master."[45]

This conception of government, in turn, was married to an expansive, generous, restless temperament—"a first-class temperament," in Justice Oliver Wendell Holmes's famous phrase, one that Holmes thought compensated for Roosevelt's "second-class intellect." Among the most vivid evidences of the Rooseveltian temperament was a commencement speech he gave at Milton Academy in Massachusetts in May 1926. He conspicuously did not assume the conventional commencement speaker's hectoring voice of sober authority, reminding the graduates of the end of their youthful innocence and their imminent entry into the vale of tears of adult responsibility. His theme, rather, was change—the accelerating and dizzying pace of change in the still-new century—and the need to match new conditions with new thinking, even new values. He beckoned his young listeners not to the sober stations of mature duty but to the soaring challenges of creative invention. A man born forty or fifty years earlier, said the forty-four-year-old Roosevelt, had been typically "brought up in a Victorian atmosphere of gloomy religion, of copybook sentiment, of life by precept, he had lived essentially as had his fathers before him." But then, said Roosevelt, came "sudden changes":

> [H]uman voices were carried to him over a tiny copper wire, juggernauts called trolley cars lined his peaceful roads, steam was replacing sails, sputtering arc-lights were appearing in the comfortable darkness of his streets, machine-made goods were forcing out the loving craftsmanship of the centuries. But, more dangerous, the accepted social structure was becoming demoralized. Women—think of it, Women!—were commencing to take positions in offices and industrial plants, and demanding—a very few of them—things called political rights. . . . In politics, too, men were speaking of new ideals and new parties, Populist and Socialist, were making themselves heard throughout the land. . . . [T]he lives of the great majority of people are more different from the lives of 1875 than were our grandfathers' lives from those of the year 1500. . . . [T]here has occurred an even more rapid condition of change in the past ten years.

The problems of the world, Roosevelt concluded, were "caused as much by those who fear change as by those who seek revolution. . . . In government, in science, in industry, in the arts, inaction and apathy are

45. Ernest K. Lindley, *Franklin D. Roosevelt: A Career in Progressive Democracy* (Indianapolis: Bobbs-Merrill, 1931), 325.

the most potent foes." Two obstacles, perversely complementary in their asymmetry, impeded progress. One was "the lack of cohesion on the part of the liberal thinkers themselves," who shared a common vision but disagreed on methods of realizing it. The other was "the solidarity of the opposition to a new outlook, [which] welds together the satisfied and the fearful."[46]

This handful of policies, this unapologetic embrace of the state, and this eager receptivity to change defined an attitude, not a program, and they exposed Roosevelt to the charge that he had more personality than character, more charm than substance. The *New Republic* found him "not a man of great intellectual force or supreme moral stamina." The journalist Walter Lippmann wrote to a friend in 1931 that after "many long talks in the last few years" he had concluded that Roosevelt was "a kind of amiable boy scout." In a column in January of 1932 Lippmann offered a portrait of Roosevelt that was destined to become notorious. "Franklin D. Roosevelt," wrote Lippmann, "is a highly impressionable person, without a firm grasp of public affairs and without very strong convictions. . . . [He] is an amiable man with many philanthropic impulses, but he is not the dangerous enemy of anything. He is too eager to please. . . . Franklin D. Roosevelt is no crusader. He is no tribune of the people. He is no enemy of entrenched privilege. He is a pleasant man who, without any important qualifications for the office, would very much like to be president."[47]

Roosevelt's performance in the electoral campaign of 1932 did little to dispel that kind of skepticism. He had once professed to be an internationalist, faithful to the precepts of his former chief, Woodrow Wilson, but in February 1932 he publicly repudiated the idea that the United States should join the League of Nations. That move was widely understood as naked and cynical appeasement of the powerful Democratic kingmaker, the archisolationist William Randolph Hearst. At Columbus, Ohio, in August, Roosevelt lampooned Hoover's moratorium, further evidence of his apparent apostasy from Wilsonian internationalism. He outlined his agricultural polices at Topeka, Kansas, on September 14, but the speech was in fact empty of content, designed, as one aide put it, to win the Midwest "without waking up the dogs of the East."[48]

46. Franklin D. Roosevelt, *Whither Bound?* (Boston: Houghton Mifflin, 1926), 4–15.
47. Schlesinger 1:291; Schwarz, *Interregnum of Despair*, 189; Walter Lippmann, *Interpretations, 1931–32* (New York: Macmillan, 1932), 260–62.
48. Raymond Moley, *After Seven Years* (New York: Harper and Brothers, 1939), 45.

Perhaps most telling, the man who had challenged Milton's graduates to welcome change and to seize the future now seemed to have embraced a different theory of history, one that emphasized stasis and closure. He cautioned the members of San Francisco's Commonwealth Club on September 23: "Our industrial plant is built; the problem just now is whether under existing conditions it is not overbuilt. Our last frontier has long since been reached." Hoover damned that sentiment as a denial of "the promise of American life . . . the counsel of despair."[49] At Oglethorpe University on May 22 Roosevelt called for "social planning" and bold experimentation; on another occasion he criticized Hoover as being "committed to the idea that we ought to center control of everything in Washington as rapidly as possible."[50] At Pittsburgh on October 19 he attacked Hoover's deficits and called for sharp reductions in government spending. Marriner Eccles opined that "given later developments, the campaign speeches often read like a giant misprint, in which Roosevelt and Hoover speak each other's lines."[51]

Even Roosevelt's own speechwriters were confused. Rexford Tugwell, one of Roosevelt's original Brain Trusters, complained that he and Roosevelt's other advisers had "started out to explain things and to deduce from the explanation what ought to be done. We were reduced now to something quite different. We were contriving ingenious accommodations to prejudice and expediency."[52] Roosevelt's mind, said another Brain Truster, Raymond Moley, "was neither exact nor orderly." On one occasion, speechwriter Moley was left "speechless" when Roosevelt, presented with two absolutely incompatible drafts of addresses on tariff policy—one calling for blanket reductions, the other for bilateral agreements—blandly instructed Moley to "weave the two together." Roosevelt, sniped Hoover, was as changeable as "a chameleon on plaid."[53]

On election day Roosevelt won by default. He held the solid South and ran strongly in the West. In a significant harbinger of the changes that were about to redefine the nature of American politics, he not only retained the support of the urban immigrant voters who had cast their ballots for Al Smith in 1928 but actually improved on Smith's margins among those crucial groups by some 12 percent. Yet Roosevelt's victory

49. *PPA*, (1938), 742. Hoover's remark is from his *Memoirs: The Great Depression*, 340.
50. Leuchtenburg, 10.
51. Marriner S. Eccles, *Beckoning Frontiers* (New York: Knopf, 1951), 95.
52. Tugwell, *Brains Trust*, 385.
53. Moley, *After Seven Years*, 56, 11, 48.

was less an affirmation of his policies than a repudiation of Hoover's. He remained inscrutable, his exact intentions a mystery. Tugwell, looking back years later, speculated about the purposes that might at that moment have lain deep in Roosevelt's mind. "I define these now, with the benefit of hindsight," wrote Tugwell, "as a better life for all Americans, and a better America to live it in. I think it was that general. There were items in it, but only a few he saw as fixed. One of these was security; if Europeans could have that, so could Americans. Another was a new framework for industrialism, and still another was a physically improved country. But those, as I see it, were about all."[54]

William Allen White, watching Roosevelt from a greater distance than Tugwell, also speculated on what kind of leader might emerge from the fog that surrounded the president-elect. "Your distant cousin is an X in the equation," he wrote to Theodore Roosevelt Jr. on February 1, 1933. But White sensed a momentous potential. "He may develop his stubbornness into courage, his amiability into wisdom, his sense of superiority into statesmanship. Responsibility," White prophetically concluded, "is a winepress that brings forth strange juices out of men."[55]

54. Tugwell, *Brains Trust*, 157–58.
55. Davis 2:392.

4

Interregnum

The country needs and, unless I mistake its temper, the country demands bold, persistent experimentation. It is common sense to take a method and try it: If it fails, admit it frankly and try another. But above all, try something.

— Franklin D. Roosevelt,
speech at Oglethorpe University, May 22, 1932

Roosevelt was now president-elect. But Herbert Hoover was still president and would remain so for four months. The ratification of the Twentieth Amendment to the Constitution in February 1933 moved the start of the presidential term to January 20 of the year following election, but the amendment would take effect only in 1937. Roosevelt's inaugural thus fell under the old rules and would not take place until March 4.[1]

History, meanwhile, refused to mark time to the antiquated cadences of the American electoral system. In the agonizing interval between Roosevelt's election in November 1932 and his inauguration in March 1933, the American banking system shut down completely. The global economy slid even deeper into the trough of the Depression. The world also became a markedly more dangerous place. Adolf Hitler was installed as chancellor of Germany, after massive unemployment had seeded despair into millions of German households and after months of bloody clashes between Communist and Nazi gangs had left scores of people dead in the streets of German cities. Japan, hell-bent on the

---

1. The amendment also changed the schedule for meetings of Congress, which was now mandated to begin its annual session on January 3. Theretofore, newly elected Congresses had to wait a full thirteen months, from November of election year until December of the succeeding year, to be seated. Roosevelt accelerated the seating of the new Congress elected in 1932 by calling it into special session in March 1933.

104

conquest of Manchuria, cast off all diplomatic restraint and formally announced its intention to quit the League of Nations. The vexed issue of World War I debts, temporarily allayed by Hoover's moratorium of 1931, once again stirred to troublesome life. These lowering clouds of political violence, war, and global economic turbulence cast their shadows over the rest of the decade, and beyond.

Scarcely a week after the election, as Roosevelt sifted contentedly through messages of congratulation in the governor's mansion in Albany, he received a lengthy telegram from Hoover. The British government, Hoover explained, was urgently requesting yet another review of the international debt question. To add point to their request the British proposed to suspend payment of their $95 million debt-service installment due on December 15. Congress had only reluctantly agreed to Hoover's moratorium of the preceding year, and "if there is to be any change in the attitude of the Congress," Hoover explained to Roosevelt, "it will be greatly affected by the views of those members who recognize you as their leader and who will properly desire your counsel and advice." Other questions about foreign relations were also pending, including plans for a World Economic Conference in London during the coming winter and the status of the Disarmament Conference already in progress in Geneva. Accordingly, Hoover asked for "an opportunity to confer with you personally at some convenient date in the near future."

Hoover's action in seeking the advice of his victorious opponent was unprecedented. It had all the appearance of a magnificent gesture of statesmanship. It also contained sinister political implications. The debt issue was the tar-baby of American politics. To touch it was to glue oneself to a messy, intractable problem that had defied the genius of statesmen for a decade. Most academic economists, as well as the Wall Street financial community, not to mention virtually all Europeans, favored outright cancellation of the war debts. Yet Congress and most Americans beyond the Atlantic seaboard continued to regard the debts as immutable financial and moral obligations—and as safeguards that served to remind those interminably quarrelsome Europeans that they could not expect to finance another war in the United States. Secretary of State Stimson noted in his diary: "Every Congressman is shooting his mouth off in the newspapers with fulminations against any concession of any installment, or any amount whatever."[2] Hoover had officially

2. Frank Freidel, *Franklin D. Roosevelt: Launching the New Deal* (Boston: Little, Brown, 1973), 28.

pledged himself against outright cancellation, and his telegram to Roosevelt had stressed that point. But as the architect of the moratorium, Hoover had also shown some flexibility, and thereby incurred the wrath of legions of isolationists. He was now suggesting that the debts might be useful bargaining levers to pry economic and military concessions out of Europe. "[W]e should be receptive," said Hoover in his telegram, "to proposals from our debtors of tangible compensation in other forms than direct payment in expansion of markets for the products of our labor and our farms." And, he added, "substantial reduction of world armament . . . has a bearing upon this question."[3] Hoover was proposing, in short, that American diplomacy should forge a strong link between the upcoming London Economic Conference and the Geneva Disarmament Conference, using the agenda of the former to shape the proceedings of the latter. This was an elaborate scheme, and an ingenious one.

But Roosevelt and his advisers quickly concluded that this apparently well-intentioned proposal concealed some explosive political dynamite. If the incoming Democratic administration agreed to let the outgoing Republicans begin negotiations along the lines Hoover was suggesting, Roosevelt's aide Rexford Tugwell wrote, "we will have to hold the bag with a hostile country and congress after they are gone."[4] From this perspective, the president's invitation to involve the president-elect in this delicate diplomacy would simply shift from Hoover's shoulders to Roosevelt's the weighty and unwelcome responsibility for the immensely unpopular policy of canceling the debts. "And if anything was clear to us," said Raymond Moley, "it was that Roosevelt must not be saddled with that responsibility."[5]

So Hoover's proposal carried with it large political risk. At the same time, according to the theory of the Depression embraced by Roosevelt and his advisers, it promised small economic reward. Hoover subscribed to a view of the Depression as stemming from international causes, especially the distortions resulting from the World War. His reverent and dogged devotion to the gold standard, the balance wheel in the international trade and financial system, owed directly to that diagnosis of the Depression's origins. His relentless and even courageous effort to resolve the international debt problem rested on the same premises.

3. *PPA* (1928–32), 873–76.
4. Freidel, *Launching*, 131n.
5. Raymond Moley, *After Seven Years* (New York: Harper and Brothers, 1939), 70.

Roosevelt, by contrast, professed to find the sources of the Depression in the United States, in structural deficiencies and institutional inadequacies that a vigorous and far-reaching reform program might remedy. This view may have owed as much to the search for a legitimating rationale for reform, or to a search for *any* policy instrument more useable than the spongy tools of international diplomacy, as it did to the rigors of economic analysis. But for whatever amalgam of reasons, international concerns were decidedly subordinate to nationalist priorities in Roosevelt's thinking at this time, and foreign relations were virtually irrelevant as a subject of economic policy. In his inaugural address Roosevelt would flatly declare that "our international trade relations, though vastly important, are in point of time and necessity secondary to the establishment of a sound national economy."[6] In June 1933 he was to remind his secretary of state, then attending the World Economic Conference in London, "that far too much importance is attached to exchange stability by banker-influenced cabinets. In our case it concerns only about 3 per cent of our total trade as measured by production."[7]

All those considerations conspired to ensure that Hoover's invitation to Roosevelt to share in the shaping of economic diplomacy had no chance of being accepted. As Moley put it, Hoover "could scarcely have chosen a field in which there was less probability of sympathetic cooperation between the two administrations." Roosevelt and his inner circle "were agreed that the heart of the recovery program was and must be domestic."[8] That was, in fact, Hoover's greatest worry about his successor: that Roosevelt's domestic priorities would encourage policies of economic nationalism, perhaps including abandonment of the gold standard, dollar devaluation, and inflation. Roosevelt and his advisers had no such clear-cut agenda in late 1932, but before another year had passed, events would confirm Hoover's fears.

In the meantime, Roosevelt could hardly ignore Hoover's invitation to consult, even if he never intended to adopt Hoover's specific suggestions. Insisting that the meeting be "wholly informal and personal," Roosevelt agreed to stop off in Washington on his way to Warm Springs, Georgia, on November 22, 1932.[9]

On the appointed day, accompanied only by his increasingly ubiq-

6. PPA (1933), 14.
7. Freidel, *Launching*, 472.
8. Moley, *After Seven Years*, 68, 70.
9. PPA (1928–32), 876.

uitous adviser Raymond Moley, Roosevelt was ushered into the White House Red Room, where President Hoover and Treasury Secretary Ogden Mills were waiting.[10] The air hung heavy with sullen tension. Hoover had insisted that Mills attend the meeting because he had been warned by so many people that Roosevelt would shift his words that he wanted a reliable witness present.[11] Moley thought that no two people in the country distrusted Roosevelt "as a human being and as President-elect" more than Hoover and Mills. Their manner suggested that they also regarded Moley with cold contempt. At a press conference before the meeting, Mills had publicly needled Moley as an unworldly professor inadequate to the complex demands of high statecraft. Moley now found Mills in person to be arrogant and condescending, even toward Hoover. The president, grave but jittery, stiffly addressing his treasury secretary as "Mills" and fixing his eye first on the carpet and then on Moley—but seldom on Roosevelt—smoked a fat cigar. All the others nervously lit cigarettes, and the atmosphere in the room thickened.

Roosevelt greeted Mills, his Harvard classmate and Hudson Valley neighbor, with a cheery "Hello, Ogden!" and kept up a gay and nonchalant front. But FDR, wary of his recently defeated adversary, also cupped in his hand several cards on which Moley had jotted questions that needed asking, including one about possible "secret agreements" that Hoover might have already made with British and French officials. Roosevelt may also have had in mind the sour memory of his last visit to the White House. At a presidential reception for governors the preceding April, Hoover, whether from callous design or thoughtless insensitivity, had kept Roosevelt waiting in a receiving line for nearly an hour. For a man whose bulky weight was supported entirely by the heavy hip-to-ankle steel braces that encased his useless legs, the ordeal was agonizing and humiliating. Roosevelt, for all his generous temperament, would have been less than human if the episode had not shaded his attitude toward Hoover.

In this awkward setting on November 22, Hoover spoke first, and at length. It was a typical Hoover performance, the sort that had impressed countless others in his business and political career. "Before he had finished," Moley later reflected, "it was clear that we were in the presence of the best-informed individual in the country on the question of

10. The following account of the meeting of November 22, 1932, draws heavily on Moley's description in *After Seven Years*, 67–77.
11. Stimson Diary, November 16, 1932.

the debts. His story showed a mastery of detail and a clarity of arrangement that compelled admiration."

But it did not compel agreement from Roosevelt. Nor did a second meeting on the same subject on January 20, 1933. The only concrete result of these failed attempts at cooperation was the deepened conviction of Hoover and his associates that Roosevelt was a dangerously lightweight politician. Henry Stimson thought that Hoover's mastery of the debt issue, compared with Roosevelt's display of vacuous bonhomie, made FDR "look like a peanut." Hoover deemed Roosevelt "amiable, pleasant, anxious to be of service, very badly informed and of comparatively little vision" and told Stimson that he had spent most of his time in conversation with Roosevelt "educating a very ignorant . . . well-meaning young man."[12]

Hoover was not finished with trying to educate that well-meaning young man, nor with attempting to secure his cooperation on economic policy. Late in the evening of February 18, 1933, as Roosevelt sat watching skits by New York political reporters in a banquet room of the Hotel Astor in central Manhattan, a Secret Service agent handed him a large brown-paper envelope. It contained a remarkable ten-page handwritten letter from Hoover. The banking system, said Hoover, was teetering on the brink of complete collapse. Gold was being shipped out of the country in dangerous amounts; capital was fleeing abroad, seeking safe haven; depositors were withdrawing their funds from banks and hoarding them at home; prices were falling and unemployment increasing dramatically. "The major difficulty," Hoover explained, "is the state of the public mind, for there is a steadily degenerating confidence in the future which has reached the height of general alarm." Hoover went on, provocatively, to claim that his own policies had substantially righted the foundering economy in the summer of 1932, only to see it succumb to renewed depression in the last several months. Still more provocatively, Hoover ascribed the latest crisis to Roosevelt's election and the unsettling prospect it raised of unbalanced budgets, inflation, abandonment of the gold standard, political experimentation, and even "dictatorship." "I am convinced," Hoover concluded, "that a very early statement by you upon two or three policies of your Administration would

12. Freidel, *Launching*, 34–35, 45. After several meetings of his own with Roosevelt, Stimson would change his opinion. He was deeply impressed with the "brave way" in which Roosevelt handled his disability, and found his intellectual range and analytic power "astounding" (118, 277). In 1940, at the age of seventy-two, Stimson was to join Franklin Roosevelt's administration as secretary of war.

serve greatly to restore confidence and cause a resumption of the march of recovery."[13]

The letter was astonishing in both tone and content. Roosevelt dismissed it as "cheeky" and made no reply for nearly two weeks. Its political implications were clear enough. Hoover acknowledged as much a few days later when he wrote to a Republican senator: "I realize that if these declarations be made by the President-elect, he will have ratified the whole major program of the Republican Administration; that is, it means the abandonment of 90% of the so-called new deal."[14] For their part, Roosevelt and his advisers were no less mindful of the political ramifications of the continuing banking crisis. Tugwell indiscreetly admitted to a Hoover sympathizer on February 25 that the Roosevelt camp "were fully aware of the bank situation and that it would undoubtedly collapse in a few days, which would place the responsibility in the lap of President Hoover." When this conversation was reported to Hoover, he exploded that Tugwell "breathes with infamous politics devoid of every atom of patriotism."[15]

Both sides, in fact, were stepping a dangerous political dance around the gathering economic crisis. Hoover seemed, as he had in the preceding electoral campaign, more interested in vindicating himself in the historical record than in genuinely enlisting his successor in helpful policies. On his side, as Moley later commented, Roosevelt "either did not realize how serious the situation was or . . . preferred to have conditions deteriorate and gain for himself the entire credit for the rescue operation. In any event," Moley somewhat cynically concluded, "his actions during the period from February 18th to March 3d would conform to any such motive on his part."[16]

As Hoover's last days in office slipped away, he continued to dun Roosevelt with requests for some reassuring public statement, but the president-elect kept his own counsel. The outgoing president, drained of power and nerve, was unable to lead; the incoming president, as yet, was unwilling. The country, numb and nearly broken, anxiously awaited deliverance from this deadening paralysis. As Roosevelt's entourage filtered into Washington in preparation for the inaugural ceremonies, vir-

13. William Starr Myers and Walter H. Newton, *The Hoover Administration: A Documented Narrative* (New York: Charles Scribner's Sons, 1936), 338–40.
14. Schlesinger 1:477; Myers and Newton, *Hoover Administration*, 341.
15. Myers and Newton, *Hoover Administration*, 356.
16. Herbert Hoover, *The Memoirs of Herbert Hoover: The Great Depression, 1929–1941* (New York: Macmillan, 1952), 215.

tually all the banks in the nation were barred shut. American capitalism seemed to be creaking to a dead halt. The thought tormented many Americans that they were witnessing the end of a historic era, an era of progress and confidence whose whimpering climax boded nothing good for the future. "When we arrived in Washington on the night of March 2," Moley wrote, "terror held the country in grip."[17] Could Roosevelt break that grip? The scale of the crisis, the completeness of Hoover's failure, and his own studious refusal to make any policy commitments during the interregnum meant that the field of political action lay before him swept of all obstructions. The power to command that field was now about to pass into his hands. What would he do?

SOME OBSERVERS, awed by Hitler's decisive march to power in Berlin, or by the enviable efficiency of Benito Mussolini's regime in Rome or Josef Stalin's in Moscow, urged that the dictators be imitated in America. Al Smith, once Roosevelt's political mentor but now an increasingly venomous critic, compared the crisis of early 1933 to the ultimate emergency of war. "What does a democracy do in a war?" Smith asked. "It becomes a tyrant, a despot, a real monarch. In the World War," he said with much exaggeration, "we took our Constitution, wrapped it up and laid it on the shelf and left it there until it was over." The Republican governor of Kansas declared that "even the iron hand of a national dictator is in preference to a paralytic stroke." The respected columnist Walter Lippmann, visiting Roosevelt at Warm Springs in late January 1933, told him with great earnestness: "The situation is critical, Franklin. You may have no alternative but to assume dictatorial power."[18]

But the affable sphinx of Hyde Park gave little clue about his reaction to such suggestions. Even his closest advisers at this time, the members of the fabled Brain Trust, marveled at Roosevelt's capacity for what Tugwell called "almost impenetrable concealment of intention."[19] Tugwell, attentively scrutinizing his chief during the electoral campaign, remarked to Moley that Roosevelt had the mobile and expressive face of an actor. His features were utterly responsive to his will, finely molding themselves to his constantly shifting purposes of persuasion, negotiation, or obfuscation, never ceasing to charm but never opening fully to reveal

17. Moley, *After Seven Years*, 143.
18. Davis 3:36; 2:3.
19. Rexford G. Tugwell, *The Brains Trust* (New York: Viking, 1968), 62.

the soul within. He could cast off one mood and assume another as easily as a mummer wiped off greasepaint. "There was another Roosevelt behind the one we saw and talked with," Tugwell later wrote; "I was baffled, unable to make out what he was like, that other man."[20]

Moley shared much of that assessment. Of course Roosevelt had an actor's manner, Moley replied to Tugwell, "and a professional actor's at that; how did I suppose he'd created and maintained the image of authority?" Moley thought that FDR had deliberately crafted his public persona in the course of a carefully constructed political career that had long aimed at the White House. "[I]t was a lifetime part that he was playing," Moley said to Tugwell, and added thoughtfully that "no one would ever see anything else."[21]

What visitors to Roosevelt did see, as they streamed by the hundreds to consult with him in Albany, Manhattan, or Warm Springs during the crowded early weeks of 1933, was a man of irrepressible vitality. He had an athlete's torso, big shoulder muscles bunched under his jacket. His vibrant good cheer was contagious. He radiated warmth and exuberance that washed over others as soon as they entered the room. He greeted visitors with easy familiarity, his upper body vigorously animated above the limp trousers and curiously unworn shoes that rested immobile below. He gestured and spoke with good-natured, head-tossing brio. His hands incessantly flourished a quill-tipped cigarette holder that flashed from his uplifted, jut-jawed face with its irregular, preorthodontic teeth to the exclamation point of a sentence—one of his endless, cascading sentences—as if he were inscribing his words upon the air.

Talk was Roosevelt's passion and his weapon. None of his associates ever knew him to read a book. It was in conversation that he gained his prodigious if disorderly store of information about the world. Drawing on that store, as Tugwell recorded, Roosevelt "could see more in an hour's drive than anyone I had ever known. He noted crops, woodlands, streams and livestock. To ride with him was to be deluged with talk, half-practical, half-fanciful."[22] Moley was astonished at the amount of intellectual ransacking Roosevelt could crowd into an evening's discussion. Sitting with his advisers as a student, as a cross-examiner, as a judge, Roosevelt would listen attentively for a few minutes and then

20. Tugwell, *Brains Trust*, 27.
21. Tugwell, *Brains Trust*, 27.
22. Rexford G. Tugwell, *Roosevelt's Revolution: The First Year, a Personal Perspective* (New York: Macmillan, 1977), 160.

begin to break in with sharp, darting questions. He took in everything as a sponge absorbs water. This uncritical receptivity sometimes frightened Moley, who noted that "so far as I know he makes no effort to check up on anything that I or anyone else has told him."[23]

Herbert Hoover forged his policies in the tidy, efficient smithy of his own highly disciplined mind. Once he had cast them in final form, he could be obstinate. Especially in his last months in the White House, he had grown downright churlish with those who dared to question him. Roosevelt's mind, by contrast, was a spacious, cluttered warehouse, a teeming curiosity shop continuously restocked with randomly acquired intellectual oddments. He was open to all number and manner of impressions, facts, theories, nostrums, and personalities. He listened to everybody and anybody. Tugwell thought he especially enjoyed talking to fanatics, particularly inflation-preaching monetary heretics like Yale's Professor Irving Fisher. The countless visitors who trooped to see FDR between election and inauguration ranged from congressional barons to local farmers, from haughty industrialists to mendicant job-seekers, from silky Morgan partners to the rough-hewn old Populist Jacob Coxey, leader of "Coxey's Army," which had marched on Washington in 1894 to demand government jobs. To all of them Roosevelt gave attentive audience. As his visitors talked, FDR would nod in apparent approval, often interjecting, "Yes, yes, yes." Many who spoke with him took this to mean agreement when it merely signified that Roosevelt understood the point being made or, possibly, that he wanted to avoid the unpleasantness of open argument. Roosevelt would in time become notorious for his unwillingness to deal with disagreement face to face. From this unwillingness would come his maddening administrative habits of trying to avoid firing anyone and of putting several people of incompatible views to work on the same project, none of whom knew what the others were doing. "When I talk to him," said the volatile demagogue Huey Long of Louisiana, "he says 'Fine! Fine! Fine!' But Joe Robinson [the somewhat plodding and thoroughly conventional Democratic majority leader in the Senate, and Long's implacable antagonist] goes to see him the next day and again he says 'Fine! Fine! Fine!' Maybe he says 'Fine!' to everybody."[24]

More often, Roosevelt did the talking—all of it. His compulsive garrulity may have originated as a calculated device to divert a listener's

23. Moley, *After Seven Years*, 11, 20.
24. Schlesinger 1:452.

attention from his physical handicap. It may have been merely one more of his abundant techniques of personal and political mastery over others. But from whatever ultimate source, a Niagara of verbiage would usually fall upon a visitor even as he walked through the door to greet Roosevelt and would tumble on without stop until it was time to leave. Anecdotes, rhetorical questions that Roosevelt answered himself, gossip about other public figures, jokes, pseudo-intimate revelations about the inner workings of policymaking—all flowed from Roosevelt's mouth, flooding the room with words and utterly drowning his interlocutor, who would depart with whatever had been on his mind still unspoken, perhaps even forgotten, but with the glow of having soaked briefly in the warm bath of Roosevelt's charm. When Nevada senator Key Pittman came to Warm Springs to lobby the president-elect for a government silver-buying program, Roosevelt parried with an hour-and-a-half-long story about digging for buried silver in Nova Scotia as a boy. Through this wall of words Pittman could insert no further mention of silver into the conversation.[25]

Whether listening or talking, in public or private, Roosevelt projected a sense of utter self-confidence and calm mastery. He was "all light and no darkness," one observer wrote; a man of "slightly unnatural sunniness," said the literary critic Edmund Wilson.[26] Those traits had their origins in the unearned legacy of his privileged upbringing. Roosevelt was born in 1882 into a family of seasoned, stable wealth dwelling on their rambling estate at Hyde Park, along the Hudson River above New York City. The neighbors included scions of the old American plutocracy like Frederick Vanderbilt and Vincent Astor, toward whom the blue-blooded Roosevelts felt a kind of genteel disdain. Roosevelt's father, James, cared for his Hyde Park property with the proud solicitude of an English country squire and passed on to his son a sense of reverential responsibility for the land. James was fifty-three when Franklin was born; the boy's mother, Sara Delano Roosevelt, was just twenty-seven. The patrician father and doting mother conferred on their only son the priceless endowment of an unshakable sense of self-worth. They also nurtured in him a robust social conscience. They sent him at the age of fourteen to the Groton School in Massachusetts, an austere and demanding bastion of high Protestant earnestness. There, in this heyday of the Social

25. Freidel, *Launching*, 77.
26. Milton MacKaye, "Profiles: The Governor—II," *New Yorker*, August 22, 1931, 28; Edmond Wilson, "The Hudson River Progressive," *New Republic*, April 5, 1933, 219–20.

Gospel movement, the Reverend Endicott Peabody instilled in his young charges the lessons of Christian duty and the ethic of public service. As the new century opened, young Franklin went on to Harvard. During his freshman year, when the boy was just on the cusp of his own manhood, his father died. Franklin attended lectures by Frederick Jackson Turner, the famed historian of the frontier, and Josiah Royce, the philosopher of communitarianism. He was a middling student but distinguished himself as editor of the campus newspaper, the *Crimson*. The one disappointment of his undergraduate years was his failure to be elected to membership in Porcellian, a snooty club whose rejection stung him deeply and may have contributed something to his later animus against the American upper crust, an animus that would in time earn him a reputation in the wood-paneled clubrooms of America's self-styled aristocracy as a "traitor to his class."

In his senior year at Harvard he became engaged to Eleanor Roosevelt, the niece of his fifth cousin Theodore Roosevelt, then president of the United States. They were married in 1905. Endicott Peabody presided over the ceremony. Cousin Teddy gave the bride away. In the following decade Eleanor bore six children. After the last was born, in 1916, she withdrew to a separate bedroom and maintained one for the remainder of her married life.

Franklin's one year at Columbia Law School proved sufficient to allow him to pass the state bar examination, and he joined a prestigious New York City law firm. Politics, however, was his passion. Inspired by the example of Cousin Theodore, he won a seat in the New York state senate in 1910. He campaigned for Woodrow Wilson in 1912 and was rewarded with Teddy's old post, the assistant secretaryship of the navy. He was the Democrats' vice-presidential nominee in 1920. Then came the illness that changed his life, the long and vain struggle to rehabilitate his broken body, and election in 1928 as governor of New York.

Though Roosevelt was never a systematic thinker, the period of lonely reflection imposed by his convalescence allowed him to shape a fairly coherent social philosophy. By the time he was elected governor, the distillate of his upbringing, education, and experience had crystallized into a few simple but powerful political principles. Moley summarized them this way: "He believed that government not only could, but should, achieve the subordination of private interests to collective interests, substitute co-operation for the mad scramble of selfish individualism. He had a profound feeling for the underdog, a real sense of the critical imbalance of economic life, a very keen awareness that political democracy could not exist side by side with economic plutocracy." As Roosevelt himself put it:

> [O]ur civilization cannot endure unless we, as individuals, realize our responsibility to and dependence on the rest of the world. For it is literally true that the "self-supporting" man or woman has become as extinct as the man of the stone age. Without the help of thousands of others, any one of us would die, naked and starved. Consider the bread upon our table, the clothes upon our backs, the luxuries that make life pleasant; how many men worked in sunlit fields, in dark mines, in the fierce heat of molten metal, and among the looms and wheels of countless factories, in order to create them for our use and enjoyment. . . . In the final analysis, the progress of our civilization will be retarded if any large body of citizens falls behind.[27]

Perhaps deep within himself Roosevelt trembled occasionally with the common human palsies of melancholy or doubt or fear, but the world saw none of it. On February 15, 1933, he gave a memorable demonstration of his powers of self-control. Alighting in Miami from an eleven-day cruise aboard Vincent Astor's yacht *Nourmahal*, FDR motored to Bay Front Park, where he made a few remarks to a large crowd. At the end of the brief speech, Mayor Anton J. Cermak of Chicago stepped up to the side of Roosevelt's open touring car and said a few words to the president-elect. Suddenly a pistol barked from the crowd. Cermak doubled over. Roosevelt ordered the Secret Service agents, who were reflexively accelerating his car away from the scene, to stop. He motioned to have Cermak, pale and pulseless, put into the seat beside him. "Tony, keep quiet—don't move. It won't hurt you if you keep quiet," Roosevelt repeated as he cradled Cermak's limp body while the car sped to the hospital.[28]

Cermak had been mortally wounded. He died within weeks, the victim of a deranged assassin who had been aiming for Roosevelt. On the evening of February 15, after Cermak had been entrusted to the doctors, Moley accompanied Roosevelt back to the *Nourmahal*, poured him a stiff drink, and prepared for the letdown now that Roosevelt was alone among his intimates. He had just been spared by inches from a killer's bullet and had held a dying man in his arms. But there was nothing— "not so much as the twitching of a muscle, the mopping of a brow, or even the hint of a false gaiety—to indicate that it wasn't any other eve-

27. Moley, *After Seven Years*, 14; PPA (1928–32), 75–76, 15.
28. Freidel, *Launching*, 168–73.

ning in any other place. Roosevelt was simply himself—easy, confident, poised, to all appearances unmoved." The episode contributed to Moley's eventual conclusion "that Roosevelt had no nerves at all." He was, said Frances Perkins, "the most complicated human being I ever knew."[29]

Unflappably cool in the face of personal danger, Roosevelt was also mystifying with respect to the particular antidepression policies that his new administration would pursue. "The fact is," Moley conceded, "that I found it impossible to discover how deeply Roosevelt was impressed with the seriousness of the crisis." While Moley and Treasury Secretary–designate William Woodin fretted over the accumulating reports of gold withdrawals and bank closings, Roosevelt remained serenely unperturbed, a monument of inscrutability, exuding "nothing but the most complete confidence in his own ability to deal with any situation that might arise."[30]

Exactly what the situation might be when Roosevelt took office on March 4 was part of the mystery. Two days after the election, on November 10, 1932, his aide Adolf Berle had sketched a tentative legislative program for the new administration. Berle cautioned that "it must be remembered that by March 4 next we may have anything on our hands from a recovery to a revolution. The chance is about even either way." He added, however, "I think the economic situation may change very much for the worse during that time, so that many of the following suggestions may have to be shifted as we go along."[31] The central task of the New Deal, Berle's memorandum implied, might be either social reform in a restored economy, or political stabilization in a disintegrating society, or, most likely and most urgently, economic recovery itself. Circumstances, not human will, said Berle, would set the priorities. In fact, these three purposes—social reform, political realignment, and economic recovery—flowed and counterflowed through the entire history of the New Deal. They often undercut and intersected one another, creating riptides of turbulence and eddies of stagnation. None would be achieved to the degree desired by its particular champions. Most notably, the goal of economic recovery would remain stubbornly elusive for eight more years. But perhaps precisely *because* the economic crisis of

29. Moley, *After Seven Years*, 139, 191; Frances Perkins, *The Roosevelt I Knew* (New York: Viking, 1946), 3.
30. Moley, *After Seven Years*, 143.
31. Freidel, *Launching*, 73n.   .

the Great Depression was so severe and so durable, Roosevelt would have an unmatched opportunity to effect major social reforms and to change the very landscape of American politics.

If Roosevelt's specific policies remained ill-defined and puzzling, little mystery surrounded his general intentions. Some things were well and widely understood: that he shared his cousin Theodore's belief in the supremacy of the public interest over private interests and in the government's role as the active agent of the public interest; that he meant to preside over a government even more vigorously interventionist and directive than Hoover's; that he intended to use government power to redress what he judged to be harmful and unfair imbalances in the American economy, especially the huge income gap between the agricultural and industrial sectors; that he had long been seeking for ordinary Americans some measure of the economic security and predictability of life's material circumstances that his own patrician class took for granted; that he had a lover's passion for the cause of conservation; that he was a champion of public waterpower. It was also clear that his confessedly liberal outlook alienated many in his own party and by the same token appealed to progressive Republicans, stimulating much political gossip about the possible emergence of a new, liberal party. Beyond that, all was speculation.

If Roosevelt had a plan in early 1933 to effect economic recovery, it was difficult to distinguish from many of the measures that Hoover, even if sometimes grudgingly, had already adopted: aid for agriculture, promotion of industrial cooperation, support for the banks, and a balanced budget. Only the last item was dubious. Roosevelt had pledged himself in the electoral campaign to fiscal orthodoxy and had denounced Hoover's budget deficits, but doubts about the strength of Roosevelt's own commitment to fiscal discipline persisted. Hoover worried that FDR would unleash the hounds of inflation, inflicting on the United States the kind of monetary calamity that had befallen Germany scarcely a decade earlier. The German hyperinflation of 1923, as well as the more moderate but still unsettling doubling of American prices between 1914 and 1920, was still fresh in memory. Those examples put sound-money men on their guard. Moreover, Roosevelt was a Democrat, and the Democratic Party, since at least the time of William Jennings Bryan in the late nineteenth century, had been home to a large proinflationary constituency. Based mostly in the chronically indebted agricultural regions of the South and West, the inflationary element in the Democratic Party was a never-dormant dog roused to noisy life by the Depression crisis.

Suspicions about Roosevelt's intentions on this point ran deep within the sound-money wing of the Democratic Party and even within his own inner circle. Largely because Roosevelt refused to lay those suspicions to rest, his first choice as secretary of the treasury, Virginia senator Carter Glass, author of the Federal Reserve Act of 1914 and probably the country's leading expert on the banking system, refused to accept appointment in Roosevelt's cabinet. Even Moley, whose job it was to persuade Glass to accept, went about the task halfheartedly. While not knowing the exact nature of Roosevelt's plans, Moley knew enough about Roosevelt's "experimental, tentative, and unorthodox temperament" not to rule out monetary tinkering.[32]

FROM ALL SIDES, pressures played upon FDR to commit himself to this or that Depression remedy or structural reform. His passive, noncommittal posture in these preinaugural days, along with the ever-deepening crisis, guaranteed the wild plurality of policies that would be pressed upon him and the sometimes desperate fervor with which they would be urged.

Pressure came first of all from his own political staff, the body of economic and legal experts assembled during the campaign and known colloquially as the Brain Trust (originally styled the Brains Trust). Though much magnified in the history books, the Brain Trust was a small and decidedly transient group of advisers whose most lasting legacy lay more in the realm of literary descriptions of the early New Deal than it did in the domain of durable policy results. The founding member of the group was Raymond Moley, in 1932 a forty-six–year old professor of government at Barnard College of Columbia University, specializing in criminal justice. Roosevelt first met him in 1928 and as governor of New York enlisted Moley's help in drafting several proposals for reform of the state prison and judicial systems. In the spring of 1932, as Roosevelt geared up for the presidential campaign, Moley responded eagerly to the candidate's request for expert professional advice on a variety of national issues. Moley began the practice of taking various academic colleagues to Albany on the late afternoon train from New York. After a meal of chronically indifferent quality, during which Roosevelt might

32. Moley, *After Seven Years*, 118ff.

murmur wistfully to his culinarily apathetic wife of dishes he wished he were eating, the group would retire to the cavernous, fusty drawing room. The discussants heaved about in the overstuffed sofa cushions, firing learned volleys across the well-worn Turkish rug, while Roosevelt listened, interrogated, opined, and absorbed. At midnight the session would end abruptly as the visitors dashed for the train back to New York.

Over the course of several weeks, Roosevelt appeared to find the counsel of three of these academic visitors particularly congenial. In addition to Moley, they were Rexford Guy Tugwell, a Columbia University economist, and Adolf A. Berle Jr., a professor at Columbia Law School. Together with longtime Roosevelt political confidante Samuel I. Rosenman, counsel to the governor, Basil "Doc" O'Connor, Roosevelt's law partner, and the financier Bernard Baruch's colorful protégé, Hugh Johnson, they constituted what Roosevelt called his "privy council" until a *New York Times* reporter coined the name "Brains Trust" in September.

The academic members of this group shared several beliefs, in addition to their personal attachment to Roosevelt. (It was Roosevelt's "vibrant aliveness, his warmth, his sympathy, his activism," that first attracted him, Moley wrote. "The rest did not precede, it followed those bare facts.")[33] Three of those beliefs were of particular significance. First, the Brain Trusters agreed that the causes as well as the cures of the Depression lay in the domestic arena. It was futile and pernicious to seek remedies, as Hoover had done, in the international realm.

Second, they all considered themselves inheritors of that tradition of progressive thought best expressed in Charles Van Hise's classic work of 1912, *Concentration and Control: A Solution of the Trust Problem in the United States*. Both Berle and Tugwell in 1932 were in the process of making important contributions to that intellectual tradition with works of their own. Berle, together with Gardiner C. Means, published *The Modern Corporation and Private Property* in 1932, a book that argued for a redefinition of property rights and more vigorous government regulation of the economy. Tugwell's *Industrial Discipline and the Governmental Arts* appeared in 1933. The thread that bound these several treatises together in a common intellectual lineage was the argument summarized in Van Hise's title: that concentration of economic power in huge industrial enterprises was a natural and beneficial feature of modern, advanced societies; and that these enormous concentrations of

33. Moley, *After Seven Years,* 9.

private power necessitated the creation of commensurately powerful public controls, or governmental regulatory bodies. Berle and Tugwell carried Van Hise's thinking a step further when they argued that it was government's right and responsibility not merely to regulate discrete economic sectors but to orchestrate the economy's various parts according to an overall plan.

Third, these ideological commitments implied hostility to what the Brain Trusters identified as "the Wilson-Brandeis philosophy" of trust-busting, or what Moley mocked as the quaint belief "that if America could once more become a nation of small proprietors, of corner grocers and smithies under spreading chestnut trees, we should have solved the problems of American life."[34]

The Brain Trusters regarded Louis Brandeis as Woodrow Wilson's "dark angel," the man whose trust-busting advice, Tugwell thought, had mischievously derailed the early twentieth-century reform movement and stalled the development of appropriate industrial policies for nearly two decades. Brandeis, appointed by Wilson to the Supreme Court in 1916, still sat on the high bench in 1932 (and would until 1939). He was consequently removed from direct influence over economic policy. But he had a faithful deputy and ideological kinsman in Felix Frankfurter, the brilliant, Vienna-born Harvard Law professor who would soon become a kind of one-man employment agency whose protégés filled many sensitive New Deal appointments. Frankfurter, too, was a frequent visitor to Albany in 1932, Tugwell ruefully noted, and "Frankfurter came from Brandeis."[35]

That the Columbia "planners" and the Harvard trust-buster were simultaneously pouring their policy potions into Roosevelt's ear was an early indication of the wide-ranging, apparently indiscriminate eclecticism that marked FDR's mental habits. In fact, despite their broad agreement on many things, the Brain Trusters themselves often disagreed about specific policies. On the most urgent issue before them, "concerning what might be done about the Depression," as Tugwell frankly conceded, "there was no agreement."[36] Berle, a Hoover supporter in 1928, applied his meticulous legal intelligence primarily to thinking about reforms in the banking system and securities markets. His basic approach closely resembled Hoover's, though he also inclined toward inflationary ideas, which neither Hoover

34. Moley, *After Seven Years,* 24.
35. Tugwell, *Brains Trust,* 59–60.
36. Tugwell, *Brains Trust,* xxv.

nor Berle's fellow Brain Trusters could countenance. Moley took another leaf from Hoover's book and promoted the idea of voluntary business-government cooperation to reduce wasteful competition.

Tugwell, whom Moley compared to a "cocktail" because "his conversation picked you up and made your brain race along," was the most politically radical of the group, as well as the most personally dashing and the most intellectually daring.[37] In the freewheeling discussions in the governor's Albany drawing room, his leaping mind frequently outpaced the others, vaulting elegantly from deep analysis to sweeping conclusions. His primary interest lay neither in reform of financial institutions nor inflation nor even industrial self-regulation but in drastic restructuring of the entire American economy under government direction. In eloquent and witty phrases, artfully deploying a master teacher's repertoire of similes and metaphors to make his points concrete and accessible, he urged upon Roosevelt an "underconsumptionist" explanation of the Depression. The owners of industry, he said, had failed to pass on a fair share of the spectacular productivity gains of the 1920s to labor in the form of higher wages or to consumers in the form of lower prices. Thus a vicious cycle had set in: workers' buying power had failed to keep pace with the productive capacity of the industrial economy, inventories had piled up, and plants eventually had to be closed and workers laid off. What was far worse, the persistent agricultural depression had denied to industrial producers a huge fraction of the consumer demand they would have enjoyed if the American economy were better balanced. "Balance" was fast becoming a buzzword in New Deal circles, and it nowhere buzzed more insistently than in Tugwell's agile, questing mind.

Deep in the substratum of Tugwell's thinking about "underconsumption" rested a largely unexcavated layer of assumptions about the historical state of development of industrial economies, particularly that of the United States. Sometimes called the "mature economy" or "stagnationist" thesis, this notion implied that the era of economic expansion had effectively ended. Technological boundaries had been reached. No great innovations of the sort that had produced the giant automobile industry were in sight. The end of immigration and declining birth rates spelled slowed or even negative population growth. Thus advanced societies need no longer concentrate on organizing themselves to produce goods more efficiently or in greater quantity. Their cardinal problem, rather, was "overproduction"—the natural reciprocal of "underconsumption."

37. Moley, *After Seven Years*, 15.

Roosevelt had given voice to that thesis in a memorable campaign speech, drafted by Adolf Berle, before the Commonwealth Club of San Francisco on September 23. "A mere builder of more industrial plants, a creator of more railroad systems, an organizer of more corporations, is as likely to be a danger as a help," said Roosevelt. "The day of the great promoter or the financial Titan, to whom we granted everything if only he would build, or develop, is over. Our task now is not discovery, or exploitation of natural resources, or necessarily producing more goods. It is the soberer, less dramatic business of administering resources and plants already in hand, of seeking to reestablish foreign markets for our surplus production, of meeting the problem of underconsumption, of adjusting production to consumption, of distributing wealth and products more equitably."[38]

Much controversy has surrounded this speech. Many historians claim that it contained more of Berle's thinking than Roosevelt's, striking, as it did, what was for Roosevelt an uncharacteristic note of entropy and pessimism. But however untypical of Roosevelt's temperament, the speech accurately reflected theories of history and economic principles that FDR had repeatedly heard discussed in his evenings with the Brain Trusters. It also fitted consistently with points he had made in other campaign speeches, notably at Oglethorpe University on May 22, when he had spoken of the "haphazardness" and "gigantic waste" in the American economy, its "superfluous duplication of productive facilities," had predicted that "our physical economic plant will not expand in the future at the same rate at which it has expanded in the past," and had called therefore for thinking "less about the producer and more about the consumer." The philosophical premises of the Commonwealth Club and Oglethorpe speeches—emphasizing consumption more than production, the economics of distribution rather than the economics of wealth creation, issues of equity over issues of growth—would be clearly discernible in much of the New Deal.[39]

Tugwell's analysis led logically to policies that would significantly redistribute income in American society. The Depression had begun in the agricultural sector, Tugwell insisted, and the agricultural sector was the place to begin the process of recovery, with some kind of program that would put more money into the hands of farmers. Tugwell would come in time to consider Roosevelt's gushy romanticism about rural life

38. PPA (1928–32), 751–52.
39. PPA (1928–32), 639–47.

one of FDR's most aggravating traits, but for now his sympathy for farmers seemed to make Roosevelt receptive to Tugwell's talk of "balance" and of the need, above all, first and foremost, to tilt the economic scales in favor of agriculture. Yet even such a persuasive mentor and such a perceptive student of Roosevelt's personality as Tugwell could not be sure that he was convincing FDR of the causal relationship between the depression in agriculture and the general depression. "We could throw out pieces of theory," Tugwell reflected; "we could suggest relations; and perhaps the inventiveness of the suggestion would attract his notice. But the tapestry of the policy he was weaving was guided by an artist's conception which was not made known to us."[40]

The Brain Trusters, especially the ever-present Moley, attracted much public notice in late 1932 and early 1933. They were a novelty in American political culture. Academic experts had played a role in the earlier progressive reform effort, but none so conspicuously or at so high a level as Moley, Tugwell, and Berle. They were newcomers to public life, amateurs, professors, refugees from the ivory tower, idea men. Those very characteristics made them objects of the public's fascination. The same facts made them objects of suspicious regard by the professional Democratic politicians who considered Roosevelt's imminent presidency their own precious personal possession, their salvation from years in the outer political darkness. "Tell the Governor that he is the boss and we will follow him to hell if we have to," vice-presidential candidate John Nance Garner instructed a messenger to Roosevelt during the campaign, "but if he goes too far with some of these wild-eyed ideas we are going to have the shit kicked out of us."[41] Moley, the nominal chairman of the Brain Trust, served for a season as Roosevelt's alter ego, his high factotum and dark familiar. He became the special focus of the party professionals' anxieties. A joke circulated to the effect that one needed to go through Roosevelt to get an appointment with Moley. Congressman Sam Rayburn of Texas accosted Moley in a railroad dining car in December 1932 and muttered menacingly, "I hope we don't have any god-damned Rasputin in this administration."[42]

RAYBURN NEEDN'T HAVE WORRIED. Neither Moley nor the Brain Trusters as a group, nor the unctuously insinuating Frankfurter, had

40. Schlesinger 1:401.
41. Schlesinger 1:416.
42. The episode is recounted both in Moley's *After Seven Years*, 83, and more colorfully in Schlesinger 1:451.

a monopoly on Roosevelt's ear. A host of other claimants also paid him
court and pressed their cases. Among them was the Democratic congressional leadership, of which Rayburn, powerful chairman of the House
Committee on Interstate and Foreign Commerce, was a prominent member. For the most part, the barons of Congress had been unenthusiastic,
even hostile, toward Roosevelt's nomination. Preponderantly from the
South, perennially reelected as beneficiaries of the Democratic Party's
post-Reconstruction political monopoly on that region, many of them
well advanced in years and antediluvian in their thinking, they had patiently accumulated seniority, quietly marking time against the day when
their party's majority status would confer upon them the coveted committee chairmanships that were the crowning achievement of a congressional
career. The Democrats had won control of the House by a slim margin in
1930. Roosevelt's landslide victory in 1932 gave them a nearly two-to-one
numerical advantage in the House and a comfortable fifteen-seat majority
in the Senate.[43] The old-line Democrats' hour of triumph had at last arrived. They had small desire to share it with Roosevelt.

As in the region from which they came, little had changed in the lives
and outlooks of these graying southerners since the long-ago days when
they had first entered politics. Many of them still clung to the political
faith of their fathers, to simple Jeffersonian maxims about states' rights and
the least possible federal government. They reverenced a balanced budget
as the holiest of civic dogmas. After years of passivity, lack of responsibility,
and the habitual naysaying typical of a minority party, they were ill suited
to creative legislating. No group of legislators, Tugwell thought, "can ever
have been less fitted to cope with a crisis requiring movement, adaptabil-
ity, and imagination."[44] Many of Herbert Hoover's cautious innovations
had unsettled them. The unpredictable, experimentally inclined Roosevelt, surrounded by his freethinking professorial claque, was downright
unnerving. Their major and almost exclusive common ground with the
new president lay in their shared concern for agriculture, the economic
foundation of the still premodern South.

These party elders joined the procession to Roosevelt's desk in late
1932 and early 1933 to urge upon him the hoary canons of economic

43. With only fitful exceptions, the Democratic Party would control both houses of
    Congress for most of the remainder of the century, reversing decades of Republican
    dominance. Until the Republicans won control of both houses in 1994, they pre-
    vailed in the Senate only in 1947–48, 1953–54, and 1980–86, and Democrats lost
    control of the House for only two sessions in the six decades after 1933, in 1947–
    48 and 1952–53.
44. Tugwell, *Roosevelt's Revolution*, 71.

and political orthodoxy. In the appropriately obsolescing forum of the Republic's last lame-duck congressional session (like all its predecessors, the Congress elected in 1930 met for a final session *after* the subsequent election, in November 1932), they also staged hearings before the Senate Finance Committee, billed by the press as a "Depression clinic" to educate the new president in the proper means to deal with the crisis. For weeks, representatives of the nation's industrial, commercial, and financial elites paraded into the Senate hearing room and hymned the praises of government frugality, stiffer taxes, and the sacred balanced budget. This was the most conventional of the conventional wisdom, and it differed from Hoover's program only in its more emphatic conservatism.

Conspicuous among the conservative voices heard in these weeks was that of Bernard Baruch, head of the War Industries Board in Woodrow Wilson's government and the consummate Democratic Party insider. A fabulously wealthy Wall Street speculator, Baruch lavished money on Democrats whom he deemed sympathetic to his own big-business outlook. He was said to have contributed some $200,000 to the 1932 campaign; Roosevelt thought that he "owned" at least sixty congressmen. His advice to FDR was Spartan in its stark simplicity: "Balance budgets. Stop spending money we haven't got. Sacrifice for frugality and revenue. Cut government spending—cut it as rations are cut in a siege. Tax—tax everybody for everything."[45]

Dozens of Baruch's economic co-religionists made the same professions in these weeks, including another powerful Wall Street operator and Democratic Party financier, Joseph P. Kennedy. These men spoke with the loud and authoritative voice of money—political money, the kind that paid for campaigns and got congressmen, senators, and presidents elected. Roosevelt could not ignore them, even while he maneuvered to keep Baruch out of his cabinet and to keep the bullishly ambitious Kennedy in check. If Baruch and Kennedy were statesmen, Tugwell thought, "my definition of the public interest was all wrong. Roosevelt, however, furnished them with the public impression of intimacy, whatever his private reservations."[46]

THE CONSERVATIVE DEMOCRATIC LEADERS in Congress took some comfort from Roosevelt's necessary attendance to the likes of Ba-

45. Freidel, *Launching*, 57.
46. Tugwell, *Brains Trust*, 152.

ruch and Kennedy and from his apparently respectful attention to their own austere advice, but they were deeply agitated at his open flirtation with progressive members of the Republican Party. Several progressive Republicans had publicly repudiated Hoover and supported Roosevelt in the presidential campaign. Roosevelt found many of them, like Nebraska's George Norris, New Mexico's Bronson Cutting, and California's Hiram Johnson, much more politically congenial than he did the more conservative members of his own Democratic Party. He invited first Johnson and then Cutting to join his cabinet as secretary of the interior. After both had declined, he named to the post another progressive Republican, the rotund and crusty fifty-nine-year-old Harold Ickes of Chicago (whom he had never met, and whose name he mispronounced "Ikes" at their first encounter—the correct pronunciation rhymes with "dickies"). He appointed still another progressive Republican, Iowa's dreamy and mystical Henry A. Wallace, as secretary of agriculture.

These were key appointments in terms of both policy and politics. The secretaries of interior and agriculture would have major responsibilities for shaping conservation measures and farm relief, two matters close to Roosevelt's heart and near the top of his list of priorities on assuming office. What was more, these appointments signaled Roosevelt's intention to assemble a new political coalition, one that would transcend the regional and ideological boundaries of the historic Democratic Party and be supportive of liberal initiatives. Roosevelt was here aiming, in effect, to repeat and consolidate in 1936 Woodrow Wilson's fleeting accomplishment of 1916. In that year Wilson had won election to a second term by attracting into the fold of the Democratic Party many of the Progressive or "Bull Moose" voters who had cast their ballots for Theodore Roosevelt in 1912. But Wilson's marriage of the forward-looking, antimachine progressive reform movement of the Northeast and West to the traditional Democratic Party, with its already incongruous bases in the backwater agrarian South and the machine-oiled immigrant ghettoes of the industrial cities, had not lasted beyond his second term. Indeed, it had endured a scant two years. It buckled under wartime pressure in the election of 1918, when Republicans won both houses of Congress, and collapsed entirely in 1920, when the Democrats lost the White House as well, ushering in a decade of Republican dominance in the nation's affairs.

By 1932, however, the opportunity vividly loomed of permanently institutionalizing Wilson's transient electoral achievement. The economic debacle, and Hoover's humiliating failure to cope with it, gave to the Democratic Party the kind of political opening that FDR had long anticipated would be necessary to crack the Republican ascendancy. Roosevelt meant to seize that opportunity and to use it imaginatively. He intended not merely to expand the Democratic Party numerically but to transform it demographically and ideologically. Central to this strategy was the South. It remained safely solid for the Democrats, the political bedrock on which all durable Democratic coalitions must be erected. But the South was an anchor as well as a base, a potential drag on any effort to innovate. The iron grip of its congressional delegation on the levers of legislative power necessitated caution and deference. In time Roosevelt would try to reshape the political and economic culture of the South, to rouse it from the slumber of tradition and nudge it into the modern, industrial era. For the moment he tried simply to avoid giving it offense while he cultivated the urban industrial workers in the great immigrant cities, as well as the old Bull Moose progressives.

The steady process of urbanization had amplified the electoral power of the city-based vote, largely made up of immigrant ethnic communities sorely afflicted by the galloping unemployment in the heavy industrial sector. Their representatives, conspicuously New York's Robert Wagner, had led the drive in Congress for federal unemployment relief and public works legislation. Together with hydroelectric power, the talismanic issue for liberal Republicans like George Norris, these items were to form a large part of Roosevelt's own early New Deal legislative agenda. Their contribution to economic recovery, at least in the short run, was arguable, but they surely facilitated the kind of long-term political realignment of which Roosevelt dreamt.

Roosevelt did not dream this dream alone. To the conservative elders of the Democratic Party, shocked by Roosevelt's nomination, his vision of the party's future was an unwelcome if perhaps inescapable nightmare. Yet others cheered the prospect. In a conversation with Louis Brandeis, Roosevelt declared that "his administration must be liberal and that he expected to lose part of his Conservative supporters. I told him 'I hoped so,'" Brandeis reported to Felix Frankfurter, "that he must realign . . . part of the forces in each party." Moley, too, hailed "the opportunity we now have for a liberal party . . . what ought to be the most significant party alignment in history."[47]

Contributing to that opportunity, and complicating it, was the composition of the Seventy-third Congress elected with Roosevelt in 1932.

47. Freidel, *Launching*, 64, 70.

More than half of its members had been voted into office since 1930 — 14 new senators and 144 new representatives in 1932 and a comparable number two years earlier. Overwhelmingly they were "Depression babies," their political careers born in the crisis and their futures dependent on doing something about it, and doing it pronto. Though much of the Democratic congressional leadership remained old-guard, southern, agrarian, and conservative, the rank-and-file Democratic majorities in both houses were largely made up of fresh, northern, urban-industrial representatives of at least potentially liberal bent. At a minimum they were impatient with inaction, prodded by their constituents to take arms against the Depression, and not likely to be silenced by appeals to tradition. They were, as yet, an unformed and unreckoned force, one that Roosevelt might mold to his purposes of remaking his party — or one whose very strength and impetuosity might force the president's hand.

Inflation was one policy that might bring this disparate assemblage of congressional Democrats together. An induced rise in prices would lift the burden of debt, raise asset and commodity values, liquefy the credit system, and prompt a new economic start — or so the argument ran. New voices joined the traditional inflationary chorus in Congress, and their demands swelled to a booming crescendo by early 1933. To the Brain Trusters' dismay, Roosevelt seemed charmed by their music. He annoyed his economic advisers, Tugwell wrote, "by persistently coming back to monetary devices taken by themselves. We were at heart believers in sound money. Greenbackism was part of the populist tradition that we hoped had been left behind. We knew well enough that it hadn't; its advocates were loud and growing louder; all the old schemes for cheapening money were apparently still alive, and there were many new ones. The Governor wanted to know all about them. We shuddered and got him the information."[48]

THIS WAS THE CONFUSING ARRAY of policy advice besetting the president-elect and the unstable constellation of political forces taking shape in Washington on inauguration day. Roosevelt confronted budget-balancers and inflators, regulators and trust-busters, traditionalist southerners and restless urban liberals. To discipline the unpredictable new Congress to his will, Roosevelt calculatingly withheld the distribution of some one hundred thousand patronage jobs to deserving Democrats until after the special legislative session that he requested to convene

48. Tugwell, *Brains Trust*, 97–98.

on March 9, 1933, had adjourned. Consequently, well into the early months of Roosevelt's presidency, most of the government bureaus and departments were still staffed with Republican holdovers from the Hoover administration. Thus did Moley record his impression that Roosevelt and his entourage "stood in the city of Washington on March 4th like a handful of marauders in hostile territory."[49]

49. Moley, *After Seven Years*, 128.

5

The Hundred Days

Philosophy? Philosophy? I am a Christian and a Democrat — that's all.
— Franklin D. Roosevelt, responding to the question
"What is your philosophy?"

Washington in 1933 was still a spacious, unhurried city with a distinctly southern flavor. As yet unjacketed by suburbs, it slept dreamily amid the gently undulating Virginia and Maryland woodlands, its slow rhythms exemplified by the World War "temporary" buildings that were still scattered about town and by the unfinished columns of what would eventually be the Department of Labor. It was not yet an imperial city, the vibrant center of political and economic command that Roosevelt was to make it.

On the Saturday morning of inauguration day, the streets of the normally languid capital began to fill with boisterous Democrats, eager to celebrate the end of their long exile from political power. Bedecked with bunting, athrob with rollicking political junketeers, Washington tried to muster a mood to defy the gray, overcast weather, and one that would hold at bay, for a hopeful moment, the pall of gloom and anxiety enveloping the entire nation. For behind the festive trappings, Washington on March 4, 1933, was a city under siege. And in the cities and hamlets beyond the capital, millions of Americans cowered apprehensively.

The siege had begun, in the manner made sickeningly familiar in the preceding three years, with yet another banking panic. This one started in Michigan, where the governor had declared an eight-day banking "holiday" on February 14, to protect the reeling banks in his state from collapsing. This drastic action in a key industrial state set off tremors throughout the country. Public apprehension about the banking system and disillusionment with bankers were amplified at this moment by revelations emanating from the Senate Banking and Currency Committee hearing room, where committee counsel Ferdinand Pecora was daily extracting scandalous admissions of malfeasance, favoritism, tax avoidance, and corruption from the princes of Wall Street. Over Hoover's strenuous objections, Congress further undermined confidence in the banks by publishing the names of institutions receiving RFC loans, a policy that amounted to broadcasting an official roster of the shakiest, most endangered banks.

After having suffered through three years of depression and witnessing more than five thousand bank failures in the last three years, Americans reacted this time with hair-trigger haste and last-ditch desperation. By the thousands, in every village and metropolis, they scurried to their banks, queued up with bags and satchels, and carted away their deposits in currency or gold. They hoarded these precious remnants of their life savings under the mattress or in coffee tins buried in the back yard. Wealthier depositors shipped gold out of the country. Stock prices plummeted again, though not from their 1929 heights.

This latest bank panic had prompted Hoover's "cheeky" appeal to Roosevelt on February 18 to make a gesture that would soothe the jittery financial world. Receiving no reply, Hoover had again beseeched Roosevelt on February 28 to make some reassuring statement. "A declaration even now on the line I suggested," Hoover pleaded, "would save losses and hardships to millions of people." He went on to suggest that Roosevelt convene a special session of Congress as soon as possible after inauguration day.[1] Again, Roosevelt demurred. Without the president-elect's concurrence, the lame-duck president would not act. From Washington came only silence.

But in bank lobbies throughout the country, there was no silence. Shouting depositors jostled and shoved up to the tellers' wickets, demanding their cash. In state after state, the banking system quivered, buckled, and was saved from final failure only by gubernatorially decreed holiday. Maryland's banks were closed for three days by executive order on February 24. Similar closings followed in Kentucky, Tennessee, California, and elsewhere. On the morning of inauguration day, the New York Stock Exchange abruptly suspended trading; so did the Chi-

---

1. Frank Freidel, *Launching the New Deal* (Boston: Little, Brown, 1973), 188; William Starr Myers and Walter H. Newton, *The Hoover Administration: A Documented Narrative* (New York: Charles Scribner's Sons, 1936), 360.

cago Board of Trade. By then governmental proclamation had shut every bank in thirty-two states. Virtually all banks in six others were closed. In the remaining states, depositors were limited to withdrawing a maximum of 5 percent of their money, in Texas no more than ten dollars in a day. Investors had ceased to invest and workers had ceased to work. Some thirteen million willing pairs of hands could find no useful employment. Many had fidgeted idly for three years. Now they wrung in anxious frustration or steepled hopefully together in prayer. History's wealthiest nation, the haughty citadel of capitalist efficiency, only four years earlier a model of apparently everlasting prosperity, land of the pilgrims' pride, of immigrant dreams and beckoning frontiers, America lay tense and still, a wasteland of economic devastation.[2]

On inaugural eve, Friday, March 3, Hoover made one last effort to secure Roosevelt's cooperation. The outgoing president's gesture was fatuous in its lateness and doomed to futility by its manner of presentation. Refusing to extend to his successor the customary invitation to a pre-inaugural White House dinner, Hoover grudgingly agreed to receive the Roosevelts for afternoon tea. He then turned this already attenuated social occasion into an awkward last-minute appeal to Roosevelt to use the doubtful authority of the World War Trading with the Enemy Act to regulate overseas gold shipments and bank withdrawals. The encounter ended badly. Hoover responded to Roosevelt's courteous suggestion that Hoover need not feel obliged to make the traditional return call on the president-elect by saying icily: "Mr. Roosevelt, when you are in Washington as long as I have been, you will learn that the President of the United States calls on nobody." A fuming Roosevelt hustled his irate family out of the room. Aside from their necessary proximity in the following day's inaugural formalities, the two men never saw each other again.[3]

ROOSEVELT BEGAN INAUGURAL DAY by attending a brief service at St. John's Episcopal Church. His old Groton School headmaster, Endicott Peabody, prayed the Lord to "bless Thy servant, Franklin, chosen to be president of the United States." After a quick stop at the Mayflower Hotel to confer urgently with his advisers on the still-worsening banking crisis, Roosevelt donned his formal attire and motored to the White House. There he joined a haggard and cheerless

2. Davis 3:26.
3. Freidel, *Launching*, 192–93.

Hoover for the ride down Pennsylvania Avenue to the inaugural platform on the east side of the Capitol.

Braced on his son's arm, Roosevelt walked his few lurching steps to
the rostrum. Breaking precedent, he recited the entire oath of office,
rather than merely repeating "I do" to the chief justice's interrogation.
Then he began his inaugural address, speaking firmly in his rich tenor
voice. Frankly acknowledging the crippled condition of the ship of state
he was now to captain, he began by reassuring his countrymen that "this
great nation will endure as it has endured, will revive and will prosper.
. . . "The only thing we have to fear," he intoned, "is fear itself." The
nation's distress, he declared, owed to "no failure of substance." Rather,
"rulers of the exchange of mankind's goods have failed through their
own stubbornness and their own incompetence, have admitted their
failure, and have abdicated. . . . The money changers have fled from
their high seats in the temple of our civilization. We may now restore
that temple to the ancient truths." The greatest task, he went on, "is to
put people to work," and he hinted at "direct recruiting by the Government" on public works projects as the means to do it. He then touched
on the notion of "balance" as he had heard the Brain Trusters discuss
it, promising "to raise the value of agricultural products and with this
the power to purchase the output of our cities." He added a flourish of
his own about the desirability of redistributing population from the cities
to the countryside. He mentioned the need to prevent mortgage foreclosures, to regulate key industries, and especially to cut government
budgets. He called for "strict supervision of all banking and credits and
investments." He stressed the primacy of domestic over international
concerns. He obliquely hinted at inflationary measures in a pledge to
ensure "an adequate but sound currency." (One hard-money congressman complained that this meant Roosevelt was "for sound currency, but
lots of it.")[4] He announced that he was calling a special session of Congress to address these issues. Then, guardedly but nevertheless ominously, he declared that if Congress should fail to act, "I shall ask the
Congress for the one remaining instrument to meet the crisis—broad
Executive power to wage a war against the emergency, as great as the
power that would be given to me if we were in fact invaded by a foreign
foe."[5]

Just weeks before his inaugural, while on his way to board the *Nour-*

4. Leuchtenburg, 42.
5. *PPA*, (1933), 11–16.

mahal in Florida, Roosevelt had spoken restlessly of the need for "action, action." President at last, he now proceeded to act with spectacular vigor.

The first and desperately urgent item of business was the banking crisis. Even as he left the Mayflower Hotel to deliver his inaugural condemnation of the "money changers," he approved a recommendation originating with the outgoing treasury secretary, Ogden Mills, to convene an emergency meeting of bankers from the leading financial centers. The next day, Sunday, March 5, Roosevelt issued two proclamations, one calling Congress into special session on March 9, the other invoking the Trading with the Enemy Act to halt all transactions in gold and declare a four-day national banking holiday—both of them measures that Hoover had vainly urged him to endorse in the preceding weeks. Hoover's men and Roosevelt's now began an intense eighty hours of collaboration to hammer out the details of an emergency banking measure that could be presented to the special session of Congress. Haunting the corridors of the Treasury Department day and night, private bankers and government officials both old and new toiled frantically to rescue the moribund corpse of American finance. In that hectic week, none led normal lives, Moley remembered. "Confusion, haste, the dread of making mistakes, the consciousness of responsibility for the economic well-being of millions of people, made mortal inroads on the health of some of us . . . and left the rest of us ready to snap at our own images in the mirror. . . . Only Roosevelt," Moley observed, "preserved the air of a man who'd found a happy way of life."[6]

Roosevelt's and Hoover's minions "had forgotten to be Republicans or Democrats," Moley commented. "We were just a bunch of men trying to save the banking system."[7] William Woodin, the new treasury secretary, and Ogden Mills, his predecessor, simply shifted places on either side of the secretary's desk in the Treasury Building. Otherwise, nothing changed in the room. The kind of bipartisan collaboration for which Hoover had long pleaded was now happening, but under Roosevelt's aegis, not Hoover's—and not, all these men hoped, too late. When the special session of Congress convened at noon on March 9, they had a bill ready—barely.

The bill was read to the House at 1:00 P.M., while some new representatives were still trying to locate their seats. Printed copies were not

6. Raymond Moley, *After Seven Years* (New York: Harper and Brothers, 1939), 191.
7. Moley, *After Seven Years*, 148.

ready for the members. A rolled-up newspaper symbolically served. After thirty-eight minutes of "debate," the chamber passed the bill, sight unseen, with a unanimous shout. The Senate approved the bill with only seven dissenting votes—all from agrarian states historically suspicious of Wall Street. The president signed the legislation into law at 8:36 in the evening. "Capitalism," concluded Moley, "was saved in eight days."[8]

The Emergency Banking Act furnished a startling demonstration of Roosevelt's penchant for action and of the Congress's willingness, at least for the moment, to submit to his leadership. But it did not signal any intention radically to reorder the American capitalist system. The act legitimated the actions Roosevelt had already taken under the terms of the Trading with the Enemy Act, conferred on the president broad discretionary powers over gold and foreign exchange transactions, empowered the RFC to subscribe to the preferred stock of banks, expanded the capacity of the Federal Reserve Board to issue currency, and authorized the reopening of banks under strict government supervision. It was a thoroughly conservative measure, which had been drafted largely by Hoover administration officials and private bankers. As one congressman later commented, "The President drove the money-changers out of the Capitol on March 4th—and they were all back on the 9th." Unorthodoxy at this moment, Moley explained, "would have drained the last remaining strength of the capitalist system," a result as distant from Roosevelt's mind as it was from Hoover's, not to mention that of the Congress.[9]

For technical reasons the banking holiday was extended through the following weekend, making Monday, March 13, the day scheduled for the government-supervised reopening of the banks. On the preceding Sunday evening, at 10:00 P.M. eastern time, tens of millions of Americans tuned their radio sets to listen to the first of Roosevelt's Fireside Chats. Working from a draft prepared by Hoover's undersecretary of the treasury, Arthur Ballantine, Roosevelt explained in simple terms what had been accomplished in Washington. He told his listeners "that it is safer to keep your money in a reopened bank than under the mattress."[10] In a voice at once commanding and avuncular, masterful yet intimate, he soothed the nervous nation. His Groton-Harvard accent might have been taken as snobbish or condescending, but it conveyed instead that

8. Moley, *After Seven Years*, 155.
9. Leuchtenburg, 44; Moley's remark is in *After Seven Years*, 155.
10. PPA (1933), 64.

same sense of optimism and calm reassurance that suffused his most intimate personal conversations.

On Monday the thirteenth the banks reopened, and the results of Roosevelt's magic with the Congress and the people were immediately apparent. Deposits and gold began to flow back into the banking system. The prolonged banking crisis, acute since at least 1930, with roots reaching back through the 1920s and even into the days of Andrew Jackson, was at last over. And Roosevelt, taking full credit, was a hero. William Randolph Hearst told him: "I guess at your next election we will make it unanimous." Even Henry Stimson, who so recently had thought FDR a "peanut," sent his "heartiest congratulations."[11]

The common people of the country sent their congratulations as well—and their good wishes and suggestions and special requests. Some 450,000 Americans wrote to their new president in his first week in office. Thereafter mail routinely poured in at a rate of four to seven thousand letters per day. The White House mailroom, staffed by a single employee in Hoover's day, had to hire seventy people to handle the flood of correspondence. Roosevelt had touched the hearts and imaginations of his countrymen like no predecessor in memory.

HE MEANT TO MAINTAIN that contact—and use it. Roosevelt rightly believed that the majority of the country's newspapers were in the hands of political conservatives, who could not be counted upon to support him in the court of public opinion. It was partly for that reason that he made such calculating use of the new electronic medium of the radio, through which he could speak directly to the public without editorial interference. And if publishers and editors could be expected to oppose him, he could nevertheless cultivate reporters.

Roosevelt's first press conference was a personal and political triumph. One hundred twenty-five White House reporters, sensing that the focus of power in Washington was shifting from Capitol Hill to the White House, in the process upgrading the prestige of their previously tedious assignment, crowded into the Oval Office on the morning of March 8. Roosevelt greeted them with his customary warmth. He made them feel like part of his family. He bantered and joked. Most important, he announced welcome changes in the rules governing presidential press conferences. He hoped to meet with reporters, he said, twice a week, at times convenient to both morning and evening editions. The contrast with Hoover,

11. Schlesinger 2:13.

who had held virtually no press conferences for over a year, was sharp. So too was Roosevelt's declaration that he would not require written questions to be submitted in advance, as had been the custom for more than a decade. He would not answer hypothetical questions, he said, nor permit direct quotation unless issued by his own staff in writing. His own statements would fall into three categories: news that could be attributed to a White House source; "background information" that reporters could use at their own discretion but without direct attribution; and "off-the-record" comments that were to be regarded as privileged and not for publication in any form. This last category was the master stroke. It invited the working press into an intimate, almost conspiratorial proximity to the seat of power, subtly enfolding them within the orbit of the presidential will. Flattered and exhilarated, the reporters broke spontaneously into applause. Roosevelt sat back in his chair, beaming.

On March 10, Roosevelt sent his second emergency measure to Congress, requesting authority to cut some $500 million from the federal budget. "For three long years the Federal Government has been on the road toward bankruptcy," he declared. He called for the elimination of some government agencies, reductions in the pay of both civilian and military employees of the government, including congressmen, and, even more controversial, a nearly 50 percent slash in payments to veterans, an item that then accounted for almost one-quarter of the $3.6 billion federal budget. Many congressmen balked at this attack on one of the most popular federal spending items. Noting that remnants of the Bonus Army were still encamped near Washington, and remembering Herbert Hoover's severe embarrassment at its hands, ninety-two Democrats, mostly agrarian radicals and big-city "machine" representatives, broke ranks and voted against the president. The bill carried in the House only with heavy conservative support. It moved swiftly through the Senate only because the Democratic leadership had adroitly scheduled just behind it on the legislative calendar a popular measure to legalize beer, thus forestalling extended debate.

Roosevelt signed the Economy Act on March 20 and the Beer-Wine Revenue Act two days later. The latter measure anticipated the repeal of Prohibition. The lame-duck Congress had passed a bill repealing the Twentieth Amendment on February 20, 1933. The requisite three-quarters of the states would ratify the measure by December 5, when the Twenty-first Amendment became law, ending the Prohibition experiment and signaling another setback for the mostly rural Protestant forces that had tried to make America dry.

In two breathless weeks the new administration had ended the banking crisis, drastically cut federal expenditures, and provided for new revenue with the relegalization of beer and light wines. In the process the president had taken on and vanquished two of the most powerful political lobbies in Washington: the veterans and the prohibitionists. He had also, apparently, jolted the country out of its stagnant, sour resignation and rekindled the nation's confidence in itself. Here at last was a leader who could lead, and a Congress that could be made to follow. Roosevelt continued to bend his party to his will by withholding the distribution of the patronage jobs for which Democrats thirsted. By that device, one observer noted, the president's "relations to Congress were to the very end of the session tinged with a shade of expectancy which is the best part of young love." Whether that relationship would evolve into a stable and productive marriage remained an open question.[12]

Where, exactly, was Roosevelt leading? His banking bill was essentially a product of Hoover's Treasury Department. His economy bill fulfilled the promise of his Pittsburgh campaign speech and slashed federal spending more deeply than Hoover had dared. The beer bill, opening new sources of revenue to the federal government, accomplished the dearest political objective of the archconservative Raskob forces in the Democratic Party. This hardly looked like the sort of "new deal" that had inspired progressive hope and spread conservative apprehension since the time of Roosevelt's nomination eight months earlier.

Roosevelt had little more in mind than these three emergency measures when he summoned the special session to convene. Now, sensing the unexpected pliancy of Congress, he determined to hold it in session and to forge ahead with additional proposals, proposals that would begin to fulfill liberal expectations and give meaning and substance to the New Deal. They comprised a clutch of initiatives aimed variously at recovery and reform, and not incidentally at political realignment. Pundits soon dubbed this burst of legislative activity the Hundred Days. When it ended with the adjournment of the special session on June 16, Roosevelt had sent fifteen messages to Congress and had in turn signed fifteen bills into law. Taken together, the accomplishments of the Hundred Days constituted a masterpiece of presidential leadership unexampled then and unmatched since (unless in the "second Hundred

12. James T. Patterson, *Congressional Conservatism and the New Deal: The Growth of the Conservative Coalition in Congress* (Lexington: University Press of Kentucky, 1967), 11.

Days" over which Roosevelt presided in the great reform surge of 1935).
The original Hundred Days forged Roosevelt's principal weapons in the
battle against the Depression and shaped much of the New Deal's historical reputation. They also have defied generations of effort to appraise
their precise economic and social impact and, perhaps even more vex-
atiously, their collective ideological identity. Like the man who presided
over them, the Hundred Days, and beyond them the New Deal itself,
have puzzled historians seeking neatly encompassing definitions of this
prolifically creative era.

ROOSEVELT FIRED the first salvo in his barrage of additional legislative proposals on March 16, when he sent his farm bill to Congress.
"I tell you frankly that it is a new and untrod path" that his bill was
breaking, said Roosevelt, "but I tell you with equal frankness that an
unprecedented condition calls for the trial of new means to rescue agriculture."[13] Roosevelt here echoed Herbert Hoover's claims of innova-
tiveness for his own farm legislation in another special session of Congress just four years earlier. That both presidents were correct testifies
both to the stubbornness of the agricultural crisis and the widening
circle of political possibility that the Depression was inscribing. Roosevelt's farm bill represented new thinking indeed, and lots of it. "Seldom
if ever," said a writer for the *New York Herald Tribune*, "has so sweeping
a piece of legislation been introduced in the American Congress." Another observer declared that the bill "sought to legalize almost anything
anybody could dream up."[14]

At the core of Roosevelt's agricultural program lay the Brain Trusters'
familiar idea of "balance," of increasing farmers' income as a means of
bolstering demand for domestic industrial products. At this juncture,
redressing the imbalance between agriculture and industry constituted
the essence of Roosevelt's antidepression strategy. In notes appended to
the 1938 edition of his official papers, Roosevelt explained again that
he deemed "the continued lack of adequate purchasing power on the
part of the farmer" to be "one of the most important reasons for the
Depression."[15] This deficiency he now proposed to remedy. But how?

Agriculture was a huge and variegated sector of the American economy. It included Alabama cotton planters and Montana cattle ranchers,

13. *PPA* (1933), 74.
14. Schlesinger 2:40; Davis 3:69.
15. *PPA* (1933), 75.

Wisconsin dairymen and Dakota wheat farmers, Missouri hog raisers and New Jersey truck gardeners, California fruit growers and Wyoming sheep men, shoeless sharecroppers and lordly latifundiaries. These disparate interests spoke with no uniform voice about the nature of agriculture's grievances or what should be done about them. All that was certain was that something must be done soon. Agricultural income had plunged by almost 60 percent in the last four years alone. And the agricultural depression dated not simply from 1929. It was already nearly a decade old at the time of the Great Crash. By early 1933 banks were foreclosing on farm mortgages at a rate of some twenty thousand per month. The president of the Farm Bureau Federation, among the most conservative of agricultural organizations, warned a Senate hearing in January: "Unless something is done for the American farmer we will have revolution in the countryside within twelve months."[16]

A cacophony of farm proposals reverberated through Congress, some still echoing from the debates of the 1920s. They ranged from the old McNary-Haugen scheme of subsidized exports to Herbert Hoover's ideas about producers' cooperatives and government purchases of surplus crops, to the perennial cries for debt cancellation and inflation, and to Roosevelt's newfangled notion of "domestic allotment," which called for direct government payments to farmers who agreed *not* to produce certain crops. Domestic allotment payments were to be financed by new taxes on agricultural processors, including canners, millers, packers, and commodity brokers.

Because Hoover's Federal Farm Board had committed itself to purchase surpluses while making no effort to curtail production, it had quickly exhausted its modest financial resources. Domestic allotment sought to avoid that problem by tackling the price-depressing surpluses at their source, preventing their production in the first place. This was a drastic solution indeed. It took the logic of Roosevelt's Commonwealth Club speech about overproduction to the extreme conclusion of literally paying for nothing. The professional economist Tugwell, one of the farm bill's chief architects, conceded to his diary that "for the economic philosophy which it represents there are no defenders at all."[17]

No philosophic defenders, perhaps, but no shortage of interested advocates. Roosevelt had sketched a vague framework for his agricultural policy in his campaign speech at Topeka, Kansas, in September. There

16. Davis 3:71.
17. Leuchtenburg, 49–50.

he had unambiguously declared in favor of "national planning in agriculture." What sort of planning, and by whom, he had left unsaid. Acknowledging that "many plans have been advanced" and that no "particular plan is applicable to all crops," he had promised blandly "to compose the conflicting elements of these various plans."[18] In practice, however, Roosevelt did not compose these elements but simply aggregated them. When repeated conferences with agricultural organizations and consultations with farm leaders failed to produce consensus, Roosevelt cut the Gordian knot by proposing an omnibus bill authorizing the use of virtually *all* competing recommendations for resolving the agricultural crisis. In a hurry to enact the legislation before the spring crops were planted and before the proposed World Economic Conference took up the subject of global agricultural surpluses, the president avoided all the tough decisions about agricultural policy even as he gathered into his hands every imaginable policy instrument.

Even so, Congress balked at swallowing such a complicated and unfamiliar proposal. Roosevelt had to do some deft politicking to move the legislation along. He reassured the devotees of the McNary-Haugen scheme by indicating that he would appoint McNary-Haugenism's principal architect, Moline Plow Company president George Peek, as head of the new Agricultural Adjustment Administration (AAA). This was a recipe that guaranteed controversy and administrative confusion. Peek, a testy, combative, big-mouthed, extreme economic nationalist, loudly denounced the acreage-retirement feature of the legislation, which was the single most innovative aspect of the domestic allotment idea. He clung tenaciously to the old McNary-Haugen formula of no limits on production, a high tariff to protect the domestic agricultural market, and government assistance in dumping American surpluses abroad. These views put him on a direct collision course with domestic-allotment advocates like Secretary of Agriculture Henry Wallace and his new assistant secretary, Rexford Tugwell. They also eventually caused Peek to clash with Secretary of State Cordell Hull, who was trying to restore American foreign trade through reciprocal trade agreements that would, among other things, inhibit dumping.

For the moment the prospect of Peek's appointment mollified one important segment of the raucous and divided agricultural lobby. Others remained unsated. Roosevelt quieted another faction when he created

18. PPA (1928–32), 703.

the Farm Credit Administration, to be headed by his old friend and Hyde Park neighbor Henry Morgenthau Jr., and proposed adding farm mortgage relief provisions to the Agricultural Adjustment Act.

The most contentious players in the debate over agricultural policy were the inflationists. Powerful and persistent, gathering growing support from all across the usual ideological boundaries that divided the Congress, they pressed their cause with religious ardor. On April 17 the Senate nearly adopted a measure for the free coinage of silver. Other, wilder proposals for cheapening the currency were dropping into the hopper, including Senator Thomas P. Gore's facetious suggestion to license counterfeiters. The next day Roosevelt informed his advisers that for political reasons he had decided not to oppose an amendment to the Agricultural Adjustment Act proposed by the old Bryanite senator from Oklahoma, Elmer Thomas. The Thomas Amendment authorized the president to induce inflation by reducing the gold content of the dollar, by coining silver, or by issuing up to $3 billion of "greenbacks," fiat money not backed by precious metal of any kind.

"Hell broke loose" among Roosevelt's economic counselors when he told them of his decision, Moley remembered. Horrified, "they began to scold Mr. Roosevelt as though he were a perverse and particularly backward schoolboy." One adviser called the Thomas Amendment "harebrained and irresponsible" and predicted "uncontrolled inflation and complete chaos." Lewis Douglas, the respected budget director whom Roosevelt much admired, called the bill "thoroughly vicious" and almost resigned on the spot. "Well," he said to a friend later in the evening, "this is the end of western civilization."[19]

Roosevelt made a show of sharing his advisers' forebodings. He pleaded that he was only yielding to the inevitable, that his tactical retreat on the Thomas Amendment, which was merely permissive in character, would head off even worse mandatory inflationary measures. But the fact is that FDR had been fascinated with inflationary ideas for months. The Thomas Amendment, which put an array of powers in his hands and left the manner and timing of their exercise to him alone, fitted his purposes to a T. Preparatory to receiving the inflationary tools Congress was about to deliver him, Roosevelt on April 19 officially took the United States off the gold standard, prohibited most overseas shipments of gold, and let the exchange value of the dollar drift downward.

19. Freidel, *Launching*, 333–34; Moley, *After Seven Years*, 159–60; Davis 3:104–10.

On June 5 Congress took the next logical step and abrogated the gold clause in all public and private contracts. The way was now cleared for a "managed currency," its volume and value unfettered by gold.

The Thomas Amendment also unlocked the logjam blocking passage of the Agricultural Adjustment Act. On May 12 the president signed the act into law, barely in time for the World Economic Conference now scheduled for the following month in London, and too late to prevent the spring plantings that Roosevelt had hoped to forestall. To implement the key acreage-reduction feature of the legislation, therefore, the AAA could not simply pay for fallow fields to remain unseeded. The new agency now faced the far more daunting task of plowing up fully one-fourth of the acreage planted to certain crops. Doing so struck many as a crime against nature, a sentiment supported by reports that balky mules could not be made to violate all training and instinct and trample down rows of freshly sprouting crops. Before long, this mulish sabotage of the best-laid plans of men could be taken as an evil omen of the host of problems that would beset the most ambitious effort at national economic planning in American history.

MEANWHILE, THE STEADY legislative drumbeat of the Hundred Days continued. Relishing power and wielding it with gusto, Roosevelt next sent to Congress, on March 21, a request for legislation aimed at unemployment relief. Here he departed most dramatically from Hoover's pettifogging timidity, and here he harvested the greatest political rewards. He proposed a Civilian Conservation Corps (CCC) to employ a quarter of a million young men on forestry, flood control, and beautification projects. Over the next decade, the CCC became one of the most popular of all the New Deal's innovations. By the time it expired in 1942, it had put more than three million idle youngsters to work at a wage of thirty dollars a month, twenty-five of which they were required to send home to their families. CCC workers built firebreaks and lookouts in the national forests and bridges, campgrounds, trails, and museums in the national parks. Roosevelt also called for a new agency, the Federal Emergency Relief Administration (FERA), to coordinate and eventually increase direct federal unemployment assistance to the states. And he served notice, a bit halfheartedly, that he would soon be making recommendations about a "broad public works labor-creating program."[20]

20. PPA (1933), 80–81.

The first two of these measures—CCC and FERA—constituted important steps along the road to direct federal involvement in unemployment relief, something that Hoover had consistently and self-punishingly resisted. Roosevelt showed no such squeamishness, just as he had not hesitated as governor of New York to embrace relief as a "social duty" of government in the face of evident human suffering. As yet, Roosevelt did not think of relief payments or public works employment as means of significantly increasing purchasing power. He proposed them for charitable reasons, and for political purposes as well, but not principally for economic ones.

Roosevelt's New York experience taught him a lasting lesson about the political value of enlarging the federal role in relief. Since his days in the state senate before World War I, and culminating in an explosive controversy involving Jimmy Walker, the flamboyantly corrupt mayor of New York during FDR's governorship, Roosevelt's political nemesis in state politics had been Tammany Hall, the ultimate, ball-jointed, air-cushioned, precision-tooled, self-oiling, thousand-kilowatt urban political machine. Like all such machines, it was an engine of corruption, but it also delivered valuable social services to its army of faithful voters. Musing on this unholy marriage of welfare and graft during the campaign, Roosevelt ventured to Tugwell "that just possibly Tammany could be undercut by taking from it the responsibility for the unemployed. What would happen to the organization," Roosevelt wondered, "if handouts didn't have to be made . . . ? Tammany might be ruined if relief was really organized. People on relief would have no use for Tammany's services. They'd be independent."[21] Even more intriguing, perhaps their dependency could be made to shift from the local boss to the national, Democratic, administration. Like Alexander Hamilton's scheme to secure the loyalty of creditors to the new national government by federal assumption of state debts, so would Roosevelt artfully transfer the primary political allegiance of the unemployed from their local political club to Washington, D.C., in the process breaking forever the historical drive shaft of the urban political machine.

These first modest steps at a direct federal role in welfare services also carried into prominence another of Roosevelt's associates from New York, Harry Hopkins, whom Roosevelt would soon name as federal relief administrator. A chain-smoking, hollow-eyed, pauper-thin social worker, a tough-talking, big-hearted blend of the sardonic and sentimental, Hop-

21. Tugwell, *Brains Trust*, 368.

kins represented an important and durable component of what might be called the emerging political culture of the New Deal. In common with Brain Truster Adolf Berle, future treasury secretary Henry Morgenthau Jr., and Labor Secretary Frances Perkins, Hopkins was steeped in the Social Gospel tradition. Earnest, high-minded, and sometimes condescending, the Social Gospelers were middle-class missionaries to America's industrial proletariat. Inspired originally by late nineteenth-century Protestant clergymen like Walter Rauschenbusch and Washington Gladden, they were committed to the moral and material uplift of the poor, and they had both the courage and the prejudices of their convictions. Berle and Morgenthau had worked for a time at Lillian Wald's Henry Street settlement house in New York, Perkins at Jane Addams's Hull House in Chicago, and Hopkins himself at New York's Christadora House. Amid the din and squalor of thronged immigrant neighborhoods, they had all learned at first hand that poverty could be an exitless way of life, that the idea of "opportunity" was often a mockery in the precarious, threadbare existence of the working class. Together with Franklin Roosevelt, they meant to do something about it. The appointment of Perkins as secretary of labor gave some clue as to how their patrician patron intended to get the job done. Perkins was not the traditional male labor leader appointed to head this most macho of government bureaus; she was a woman social worker. In common with Roosevelt, as Arthur M. Schlesinger Jr. has observed, Perkins tended "to be more interested in doing things for labor than enabling labor to do things for itself; and her emphasis as Secretary was rather on the improvement of standards of work and welfare than on the development of labor self-organization."[22]

As for public works, Roosevelt remained skeptical. Progressives in Congress still clamored for a $5 billion construction program, but Roosevelt reiterated Hoover's insistence that public works be self-liquidating. He also endorsed Hoover's conclusion that only about $900 million worth of acceptable projects were on the shelf. "Do not write stories about five or six billion dollars of public works, " he cautioned reporters on April 19. "That is wild."[23] When Perkins pressed a $5 billion list of proposed projects on him at a White House meeting on April 29, he countered by going through the New York projects item by item, pointing out in well-informed detail how unsound most of them were. In the

22. Schlesinger 2:300.
23. PPA (1933), 141.

end Roosevelt caved in to political pressure and allowed an appropriation for $3.3 billion to be made for the new Public Works Administration. But he also took steps to ensure that the PWA would be cheese-paring and tightfisted in its disbursement of those funds.

Roosevelt further demonstrated his continuing commitment to maintain at least the appearance of fiscal orthodoxy when he established a separate "emergency budget" for relief and employment expenditures. The regular budget he would balance, he promised, but he did not think it fair "to put into that part of the budget expenditures that relate to keeping human beings from starving in this emergency. . . . You cannot let people starve, but this starvation crisis is not an annually recurring charge."[24] Though mocked by Roosevelt's critics as an accounting trick, the very idea of an emergency budget accurately registered his persistent respect for the conventional budgetary wisdom, as well as his belief, reminiscent of Hoover's repeatedly dashed hopes, that the crisis might soon be over.

ROOSEVELT'S TENACIOUS FRUGALITY, especially on public works, aggravated his progressive allies, but they found much to celebrate in his public power policies. Here was an area to which Roosevelt, so rarely a deep analyst of any subject, had uncharacteristically devoted painstaking attention. His knowledge of the complicated accounting and valuation procedures employed in the public utilities industry, thought Tugwell, "was worthy of a lifelong student."[25] His advanced views on this subject endeared him to progressives. Accompanied by the great paladin of public power, George Norris, Roosevelt had paid an emotional visit to Muscle Shoals, Alabama, in January 1933. Wilson Dam at Muscle Shoals on the Tennessee River had been built by the federal government during World War I to facilitate nitrate production for the manufacture of explosives; completed too late for wartime use, it had been a bone of political contention ever since. Private utilities interests, fighting hammer and claw and with the help of Presidents Coolidge and Hoover, had repeatedly blocked Norris's scheme for federal operation of the dam's hydroelectric generating capacity. Roosevelt now saw the great dam, symbol of progressive frustrations and progressive hopes, for the first time. He was struck by the sight and sound of the foaming waters roaring unused over its massive spillways. In the vast surrounding

24. Freidel, *Launching*, 251–52.
25. Tugwell, *Brains Trust*, 74.

valley of the Tennessee, families nightly lit their cabins with kerosene lamps and cooked on wood stoves. To Roosevelt, the contrast was intolerable.

"Is he really with you?" a reporter asked Norris on his return to Washington. "He is more than with me," the elderly senator replied, "because he plans to go even farther than I did."[26] On April 10 Roosevelt put Congress on notice just how far he intended to go. "[T]he Muscle Shoals development is but a small part of the potential public usefulness of the entire Tennessee River," Roosevelt said. He requested the creation of a Tennessee Valley Authority (TVA), a public corporation charged to generate and distribute hydroelectric power from Muscle Shoals, to build more dams for flood control and additional generating capacity, to produce fertilizers, to combat soil erosion and deforestation, to dig a 650-mile navigable waterway from Knoxville on the upper reaches of the Tennessee River system to Paducah on the Ohio, to upgrade health and educational services in the depressed valley, to promote conservation and the development of recreational facilities, and to attract new industries to the region. Roosevelt's vision of what the TVA might do was breathtaking in its imaginative reach. Even Norris was struck by its audacity. "What are you going to say when they ask you the political philosophy behind TVA?" Norris asked FDR. "I'll tell them it's neither fish nor fowl," Roosevelt answered, "but, whatever it is, it will taste awfully good to the people of the Tennessee Valley." And whatever it was, Roosevelt did not intend it to be a purely regional dish, served only within the boundaries of the Tennessee River watershed. "If we are successful here," Roosevelt told the Congress, "we can march on, step by step, in a like development of other great natural territorial units within our borders."[27]

TVA, duly created by Congress on May 18, delighted the progressives. It ratified beyond their dearest expectations the wisdom of their campaign support for Roosevelt. It also fitted perfectly with FDR's political intentions for the South. The Tennessee River cut through seven states of the impoverished, underdeveloped region. TVA would bring jobs, investment, and the promise of prosperity to a sprawling area that had stagnated since the Civil War. At a stroke, Roosevelt had thus earned the gratitude of the two most disparate elements in the unlikely political coalition he was trying to assemble: traditional southern Democrats and

26. Schlesinger 2:324.
27. PPA (1933), 122–23; Freidel, *Launching*, 351.

forward-looking Republican progressives. He had also taken a giant step in the direction of modernizing the South, laying the foundations for the region's federally sponsored advance into the industrial era. Surprisingly little remarked at its inception, TVA would become the forward edge of the great transforming blade of federal power that would within two generations resculpt the cotton belt into the sun belt.[28]

ON APRIL 4, 1933, Moley and Roosevelt reviewed with satisfaction the president's astonishingly successful legislative record to date. Congress had passed the banking, budget, and beer bills and had created the Civilian Conservation Corps, especially gratifying to the conservation-minded president. The farm and unemployment relief bills were making their way through the Capitol Hill machinery, as was another Roosevelt proposal for reform of the securities markets. The president was scheduled to ask for TVA within the following week and for legislation to shore up the sagging home-mortgage industry shortly thereafter. This constituted a record of considerable achievement. Roosevelt had ridden the Congress like a skilled jockey, the staccato whip-touches of his several brief, urgent messages stirring the balky House and Senate to unprecedented movement. But now, the bit firmly in its teeth, Congress theatened to buck the president and run away with its own agenda.

Virtually everything accomplished thus far consisted of emergency remedial and long-range reform measures. The banking bill, together with the pending securities and mortgage legislation, would stanch the bleeding from the nation's financial system. The budget bill aimed to restore confidence in the investing community. The beer bill modestly increased tax revenues, to the same purpose. But none of the measures thus far enacted provided positive fiscal stimulus to the economy. All to the contrary, the net effect of Roosevelt's budget cutting and tax hiking was decidedly deflationary. Even the relief bill was scaled to the prevention of human suffering, not to the revival of consumer demand. The farm program should in time furnish some economic stimulus, and so might TVA, but it would be months, maybe years, before their effects were visible. None of these measures would make any significant contribution in the short run to the urgent goal of economic recovery. With the economy prostrate and thirteen million people still unemployed, the

28. See Bruce Schulman's development of this theme in *From Cotton Belt to Sunbelt* (New York: Oxford University Press, 1991).

pressure in Congress to take swift and dramatic action was growing irresistible.

Roosevelt appreciated these facts and had been casting about for some means to stimulate industrial activity. But spokesmen for industry, supposedly a more coherent and well-organized economic sector than agriculture, were proving unable to agree on what steps should be taken or even to arrive at the kind of rough consensus on a range of possible measures that the farm leaders had managed eventually to reach. Within the government, Roosevelt's advisers were split between adherents to the Brandeisian antitrust tradition and proponents of the Van Hise philosophy of regulatory control. They too could not find common ground. Roosevelt and Moley accordingly decided at their meeting on April 4 that thinking in both the business community and in government circles on the subject of industrial recovery policy had not yet crystallized sufficiently to justify any further moves at the time. They agreed that nothing should be done yet.

In the meantime Congress, as with inflation and the Thomas Amendment, had been taking the subject of industrial policy into its own hands. Roosevelt's do-nothing decision of April 4, Moley wrote, "went out the window on April 6th."[29] On that day the Senate passed the "thirty-hour bill" sponsored by Alabama senator Hugo Black. A work-spreading device, Black's bill prohibited from interstate commerce any goods manufactured in a plant whose employees worked more than a thirty-hour week. This requirement would supposedly create some six million new jobs. Here at last, it seemed, someone was smiting the dragon of Depression with the kind of quick, clean stroke to the heart for which the long-suffering country was praying.

But Roosevelt was worried. He concurred with his attorney general's opinion that the Black bill was unconstitutional. Moreover, he deemed it unworkable in many of the rural and agricultural industries with which he was most familiar, like canneries and dairies. Black's proposal could not be adapted "to the rhythm of the cow," he told Frances Perkins, a phrase that he repeatedly invoked in his criticisms of the thirty-hour idea.[30] He also believed, correctly, that reducing the workweek without maintaining wages would simply punish workers by shrinking their paychecks. Yet to maintain wages while adding six million workers to the nation's payrolls might bankrupt already faltering businesses.

29. Moley, *After Seven Years*, 186.
30. Frances Perkins, *The Roosevelt I Knew* (New York: Viking, 1946), 194.

For all these reasons, Roosevelt felt obliged to oppose the Black bill, despite his sympathy with its goal of reducing unemployment. But he had, at first, nothing to put in its place. In what was fast becoming notorious as a standard Rooseveltian practice, he assigned several different people, none of whom had much knowledge of the others' activity, to draft proposals for an industrial recovery bill. Through the month of April they worked feverishly. In the end Roosevelt ordered the advocates for the several competing schemes that this process cast up to shut themselves together in a room and not come out until they had settled their differences.

Out of this hurried, chaotic, initially defensive and ultimately compromised endeavor came Roosevelt's message to the Congress of May 17, calling for a National Industrial Recovery Act (NIRA). The proposed legislation embodied three major elements. One, incorporated in the famous Section 7(a), was the most direct successor to the now-buried Black bill. It provided for federal regulation of maximum hours and minimum wages in various industries. Even more consequentially, and somewhat surprisingly, it stipulated the right of industrial workers "to organize and bargain collectively through representatives of their own choosing"—a historic shift away from the government's traditional refusal to guarantee labor's highest objective, the right to unionize.

A second part of the bill created the National Recovery Administration (NRA). The NRA was to be charged with overseeing a vast process of government-sanctioned cartelization. Production in whole industries would be controlled, and prices and wages would be raised, by government-sanctioned industrial compacts; the antitrust laws were largely to be suspended. The rationale, Roosevelt explained in a phrase that once again recollected his Commonwealth Club address, was "to prevent unfair competition and disastrous overproduction." To Moley he privately acknowledged that he was "taking an enormous step away from the philosophy of equalitarianism and laissez-faire.... If that philosophy hadn't proved to be bankrupt," Roosevelt added, "Herbert Hoover would be sitting here right now."[31]

The bill's third major component created the Public Works Administration (PWA) to undertake an ambitious public construction program. If the NRA was the chassis of the legislation, creating a framework within which American industry might be reformed and regulated, then the PWA was the engine, or at least the starting motor. Reducing hours,

31. PPA (1933), 202; Moley, After Seven Years, 189.

spreading work, and stabilizing wages would have no appreciably positive economic effect, and might even inflict additional economic damage, unless aggregate purchasing power was somehow increased. Thus NRA and PWA were necessarily complementary. The new spending engendered by PWA, along with the eventual boost to agricultural income envisioned in the AAA legislation, would increase the total volume of purchases. NRA would equitably spread the benefits of rising income between labor and capital. NRA and AAA together would ensure balance between industry and agriculture. That, at least, was the theory, such as it was. Crucial to its successful application was the quick release of money into the economy through a rapidly adopted public works program. The figure finally settled on for PWA spending was $3.3 billion.

In accepting that figure, Roosevelt yielded to the will of Congress, over his own best judgment. He remained skeptical that PWA would prove an effective mechanism for generating employment, and he had given up none of his objections to its budget-busting implications. Consequently, his message to Congress accompanying the NIRA bill called for $220 million in new taxes, sufficient to service the interest payments on the sum the government would be forced to borrow to pay for the public works program.

The NRA would soon become the most conspicuous of all the freshly minted New Deal agencies, and it has long stood at the center of all efforts to explain the early New Deal's economic philosophy and anti-depression strategy. Thus it is worth remembering the adventitious circumstances of the NRA's birth. Conceived as a means to block the thirty-hour bill, NRA fused emergency relief measures with a version of the venerable Van Hise regulatory reform program, a concept long fermented in the wood of academic lecture halls but little tested in practice. The National Industrial Recovery Act, said Moley, was "a thorough hodge-podge of provisions designed to give the country temporary economic stimulation and provisions designed to lay the groundwork for permanent business-government partnership and planning, of provisions calculated to satisfy the forces behind the Black bill and provisions calculated to achieve workable wage-hour agreements." Lumping all of these provisions together in a single piece of legislation, Moley later reflected, produced a "confused, two-headed experiment." It was, he concluded, "a mistake."[32] This ramshackle, hastily assembled contrap-

32. Moley, *After Seven Years*, 190, 184.

tion was now rolled up to take its place alongside AAA in the battery of New Deal heavy artillery deployed in the war against the Depression.

In a final rush of legislative activity, Congress passed the National Industrial Recovery Act and adjourned on June 16. On the same day, it adopted the Glass-Steagall Banking Act, which divorced commercial from investment banking, and, over Roosevelt's objections, instituted federal insurance of bank deposits, the Farm Credit Act, and a railroad regulation bill.

So ENDED the Hundred Days Congress. As Roosevelt signed the final bills that arrived from Capitol Hill on June 16, he remarked that "more history is being made today than in [any] one day of our national life."[33] By any standard, the achievements of the Hundred Days were impressive. The New Deal had decisively halted the banking panic. It had invented wholly new institutions to restructure vast tracts of the nation's economy, from banking to agriculture to industry to labor relations. It had authorized the biggest public works program in American history. It had earmarked billions of dollars for federal relief to the unemployed. It had designated the great Tennessee watershed as the site of an unprecedented experiment in comprehensive, planned regional development. No less important, the spirit of the country, so discouraged by four years of economic devastation, had been infused with Roosevelt's own contagious optimism and hope. In the process, Roosevelt himself had dumfounded those critics who believed they had taken his measure months before and found him then so sorely wanting. Even some old acquaintances wondered if he were the same man. The oath of office, wrote one journalist, "seems suddenly to have transfigured him from a man of mere charm and buoyancy to one of dynamic aggressiveness."[34]

But for all the excitement of the Hundred Days and the rising stature of Roosevelt's reputation, the Depression still hung darkly over the land. The precise battle plan of the New Deal's attack on it remained difficult to define. Little coherent pattern could be detected in the unlikely mixture of policies that had been adopted. They ranged from orthodox budget cutting to expansive spending for relief and public works, from tough controls on Wall Street to government-supervised cartelization, from deliberate crop destruction to thoughtful conservation, from mortgage protection for the middle class to union protection for labor. "It simply has

33. Leuchtenburg, 61.
34. Leuchtenburg, 61.

to be admitted," Tugwell later wrote, "that Roosevelt was not yet certain what direction he ought to take and was, in fact, going both ways at once."[35]

Some of these measures aimed at economic recovery, but at least as many were meant to provide only palliative relief or to enact reforms long-standing on somebody's agenda but only obliquely related to combating the Depression. Some, like TVA, were Roosevelt's idea. Some, like the banking bill, were largely Hoover's. Others, like AAA and NRA, had been devised for the most part by the constituencies affected by them. Still others, like the labor provisions of the NIRA and the Thomas Amendment to the AAA legislation, had originated in Congress. About the only defensible statement that could be made about them in the aggregate was that they accurately reflected Roosevelt's penchant for action, his inclination to experiment, and his receptivity to all kinds of innovation. To look upon these policies as the result of a unified plan, Moley later wrote, "was to believe that the accumulation of stuffed snakes, baseball pictures, school flags, old tennis shoes, carpenter's tools, geometry books, and chemistry sets in a boy's bedroom could have been put there by an interior decorator."[36]

And yet, amid the chaos of the Hundred Days, and indeed through the tense stand-off of the interregnum that preceded it, one thread flashed and dove like a scarlet skein shot through brocade: inflation. Roosevelt had long flirted with inflation as a Depression remedy. In early April he called it "inevitable."[37] By June he deemed it positively desirable.

The historic check on a nation's impulse to inflate had been the gold standard, under which inflating prices attracted imports, which were paid for in gold shipments, thus contracting the monetary base, depressing prices, and nipping the inflationary cycle in the bud. It was precisely the swift power and elegant automaticity of the gold standard that had forced the decision in Britain to go off gold in September 1931. Faced with the choice of protecting the exchange value of the pound by staying on gold or protecting the domestic prices of British products, Britain had abandoned gold. Though FDR seemed slow to grasp the point, the United States faced exactly the same choice in 1933.

35. Rexford G. Tugwell, *Roosevelt's Revolution: The First Year, a Personal Perspective* (New York: Macmillan, 1977), 59.
36. Moley, *After Seven Years*, 369–70.
37. Schlesinger 2:196.

At his press conference on April 19, FDR had declared that he "absolutely" intended to return the United States to the gold standard and added that "one of the things we hope to do is to get the world as a whole back on some form of gold standard."[38] In well-publicized conferences with British prime minister Ramsay MacDonald and French premier Edouard Herriot later in the month, he further gave the impression that the United States would look to the now imminent World Economic Conference to stabilize international exchange rates and reestablish the international gold standard. In an even more lavishly publicized appeal to fifty-four heads of state on May 16, Roosevelt had eloquently called for "stabilization of currencies."[39]

The world was astonished, therefore, when shortly after the World Economic Conference convened Roosevelt scuttled it with his infamous "bombshell message" of July 3. He brusquely declared to the delegates who were waiting upon his word in London that the United States would not be a party to efforts at exchange-rate stabilization, nor would it return in the foreseeable future to gold. Without American participation, there was little the conferees could do to patch up the wounded international economic system. Roosevelt appeared not to care. He had other, exclusively nationalistic, priorities in mind. "Old fetishes of so-called international bankers," he lectured the London delegates, "are being replaced by efforts to plan national currencies."[40] Roosevelt's message not only destroyed the London conference. It also definitively killed any further prospect of international cooperation in the fight against the global depression. Among those observers of the London proceedings who drew the lesson that the United States intended to play no consequential international role was Adolf Hitler. Like Japan in Manchuria, Hitler concluded, Germany could do what it wanted in Europe without fear of American reprisal. Here, five years before the western European democracies' infamous capitulation at Munich to Hitler's demand that he be allowed to absorb part of Czechoslovakia, the Western powers had shown that they had little stomach for concerted action in the face of danger.

Vats of ink have been drained in efforts to explain Roosevelt's surprise attack on the London conference. The full story is rich in theatrics and mystery. It includes the appointment of a colorful and comically dis-

---

38. *PPA* (1933), 140.
39. *PPA* (1933), 186.
40. *PPA* (1933), 265.

cordant American delegation, headed by the dignified, white-maned secretary of state, Cordell Hull, a sound-money man and fervent internationalist, and counting among its members the silver fanatic and narrow protectionist Key Pittman, Senate Foreign Relations Committee chairman and, in London, a high-living, madly carousing, knife-brandishing drunk. It contains elements of gaudy melodrama involving the dying Secretary of the Treasury Woodin, who fainted during a tense transatlantic telephone consultation. It encompasses the tragic tale of Raymond Moley, borne by navy ship and aircraft to high-seas conferences with Roosevelt, who was piloting his small sailboat along the fog-shrouded coast of New England, allegedly studying advanced treatises on monetary theory while his boat nightly swung around its anchor. Emerging from these dramatic meetings, Moley was dispatched to London, his progress across the Atlantic nervously followed in the world press. He was ostensibly sent to rescue the conference with an affirmation of Roosevelt's belief in international cooperation, but he had the ground abruptly and astoundingly cut from beneath him by Roosevelt's message, which, faithful to the protocols of tragedy, was heavily grounded in Moley's own nationalistic analysis of the Depression. In the process, Moley mortally antagonized his immediate superior, Cordell Hull, marking the beginning of the end of his meteoric political career. He was soon forced to resign his position as assistant secretary of state and drifted gradually into estrangement from the New Deal and sometimes acrid criticism of Franklin Roosevelt.

The denouement in London came with the conference's stormy adjournment, amid denunciations of FDR from all sides. Prime Minister Ramsay MacDonald expressed "the most bitter resentment" against the man who had personally assured him in Washington only weeks earlier that he favored stabilization. A British journalist called Roosevelt a "laughing stock" and damned his message as a document that "will be filed for all times as a classic example of conceit, hectoring, and ambiguity." John Maynard Keynes, the British economist busy developing his own revolutionary ideas about managed currencies, was virtually alone in his praise. The president's action, he wrote, was "magnificently right."[41]

But the histrionic pageantry of this episode should not be allowed to

---

41. Schlesinger 2:195–232; Davis 3:182–98; Moley, *After Seven Years*, 196–269; Herbert Feis, *1933: Characters in Crisis* (Boston: Little, Brown, 1966), 95–258.

obscure a central truth: the essential logic of Roosevelt's recovery program was inflationary and had been so from the outset. Inflation and the gold standard were incompatible. In this sense, the World Economic Conference was doomed to failure before it even convened.

Heavy majorities in Congress, especially in Roosevelt's own Democratic Party, demanded inflation. The debt-freighted agricultural sector, central to Roosevelt's antidepression strategy and sentimentally dear to him, demanded inflation. The NRA's price-fixing and wage-boosting programs demanded inflation. Inflation would make it easier to service the indebtedness required to pay for federal relief, not to mention the unwelcome debt that the PWA's public works program had forced upon Roosevelt. Inflation was necessary to virtually all parts of the president's early New Deal agenda. Roosevelt had for months displayed a persistent interest in inflationary ideas. And inflation could not be accomplished if the United States agreed to play by the rigid, anti-inflationary rules of the gold standard regime. However much Roosevelt may have believed his own statements in April about returning to gold, the inescapable anti–gold standard logic of his program must at some point have impressed itself upon him. By July 3, 1933, if not sooner, it surely had. There was by then no more chance that FDR would return to gold than there had been a chance that he would accept Hoover's invitation to cooperate on the debt question during the interregnum — and for the same reason. As FDR had proclaimed in his inaugural address, he believed America's international economic commitments to be "secondary to the establishment of a sound national economy." He sounded the same theme in his "bombshell message" on July 3: "The sound internal economic system of a Nation is a greater factor in its well-being than the price of its currency in changing terms of the currencies of other Nations."[42]

Among the consequences that flowed from that parochial belief was America's refusal to play a part in stemming the tide of economic nationalism and vicious militarism, of Nazism and Fascism and Japanese aggression, that were as much the products of the global depression as Chicago breadlines and Kansas City Hoovervilles. Keynes notwithstanding, Roosevelt was here something sadly less than "magnificently right." But in deed if not word, from his rejection of Hoover's invitation to collaborate on the international debt issue to his repudiation of inter-

42. *PPA* (1933), 264–65.

national economic cooperation in London, Roosevelt, whatever else might be said, was with respect to American foreign policy magnificently consistent: he was for the time being a thoroughgoing isolationist.

ROOSEVELT DID NOT LACK for evidence that the world was growing more dangerous. In the month of his inaugural, Japan burned its diplomatic bridges and gave notice of its intent to quit the League of Nations in 1935. Roosevelt's ambassador in Tokyo soberly informed the president that "this step indicates the complete supremacy of the military."[43] On February 27 arsonists set fire to the German Reichstag building in Berlin. Hitler seized the occasion to demand absolute dictatorial power. The Reichstag gave it to him on March 23. Hitler proceeded to abolish the German federal system, concentrating all political power in his hands in Berlin. He dissolved the trade unions and closed the fist of Nazi control over the universities and churches. Nazi students stoked huge bonfires with books deemed offensive to der Führer. Nazi mobs fell upon Jews in the streets. On April 1 the Nazi Party announced a boycott of all Jewish businesses, as a preliminary to expelling Jews from government, the professions, and the arts.

Hitler, Roosevelt confided to French ambassador Paul Claudel, was "a madman." He knows some of Hitler's counselors personally, the president went on, and they "are even madder than he is."[44] Urged on by American Jewish leaders, Roosevelt expressed his dismay about Nazi anti-Semitism to Reichsbank president Hjalmar Schacht, but to no avail. Schacht, in fact, like so many visitors to Roosevelt's office, came away with the vague impression that the genial Roosevelt had no terribly serious disagreement with him or with the policies he represented.

Then, on May 16, Roosevelt had issued his "Appeal to the Nations of the World for Peace and for the End of Economic Chaos." Calling attention to the ongoing Disarmament Conference in Geneva and the upcoming World Economic Conference in London, Roosevelt declared that "if any strong Nation refuses to join with genuine sincerity in these concerted efforts for political and economic peace, the one at Geneva and the other at London, progress can be obstructed and ultimately blocked. In such event the civilized world, seeking both forms of peace, will know where the responsibility for failure lies."[45] Praising Roosevelt's

43. Freidel, *Launching*, 366–67.
44. Freidel, *Launching*, 377.
45. *PPA*, (1933), 187–88.

speech, the *San Francisco Chronicle* said: "This is the end of isolation, or it is nothing."[46]

It was nothing. Within months Hitler torpedoed the disarmament talks at Geneva and began to build the fearsome Nazi *Wehrmacht*. Roosevelt, mocking his own words of May 16, sank the economic conference at London. The two forums whose agendas Hoover had urged Roosevelt to link, and that Roosevelt himself had so piously praised as the sites of efforts for international peace, stood separately silent. A thin but plausible opportunity to arrest the plunge into chaos and bloodshed, to restore international economic health and maintain political stability, had died, and the world might well have asked where the responsibility lay.

At the end of August D'Arcy Osborne, chargé d'affaires at the British embassy in Washington, summed up his impressions of the New Deal for his home office. Roosevelt's "first much advertised entry into the field of foreign politics," he observed, "was somewhat of a fiasco. . . . From President downwards immediate interest and sentiment of the country is concentrated on recovery programme and its domestic results, and this implies a nationalistic inspiration and orientation of foreign policy. . . . Situation here seems to render isolation and nationalism inevitable."

So the world slid further down the ugly helix of economic isolationism and military rearmament toward the ultimate catastrophe of global war. Roosevelt had shown no more vision than the other desperately self-protective nationalists in 1933, perhaps even somewhat less. Having bled awhile, America laid down its international commitments. Who could say if it would rise to fight again? Falsely thinking themselves safe behind their ocean moats, Americans prepared to take up arms alone in the battle against the Depression, girded now with the abundant weapons crafted in the Hundred Days, not least the inflationary powers for whose free exercise the collapse in London cleared the way. They had a resourceful if mysterious leader. He might just carry them through the crisis. "But generally speaking," D'Arcy Osborne concluded, "situation here is so incalculable and President himself so mercurial and his policies so admittedly empirical that all estimates and forecasts are dangerous."[47]

46. Freidel, *Launching*, 404.
47. Freidel, *Launching*, 498.

6

The Ordeal of the American People

I saw old friends of mine — men I had been to school with — digging ditches and laying sewer pipe. They were wearing their regular business suits as they worked because they couldn't afford overalls and rubber boots. If I ever thought, "There, but for the grace of God —" it was right then.

— Frank Walker, president of the
National Emergency Council, 1934

"What I want you to do," said Harry Hopkins to Lorena Hickok in July 1933, "is to go out around the country and look this thing over. I don't want statistics from you. I don't want the social-worker angle. I just want your own reaction, as an ordinary citizen.

"Go talk with preachers and teachers, businessmen, workers, farmers. Go talk with the unemployed, those who are on relief and those who aren't. And when you talk with them don't ever forget that but for the grace of God you, I, any of our friends might be in their shoes. Tell me what you see and hear. All of it. Don't ever pull your punches."[1]

The Depression was now in its fourth year. In the neighborhoods and hamlets of a stricken nation millions of men and women languished in sullen gloom and looked to Washington with guarded hope. Still they struggled to comprehend the nature of the calamity that had engulfed them. Across Hopkins's desk at the newly created Federal Emergency Relief Administration flowed rivers of data that measured the Depression's impact in cool numbers. But Hopkins wanted more — to touch the human face of the catastrophe, taste in his own mouth the metallic smack of the fear and hunger of the unemployed, as he had when he

1. Richard Lowitt and Maurine Beasley, eds., *One Third of a Nation: Lorena Hickok Reports on the Great Depression* (Urbana: University of Illinois Press, 1981), ix–x.

worked among the immigrant poor at New York's Christadora settlement house in 1912. Tied to his desk in Washington, he dispatched Lorena Hickok in his stead. In her he chose a uniquely gutsy and perceptive observer who could be counted on to see without illusion and to report with candor, insight, and moxie.

Hopkins and Hickok were cast from similar molds. Both were children of the Midwest who had blossomed in New York's teeming metropolis. Both remembered their own austere childhoods on the prairie and found nothing that was romantic — and, for that matter, little that was potentially revolutionary — in the grit of hardship. Both hid soft hearts within shells of jaunty acerbity. Hopkins, forty-three years old in 1933, gaunt and chronically disheveled, was a harnessmaker's son with a lasting devotion to racehorses. Like the track touts with whom he frequently kept company, he affected a hell's-bells air that caused others to appraise him as both shrewd and faintly ominous. Yet compassion suffused his nature, tempered by a piercing intelligence that would one day lead Winston Churchill to dub him "Lord Root of the Matter."[2]

Hickok, forty in 1933, had struggled up from a painful childhood on the bleak northern plains to become, in her own unapologetic words, "just about the top gal reporter in the country." A colleague once described her as "endowed with a vast body, beautiful legs and a peaches-and-cream complexion." Five foot eight and nearly two hundred pounds, she was big, boisterous, unconventional, and irreverent. She could smoke, drink, play poker, and cuss as well as any of her male colleagues, and she could write better than most of them. After working as a feature writer in Milwaukee and Minneapolis she moved to New York, where the Associated Press assigned her in 1928 to hard-news stories, then an unusual beat for a woman journalist. In 1932 she covered the sensational Lindbergh-baby kidnaping story. Later that year she accepted the assignment that changed her life: covering Eleanor Roosevelt during the presidential campaign.[3]

Hickok did not merely report about her new subject. She grew attached to Eleanor Roosevelt in ways that eventually strained the rules of journalistic objectivity. She began clearing her stories with Eleanor herself or with Franklin's chief adviser, Louis Howe. By campaign's end

2. Robert E. Sherwood, *Roosevelt and Hopkins* (New York: Grosset and Dunlap, 1948, 1950), 1–5. See also Schlesinger 2:266.
3. Blanche Wiesen Cook, *Eleanor Roosevelt: A Life*, vol. 1, 1884–1933 (New York: Viking, 1992), 468.

Hickok had effectively ceased to be a reporter and had become Eleanor's press agent, as well as her deeply intimate companion.[4]

Hickok resigned from the Associated Press in June 1933, took a month-long motoring holiday through New England and eastern Canada with Eleanor, and started off on her new assignment from Hopkins. She set out to interview plain folk and local big shots, housewives and working stiffs, cotton lords and miners, waitresses and mill hands, tenant farmers and relief administrators. At night she holed up in spare hotel rooms and pecked out her impressions on a portable typewriter. Soon her reports started arriving in Hopkins's Washington office, from the sooty coal districts of Pennsylvania and West Virginia and Kentucky in August, from stoically suffering New England villages in September, from the wheatfields of North Dakota in October. They continued to come for nearly two more years, from the cotton belt of Georgia, the Carolinas, Alabama, and Texas, and from the ranches, mining camps, fruit orchards, and raw cities of the Far West. She saw with a seasoned reporter's eye and wrote in an earthy, no-foolin' style that managed to be at once unsentimentally cool and warmly sympathetic. "Mr. Hopkins said today," an admiring Eleanor wrote her in December 1933, "that your reports would be the best history of the Depression in future years."[5]

From the charts and tables accumulating on his desk even before Hickok's letters began to arrive, Hopkins could already sketch the grim outlines of that history.[6] Stockholders, his figures confirmed, had watched as three-quarters of the value of their assets had simply evaporated since 1929, a colossal financial meltdown that blighted not only the notoriously idle rich but struggling neighborhood banks, hard-earned retirement nest eggs, and college and university endowments as well. The more than five thousand bank failures between the Crash and the

4. By some accounts, the relationship between Eleanor Roosevelt and Lorena Hickok even transgressed conventional standards of sexual propriety, though whether their warmly intimate relationship was physically consummated remains conjectural. See Cook, *Eleanor Roosevelt*, and a rejoinder by Geoffrey Ward, "Outing Eleanor Roosevelt," *New York Review of Books*, September 24, 1992, 15.

5. Eleanor Roosevelt to Lorena Hickok, December 7, 1933, quoted in Lowitt and Beasley, *One Third of a Nation*, xxxiii.

6. Much of the discussion of the Depression's impact that follows is drawn from Lester V. Chandler, *America's Greatest Depression, 1929–1941* (New York: Harper and Row, 1970); Anthony J. Badger, *The New Deal: The Depression Years* (New York: Farrar, Straus and Giroux, 1989); and Harry L. Hopkins, *Spending to Save: The Complete Story of Relief* (New York: Norton, 1936).

New Deal's rescue operation in March 1933 wiped out some $7 billion in depositors' money. Accelerating foreclosures on defaulted home mortgages—150,000 homeowners lost their property in 1930, 200,000 in 1931, 250,000 in 1932—stripped millions of people of both shelter and life savings at a single stroke and menaced the balance sheets of thousands of surviving banks. Several states and some thirteen hundred municipalities, crushed by sinking real estate prices and consequently shrinking tax revenues, defaulted on their obligations to creditors, pinched their already scant social services, cut payrolls, and slashed paychecks. Chicago was reduced to paying its teachers in tax warrants and then, in the winter of 1932–33, to paying them nothing at all.

Gross national product had fallen by 1933 to half its 1929 level. Spending for new plants and equipment had ground to a virtual standstill. Businesses invested only $3 billion in 1933, compared with $24 billion in 1929. Some industries, to be sure, were effectively Depression-proof; shoe and cigarette manufacturers, for example, experienced only minor slumps. Other industries, however, dependent on discretionary spending, had all but gone out of business. Only one-third as many automobiles rolled off the assembly lines in 1933 as in 1929, a slowdown that induced commensurate shrinkage in other heavy industries. Iron and steel production declined by 60 percent from pre-Crash levels. Machine-tool makers cut their output by nearly two-thirds. Residential and industrial construction shriveled to less than one-fifth of its pre-Depression volume, a wrenching contraction that spread through lumber camps, steel mills, and appliance factories, disemploying thousands of loggers, mill hands, sheet-metal workers, engineers, architects, carpenters, plumbers, roofers, plasterers, painters, and electricians. Mute shoals of jobless men drifted through the streets of every American city in 1933.

Nowhere did the Depression strike more savagely than in the American countryside. On America's farms, income had plummeted from $6 billion in what for farmers was the already lean year of 1929 to $2 billion in 1932. The net receipts from the wheat harvest in one Oklahoma county went from $1.2 million in 1931 to just $7,000 in 1933. Mississippi's pathetic $239 per capita income in 1929 sank to $117 in 1933.

Unemployment and its close companion, reduced wages, were the most obvious and the most wounding of all the Depression's effects. The government's data showed that 25 percent of the work force, some thirteen million workers, including nearly four hundred thousand women, stood idle in 1933. The great majority of the men and many of the women were heads of households, the sole breadwinners for their families.[7] Yet if misery was widespread, its burdens were not uniformly distributed. Differences in gender, age, race, occupation, and region powerfully mediated the Depression's impact on particular individuals. To borrow from Tolstoy, every unhappy family was unhappy in its own way. Different people suffered and coped, and occasionally prevailed, according to their own peculiar circumstances.

Working women at first lost their jobs at a faster rate than men—then reentered the work force more rapidly. In the early years of the Depression, many employers, including the federal government, tried to spread what employment they had to heads of households. That meant firing any married woman identified as a family's "secondary" wage-earner. But the gender segregation in employment patterns that was already well established before the Depression also worked to women's advantage. Heavy industry suffered the worst unemployment, but relatively few women stoked blast furnaces in the steel mills or drilled rivets on assembly lines or swung hammers in the building trades. The teaching profession, however, in which women were highly concentrated and indeed constituted a hefty majority of employees, suffered pay cuts but only minimal job losses. And the underlying trends of the economy meant that what new jobs did become available in the 1930s, such as telephone switchboard operation and clerical work, were peculiarly suited to women.

Unemployment fell most heavily on the most predictably vulnerable: the very young, the elderly, the least educated, the unskilled, and especially, as Hickok was about to discover, on rural Americans. It fell with compound force on blacks, immigrants, and Mexican-Americans. Workers under twenty or over sixty were almost twice as likely as others to be out of a job. Hopkins's studies showed that one-fifth of all the people on the federal relief rolls were black, a proportion roughly double the African-American presence in the population. Most of them were in the rural South.

Some of the jobless never appeared on the relief rolls at all because they simply left the country. Thousands of immigrants forsook the fabled American land of promise and returned to their old countries. Some one hundred thousand American workers in 1931 applied for jobs in what appeared to be a newly promising land, Soviet Russia.[8] More than

7. Nearly four million of the nation's approximately thirty million households were headed by women in 1930. See James T. Patterson, *America's Struggle against Poverty, 1900–1980* (Cambridge: Harvard University Press, 1981), 29, and *HSUS*, 41.
8. Leuchtenburg, 28.

four hundred thousand Mexican-Americans, many of them U.S. citizens, returned to Mexico in the 1930s, some voluntarily but many against their will. Immigration officials in Santa Barbara, California, herded Mexican farm workers into the Southern Pacific depot, packed them into sealed boxcars, and unceremoniously shipped them southward.[9]

The typical unemployed urban worker on relief, Hopkins found, "was a white man, thirty-eight years of age and the head of a household. . . . [H]e had been more often than not an unskilled or semi-skilled worker in the manufacturing or mechanical industries. He had had some ten years' experience at what he considered to be his usual occupation. He had not finished elementary school. He had been out of any kind of job lasting one month or more for two years, and had not been working at his usual occupation for over two and a half years."[10] Hopkins stressed particularly the problems of the elderly, who, he concluded, "through hardship, discouragement and sickness as well as advancing years, [have] gone into an occupational oblivion from which they will never be rescued by private industry."[11] That line of thinking, driven by the specter of permanent, structural unemployment as a result of accelerating technological change, and looking toward removing supposedly obsolescent elderly workers from the wage-labor markets altogether, would in time lead to the landmark Social Security Act of 1935.

Hopkins's statistical data revealed still other aspects of the Depression's impact. Facing an uncertain future, young people were postponing or canceling plans to marry; the marriage rate had fallen since 1929 by 22 percent. The Depression's gloom seeped even into the nation's bedrooms, as married couples had fewer children—15 percent fewer in 1933 than in 1929. Even the divorce rate declined by 25 percent, as the contracting economy sealed the exits from unhappy marriages. Unemployment could also powerfully rearrange the psychological geometry of families. "Before the depression," one jobless father told an interviewer, "I wore the pants in this family, and rightly so. During the depression, I lost something. Maybe you call it self-respect, but in losing it I also lost the respect of my children, and I am afraid that I am losing my wife." "There certainly was a change in our family," said another victim of unemployment, "and I can define it in just one word—I relinquished power in the family. I think the man should be boss in the family. . . .

9. On Mexican-Americans, see Ronald Takaki, *A Different Mirror* (Boston: Little, Brown, 1993), 333–34; and Albert Camarillo, *Chicanos in a Changing Society* (Cambridge: Harvard University Press, 1979), 163.
10. Hopkins, *Spending to Save*, 161.
11. Hopkins, *Spending to Save*, 163.

But now I don't even try to be the boss. She controls all the money. . . . The boarders pay her, the children turn in their money to her, and the relief check is cashed by her or the boy. I toned down a good deal as a result of it." Said another: "It's only natural. When a father cannot support his family, supply them with clothing and good food, the children are bound to lose respect. . . . When they see me hanging around the house all the time and know that I can't find work, it has its effect all right."[12]

When Hickok sallied forth to reconnoiter the Depression's human toll in 1933, the country was, to be sure, wallowing in the deepest trough of the unemployment crisis. But despite the New Deal's exertions and innovations, and contrary to much later mythology, in no subsequent year in the 1930s would the unemployment rate fall below 14 percent. The average for the decade as a whole was 17.1 percent. The Depression and the New Deal, in short, were Siamese twins, enduring together in a painful but symbiotic relationship that stretched to the end of the decade. The dilemmas and duration of that relationship helped to account for both the failures and the triumphs of the New Deal.

In Pennsylvania, Hickok's first destination, Governor Gifford Pinchot had reported in the summer of 1932 that some 1,150,000 persons were "totally unemployed." Many others were on "short hours." Only two-fifths of Pennsylvania's normal working population, Pinchot concluded, had full-time work. Elsewhere, the Ford Motor Company in Detroit had laid off more than two-thirds of its workers. Other giant industries followed suit. Westinghouse and General Electric in 1933 employed fewer than half as many workers as in 1929. In Birmingham, Alabama, another of Hickok's destinations, Congressman George Huddleston reported that only 8,000 of some 108,000 workers still had full-time employment in 1932; 25,000 had no work at all, and the remaining 75,000 counted themselves lucky to toil a few days per week. "Practically all," said Huddleston, "have had serious cuts in their wages and many of them do not average over $1.50 a day."[13]

Later investigators calculated that nationwide the combined effects of unemployment and involuntary part-time employment left half of America's usual work force unutilized throughout the Depression decade—a

---

12. Mirra Komarovsky, *The Unemployed Man and His Family: The Effect of Unemployment Upon the Status of the Man in Fifty-nine Families* (New York: Dryden, 1940), 41, 31, 98.
13. Hopkins, *Spending to Save*, 92; Chandler, *America's Greatest Depression*, 43.

loss of some 104 million person-years of labor, the most perishable and irreplaceable of all commodities. Similar calculations suggest that the "lost output" in the American economy of the 1930s, measured against what would have been produced if 1920s rates of employment had held, amounted to some $360 billion dollars—enough at 1929 prices to have built 35 million homes, 179 million automobiles, or 716,000 schools.

Like Hopkins, observers then and later have struggled to make human sense out of these numbingly abstract numbers. One thinking exercise goes as follows: imagine that on New Year's Day 1931, when the depression was not yet "Great," one hundred thousand people, all of them gainfully employed, most of them the sole means of livelihood for their families, sat beneath the beaming California sun in the Rose Bowl, filling the eight-year-old Pasadena stadium to capacity to watch Alabama's Crimson Tide play the Washington State Cougars in the sixteenth annual Rose Bowl Game.[14] When the game ended, the loudspeakers announced that every person in attendance that day had just lost his or her job. On exiting, the stunned fans were handed further notices. Sixty-two thousand were informed that they would not be employed for at least a year to follow; forty-four thousand of those were given two-year layoffs; twenty-four thousand, three years; eleven thousand received the grim news that they would be unemployed for four years or more (an approximation of the patterns in the unemployment statistics for the decade of the 1930s). Then imagine that this spectacle was repeated at the Rose Bowl, without even the consolation of a football game, the following week—and the week after that, and again after that, for 130 weeks. At the rate of a hundred thousand persons summarily laid off in successive weeks it would take two and one-half years, until July 1933, the date of Hickok's departure on her assignment for Hopkins, to reach the sum of thirteen million unemployed.

But even such mental exercises as that run up against what Hopkins called "the natural limit of personal imagination and sympathy. You can pity six men," Hopkins sagely noted, "but you can't keep stirred up over six million."[15] It was to compensate for those natural deficiencies of the

14. In fact, a less-than-capacity crowd of seventy thousand saw Alabama defeat Washington State 24–0 on January 1, 1931. On that same day, Franklin D. Roosevelt delivered his second inaugural address as governor of New York. In yet another reminder that few Americans at this date sensed the dimensions of the crisis that was developing, Roosevelt devoted most of his speech to decrying the inefficiencies of local government.
15. Hopkins, *Spending to Save*, 111.

imagination that he was sending Lorena Hickok on her mission. From her reportage he hoped to vivify real faces and voices out of the statistical dust. She did not disappoint him.

Hickok set out in quest of the human reality of the Depression. She found that and much more besides. In dingy working-class neighborhoods in Philadelphia and New York, in unpainted clapboard farmhouses in North Dakota, on the ravaged cotton farms of Georgia, on the dusty mesas of Colorado, Hickok uncovered not just the effects of the economic crisis that had begun in 1929. She found herself face to face as well with the human wreckage of a century of pell-mell, buccaneering, no-holds-barred, free-market industrial and agricultural capitalism. As her travels progressed, she gradually came to acknowledge the sobering reality that for many Americans the Great Depression brought times only a little harder than usual. She discovered, in short, what historian James Patterson has called the "old poverty" that was endemic in America well before the Depression hit. By his estimate, even in the midst of the storied prosperity of the 1920s some forty million Americans, including virtually all nonwhites, most of the elderly, and much of the rural population, were eking out unrelievedly precarious lives that were scarcely visible and practically unimaginable to their more financially secure countrymen. "The researches we have made into standards of living of the American family," Hopkins wrote, "have uncovered for the public gaze a volume of chronic poverty, unsuspected except by a few students and by those who have always experienced it." From this perspective, the Depression was not just a passing crisis but an episode that revealed deeply rooted structural inequities in American society.[16]

The "old poor" were among the Depression's most ravaged victims, but it was not the Depression that had impoverished them. They were the "one-third of a nation" that Franklin Roosevelt would describe in 1937 as chronically "ill-housed, ill-clad, ill-nourished."[17] By suddenly threatening to push millions of other Americans into their wretched condition, the Depression pried open a narrow window of political opportunity to do something at last on behalf of that long-suffering one-third, and in the process to redefine the very character of America.

DEPARTING FROM WASHINGTON in a car acquired with Eleanor's help and nicknamed "Bluette," Hickok headed first for the hills and

---

16. Patterson, *America's Struggle against Poverty*, 41; Hopkins, *Spending to Save*, 111.
17. *PPA* (1937), 5.

ravines of the Appalachian soft-coal district, a dismally hardscrabble region stretching through western Pennsylvania, West Virginia, and Kentucky. She was starting at the bottom. "In the whole range of Depression," said Gifford Pinchot, "there is nothing worse than the condition of the soft coal miners."[18] Soft, or bituminous, coal had been for nearly two centuries the basic fuel that powered the global industrial revolution, but even before World War I the coal-burning era was everywhere on the wane. Diesel engines had replaced coal-fired boilers in steamships and locomotives. Coalbins were disappearing from basements as Americans abandoned smudgy coal furnaces for clean-burning gas or oil or smokeless electric heating systems. Plagued by competition from these new energy sources, especially the recently tapped oil fields in southern California, Oklahoma, and the vast Permian Basin in West Texas, coal displayed through the 1920s all the classical symptoms of a sick industry: shrinking demand, excess supply, chaotic disorganization, cutthroat competition, and hellish punishment for workers.

The Depression exacerbated this already calamitous cycle. Operators fought more savagely than ever to stay alive by cutting prices and paychecks. At one point some of them even begged the government to buy the mines "at any price. . . . Anything so we can get out of it."[19] Coal that had fetched up to $4 a ton in the mid-1920s sold for $1.31 a ton in 1932. Miners who had earned seven dollars a day before the Crash now begged the pit-boss for the chance to squirm into thirty-inch coal seams for as little as one dollar. Men who had once loaded tons of coal per day grubbed around the base of the tipple for a few lumps of fuel to heat a meager supper — often nothing more than "bulldog gravy" made of flour, water, and lard. The miner's diet, said United Mine Workers president John L. Lewis, "is actually below domestic animal standards."[20]

Stranded without work in isolated company towns, living on the owners' sufferance in company housing, in debt to the company store, cowed by insecurity and occasional strong-arm tactics into a subdued, passive frame of mind, the miners struck Hickok as a singularly pathetic lot. "Some of them have been starving for eight years," she reported to Hopkins. "I was told there are children in West Virginia who never tasted milk! I visited one group of 45 blacklisted miners and their fam-

18. Badger, New Deal, 19.
19. Frances Perkins, The Roosevelt I Knew (New York: Viking, 1946), 230.
20. James P. Johnson, The Politics of Soft Coal: The Bituminous Industry from World War I through the New Deal (Urbana: University of Illinois Press, 1979), 125.

ilies, who had been living in tents two years. . . . Most of the women you see in the camps are going without shoes or stockings. . . . It's fairly common to see children entirely naked." The ravages of tuberculosis, "black lung" disease, and asthma, as well as typhoid, diptheria, pellagra, and severe malnutrition, were everywhere apparent. Some miners' families, said Hickok, "had been living for days on green corn and string beans—and precious little of that. And some had nothing at all, actually hadn't eaten for a couple of days. At the Continental Hotel in Pineville [Kentucky] I was told that five babies up one of those creeks had died of starvation in the last ten days. . . . Dysentery is so common that nobody says much about it. 'We begin losing our babies with dysentery in September,' " one of Hickok's informants casually remarked.

Patriotic, religious, gentle, of "pure Anglo-Saxon stock," these mountain folk impressed Hickok as "curiously appealing." Yet she found both their stark destitution and their stoic resignation appalling. Here began her real education—and through her, Hopkins's and Roosevelt's—about the awful dimensions of the human damage the Depression had laid bare and about the curious apathy with which many Americans continued to submit to their fates. Sixty-two percent of the people in ten eastern Kentucky mining counties looked to federal relief for their very survival in the summer of 1933, Hickok learned. Twenty-eight thousand families, more than 150,000 souls, depended on local relief offices for grocery orders that they could present to the company store. Then, on August 12, owing to delays in the Kentucky state government's provision of funds to match the federal government's appropriations, even that minimal assistance stopped. Little groups of people, many of them illiterate, straggled to closed relief agencies, stared helplessly at written notices announcing the end of aid, and silently shuffled away. Given their desperate plight, "I cannot for the life of me understand," Hickok mused, "why they don't go down and raid the Blue Grass country."[21]

Hickok's observations about relief and its social and political impact particularly intrigued Hopkins. His Federal Emergency Relief Administration had been charged in May 1933 with dispensing some $500 million of federal relief money. Half went to the states on a matching basis, one federal for three state dollars. Hopkins had discretion to distribute the remaining $250 million on the basis of "need." Congress and various governors tried in vain to learn the "formula" by which Hopkins dispensed his discretionary moneys. Governor Martin Davey of Ohio at one point issued a warrant for Hopkins's arrest should he ever set foot in the state. Later studies suggest that Hopkins indeed had a formula, and it was one that he and FDR had learned from the old urban political machines. FERA checks flowed disproportionately to certain "swing" states, outside the already secure solid South, in an effort to win votes and cultivate political loyalty.[22]

With FERA the federal government took its first steps into the business of direct relief and began, however modestly, to chart the path toward the modern American welfare state. FERA's brief history vividly exposed both the practical difficulties and the political and philosophical conflicts that beset welfare programs ever after. Its odd and unwieldy administrative architecture reflected the peculiar characteristics of the American federal system and underlined, too, the strikingly sparse administrative capacity of the federal government over which Franklin Roosevelt presided in 1933. That puny capacity was a legacy of historic Jeffersonian wariness of centralized power, among the most deeply rooted values in American political culture. Beginning with FERA and other innovative federal policies in 1933, the New Deal would change that culture, but the tortured evolution of the American welfare system, even by means artfully contrived and often sharply attenuated, would be among the most controversial of Roosevelt's legacies.

Hopkins made a conspicuous show of executive energy by allocating over $5 million during his first two hours in office in May 1933. But his very need for speed drove Hopkins into awkward and contentious relationships with state and local welfare agencies. FERA was an emergency body, hastily established and rushing without precedent or staff to cope with a vast national crisis. Its skeletal Washington office, never numbering more than a few hundred people, necessarily relied on state and county officials to screen relief applicants and distribute benefits. Though by 1933 most states had exhausted their capacity to cope with the Depression's needy, many of them nevertheless balked at participating in the federal relief program. Some, like Kentucky, pleaded that constitutional constraints blocked them from allocating the required matching funds. "Those states which took advantage of their real or alleged constitutional limitations [on borrowing for relief purposes]," Hopkins noted acerbically, "laid a crushing burden upon their local communities," whose usual source of revenue, real estate taxes, was drastically contracting.

Yet most state officials, whatever their reservations in principle about

22. Gavin Wright, "The Political Economy of New Deal Spending: An Econometric Analysis," *Review of Economics and Statistics* 56 (1974): 262–81.

federal intrusion into the traditionally local administration of welfare, joined hands of necessity with FERA. Some shrewdly saw political opportunity in the sudden infusion of federal dollars, to Hopkins's continuing aggravation. "Our chief trouble in Pennsylvania," Hickok reported to her chief at the very outset of her tour, "is politics. From the township to Harrisburg, the state is honeycombed with politicians all fighting for the privilege of distributing relief funds."[23] The danger of letting local pols manipulate FERA funds for their own partisan advantage compelled FERA to impose distasteful restrictions. Work relief was rare; straight cash payments, rarer still. Instead, driven by fiscal prudence and political wariness, FERA reluctantly instructed local agencies to set up commissaries to dispense food and clothing, a practice Hopkins branded the "most degrading" of all forms of relief. Scarcely less resented by recipients was the grocery order, exchangeable for designated items at the local store. Beans and rice were allowed, but no razors or tobacco or pencils or tablets. Hopkins detested these demeaning practices. "It is a matter of opinion," he drily remarked, "whether more damage is done to the human spirit by a lack of vitamins or complete surrender of choice."[24]

Beyond the realms of bureaucracy and politics, FERA encountered still more intractable difficulties in the domains of social attitudes and deeply embedded cultural values, those sometimes dark regions of the human spirit whose vitality was always Hopkins's primary concern. In the relief business, said Hopkins, "our raw material is misery."[25] Yet for all its familiarity in human annals, and despite its envelopment of millions of Americans in the Depression era, misery assuredly did not evoke universal sympathy, nor agreement about its remedy. The Depression was a wholesale social catastrophe that fell indiscriminately on vast sectors of American society. Yet the belief persisted among many Americans that the needy, new poor and old poor alike, were personally culpable for their plight, sinners against the social order, reprobates and ne'er-do-wells, spongers and bums with no legitimate claim on the public's sympathy or purse.

Local welfare administrators were sometimes among the most tenacious exponents of that view. They treated welfare applicants accordingly, especially when class, religious, or ethnic differences separated

23. Lowitt and Beasley, *One Third of a Nation,* 8.
24. Hopkins, *Spending to Save,* 105.
25. Hopkins, *Spending to Save,* 125.

applicants from administrators. In Calais, Maine, where most reliefers were out-of-work Catholic French-Canadians and most officials were Protestant Yankee blue-bloods, Hickok reported that "the people on relief in that town are subjected to treatment that is almost medieval in its stinginess and stupidity." In North Dakota, where a combination of drought, hail, grasshoppers, and collapsed markets had bankrupted nearly every farmer in the state, Hickok found the state relief committee dominated by officials who "think there is something wrong with a man who cannot make a living. . . . I find them rather like the people in Maine . . . They talk so much about 'the undeserving' and 'the bums'." A relief director in Savannah told Hickok flatly: "Any Nigger who gets over $8 a week is a spoiled Nigger, that's all. . . . The Negroes . . . regard the President as the Messiah, and they think that . . . they'll all be getting $12 a week for the rest of their lives." In Tennessee, she encountered relief workers "whose approach to the relief problem is so typical of the old line social worker, supported by private philanthropy and looking down his—only usually it was HER—nose at God's patient poor, that it made me gag a little."[26]

"Under the philosophy of this ancient practice," Hopkins lamented, the relief applicant was thought to be "in some way morally deficient. He must be made to feel his pauperism. Every help which was given him was to be given in a way to intensify his sense of shame. Usually he was forced to plead his destitution in an offensively dreary room"—the notorious "intake" facility where applicants were first screened for eligibility.[27]

"Mr. Hopkins, did you ever spend a couple of hours sitting around an intake?" Hickok asked from Texas in the spring of 1934. "[I]ntake is about the nearest thing to Hell that I know anything about. The smell alone—I'd recognize it anywhere. And take that on top of the psychological effect of having to be there at all. God!. . . . If I were applying

26. Lowitt and Beasley, One Third of a Nation, 37, 67, 154, 277. Even Hickok's capacious sympathies had their limits, etched by the easy racial stereotyping common to the era. As she wrote from Georgia: "More than half the population of the city is Negro—and SUCH Negroes! Even their lips are black, and the whites of their eyes! They're almost as inarticulate as animals." She worried that blacks in the South and Mexicans in the West had such low standards of living that they might choose to become a permanently dependent welfare class. She mused about a double standard of relief, with one level of support for "Mexicans and Negroes" and another for those "with white standards of living": "Two standards of relief. The idea will sound horrible in Washington, but—I'm beginning to wonder" (151–52, 238–40).
27. Hopkins, Spending to Save, 100.

for relief, one look at the average intake room would send me to the river."[28]

The humiliation of presenting oneself at the intake was only the beginning. Next came a "means test," entailing a detailed examination of the applicant's private life. The typical relief applicant under FERA received a home visit from a social worker who inquired about income, savings, debts, relatives, health, and diet. Then came inquiries about the applicant's circumstances "to clergymen, to school teachers, to public nurses or to whatever society might possibly assist them. . . . It is no wonder," Hopkins later commented disgustedly, "that when men knew or feared this was in store for them they kept secret from their wives and families that they had received their dismissal slips. . . . If we had not become so accustomed, and, in a sense, so hardened to the fact of poverty, we should even now be astounded at our effrontery."[29]

Hopkins saw the Depression as a social disaster, not the simple aggregation of countless individual moral failings. "Three or four million heads of families don't turn into tramps and cheats overnight," he said, "nor do they lose the habits and standards of a lifetime. . . . They don't drink any more than the rest of us, they don't lie any more, they're no lazier than the rest of us. . . . An eighth or a tenth of the earning population does not change its character which has been generations in the moulding, or, if such a change actually occurs, we can scarcely charge it up to personal sin."[30]

Still, the attitudes against which Hopkins inveighed ran stubbornly deep. Indeed, contempt for the Depression's victims, ironically enough, often lodged most deeply in the hearts and minds of the victims themselves. Social investigators in the 1930s repeatedly encountered feelings of guilt and self-recrimination among the unemployed, despite the transparent reality that their plight owed to a systemic economic breakdown, not to their own personal shortcomings. The Depression thus revealed one of the perverse implications of American society's vaunted celebration of individualism. In a culture that ascribed all success to individual striving, it seemed to follow axiomatically that failure was due to individual inadequacy.

Self-indictment was especially pronounced among many of the newly poor—the white-collar classes who had been the chief acolytes and ben-

28. Lowitt and Beasley, *One Third of a Nation*, 221–22.
29. Hopkins, *Spending to Save*, 101–2.
30. Hopkins, *Spending to Save*, 125, 100, 110; Badger, *New Deal*, 200.

eficiaries of the individualistic creed. Their sudden descent from security, self-sufficiency, and pride to uncertainty, dependency, and shame left many of them neither angry nor politically radicalized but, as Hickok said, simply "dumb with misery." "The whole white collar class," a newspaper editor told her in New Orleans, "are taking an awful beating. . . . They're whipped, that's all. And it's bad." As for seeking relief, the difficulty, said Hickok, "is in getting white collar people to register at all. God, how they hate it." An engineer told her, "I simply had to murder my pride." "We'd lived on bread and water three weeks before I could make myself do it," an insurance man confessed. "It took me a month," an Alabama lumberman explained; "I used to go down there every day or so and walk past the place again and again. I just couldn't make myself go in." A twenty-eight-year-old college-educated woman in Texas, unemployed after eight years as a teacher, spoke the thoughts of many middle-class Americans down and out in the Depression: "If . . . I can't make a living," she shrugged, "I'm just no good, I guess."[31]

"I have seen thousands of these defeated, discouraged, hopeless men and women, cringing and fawning as they come to ask for public aid," said the mayor of Toledo, Ohio. "It is a spectacle of national degeneration."[32] Hopkins agreed. By October 1933 he was sorely disillusioned with FERA's stopgap, ragtag relief effort, with its mortifying means test and niggardly, condescending local administrators. He had in any case effectively exhausted the original $500 million FERA appropriation. Yet an economic recovery that would absorb the millions of unemployed was nowhere in sight. If the nation were to make it through the oncoming winter, a new relief program was necessary.

Hopkins's answer was the Civil Works Administration (CWA), launched with Roosevelt's blessing on November 9. CWA relied for its funding on an allocation from the budget of the Public Works Administration and for its administrative apparatus on still other agencies in the pint-sized federal bureaucracy. Army warehouses supplied tools and materials for CWA projects. The Veterans Administration, one of the few federal agencies with a truly national disbursement system in place, became CWA's paymaster. With model efficiency, it issued paychecks to some eight hundred thousand workers within two weeks of the CWA's creation. By January 1934 CWA had put 4.2 million men and women to work.

31. Lowitt and Beasley, *One Third of a Nation,* 205, 220, 206–7, 223.
32. Schlesinger 2:268.

The operative word was "work." At Hopkins's insistence, CWA was not only a purely federal undertaking; it was also, more importantly, a *work*-relief program. It did not condescend to clients; it hired employees. Half were taken from the relief rolls and half from the needy unemployed, without subjection to a means test. CWA paid the prevailing minimum wage, regionally adjusted: forty cents an hour for unskilled labor in the South, forty-five cents in the central states, and sixty cents in the North. "Wages were what we were after," said Hopkins, and in its five-month existence CWA handed out paychecks totaling $833,960,000. CWA focused on light construction and maintenance projects that could be mounted swiftly. Its workers upgraded roads and bridges, laid sewer pipe, spruced up forty thousand schools, refurbished hospitals, and installed 150,000 outhouses for farm families. "Long after the workers of CWA are dead and gone and these hard times forgotten, their effort will be remembered by permanent useful works in every county of ever state," Hopkins proudly noted.[33]

"Three loud cheers for the CWA!" Hickok wrote to Hopkins from Lincoln, Nebraska, in November 1933. "[I]t's the smartest thing that has been tried since we went into the relief business. It is actually getting out some of that Public Works money," she added, in a pointed reminder that Interior Secretary Harold Ickes, whose Public Works Administration had been intended as the New Deal's premier "pump-priming" agency, had thus far proved unable to find the pump handle. Most important, Hickok and Hopkins agreed, by giving people gainful employment, CWA in federal hands removed the stigma of relief. It dignified men and women with a paycheck instead of mortifying them with a handout. "We aren't on relief any more," one woman said proudly. "My husband is working for the Government."[34]

Just that kind of reaction—not to mention the nearly $200 million monthly price tag for CWA—worried President Roosevelt. Working for the government might become a habit with the country, he brooded, just as Hoover had worried earlier. In January 1934 Roosevelt told his advisers: "We must not take the position that we are going to have permanent Depression in this country." Shortly thereafter he ordered the termination of CWA, effective on March 31. For the remainder of 1934 the federal government substantially abandoned the distasteful task

33. Hopkins, *Spending to Save*, 117, 120.
34. Hopkins, *Spending to Save*, 114.

of relief and tried to come to grips with the even more daunting task of recovery.[35]

RECOVERY REMAINED maddeningly elusive. "Balance" still seemed the key. Following the Hundred Days, Roosevelt counted primarily on two measures to effect the equilibrium between industry and agriculture thought to be essential to economic health. One was an unorthodox and controversial gold-buying scheme, aimed at depreciating the dollar and thus easing debt burdens, particularly for farmers. The other was an elaborate scheme to micromanage the farm sector through the newly created Agricultural Adjustment Administration.

For much of 1933 and 1934, however, both monetary and agricultural policy were overshadowed by the aggressively publicized endeavors of another agency: the National Recovery Administration. Though it was created virtually as an afterthought on the one hundredth day of the special congressional session that ended on June 16, 1933, the NRA almost instantly emerged as the signature New Deal creation. "In some people's minds," Frances Perkins later observed, "the New Deal and NRA were almost the same thing."[36]

The NRA owed much of its towering profile in the public mind to the extravagantly colorful personality of its chief, Hugh S. Johnson. Raised in frontier Oklahoma, Johnson was fifty-one years old in 1933, a West Point graduate who rose to the rank of brigadier general before resigning in 1919 to pursue a business career. His seamed and jowly face floridly testified to the rigors of the professional soldier's life as well as the ravages of drink. Melodramatic in his temperament, mercurial in his moods, ingeniously profane in his speech, Johnson could weep at the opera, vilify his enemies, chew out his underlings, and rhapsodize about the virtues of NRA with equal flamboyance. On accepting his appointment in June 1933 he declared: "It will be red fire at first and dead cats afterward"—one of the printable specimens of his sometimes mystifyingly inventive prose.[37]

Johnson envisioned the NRA, in Arthur M. Schlesinger Jr.'s phrase, "as a giant organ through which he could play on the economy of the country."[38] His model was the War Industries Board (WIB) of 1917–18,

---

35. Leuchtenburg, 122.
36. Perkins, Roosevelt I Knew, 210.
37. Hugh S. Johnson, The Blue Eagle from Egg to Earth (Garden City, N.Y.: Doubleday, Doran, 1935), 208.
38. Schlesinger 2:103.

chaired by his idol and business associate Bernard Baruch. Johnson himself had served as director of the WIB's Purchase and Supply Branch, representing the military purchasing bureaus to the various commodity sections of the WIB. Franklin Roosevelt had also conjured the World War experience in announcing the NRA's birth on June 16. "I had part in the great cooperation of 1917 and 1918," the president declared, and he called on the country to recollect the war crisis and the spirit of national unity it evoked. "Must we go on in many groping, disorganized, separate units to defeat," the president asked, extending the military metaphor, "or shall we move as one great team to victory?"[39]

But if the NRA was patterned on the War Industries Board, a crucial element was missing: the war. To be sure, a psychological sense of crisis prevailed in 1933 that was comparable to the emergency atmosphere of 1917; the difference was not mood but money. The federal government had borrowed over $21 billion dollars in just two years to fight World War I, a figure that exceeded the sum of New Deal deficits from 1933 down to the eve of World War II.[40] The National Industrial Recovery Act that established the NRA had also authorized the Public Works Administration to borrow $3.3 billion for pump-priming expenditures to infuse new purchasing power into the economy. NRA and PWA were to be like two lungs, each necessary for breathing life into the moribund industrial sector. But as Herbert Hoover had discovered, it took time, lots of it, to start up construction projects of any significant scale—time for site surveys, architectural designs, and engineering studies to be completed before actual construction could start. What was more, Roosevelt's own sense of fiscal caution, not unlike Hoover's, had led him to deprive the energetic but erratic Johnson of control over PWA and assign it instead to the irascible interior secretary, Harold Ickes. "Honest Harold," Ickes was soon dubbed, for the scrupulous care and agonizing deliberateness with which he dispensed PWA funds. Penny-pinching and cautious to a fault, Ickes was hypervigilant to forestall accusations of waste or fraud. He spent just $110 million of PWA money in 1933. "He still has to learn," said one of Ickes's exasperated assistants, "that the Administrator of a $3 billion fund hasn't time to check every typewriter acquisition." Under Ickes's obsessively prudent management, PWA contributed nothing in 1933 to economic stimulus, rendering

39. Johnson, *Blue Eagle*, 440, 443.
40. *HSUS*, 1104–5.

NRA effectively dead on arrival as a recovery measure. "Once deprived of the second lung," an NRA official wrote, "the economy had to bear too great a burden on the NRA lung—inasmuch as the PWA was scarcely palpitating for almost half a year after the NRA was organized."[41]

If Johnson, the would-be master economic organist, found himself from the outset seated at a magnificent musical instrument that lacked wind-box or bellows, he nevertheless proceeded to bang away at the keyboard of the NRA with missionary zeal and maniacal energy. There was no truer believer in the philosophy of industrial coordination that NRA was charged with implementing. "I regard NRA as a holy thing," he said. He credited his mentor, Bernard Baruch, with the best formulation of the NRA's economic creed. "The government has fostered our over-capacitated industrial combinations, and even encouraged these combinations to increase production," Baruch explained to a Brookings Institution gathering in May 1933.

> But it seems public lunacy to decree unlimited operation of a system which periodically disgorges indigestible masses of unconsummable products. In today's desperate struggle for the scant remaining business, cost and price have become such factors that, in the unstable fringes which surround each industry, a few operators have taken the last dangerous step in economic retrogression—the attainment of low costs by the degradation of labor standards.... Lower wages—lower costs—lower prices—and the whole vicious cycle goes on.[42]

The NRA, in Baruch's and Johnson's view, could arrest this cycle by government-sponsored agreements to curb ruinous overproduction, allocate production quotas, and stabilize wages. The last item was particularly important. If there was any defensible economic logic to NRA at all, it consisted in the idea that recovery could not come about so long as shrinking payrolls continued to leach purchasing power out of the ailing economy.

The essence of Baruch's and Johnson's thinking resided in their shared hostility to competition. "The murderous doctrine of savage and wolfish competition," Johnson called it, "looking to dog-eat-dog and devil take the hindmost," had impelled even humane and fair-minded employers to slash wages and lay off workers by the millions. In contrast, Johnson intoned, "the very heart of the New Deal is the principle of

41. Badger, *New Deal*, 83; Schlesinger 2:109.
42. Johnson, *Blue Eagle*, x.

concerted action in industry and agriculture under government supervision."[43]

These ideas may have made up the heart of the New Deal in 1933, but they were themselves scarcely new. Not only had they informed the WIB experience in the World War, but they had also found expression in Secretary of Commerce Hoover's promotion of trade associations and labor unions in the 1920s, as well as in President Hoover's meetings with business leaders in the first flush of crisis in 1929 and his highly publicized appeals for maintenance of wage rates in the first two years of the Depression. Roosevelt had embraced similar ideas in his address to San Francisco's Commonwealth Club during the 1932 campaign, when he called for "administering resources and plants already in hand . . . , adjusting production to consumption."[44] In May 1933 the new President had sounded the same note again when he complained to his advisers about the problem of "foolish overproduction."[45] That foolishness, and the cutthroat competition it engendered, NRA now sought to end.

In few industries was overproduction more problematic than in cotton textiles. Like soft coal, textile manufacturing had been sick for a long time before the Depression descended. An "old" industry, in America as elsewhere among the first to employ the factory system of production, cotton textile manufacturing had migrated in the years after Reconstruction out of its original New England home and into the South. "Bring the mills to the cotton," southern promoters had preached, seeking to raise an industrial "new South" out of the wreckage of the Civil War. By 1930 they had succeeded beyond all expectations—the South then spun two-thirds of the nation's cotton cloth—but the textile industry had become ferociously competitive, chronically beset by excess capacity, price-gouging, and the by now familiar tribulations visited upon labor.

Textile workers had long been a harshly abused lot. The greatest attraction of the South for investors had in fact not been proximity to the cotton fields but proximity to an abundance of low-wage, nonunionized labor. Keeping labor cheap and unorganized had become almost a religion among the southern mill owners. The Appalachian foothills from Alabama through the Carolinas were pocked with cheerless company mill towns where white "hillbillies," wrenched from their isolated

43. Johnson, *Blue Eagle*, 169.
44. *PPA* (1928–32), 751–52.
45. Davis 3:137.

mountain homesteads, crowded into what Lorena Hickok described as "blocks and blocks of shabby, tumbledown little houses."[46] Whole families, including children as young as seven, worked grueling hours. Sometimes they toiled through the night amid the whirling spindles and clouds of lint, earning subsistence wages, often paid in scrip good only at the company store. Like their cousins who had stayed in the hills to dig coal, the "lintheads," long oppressed by dependency, want, and fear, saw their lives go from unspeakably bad to unimaginably worse as the Depression deepened. Wages sank to as low as five dollars for a fifty-five-hour week. Thousands of mill workers were laid off altogether. Those who remained on the job submitted resentfully to the hated "stretch-out," the mill hands' term for the practice of forcing fewer and fewer workers to tend more and more of the spindles clattering in their relentless ranks on the shop floor. "They'd just add a little bit more to it," said one woman mill hand, "and you was always in a hole, trying to catch up." "There's many a times I dreamt about it," said another; "I just sweated it out in my dreams like I did when I was on the job, wanting to quit, and knew I couldn't afford to."[47] Cries for abolition of the stretch-out, along with demands for union recognition, touched off a violent confrontation between workers and management in 1929, ending in the gunshot deaths of the police chief and a woman union organizer in Gastonia, North Carolina. Now, four years later, an edgy tension shivered over the Piedmont as falling prices and deteriorating work conditions once again pushed mill owners and workers alike to the breaking point.

Not surprisingly, the textilemakers' trade association, the Cotton Textile Institute, had a draft code ready for submission to Johnson on the day the National Industrial Recovery Act was signed into law. The NRA promised to do for the cottonmakers what they had proved unable to do for themselves: end cutthroat price discounting and stabilize their destructively competitive industry by setting production quotas for individual mills. In return for government-supervised limitations on output—indeed, as the mechanism for enforcing those limitations—the manufacturers agreed to the forty-hour week as the maximum they would ask from their workers. They further agreed to set minimum wage

46. Lowitt and Beasley, *One Third of a Nation*, 176.
47. Jacquelyn Dowd Hall et al., *Like a Family: The Making of a Southern Cotton Mill World* (New York: Norton, 1987), 212.

standards. In what was hailed as a historic breakthrough, they also pledged to abolish child labor altogether. In addition, pursuant to Section 7(a) of the NIRA, the cotton producers agreed, at least in principle, to accept the principle of collective bargaining.

Thunderous applause filled the room when the textile barons announced their intention to end child labor. "The Textile Code had done in a few minutes what neither the law nor constitutional amendment had been able to do in forty years," Johnson crowed. He exulted that the textile accord "showed the way and set the tempo for the execution of the entire recovery act."[48]

Johnson later claimed that the NRA eventually put nearly three million people to work and added $3 billion to the national purchasing power, but for neither the first time nor the last, Johnson was whistling "Dixie." Much of the modest rise in production and employment in the spring of 1933 owed not to the salutary ministrations of NRA but to nervous anticipation of its impact. A wavelet of preemptive building and buying rippled through the economy between March and July, as businesses sought to build inventories and consummate purchases before government-imposed wage and price rules went into effect. And as the summer months dragged on, the Cotton Textile Code seemed less of a pathbreaking precedent and more of a singular event, as the other "Big Ten" industries—coal, petroleum, iron and steel, automobiles, lumber, the garment trades, wholesale distributors, retailers, and construction—refused to follow suit.

Johnson faced this persistent industrial recalcitrance with his trademark mix of bluster, bravado, and baloney. "Away slight men!" he railed to a group of businessmen in Atlanta. "You may have been Captains of Industry once, but you are Corporals of Disaster now." Pleading for minimum wage standards, he declaimed that "men have died and worms have eaten them but not from paying human labor thirty cents an hour." The "chiselers" who tried to shave NRA standards, he thundered, were "guilty of a practice as cheap as stealing pennies out of the cup of a blind beggar."[49]

Frustrated by his lack of accomplishment after the magnificent overture of the Cotton Textile Code, Johnson cast about for ways to make

48. Johnson, *Blue Eagle*, 233, 230, ix. In somewhat muted form, Johnson's extravagant claims for the NRA echo in many of the standard histories of the New Deal. See, for example, Schlesinger 2:174, and Leuchtenburg, 69.
49. Schlesinger 2:120; Johnson, *Blue Eagle*, 263.

more economic music. He soon encountered difficulties even graver in their implications than Roosevelt's regrettable segregation of PWA and its pump-priming money. Johnson's staff advised him that NRA would not withstand a legal challenge to its enforcement powers. The licensing provisions by which the NIRA legislation provided for government enforcement of the codes, he was told, were almost certainly unconstitutional. Johnson would never use them. Instead, he turned to the techniques of propaganda and moral suasion and once again looked to his war experience for guidance. "There have been six similar mass movements of this nation depending for support on almost unanimous popular participation," he explained, in a comparison as historically telling as it was mathematically dubious: "the Selective Draft, the Liberty Loan Campaign, the Food Administration, the War Industries Board Mobilization of Industry in 1917 and 1918, and the Blue Eagle Drive in 1933." All save the last dated from World War I. Johnson himself had a hand in two of them, the draft and the WIB. All of them, including the peculiarly administered wartime draft, embodied the reflexive American preference for voluntary rather than statutory means to social ends, for invoking mass sentiment rather than the majesty of the law, even when confronted with emergencies on the scale of war and Depression.[50]

Fired by this inspiration, Johnson launched an audacious propaganda campaign in July. He asked employers voluntarily to sign a blanket code, the President's Reemployment Agreement, pledging themselves to pay a minimum wage of forty cents per hour for a thirty-five–hour maximum week. He implored consumers to trade only with establishments that displayed the symbol of participation, the stylized Blue Eagle. Devised by Johnson himself and patterned on Native American thunderbird designs, the Blue Eagle, along with its accompanying legend, "we do our part," was destined to become a ubiquitous Depression-era logo. The president kicked off the Blue Eagle campaign with a Fireside Chat at the end of July. Once again invoking the wartime ideal of cooperation in a time of crisis, Roosevelt declared that "those who cooperate in this program must know each other at a glance. That is why we have provided a badge of honor for this purpose, a simple design with a legend, 'We do our part,' and I ask that all those who join with me shall display

50. For extended discussion of the voluntarist ethos in World War I mobilization, see David M. Kennedy, *Over Here: The First World War and American Society* (New York: Oxford University Press, 1980); and Robert D. Cuff's pioneering study, *The War Industries Board: Business-Government Relations during World War I* (Baltimore: Johns Hopkins University Press, 1973).

that badge prominently. . . . There are adequate penalties in the law," the president assured his listeners, but "opinion and conscience" were "the only instruments we shall use in this great summer offensive against unemployment." Johnson put the same matter more pungently: "May God have mercy on the man or group of men who attempt to trifle with this bird."[51]

Blue Eagle badges soon blossomed on store windows and theater marquees, on newspapers and delivery trucks. As in World War I, "four-minute men" stepped forward to preach the Blue Eagle gospel on stages and street corners. Posters proclaimed it from buses and billboards. A monster Blue Eagle parade in New York City in September drew almost two million persons into the streets. The Blue Eagle was meant to symbolize unity and mutuality, and it no doubt did for a season, but Johnson's ubiquitous "badge of honor" also clearly signaled the poverty of the New Deal's imagination and the meagerness of the methods it could bring to bear at this time against the Depression. Reduced to the kind of incantation and exhortation for which they had flayed Hoover, the New Dealers stood revealed in late 1933 as something less than the bold innovators and aggressive wielders of government power that legend later portrayed.

While the Blue Eagle ballyhoo went on, Johnson plunged ahead with his campaign to create code authorities in the major industrial sectors. By September he had largely succeeded, but with lamentably predictable results. Deprived of any formal means to compel compliance, Johnson necessarily acquiesced in codes that amounted to nothing less than the cartelization of huge sectors of American industry under the government's auspices. Various trade associations, like the Iron and Steel Institute or the National Automobile Chamber of Commerce, cloaked now with the vague mantle of governmental authority, effectively became the code authorities for their respective industries. They ignored the antitrust laws with impunity and enforced production quotas and price policies on their members. Typically, the largest producers dominated the codemaking bodies, producing squeals of complaint from smaller operators, labor, and consumers. Though the NRA contained both a Labor Board and a Consumer Advisory Board, and though in theory both those interests were supposed to be represented in code-making and code administration, in fact fewer than 10 percent of the

51. Johnson, *Blue Eagle*, 260, 263.

code authorities had labor representation and only 1 percent had consumer members.[52]

The cotton code foreshadowed many of the problems that bedeviled the NRA in later 1933 and 1934 and, more broadly, suggested some of the difficulties endemic to all government regulation of free-market economies. By stipulating that cotton spindles could not run more than two forty-hour shifts per week, the cotton code sanctioned massive layoffs in the mill towns. The mill operators effected many of those layoffs by ceasing to employ children, thus exposing the hard business logic beneath their apparently magnanimous concession to the cause of ending child labor. For those workers who remained, the owners often evaded minimum wage rules by reclassifying jobs into exempt categories such as "learners" or "cleaners." In late August a textile union representative reported that "no mills I know of are living up to the code."[53] Equally troublesome, code-sanctioned price-fixing, usually mandated with a rule prohibiting sale below the cost of production, however that might be calculated, had begun by late 1933 to raise consumer prices, in some cases pushing them 20 percent above 1929 levels.

The codes did impose a semblance of order on the chaos that beset many industries in 1933. It did so especially in those historically troubled sectors like textiles, coal, oil, and the retail trades, which were fragmented into myriad little enterprises that had been unable to cooperate sufficiently to stabilize their markets. But in other sectors, like steel and automobiles, where heavy capital requirements had long since bred oligopolistic market structures, allowing a relative handful of producers to concert their price and wage policies, the codes were largely redundant or irrelevant. And for virtually all industries, even the light hand of government authority that Johnson was able to lay upon them held deeply disturbing implications. Almost overnight, NRA mushroomed into a bureaucratic colossus. Its staff of some forty-five hundred oversaw more than seven hundred codes, many of which overlapped, sometimes inconsistently. Corkmakers, for example, faced an array of no fewer than thirty-four codes. Hardware stores operated under nineteen different codes, each with its own elaborate catalogue of regulations. In just two years NRA regulators drafted some thirteen thousand pages of codes and issued eleven thousand interpretive rulings. No mat-

52. Bernard Bellush, *The Failure of the NRA* (New York: Norton, 1975), 47.
53. Bellush, *Failure of the NRA*, 55.

ter how constricted their formal legal power, nor how cleverly they strove to exercise what power they had, the mere appearance on the field of that unprecedented bureaucratic horde struck terror into the breasts of many businessmen. "The excessive centralization and the dictatorial spirit," wrote the journalist Walter Lippmann, "are producing a revulsion of feeling against bureaucratic control of American economic life."[54]

By early 1934 discontent with NRA prompted Johnson, in a typical grandstand stunt, to convene a "Field Day of Criticism." On February 27 more than two thousand people crowded into the Department of Commerce's cavernous auditorium, their hands clutching sheets of notes itemizing NRA's offenses. So abundant were their grievances that Johnson was obliged to extend the gripe session. For four days witnesses vented their complaints about high prices, red tape, and mistreatment of labor. A black spokesman detailed the effects of the NRA's acceptance (like CWA's) of regional wage differentials on blacks, the lowest-paid workers in the low-wage South.

Meanwhile, congressional accusations that NRA was promoting monopoly compelled Roosevelt to appoint a National Recovery Review Board, improbably chaired by Clarence Darrow, the renowned and idiosyncratic criminal lawyer. Darrow took it upon himself to champion the "little fellow," the small businessman who was allegedly oppressed by the industrial titans who sat in control of the various code authorities. Johnson retorted that the "little fellow" was often a "stingy, sleazy . . . greasy" operator whose principal complaint was that he "does not want to pay code wages for code hours." The glare of NRA's publicity, said Johnson, had revealed "black men working in a steaming lumber swamp for seven and five cents an hour. . . . Children toiling in factories for very little more. . . . Women in sweat shops and garret slums bending night and day over garments. . . . Who is the real Little Fellow," Johnson asked, "the black man in the swamp—the child in the factory—the women in the sweat shop—or is it the small enterprise that says it cannot exist in competition unless it practices those barbarisms?"[55] There was much truth in what Johnson said, but Darrow's slapdash report, the seventy-seven-year-old lawyer's last and rather embarrassing hurrah, nevertheless affirmed that the NRA did indeed sustain monopolistic practices, then inconsistently suggested both antitrust prosecutions and socialized ownership as remedies.

54. Schlesinger 2:121.
55. Johnson, *Blue Eagle*, 275–76.

No criticisms of NRA stung more sharply or more plainly revealed NRA's defects than those that focused on Johnson's policies toward labor. Business owners quickly figured out how to turn NRA codes to their advantage in setting production levels and prices, but when it came to labor regulations, management balked. Section 7(a) of the National Industrial Recovery Act obliged management to engage in good-faith collective bargaining with workers. What that requirement might mean in practice remained to be seen. Some labor leaders, notably John L. Lewis, the histrionically gifted head of the United Mine Workers, likened 7(a) to Lincoln's Emancipation Proclamation. Galvanized by the prospects that 7(a) opened up, Lewis dispatched his minions through the coal districts in the summer of 1933. "The President wants you to join a union," they urged, and within months the UMW membership quadrupled, to some four hundred thousand. But in other industries, like steel and automobiles, employers insisted that they could comply with 7(a) simply by themselves setting up a company union, a body they could tightly control. The effect of establishing a company union, Arthur M. Schlesinger Jr. aptly notes, was "to create a bargaining tableau without creating anything approaching equality of bargaining power."[56] In some steel plants, workers flaunted their contempt for company unions by throwing old washers into the barrels provided for the deposit of their union "dues."[57]

Conflicts erupted everywhere over what form of union would prevail. A season of labor unrest swept in with the warm summer weather in 1933 as other labor organizers moved to follow Lewis's energetic lead. In August Johnson set up a new body, the National Labor Board (NLB), to mediate the proliferating labor-management clashes. The NLB soon devised the so-called Reading Formula, providing for supervised elections in which workers could choose their own representatives for collective bargaining. The NLB held that a majority of workers could determine the sole bargaining agent for all the workers in a given shop. Johnson quickly undercut that ruling, however, by issuing a contrary opinion that left employers free to practice the ancient tactics of divide and conquer by recognizing any number of workers' representatives — including company unions. No mechanism existed to resolve this standoff between the NRA chief and his own labor body. It soon became

56. Schlesinger 2:145.
57. Lizabeth Cohen, *Making a New Deal* (Cambridge: Cambridge University Press, 1990), 305.

apparent that the NLB was essentially helpless in the face of evasion or outright defiance of its rulings. "Industry generally is in revolt against NRA and is throwing down the gauntlet to the President," Hickok reported in May 1934.[58] Workers, promised so much but given so little by 7(a), grew increasingly disillusioned. "It has almost shaken their faith in the United States Government," one witness testified at Johnson's Field Day of Criticism.[59]

By late 1934, harassed by complaints from businesses big and small, as well as from workers and consumers and even from his own colleagues at the NRA, Johnson was growing more and more frenetically erratic. He disappeared for days at a time on monumental benders, reemerging wreathed in fogs of fustian to compare himself with Moses and the NRA codes with the Decalogue. Roosevelt at last secured his resignation, and he bade his staff a tearful farewell on October 1. The NRA struggled along for a few more months, rid of its egregious leader but still saddled with a host of intractable problems. It succumbed to a unanimous Supreme Court declaration of its unconstitutionality in May 1935.[60]

Johnson had failed utterly to coax out of the instrument of the NRA the mighty chords of industrial harmony that he had yearned to play. To be sure, Ickes's tightfisted control of PWA monies had hamstrung NRA from the outset as an engine of recovery, but the explanation for NRA's problems goes deeper than that. FERA and CWA, after all, did between them pump more than $1.3 billion into the economy in 1933–34, a good fraction of the original PWA appropriation and some of it, in fact, taken from the PWA budget. It was not simply want of money but the want of historical perspective, of adequate means, and of effective ideas that accounted for NRA's sorry record. Over all of NRA's history fell the shadow of the old mercantilist dream that a class of informed and disinterested mandarins could orchestrate all the parts of the economy into an efficient and harmonious whole. That dream had begun to fade with the dawn of the industrial revolution in the eighteenth century. The fantastic complexities of modern, twentieth-century economies were rendering it almost entirely chimerical. Worse, lacking proper enforcement powers, Johnson's codemakers, like their predeces-

---

58. Lowitt and Beasley, *One Third of a Nation*, 263.
59. Bellush, *Failure of the NRA*, 75.
60. The case was *Schechter Poultry Corporation v. United States* (295 U.S. 495). For further discussion, see p. 328.

sors at the War Industries Board in 1917–18, sought in vain to assert an ill-defined public interest against the quite concrete private interests, especially the interests of capital, to which they were repeatedly forced to concede. Worse still, NRA rested upon the assumption, widespread in the early New Deal years, that overproduction had caused the Depression and that in scarcity lay salvation. That premise precluded any serious search for economic growth, made stability the touchstone of policy, and underwrote the kinds of restrictionist practices traditionally associated with monopolies.

The best that could be said of NRA was that it held the line for a time against further degradation of labor standards and that it energized a much-needed and long-suppressed labor organizing drive. However fitful its progress in 1933 and 1934, that drive would soon swell to huge proportions. Within a few years it would revolutionize labor-management relations and dramatically improve the living standards of much of the American working class.

As 1934 drew to a close and the third year of the New Deal was about to open, recovery was still nowhere in sight. The curious passivity of the American people that had perplexed so many observers was waning, yielding to a mounting sense of grievance and a restless demand for answers. Especially in the ravaged countryside that had been both Hoover's and Roosevelt's first concern, things had gone from bad to worse. Up the great valley of the Mississippi and across the northern plains, as well as in the grim working-class neighborhoods of the Northeast's industrial cities, the murmur of discontent was at last threatening to swell into a cry for revolution.

7

Chasing the Phantom of Recovery

I am a farmer. . . . Last spring I thought you really intended to do some-
thing for this country. Now I have given it all up. Henceforward I am
swearing eternal vengeance on the financial barons and will do every
single thing I can to bring about communism.
> —An Indiana farmer to Franklin D. Roosevelt,
> October 16, 1933

In October 1933 Lorena Hickok steered Bluette westward into America's
agrarian heartland and back to the scenes of her own childhood.

The Depression "is 10 or 12 years old out here," she reminded Hopkins from Iowa. "These plains are beautiful," she wrote Eleanor Roosevelt from North Dakota. "But, oh, the terrible, crushing drabness of life
here. And the suffering, for both people and animals. . . . Most of the
farm buildings haven't been painted in God only knows how long . . . !
If I had to live here, I think I'd just quietly call it a day and commit
suicide. . . . The people up here . . . are in a daze. A sort of nameless
dread hangs over the place."[1]

As the NRA enclosed more and more sectors within its code agreements, prices for industrial products stabilized, then rose modestly. But
in agriculture, the sector the New Deal had identified as most in need
of revitalization and on which it pinned its chief hopes for recovery,
prices remained stuck at less than 60 percent of 1929 levels. Farmers
felt betrayed. In the farm counties of Minnesota in November, Hickok
noted "the bitterness toward NRA. . . . NRA is not at all popular, to be
sure. Well, how *could* it be?" she asked. The prices that farmers paid
"*did* go up faster than their incomes."[2] Astonishingly, the New Deal in

---

1. Richard Lowitt and Maurine Beasley, eds., *One Third of a Nation: Lorena Hickok
   Reports on the Great Depression* (Urbana: University of Illinois Press), 73.
2. Lowitt and Beasley, *One Third of a Nation*, 74, 117.

1933 seemed to be exacerbating, not redressing, the problem of "balance" in the American economy. "We have been patient and long suffering," said a farm leader in October 1933. "We were promised a New Deal. . . . Instead we have the same old stacked deck."[3]

In Morton County, North Dakota, Hickok came out of a meeting in "a shabby little country church" to find several denim-clad farmers, wearing all the clothes they owned, huddled inside her car for warmth. As winter closed its grip over the northern plains, farmers were burning cow manure ("buffalo chips") and rushes cut from dried lake beds for fuel. Even the animals suffered. "The plight of the livestock," Hickok wrote, "is pitiable." Milk cows were drying up for lack of feed. Farmers eligible for relief road work did not have teams healthy enough to pull road scrapers. "Half-starved horses have dropped in the harness," Hickok related, "right on the road job. . . . They've even harvested Russian thistle to feed to their horses and cattle. Russian thistle, for your information," she explained to Hopkins, "is a thistle plant with shallow roots that dries up in the fall and is blown across the prairies like rolls of barbed wire. The effect on the digestive apparatus of an animal . . . would be, I should imagine, much the same as though it had eaten barbed wire." In neighboring South Dakota several days later, she found farm wives feeding Russian thistle soup to their children.[4]

South Dakota, she reported to Hopkins, is the " 'Siberia' of the United States. A more hopeless place I never saw. Half the people — the farmers particularly — are scared to death. . . . The rest of the people are apathetic." She poured out her feelings to Eleanor Roosevelt: "Oh, these poor, confused people, living their dreary little lives. . . . And — my God, what families! I went to see a woman today who has ten children and is about to have another. She had so many that she didn't call them by their names, but referred to them as 'this little girl' and 'that little boy.' " Far out on the wind-scoured prairie Hickok visited

> what had once been a house. No repairs have been made in years. The kitchen floor was all patched up with pieces of tin. . . . Great patches of plaster had fallen from the walls. Newspapers had been stuffed in the cracks about the windows. And in that house two small boys . . . were running about without a stitch on save some ragged overalls. No shoes or stockings. Their feet were purple with cold. . . . This, dear lady, is the stuff that farm strikes and agrarian revolutions are

3. Davis 3:89.
4. Davis 3:55–60, 91, 96.

made of. Communist agitators are in here now, working among these people.

The country west of the Missouri River, she opined, bluntly debunking the sacred tenets of frontier boosterism, "never should have been opened up."[5]

The plight of the prairie folk was even worse than Hickok had remembered from her girlhood. The gritty reality and unrelieved scale of rural poverty clearly staggered her. She may well have read *Tobacco Road*, Erskine Caldwell's best-selling 1932 tale of lust and squalor in backcountry Georgia, or while visiting Eleanor in New York she may even have seen the stage adaptation of Caldwell's novel, then playing to packed houses on Broadway. But no fiction, not even John Steinbeck's melodramatic *Grapes of Wrath* later in the Depression decade, could do full justice to the desolate facts of American rural life.

Only 16 percent of farm households earned incomes above the national median of fifteen hundred dollars per year in the mid-1930s. More than half of all farm families had annual incomes of less than a thousand dollars. In 1934 the per capita income of farm households was just $167. In that same year, even after the efforts of CWA, only one farmhouse in ten had an indoor toilet; only one in five had electricity. Frequent pregnancies, medically unattended childbirths, malnutrition, pellagra, malaria, hookworm, and other parasites exacted heavy tolls in human life and energy. More than thirteen hundred rural counties, containing some seventeen million souls, had no general hospital, and most of them lacked even a public health nurse. Illiteracy was twice as common in rural districts as in cities. Nearly one million rural children between the ages of seven and thirteen did not attend school at all. In this generally dismal picture, the southeastern states were the most dismal by far. Sharecroppers and tenants, an agrarian class peculiarly concentrated in the old South, were probably the poorest Americans. One study of *employed* sharecroppers in four southern states revealed average annual cash incomes of $350 for white families and $294 for black.[6]

Hickok found the Midwest "depressing" in the winter of 1933–34, but even the sobering scenes of want and deprivation that she confronted in the Dakotas could not prepare her for what she saw in the South in early 1934. "I just can't describe to you some of the things I've seen and

5. Davis 3:83, 90, 60–61, 83–85.
6. Anna Rochester, *Why Farmers Are Poor* (New York: International Publishers, 1940), 11–13; *HSUS*, 483.

heard down here these last few days. I shall never forget them—never as long as I live," she wrote to Hopkins from Georgia in January. Southern farm workers, "half-starved Whites and Blacks," she reported, "struggle in competition for less to eat than my dog gets at home, for the privilege of living in huts that are infinitely less comfortable than his kennel." The Depression had certainly blighted the region, Hickok acknowledged, but she was shrewd enough to note that she was also seeing the ghastly accumulation of generations of poverty, neglect, and racial oppression. "If there is a school system in the state, it simply isn't functioning," she wrote. "It can't. The children just can't go to school, hundreds of them, because they haven't the clothes. The illiterate parents of hundreds of others don't send them. As a result you've got the picture of hundreds of boys and girls in their teens down here in some of these rural areas who can't read or write. I'm not exaggerating. . . . Why, some of them can barely talk!"[7]

In the citrus groves of Florida she found seasonal farm workers living in a state of virtual "peonage," even while the nearby tourist hotels were "comfortably filled." The Florida citrus growers, she fumed, "have got the world licked . . . for being mean-spirited, selfish, and irresponsible." In North Carolina in February she gave full vent to her indignation at the historical crimes of the sharecropping system—and hinted at the kind of threat that even the modest, hesitant programs of the early New Deal were already beginning to pose to southern mores:

> The truth is that the rural South never has progressed beyond slave labor. . . . When their slaves were taken away, they proceeded to establish a system of peonage that was as close to slavery as it possibly could be and included Whites as well as Blacks. During the Depression, the paternalistic landlord was hard put to it to "furnish" his tenants [provide a credit for seed, tools, and food]. He was darned glad to have us take over the job. But now, finding that CWA has taken up some of this labor surplus . . . he is panicky, realizes that he may have to make better terms with his tenants and pay his day labor more, and is raising a terrific howl against CWA. Whatever we do down here that may take up that rural labor surplus is going to make these farmers yell.[8]

Some of those landlords, and their political protectors, yelled directly to President Roosevelt. When a farm laborer on relief wrote to Georgia governor Eugene Talmadge that "I wouldn't plow nobody's mule from

7. Lowitt and Beasley, *One Third of a Nation*, 158–59.
8. Lowitt and Beasley, *One Third of a Nation*, 164–65, 186–87.

sunrise to sunset for 50 cents a day when I could get $1.30 for pretend-
ing to work on a DITCH," Talmadge forwarded the letter to the White
House. "I take it . . . that you approve of paying farm labor 40 to 50
cents per day," Roosevelt heatedly replied. "Somehow I cannot get it
into my head that wages on such a scale make possible a reasonable
American standard of living."[9]

Throughout the South, time and again Hickok heard the same complaints: that CWA, unlike NRA, refused to recognize historic black-white
wage differentials; that the prospect of federal relief payments was sucking low-wage agricultural workers, blacks especially, into cities like
Savannah, where they threatened to become a permanent welfare class;
that "the Federal Government came down here and put all the bums
to work at more money than labor had ever been paid down here before"; that the insistence of many federal officers on "mistering the niggers" had stirred up southern blacks and threatened to explode the region's volatile race system.[10] These criticisms exposed the depths of the
region's economic backwardness, as well as the difficulties that attended
any policy that might perturb the tense membrane of class and race
relations in the South.

Farther west, in the region at whose center the Texas and Oklahoma
panhandles touched, nature and man had conspired by the 1930s to
breed an ecological and human catastrophe called the Dust Bowl. The
pioneers who first ventured out onto the high southern plains had called
themselves "sod-busters," and they had proceeded to break the very back
of the land. By the 1920s, their tractors were clawing the skin off the
earth, scratching at its fragile face to plant ever larger crops, more cotton
and wheat to carry to market as prices per bale and bushel steadily fell.
They seamed the land with furrows down which washed acres of topsoil
when the rains came. When the rain stopped in 1930, the wounded
earth cracked open and dry grass crunched under men's boots. By 1934
in some areas the tortured soil lacked any detectable moisture to a depth
of three feet. The wind lifted the surface powder into the skies, creating
towering eight-thousand-foot waves known as "black blizzards." Great
earthen clouds rose up off the land and bore down on cities to the east.
One dust storm so darkened Great Bend, Kansas, that a resident
claimed, "Lady Godiva could ride thru the streets without even the

9. Schlesinger 2:274. Roosevelt dictated this reply to Talmadge but sent the letter over
Harry Hopkins's signature.
10. Lowitt and Beasley, *One Third of a Nation*, 154; Leuchtenburg, 138.

horse seeing her." The Kansas newspaperman William Allen White likened it to the ashes that had buried Pompeii. In the tradition of the frontier tall tale, one joke had it that a Dust Bowl farmer fainted when a drop of water hit him in the face; he revived only when three buckets of sand were tossed over him.

The Dust Bowl coughed out thousands of "exodusters" in the Depression years. They were usually known as "Okies," but though more than three hundred thousand people were blown out of Oklahoma, more thousands came from Texas, Kansas, and Colorado. They were as much the victims of their own farming practices as they were of nature's cruelty. "Grab and greed," said the journalist Carey McWilliams, punished them as much as dust and tractors. They went to California, mostly, though to other places, too, and they soon became symbols of the decade's worst ravages. Their story had the makings of an inverted version of the epic American tale. They were refugees from the fabled heartland, outbound from the prairies that had beckoned their ancestors westward, sad testimonials to the death of the dream of America as an uncovered ore bed of inexhaustible bounty, no longer hopeful pioneers but woebegone refugees. The photographer Dorothea Lange and her husband, economist Paul Taylor, captured their gaunt faces and recorded their spare histories in *An American Exodus: A Record of Human Erosion*, published in 1938. The following year John Steinbeck bestowed literary immortality on the Okie migrants in his best-selling novel *The Grapes of Wrath*, made into a popular movie in 1940.[11]

The Midwest, besides the South the nation's other great agricultural region, meanwhile rumbled with problems of its own. Unlike the South, where a relatively small number of baronial landlords owned vast tracts of land, family farms predominated in the sprawling corn, wheat, cattle, and dairy belts that stretched across the broad midcontinent, through the Palouse country of the Pacific Northwest, and into the verdant Puget-Willamette trough in western Washington and Oregon. (In California, the state with the nation's largest agricultural output, landholding patterns more closely resembled those in the South.) Typically encumbered by debt, family farms began to go under the auctioneer's hammer as banks first foreclosed on the properties that secured defaulted

11. Donald Worster, *Dust Bowl: The Southern Plains in the 1930s* (New York: Oxford University Press, 1979); and James N. Gregory, *American Exodus: The Dust Bowl Migration and Okie Culture in California* (New York: Oxford University Press, 1989).

mortgages, then tried to recoup some value by offering the repossessed farms for sale to the highest bidder. Throughout the midwestern heartland, groups of neighbors gathered at auctions to intimidate would-be buyers from bidding. These occasionally violent tactics restored farms to their original owners, sometimes for token payments of as little as one cent. By 1933 a noisy organization, the Farmers Holiday Association, led by Milo Reno, a prairie populist and rousing orator in the William Jennings Bryan mold, clamored for an end to foreclosures and for government-sanctioned codes to control production and guarantee prices in the agricultural sector, just as NRA was doing for industry.

Rough vigilante justice often accompanied these efforts. In Le Mars, Iowa, in April 1933 a mob of farmers, their faces masked with blue kerchiefs, abducted a judge who refused to suspend foreclosure proceedings, threatened him with lynching, tore off his clothes, and left him beaten, muddy, and humiliated in a roadside ditch. The governor of Iowa soon placed half a dozen counties under martial law. Hickok reported the disruption of a foreclosure sale in South Dakota when "the Farm Holiday crowd" disarmed sheriff's deputies and "ended up by tearing the sheriff's clothes off and beating him quite badly."[12]

In October 1933 Reno called for a "farm strike" unless his demands were met: currency inflation, a moratorium on foreclosures, and, most important, price supports for farm products. For good measure, Reno threw in a slap at "the money-lords of Wall Street." At a raucous meeting in Des Moines, Iowa, on October 30, the governors of North and South Dakota, Iowa, Minnesota, and Wisconsin endorsed Reno's program. North Dakota governor William Langer had already threatened to use his state's National Guard to enforce an embargo on the shipment of any wheat out of North Dakota for a price below the "cost of production." Even as the five governors made their way as a group from Des Moines to Washington to press these demands, more violence flared across the upper Mississippi Valley. Striking farmers overturned milk vats, blocked roadways, and throttled delivery of cattle and hogs to the great stockyards in Omaha. Meanwhile, inflationists like Oklahoma's Elmer Thomas threatened a march of a million men on Washington to force the administration's hand. "The West is seething with unrest," Roosevelt acknowledged, and farmers "must have higher values to pay off their debts."[13]

12. Lowitt and Beasley, *One Third of a Nation*, 79.
13. Schlesinger 2:236–37.

The thunder rolling up out of the farm belt prompted Roosevelt to begin pursuing in earnest the inflationary policies for which his withdrawal from the London Economic Conference had prepared the way. The president embraced the highly questionable theory of Cornell professor George F. Warren that substantial government purchases of gold would spur inflation and thereby both reduce debt burdens and raise commodity prices. Orthodox bankers and mainstream economists were aghast. Roosevelt waved their objections aside. "I wish our banking and economist friends would realize the seriousness of the situation from the point of view of the debtor classes . . . and think less from the point of view of the 10 percent who constitute the creditor classes," he said to his treasury secretary. In late October Roosevelt announced in a Fireside Chat that the Reconstruction Finance Corporation would begin to purchase U.S.-mined gold at "prices to be determined from time to time after consultation with the Secretary of the Treasury and the President. . . . We are thus continuing to move toward a managed currency."[14]

There ensued one of the most bizarre episodes in the history of American finance. Each morning for the next several weeks, Roosevelt over his breakfast eggs would name the price at which the government would buy gold that day. Hard-money men quit the administration in disgust. Roosevelt personally fired one prominent dissenter, Treasury Undersecretary Dean Acheson.

When the gold-purchase program ended in January 1934, the price of gold had risen from $20.67 an ounce to $35. The dollar had lost some 40 percent of its foreign exchange value as measured in gold, a devaluation that might in theory have bolstered American exports but that in fact exported nothing but more financial turmoil to America's few remaining trading partners. Domestic commodity prices, meanwhile, actually declined slightly in late 1933. Like a cracker-barrel argument, the gold-buying scheme had proceeded from dubious premises to a sputtering conclusion. Watching from England, John Maynard Keynes sniped that Roosevelt's manipulation of the currency "looked to me more like a gold standard on the booze than the ideal managed currency of my dreams." Shortly thereafter, Keynes called on Roosevelt at the White House. "I saw your friend Keynes," the bemused president said to Labor Secretary Frances Perkins. "He left a whole rigmarole of figures. He must be a mathematician rather than a political economist." As

14. Schlesinger 2:240.

for Keynes, he somewhat undiplomatically remarked to Perkins that he had "supposed the President was more literate, economically speaking."[15]

Gold buying did satisfy Roosevelt's itch for action, even ill-founded action. The gold scheme served the president's political purposes as well. "Gentlemen," he lectured a group of skeptical government officials in late October, "if we continued a week or so longer without my having made this move on gold, we would have had an agrarian revolution in this country."[16] Roosevelt exaggerated the revolutionary proportions of whatever was astir in the American countryside in 1933. To be sure, Lorena Hickok was reporting that Communist organizers were trying to influence the Farmers Holiday movement; that Sioux City, Iowa, was "a hotbed of the 'reds' "; and that growers in California's Imperial Valley were "simply hysterical" about Communists.[17] But a few outbreaks of hooliganism and scattered milk-spillings did not a revolution make. The Farmers Holiday Association, never more than a splinter group of the National Farmers Union, itself the smallest of the farm organizations, had crested in power and influence with the Des Moines meeting of October 30, and it soon faded away. What in the end impressed Hickok more than the revolutionary potential of a host of pitchfork-wielding angry farmers was, in fact, the torpor and dispiritedness that still hung over much of the farm belt like a sultry summer haze. "I was told in Bismarck," she reported on the very day of the Des Moines meeting, "that in the country I visited this afternoon I would find a good deal of unrest—'farm holiday' spirit. I can't say that I did. They seemed almost too patient to me."[18]

Whatever else might be said about it, the gold-buying scheme kept

15. Keynes, "Open Letter to President Roosevelt," New York Times, December 31, 1933, sec. 8, 2; Frances Perkins, The Roosevelt I Knew (New York: Viking, 1946), 225–26. The inflationists had one more inning, when they succeeded in passing the Silver Purchase Act in June 1934. It committed the government to buy silver from domestic producers until government silver holdings reached a value of one-third of gold reserves—a considerable improvement on the whole Bryanite "16-to-1" ratio. The government only monetized a portion of its silver holdings, however, in the form of coins and small-denomination "silver certificates," which circulated for nearly thirty more years. The Silver Purchase Act in the end represented less of a triumph for the inflationists than it did a stunning victory for the silver-mining industry, which had seized the opportune political moment to guarantee government purchases of its product at wholly artificial prices.

16. Schlesinger 2:242.

17. Lowitt and Beasley, One Third of a Nation, 79, 107, 306.

18. Lowitt and Beasley, One Third of a Nation, 58.

the farm belt relatively quiescent long enough for the New Deal's major agricultural programs to begin to work their effects. By the end of 1933 Farm Credit Administration refinancing contracts began to salvage family farms threatened with foreclosure. Soon the Agricultural Adjustment Administration's benefit payments and commodity loans began flowing into the farm belt as well. Like the industrial sector under NRA, agriculture began slowly to stabilize. But full-blown recovery would long elude the nation's farmers, especially the very poorest among them.

Gold buying also reflected the spirit of beggar-thy-neighbor economic isolationism that informed the early New Deal and indeed infested virtually all the globe's chancelleries in the depths of the Depression. When pugnaciously nationalistic AAA administrator George Peek advocated dumping America's mounting agricultural surpluses abroad, the otherwise internationally minded secretary of agriculture, Henry A. Wallace, cut him off with a scarcely less nationalistic retort: "We ought to act for the moment," Wallace explained, "as if we were a self-contained agricultural economy."[19] Wallace's statement held profound implications. Economic rescue, it suggested, depended on economic isolation. Only in such isolation could American farmers come to grips with the demons of overproduction that had plagued and impoverished them for more than a decade.

The farmers' plight furnished a classical illustration of how Adam Smith's legendary invisible hand might in certain circumstances be unable to orchestrate the general welfare out of a myriad of competing self-interests. As a group, American farmers annually brought more crops to market than the market could absorb at prices farmers found acceptable. Individual farmers, logically enough, tried to sustain their income levels by compensating for lower unit prices with higher volume. They tilled more acres, laid on more fertilizer, bought more tractors and seed drills and harvesters, and carried even larger crops to market. But the sum of those individual decisions inundated markets still further and further depressed prices. Collective misery, not the common good, was the bitter fruit of free-market striving by farmers.

How to break this vicious cycle was a problem that had stumped agricultural policymakers for more than a decade before 1933. George Peek and other partisans of the McNary-Haugen legislation in the 1920s had sought to dispose of American crop surpluses abroad, moving them to foreign markets with government subsidies if necessary. President

19. Schlesinger 2:55.

Hoover had tried to induce farmers' cooperatives to create more orderly agricultural markets, and he had created the Federal Farm Board to support price levels with government purchases of surplus crops. But in the troubled international economic environment of 1933, in which all nations desperately sought refuge in policies of protectionism and autarky, Peek's search for foreign markets was doomed from the outset. So too, as the example of Hoover's swiftly bankrupted Farm Board had dismally proved, was any agricultural remedy that failed to grasp the nettle of curtailing farm output.

New Dealers believed that much more than the well-being of farmers was at stake in agricultural policy. Most of them took Secretary Wallace's idea about the "self-contained agricultural economy" one step further. Not just agriculture but the entire American economy, they believed, was a virtually self-contained entity. Its continental scale and varied physical endowment made it less dependent on foreign trade than that of virtually any other modern state. Roosevelt's policies on exchange stabilization and gold had insulated it more effectively than ever. And inside the sealed vessel of the American economy, New Dealers claimed, recovery depended above all on striking a new "balance" between productive capacity and consuming power by changing the terms of trade between industry and agriculture. No idea pulsed more vibrantly at the very heart of the New Deal in 1933 than the conviction that on the success of AAA's effort to stimulate consumer demand by raising farm incomes rode the hopes not only of the nation's farmers but of the nation itself.

Given the manifest imbalances in the American economy in the years after World War I—not to mention the national mythology about sturdy yeomen and noble sons and daughters of the soil as the backbone of the Republic—the idea that farmers held the key to recovery had an unarguable appeal. Farmers were, after all, still some 30 percent of the work force. Many Americans easily recalled the not-so-distant era when farmers made up a majority of the American population. Farm spokesmen artfully played the chords of national memory as they rehearsed the woes of the countryside in the Depression. Those woes were real enough. The "parity ratio"—the ratio between the prices that farmers received for the basket of goods they sold to the prices they paid for the basket of goods they bought—had never regained its World War I level throughout the decade of the 1920s. After 1929 it had plummeted disastrously. At the end of the 1920s the parity ratio stood at 92 percent of what it had been in the relatively prosperous baseline period of 1910–

14. By 1932 it had sunk to 58 percent. The total of farm income in 1932 was less than one-third of what it had been in the already bad year of 1929.[20]

There was no denying the destitution and squalor that lay over much of the American countryside in the 1930s. Nor was there any denying the proposition that an economically healthy agricultural sector would be good both for those who lived and worked in it as well as for their urban cousins who sold them clothing, machinery, books, and utensils. But there was more than a little that was quaintly anachronistic about the New Dealers' faith in agricultural revival as the master key to general prosperity, and there was much that was grossly opportunistic in the response of the farmers themselves to the New Deal.

The relative importance of agriculture in the American economy, and the relative size of the farm work force, had been shrinking for a long time before the Depression arrived. Global competition, mechanization, increasing agricultural productivity, and industrial growth underwrote a steady country-to-city migration that had been swelling for a century or more—not only in America but in virtually all the Western world, as the millions of displaced peasants from the valleys of the Vistula and the Danube and the hills of the Carpathians and the Apennines who had swarmed for decades into American cities extravagantly attested. In America as elsewhere in the mid-twentieth century, the long-term dynamics of increasing consumer demand and economic vitality were most prodigiously at work not in the countryside but in the industrial cities. The Populist movement at the end of the nineteenth century bore colorful if rueful witness to those developments. When William Jennings Bryan taunted urbanites in 1896 that if they were to "destroy our farms . . . the grass will grow in the streets of every city in the country," he was invoking a homely but already obsolescent economic verity. Populism had in fact been energized by the well-founded anxiety that the countryside was being steadily eclipsed, that population, power, and economic leadership were all flowing ever more rapidly into the cities.

It was to industry and the cities, to the steel-hearths and assembly lines and chemical and electronic laboratories, that a better sense of history might have guided the main efforts of policymakers seeking economic recovery in 1933. Those sectors held the potential for new technologies that promised a future of enormous economic vitality. But nostalgia, intellectual inertia, and political pressure beckoned the New

20. *HSUS*, 489.

Dealers backward, to the cornfields and hay-meadows and pastoral idylls of national mythology—and into the welcoming arms of a lean and hungry agricultural lobby. The Populists in the 1890s had struggled to wring from the agrarian myth some political concessions to soften the consequences of agriculture's inexorable economic diminution, and they had lost. But in the crisis of the 1930s, Bryan's avatars rose again. They rang all the changes of the same agrarian myth and won concessions beyond the Great Commoner's most sumptuous dreams. The New Deal laid the groundwork for a system of farm subsidies that in the end mocked the pieties of frontier individualism and made the agricultural sector a virtual ward of the state. Save only swaddled infants in their mothers' arms, no members of American society would emerge from the New Deal more tenderly coddled than farmers, especially those large-scale commercial growers to whom most New Deal agricultural benefits accrued.

THE PATTERN of agricultural policy that the New Deal bequeathed to later generations owed much to the peculiar conjunction in the 1930s of the history of Populist agitation, the urgent economic crisis, an aggressive agricultural constituency—and a singularly preexisting federal institutional framework. Uniquely among government entities at the Depression's onset, the Department of Agriculture in 1933 was what has been described as "an island of state strength in an ocean of weakness."[21] Both FERA and CWA in the relief field, and NRA in the industrial field, were conceived as temporary emergency measures and started out from scratch as independent agencies, but AAA immediately found a natural and comfortable home in an established cabinet department. Founded in 1889, the first cabinet-level agency created in the new American epoch that dawned after the Civil War—aptly enough in the still predominantly agricultural republic of the late nineteenth century—the Department of Agriculture represented the first halting steps in the United States toward national direction of a major economic sector. Farmers thus had a longer history than any other group of making claims on the federal government. Comparable claims emerged only much later and even more haltingly from industry and labor. Those groups received cabinet-level attention in a single Department of Commerce and Labor in 1903. Even after its separation into

21. Theda Skocpol and Kenneth Finegold, "State Capacity and Economic Intervention in the Early New Deal," *Political Science Quarterly* 97, no. 2 (Summer 1982): 271.

two distinct departments in 1913, they remained weak agencies, starved for reliable data, unsure of their mandates, thinly staffed, and lacking articulate, well-organized clienteles. Part of Herbert Hoover's notoriety in the 1920s was due to his efforts to make the Department of Commerce a modern agency, one that could bring governmental power meaningfully to bear in the industrial sector.

In the agricultural field the picture was different. By the 1930s Agriculture had an effective data-gathering arm in the Division of Crop and Livestock Estimates, a body of trained personnel in the Bureau of Agricultural Economics, a network of local institutional partners in the land-grant colleges, an in-place field administration in the Extension Service, and, not least, a vocal, experienced, and aggressive constituent pressure group, one particularly attentive to the needs of the largest commercial growers, in the American Farm Bureau Federation. These arrangements set the stage for an unusually intimate and durable relationship between the federal government and the nation's farmers.[22]

Historically, the Department of Agriculture had exercised itself to help farmers increase production. Researchers at the land-grant colleges developed more fruitful strains of wheat and corn, more bug-resistant cotton plants and grapevines, more prolific breeds of pigs and cows; the Extension Service's county agents promulgated these discoveries across the land. But in the agriculturally bountiful yet stubbornly depressed 1920s some agrarian economists, notably M. L. Wilson of Montana State College, began to rethink the wisdom of the gospel of bounty. A visit to Russia's "virgin-soil" wheat lands, where oceanic expanses of grainfields undulated from horizon to horizon, deeply impressed upon Wilson the burgeoning capacity of the planet's agricultural producers. If American farmers were to survive, he concluded, they must protect their own domestic market, then adjust production to consumption. These were the basic premises on which the idea of AAA rested.

At its core, the thinking that underlay AAA derived from the same conviction about the salutary effects of scarcity that had produced the NRA industrial codes. But willfully inducing scarcity rasped against the grain of attitudes and habits evolved since time immemorial among those who wrung their livelihood from the soil. While industrial manufacturers had slashed their output by 42 percent in the first four years

---

22. For further discussion of the federal government's role in fostering the American Farm Bureau Federation, see David M. Kennedy, *Over Here: The First World War and American Society* (New York: Oxford University Press, 1980), chap. 2.

of the Depression, farmers had persisted in their timeworn habit of bringing ever more food and fiber to market, thus abetting and even accelerating the downward slide of prices.

Given those millennia-old habits of the husbandman, Professor Wilson's program for agricultural revival was radical indeed. At its heart, as legislated in the Agricultural Adjustment Act, was the Domestic Allotment Plan. It proposed to levy a tax on agricultural processors and use the proceeds to pay farmers for letting acreage lie fallow or shifting it to nonsurplus crop lines. This "benefit payment" program was designed to prevent the planting of potentially surplus crops in the first place. It was soon supplemented by a "commodity loan" program that aimed to prevent storable crops that had already been harvested from reaching the market until prices had risen. The Commodity Credit Corporation, spun off from the Reconstruction Finance Corporation and funded through the RFC appropriation, offered farmers nonrecourse loans at rates above the market price of their crops. If prices rose, the farmer could repay the loan, redeem his crop, and sell it. If not, the government kept the crop, and the farmer kept his money.[23] Begun almost as an afterthought as part of the rescue operation for cotton in October 1933, the Commodity Credit Corporation essentially reinstated Hoover's old Farm Board, albeit in a context of production controls that would supposedly keep it from being swamped with limitless surpluses. Substantial surpluses accumulated nonetheless. By the eve of World War II the corporation held in its warehouses and elevators a third of a billion dollars' worth of unmarketable cotton and somewhat lesser quantities of corn and wheat.[24]

Despite Roosevelt's effort to shepherd the farm bill swiftly through Congress during the Hundred Days, it had been presented for his signature only on May 12, well after spring planting had begun. Seeds had already sprouted in thousands of cotton patches throughout the South and in the rolling wheatfields of the West. Millions of pigs had farrowed in broodsheds and barnyards across the corn belt. By an ironic and short-lived mercy, drought spared Secretary of Agriculture Henry A. Wallace

23. Some surplus foodstuffs were purchased by the Federal Surplus Relief Corporation for distribution by relief agencies, foreshadowing the Food Stamp Program established in 1939. In light of later controversy over the Food Stamp Program it is worth noting that its principal origins lay in the quest for agricultural profitability, not in concern for the undernourished urban poor.

24. *HSUS*, 488.

from resorting to drastic measures to curtail the wheat crop.[25] But to prevent cotton and hogs from glutting their respective markets, Wallace found himself in 1933 charged with the distasteful task of persuading farmers to plow up some ten million acres of sprouting cotton and to slaughter some six million squealing piglets.

Crop prevention might have been unorthodox, but outright crop destruction struck many farmers as criminal, perhaps even sacrilegious. Wallace himself conceded that the cotton plow-up and the "pig infanticide" "were not acts of idealism in any sane society. . . . To destroy a standing crop goes against the soundest instincts of human nature." Milo Reno said flatly that "for the government to destroy food and reduce crops . . . is wicked." In fact, cotton was the only crop plowed up and hogs the only livestock deliberately slaughtered, but the drama of their destruction fixed the image of the AAA in the minds of many Americans and emphatically underscored the novelty of its methods. The Department of Agriculture and the AAA, Lorena Hickok was told in Minnesota in October 1933, "are trying to do a lot of funny things." From Nebraska a few weeks later she reported that "Wallace IS unpopular out here — even among the gang that still believes in giving the Administration a chance." A prominent farm leader voiced the sentiments of many Americans when he said: "That we should have idle and hungry and ill-clad millions on the one hand, and so much food and wool and cotton upon the other that we don't know what to do with it, this is an utterly idiotic situation, and one which makes a laughing stock of our genius as a people."[26]

Wallace shrugged off these criticisms and soldiered ahead with his crusade to restore vitality to American agriculture. Rumpled and tousle-haired, plain-spoken and unpretentious, forty-five years old in 1933, Wallace then and later was a magnet for controversy. To his partisans he was an agrarian intellectual, a scientist and a visionary, like his father before him an editor of the respected farm journal *Wallace's Farmer*. Again like his father, who had been Warren G. Harding's secretary of agriculture, the younger Wallace was an agricultural statesman who moved easily between the corn cribs and feedlots of his native Iowa and

25. The wheat harvest dropped from an annual average of some 864 million bushels in 1928–32 to about 567 million bushels in 1933–35; AAA accounted for less than 7 percent of that reduction, while the weather was responsible for the rest. Schlesinger 2:70.

26. Schlesinger 2:63, 61, 65; Lowitt and Beasley, *One Third of a Nation*, 54, 106; Anthony J. Badger, *The New Deal*, (New York: Farrar, Straus and Giroux, 1989), 163.

the salons and committee rooms of Washington. To his detractors he was a dreamy rustic, an awkward and swankless bumpkin, a pixilated hayseed who dabbled in fad diets, consulted Navajo shamans, and proved a sucker for the enchantments of spiritual snake-oil merchants like his confidante and guru, the emigré Russian mystic Nicholas Roerich.

Whatever his abundant personal idiosyncrasies, Wallace had an uncommonly deep and thorough understanding of American agriculture. He was at bottom a man of the soil. Yet despite his sometimes moony rhapsodizing about the virtues of the bucolic life, he never retreated from his conviction that farming was a business, nor did he apologize for his insistence that it should be a profitable business. He denounced those who bemoaned the AAA's policy of raising farm prices through planned scarcity as "standpat sentimentalists who weep that farmers should practice controlled production [but] do not suggest that clothing factories go on producing *ad infinitum*, regardless of effective demand for their merchandise, until every naked Chinaman is clad. . . . We must play with the cards that are dealt," he said. "Agriculture cannot survive in a capitalist society as a philanthropic enterprise."[27] But it could survive, as Wallace's policies ultimately demonstrated, as a thoroughly subsidized enterprise, suckled in perpetuity on the public teat.

To implement its novel policies with maximum speed, AAA turned to the network of Extension Service agents already in place in virtually every rural county in America. The county agents, in turn, arranged for the formation of local production-control committees in whom effective administrative authority over AAA programs came to reside. It pleased Henry Wallace to describe these bodies as exemplars of "economic democracy," but the reality was somewhat different. Given their history of close collaboration with the largest commercial farmers, the agents, predictably enough, tended to select the richest, most substantial growers in each locality to sit on the committees. The power of the committees was considerable. By 1934 nearly four thousand local committees set production quotas, monitored acreage-reduction contracts, and disbursed government payments.

Like the NRA, AAA was at least nominally a voluntary program. In theory, any individual farmer could elect to sign up for the acreage-reduction or crop-loan programs or to produce as much as he liked and take his chances in the open market. In practice, however, too many

27. Schlesinger 2:63.

nonsigners would undermine the whole surplus-reducing logic of AAA. Not surprisingly, the local committees therefore exerted themselves strenuously to bring their neighbors into the AAA fold. Sometimes they resorted to vigilante intimidation. In two sectors—cotton and tobacco—the effort to induce voluntary compliance gave way in 1934 to compulsory, statutory measures, requested by a majority of the producers themselves. The Bankhead Cotton Control Act and its companion measure, the Kerr-Smith Tobacco Control Act, licensed thousands of individual growers and levied a punitive tax on crops produced in excess of stipulated quotas.

These policies, helped by punishing droughts in the wheat and corn belts, achieved modest economic success. Cotton prices improved from less than seven cents a pound in 1932 to better than twelve cents a pound in 1934. Wheat went from its 1932 low of thirty-eight cents a bushel to eighty-six cents in 1934. Corn moved from thirty-two cents a bushel to eighty-two cents in the same period. Overall, net farm income rose by 50 percent between 1932 and 1936. The parity ratio, thanks partly to higher crop prices but largely to several billion dollars in processing-tax transfer payments to nonproducing farmers, improved from fifty-eight in 1932 to touch ninety-three in 1937, before slumping again to eighty-one by the eve of World War II.[28] Yet those numbers masked persistent and even worsening travails for many millions of Americans in the countryside.

Nowhere were those travails more grotesque than in the cotton South, haunted still by the racial anxieties and class antagonisms that were the malignant residue of the region's troubled history. The cotton belt was home in the 1930s to one-third of the farm population, some two million families, nearly nine million souls whose livelihoods were staked by iron necessity to the white staple. Most were tenant farmers and sharecroppers. They owned no land of their own but lived precariously from season to season by tendering the landlord a lien on their crop in return for a "furnish," usually a credit good for seed, tools, food, and clothing at a store often owned by the landlord himself. Rarely if ever did a tenant earn enough to pay off his debts and escape the system. Since the end of the Civil War this semifeudal system had swollen in the South to hold in its suffocating embrace more than a million white households and well over half a million black families. They were trapped in the system of virtual peonage that had so disturbed Lorena

28. *HSUS*, 511, 517, 483, 489.

Hickok when she first encountered it in Georgia and the Carolinas in early 1934. The croppers lived in hopeless poverty, indebtedness, and fear, fear that was especially paralyzing if they were black. Their only effective recourse against exploitative landlords was to move, as many of them did every year, wearily exchanging one master for another. It was, as Hickok said, a form of slavery in all but name.

She was not alone in the 1930s in describing the life of the southern sharecropper as something that "seemed to belong to another land than the America I knew and loved." After *Fortune* magazine sent the young poet James Agee and the photographer Walker Evans to Alabama to report on tenant farmers, the magazine found their account of the suffering they had seen too harrowing to publish—a rejection that eventually led to its release in book form as *Let Us Now Praise Famous Men*, one of the most sobering artistic achievements of the decade. The writer Erskine Caldwell, no stranger to the harsh grindstone of southern tenant life, recorded scenes of almost unimaginable degradation. Visiting a Georgia sharecropper's cabin that held three families jammed into two rooms, he saw a gaunt six-year-old boy licking the wrappings of a meat package, while "on the floor before an open fire lay two babies, neither a year old, sucking the dry teats of a mongrel bitch." An English journalist in the same year wrote that she "had traveled over most of Europe and part of Africa, but I have never seen such terrible sights as I saw yesterday among the sharecroppers of Arkansas." Henry Wallace himself in the following year declared that on a trip through the cotton states from Arkansas to the East Coast he had witnessed "a poverty so abject" that "I am tempted to say that one third of the farmers of the United States live under conditions which are so much worse than the peasantry of Europe that the city people of the United States should be thoroughly ashamed."[29]

The Depression fell with especially sharp brutality on sharecroppers. The AAA's policies, however unintentionally, cruelly exacerbated their plight. The basic mechanism by which the AAA reduced cotton surpluses was by reducing the acreage planted to cotton. It accomplished this by writing contracts with landlords, in which benefit payments ef-

29. Theodore Saloutos, *The American Farmer and the New Deal* (Ames: Iowa State University Press, 1982), 66, 187; Schlesinger 2:375–76. For a perceptive discussion of Agee and Evans's book, see Richard H. Pells, *Radical Visions, American Dreams* (New York: Harper and Row, 1973), 246ff.

fectively served as rent for land taken out of production. Since most of the withdrawn acreage was worked by tenants and croppers, AAA at a stroke deprived them of their already meager means of earning their daily bread. In theory, landlords were supposed to share their benefit payments with their tenants. In practice, few of them did. The planters pocketed 90 percent of the AAA benefit payments in 1933 and left their hapless croppers to shift for themselves. Browbeaten by generations of intimidation backed as needed by noose and fire, few tenants could find the courage or the means to make effective protest. When black and white tenants in Arkansas, where six out of ten farms were held in tenancy, organized the Southern Tenant Farmers Union (STFU) in July 1934, reprisals were swift and savage. "Riding bosses" descended on STFU meetings with whips and guns, hounded and beat organizers, and inveighed against the pernicious influence of "outside agitators," including the prominent socialist Norman Thomas. Pummeled off a speaker's platform by sheriff's deputies in the town of Birdsong, Thomas was emphatically told, "We don't need no Gawd-damned Yankee Bastard to tell us what to do with our niggers."[30]

Many displaced croppers headed for the cities, where FERA checks or CWA jobs might tide them over. Others took to the roads, joining the itinerants pathetically westering in their jalopies like human tumbleweeds, their image forever etched in American memory by Steinbeck's touching portrayal of the Joad family in *Grapes of Wrath*. But as Norman Thomas insisted, while Steinbeck's Joads had been tractored off the land in the Dust Bowl, in the cotton South "it wasn't just the tractor turning up the land that drove people out; it was the deliberate displacement of the AAA."[31] In his masterful study of race relations in America, the Swedish economist Gunnar Myrdal described the AAA as a kind of American enclosure movement:

> Landlords have been made to reduce drastically the acreage of their main labor-requiring crops. They have been given a large part of the power over the local administration of this program. They have a strong economic incentive to reduce their tenant labor force, a large part of which consists of politically and legally impotent Negroes. Yet they have been asked not to make any such reduction. It would certainly not be compatible with usual human behavior, if this request generally

30. Schlesinger 2:378.
31. Davis 3:476.

had been fulfilled. Under the circumstances, there is no reason at all to be surprised about the wholesale decline in tenancy. Indeed, it would be surprising if it had not happened.[32]

Hounded out of Arkansas, a shaken Thomas went to Washington, secured an appointment with the president, and brought with him to the White House a copy of the AAA cotton contract. Pushing it across the desk toward Roosevelt, he pointed out Section 7, which required planters to make good-faith efforts to continue to employ tenants whose land was removed from production. "That can mean anything or nothing, can't it, Norman?" the president genially responded. Thomas was outraged. He described the plight of the southern sharecroppers as "potentially the most dangerous situation I have seen in America." He demanded that the president make a stand for social justice in the South by supporting the federal antilynching bill introduced in the Senate in January 1934. Only by making lynching a federal crime could the reign of terror that brooded over the South be broken. A presumptive majority favored the bill, Thomas argued; but it could reach the floor of the Senate for a vote only if the president lent his support for a motion to invoke the cloture rule and end a threatened southern filibuster. The argument discomforted Roosevelt. Just weeks earlier he had explained to NAACP secretary Walter White that he could not support the antilynching bill because "Southerners, by reason of the seniority rule in Congress, are chairmen or occupy strategic positions on most of the Senate and House committees. If I come out for the anti-lynching bill now, they will block every bill I ask Congress to pass to keep America from collapsing. I just can't take that risk." Supporting the STFU would especially complicate his relationship with Arkansas's own Joseph Robinson, the Senate majority leader; crucial to Roosevelt's legislative program, he had been slandered by the STFU's newspaper as "Greasy Joe." Roosevelt shared this calculated political reasoning with Thomas. "Now come, Norman," he said, "I'm a damned sight better politician than you are. I know the South, and there is arising a new generation of leaders and we've got to be patient."[33]

The patience the president counseled did not assuage Thomas, nor did it satisfy principled reformers within the New Deal administration. The plight of the southern sharecroppers, blacks especially, became the sharpest point of contention between two factions that struggled in the

32. Gunnar Myrdal, *An American Dilemma* (New York: Harper and Row, 1944), 258.
33. Davis 3:483–84; Schlesinger 2:37.

Department of Agriculture for control of the New Deal's agricultural policies and, through those policies, for the power to shape the future of rural American life. On the one side were the career agricultural bureaucrats, many of them ensconced in the department since the time of the first Secretary Wallace in the Harding era. Thoroughly marinated in the commercial culture of the Farm Bureau and the Extension Service, they clung to a single-minded conception of agriculture as a business enterprise and to a no less restrictive notion of their own responsibilities as public servants. "The job's simple," said George Peek, the first director of AAA and the old guard's great champion. "It's just to put up farm prices."[34]

Arrayed against "Henry's father's gang" was a group of young New Dealers, many of them bookish intellectuals and Ivy League lawyers with no practical knowledge of agriculture nor actual experience with rural life. One of them famously betrayed his city-slicker roots when he inquired about the welfare of the macaroni growers. Peek ridiculed them as "boys with their hair ablaze," but those blazing boys were in fact dedicated, conscience-driven reformers. They aimed at nothing less than leveraging the opportunity given them by the Depression crisis not just to bring prosperity to the biggest farmers but to bring justice and decent standards of living to all rural Americans, farm workers as well as landowners, black as well as white.

The reformers were concentrated in the legal division of AAA, headed by general counsel Jerome N. Frank. He assembled an unusually talented group of young lawyers, including Abe Fortas, Adlai Stevenson, and Alger Hiss, all of whom looked to Frank and to Assistant Secretary of Agriculture Rexford Tugwell for guidance and support.[35] In January 1935 Frank sent Mary Connor Myers to Arkansas to investigate the SFTU's claims about violations of Section 7. "Have heard one long story

34. Schlesinger 2:46.
35. Some other members of Frank's staff, perhaps including Hiss but certainly not including Frank himself, were organized in 1933 into a secretive Communist group. They met clandestinely, though more for radical conversation than political conspiring, in a Washington music studio run by the sister of the chief organizer, Hal Ware. Among them were Lee Pressman, Jon Abt, and Nathan Witt. Ware, son of the redoubtable agitator Ella Reeve "Mother" Bloor, had a vaguely defined consulting relationship with the Department of Agriculture and did nurture Communist elements in the Farmers Holiday movement. Aside from that extremely marginal and inconsequential activity, none of these closet radicals exerted any significant communist influence on AAA policy. For more on this group, see Whittaker Chambers, *Witness* (New York: Random House, 1952).

of human greed," she wired back to Frank. It was apparent to her that many planters regarded payments to croppers, in the words of one land-lord, "as little more than a gracious gesture," if they bothered to make the gesture at all.[36] Frank instructed Alger Hiss to draw up a new guide-line strengthening Section 7.

Hiss, an urbane twenty-eight-year-old Harvard law graduate, by his own admission not very knowledgeable about the cotton economy, was also innocent of the explosive volatility of the race issue in the South. He had drafted the original cotton code almost immediately on his ar-rival in Washington in 1933, and soon got a rough education in the mores of the region that his directive threatened to upset. When South Carolina senator Ellison "Cotton Ed" Smith learned that Hiss's contracts provided for checks going directly to tenants, he stormed into Hiss's office. "Young fella," he blustered, "you can't do this to my niggers, paying checks to them. They don't know what to do with the money. The money should come to me. I'll take care of them. They're mine." Following confrontations like that, Hiss had few illusions about AAA's impact on southern tenant farmers. "After the first year of the cotton program," he later explained, "it was clear that, for all its idealism, it was hurting and might further hurt the tenants because if a landowner was going to reduce production by a third, he had a third too many tenants or sharecroppers. Most of them depended on the little huts that were supplied and the garden patches where they were allowed to raise vegetables for themselves." The new agreement that Hiss now drew up in early 1935 "provided that no signer of a contract, no owner of land, could get rid of his tenants. He had to retain the same number of tenants. There were clauses that indicated they should be the same individuals. . . . They had a right to live in the huts that they'd been living in and to continue to have use of work animals and garden plots." In a monumental understatement, Hiss added that "this caused real turmoil."[37]

In the absence of AAA director Chester Davis, who had replaced Peek in December 1933 but shared many of Peek's views on farm policy, Frank caused Hiss's guideline to be promulgated as an administrative directive on February 1, 1935. It was a triumphant moment for the AAA

36. Donald H. Grubbs, *Cry from the Cotton: The Southern Tenant Farmers' Union and the New Deal* (Chapel Hill: University of North Carolina Press, 1971), 48–49, 22.
37. Katie Louchheim, ed., *The Making of the New Deal: The Insiders Speak* (Cam-bridge: Harvard University Press, 1983), 238–39.

liberals, a moment when, as Hiss recollected, they felt that they "were representing Secretary Wallace's view." But their triumph was short-lived. Wallace soon let them down, and hard. Davis rushed back to Washington, canceled the directive, and demanded that Wallace allow him to fire Frank and several members of Frank's overzealous staff. Wallace acceded, Roosevelt made no objection, and the liberals were summarily purged. Friendless and powerless, the displaced sharecroppers and tenants of the cotton belt were left to their own weak devices. Curiously, Hiss was spared from Davis's ax, but "from then on," Hiss later reflected, "my interest in Triple-A lessened and the fire went out of the whole thing."[38]

Thus AAA, like NRA, proved most effective not in promoting recovery, nor in protecting what Hugh Johnson called the "little fellow," but in salvaging the bacon of the biggest commercial interests, in this case the southern cotton lords. And while NRA had galvanized leaders like John L. Lewis to invigorate a labor movement that would soon convulse entire industries and revolutionize the status of American industrial workers, no really effective champions of the farmers displaced by AAA's policies ever emerged after Frank's liberals were purged. Tractored and AAA-ed off the land, they accumulated like dried weeds in the fence-corners of the American countryside, especially in the South. They remained a dazed and almost motionless mass, saved for the while from starvation by federal relief agencies but devoid of land, work, or prospects. "By some means or other," Lorena Hickok candidly observed, "these people have to be removed from the labor market. . . . The only way out is to remove from the labor market enough poor Whites and Blacks so that members of both races who are left will have some sort of chance."[39] On the far western edge of the cotton belt, in the sere wasteland of the Oklahoma-Texas-Kansas Dust Bowl, stark necessity had already put thousands of these pioneers of misfortune into motion. For the remainder of the 1930s millions of others continued to languish hopelessly in the old Southeast. It would take a war, in the next decade, to shake them loose.

BY EARLY 1935, as the New Deal approached the beginning of its third year, the liberals purged from AAA were not alone in their disillusionment. The fire of enthusiasm for Roosevelt's Hundred Days

38. Loucheim, *Making of the New Deal*, 239–40.
39. Lowitt and Beasley, *One Third of a Nation*, 158.

policies was flickering low for many who had cheered him in 1933. Brain Truster Raymond Moley, both the agent and the victim of Roosevelt's renunciation of internationalism at the London World Economic Conference in June 1933, left his government post a few months later. The gold-buying scheme had cost the president the service of several monetary traditionalists. Hugh Johnson had departed NRA. George Peek was gone from AAA. Budget director Lewis Douglas, already rattled by the abandonment of the gold standard in 1933, grew increasingly disenchanted with Roosevelt's fiscal unorthodoxy and resigned in August 1934.

In that same month, disaffected conservatives within the president's Democratic Party formed the American Liberty League. Its members included Al Smith, former Democratic Party chairman John J. Raskob, onetime Democratic presidential nominee John W. Davis, and a raft of corporate leaders like Alfred P. Sloan of General Motors and Sewell Avery of Montgomery Ward. Growing ever more shrill in their denunciation of the New Deal, they represented what Herbert Hoover scornfully called the "Wall Street model of human liberty." (Hoover pointedly declined an invitation to join.)[40]

The birth of the Liberty League marked the beginning of organized, articulate opposition to the New Deal on the right, including the right wing of the president's own party. But the worm of doubt about the New Deal's effectiveness and even its ultimate purposes also began to gnaw at others, including liberals. As 1935 opened, some ten million persons, more than 20 percent of the work force, still remained jobless. The country seemed to flounder, without a workable remedy to the afflictions from which it had been suffering now for half a decade. Even Lorena Hickok succumbed to the mood of disaffection. As early as April 1934 she confided to Hopkins from Texas: "At no time previously, since taking this job, have I been quite so discouraged." When a Texas businessman

---

40. The Liberty Leaguers hyperbolically fulminated against state socialism and the dictatorial ambitions of Roosevelt. No doubt their anxieties would have been exacerbated had they known that one of the president's closest advisers, Adolf Berle, had adopted the joking habit of addressing all correspondence to the president "Dear Caesar" and that the guests at Roosevelt's annual birthday dinner, given by the Cuff Links Club, composed of some of FDR's oldest supporters, to whom he had given gold cuff links in thanks for support in his vice-presidential bid of 1920, came in Roman garb. FDR himself was usually attired in a royal purple toga, crowned with laurel, and played to the hilt the role of imperious master of the revels. See Davis 3:347–48.

unapologetically told her that he favored fascism for the United States, she confessed to Hopkins that "honestly, after nearly a year of traveling about this country, I'm almost forced to agree with him. If I were 20 years younger and weighed 75 pounds less, I think I'd start out to be the Joan of Arc of the Fascist movement in the United States. . . . I've been out on this trip now for a little more than two weeks. In all that time I've hardly met a single person who seemed confident and cheerful. Relief loads are mounting, They can't see any improvement. . . . Nobody seems to think any more that the thing is going to WORK."[41]

In a summary report to Hopkins on New Year's Day 1935, Hickok rehearsed her worries about a "stranded generation": men over forty with half-grown families, people who might never get their jobs back. "Through loss of skill, through mental and physical deterioration due to long enforced idleness, the relief clients, the people who have been longest without work, are gradually being forced into the class of un-employables — rusty tools, abandoned, not worth using any more. . . . And so they go on — the gaunt, ragged legion of the industrially damned. Bewildered, apathetic, many of them terrifyingly patient."[42]

But the mysterious patience of the American people in the face of adversity that had so consistently impressed Hickok and others was show-ing signs of rubbing thin. Evidence of a polarization in the electorate and of a momentous shift in the American center of political gravity was becoming increasingly apparent. The frustration born of raised hopes and stalled progress began to manifest itself ever more stridently as 1934 wore on and recovery remained beyond reach. Frustration some-times sought unconventional outlets. Louisiana's outrageous Senator Huey P. Long launched his Share Our Wealth Society in January 1934 with promises "to make every man a king" through wholesale (and wholly fantastic) redistribution of the national patrimony. In the same month, California physician Dr. Francis Townsend established Old Age Revolving Pensions, Ltd., to promote his fetching nostrum of paying two hundred dollars monthly to all Americans over sixty. Led by militant longshoremen, a general strike briefly paralyzed San Francisco in July 1934. Other strikers shut down the textile mills from New England to the Carolinas in September. The crusading novelist Upton Sinclair ran for governor in California on a utopian "production-for-use" commu-nitarian platform; he polled nearly a million votes in the November

41. Lowitt and Beasley, One Third of a Nation, 218.
42. Lowitt and Beasley, One Third of a Nation, 361–63.

election. Just days later, the Reverend Charles Coughlin, the eccentric but widely popular "radio priest" from Royal Oak, Michigan, announced the formation of the National Union for Social Justice as a vehicle to promote his own peculiar blend of inflation and anti-Semitism.

In November 1934 this bubbling discontent wrought an unprecedented political result. It had been—and remains—a truism of American politics that the presidential party loses congressional seats in off-year elections, but in the new Congress that was to be installed in January 1935, it was the Republicans who lost, going from 117 to 103 seats in the House and from 35 to 25 seats in the Senate. Democrats would now enjoy two-thirds majorities in both chambers. Roosevelt had set the stage for the sweeping Democratic victories in a June 1934 Fireside Chat, when he asked his listeners to "judge recovery" by "the plain facts of your individual situation. Are you better off than you were last year?" In fact, recovery remained out of reach, and few Americans were appreciably better off then they had been a year earlier, but Roosevelt's Democrats benefited less from what they had done than from the fact that they had done something. How long the American people would be satisfied with mere action, without measurable results, remained anybody's guess.

Enfolded in the numbers that defined the huge Democratic majorities was a development of significant political consequence: the party was growing ever more rapidly from its traditional southern base to embrace new constituencies in the great industrial cities of the North and the commercial centers of the West. Almost the only Republican gains in the 1934 congressional elections were in upstate New York, in rural Protestant districts in central and southern Ohio, Indiana, and Illinois, and on the Great Plains—all areas that were inexorably shrinking in demographic and economic importance. The fastest-growing population groups in America—Catholic and Jewish immigrants and their voting-age second-generation children—were moving en masse into the Democratic Party. So were blacks in those northern precincts where they could vote. The future of African-American political loyalties was strongly signaled in Chicago, where the black Democrat Arthur W. Mitchell defeated the black Republican Oscar De Priest to become the first black Democrat ever elected to Congress. How would these swelling constituencies, for so long made to feel like outsiders, ground down by half a decade of Depression, and now freshly and hugely enfranchised, wield their new power? That very question worried the old-guard Democratic leaders in the House, who began immediately to seek ways to control the potentially unruly majority they now commanded. When the new Congress convened in early 1935, the leadership raised from 145 to 218 the number of signatures required for a discharge petition, the motion that could compel a committee to release a bill for discussion on the House floor. Even that transparent effort to corral the new Congress's radicalism might prove insufficient—especially if the president turned radical himself.[43]

Roosevelt now stood in a position analogous to Lincoln's after the failure of the Peninsula Campaign. Had George McClellan's troops taken Richmond in the summer of 1862, the Union would in all likelihood have been restored with slavery intact, given Lincoln's stated purpose at the time that his sole war aim was to restore the Union and nothing more. By retreating from Richmond and leaving Lee and the Confederacy to fight another day, McClellan ensured that the war would escalate, that it would go on until slavery was rooted out and the social and economic order of the old South undone. As Roosevelt in the early weeks of 1935 contemplated the New Deal's disappointing economic performance, he might have reflected on what that long-ago military defeat had done for Lincoln. For had Hugh Johnson and Henry Wallace been swiftly successful in restoring prosperity by 1934, the most ambitious reform aspirations of the New Deal might never have come to pass. It was, ironically enough, the continuing economic crisis that helped elect the reform-minded Democratic majority in 1934 and gave Roosevelt his opportunity not just to revitalize the economy but to reshape the very contours of American life.

Driving with his staff to a racetrack near Washington just after the November 1934 elections, Harry Hopkins was keen with anticipation. Perhaps lacking a detailed sense of history past but sensing unerringly that much history could now be made, he burst out: "Boys—this is our hour. We've got to get everything we want—a works program, social security, wages and hours, everything—now or never. Get your minds to work on developing a complete ticket to provide security for all the folks of this country up and down and across the board."[44] As much as any statement, Hopkins's exclamation defined a charter for 1935, a year that would witness the fullest triumph of the New Deal's reform agenda.

43. See the brief but excellent summary in Michael Barone, *Our Country: The Shaping of American from Roosevelt to Reagan* (New York: Free Press, 1990), 69–78.
44. Robert E. Sherwood, *Roosevelt and Hopkins: An Intimate History* (New York: Grosset and Dunlap, 1948, 1950), 65.

8

The Rumble of Discontent

I wish there were a few million radicals.
                    —Louisiana senator Huey P. Long, April 1935

As 1935 opened, what history was to remember as the New Deal had
not yet happened. Franklin Roosevelt had given the country an abundance of the "bold, persistent experimentation" that he had promised
in the presidential campaign of 1932, as well as a stiff dose of the "action
along new lines . . . action, action" that he had urged upon his advisers
just before taking office in 1933. The sheer activism of the new administration no doubt helped to shore up the national spirit in a season of
despair, as did Roosevelt's own carbonated optimism—"it seemed to
generate from him as naturally as heat from fire," one awed presidential
dinner guest wrote.[1] But nations—and their leaders—can subsist on
solely spiritual nourishment little longer than they can live on bread
alone. Despite the exhilaration of the Hundred Days, despite the exertions of the NRA and the AAA, despite the reopening of the banks and
the efforts of federal relief agencies, despite all the ingenuity and exuberance of Roosevelt and his New Dealers, the Depression persisted.
After two full years of the New Deal, one in five American workers
remained jobless. The tonic effect of Roosevelt's inaugural declaration
that "the only thing we have to fear is fear itself" had long since worn
off. To many of those who had put their faith in Roosevelt in 1932, and
especially to those who had always hoped for something more dramatic
than his prudent and piecemeal reformism, the New Deal appeared,
even before it reached its second anniversary, to be a spent political

1. Jerre Mangione, *The Dream and the Deal: The Federal Writers Project, 1933–1945*
   (Boston: Little, Brown, 1972), 11.

218

force. If the buoyant president had a coherent vision of a future that he deemed it his destiny to bring about, it remained scarcely visible to the American people.

On many sides, impatience with Roosevelt's admittedly energetic but apparently ineffective leadership deepened through 1934. On the right, conservative Republicans like Herbert Hoover and disaffected Democrats like Al Smith nattered crankily about the loss of individual liberty and the corruption of American ideals. Some of them gathered in the American Liberty League. Others worked to make the Republican Party the vessel of ultimate salvation from Roosevelt's alleged follies. For the moment they bided their time and awaited the catastrophe that they believed inevitably lay ahead.

Disillusionment with Roosevelt ran deepest and most dangerously on the left, especially among jobless workers and busted farmers, among reformers and visionaries who had been led to giddy heights of expectation by Roosevelt's aggressive presidential beginning, and among radicals who saw in the Depression the clinching proof that American capitalism was defunct, beyond all hope of salvation or melioration. The prolonged agonies and frustrations of those unquiet souls incubated countless prescriptions to lift the nation's afflictions as the Depression stubbornly lingered. Many of the nostrums that sprouted in the soil of the Depression's misery tested the limits of orthodoxy. Some tested the boundaries of credibility. Together, they tested the very fabric of American political culture—and eventually helped to stretch it.

ROOSEVELT'S DREAM of advancing liberalism by forging a new electoral union of forward-thinking Democrats and progressive Republicans threatened to degenerate into a nightmare in which the various progressive forces in the country might so fragment as to lose all capacity for common political action. The very plurality of the "different so-called progressive and liberal organizations that are cropping up all over the country," one adviser warned in early 1935, threatened the president's political viability and even the effectiveness of the liberal cause.[2] The Senate Progressive Republicans like California's Hiram Johnson, New Mexico's Bronson Cutting, and Wisconsin's Robert La Follette Jr.,

2. The remark was made by David K. Niles, a former operative in the La Follette presidential campaign of 1924, director of the liberal Ford Hall Forum in Boston, and associate of Felix Frankfurter. Niles's worries led to a meeting between Roosevelt and a group of progressive Republican senators at the White House on May 14, 1935. An account is in Davis 3:508ff.

as well as Montana's Burton Wheeler, were growing restive. Mostly from rural states, mostly in favor of inflation, and mostly isolationist in foreign policy, they increasingly chafed at Roosevelt's cautious monetary policies, at the smallness and hesitation of his steps away from fiscal orthodoxy, at his alleged mollycoddling of big business and Wall Street, and at disturbing signs of his renascent internationalism. Wheeler, a nominal Democrat who had been La Follette's father's running mate on the Progressive ticket in 1924, was openly discussing the need for a third party in 1936. In Wisconsin, the redoubtable La Follette and his brother, Philip, like their father before them, broke with the state Republican Party in May 1934 and launched a new Progressive Party, with Roosevelt's quiet support. Yet Philip La Follette soon declared: "We are not liberals! Liberalism is nothing but a sort of milk-and-water tolerance. . . . I believe in a fundamental and basic change. I think a cooperative society based on American traditions is inevitable."[3]

La Follette never explained precisely what that "cooperative society" might look like, but in neighboring Minnesota, Farmer-Labor Party leader Floyd Bjerstjerne Olson, governor since 1932, was giving extravagant definition to his own vision of a "cooperative commonwealth." Though Roosevelt had assisted his election in 1932 and tacitly backed him for reelection in 1934, Olson, like the La Follettes, loudly declaimed: "I am not a liberal. I am a radical. You bet your life I'm a radical. You might say I'm radical as hell!" Lorena Hickok reported in late 1933 that "this boy Olson is, in my opinion, about the smartest 'Red' in this country." Olson blustered to Hickok: "You go back to Washington and tell 'em that Olson is taking recruits for the Minnesota National Guard, and he isn't taking anybody who doesn't carry a Red card."[4] A former Wobbly and a child of the quasi-socialist Non-Partisan League that had swept the northern wheat belt in the World War I era, Olson was American radicalism's native son, a big, laughing, broad-shouldered, sandy-haired man with deep roots in the populist soil that covered much of the nation's agrarian heartland. Like his People's Party antecedents of the 1890s, he demanded government ownership of key industries.

Ideas like that appealed strongly to the intellectuals associated with the League for Independent Political Action, founded in 1929 by the

---

3. Schlesinger 3:107.
4. Leuchtenburg, 96; Schlesinger 3:99; Richard Lowitt and Maurine Beasley, eds., *One Third of a Nation: Lorena Hickok Reports on the Great Depression* (Urbana: University of Illinois Press, 1981), 136–37.

University of Chicago economist Paul H. Douglas and the dean of American philosophers, John Dewey. "Capitalism must be destroyed," the league declared. Dewey himself said of the New Deal's effort to create a "controlled and humanized capitalism" that "no such compromise with a decaying system is possible." The league advocated socialism in all but name—a controlled and humanized socialism, it might be charitably called, committed to tempering its collectivist regime with tolerance for differences and respect for individual freedoms, but dedicated nonetheless to a systemic egalitarianism under pervasive state control. Dewey and the league carried forward a thread of political thought that ran far back into the American past. Their nemesis was laissez-faire capitalism. Their Bible was Edward Bellamy's utopian tract of 1888, *Looking Backward*, which portrayed a regimented, antiseptic, but serene future society eternally prospering under a system of benevolent direction by the central state. Their forum was the magazine *Common Sense*, founded in 1932 by Yale graduate Alfred Bingham, who considered himself the chief steward of the progressive-era tradition of national economic planning and state direction of the economy. Their special hero, for a season, was Floyd Olson. In him they saw a practicing politician who seemed open to some decidedly unconventional political ideas. Olson thrilled the league's somewhat dreamy loyalists when he talked about production for use, not for profit, and declared that "American capitalism cannot be reformed." "A third party must arise," Olson wrote in *Common Sense* in 1935, "and preach the gospel of government and collective ownership of the means of production and distribution." "Whether there will be a third party in 1936," Olson told an interviewer, "depends mainly on Mr. Roosevelt." As for its leadership: maybe Bob La Follette or Burton Wheeler; "I think I'm a little too radical," Olson conceded. "How about 1940?" the interviewer persisted. "Maybe by then I won't be radical enough," Olson replied.[5] Partisans of the league loved this line of thinking. So did the handful of sincere citizens, notably the indefatigable crusader Norman Thomas, who remained in the American Socialist Party.

But for some, Olson and even the Socialists were not then radical enough, nor ever would be. Members of the Communist Party of the United States of America (CPUSA) believed that nothing less than the reconstruction of American society on the Soviet model would consti-

---

5. Schlesinger 3:104. In fact, by 1940 Olson would be dead. He died in 1936, at the age of forty-four.

tute a proper use of the opportunity the Depression presented. Now, in the moment of capitalism's unarguable collapse, was the time to catalyze the inevitable revolution that Marxist theory predicted. Party doctrine in 1933–34 dictated no compromise and no cooperation with "bourgeois democracy." The party's official organ, the *Daily Worker*, damned the NRA as a "fascist slave program." CPUSA general secretary Earl Browder said in 1934 that "Roosevelt's program is the same as that of finance capital the world over. . . . [I]t is the same," he declared with much hyperbole and no shame, "as Hitler's program."[6]

Disgruntled members of Eugene Debs's Socialist Party had broken away to form the CPUSA in 1919. Riven through the 1920s by faction-fighting between Trotskyists and Stalinists, and hobbled by endless doctrinal arguments with other leftist groups like the socialists, the party eventually united in 1932 behind presidential candidate William Z. Foster. Foster and his African-American running mate, James Ford, polled some 102,000 votes. That was an all-time electoral high for the party, but far less than the 884,000 thousand votes cast for Norman Thomas, and a number that was dwarfed by the 22.8 million ballots for Roosevelt. The Foster-Ford ticket nevertheless attracted some notable sympathizers, including the novelists John Dos Passos and Sherwood Anderson, the philosopher Sidney Hook, the literary critic Edmund Wilson, and the Harlem poet Langston Hughes, all of whom signed a manifesto declaring that "as responsible intellectual workers we have aligned ourselves with the frankly revolutionary Communist Party."[7]

The party dedicated itself in the early Depression years to staging political demonstrations (often the occasions for bloody melees pitting rock-throwing demonstrators against truncheon-wielding police), organizing Unemployment Councils to push for more generous relief payments, leading rent strikes and hunger marches, trying to unionize workers through the Trade Union Unity League, and recruiting members in the African-American community. When nine young black men were arrested and charged with gang-raping two white girls in a boxcar near Scottsboro, Alabama, in 1931, the party's legal arm, the International Labor Defense, took up their defense. The party energetically exploited its role in the case of the "Scottsboro Boys" to win support in the black community but enjoyed only modest success, especially since all nine

6. Schlesinger 3:190.
7. Harvey Klehr and John Earl Haynes, *The American Communist Movement: Storming Heaven Itself* (New York: Twayne, 1992), 67.

defendants were convicted by an all-white Alabama jury and sentenced to the electric chair.[8] The party's difficulties among African-Americans also stemmed in no small part from a 1928 Comintern resolution defining American Negroes as a subject nation and calling for black self-determination—a notion so incendiary to southern whites that most black American Communists refused to endorse it. Blacks never amounted to more than 10 percent of the party's membership.

But though they made some inroads among industrial workers, raised some hell in the streets, and fought, often courageously, for the rights of black Americans, the American Communists remained a small and isolated group. Three-fifths of them were foreign born, with especially heavy representation among Finns in the upper Midwest and Jews in the big cities. One-third of all members were New Yorkers, with other concentrations in Cleveland, Detroit, Chicago, and San Francisco. All told, the party counted fewer than thirty thousand members in 1934. After five years of depression, and with millions still unemployed, that number testified bluntly to the great distance that separated Communist doctrine and tactics from American political reality.

Yet the isolation of the Communists still left plenty of room for radicalism—a peculiarly American style of radicalism—in the churning political cauldron of the Depression decade. Whether the New Deal could contain and channel that radicalism, or whether it would be swept away by it, was a question that nagged at many New Dealers. "The country is much more radical than the Administration," Interior Secretary Harold Ickes noted in his diary on September 15, 1934. Roosevelt, he thought, "would have to move further to the left in order to hold the country. . . . If Roosevelt can't hold the country within reasonable safe limit [sic], no one else can possibly hope to do so. . . . [A] breakdown on the part of the Administration would result in an extreme radical movement, the extent of which no one could foresee."[9]

The practical difficulties that attended such a presidential move to the left soon presented themselves in California, then as later a fertile hatchery of novelties both political and social. What the visiting Englishman James Bryce wrote about California in the 1880s still held true half a century later: "It is thoroughly American, but most so in those

8. The ILD carried the case on appeal to the U.S. Supreme Court, which in 1935 reversed the original convictions and ordered a new trial. Charges against four of the defendants were eventually dropped, but the remaining five were again found guilty. None was executed, but the last defendant remained in prison until 1950.
9. Ickes Diary 1:195–96.

points wherein the Old World differs from the New.. . . . Changes of public sentiment are sudden and violent. . . . [T]he masses are impatient, accustomed to blame everything and everybody but themselves for the slow approach of the millennium, ready to try instant, even if perilous, remedies for a present evil."[10] Among the last outposts of the American frontier, California held a disproportionate share of the frontier's usual assortment of rootless, restless souls, including sun-seekers from the Midwest, refugees from the Dust Bowl, immigrants from Mexico and the far shores of the Pacific, and drifters of every purpose and credo. As on all previous frontiers, these fluid and questing masses were ready recruits for promoters of material prosperity and merchants of spiritual solace. In the 1920s they had flocked by the tens of thousands to Los Angeles to hear the Four-Square Gospel of the melodramatic revivalist Aimee Semple McPherson.

In this California atmosphere of perpetual social and psychological ferment, the Depression summoned forth not one but two new prophets. Both were no less alluring in their assurances of earthly salvation than was McPherson in her costumed pageants evoking the heavenly reward that awaited the righteous.

The first was an obscure sixty-six-year-old physician, Dr. Francis Everett Townsend. In September 1933 he sent a letter to his local newspaper in the sun-washed community of Long Beach, where he had intermittently practiced medicine and dabbled in real estate since 1919. In a homely allusion to the tactics of the AAA, he said that "it is just as necessary to make some disposal of our surplus workers, as it is to dispose of our surplus wheat or corn."[11] (He sensitively refrained from invoking the examples of surplus cotton and pigs.) The particular surplus workers the sexagenarian Townsend had in mind were the elderly. As shortly refined, Townsend's plan called for monthly payments of two hundred to all persons over the age of sixty who agreed both to retire from active employment and to spend the money in the month they received it. A national 2 percent value-added tax, assessed at every transaction as a product made its way from raw material to final market, was to finance the scheme. The effects of his plan, Townsend claimed, were almost endlessly beneficial: it would directly aid the deserving elderly, raise wages by shrinking the labor pool, and stimulate recovery through the

10. James Bryce, *The American Commonwealth*, 3d ed. (New York: Macmillan, 1895), 2:425.
11. Schlesinger 3:31.

forced circulation of all those monthly checks. It seemed too good to be true, and it was.

Analysts then and later have agreed that Townsend's plan was as economically daft as it was politically seductive. Fully funding the recommended monthly payments to the 9 percent of the American population over the age of sixty would soak up half the national income and double the national tax burden. Simply transferring purchasing power from the taxed young to the consuming old would do little to increase aggregate consumption. And the value-added tax mechanism might well promote the growth of monopolies, as firms integrated to avoid taxable transactions with suppliers and contractors.

Despite these objections, Townsend fever spread rapidly. Within weeks after the gray-haired doctor's letter, Townsend Clubs sprouted like mushrooms after a spring rain, first in the always fertile social humus of California, then throughout the rest of the country. In meetings redolent of old-time Gospel revivalism, the Townsendites circulated and signed petitions demanding a federal law to make Dr. Townsend's dream a reality. In January 1934 Townsend formally incorporated this sprawling movement as Old Age Revolving Pensions, Ltd. A year later, he launched a newsletter, the *Townsend National Weekly*. By then the number of Townsend Clubs was approaching five thousand, with over two million members. As many as twenty-five million Americans had signed Townsend's petitions. The California congressional delegation was largely beholden to Townsendite support in the elections of 1934. One grateful recipient of that support introduced a bill containing Townsend's recommendations when the new congressional session opened in January 1935. That bill conflicted directly with the as yet unintroduced Social Security bill that the Roosevelt administration was preparing.

In the same month during which Dr. Townsend was inscribing his way to notoriety with his fateful letter to the *Long Beach Press-Telegram*, an already notorious figure was writing his own way onto the center of the California political stage. Upton Sinclair, celebrated muckraker, author of nearly four dozen books, cudgel of capitalism, lifelong member of the Socialist Party, addict of causes, romantic and eccentric champion of the underdog, a man who subsisted largely on a diet of brown rice, fruit, and celery, a conscience-driven sentimentalist whom H. L. Mencken described as believing in more things than any other man in the world, published a characteristically impassioned pamphlet entitled *I, Governor of California and How I Ended Poverty*. Like his hero Edward Bellamy, Sinclair cast his political vision in the form of a utopian fantasy (his pamphlet's subtitle was *A True Story of the Future*). In the limpid prose that had endeared him to two generations of readers, Sinclair described his campaign and election and his swift implementation of the program he called EPIC—End Poverty in California. The genius of EPIC consisted in a proposal that Floyd Olson and the League for Independent Political Action could find congenial: the state would seize idle lands and factories and turn them over to farmers' and workers' cooperatives for production-for-use. In time, Sinclair predicted, these "public industries" would drive private industry out of business and usher in "The Cooperative Commonwealth."[12] In pursuit of that goal, Sinclair changed his party registration and declared himself a candidate for the Democratic nomination for governor.

To the astonishment of many party regulars, a groundswell of support, propelled by the desperate yearnings of Depression-plagued Californians, carried Sinclair to victory in the Democratic Party primary election in August 1934. Sinclair's candidacy created an instant dilemma for Franklin Roosevelt. Here was a bona fide gubernatorial nominee who was a Democrat, but one whose politics were wildly to the left of the president's and fantastically unsettling to most members of the president's party. Sinclair demanded a public presidential endorsement. The Roosevelt charm mollified Sinclair for a time after a personal meeting at Hyde Park in early September 1934. The president, Sinclair told reporters, was "one of the kindest and most genial and frank and open-minded and lovable men I have ever met."[13] But Roosevelt was not about to embrace what he regarded as Sinclair's lunatic proposals for confiscation of private property and the abolition of the profit system. The president kept his public silence on Sinclair's candidacy and abandoned the quixotic novelist to the ferocious assaults of California Republicans, orchestrated largely by movie magnate Louis B. Mayer. In a campaign unusually savage even by California's mud-and-circuses standards, Sinclair went down to decisive defeat. He salvaged what he could from the sorry episode by making it the subject of a new book: *I, Candidate for Governor: And How I Got Licked*.

EPIC had been endorsed by intellectuals like John Dos Passos and Theodore Dreiser, as well as by International Ladies Garment Workers Union leader David Dubinsky. They were sorely disappointed by the

---

12. Schlesinger 3:111–23; Davis 3:2–5, 423ff.
13. Davis 3:409.

outcome in California. Sinclair's defeat struck many on the left as emblematic of the problems with politics as usual, with the traditional political parties, and with Franklin Roosevelt himself, especially since Roosevelt's own efforts to grapple with the Depression had produced little result. "Failure is a hard word," declared the radical periodical *Common Sense* in late 1934, giving voice to the thoughts of many on the increasingly fractious and agitated left. "Yet we believe the record indicates that nothing but failure can be expected from the New Deal."[14]

As that sentiment spread, the possibility loomed that a leader might arise, someone more worldly than the moonstruck Sinclair, more broad-gauged than the single-issue Townsend, more focused and disciplined than the sometimes feckless Olson, more earthy than the cerebral crowd around *Common Sense*, more in the American grain than the Socialists or the Communists—someone who could piece together a new political vessel to hold all the boiling discontents of a people increasingly confounded by the Depression. Politics, no less than nature, abhors a vacuum. Roosevelt had easily filled the space evacuated by Hoover's policy failures, but what might rush into the void created by the apparent failure of the New Deal? Perhaps this was one of those moments—rare in American history but its possibilities apparent even in other advanced democracies, as the Nazi ascendancy in Germany vividly illustrated—when a mass movement might wrest the initiative from the established political authorities and impose its own agenda on the nation.

WHO MIGHT LEAD such a movement? Extraordinary times generated extraordinary candidates, and in extraordinary profusion. Of the legions of radicals and demagogues and nostrum-mongers and just plain crackpots who flourished in the heated atmosphere of the Depression, none seemed at first a more unlikely messiah than the Reverend Charles Edward Coughlin, a Canadian-born Roman Catholic priest.

In 1926, at the age of thirty-four, Coughlin became the pastor of a tiny new parish in the Detroit suburb of Royal Oak, its church designated as a shrine to the recently canonized St. Therese of the Little Flower of Jesus. Numbering but twenty-five Catholic families, Coughlin's modest flock seemed an improbable power base from which to reach for national attention. And the bleak, gritty community of Royal Oak lay far from the hubs of national influence.

Yet Coughlin's little congregation, composed mostly of autoworkers

14. *Common Sense*, September 1934, 2, quoted in Leuchtenburg, 95.

just prosperous enough to move to suburbia from the soot and clang of Detroit's inner city, represented a rising force in American political life. These lower-middle-class Catholics, many of them scarcely a generation removed from their ancestral old countries, were grateful but wary beneficiaries of 1920s prosperity. They were not the poorest Americans, but rather those who had managed to step up just a rung or two on the ladder of social mobility. They were the kinds of people who proudly decorated their front parlors with framed photographs from the color rotogravure section of the Sunday newspaper, took an occasional vacation, bought a car on the installment plan, looked forward to one day owning their own home free and clear. The Depression had not so much impoverished them as it had swiftly checked their brave march toward realizing the American dream. In Royal Oak and in scores of other neighborhoods in and around the great industrial cities of the Northeast and upper Midwest, they huddled in their tightly knit ethnic enclaves, fretted about their precarious economic status, and fumed at what they felt was the implacable hostility of the Protestant majority. Coughlin had his own reminder of that hostility when the Ku Klux Klan welcomed him to Royal Oak by burning a cross on his church lawn. Leaders like Boston's James Michael Curley had already made careers out of quickening the anxieties and playing on the resentments of people like Coughlin's parishioners, but Curley and other Catholic mayors, like Tammany Hall's Jimmy Walker in New York and Chicago's Anton Cermak, were local figures. Coughlin aimed for national stature. The vehicle that would take him there, he believed, was a wondrous, newfangled technology scarcely a decade old: the radio.

The political and social effects of radio were only beginning to be felt in the late 1920s, let alone understood. For several years following the first commercial broadcasts on Detroit station WWJ in 1920, most radio stations operated at low power, usually under a hundred watts. Signals could be reliably transmitted only a few miles. Stations, many of them sponsored by local churches, labor unions, or ethnic organizations, served markets scarcely larger than neighborhoods. Much programming—religious services, talk shows, vaudeville entertainments, and "nationality hours" featuring news of Poland or Italy—catered to discrete ethnic communities in their native, old-world tongues. Radio thus made its debut as a technology that strengthened local institutions. But the new medium swiftly developed into an electronic floodgate through which flowed a one-way tide of mass cultural products that began to swamp the values and manners and tastes of once-isolated localities. The first five-thousand-watt transmitters appeared in 1925, and ten-thousand–watt stations were broadcasting by 1928. Networks soon provided platforms for commercially sponsored and nationally syndicated programs, beginning with *Amos 'n' Andy*, a perennially popular comedy show that first went on the air in 1928.

Radio assaulted the insularity of local communities. It also, not incidentally, catalyzed the homogenization of American popular culture. And it promised to revolutionize politics. Scholars later employed the term "disintermediation" to describe the potential political effects of radio (and eventually, of course, television). Radio provided a means to concentrate and exercise power from the top, to bypass and shrink the influence of leaders and institutions that had previously mediated between individuals and local communities on the one side and the national political parties and the national government on the other. And as in the realm of culture, in the political realm radio was for all practical purposes a one-way conduit. Powerful voices flowed out over the airwaves and washed over listeners by the millions. Few of those listeners could answer back. The radio created a political environment unimaginably distant from the give-and-take of the town meeting, which Thomas Jefferson had praised as "the best school of political liberty the world ever saw." Radio might be a medium of awesome power for good or ill. Franklin Roosevelt was among the first to sense its political possibilities. Father Charles Coughlin was another.[15]

Coughlin started modestly enough, when a microphone attached to his pulpit on October 17, 1926, carried the words of his Sunday sermon to the listening audience of Detroit station WJR. Within three years stations in Chicago and Cincinnati were also carrying his message. In 1930 he struck a deal with the Columbia Broadcasting System to transmit his sermons nationwide. By the time the Depression had fully engulfed the country, tens of millions of Americans regularly gathered around their radio receivers on Sunday afternoons to listen to the "Radio Priest." In ethnic neighborhoods in the stricken industrial belt, residents could walk for blocks on a summer Sunday and never miss a word of Father Coughlin's voice radiating out of open parlor windows.

And what a voice it was! Lightly brushed with brogue, melodic and soothing, it was a voice, the novelist Wallace Stegner said, "of such

---

15. Lizabeth Cohen, *Making a New Deal: Industrial Workers in Chicago, 1919–1939* (Cambridge: Cambridge University Press, 1990), 129ff., offers an excellent discussion of the earliest impact of radio.

mellow richness, such manly, heart-warming, confidential intimacy, such emotional and ingratiating charm, that anyone turning past it on the radio dial almost automatically returned to hear it again." It was, Stegner concluded, "without doubt one of the great speaking voices of the twentieth century. . . . It was a voice made for promises."[16]

It was also a voice that increasingly spoke not of religion but of politics. Coughlin's earliest broadcasts addressed such topics as the meaning of the sacraments and the evils of birth control, but he struck out in a new direction when his sermon of January 12, 1930, ferociously attacked Communism—then threatening to win converts among the swelling ranks of Detroit's unemployed autoworkers. Before long, loosely adopting the Catholic social-justice doctrines expressed in the papal encyclicals *Rerum Novarum* (1891) and *Quadragesimo Anno* (1931), Coughlin was hurling invective at Herbert Hoover, denouncing international bankers, railing at the gold standard, demanding inflation—above all, inflation through the monetization of silver—and declaiming on the virtues of nationalizing the entire American banking system. "I knew damn well," he irreverently reflected, uncloaking the megalomania that would eventually help to undo him, "that the little people, the average man, was suffering. I also knew that no one had the courage to tell the truth about why the nation was in such mortal danger. I knew that if anyone was going to inform the American citizenry, it would have to be me."[17] Millions of listeners lapped up his message. By 1932 Coughlin's fan mail, much of it stuffed with cash, required the attention of 106 clerks and four personal secretaries. Two years later, he was receiving more mail than any other person in the United States, including the president.

Little of this, especially Coughlin's readiness to rain verbal blows on an already reeling Herbert Hoover, was lost on Franklin Roosevelt. In May 1931 a relative in Detroit wrote to Roosevelt that Coughlin "has a following just about equal to that of Mr. Ghandi. . . . He would like to tender his services. . . . He would be difficult to handle and might be full of dynamite, but I think you had better prepare to say 'yes' or 'no.'"

Roosevelt hesitated at first, but no politician aspiring to the presidency

16. Alan Brinkley, *Voices of Protest: Huey Long, Father Coughlin, and the Great Depression* (New York: Knopf, 1982), 90. For much of my account of both Coughlin and Huey Long, and especially for my understanding of the ideology they represented, I am deeply indebted to Brinkley's study.

17. Michael R. Beschloss, *Kennedy and Roosevelt: An Uneasy Alliance* (New York: Norton, 1980), 114.

could afford to ignore those dazzling Coughlin numbers. More specifically, Roosevelt doubtless saw in Coughlin a bridge to the Catholic immigrant communities that he hoped to bring into his national electoral coalition. Accordingly, Roosevelt cultivated Coughlin through two dependable Irish-Catholic intermediaries: the financier Joseph P. Kennedy and the liberal Detroit mayor, Frank Murphy. At their urging, the priest—"Padre," Roosevelt intimately called him—visited candidate Roosevelt twice in 1932 and sent him a sycophantish telegram upon Roosevelt's receipt of the Democratic nomination: "I am with you to the end. Say the word and I will follow."[18]

In the ensuing campaign, Coughlin sulfurously condemned Hoover, to Roosevelt's undoubted delight and certain benefit. In the early months of the New Deal the "padre" further ingratiated himself to Roosevelt with florid endorsements of the new president's political program. "The New Deal is Christ's deal!" he intoned. The country faced the choice, said Coughlin, of "Roosevelt or ruin." Intoxicated with his apparent access to power, Coughlin took to dropping in unannounced at the White House, joking chummily with Roosevelt's staff, lacing his remarks to reporters with intimate references to "the Boss," and presumptuously suggesting lists of good Catholics who should receive ambassadorial appointments. This false familiarity got to be too much for the president. "Who the hell does he think he is?" Roosevelt asked an aide. "He should run for the Presidency himself."[19]

Given the country's religious prejudices, Coughlin's Roman collar made such a run improbable. Given the Constitution, his Canadian birth made it impossible. But neither religious scruple nor legal impediment could compromise the Radio Priest's campaign against the Money Power—that old American nemesis, ensconced in Wall Street, entwined with the dread international bankers, its machinations, Coughlin darkly hinted, cunningly orchestrated by a sinister Jewish directorate. As the Depression persisted, as Roosevelt rehabilitated rather than expropriated the banks, and especially as he failed to pursue inflationary policies with sufficient vigor, Coughlin grew increasingly critical of the New Deal. When the Treasury Department in early 1934 sought to check the silverites by publishing a list of silver speculators that included the name of Coughlin's own private secretary, Coughlin raged against the enemies

18. Charles J. Tull, *Father Coughlin and the New Deal* (Syracuse: Syracuse University Press, 1965), 15.
19. Beschloss, *Kennedy and Roosevelt*, 116.

of "gentile silver" and challenged the Democratic Party, on pain of "political death," to explain "why there is want in the midst of plenty." Now more than ever, he pointedly announced, "I am in favor of *a* New Deal."[20]

Coughlin soon went further. The old political parties, he declared late in 1934, "are all but dead" and should "relinquish the skeletons of their putrefying carcasses to the halls of a historical museum."[21] On November 11, 1934, he announced the birth of a new political body, which he christened the National Union for Social Justice. Its platform of "Sixteen Principles" encompassed pleas for monetary reforms, as well as calls for the nationalization of key industries and protection of the rights of labor. Though it had scant organizational structure and an indeterminate membership—estimates ran as high as eight million—the National Union represented a potentially formidable new political force, one that might mobilize the immigrant industrial workers who by now had been seething in unwanted idleness for five years. In all but name, it was a new political party, or certainly aspired to be. In all but its demographic base, it resurrected the Populist movement of the 1890s, complete with monetary obsessions, conspiracy theories, cranky anti-internationalism, and innuendoes of anti-Semitism. Moving ever farther away from Roosevelt, whom he shortly accused of having "out-Hoovered Hoover" and protecting "plutocrats" as well as "communists," Coughlin soon seized an opportunity to field-test this new political machine.

On January 16, 1935, Roosevelt asked for approval of a treaty providing for American affiliation with the World Court, seated at The Hague. Many members of the president's official family thought from the outset that the proposal to join the Court was a political error. "I have been surprised all along that the President should make this such an issue as he has made it," Harold Ickes wrote in his diary. "I am confident that the sentiment of the country is overwhelmingly opposed to going into the League Court. . . . [I]f this proposition were put to a vote of the people, it would be defeated two to one."[22] But to Roosevelt, the proposal represented a small gesture that might temper the isolationist image he had projected at the time of the London Economic Conference. Roosevelt was growing increasingly convinced that the international situation was deteriorating dangerously, as evidenced by Japan's recent

20. Brinkley, *Voices of Protest*, 123.
21. Schlesinger 3:24.
22. Ickes Diary 1:284.

repudiation of the naval limitation agreements of the preceding decade and Tokyo's apparent determination to plunge ahead with the construction of a huge new battle fleet. In the face of such challenges, America could ill afford to stand by idly, Roosevelt reasoned. He hoped to send a modest signal to the world that he had not fully repudiated his own internationalist convictions, forged in the service of Woodrow Wilson, abandoned temporarily in 1932 and 1933, but awakened again in the gathering world crisis of the mid-1930s. Adherence to the Court might also serve an educational purpose at home, weaning Americans ever so slightly from the complacent parochialism they had reembraced after the debacle of the Great War. After careful polling of the huge Democratic majority in the new Senate, and with assurances that American sovereignty would be in no way imperiled by Court membership, Roosevelt went ahead, confident of success.

Coughlin had other ideas. On Sunday, January 27, he preached over the airwaves on "the menace of the World Court," denouncing Roosevelt's proposal as well as "the international bankers" who were the alleged beneficiaries of the president's nefarious ploy. He urged his listeners to send telegrams to their senators demanding a "no" vote. Prodded also by the isolationist Hearst press, Coughlin's vast audience responded with an avalanche of telegrams, wheelbarrowed by the hundreds of thousands into the Senate Office Building on the morning of Monday, January 28. The following day the Senate failed to muster the two-thirds vote necessary to ratify the Court treaty. "I do not intend to have these gentlemen whose names I cannot even pronounce, let alone spell, passing upon the rights of the American people," declared Louisiana senator Huey Long. The Court proposal, seemingly a sure thing just days earlier, died. Roosevelt was stunned. "The radio talks of people like Coughlin turned the trick against us," he gloomily wrote to a friend.[23]

The World Court fight provided a lightning demonstration of Coughlin's power and dealt a stinging blow to Roosevelt. "The legend of invulnerability fades fast," wrote the columnist Arthur Krock. Roosevelt's considerable political reputation had perceptibly shrunk, not to mention his hard political influence, especially in the increasingly urgent realm of diplomacy. If even the modest and largely symbolic act of associating

23. T. Harry Williams, *Huey Long* (New York: Knopf, 1969), 800; Elliott Roosevelt, ed., *FDR: His Personal Letters, 1928–1945* (New York: Duell, Sloan, and Pearce, 1950), 451.

with the international tribunal at The Hague could be so summarily rejected, there seemed little prospect that Roosevelt could nudge his countrymen away from their historic isolationism and toward any kind of meaningful commitment to join with the other democracies in resisting the rising menace of dictatorship and aggression. Roosevelt was especially bitter about the senators who had been swayed by Coughlin's campaign. "As to the 36 Gentlemen who voted against the principle of a World Court," he wrote to Senate Majority Leader Joseph Robinson, "I am inclined to think that if they ever get to Heaven they will be doing a great deal of apologizing for a very long time—that is if God is against war—and I think he is."[24]

No less dispiriting to FDR than the actual defeat on the World Court treaty was the manner of its accomplishment. As Coughlin moved to consolidate and wield his political influence, he exhibited a wicked genius for unsealing some of the dankest chambers of the national soul. He played guilefully on his followers' worst instincts: their suspicious provincialism, their unworldly ignorance, their yearning for simple explanations and extravagant remedies for their undeniable problems, their readiness to believe in conspiracies, their sulky resentments, and their all too human capacity for hatred. The National Union for Social Justice remained an inchoate entity in early 1935, and Coughlin's sustainable political strength was still a matter of conjecture. But if the Radio Priest could succeed in shepherding his followers into an alliance with some of the other dissident protest movements rumbling across the land, those led by Townsend and Sinclair in California, by Olson and the La Follettes in the upper Midwest, and, especially, by the mercurial senator from Louisiana, Huey Pierce Long, there was no telling what disruptive furies might be unleashed.

Of all those figures, Long was the shrewdest operator and the most thoroughly professional politician. He had brains, money, ambition, extravagant oratorical skills, a gift for political theater, and a lupine instinct for the nation's political jugular. He was the radical most likely to succeed. Long was also an extreme example of a political species native to American democracy, a species recognizable by its distinctive tongue. Long spoke a language more passionate and colorful than others of his genus, but like Coughlin he spoke nevertheless in the familiar accents of American populism. Populism was an American-made idiom. It was

24. Edgar B. Nixon, ed., *Franklin D. Roosevelt and Foreign Affairs* (Cambridge: Belknap Press of Harvard University Press, 1969), 2:381.

audible to listeners as far back as Alexis de Tocqueville in the days of Andrew Jackson. It swelled to a roar in the People's Party upheavals of the 1890s and never fully subsided. Often cast in the rough cadences of untutored, rural American speech, the populist dialect gave voice to the fears of the powerless and the animosities of the alienated. It spoke of equality and freedom, but the greater of these was equality. Equality, Tocqueville wrote, was the principal "passion" of the Americans. In pursuit of equality, the Americans were "ardent, insatiable, incessant, invincible; they call for equality in freedom; and if they cannot obtain that, they still call for equality in slavery. They will endure poverty, servitude, barbarism, but they will not endure aristocracy."[25] Populism contrasted the virtues of "the people" to the vices of shadowy elites whose greedy manipulations oppressed the poor and perverted democracy. It was always a language of resentment, of raw class antagonism, edged with envy and grudge. In the charged atmosphere of the 1930s, it could easily become a language of reprisal.[26]

Long had mastered the populist tongue to a degree that few could match, before or since. Other than Franklin Roosevelt himself, no figure flashed more incandescently across the Depression-darkened American political landscape. Fulminating against wealth and Wall Street, incanting the excellences and the tribulations of the common man, Long strutted across the national stage full of sound and fury. For a long, tense season, it seemed that the traditional political system could contain neither him nor the pent-up rancor that he threatened to release.

Long hailed from Winn Parish, a pine-covered, red-soil district in the north central Louisiana uplands. Winn was a place of one-man-and-a-mule farms, small lumber mills, and scant graces. It was peopled mainly with plain-living white Southern Baptists with little to boast of on this earth save their reputation for cussedness. For generations, they had suspicioned outsiders and writhed under the twin burdens of poverty and powerlessness, the weight of the first attributed directly to the persistence of the latter. Many of their forebears had been Unionists in secessionist Louisiana; others had spearheaded Louisiana's Populist movement in the 1890s; still others had voted heavily for Socialist presidential candidate Eugene Debs in 1912. None of these fitful gestures

25. Alexis de Tocqueville, *Democracy in America* (New York: Vintage, 1945), 2:102–3.
26. For an extended discussion of the populist strand in American political culture, see Michael Kazin, *The Populist Persuasion: An American History* (New York: Basic, 1995).

of defiance had improved their lot. Winn endured as a changeless hummock of contrariness in one of the poorest and most corrupt states of the Union. On the eve of the Depression, one-fifth of the adult white men in the state, and a much higher proportion of blacks, were illiterate. Despite Louisiana's rich natural endowments of oil and gas, an oligarchy of self-satisfied businessmen and haughty planters kept the state's per capita income lower than in all but nine other states.

Long had been born in 1893, when the Populist movement was cresting in popularity. More than the signs of the zodiac, the earthly place and historical moment of his birth marked him. He was the legatee of a rank heritage of sour resentment and frustrated radicalism. Few men more naturally came by the temperament of the aginner.

Long first ran for public office in 1918, standing successfully for the post of state railroad commissioner. Throughout the 1920s Commissioner Long made a reputation as a champion of the people and the scourge of the big corporations, especially the Standard Oil Company, that ruled the state with baronial sway. In 1928 he campaigned for governor on a slogan that distilled the essence of the old populist dream of unchained affluence and radical leveling: "Every man a king, but no one wears a crown." Capitalizing on the state's festering economic grievances, Long won handsomely. Now, Long told his followers on election night, "We'll show 'em who's boss. . . . You fellers stick by me. . . . We're just getting started."[27]

Just getting started indeed. Governor Long went to work with single-minded intensity. He jacked up taxes on oil and gas producers and used the revenue for badly needed improvements to the state's highway system, free textbooks for schoolchildren, and new hospitals and public buildings. Meanwhile he closed his grip over the state's political apparatus, making Louisiana the closest thing to a dictatorship that America has ever known.

Elected to the U.S. Senate in 1930, Long refused to vacate the governorship for nearly two more years, holding both offices simultaneously. Arriving at last to take up his Senate seat in June 1933, he called at the White House to see Franklin Roosevelt. "Frank," Long called the president, whose Harvard airs and polished manners galled the populist from Winn. In a studied gesture of brazen disrespect, Long cheekily neglected to doff his straw hat, removing it only for an occasional emphatic tap on Roosevelt's immobile knee. On this occasion and countless others,

27. Brinkley, *Voices of Protest*, 22.

Long exuded contempt for the national political establishment, for the moguls and insiders and "high hats" who looked down their noses at the likes of Winn Parish's honest rednecked yeomen. "All I care," he said, "is what the boys at the forks of the creek think of me."[28]

They loved him. Louisianans allowed Long and his lieutenants to seize unprecedented power. Through graft and coercion Long filled a bulging political war chest. Secure in his home state and robustly financed, Long strode into the national arena in the role of hillbilly hero and played it with gusto. He wore white silk suits and pink silk ties, womanized openly, swilled whiskey in the finest bars, swaggered his way around Washington, and breathed defiance into the teeth of his critics. The president's mother called him "that *awful* man." His friends called him "Kingfish," after a character on the radio program *Amos 'n' Andy.* ("*Der* Kingfish," said Long's critics, seeing parallels with another dangerous demagogue.) The *New York Times* called him "a man with a front of brass and lungs of leather." Franklin Roosevelt called him "one of the two most dangerous men in the country." (The other, said Roosevelt, was Army Chief of Staff Douglas MacArthur.)[29]

Like Father Coughlin, Long at first supported the New Deal, especially its early emphasis on inflation. But the Economy Act and especially the NRA convinced him that Roosevelt was just another contemptible high-hatter, in bed with the Money Power and the big corporations and the entrenched elites of the loathsome Eastern Establishment. Like Father Coughlin, he was soon ready openly to repudiate the Roosevelt program. And like Father Coughlin, indeed like Roosevelt himself, he relied on the radio to reach his audience and build his political base.[30]

Like Upton Sinclair, Long also relied on the written word to spread his message. In October 1933 he published an autobiography, *Every Man a King*, and in 1935, in direct imitation of Sinclair, *My First Days in the White House.* Neither book impressed the critics, one of whom sneered that Long was "unbalanced, vulgar, in many ways ignorant, and quite reckless." Long, however, cared little for the encomia of the literati. His books, says historian Alan Brinkley, were "intended for men

28. Brinkley, *Voices of Protest*, 75.
29. Schlesinger 3:61; Brinkley, *Voices of Protest*, 56–58.
30. Like Father Coughlin, too, Long found himself the object of counterattacks from the Roosevelt administration. The president blocked all federal patronage to the Long machine in Louisiana and ordered an Internal Revenue Service investigation of Long and his political associates.

and women not in the habit of reading books." Those who were in the habit could read thinly fictionalized accounts of characters based on Long in Sinclair Lewis's *It Can't Happen Here* (1935), a cautionary tale about the possibilities of a native American fascism, and later in Robert Penn Warren's *All the King's Men* (1946), a sensitive novel about the psychology of power and corruption.[31]

In 1934 Long launched the Share Our Wealth Society. He took to the airwaves to describe its simple platform: he would make "every man a king" by confiscating large fortunes, levying steeply progressive income taxes, and distributing the revenue to every American family in the form of a "household estate" of five thousand dollars—enough, he suggested, for a home, an automobile, and, significantly, a radio. In addition, each family would be guaranteed a minimum annual income of twenty-five hundred dollars per year (nearly double the median family income at the time).[32] Nor was that all: Long added promises of shorter working hours, improved veterans' benefits, educational subsidies for the young, and pensions for the elderly. ("This attracted a lot of Townsendites to us," crowed one of Long's minions.)[33] He pitched his program in terms long familiar in Winn Parish, painting a picture of an American Eden corrupted by the serpent of monopoly power:

> God invited us all to come and eat and drink all we wanted. He smiled on our land and we grew crops of plenty to eat and wear. He showed us in the earth the iron and other things to make everything we wanted. He unfolded to us the secrets of science so that our work might be easy. God called: 'Come to my feast!' [But then] Rockefeller, Morgan, and their crowd stepped up and took enough for 120,000,000 people and left only enough for 5,000,000 for all the other 125,000,000 to eat. And so many millions must go hungry and without those good things God gave us unless we call on them to put some of it back.[34]

Contemporary analysts estimated that even if all existing wealth were in liquid form and could be cashed out and distributed, confiscating all fortunes larger than a million dollars (more than Long called for) would produce not five thousand dollars per family but a mere four hundred. The heavy taxes necessary to guarantee a minimum income to all of twenty-five hundred per year would leave no individual's annual income

31. Brinkley, *Voices of Protest*, 70.
32. *HSUS*, 303, gives median family income as $1,231 in 1939.
33. Schlesinger 3:63.
34. Brinkley, *Voices of Protest*, 70.

above three thousand dollars. Long cared little for such arithmetic. He knew that though the Share Our Wealth scheme, like the Townsend Plan, might be the stuff of shoddy economic fantasy, it was shiny, twenty-four-carat political gold. "Be prepared for the slurs and snickers of some high ups," he cautioned his listeners. "Let no one tell you that it is difficult to redistribute the wealth of this land. It is simple."[35]

As 1935 opened, Long stepped up his radio appearances. On January 9 he told a national audience that he had "begged and pleaded and did everything else under the sun" to "try to get Mr. Roosevelt to keep his word that he gave us." But now he had given up. "Hope for more through Roosevelt? He has promised and promised, smiled and bowed. . . . There is no use to wait three more years. It is not Roosevelt or ruin, it is Roosevelt's ruin." Long boldly pressed the attack, indicting not just the president's policies but also his person: "When I saw him spending all his time of ease and recreation with the big partners of Mr. John D. Rockefeller, Jr., with such men as the Astors and company, maybe I ought to have had better sense than to have believed he would ever break down their big fortunes to give enough to the masses to end poverty." Before long, the Kingfish took to calling Roosevelt the "Knight of the *Nourmahal*" (Vincent Astor's yacht, on which FDR frequently vacationed).[36]

Long's broadcasts regularly elicited more than a hundred thousand letters of support. Within a year the nationally organized Share Our Wealth Society claimed five million members, perhaps an exaggeration but at least roughly suggestive of the national audience Long was awakening. Long began to reach out to other dissidents. "Father Coughlin has a damn good platform," said Long, "and I'm 100 percent for him. . . . What he thinks is right down my alley." What Coughlin and Long thought made sense to many Americans mystified by the Depression and chafing still at the persistent spectacle of want amidst plenty. In Wisconsin, the La Follettes' official organ, the *Progressive*, editorialized that it did not agree "with every conclusion reached by Father Coughlin and Senator Long, [but] when they contend . . . that the tremendous wealth of this country should be more equitably shared for a more abundant life for the masses of the people, we agree heartily with them."[37] Long made overtures to the Townsendites and the survivors of the EPIC

35. Schlesinger 3:64; Brinkley, *Voices of Protest*, 73.
36. *New York Times*, January 10, 1935, 1; Davis 3:502.
37. Schlesinger 3:249; Brinkley, *Voices of Protest*, 232.

fiasco in California. In the spring of 1935 Milo Reno introduced him to a Farmers Holiday Association convention in Des Moines. "Do you believe in the redistribution of wealth?" Long asked. The crowd of more than ten thousand roared back a unanimous "Yes!" "I could take this state like a whirlwind," Long exulted. In Philadelphia Long spoke to an enthusiastic crowd in March 1935. Surveying the scene, Philadelphia's former mayor said: "There are 250,000 Long votes."[38] "I'll tell you here and now," Long said to reporters a few months later, "that Franklin Roosevelt will not be the next President of the United States. If the Democrats nominate Roosevelt and the Republicans nominate Hoover, Huey Long will be your next President."[39]

In the Roosevelt circle, this blustering was taken seriously. On the evening of March 4, 1935, on a nationwide NBC radio broadcast marking the second anniversary of Roosevelt's inauguration, Hugh Johnson, still a Roosevelt loyalist despite being sacked from the directorship of the NRA just months earlier, loosed his intimidating powers of invective against the "great Louisiana demagogue and this political padre." Long and Coughlin spoke, Johnson complained, "with nothing of learning, knowledge nor experience to lead us through a labyrinth that has perplexed the minds of men since the beginning of time. . . . These two men are raging up and down this land preaching not construction but destruction—not reform but revolution." And, Johnson warned, they were finding a receptive audience. "You can laugh at Father Coughlin, you can snort at Huey Long—but this country was never under a greater menace."[40]

Louis Howe, Roosevelt's most trusted and loyal adviser, closely monitored the Coughlin and Long phenomena. In early 1935 he sent the president a copy of a letter from a Montana banker, "who, of all people, has been converted by Huey Long. . . . It is symptoms like this I think we should watch very carefully," Howe admonished.[41] Soon thereafter Postmaster General and Democratic Committee chairman James Farley commissioned a secret poll to "find out if Huey's sales talks for his 'share the wealth' program were attracting many customers. . . . We kept a careful eye on what Huey and his political allies . . . were attempting to do." The results surprised and dismayed Farley. The poll indicated that Long,

38. Brinkley, *Voices of Protest*, 237, 170.
39. Brinkley, *Voices of Protest*, 81.
40. Brinkley, *Voices of Protest*, 6.
41. E. Roosevelt, *FDR: His Personal Letters*, 460.

running for the presidency on a third-party ticket, could attract as many as four million votes, about 10 percent of the anticipated total in 1936. Farley's poll also demonstrated that Long was succeeding in making himself a national figure, with strength in the North as well as the South, in industrial centers as well as rural areas. "It was easy to conceive a situation," Farley concluded, "whereby Long, by polling more than 3,000,000 votes, might have the balance of power in the 1936 election. For example, the poll indicated that he would command upward of 100,000 votes in New York State, a pivotal state in any national election; and a vote of that size could easily mean the difference between victory or defeat. . . . [T]hat number of votes . . . would come mostly from our side, and the result might spell disaster." Roosevelt shared that assessment. "Long plans to be a candidate of the Hitler type for the presidency in 1936," he told William E. Dodd, his ambassador to Germany. "He thinks he will have a hundred votes in the Democratic convention. Then he will set up as an independent with Southern and mid-western Progressives. . . . Thus he hopes to defeat the Democratic party and put in a reactionary Republican. That would bring the country to such a state by 1940 that Long thinks he would be made dictator. There are in fact some Southerners looking that way, and some Progressives are drifting that way. . . . Thus it is an ominous situation."[42]

Long, said a worried Democratic senator, "is brilliant and dangerous. He is industrious and has much capacity. The depression has increased radicalism in this country—nobody knows how much. Long is making every preparation to unite it politically in 1936. . . . We are obliged to propose and accept many things in the New Deal that otherwise we would not because we must prevent a union of discontent around him. The President is the only hope of the conservatives and the liberals; if his program is restricted, the answer may be Huey Long."[43]

Comments like that have led many historians to argue that Roosevelt, who was about to propose several dramatic reform proposals in 1935, did so principally in response to pressure from Long and Coughlin. Without the demagogues, the argument implies, there might never have been a genuine New Deal, and what liberalism was in it was wrung from a reluctant, temperamentally conservative Roosevelt only under

42. James A. Farley, *Behind the Ballots: The Personal History of a Politician* (New York: Harcourt, Brace, 1938), 249–50; William E. Dodd Jr. and Martha Dodd, eds., *Ambassador Dodd's Diary, 1933–1938* (New York: Harcourt, Brace, 1941), 213–14.
43. *New York Times*, January 10, 1935, 10.

threat of his own political extinction. Even Roosevelt's son Elliott claimed that the entire epochal legislative program of 1935—the landmark laws that constituted what is sometimes, and somewhat misleadingly, labeled the "Second New Deal," including the Emergency Relief Appropriation Act, the Banking Act, the Wagner National Labor Relations Act, the Public Utility Holding Companies Act, the Social Security Act, and the Wealth Tax Act—were "designed to cut the ground from under the demagogues."[44]

That judgment is surely exaggerated. Many of the measures that came to pass in 1935—most notably the Social Security Act, the most consequential of New Deal achievements—had been on deck well before "the demagogue and the padre" had their innings. Roosevelt and Harry Hopkins had been seeking major revisions in relief policy since the winter of 1933–34. Banking reform had been on the New Deal's agenda since the first of the Hundred Days. Senator Robert Wagner had been pushing for years to enact policies like those embodied in the National Labor Relations Bill. Utilities reform had been among Roosevelt's highest priorities when he was governor of New York. As for Social Security, Roosevelt had endorsed the basic concept at least as early as 1930. Only the Wealth Tax Act truly answers to the description of a Roosevelt political initiative undertaken in direct response to the Coughlin and Long agitation.

YET IF COUGHLIN AND LONG did not force the Second New Deal on a resisting Roosevelt, they did threaten to hijack it. The president was obliged to dig in and defend his program against the danger that a radical groundswell might run it off the road of financial soundness and political prudence. "I am fighting Communism, Huey Longism, Coughlinism, Townsendism," Roosevelt told a journalist in early 1935, but he was not at this point battling them by stealing their thunder. He had long since stocked his own legislative arsenal with thunder enough. In his pitch for the Wealth Tax Act and in the presidential campaign of 1936, Roosevelt did in the end arguably fight fire with fire by mimicking some of the radicals' most confrontational rhetoric. But for the present he was working, he explained, "to save our system, the capitalist system," from "crackpot ideas." Steady on course, no veering leftward, or rightward either, for that matter—that was the strategy for 1935.[45]

44. E. Roosevelt, FDR: His Personal Letters, 444.
45. E. D. Coblentz, William Randolph Hearst (New York: Simon and Schuster, 1952), 178.

Roosevelt based that strategy on shrewd political calculations. Writing to his former associate from the Woodrow Wilson years, Colonel Edward M. House, Roosevelt in February 1935 offered a detailed analysis of the political opposition he faced. It embraced old-guard conservative Republicans, "more liberal Republicans," and "Progressive Republicans like La Follette, Cutting, Nye, etc., who are flirting with the idea of a third party ticket anyway with the knowledge that such a third ticket would be beaten but that it would defeat us, elect a conservative Republican and cause a complete swing far to the left before 1940. All of these Republican elements," Roosevelt continued, "are flirting with Huey Long and probably financing him. A third Progressive Republican ticket and a fourth 'Share the Wealth' ticket they believe would crush us. . . . There is no question that it is all a dangerous situation," Roosevelt conceded. But he coolly added the keen insight that "when it comes to Show-down these fellows cannot all lie in the same bed."[46]

Roosevelt may also have sensed something about the Long and Coughlin constituencies that the historian Alan Brinkley later put at the heart of his analysis of their Depression-era appeal. The men and women attracted to Long and Coughlin, Brinkley speculates, were not the most desperately poor. They seemed, rather, to be people who "had more to protect: a hard-won status as part of the working-class elite, a vaguely middle-class life-style, often a modest investment in a home. . . . They were people with something to lose. . . . What they shared was an imperiled membership in a world of modest middle-class accomplishment."[47] They were, in other words, from that petite bourgeois social stratum that Alexis de Tocqueville had long ago described as the "eager and apprehensive men of small property." They constituted the characteristic class shaped by the fluid, unstable conditions of American democracy. "They love change," Tocqueville observed, "but they dread revolutions. . . . They continually and in a thousand ways feel that they might lose by one."[48] They were never, in short, not even in the Depression, the stuff from which genuinely revolutionary movements might be forged. They might occasionally drink the demagogues' intoxicating rhetorical brew, but in the end they did their basic political business on plain water.

The real menace the demagogues posed was not that they might

46. E. Roosevelt, FDR: His Personal Letters, 452–53.
47. Brinkley, Voices of Protest, 202–3.
48. Tocqueville, Democracy in America, 2:265–78.

revolutionize this recalcitrant mass and use it to shove the country rudely to the left but that they might succeed for a time in so coarsening public opinion, so souring the political atmosphere, and so fracturing the traditional parties that were the usual vehicles of governance that a lengthy period of political paralysis would ensue. Not social revolution but stasis was the worst plausible outcome of the radical agitation. This was the danger Roosevelt saw in early 1935, but he was sure he could head it off. Indeed, it was a mark of Roosevelt's reflexive political genius that instead of simply bending with the pressure from his left, he capitalized on it. He could now credibly argue to conservative stand-patters that his own program, radical enough by any objective standard, was a prudent bulwark against the irresponsible radicalism of the demagogues. If others offered a politics of resentment, he would offer a politics of possibility. If Coughlin and Long appealed to the dark side of people's souls, Roosevelt would follow the example of Lincoln and speak to the better angels of their nature. "Some well-timed, common sense campaigning on my part this spring or summer will bring people to their senses," the president confidently predicted.[49]

Roosevelt had in fact been building up to that campaign for more than a year, in a remarkable series of addresses, including several Fireside Chats broadcast nationally on the radio. Despite the frequently repeated accusation that the New Deal lacked a coherent philosophy and that Roosevelt had no capacity for ordered, systematic thought, those addresses, taken together, etched at least the outlines of a structured and durable social philosophy that constituted the ideological heart of the New Deal. Roosevelt minted that philosophy from the feelings of seigneurial solicitude for his country that lay at the core of his patrician temperament. "[F]rom the bottom of his heart he wants [people] to be as happy as he is," Raymond Moley wrote. "He is outraged by hunger and unemployment, as though they were personal affronts in a world he is certain he can make far better, totally other, than it has been." Rexford Tugwell spoke in a similar vein when he described the fundamental purposes that lay deep in Roosevelt's mind when he first assumed the presidency: "a better life for all Americans, and a better America to live it in."[50]

In 1934 and 1935 Roosevelt took up the task of translating those sen-

---

49. E. Roosevelt, FDR: His Personal Letters, 453.
50. Rexford G. Tugwell, The Brains Trust (New York: Viking, 1968) 157–58; Raymond Moley, After Seven Years (New York: Harper and Brothers, 1939), 390.

timents and generalities into a concrete political credo. Long and the other radicals provided the occasion for Roosevelt to articulate fully and specifically just what it was that the New Deal was about. In the campaign of 1932 he had, perhaps deliberately, remained vague and inscrutable, though in retrospect the germ of his mature political thought can be found in some of his 1932 campaign addresses, especially his speech to San Francisco's Commonwealth Club. In 1933 he had pursued a bewildering array of sometimes contradictory policies and, perhaps inevitably, had little opportunity to define what architecture, if any, held them all together in his head. But as 1934 lengthened, Roosevelt at last proceeded to elaborate for his countrymen his vision of the future into which he hoped to lead them. He gave the nation a presidential civics lesson that defined nothing less than the ideology of modern liberalism. He breathed new meaning into ideas like liberty and freedom. He bestowed new legitimacy on the idea of government. He introduced new political ideas, like social security. He transformed the country's very sense of itself, and of what was politically possible, in enduring ways. Before he was finished, Franklin Roosevelt had changed the nation's political mind and its institutional structure to a degree that few leaders before him had dared to dream, let alone try, and that few leaders thereafter dared to challenge.

He began with history and with the changing role of government. As in his "Whither Bound" address to the Milton Academy graduates in 1926, change was his keynote—its inevitability and the equally inevitable obligation to adjust to it, to heal its ruptures and seize its opportunities. "[I]n the earlier days," he said in a special message to Congress on June 8, 1934, when he foreshadowed the social security program he intended to develop, "the interdependence of members of families upon each other and of the families within a small community upon each other" provided fulfillment and security. But those simple frontier conditions had now disappeared. "The complexities of great communities and of organized industry make less real these simple means of security. Therefore, we are compelled to employ the active interest of the Nation as a whole through government in order to encourage a greater security for each individual who composes it." The federal government was established under the Constitution, he recollected, "to promote the general welfare," and it was now government's "plain duty to provide for that security upon which welfare depends."

Security was the touchstone, the single word that summed up more of what Roosevelt aimed at that than any other. "Among our objectives," he declared, "I place the security of the men, women and children of the Nation first." People wanted, indeed, they had a "right"—a significant escalation of the rhetoric of political claims—to three types of security: "decent homes to live in," "productive work," and "security against the hazards and vicissitudes of life."

Figuratively nodding to his political right, in a Fireside Chat just three weeks later he explained in his reassuring, sonorous voice that some people "will try to give you new and strange names for what we are doing. Sometimes they will call it 'Fascism,' sometimes 'Communism,' sometimes 'Regimentation,' sometimes 'Socialism.' But, in so doing, they are trying to make very complex and theoretical something that is really very simple and very practical. . . . Plausible self-seekers and theoretical die-hards will tell you of the loss of individual liberty. Answer this question out of the facts of your own life. Have you lost any of your rights or liberty or constitutional freedom of action and choice?" He made no apology for his conception of government as a shaping agent in modern American life. Speaking extemporaneously at the site of Bonneville Dam on the Columbia River in the summer of 1934, he said flatly that "the power we shall develop here is going to be power which for all time is going to be controlled by Government."[51]

In a subsequent Fireside Chat in September, Roosevelt deepened his argument for positive government, quoting at length from the revered progressive-era statesman Elihu Root:

> The tremendous power of organization [Root had said] has combined great aggregations of capital in enormous industrial establishments . . . so great in the mass that each individual concerned in them is quite helpless by himself. . . . [T]he old reliance upon the free action of individual wills appears quite inadequate. . . . [T]he intervention of that organized control we call government seems necessary.

The "organized control we call government"—there was the heart of the matter. "Men may differ as to the particular form of governmental activity with respect to industry or business," Roosevelt commented, "but nearly all are agreed that private enterprise in times such as these cannot be left without assistance and without reasonable safeguards lest it destroy not only itself but also our process of civilization." Invoking another American icon, Roosevelt said: "I believe with Abraham Lincoln, that

51. PPA (1934), 287ff., 312ff., 325ff.

'The legitimate object of Government is to do for a community of people whatever they need to have done but cannot do at all or cannot do
so well for themselves in their separate and individual capacities.'" In
his own words, he added: "I am not for a return to that definition of
liberty under which for many years a free people were being gradually
regimented into the service of the privileged few. I prefer and I am sure
you prefer that broader definition of liberty under which we are moving
forward to greater freedom, to greater security for the average man than
he has ever known before in the history of America."[52]

In his annual message to Congress on January 4, 1935, Roosevelt
frankly declared that "social justice, no longer a distant ideal, has become a definite goal." He began to detail the specific proposals that
would make that goal a reality. "As our measures take root in the living
texture of life," he declared, "the unity of our program reveals itself to
the Nation."[53]

The unifying design of that program took different forms in different
sectors of the nation's life, but the overall pattern of the Second New
Deal taking shape in 1935 was becoming clear. In the social realm, the
dominant motif was security; in the economic realm, regulation (which
was security by another name); and in the physical realm, planned development. In all those domains the common objective was stability. No
other aspiration more deeply informed the Second New Deal, and no
other achievement better represented the New Deal's lasting legacy.
Roosevelt now sought not simply recovery, nor merely relief, nor even
the perpetual economic growth that would constitute a later generation's
social and political holy grail. Roosevelt sought instead a new framework
for American life, something "totally other" than what had gone before,
in Moley's phrase, something that would permit the steadying hand of
"that organized control we call government" to sustain balance and equity and orderliness throughout American society. Roosevelt's dream was
the old progressive dream of wringing order out of chaos, seeking mastery rather than accepting drift, imparting to ordinary Americans at least
some measure of the kind of predictability to their lives that was the
birthright of the Roosevelts and the class of patrician squires to which
they belonged. It was a dream nurtured in the minds of countless reformers over a century of unbridled and unsettling industrial revolution;

52. *PPA* (1934), 413ff.
53. *PPA* (1935), 16.

a dream quickened in the progressive reform era of Roosevelt's youth, not least by his own cousin Theodore; a dream raised to insistent urgency by the catastrophe of the Depression. It was a dream now brought within reach of realization by that same Depression and by the sense of possibility and the political fluidity it induced.[54]

54. Much scholarly energy has gone into analyzing the ideology of the Second New Deal of 1935 and trying to distinguish it from the First New Deal of 1933. Arthur M. Schlesinger Jr. (Schlesinger 3, esp. 385–408) advanced the thesis that the macroeconomic planners in the New Nationalist tradition who dominated the First New Deal now gave way to the microeconomic trust busters and regulators of the Brandeisian–Woodrow Wilson persuasion, allied with proto-Keynesians increasingly convinced of the stimulatory power of deficit spending. Much of the argument over this subject has been an exercise in historiographical hairsplitting. My own view discounts the ideological coherence of the First New Deal and therefore posits no sharp conceptual break in 1935. It is also my view that not economic policy strictly defined but social security policy broadly construed — as embodied principally in the legislation of that name, as well as in the Emergency Relief Appropriation Act — constituted the heart of the Second New Deal and that the social security measures of 1935 represented no significant repudiation of previous policies. Rather, they evolved organically out of the social thought of the previous two decades as well out of the circumstances of the Depression.

9

A Season for Reform

The social objective . . . is to do what any honest government of any country would do: to try to increase the security and happiness of a larger number of people in all occupations of life and in all parts of the country . . . to give them assurance that they are not going to starve in their old age.
— Franklin D. Roosevelt, press conference of June 7, 1935,
responding to the question "What would you say was the
social objective of the administration?"

While Roosevelt cruised through the Bahamas on Vincent Astor's *Nourmahal* in the early spring weeks of 1935, the first part of his ambitious legislative program for the year, the Emergency Relief Appropriation Bill, sailed through the new Congress. He called it the "Big Bill," and not without reason. The bill asked for the largest peacetime appropriation to date in American history. It authorized more spending than the sum of all federal revenues in 1934. Four billion dollars in new funds, along with $880 million reallocated from previously authorized appropriations, were to be used for work relief and public works construction.

The word "emergency" in the bill's title was more than a little misleading. Roosevelt and the bill's principal architects in fact believed that they were addressing not a transient disruption in the labor markets but a long-term, perhaps permanent, deficit in the ability of the private economy to provide employment for all who sought it. In the masterwork he was then drafting, John Maynard Keynes would place that dread prospect—what Keynes called "equilibrium at less than full employment"—at the center of his analysis.[1] The social scientists who had compiled

1. John Maynard Keynes, *The General Theory of Employment, Interest, and Money* (New York: Harcourt, Brace, 1936).

249

Herbert Hoover's *Recent Social Trends* had worried half a decade earlier that long-term "technological unemployment" threatened to permanently engulf huge sectors of the work force, particularly the less skilled and the elderly. Some observers needed no sophisticated theory to suggest that deep structural changes in the economy were making what had once been almost unimaginable now seem like a distinct possibility. Lorena Hickok had opined to Harry Hopkins as early as the spring of 1934 that "it looks as though we're in this relief business for a long, long time. . . . The majority of those over 45 probably will NEVER get their jobs back."[2] Hopkins himself was soon speaking of workers who had passed into "an occupational oblivion from which they will never be rescued by private industry. . . . Until the time comes, if it ever comes," he argued, "when industry and business can absorb all able-bodied workers—and that time seems to grow more distant with improvements in management and technology—we shall have with us large numbers of the unemployed. Intelligent people have long since left behind them," Hopkins continued, "the notion that . . . the unemployed will disappear as dramatically as they made their appearance after 1929. . . . For them a security program is the only answer."[3] Roosevelt, too, had forewarned the Congress in early 1934 that government might have to become the employer of last resort and remain so into an indefinite future. "For many years to come," he said, "we shall be engaged in the task of rehabilitating many hundreds of thousands of our American families." The need for relief would continue "for a long time to come," he added in his Fireside Chat of June 28, 1934. "We may as well recognize that fact."[4]

The Big Bill met that fact head-on. Explaining the bill in his annual message to Congress on January 4, 1935, Roosevelt, instructed by Hopkins's experience with FERA and CWA, drew a sharp distinction between "relief" and "work relief." He declared emphatically: "The Federal Government must and shall quit this business of relief," by which he meant "the giving of cash, of market baskets, of a few hours of weekly work cutting grass, raking leaves or picking up papers in the public parks." In words that might have been uttered by Herbert Hoover, Roosevelt said that this sort of relief "induces a spiritual and moral disinte-

2. Richard Lowitt and Maurine Beasley, eds., *One Third of a Nation: Lorena Hickok Reports on the Great Depression* (Urbana: University of Illinois Press, 1981), 233.
3. Harry Hopkins, *Spending to Save* (New York: Norton, 1936), 180–81.
4. *PPA* (1934), 291, 313.

gration fundamentally destructive to the national fibre. To dole out relief
in this way is to administer a narcotic, a subtle destroyer of the human
spirit." *Work,* on the other hand, nurtured "self-respect . . . self-reliance
and courage and determination." Therefore the federal government—
"the only governmental agency with sufficient power and credit to meet
this situation"—would offer employment to the approximately 3.5 million jobless but employable persons then on the relief rolls. (Another
five million unemployed were not on relief and fell outside the scope
of Roosevelt's proposal.) As for the estimated 1.5 million unemployable
relief recipients—the ill, the aged, the physically handicapped—they
had been cared for in pre-Depression days by local governments and
agencies, said Roosevelt, and "it is my thought that in the future they
must be cared for as they were before. . . . [C]ommon sense tells us," he
added, "that the wealth necessary for this task existed and still exists in
the local community." Perhaps it did, but to mobilize it local communities were levying new taxes, especially regressive sales taxes, which
twenty-one states had newly imposed since 1932. This was but one of
many ways in which the Depression drove the growth of government at
all levels, not just at the federal center in Washington.[5]

Roosevelt laid down certain criteria to guide the expenditure of work-
relief funds. Projects should be permanently useful and preferably self-
liquidating; they should be labor-intensive and pay a "security wage"
greater than the dole but less than private employment; they should
compete "as little as possible with private enterprises."[6] Congress agreed,
with one telling reservation. At the insistence of the old isolationist Senator William E. Borah of Idaho, the Senate inserted a proviso that "no
part of the appropriations . . . shall be used for munitions, warships, or
military and naval materiel." With that restriction, the Emergency Relief
Appropriation Act became law on April 8, 1935.[7]

An omnibus measure, the act breathed new life into existing agencies
like the Civilian Conservation Corps and the Public Works Administration and created new bodies besides. Though critics continued to charge

5. See James T. Patterson, *The New Deal and the States: Federalism in Transition*
   (Princeton: Princeton University Press, 1969), passim; and the same author's *America's Struggle against Poverty, 1900–1980* (Cambridge: Harvard University Press,
   1981), 62.
6. *PPA* (1935), 19–23.
7. Robert E. Sherwood, *Roosevelt and Hopkins* (New York: Grosset and Dunlap, 1950),
   67.

that the PWA under the ever-cautious Ickes was still dispensing money from a medicine dropper, Ickes in the end became, in William Leuchtenburg's phrase, "a builder to rival Cheops."[8] His PWA workers built roads and schools and courthouses and hospitals. They built the Triborough Bridge and the Lincoln Tunnel and La Guardia Airport in New York, the Skyline Drive in Virginia, and the Overseas Highway in the Florida Keys, as well as the San Francisco–Oakland Bay Bridge in California — and, using monies from the original PWA appropriation in 1933, the aircraft carriers *Yorktown* and *Enterprise* in Newport News and the light cruiser *Vincennes* in the Bethlehem Steel shipyard in Quincy, Massachusetts.

The Big Bill also spawned a prolific brood of new governmental agencies, most of them established by executive order under the unprecedentedly broad authority that the Emergency Relief Appropriation Act had conferred upon the president. The Rural Electrification Administration (REA) under Morris Llewellyn Cooke brought cheap power to the countryside, mostly by midwifing the emergence of hundreds of nonprofit, publicly owned electrical cooperatives. When REA began its work, fewer than two farms in ten had electricity; a little more than a decade later, thanks to low-cost REA loans that built generating plants and strung power lines down country lanes and across field and pasture, nine out of ten did. The National Youth Administration, under Aubrey Williams, provided part-time jobs to needy high school and college students — thus encouraging youths to stay in school and out of the regular employment markets. The Resettlement Administration, under former Brain Truster Rexford Tugwell, built three "greenbelt" suburban towns — Greenbelt, near Washington, D.C.; Greenhills, near Cincinnati; and Greendale, near Milwaukee — though its brief experiment in urban planning collapsed when it was absorbed into a new agency, the Farm Security Administration, in 1937.

The largest agency born of the Emergency Relief Appropriation Act was the Works Progress Administration (WPA; after 1939, Works Projects Administration). It was headed by the driven, savvy Harry Hopkins, a man Hugh Johnson described as having "a mind like a razor, a tongue like a skinning knife, a temper like a Tartar and a sufficient vocabulary of parlor profanity . . . to make a mule-skinner jealous."[9] WPA employed more than three million people in its first year and in the eight years

8. Leuchtenburg, 133.
9. Sherwood, *Roosevelt and Hopkins*, 80.

of its life put 8.5 million persons to work at a total cost of some $11 billion. WPA construction workers built half a million miles of highways and nearly a hundred thousand bridges and as many public buildings, erected the Dock Street Theater in Charleston and Timberline Lodge on the slopes of Oregon's Mount Hood, and laid out some eight thousand parks.

The WPA was from the outset a magnet for controversy. It was a federal program, but one that recognized the timeworn principle that "all politics is local." Roosevelt used it to build up those local bosses who would, in turn, support his national programs. Republicans complained that it was simply a gigantic federal patronage machine, operated for the sole benefit of the Democratic Party. That criticism was not unfounded, though it was not only Democrats whom Roosevelt favored with WPA patronage. In keeping with Roosevelt's larger purpose of creating a new, liberal political coalition, some progressive Republicans were also the beneficiaries of his WPA largesse. In New York City, where nearly a quarter of a million people were on the WPA rolls in 1936, the President allowed Republican mayor Fiorello La Guardia a large voice in dispensing WPA jobs. Elsewhere, however, Roosevelt often chose to work closely with the most entrenched of the old-line Democratic bosses. In Memphis, Tennessee, Democratic mayor Edward H. Crump exacted political contributions from WPA workers as the price of employment. WPA as well as PWA money flowed into the grasping hands of Missouri senator Harry S Truman's political sponsor, the Democratic Pendergast machine in Kansas City. In Illinois, WPA workers were instructed how to vote by the Chicago Democratic boss Edward J. Kelley. Kelley repaid the favor with unstinting support for the president. "Roosevelt is my religion," he said. In New Jersey, all WPA jobholders were required to tithe 3 percent of their meager paychecks to the Democratic machine of Frank Hague. His legions of enemies dubbed Hague the "Hudson County Hitler." Roosevelt found him personally disgusting but politically useful.[10]

Still other controversies beset WPA, many of them fueled by a new militancy about the rights of the disadvantaged, others nourished by traditional skepticism about the "undeserving poor." The left-wing magazine *Nation* carped that WPA proffered help to workers in America's "crippled capitalist system" only after requiring them to toil "at de-

10. Lyle W. Dorsett, *Franklin D. Roosevelt and the Big City Bosses* (Port Washington, N.Y.: Kennikat, 1977), passim.

pressed wages in a federal work gang." But when WPA workers in New York, led by the Communist-inspired Workers Alliance, struck for higher wages, more fortunate New Yorkers were infuriated. Three-quarters of them told pollsters that the strikers should be summarily fired. The WPA, they said, was a "form of charity, and the workers should be glad of what they get." Other controversies reflected the great regional and racial differences in American society. To be qualified for WPA employment, a worker could not refuse private employment at pay scales prevailing in his or her community. But defining the "prevailing wage" was not easy. Nationally, the average WPA wage in 1936 was fifty-two dollars a month, but in the deepest southern states, it was as low as twenty-three dollars a month. And since the "prevailing" scale of pay for blacks in the South was lower than that for whites, Negroes refusing a three-dollar-per-week private job might be denied WPA eligibility, while whites were not. A similar differential applied to the pay scales of Hispanic women in the Southwest, who were typically offered only part-time WPA jobs so they would not receive a higher wage than a full-time private employer was willing to pay. Yet Hopkins strove to keep discrimination to a minimum, and black leaders appreciated his effort. For all its timidity, the federal government was emerging as African-Americans' most reliable political ally. The NAACP resisted all proposals to place even more control in local hands. "The gover'ment is the best boss I ever had," said one black WPA worker in North Carolina.[11]

Encouraged by Eleanor Roosevelt, Hopkins also established projects that gave work to thousands of artists, musicians, actors, and writers. "Hell, they've got to eat just like other people," Hopkins replied to the inevitable critics.[12] The Federal Art Project employed painters and sculptors to teach their crafts in rural schools. It commissioned muralists to fresco post offices with depictions of ordinary American life; many of

11. *Nation*, February 13, 1935, 172; Patterson, *America's Struggle against Poverty*, 66; Donald Stevenson Howard, *The WPA and Federal Relief Policy* (New York: Russell Sage Foundation, 1943), 181–82, 291–96.

12. Jerre Mangione, *The Dream and the Deal: The Federal Writers' Project, 1935–1943* (Boston: Little, Brown, 1972), 4. Hopkins also glimpsed the employment and economic potential in the arts, entertainment, and sports industries that would grow so large in the post–World War II era. "Few things could add such a permanent volume of employment," he wrote, "as would a program of educating the public to use the services and participate in the pleasures of the culture we possess. I use the word culture as including everything from basketball to a violin performance." Hopkins, *Spending to Save*, 175.

them painted in the simple pictorial style of Breughel's portraits of Flemish peasants, enriched by the influence of the modern Mexican muralists, especially Diego Rivera. Franklin Roosevelt, in a sympathetic and sensitive appraisal of these sometimes controversial murals, thought some of them good, "some not so good, but all of it native, human, eager, and alive—all of it painted by their own kind in their own country, and painted about things that they know and look at often and have touched and loved."[13]

The Federal Music Project sponsored dozens of symphony orchestras and jazz groups. Its fifteen thousand musicians gave some 225,000 performances, including free concerts in New York's Central Park. Its researchers sought out traditional Appalachian banjo pickers and New England gut-bucket strummers and Texas fiddlers and Tennessee yodelers and Indiana jug bands, recording a unique aural archive of America's musical history.

The Federal Theater Project staged classics like Shakespeare's *Twelfth Night* and *Macbeth* (with an all-black cast). It also produced contemporary works like *It Can't Happen Here*, an adaptation of Sinclair Lewis's provocative best-selling novel of 1935, portraying the rise to power of an American fascist movement. Lewis himself played the role of his hero, Doremus Jessup, in the New York production. Taking to the road, the Theater Project brought plays and vaudeville acts and marionette shows to countless small towns. It developed an innovative production called the Living Newspaper, dramatizing headline news stories with such plays as *Triple A Ploughed Under*, *Power*, and *One Third of a Nation*. Federal Theater Project audiences totaled more than thirty million before the program was abolished in 1939 amid charges that it spread pro–New Deal propaganda and that it scandalously encouraged black and white mixing in its stage productions.

The Federal Writers Project, the fourth and most famous in the quartet of WPA arts programs collectively known as Federal One, put writers to work on the American Guide Series, an immensely popular set of guidebooks to each of the states, major cities, and interstate highway routes. The WPA guides, the critic Alfred Kazin wrote, "resulted in an extraordinary contemporary epic. . . . Road by road, town by town, down under the alluvia of the industrial culture of the twentieth century," the guides reflected the depression era's suddenly acute hunger to know "the whole of

13. Leuchtenburg, 128.

the American past, a need to give . . . New Deal America a foundation in the American inheritance."[14] Writers Project investigators also interviewed former slaves and chronicled their fading memories in poignant narratives that vividly preserved the human face of the peculiar institution. Federally funded folklorists recorded the bleak life histories of black sharecroppers and Appalachian lintheads and published many of them in a remarkable collection of reminiscences, *These Are Our Lives*, in 1939.

The artistic and literary outpouring of the Depression years, much of it fostered by Federal One, constituted what Kazin was soon to call "one of the most remarkable phenomena of the era of crisis. . . . Whatever form this literature took—the WPA guides to the states and roads . . . the half-sentimental, half-commercial new folklore . . . ; the endless documentation of the dispossessed in American life—it testified to an extraordinary national self-scrutiny. . . . Never before did a nation seem so hungry for news of itself."[15]

To a remarkable degree, Americans wanted that news straight, not sauced in the artifice of fiction but served plain in documentary reporting and, especially, in the unmediated images of photography and film. (*Life* magazine, devoted entirely to photographic reporting, marked the surging popularity of this medium on its first appearance in 1936.) In a stunning parade of books, in both words and photographs, Americans saw the many faces of their country as never before: not only in the WPA slave narratives and in *These Are Our Lives* but also in the portraits of tenant farmers by Walker Evans and James Agee in *Let Us Now Praise Famous Men* and by Erskine Caldwell and Margaret Bourke-White in *You Have Seen Their Faces*; in Dorothea Lange and Paul S. Taylor's Dust Bowl saga, *An American Exodus*; in the earthy social reporting of Edmund Wilson's *The American Jitters* and Louis Adamic's *My America*; in the simple place-name litany and stark images of prairie and river and forest in Pare Lorentz's films *The Plow That Broke the Plains* and *The River*.

Much of this artistic commentary was openly critical of the America it revealed. But Kazin and others noticed something else about it, too— its persistent subtext of patriotic nationalism, its "powers of affirmation," its commitment "to love what it knew."[16] It was as if the American

14. Alfred Kazin, *On Native Grounds* (Garden City, N.Y.: Doubleday, 1942), 393.
15. Kazin, *On Native Grounds*, 378–79.
16. Kazin, *On Native Grounds*, 378–79. See also William Stott, *Documentary Expression in Thirties America* (New York: Oxford University Press, 1973); and Richard Pells, *Radical Visions, American Dreams* (New York: Harper and Row, 1973).

people, just as they were poised to execute more social and political and economic innovation than ever before in their history, felt the need to take a long and affectionate look at their past before they bade much of it farewell, a need to inventory who they were and how they lived, to benchmark their country and their culture so as to measure the distance traveled into the future that Franklin Roosevelt was promising.

IF ROOSEVELT had had his way, the Big Bill would have been bigger still. He saw it as part of a single, integrated plan to provide present relief, future stability, and permanent security. Though Roosevelt developed his complex scheme with infinitely more financial precision than did Dr. Francis Townsend, much of the president's thinking about security—what would soon come to be called "social security"—rested on a premise little different from that of the Long Beach physician: that overcompetition in the labor markets depressed wages, spread misery rather than income, cramped the economy's aggregate purchasing power, and worked special hardship on the elderly. Like Townsend, Roosevelt was determined to find some means to "dispose of surplus workers," in particular those over the age of sixty-five. As the president saw things, the federal government would provide immediate relief to able-bodied workers by becoming the employer of last resort, even while returning traditional welfare functions to the states. Unemployment insurance would mitigate damage from future economic downturns by sustaining both the living standards of individual workers and the overall consuming power of the economy. And most important, for the lasting future, wage competition would be reduced, net purchasing power further stabilized, and the elderly made secure by removing older workers from the labor force altogether, through a system of government-guaranteed old-age pensions. "If Dr. Townsend's medicine were a good remedy," the prestigious columnist Walter Lippmann had mocked, "the more people the country could find to support in idleness the better off it would be."[17] Yet a version of that apparently outlandish idea did indeed inform Roosevelt's thinking. Warmhearted humanitarian considerations surely argued against elder labor, no less than they did against child labor. But removing both the young and the old from the work force had a cold economic logic too. Depression America had productive work only for so many, the president reasoned. Forcibly idling some was the price of securing a living wage for others.

17. Leuchtenburg, 105.

Such was the grand design in Roosevelt's mind. He regarded all three of those elements—work relief, unemployment insurance, and old-age pensions—as parts of a unitary whole, a comprehensive strategy to put the country on a pathway to sustainable economic and social stability. But on the advice of aides worried about legislative efficiency as well as constitutional challenges, he split the multipart package in two. The Emergency Relief Appropriation Act addressed only the most immediate of his goals. Most of the agencies it spawned were destined to survive less than a decade. The longer-term features of Roosevelt's grand design—unemployment insurance and old-age pensions—were incorporated in a separate piece of legislation, a landmark measure whose legacy endured and reshaped the texture of American life: the Social Security Act.

No other New Deal measure proved more lastingly consequential or more emblematic of the very meaning of the New Deal. Nor did any other better reveal the tangled skein of human needs, economic calculations, idealistic visions, political pressures, partisan maneuverings, actuarial projections, and constitutional constraints out of which Roosevelt was obliged to weave his reform program. Tortuously threading each of those filaments through the needle of the legislative process, Roosevelt began with the Social Security Act to knit the fabric of the modern welfare state. It would in the end be a peculiar garment, one that could have been fashioned only in America and perhaps only in the circumstances of the Depression era.[18]

No one knew better the singular possibilities of that place and time than Secretary of Labor Frances Perkins. To her the president in mid-1934 assigned the task of chairing a cabinet committee to prepare the social security legislation for submission to Congress. (Its other members were Treasury Secretary Henry Morgenthau, Attorney General Homer Cummings, Agriculture Secretary Henry Wallace, and Relief Administrator Harry Hopkins.) "[T]his was the time, above all times," Perkins wrote, "to be foresighted about future problems of unemployment and unprotected old age." The president shared this sense of urgency—and opportunity. Now is the time, he said to Perkins in 1934, when "we have to get it started, or it will never start."[19]

18. For a discussion of the uniqueness of the American welfare system, see Christopher Leman, "Patterns of Policy Development: Social Security in the United States and Canada," *Public Policy* 25, no. 2 (Spring 1977): 261–91.
19. Frances Perkins, *The Roosevelt I Knew* (New York: Viking 1946), 281.

Perkins brought to her task the commonsensical practicality of her New England forebears, the sometimes patronizing compassion of the social worker milieu in which she had been steeped at Jane Addams's Hull House as a young woman, and a large fund of political know-how compiled in her career as a labor lobbyist and industrial commissioner in New York. In her signature felt tricorn hat, topping an oval face punctuated by what one overawed labor chieftain called her "basilisk eyes," Perkins had evolved from a romantic Mount Holyoke graduate who tried to sell "true love" stories to pulp magazines into a mature, deadly serious battler for the underprivileged. Plain-spoken, plainly dressed, and disarmingly direct, she was thought by some to possess more earnestness than wit. Her frequently leaden garrulity in cabinet meetings irritated more than one of her male colleagues. One misogynistic wag called her "a colorless woman who talked as if she swallowed a press release." Another even more gratuitously accused her of wearing dresses "designed by the Bureau of Standards."[20]

"Madame Secretary," Perkins preferred to be called, proud of her status as the first woman cabinet member. She owed her position not only to her long comradeship-in-arms with Al Smith and Franklin Roosevelt in New York's reform battles but also to the spreading influence of an organized women's faction in the Democratic Party. Led by Mary "Molly" Dewson, head of the party's Women's Division, the group had successfully lobbied for Perkins's appointment after Roosevelt's election in 1932. In common with Dewson and other progressive reformers of her generation, especially the women among them, Perkins had been deeply affected by the 1911 fire at New York City's Triangle Shirtwaist Company, in which 146 women workers were incinerated in a burning factory whose emergency exits had been bolted shut. She directed the State Factory Commission investigation of that tragedy, which resulted in legislation mandating workplace safety and protection for workers, especially women. The Triangle Fire and its aftermath had given powerful impetus to the progressive-era movement for governmental supervision of industry, and its lessons were seared into the minds of many New Dealers. (Franklin Roosevelt alluded to it explicitly in a press conference on May 3, 1935, explaining the necessity of industrial regulation; Robert Wagner could recall minute details of the Triangle tragedy a quarter century later.) Certainly the Triangle Fire episode shaped

20. *New York Times*, May 15, 1965, 31; Lillian Holmen Mohr, *Frances Perkins* (Croton-on-Hudson, N.Y.: North River, 1979), 117.

Frances Perkins's lifelong approach to such issues. It deepened her conviction that many employers, left to their own devices, could not be counted upon to deal squarely with their employees. It also reinforced her belief that enlightened middle-class reformers could do more and better for the working classes through wise legislation than workers could do for themselves through union organization—and could do it more efficiently, without nasty industrial conflict and protracted social disruption.

A similar calculus of preemption had led Otto von Bismarck to push compulsory social insurance laws through the German Reichstag in the 1880s, and it had prompted the ruling parties in many other European countries to follow suit in the next half century. But until the 1930s no comparable movement gathered sufficient support, either from rulers or reformers, in the individualistic, laissez-faire United States. Meanwhile the American labor movement, led by the stubborn Samuel Gompers, with his deep antipathy to relying on government for anything other than protection of labor's right to organize, set its face against such schemes. Even after Gompers's death in 1924, until as late as 1932, his American Federation of Labor spurned blanket legislation to aid the toiling classes and continued to insist on bargaining for benefits piecemeal, union by union and shop by shop. The result was that the United States, virtually alone among modern industrial countries, confronted the Depression with no national system in place to compensate for the lost wages of unemployment or make provision for the old. Just a single American state, Wisconsin, had a publicly financed unemployment insurance program, and it was created only in 1932, its implementation delayed until 1934. As for pensions, more than a dozen states had old-age insurance laws on the books by the eve of the Depression, but they were so woefully underfunded that by one estimate only about twelve hundred of the nation's indigent elderly received payments from state plans in 1929, and their checks totaled a paltry $222,000 for the year, less than two hundred dollars for each recipient. Many military veterans and federal civil servants, as well as public employees like police, firefighters, and teachers, were covered by pensions, as were about 15 percent of workers in private industry. Yet the Depression badly stressed the ability of municipalities and corporations to honor pension obligations even to those lucky few. Many private plans simply folded in the years after the Crash. Others sharply curtailed benefits.[21]

21. Davis 3:442; W. Andrew Achenbaum, *Old Age in the New Land* (Baltimore: Johns Hopkins University Press, 1978), 129.

For the great majority of workers, who lacked any pension coverage whatsoever, the very thought of "retirement" was unthinkable. Most elderly laborers worked until they dropped or were fired, then threw themselves either on the mercy of their families or on the decidedly less tender mercies of a local welfare agency. Tens of thousands of elderly persons passed their final days in the 1920s in nearly thirteen hundred city- and county-supported "old-age homes." Of the 8 percent of the population who were over the age of sixty-five in 1935—a proportion that had more than doubled since the turn of the century and would rise to more than 12 percent by the century's end—nearly half were on some form of relief. As dietary and medical improvements steadily lengthened the life span and swelled the elderly cohort, that problem could only grow worse.

The problem of old-age relief had a lengthy history. The Progressive Party platform of 1912 had called for old-age pensions. A number of lobbies, including the American Association for Labor Legislation, the American Association for Old Age Security, and the Fraternal Order of Eagles, had been agitating for old-age insurance well before Dr. Townsend sent his fateful letter in 1934. Roosevelt had voiced his support for the idea at a Governors Conference in Salt Lake City in 1930. The Democratic Party platform of 1932 pledged Roosevelt's party to "unemployment and old-age insurance under State laws."

Pursuant to that goal, New York senator Robert Wagner and Maryland representative David J. Lewis cosponsored an unemployment insurance bill when the new congressional session opened in 1934. The Wagner-Lewis bill took its place alongside the Dill-Connery old-age pension bill, which had been working its way through Congress since 1932 and was now favorably reported out of committee. Together the two bills went a long way toward redeeming the Democratic platform promises of 1932. Yet to the chagrin of their sponsors the president distanced himself from both measures. Frances Perkins knew why. The president intended to seize ownership of these issues for himself. He would send a special message to Congress, appoint a presidential commission to draft the legislation, and use its deliberations to educate the public about social insurance, not least about his own commitment to it. "If possible," Perkins explained to a young aide temporarily discouraged by the president's diffidence, "it will be a campaign issue."[22]

At the outset the president entertained extravagantly far-reaching ideas

22. Thomas E. Eliot, *Recollections of the New Deal* (Boston: Northeastern University Press, 1992), 88.

about the welfare system he envisioned. "[T]here is no reason why everybody in the United States should not be covered," he mused to Perkins on one occasion. "I see no reason why every child, from the day he is born, shouldn't be a member of the social security system. When he begins to grow up, he should know he will have old-age benefits direct from the insurance system to which he will belong all his life. If he is out of work, he gets a benefit. If he is sick or crippled, he gets a benefit. . . . And there is no reason why just the industrial workers should get the benefit of this," Roosevelt went on. "Everybody ought to be in on it—the farmer and his wife and his family. I don't see why not," Roosevelt persisted, as Perkins shook her head at this presidential woolgathering. "I don't see why not. Cradle to the grave—from the cradle to the grave they ought to be in a social insurance system."[23]

That may have been the president's ideal outcome, but he knew as well as anyone that he would have to temper that vision in the forge of political and fiscal reality. Much of the country, not least the southern Democrats who were essential to his party's congressional majority, remained suspicious about all forms of social insurance. So Perkins, with dour Yankee prudence, went to work in a more practical vein. In the summer of 1934 she convened the Committee on Economic Security (CES), an advisory body of technical experts who would hammer out the precise terms of the social security legislation. She instructed the CES in words that spoke eloquently about her sensitivity to the novelties and difficulties of what they were about to undertake. "I recall emphasizing," she later wrote, "that the President was already in favor of a program of social insurance, but that it remained for them to make it practicable. We expected them," she recollected, in a passage that says volumes about her shrewd assessment of American political culture in the 1930s, "to remember that this was the United States in the years 1934–35. We hoped they would make recommendations based upon a practical knowledge of the needs of our country, the prejudices of our people, and our legislative habits."

The needs of the country were plain enough. But what of those prejudices and habits? What, in particular, of that phrase "under state laws" in the Democratic platform? Few items more deeply vexed the CES planners. Given the mobility of American workers and the manifest desirability of uniformity in national laws, most of the CES experts insisted that a centralized, federally administered system of social insur-

23. Perkins, *The Roosevelt I Knew*, 282–83.

ance would be the most equitable and the easiest to manage. They deemed a miscellany of state systems to be utterly impractical. Yet deeply ingrained traditions of states' rights challenged that commonsense approach, as did pervasive doubts about the federal government's constitutional power to act in this area.

Thomas Eliot, the young, Harvard-educated general counsel to the CES who played a major role in drafting the final bill, worried above all about "the omnipresent question of constitutionality." The lower federal courts, Eliot knew, had already handed down hundreds of injunctions against other New Deal measures. Constitutional tests of NRA and AAA were working their way to the Supreme Court. There, four justices—the "Battalion of Death" that included Justices McReynolds, Butler, VanDevanter, and Sutherland—were notoriously hostile to virtually any expansion of federal power over industry and commerce, not to mention the far bolder innovation of federal initiatives respecting employment and old age. Eliot brooded that "I could not honestly assure the committee that a national plan . . . would be upheld by the Supreme Court."

Political calculations in that agitated year of 1934 also played a part in driving the planners away from a purely federal welfare system. When the idea of federalizing the whole social insurance program was mentioned to the president, he quickly replied, "Oh no, we've got to leave all that we can to the states. All the power shouldn't be in the hands of the federal government. Look—just think what would happen if all the power *was* concentrated here, and *Huey Long* became president!"[24]

Against their better judgment, the CES experts therefore resigned themselves to settling for a mixed federal-state system. Perkins took what comfort she could from the reflection that if the Supreme Court should declare the federal aspects of the law to be unconstitutional, at least the state laws would remain. Though they would not be uniform, they would be better than nothing.

Under those constraints, the CES began its momentous task. Roosevelt at first charged the group to devise workable legislation not only for unemployment insurance and old-age pensions but also, reflecting the president's most unrestrained ambitions, for a national system of health care. The political obstacles in the path to that last objective doomed it virtually from the outset. Health-care provisions were to survive in the final act only as a residue, in the form of small grants-in-aid to the states

24. Eliot, *Recollections of the New Deal*, 95–98.

for rural public health programs and services for the physically handicapped.

Unemployment insurance posed a huge conundrum. The president's desire "to leave all that we can to the states," as well as the constitutional doubts that overhung any federal initiative, created a tightly confining matrix within which the CES planners were compelled to work. The Wisconsin plan, requiring individual employers to build up reserve funds for unemployment relief, was already on the books. A few other states were considering comparable laws, often with important variations such as requiring contributions from employees as well as employers or creating a single, state-managed fund rather than segregated reserves managed by individual firms. But in the absence of a national system, states that enacted any such laws put themselves at a disastrous competitive disadvantage. "Some way must be found," Eliot fretted, "to induce *all* the states to enact these laws—but what way? How?"[25]

Supreme Court Justice Louis D. Brandeis had an answer. He had a long and passionate interest in the cause of unemployment insurance. As early as 1911 he had written that "the paramount evil in the workingman's life is irregularity of employment." (This judgment was echoed in Robert and Helen Merrell Lynd's classic study *Middletown* a decade later, when they cited "irregularity of employment" as the major factor that defined the difference between the life trajectories of the working class and the middle class.) Now, as a sitting Supreme Court justice, Brandeis could not himself openly intervene in the bill-drafting process. But through the intermediary of his daughter Elizabeth, married to Paul A. Raushenbush, the director of the Wisconsin unemployment insurance plan, the seventy-seven-year-old jurist maneuvered from behind the scene to exercise a profound influence over the drafting of the Social Security Act.

In the summer of 1933 the Raushenbushes visited the Brandeis summer home on Cape Cod. Gratified by the recently enacted Wisconsin law, they wondered how it might become a model for national legislation. The shrewd old justice provocatively suggested that they read the Supreme Court's decision in a 1926 case, *Florida v. Mellon*. That case originated in a campaign to sell Florida real estate to sun-seeking wealthy northern retirees by reminding them that Florida had no inheritance tax. The frost-belt states whose revenues depended in part on taxing the estates of those potentially migratory millionaires thereupon

25. Eliot, *Recollections of the New Deal*, 75.

sought ways to check what they regarded as Florida's unfair competitive advantage. They prevailed upon Congress to enact a federal estate tax, with a proviso that the estates of decedents from a state with its own inheritance tax could deduct from their federal tax obligation the amount owed the state. Poof, went the Sunshine State's tax advantage. But Florida objected on the grounds that the federal law unconstitutionally compelled states to impose inheritance taxes, on pain of losing taxable revenues to the federal government. The Supreme Court unanimously dismissed Florida's claim and let the federal law stand.

This tax-offset device, Brandeis cleverly insinuated into the heads of his daughter and son-in-law, was the mechanism by which the states could be constitutionally coerced into enacting unemployment insurance laws. *Florida v. Mellon* thus helped to write a new chapter in the history of American federalism. In common with other New Deal–era developments, it provided yet another means by which the expansion of federal power did not come at the expense of diminished state power but worked, rather, to induce the growth of government at the state level as well.

In early January 1934 Elizabeth Brandeis Raushenbush shared her thoughts on this line of reasoning with Secretary Perkins. At Perkins's urging, an exhilarated Eliot incorporated the tax-offset feature into the unemployment insurance portion of the Social Security bill. States would face the choice of devising their own unemployment insurance schemes or watching tax revenues flow away to Washington to finance a federal unemployment program. This device removed the constitutional roadblock, but at the price of engendering a profligately disparate system that threatened to hinder labor force mobility. Forty-eight states would run forty-eight different unemployment compensation plans with minimal national standards and with benefits that were neither uniform nor portable.

If the tax-offset device displaced the constitutional obstacle to unemployment insurance, the problem of old-age insurance remained. And a huge problem it was. With that part of the bill, Perkins remembered more than a decade later, "we had an even more difficult time. . . . It is difficult now to understand fully the doubts and confusions in which we were planning this great new enterprise in 1934. The problems of constitutional law seemed almost insuperable." A special sense of urgency shadowed this part of the CES's deliberations. "One hardly realizes nowadays how strong was the sentiment in favor of the Townsend Plan and other exotic schemes," Perkins later wrote. "We must remember, those were the days of the 'share-the-wealth' schemes." Old-age insurance, Perkins concluded, was "politically almost essential."[26]

In lengthy lunchtime meetings in Perkins's office, at which Henry Wallace, then in a vegetarian phase, politely declined the proffered sandwiches, the planners wrestled through the autumn of 1934 with the old-age insurance features of the bill. They grappled mostly with the stringent conditions that the president had laid down in his special message of June 8. Any federal pension system, he had stipulated, must be based on private insurance principles. Specifically, he had said, "the funds necessary to provide this insurance should be raised by contribution rather than by an increase in general taxation." His usual fiscal conservatism led Roosevelt to that position, as did Witte's pointed warning that without a contributory system "we are in for free pensions for everybody with constant pressure for higher pensions, far exceeding anything that the veterans have ever been able to exert." Taking his own measure of "the prejudices of our people," Roosevelt clearly intended to establish his social security system not as a civil right but as a property right. That was the American way.

The contributory requirement enormously complicated the planners' task. "[W]hat in the world," Eliot asked himself, "could be devised to carry out the president's wish for a contributory old age insurance program that would pass judicial muster?" The president's insistence that workers themselves should contribute to their own individual old-age pension accounts through a payroll tax seemed to offer an open invitation to judicial nullification. "[W]ouldn't the Court say," Eliot worried, "that a law levying a payroll tax and spending the proceeds in paying old age benefits was really nothing else but a federal insurance scheme to provide annuities to the elderly, and that the Constitution gave Congress no authority to go into the insurance business?"[27]

Nor was that the only problem with the president's preferred scheme for old-age insurance. It also largely neutered the income-redistribution effects of the legislation. It meant that, virtually alone among modern nations, the United States would offer its workers an old-age maintenance system financed by a regressive tax on the workers themselves. What was more, in the short run, building a Social Security reserve fund by withdrawing money through taxation from the otherwise spend-

26. Perkins, *The Roosevelt I Knew*, 278–95.
27. Patterson, *America's Struggle against Poverty*, 73; Eliot, *Recollections of the New Deal*, 96, 97.

able incomes of workers would be sharply deflationary, hardly a welcome effect in the midst of the Depression.

Perkins explained all these objections to the president. "We can't help that," Roosevelt curtly replied. He explained his basic principle to Perkins and a soberly impressed Eliot at a meeting in August 1934: "He wanted the use of gov't [sic] funds limited as much as possible, preferring 'contributions,'" Eliot wrote. "No dole," Roosevelt emphasized, "mustn't have a dole." "No money out of the Treasury," he declared on another occasion. He understood as clearly as any the inequity and economic dysfunctionality of the contributory payroll tax, but he understood equally those "legislative habits" and "prejudices" about which Perkins had reminded the CES. "I guess you're right on the economics," Roosevelt explained to another critic some years later, "but those taxes were never a problem of economics. They are politics all the way through. We put those payroll contributions there so as to give the contributors a legal, moral, and political right to collect their pensions and their unemployment benefits. With those taxes in there, no damn politician can ever scrap my social security program."[28]

Those same "popular prejudices" cast their shadow over the CES's deliberations in other ways. What should be the size of the benefit paid to retirees? "The easiest way," Perkins wrote, "would be to pay the same amount to everyone," a way that would also imply some income redistribution. "But," she added, "that is contrary to the typical American attitude that a man who works hard, becomes highly skilled, and earns high wages 'deserves' more on retirement than one who had not become a skilled worker." Therefore, the planners again swallowed their better judgment and decided on the more complicated system of paying benefits in proportion to previous earnings, yet another borrowing from the private insurance model on which Roosevelt insisted.

A final problem remained, one whose technical complexities intersected with political considerations to work a long and vexatious effect on the Social Security program. Workers then older than forty-five years of age would have only a limited number of years to pay into the system—for the earliest retirees a maximum of three years, as it turned out, since the first payroll deductions were scheduled to begin in 1937 and the first distributions were ultimately paid in 1940. The planners therefore recommended granting those first beneficiaries retirement pay-

28. Perkins, *The Roosevelt I Knew*, 281; Eliot, *Recollections of the New Deal*, 98, 102; Schlesinger, 2:308–09.

ments that would far exceed the value of their accumulated contributions, an arrangement that had a sizeable income-redistribution effect, albeit an exclusively intergenerational one. According to standard accounting procedures, payments to that first generation of recipients would create an accrued liability in the Social Security reserve fund that would have to be covered by general revenues at some future date — according to some estimates as early as 1965, and surely by 1980. That anticipated shortfall flatly contradicted the private insurance guidelines the president had laid down, including his strictures against money out of the treasury.

But the alternatives, Perkins explained to FDR, were to levy such high initial taxes "as to be almost confiscatory," to give this group "ridiculously small benefits," or to postpone the start-up of payments for many years, perhaps a dozen or more. The first alternative made no economic sense in the depressed circumstances of 1935. Roosevelt squelched the other two choices as politically unacceptable. "We have to have it," he told her. "The Congress can't stand the pressure of the Townsend Plan unless we have a real old-age insurance system, nor can I face the country."[29] But neither would he tolerate an accrued liability. "Ah," he exclaimed, when Perkins presented the CES's draft proposal, "but this is the same old dole under another name. It is almost dishonest to build up an accumulated deficit for the Congress of the United States to meet in 1980. We can't do that. We can't sell the United States short in 1980 any more than in 1935."[30]

How to break this impasse? Treasury Secretary Henry Morgenthau had the solution. He made two proposals. First, he recommended a modest increase in the rate of the contributory payroll tax so as to build a large reserve fund that would permanently preclude the need for future general revenues. To avoid "confiscatory" rates, Morgenthau also recommended a second, still more consequential, amendment to the

29. Perkins, *The Roosevelt I Knew*, 194,
30. Perkins, *The Roosevelt I Knew*, 294. The CES, in an open letter to the president dated January 17, 1935, had noted that "Government contributions" would be necessary "after the system has been in operation for thirty years" — or 1965. *PPA* (1935), 53. Why Roosevelt sometimes thought in terms of 1980 rather than 1965 is not clear. Further confusion about this issue is evident in Roosevelt's special Social Security message to Congress of January 17, 1935, when he remarked that "for those who are now too old to build up their own insurance," it would be necessary to make payments from general funds "for perhaps 30 years to come." *PPA* (1935), 45–46. The president heard Morgenthau's misgivings about how to finance the pensions of the over–forty-five group only after he had delivered his January 17 message.

draft bill. He insisted on excluding from old-age coverage farm laborers, domestic servants, and workers in establishments with fewer than ten employees. "This was a blow," Perkins said. "But there were enough people afraid of the deflationary effects of this large money collection, enough people afraid of too large a system, and enough people confused about the desirability of social legislation by the Federal Government, to make it a foregone conclusion that if the Secretary of the Treasury recommended limitation, limitation there would be."[31]

So Perkins grudgingly acquiesced in Morgenthau's amendments. By this time she was grateful to accomplish anything at all. So many clashing interests and contrary ideas had contended in shaping the Social Security bill that Perkins likened her task to "driving a team of highstrung unbroken horses." Yet she could not help but regret the degree to which Roosevelt's original vision had been compromised. "The thing had been chiseled down to a conservative pattern," she rightly remarked. Health care had been dropped. Unemployment insurance fell far short of a consistent national plan. Contributory taxes for old-age insurance had been retained and even expanded beyond the planners' intentions. And 9.4 million of the least secure, most needful workers—a disproportionate number of them black farm laborers and black female domestics—had at a stroke been denied old-age coverage altogether.

All of this was lamentable to the group that crafted the legislation, but they deemed the most lamentable feature of the Social Security bill to be the virtual sacralization of the contributory principle and the consequent reinforcement of the private insurance model of social security that took root in the public mind. The "contributions" were in fact nothing more nor less than taxes by another name. But in the climate of Depression America, they could scarcely be called that in public. "The apparent analogy with private insurance," one expert wrote, made Social Security "acceptable to a society which was dominated by business ethics and which stressed individual economic responsibility." Eliot voiced the disappointment of many on the CES planning group in a statement years later:

> In 1935 . . . all the members of the committee and its large staff of experts agreed on the contributory principle: the ultimate beneficiary should contribute a part of the cost of his eventual old age annuity. . . . But they assumed that before long . . . income taxes would supplement the employee's contributions. . . . All, that is, except the Secretary

31. Perkins, *The Roosevelt I Knew*, 298.

of the Treasury, Henry Morgenthau, [who] persuaded the President that the rates of payroll and earnings taxes should be raised, to make the system forever "self-supporting." The rest of the Committee and the staff greatly regretted this, for the earnings tax, while necessary to effectuate the contributory principle, is a regressive tax and should be held at a very low rate.[32]

THE PRESIDENT at last faced the country on January 17, 1935, and unveiled his Social Security program. Though it fell far short of his grandest design, it did offer to some twenty-six million workers at least a measure of "security against the hazards and vicissitudes of life." For all its limitations, Perkins shrewdly assessed the final bill as "the only plan that could have been put through Congress."[33]

"We pay now for the dreadful consequence of economic insecurity — and dearly," the president said in his special message to Congress accompanying the draft Social Security bill. "No one can guarantee this country against the dangers of future depressions," Roosevelt conceded, "but we can reduce those dangers. We can eliminate many of the factors that cause economic depressions, and we can provide the means of mitigating their results. This plan for economic security is at once a measure of prevention and a method of alleviation." In a thinly veiled reference to the Townsend and Long schemes, he described his own proposal as proceeding from "sound caution and consideration of all of the factors concerned: the national credit, the rights and responsibilities of States, the capacity of industry to assume financial responsibilities and the fundamental necessity of proceeding in a manner that will merit the enthusiastic support of citizens of all sorts." Now was not the time,

32. Patterson, *America's Struggle against Poverty*, 74, 75; Eliot, *Recollections of the New Deal*, 103. Eliot also points out that in 1939 Congress amended the act, partly in a deliberate move to reduce the size of the accumulating "trust fund," which was then growing at a rate projected to reach $50 billion by 1980. Since that sum exceeded the federal debt outstanding in the late 1930s, the prospect loomed that the Social Security reserve might eventually have to be invested in the stocks and bonds of private corporations — creating a kind of back road to socialism that would have assuredly been an ironic result of the elaborate maneuvering in the original Social Security legislation to avoid even the appearance of socialism. The rate of growth of the reserve was slowed by lowering the payroll tax and extending coverage, principally to survivors of beneficiaries. Only in the 1950s were agricultural and domestic workers finally covered, and the system at last approached the universal coverage that Roosevelt had originally dreamed of.

33. PPA (1935), 17; Perkins, *The Roosevelt I Knew*, 284.

he warned, to jeopardize the "precious" goal of security "by attempting to apply it on too ambitious a scale."[34]

Roosevelt had prepared the ground well. His transparent allusions to less responsible schemes helped convince congressional doubters that the president's measured radicalism was far preferable to the dread Long and Townsend alternatives—or the even more dread option of a bill introduced by Minnesota representative Ernest Lundeen, which called for unemployment compensation at full wages to all jobless workers, paid for out of general tax revenues and administered by local workers' councils. After lengthy hearings through an exceptionally crowded legislative season, the Social Security Act became law on August 14, 1935.

The final act provided for unemployment insurance and old-age pensions, its principal features, and also authorized nearly $50 million in federal grants to the states for the immediate relief of the indigent elderly, another $25 million for Aid to Dependent Children, and modest sums for public health services. To finance the unemployment plan, the act levied a federal tax of 1 percent on employers of eight or more workers, rising to 2 percent in 1937 and 3 percent thereafter. States were to administer their own plans and could utilize the tax-offset feature of the law to recapture up to 90 percent of the federal levy, with most of the remaining 10 percent earmarked for administrative expenses. Old-age pension accounts were funded by employee "contributions" of 1 percent in 1937, rising in three-year stages to 3 percent in 1949, and matched by a like tax on employers. Depending on a worker's lifetime employment record and average wage, payments in retirement would range from ten to eighty-five dollars per month. Only the appropriations for the indigent elderly, seen as a transitional expense until Social Security coverage became more nearly universal, and for Aid to Dependent Children (ADC) were to come from general tax revenues. ADC—later Aid to Families with Dependent Children, or AFDC—was a "new departure," the CES report frankly acknowledged, but one that was "imperative" for "rearing fatherless families," a particular concern in a decade when so many work-seeking fathers had abandoned their families and taken to the road.[35]

With what Perkins called these "practical, flat-footed first steps," the groundwork for the modern American welfare state was laid. For all the

34. *PPA* (1935), 43–46.
35. *PPA* (1935), 55.

caution that attended its origins, Perkins said, Roosevelt always regarded the Social Security Act as the "cornerstone of his administration." On that admittedly modest foundation an imposing edifice was eventually raised.[36] In the next few years, all the states passed unemployment compensation laws of their own, to take advantage of the law's tax-offset feature and "keep the money at home." Though levels of benefits varied widely from state to state, the typical plan provided sixteen weeks of unemployment checks at half pay, up to a maximum of fifteen dollars per week, roughly equivalent to the average WPA wage. Most plans provided no further relief to an unemployed worker who still remained jobless after the initial period of coverage expired—other than to seek a WPA job. Similarly, several states expanded and upgraded their services to the indigent elderly and to dependent children, so as to receive their share of the federal grants for those purposes legislated in the 1935 act. Here, too, there was much variation among the states. Until 1939, ten states declined to join these categorical assistance plans at all. Those that did received federal moneys for old-age assistance on a one-for-one matching basis, up to a federal maximum of fifteen dollars per recipient per month. Combined federal-state payments to the indigent elderly in 1936 ranged from $3.92 in Mississippi to $31.36 in California, for a national average of $18.36 per month. Reflecting Roosevelt's notion that the "local community" had first responsibility and adequate resources to deal with "unemployable" relief recipients, the federal government contributed to ADC on a one-for-two federal-to-state basis, up to a federal maximum of twelve dollars for the first child and eight dollars for younger children. By 1939, when about seven hundred thousand children benefited from ADC, average monthly payments per family were about $32, ranging from $8.10 in Arkansas to $61.07 in Massachusetts. At the federal level, meanwhile, a vast new bureaucracy came into being. It employed over twelve thousand people in 202 regional offices and in Washington, D.C., where a central card file holding the records of some twenty-six million Social Security registrants covered an acre of floor space.[37]

On January 17, 1940, a seventy-six-year-old Vermonter, Ida M. Fuller, received the first Social Security check, for $41.30. Half a century later, forty million beneficiaries received monthly payments averaging over

36. Perkins, The Roosevelt I Knew, 284, 301.
37. Patterson, America's Struggle against Poverty, 67–77; Achenbaum, Old Age in the New Land, 127–41; New York Times, August 27, 1935, 10.

five hundred dollars. Accounting for more than $400 billion in annual expenditures by century's end, Social Security and its add-on programs, including Medicare, had become the largest item in the federal budget. With good reason does one Roosevelt biographer declare the Social Security Act "the most important single piece of social legislation in all American history, if importance be measured in terms of historical decisiveness and direct influence upon the lives of individual Americans."[38]

YET EVEN AS THE SPRAWLING Social Security administrative apparatus began to take shape, doubts were multiplying about the permanence of Roosevelt's innovative plan, and about the survivability of many other New Deal achievements as well. On May 6, 1935, the Supreme Court declared unconstitutional the Railroad Retirement Act of 1934, using language that seemed to threaten, as Eliot had feared, the old-age insurance features of the Social Security bill. Worse, on May 27 a unanimous Court nullified the National Industrial Recovery Act, in terms so sweeping as to put at risk virtually all the New Deal legislation of the preceding two years. Roosevelt called it the most troubling judicial decision since the Dred Scott case, because it brought "the country as a whole up against a very practical question. . . . Does this decision mean that the United States Government has no control over any national economic problem?" The Court's action, the president fumed, was hopelessly anachronistic. "We have been relegated to the horse-and-buggy definition of interstate commerce," he declared angrily.[39]

But rather than slowing Roosevelt's political momentum, the Supreme Court's actions seemed instead to galvanize him. On June 4 he urged the Congress to remain in extraordinary session through the sweltering summer—most government buildings, including all but a few rooms in the Capitol, still lacked air-conditioning—in order to pass four pieces of "must" legislation: in addition to the Social Security bill, they included Senator Wagner's bill to create a national labor relations board, urgently necessary for industrial peace now that the Court had voided the labor provisions of NRA; a bill to break up large public utility holding companies; and a bill to increase the power of the Federal Reserve System's Open Market Committee, making it a more effective instrument for controlling the money supply.

38. Davis 3:437.
39. PPA (1935), 200–222.

The last measure was the least controversial. When the Federal Reserve System had been created in pre–World War I days, little attention had been given to the effects of its transactions in government securities, which amounted then to a negligible sum. When the war then ballooned the national debt, the Fed set up the Open Market Committee to buy and sell government debt instruments. It soon became apparent that the committee's operations could exert a powerful influence on the money supply and the availability of credit, as well as on the interest rates at which the treasury could borrow. The committee, however, was at first an informal body. Even after being granted statutory recognition in the Banking Act of 1933, it remained under the control of the private bankers, largely based in New York, who represented the Fed's member institutions. Those institutions in any case were still free to conduct their own open-market sale and purchase of government securities. Roosevelt's banking bill proposed bringing the Open Market Committee under the direct and exclusive authority of the Federal Reserve's Board of Governors, a move aimed at enhancing central control over the nation's money markets, easing treasury funding operations, and improving the Federal Reserve's capacity to modulate swings in the business cycle. The president signed the bill on August 24, 1935. The Fed now had more of the trappings of a true central bank than any American institution had wielded since the demise of the Bank of the United States in Andrew Jackson's day. Working through the enervating humidity of a Washington summer, Congress further obliged the president and passed all of his other "must" bills substantially as he submitted them.

The record of that 1935 congressional session was remarkable by any measure, as Roosevelt acknowledged in a letter of appreciation when Congress adjourned at on August 24: "When a calm and fair review of the work of this Congress is made," he said, "it will be called a historic session," a judgment that time has ratified. Indeed, as Roosevelt said just days earlier, at the signing ceremony for the Social Security Act, "[i]f the Senate and the House of Representatives in this long and arduous session had done nothing more than pass this Bill, the session would be regarded as historic for all time."[40] The measures enacted in 1935 held the potential to transform American social and economic life. The Wagner Act, in particular, might prove second only to the Social Security Act in its power to reshape the workplace and, not incidentally,

40. PPA (1935), 325.

to determine the political future of the Democratic Party. Yet over all those prospects there still lay the shadow of constitutional challenge.[41]

There also remained the questions of Long and Coughlin. Robert La Follette and other progressives had advised the president in the spring of 1935 that "the best answer to Huey Long and Father Coughlin would be the enactment into law of the Administration bills now pending."[42] Those bills, the four on Roosevelt's June 4 "must" list, had now been enacted. Long and Coughlin supposedly had their answer. But for reasons that have long intrigued historians, the president was not content to leave matters there.

To the sharp surprise and considerable discomfort of his own mostly southern conservative legislative leaders, Roosevelt added a fifth measure to his "must" list in late June: tax reform. Just six months earlier, the president had declared the federal revenue system to be in no need of amendment. But on June 19 he told the Congress: "Our revenue laws have operated in many ways to the unfair advantage of the few, and they have done little to prevent an unjust concentration of wealth and economic power. . . . Social unrest and a deepening sense of unfairness are dangers to our national life which we must minimize by rigorous methods." Accordingly, he asked for "very high taxes" on large incomes and for stiffer inheritance taxes, since "the transmission from generation to generation of vast fortunes . . . is not consistent with the ideals and sentiments of the American people."[43] In addition, he requested a graduated corporate income tax and taxes on intercorporate dividends—a blow at the holding companies also under attack in the public utilities holding company bill. He called it a "wealth tax." Others soon dubbed it a "soak-the-rich" bill. As Roosevelt's message was read in the Senate, Huey Long strutted about the chamber, pointing to himself as the original inspiration of the president's tax proposals. Long concluded the recital with a fervent "Amen!"

But there was more rhetoric than revenue in the president's tax proposal—and some high-stakes politicking as well. Morgenthau acknowledged as much when he told a Treasury Department subordinate that the tax bill was one issue that FDR "could well afford to be defeated

41. For a discussion of the Wagner Act and its implications, see chap. 10. The Public Utilities Holding Company Act and other items of economic legislation are discussed in chaps. 11 and 12.
42. Ickes Diary 1:363.
43. PPA (1935), 270–76.

on." The president, he explained, simply had to "make his record clear." The tax proposal, Morgenthau went on, "is more or less a campaign document." As a congressman put it, "This is a hell raiser, not a revenue raiser." The president uncomplainingly acquiesced in congressional tinkering with the bill, passed in the waning hours of the session, so that it promised to generate only about $250 million in additional funds, a piddling sum. The final law imposed a tax of 79 percent on incomes over $5 million, a rate that appeared to be downright confiscatory but in fact covered precisely one individual—John D. Rockefeller. The basic rate remained at 4 percent, and in an era when three-quarters of all families earned less than two thousand dollars per year, well below the minimum taxable level for a married couple, fewer than one American household in twenty paid any federal income tax at all. A couple with an income of four thousand dollars would have been in the top tenth of all income receivers; if they had two children, they would have paid a tax of sixteen dollars. A similar family making twelve thousand dollars—placing them in the richest 1 percent of households—would pay less than six hundred dollars. As the closest student of Depression-era tax policy says, there were two tax systems in the New Deal, "one a revenue workhorse, the other a symbolic showpiece." The "wealth tax" of 1935 was decidedly more showpiece than workhorse.[44]

It was not revenue but politics that drove Roosevelt's tax strategy. Here he was indeed "stealing Huey Long's thunder," as he frankly admitted to Raymond Moley in the spring of 1935. And in the process of seeking to make Long's supporters his own, he also drew to himself the bitter enmity of Long's opponents. "It was on that day," said Moley, referring to Roosevelt's June 19 tax message, "the split in the Democratic Party began."[45] It was on that day, too, that the hatred of the rich toward Roosevelt began to congeal into icy contempt for the Hudson River squire, denounced now as "a traitor to his class." (A cartoon of the era depicted an affluent crowd on its way to the movie theater "to hiss Roosevelt.") William Randolph Hearst branded Roosevelt's tax proposal "Communism." He instructed his editors to call the tax bill the "soak-the-successful" bill and to begin substituting "Raw Deal" for "New

---

44. Mark H. Leff, *The Limits of Symbolic Reform: The New Deal and Taxation, 1933–1939* (Cambridge: Cambridge University Press, 1984), 91–96, 2.

45. Raymond Moley, *After Seven Years* (New York: Harper and Brothers, 1939), 312. The tax message, which Roosevelt dragooned a reluctant Moley to help draft, sealed Moley's own alienation from Roosevelt and the New Deal.

Deal" in news coverage of the administration. Privately he took to calling the president "Stalin Delano Roosevelt."

For his part, Roosevelt seemed almost to enjoy the passions he had aroused among the well-to-do. Reading aloud to Ickes from one of the barbed passages in his tax message, he looked up with a smile and said, "That is for Hearst." Some months later, FDR spoke at the Harvard University Tercentenary Celebration. Perhaps the visit awakened his long-ago rejection from Porcellian, a memory that may have inflamed his new itch to provoke the smug rich. At the university's bicentennial in 1836, he pointed out, "many of the alumni of Harvard were sorely troubled concerning the state of the Nation. Andrew Jackson was President. On the two hundred fiftieth anniversary of the founding of Harvard College, alumni again were sorely troubled. Grover Cleveland was President. Now, on the three hundredth anniversary," he concluded with relish, "I am the President."[46]

When Congress finally adjourned at the end of August, Roy Howard, head of the Scripps-Howard newspaper chain and generally friendly to the administration, wrote the president with an earnest suggestion. "I have been seeking reasons for the doubts and uncertainties of those business men who are skeptics, critics, and outright opponents of your program," Howard said. "[T]hroughout the country many business men who once gave you sincere support are now, not merely hostile, they are frightened." They had become convinced, Howard went on, "that you fathered a tax bill that aims at revenge rather than revenue — revenge on business. . . . That there can be no real recovery until the fears of business have been allayed through the granting of a breathing spell to industry." For the "orderly modernization of a system we want to preserve," Howard urged, there must be "a recess from further experimentation until the country can recover its losses."[47]

A week later the president replied, releasing both Howard's letter and his own response to the press. He rehearsed "the essential outline of what has been done," vigorously defending his measures "to seek a wise balance in American economic life, to restore our banking system to public confidence, to protect investors in the security market, to give labor freedom to organize and protection from exploitation, to safeguard and develop our national resources, to set up protection against the

46. Ickes Diary 1:384; Frank Freidel, *Franklin D. Roosevelt: A Rendezvous with Destiny* (Boston: Little, Brown, 1990), 206.
47. PPA (1935), 353.

vicissitudes incident to old age and unemployment, to relieve destitution and suffering and to relieve investors and consumers from the burden of unnecessary corporate machinery." It was a creditable record, Roosevelt said with much pride and not a little heat. But, he conceded, his basic program "has now reached substantial completion and the 'breathing spell' of which you speak is here—very decidedly so."[48]

With respect to substantive legislation, Roosevelt's "breathing spell" proved longer than he could have anticipated. With just a handful of exceptions, the legislative record of the New Deal was complete by August 1935. But when it came to attacks on business, the breathing spell proved much shorter than Roosevelt led Howard to expect. With his employment and security legislation, Roosevelt had apparently battened the New Deal against challengers from the left. The political threat from that quarter further dissipated in early September when Huey Long fell to an assassin's bullets in the marble corridor of the Louisiana Capitol at Baton Rouge. "I wonder why he shot me?" Long gasped, before lapsing into a coma. The question was never satisfactorily answered, as Long's bodyguards emptied their guns into the assassin's body. After lingering for nearly two days, passing in and out of consciousness, Long died on September 10. His last words were "God, don't let me die! I have so much to do!"[49]

But Roosevelt seemed to believe that neither his legislative record nor even Long's death could fully neutralize the forces of radicalism. When Ickes told him yet again, on December 10, 1935, "that I believed the general sentiment of the country to be much more radical than that of the Administration," Roosevelt readily agreed.[50] Despite his promise of a "breathing spell," Roosevelt went vigorously back on to the attack against business. From some mixture of principled conviction, personal pique, and political calculation, Roosevelt withdrew the hand of cooperation that he had extended to capital in 1933 and had proffered again in his open letter to the Scripps-Howard chief. Instead he now brandished the mailed fist of open political warfare. The undertone of truculence in his conciliatory reply to Howard swelled to a crescendo as the 1936 presidential campaign took shape.

Roosevelt effectively opened his antibusiness campaign with his annual message to Congress on January 3, 1936. Departing from prece-

48. PPA (1935), 354–57.
49. T. Harry Williams, *Huey Long* (New York: Knopf, 1969), 866, 876.
50. Ickes Diary 1:480.

dent, he delivered his address in the evening, to ensure the largest possible radio audience. Further breaking with tradition, he used the occasion not to describe the state of the Union but to make a blatantly political speech, pillorying his vaguely defined but nonetheless recognizable foes on the right. "We have earned the hatred of entrenched greed," the president declared. "They seek the restoration of their selfish power. . . . Give them their way and they will take the course of every autocracy of the past—power for themselves, enslavement for the public."[51] Huey Long himself could scarcely have put it more pungently. Republicans in the House chamber guffawed loudly when Roosevelt in conclusion referred to "this message on the state of the union." Even the left-leaning *Nation* was unsettled. "The President," it declared, "showed himself complete master of the grammar of vituperation." The magazine went on to condemn the president for turning "what was supposed to be a thoughtful discussion of the nation's ills and ways of treating them into a political diatribe."[52]

Diatribe was one thing. Money was another. Roosevelt soon pressed for further tax reform, reopening the wounds inflicted by his 1935 "wealth tax." On March 3, 1936, he sent Congress a supplemental budget message asking for a tax on undistributed corporate profits. This time, the government's revenue needs were real enough. The Supreme Court's elimination of the AAA had deprived the treasury of some $500 million in anticipated tax receipts. And over Roosevelt's veto, Congress had passed the long-stalled "bonus bill" in late January, calling for payments to World War I veterans of nearly $2 billion in 1936, instead of 1945. The bonus payment created a requirement for a $120 million carrying charge in each of the following nine years, to service the debt incurred to make the lump-sum distribution to the veterans. But in choosing to raise the needed revenues by taxing undistributed corporate profits, Roosevelt was threatening to shove the hand of government into the innermost workings of private businesses. Advocates of the scheme argued that a tax on retained earnings would create incentives to distribute profits in the form of higher wages or dividends, thus stimulating consumption. The tax also fitted nicely with views that Tugwell had expressed in *Industrial Discipline and the Governmental Arts* in 1933: that retained corporate earnings were one mechanism by which industrial managers loosed themselves from the discipline of the money mar-

51. *PPA* (1936), 13–16.
52. *Nation*, January 15, 1936, 60, 65.

kets and funded bad investment decisions or built redundant industrial facilities, thus exacerbating the structural problem of excess industrial capacity. Opponents countered that the tax would crimp management's ability to save against a rainy day, would enslave businessmen to the bankers, and, most important, would make it difficult for managers to plan for the kind of expansion that fostered economic growth. Business hated the undistributed corporate profits tax. Congress in the end harkened to the critics and significantly watered down FDR's original proposal, setting the tax rate at 7 to 27 percent and largely exempting small enterprises. But the final law did establish the principle that retained earnings could be taxed. In corporate boardrooms from Wall Street to the Golden Gate, fear and loathing of Roosevelt deepened.

More was to come. On June 27, 1936, Roosevelt accepted the Democratic Party's presidential nomination in a memorable speech broadcast nationwide from Philadelphia's Franklin Field.[53] "Philadelphia is a good city in which to write American history," he began, and proceeded to compare the patriots' struggle against political autocracy in 1776 to his own struggle against "economic royalists" 160 years later. "Necessitous men are not free men," he intoned, and argued that economic inequality made political equality meaningless. Before the New Deal, he charged, "[a] small group had concentrated into their own hands an almost complete control over other people's property, other people's money, other people's labor — other people's lives. For too many of us life was no longer free; liberty was no longer real; men could no longer follow the pursuit of happiness.

"Against economic tyranny such as this," Roosevelt went on, "the American citizen could appeal only to the organized power of Government." Then, in a lyrical peroration that would long echo in American political oratory, he said:

> Governments can err, Presidents do make mistakes, but the immortal Dante tells us that divine justice weighs the sins of the cold-blooded and the sins of the warm-hearted in different scales.

53. The occasion was memorable for more than the speech. It also marked one of the few times that Roosevelt's physical handicap was publicly and humiliatingly displayed. On his way to the platform, Roosevelt reached out to shake the hand of the elderly poet Edwin Markham. The locking device on his steel leg brace sprang open, and Roosevelt fell helplessly to the ground. An aide forced the brace back into position; Roosevelt snapped, "Clean me up," and proceeded to the rostrum. Few people beyond the president's immediate entourage saw the incident. An account is in Schlesinger 3:583–84.

> Better the occasional faults of a Government that lives in a spirit of charity than the consistent omissions of a Government frozen in the ice of its own indifference.
>
> There is a mysterious cycle in human events. To some generations much is given. Of other generations much is expected. This generation of Americans has a rendezvous with destiny.[54]

This was too much for Moley. At dinner with Roosevelt in the White House family dining room three days before the Philadelphia speech, Moley's suggestion that the president strike a conciliatory tone in his upcoming address touched off a bitter exchange between the two men. Roosevelt twitted Moley about his "new, rich friends." Moley responded with heat, and Roosevelt grew snappish. "For the first and only time in my life, I saw the President forget himself as a gentleman," one of the other dinner guests recalled. "We all felt embarrassed. . . . It was an ordeal for all of us, and we were relieved when dinner finally broke up."[55]

Moley's friendship with the president effectively ended that evening. Other former allies had already parted company with Roosevelt. Al Smith told a Liberty League banquet at Washington's Mayflower Hotel in January 1936 that he would probably "take a walk" during the November elections. He compared the New Dealers to Marx and Lenin as well as to Norman Thomas. He accused Roosevelt of handing the government over to dreamy professors and bleeding-heart social workers. "Who is Ickes?" he asked. "Who is Wallace? Who is Hopkins, and, in the name of all that is good and holy, who is Tugwell, and where did he blow from?"[56]

Undeterred by this attack from his old political comrade, Roosevelt turned up the heat. When the Republicans gave their presidential nomination to the bland and genial Kansas governor, Alf Landon, touted as the "Kansas Coolidge" but in fact a mildly liberal legatee of the old Bull Moose tradition, Roosevelt largely ignored him. He especially ignored the Republican platform's pledge to "use the tax power for raising revenue and not for punitive or political purposes." He campaigned instead against "greed" and "autocracy." Business interests returned the fire. They drove Roosevelt to a cold fury late in the presidential campaign, when some employers distributed messages in paychecks charging

54. PPA (1936), 230–36.
55. Samuel I. Rosenman, Working with Roosevelt (New York: Harper and Brothers, 1952), 105; see Moley's own account in After Seven Years, 345.
56. Leuchtenburg, 178.

that the new Social Security system would require all participants to wear stainless-steel identification dogtags around their necks and that there was "no guarantee" that workers would ever see their payroll-tax deductions, scheduled to begin on January 1, 1937, returned to them as old-age pensions. Enraged, Roosevelt began to compare himself with Andrew Jackson, the president who had first demonstrated the political power of the populist style. "It is absolutely true," Roosevelt said, that Jackson's opponents "represented the same social outlook and the same element in the population that ours do."[57]

Ending his presidential campaign with a long speechmaking swing around the Northeast, especially the industrial districts of Pennsylvania, New England, and New York, Roosevelt brought his political jihad to a rousing climax in New York's Madison Square Garden on the evening of October 31, 1936. Leaning into the microphone after an uproarious thirteen-minute ovation, Roosevelt indicted his "old enemies": the sponsors and beneficiaries of "business and financial monopoly, speculation, reckless banking, class antagonism, war profiteering"—in short, "organized money." In a voice that even a sympathetic historian calls "hard, almost vengeful," Roosevelt went on: "Never before in all our history have these forces been so united against one candidate as they stand today. They are unanimous in their hate for me—and I welcome their hatred." The crowd erupted. "I should like to have it said of my first Administration," Roosevelt continued, "that in it the forces of selfishness and of lust for power met their match. I should like to have it said . . ." The crowd exploded with anticipation. "Wait a moment! I should like to have it said of my second Administration that in it these forces met their master." Bedlam broke out on the arena floor as the partisan audience roared its approval. But the spectacle at Madison Square Garden troubled other observers of the president's campaign. "Thoughtful citizens," Moley reflected, "were stunned by the violence, the bombast, the naked demagoguery of these sentences. No one who has merely read them can half know the meaning conveyed by the cadences of the voice that uttered them. . . . I began to wonder," Moley reflected, "whether he wasn't beginning to feel that the proof of a measure's merit was the extent to which it offended the business community."[58]

57. Leff, *Limits of Symbolic Reform*, 189; Schlesinger 3:637.
58. *PPA* (1936), 566–73; Moley, *After Seven Years*, 352. 313. Good accounts of the occasion are in Schlesinger 3:638–39; Leuchtenburg, 184; and Davis 3:644–45.

Why did Roosevelt do it? Moley asked himself. Why did the president go out of his way in 1935 and 1936 to antagonize businessmen? Why did he reject Roy Howard's counsel that "there can be no real recovery until the fears of business have been allayed" and instead insist on gratuitously provoking business and thickening its anxiety? Those questions elude easy answers if, like Moley and Howard, one assumes that economic recovery was Roosevelt's highest priority. But if one recognizes that lasting social reform and durable political realignment were at least equally important items on Roosevelt's agenda, then some of the mystery lifts. Politically, Roosevelt had little to lose by alienating the right in 1936. The reforms of 1935 had already estranged many conservatives from the New Deal. A Gallup poll in 1936 showed that while 53 percent of potential voters favored Roosevelt's reelection, only 31 percent of those listed in *Who's Who* did, a fair index of disaffection among the upper crust. The real danger was that Roosevelt might fail to contain and channel the restive forces swarming on his left. There, in the immigrant wards of the smokestack towns washed by the voice of the Radio Priest, and in the blighted rural districts where one-gallus farmers stirred to the dream of Every Man a King, were the makings of a permanent Democratic political majority that would safeguard the New Deal and possibly even expand it—or of endless unrest that would make it impossible for Roosevelt or anyone else to govern responsibly.[59]

Not the least of Roosevelt's worries was the Union Party, cobbled together in June 1936 by Townsendites, Father Coughlin, and the self-anointed successor to the assassinated Huey Long, a former Disciples of Christ preacher and onetime field organizer for Long's Share Our Wealth clubs, Gerald L. K. Smith. As a stump speaker, Smith outshone even the legendary Long himself. Tall, handsome, and energetic, Smith, said H. L. Mencken, was "the gutsiest and goriest, loudest and lustiest, the deadliest and damndest orator ever heard on this or any other earth . . . the champion boob-bumper of all epochs." He mesmerized audiences with his cry to "pull down these huge piles of gold until there shall be a real job, not a little old sow-belly, black-eyed pea job but real spending money, beefsteak and gravy, Chevrolet, Ford in the garage, new suit, Thomas Jefferson, Jesus Christ, red, white, and blue job for every man." He routinely closed his political rallies with a prayer: "Lift us out of this wretchedness O Lord, out of this poverty, lift us who stand here in slavery tonight. . . . Out of the

59. John M. Allswang, *The New Deal and American Politics* (New York: John Wiley and Sons, 1978), 57.

land of bondage into the land of milk and honey where every man is a king but no one wears a crown. Amen." When the Union Party nominated North Dakota congressman William Lemke for president, Coughlin declared he would produce at least nine million votes for Lemke or quit broadcasting. No one took that claim seriously, but in some states, Democratic pollsters warned, the Union Party might win up to 20 percent of Irish-Catholic votes, enough to sap the political strength of the working-class constituency on which Roosevelt's reelection depended.[60]

To bind the potentially explosive left to him and to reduce its capacity for radical mischief, rhetorical attacks on business were a cheap price to pay. To combat "crackpot ideas," Roosevelt had told a reporter during the "wealth tax" debate in 1935, "it may be necessary to throw to the wolves the forty-six men who are reported to have incomes in excess of one million dollars a year. This can be accomplished through taxation." But in fact Roosevelt's tax proposals had been more bluff than bludgeon. In reality all of Roosevelt's antibusiness "radicalism" in 1936 was a carefully staged political performance, an attack not on the capitalist system itself but on a few high-profile capitalists. This may have been class warfare, as Roosevelt's critics howled, but it was only a war of words. Roosevelt's scathing indictments of business in the 1936 campaign did not so much add insult to injury as they substituted insult *for* injury.[61]

Roosevelt's performance may have carried a low political cost, but it exacted a high price of another sort. Former Brain Truster Adolf Berle reckoned that price in psychological terms as "shattered morale" in the business community, but Berle also recognized that the state of business morale—what Hoover had called business "confidence"—had hard implications for economic recovery. "In the absence of a large Government ownership program," Berle reflected, there was no "class or group to whom we may turn for economic leadership."[62] Yet for the moment Roosevelt seemed willing to slacken his pursuit of recovery in order to consolidate his political gains.

ON NOVEMBER 3, the nation voted. The results extravagantly demonstrated the political shrewdness of Roosevelt's strategy. In the im-

60. Alan Brinkley, *Voices of Protest: Huey Long, Father Coughlin, and the Great Depression* (New York: Knopf, 1982), 173; Williams, *Huey Long*, 699–700; Leuchtenburg, 181–83.

61. Leff, *Limits of Symbolic Reform*, chap. 3, insightfully explores this theme.

62. Beatrice Bishop Berle and Travis Beal Jacobs, *Navigating the Rapids, 1918–1971: From the Papers of Adolf A. Berle* (New York: Harcourt Brace Jovanovich, 1973), 171.

migrant wards of the great industrial cities, where many people had never bothered to cast a ballot before the Depression, and where political loyalties had traditionally shifted mercurially, turnout rose nearly a third over 1932, and voters went overwhelmingly for Roosevelt and the Democrats. This was no accident. Roosevelt had assiduously wooed those voters, and his wooing took many forms. FDR's huge electoral majority of nearly twenty-eight million votes flowed from his rhetorical blasts at the right and from gratitude for unemployment relief and the prospective benefits of Social Security. He had also freely and consciously spent the oldest coin of political exchange: patronage. The New Deal had dispensed CWA and WPA jobs not only to the materially needy but to the politically needed. Roosevelt had disbursed still other favors. One out of four of his judicial appointments had gone to Catholics, more than a sixfold increase from the level of Catholic appointments to the federal bench in the decade of his Republican presidential predecessors. Where they could vote, African-Americans, too, registered their political gratitude not only for WPA jobs but for the highly publicized solicitude of Eleanor Roosevelt. Labor unions, especially the rapidly growing industrial unions robustly flexing their muscles after the passage of the Wagner Act, both contributed to Roosevelt's campaign war chest and turned out the vote for him in huge numbers. The very nature of many New Deal initiatives created political loyalty in direct, palpable ways.

As the political analyst Michael Barone later put it: "The New Deal changed American life by changing the relationship between Americans and their government. In 1930 the federal government consumed less than 4% of the gross national product; except for the Post Office, it was remote from the life of ordinary people. By 1936 the federal government consumed 9% of GNP and through WPA employed 7% of the work force; it was a living presence across the country." That presence meant votes. The four million homeowners whose property had been saved by the Home Owners Loan Corporation, for example, and the many millions more whose bank savings had been secured by the Federal Deposit Insurance Corporation also owed a weighty political debt to Franklin Roosevelt.[63]

63. Michael Barone, *Our Country: The Shaping of America from Roosevelt to Reagan* (New York: Free Press 1990) 95–96. According to Moley, Roosevelt's political adviser and Bronx Democratic boss Edward J. Flynn had laid out the basic campaign strategy at least as early as 1935, when he allegedly told Roosevelt that "there are two or three million more dedicated Republicans in the United States than there are Democrats. The population, however, is drifting into the urban areas. The election

The electoral results were unprecedented. Roosevelt, it was instantly clear, had established the basis for a new and potentially lasting political coalition. He had succeeded in drawing to himself enormous majorities in the working-class industrial cities, all but two of which went Democratic. The Union Party polled a miserable 882,000 votes—powerful testimony to the effects of Roosevelt's successful co-optation of both the program and the rhetoric of the left, as well as to the absence of Huey Long from the scene. Scarcely less pathetic was the Republican showing. Landon gathered sixteen million popular votes but won the electoral votes of only two states, prompting wags to retool the old political saw about the predictive power of Maine's presidential preference. Democrats now gloated that "as Maine goes, so goes Vermont." Among the casualties of the Roosevelt landslide was the venerable *Literary Digest* electoral poll (and soon the *Literary Digest* itself), which had fairly accurately predicted the outcomes of several preceding presidential elections and had forecast a Landon victory in 1936. But the *Digest* this time made the fatal error of polling persons whose names appeared in telephone books and automobile registration lists, unwittingly skewing its sample toward relatively well-off voters.[64]

For Roosevelt, the election was a glorious, ringing triumph. His 523–8 electoral college margin over Landon was the most lopsided result in more than a century, since James Monroe's 231–1 advantage over John Quincy Adams in 1820. In the House the Democrats took 331 seats, leaving the Republicans with but 89. Democrats would hold 76 seats in the new Senate, a crowd so large that twelve freshman Democrats would have to sit on the traditionally Republican side of the aisle. A heavy majority of governorships were now also in the hands of the Democrats. What William Allen White had said of Roosevelt after the 1934 congressional elections was now more true than ever: "He has been all but crowned by the people."[65]

---

of 1932 was not normal. To remain in power we must attract some millions, perhaps seven million, who are hostile or indifferent to both parties. They believe the Republican Party to be controlled by big business and the Democratic Party by the conservative South. These millions are mostly in the cities. They include racial and religious minorities and labor people. We must attract them by radical programs of social and economic reform." Moley, *The First New Deal* (New York: Harcourt, Brace and World, 1966), 379.

64. Peverill Squire, "Why the 1936 Literary Digest Poll Failed," *Public Opinion Quarterly* 52 (1988): 125–33.

65. Davis 3:422.

What would Roosevelt do with that clamorous mandate, and with all that political power? The nation soon had its answer. Some three-quarters of a century earlier, Abraham Lincoln had in his second inaugural address turned away from the immediate political crisis of secession that had preoccupied his first inaugural and dwelt on the stubborn moral evil of slavery. He vowed to prosecute the war "until every drop of blood drawn with the lash shall be paid by another drawn with the sword." So now did Roosevelt in his second inaugural play down the emergency of the Depression. He spoke instead of the enduring evils that he proposed in his second term to vanquish. The first president to be inaugurated in January, Roosevelt looked out over the rain-drenched crowd facing the Capitol's east facade on January 20, 1937, and laid out the manifesto for his second administration:

> In this nation I see tens of millions of citizens who at this very moment are denied the greater part of what the very lowest standards of today call the necessities of life.
> I see millions of families trying to live on incomes so meager that the pall of family disaster hangs over them day by day.
> I see millions whose daily lives in city and on farm continue under conditions labeled indecent by a so-called polite society half a century ago.
> I see millions denied education, recreation, and the opportunity to better their lot and the lot of their children.
> I see millions lacking the means to buy the products of farm and factory and by their poverty denying work and productivity to many other millions.
> I see one-third of a nation ill-housed, ill-clad, ill-nourished.
> It is not in despair that I paint you that picture [Roosevelt concluded] I paint it for you in hope — because the Nation, seeing and understanding the injustice in it, proposes to paint it out. . . . The test of our progress is not whether we add more to the abundance of those who have much; it is whether we provide enough for those who have too little.[66]

It was a noble purpose and a handsome test of progress, enunciated with clarity and passion by an American leader empowered like none before him to make his vision a reality. But as the new year of 1937 opened, Roosevelt faced a future that held perils beyond even his wizardly reckoning.

66. *PPA* (1937), 1–6.

10

Strike!

*My boyhood was a pretty rough passage. I came through it, yes. But
that was luck, luck, luck! Think of the others!*
— New York senator Robert F. Wagner

Despite Roosevelt's fulminations against business, and despite the fumbling performance of the NRA and AAA, as early as 1935 the economy
had begun to show at least modest signs of recovery. In the hollows of
Appalachia, miners were retimbering coal shafts dank and rubbled from
years of disuse. Workers oiled rusty spindles in long-shuttered textile
mills from Massachusetts to the Carolinas. The clang of stamping
presses and the buzz of machine tools split the stillness that had descended in 1929 over the great industrial belt between the Ohio River
and the Great Lakes. Stevedores were once again winching cargoes onto
the docks of Puget Sound and San Francisco Bay. Tugs taken out of
mothballs nudged barge-rafts up the Mississippi from New Orleans.
Along the Monongahela and the Allegheny, banked forge and foundry
furnaces were coughing back to life. Haltingly, hopefully, America was
going back to work.

Official figures confirmed the extent of the revival. Gross national
product for 1935 stood at nearly $88 billion, well above the low point
of some $73 billion in 1933, though still below the 1929 high of $104
billion. A more sensitive gauge of economic performance, measuring
the volume of industrial output on a monthly basis, confirmed the steady
and even accelerating pace of improvement. On a 1929 base of 100,
the Federal Reserve Board's Index of Industrial Production climbed
from less than 50 in 1933 to 70 in 1934 and was rising above 80 as 1935
drew to a close. These favorable trends gathered still more momentum
throughout 1936 and on into early 1937. By the time of Roosevelt's tri-

umphal reelection in November 1936, the ranks of the unemployed had shrunk by nearly four million from the 1933 total of some thirteen million. Within weeks of his inauguration at the end of January 1937, almost two million additional workers had found jobs (though the unemployment rate in 1937 remained at 14 percent and never went lower for the remainder of the decade). Gross national product totaled almost $100 billion for 1936 and would actually exceed the 1929 figure in 1937 (though only barely and briefly).[1]

This economic revival, however tenuous, set the stage for the American labor movement's crusade to realize its most elusive goal: organizing the millions of unskilled workers in the great mass-production sectors, especially steel and automaking, into powerful industrial unions. That objective had lain beyond labor's grasp since the Knights of Labor had sputtered to an inglorious death some fifty years earlier. It had receded even further from reach as the Depression had perversely immunized firms without customers from labor's most potent weapon, the threat of work stoppage. But prosperity, especially the first prosperity after such a long interval of depression, rendered many firms vulnerable once again to the tactics of slowdown and strike.

Other elements essential to accomplishing labor's goals were also falling into place. Thanks to the Norris–La Guardia Act of 1932, which had bound the federal judiciary from issuing injunctions in labor disputes, capital could no longer look to the federal courts for help. Successful labor organizing now depended as never before on friendly, or at least neutral, state governments. Many governors in the past had proved all too willing to send in the militia to break picket lines and escort scabs into struck mills, mines, and factories. But by 1937, due largely to the active campaigning and generous funding of John L. Lewis's United Mine Workers, liberal Democrats, sympathetic to labor, held the governorships of several key industrial states. Herbert Lehman presided in New York. George Earle sat in the statehouse in steelmaking Pennsylvania, where the long-silent mills were now thundering at 90 percent of capacity and beginning to generate profits for the first time in half a decade. And on January 1, 1937, Frank L. Murphy took the oath of office as governor of Michigan, where the huge automobile plants that had lain vacant and forlorn since 1929 from Detroit to Flint and beyond were stirring back to life, gearing up for an anticipated

1. Lester V. Chandler, *America's Greatest Depression, 1929–1941* (New York: Harper and Row, 1970), 4–7, 129–32.

production run of some four million cars in the year ahead, nearly double their average annual output in the first half of the decade.

Labor also had reason to hope that as Franklin Roosevelt began his second term the federal government would not merely stand aside but would look benevolently on its purposes. Labor's Non-Partisan League, largely a John L. Lewis creation, had campaigned vigorously for Roosevelt's reelection. Lewis's United Mine Workers treasury alone had furnished the Roosevelt campaign with some $500,000 in funds in 1936. Lewis pointedly reminded the president that labor had turned out the vote for him and his party in the mining and mill districts from the Alleghenies to Chicago. Labor had helped Roosevelt to win traditionally Republican Pennsylvania, which he had lost to Hoover in 1932, and working-class votes helped to produce a 67 percent victory margin in Indiana. Lewis himself, though a lifelong Republican, had emphatically endorsed Roosevelt in 1936. For good measure he had denounced Alf Landon in front of a cheering crowd of coal miners in Pottsville, Pennsylvania, as "just as empty, as inane, and innocuous as a watermelon that had been boiled in a bathtub." For these services, political, financial, and rhetorical, Lewis believed that Roosevelt owed him one — a big one. "We must capitalize on the election," Lewis told his associates in late 1936. Labor had been "out fighting for Roosevelt and every steel town showed a smashing victory for him." Now was the time to demand that the favor be returned.[2]

Most important, the Wagner National Labor Relations Act of 1935 had put a mighty weapon at labor's disposal. The act created at least a skeletal legal framework guaranteeing workers' right to organize and requiring employers to bargain with duly recognized union representatives. It empowered the National Labor Relations Board (NLRB) to supervise elections in which workers might choose their union representatives. It prohibited such "unfair labor practices" by employers as discrimination against union members, refusal to bargain, and, most telling, management sponsorship of company unions.

But the Wagner Act was not by itself sufficient to realize labor's ends. For one thing, the act at first commanded no servile assent from employers. Invigorated by a widely bruited opinion of the American Liberty League that the act was unconstitutional and would soon be formally

2. Melvyn Dubofsky and Warren Van Tine, *John L. Lewis: A Biography* (New York: Quadrangle/New York Times, 1977), 252; Robert H. Zieger, *American Workers, American Unions, 1920–1985* (Baltimore: Johns Hopkins University Press, 1986), 46.

declared so by the Supreme Court, many employers announced that they would openly defy its provisions. For another, even should the law be constitutionally approved, workers must still take the initiative to organize themselves. And once organized, they were guaranteed no particular results by the Wagner Act, which stopped short of compelling employers to reach *agreement* with their employees. As Massachusetts senator David Walsh said during the debate on the Wagner bill:

> Let me emphasize again: When the employees have chosen their organization, when they have selected their representatives, all the bill proposes to do is to escort them to the door of their employer and say, "Here they are, the legal representatives of your employees." What happens behind those doors is not inquired into, and the bill does not seek to inquire into it. . . . The employer . . . is obliged to sign no agreement; he can say, "Gentlemen, we have heard you and considered your proposals. We cannot comply with your request," and that ends it.[3]

Yet for all its limitations, the Wagner Act opened a world of possibility to American labor. Together with the favorable political climate and the vulnerability of the steel manufacturers and automakers to any disruption of their first prospective profits in years, the act helped initiate a historic organizing drive that rearranged the balance of power between American capital and labor. Labor's awakening also secured a broad working-class constituent base that would help to make the Democrats the majority party for a long time to come. Ironically, some of the tactics that were to win labor's victories would in the end also help to hasten the closing of the New Deal era of reform.

If the stage was now set at the end of 1936, it remained for workers themselves to raise the curtain. There had already been a handful of successful, though turbulent, overtures—and many more heartbreaking false starts. The few successes had been cued, as had the several failures been miscued, by the passage of the National Industrial Recovery Act in 1933. The act's Section 7(a), by ostensibly guaranteeing labor's right to collective bargaining, had struck a spark of hope that ignited the heaps of combustibles littered across the American social and economic landscape in 1933. For the remainder of that first New Deal year and into the next, workers seized the chance to redress grievances accumulated over decades of unbridled industrialization and exacerbated by years of

---

3. Milton Derber and Edwin Young, eds., *Labor and the New Deal* (Madison: University of Wisconsin Press, 1957), 148.

economic collapse: poor wages, arbitrary work rules, no job security and, above all, no union. Some employers, notably General Electric president Gerard Swope, a progressive businessman who was among the architects of the NRA, welcomed and even encouraged the unionization of their employees. More employers, if they honored 7(a) at all, did so by establishing company unions, so-called Employee Representation Plans (ERPs), which were in fact the docile and housebroken creatures of management.[4] When workers persisted in their efforts to realize the promise of 7(a) and gain recognition of their own independent unions, most employers resisted, at times savagely. The federal government itself waffled in its own interpretation of 7(a), sometimes favoring workers, sometimes employers. In this fluid and volatile environment, what can only be called open class warfare, often orchestrated by bellicose radicals, erupted in scores of communities in 1933 and 1934.

In Toledo, Ohio, A. J. Muste's unapologetically radical American Workers Party forged an unusual alliance of both employed and unemployed workers to force the Electric Auto-Lite Company to recognize a new, NRA-spawned union. For several days in May 1934, knots of strikers and National Guardsmen battled through the streets of the city, repeatedly clashing in bare-knuckle brawls. On May 24 the skittish and poorly trained guardsmen botched a bayonet charge into the strikers' ranks. In desperation, they then fired a volley of rifle fire into the crowd. Two men died of gunshot wounds. Chastened, Auto-Lite's management submitted to arbitration that eventually secured the union's right to be recognized.

Elsewhere, even human life proved an insufficient price to purchase labor's goals. In southern California's lush Imperial Valley, the Communist-led Cannery and Agricultural Workers Industrial Union (CAW) set out to organize the stoop-laborers who sweated under the California sun in the Golden State's giant agribusiness "factories in the field." The California field hands, as well as the packers in the canning sheds, worked under conditions that one investigator thought "competed favorably with slavery." Given the color line that separated white growers from their mostly Mexican and Filipino workers, the Imperial Valley recollected slavery in other ways as well. In what was to become a tragically familiar pattern, the growers responded by denouncing the CAW

---

4. Company unions were the fastest-growing of all unions between 1932 and 1935, jumping from 1.25 million to 2.5 million members, who accounted for some 60 percent of all organized workers. Derber and Young, *Labor and the New Deal*, 288.

as a Communist conspiracy. They sent in toughs who strong-armed union officials and killed three unarmed strikers with rifle fire. Without consistent support from either Sacramento or Washington, the federal official sent to mediate the dispute soon resigned in disgust. The Imperial Valley, he declared on his departure in June 1934, "is governed by a small group which, in advertising a war against communism is sponsoring terrorism, intimidation and injustice. . . . It is time the Imperial Valley awakens to the fact that it is part of the United States." The CAW was licked. It withdrew from the valley and soon expired, leaving behind only a militantly antiunion growers' association, the Associated Farmers of California, Inc., and a lasting lesson in the obstacles to unionizing the farm sector. The framers of the Wagner Act acknowledged those obstacles when they specifically exempted agricultural workers from its provisions.[5]

Another explosive labor disturbance rocked California just days after the valley's tense feudal order was bloodily restored. San Francisco longshoremen, protesting shippers' control of the hated "shape-up," where mobs of men milled about at dawn near the Ferry Building and implored an imperious foreman for the favor of a day's employment, had shut down the port of San Francisco for nearly two months. The Industrial Association, a business body formed in 1921 to suppress San Francisco unions, determined to break the strike by force. The association made its move on the morning of July 5, 1934. Under heavy police escort, several red trucks threaded their way past the Ferry Building along the Embarcadero, the broad thoroughfare fronting San Francisco's docklands, to deliver their cargoes of strikebreakers to the idle wharves. The drivers proceeded in cautious convoy, nervously avoiding eye contact with the stevedores manning the picket line that straggled along the fog-laden Embarcadero. Before long the strikers' sullen anger exploded into unshirted rage. Shouting obscenities, men swarmed toward the trucks, flinging rocks and pieces of iron pipe. Police shotguns and revolvers barked; nightsticks flailed; teargas billowed through the streets; bullets shattered windows, showering the crowd with shards of glass. When the fighting finally subsided, two strikers lay dead from gunfire.

At the slain strikers' funeral several days later, thousands of sympa-

5. Lloyd H. Fisher, *The Harvest Labor Market in California*, quoted in Irving Bernstein, *Turbulent Years: A History of the American Worker, 1933–1941* (Boston: Houghton Mifflin, 1970), 145, 168. The federal official was General Pelham D. Glassford, who had been the Washington, D.C., chief of police at the time of the Bonus March in 1932.

thizers slowly shuffled for hours, eight abreast, behind the flatbed trucks bearing the coffins down Market Street. This massive display of community support inspired strike leader Harry Bridges, a wiry Australian firebrand and head of the International Longshoremen's Association (ILA). Bridges made no secret of his association with Communists. He now called for the ultimate weapon in labor's arsenal. It was a fearsome instrument that amounted to a declaration of class war: a general strike. More than 130,000 workers honored Bridges's summons. For four days beginning on July 16, San Francisco became a virtual ghost town, its streets empty, its shops closed, its freight terminals blockaded, its supplies of fuel oil and gasoline shut off. In the end faction-fighting between AFL transit and construction unions and Bridges's ILA crippled the strike, and the City by the Bay returned to its usual routines. The workers eventually secured a contract that abolished the shape-up, but San Francisco, abashed by employer brutality and bruised by the hard punch of labor's muscle, had learned a sobering lesson about the depths of class hatreds.

Other communities were soon to receive the same rough education. Along with St. Paul, its twin city on the opposite bank of the upper Mississippi, Minneapolis had long teetered on the edge of violent class confrontation. Ethnic divisions aggravated seething class antagonisms. Old-stock Yankee grandees controlled the giant flour mills that processed the northern prairie's great grain harvests. They owned the railroads that carried the flour, timber, and Mesabi Range iron ore to market. They ran the banks that financed the Twin Cities' global commodities trade. Those same pillars of the community also bankrolled the Citizens Alliance. Like San Francisco's Industrial Association, the alliance was a pugnaciously antilabor body. In 1934 it outfitted what amounted to a private army to keep the predominantly Scandinavian and Irish working class in place.

The Depression had dealt especially cruelly with the Twin Cities. The agricultural collapse shut down many mills. The slumping steel industry cut back its orders for Mesabi iron, spelling doom both for the mines and for the railroads that moved the ore. A nationwide standstill in construction slashed the demand for lumber. Unemployed lumberjacks and miners, along with foreclosed farmers, drifted into Minneapolis and St. Paul and quickly landed on the relief rolls. By the spring of 1934, a third of the people in Hennepin County depended on public support for their daily bread. The huge and growing pool of the unemployed put relentless downward pressure on the wages of those still clinging to their jobs. Truck drivers suffered particularly badly. They earned as little as twelve dollars weekly and were sometimes paid not in cash but in bruised vegetables.[6]

Led by the radical Dunne brothers, founding members of the Trotskyist Communist League of America, Teamster Local 574 demanded better wages and union recognition for its truck drivers. Like Bridges in San Francisco, the Dunnes in Minneapolis made achieving "closed shop" rules their highest priority—that is, agreement by employers to hire only union members, an arrangement that would give the union, not the bosses, control of the labor pool and hence powerful leverage over wages and work conditions. Like the Industrial Association in San Francisco, the Citizens Alliance would have none of it. When the trucking firms flatly refused to negotiate in the spring of 1934, the Dunnes vowed to stop every wheel in the city. They issued lengths of galvanized pipe and baseball bats to the striking teamsters. For its part, the Citizens Alliance organized a posse of vigilantes called the Citizens Army and armed it to the teeth.

A ragged skirmish in May left two Citizens Army soldiers dead and brought a tense truce, but neither side made meaningful concessions, despite the efforts of federal mediators. Both camps were spoiling for a fight that would break the deadlock. On Bloody Friday, July 20, they got it. A crowd of teamsters cut off a truck that was provocatively trying to move under police escort through a picket line. As if on cue, the police opened fire, pouring round after round of buckshot into the backs of the scattering teamsters. They wounded sixty-seven workers and killed two. Pandemonium convulsed Minneapolis. Governor Floyd Olson, self-described radical and a darling of the intellectual left, declared martial law. The following month, the trucking firms grudgingly accepted the teamsters' closed-shop demands. The Dunnes had won a smashing victory, though at a terrible human cost. In the process, they had laid bare the limits of Olson's vaunted "radicalism" and exposed the weakness of the civil authorities in the face of a disturbance such as the Dunnes were prepared to inflict and the Citizens Army was prepared to accept. They had also made Teamsters Local 574 into a powerful bastion of radicalism within the American labor movement.

In September 1934 even greater violence swept the textile districts from New England to the southern piedmont, as the United Textile Workers (UTW) struck to force mill operators to honor the wage, work-

6. Bernstein, *Turbulent Years*, 229–30.

sharing, and collective bargaining provisions of the Cotton Textile Code, the first and much-ballyhooed industry-wide NRA code signed in July 1933. The strike stretched through some twenty states and posed insuperable logistical problems for its organizers. It was probably doomed from the start. Poorly disciplined worker demonstrations in several New England mill towns degenerated into rioting that claimed two lives and left scores wounded. While federal officials dithered ineptly to resolve the dispute, more blood flowed. A union sympathizer and a deputy were killed in Trion, Georgia, on September 5. On the following day six strikers fell to police guns in South Carolina. Battered everywhere and badly bloodied by the murderous response in the South, the UTW called it quits in October. "We won't have our people going up against machine guns," said a union official. President Roosevelt pleaded for the reemployment of strikers without reprisals, but a reporter wrote from North Carolina in November that the workers continued to "live in terror of being penalized for joining unions." As for the employers, she said, they "live in a state of mingled rage and fear against this imported monstrosity: organized labor." Management's mood was well captured in a trade publication's brazen declaration that "a few hundred funerals will have a quieting influence."[7]

FRANKLIN ROOSEVELT was widely perceived as the patron of labor's awakening, and for a long season he was surely the political beneficiary of labor's growing assertiveness. Labor organizers knew the power of the Roosevelt magic and exploited it shamelessly. John L. Lewis shrewdly invoked the Roosevelt mystique in his organizing drive among coal miners in 1933, when he trumpeted that "the President wants you to join a union." Millions of working-class Americans came to see Roosevelt not simply as their president but as their special advocate, even their personal friend. Scrawling unschooled prose onto lined tablet paper, they reached out by the thousands to touch the presidential hem. "I am a long ways from you in distance yet my faith is in you my heart with you and I am for you sink or swim," a South Carolina textile mill hand wrote to Roosevelt. Strikers surrounding the vast Goodyear tire factory in Akron, Ohio, in 1936 named one of the strong points along their eleven-mile picket line "Camp Roosevelt." (A second was named "Camp John L. Lewis," and a third, with somewhat less ideological punctilio, "Camp Mae West.") Lewis coached his field organ-

7. Bernstein, *Turbulent Years*, 311, 315; Leuchtenburg, 113.

izers to close their speeches by leaning forward, holding high their crossed middle and index fingers, and intoning confidentially: "And I tell you, boys, John L. Lewis and President Roosevelt, why they're just like that!" One North Carolina mill worker summed up the pro-Roosevelt sentiments of many when he said that "Mr. Roosevelt is the only man we ever had in the White House who would understand that my boss is a sonofabitch."[8]

But Roosevelt was in fact a rather diffident champion of labor, and especially of organized labor unions. If he was the worker's patron, it was also true that his fundamental attitude toward labor was somewhat patronizing. Like Secretary of Labor Perkins, he was more interested in giving workers purchasing power than in granting them political power. He believed that passing pension and unemployment laws, as well as wage and hour legislation, rather than guaranteeing collective bargaining rights, was the best way to improve the workers' lot.[9] It was hardly surprising, therefore, that he had offered only episodic and inconsistent guidance to the NRA administrators charged with implementing 7(a). In March 1934 he personally broke the back of a drive to unionize the automobile industry. He imposed a settlement that disallowed the principle of majority rule in determining labor's bargaining representative and that endorsed the hated company unions, thus perpetuating management's ability to divide labor's ranks and dominate the bargaining process. Three months later, the president defied his liberal allies in Congress and supported a bill that established a decidedly weak successor to the NRA's ineffectual National Labor Board. "The New Deal," progressive Republican Senator Bronson Cutting complained, "is being strangled in the house of its friends."[10] As for the Wagner National Labor Relations Act, Roosevelt only belatedly threw his support behind it in 1935, and then largely because he saw it as a way to increase workers' consuming power, as well as a means to suppress the repeated labor

8. Jacquelyn Dowd Hall et al., *Like a Family: The Making of a Southern Cotton Mill World* (New York: Norton, 1987), 291; Robert H. Zieger, *The CIO, 1935–1955* (Chapel Hill: University of North Carolina Press, 1995), 32; Eric F. Goldman, *Rendezvous with Destiny* (New York: Knopf, 1952), 345.

9. The Walsh-Healy Government Contracts Act of 1936 well reflected Roosevelt's preferred approach. That act relied on the government's contracting power, not labor's bargaining power, to improve wages and working conditions. It provided that all government contractors should pay a minimum wage as determined by the secretary of labor and should observe the eight-hour day and the forty-hour week. It also prohibited child and convict labor on government contracts.

10. Bernstein, *Turbulent Years*, 204.

disturbances that, as the act claimed, were "burdening or obstructing commerce."[11] Small wonder, then, that the administration found itself bamboozled and irritated by the labor eruptions of Roosevelt's first term and that it moved only hesitantly and ineffectively to channel the accelerating momentum of labor militancy.

No less alarming to prolabor progressives like Cutting (and Minnesota's Floyd Olson), the house of labor was deeply divided. The self-contented craft unionists who ran the American Federation of Labor as a kind of working-class gentleman's club for skilled tradesmen were at dagger's points with the likes of radicals such as A. J. Muste, Harry Bridges, and the Dunne brothers. The desire of the traditional labor chieftains and their liberal allies to spike working-class radicalism formed no small part of the motivation behind the passage of the Wagner Act. "I am for it as a safety measure," federal mediator Lloyd Garrison testified to the Senate Labor Committee in 1935, "because I regard organized labor in this country as our chief bulwark against Communism and revolutionary movements."[12] In the alarmed eyes of men like Cutting, Olson, Garrison, and even Wagner himself, the Communists were hard, unyielding men, brined in Marxist doctrine, contemptuous of mere "reform," intoxicated with the dream of revolution, howling barbarians at the gates of American civilization. Though exaggerated, that picture was not without foundation. Many radicals, peering into the gloom of Depression America, glimpsed the approaching socialist millennium amidst the social and economic wreckage that cluttered the national landscape. They saw themselves not simply as samaritans who were comforting the working stiff but as men and women who were manipulating the very levers of history, hastening the final conflict that would kill off capitalism once and for all and usher in the promised proletarian utopia. To grasp that great prize they would pay virtually any price, come hell or armed struggle.

JOHN L. LEWIS had more modest aims, but they were ambitious enough. Asked by a reporter in 1937 what labor should have, the United Mine Workers chief quickly replied, "The right to organize," and added: "shorter hours, the prohibition of child labor, equal pay for men and women doing substantially the same kind of work," and a guarantee

11. *U.S. Statutes at Large* 49:449, cited in Howard Zinn, *New Deal Thought* (Indianapolis: Bobbs-Merrill, 1966), 196.
12. Bernstein, *Turbulent Years*, 332.

"that all who are able to work and willing shall have the opportunity for steady employment." The reporter pressed on: What about a living wage? "No," Lewis roared, pounding his fist on his desk. "Not a living wage! We ask more than that. We demand for the unskilled workers a wage that will enable them to maintain themselves and their families in health and modern comfort, to purchase their own homes, to enable their children to obtain at least a high-school education and to provide against sickness, disability and death."[13] Lewis, in short, dreamed a realistic, achievable dream for American labor, the dream that workers could enjoy middle-class standards of living, and he described it in terms not unlike those that defined Franklin Roosevelt's own social vision. As Lewis and Roosevelt both saw things, capitalism need not be uprooted, but its fruits must be more equitably distributed.

Dour-visaged, thickly eyebrowed, richly maned, his 230-pound bulk always impeccably tailored, Lewis was a man of ursine appearance and volcanic personality, a no-holds-barred advocate for labor and a fearsome adversary. Businessmen, as well as his own plentiful rivals in the labor movement, denounced him as a berseker and a demagogue. But like FDR, Lewis could credibly present himself in the mid-1930s as a responsible alternative to the far more disruptive radicals stirring menacingly to his left. It was both men's style, Lewis's even more than Roosevelt's, to wax rhetorically extreme but to pursue decidedly moderate policies. Both believed that if peaceful change were rendered impossible, violent revolution would be rendered inevitable. "American labor," Lewis testifed to a Senate Committee in 1933, "stand[s] between the rapacity of the robber barons of industry of America and the lustful rage of the communists, who would lay waste to our traditions and our institutions with fire and sword."[14]

Lewis had been born to Welsh immigrant parents in an Iowa coal-mining town in 1880. As a young man he had followed his father and brothers into the mines, learning firsthand what it was like to descend into the earth's bowels at first light and spend all the sunshine hours pickaxing a coal face illumined only by the wan beam of his headlamp. The young Lewis had also for a time managed the Lucas, Iowa, Opera House and occasionally acted on its stage. It was there, presumably, that he began to fashion his extravagantly thespian persona, which by the 1930s was a carefully wrought specimen of performance art. "My stock

13. *New York Times Magazine*, March 21, 1937, 3.
14. Dubofsky and Van Tine, *John L. Lewis*, 183.

in trade is being the ogre," he once said. "That's how I make my way." To Frances Perkins he estimated that his scowl was worth a million dollars.[15] His stentorian voice could shake an auditorium or bathe an outdoor crowd without help from electrical amplification. He cultivated a grandiloquent, rococo style of speech that was viscous with borrowings from the Bible and the Bard, not to mention elaborate syntactical embroideries of his own artful invention. His ego stretched as far as the undulating Iowa corn fields of his youth, and he made no apology for his incessant self-aggrandizement. "He who tooteth not his own horn," he declared in his trademark vernacular, "the same shall not be tooted."[16]

Lewis might have been the delight of the caricaturists, but he was a deadly serious, eminently practical, and extraordinarily effective labor leader — or, as he preferred to think of himself, "executive." No one inscribed his mark more deeply, or flamboyantly, into the annals of labor history in the 1930s. More keenly than any other man, Lewis understood that the peculiar constellation of political and economic conditions in the mid-1930s presented American labor with a unique opportunity. He was on fire to seize it.

Lewis had used the opening provided by NRA to triple the membership of his own United Mine Workers (UMW) in 1933. He then hoped to employ the UMW, with its bulging treasury and its cadre of seasoned organizers, as an engine to drive the process of industrial unionization in other sectors, especially steel and autos. But first he had to convince the UMW's parent organization, the AFL, to abandon its traditional practice of organizing skilled craftsmen along guild lines and to take up instead the unfamiliar task of organizing unskilled workers on an industry-wide basis. He faced formidable resistance.

Many of the complacent princelings of the AFL contemplated Lewis's plans for industrial unionism with a distaste that bordered on horror. They recollected the circumstances of the AFL's birth in the turbulent 1880s, when Samuel Gompers had led a handful of craft unionists out of the Knights of Labor. Gompers's express purpose was to protect the economic interests of the "aristocrats of American labor," like the skilled carpenters, machinists, and steamfitters, by dissociating them from the undifferentiated mass of workers that the Knights had unsuccessfully tried to weld together. The AFL had done well for its elite and exclu-

15. Dubofsky and Van Tine, *John L. Lewis*, 282.
16. Schlesinger 2:138.

sionary member guilds in the half century since Gompers had left the Knights, although its members never added up to more than 10 percent of American workers. Yet it was the federation's very exclusivity, according to its own canonical doctrines, that accounted for its success. The masses of unskilled factory workers whom Lewis now proposed to escort aboard labor's ark conjured visions of a return to the broadly inclusionary, ramshackle organization of the Knights, which most AFL leaders regarded as hopelessly utopian and utterly ineffectual as a guarantor of labor's interests.

More than the purely economic privileges of labor's aristocracy was at stake. With notable exceptions like the heavily Jewish garment and clothing workers, the AFL unions tended to be populated by people of English, Irish, and German stock. Their forebears were well established in the country by the late nineteenth century or earlier. The ranks of the unskilled, on the other hand, were disproportionately composed from the great waves of southern and eastern European "new" immigrants who had landed on American shores in the three decades following the AFL's founding. Teamster president Dan Tobin sneered at those latter-day immigrants as "the rubbish at labor's door." Such ethnic antagonisms, coupled with the distinct economic interests that divided skilled from unskilled workers, created yawning cultural and political chasms that badly fissured the American working class. Many of the old-line AFL chieftains would have no truck with the ethnically exotic, unwashed *Lumpen* that Lewis now hoped to mobilize. "My wife can always tell from the smell of my clothes what breed of foreigners I've been hanging out with," one AFL organizer said contemptuously.[17]

By late 1935 Lewis was fed up with the AFL's clubby disdain for the cause of industrial unionism. A year earlier, in San Francisco, the federation's annual convention had resolved to commence organizing in the industrial field, but little organizing had actually taken place. Lewis therefore arrived at the 1935 AFL convention in high dudgeon and poised for full rhetorical flight. "At San Francisco they seduced me with fair words," he proclaimed to the assembled delegates in Atlantic City when he took to the rostrum on October 16. "Now, of course, having learned that I was seduced, I am enraged and I am ready to rend my seducers limb from limb. . . . Heed this cry from Macedonia that comes from the hearts of men," he pleaded. If the AFL did not take up the

17. Dubofsky and Van Tine, *John L. Lewis*, 203; Melvyn Dubofsky, *American Labor since the New Deal* (Chicago: Quadrangle, 1971), 9.

cause of industrial unionism, he warned, a golden opportunity for labor would be lost and "high wassail will prevail at the banquet tables of the mighty."[18]

Despite Lewis's operatic oratory, the convention overwhelmingly rejected a resolution supporting industrial unionism. Lewis was infuriated. When carpenters' union president Big Bill Hutcheson called Lewis a "bastard" in the course of a haggle over parliamentary rules, Lewis's wrath exploded. With a swift jab to the jaw, he sent Hutcheson crashing over a table, blood streaking his face from forehead to chin. Then, an observer related, "Lewis casually adjusted his collar and tie, relit his cigar, and sauntered slowly through the crowded aisles to the rostrum."[19]

Given Lewis's penchant for the theatrical, the punch that decked Hutcheson may well have been a premeditated blow, an artfully staged declaration of the civil war in labor's ranks that Lewis now proposed to wage without mercy. Just three weeks later, he widened his breach with the craft unionists. Together with David Dubinsky of the International Ladies Garment Workers Union (ILGWU) and Sidney Hillman of the Amalgamated Clothing Workers (ACW), he announced on November 9, 1935, the formation of a new labor body, the Committee for Industrial Organization (CIO). Lewis pledged five thousand from the UMW treasury to get the CIO up and running. Dubinsky and Hillman contributed like amounts from their respective unions. For the moment the CIO remained within the AFL, but given its purposes and Lewis's personality, its eventual breakaway was all but inevitable. Lewis took another step in that direction on November 23, when he resigned his AFL vice-presidency.

THE CIO'S FIRST OBJECTIVE was steel, a historically impregnable citadel of antiunionism. Lewis called steel the "Hindenburg Line" of American industry. Cracking that line, he believed, was the key to the success of industrial unionism everywhere. Steel posed a mountainous challenge. Because steel production was divided into many discrete stages, steelworkers were parceled out into numerous small work gangs, physically separated and often ethnically segregated, making mass organization difficult. The acrid memory of past labor defeats hung like soot over the steel districts. In 1892 a strike over recognition of the Amalgamated Association of Iron and Steel Workers had been broken

18. Bernstein, *Turbulent Years*, 392.
19. Dubofsky and Van Tine, *John L. Lewis*, 220.

in a legend-leaving clash that killed ten steelworkers at Homestead, Pennsylvania. Another huge effort to unionize steel was utterly crushed in 1919, not least by management's cynical exploitation of the ethnic and racial tensions that seamed the polyglot steel work force.[20]

A handful of enormous corporations dominated the steel industry— U.S. Steel with 222,000 employees, Bethlehem with 80,000, Republic with 49,000. U.S. Steel alone, known in the trade simply as "Big Steel," with its mammoth milling and fabricating facilities concentrated around Pittsburgh, Chicago, and Birmingham, could produce more steel than Germany, the world's second-largest steelmaking *country*. In the stark company towns that pocked the steel regions, Big Steel and the other, so-called Little Steel companies, all ruled with feudal sway. They defied labor organizers and even federal authorities with impunity. In Homestead, haunted by the specters of 1892, no union meeting had been held since 1919. In 1934 U.S. Steel's minions in Homestead had successfully prevented Labor Secretary Frances Perkins from speaking in the town's public park.

But Lewis could see that things were changing in 1936, thanks to labor's growing political clout as well as the nascent economic recovery and, not least, because the public mood was swinging in labor's favor. Since the Depression's onset, many middle-class readers had encountered poignant, sympathy-inducing accounts of working-class life in "proletarian novels" like Tom Kromer's *Waiting for Nothing* (1935) and Edward Anderson's *Hungry Men* (1935). Much art and literature reflected the leftish cultural mood of the Depression decade, when workers could plausibly be cast as heroes and capitalists as villains. Two monumental trilogies instructed large reading audiences about the stark realities of workers' culture: James T. Farrell's unsparing chronicle of an Irish immigrant family in Chicago, *Studs Lonigan* (1932–35) and John Dos Passos's phenomenally comprehensive and inventive contraption, *USA* (1930–36). Erskine Caldwell's *Tobacco Road* (1932) and John Steinbeck's *Tortilla Flat* (1935) and *In Dubious Battle* (1936) etched indelible portraits of the wretched lives of agricultural workers, still more than 20 percent of the work force. Throughout 1935 New York theatergoers were nightly brought to their feet, yelling, "Strike! Strike!" as the curtain closed on the Group Theatre's production of Clifford Odets's agitprop

20. For an account of the 1919 steel strike, see David M. Kennedy, *Over Here: The First World War and American Society* (New York: Oxford University Press, 1980), 270–79.

one-acter *Waiting for Lefty*, arguably the best work of proletarian literature to come out of the 1930s. Films like King Vidor's elegaic *Our Daily Bread* further deepened a vein of sympathy for workers, especially the unemployed.

In June 1936 the U.S. Senate considerably widened the stage for prolabor propaganda. It charged a committee chaired by Wisconsin's Senator Robert M. La Follette Jr. "to make an investigation of violations of the rights of free speech and assembly and undue interference with the right of labor to organize and bargain collectively."[21] The La Follette Committee became a mighty organ of publicity, pumping out exposés of the criminal underside of corporate labor relations policies—including espionage, naked intimidation, and armed thuggery. These revelations further fostered a climate of opinion favorable to labor and, at least for a season, restrained management from its customary reliance on the mailed fist. And of course the Wagner Act's creation of the NLRB institutionalized the government-labor partnership, a crucial political datum that was plain to all observers.

In a moving demonstration of labor's mounting confidence, two thousand steelworkers and coal miners gathered on a sunny July Sunday in 1936 at the old Homestead battleground to pay homage to the martyrs of 1892. The lieutenant governor of Pennsylvania, who was also a UMW vice-president, gazed out over the picnicking crowd and declared the steel towns open to union organizers. On behalf of Governor George Earle, he promised public relief payments to workers and their families in the event of a strike—in effect, a taxpayers' subsidy for a labor action. At the graveside of the men slain in 1892, a UMW official offered a brief prayer: "We have come to renew the struggle for which you gave your lives. We pledge all our efforts to bring a better life for the steel workers. We hope you have found peace and happiness. God rest your soul."[22]

In this atmosphere the CIO's great steel organizing drive began. Hurling defiance at the do-nothing AFL, in June 1936 Lewis launched the Steel Workers Organizing Committee (SWOC), with his faithful lieutenant, UMW vice-president Philip Murray, as its head. This was the last straw for the AFL leadership. They accused Lewis of dividing labor's ranks by organizing a rival union—the unforgivable sin of "dual unionism"—and drubbed the CIO member unions out of the AFL, thus es-

21. Bernstein, *Turbulent Years*, 451.
22. Bernstein, *Turbulent Years*, 434.

calating labor's fratricidal war.[23] Lewis responded with characteristic flame and sulfur and threw in some gratuitous aspersions on his adversaries' manhood. "It is inconceivable," he wrote to AFL president William Green, "that you intend . . . to sit with the women under an awning on the hilltop, while the steel workers in the valley struggle in the dust and agony of industrial warfare."[24] The CIO, Lewis announced, would contribute up to $500,000 to finance the steel drive. That figure soon swelled to more than $2.5 million, most of it from the coffers of the UMW. In addition to Murray, the UMW also contributed twelve trained organizers to SWOC, the nucleus of a field staff that grew to 433. Dubinsky's ILGWU and Hillman's ACW seconded other experienced men to the committee. Before long SWOC organizers were motoring into steel towns from Pennsylvania to Illinois to Alabama, often accompanied by automobiles marked "Car of the United States Senate, La Follette Civil Liberties Committee Investigators."[25]

Significantly, the CIO's and SWOC's top leadership, with the conspicuous exception of Lewis himself, were themselves immigrants — as was Robert Wagner, the legislative craftsman of the epochal labor law that bore his name. They were men viscerally in touch with the fiber and rhythms of the lives of the workers they sought to organize. At the age of nine, Wagner had been the youngest of six children who migrated with their parents to New York in 1886 from the Rhineland village of Nastatten. The ILGWU's David Dubinsky had been born David Dobnievski in Brest-Litovsk in Russian Poland in the fateful year of 1892. He had traveled in steerage to New York City in 1911. Sidney Hillman was born as Simcha Hillman in the Lithuanian shtetl of Zagare in 1887 and arrived in New York twenty years later, after giving up his studies for the rabbinate. In 1936 Dubinsky and Hillman, favoring practical results over doctrinal purity, organized a mass defection from Norman Thomas's Socialist Party to Roosevelt's Democrats, effectively destroying the Socialists as a political force.

As for SWOC chairman Philip Murray, it was his special quality, a journalist wrote, "to touch the love and not the fears of men." But Murray knew their fears, too — the fears of joblessness and employer intimidation, the fears bred of being a stranger in a strange land, part

23. The CIO would formally acknowledge its departure from the AFL in October 1938, when it officially changed its name to the Congress of Industrial Organizations. The AFL and the CIO then remained separate bodies until their merger in 1955.
24. Dubofsky and Van Tine, *John L. Lewis*, 238.
25. Bernstein, *Turbulent Years*, 455.

of the flotsam torn loose by the tidal wave of industrial revolution that swept tens of millions of Europeans across the Atlantic in the years around the turn of the century. Murray's own family were immigrants twice over. His father had taken them out of Catholic Ireland to seek work in the coal mines of Scottish Blantyre. Murray was born in Glasgow in 1886 and never lost his soft Glaswegian burr. In 1902, when Phil was sixteen, the Murrays moved again, this time to the coal districts of Pennsylvania, their second uprooting in a generation. These forced removals deeply shaped Murray. In common with Wagner, Dubinski, Hillman, and Lewis, too, he was no ideologue, no bookish theorist who dealt in abstractions like "proletariat," no slave to doctrines that were unchecked by the feel of flesh and blood and the habits of fellow-feeling. Each of these men knew in his own marrow the disquiet of impermanency, the dread of tomorrow, and above all the yearning for security that daily squeezed at the hearts of the men and women in America's factories, mills, and mines. The "quest for security," Hillman declared in 1934, was "the central issue in this life of modern man."[26]

Under Murray's leadership and with the blessing of Lewis, Dubinsky, and Hillman, SWOC was determined to avoid the fate of previous attempts to unionize the steel industry, which had foundered on the rocks of ethnic and racial rivalry. History was on their side by 1936. The cessation of mass immigration in the early 1920s had given America's several immigrant communities time to stabilize. By the 1930s they contained a much larger proportion of native-born Americans who spoke English as their mother tongue than had been true in 1892 or 1919.

What was more, the pervasive influence of the new mass popular entertainments that began to flourish in the 1920s, including movies and radio, had nurtured in the immigrant neighborhoods at least the rudiments of a common culture that, for better or worse, proved powerfully corrosive to their separate old-world identities. Then the Depression had dealt a mortal blow to the fragile infrastructure of ethnic banks, neighborhood grocery stores, and nationality-based charity societies that had sustained ethnic separateness for generations. The Depression had also powerfully catalyzed a sense of common economic grievance that transcended the particular loyalties of the nation's diverse immigrant groups. For the first time since the age of mass immigration had begun some fifty years earlier, culturally variegating the American labor force

26. Steve Fraser and Gary Gerstle, eds., *The Rise and Fall of the New Deal Order, 1930–1980* (Princeton: Princeton University press, 1989), 78.

to a degree unknown in other industrial countries, the possibility hovered just over the horizon that a unified American working *class* could be forged out of America's heterogeneous ethnic enclaves.[27]

Sensing that possibility, SWOC began its organizing campaign in the fraternal and religious organizations that ministered to the various steel communities. SWOC field workers spoke reassuringly to apprehensive little groups gathered in the bare meeting halls of Lithuanian Lodges, Polish Mutual Benefit Societies, and Czech Sokols, as well as in Hungarian churches and Italian men's clubs. Black workers constituted a special case. Many blacks had found their first industrial employment as strikebreakers in the steel strike of 1919. They thereby earned the lasting resentment of the striking whites, whose proferred hand they now hesitated to grasp. They had also secured the grudging patronage of the steel companies, whose wrath they now were disinclined to provoke. SWOC consequently made little headway among blacks, though it continued to enunciate the principle, as did the CIO in general, of racial equality in union membership.[28]

In a gesture that served notice to the steelmakers that labor now meant to be recognized as an equal partner with capital, Lewis and Murray set up SWOC's headquarters in Pittsburgh's Grant Building, where several steel corporations had their home offices. Directed from Murray's thirty-sixth-floor Pittsburgh office and fueled by UMW money, SWOC organizers fanned out into the steel districts in the summer and fall of 1936. By the end of the year they had taken over the old Amalgamated Association of Iron, Steel, and Tin Workers (AA), a nearly lifeless AFL

27. For a brilliant and detailed analysis of the ways in which mass culture and the Depression forged a new class consciousness out of the ethnically divided American labor force, see Lizabeth Cohen, *Making a New Deal: Industrial Workers in Chicago, 1919–1939* (New York: Cambridge University Press, 1990).

28. Black groups like the NAACP and the Urban League had worried that the Wagner Act itself might perversely reinforce racism. To the extent that the act allowed unions to secure "closed shops," where only union members could be employed, unions could in theory bar blacks from membership and hence from employment. Senator Wagner and the act's other sponsors, however, failed to accept suggested amendments that would have defined racial discrimination by a union as an "unfair labor practice." Thus the CIO's inclusionary policy, for all its difficulties in practice, was not driven by legal requirement but by the organization's own sense of racial justice and of effective industrial unionizing strategies. Not all CIO unions consistently followed inclusionary policies; in future years, unions themselves would be major battlegrounds in the struggle for racial equality. See Bernstein, *Turbulent Years*, 189–90, 454.

affiliate, and filled its hollow organizational shell with dedicated industrial unionists. SWOC and AA organizers next systematically undertook to capture control of the various company unions, or ERPs, that management had summoned into being since 1933.

The steelmakers fought back. Invoking the American Liberty League's pronouncement on the Wagner Act's unconstitutionality, they tried to sustain the ERPs, in clear violation of the act's strictures against company unions, by offering ERP-covered workers seductively generous wage increases. SWOC organizers countered that the real issue was long-term union independence, not short-term pay. Both sides dug in for the siege of Fortress Steel. Pittsburgh's Grant Building, where Murray and the steel executives routinely rode the elevators together in stiff silence, seemed likely to become the epicenter of a titanic confrontation that would paralyze the steel industry, idle thousands of workers, snarl the economy, and perhaps touch off yet another round of violence. As winter closed over the industrial heartland at the end of 1936, a mood of nervous apprehension gripped the steel regions. The possibility loomed of a strike even more rancorous and bloody than the great upheavals of 1892 and 1919.

THE FATEFUL ERUPTION, however, came not in the steel towns around Pittsburgh but in Flint, Michigan — in autos, not in steel. It began on the evening of December 30, 1936, when a young woman at the United Auto Workers' Flint office switched on a two-hundred-watt red bulb, the signal for a meeting. The simple flick of that light switch set off a chain of events that forever altered the place of labor in American society.

Flint, some sixty-five miles north of Detroit, was a gritty monument to the transfiguring power of the industrial revolution. Just three decades earlier, Flint had been a quiet country village, devoted principally to making carriages and buggies. By the 1920s it had become a boom town, a pulsing industrial organism that pumped its myriad products through the labyrinthine arteries of the greatest of all mass-production industries, that signature creation of American consumer capitalism: automobile manufacturing. In 1936 Flint was ailing, to be sure, but it remained the solar plexus of the General Motors Corporation's colossal automaking empire.

Even bigger than Big Steel, GM was the world's largest manufacturing corporation. Its quarter million employees made nearly half of all American cars in 1936. Virtually all the rest were manufactured by just two other firms, Ford and Chrysler. GM dominated an industry even more oligopolistic than steel, and since oligopolies by their very nature impede price flexibility, the "Big Three" American carmakers traditionally sought to bolster their profit margins not by raising prices but by cutting costs, especially labor costs. Hourly wage rates for autoworkers were high, but their gross incomes were low, thanks to the industry's practice of periodically shutting down the production lines to accommodate annual model changes. The Ford Motor Company exacerbated the effects of that practice by its policy of rehiring seasonally laid-off workers, regardless of skill or seniority, at the starting rate. Autoworkers, in common with mass-production workers everywhere, also chafed at their enthrallment to the despotic tempo of the assembly line, especially the hated speed-up. They graveled, too, under the often arbitrary control of foremen who hired and fired and promoted and penalized at whim. And the Great Depression, of course, by virtually extinguishing the market for new cars, had visited upon autoworkers especially appalling rates of unemployment.

These accumulated grievances, compounded by the Depression, made the autoworkers peculiarly ripe for industrial unionism. So did the physical circumstances of auto production, where huge gangs, effectively undifferentiated by skill, worked together under one roof on enormous factory floors. At Ford's River Rouge complex alone, the world's largest integrated industrial plant, some ninety-five thousand lunch bucket–toting workers poured daily through the factory gates at peak employment. And as in steel, so too in the automotive sector did the timing seem propitious for an organizational campaign. The Big Three in late 1936 were gearing up for their largest production runs in years, rendering them especially vulnerable to the threat of work stoppage.

But labor organizers faced daunting obstacles in the auto industry. As the La Follette Committee revealed to an indignant nation, Ford Motor Company's blandly named Service Department, headed by a pint-sized ex-pugilist named Harry Bennett, ruthlessly suppressed even the faintest stirrings of union sentiment. Workers suspected of union sympathy were summarily dismissed or physically harrassed on the shop floor — "shaking 'em up in the aisles," Bennett called it. Bennett built Ford Service into a paramilitary force of some three thousand armed men who stalked and threatened "disloyal" employees and inflicted physical injuries without scruple or remorse. His minions, said Bennett, were all "tough sons-of-bitches, but every one a gentleman." At General Motors, antiunion tactics were more subtle but no less effective. In 1934 and 1935 GM spent nearly $1 million to field a force of wiretappers, infiltrators, and finks that the La Follette Committee condemned as "a far-flung industrial Cheka . . . the most colossal supersystem of spies yet devised in any American corporation."[29]

Among the consequences of the automakers' wholesale suppression of independent unions were the need for labor organizers to work under the cloak of secrecy and the need for tactics that did not depend on mass participation, as the traditional techniques of walkout and picket line required. Those stark necessities mothered a simple invention: the sit-down strike. Legend to the contrary, the great sit-down strike of 1937 in Flint did not spring from a spontaneous explosion of mass worker sentiment. It depended, rather, on the carefully laid plans and skillful execution of a cadre of highly disciplined leaders, many of them Communists. Nor was the sit-down strike, strictly speaking, an American invention. Though the tactic had been sporadically employed in strikes in the Ohio Valley's rubber industry in 1936, its efficacy was spectacularly established in 1937 in France, when a million workers took possession of scores of factories, helped bring Leon Blum to power, and wrung new social and labor legislation out of Blum's socialist government. That awesome display of the sit-down's power inspired American unionists. It also frightened many in the great property-owning American middle class.

The logic of the sit-down strike called for identifying a critical pressure point in the ganglia of the huge automaking system and pinching off production at that strategic site. Fisher Body Plant Number One in Flint was just such a point. It contained one of only two sets of body dies for GM's 1937 model Pontiacs, Oldsmobiles, Buicks, and Cadillacs (the other set of dies, for Chevrolets, was in the Fisher plant in Cleveland). If Fisher Number One could be taken off line, GM's output could be choked to a trickle. Accordingly, United Auto Workers (UAW) organizers, working nervously in an environment they knew to be honeycombed with spies and stool pigeons, were preparing in late 1936 to seize control of Fisher One, as well as Fisher Cleveland, early in the new year.

Events soon accelerated this timetable. In the fading late afternoon light of December 30, a UAW member inside Fisher One noticed that railroad cars had rolled up to the plant's loading dock, where men were

29. R. L. Tyler, *Walter Reuther*, (N.p.: William B. Eerdmans, 1973), 39; Bernstein, *Turbulent Years*, 516–517.

preparing the critical dies for shipment. He phoned the information to the UAW office across the street, causing the red meeting light to go on. At 8:00 P.M., swing-shift workers on their meal break crowded into the UAW hall. Union officials instructed the men to return to the Fisher One plant, sit down, and stay put. The leaders waited anxiously when the starting whistle blew. There was no responsive throb of machinery. "She's ours!" a worker shouted from a third-story window. The dies would not move. The plant was shut down—and occupied.[30]

The Flint sit-down strike amounted to nothing less than the forcible seizure by workers of the means of production—a recognizable enactment of a core tenet of socialism, though the Flint strikers stopped well short of demanding permanent ownership of the seized plant. What they did demand, quite simply, was that the General Motors Corporation recognize the United Auto Workers as the sole legitimate bargaining agent for GM employees. There were other demands—for a grievance procedure, a shorter workweek, and a minimum wage scale—but union recognition was the essential item. The Flint sit-down, historian Robert H. Zieger has rightly concluded, "epitomized the two polar, yet complementary, tendencies within the CIO, namely the anger and resentment of large portions of the working class and the modesty of their goals."[31]

GM denounced the sit-down as an unlawful trespass. The giant automaker mounted a publicity campaign to tarnish the strike as the work of Communists and "outsider agitators" and secured an injunction ordering the strikers to evacuate Fisher One. Ignoring the court order, the UAW proceeded to seize additional, adjacent plants. Fisher Two was secured on January 11 following a clash with police that came to be known as the "Battle of the Running Bulls." After staging a clever diversion, unionists on February 1 took over Chevrolet No. 4, a huge installation capable of producing a million engines per year. Inside the plants, Reuther's UAW "captains" organized men into squads of fifteen, insisted on strict adherence to hygiene and safety rules, arranged for food to be delivered, and organized recreational activities to while away the time. Group singing was especially popular and caught the exultant mood of labor's new-found potency:

> When they tie the can to a union man,
> Sit down! Sit down!

30. This account of the automobile sit-down strike is heavily indebted to Bernstein, *Turbulent Years*, chap. 11.
31. Zieger, *CIO*, 46.

When the speedup comes, just twiddle your thumbs,
Sit down! Sit down!
When the boss won't talk, don't take a walk.
Sit down! Sit down![32]

As the sit-down spread, pressure mounted on Governor Frank Murphy to send in the National Guard. Murphy had no doubt that the strike was illegal. He also had no taste, as he exclaimed to a friend, for "going down in history as Bloody Murphy! If I send those soldiers right in on the men," he explained, "there'd be no telling how many would be killed. It would be inconsistent with everything I have stood for in my whole political life." After the Battle of the Running Bulls, Murphy did in fact mobilize the Michigan Guard, but only to keep order, not to break the strike. "The state authorities," the governor declared, "will not take sides. They are here only to protect the public peace . . . And for no other reason at all." Following the lead of Governor Earle in Pennsylvania, Murphy also authorized relief payments for the families of the strikers. For virtually the first time in the history of American industrial conflicts, state officials determined to sit on their hands, leaving labor and capital to negotiate their own way out of the impasse. Discipline and raw economic power, not legal injunction or political intervention, would determine the outcome.[33]

Discipline was no problem, thanks to the tireless and careful leadership of Walter Reuther, the president of UAW Local 174 and a key tactician of the sit-down strike. Reuther had been born to German immigrant parents in Wheeling, West Virginia, in 1907. In 1927 he went to Detroit and got his first job at the Ford Motor Company. Because he worked the swing shift, he could take classes at Detroit's municipal university (later Wayne State University), where he joined the League for Industrial Democracy and plunged into the sectarian jungle of leftist politics. In 1933 Ford laid him off. Reuther and his brother, Victor, cashed in their meager savings and set out to see the world. In Germany, Nazi guides showed them the burned Reichstag building. They worked for a time at a Soviet auto plant in Gorki, helping to make the familiar Model A from dies the Soviets had purchased from Ford. In 1936 Reuther was elected to the board of the infant UAW. He was by then a seasoned organizer and was determined to make the UAW into a powerful industrial union.

John L. Lewis, absorbed in planning for the steel strike, was caught

32. Tyler, *Walter Reuther*, 38.
33. Bernstein, *Turbulent Years*, 541, 534.

off guard by the UAW's initiative but soon scrambled to get control of events in Flint. He denounced GM's owners—singling out the duPont family, the corporation's biggest shareholders, and, not incidentally, the chief financial backers of the Liberty League—as "economic royalists." Reminding Franklin Roosevelt of his debt to labor, Lewis declared that those "economic royalists now have their fangs in labor, and the workers expect the Administration in every reasonable and legal way to support the auto workers in their fight with the same rapacious enemy." On February 3 he left Washington's Union Station to assume personal command over the UAW side of negotiations in Michigan. In a characteristically gratuitous flourish, he intoned to reporters: "Let there be no moaning at the bar when I put out to sea."[34]

Roosevelt, behind the scenes, urged the General Motors executives to reach a settlement that recognized the union. Murphy meanwhile worked on Lewis to temper the strikers' demands. The sit-down was hurting GM badly. Its output plummeted from some 50,000 cars in December 1936 to a mere 125 during the first week in February 1937. The corporation secured a second antistrike injunction in late January but was in fact edging toward agreement with the UAW's demands, especially its central demand for union recognition. Lewis, however, seemed inclined to hold out for more. How to move him the last few inches toward final accord? Murphy, citing the injunction, warned Lewis that as governor of Michigan he had no alternative but to perform his sworn duty faithfully to execute the law. He would have to send in the Guard. What, he asked, would Lewis then do? Lewis in later years gave many versions of his reply. According to one, probably embellished by time and Lewis's promiscuous imagination, he told Murphy:

> You want my answer, sir? I give it to you. Tomorrow morning, I shall personally enter General Motors plant Chevrolet No. 4. I shall order the men to disregard your order, to stand fast. I shall then walk up to the largest window in the plant, open it, divest myself of my outer raiment, remove my shirt, and bare my bosom. Then when you order your troops to fire, mine will be the first breast that those bullets will strike!
>
> And as my body falls from that window to the ground, you listen to the voice of your grandfather [executed for rebellion in nineteenth-century Ireland] as he whispers in your ear, "Frank, are you sure you are doing the right thing?"[35]

34. Dubofsky and Van Tine, *John L. Lewis*, 263–64, 267.
35. Bernstein, *Turbulent Years*, 548.

However colorful this exchange, it was almost certainly of no consequence. Murphy was bluffing. He had already made it clear that he would not send in troops. And General Motors, watching its market share shrink as rivals Chrysler and Ford boosted production to take advantage of the GM shutdown, desperately needed a resolution to the strike. On February 11, after forty-four days of dramatic stand-off, Lewis walked into the GM Building, immediately across Detroit's Grand Boulevard from the Fisher Building where Father Coughlin made his broadcasts. He signed an agreement by which GM recognized the UAW as the exclusive representative of the men in the struck factories. Other UAW demands went unmet for the moment, but the central point had been won. The men marched out of the shut plants to an uproarious celebration. Industrial unionism had established a major beachhead in a core American industry.

The lessons of Flint were not lost on the steelmakers. Given the manifest unwillingness of government to throw its weight to the side of management, the sit-down was an industrial weapon of awesome power. Accordingly, on March 2, 1937, U.S. Steel announced that it would recognize the Steel Workers Organizing Committee. That announcement was astonishing enough. No less astonishing, Big Steel added that it was also granting a pay hike, as well as an eight-hour day and a forty-hour week, with overtime clocked on a "time-and-half" basis. Incredibly, Fortress Steel, the "Hindenburg Line" of antiunionism, had surrendered without a struggle. Like GM, it had caved in to labor's economic power, not to the government's political power. The National Labor Relations Board, still intimidated by the overhanging threat of judicial nullification, had played no direct part in the breakthroughs in autos and steel. To be sure, the board's very existence signaled the changing political climate in which labor-management confrontations would now have to be resolved, but in these two landmark cases, government's most important contribution to the CIO's success had been, quite simply, to stay out of the way.

Lewis's dream of industrial unionism now became a reality at a stunning speed. UAW membership exploded, from 88,000 at the end of the sit-down to 166,000 a month later and more than 200,000 by the end of the year. SWOC signed up more than 300,000 members within two months after U.S. Steel's capitulation. By August 1937 the CIO as a whole claimed to have over 3.4 million members, more than the AFL.

The twin victories in autos and steel infused the CIO with the spirit of a folk movement, radiating camaraderie and idealism and promising to carry all before it. The feeling spread among workers that after generations of frustration, they had at last liberated themselves from legal and political repression, from the ethnic prejudices that divided them, and from the dispiriting memories of their past failures. One worker gave eloquent voice to the intoxicating mood of class solidarity that filled the air: "Once in the Ford plant," he said, "they called me 'dumb Polack,' but now with UAW they call me brother."[36] In this radiantly shining moment, almost anything seemed possible. "The CIO," a writer in the *Nation* concluded, "is changing both the structure and orientation of American labor. . . . It is gradually killing off the AFL. . . . It is profoundly affecting our two major political parties. It is transforming the relationship of government to industry."[37]

YET THE CIO'S MOMENT of euphoria was brief. Its agenda remained limited, for the time being, to little more than union recognition. Its organizational structure was fragile and uncertain, hostage to the mercurial moods of John L. Lewis. Internal faction-fighting soon sapped much of the CIO's vitality, particularly in a protracted struggle over Communist influence in the UAW. American communists had long worked through the Trade Union Unity League, a rival body to the AFL, but the CPUSA officially abandoned that policy in 1934. In the following year Josef Stalin directed Communists everywhere to adopt the "Popular Front" strategy of making common cause with all parties on the left, including socialists and orthodox trade unionists, in the struggle against fascism. The asendancy to leadership in the CPUSA of Earl Browder, a Kansas-born accountant and former Socialist, signaled the shift. American Communists now abandoned their efforts to organize separate trade unions and sought cooperative relations with existing labor organizations. Scores of well-trained and dedicated Communist organizers thus became available to the CIO just as it came into being. Lewis welcomed the "red and rebellious" into the mass movement he was trying to mount and made aggressive use of their organizing talents. When the old Socialist David Dubinsky questioned the wisdom of that strategy, Lewis waved his objections away. "Who gets the bird?" Lewis asked, "the hunter or the dog?"[38]

That question was not so easily answered. Though Communists never

36. Zieger, *American Workers*, 68.
37. Dubofsky and Van Tine, *John L. Lewis*, 278.
38. Dubofsky and Van Tine, *John L. Lewis*, 289.

captured the great member-rich, core-industry prizes of the UAW or the steelworkers' union, they did acquire substantial strength in the merchant seamen's and transit workers' unions, and for a long while effectively controlled the United Electrical, Radio, and Machine Workers. The political and ideological struggles within the CIO aggravated and widened the schism with the AFL. The AFL launched a kind of "counterreformation" in 1938, presenting itself to employers—and to workers—as a safer bet than the allegedly radical-infested CIO. "Every CIO representative is looked upon as a walking strike," said one AFL official, an image that frightened both managers and the men and women on the shop floor alike.[39] When Texas congressman Martin Dies opened hearings before the House Committee for the Investigation of Un-American Activities in June 1938, among the first witnesses was the blunt-spoken AFL official John Frey, who attacked the CIO as a seminary of Communist sedition. At one point the AFL even sponsored boycotts of CIO-made goods. These tactics worked. By the end of the decade, the relatively conservative AFL had succeeded in unionizing workers outside the steel and auto industries and regained its position as the largest American labor organization.

If the aroma of radicalism clinging to the CIO repelled many, so, increasingly, did its reputation for a kind of undisciplined, wildcat unionism, permitting unauthorized work stoppages to break out repeatedly. The sit-down tactic in particular was so easily emulated that scattered groups of workers began employing it indiscriminately after the spectacular victory at Flint. GM, which had recognized the UAW in February 1937 precisely in order to end the Flint sit-down, complained to UAW officials that 170 of its other facilities were interrupted by similar actions in the next three months. As those disruptions spread, the public sympathy that had been so crucial to labor's gains began to erode. Indeed, the radical potential of the sit-down tactic had always rattled many middle-class Americans. Two-thirds of respondents in a Gallup poll in February 1937 believed that GM was right not to negotiate with the sit-downers, and strong majorities sympathized with the employers. Senator James Byrnes of South Carolina spoke the sentiments of many when he denounced the sit-down tactic in April, inducing the Senate to vote 75–3 for a nonbinding resolution declaring the sit-down illegal. Two years later, in the case of *NLRB v. Fansteel Metallurgical Corporation*, the

39. Zieger, *CIO*, 67.

Supreme Court unambiguously outlawed the sit-down as "a high-handed proceeding without shadow of a legal right."[40]

Emboldened by these shifts in the winds of public, congressional, and legal opinion, some employers reverted to the old tactics of checking unionization with unbridled force. On many fronts, the CIO was stopped in its tracks. When five UAW organizers, including Walter Reuther, tried on May 26, 1937, to distribute handbills to workers crossing an overpass to enter Ford's River Rouge complex, Bennett's goons beat them bloody. When Henry Luce's *Time* magazine opined that the publicity from the attack had inflicted more harm on Ford Motors than on Reuther, Henry Ford withdrew all advertising from Luce's publications, *Time, Life,* and *Fortune,* for the next year and a half. Ford held out against the UAW for four more years. So did several other major employers, including International Harvester, Westinghouse, Maytag, Allis-Chalmers, Weyerhauser, the big meatpackers, and, most notoriously, Little Steel. Only the advent of war as the next decade opened would bring gains as dramatic as those of the first half of 1937.[41]

Little Steel proved the CIO's Waterloo. The "Battle of the Overpass" was but a preview of a far bloodier encounter at Republic Steel Company's South Chicago plant just four days later, on Memorial Day 1937. Republic had been run since 1929 by Thomas Mercer Girdler, a gruff steelman as implacably dedicated to protecting the privileges of capital as Lewis was to asserting the cause of labor. Here, if ever, Lewis's near-irresistible force collided with an all but unmovable object. Girdler had earned a ruthless reputation in the 1920s as the superintendent of the Jones and Laughlin plant at Aliquippa, Pennsylvania, known to steelworkers as "Little Siberia" because of the systematic terror with which Girdler kept his workers in line and unions out. Girdler now assumed the leadership of the Little Steel group's campaign to avoid Big Steel's fate at the hands of the SWOC.

Girdler and Little Steel adopted what came to be called the "Mohawk Valley Formula," a union-busting strategy that had originated at the Remington Rand Corporation's plants in upstate New York in 1936. The Mohawk Valley Formula called for branding union organizers as Com-

40. George H. Gallup, *The Gallup Poll: Public Opinion, 1935–1971* (New York: Random House, 1972), 1:41, 48–49, 52, 55; *NLRB v. Fansteel Metallurgical Corp.,* 306 U.S. 240 (1939).
41. Tyler, *Walter Reuther,* 40.

munists, forming a Citizens Committee to deny unionists community sympathy, securing the support of local police, and fostering organizations of "loyal employees." To these items Girdler added some refinements of his own, including arming Republic Steel's private police force of nearly four hundred men with pistols, shotguns, rifles, and gas grenades. Lewis called Girdler "a heavily armed monomaniac, with murderous tendencies, who has gone berserk." Girdler did not flinch. Rather than "surrender" like U.S. Steel, he announced, he would shut his plants and "raise apples and potatoes." Girdler cannily conceded all the wage and work-condition clauses of SWOC's agreement with U.S. Steel but adamantly refused union recognition. There he drew the line. If labor wanted Little Steel, Girdler, like Grant before Richmond, was prepared to fight it out on that line if it took all summer.[42]

On the summery afternoon of Memorial Day the dreaded confrontation came. A crowd of several hundred picnicking union sympathizers, including women and children, marched toward Republic's South Chicago mill to express their support for UAW pickets pacing peacefully in front of the mill gates. A police cordon moved across the route of the march and ordered the crowd to disperse. Milling and jostling, the two groups faced off for several moments along a quavering three-hundred-foot front. A marcher some twenty feet back lobbed a stick toward the line of confrontation. Suddenly the crack of police pistol shots rent the air. The police rushed forward, firing and laying truncheons and ax handles into the fleeing and the fallen alike. A Paramount Newsreel cameraman captured the chaotic scene in a film thought to be too inflammatory for public release but privately screened for the La Follette Committee. It recorded a maniacal police riot that left ten men dead, seven of them shot in the back. Thirty others, including one woman and three children, suffered gunshot wounds. Nine were permanently disabled. "Can it be true," Lewis asked the following day, "that striking workmen may be shot down at will by the very agents of the law? Is labor to be protected or is it to be butchered?"[43]

More violence quickly followed, trying the patience even of labor's friends. Prolabor Governor Earle was forced to impose martial law on Johnstown, Pennsylvania, in June. Governor Martin Davey had to do the same in Youngstown, Ohio, following the shooting deaths of two steelworkers on June 19. On July 11 police opened fire outside a union

42. Bernstein, *Turbulent Years*, 481.
43. Zieger, *CIO*, 62.

headquarters in Masillon, Ohio, killing three. The summer of 1937 saw the deaths of eighteen workers, all, at least in the short run, in vain. Little Steel did not budge. Public opinion, meanwhile, grew increasingly disquieted at labor's mounting militancy, at the runaway spate of sit-downs, and especially at the apparently ceaseless turbulence that attended the CIO's struggle to conquer Little Steel.

Pressure mounted on Roosevelt to intervene, or at least to make his sympathies clear. He was, he knew, damned if he did and damned if he didn't. How could he take the side of labor without appearing to sanction the increasingly unpopular sit-downs, or even appearing to acquiesce in violence? But how could he condemn labor without affronting the millions of workers who had voted for him in 1936? Asked for his opinion at a press conference on June 29, 1937, he gave a reply that was couched obliquely but probably reflected accurately enough his own exasperation with labor as well as management. "The majority of the people are saying just one thing," Roosevelt declared, quoting a line from *Romeo and Juliet*: "A plague on both your houses." A radio address on the following Labor Day yielded John L. Lewis's retort, cobbled together from his own richly stocked lexical inventory: "Labor, like Israel, has many sorrows. Its women weep for their fallen, and they lament for the future of the children of the race. It ill behooves one who has supped at labor's table and who has been sheltered in labor's house to curse with equal fervor and fine impartiality both labor and its adversaries when they become locked in deadly embrace." With that, the historian Irving Bernstein concludes, "a brief and not very beautiful friendship had come to an end."[44]

THE ROOSEVELT-LEWIS ALLIANCE had lasted five years. It had brought forth a prolific brood of new unions, though many students of labor's flowering in the 1930s have charged that Roosevelt's claims to paternity were weak. As one labor historian has concluded, "one carries away a distinct impression of *inadvertency* in the role the New Deal played in the expansion of the labor movement."[45] Inadvertency, perhaps, but indispensability as well. In the agricultural and service sectors, where the NLRB's writ did not run, the union movement remained

44. *Complete Press Conferences of Franklin D. Roosevelt* (New York: Da Capo, 1972), 9:467; Dubofsky and Van Tine, *John L. Lewis*, 327; Bernstein, *Turbulent Years*, 496.
45. David Brody, *Workers in Industrial America: Essays on the Twentieth-Century Struggle* (New York: Oxford University Press, 1980), 145.

stalled before insurmountable obstacles to effective organizing. But in the industrial sectors that lay under the hand of New Deal policy, labor's gains were dramatic. The simple prospect of that hand's intervention changed the power equation between capital and labor. In fact, the CIO's largest gains in membership came in the period between 1935 and 1937, when the NLRB was hemmed in by the threat of judicial extinction. When the Wagner Act's constitutionality was at last affirmed in the *Jones and Laughlin* case (see p. 335), the NLRB's work load ballooned to thousands of cases per month. But the big organizing successes at GM and U.S. Steel were by then already well secured.

From some three million union members in 1933, the ranks of organized labor swelled to more than eight million by end of the decade—some 23 percent of the nonagricultural work force. Union membership was heavily concentrated in the mature industries of manufacturing, transportation, and mining and in the northeastern and Pacific Coast states, especially those states where prolabor governors presided. In the South, still predominantly agricultural and still wedded to the idea that cheap labor was its biggest competitive asset, only one worker in ten belonged to a union as the decade of the 1930s closed.

From a skeletal staff of 14 lawyers in 1935, the NLRB grew to employ some 226 lawyers four years later. Though criticized then and later as another example of bloated bureaucracy, the NLRB in fact provided a mechanism that quelled the raucous labor upheavals of the 1930s and served thereafter as an orderly forum where disputes between management and labor—or between competing unions—could be peaceably resolved. The kind of violence that long dogged the history of American industrialization and exploded with savage ferocity in the Depression years largely disappeared. With the passage of the Wagner Act, the locus of labor conflict shifted from the streets to the NLRB's hearing rooms—and to the courts, as labor relations became enmeshed in one of the most elaborately articulated bodies of law in the American statute books. Bloody clashes at the factory gate gave way to decorously argued points of order in front of a federal mediator or a judge. Both sides gained as well as lost. Capital gave up some of its prerogatives but won a measure of industrial peace. Labor subjected itself to the sometimes meddlesome tutelage of the regulatory state but achieved a degree of parity with management at the bargaining table and, no less important, unprecedented prosperity and security as well.

Unions made a difference. In the organized industries, wages rose after 1935 in measurably greater degree than in unorganized sectors.

Lewis's coal miners made ninety cents an hour in 1940, one-third higher than the average industrial wage of seventy-four cents. Autoworkers by 1941 earned $1.04 an hour. Union insistence on the seniority principle also rendered employment more predictable, conferring especially valuable protection on older workers, who naturally had longer terms of service. Union-negotiated grievance procedures checked the petty tyranny of foremen and supervisors. Men, who composed some three-quarters of the work force, were the principal beneficiaries of these gains. For the fourteen million women workers, mostly in the largely unorganized service sector, for the many millions of agricultural laborers, and for almost all workers of whatever description in the South, comparable benefits would be a long time coming. The heavily female garment trades paid sixty cents per hour in 1940; retail clerks made thirty-five to fifty cents; textile mill workers, forty-six cents. But for employed workers generally—always the majority, even in the 1930s, it is worth remembering—and especially for manufacturing workers, the conditions of life and work were markedly better at the decade's end than at its beginning, and the improvement was due in no small measure to the success of the union movement. In 1941 the average yearly income for a manufacturing worker was $1,449. A steelworker with a statistically typical family of 2.5 children could afford a new coat for himself and his wife every six years and could buy a new pair of shoes for each child every two years. Mother could purchase two housedresses, and father one workshirt, every year. They could afford a used car and the rent for a five-room apartment. Their household budget was well below the two thousand that experts deemed necessary for a comfortable standard of living, but it was a sum that looked almost princely to people who had scraped and fretted through the Depression decade.[46]

Whether through inadvertence or intention, Roosevelt and the Democratic Party were surely the rich beneficiaries of these changes in workers' circumstances. Before the 1930s many workers, especially if they were of immigrant stock, had rarely troubled to vote and had in any case fickle, unreliable political loyalties. To be sure, urban machines like Anton Cermak's in Chicago had begun to weld immigrant workers to the Democratic Party well before the New Deal appeared on the scene. But it was only in the 1930s, thanks largely to organized labor's achievements and Roosevelt's uncanny ability to associate himself with those achievements, that labor became a sizable and dependable com-

46. Zieger, CIO, 111ff.

ponent of the Democrats' constituency. When they next had the chance to vote for him, in the presidential election of 1940, workers went so heavily for Roosevelt that he increased his victory margin in the big industrial cities to a formidable 59 percent.[47]

In the process of becoming reliable Democrats, workers also buried once and for all the always evanescent dream of an exclusively workingpeople's party. Just as workers eschewed the overthrow of capitalism to embrace bread-and-butter unionism, so did they repudiate radical politics and attach themselves to one of the existing mainstream parties. In the process, they wrote the epitaph for American socialism and stifled American Communism in its cradle.

A heightened sense of class consciousness did indeed emerge in the United States in the Depression years, but it was of a stubbornly characteristic American type. It did not frontally challenge existing institutions but asked—demanded—a larger measure of participation in them. In the end the trade union movement, the Democratic Party, and the big corporations as well all proved sufficiently resilient to allow for that participation. As for the workers themselves, a poll in 1939 revealed that they had few illusions about their situation. Fully half of the respondents identifed themselves as belonging to the lower or lower-middle income categories. But when asked to which social class they belonged, 88 percent replied "middle." Those opinions suggested that workers realistically appraised their economic circumstance but also clung to their faith in an inclusive, egalitarian democracy and to the hope for social mobility. Even in the midst of the country's greatest depression, for millions of working-class citizens the American dream had survived. Indeed, for many it was on the way to becoming a greater reality than ever before.[48]

---

47. Michael Barone, *Our Country: The Shaping of America from Roosevelt to Reagan* (New York: Free Press, 1990), 144.
48. Zieger, *CIO*, 116.

11

The Ordeal of Franklin Roosevelt

Once you build a house you always have it. On the other hand, a social or an economic gain is a different matter. A social or an economic gain made by one Administration, for instance, may, and often does, evaporate into thin air under the next Administration.

— President Franklin D. Roosevelt,
radio address, November 4, 1938

Pride, the ancient wisdom proclaims, goeth before a fall. Franklin Roosevelt in early 1937 had reason to be the proudest of men. He had wrung landmark reforms from Congress in 1935. He had won reelection in 1936 by a larger margin than any president in more than a century. He had ushered new constituencies into the Democratic Party, forging an electoral coalition of formidable power and durability. And as the first year of his second term opened, the economy he had pledged to revive continued to show signs of shaking off its Depression narcosis. Roosevelt understandably took satisfaction in these political achievements and took credit, as is the politician's habit, for the country's economic reawakening as well. He boasted in his second inaugural address, not without reason or pride, that "our progress out of the depression is obvious." And yet before the year 1937 was out, both the economy and the president's political fortunes would tumble to depths not touched since Herbert Hoover's presidency.[1]

Even in the heady moments of early 1937, a quaver of foreboding crept into the president's celebration of economic recovery. His agenda had from the outset embraced more than simply restoring the economy to good health. He also aimed to enact durable reforms, to reshape the topography of American economic and social life both to prevent future

1. *PPA* (1937), 2.

323

depressions and permanently to improve the lot of the millions who were ill housed, ill clad, and ill nourished. Toward those goals he had made notable progress in his first term, not least with the passage of the Social Security and National Labor Relations Acts.

But those accomplishments were not yet secure, nor were his larger purposes yet fully gained. Economic recovery, he worried, though surely welcome for its own sake, might therefore be politically premature. It might dissipate the fleeting public mood that had permitted him the rare scope for presidential initiative that he had enjoyed in his first term. Future congresses might dismantle the fragile edifice of reforms thrown up hastily in the emergency atmosphere of the Depression crisis. Future presidents, even liberal presidents, might prove unable to orchestrate their party and to wield executive power as effectively as Roosevelt had between 1933 and 1936.

Most ominous, the threat of judicial nullification loomed over virtually every New Deal measure thus far enacted. The Supreme Court had already gutted many of the reform initiatives of the Hundred Days, notably NRA and AAA. Lawsuits challenging the constitutionality of all the major legislative acts of 1935 — Social Security, the National Labor Relations Act, the Public Utilities Holding Company Act — were grinding through the judicial system as 1937 opened. The president had no reason to believe that the Supreme Court would in the end give its approval to his myriad innovations, particularly if they no longer seemed necessary to effecting recovery.

And so much remained undone. There was still that "one-third of a nation" whose needs had only begun to be addressed. The achievements of his first term, Roosevelt said in his inaugural address, "were won under the pressure of more than ordinary circumstance . . . under the goad of fear and suffering." Then, he said, "the times were on the side of progress." But now, he warned, "symptoms of prosperity may become portents of disaster! Prosperity already tests the persistence of our progressive purpose."[2]

Prosperity as disaster? This was rank heresy for a politician to voice at any time. In the midst of the Great Depression it seemed to invite political anathema. Yet this was neither the first time nor the last that Roosevelt reflected on the complex relationship between economic crisis and political reform. As early as 1924, he had written to fellow Democrats that the hour of opportunity for liberalism would not arrive "until-

2. PPA (1937), 4.

the Republicans had led us into a serious period of depression and unemployment."[3] As it happened, catastrophic depression and massive unemployment, on scales Roosevelt neither anticipated nor wished, had furnished more occasion for liberal achievement than he had dared to anticipate. Now those scourges seemed to be lifting. With their disappearance the season of political reform might also be coming to a close.

Again and again in 1937, in private settings as well as public, Roosevelt returned to this theme. In his annual message to Congress in early January, he put the legislators on notice that "[y]our task and mine is not ending with the Depression," foreshadowing the even stronger warning he enunciated in his inaugural address a few weeks later.[4] In February he confided in a personal letter to Felix Frankfurter his fear that "the return of prosperity, at this moment, may blunt our senses."[5] In a Fireside Chat a few months later he declared that government could not "stop governing simply because prosperity has come back a long way."[6]

As his second term began, Roosevelt was therefore determined to strike boldly. In the waning moment before prosperity had fully returned, he must protect the New Deal and prepare the way for further reform. He struck on three fronts: at the judiciary, at Congress, and, eventually, at elements within his own party, particularly its entrenched southern wing.

FATEFULLY, HE BEGAN with the judiciary. In a singular and eventually disastrous political miscalculation, Roosevelt opened his new term by launching a surprise attack on one of the most sacred American institutions, the Supreme Court.

On February 5, 1937, Roosevelt startled Congress with a special message. He asked for a statute that would allow the president to appoint one additional justice to the Supreme Court, up to a total of six new appointments, for every sitting justice who declined to retire at age seventy. Additionally, he requested authority on a like basis to name up to forty-four new judges to the lower federal courts. These changes were necessary, Roosevelt explained, to promote judicial efficiency by clearing crowded dockets.

3. Frank Freidel, *Franklin Roosevelt: The Ordeal* (Boston: Little, Brown, 1954), 183.
4. *PPA* (1936), 642.
5. Max Freedman, ed., *Roosevelt and Frankfurter: Their Correspondence, 1928–1945* (Boston: Little, Brown, 1967), 382.
6. *PPA* (1937), 431.

There was nothing sacrosanct about the nine-justice Court that Roosevelt sought to enlarge. At various times in the Court's history Congress had specified five, six, seven, and ten justices as the high bench's statutory complement. But Roosevelt awkwardly tried to justify his proposed changes with unsupportable charges of inefficiency and with gratuitous, unpersuasive innuendoes about the senility of the current justices. "[A]ged or infirm judges — a subject of delicacy," Roosevelt conceded — were inclined "to avoid an examination of complicated and changed conditions. Little by little, new facts become blurred through old glasses fitted, as it were, for the needs of another generation; older men, assuming that the scene is the same as it was in the past, cease to explore or inquire into the present or the future."[7]

There was a wisp of truth in what Roosevelt said. The average age of the current justices was seventy-one. Louis Brandeis was the oldest at eighty. Ironically, the elderly Brandeis, along with Benjamin Cardozo (sixty-six) and Harlan Fiske Stone (sixty-four), made up the Court's most consistently liberal bloc. The notoriously conservative "Four Horsemen" were all septuagenarians: James C. McReynolds (seventy-five), George Sutherland (seventy-four), Willis Van Devanter (seventy-seven), and Pierce Butler (seventy). Chief Justice Charles Evans Hughes was seventy-five; he and Owen J. Roberts, the Court's youngster at sixty-one, made up the swing votes that held the balance of power.

But neither efficiency nor age was the real issue, and Roosevelt knew it. So did the country. The normally pro–New Deal *New York World-Telegram* condemned Roosevelt's scheme as "too clever, too damned clever." Even Roosevelt's loyal associate Samuel Rosenman later lamented "the cleverness, the too much cleverness" of Roosevelt's plan.[8] Roosevelt was proposing to fiddle with one of the most respected and immutable American institutions, one designed by the Founders and enshrined in national mythology as the ballast whose unshifting weight could be counted upon to steady the ship of state. It did the president's cause incalculable harm that he opened the national discussion about this explosive issue on a transparently disingenuous note.

Yet the causes of Roosevelt's exasperation with the Court were genuine enough. He had appointed not one of the nine sitting justices; he was at that moment the first president since Andrew Johnson not to have made a Supreme Court nomination. His Democratic predecessor and

7. *PPA* (1937), 44.
8. Davis 51, 97.

former chief, Woodrow Wilson, had appointed the liberal Brandeis and the conservative McReynolds. Republican presidents had named all the others, just as they had named a heavy majority (nearly 80 percent) of judges then sitting at all levels of the federal judiciary.[9] Though its members were not monolithic in their thinking, the "Court of Methuselahs" regularly produced majorities, with the Four Horsemen as their nucleus, for decisions that threatened everything the New Deal was trying to accomplish.

In the broadest sense, the Court's power derived from the doctrine of judicial review, a concept not defined in the Constitution but first asserted by John Marshall in *Marbury v. Madison* in 1803, when he claimed for the Supreme Court the ultimate authority to define the meaning of the Constitution and set limits to legislative action. The doctrine lay dormant for half a century thereafter, not revived again until the Dred Scott case in 1857. But in the decades following the Civil War, as both state legislatures and the federal Congress tried to assert some control over the rapidly industrializing economy, the Court was increasingly inclined to stay the legislators' hands. The specific restraint it invoked most often was one fashioned from the elusive concept of substantive due process.

Substantive due process amounted in practice to the proposition that some "substantive" rights were so inviolable—especially property and contract rights—that they lay beyond the reach of any imaginable "process," or law. Though in explaining its decisions the Court cited various specific points of the law, such as restrictions on the commerce power or freedom of contract, the environing idea that since the 1890s had shaped the Court's basic attitude toward economic legislation was the principle of laissez-faire, or noninterference in the market economy. Applying that principle made the judiciary the most powerful arm of government, though its power was wholly the power to veto. Reformers from Theodore Roosevelt onward, including on occasion jurists like Brandeis and Stone, had decried this meddlesome judicial activism, beseeching the black-robed, unelected justices to defer to the will of democratically elected legislatures. But they pleaded in vain. In the

9. Hughes and Van Devanter had been appointed by President Taft, Sutherland and Butler by Harding, Stone by Coolidge, and Cardozo and Roberts by Hoover, who had also elevated Hughes to the position of chief justice. In 1933 approximately 191 of the 266 federal judges were Republican appointees. William E. Leuchtenburg, *The Supreme Court Reborn: The Constitutional Revolution in the Age of Roosevelt* (New York: Oxford University Press, 1995), 79, n. 5.

1920s alone, no fewer than nineteen socioeconomic statutes had fallen to the judicial ax, including laws that prohibited child labor and defined minimum wages for women workers. In the 1930s the flood of New Deal legislation made a titanic duel with the judiciary all but inevitable.

The Court had already thrown down the gauntlet to the New Deal. On "Black Monday," May 27, 1935, in *Schechter Poultry Corporation v. United States*, known ever after as the "sick chicken" case, the justices had unanimously declared the National Industrial Recovery Act to be unconstitutional. Congress, said the Court, had impermissibly delegated its inalienable lawmaking authority to the National Recovery Administration—"delegation run riot," said Justice Cardozo. The opinion not only voided the NRA but jeopardized the very concept of rulemaking independent regulatory agencies like the Securities and Exchange Commission or the National Labor Relations Board. For good measure, the Court also went out of its way to define the Schechter brothers' Brooklyn kosher-poultry business as exclusively *intra*state in character. The decision thus put the Schechters' violation of NRA wage and hour codes, not to mention their sale of diseased poultry, beyond the reach of federal power, which was constitutionally confined to the regulation of *inter*state commerce.[10]

The *Schecter* decision stunned Roosevelt. What was at stake, he instantly recognized, was nothing less than what the *New Republic* called "the very foundation of national power in a modern industrial society." Could the government act in the face of the greatest economic calamity in American history, or was it to be forever hog-tied by the strictures of the Constitution? "We have been relegated to the horse-and-buggy definition of interstate commerce," Roosevelt complained. "I tell you, Mr. President," Attorney General Homer Cummings fulminated, "they mean to destroy us. . . . We will have to find a way to get rid of the present membership of the Supreme Court."[11]

Worse soon followed. In the first week of 1936 the Court took up residence in its new classic-revival temple on Capitol Hill. "It is a mag-

---

10. *Schechter Poultry Corporation v. United States*, 295 U.S. 495 (1935). On the same day as the *Schechter* decision, the Court also handed down two other decisions harmful to the New Deal. In *Louisville Bank v. Radford* (295 U.S. 555), the Court invalidated the Frazier-Lemke mortgage moratorium act. In *Humphrey's Executor v. United States* (291 U.S. 602), it sharply circumscribed the president's power to remove members of regulatory commissions.

11. Leuchtenburg, *Supreme Court Reborn*, 43, 85, 88.

nificent structure," said a *New Yorker* writer, "with fine big windows to throw the New Deal out of."[12] On January 6, in the case of *United States v. Butler*, the Court by a six-to-three vote tossed out the Agricultural Adjustment Act. The tax on processors that went to pay farmers who limited crop production, the Court declared, unconstitutionally encroached on regulatory powers reserved to the states by the Tenth Amendment. Justice Stone in dissent said that the majority's decision in the AAA case proceeded from "a tortured construction of the Constitution. . . . Courts are not the only agency of government that must be assumed to have capacity to govern," he admonished, in what was by then a familiar criticism.[13] In March 1936, again citing the Tenth Amendment as well as limitations on the commerce power, the Court struck down the Guffey Bituminous Coal Conservation Act, a "little NRA" law enacted after *Schechter* to shore up the chronically ailing coal industry.

Then came the crowning blow. Just weeks later, in *Morehead v. New York ex rel. Tipaldo*, Owen Roberts joined the Four Horsemen to form a scant five-to-four majority that invalidated a New York minimum wage law as an unconstitutional infringement on freedom of contract. The Court's other decisions in the 1936 term had circumscribed federal power, largely in the name of states' rights. Now the *Tipaldo* decision sharply curtailed the regulatory powers of the states themselves.

For the critics of substantive due process, *Tipaldo* was the final insult. Justice Stone dissented with unusual vigor. "There is grim irony," he wrote, "in speaking of the freedom of contract of those who, because of their economic necessities, give their services for less than is needful to keep body and soul together." Privately, Stone wrote to his sister that the *Tipaldo* decision climaxed "one of the most disastrous" terms in the Court's history. "[*Tipaldo*] was a holding by a divided vote that there was no power in a state to regulate minimum wages for women. Since the Court last week said that this could not be done by the national government, as the matter was local, and now it is said that it cannot be done by local governments even though it is local, we seem to have tied Uncle Sam up in a hard knot." For his part, Roosevelt trenchantly remarked that with the *Tipaldo* decision the Court had for all practical

12. *New Yorker* quoted in Irving Bernstein, *Turbulent Years: A History of the American Worker, 1933–1941* (Boston: Houghton Mifflin, 1970), 639.
13. *Butler v. United States*, 297 U.S.1 (1936).

purposes marked off a "no man's land where no Government — State or Federal — can function."[14]

Reflecting the accumulating frustration with the Court's dogged devotion to judicial nullification, more than one hundred bills were introduced in Congress in 1936 to redefine the balance of power between the legislative and judicial branches of government. After *Tipaldo*, even Herbert Hoover called for a constitutional amendment to restore to the states "the power they thought they already had," and the Republican platform of 1936 strongly advocated such an amendment.[15]

Against this background, Franklin Roosevelt's aggravation with judicial obstruction was neither unwarranted nor singular. Nor was it precipitate. As early as November 1935, Harold Ickes had recorded in his diary: "Clearly, it is running in the President's mind that substantially all of the New Deal bills will be declared unconstitutional by the Supreme Court. This will mean that everything that this Administration has done of any moment will be nullified."[16] Throughout 1935 and 1936, at Roosevelt's urging, Justice Department lawyers had struggled to draft a constitutional amendment to curb the Court's power. But they wrestled in vain with a grotesquely cumbersome formula that would have conferred explicit powers of judicial review on the Court, while providing, after an intervening election, for legislative override of Court findings of unconstitutionality — a kind of indirect popular referendum, designed by Rube Goldberg. By early 1937 two years of effort had not yielded an acceptable draft.

The amendment process was in any case designedly difficult, requiring two-thirds approval in each house of Congress and ratification by three-fourths of the states. It was also time-consuming. The example of the amendment prohibiting child labor, first approved by Congress in 1924 but still unpassed by the requisite number of states thirteen years later, weighed heavily in the president's thinking. Time, Roosevelt knew, was of the essence. Cases testing the validity of the National Labor Relations Act, the Social Security Act, and a bundle of state minimum wage and unemployment compensation laws were already on the Court's docket by the end of 1936. Unless something were done, the new year might bring a constitutional Armageddon. The distinct possibility

---

14. *Morehead v. New York ex rel. Tipaldo*, 298 U.S. 587 (1936), 632; Leuchtenburg, *Supreme Court Reborn*, 159, 100.

15. Leuchtenburg, *Supreme Court Reborn*, 100–101.

16. Ickes Diary 1:495.

loomed that when the Court reconvened in January the entire New Deal might be summarily repealed by wholesale judicial annihilation—a bitterly ironic sequel to Roosevelt's smashing 1936 electoral victory. Roosevelt was understandably appalled at this prospect. "When I retire to private life on January 20, 1941," he said, dramatically revealing his own estimate of the gravity of the impending crisis, "I do not want to leave the country in the condition Buchanan left it to Lincoln."[17]

SMALL WONDER, THEN, that Roosevelt pursued Attorney General Cummings's suggestion to "get rid of the present membership of the Supreme Court." Given the decades-long agitation against "judicial supremacy," and among the array of nostrums prescribed at the time for judicial reform, the plan that Roosevelt advanced on February 5 stood out not for its boldness but for its mildness. It defined no new constitutional role for the Court and thus left the time-honored system of checks and balances unperturbed. It did not in fact propose literally to "get rid" of the Court's sitting justices but asked merely for an expansion, under stipulated conditions, of the Court's personnel, and asked for that expansion in the larger context of streamlining the entire federal judiciary. Roosevelt's Court plan was no wanton blunder. It was a calculated risk, and not an unreasonable one. He was wagering a modest challenge to the tradition of an independent judiciary against the prospect of the entire New Deal's judicial extinction.

But Roosevelt woefully underestimated the strength of popular devotion to the Court's traditional role. He also miscalculated badly in his choice of tactics and timing. From the moment of its unveiling, his Court plan stirred a nest of furies whose destructive power swiftly swelled to awesome proportions, well beyond the president's ability to control.

What the president called judicial reform a mighty host of critics throatily assailed as "Court-packing." "If the American people accept this last audacity of the President without letting out a yell to high heaven, they have ceased to be jealous of their liberties and are ripe for ruin," wrote the columnist Dorothy Thompson. A fatal elision took root in the public's mind between the Court plan, the contemporaneous sit-down strikes, and the president's role in each. Somehow, Roosevelt managed to be perceived as both the acknowledged perpetrator of one affront to traditional notions of constitutional order (by attacking the Court) and the indulgent patron of another (by remaining silent on the sit-

17. *Time*, March 8, 1937, 13.

downs). Americans overwhelmingly told pollsters that they disapproved of the sit-down strikers. Before 1937 was out, 45 percent of respondents in one Gallup poll deemed the administration "too friendly" to labor.[18]

Nor did it help matters that just weeks before his Court message, Roosevelt had asked Congress for legislation to reorganize the executive branch. The executive reorganization bill was a sensible proposal, incorporating the recommendations of independent experts to bring the federal executive into line with the principles of modern management science. But in company with the Court-reform bill, it opened Roosevelt to charges of seeking "dictatorship" by weakening other branches of government and aggrandizing the power of the presidency. Ominously, a Gallup poll in the weeks just after the bombshell Court message—when the furor over the sit-downs was at its height—showed a solid majority (53 percent) opposed to the president's Court proposal.[19]

Roosevelt seemed to have been deserted by the political muses who had guided him so surely throughout his career. He unaccountably compounded his already abundant errors by shrouding his intentions in secrecy until the last minute, robbing himself of the indispensable congressional support that might have come with the lawmakers' sense of participation in the plan's development. The first that congressional leaders heard of the Court scheme was on the morning of February 5, when Roosevelt gave them a perfunctory briefing at the White House just hours before his special message went up to Capitol Hill. Kentucky senator Alben W. Barkley, usually a staunch Roosevelt supporter, later reflected that in this case Roosevelt was a "poor quarterback. He didn't give us the signals in advance of the play." In Vice-President Garner's car headed back to the Capitol, House Judiciary Committee chairman Hatton Sumners of Texas turned to the others. "Boys," he said, "here's where I cash in." When the bill was read later that day in the Senate, Garner stood in the lobby, ostentatiously holding his nose and turning his thumb down.[20] A few weeks later, disgusted alike with Roosevelt's silence on the sit-down strikes and with the Supreme Court bill, Garner betook himself on an extended vacation to Texas. His departure deprived Roosevelt of crucial leadership in the Congress, where Garner had long

18. *Literary Digest*, February 20, 1937, 3; George H. Gallup, *The Gallup Poll: Public Opinion, 1935–1971* (New York: Random House, 1972), 1:69.
19. Gallup, *Gallup Poll*, 1:50.
20. James T. Patterson, *Congressional Conservatism and the New Deal: The Growth of the Conservative Coalition in Congress, 1933–1939* (Lexington: University of Kentucky Press, 1967), 87–92.

An End and a Beginning

Armistice Day, November 11, 1918. These Philadelphians cheering the end of the Great War did not yet understand how dark a shadow the war was to cast over their future. The peace agreement that President Woodrow Wilson helped to negotiate left many questions unsettled and sowed the seeds of an even greater war scarcely a generation later. The mood of celebration in America eventually gave way to disillusionment with foreign entanglements and a reinvigorated isolationism. (NATIONAL ARCHIVES W&C 715)

American Life on the Eve of the Depression

Doing the washing, Iowa, 1922. (NATIONAL ARCHIVES RG 33SC-1241)

A kitchen in Maryland, 1929. Rural America was virtually another country in the 1920s, lacking amenities like indoor plumbing and electricity that were common in cities. This Iowa woman had probably pumped water from a well to do her laundry; the Maryland family whose kitchen is shown here cooked and heated their house with a wood stove and lit their spare rooms with oil lamps or candles. (NATIONAL ARCHIVES 33SC-11870)

"Little Italy," Chicago, in the pre-Depression era. Well into the 1920s and beyond, many immigrants lived in insular, parochial communities on the margins of American society. (CHICAGO HISTORICAL SOCIETY ICHI-24279)

In black America: Mississippi sharecroppers near Vicksburg, Mississippi, 1936. More than 80 percent of African-Americans dwelled in the South until the eve of World War II. Segregated, disenfranchised, and largely confined to sharecropping, they were the poorest of the poor in the nation's most economically backward region, and no strangers to suffering, well before the Depression descended. (LIBRARY OF CONGRESS LC-USF34T01-9575)

Restaurant, Lancaster, Ohio, 1938. Racial segregation in pre–World War II America was not confined to the South, as this Ohio restaurant unapologetically advertised. (LIBRARY OF CONGRESS LC-USF 3301-6392-M4)

A Stricken People

Panic. After the great stock market crash of 1929, frightened depositors rushed to withdraw their funds before their banks failed, driving the economic spiral even more steeply downward. (FRANKLIN D. ROOSEVELT LIBRARY 7420 [1007])

Breadline, New York City, 1932. The swelling ranks of the unemployed had overwhelmed local charities and governments by 1932, making some kind of federal relief effort all but inevitable. In the process of implementing that effort, the federal government transformed its role in American society. (FRANKLIN D. ROOSEVELT LIBRARY 97107 [1])

"Okies," California, 1935. Thousands of refugees from the drought-plagued Oklahoma-Texas-Kansas "Dust Bowl" headed west in the Depression years, with misery as their unshakeable companion. (FRANKLIN D. ROOSEVELT LIBRARY 53227 [575])

Cotton pickers, Arizona, 1940. Migrant agricultural workers lived a hand-to-mouth existence on the road, making do in crude shelters like this one, with no sanitation, no water, no electricity, and no prospects. (NATIONAL ARCHIVES 83-G-44357)

THERE IS A SANTA CLAUS!

The Great Engineer, 1929. In the early months of the Depression, President Herbert Hoover was widely regarded as a vigorous, effective battler against the economic crisis. (LIBRARY OF CONGRESS LC-USZ62-38795)

The humiliation of Hoover, 1932. After more than three years of Depression, Hoover's reputation had taken a brutal beating. (LIBRARY OF CONGRESS LC-USZ62-19646)

The changing of the guard, 1933. Hoover's and Roosevelt's faces on their way to FDR's inauguration reflected their different temperaments as well as their different political fortunes. (FRANKLIN D.
ROOSEVELT LIBRARY)

The Coming of the New Deal

The blue eagle. The National Recovery Administration's symbol was ubiquitous in the early New Deal years—until the NRA was struck down by the Supreme Court in 1935. The NRA was the most ambitious federal economic program in history, but it did not bring recovery. (FRANKLIN D. ROOSEVELT LIBRARY 7163)

The Civilian Conservation Corps. The CCC was among the most popular of the New Deal's programs. It put thousands of young men to work restoring the nation's blighted forests and building outdoor recreational facilities. (FRANKLIN D. ROOSEVELT LIBRARY 7420 [273])

Work Projects Administration artists at work. WPA artists enhanced many public spaces in the Depression years. These muralists worked on "The Role of the Immigrant in the Industrial Development of America" for the dining room of the historic immigrant-receiving center on New York's Ellis Island. (NATIONAL ARCHIVES RG 69-AG-413)

The National Youth Administration. These young women at an NYA center in Phoenix, Arizona, in 1936 were being schooled for jobs as domestic servants. Taking America as it found it, the NYA dared not disturb deeply entrenched habits of racial and occupational segregation—a pattern to which many New Deal programs conformed. (FRANKLIN D. ROOSEVELT LIBRARY 5251 [107])

Social Security. Elderly Americans like this couple began to receive their first Social Security checks in 1940. Social Security laid the foundation of the modern American welfare state, and has proved among the most consequential and durable of all the New Deal's reforms. (NATIONAL ARCHIVES RG 47-GA-4-2529-2-1-C)

A Different Kind of President

The common touch. FDR chats with a North Dakota farmer in 1936. Roosevelt touched the hearts of his countrymen like no predecessor in memory. His "fireside chats" on the radio brought his voice and his warm, avuncular personality into millions of homes, revolutionizing the relationship of ordinary Americans with the presidency. (FRANKLIN D. ROOSEVELT LIBRARY)

"Come along. We're going to the Trans-Lux to hiss Roosevelt." By 1936, many well-to-do Americans condemned Roosevelt as a "class traitor" whose policies exacerbated class divisions and punished the successful. Both accusations were grossly overdrawn. (DRAWING BY PETER ARNO, © 1936, THE NEW YORKER MAGAZINE)

"Yes, You Remembered Me." Roosevelt's New Deal won the political loyalty of millions of working-class voters and helped the Democrats achieve huge electoral majorities in 1936. Yet within months of that enormous victory, Roosevelt found himself politically on the defensive. He faced a resurgent conservative bloc in Congress, a new economic crisis, and a badly deteriorating international situation. The New Deal was effectively finished even before Roosevelt began his second term in 1937. (LIBRARY OF CONGRESS LC-USZ62-34309; © NEW YORK DAILY NEWS, I.P., REPRINTED WITH PERMISSION)

The Specter of Class War

Picket line, Greensboro, Georgia, 1934. The New Deal gave a mighty impetus to union-organizing campaigns, but often proved unable to control the forces it had unleashed. These textile workers were part of an industry-wide shut-down that eventually produced scores of arrests and the deaths of fourteen strikers. It ended with an uneasy settlement that pleased neither side. (LIBRARY OF CONGRESS LC-USF33-20936-MZ)

Minneapolis, 1934. A virtual civil war rocked Minneapolis in the summer of 1934. This clash between striking truck drivers and police left more than sixty strikers wounded and two dead. (FRANKLIN D. ROOSEVELT LIBRARY 72142)

The Battle of the Overpass. Goons from the Ford Motor Company's "Service Department"—in reality a private police force dedicated to suppressing trade unions at Ford—assaulted a group of union organizers trying to distribute handbills outside Ford's River Rouge plant on May 26, 1937. Just four days later, one of the bloodiest confrontations in American labor history, the so-called Memorial Day Massacre, left ten men dead outside Republic Steel's Chicago works. (FRANKLIN D. ROOSEVELT LIBRARY 7819 [4])

Eleanor Roosevelt. The First Lady visits a WPA-sponsored Negro nursery school in Des Moines, Iowa, in 1936. She served as the New Deal's conscience and as the President's ambassador to black America. (FRANKLIN D. ROOSEVELT LIBRARY 64141)

Harry Hopkins. A former social worker, he administered the New Deal's vast relief programs and eventually became Roosevelt's most trusted adviser and confidant during World War II. (LIBRARY OF CONGRESS LC-USZ6 2-36963)

FDR, Interior Secretary Harold Ickes, and Agriculture Secretary Henry A. Wallace. Ickes and Wallace were both former Republicans. Their appointments reflected Roosevelt's strategy of trying to build a new liberal coalition that would absorb Republican progressives. Ickes served into the Truman administration, but Wallace proved too left-wing for many traditional Democrats. Sorely aggrieved when Roosevelt named Wallace as his vice-presidential running mate in 1940, they forced Wallace off the ticket in 1944, paving the way for Harry S. Truman's nomination. (LIBRARY OF CONGRESS LC-USZ6 2-98147)

Huey P. Long. The Louisiana senator seemed poised to mount a radical challenge to the New Deal, but he was cut down by an assassin's gun in September 1935. (LIBRARY OF CONGRESS LC-USZ6 2-111013)

John L. Lewis. A virtuoso of bombast and invective, Lewis galvanized the movement for industrial unionism and helped deliver the labor vote for Roosevelt in 1936. Four years later, strenuously disagreeing with FDR's pro-British foreign policies, he endorsed Wendell Willkie for the presidency. (UPI/CORBIS-BETTMANN)

Father Charles E. Coughlin. Like Roosevelt, Coughlin was a master of the new medium of radio. An early supporter of the New Deal, he later became a bitter critic. His anti-Semitic rantings eventually caused the Catholic church to silence him. (LIBRARY OF CONGRESS LC-USZ6 2-111027)

Adolf Hitler. The Nazi leader at a party rally in Nuremberg in 1928. In January 1933 he would assume the German chancellorship, just two months before Roosevelt's inauguration as president. All the New Deal was played out under the lengthening shadow of the Nazi menace. In 1939 Hitler would plunge the world—including, eventually, a reluctant United States—into history's most awful war. (NATIONAL ARCHIVES 242-HAP-1928 [46])

been a representative and now served as presiding officer of the Senate. "This is a fine time to jump ship. . . . Why in hell did Jack have to leave at this time for?" Roosevelt fumed to Jim Farley. "I don't think the President ever forgave Garner," Farley concluded.[21]

Sumners and Garner were not the only defectors. Many southern Democrats abandoned the president, fearing that a more liberal Court might open the door to a second Reconstruction that would challenge white supremacy. Roosevelt may have anticipated defections of that sort, but to his chagrin his Court-reform proposal also alienated many of his formerly reliable progressive allies like Montana's Senator Burton Wheeler. Though they shared Roosevelt's frustration with the current Court's conservatism, they objected on principle to any compromising of the judiciary's independence. In a surprising and major embarrassment to the president, many Democratic liberals also hotly denounced the Roosevelt plan. New York Democratic governor Herbert Lehman, whom FDR had once described as "my strong right arm," was among them. "Last week," a newsmagazine reported when Lehman announced his opposition to the Court plan, "the strong right arm gave [Roosevelt] a jolting blow between the eyes." As for Wheeler, he emerged as the Court plan's chief opponent in the Senate. During "the hysteria of the First World War," Wheeler claimed with some hyperbole, "I saw men strung up. Only the federal courts stood up at all, and the Supreme Court better than any of them." Republicans kept their peace, quietly savoring the Democratic fratricide.[22]

Wheeler orchestrated a brilliant series of ripostes to the president's proposal. He produced a devastatingly cogent letter from Chief Justice Hughes, a venerable, bearded figure of imperturbable dignity and the object of iconic popular veneration as the spirit of the laws incarnate. Hughes conclusively rebutted Roosevelt's specious claims about judicial inefficiency. To the president's proposal to enlarge the bench, Hughes delivered a magisterial rebuke: "More judges to hear, more judges to confer, more judges to discuss, more judges to be convinced and to decide," said Hughes, hardly constituted a formula for more expeditious litigation.[23]

By early March Roosevelt abandoned his arguments about ineffi-

21. James A. Farley, *Jim Farley's Story: The Roosevelt Years* (New York: McGraw-Hill, 1948), 84.

22. *Digest* 1, no. 3 (July 31, 1937): 5; Studs Terkel, *Hard Times: An Oral History of the Great Depression* (New York: Pantheon, 1970), 271.

23. Leuchtenburg, *Supreme Court Reborn*, 133.

ciency and senescence and began to make his case squarely on the grounds of judicial philosophy, something he would probably have been better advised to do from the outset. By this time it was too late. The president's deviousness and the responses his original message had reflexively evoked had put a framework around the Court-reform story from which it proved impossible to escape: Roosevelt was seeking dictatorial power, his critics charged, perhaps not for himself, but in ways that a future president could easily abuse. As Wheeler said in a radio address: "Create now a political Court to echo the ideas of the executive and you have created a weapon; a weapon which in the hands of another President could . . . cut down those guarantees of liberty written by the blood of your forefathers."[24]

Congress, including large elements of the president's own party, was by now in open rebellion against the Court-reform plan. The Court itself delivered the killing blows, though in laying Roosevelt's plan to rest it also opened a new constitutional era. On Easter Monday, March 29, the Court handed down an opinion in a case that at once tolled the knell for Roosevelt's proposal, even as it heralded the dawn of a judicial revolution. Like many great cases, this one had its origins in the commonest grit of everyday life. Elsie Parrish was a chambermaid who had swept rugs and cleaned toilets for nearly two years in the Cascadian Hotel in Wenatchee, Washington, a dusty farm town on the Columbia River plateau. Upon her discharge in 1935, she asked for $216.19 in back pay, which she was owed under the terms of a Washington State minimum wage law enacted in 1913. West Coast Hotel Corporation, the Cascadian's parent company, offered to settle for seventeen dollars. Elsie Parrish sued for the full amount. The corporation thereupon challenged the constitutionality of the Washington law.

Chief Justice Hughes himself delivered the majority opinion in *West Coast Hotel v. Parrish.* The Court had decided in favor of Elsie Parrish, Hughes declared, speaking with Olympian authority in language that signaled a new willingness to defer to legislatures on economic matters. Slowly, the significance of Hughes's pronouncement sank in. Astonishingly, the justices had voted by a five-to-four majority to uphold the Washington State minimum wage law—a statute effectively identical to the New York law that the same Court had invalidated by the same margin in *Tipaldo* only a year earlier!

24. Burton K. Wheeler, *Yankee from the West* (Garden City, N.Y.: Doubleday, 1962), 325.

The decision in *Parrish* amounted to "the greatest constitutional somersault in history," declared one commentator. "On Easter Sunday," said another, "state minimum wage laws were unconstitutional, but about noon on Easter Monday, these laws were constitutional." The key to this breathtaking reversal was the shift of a single vote. Justice Roberts had sided with the conservative quartet in *Tipaldo*, but now he followed Hughes and joined the liberal trio. It was later revealed that Roberts cast his critical vote in the *Parrish* case in the justices' conference of December 19, 1936 — more than seven weeks *before* Roosevelt's February 5 message to Congress. But if Roberts did not change course because of the specific storm unleashed by Roosevelt's Court-packing plan, it stretches credulity to conclude that he, and Hughes, were not influenced by the high-pressure front that had been building for many months, indeed years, over the Court's obstructionist tactics. In any case, Roberts's action decisively shifted the Court's ideological center of gravity. "By nodding his head instead of shaking it," an observer noted, "Owen Roberts, one single human being, had amended the Constitution of the United States." Pundits immediately called Roberts's judicial pirouette "the switch in time that saved nine," a deft maneuver that spiked Roosevelt's Court reform while ushering in a new jurisprudential regime.[25]

Parrish dealt with a state law, not a federal one, but it proved a fateful harbinger. On April 12 the chief justice again spoke for the same five-to-four majority when he delivered the Court's opinion in the case of *NLRB v. Jones and Laughlin*, a crucial test of the Wagner National Labor Relations Act. The case stemmed from a complaint to the NLRB that ten workers had been dismissed from the Jones and Laughlin Steel Company's infamous "Little Siberia" works in Aliquippa, Pennsylvania, because they were union members — a clear violation of the Wagner Act's prohibition on unfair labor practices. Jones and Laughlin contended that the National Labor Relations Act was unconstitutional, and therefore the NLRB had no authority to receive or act upon the workers' grievance.

Once again Hughes, in all his white-bearded majesty, read the majority opinion. He spoke "magnificently," two reporters noted, with "an

25. Leuchtenburg, *Supreme Court Reborn*, 166, Roberts's action has been understandably controversial. For a summary review of the controversy, see Richard D. Freidman, "A Reaffirmation: The Authenticity of the Roberts Memorandum, or Felix the Non-Forger," *University of Pennsylvania Law Review* 142, no. 6 (June 1994): 1985.

overtone of infallibility which made the whole business sound like a rehearsal for the last judgment."[26] The Wagner Act's constitutionality depended on a broad construction of the commerce power, which the Court had been unwilling to recognize in its *Schechter* and Guffey Coal Act decisions. Now Hughes ignored those precedents, enunciated just months earlier by the same Court, and ruled that the Wagner Act fell within a constitutionally legitimate definition of the commerce power. "When I hear Wagner Bill went constitutional, I happy," said a steelworker in Little Siberia. "I say good, now Aliquippa become part of the United States."[27] Just six weeks later, the same majority of Brandeis, Cardozo, Stone, Hughes, and Roberts voted to uphold the unemployment insurance features of the Social Security Act, and the even more comfortable majority of seven to two sustained the act's old-age pension provisions.[28]

These several decisions, along with Hughes's letter and Justice Van Devanter's announcement on May 18 of his intention to retire, buried the Court-reform plan. Against all odds, Roosevelt perversely persisted for a time, but when his loyal Senate majority leader, Joseph Robinson, dropped dead from a heart attack on July 14, Roosevelt knew he was whipped. Indeed, the rage of the president's opponents was by then so great that they blamed him for the stress that killed Robinson! The bill's only statutory residue was a severely diluted Judicial Procedure Reform Act, passed in August, which tinkered with lower-court procedures but made no provision for new justices.

Father Time, not legislation, eventually allowed Roosevelt to compose a Court more congenial to his views. He named Alabama senator Hugo Black to fill Van Devanter's seat, weathering a nasty squall over Black's former membership in the Ku Klux Klan, and he made seven more appointments over the next eight years. Even the archconservative Justice McReynolds, who allegedly vowed that he would "never resign as long as that crippled son of a bitch is in the White House," slipped out of his robe in 1941.[29]

Even before Roosevelt was able to staff the high bench with a majority

26. Joseph Alsop and Turner Catledge, *The 168 Days* (Garden City, N.Y.: Doubleday, Doran, 1938), 146–47.
27. Robert H. Zieger, *The CIO, 1935–1955* (Chapel Hill: University of North Carolina Press, 1995), 131.
28. *Steward Machine Co. v. Davis*, 301 U.S. 548 (1937), and *Helvering v. Davis*, 301 U.S. 619 (1937).
29. Leuchtenburg, *Supreme Court Reborn*, 115.

of his own appointees, he had wrought a momentous judicial transformation. He lost the battle to expand the Court but won the war for a shift in constitutional doctrine. "We obtained 98 percent of all the objectives intended by the Court plan," Roosevelt observed in late 1938.[30] The "nine old men"—or at least the youngest of them, Owen Roberts, in company with Hughes—had proved nimble enough to shift their ideological ground. In the course of countering Roosevelt's Court-packing plan, they gave birth to what has been rightly called "the Constitutional Revolution of 1937."[31] The New Deal, especially its core program enacted in 1935, was now constitutionally safe. And for at least half a century thereafter the Court did not overturn a single piece of significant state or national socioeconomic legislation. In the economic realm, at least, substantive due process was dead. As one authority concluded in 1941:

> The Court has discarded the idea that the laissez-faire, noninterventionist conception of governmental action offers a feasible approach to the problem of adapting the Constitution to the needs of the Twentieth Century. Rendered into the idiom of American constitutional law, this means that *the National Government is entitled to employ any and all of its powers to forward any and all of the objectives of good government.* This fundamental point being established . . . the principal doctrines of American constitutional theory, those which have furnished the matrix of the vastly extended judicial review which developed after 1890, have become largely otiose and superfluous.[32]

ROOSEVELT HAD WON THE WAR, but his success furnished a textbook example of a Pyrrhic victory. The resolution of the Court battle helped to secure the New Deal's achievements to date and cleared the constitutional pathway for further reforms. Ironically, however, the struggle had inflicted such grievous political wounds on the president that the New Deal's political momentum was exhausted by mid-1937. The way was open, but Roosevelt lacked the means to go forward. Most fatefully, the Court battle had exposed deep fissures in the ranks of the Democratic Party. With the president's blood on the water, Democrats who had stewed privately under Roosevelt's leadership now openly unfurled the standard of revolt. "What we have to do," North Carolina's

30. *PPA* (1938), 490.
31. Leuchtenburg, *Supreme Court Reborn*, 168.
32. Edwin S. Corwin, *Constitutional Revolution, Ltd.* (Claremont, Calif.: Pomona College, Scripps College, Claremont Colleges, 1941), 112–13; italics in original.

Senator Josiah Bailey wrote to his Virginia colleague Harry Byrd, "is to preserve, if we can, the Democratic Party against his efforts to make it the Roosevelt party."[33] "Who does he think he is?" Burton Wheeler remarked of Roosevelt. "He used to be just one of the barons. I was the baron of the northwest, Huey Long was the baron of the south. He's like a king trying to reduce the barons."[34] Now those Democratic barons made Capitol Hill their American Runnymede. In the chambers of the House and especially of the Senate, they gathered in 1937 not to do Roosevelt's bidding but to hurl defiance at their chief. Despite his party's command of congressional majorities far larger than those of his first term, never again would Roosevelt succeed in controlling the legislative process as he had in 1933 and again in 1935, when, it was increasingly clear, the New Deal had reached its climax. As Henry Wallace later remarked, "The whole New Deal really went up in smoke as a result of the Supreme Court fight."[35]

Yet too much can be made of the contest over the Court as the *cause* of the New Deal's attenuation in Roosevelt's second term. The opposition to Roosevelt that surfaced in 1937 may have crystallized around the Court-reform issue, but it was not Court reform that created that opposition in the first place. The Democratic Party that Roosevelt had inherited in 1933 was still in many ways the ramshackle, disarticulated assemblage of factions that had deadlocked at Madison Square Garden in 1924, unable to calm the feuds among its urban and rural, wet and dry, immigrant and old-stock, northern and southern wings. That party had always been an unlikely vehicle for the kind of reform cargo that Roosevelt had somewhat miraculously managed to make it carry, and until now he had done little to overhaul it. Since at least the time of the president's "wealth tax" proposal in 1935, that vehicle had been threatening to fall apart. The origins of its instability lay partly in the familiar conflict between the party's southern and northern wings. But that sectional tension masked a still deeper sectoral conflict between urban and rural interests. In a close analysis of congressional voting patterns in the mid-1930s, historian James Patterson found that the most powerful determinant of anti–New Deal sentiment among Democrats was "an anti-metropolitan ideology" that generated opposition to Roo-

33. John M. Allswang, *The New Deal and American Politics* (New York: John Wiley and Sons, 1978), 120.
34. Patterson, *Congressional Conservatism and the New Deal*, 115.
35. Leuchtenburg, *Supreme Court Reborn*, 464.

sevelt not only in the rural South but also in rural New England and the rural Midwest and West. As in physics, so in politics: for every action there is a reaction, perhaps not equal nor precisely opposite, but reliably contrary nonetheless. Thus as Roosevelt became ever more closely identified with urban, industrial workers, and as their representatives increasingly forced measures like Social Security and labor legislation onto the congressional agenda, a counterpressure began to build. It was, Patterson asserts, "the urban nature of the [New Deal] measures themselves" that most agitated Roosevelt's opponents. Even without the Court fight, Patterson concludes, "sizable conservative opposition to measures of this sort would have developed."[36]

It was only logical, moreover, that Congress should become the staging ground for that opposition. Because of the peculiarities of the American representational system, and given the persistently rural character of much of American society, 54 out of 96 senators and 225 of 435 representatives had been sent to Congress by predominantly rural constituencies. And virtually all representatives, urban and rural alike, chafed at Roosevelt's vigorous expansion of executive power.[37]

By 1937 that conservative coalition, an emergent alliance of congressional Democrats and Republicans, was sizeable indeed and itching to flex its muscle. Robust as it was, it had insufficient strength as yet to take the offensive, but its powers to impede by exercising a kind of legislative veto were formidable. Accordingly, when Congress in 1937 recaptured the legislative initiative from the president, it proceeded to do very little legislating. A militant minority in the Congress emulated the tactics of another militant minority in Flint and staged a legislative sit-down. Conservatives already occupied key parts of the Capitol precincts at the end of Pennsylvania Avenue. What the Fisher die plants were to GM, committee chairmanships were to Congress: strategic positions whose possession conferred command over the entire enterprise, lawmaking no less than carmaking. And thanks to seniority rules, representatives and senators from the one-party South were in possession of a disproportionate share of committee chairmanships. From those pivotal seats, they could see to it that very little legislative product left Capitol Hill in 1937. The regular congressional session in the first part of the year was almost wholly absorbed with the Court struggle and its sequellae — selecting Kentucky's Alben Barkley to replace the dead Sen-

36. Patterson, *Congressional Conservatism and the New Deal*, 160–62.
37. Patterson, *Congressional Conservatism and the New Deal*, 333.

ate majority leader, Joseph Robinson, and confirming Hugo Black's appointment to the Court. The Wagner-Steagall National Housing Act, a
weak measure passed in 1937 that only timidly encouraged the development of public housing projects, represented the sole, pallid vestige
of the New Deal spirit that had pulsed so strongly through the Capitol's
chambers just months earlier.

Frustrated at this unproductive result, Roosevelt summoned the Congress into special session on November 15. The president asked again
for action on his executive reorganization bill, as well as a new farm bill
(to replace the fallen AAA), wages-and-hours standards, and legislation
to create regional bodies for the management and development of natural resources—"Seven Little TVAs." To many observers, the president
seemed dispirited, discouraged, hardly the same man who had soothed
the nation's fears and ringmastered the fabled Hundred Days special
session in 1933. "[T]he President is showing the strain," Ickes noted in
his diary. "He looks all of 15 years older since he was inaugurated in
1933. I don't see how anyone could stand the strain he has been under."[38] As events proved, the contrast with 1933 could not have been
more stark. When the special session adjourned on December 21, not
a single one of Roosevelt's measures had been passed.

Worse, in the special session's final days a bipartisan group, dominated
by southern Democrats, issued a ten-point "Conservative Manifesto."
Principally drafted by Senator Josiah Bailey, it denounced the sit-down
strikes, demanded lower federal taxes and a balanced budget, defended
states' rights as well as the rights of private enterprise against government
encroachment, and warned of the dangers of creating a permanently
dependent welfare class. For Roosevelt, this anti–New Deal blast, not
more New Deal–style legislation, was the bitter fruit of the special congressional session.

The manifesto constituted a kind of founding charter for modern
American conservatism. It was among the first systematic expressions of
an antigovernment political philosophy that had deep roots in American
political culture but only an inchoate existence before the New Deal.
Then, as Calvin Coolidge famously remarked, most people would
scarcely have noticed if the federal government had gone out of existence, but by the late 1930s the New Deal had begun to alter the scale
of federal institutions and extend the reach of federal authority. This
emergence of a large, interventionist government, accomplished in an

38. Ickes Diary 2:246.

atmosphere of crisis by a series of aggressive presidential initiatives, now began to provoke a powerful though not yet wholly coherent conservative counterattack. The crystallization of this new conservative ideology, as much as the New Deal that precipitated its articulation, was among the enduring legacies of the 1930s.

This resurgent conservatism gathered in supporters of many types: Republican partisans and others nervous about executive power; managers and middle-class property owners fearful of labor's new assertiveness and the federal government's role in nurturing it; investors worried about New Deal ambitions to wring higher wages, lower prices, and more tax revenue out of corporate profits; businesspeople resentful of proliferating federal regulations; all kinds of taxpayers anxious about shouldering relief burdens; farmers chafing under agricultural controls; and, not least, white southerners exquisitely sensitive to any possible challenge to racial segregation.

Since Reconstruction Days the solid South had been the foundational constituency of the Democratic Party. The South's peculiar racial sensitivities provided the occasion in early 1938 for a stunning demonstration of the power of that region's elected representatives to stymie the legislative process and to write finis to the New Deal chapter in American history. Southern Democrats had reluctantly agreed at their party's convention in the summer of 1936 to give up the two-thirds majority rule for selecting presidential nominees, a device that had traditionally granted the South an effective veto over any candidate judged unsafe on the race issue. (South Carolina's Senator Ellison "Cotton Ed" Smith had walked out of the convention when a black clergyman delivered an invocation. "By God, he's as black as melted midnight!" Smith exploded. "Get outa my way. This mongrel meeting ain't no place for a white man!" he announced as he departed. "I don't want any blue-gummed, slew-footed Senegambian praying for me politically." Smith exited a second time when Chicagoan Arthur Mitchell, the first black Democrat ever elected to Congress, seconded Roosevelt's nomination.)[39] Later that year Roosevelt's overwhelming victory margin dramatized the unsettling truth that a Democratic president could be elected without a single southern electoral vote. Then in 1937 many white southerners had looked on in alarm as the Supreme Court genuflected to Roosevelt's will, compromising another institution that had often served as a bulwark of the region's racial

39. Allan A. Michie and Frank Rhylick, *Dixie Demagogues* (New York: Vanguard, 1939), 266, 281.

regime. As the South's influence over the federal executive and judiciary weakened, Congress became an especially contested battleground.

A tense battle line formed in April 1937, when a hushed House listened to Michigan representative Earl Cory Michener read the press accounts of a grisly lynching in Duck Hill, Mississippi. A mob had seized two handcuffed black men from the Winona County sheriff, chained them to a tree, mutilated their bodies with blowtorches, shotgunned them, doused the corpses with gasoline, and set them afire. It was but the latest in a nauseating parade of lynchings that had claimed more than one hundred lives since 1930, all of them horrifying testimonials to the price in blood and tears of maintaining the South's segregationist order. Three days later, the House voted favorably on an antilynching bill first introduced in 1934. The bill established federal penalties for local law enforcement officers delinquent in preventing lynchings and provided for federal prosecution of lynchers if local authorities proved unwilling. For southerners, the bill unleashed all their worst fears of a revived Reconstruction Era. Reconstruction was no historical bygone so far as many white southerners were concerned. It was a living and festering memory, one whose distorted image of vindictive northern interlopers and corrupted black legislators had been reinforced in the popular mind by films like D. W. Griffith's sensational *Birth of a Nation* a generation earlier and by a steady stream of factually dubious but highly influential scholarly writing produced by the historian William A. Dunning and the students he trained at Columbia University. Inflamed at the prospect of renewed federal interference with the South's racial system, every southern representative but one, Maury Maverick of Texas, voted in the negative on the antilynching bill.

In the Senate, with its tradition of unlimited debate and thus the possibility of filibuster, the South drew up its principal line of defense. North Carolina's Bailey defined the southern position: "[T]he proposed lynching bill," he wrote, "is the forerunner of a policy studiously cultivated by agitators, not for the purpose of preventing lynching, but for the purpose of introducing the policy of Federal interference in local affairs. The lynching bill would promptly be followed by a civil rights bill, drawn upon lines of the bill which Thad Stevens tried to put upon the South. . . . I give you warning," Bailey proclaimed menacingly, figuratively nodding at the White House, "that no administration can survive without us."[40]

40. Harvard Sitkoff, *A New Deal for Blacks* (New York: Oxford University Press, 1978), 291.

Nor could any legislative business be transacted in the face of such resistance. When the bill was introduced at the opening of the congressional session in 1938, southern senators mounted a wrathful filibuster. South Carolina's James Byrnes, on most other matters one of Roosevelt's most reliable congressional lieutenants, declared that the South had "been deserted by the Democrats of the North." Mississippi's Pat Harrison, another Roosevelt ally in the early New Deal years, raised the prospect of miscegenation, the deepest pathological dread haunting the minds of segregationists. His fellow Mississippian Theodore Bilbo dusted off a nineteenth-century scheme for repatriating American blacks to Africa. Louisiana's Allen J. Ellender declared: "I believe in white supremacy, and as long as I am in the Senate I expect to fight for white supremacy." Sentiments like those, and nothing else, emanated from southerners in the Senate for six weeks, stopping the nation's lawmaking machinery cold. The legislative paralysis ended only when the antilynching bill was at last withdrawn on February 21.[41]

Despite pleas from black leaders and from his wife, Roosevelt declined to give the antilynching bill anything more than nominal support. "I did not choose the tools with which I must work," Roosevelt had earlier explained to NAACP executive secretary Walter White. "Had I been permitted to choose them I would have selected quite different ones. But I've got to get legislation passed by Congress to save America. The Southerners by reason of the seniority rule in Congress are chairmen or occupy strategic places on most of the Senate and House committees. If I come out for the antilynching bill now, they will block every bill I ask Congress to pass to keep America from collapsing. I just can't take that risk."[42]

Roosevelt's refusal to champion the antilynching bill marked the limits of his inclination to challenge the conservative southern grandees of his party. A frontal assault on the South's racial system, Roosevelt judged and the six-week filibuster confirmed, would irretrievably alienate the white southern political establishment, fracture his party beyond repair, and indefinitely deadlock the Congress.

IT WOULD BE TOO MUCH to suggest that anti–New Deal southern senators filibustered the antilynching bill merely to remind Roosevelt of the formidable powers of obstruction that remained to them. The bill, after all, had not been on the president's "must" list, and racial

41. Sitkoff, New Deal for Blacks, 292–93.
42. Walter White, A Man Called White (New York: Viking, 1948), 169–70.

anxiety assuredly trumped political signaling as the filibuster's prime motivator. But it was true nonetheless that the antilynching filibuster vividly illustrated the capacity to impede that was inherent in the American constitutional system of checks and balances, as reinforced by the rules of the Senate. The filibuster thus provided further proof, if proof were needed, of how justified were Roosevelt's fears for the future of the New Deal. It also highlighted the unique vexations that continued to enchain the South in economic backwardness and isolation.

It would also be too much to suggest that it was the antilynching filibuster that prompted Roosevelt to unsheath the sword of political retribution against southern conservatives in the 1938 electoral season. But it is true that the fate of the antilynching bill set the tone for the remainder of the legislative session of 1938, and it was surely that session's barren legislative record that convinced Roosevelt that he must try to purge his party of conservatives.

The president proved little more able in 1938 than he had in the previous year to impose his will on the Congress. Of the four presidential proposals that had been outstanding since early 1937, the farm bill passed at last in 1938, but it amounted to little more than a revival of the old AAA mechanisms, with some technical tinkering, now that the Supreme Court had registered its amenability to such legislation. In any event, farm legislation constituted no offense against the "antimetropolitan" ideology that animated the conservative coalition. On two other measures, the president lost. Congress rebuffed executive reorganization, only to resuscitate it in much weaker form in 1939. The "Seven TVAs" regional planning authority legislation was deader than a tent peg, never to be revived in any form. These defeats took their toll on Roosevelt. "It looks as if all the courage has oozed out of the President," Ickes wrote in his diary as the 1938 stalemate dragged on. "He has let things drift. . . . Ever since the Court fight, he has acted to me like a beaten man."[43]

Only a wages-and-hours bill, the fourth of Roosevelt's holdover measures from 1937, survived the legislative gauntlet as a feeble reminder of the president's once-irresistible powers. The Fair Labor Standards Act of 1938 (FLSA) was a direct lineal descendant of the NRA of 1933. It prohibited child labor and required employers in industry (but not in agriculture, domestic service, or certain other service categories) to adopt in stages a forty-cent hourly minimum wage and a forty-hour week. The

43. Ickes Diary 2:326, 339–49.

act displayed yet again Roosevelt's preferred policies toward labor, which were to confer benefits by statute rather than by collective bargaining — and in so doing, some liberals thought, to dampen incentives for forming unions in the first place. For just that reason, the bill troubled many labor leaders, though they hesitated to oppose it openly. One AFL spokesman remarked privately that the act was "bad medicine for us, to give those jerks something for nothing and then they won't join the cause."[44]

"That's that," Roosevelt was heard to sigh on June 25 as he put his signature to the bill — an expression to which history has attached even more finality than the president could have intended. The Fair Labor Standards Act, as it turned out, was the last New Deal reform ever to be inscribed in the statute books. With the pen that affixed his name to the bill, Roosevelt in effect drew a circle around all the New Deal that there was going to be, at least in his own lifetime.

The president's support for the Fair Labor Standards Act also widened the breach between Roosevelt and the conservative southern Democratic oligarchy and testified to Roosevelt's growing willingness to confront them directly. "Southern Senators," Attorney General Cummings noted in his diary, "actually froth at the mouth when the subject [of minimum wage legislation] is mentioned." South Carolina's Cotton Ed Smith declared that the law was unnecessary because a man could support a family for fifty cents a day in his home state. It was a high principle of orthodox southern thinking that low wages were the South's major — perhaps only — advantage in competition with more efficient northern industries. Not without reason did Walter Lippmann describe the Fair Labor Standards Act as "a sectional bill thinly disguised as a humanitarian reform." Nearly 20 percent of southern industrial workers earned below the new minimum wage. Elsewhere in the country, fewer than 3 percent did. Unmistakably, the new law would lay its hand much more heavily on the South than on other regions.[45]

But as Roosevelt saw matters, it was precisely the South's miserably low wages that accounted for much of the region's economic plight. In company with a small band of southern liberals, including Alabama's

44. Joseph P. Lash, *Dealers and Dreamers: A New Look at the New Deal* (New York: Doubleday, 1988), 338.
45. Bruce J. Schulman, *From Cotton Belt to Sunbelt: Federal Policy, Economic Development, and the Transformation of the South, 1938–1980* (New York: Oxford University Press, 1991), 54; the same source gives the figures on regional wage differentials at 259, n. 11.

Hugo Black and his senatorial replacement Lister Hill, Florida's Senator Claude Pepper, and Texas Congressman Lyndon Baines Johnson, Roosevelt believed that raising southern wages was a cudgel with which to bludgeon the South into the modern era. Ending the South's historic low-wage regime would force mechanization and bring greater efficiency to southern businesses. The cheap-labor textile mills that dotted the Piedmont, wheezing along with fifty-year-old spindles, were "highly, completely inefficient. That type of factory ought not to be in existence," Roosevelt unequivocally declared.[46] Moreover, Roosevelt explained, "Cheap wages mean low buying power . . . and let us remember that buying power means many other kinds of better things, better schools, better health, better hospitals, better highways."[47]

Having secured the FLSA, Roosevelt continued to press his case for uplifting the nation's poorest region. Calling the South "the Nation's number one economic problem," he commissioned *The Report on Economic Conditions of the South*, released amid great fanfare in August 1938. Disguised as an objective analysis of the southern economy, the *Report* was in fact a manifesto for the southern liberals' program for regional development. They looked to the federal government to develop the region's human and physical resources, break down the South's "colonial" thralldom to northern capital and manufacturing, and integrate the former Confederacy into the national economy. In short, they envisioned a kind of regionally targeted New Deal.

Before economic reform, however, Roosevelt and his liberal allies needed political reform. If the plan for regional development outlined in the *Report* were to have any chance of success, there had to be more pro–New Deal southern politicians like Hill, Pepper, and Johnson and fewer reactionaries like Bailey, Bilbo, and Smith. The *Report* in fact had its origins in Roosevelt's request to Clark Foreman, a liberal white Georgian who served as Harold Ickes's special assistant for Negro affairs, for advice on how to beat archconservative Georgia senator Walter George in the upcoming 1938 Democratic primary election. The *Report* was, in Foreman's words, "a part of the President's program to liberalize the Democratic Party."[48]

Emboldened by the liberal Claude Pepper's victory in the May 1938

46. PPA (1938), 196.
47. Schulman, *From Cotton Belt to Sunbelt*, 64.
48. Schulman, *From Cotton Belt to Sunbelt*, 52.

Florida senatorial primary, FDR determined to intervene in a series of primary elections. In a late June Fireside Chat he declared war on the "Copperheads" who, like their Civil War counterparts, valued peace more than justice. "An election cannot give a country a firm sense of direction," said Roosevelt, "if it has two or more national parties which merely have different names but are as alike in their principles and aims as peas in the same pod."[49] He meant to make the Democratic Party the liberal party, the party of a permanent New Deal. Now was the moment to make that goal, long fermenting in Roosevelt's mind, into a reality. It required, above all, transforming the party's historic base in the South.

Proceeding by train through sweltering Dixie in the late summer, Roosevelt recited the *Report*'s damning litany of southern deficiencies in wages, education, housing, credit facilities, and manufacturing capacity. He summoned southern voters to repudiate politicians who tolerated such conditions. In South Carolina he declared that no man or family could live on fifty cents a day—a pointed rebuke to Cotton Ed Smith. In his "second home state of Georgia" on August 11 he confronted Senator Walter George in a dramatic face-to-face encounter. Appearing on the same platform with George in the small town of Barnesville, Roosevelt taunted the senator with a candor that edged on insult. George, conceded the president, was "a gentleman and a scholar," but he "cannot possibly . . . be classified as belonging to the liberal school of thought. . . . [O]n most public questions he and I do not speak the same language." With that, Roosevelt endorsed George's primary election challenger, a reluctant young attorney named Lawrence Camp, who fidgeted uneasily in his chair while a few mixed cheers and boos floated up from the stunned crowd. George, who had sat in Tom Watson's old Senate seat since 1922, a man so haughty that his own wife addressed him as Mr. George, rose to his feet and replied stiffly: "Mr. President, I want you to know that I accept the challenge."[50]

Roosevelt went on to Maryland, where he attacked another implacably anti–New Deal Democrat, Senator Millard Tydings. The president also spoke out on behalf of his liberal allies, including Maverick in Texas and especially Murphy in Michigan and Earle in Pennsylvania, the governors who had played such pivotal roles in the great labor upheavals

49. *PPA* (1938), 395.
50. Davis 4:279.

of the preceding year. In a nationally broadcast Fireside Chat on election eve, Roosevelt summarized his case with a highly partisan recapitulation of modern American political history:

> We all remember well known examples of what an ill-advised shift from liberal to conservative leadership can do to an incompleted liberal program. Theodore Roosevelt, for example, started a march of progress during his seven years in the Presidency, but after 4 years of President Taft, little was left of the progress that had been made. Think of the great liberal achievements of Woodrow Wilson's New Freedom and how quickly they were liquidated under President Harding. We have to have reasonable continuity in liberal government in order to get permanent results.[51]

Later observers read into those remarks an adumbration of Roosevelt's intention to run for a third presidential term. Whether or not that purpose was already forming in the president's mind, he struck a note in that Fireside Chat consistent with much that he had been saying since his second inaugural address: that the achievements of the New Deal, not to mention the prospects for its extension, were endangered by conservative reaction.

Election day laid bare the depths of that reaction and the danger it held. In the South, Roosevelt failed utterly in his effort to liberalize the Democratic Party. He succeeded only in further alienating the Democratic southern leadership. George in Georgia and Smith in South Carolina were reelected decisively, as was Tydings in Maryland. All denounced Roosevelt as a meddlesome Yankee carpetbagger. George called the president's attack at Barnesville part of "a second march through Georgia." Smith stood before a statue of Confederate hero Wade Hampton and declared that "no man dares to come into South Carolina and try to dictate to the sons of those men who held high the hands of Lee and Hampton." Asked after the election if Roosevelt was not his own worst enemy, Smith snapped, "Not as long as I am alive." Surveying the wreckage of his electoral forays into the South, Roosevelt reflected glumly: "It takes a long, long time to bring the past up to the present."[52]

Elsewhere, Rooseveltian liberals fell like dead timber before the rising conservative wind. Maverick lost in Texas. So did Earle in Pennsylvania

51. PPA (1938), 585.
52. Schulman, *From Cotton Belt to Sunbelt*, 53.

and Murphy in Michigan. So, for that matter, did the Democratic congressional candidate in the district that included Flint, a bitter coda to the sit-down drama. New York's Governor Lehman barely survived a challenge from a dashing young district attorney, Thomas E. Dewey. The Republicans scored their biggest gains since 1928. They won thirteen governorships, doubled their strength in the House, and gained eight new seats in the Senate. The election was a humiliating rebuke to the president and delivered a knockout punch to the New Deal. Astonishingly, the great mountain of political capital that Roosevelt had amassed in 1936 had eroded away in the space of just two years. He had hoped to use that capital to make the Democratic Party a New Deal party and to make the United States permanently a New Deal country. But the South emerged more anti–New Deal and anti-Roosevelt than ever, and outside the South Republicans had eaten deeply into Democratic strength.

The conservative coalition in Congress now had sufficient mass and muscle to go on the offensive. Taking a leaf from the book of the La Follette Civil Liberties Committee, Texas congressman Martin Dies's House Un-American Activities Committee conducted sensational public hearings alleging Communist influence in the labor movement as well as in various New Deal projects. Dies's revelations helped kill the Federal Theater Project in 1939, the first of several New Deal agencies to be dismantled in the next half dozen years. Allegations that the WPA had been put to political use in Alben Barkeley's reelection campaign in Kentucky, as well as in other states, encouraged Congress to slash its appropriations and to pass the Hatch Act, prohibiting federal employees, including workers on federal relief projects, from participating in political campaigns. A reporter further inflamed sentiment against the WPA when he quoted WPA administrator Harry Hopkins as saying in August 1938: "We shall tax and tax, and spend and spend, and elect and elect." Hopkins almost certainly never said anything of the kind, but the phrase struck a responsive chord among those disposed to believe it and was still cited as biblical writ by anti–New Deal critics many decades later.[53]

By the end of 1938 liberal reformers were everywhere in retreat. As the next electoral season of 1940 loomed, noted an observer, the New Deal "has been reduced to a movement with no program, with no ef-

---

53. The definitive account of what Hopkins did not say is in Robert E. Sherwood, *Roosevelt and Hopkins* (New York: Grosset and Dunlap, 1950), 102–4.

fective political organization, with no vast popular party strength behind it, and with no candidate."[54]

POLITICAL CHECKMATE went hand in hand with policy stalemate, as a renewed economic crisis calamitously revealed. In May 1937 the economic recovery building since 1933 had crested, well short of 1929 levels of employment. By August the economy was once again sliding measurably downward; in September, rapidly downward. In October the stock market cracked. The dread specter of 1929 once again haunted the country. "We are headed right into another Depression," Morgenthau warned the president, and he was right.[55] Conditions deteriorated with astonishing speed, swiftly eclipsing the rate of economic decay that had destroyed Herbert Hoover. Within weeks, stocks gave up more than a third of their value. Corporate profits plunged nearly 80 percent. Steel production in the year's last quarter sank to one-fourth of its mid-1937 level, pacing a 40 percent decline in overall industrial output. In Detroit the relief rolls in early 1938 ballooned to four times their 1937 size. Union organizing, crimped once again by a weakening economy, ground to a halt. By the end of the winter of 1937–38, more than two million workers had received layoff notices. They expanded the already crowded ranks of the unemployed to more than ten million souls, or 19 percent of the work force, numbers that evoked grim comparison with the Hoover years.

Critics called it the "Roosevelt Recession." It was a depression within a depression, the first economic downturn since Roosevelt had taken office. The president paid a stiff political price for it at the polls in 1938. What caused it? Equally important, what did Roosevelt, with the example of Hoover before him, and with more than four years of his own Depression-fighting experience behind him, do about it?

The recession touched off an acrimonious, prolonged, and in the end maddeningly inconsequential policy debate within the Roosevelt administration. Seldom has so much intellectual and political energy been expended with such slender result. Yet the peculiar array of explanations and nostrums that contended in this episode, and the particular equilibrium in which they finally came to rest, reveal much about the character and the historical significance of the New Deal.

54. James MacGregor Burns, *Roosevelt: The Lion and The Fox* (New York: Harcourt, Brace, 1956), 375.
55. Alan Brinkley, *The End of Reform: New Deal Liberalism in Depression and War* (New York: Knopf, 1995), 17.

The downturn was perhaps due in part to nothing more than the familiar rhythms of the business cycle, which dictated some inevitable measure of contraction after four years of expansion. But in the newly politicized economic atmosphere of 1937, when government as never before was claiming responsibility for economic performance, such explanations got short shrift.

One school of thought laid the blame for the recession on the administration's antibusiness policies or, somewhat more benignly, on the inevitable uncertainties brewed by the New Deal's "regime change" in the rules of the economic game. Repeated budget deficits, escalating regulatory burdens, threats of higher taxes, mounting labor costs, and, most important, persistent anxiety about what further provocations to business the New Deal had in store, so the argument ran, sapped the confidence of investors and inhibited the commitment of capital to new enterprises. The proof of this thesis seemed to be in the numbers: net new private investment in the mid-1930s was running at only about one-third of its rate a decade earlier. Capital, in short, was hibernating. Lammot du Pont explained why in 1937:

> Uncertainty rules the tax situation, the labor situation, the monetary situation, and practically every legal condition under which industry must operate. Are taxes to go higher, lower or stay where they are? We don't know. Is labor to be union or non-union? . . . Are we to have inflation or deflation, more government spending or less? . . . Are new restrictions to be placed on capital, new limits on profits? . . . It is impossible to even guess at the answers.[56]

These views were not simply the property of conservative business interests. They also found support within the administration. "You could not have a government," former Brain Truster Adolf Berle wrote, "perpetually at war with its economic machinery." Business was demoralized, said Berle, and for obvious reasons: "[p]ractically no business group in the country has escaped investigation or other attack in the last five years . . . [T]he result has been shattered morale. . . . It is, therefore, necessary to make that group pull itself together."[57] At a cabinet meeting

56. Quoted in Robert Higgs, "Regime Uncertainty: Why the Great Depression Lasted So Long and Why Prosperity Resumed after the War," *Independent Review* 1, no. 4 (Spring 1997): 576.
57. Brinkley, *End of Reform*, 20; Beatrice Bishop Berle and Travis Beal Jacobs, *Navigating the Rapids, 1918–1971: From the Papers of Adolf A. Berle* (New York: Harcourt Brace Jovanovich, 1973), 171.

in early November 1937, Treasury Secretary Morgenthau and Postmaster General Farley both urged this diagnosis on the president and begged him to apply the appropriate remedy: a balanced budget, along with a general detente in the administration's relationship with business. "Oh, for God's sake, Henry," said Roosevelt exasperatedly to Morgenthau, "do you want me to read the record again?" The public utilities companies, Farley argued, were especially critical. They were hugely capital-intensive enterprises, capable of generating enormous new jobmaking investments in dams, power plants, and transmission lines, but they had been knocked off balance by the Public Utilities Holding Company Act of 1935, aimed at drastic restructuring of the industry. Uncertain of their future, the utilities companies had choked their new investment to a trickle. They "would spend a lot of money," Farley said, "if they knew where they are heading." Roosevelt replied petulantly that in his view the utilities were overcapitalized, greedy for returns on bloated evalua-tions of their stock. "Every time you do anything for them, they want something else," Roosevelt said. "You can't get anywhere with any of them."[58]

Roosevelt went on in later weeks to speculate that the slowdown in investment was not economically explicable but was, rather, part of a political conspiracy against him, a "capital strike" designed to dislodge him from office and destroy the New Deal by inducing another eco-nomic breakdown that would subject him to Hoover's fate. In a reprise of his tactics in the "wealth tax" battle of 1935 and the electoral cam-paign of 1936, Roosevelt loosed Assistant Attorney General Robert Jack-son, along with Ickes, to give a series of blistering speeches in December 1937. Ickes inveighed against Henry Ford, Tom Girdler, and the "Sixty Families" (a phrase borrowed from the title of Ferdinand Lundberg's muckraking exposé) who, he charged, made up "the living center of the modern industrial oligarchy which dominates the United States." Left unchecked, Ickes thundered, they would create "big-business Fascist America—an enslaved America." For his part, Jackson decried the slump in private investment as "a general strike—the first general strike in America—a strike against the government—a strike to coerce political action." Roosevelt even ordered an FBI investigation of possible criminal conspiracy in the alleged capitalist strike, but it revealed nothing of substance.[59]

58. Farley, *Jim Farley's Story*, 105.
59. Brinkley, *End of Reform*, 45–46; Brinkley, "The New Deal and the Idea of the State," in Steve Fraser and Gary Gerstle, *The Rise and Fall of the New Deal Order* (Prince-ton: Princeton University Press, 1989), 113, n. 8.

The theory of a conspiratorial capital strike had little basis in fact, but it nevertheless fell on receptive ears among a group coming to be known simply as the "New Dealers." The New Dealers were a kind of party within a party, or, more precisely, a faction within the administration. They were mostly young men, and mostly protégés of Harvard Law professor Felix Frankfurter, though from time to time they also enjoyed the patronage of Harold Ickes, Henry Wallace, and Frances Perkins in the cabinet and occasionally Harry Hopkins at the WPA and Marriner Eccles at the Federal Reserve. With exceptions like William O. Douglas, who chaired the Securities and Exchange Commission, they were scattered through the middle ranks of the federal bureaucracy, in obscure posts that belied the influence they wielded: Thomas G. Corcoran at the Reconstruction Finance Corporation; Benjamin V. Cohen at the National Power Committee in the Interior Department; Isador Lubin at the Bureau of Labor Statistics; Lauchlin Currie at the Federal Reserve; Mordecai Ezekiel in the Agriculture Department; Leon Henderson at the WPA; Jerome Frank at the SEC. They numbered perhaps two to three hundred people, mostly young lawyers and economists. Corcoran, a gifted speechwriter and legislative draftsman and a canny political tactician, was a wily operator who gave definition to the emerging political type of the "Washington insider." As much as anyone, he served as the leader of this informal group. He was also their chief recruiting officer, consulting closely with his mentor, Frankfurter, to identify and place new talent. To his home in Georgetown, dubbed the "Little Red House" by conservative pundits, the New Dealers came to eat and drink and hone their wits in argument.

Many of the New Dealers had arrived in Washington in the earliest days of the Roosevelt administration. They were talented and hungry youngsters for whom government employment in those lean times was the best, or perhaps the only, job opportunity available. But it was not just the accident of employment that bound the New Dealers together. Though they represented a broad range of opinions and sometimes clashed over specific policies, they shared certain core beliefs: a deep suspicion of businessmen and a fierce faith in government as the agency of justice and progress. Some of them blamed the 1937 recession, and indeed all the ills of the Depression decade, on the insidious influence of "monopolies," for which evil the appropriate remedy was vigorous enforcement of the antitrust laws. For others, the NRA had embodied the dream of a vast governmental superagency that could wring order out of the vast, seething, wasteful chaos of American capitalism.

An aura of youthful glamour and political idealism emanated from the New Dealers, but the strong scent of mandarinism clung to them as well. None held elected office — ever. They took their inspiration from books like James Landis's *The Administrative Process* (1938) and Thurman Arnold's *Symbols of Government* (1935) and *The Folklore of Capitalism* (1937), all of which argued for more plentiful and more powerful government agencies, administered by technicians with wide discretionary authority, who would be charged with overseeing and fine-tuning the increasingly complex industrial economy. What America needed, Arnold declared in *The Folklore of Capitalism*, was "a religion of government."[60]

Above all, many of the New Dealers were especially enthusiastic about the novel economic doctrines of John Maynard Keynes, published in 1936 as *The General Theory of Employment, Interest, and Money*. They found particularly congenial Keynes's claim that government's role in promoting consumption, rather than directly stimulating investment, was the key to economic health. Governments, Keynes argued, must be willing to sustain purchasing power with "compensatory" fiscal policies, including heavy government borrowing, to offset downward swings in the business cycle. In this view, government deficits were necessary and powerful tools of economic recovery, not signs of fiscal malfeasance. Accordingly, deficits should be embraced boldly, without stint or apology, as the occasion demanded. This advice, of course, was the most outrageous heresy among orthodox economists and was still anathema, at least in theory, to most statesmen — including, as it turned out, to Franklin Roosevelt. But the renewed economic crisis of 1937–38, coming after almost a decade of the Great Depression, opened the field to heresies of all kinds, and the New Dealers were nothing if not heterodox.

To their defenders, the New Dealers were selfless civil servants, paladins of the public interest, the inheritors of the progressive tradition that placed its faith in disinterested expertise as the surest safeguard of democracy in the modern world. To their detractors, like former AAA administrator George Peek, they were a "plague of young lawyers" who had "crossed the border line of sanity," arrogant manipulators of the increasingly elaborate and arcane New Deal–spawned governmental apparatus whose mysteries only this new class of secular priests could penetrate.[61] Even Harry Hopkins, their sometime champion, said of them

---

60. Thurman Arnold, *The Folklore of Capitalism* (New Haven: Yale University Press, 1937), 389.

61. George N. Peek, *Why Quit Our Own?* (New York: D. Van Nostrand, 1936), 12, 20. Many of the New Dealers went on to lucrative private careers, often in Washington

in 1939 that "there are people in this town who don't want recovery. ... There are a lot of the younger fellows sitting around who talk things over who don't want recovery, because they want the government to stay on the top deck."[62]

Not surprisingly, the New Dealers sought the principal cause of the recession in government policy and the cure in the same place. In a memorandum that was destined to assume the status of a kind of New Dealers' Nicene Creed, Currie, with the help of Henderson and Lubin, drafted an analysis of the recession and a program for coping with it. Together, they presented it to the president in early November.

As the three New Dealers saw things, the government had committed several economic crimes in late 1936 and early 1937. First the Federal Reserve, inexplicably worried about inflation even in the midst of high unemployment, contracted the money supply by sterilizing gold imports and raising member bank reserve requirements. Then came a sharp reversal in the federal government's fiscal policy. In 1936, thanks largely to the payment of the veterans' bonus that had passed over Roosevelt's veto, as well as to continuing WPA and PWA expenditures, the New Deal had poured nearly $4 billion in excess of tax receipts into the economy. These deficits, virtually equivalent to the entire federal budget in 1933, had stimulated consumption and spurred economic recovery. But in 1937 the one-time bonus payment had disappeared, and the new, regressive Social Security taxes bit some $2 billion out of the national income without yet returning anything as benefits (the first of which would be paid only in 1940). Worst of all, Roosevelt worried as ever about balancing the budget. Eager to make the political statement that with the end of the Depression in sight relief could be cut back, he ordered deep reductions in both WPA and PWA expenditures in the summer of 1937. For the first nine months of 1937, the federal budget was actually in the black, by some $66 million. So: government deficits had underwritten the 1933–37 recovery; the reduction of the deficits had caused the recession; ergo, the New Dealers argued, the antidote was obvious. The federal government must resume large-scale spending: Q.E.D.

---

law firms, selling to corporate clients their special expertise in the workings of the very government agencies they had helped to build. Corcoran's career served as the prototype for this new type of legal practice, which virtually required some sort of apprenticeship in government service. See Peter H. Irons, *The New Deal Lawyers* (Princeton: Princeton University Press, 1982).

62. John Morton Blum, *From the Morgenthau Diaries: Years of Urgency, 1938–1941* (Boston: Houghton-Mifflin, 1965), 26.

Marriner Eccles, Currie's boss and a vociferous champion of spending, later chronicled the fate of that tidy syllogistic analysis. At a meeting at the White House on November 8, 1937, he recalled, "the pattern of discussion was provided by a now famous memorandum prepared by Isador Lubin, Leon Henderson, and Lauchlin Currie, indicating how a reduction in government spending had helped to precipitate the recession. There were indications that Roosevelt was impressed by the argument advanced to him." At a subsequent meeting on the afternoon of November 10, Roosevelt again agreed that what was needed was "a resumption of government spending and not a curb on it."

But then, to Eccles's astonishment, on the evening of that same November 10, Treasury Secretary Morgenthau, with Roosevelt's evident blessing, addressed an audience of business leaders in New York and pledged a balanced budget—a statement that elicited honks of laughter from some of his auditors. But what bothered Eccles was not the incredulity of businessmen about the promise of a balanced budget. It was the fact that the president on the exact same day had "assented to two contradictory policies"—deficit spending in the afternoon and a balanced budget in the evening. This legerdemain led Eccles to what he conceded was an "ungenerous" conclusion. "The contradictions between the afternoon and evening positions made me wonder," Eccles recalled, "whether the New Deal was merely a political slogan or if Roosevelt really knew what the New Deal was."[63]

What the New Deal was—the question has echoed down the years and at no time sounded more urgently than in this crisis within a crisis in 1937–38. Yet to Eccles's continuing dismay, Roosevelt moved with glacial slowness toward resolving the contradictions that beset his administration's policies. In his message to the special session of Congress that convened on November 15, the president scarcely mentioned the recession. For nearly five more months the debate within the administration churned on, pitting budget-balancers against spenders, business conciliators and confidence-builders against regulators and trust-busters. It was, says historian Alan Brinkley, "an intense ideological struggle—a struggle among different conceptions of the economy, among different views of the state, and among different . . . political traditions. . . . It was a struggle to define the soul of the New Deal."[64]

Ironically enough, victory in the struggle for the New Deal's soul

63. Marriner S. Eccles, *Beckoning Frontiers* (New York: Knopf, 1951), 304.
64. Brinkley, *End of Reform*, 18.

would not in the end be worth much, since the New Deal, bleeding from the Court battle and jacketed by newly militant conservatives, was in the process of giving up the ghost. That very prospect, exacerbated by the prolonged paralysis of the Roosevelt administration as 1937 passed into 1938, excited anxieties well beyond the United States.

In a widely publicized open letter to Roosevelt in 1933, the British economist John Maynard Keynes had praised the American president as "the trustee for those in every country who seek to mend the evils of our condition by reasoned experiment within the framework of the existing social system. If you fail, rational change will be gravely prejudiced throughout the world, leaving orthodoxy and revolution to fight it out."[65] Now, four years later, as the American economy slid toward the lip of a catastrophe potentially even greater than that of 1929, Keynes wrote the president again, this time privately. "I am terrified," he confided, "lest progressive causes in all the democratic countries should suffer injury, because you have taken too lightly the risk to their prestige which would result from a failure measured in terms of immediate prosperity." He praised Roosevelt's reforms, citing the New Deal's agricultural policies, the SEC, the promotion of collective bargaining, and the wages-and-hours bill. But without economic recovery, Keynes feared, all those gains and more would be lost.

The president had to decide, Keynes insisted, on the balance of private and public means that might be mobilized to stimulate the economy. New investment in housing, public utilities, and the railroads would create jobs, generate income, and restore economic vitality by increasing aggregate demand. But where was the money for that new investment to come from? Keynes made no secret of his own preferences: "[D]urable investment must come increasingly under state direction." He favored public ownership of the utilities, nationalization of the railroads, and direct subsidies for "working class houses," as in Britain. Housing, above all, said Keynes, was "by far the best aid to recovery" because of the large and geographically dispersed potential demand. "I should advise putting most of your eggs in this basket," Keynes urged. But in the case of the railroads and utilities, and by implication other industries, Keynes acknowledged that in America "public opinion is not yet ripe" for public ownership. Therefore, he asked sharply, "what is the object of chasing the utilities round the lot every other week?" Businessmen, Keynes concluded, "have a different set of delusions from

65. *New York Times*, December 31, 1933, sec. 8, 2.

politicians; and need, therefore, different handling. . . . It is a mistake to think that they are more immoral than politicians. If you work them into [a] surly, obstinate, terrified mood . . . , the nation's burdens will not get carried to market; and in the end public opinion will veer their way."[66]

This was stern stuff, delivered with a note of professorial hauteur that could not have charmed Franklin Roosevelt. But it was also useable stuff, even commonsensical stuff, despite Roosevelt's belief that Keynes was good for little except arcane, abstract theorizing. The British economist's advice pointed clearly to a two-pronged policy of mollifying business and thereby reinvigorating private investment, while in the meantime "priming the pump" with substantial government outlays, especially in the field of housing. This combination of government stimulus to consumption and resumed private capital formation seemed a sensible formula for effecting a recovery that could be durable and self-sustaining. Its logic would, in time, constitute the operational heart of "Keynesian economics." It was not a conceptually difficult formula to grasp. Indeed, many American policymakers like Eccles, and even, in a limited way, Herbert Hoover, had intuited the essence of these ideas well before Keynes famously put them to paper. To reverse Keynes's notorious dictum to the effect that practical men are but the unwitting slaves of some defunct economist, it may be equally true that many economists in the last analysis simply wrap the mantle of academic theory around the practical dictates of instinct and necessity. Surely what the world eventually came to know as "Keynesianism" grew as much from the jumble of circumstance, politics, and adaptation as it did from the pages of the textbooks. So what, in the end, did Roosevelt, supposedly a keen student of circumstance, a master of politics, and a genius of adaptation, do?

The answer is that he did a little of everything and a lot of mischief. In April 1938 he acceded to the importunings of the spenders and requested an emergency appropriation of some $3 billion. Many historians have hailed that decision as establishing the first deficit deliberately embraced for purposes of economic stimulus. But in a $100 billion economy, with more than ten million persons unemployed, $3 billion was a decidedly modest sum, not appreciably larger than most earlier New Deal deficits, considerably less than the unintended deficit of 1936, and far short of the kind of economic boost that Keynes envisioned as nec-

66. Keynes's letter to Roosevelt of February 1, 1938, is reprinted in Howard Zinn, *New Deal Thought* (Indianapolis: Bobbs-Merrill, 1966), 403–9.

essary to overcome the Depression once and for all. Moreover, Roosevelt chose virtually the same moment to renew his perturbations of the business climate by launching the so-called Temporary National Economic Committee (TNEC, with Leon Henderson as its executive secretary), charged with conducting, amid glaring publicity, a joint congressional-executive probe of "monopolies." For good measure, he appointed Thurman Arnold head of the Justice Department's Anti-Trust Division. Arnold proceeded to expand the division's staff from a few dozen lawyers to nearly three hundred. They brought a flurry of antitrust suits, designed less to eradicate monopoly, as Arnold later explained, than to remind businessmen, as Theodore Roosevelt had done at the century's opening, that not they but the government held ultimate power. As for the TNEC, said *Time*, after three years of investigation, "a terrific broadside might have been expected. Instead, the committee rolled a rusty BB gun into place [and] pinged at the nation's economic problems."[67]

These decisions spelled a messy conclusion to the protracted policy debate of 1937–38. They also signaled what some critics have identified as a defining historical moment, a quiet revolution that fundamentally transformed the assumptions, aspirations, and techniques of modern American liberalism. In this view, Roosevelt's deliberate embrace of deficit spending—and, more generally, the New Dealers' enthusiasm for the Keynesian economic theory that informed and ratified that policy— tolled the knell for an older reform tradition. The progressives of an earlier day, and even the liberals of Franklin Roosevelt's own generation, so this argument runs, had been preoccupied with effecting structural economic reform, achieving distributive justice, and guaranteeing full citizenship to all Americans. The new generation of liberals coming of age in the late 1930s supposedly repudiated that reforming heritage in order to reach an accommodation with their traditional nemesis, capitalism. In the process they abandoned the strategy of direct governmental interventions to secure equality and protect the disadvantaged, and instead established a new political religion devoted to the god of economic growth. "With reasonably full employment, adequate purchasing power, and near capacity production," one of them explained in 1938, "many problems now appearing to call for government intervention or control might solve themselves."[68] If earlier liberals conceived of the economy as a mechanism that needed fixing, the Keynesians

---

67. Fraser and Gerstle, *Rise and Fall of the New Deal Order*, 92.
68. Beardsley Ruml quoted in Dean L. May, *From New Deal to New Economics: The American Liberal Response to the Recession of 1937* (New York: Garland, 1981), 160.

thought of the economy as an organism that needed feeding but that should otherwise be left to its own devices. The political theorist Michael Sandel has spelled out the alleged deficiencies of this new ideology:

> Keynesian fiscal policy is neutral . . . in its assumption that government should not form or revise, or for that matter even judge, the interests and ends its citizens espouse; rather, it should enable them to pursue those interests and ends, whatever they may be, consistent with a similar liberty for others. It is this assumption above all that distinguishes the political economy of growth from the political economy of citizenship, and links Keynesian economics to contemporary liberalism.[69]

Yet so far as the economy was concerned in 1938, Roosevelt's actions looked for the moment to be something considerably less than revolutionary. The president may have planted the seeds of the "Keynesian Revolution" in American fiscal policy, but it would be some time before they would fully flower. In the meantime, Roosevelt seemed to have wrought the worst of all worlds: insufficient government spending to effect recovery, but sufficient government sword-rattling to keep private capital cowed. "The President won't spend any money," an exasperated Jerome Frank exclaimed. "Nobody on the outside will believe the trouble we have with him. Yet they call him a big spender. It makes me laugh."[70] As for private businessmen, they still hesitated to make new investments. Why, the president mused one night at dinner, did they lack confidence in the economy? Because, Eleanor replied tellingly, "They are afraid of you."[71] Deprived of adequate public or private means of revival, the economy sputtered on, not reaching the output levels of 1937 until the fateful year of 1941, when the threat of war, not enlightened New Deal policies, compelled government expenditures at levels previously unimaginable.

Various explanations have been offered for Roosevelt's belated choice in 1938 of these weak and contradictory instruments of economic policy. In part, he may have simply succumbed to the politician's natural urge to do a little something for everybody. Probably he also felt, as his political capital melted away under the heat from the Court fight in 1937

69. Michael J. Sandel, *Democracy's Discontent: America in Search of a Public Philosophy* (Cambridge: Belknap Press of Harvard University Press, 1996), 267.
70. Lash, *Dealers and Dreamers*, 322.
71. Frank Freidel, *Franklin D. Roosevelt: A Rendezvous with Destiny* (Boston: Little, Brown, 1990), 257.

and the worsening economic crisis in 1938, that a *little* something was all he could do in the face of waning presidential influence and waxing congressional autonomy. Despite the lamentations of later critics, the fact was that further structural reform was for the moment a political impossibility. Deficit spending was about the only policy on which the fractious Congress, liberals and conservatives alike, could unite, and even then Congress didn't want too much of it. Neither, apparently, did Roosevelt. He was a decidedly reluctant and an exceedingly moderate Keynesian. He was still hemmed in by intellectual limitations, scarcely more able than Herbert Hoover had been to think his way out of the box of orthodoxy and boldly repudiate the dogma of the balanced budget. And perhaps at some level deep within Roosevelt's mind he may have shared a version of the perversely inhibiting sentiment that Harry Hopkins ascribed to the band of New Dealers who now seemed to have the president's ear: the feeling that with full recovery the government would no longer be on the top deck, and the door would shut forever against the possibility of further reform.

WHAT WAS THE NEW DEAL? Marriner Eccles had wondered. Whatever it was, Roosevelt conclusively demonstrated in 1938 that it was not a recovery program, at any rate not an effective one. There was a paradox here, and no little danger. Serious structural reform seemed possible only in the context of economic crisis, but the prolongation of that crisis, as Keynes warned, would in the end jeopardize all that Roosevelt had achieved, and thereby jeopardize the cause of liberalism everywhere.

Liberal democracy was everywhere in peril in 1938. Mussolini and Hitler had long since closed the fist of dictatorship over Italy and Germany. In Spain a civil war pitting fascists against republicans had been raging for two years. Italy had conquered Ethiopia in 1936. Japan had invaded China in the summer of 1937. In March 1938, even as Roosevelt groped for policies to right the economy and save the New Deal, Hitler annexed Austria to the German *Reich*. Reports arrived almost immediately of Nazi reprisals against Viennese Jews. Before the year was out, Hitler absorbed the Czechoslovakian Sudetenland as well, then forced the European democracies at Munich to legitimate his grab. In November 1938 he loosed his Nazi thugs against Germany's Jews in an orgy of violence known as *Kristallnacht*, the night of the broken glass.

It was against this backdrop of gathering global menace that Roosevelt spoke to the nation in a Fireside Chat on April 14, 1938, to announce at last the request for increased spending that constituted part of his hesitant and contradictory response to the deepening American economic crisis. "Security is our greatest need," the president intoned into the microphones on his White House desk. Then he alluded to the Nazi ingestion of Austria just a month earlier: "Democracy has disappeared in several other great nations," he said, "not because the people of those nations disliked democracy, but because they had grown tired of unemployment and insecurity, of seeing their children hungry while they sat helpless in the face of government confusion and government weakness through lack of leadership in government." Some listeners might have wondered if he was not talking about his own government and his own leadership. "History proves," Roosevelt concluded, "that dictatorships do not grow out of strong and successful governments, but out of weak and helpless ones."[72]

Yet Roosevelt himself stood before the world in 1938 as a badly weakened leader, unable to summon the imagination or to secure the political strength to cure his own country's apparently endless economic crisis. In the ninth year of the Great Depression and the sixth year of Roosevelt's New Deal, with more than ten million workers still unemployed, America had still not found a formula for economic recovery. From such a leader, what could the democracies hope? From such a troubled nation, what did the dictators have to fear?

72. *PPA* (1938), 242.

12

What the New Deal Did

At the heart of the New Deal there was not a philosophy but a temperament.
— Richard Hofstadter, *The American Political Tradition*, 1948

Not with a bang, but a whimper, the New Deal petered out in 1938. Roosevelt's annual message to Congress in January 1939 was his first in which he did not propose new social and economic programs. "We have now passed the period of internal conflict in the launching of our program of social reform," he announced. "Our full energies may now be released to invigorate the processes of recovery in order to preserve our reforms."[1] As it happened, recovery awaited not the release of more New Deal energies but the unleashing of the dogs of war. Yet the end of reform scarcely meant the end of social and economic change, nor even the end of pursuing those goals the New Deal had championed, especially the goal of security. When the war brought recovery at last, a recovery that inaugurated the most prosperous quarter century America has ever known, it brought it to an economy and a country that the New Deal had fundamentally altered. Indeed, the achievements of the New Deal years surely played a role in determining the degree and the duration of postwar prosperity.

The era of reform might have ended in 1938, but it is worth remembering just how much reform had already taken place by that date. Into the five years of the New Deal was crowded more social and institutional change than into virtually any comparable compass of time in the nation's past. Change is always controversial. Change on the scale the New Deal wrought has proved interminably controversial. Debate about the

1. PPA (1939), 7.

363

New Deal's historical significance, its ideological identity, and its political, social, and economic consequences has ground on for more than half a century. Roosevelt's reforms have become an unavoidable touchstone of American political argument, a talisman invoked by all parties to legitimate or condemn as the occasion requires, an emblem and barometer of American attitudes toward government itself. So just what, exactly, *did* the New Deal do?

It might be well to begin by recognizing what the New Deal did not do, in addition to its conspicuous failure to produce economic recovery. Much mythology and New Deal rhetoric notwithstanding, it did not substantially redistribute the national income. America's income profile in 1940 closely resembled that of 1930, and for that matter 1920.[2] The falling economic tide of the Depression lowered all boats, but by and large they held their relative positions; what little income leveling there was resulted more from Depression-diminished returns to investments, not to redistributive tax policies. Nor, with essentially minor exceptions like the TVA's electric-power business, did the New Deal challenge the fundamental tenet of capitalism: private ownership of the means of production. In contrast with the pattern in virtually all other industrial societies, whether Communist, socialist, or capitalist, no significant state-owned enterprises emerged in New Deal America.

It is also frequently said that the New Deal conformed to no preexisting ideological agenda and that it never produced a spokesman, not even Franklin Roosevelt, who was able systematically to lay out the New Deal's social and economic philosophy. Then and later, critics have charged that so many inconsistent impulses contended under the tent of Roosevelt's New Deal that to seek for system and coherence was to pursue a fool's errand. That accusation has echoed repeatedly in assessments that stress the New Deal's mongrel intellectual pedigree, its improbably plural constituent base, its political pragmatism, its abundant

2. See, for example, Mark H. Leff, *The Limits of Symbolic Reform: The New Deal and Taxation, 1933–1939* (Cambridge: Cambridge University Press, 1984); U.S. Bureau of the Census, *Income Distribution in the United States* (Washington: US GPO, 1966); Simon Kuznets, "Long Term Changes in the National Income of the United States of America since 1870," in Kuznets, ed., *Income and Wealth Series II* (Cambridge: Bowes and Bowes, 1952); Jeffrey G. Williamson and Peter H. Lindert, *American Inequality: A Macroeconomic History* (New York: Academic, 1980); Robert Lampman, *The Share of Top Wealth-Holders in National Wealth* (Princeton: Princeton University Press, 1962).

promiscuities, inconsistencies, contradictions, inconstancies, and failures.[3] What unity of plan or purpose, one might ask, was to be found in an administration that at various times tinkered with inflation and with price controls, with deficit spending and budget-balancing, cartelization and trust-busting, the promotion of consumption and the intimidation of investment, farm-acreage reduction and land reclamation, public employment projects and forced removals from the labor pool? "Economically," one historian concludes with some justice, "the New Deal had been opportunistic in the grand manner."[4]

And yet, illumined by the stern-lantern of history, the New Deal can be seen to have left in place a set of institutional arrangements that constituted a more coherent pattern than is dreamt of in many philosophies. That pattern can be summarized in a single word: security — security for vulnerable individuals, to be sure, as Roosevelt famously urged in his campaign for the Social Security Act of 1935, but security for capitalists and consumers, for workers and employers, for corporations and farms and homeowners and bankers and builders as well. Job security, life-cycle security, financial security, market security — however it might be defined, achieving security was the leitmotif of virtually everything the New Deal attempted. Unarguably, Roosevelt sought to enlarge the national state as the principal instrument of the security and stability that he hoped to impart to American life. But legend to the contrary, much of the security that the New Deal threaded into the fabric of American society was often stitched with a remarkably delicate hand, not simply imposed by the fist of the imperious state. And with the notable exceptions of agricultural subsidies and old-age pensions, it was not usually purchased with the taxpayers' dollars. Nowhere was the artful design of the New Deal's security program more evident than in the financial sector.

AT THE TIP of Manhattan Island, south of the street laid out along the line where the first Dutch settlers built their wall to defend against marauding Indians, beats the very heart of American capitalism. Deep in the urban canyons of the old Dutch city sits the New York Stock Exchange,

3. The classic study of the New Deal's tangled intellectual genealogy in the realm of economic policy is Ellis W. Hawley, *The New Deal and the Problem of Monopoly* (Princeton: Princeton University Press, 1966).
4. James MacGregor Burns, *Roosevelt: The Lion and the Fox* (New York: Harcourt, Brace, 1956), 322.

whence had come the first herald of the Depression's onset. As the Great Crash of 1929 reverberated through the financial system, annihilating billions of dollars in asset values and forcing bank closures, it raised a mighty cry for the reform of "Wall Street," a site that early and late has been beleaguered by threatening hordes incensed at its supposedly inordinate power. The New Deal heeded that cry. Among its first initiatives was the reform of the American financial sector, including the banks and the securities markets. What did it accomplish?

Faced with effectively complete collapse of the banking system in 1933, the New Deal confronted a choice. On the one hand, it could try to nationalize the system, or perhaps create a new government bank that would threaten eventually to drive all private banks out of business. On the other hand, it could accede to the long-standing requests of the major money-center banks—especially those headquartered around Wall Street—to relax restrictions on branch and interstate banking, allow mergers and consolidations, and thereby facilitate the emergence of a highly concentrated private banking industry, with just a few dozen powerful institutions to carry on the nation's banking business. That, in fact, was the pattern in most other industrialized countries. But the New Deal did neither. Instead, it left the astonishingly plural and localized American banking system in place, while inducing one important structural change and introducing one key new institution.

The structural change, mandated by the Glass-Steagall Banking Act of 1933, was to separate investment banks from commercial banks, thus securing depositors' savings against the risks of being used for highly speculative purposes. The same Act created a new entity, the Federal Bank Deposit Insurance Corporation (FBDIC, later simply FDIC). Guaranteeing individual bank deposits up to five thousand dollars (later raised) and funded by minimal subscriptions from Federal Reserve member institutions, the FDIC forever liberated banks and depositors from the fearful psychology of bank "runs," or panics. These two simple measures did not impose an oppressively elaborate new regulatory apparatus on American banking, nor did they levy appreciable costs on either taxpayers or member banks. But they did inject unprecedented stability into the American banking system. Bank failures, which had occurred at the rate of hundreds per year even before the Depression's descent, numbered fewer than ten per year in the decades after 1933.

If speculation and lack of depositor confidence had been the major problems of the banking system, the cardinal affliction of the closely related securities industry had been ignorance. Pervasive, systemic ignorance blanketed Wall Street like a perpetual North Atlantic fog before the New Deal, badly impeding the efficient operation of the securities markets and leaving them vulnerable to all kinds of abuses. Wall Street before the 1930s was a strikingly information-starved environment. Many firms whose securities were publicly traded published no regular reports or issued reports whose data were so arbitrarily selected and capriciously audited as to be worse than useless. It was this circumstance that had conferred such awesome power on a handful of investment bankers like J. P. Morgan, because they commanded a virtual monopoly of the information necessary to making sound financial decisions.[5] Especially in the secondary markets, where reliable information was all but impossible for the average investor to come by, opportunities abounded for insider manipulation and wildcat speculation. "It's easy to make money in this market," the canny speculator Joseph P. Kennedy had confided to a partner in the palmy days of the 1920s. "We'd better get in before they pass a law against it."[6]

The New Deal did pass a law against it, then assigned Joseph P. Kennedy to implement that law, a choice often compared to putting the fox in the henhouse or setting a thief to catch a thief. In 1934 Kennedy became the first chairman of the new Securities Exchange Commission (SEC), one of just four new regulatory bodies established by the New Deal.[7] The SEC's powers derived from statutes so patently needed but so intricately technical that Texas congressman Sam Rayburn admitted he did not know whether the legislation "passed so readily because it was so damned good or so damned incomprehensible." Yet some years later, Rayburn acknowledged that the SEC, thanks in part to the start it got from Kennedy, was "the strongest Commission in the government."A study of the federal bureaucracy overseen by Herbert Hoover called the SEC "an outstanding example of the independent commission at its best."[8]

5. For a vivid description of the workings of the pre–New Deal financial marketplace, see Ron Chernow, *The House of Morgan* (New York: Atlantic Monthly, 1990).

6. Kennedy quoted in Michael R. Beschloss, *Kennedy and Roosevelt: An Uneasy Alliance* (New York: Norton, 1980), 60.

7. The others were the National Labor Relations Board, the Civil Aeronautics Authority, and the Federal Communications Commission. Some existing agencies were also considerably strengthened, notably the Federal Power Commission, the Federal Trade Commission, the Interstate Commerce Commission, and the Federal Reserve Board.

8. Congressman Sam Rayburn and the Hoover Commission Report quoted in Thomas K. McCraw, *Prophets of Regulation* (Cambridge: Belknap Press of Harvard University Press, 1984), 175, 153–54.

For all the complexity of its enabling legislation, the power of the SEC resided principally in just two provisions, both of them ingeniously simple. The first mandated disclosure of detailed information, such as balance sheets, profit and loss statements, and the names and compensation of corporate officers, about firms whose securities were publicly traded. The second required verification of that information by independent auditors using standardized accounting procedures. At a stroke, those measures ended the monopoly of the Morgans and their like on investment information. Wall Street was now saturated with data that were relevant, accessible, and comparable across firms and transactions. The SEC's regulations unarguably imposed new reporting requirements on businesses. They also gave a huge boost to the status of the accounting profession. But they hardly constituted a wholesale assault on the theory or practice of free-market capitalism. All to the contrary, the SEC's regulations dramatically improved the economic efficiency of the financial markets by making buy and sell decisions well-informed decisions, provided that the contracting parties consulted the data now so copiously available. This was less the reform than it was the rationalization of capitalism, along the lines of capitalism's own claims about how free markets were supposed to work.

The New Deal's housing policies provide perhaps the best example of its techniques for stabilizing a major economic sector by introducing new elements of information and reliability. By its very nature, the potential demand for housing was large, widespread, and capable of generating significant employment in countless localities. John Maynard Keynes was not alone in recognizing that housing was a sector with enormous promise for invigorating the economy. Well before Keynes urged Roosevelt to put his eggs in the housing basket, Herbert Hoover had patronized the Better Homes for America Movement in the 1920s. In 1931, as new home construction plunged by 95 percent from its pre-1929 levels, he had convened a national presidential conference on Home Building and Home Ownership. Its very title, especially the latter phrase, advertised Hoover's preferred approach to the housing issue.[9]

As in the banking sector, the New Deal faced a choice in the housing field. It could take Keynes's advice and get behind proposals from congressional liberals like Robert Wagner for large-scale, European-style public

9. For a study of Hoover's policies, see Karen Dunn-Haley, *The House That Uncle Sam Built: The Political Culture of Federal Housing Policy, 1919–1932*, Ph.D. dissertation, Stanford University, 1995.

housing programs, or it could follow Hoover's lead and seek measures to stimulate private home building and individual home ownership. Despite its experimentation with government-built model communities like the so-called Greenbelt Towns (of which only three were built) and its occasional obeisance to public housing programs (as in the modestly funded Wagner-Steagall National Housing Act of 1937), the New Deal essentially adopted — and significantly advanced — Hoover's approach. Two new agencies, the Home Owners Loan Corporation (HOLC) and the Federal Housing Administration (FHA), supplemented by the Veterans Administration's housing program after World War II and the creation of the Federal National Mortgage Association (Fannie Mae) under the auspices of the RFC in 1938, implemented the New Deal's housing program.[10]

The HOLC began in 1933 as an emergency agency with two objectives: to protect defaulting homeowners against foreclosure and to improve lending institutions' balance sheets by refinancing shaky mortgages. With much publicity, the HOLC stopped the avalanche of defaults in 1933, but its lasting legacy was a quieter affair. Just as the SEC introduced standardized accounting practices into the securities industry, the HOLC, to facilitate its nationwide lending operations, encouraged uniform national appraisal methods throughout the real estate industry. The FHA, created in 1934 to insure long-term mortgages in much the manner that the FDIC insured bank deposits, took the next logical step and defined national standards of home construction. The creation of Fannie Mae completed the New Deal's housing program apparatus. Fannie Mae furnished lending institutions with a mechanism for reselling their mortgages, thus increasing the lenders' liquidity and making more money available for subsequent rounds of construction. Taken together, the standardization of appraisal methods and construction criteria, along with the mortgage insurance and resale facilities the New Deal put in place, removed much of the risk from home-lending.

The FHA and Fannie Mae themselves neither built houses nor loaned money, nor did they manage to stimulate much new construction in the 1930s. However, they arranged an institutional landscape in which unprecedented amounts of private capital could flow into the home construction industry in the post–World War II years. The New Deal's hous-

10. The discussion of housing here is much indebted to Kenneth T. Jackson's pioneering work, *Crabgrass Frontier: The Suburbanization of the United States* (New York: Oxford University Press, 1985). Parallel programs, legislated by the Farm Mortgage Refinancing Act of 1934 and the Frazier-Lemke Federal Farm Bankruptcy Acts of 1934 and 1935, gave similar relief to farm owners.

ing policies, cleverly commingling public and private institutions, demonstrated that political economy need not be a zero-sum game, in which the expansion of state power automatically spelled the shrinkage of private prerogatives. Once the war was over, this New Deal "reform" proved not to have checked or intimidated capital so much as to have liberated it. And eventually it revolutionized the way Americans lived.

Before the New Deal, only about four Americans in ten lived in their own homes. Homeowners in the 1920s typically paid full cash or very large down payments for their houses, usually not less than 30 percent. The standard mortgage was offered by a local institution with a highly limited service area, had only a five-to-ten-year maturity, bore interest as high as 8 percent, and required a large "balloon" payment, or refinancing, at its termination. Not surprisingly, under such conditions a majority of Americans were renters.

The New Deal changed all that. Uniform appraisal procedures made lenders much more confident in the underlying value of mortgaged properties. FHA insurance made them less nervous about loans going sour. Consequently, lenders began to accept down payments of 10 percent and to offer thirty-year fully amortized mortgages with level monthly payments. Interest rates on mortgages also came down as the element of risk diminished. Finally, nationally standardized appraisal and construction standards, along with Fannie Mae's national market for mortgage paper, allowed funds to flow out of regions of historic capital surplus to regions of historic capital deficit—that is, from city to suburbs and from the Northeast to the South and West.

The New Deal, in short, put in place an apparatus of financial security that allowed private money to build postwar suburbia and the sun belt. Private money built private homes. Four decades after the New Deal, nearly two-thirds of Americans lived in owner-occupied houses. Only 1 percent, usually the poorest of the poor, lived in public housing. By contrast, in John Maynard Keynes's England, nearly half the population lived in public housing in the early postwar years, as did more than a third of the population of France.[11]

IN THE FINANCIAL AND HOUSING SECTORS, the New Deal built structures of stability by the inventively simple devices of standardizing

11. Jackson, *Crabgrass Frontier*, 224. Jackson also demonstrates that both the private and public housing programs encouraged by the New Deal frequently reinforced and even exacerbated racial segregation in housing. It is also worth noting that by the 1990s Britain had substantially abandoned the public housing model, and a majority of Britons had become homeowners.

and promulgating relevant information and by introducing industry-wide self-insurance schemes that calmed jittery markets and offered dependable safeguards to capital. In many other sectors, the New Deal's technique was somewhat less artful; it was, simply, to suppress competition, or at least to modulate its destructive effects. But everywhere the objective was the same: to create a uniquely American system of relatively riskless capitalism.

The New Deal applied its crudest version of the anticompetitive approach to the chronically volatile agricultural sector. There it contained destabilizing competition with the ham-handed device of simply paying producers not to produce, keeping price-depressing surpluses off the market altogether. Some of the same logic of mandatory and even subsidized reduction of competition was also apparent in the New Deal's treatment of labor markets. Franklin Roosevelt declaimed about social justice in his campaigns for the Social Security Act and the Fair Labor Standards Act, and he achieved much justice, too. But those acts also shaped a manpower policy that had nearly as much to do with stability, plain and simple, as it did with social justice. Prohibitions on child labor, combined with virtually obligatory retirement by age sixty-five, statutorily shrank the size of the labor pool and therefore reduced wage competition. Retirees were, in effect, paid not to work, just as farmers were paid not to produce (though all but the first generation of Social Security pensioners were ostensibly paid from their own forced-savings accounts, while farmers unapologetically drew their subsidies from general treasury revenues). The Fair Labor Standards Act, as well as the industry-wide bargaining power of the new CIO unions, also built broad floors under wages and thereby further reduced the ability of employers and employees alike to compete by lowering labor costs.

In some sectors, new regulatory commissions provided orderly forums where the rules of competition could be agreed on and the clash of interests accommodated in a peaceful manner. The National Labor Relations Board provided a compelling example of that technique. Elsewhere, as in large infrastructural industries like transportation, communications, and energy, as well as in the wholesale distribution and retail marketing sectors, the New Deal sought stability by directly curtailing price and cost competition, often by limiting new entrants. The Civil Aeronautics Board, created in 1938, performed those functions for the infant airline industry; the Interstate Commerce Commission for the older railroad industry, and, after the passage of the Motor Carrier Act of 1935, for truckers as well. The Federal Communications Commission, born in 1934, did the same for telephones, radio, and, later, television; the Federal Power Commission, though with more difficulty, for oil and gas production. The Federal Trade Commission, newly empowered by two New Deal "fair trade" laws, was charged with limiting price competition in the retail and wholesale trades. (The Robinson-Patman Act of 1936 prohibited chain stores from discounting below certain stipulated levels, a way of insulating "mom-and-pop" corner stores against aggressive price pressure from the high-volume giants. The Miller-Tydings Act of 1937 legalized price-maintenance contracts between wholesalers and their distributors, a way of stabilizing the prices of nationally marketed name-brand goods.)

The creation of this array of anticompetitive and regulatory instruments has often been criticized as an inappropriate response to the Great Depression. The economic historian Peter Temin, for example, writes that "the New Deal represented an attempt to solve macroeconomic problems with microeconomic tools."[12] That judgment rests on the assumption that solving the macroeconomic problem of insufficient demand and high unemployment by inducing economic recovery was the New Deal's highest priority. Certainly Roosevelt said on countless occasions that such was his goal. But if actions speak louder than words, then it may be fair to conclude that perhaps not in stated purpose, but surely in actual practice, the New Deal's premier objective, at least until 1938, and in Roosevelt's mind probably for a long time thereafter, was not economic recovery but structural reform. In the last analysis, reform was the New Deal's lasting legacy.

The pattern of economic reforms that the New Deal wove arose out of concrete historical circumstances. It also had a more coherent intellectual underpinning than is customarily recognized. Its cardinal aim was not to destroy capitalism but to devolatilize it, and at the same time to distribute its benefits more evenly. New Deal regulatory initiatives were precipitated from decades of anxiety about overcapacity and cutthroat competition, the very issues that had so disrupted the first great national industry, the railroads, in the nineteenth century and led to the creation of the country's first regulatory commission, the Interstate Commerce Commission (ICC), in 1887. Against that background, the Depression appeared to signal the final, inevitable collapse of an economy that had been beset for at least fifty years by overproduction and an excess of competition. The regulatory regime that the New Deal put in

---

12. Temin's remark is in Gary M. Walton, ed., *Regulatory Change in an Atmosphere of Crisis: Current Implications of the Roosevelt Years* (New York: Academic, 1979), 58.

place seemed, therefore, but a logical extension of the kind of competition-controlling remedies that the ICC had first applied to the railroads half a century earlier and a fitting climax to five decades of sometimes wild economic turbulence.

Those views found their most systematic formulation in Franklin Roosevelt's 1932 campaign address at San Francisco's Commonwealth Club. As much as any single document can, that speech served as a charter for the New Deal's economic program:

> The history of the last half century is in large measure a history of a group of financial Titans. . . .
>
> As long as we had free land; as long as population was growing by leaps and bounds; as long as our industrial plants were insufficient to supply our own needs, society chose to give the ambitious man free play and unlimited reward provided only that he produced the economic plant so much desired. During this period of expansion, there was equal opportunity for all and the business of government was not to interfere but to assist in the development of industry.
>
> [But now] our industrial plant is built; the problem just now is whether under existing conditions it is not overbuilt. Our last frontier has long since been reached, and there is practically no more free land. . . . We are now providing a drab living for our own people. . . .
>
> Clearly, all this calls for a re-appraisal of values. A mere builder of more industrial plants, a creator of more railroad systems, an organizer of more corporations, is as likely to be a danger as a help. The day of the great promoter or the financial Titan, to whom we granted everything if only he would build, or develop, is over. Our task now is not discovery, or exploitation of natural resources, or necessarily producing more goods. It is the soberer, less dramatic business of administering resources and plants already in hand, of seeking to reestablish foreign markets for our surplus production, of meeting the problem of underconsumption, of adjusting production to consumption, of distributing wealth and products more equitably, of adapting existing economic organizations to the service of the people. The day of enlightened administration has come. . . . As I see it, the task of government in its relation to business is to assist the development of . . . an economic constitutional order."[13]

The National Recovery Administration, of course, with its measures to stabilize production and limit price and wage competition, was the classic institutional expression of that philosophy. But even after the

13. *PPA* (1928–32), 742–56.

NRA's demise in 1935, the thinking that had shaped it continued to inform New Deal efforts to erect a new "economic constitutional order."

That thinking rested on three premises, two of them explicit, the other usually implicit. The first was the notion, so vividly and repeatedly evident in Roosevelt's Commonwealth Club Address, that the era of economic growth had ended. With his references to the closing of the frontier, Roosevelt, echoing Frederick Jackson Turner's celebrated thesis about the 1890s, suggested that the Depression did not mark a transient crisis but heralded instead the death of an era and the birth of a new historical epoch. Many other New Dealers, from Rexford Tugwell to the young Keynesians who rose to prominence in the second Roosevelt administration, shared this view. It deeply colored their thought right down to the end of the Depression decade. "The economic crisis facing America is not a temporary one," the economist Lauchlin Currie wrote to his boss, Marriner Eccles, in 1939. "The violence of the depression following 1929," Currie continued, "obscured for some time the fact that a profound change of a chronic or secular nature had occurred."[14] That change, Currie concluded, was the emergence of a "mature" economy, one whose capacity for growth was largely exhausted. The best that could be hoped for, therefore, was to restore the gross levels of production of the late 1920s and to effect a more equitable distribution of consuming power so as to sustain those levels indefinitely. Roosevelt himself said consistently that his "goal" was to raise national income to "ninety or one hundred" billion dollars. "When, the Lord only knows," he remarked to reporters as late as October 1937, "but that is a perfectly sound goal."[15] Measured against a national income of nearly $87 billion in 1929, it was also a perfectly modest goal, a goal inspired by visions of economic restoration, not economic expansion.

The second premise that informed New Deal policy was closely related to the first and was also evident in Roosevelt's Commonwealth Club address. It was the idea that the private sector, left to its own devices, would never again be capable of generating sufficient investment and employment to sustain even a 1920s-level economy. That premise was the starting point for Harry Hopkins's Works Progress Administration. Both he and Roosevelt presumed that WPA would be a

14. Currie quoted in Alan Brinkley, *The End of Reform: New Deal Liberalism in Recession and War* (New York: Knopf, 1995), 122.

15. *PPA* (1937), 476; see also Roosevelt's annual message to Congress of January 3, 1938, *PPA* (1938), 3.

permanently necessary government employment program. ("The time
. . . when industry and business can absorb all able-bodied workers," said
Hopkins in 1936, "seems to grow more distant with improvements in
management and technology.")[16] The same assumption about the long-
term structural inadequacies of the private sector in "mature" economies
formed much of the intellectual core of Keynesian analysis. Even before
Keynes gave the idea full articulation, this motif ran like a bright thread
through the writings of the professional practitioners of the dismal science in the 1930s. Alvin Hansen, a Harvard economist destined to become America's leading Keynesian, gave forceful expression to this notion in 1938 in *Full Employment or Stagnation?*, a book that helped to
popularize the concept of "secular stagnation" while also arguing that
government spending was indispensable to make up for the permanent
deficiencies of private capital.[17]

The third premise that molded the economic thinking and policies
of the New Deal was the assumption, less consciously held than the
other two but powerfully determinative nonetheless, that the United
States was an economically self-sufficient nation. That concept of economic isolationism had underlain Roosevelt's frank declaration in his
first inaugural address that "our international trade relations . . . are in
point of time and necessity secondary only to the establishment of a
sound national economy." It had formed the basis of his inflationary
schemes of 1933 and 1934. It formed the filament on which a series of
New Deal measures, from crop supports to minimum wage and price-
fixing legislation, was strung. When Roosevelt spoke of "balance" between American industry and agriculture, or when he posited the requirement "that the income of our working population actually expands
sufficiently to create markets to absorb that increased production," he
was clearly envisioning an America for which foreign markets, not to
mention foreign competitors, did not exist.[18]

FROM THOSE INTELLECTUAL BUILDING BLOCKS, composed of a
theory of history, a conception of the nature of modern economies, and
an appraisal of America's unique position in the world, the New

16. Harry Hopkins, *Spending to Save* (New York: Norton, 1936), 180–81.
17. Alvin H. Hansen, *Full Employment or Stagnation?* (New York: Norton, 1938). Wit-
    nessing the economic impact of World War II, Hansen later revised his views on
    secular stagnation. "All of us had our sights too low," he wrote in 1944. See Alvin
    H. Hansen, "Planning Full Employment," *Nation*, October 21, 1944, 492.
18. *PPA* (1933), 14, (1937), 496.

Deal erected an institutional scaffolding designed to provide unprecedented stability and predictability for the American economy. In time, that edifice would serve as the latticework on which the postwar economy grew like kudzu, the "mile-a-minute vine" that carpets much of the South. To be sure, the unparalleled economic vitality of the post-1940 decades was attributable to many factors, not least the gusher of deficit spending triggered by World War II, as well as the long exemption from foreign competition that the results of the war conferred on the United States. But the elements of financial reliability, modulated competition in commodity, transportation, communication, retail, and labor markets, well-ordered relations between management and labor, and government support of at least minimal levels of aggregate demand—developments that owed much to the New Deal—must surely figure largely in any comprehensive explanation of the performance of the American economy in the postwar quarter century.

Yet economic growth as a later generation would know it formed little part of the New Deal's ambition, even after FDR's timid, attenuated acceptance of Keynesian deficits in 1938. Roosevelt remained reluctant to the end of the 1930s to engage in the scale of compensatory spending adequate to restore the economy to pre-Depression levels, let alone expand it. Nor would he relax his attacks on business sufficiently to encourage capital to take full advantage of the stabilizing elements his own government was putting in place. Ironically, he succeeded in building structures of stability while maintaining throughout the 1930s, so far as businessmen were concerned, an atmosphere of uncertainty. Capital can live with restrictions, but it is terrorized by insecurity. "Business is now hesitant about making long term plans," the head of the New York Federal Reserve Board wrote to Marriner Eccles in 1937, "partly because it feels it does not know what the rules of the game are going to be."[19] That sentiment was widely shared in the business community. It was not so much the regulations that the New Deal imposed that intimidated businessmen in the 1930s; it was the fear of what new and unknown provocations Roosevelt might yet unleash. When at last Roosevelt declared the New Deal's reform phase at an end, and when the war compelled government spending on an unexampled scale, capital was

19. Quoted in Richard Polenberg, "The Decline of the New Deal, 1937–1940," in John Braeman et al., eds., *The New Deal: The National Level* (Columbus: Ohio State University Press, 1975), 255.

unshackled, and the economy energized, to a degree that he and other New Dealers could scarcely have imagined in the Depression decade. And ever after, Americans assumed that the federal government had not merely a role, but a major responsibility, in ensuring the health of the economy and the welfare of citizens. That simple but momentous shift in perception was the newest thing in all the New Deal, and the most consequential too.

HUMANKIND, OF COURSE, does not live by bread alone. Any assessment of what the New Deal did would be incomplete if it rested with an appraisal of New Deal economic policies and failed to acknowledge the remarkable array of social innovations nourished by Roosevelt's expansive temperament.

The world is not a finished place, the philosopher William James once said, nor ever will be. Neither was the New Deal a finished thing, though in later years some scholars lamented its incompleteness, its alleged political timidity, and its supposedly premature demise.[20] But what needs emphasis, in the final accounting, is not what the New Deal failed to do but how it managed to do so much in the uniquely malleable moment of the mid-1930s. That brief span of years, it is now clear, constituted one of only a handful of episodes in American history when substantial and lasting social change has occurred—when the country was, in measurable degree, remade. The American political system, after all, was purpose-built in the eighteenth century to prevent its easy manipulation from the national capital, to bind governments down from mischief, as Jefferson said, by the chains of the Constitution, especially by the notoriously constraining system of checks and balances. It is hardly surprising, therefore, that political stasis defines the "normal" American condition. Against that backdrop, what stands out about the New Deal are not its limitations and its temerity but the boldness of its vision and the consequent sweep of its ultimate achievement.

For all his alleged inscrutability, Franklin Roosevelt's social vision was

20. Works that generally share a critical posture toward the New Deal include Barton J. Bernstein, "The Conservative Achievements of Liberal Reform," in Bernstein, ed., *Towards a New Past* (New York: Pantheon, 1968); Howard Zinn, *New Deal Thought* (Indianapolis: Bobbs-Merrill 1966); Paul Conkin, *The New Deal*, 3d ed. (Arlington Heights, Ill.: Harlan Davidson, 1992); Brinkley, *End of Reform*; and Michael Sandel, *Democracy's Discontent: America in Search of a Public Philosophy* (Cambridge: Belknap Press of Harvard University Press, 1996).

clear enough. "We are going to make a country," he once said to Frances Perkins, "in which no one is left out."[21] In that unadorned sentence Roosevelt spoke volumes about the New Deal's lasting historical meaning. Like his rambling, comfortable, and unpretentious old home on the bluff above the Hudson River, Roosevelt's New Deal was a welcoming mansion of many rooms, a place where millions of his fellow citizens could find at last a measure of the security that the patrician Roosevelts enjoyed as their birthright.

Perhaps the New Deal's greatest achievement was its accommodation of the maturing immigrant communities that had milled uneasily on the margins of American society for a generation and more before the 1930s. In bringing them into the Democratic Party and closer to the mainstream of national life, the New Deal, even without fully intending to do so, also made room for an almost wholly new institution, the industrial union. To tens of millions of rural Americans, the New Deal offered the modern comforts of electricity, schools, and roads, as well as unaccustomed financial stability. To the elderly and the unemployed it extended the promise of income security, and the salvaged dignity that went with it.

To black Americans the New Deal offered jobs with the CCC, WPA, and PWA and, perhaps as important, the compliment of respect from at least some federal officials. The time had not come for direct federal action to challenge Jim Crow and put right at last the crimes of slavery and discrimination, but more than a few New Dealers made clear where their sympathies lay and quietly prepared for a better future. Urged on by Eleanor Roosevelt, the president brought African-Americans into the government in small but unprecedented numbers. By the mid-1930s they gathered periodically as an informal "black cabinet," guided often by the redoubtable Mary McLeod Bethune. Roosevelt also appointed the first black federal judge, William Hastie. Several New Deal Departments and agencies, including especially Ickes's Interior Department and Aubrey Williams's National Youth Administration, placed advisers for "Negro affairs" on their staffs.

In the yeasty atmosphere of Roosevelt's New Deal, scores of social experiments flourished. Not all of them were successful, not all of them destined to last, but all shared the common purpose of building a country from whose basic benefits and privileges no one was excluded. The

21. Frances Perkins, *The Roosevelt I Knew* (New York: Viking, 1946), 113.

Resettlement Administration laid out model communities for displaced farmers and refugees from the shattered industrial cities, though only a handful of those social experiments survived, and they soon lost their distinctive, utopian character. The Farm Security Administration maintained migrant labor camps that sheltered thousands of families like John Steinbeck's Joads. The Tennessee Valley Authority brought electricity, and with it industry, to the chronically depressed upper South. The Bonneville Power Authority made a start on doing the same for the Columbia River Basin in the long-isolated Pacific Northwest. The New Deal also extended the hand of recognition to Native Americans. The Indian Reorganization Act of 1934—the so-called Indian New Deal—ended the half-century-old policy of forced assimilation and alienation of tribal lands and encouraged tribes to establish their own self-governing bodies and to preserve their ancestral traditions. Though some Indians denounced this policy as a "back-to-the-blanket" measure that sought to make museum pieces out of Native Americans, the act accurately reflected the New Deal's consistently inclusionary ethos.

The New Deal also succored the indigent and patronized the arts. It built roads and bridges and hospitals. It even sought a kind of security for the land itself, adding some twelve million acres of national parklands, including Olympic National Park in Washington State, Isle Royal in Lake Superior, the Everglades in Florida, and King's Canyon in California. It planted trees and fought erosion. It erected mammoth dams—Grand Coulee and Bonneville on the Columbia, Shasta on the Sacramento, Fort Peck on the Missouri—that were river-tamers and nature-busters, to be sure, but jobmakers and region-builders, too.

Above all, the New Deal gave to countless Americans who had never had much of it a sense of security, and with it a sense of having a stake in their country. And it did it all without shredding the American Constitution or sundering the American people. At a time when despair and alienation were prostrating other peoples under the heel of dictatorship, that was no small accomplishment.

The columnist Dorothy Thompson summed up Franklin Roosevelt's achievements at the end of the Depression decade, in 1940:

> We have behind us eight terrible years of a crisis we have shared with all countries. Here we are, and our basic institutions are still intact, our people relatively prosperous, and most important of all, our society relatively affectionate. No rift has made an unbridgeable schism between us. The working classes are not clamoring for [Communist Party

boss] Mr. Browder and the industrialists are not demanding a Man on Horseback. No country in the world is so well off.[22]

In the last analysis, Franklin Roosevelt faithfully discharged his duties, in John Maynard Keynes's words of 1933, as "the trustee for those in every country" who believed in social peace and in democracy. He did mend the evils of the Depression by reasoned experiment within the framework of the existing social system. He did prevent a naked confrontation between orthodoxy and revolution. The priceless value of that achievement, surely as much as the columns of ciphers that recorded national income and production, must be reckoned in any final accounting of what the New Deal did.

22. *New York Herald Tribune*, October 9, 1940, rpt. in Arthur M. Schlesinger Jr., *The History of American Presidential Elections, 1789–1968* (New York: Chelsea House, 1971), 4:2981–93.

13

The Gathering Storm

To hell with Europe and the rest of those nations!
— Minnesota senator Thomas Schall, 1935

For all its agony of carnage and destruction, the Great War of 1914–18 settled little. In time, it would come to be seen as but the opening chapter in the twentieth century's own Thirty-Year War, a conflict that endured thirty-one years, to be exact, from 1914 to 1945, and at the price of some sixty million lives forever transformed the world. To be sure, the First World War had shattered the Austro-Hungarian empire and left Germany defeated. But the treaty signed in the Hall of Mirrors at Versailles on June 28, 1919, neither extinguished the ambitions that had ignited the war nor quieted the anxieties it had spawned. Victors and vanquished agreed only that the conflict had been a dreadful catastrophe, a blood-spilling, man-killing, nation-eating nightmare of unprecedented horror. All were determined to avoid its reoccurrence. More precisely, each nation was determined to avoid the repetition of its own role in it.

For two countries, Italy and Japan, it was not so much the war itself as its disappointing outcome that rankled. The Italians and the Japanese alike felt cheated at Versailles out of their victors' just desserts and eventually fell under rulers dedicated to redressing that grievance, by force of arms if necessary. Italy's Fascist leader Benito Mussolini came to power in 1922. *Il Duce* dreamed of a new Roman empire in Africa and the eastern Mediterranean. Militarists in Japan cast covetous eyes on China, especially the rich northern region of Manchuria, and ultimately on Southeast Asia and the Dutch East Indies as well.

Russia, revolutionized by the Bolsheviks in 1917, had made its own peace with Germany at Brest-Litovsk in March 1918 and then found itself shut out entirely from the negotiations at Paris that shaped the Versailles Treaty. The chief lesson the new Soviet regime took from the war was the usefulness, indeed the necessity, of a wily neutrality. Feared and isolated by the Western democracies, the Soviets under Josef Stalin dedicated themselves to building "socialism in one country" while waiting for the reeruption of the capitalist fratricide that Marxist-Leninist theory confidently predicted.

France, able to repel the German invaders of 1914 only with the help of British and, at the eleventh hour, American allies, drew two conclusions from its war experience: that the French frontier with Germany must be massively fortified, so that any future war would not be fought on French soil; and that France could not successfully grapple alone against German power. Neither of those prescriptions proved very useful in practice. French war minister André Maginot ordered the construction along the French-German frontier of the supposedly impregnable network of forts that bore his name. But the Maginot Line came in time to symbolize the futility of static tactics in the dawning era of mobile warfare and, more broadly, the stolid vacuity and rigidly defensive logic of interwar French military thinking—a classic instance of military planners fighting the last war. As for allies, the French suffered bitter disappointment when the Americans failed to honor Woodrow Wilson's promise at Versailles that they would sign a treaty pledging the United States to guarantee France's security. Britain, France's other former comrade-in-arms against the kaiser's Germany, proved scarcely more dependable. Anxious and adrift, France played an uncertain, negligible international role in the postwar decades.

Bled to the point of exhaustion by four years of trench warfare, Britain after 1918 resolved not to allow a local irritation in Europe, like the clash between Austria-Hungary and Serbia that had touched off the Great War, to metastasize into another great-power bloodbath. In a single battle on the Somme River in 1916, 420,000 Britons had perished; at Passchendaele a year later, another 245,000 died. After such horrendous losses Britain vowed never again to hurl a large ground force against an enemy's main strength on the European continent. In any future conflict, Britain would rely principally on sea power and air power and leave most of the ground fighting to others. But public sentiment in Britain, as in France, was above all staunchly committed to avoiding another war altogether. "This house will in no circumstance fight for its King and its Country," the students of the Oxford Union notoriously voted in February 1933. Two years later, thousands of young, pacifistic Britons joined the Peace Pledge Union to oppose their government's then-modest rearmament measures.

In defeated Germany, Adolf Hitler distilled the war's lessons for his country into a prescription for victory next time. Virtually alone among the Great War's survivors, ex-corporal Hitler ravened for more war still. He calculated that the very inconceivability of another war in the eyes of most statesmen—particularly in France and Britain, not to mention the faraway United States—would for a long time blind them to his own intentions and rob them of the will and the means to resist him.

Those intentions were as simple as they were grotesque: to secure living space (*Lebensraum*), into which a racially purified German people could expand indefinitely. Purged of what Hitler identified as the Jewish incubus in their midst, the "master race" would sweep aside the "inferior" Slavic peoples and the many millions of additional Jews who dwelled to Germany's east, claim new sod for the German plow, and create a greater *Reich* that would last a thousand years. That grand racialist geopolitical vision, Hitler reckoned, could be realized only by war—but not by employing the tactics of the Great War of 1914–18. Hitler, too, learned from history. The defeat of 1918 confirmed that in a protracted war of Germany against all, Germany could not win. Hitler therefore determined to fight his war in stages, one foe at a time, with swift, overpowering blows delivered serially against isolated enemies. He would seek allies where he could and maneuver when possible behind the cloak of diplomacy. He would take full advantage of modern technology, especially rapid means of transporting troops and firepower, and the fearsome striking power of armored divisions. Hitler's strategy cunningly exploited the greatest weaknesses of his adversaries: their morbid fear of renewed fighting, their inability to make common cause, their reluctance to rearm, their slavish devotion to outmoded doctrines of warfare.

Hitler moved first to consolidate his power within Germany itself. Within months of his installation as chancellor in January 1933, he contrived to eliminate all opposition and turn Germany into a totalitarian regime, with himself as its supreme and sole leader: *der Führer*. In the charged atmosphere following the burning of the Reichstag building on the night of February 27, 1933, his government issued emergency decrees effectively suppressing freedom of speech and assembly. The following week, just as Franklin Roosevelt was being inaugurated in Washington, D.C., the German people gave his Nazi Party nearly 44 percent of the votes in the last parliamentary election in which they would be allowed to participate for the next dozen years. Emboldened, Hitler invoked the emergency decrees and stepped up the arrests of those Communist deputies who were his principal parliamentary opposition. Now a majority in the Reichstag, on March 23 the Nazis passed an Enabling Law that invested all legislative power in Hitler's hands. While Franklin Roosevelt was coaxing the Hundred Days' legislation out of the American Congress in the spring of 1933, Hitler was dissolving the trade unions, putting his Nazi cronies in control of the various federal states, and Nazifying the press and the universities. On July 14 the government declared the Nazis the only legal political party in Germany. Hitler now ruled without opposition. A reign of terror descended over Germany, enforced with remorseless efficiency by the Geheime Staatspolizei, or Gestapo. A year later, while Roosevelt was contending with conservative dissidents like those in the Liberty League, Hitler dispatched his main Nazi rival, SA leader Ernst Röhm, by having him summarily executed. The following year, the year of Social Security and the Wagner Act, Hitler codified his policies against the Jews in the Nuremberg Decrees, which stripped German Jews of their citizenship, excluded them from the professions and military service, and prohibited marriage between Jews and "Aryans."

Hitler matched the pace of his drive toward dictatorship at home with the accelerating tempo of his foreign provocations. In October 1933 he withdrew Germany from the League of Nations and from the Disarmament Conference in Geneva. On March 16, 1935, speaking at the magnificently ornate Berlin Opera House, the last surviving field marshal of the Imperial German Army at his side, he renounced the disarmament clauses of the Versailles Treaty, revealed the existence of a clandestinely built German air force, and ordered a vast program of rearmament, including the raising of a half-million-man conscript army.

One year later, on March 7, 1936, Hitler marched thirty-five thousand German troops into the Rhineland, in flagrant violation of treaty promises that the strategic Rhine buffer zone that lay between France and the German industrial heartland of the Ruhr would remain forever demilitarized. The remilitarization of the Rhineland was Hitler's most brazen gamble to date. He later acknowledged that he would have been compelled to withdraw had he met armed resistance.[1] But Italy was

---

1. "The forty-eight hours after the march into the Rhineland were the most nerve-racking in my life," Hitler later admitted. "If the French had then marched into the

otherwise engaged, Britain had no stomach for standing firm, and France, left to its own devices, could only acquiesce. The Ruhr now lay safely insulated from French attack. Hitler was well on his way toward assuming a commanding military position in Europe.

Hitler proceeded to cement an alliance with Fascist Italy in the so-called Rome-Berlin Axis agreement and to join hands with Japan in the Anti-Comintern Pact, both consummated in November 1936. Like a drunken reveler calling for madder music and stronger wine, *der Führer* grew ever bolder. When civil war erupted in Spain in July 1936, Hitler and Mussolini both sent aircraft to bolster General Francisco Franco's rebels. Two years later, Hitler annexed Austria, incorporating it into the *Reich* as the German province of Ostmark. On March 14, 1938, Hitler motored triumphantly through Vienna, the city where he had lived in lonely poverty as a youth. Cowering before Hitler's bullying, the other European powers swallowed this latest violation of the Versailles Treaty as meekly as they had the others.

As the spectacle of swelling Nazi power unfolded in Europe, most Americans looked on with an air of detached indifference. In the war of 1914–18 that had set the stage on which Hitler now strutted, no people had been more reluctant combatants, and few more disappointed with the result, than the Americans. The United States had abandoned its historic policy of isolationism and entered the European conflict only when the war was already two and one-half years old, in April 1917. By the time an American army could be raised, trained, transported, and deployed, the fighting in Europe had already slaughtered millions. American troops fought only two major battles under American command, at St. Mihiel and the Meuse-Argonne, both in the closing weeks of the war. Though the latter in particular exacted a heavy toll in American lives, neither contributed significantly to Germany's defeat. Even as a co-belligerent alongside England and France, Woodrow Wilson stopped short of becoming their formal "ally." The official name of the anti-German coalition after the United States had joined it in April 1917 was "the Allied *and Associated* Powers," nomenclature that testified awk-

---

Rhineland, we would have had to withdraw with our tails between our legs, for the military resources at our disposal would have been wholly inadequate for even a moderate resistance." William L. Shirer, *The Rise and Fall of the Third Reich* (New York: Simon and Schuster, 1960), 293.

wardly but unmistakably to the Americans' continuing desire to keep their distance from the conflicts of Europe. And as in war, so in peace. No nation had more definitively repudiated the settlement inked at Versailles, despite the fact that an American president had been among its principal draftsmen. In the postwar decade, Americans said no to Woodrow Wilson's League of Nations, no to the French security treaty, no to freer trade policies, no to pleas from France and Britain to forgive their wartime loans from the U.S. Treasury, and no to further unlimited immigration from Europe, when Congress passed the highly restrictive immigration quota laws of 1921 and 1924.

No people came to believe more emphatically than the Americans that the Great War was an unalloyed tragedy, an unpardonably costly mistake never to be repeated. More than fifty thousand American doughboys had perished fighting on the western front, and to what avail? So far from being redeemed by American intervention, Europe swiftly slid back into its historic vices of authoritarianism and armed rivalry, while America slid back into its historic attitude of isolationism. Isolationism may have been most pronounced in the landlocked Midwest, but Americans of both sexes, of all ages, religions, and political persuasions, from all ethnic groups and all regions, shared in the postwar years a feeling of apathy toward Europe, not to mention the rest of the wretchedly quarrelsome world, that bordered on disgust. "Let us turn our eyes inward," declared Pennsylvania's liberal Democratic governor George Earle in 1935. "If the world is to become a wilderness of waste, hatred, and bitterness, let us all the more earnestly protect and preserve our own oasis of liberty."[2]

Both the accident of geography and old habits of mind underlay that attitude. America had grown to national maturity on a remote continent in the absence of threats from abroad, a luxury history has afforded to few nations. That peculiar circumstance bred in Americans the dangerous illusion that they could choose whether and when to participate in the world. The idea of isolation was as old as America itself. From John Winthrop's declaration that Americans dwelt in a "city upon a hill" through George Washington's admonition to beware "the insidious wiles of foreign influence," Thomas Jefferson's repudiation of "entangling alliances," Mark Twain's satirical anti-European diatribes in *The Innocents Abroad* and *A Connecticut Yankee in King Arthur's Court*, and Henry James's sensitive "transatlantic novels," down even to F. Scott's Fitzger-

2. Leuchtenburg, 197n.

ald's poetic conclusion to his 1925 novel *The Great Gatsby*, with its lyrical invocation of the "fresh green breast of the New World," Americans had thought of themselves as not simply distant from the Old World but different from it as well. That difference, indeed, defined for many the essence — and the superiority — of the American national identity. International involvement was therefore worse than useless. It risked contaminating the very character of the nation. "Rejection of Europe," the novelist John Dos Passos once wrote, "is what America is all about."

In the Great War — what Americans often tellingly called "the European War" — the United States had haltingly abandoned that centuries-old cultural wisdom, only to reembrace it with deepened conviction in the war's aftermath. Popular writers like Dos Passos and e. e. cummings fed the public's sense of disillusion with the war in books like *Three Soldiers* (1921) and *The Enormous Room* (1922). Antiwar fiction reached a crescendo in 1929 with the publication of Ernest Hemingway's *A Farewell to Arms* and Erich Maria Remarque's international best-seller, *All Quiet on the Western Front*. A spate of revisionist histories of American involvement in the war also drove the isolationist moral home to a broad reading audience. Taken together, books like Harry Elmer Barnes's *Genesis of the World War* (1926), C. Hartley Grattan's *Why We Fought* (1929), Walter Millis's *Road to War* (1935), and Charles C. Tansill's *America Goes to War* (1938) composed a formidable brief that indicted the folly of America's departure in 1917 from its historic policy of isolation. The war had been fought, those authors argued, not to make the world safe for democracy but to make it safe for Wall Street bankers and grasping arms manufacturers. The American public had been duped by British propaganda, and Woodrow Wilson had been trapped by his stubborn Presbyterian moralism and slavish, unrealistic devotion to the principle of "neutral rights." The only winners were the "merchants of death" — the financiers and munitions-makers who harvested obscene profits from the war. Ordinary Americans had no appreciable interests at stake in 1917, so the argument ran, and the country should have stayed out of the fray.

The indictment was grossly overdrawn, but it fell on receptive ears, especially in the antibusiness atmosphere of the Great Depression. The isolationist implications of that message drew powerful reinforcement in the mid-1930s from the accusations emanating from the Senate's Special Committee Investigating the Munitions Industry. Chaired by progressive Republican North Dakota senator Gerald Nye, the committee owed its existence to a growing American peace movement that through petitions, pamphlets, and demonstrations had become a force to be reckoned with. Spurred especially by a sensational exposé that appeared in *Fortune* magazine in March 1934 entitled "Arms and the Men," by publication soon thereafter of H. C. Engelbrecht's and F. C. Hanighen's *Merchants of Death*, a Book-of-the-Month Club selection, and by the indefatigable lobbying of the Women's International League for Peace and Freedom, the Nye Committee served for two years after its formation in April 1934 as the country's principal platform for isolationist preachments. It served, too, as a pulpit for indignant condemnations of the crimes of big business, which had somehow, the committee insinuated (though never proved), covertly forced the Wilson administration into war.

President Roosevelt at first encouraged the Nye Committee, not least because its revelations discredited the corporate titans and the bankers, the du Ponts and the Wall Street investment houses, that were then among his fiercest political adversaries. In time the president would have reason to regret the strengthened sentiment of inward-looking nationalism that the Nye Committee helped to foster. But when the Nye group began its labors, Roosevelt himself showed every sign of swimming with the same isolationist tide that had swept up his countrymen in the years after the Great War.

In the 1932 presidential campaign, Roosevelt had disavowed his earlier support for American membership in the League of Nations. In his inaugural address he had declared that "our international trade relations, though vastly important, are in point of time and necessity secondary to the establishment of a sound national economy." He gave concrete meaning to that principle when he scuttled the London Economic Conference in June 1933 and embarked thereafter on the highly nationalistic monetary policy of abandoning the gold standard and devaluing the dollar. Many New Deal measures, such as the NRA's wage-pegging and price-setting and the AAA's efforts to raise agricultural prices, depended on keeping the American economy insulated from foreign competition. In keeping with the temper of the times and with his own budget-cutting agenda, Roosevelt also moved swiftly after his inauguration to shrink the already skeletal 140,000-man army. Army Chief of Staff Douglas MacArthur remonstrated vehemently. Meeting with Roosevelt at the White House, MacArthur later recalled, "I spoke recklessly and said something to the effect that when we lost the next war, and an American boy, lying in the mud with an enemy bayonet through his belly and an enemy foot on his dying throat, spat out his last curse, I wanted the name not to be MacArthur, but Roosevelt." A livid president shouted that MacArthur could not talk that way to the commander-in-chief. MacArthur, choked with emotion, hurried outside and vomited on the White House steps. The army's budget stayed cut.[3]

To be sure, Roosevelt also made internationalist gestures in the early New Deal years, suggesting that he had not entirely lost touch with the ideals that he had espoused as Woodrow Wilson's assistant secretary of the navy. Few presidents, indeed, brought to their conduct of foreign affairs a more sophisticated internationalist background. Roosevelt had been reared in that cosmopolitan, Anglophilic social class that took for granted the organic unity of the Atlantic world, a cultural affinity that rasped against the grain of popular American attitudes. His education on two continents had given him a working knowledge of the German and French languages, as well as an intuitive understanding of foreign affairs rivaled among modern presidents only by his cousin Theodore. Like Theodore, he favored the navy as his instrument for projecting American power, though his naval enthusiasm was attenuated after 1933 by financial and legal constraints. Unable to secure large shipbuilding appropriations directly from the Congress, Roosevelt did direct some money from public works appropriations toward constructing a modern fleet, but only up to the rather modest strength allowed by the naval-limitation treaties signed at Washington in 1922 and London in 1930. Though Franklin Roosevelt's White House had no national security adviser or formal foreign policy decision-making apparatus, the president relished interrogating foreign visitors and was a keen consumer of information from several American diplomats. They included especially William C. Bullitt, his ambassador to Russia and later to France, and the president's fellow Grotonian, Sumner Welles, who served as assistant secretary of state for Latin America and, after 1937, undersecretary of state. The brash Bullitt and the silky Welles cordially detested one another, but they agreed that the United States must take a more active role in the world and encouraged the same attitude in their chief. Roosevelt also anointed Cordell Hull, a relentless advocate of free trade, as his secretary of state. He supported Hull's campaign for the Reciprocal Trade Agreements Act in 1934, as well as Hull's subsequent efforts to negotiate reciprocity treaties incorporating the trade-expanding uncon-ditional most-favored-nation principle. Defying the venomous invective of conservatives—and the scolding of his own mother—Roosevelt

3. Douglas MacArthur, *Reminiscences* (New York: McGraw-Hill, 1964), 101.

extended the hand of diplomatic recognition to Soviet Russia in November 1933, a move designed both to broaden American trade opportunities and to strengthen Soviet resistance to possible future Japanese expansionism in China (in both of which hopes Roosevelt was ultimately disappointed). He made partial amends for his destructive role in helping to sink the 1933 London Economic Conference when he concluded an exchange stabilization agreement with Britain and France in 1936.

But for a long season, Roosevelt seemed more committed to a kind of abstract, prospective internationalism than to anything concrete in the here and now. As a Wilsonian, he no doubt hoped that a world of liberalized trade and international cooperation would one day emerge from the sorry mess that war and depression had inflicted on the planet. But during his first term, the mood of the country, as well as Roosevelt's personal priorities and the practical realities of New Deal politics, dictated that he promote no serious American effort to bring that better world about. No politician as sensitively attuned to the popular temper as Roosevelt was could have failed to register the isolationist spirit that pervaded Depression-era America. Moreover, domestic reform, along with economic recovery, was Roosevelt's own most urgent preoccupation. All other political desiderata shriveled to trivial proportions in comparison. And indispensable to the success of the New Deal, and to Roosevelt's longer-range goal of creating a durable liberal political coalition, was the support of a band of progressive Republican senators, including Gerald Nye and his North Dakota colleague Lynn Frazier, George Norris of Nebraska, Robert La Follette Jr. of Wisconsin, William Borah of Idaho, Hiram Johnson of California, and Bronson Cutting of New Mexico. These men were implacable isolationists. Norris, along with La Follette's father, was among the half-dozen senators who had voted against American entry into the First World War in 1917. Borah and Johnson had constituted themselves as a "truth squad" that shadowed Woodrow Wilson around the country in 1919 to undermine his appeals for ratification of the Versailles Treaty. As the historian Robert Dallek has succinctly said of Roosevelt at this time, "a struggle with his progressive Republican friends for minor foreign policy goals at the likely expense of domestic advance was something he would not do."[4] Indeed, to curry favor with this group Roosevelt acquiesced in legislation sponsored by Hiram Johnson in 1934 that prohibited loans to governments that were in default on their existing obligations to the U.S. Treasury—a

4. Dallek, 71.

measure that would in time threaten to stifle Roosevelt's efforts to get American aid into the hands of Hitler's foes.[5]

Even the modest foreign policy initiatives that Roosevelt undertook in his first term suggested that he had only a limited internationalist agenda. He persisted in Herbert Hoover's "Good Neighbor" policy toward Latin America, honoring Hoover's agreement to withdraw the U.S. occupation force from Haiti. When the marine buglers sounded their final notes at Port-au-Prince in 1934, the last Yankee garrison in the Caribbean folded its tents, ending (for a while) more than three decades of armed American intervention south of the border.[6] Roosevelt instructed Hull to vote in favor of a resolution at the Pan-American Conference in Montevideo, Uruguay, in December 1933, proclaiming that "no state has the right to intervene in the internal or external affairs of another." That statement explicitly repudiated the bellicose "corollary" that cousin Theodore had attached to the Monroe Doctrine in 1904, when TR had claimed the right for the United States to exercise international police power in the Western Hemisphere. Roosevelt followed up in 1934 by releasing Cuba from the terms of the Platt Amendment of 1901, whereby the Cuban constitution had conceded the right of intervention to the United States. Mexico put this good neighborliness to a stiff test in 1938 when it nationalized its oil industry, expropriating the property of several American firms. But Roosevelt, faithful to the Good Neighbor creed, rejected demands that he intervene and successfully negotiated acceptable compensation for the confiscated American holdings.

All this assuredly pleased the Latin Americans. They cheered Roosevelt warmly when he toured the Caribbean in 1934 and sailed to South America in 1936, the first American president to travel to the

5. The attorney general interpreted the Johnson Act to mean that token payments would be insufficient to prevent a declaration of default. The long-suffering European debtors, save only Finland, thereupon defaulted outright on June 15, 1934, thus cutting themselves off from any future American credits. This situation vastly complicated Roosevelt's efforts at the beginning of the next decade to provide Britain with the means to purchase arms in the United States.

6. Since the Spanish-American War of 1898, the United States had repeatedly dispatched troops to Nicaragua and Cuba, as well as to the Dominican Republic from 1916 to 1924, and to Haiti, where they had been stationed since 1914. After the withdrawal from Haiti, American forces remained in the Caribbean at the Guntánamo naval base in Cuba and in the Panama Canal Zone, though strictly speaking, in neither of those places did they constitute an occupational force that dictated to the governments of Cuba and Panama respectively.

southern continent. But in Rome and Paris and London and Moscow, and especially in Berlin and Tokyo, the Good Neighbor policy could be seen simply as another calculated American abandonment of unwanted foreign burdens. In company with the torpedoing of the London Economic Conference, the farewell to the gold standard, and the passage of the Johnson Act, Roosevelt's overtures to the Latin Americans seemed to be part of a systematic American retreat from the world, one that would leave the United States with some enhanced moral influence in the Western Hemisphere, perhaps, but few formal obligations there and none elsewhere. Roosevelt strengthened that impression in March 1934 when he signed the Tydings-McDuffie Act, promising independence to the Philippines at the end of a ten-year transitional period—a strong signal that the United States intended to terminate its four-decade-old imperial fling in Asia.

Watching these events from Berlin, Adolf Hitler feared nothing from the United States as he began methodically to unspool his expansionist schemes. In Hitler's reading of history, America had been an irrelevant latecomer in the Great War. Its presence on the battlefield formed no part of his explanation for Germany's defeat, which he attributed to a "stab in the back" by effete politicians in Berlin. Neither then nor later, he thought, did Germany need to worry about American military power. At some distant date, Hitler occasionally imagined, he might have to confront the United States, and he dabbled with contingency plans for a blue-water navy and a long-range air arm that could carry the eventual battle to North America. But for the foreseeable future the Americans simply did not figure in his calculations. They were, he concluded in his own peculiar reading of the American people and past, a mongrel race, doomed to the trash heap of history when the timid shopkeepers of the North had defeated the race-proud lords of the plantation in the Civil War and proceeded to open the national bloodstream to indiscriminate immigrant inflows and, worse, black contamination. Even Aryan peoples could be corrupted by infection with the bacillus of American mediocrity. "Transport a German to Kiev," Hitler said, "and he remains a perfect German. But transplant him to Miami, and you make a degenerate out of him—in other words, an American." As time went on, *der Führer* found confirming proof of these views in Roosevelt's continuing inability to overcome the Depression, a demonstration of political helplessness that Hitler scornfully contrasted with his own unarguable economic success in Germany. He bizarrely seized on the panic set off by Orson Welles's elaborate radio-show hoax in 1938, which led millions of Americans to believe that Martians had invaded the country, as further ratification of his low estimate of American intelligence. When he later watched the film *The Grapes of Wrath*, he concluded that its portrait of a destitute and conflicted country accurately depicted America as it ever was and ever would be. "America," he sneered in 1939, "is not dangerous to us."[7] Though forged in the overheated smithy of Hitler's lurid brain, that conclusion was for the time being not without foundation in fact.

AFTER THE SENATE had refused Roosevelt's request for American participation in the World Court in January 1935, the president lamented to a friend that "we face a large misinformed public opinion." Because that opinion seemed so entrenched, he predicted to his ambassador to Germany, "we shall go through a period of non-cooperation in everything, I fear, for the next year or two." To another correspondent he said glumly that "today, quite frankly, the wind everywhere blows against us."[8] As it happened, much more than "a year or two" had to pass before that isolationist wind abated. Beginning in early 1935, American isolationism hardened from mere indifference to the outside world into studied, active repudiation of anything that smacked of international political or military engagement—or even, under some circumstances, economic engagement. From about the same time may be dated the origins of Roosevelt's own growing conviction that the weight of the United States must somehow be put into the scales to counterbalance the aggressive designs of the dictators and the militarists. Ironically, just as the president's internationalist convictions began to deepen, the isolationist mood of his countrymen started to congeal all the more stubbornly. What emerged was a stalemate in foreign policy no less intractable than the stalemate that paralyzed the movement for domestic reform after 1936. Indeed, at many points it seemed that Roosevelt himself was less the principled opponent of the isolationists than their willing captive.

Before the year 1935 was out, Congress codified isolationist sentiment into the first of five formal neutrality laws that aimed to insulate the United States from the war-storms then brewing across the globe from

7. Gerhard Weinberg, "Hitler's Image of the United States," *American Historical Review* 69 (July 1964): 1006–21.
8. Edgar B. Nixon, ed., *Franklin D. Roosevelt and Foreign Affairs* (Cambridge: Belknap Press of Harvard University Press, 1969), 2:386–87; Elliott Roosevelt, ed., *FDR: His Personal Letters, 1928–1945* (New York: Duell, Sloan and Pearce, 1950), 1:450–51.

Europe to Asia. A long-simmering dispute between Italy and Ethiopia provided the occasion for the first of the neutrality statutes enacted between 1935 and 1939. As Mussolini blustered against the Ethiopians and prepared to avenge the humiliating Italian defeat at Adowa four decades earlier, Europe seemed to teeter in early 1935 on the brink of a general war. These were "hair-trigger times," Roosevelt wrote in March, worse even than the fateful summer of 1914, "because at that time there was economic and social stability."[9] While Europeans trembled at the prospect of imminent war, Americans demonstrated for perpetual peace. On April 6, the eighteenth anniversary of American entry into the Great War, fifty thousand veterans staged a "march for peace" in Washington, D.C. They laid commemorative wreaths on the graves of three of the fifty representatives who had voted against the declaration of war in 1917. Three days later some 175,000 college students mounted a one-hour "strike for peace" on campuses across the country. They demanded the abolition of Reserve Officer Training Corps (ROTC) programs and called for "schools, not battleships." One student leader warned that the strike was "a dress rehearsal of what students intended to do should war be declared."[10] On Capitol Hill, the House chamber reverberated with pacifist oratory. Representatives vied with one another to toughen the neutrality bill then making its way through the legislative mill. Roosevelt himself, to the surprise of Senator Nye, had endorsed neutrality legislation in a meeting with the Munitions Committee on March 19, just three days after Hitler's dramatic rearmament announcement at the Berlin Opera House.

The bill that finally emerged required the president, after proclaiming that a state of war existed between foreign states, to impose an embargo on the shipment of arms to *all* the belligerents. It also empowered the president to declare that American citizens traveled on belligerent vessels at their own risk. The statute was clearly precipitated out of the political atmosphere created by what one senator called "that fool munitions committee."[11] It sought to avoid the perceived mistakes of Woodrow Wilson by removing the possibility that either the economic or the emotional provocations of 1914–17 could be repeated—a clear case of fighting, or trying not to fight, the last war. In effect, the statute formally

9. Nixon, *Franklin D. Roosevelt and Foreign Affairs*, 2:437.
10. Dallek, 101.
11. Pittman used the term in a telephone conversation with presidential assistant Stephen T. Early on August 19. Nixon, *Franklin D. Roosevelt and Foreign Affairs*, 2: 608.

renounced certain "neutral rights," even with their rather substantial attendant economic benefits, as the price the United States was willing to pay for peace.

Roosevelt would have preferred a slightly different bill, one that would have given him the discretionary authority to impose an arms embargo selectively, against an aggressor nation, rather than automatically and indiscriminately applying it to all belligerents. But Senate Foreign Relations Committee chairman Key Pittman of Nevada warned him that he would be "licked as sure as hell" if he insisted on the right to designate the aggressor. With his epochal domestic reform program at risk of being filibustered to death by a showdown over neutrality legislation in that momentous summer of 1935, Roosevelt took Pittman's advice. He agreed to be shackled by the mandatory features of the law. "[T]he inflexible provisions might drag us into war instead of keeping us out," he warned while signing the bill on August 31, but signed it nonetheless, while telling reporters that it was "entirely satisfactory" and would in any event expire in six months, when Congress reconvened in February 1936.[12]

On October 3, 1935, just weeks after Roosevelt signed the Neutrality Act, Mussolini's troops at last crossed from Italian Somalia in the Horn of Africa into the parched mountains of Ethiopia. The infantry were preceded by bombers that blasted mud-hut villages and strafed defenseless horsemen. The widely publicized boast of Mussolini's son that he exulted in the "magnificent sport" of watching his victims blow up like "a budding rose unfolding" helped to clinch American sympathy for the hapless Ethiopians and their diminutive emperor, Haile Selassie. But moral sympathy did not mean material support. The League of Nations voted on October 10 to take collective action against Italian aggression. When the league appeared ready to embargo oil shipments to Italy, a move that would have stopped Mussolini's war machine in its tracks, the league's Coordination Committee inquired if nonmember states would cooperate in the embargo. The United States, then the producer of more than half the world's oil, was the key to this strategy. But Roosevelt demurred. Oil was not among the "arms, ammunition or implements of war" enumerated in the Neutrality Act's list of goods to be embargoed. Putting it on the list, and applying the embargo to only one of the belligerents, would require a presidential initiative that would have violated the letter as well as the spirit of the statute that Roosevelt

12. Nixon, *Franklin D. Roosevelt and Foreign Affairs,* 2:632–33, 623.

had just signed. Moreover, Roosevelt appreciated that any semblance of cooperation with the diplomats in Geneva would expose him to attack by isolationists as the pliant creature of the league. In the current American political climate, that charge was anathema. "I'm walking a tight rope," Roosevelt confided to Democratic Party chairman Jim Farley; "I realize the seriousness of this from an international as well as a domestic point of view."[13] Alignment with the league might help to halt Mussolini, but it would almost certainly defeat Roosevelt's hope of wringing more discretionary authority out of the Congress when the Neutrality Act came up for revision in February 1936. What was more, such action might hand the isolationists a sword with which they could slash at Roosevelt in the next year's presidential election. Under the circumstances, Roosevelt contented himself with announcing a "moral embargo" on the shipment of oil and other raw materials to Italy. The moral embargo, not surprisingly, proved to be a thinner-than-paper barrier. American shipments of oil to Italy, as well as of copper, scrap iron, and other critical raw materials, nearly tripled in the following months.

The United States thus posed no significant obstacle to *Il Duce's* imperial ambitions in Africa. But whether American cooperation would have sufficiently braced the league and stopped the Italian invasion is dubious. In any apportionment of responsibility for the subjugation of Ethiopia, the Europeans must shoulder most of the blame. London and Paris, still traumatized by the memories of the Great War and inordinately fearful of "losing" Mussolini to Hitler, muffled their protests. They never did impose the oil embargo. They also conspicuously refrained from closing the Suez Canal, which at a stroke would have marooned Mussolini's troops in Ethiopia and doomed his military adventure to failure. In December 1935 the British and French governments even briefly endorsed an agreement between Sir Samuel Hoare and Pierre Laval, their respective foreign ministers, that handed over most of Ethiopia to Mussolini. The public outcry in Britain against this cynical ploy forced its retraction, as well as Hoare's resignation. But in Rome and Berlin, the fact that the Hoare-Laval deal had been advanced at all confirmed the weakness of the democracies. In the United States, the deal deepened the contempt that many Americans, including Roosevelt, felt for European diplomats. "I am not profoundly impressed with European ideology," Roosevelt's ambassador to Turkey wrote archly. "I

13. James Farley, *Jim Farley's Story: The Roosevelt Years* (New York: Whittlesey House, 1948), 55–56.

feel just the way you do," Roosevelt replied. "What a commentary on world ethics these past weeks have shown." At tea in the White House with the visiting archbishop of York, Roosevelt went out of his way to say that his disgust with the "attempt on the part of Great Britain and France to dismember Ethiopia" had snuffed out any inclination on his part to cooperate with the league. The Hoare-Laval scheme, Roosevelt told the clergyman, was simply "outrageous."[14] The Italians completed their conquest of Ethiopia in May, without significant further remonstrance from the league or its member states. Soon thereafter Mussolini withdrew from the impotent league. On November 1, 1936, the Rome-Berlin Axis agreement was announced. Three weeks later, Germany and Japan signed the Anti-Comintern Pact.

The crisis in barren and remote Ethiopia was a turning point. The inability of the powers to stop Mussolini's war of aggression, Winston Churchill later reflected, "played a part in leading to an infinitely more terrible war. Mussolini's bluff succeeded, and an important spectator drew far-reaching conclusions from the fact. Hitler had long resolved on war for German aggrandizement. He now formed a view of Great Britain's degeneracy which was only to be changed too late for peace and too late for him. In Japan, also, there were pensive spectators. . . . [I]t was a grievous deed to recoil. . . . Unless [the British] were prepared to back words and gestures by action, it might have been better to keep out of it all, like the United States, and let things rip and see what happened."[15]

Letting things rip and seeing what happened served as a fair description of American foreign policy for much of the rest of the 1930s. Congress extended the Neutrality Act for fourteen additional months in February 1936, without acceding to Roosevelt's requested revision allowing greater presidential discretion. The new law even added prohibitions on loans or credits to nations at war, a largely redundant feature given the strictures of the 1934 Johnson Act, but a provision that reminded the world of America's determination to wash its hands of whatever mischief the dictators might be plotting.

THE ETHIOPIAN EPISODE had exposed for all who cared to notice both the dithering of the European democracies and the studied irrelevance of the United States in the face of an international crisis.

---

14. Nixon, *Franklin D. Roosevelt and Foreign Affairs*, 3:112, 130; Ickes Diary 1:484.
15. Churchill 1:177, 183.

The road now lay wide open to further aggressions. In January 1936 Japan walked out of the London Naval Conference that was trying to sustain the British-American-Japanese ship-tonnage ratios of 5:5:3 that had been agreed in the naval limitation treaties of 1922 and 1930. The Imperial Japanese Navy began laying keels for a modern battle fleet designed to turn the western Pacific into a Japanese lake. Hitler proceeded with his own rearmament program and militarized the Rhineland in March.

On July 17, 1936, the European scene grew still more ominous. General Francisco Franco raised a Spanish army revolt in Morocco, crossed to Cadiz, and inflamed Spain in a bloody civil war that was to endure for three years. Franco sought by force of arms to reverse the electoral victory of the left-leaning republican government that had come to power in Madrid just months earlier, following riotous clashes between Spanish fascists and leftists. Both sides soon appealed for aid to their ideological sympathizers abroad: the republicans to Stalin in Moscow and to the newly elected Popular Front government of Léon Blum in Paris; Franco and the fascists to Berlin and Rome. Hitler and Mussolini responded readily, sending airplanes and pilots and, later, tens of thousands of infantrymen. Stalin sent tanks and aircraft and military "advisers," though Russia's distance from the Iberian peninsula seriously hampered his ability to supply the republicans. But Blum's government in Paris, though well positioned to help and drawn by political affinity toward the republicans, succumbed to pressure from the ever-cautious British and in the end declined to send any aid at all. Instead, Blum joined with London in a Nonintervention Committee that sought to "localize" the Spanish conflict by embargoing arms shipments to both sides. International law recognized that in the event of internal rebellion neutral states had a right to supply a legitimate government such as the republican regime in Madrid, but London and Paris were clearly willing to give up that right. They would sacrifice a sister republic rather than risk a wider war. While the democracies stood fastidiously aside, the conflict in Spain developed into what the American ambassador to Madrid, Claude Bowers, correctly called "a foreign war of the Fascist Powers against the Government of Spain."[16]

Most Americans could not have cared less. A Gallup poll in January 1937 found that two-thirds of the American public had no opinion about

16. Dallek, 140.

the events in Spain.[17] With only one dissenting vote, on January 6 Congress passed the third of the neutrality laws. It took the form of a joint resolution explicitly extending the arms embargo, originally drafted with international conflicts in mind, to the civil war in Spain. Roosevelt offered no objection. Poised to launch his campaign for Supreme Court reform, he was in no mood to borrow additional trouble over a distant squabble about which the American public cared little. As with the nonintervention formula embraced by London and Paris, the resolution's practical effect was to deny the republicans the means to defend themselves, while the dictators in Rome and Berlin continued to send supplies to Franco.

Not all Americans shared in the general apathy about Spain. The republican government's aggressively anticlerical policies had badly upset the Roman Catholic hierarchy, which therefore generally favored Roosevelt's course of action — or inaction. On the political left, some impassioned idealists saw Spain as the arena in which the great moral confrontation between fascism and democracy was being fought. Several thousand young Americans traveled to France with passports stamped "not valid for travel in Spain," then slipped over the Pyrenees and shouldered arms alongside their republican comrades. In February 1937 the Abraham Lincoln Battalion, an ill-trained and ill-used force of some 450 American volunteers, was recklessly thrown into battle in the Jarama Valley near Madrid, where 120 died and another 175 were wounded. For many on the left, the Spanish Civil War was the unhealing wound in the heart, the occasion when the cause of justice was betrayed not only by the cowardice of the democracies but also by the cynical callousness of the Communists who controlled much of the republican military effort. The spirit of despair and the sense of looming disaster that the war bred among many were later well captured in Ernest Hemingway's novel about the conflict, *For Whom the Bell Tolls* (1940).

With substantial German and Italian help, Franco overcame the last of the republican opposition in early 1939. Britain and France quickly recognized his government. So did Roosevelt, though with evident distaste. His government's Spanish policy had been "a grave mistake," he conceded to his cabinet, a recognition that came too late to do any good. Republican Spain, he said, should have been allowed to buy arms to "fight for her life against Franco — to fight for her life and for the

17. George H. Gallup, *The Gallup Poll: Public Opinion, 1935–1971* (New York: Random House, 1972), 1:49.

lives of some of the rest of us well," Roosevelt added, "as events will very likely prove."[18]

THE NEUTRALITY LAW OF 1935, renewed for fourteen months in February 1936, was due to expire on May 1, 1937. Given the increasingly unsettled state of the world, Congress in 1937 resolved to enact "permanent" neutrality legislation. Roosevelt still preferred to have a degree of flexibility, but in the midst of his bitter confrontation with the Congress over Court reform and with the country convulsed by controversy over the sit-down strikes, he was in no position to impose his will. Nor was the Congress, where the charge of "dictatorship" was being leveled at Roosevelt's Court proposal and at his executive reorganization bill, in any mood to expand the scope of presidential authority. The Neutrality Act of 1937, the fourth of the neutrality laws, reaffirmed the mandatory ban on arms and loans to countries at war, as well as to disputants in civil wars (with an exception for Latin America, where the United States clearly wished to persist in its traditional policy of upholding legitimate regimes). It toughened the sanctions against American passengers on belligerent vessels by making such travel illegal. The question of selling "nonmilitary" commodities like oil and copper to belligerent states, even when they were clearly the aggressors, remained vexed. As they had demonstrated during the Ethiopian crisis, American businesses were reluctant to give up such lucrative commercial opportunities. On the other hand, isolationists were determined not to walk again down the path that had led to war in 1917, when German U-boat attacks on American ships, and the alleged desire to protect American loans, had apparently made war inevitable. The result was a compromise, known as "cash-and-carry." It stipulated that shipments to belligerents of raw materials and other items not explicitly military in nature might be permitted, but only if the buyers paid in cash and carried the goods away from American ports in their own ships. This provision was limited to two years.

The new statute accurately reflected the anti-internationalist American mood. It also dictated the formal, statutory framework within which Franklin Roosevelt would be compelled to conduct American foreign

18. Dallek, 180. Roosevelt did for a time conspire in covert shipments of materials through France to the Madrid regime, acting through his brother-in-law G. Hall Roosevelt. The scheme collapsed when the French government definitively sealed the French-Spanish border in mid-1938. See Frank Freidel, *Franklin D. Roosevelt: A Rendezvous with Destiny* (Boston: Little, Brown, 1990), 271–72.

policy for the remainder of the decade. With stout legal thread, Congress had spun a straitjacket that rendered the United States effectively powerless in the face of the global conflagration that was about to explode.

With Mussolini now in possession of Ethiopia, Hitler entrenched in the Rhineland, Franco advancing in Spain, and the Americans formally proclaiming their "permanent" neutrality, Japan lit the next match. A minor clash between Chinese and Japanese troops at the Marco Polo Bridge near Peking (Beijing) touched off full-scale war between Japan and China in July 1937. Japan was by then spoiling for the fight. Japanese units soon landed at Shanghai, entered the teeming valley of the Yangtze, and headed for the Nationalist Chinese capital at Nanking (Nanjing), which fell on December 12. For the next several weeks, Japanese troops rampaged through the city and its surroundings. In an orgy of rape, bayoneting, beheading, and machine-gunning, they murdered as many as two hundred thousand Chinese, providing a harrowing preview of the atrocities that modern warfare could visit upon civilians. What came to be known as the Rape of Nanking left Americans agape at its cruel ferocity but little inclined to do anything meaningful to halt the Japanese juggernaut.[19]

As in Ethiopia, American sympathies instinctively went out to the victims of aggression. A Gallup poll in late 1937 found 59 percent of respondents favored China, while only 1 percent backed Japan.[20] Thanks to generations of American missionaries in China and to the editorial interest of Henry Luce, the son of one of those missionary couples and the publisher of *Time* magazine, China had long enjoyed an emotional hold on American hearts. That grip was tightened in the 1930s by the runaway popularity of Pearl Buck's sentimental novel *The Good Earth*. By uncanny coincidence, Buck's book was first published in 1931, just as the Japanese were seizing Manchuria. Some two million Americans had read it by 1937, when the film version appeared at virtually the same time the Sino-Japanese war broke out. The film was seen by more than twenty million Americans. "In a way that never could have been accomplished by event or propaganda," Harold Isaacs later wrote, Buck's touching portrayal of a Chinese peasant and his wife "humanized the people who became Japan's principal victims. . . . Although it did not

---

19. See Iris Chang, *The Rape of Nanking: The Forgotten Holocaust of World War II* (New York: Basic, 1997).
20. Cantril, 1081–82.

deal with the war itself, it gave the quality of individual recognition to the figure of the heroic Chinese peasant or peasant-soldier who offered battle to the Japanese against such great odds."[21]

But as in Ethiopia and Spain, moral sympathy did not easily translate into material support. Even when Japanese pilots sank the United States gunboat *Panay* during the assault on Nanking on December 12, the American response was muted. In an earlier era, the sinking of the *Panay* would have raised an unshirted outcry for retaliation. Japanese warplanes bombed the *Panay* in broad daylight as it lay at anchor in the confined waters of the Yangtze channel. Two eighteen-by-fourteen-foot American flags were conspicuously laid out on its top deck. Film shot by a Universal Newsreel cameraman who happened to be aboard clearly belied the Japanese claim that the pilots had been flying too high to discern the ship's markings. The film also showed Japanese planes repeatedly strafing escaping survivors. By the time the *Panay* settled to the bottom of the turbid Yangtze, two people aboard had been killed and some thirty wounded. But the *Panay* was not to be a modern *Maine*, nor even a *Lusitania*. Its sinking produced a cry for withdrawal, not for war. "We should learn that it is about time for us to mind our own business," Texas Democrat Maury Maverick declared in the House.[22] A few months later, a *Fortune* magazine poll showed that a majority of Americans favored getting the United States out of China altogether.[23] When Japan tendered an official apology for the *Panay* incident and paid some $2 million in reparations, the crisis swiftly blew over.

The principal residue of the *Panay* affair in Congress was not more bellicosity but more pacifism. The incident boosted Indiana Democratic representative Louis Ludlow's three-year-old campaign for a constitutional amendment requiring a national referendum for a declaration of war (except in case of invasion). A transparently silly idea, accurately likened by critics to convening a town meeting before authorizing the fire department to put out a blaze, Ludlow's amendment enjoyed strong

21. Harold R. Isaacs, *Scratches on Our Minds: American Images of China and India* (New York: John Day, 1958), 157.
22. An explosion aboard the U.S. battleship *Maine* in Havana harbor led to war with Spain in 1898. The German sinking of the British liner *Lusitania*, with heavy loss of American lives, produced a loud clamor for war against Germany in 1915. Maverick quoted in Manny T. Koginos, *The* Panay *Incident: Prelude to War* (Lafayette, Ind.: Purdue University Studies, 1967), 46.
23. *Fortune* 17 (April 1938): 109.

public support. A Gallup poll in October 1937 registered 73 percent approval.[24] In the wake of the *Panay*, Ludlow's proposal now also found remarkable favor in the House. Its supporters, many of them Democrats, overrode the House leadership and forced the Ludlow bill out of committee on a discharge petition. After strenuous administration lobbying against it, when it came to a vote on January 10, 1938, the Ludlow Amendment was defeated only by the narrow margin of 209 to 188. The episode provided a dramatic demonstration of the formidable strength of the isolationist bloc on Capitol Hill, even in the wake of an inflammatory act such as the wanton sinking of a U.S. Navy vessel.

At the other end of Pennsylvania Avenue, Franklin Roosevelt took what consolation he could from the final Ludlow vote, but an effective policy to cope with the situation in Asia—not to mention Europe—continued to elude him. Strictly speaking, the recently passed Neutrality Act of 1937 did not apply to the Asian crisis, since neither China nor Japan bothered to issue a formal declaration of war. Roosevelt came under isolationist pressure to invoke the act by declaring that a state of war existed, but he refrained. He knew that applying the neutrality legislation's arms embargo would preclude any possibility of American military aid to China, while the cash-and-carry provisions would still allow Japan to provision itself from American sources. In the event, both sides sought supplies in the United States, though Japan, as a relatively wealthy sea power, was by far the larger purchaser of American goods—especially scrap iron and petroleum products. AMERICAN SCRAP IRON PLAYS GRIM ROLE IN FAR EASTERN WAR, the *Washington Post* headlined on August 29, 1937. JAPANESE RAIN DEATH WITH ONE-TIME JUNK. GUNS, BOMBS, AND BATTLESHIPS, ALL MADE FROM OLD METAL, SHIPPED ACROSS PACIFIC IN GROWING AMOUNTS.[25] Neutrality Act or not, pro-Chinese sympathies or not, the effect of American policy in practice was to provide assistance for Japan's war of aggression against China.

For more than four years, the Sino-Japanese "incident" dragged on, while Roosevelt struggled to find ways to aid China and restrain Japan without antagonizing the isolationists at home or further provoking what Secretary Hull called the "wild, runaway, half-insane men" in Tokyo.[26] "Minds were ransacked," the historian Herbert Feis later wrote, "in a

24. Gallup, *Gallup Poll* 1:71.
25. Herbert Feis, *The Road to Pearl Harbor* (New York: Atheneum, 1963), 11.
26. Dallek, 154.

search for effective ways of causing Japan to desist, while staying uninvolved. Unhappily none was found."[27]

When Neville Chamberlain, who some six months earlier had succeeded Stanley Baldwin as British prime minister, raised the question in December 1937 of impressing Japan with a joint U.S.-British demonstration of naval force at Britain's great Asian base of Singapore, Roosevelt squelched the idea outright. "[T]hough the President and the Secretary of State . . . had been doing their best to bring American public opinion to realize the situation," the British ambassador in Washington informed his government, "they were not yet in a position to adopt any measures of the kind now contemplated." The opportunity for showing a united Anglo-American naval front in the Pacific was lost. Chamberlain expressed his disappointment to his sister: "[I]t is always best and safest," he said, "to count on *nothing* from the Americans but words."[28]

The Americans offered ample confirmation for Chamberlain's lack of confidence in them. On October 5, 1937, Roosevelt spoke what sounded like some big words indeed. The occasion took on added drama because the president chose to speak them in Chicago, a city fed a daily diet of Roosevelt-be-damned invective by Robert R. McCormick's militantly anti–New Deal and obstreperously isolationist *Chicago Tribune*, on whose masthead McCormick emblazoned the motto THE WORLD'S GREATEST NEWSPAPER. McCormick himself, at six feet four inches, with a fifty-two-inch chest and thirty-six-inch arms, was a bullying giant of a man and a towering colossus of provincialism. He routinely pronounced upon the world in steely aphorisms that left no room for nuance or argument. The *Tribune*, with its million daily readers, and its sister radio station, whose call letters, of course, were WGN, provided McCormick with incomparable pulpits from which he trumpeted his trademark prejudices across what he called "Chicagoland"—the five-state region that stretched from Iowa to Ohio, the very heartland of American isolationism. Little escaped the copious arc of McCormick's rage. Wisconsin he declared "the nuttiest state in the Union, next to California." The northeastern United States swarmed with the "dodging, obligation-shifting idle rich . . . diluted in their Americanism by other hordes of immigrants." Foreign service officers were "he-debutantes, dead from the

27. Feis, *Road to Pearl Harbor*, 10.
28. William R. Rock, *Chamberlain and Roosevelt: British Foreign Policy and the United States, 1937–1940* (Columbus: Ohio State University Press, 1988), 54, 48.

neck up." Herbert Hoover was "the greatest state socialist in history." Franklin Roosevelt was "a Communist." McCormick, said the British ambassador to Washington, was "stubborn, slow-thinking, and bellicose." He was also enormously influential. By speaking in Chicago, Roosevelt was apparently bearding the isolationist lion in his den.[29]

"The epidemic of world lawlessness is spreading," the president declared, in what seemed to be a stout-hearted challenge to the insular prejudices of his hostile Chicagoland listeners. "When an epidemic of physical disease starts to spread, the community approves and joins in a quarantine of the patients in order to protect the health of the community against the spread of the disease. . . . War is a contagion, whether it be declared or undeclared," he said, in obvious reference to the Sino-Japanese conflict. "There is no escape," he warned his presumably skeptical audience, "through mere isolation or neutrality. . . . There must be positive endeavors to preserve peace."[30]

The "Quarantine Speech" seemed to throw down the gauntlet to the isolationists and to herald a presidential crusade to educate the American public about the necessity for international engagement. What could Roosevelt's words mean, other than a pledge of American support for a concerted plan of action against Japan? British foreign secretary Anthony Eden, who, like Winston Churchill later, made Anglo-American cooperation the supreme goal of British policy, pressed Washington for an "exact interpretation" of Roosevelt's remarks. What "positive endeavors" did the president have in mind? What, Eden wanted particularly to know, would be the American position at the nine-power meeting soon to convene in Brussels to discuss the Asian crisis? Eden advised that only a policy of active assistance to China combined with economic pressure on Japan would be effective. Was this what Roosevelt intended?

Roosevelt gave his answer through his emissary to the Brussels talks, Norman Davis. Tell the British "that there is such a thing as public opinion in the United States," the president instructed Davis. He could not afford, Roosevelt continued, "to be made, in popular opinion at home, a tail to the British kite." In London, the *Times* opined that in the last analysis "Mr. Roosevelt was defining an attitude and not a program." That description proved prophetic. The Brussels conference con-

29. Richard Norton Smith, *The Colonel: The Life and Legend of Robert R. McCormick* (Boston: Houghton Mifflin, 1997), passim.
30. PPA (1937), 406–11.

vened and adjourned in November without consequence. The last reasonable chance to settle the Sino-Japanese war by joint international action was lost. The Americans, Neville Chamberlain's sister acidly remarked, were "hardly a people to go tiger shooting with."[31]

"It's a terrible thing," Roosevelt allegedly said about the failure of his Chicago speech to make a dent in isolationist opinion, "to look over your shoulder when you are trying to lead — and find no one there." But Roosevelt's leadership in this case was neither valiant nor consistent. Though he had chosen to challenge McCormick and the isolationists in their midwestern heartland, he had shown no stomach for the kind of prolonged confrontation with them that might change the course of American foreign policy. Indeed, he scarcely waited to gauge the reaction to his Chicago address before he started backpedaling. Just one day after the Quarantine Speech, reporters asked Roosevelt if he cared to amplify his remarks. No, Roosevelt blandly replied. The reporters pressed on: Was there any conflict between what he was suggesting and the Neutrality Act? No, said Roosevelt. Did his speech imply economic sanctions against Japan? they persisted. No, insisted Roosevelt. "Look," he said, " 'sanctions' is a terrible word to use. They are out of the window." If not sanctions, then what program might the administration follow? "We are looking for a program," Roosevelt explained to the astonished journalists. "It might be a stronger neutrality."[32]

European leaders, particularly in Britain, were meanwhile looking over their own shoulders and wondering where Roosevelt was. The American president's failure to follow up on the Quarantine Speech made an especially deep imprint on Neville Chamberlain, desperately searching for his own program to cope with the dictators. Britain needed partners if it were to make an effective stand against the aggressors. No reliable partnership seemed likely with the Americans. "The main lesson to be drawn" from the failed Brussels Conference, Chamberlain told his cabinet on the day the conference adjourned, "was the difficulty of securing effective cooperation from the United States of America."

Those events at the end of 1937 formed the backdrop for the reception that Chamberlain gave in January 1938 to Roosevelt's plan for an international peace conference, an episode that excited hot argument at

---

31. Dallek, 152; Davis 4:133–36; Rock, *Chamberlain and Roosevelt*, 43.
32. Samuel I. Rosenman, *Working with Roosevelt* (New York: Harper and Brothers, 1952), 167; PPA (1937), 414ff.

the time and has remained controversial ever since. The president proposed to invite to Washington representatives from a number of small states—Sweden, the Netherlands, Belgium, Switzerland, Hungary, Yugoslavia, Turkey, and three Latin American countries to be designated—to discuss rules of international behavior, arms reduction, access to raw materials, and the rights and obligations of neutrals. After coming to such agreement as they could, these states would then promulgate their conclusions to other nations. What, the president inquired, did the British government think of this proposal?

Chamberlain, not without cause, instinctively judged the plan to be "rather preposterous . . . fantastic & likely to excite the derision of Germany and Italy." It scarcely helped that Roosevelt accompanied his inquiry with a reminder that the United States still held fast to its "traditional policy of freedom from political involvement."

Despite Chamberlain's skepticism, the British cabinet met in several urgent sessions in mid-January to consider Roosevelt's idea. The atmosphere at Whitehall was tense, because the American proposal exacerbated a tortuous policy debate already in progress. Chamberlain in December had received from his chiefs of staff a secret report emphasizing that in light of Britain's military unpreparedness, it was imperative to pursue "any political or international action that can be taken to reduce the numbers of our potential enemies and to gain the support of potential allies." But in Chamberlain's eyes, what the chiefs described as a two-pronged strategy—splitting the German-Italian-Japanese alliance *and* finding new allies—boiled down in practice to a painful choice: detaching one of the adversaries from the others by judicious concessions *or* securing a dependable ally, namely, the United States. This choice became a bitter point of contention between Prime Minister Chamberlain and Foreign Secretary Eden. Chamberlain believed in the first strategy, one that fitted the usual definitions of diplomacy as the search for workable concessions and compromises to avoid open conflict, but a strategy that was soon to be called and forever to be damned as appeasement. Eden believed in the latter, emphasizing the crucial importance of the United States. Roosevelt's overture, Eden argued, might provide the opportunity at last to clasp hands with the Americans and begin to knit a thick cable of opposition to Hitler's ambitions. Chamberlain countered that while the potential strength of the United States was undeniable, "he would be a rash man who based his calculations on help from that quarter." The "isolationists" were "so strong

& so vocal," Chamberlain noted in his diary, that the United States could not be "depended upon for help if [Britain] should get into trouble."[33]

Chamberlain's eventual reply to Roosevelt's inquiry, said Sumner Welles, was "like a douche of cold water."[34] He showed no enthusiasm whatsoever for Roosevelt's proposal. What was more, the British prime minister revealed that he was about to embark on a policy designed to wean Mussolini away from his attachment to Hitler by extending de jure recognition to the Italian occupation of Ethiopia. By feeding Mussolini at least some of what he wanted, Italy might be sated, and Britain would have one less adversary to worry about. Appeasing Mussolini, Chamberlain calculated, would pacify the Mediterranean, guarantee the Suez gateway to India and beyond, and give Britain a freer hand to deal with the Germans in Europe and the Japanese in the Pacific. Chamberlain extended recognition on April 16. Roosevelt, cautioned even by his trusted adviser Bullitt that his plan for a Washington conference would strike the rest of the world as "an escape from reality," allowed the idea to die.[35]

Chamberlain's rejection of Roosevelt's initiative and his embarkation on the road of appeasement thereafter have earned him almost universal condemnation in the history books. Eden, who had earlier proclaimed his willingness to trek from Australia to Alaska to secure American cooperation, resigned as foreign secretary in protest against Chamberlain's decision. Winston Churchill, who would in time stake his entire strategy for British survival on American aid, later wrote of these weeks that "no event could have been more likely to stave off, or even prevent, war than the arrival of the United States in the circle of European hates and fears. To Britain it was almost a matter of life and death. . . . We must regard its rejection . . . as the loss of the last frail chance to save the world from tyranny otherwise than by war. That Mr Chamberlain . . .

33. Rock, *Chamberlain and Roosevelt*, 45–70.
34. Sumner Welles, *Seven Decisions That Shaped History* (New York: Harper and Brothers, 1951), 27.
35. Bullitt to Roosevelt, January 20, 1938. Bullitt thought little more of the scheme than did Chamberlain: "It would be as if in the palmiest days of Al Capone you had summoned a national conference of psychoanalysts to Washington to discuss the psychological causes of crime." Orville H. Bullitt, ed., *For the President: Personal and Secret, Correspondence between Franklin D. Roosevelt and William C. Bullitt* (Boston: Houghton Mifflin, 1972), 252.

wave[d] away the proffered hand stretched out across the Atlantic leaves one, even at this date, breathless with amazement."[36]

But had Roosevelt's proffered hand held anything useful? The thinking behind his conference scheme was unorthodox to the point of being fanciful. How could a proclamation of principles by a gaggle of small and peripheral states realistically be expected to rein in Hitler's headlong plunge toward war? Even with American endorsement, would such a statement have meaningfully signaled "the arrival of the United States in the circle of European hates and fears"? And if one remembers how often the American hand had been proffered, only to be withdrawn, as at London in June of 1933, or Chicago in October of 1937 — or how often it had not been extended at all, as in Ethiopia in 1935, or in Spain in 1936, or in the Pacific in late 1937 — one's breath returns, and with it a measure of sympathy for Chamberlain's predicament. Judging Roosevelt to be "a dangerous and unreliable horse in any team," keenly aware of how inadequately armed and politically isolated Britain was, Chamberlain concluded, not altogether unreasonably, that he had little choice but to seek some kind of accommodation with the dictators. Appeasement had begun.[37]

But Hitler was unappeasable. Unknown to Chamberlain, *der Führer* had already announced to his senior political and military officials that "Germany's problems could be solved only by means of force."[38] In a systematic four-hour-long exposition on November 5, 1937, in the *Reichkanzlei* in Berlin, Hitler flabbergasted his subordinates with the boldness of his war plans and his detailed analysis of the probable reactions of the other powers. With methodical confidence, he predicted the responses of Britain, France, Russia, Italy, Japan, Czechoslovakia, Belgium, Holland, and Spain. Significantly, the United States figured not at all in his thinking. War must come within the next few years, he declared, perhaps as early as 1938, and no later than 1945, after which Germany would no longer enjoy uncontested superiority in armaments. First steps would be the annexation of Austria and the elimination of Czechoslovakia. Officers who questioned the wisdom of these policies were dismissed. In March 1938 Hitler executed the first part of this plan, absorbing Austria into the *Reich*.

36. Churchill 1:254–55.
37. Freidel, *Rendezvous with Destiny*, 260.
38. Shirer, *Rise and Fall of the Third Reich*, 306

WITHIN DAYS of the German takeover of Austria, reports came out of Vienna about atrocities inflicted on Jews. The reports made for grim news, but by this date they were hardly surprising. Nazi racial policies were no secret by 1938. Hitler's manic tract of 1924, *Mein Kampf*, had conjured the fantastic web connecting "international Jewry" and the "Bolshevik conspiracy" that became a central tenet of Nazi ideology. Immediately on taking power in 1933, the Nazis had begun to persecute Germany's half-million Jews. They organized boycotts of Jewish enterprises, and Nazi toughs openly abused Jews in the streets. The Nuremberg Laws in 1935 tightened the noose further, barring Jews from broad categories of employment and severely limiting their civil rights. When the Germans swallowed Austria, they imposed all those restrictions on an additional 190,000 Jews. Faced with pauperization and worse, thousands of Jews tried to flee from the spreading Nazi menace. As German troops fanned out through Vienna, three thousand Jews per day applied for visas to enter the United States. By then the American consulate in Stuttgart, Germany, authorized to issue 850 visas per month, had a backlog of some 110,000 visa applications.

The American press had long reported on Nazi mistreatment of the Jews. Dorothy Thompson's many articles and two books, *Refugees: Anarchy or Organization* (1938) and *Let the Record Speak* (1940), constituted an especially searing indictment of both Nazi misanthropy and American apathy. The virulence of Nazi anti-Semitism had no comparably malignant American analogue, not even the septic rantings of Father Coughlin against the "Jew Deal" or the scattered outpourings of a handful of other hatemongers. American society in the 1930s was not free of the stain of anti-Semitism, but most Americans, Jews and gentiles alike, generally condemned Nazi racialism. Yet while both private organizations and government officials in the United States expressed dismay over the plight of the Jews in German Europe, few understood as yet the genocidal implications of Nazi racial ideology, and fewer still found the means to make effective protest. As happened so often in this melancholy decade, sympathy stopped short of concrete support.

Sometimes sympathy stopped short even of symbolic gestures. When Hitler ruled that no German Jews would be allowed to compete in the 1936 Berlin Olympic Games, several American athletic organizations proposed to boycott the event. For nearly a year, debate over participation in the Berlin Games raged through the American sporting community, in the process educating broad sectors of the public about the depths of Nazi brutality. But in a formal vote in December 1935, the Amateur Athletic Union, America's credentialing sport bureaucracy, narrowly rejected a boycott resolution. The American Olympic Committee, headed by Avery Brundage, encouraged American athletes to participate, lending some aura of legitimacy to the Hitler regime and wasting an opportunity, as the *Washington Post* commented, "to let the Germans see what the outside world thinks of their present rulers."[39]

Divisions among America's nearly five million Jews also impeded the search for useful tools to mitigate Hitler's racial policies. Both the degree of the impending danger and the method for dealing with it were questions that excited sharp disagreement and exacerbated old tensions among American Jews. The American Jewish Congress, led by Rabbi Stephen Wise, represented the masses of East European Jews who had flooded into the United States beginning in the 1890s. Often socialist in politics, orthodox in religion, and Zionist in aspiration, they organized drives in the 1930s to boycott German goods, staged mock trials of Hitler in several American cities, and pressed for relaxation of the American immigration laws so that more Jewish refugees could enter the United States. But the American Jewish Committee, an older and more moderate body, displayed the measured caution typical of its mostly German-Jewish constituents. Their American roots reached well back into the nineteenth century. Conservative in politics, adherents of reform Judaism if they practiced their faith at all, and generally well assimilated, they opposed both the boycotts of German goods and the mock trials. They were also temperate in their advocacy of policies that would bring large numbers of additional Jews to the United States—particularly

---

39. Deborah E. Lipstadt, *Beyond Belief: The American Press and the Coming of the Holocaust, 1933–1945* (New York: Free Press, 1986), 78. See also Arthur D. Morse, *While Six Million Died: A Chronicle of American Apathy* (New York: Random House, 1968), 172ff. As it happened, the African-American athlete Jesse Owens spectacularly discredited Hitler's theories of Aryan superiority at the Games when he won four gold medals in the track and field events: for the 100-and 200-meter dashes, the broad jump, and as a member of the 400-meter relay team. Hitler conspicuously refused to shake Owens's hand, or the hands of the three other black American athletes who won gold medals: Archie Williams, John Woodruff, and Cornelius Johnson. In another highly controversial episode, the American track coach changed the lineup of the 400-meter relay team, preventing two athletes from running—Sam Stoller and Marty Glickman, the only two members of the American Olympic track team who did not get a chance to compete, and the only two Jews. See Marty Glickman, *The Fastest Kid on the Block* (Syracuse: Syracuse University Press, 1996).

more East European Jews of the sort whose recent arrival had already proved unsettling to the old German-Jewish establishment. Walter Lippmann, perhaps America's foremost political commentator of the time, exemplified German-Jewish sentiments when he wrote that "the rich and vulgar and pretentious Jews of our big American cities are . . . the real fountain of anti-Semitism." The American Jewish Committee was even wary of proposals to unify the American Jewish community in a single organization, for fear of validating anti-Semitic propaganda about the Jewish "state within a state" and touching off a barrage of reprisals. Most important, few Jews of any persuasion, in America or elsewhere, including Germany, and few gentiles either, for that matter, as yet fully comprehended the force of the systematic onslaught against Jewry that Hitler would soon unleash. How, indeed, could it be comprehended? Generations later, the moral enormity of what came to be known as the Holocaust still quivered painfully in the world's conscience, a ghastly icon of humankind's capacity for fiendishness. In the meantime, as one Jewish commentator said in 1933, "What else can we do but scream? Jewish power lies in screaming . . . we are powerless."[40]

Bounded by ignorance as much as by apathy and anti-Semitism, Roosevelt's government felt itself to be legally powerless as well. "The German authorities are treating the Jews shamefully," Roosevelt remarked as early as 1933 when he sent William E. Dodd off as his ambassador to Germany. "[W]hatever we can do to moderate the general persecution by unofficial and personal influence ought to be done," the president instructed Dodd. "But this is also not a governmental affair," Roosevelt cautioned. "We can do nothing except for American citizens."[41]

But if the United States could do little for the Jews inside Germany, could it not open its doors to those trying to leave? After the announcement of the Nuremberg Laws in September 1935, New York governor Herbert Lehman, a prominent Jewish leader and usually a close political ally of Roosevelt's, proposed doubling the number of German Jews annually admitted to the United States, from twenty-five hundred to five thousand—"almost a negligible number," Lehman noted. Roosevelt responded sympathetically that consular officials had been instructed to

40. Ronald Steel, *Walter Lippmann and the American Century* (Boston: Atlantic–Little, Brown, 1980), 192; A. Ginsburg, "Our Protest," *Forwards*, April 1, 1933, 8, quoted in Henry L. Feingold, *The Politics of Rescue: The Roosevelt Administration and the Holocaust, 1938–1945* (New York: Holocaust Library, 1970), 13.
41. William E. Dodd Jr. and Martha Dodd, eds., *Ambassador Dodd's Diary, 1933–1938* (New York: Harcourt, Brace), 1941, 5.

offer "the most considerate attention and the most generous and favorable treatment possible under the laws of the country."[42] The numbers of German-Jewish immigrants grew modestly but nevertheless stayed "negligible." Immigrants of whatever faith from Germany totaled some six thousand in 1936 and eleven thousand in 1937.[43]

Why did the potential refugee flood remain such a trickle? The explanation lay partly in the intersection of Nazi policy with those "laws of the country" about which Roosevelt reminded Lehman. Nazi regulations severely restricted the sum of money that a departing Jew could take out of Germany. As early as 1934 the amount had been reduced to the equivalent of four dollars, essentially pauperizing any Jew trying to leave the country. In the United States, immigration statutes forbade issuing visas to persons "likely to become a public charge." Herbert Hoover in 1930 had ordered consular officials to apply that clause strictly, as the American unemployment crisis worsened. Under the circumstances, few systematically impoverished German Jews could qualify for visas.

Congressman Emmanuel Celler, who represented a heavily Jewish Brooklyn district, criticized the State Department's consular service for having "a heart beat muffled in protocol," but even after the Roosevelt administration liberalized visa application rules in 1935, the problem remained.[44] Its deeper roots lay not in the technical minutiae of consular procedures but in pervasive anti-immigration attitudes and especially in the very nature of the 1924 National Origins Act that governed all American immigration policy. That law constrained Roosevelt's refugee policy as tightly as the Neutrality Acts constrained his diplomacy. It imposed a ceiling of 150,000 immigrants per year, with quotas allocated by country on the basis of a given nationality's proportional presence in the census of 1920. Quotas were not fungible among countries—that is, an unfilled quota from Britain could not be assigned to Germany. Moreover, the 1924 law took no official cognizance of "refugees" and thus made no provision for offering asylum to the victims of religious or political persecution. No American contribution to solving the looming catastrophe of European Jewry was possible without revising those nu-

---

42. Lehman to FDR, November 1, 1935, in Nixon, *Franklin D. Roosevelt and Foreign Affairs*, 3:51, 65.
43. *HSUS*, 105. By one estimate, 102,000 Jews made their way into the United States between 1933 and 1938. See I.C.B. Dear, ed., *The Oxford Companion to the Second World War* (New York: Oxford University Press, 1995), 366.
44. *New York Times*, February 4, 1938, 12.

merical restrictions or, at a minimum, amending the law to exempt from the quota system persons who were designated as refugees. Neither development seemed likely. The country had effectively barred its doors to further mass immigration in 1924. It was in no mood now, in the midst of the Great Depression, to change its mind and take the barriers down. Persistent unemployment, which had sharply worsened in the "Roosevelt Recession" of 1937–38, posed an iron obstacle to opening the gates to more immigrants of whatever description. And in the world of 1938, advertising asylum for refugees might invite a massive Jewish exodus — or expulsion — from countries like Poland and Romania, which were all too eager to declare their many millions of Jews "surplus" and be rid of them forever. Polish officials even hinted that they would happily arrange pogroms to demonstrate the urgency of their own Jewish "problem."

Shortly after the Austrian *Anschluss*, Roosevelt stretched the limits of presidential authority when he ordered the merging of the German and Austrian quotas and the special expediting of Jewish visa applications, measures that permitted some fifty thousand Jews to escape Nazi hands in the next two years. He was under no illusions about the political risks. "[T]he narrow isolationists," he confided to Governor Lehman's brother, might "use this move of ours for purely partisan objectives." At the same time, the president also called for an international conference to discuss the impending refugee crisis, while carefully noting in his invitation that "no country would be expected to receive greater number of emigrants than is permitted by its existing legislation." Lehman wired Roosevelt a single word: "Splendid!" Roosevelt answered: "I only wish I could do more." In the event, his initiative amounted to pathetically little indeed.[45]

The refugee conference convened in the French resort town of Evian-les-Bains on the shores of Lake Geneva on July 6, 1938. Even before the delegates gathered, the prospects for helpful action seemed dim. Switzerland, wary of provoking its powerful German neighbor, had asked not to be the host country. Britain agreed to attend only on condition that Palestine, the historic Jewish homeland and long the object of Zionist agitation, not be discussed. Delegates from several Latin American states, regarded by many as possible sites for Jewish resettlement, rejected all such ideas outright. "[E]lements that might endanger the solid basis of our Ibero-American personality [and] our Catholic

45. Feingold, *Politics of Rescue*, 3, 23, 24.

tradition," declared a Peruvian newspaper, would find no welcome in Latin America. Nazi propaganda chief Josef Goebbels announced that "if there is any country that believes it has not enough Jews, I shall gladly turn over to it all our Jews." Hitler declared himself "ready to put all these criminals at the disposal of these countries, for all I care, even on luxury ships." The conference ended with a whimper. Its only tangible outcome was the creation of an Intergovernmental Committee on Political Refugees (IGC). Based in London and headed by an American, Roosevelt's fellow Grotonian George Rublee, the IGC spent the next several months floundering through byzantine negotiations with the Nazis to ransom German Jews for badly-needed foreign exchange.[46]

The problem of where to relocate Germany's Jews proved an insuperable obstacle. A Nazi newspaper commented: "We are saying openly that we do not want the Jews while the democracies keep on claiming that they are willing to receive them — and then leave the guests out in the cold! Aren't we savages better men after all?" The *Richmond* (Virginia) *News Leader* was a lonely voice criticizing the Roosevelt administration for resting "content with friendly gestures and kind words. . . . [S]ome of us," the paper concluded, "are a bit ashamed of our country." But a *Fortune* survey in 1938 showed that fewer than 5 percent of Americans were willing to raise immigration quotas to accommodate refugees. More than two-thirds agreed that "with conditions as they are we should try to keep them out." The Depression had helped to reinforce an isolationism of the spirit, a kind of moral numbness, that checked American humanitarianism as tightly as political isolationism straitjacketed American diplomacy.[47]

A new eruption of Nazi ferocity soon highlighted the tragic futility of Evian. On November 7, 1938, a seventeen-year-old German Jewish refugee shot and killed a German diplomat in Paris. Reprisals followed swiftly. Hitler's government organized a pogrom that exploded all over Germany on the night of November 9–10. Nazi thugs looted Jewish homes, burned synagogues, smashed Jewish shops, killed dozens of Jews, and arrested some twenty thousand Jewish "criminals." Known as *Kristallnacht* (Crystal Night) for the pools of broken glass that littered German streets on the morning of November 10, this officially sanctioned orgy of pillage and arson and murder had not yet drained the

46. Morse, *While Six Million Died*, 344, 228, 204.
47. Morse, *While Six Million Died*, 288; *Richmond News Leader* quoted in Lipstadt, *Beyond Belief*, 96.

vials of Nazi wrath. Two days later, with lunatic cruelty, the German government announced that the property damage incurred during *Kristallnacht* would be repaired by levying a huge "atonement fine" on the Jews. At the same time, it ordered all Jewish retail establishments closed. A few weeks later, the government announced the confiscation of all Jewish assets.

These barbarities outraged many Americans. Protesters threatened to bomb the German consulate in New York City, to which Mayor Fiorello La Guardia responded by assigning an all-Jewish police detail to guard duty. Herbert Hoover, Al Smith, Alf Landon, Harold Ickes, and other prominent figures went on the radio to denounce Germany's night of horror. The German ambassador in Washington cabled Berlin that *Kristallnacht* had raised a hurricane of condemnation in the American press, which "is without exception incensed against Germany[.] . . . [E]ven the respectable patriotic circles which were thoroughly . . . anti-Semitic in their outlook also begin to turn away from us."

Roosevelt took what action he could. He recalled American ambassador Hugh Wilson from Berlin, for "consultation," and Wilson never returned to his post. (The Germans reciprocated by withdrawing their ambassador from Washington.) Again pushing the limits of presidential authority, Roosevelt by executive order extended the visas of some fifteen thousand German and Austrian nationals already resident in the United States, including the great emigré physicist Albert Einstein. Speaking to reporters five days after *Kristallnacht*, the president pointedly declared that he "could scarcely believe that such things could occur in a twentieth-century civilization." Yet the familiar political restraints stayed Roosevelt's hand from more forceful measures. "Would you recommend a relaxation of our immigration restrictions so that the Jewish refugees could be received in the this country?" a reporter asked. "That is not in contemplation," Roosevelt shot back. "We have the quota system."[48]

Kristallnacht prompted several attempts to modify the quota system. Congressman Samuel Dickstein sponsored legislation that would "mortgage" future quotas, accelerating Jewish immigration by allowing refugees in 1938 and 1939 to anticipate the quotas for 1940 and 1941. New York's Senator Robert Wagner and Representative Edith Nourse Rogers of Massachusetts introduced a bill to allow twenty thousand German children under fourteen years of age to enter outside the quota limits. Emmanuel Celler tried to secure an exemption from quota restrictions

48. PPA (1938), 597–98.

for racial or religious refugees. All these proposals were in vain. Two-thirds of respondents told pollsters in January 1939 that they opposed the Wagner-Rogers bill to admit young children. (When the question was modified to specify admitting Jewish children, opposition dropped slightly, to 61 percent). In mid-1939, the *Fortune* poll asked: "If you were a member of Congress, would you vote yes or no on a bill to open the doors . . . to a larger number of European refugees?" Eighty-five per-cent of Protestants, 84 percent of Catholics, and an astonishing 25.8 percent of Jews answered no. Americans might extend their hearts to Hitler's victims, but not their hands.[49]

Events in mid-1939 starkly demonstrated the potentially lethal impli-cations of the quota system. As Europe's Jews scrambled for the rapidly closing exits from Hitler's *Reich*, a cynical business developed in the sale of visas, especially by grasping Latin American officials, with the con-nivance of the Gestapo. Hundreds of desperate refugees clutching visas of dubious legality crammed aboard ships, seeking safe haven in the New World. Many of the destination countries simply refused to honor the visas. Mexico, Paraguay, Argentina, and Costa Rica all denied entry to arriving Jews bearing documents sold by corrupt officials at their European consulates.

One such ship, the Hamburg-American line's SS *St. Louis*, steamed into Havana harbor on May 27 with 930 Jewish refugees. The Cuban government refused to allow the passengers to disembark and was deaf to arguments that most of the exiles had no intention of remaining permanently in Cuba. More than seven hundred of them were on wait-ing lists for future admission to the United States. They planned to stay in Cuba only until their quota-allocation numbers came up—a date that might have come sooner rather than later had Samuel Dickstein's legislation passed.

American Jewish philanthropies offered to post a bond guaranteeing eventual transit to the United States, but the Cuban government was not interested. Aboard ship, two passengers committed suicide. Captain Gustav Schroeder reprovisioned his vessel and sailed away from Havana. He made half speed up the eastern seaboard of the United States while negotiators begged the State Department to allow the refugees to dis-embark at an American port. For days Schroeder steamed within sight of Miami and other American cities, shadowed by a Coast Guard cutter with orders to pick up and return to the *St. Louis* any passengers who

49. Cantril, 1081, 1150.

went overboard. On June 6 Schroeder finally set his return course eastward, bearing his doomed cargo back to Europe. He managed to distribute his passengers among Britain, France, Holland, and Belgium —
all but Britain destined to fall under German rule within two years,
exposing the Jews once more to Nazi reprisals. The bright lights of
Miami remained a sorrowing memory of how tantalizingly close they
had come to sanctuary — and salvation.

HAVING SHOWN THEMSELVES incapable of finding a solution to
the refugee crisis, the Western powers proved equally unable to resist
Hitler's next provocation. Even while he was ingesting Austria in the
spring and summer of 1938, Hitler was preparing to chew up Czechoslovakia. The feeble response of the democracies to his intensifying war
against the Jews only deepened his contempt for his adversaries. Now
was the time to strike. In Czechoslovakia in 1938 he meant to have the
war he had described to his senior officials in November 1937. "It is my
unalterable decision," he declared in a directive dated May 30, 1938,
"to smash Czechoslovakia by military action in the near future."[50] The
pretext would be the alleged desire of the more than three million ethnic Germans in Czechoslovakia's Sudeten region to join their kinsmen
in the *Reich*. Hitler, proclaiming loftily the Versailles principle of self-
determination, demanded the annexation of the Sudetenland to Germany.

The Western powers proved willing to sacrifice the Sudetenland on
the altar of appeasement. The Czech crisis, said Britain's Chamberlain,
was "a quarrel in a faraway country between people of whom we know
nothing."[51] In two meetings in southern Germany with Hitler in mid-
September 1938, the first at Berchtesgaden and the second at Bad Go-
desberg, Chamberlain agreed to a gradual, orderly transfer of the Sudetenland to German control. But Hitler greeted every concession with
a fresh escalation of his demands. He meant to have war, not simply
the Sudetenland. With each passing September day, the war he wanted
seemed more imminent. France called up half a million reservists. The
British began digging air-raid shelters in London parks. Then, in a last,
fateful concession, Chamberlain agreed to attend a third conference on
September 29 in Munich, where the fate of Czechoslovakia was to be
infamously sealed. Franklin Roosevelt sent Chamberlain a two-word ca-

50. Shirer, *Rise and Fall of the Third Reich*, 365.
51. Rock, *Chamberlain and Roosevelt*, 122.

ble: "Good man." Meanwhile the American president assured Hitler: "The Government of the United States has no political involvements in Europe, and will assume no obligations in the conduct of the present negotiations."[52]

Like a thunderclap, the settlement agreed at Munich, providing for the immediate incorporation of the Sudetenland into Germany, reverberated around the world. In the streets of London, huge crowds cheered Chamberlain's announcement that the Munich agreement meant "peace in our time." On the floor of the Mother of Parliaments, in contrast, Winston Churchill called the Munich accord "a total and unmitigated defeat. . . . This is only the beginning of the reckoning," Churchill warned. "This is only the first sip, the first foretaste of a bitter cup which will be proffered to us year by year unless . . . we arise again and take our stand for freedom as in the olden time."[53] In Prague, the stunned Czechs stared at the maps of their shrunken state, shorn by a few pen-strokes of its rich Sudeten province. They had looked on as helpless witnesses at their own national evisceration. In Berlin, Hitler felt cheated. He had sought war, but had to settle for the Sudetenland. The next time, he would not be so easily bought off.

In Washington, Roosevelt likened the British and French diplomats who had signed the Munich agreement to Judas Iscariot. As the Czech crisis unfolded, Roosevelt had dunned the Europeans with private and public appeals for peace, and he had given the British ambassador vague assurances about American participation in a possible blockade of Germany. But in fact the American president was a powerless spectator at Munich, a weak and resourceless leader of an unarmed, economically wounded, and diplomatically isolated country. He, and America, had counted for nothing in the scales of diplomacy—or worse than nothing if one agrees with the thinking of Eden and Churchill that some greater American presence would have stiffened the spines of the European democracies. For all Roosevelt's moral dudgeon at Chamberlain's supposedly craven behavior, the sobering truth was, in the words of the historian Robert Divine, that "American isolation had become the handmaiden of European appeasement."[54]

Yet the Munich crisis marked a turning point of sorts in American

52. *FRUS* (1938) 1:688, 685.
53. Roosevelt quoted in Ickes Diary 2:469. Churchill remarks from Churchill 326–28.
54. Robert A. Divine, *The Reluctant Belligerent: American Entry into World War II* (New York: John Wiley and Sons, 1965), 55.

foreign policy, or at least in Franklin Roosevelt's sense of urgency about America's role in the world. "We had to [overhaul] our entire preparedness [program] in the light of Munich," Roosevelt later reflected. Three items commanded the highest priority. "First, place more emphasis on the North-South American axis; Second, Revise the neutrality act; Third, use our diplomatic influence to hamper the aggressors."[55]

Some of these objectives proved more easily achievable than others. A United States delegation to the Conference of American States in December 1938 persuaded the other American republics to sign the Declaration of Lima, pledging consultation in case war threatened anywhere in the hemisphere. The Declaration represented one of the first tangible diplomatic rewards of the vaunted Good Neighbor policy and constituted a halting, tentative step toward hemispheric solidarity.

Revising the Neutrality Act proved to be a tougher proposition. Roosevelt at this moment, following the disastrous 1938 elections, had less influence on Capitol Hill than he had in the conference hall at Lima. Nevertheless, in his State of the Union message of January 4, 1939, Roosevelt opened the campaign for revision of the neutrality law. He now took up the task he had so long postponed: seriously educating the American people about the international menace that was looming. In a thinly veiled reference to Nazi persecution of the Jews, Roosevelt began his address with a warning that "storms from abroad directly challenge . . . religion. . . . There comes a time in the affairs of men when they must prepare to defend not their homes alone but the tenets of faith and humanity on which their churches, their governments and their very civilization are founded. The defense of religion, of democracy, and of good faith among nations is all the same fight. To save one we must now make up our minds to save all." The world had grown small, Roosevelt said, "and weapons of attack so swift that no nation can be safe." There were "many methods short of war," the president declared, that might protect America and allow the United States to use its influence for good. First among those methods was revision of the neutrality statutes. "We have learned that when we deliberately try to legislate neutrality, our neutrality laws may operate unevenly and unfairly—may actually give aid to an aggressor and deny it to the victim," the president said. "[W]e ought not to let that happen anymore."[56] But before he could begin to specify just how he proposed to prevent that

55. Freidel, *Rendezvous with Destiny*, 306.
56. PPA (1939), 1–4.

from happening, the movement for neutrality revision was badly derailed.

Less than three weeks after Roosevelt's address, an experimental American military aircraft crashed in southern California. A badly injured French officer was hauled from the wreckage, igniting a furor about alleged secret presidential agreements to sell arms in violation of the neutrality law. Roosevelt met with members of the Senate Military Affairs Committee on January 31 to quell the uproar. Yes, he said, the French were negotiating to buy American military aircraft, and they were prepared to pay in cash. This was good for American business and workers, perfectly legal, and a boost for the cause of democracy into the bargain. Then Roosevelt went on, taking the senators into his confidence. He spoke candidly about his growing conviction that America must become engaged in Europe. "So soon as one nation dominates Europe, that nation will be able to turn to the world sphere," he explained. The nations on Germany's periphery, France not least of all, were in imminent danger of subjugation, as the examples of Austria and Czechoslovakia attested. "That is why the safety of the Rhine frontier does necessarily interest us," Roosevelt said.

Despite assurances of confidentiality, a source Roosevelt identified as "some boob" leaked to the press that the president had said that "America's frontier is on the Rhine." A storm of imprecations against Roosevelt's dangerous internationalism forced him to back away from neutrality revision. The country's "foreign policy has not changed and it is not going to change," Roosevelt declared to reporters a few days later, in flat contradiction of his State of the Union remarks. An American diplomat reported to Roosevelt the mounting feeling in Europe that the president's swift and unseemly retreat from neutrality revision after the "frontier-on-the-Rhine" flap gave Hitler and Mussolini "reason to believe now that American public opinion will not tolerate any other than an attitude of the most rigid neutrality. . . . [Y]our disavowal has cleared the atmosphere concerning America as far as the dictators are concerned."[57]

At 6:00 A.M. on March 15, 1939, Hitler completed his conquest of Czechoslovakia. Armed columns poured over the Czech border and swiftly overran the rump state that was the sad and short-lived legacy of

57. Eamon de Valera quoted by John Cudahy in Cudahy to Roosevelt, February 9, 1939, in Donald B. Schewe, ed., *Franklin D. Roosevelt and Foreign Affairs* (New York: Clearwater, 1969), 13:273. Roosevelt's remark to reporters is in the same volume, 243.

Munich. By nightfall Hitler motored triumphantly through Prague, just as he had through Vienna almost a year to the day earlier.

The extinction of what was left of Czechoslovakia also extinguished Chamberlain's policy of appeasement. Within weeks his government reversed the course to which it had hewed for nearly two years and announced that Britain was now committed to the defense of Poland, Hitler's next presumptive target. That British pledge armed the mechanism that at Hitler's next probe would pitch the world into war.

Czechoslovakia's death throes also revived Roosevelt's campaign to overhaul the neutrality laws. "If Germany invades a country and declares war," Roosevelt remarked on the day following the Czech invasion, "we'll be on the side of Hitler by invoking the act." Repeal of the arms embargo was desperately needed, said Roosevelt, though he was willing to leave in place the cash-and-carry provisions of the 1937 statute, which expired just a few weeks hence, in May 1939. Roosevelt appreciated that cash-and-carry worked all wrong in the Pacific, where it favored Japan, but it worked just fine in the Atlantic, where the wealthy sea powers, Britain and France, would be its chief beneficiaries.

The administration exerted itself vigorously for repeal of the arms embargo. Secretary of State Hull lobbied indefatigably for the change. The coming clash in Europe, Hull warned, would not be just "another goddam piddling dispute over a boundary line." It would be a global struggle against barbarism. The existing legislation, Hull said, amounted to "a wretched little bobtailed, sawed-off domestic statute" that cut across the grain of international law and diplomatic practice. It "conferred a gratuitous benefit on the probable aggressors." To leave it in place, said Hull, was "just plain chuckle-headed."[58]

Even Hull's impassioned pleading proved inadequate to the task. By a narrow margin, the House voted to retain the arms embargo on June 29. In the Senate, Roosevelt faced a special problem. On the Foreign Relations Committee sat two senators, Walter F. George of Georgia and Guy M. Gillette of Iowa, whose unquenchable enmity Roosevelt had earned when he campaigned against them in the Democratic primary elections in 1938. Added to the already considerable weight of the isolationists, George's and Gillette's disinclination to do Roosevelt's bidding doomed his request to defeat. At a bitterly argumentative meeting at the

58. Joseph Alsop and Robert Kintner, *American White Paper: The Story of American Diplomacy and the Second World War* (New York: Simon and Schuster, 1940), 41–42.

White House on the evening of July 18, 1939, Roosevelt and Hull pleaded with Senate leaders to let neutrality revision move through the upper chamber. "Our decision may well affect not only the people of our own country, but also the peoples of the world," said Roosevelt. Rehearsing his failed efforts to make American influence felt, he told the senators: "I've fired my last shot. I think I ought to have another round in my belt." His listeners were unmoved. Archisolationist Senator Borah so adamantly and arrogantly dismissed Hull's warnings of imminent war that the courtly secretary of state was struck dumb with indignation. Vice-President Garner polled the participants as to whether the Senate would approve the administration's proposal. All answered no. "Well Captain," Garner said summarily to Roosevelt, "[y]ou haven't got the votes, and that's all there is to it."[59]

ROOSEVELT FARED no better with the third of his initiatives in early 1939, his effort to "use our diplomatic influence to hamper the aggressors." On April 15, 1939, he sent a widely publicized message to Hitler and Mussolini. He listed thirty-one countries by name and asked for an assurance that neither Italy nor Germany would attack them for at least ten years. Mussolini saw no reason to respond to the leader of a government restricted to "its customary role of distant spectator, " and he scoffed at the message as attributable to Roosevelt's "infantile paralysis." Nazi Air Marshal Hermann Goering sneered that "Roosevelt was suffering from an incipient mental disease." Hitler, too, at first refused to reply to "so contemptible a creature" as Roosevelt.[60]

Soon, however, der Führer saw in Roosevelt's appeal an opportunity to make political hay. The German Foreign Office on April 17 put two questions to all the states enumerated by Roosevelt, with the conspicuous exceptions of Poland, Russia, Britain, and France: Did they feel threatened by Germany? Had they authorized Roosevelt to make his proposal? Armed with their replies, Hitler rose before the Reichstag on April 28 to make what the American journalist William Shirer later described as "the most brilliant oration he ever gave, certainly the greatest this writer ever heard from him. For sheer eloquence, craftiness, irony, sarcasm and hypocrisy, it reached a new level that he was never to approach again." For more than two hours, Hitler heaped scorn on the American president. He also rehearsed many of the arguments of

59. Alsop and Kintner, *American White Paper*, 44–46.
60. Shirer, *Rise and Fall of the Third Reich*, 470; L & G, *Challenge*, 87.

the American isolationists: that Germany aimed only to redress the grievances of the Versailles Treaty, that it was the British who could not be
trusted, that Western propaganda organs painted an unfair picture of
Germany, that he alone was ever ready to come to the negotiating table.

Hitler then turned to Roosevelt's specific questions. As Shirer remembered it:

> The paunchy deputies rocked with raucous laughter as the Fuehrer
> uttered with increasing effect his seemingly endless ridicule of the
> American President. One by one he took up the points of Roosevelt's
> telegram, paused, almost smiled, and then, like a schoolmaster, uttered
> in a low voice one word, "Answer" — and gave it.

Who had scuttled the League of Nations by refusing to join? Hitler
asked. America. And how had the United States come to dominate
North America in the first place? Not at the conference table, said Hitler. Any who doubted it should look to the history of the Sioux tribes.
Gratuitously, Hitler added that he had no intention of invading the
United States. Then came the peroration, at once a sharp personal jab
at Roosevelt and a reinforcing stroke for the American isolationists:

> Mr. Roosevelt! I once took over a State which was faced by complete
> ruin. . . . I have conquered chaos in Germany, re-established order and
> enormously increased production [the implied contrast with America's
> continuing Depression stung], developed traffic, caused mighty roads
> to be built and canals to be dug, called into being gigantic new fac-
> tories. . . . I have succeeded in finding useful work once more for the
> whole of the seven million unemployed. . . .
>
> You, Mr. Roosevelt, have a much easier task in comparison. You
> became President of the United States in 1933 when I became Chan-
> cellor of the Reich. From the very outset you stepped to the head of
> one of the largest and wealthiest States in the world. . . . Conditions
> prevailing in your country are on such a large scale that you can find
> time and leisure to give your attention to universal problems. . . . [M]y
> world, Mr. Roosevelt . . . , is unfortunately much smaller.

For sheer gall, guile, and hoodwinking, the speech was a black masterpiece. American isolationists crowed that this was Roosevelt's reward
for his gratuitous meddling. "Roosevelt put his chin out, and he got a
resounding whack on it," said California's Republican senator Hiram
Johnson, to which Senator Nye laconically added: "He asked for it."
The speech also vividly demonstrated Hitler's utter contempt for the

United States. A few weeks later he declared: "Because of its neutrality laws, America is not dangerous to us."[61]

The drums of war now quickened their tempo. Mussolini invaded Albania on April 9. Britain introduced conscription a few days later. Hitler made menacing gestures toward Poland. Britain and France sent diplomatic missions to Moscow, seeking to enlist Russia in the anti-Nazi front. That effort yielded no result. Stalin had viewed the Munich agreement as a betrayal of Russian security interests, and especially at this late date he had no confidence in British or French determination to stand firm against Hitler.

The breakdown of Soviet-Western talks gave Hitler one more opportunity to exploit the divisions among his potential foes. In an announcement that stunned the world, not least the antifascist left in the Western countries, Berlin and Moscow revealed on August 23 that they had signed a nonaggression pact. Secret protocols provided for the partition of Poland and for Soviet absorption of the Baltic states, as well as territory in Finland and Bessarabia. The die was now all but cast.

The death watch for Europe began. In Washington, one State Department official likened the atmosphere to "the feeling of sitting in a house where somebody is dying upstairs." Adolf Berle noted in his diary: "I have a horrible feeling of seeing the breaking of a civilization dying even before its actual death." The last days of August, Berle wrote, "produced almost exactly the sensation you might have waiting for a jury to bring in a verdict on the life or death of about ten million people."[62]

At 3:00 A.M. on September 1, 1939, the telephone rang at Franklin Roosevelt's bedside in the White House. It was Ambassador Bullitt calling from Paris. "Mr. President," Bullitt said, "several German divisions are deep in Polish territory. . . . There are reports of bombers over the city of Warsaw."

"Well, Bill," Roosevelt replied, "it has come at last. God help us all!"[63]

---

61. Johnson to Hiram W. Johnson Jr., April 29, 1939, in Robert E. Burke, ed., *The Diary Letters of Hiram Johnson* (New York: Garland, 1983), 7:n.p. Nye quoted in L & G, *Challenge*, 89. Hitler quoted in Weinberg, "Hitler's Image of the United States," 1013.

62. Dallek, 197; Beatrice Bishop Berle and Travis Beal Jacobs, *Navigating the Rapids: From the Papers of Adolf A. Berle* (New York: Harcourt Brace Jovanovich, 1973), 244, 245.

63. Alsop and Kintner, *American White Paper*, 1.

14

The Agony of Neutrality

*If we are conquered, all will be enslaved and the United States will be
left single-handed to guard the rights of man.*
— First Lord of the Admiralty Winston S. Churchill,
November 12, 1939

While German dive-bombers screamed over Warsaw and German tanks
crunched through the stubble of the freshly harvested grain fields in
Polish Silesia, the world briefly and vainly held its breath, hoping against
all reason that the war that had come at last might somehow not really
have come at all. But on September 3, after Hitler had rejected British
and French ultimata to withdraw from Poland, futile hope expired.
Seated in front of a microphone at Number 10 Downing Street, Chamberlain announced to his countrymen on September 3 that "this country
is at war with Germany." In Paris, Prime Minister Edouard Daladier
followed suit a few hours later.[1]

In Washington, Roosevelt's first public pronouncement on September
1 was a plea to all the belligerents to refrain from "bombardment from
the air of civilian populations or of unfortified cities"—an appeal that
bespoke the terror of air power then obsessing every mind, and a declaration that eventually made for ironic reading in the light of the war's
nuclear climax at Hiroshima and Nagasaki nearly six years later. On the
evening of September 3, Roosevelt also took to the radio to deliver another of his now familiar Fireside Chats. "Until four-thirty o'clock this
morning I had hoped against hope that some miracle would prevent a
devastating war in Europe and bring to an end the invasion of Poland

1. James W. Gantenbein, ed., *Documentary Background of World War II* (New York:
Columbia University press, 1948), 409.

by Germany," the president said. Now that war had irreversibly come, Roosevelt announced, "[t]his nation will remain a neutral nation." But, Roosevelt emphatically added, "I cannot ask that every American remain neutral in thought as well. . . . Even a neutral cannot be asked to close his mind or close his conscience."[2]

The president's statement contrasted starkly with Woodrow Wilson's appeal at the outbreak of the Great War in 1914 that his countrymen should be "impartial in thought as well as in action." By late 1939 few could doubt where American sympathies lay. The mind and conscience of America were decidedly anti-Hitler. A Gallup poll in October found that 84 percent of respondents were pro-Ally and only 2 per cent pro-German. But as it had for half a decade of troubled peace, so now in wartime moral sympathy stopped well short of armed support. Though Roosevelt might have conceded, even encouraged, American alignment with Britain and France in his Fireside Chat, he also declared that "the United States will keep out of this war. . . . Let no man or woman," he said, "thoughtlessly or falsely talk of America sending its armies to European fields."[3]

Meeting with his cabinet on the afternoon of September 1, Roosevelt clung reflexively to the "methods-short-of-war" approach he had outlined some eight months earlier. Over and over he insisted, "We are not going in." When War Department planners proposed raising an army large enough to support a possible American Expeditionary Force in Europe, Roosevelt cut them off: "You can base your calculations on an army of 750,000 men [the army's strength was then about 175,000], for whatever happens, we won't send troops abroad. We need only think of defending this hemisphere."[4]

Roosevelt needed also, of course, to think about how, exactly, he might supply Britain and France with the tools to fight Hitler. Munitioning the democracies was the heart of the methods-short-of-war policy. Finding the means to do so was the major foreign policy problem with which Roosevelt had been wrestling since his unsuccessful attempt

2. *PPA* (1939), 454; Russell D. Buhite and David W. Levy, eds., *FDR's Fireside Chats* (Norman: University of Oklahoma Press, 1992), 148–51. Buhite and Levy use transcriptions of Roosevelt's actual radio addresses, which sometimes differ slightly from the official versions published in *PPA*.

3. *Public Opinion Quarterly* 4 (March 1940):102; Buhite and Levy, *Fireside Chats*, 149.

4. Joseph Alsop and Robert Kintner, *American White Paper: The Story of American Diplomacy and the Second World War* (New York: Simon and Schuster, 1940), 64–65.

to modify the first Neutrality Act in 1935. The president had long since made his own general intentions clear to European leaders, though he was notably less candid with the American people, and for that matter aggravatingly unrealistic in his signals to the Europeans. In late 1938, in the wake of the Munich debacle, he had privately promised Prime Minister Chamberlain that "in the event of war with the dictators he had the industrial resources of the American nation behind him," though he knew as well as Chamberlain did that formidable legal and political obstacles stood athwart any serious effort to make good on that promise. At about the same time, meeting secretly at Hyde Park with the French financier Jean Monnet, Roosevelt sketched an elaborate, even fantastic, scheme for evading the American Neutrality Act: in the event of war, Roosevelt suggested, American factories at Detroit and Niagara Falls would ship motors and airframes across the border to Canada, where they could be assembled and flown away as combat-fitted aircraft. Implementing that ploy would violate the presidential oath to enforce the law and would almost surely expose Roosevelt to demands by isolationists for his impeachment. That Roosevelt even entertained such notions is a measure of the desperation to which isolationist strictures had driven him.

The same obsession with air power that informed Roosevelt's plea to avoid city-bombing had also guided much of the president's thinking about American strategy. It was said of Roosevelt that he played with the navy as another man might play with toy trains. He had served as assistant secretary of the navy, adorned his White House office with prints of historic naval vessels, and routinely commandeered navy ships for presidential "vacations" at sea. Yet for all his doting upon the navy, Roosevelt was if anything an even more enthusiastic advocate of the air arm. Air power — especially air power delivered to the European democracies from American factories — seemed the ideal instrument with which the historically isolationist and chronically depressed United States could implement the short-of-war strategy. Even more effectively than ships, wide-ranging airplanes could patrol the ocean vastness and keep the fighting far from the New World's shores. Deep-penetration bombing raids could strike much farther into the enemy heartland than even the biggest naval guns could reach. A few thousand bombers, flown by several thousand airmen, could inflict damage at many times the rate of a million-man ground force, and at a lower cost in human life. And building the bombing machines for a vast air fleet would invigorate the American economy, giving employment to countless workers.

Ever receptive to novelty, Roosevelt had easily succumbed to the seductive logic of aerial warfare. At the time of the Munich crisis he had mused that "pounding away at Germany from the air" would crack the morale of the German people. "This kind of war," Roosevelt claimed, "would cost less money, would mean comparatively few casualties, and would be more likely to succeed than a traditional war by land and sea."[5] At a momentous meeting with his military advisers at the White House on November 14, 1938, Roosevelt had laid out his extraordinarily ambitious plan to develop an American aircraft industry sufficient to equip the British and French and to maintain a ten-thousand-plane American air force. To him, the lesson of Chamberlain's humiliation at Munich was clear. As William Bullitt had tersely put it, "The moral is: If you have enough airplanes you don't have to go to Berchtesgaden." Roosevelt agreed. "Had we had this summer 5,000 planes and the capacity immediately to produce 10,000 per year, even though I might have had to ask Congress for authority to sell or lend them to the countries in Europe," said Roosevelt, "Hitler would not have dared to take the stand he did." Army Air Corps General H. H. "Hap" Arnold exulted at this presidential endorsement: "Airplanes—now—and lots of them!" was Arnold's summation of Roosevelt's position. "The President came straight out for air power. . . . [Expanded American ground forces] would not scare Hitler one blankety-blank-blank bit! What he wanted was airplanes."[6] Pursuant to that aim, Roosevelt asked Congress in January 1939 for a special appropriation of $300 million for aircraft construction. That request marked the decidedly modest origins of a rearmament program that would in time pour forth an avalanche of weaponry.

As the shooting war began, the full impact of that avalanche still lay well over the horizon of the future. Roosevelt's overtures to Chamberlain and Monnet in 1938, as well as his extravagant plans to expand the American aircraft industry, had come to little by late 1939. The president's clandestine offers of aid to Britain and France precluded any deterrent effect on Hitler, as the historian Donald Watt has acidly observed, for the simple reason that "deterrence and secrecy are largely incompatible notions."[7] What was more, Roosevelt's lavish ambitions for

5. Ickes Diary 2:469.
6. Orville H. Bullitt, ed., *For the President: Personal and Secret, Correspondence between Franklin D. Roosevelt and William C. Bullitt* (Boston: Houghton Mifflin, 1972), 288; Morgenthau Diary, 273; Arnold quoted in Michael S. Sherry, *The Rise of American Air Power: The Creation of Armageddon* (New Haven: Yale University Press, 1987), 80.
7. Donald Cameron Watt, *How War Came: The Immediate Origins of the Second World War, 1938–1939* (New York: Pantheon, 1989), 130.

the air corps flummoxed most American military leaders, with the conspicuous exception of Hap Arnold. They preferred a balanced force, its ground, sea, and air arms all proportionately developed and deployed in concert. "What are we going to do with fifteen thousand planes?" Army Chief of Staff Malin Craig angrily queried. They worried even more about the president's impatience to deliver planes to the Europeans, at a time when American forces were pathetically under strength. "Don't you think so, George?" Roosevelt asked chummily of Malin's deputy chief, General George C. Marshall, at the conclusion of the presidential pitch on November 14, 1938, for delivering airplanes to Europe. "I am sorry, Mr. President, but I don't agree at all," Marshall frostily replied. It was the last time Roosevelt ever addressed Marshall, a studiously formal man, by his first name.

George Marshall was in the habit of speaking bluntly to his superiors. As a young captain with the American Expeditionary Force in France in 1917, he had dared to correct General John J. Pershing in front of a group of fellow officers. Pershing responded by making Marshall his principal aide. But despite his anointing by the legendary Pershing, Marshall, in common with almost all officers in the interwar years, had languished in the missionless peacetime army, where promotion was slow and action rare. He remained a lieutenant colonel for eleven years. He uncomplainingly accepted a series of apparently dead-end assignments: with the tiny U.S. Army garrison in Tientsin, China; with the Illinois National Guard; and even with the Civilian Conservation Corps. Yet everywhere he made a consistent impression as an outstanding soldier. His directness, his keen analytic mind, his unadorned speech, and his granitic constancy evoked admiration that bordered on reverence. More than one of his commanding officers, answering the routine efficiency report question of whether they would like to have Marshall serve under them in battle, replied that they would prefer to serve under his command — the highest of soldierly compliments. Marshall was just shy of six feet tall, ramrod-straight, invariably proper, impeccably self-controlled, and determinedly soft-spoken. Most associates saw only fleeting glimpses of his potentially volcanic temper. "I cannot allow myself to get angry," he once told his wife; "that would be fatal." In 1938, at the age of fifty-eight, Marshall became the head of the War Plans Division, then deputy chief of staff under Malin. On the signal date of September 1, 1939, Roosevelt elevated him to army chief of staff. He was by then a shrewd, even ruthless judge of men. He proceeded to winnow the army's senescent officers corps to identify the leaders who could fight and win the next war. He also determined that he could not do his job properly if he allowed himself to be seduced by the fabled Rooseveltian charm. He reportedly made a solemn vow never to laugh at the president's jokes.[8]

Marshall's stony riposte to Roosevelt on November 14, 1938, began a protracted debate between the president and his service chiefs about the competing needs of the Allied and the United States armed forces for the still-limited output of American war materiel. Many factors conspired to keep that output small: the persistent belief that the conflict was far away and somebody else's business, or that it might yet be averted altogether; the hair-trigger sensitivity of congressional isolationists to anything that hinted at a more active American international role; and the constraints of traditional fiscal orthodoxy. All those considerations had long precluded any request on Roosevelt's part for substantial military and naval budgets. The total national defense appropriation in fiscal 1940 was just $1.3 billion, a 50 percent increase over 1939, but still only about one-seventh of the federal budget. In January 1940 Roosevelt asked for a small increase to $1.8 billion for the 1941 fiscal year, and Congress immediately proceeded to whittle away even at that modest sum. In any case, the Nye Committee's sensational accusations of World War I profiteering left many corporations gun-shy about accepting orders for armaments. The 1939 defense budget provided funding for just 250 B-17 "Flying Fortresses," designed in 1935 as the premier American long-range bomber, and the army placed orders for only seventy B-17s in fiscal 1940. Actual production lagged even further behind the president's grand vision of a mighty air fleet. Exactly fifty-two B-17s were available for service as late as May 1940.[9]

As for foreign purchases, despite Roosevelt's active encouragement, European orders for aircraft remained exceedingly modest in scale. The Allies were understandably skittish about becoming reliant on a source of critical supplies that would statutorily dry up the instant formal hostilities commenced. Looking toward a protracted war, and doubly debarred (by the Johnson debt-default law and the cash-and-carry provisions of the Neutrality Act) from seeking credit in the United States, they also hesitated to exhaust their precious dollar and gold reserves.

8. Eric Larrabee, *Commander in Chief: Franklin Delano Roosevelt, His Lieutenants, and Their War* (New York: Harper and Row, 1987), 96ff.
9. Sherry, *Rise of American Air Power*, 89; Mark Skinner Watson, *United States Army in World War II: Chief of Staff: Prewar Plans and Preparations* (Washington: Department of the Army, 1950), 305.

They worried too about the political implications of provoking an isolationist backlash if they appeared to be stretching the spirit of the Neutrality Act. By mid-1939 the French and British together had contracted for only about fifteen hundred aircraft.[10] As the war began, the United States was itself unarmed and was making only a piddling contribution to munitioning the European democracies. The result, said Undersecretary of State Sumner Welles, was a "nightmare of frustration." The government "had no means whatever," Welles explained, "short of war, to which American public opinion was overwhelmingly opposed, of diverting or checking the world cataclysm and the threat to the very survival of this country."[11] The short-of-war strategy, in other words, amounted in practice to not much of a strategy at all.

Exercising the scant discretion that the law permitted him, Roosevelt delayed official recognition of the European war until September 5, 1939, to permit Britain and France to clear some previously ordered supplies from American ports. Then he issued two Neutrality Proclamations, one, like Wilson's in 1914, in accordance with traditional international law, the other mandated by the Neutrality Act of 1937. The latter declaration clamped an iron-bound embargo on all "arms, ammunition, or implements of war," including "aircraft, unassembled, assembled or dismantled," as well as "propellers or air screws, fuselages, hulls, wings, tail units [and] aircraft engines." Now the Allies could not legally buy so much as a single cartridge in the United States, let alone vast swarms of combat aircraft.

From London, Ambassador Kennedy reported that British officials were "depressed beyond words" that the Neutrality Act had been invoked. From Paris, Bullitt wrote: "It is, of course, obvious that if the Neutrality Act remains in its present form, France and England will be defeated rapidly." Repealing the act now became Roosevelt's highest priority. "I am almost literally walking on eggs," Roosevelt wrote, "saying nothing, seeing nothing, and hearing nothing" as he tried to ease neutrality revision through the treacherous legislative process. On September 13, nearly two weeks after the fighting had erupted in Poland, and after delicate politicking with key legislators, he called for a special session of Congress to convene on September 21 to consider neutrality revision.[12]

10. Craven and Cate 6:302.
11. Sumner Welles, *The Time for Decision* (New York: Harper and Brothers, 1944), 148.
12. Kennedy quoted in Dallek, 200; Bullitt's remark is in Bullitt, *For the President*, 369; Roosevelt in Elliott Roosevelt, ed., *FDR: His Personal Letters, 1928–1945* (New York: Duell, Sloan and Pearce, 1950), 2:934.

Despite the president's measured caution, the announcement of a special congressional session instantly galvanized the champions of isolation. Senator Borah broadcast a lurid warning on September 14 that tampering with the neutrality law would surely lead to eventual American belligerency (a prediction that was to prove correct). On the following day, the celebrated aviator Charles Lindbergh made the first of several impassioned radio addresses against neutrality revision. "The destiny of this country does not call for our involvement in European wars," Lindbergh said. "One need only glance at a map to see where our true frontiers lie. What more could we ask than the Atlantic Ocean on the east and the Pacific on the west . . . ? An ocean is a formidable barrier, even for modern aircraft." Lindbergh, Father Charles Coughlin, and several isolationist senators filled the airwaves with denunciations of Roosevelt's impending request to amend the 1937 statute. In a matter of days, their campaign swamped congressional offices with more than a million antirevision telegrams, letters, and postcards.[13]

After six weeks of contentious debate, Congress at last sent a revised neutrality bill to the White House. Voting on the bill illustrated the momentous shifts in political geometry that had occurred since the glory days of the New Deal. In the Senate, most of Roosevelt's erstwhile progressive Republican allies on domestic policy deserted him. In the House, southern Democrats voted 110–8 in favor of revision, vividly highlighting the degree to which the president's foreign policies now depended not on the liberal coalition that had legislated the New Deal but on the traditionally conservative southern core of his party, which was largely hostile to further domestic reform.

Roosevelt signed the revised Neutrality Act on November 4, 1939. He beamed for the newsreel cameras as he affixed his name to the document and made a show of handing the ceremonial pens to the bill's congressional sponsors. Despite this presidential bravado, however, the new Neutrality Act represented at best only a partial victory for the

13. Charles A. Lindbergh, "Appeal to Isolationism," *Vital Speeches of the Day*, October 1, 1939, 751–52; Dallek, 200ff. Lindbergh, an attractive personality celebrated as the first man to fly solo across the Atlantic, was a particularly sharp thorn in Roosevelt's side. He had visited Germany several times in the 1930s and had been decorated by the German government in 1938, prompting Roosevelt to conclude that more than simple, home-grown isolationism motivated Lindbergh's crusade against neutrality revision. "If I should die tomorrow, I want you to know this," Roosevelt exploded to Secretary Morgenthau in May 1940: "I am absolutely convinced that Lindbergh is a Nazi." Frank Freidel, *Franklin D. Roosevelt: Rendezvous with Destiny* (Boston: Little, Brown, 1990), 323.

methods-short-of-war strategy. The act did lift the arms embargo. Belligerent powers could now place orders for war material, including combat aircraft, in the United States. But congressional isolationists still had sufficient strength to exact a heavy price for that concession: they restored the 1937 law's cash-and-carry provisions, which had expired in May 1939. Credits to belligerents were absolutely prohibited, from the U.S. Treasury and from private bankers alike. Purchasers of arms and ammunition had to make full cash payment and take title before the goods left American docks, and shipments could move only in foreign vessels. Further underscoring the implacable determination of American lawmakers to avoid a war-precipitating incident, the new law forbade American merchant ships from transiting a broad "danger zone" that embraced most of the sea lanes to western European ports, neutral as well as belligerent. The North Atlantic was Britain's historic lifeline and America's traditional shield. With the flourish of his pen on November 4, Roosevelt swept that sea more cleanly of American ships than a thousand torpedoes could have done.

This limited revision of the neutrality law accurately reflected the precarious equilibrium in which American diplomacy was now suspended. Public opinion and official policy alike hung quivering between hope and fear—hope that with American help the Allies could defeat Hitler, and fear that events might yet suck the United States into the conflict. Roosevelt, for one, did not deceive himself about the terrifying implications of a Nazi triumph in Europe, but neither did he suffer any illusions about the temper of his countrymen. "What worries me," Roosevelt confided in late December 1939 to a fellow internationalist, Kansas newspaperman William Allen White, "is that public opinion over here is patting itself on the back every morning and thanking God for the Atlantic Ocean (and the Pacific Ocean). We greatly underestimate the serious implications to our own future. . . . Therefore, my sage old friend, my problem is to get the American people to think of conceivable consequences without scaring the American people into thinking that they are going to be dragged into this war."[14]

THE EERY LULL that settled over much of Europe after the German invasion of Poland compounded Roosevelt's problem in late 1939 and early 1940, as he faced the task of educating Americans about the real and present danger they faced. Fulfilling the secret protocols of

14. E. Roosevelt, FDR: His Personal Letters 2:968.

the Nazi-Soviet pact, Stalin gobbled up eastern Poland in mid-September and invaded Finland at the end of November. But those were relatively minor clashes on Europe's distant eastern periphery. In the western European heartland, the fearsome German *Wehrmacht*, the truly great menace to the peace of the Old Continent, lay mysteriously idle. The *Blitzkrieg*, or "lightning war," that had crushed Poland in three weeks gave way to six months of *Sitzkrieg*—a curious "sitting war" during which Hitler consolidated his gains but launched no new military adventures.

Hitler kept Paris and London off balance during this interval with seductive but ultimately bogus peace feelers. For their part, the Allies showed no inclination to seize the military initiative. France marked time, deluded by its faith in the supposedly impenetrable Maginot Line. Britain contented itself with leaflet raids on German cities. As the closing days of 1939 stretched to weeks and then to months, and still no blow came in the west, Europe relaxed a bit. English children who had been evacuated from London under the threat of air raids in September were returning home by Christmastime. Even so bellicose a Briton as Winston Churchill, appointed in early September as first lord of the British admiralty in Chamberlain's cabinet, continued to think of the war more as an imminent prospect than a present reality. As late as Christmas Day 1939, he telegraphed to Franklin Roosevelt: "Generally speaking, think war will begin soon now."[15]

As 1940 opened, there was still no war in the west—or only what Senator Borah sneeringly called the "Phony War," yet another saber-rattling stand-off between the blustering Nazis and the craven democracies, but nothing for the United States to worry about. Among Americans, the British ambassador reported from Washington, there was a feeling "of boredom that the tremendous drama of unlimited aerial war in Europe which they had been educated to expect is apparently not going to come off."[16]

The Phony War's strange calm appeared momentarily to enchant even Franklin Roosevelt with the mirage of a negotiated settlement before the dreaded wider war exploded. The recent history of appeasement gave him little basis for confidence that either Britain or France would

15. *C&R* 1:29. Interestingly, Churchill wrote Chamberlain on the same day that he considered Roosevelt Britain's friend, "but I expect he wants to be re-elected, and I fear that isolationism is the winning ticket." Rock, *Chamberlain and Roosevelt,* 243.

16. Rock, *Chamberlain and Roosevelt,* 224.

muster the political will to stand up to Hitler for long. Nor did he have much reason to believe that the British or the French military would prove any kind of match for the Nazi juggernaut once it started to roll. Bullitt sent several warnings from Paris that France would be subdued by German air power well before the French could build their own air arm, with or without American help. From London, Ambassador Kennedy repeatedly emphasized the morale-sapping effects of Berlin's suggestions of a settlement. Chamberlain, Kennedy believed, might yet cut a deal with Hitler. Kennedy himself, in fact, was inclined to favor such a deal as the best that outgunned and underfinanced England could hope for. "Make no mistake," Kennedy wrote the president on November 3, "there is a very definite undercurrent in this country for peace. . . . Although everybody hates Hitler, [the British] still don't want to be finished economically, financially, politically, and socially, which they are beginning to suspect will be their fate if the war goes on very long."[17]

The better to gauge the European mood, Roosevelt announced on February 9, 1940, that he was dispatching Undersecretary of State Sumner Welles on an ostensible "fact-finding" mission to Rome, Berlin, Paris, and London. The deeper purpose of Welles's trip the president did not feel free to state publicly: to explore the possibility of an American-mediated peace settlement negotiated with Hitler—surely, Roosevelt felt, a preferable course to a peace settlement dictated by Hitler.

What Welles found unnerved him. Though many Italian officials were anxiously seeking a way to avoid war, Mussolini was clearly Italy's supreme boss, and Welles concluded that there was not "the slightest chance of any successful negotiation" with Il Duce.[18] In Berlin, where he saw Polish prisoners of war glumly shoveling snow from the streets, Welles sat icily through a two-hour harangue from German foreign minister Joachim von Ribbentrop, the minister's eyes continually closed, "the pomposity and absurdity of his manner" accentuating the impression that "the man is saturated with hate for England." Welles came away from an interview with Hitler on the following day "thinking to myself as I got into the car that it was only too tragically plain that all decisions had already been made. The best that could be hoped for was delay, for what little that might be worth." In Paris, motoring through

17. Bullitt, For the President, 380, 391; Kennedy quoted in Rock, Chamberlain and Roosevelt, 236, and Dallek, 213.
18. L&G, Challenge 374.

the streets where he had spent much of his privileged childhood, Welles received abundant confirmation of the grim reports that Bullitt had been filing about the state of French morale. He saw only "sullen apathy" in people's faces. "[O]nly in the rarest instances ... did I obtain the impression of hope or vigor, or even, tragically enough, of the will to courage."

In England, the picture was different. "There was no resemblance between the impressions which I obtained in London and those which had been forced upon me in Paris," Welles later recalled. Many writers have played down Welles's sojourn in London as mere "window dressing" to mask his allegedly more serious mission to Rome and Berlin. But in fact it was Welles's visit to England that had by far the more important consequences, for the simple reason that Welles there confronted in person the stiffening English spirit of defiance — a spirit that Ambassador Kennedy's doom-laden reports had done little to convey. The British, Welles momentously concluded, "would fight to the last ditch. ... There appeared to be a determination that rather than live once more through the experiences that they had suffered since the autumn of 1938, they would see it through to the end no matter how far off that end might be, nor how bitter the progress toward it might prove." The attitudes of two men in particular made a deep impression on Welles. Anthony Eden, the once and future foreign secretary now in the Dominions Office, forcefully expressed his stark conviction "that nothing but war is possible until Hitlerism has been overthrown." Still more emphatically, Winston Churchill, once and present first lord of the admiralty and soon to become prime minister, bathed Welles in "a cascade of oratory, brilliant and always effective, interlarded with considerable wit." Wreathed in cigar smoke and gesturing with a glass of whiskey and soda (not his first of the day, Welles surmised), Churchill declaimed: "There could be no solution other than outright and complete defeat of Germany [and] the destruction of National Socialism."

Welles returned to Washington at the end of March and submitted his report to the president. His journey had demolished two illusions. On the one hand, his discussions with Mussolini and Hitler conclusively established that the quest for a negotiated peace was "a forlorn hope." On the other hand, contrary to what the history of the Chamberlain ministry and the assessments of Ambassador Kennedy had long suggested, England was not entirely devoid of the will to resist the Nazis. Welles had found among at least some leaders in England, Churchill most conspicuously, a fierce resolution to make war to the end against

Hitler. On that resolution, and especially on Churchill's ability to sustain it and to convince others, the Americans above all, of its depth and durability, much history would turn.[19]

No sooner had Welles arrived back in the United States than Hitler shattered the false calm of the European standstill. On April 9 Germany occupied Denmark, and German troops swarmed with astonishing speed across southern Norway and into several ports along the fjord-serrated Norwegian coast. An Anglo-French force scrambled to dislodge the invaders, but within weeks the Germans overran the country, and the humiliated Allies withdrew. As the Royal Navy evacuated British units from collapsing Norway in early May, Chamberlain's government finally fell. (In France, Daladier had been replaced by a new prime minister, Paul Reynaud, some seven weeks earlier.) "In the name of God, go!" one backbencher shouted at Chamberlain, quoting Cromwell's words to the Long Parliament in the seventeenth century. "You have sat too long here for any good you have been doing. Depart, I say, and let us have done with you." On May 10 Winston Churchill became prime minister. "I felt as if I were walking with Destiny," Churchill recollected, "and that all my past life had been but a preparation for this hour and for this trial."[20]

The swift subjugation of Norway was but a prelude to the long-delayed attack in the west. On May 10, the same day Churchill clasped Destiny's hand in Britain, the full ferocity of *Blitzkrieg* detonated over Holland, Belgium, and Luxembourg. German airborne troops nullified the Netherlands' historic defense of flooding the invasion routes. Luftwaffe bombers flattened the center of Rotterdam. Panzer (mechanized) divisions raced toward Brussels. On May 14, eighteen hundred German tanks roared out of the Ardennes woods, well north of the useless Maginot Line, and scythed clockwise toward the sea, cutting off the French and British columns that had advanced to check the initial German thrust into the low countries. Luxembourg was unceremoniously overrun. Holland surrendered on May 14, Belgium on May 28. On May 15, French premier Paul Reynaud telephoned Winston Churchill. "We have been defeated," he said, speaking in English. When a stunned Churchill made no reply, Reynaud went on: "We are beaten; we have

19. Welles, *Time for Decision*, 91, 99, 109, 121, 134, 77.
20. Churchill 1:659, 667.

lost the battle," a declaration that proved premature by only thirty-two days.

In that chaotic thirty-two-day interval, amid scenes of indescribable pandemonium, including exchanges of gunfire between French and British troops scurrying for the evacuation ships, Britain managed to rescue some 338,000 troops (including over a hundred thousand Frenchmen) from the northern French port of Dunkirk—making, with Norway, two evacuations of an Allied force from the European continent in as many months. Left abandoned on and about the gravelly Dunkirk beaches was all the British Expeditionary Force's heavy equipment— "the whole equipment of the Army to which all the firstfruits of our factories had hitherto been given," Churchill lamented, including ninety thousand rifles, seven thousand tons of ammunition, and 120,000 vehicles.

Churchill's distress reflected his keen understanding of the inexorable economic logic of modern warfare, when machines, and the speed and volume of their manufacture, mattered at least as much as men, and the swiftness and precision of their maneuver, in determining the battle's outcome. The pell-mell retreat from Dunkirk had stripped the British army of the bulk of its implements of war. "Many months must elapse," Churchill brooded, "before this loss could be repaired." On the sea and in the air, the Royal Navy and the Royal Air Force remained viable fighting forces. But on land, Britain was now all but defenseless.[21]

Once the departing British and French troops disappeared across the Channel, the remainder of the French army crumpled before the German onslaught with little more than a flourish of the matador's cape. The panzer columns rolled over obsolete antitank obstacles as if they were tin cans and swept across the Meuse River "as if it did not exist," an awed Bullitt reported. Even the battle-seasoned Churchill was agape at the speed and crushing completeness of the Nazi victory. "I did not comprehend," he later reflected, "the violence of the revolution effected since the last war by the incursion of a mass of fast-moving heavy armour."

On June 10, playing "the role of jackal to Hitler's lion," in Harold

21. Churchill 2:42, 141–42. One British soldier remembered moving with his artillery regiment to take up defensive positions in Yorkshire. "The total equipment of the 65th Field Regiment, Royal Artillery, at that historic moment was one commandeered civilian truck and a few dozen rifles," he recalled. Ronald Lewin, *Ultra Goes to War* (London: Grafton 1988), 73.

Ickes's trenchant phrase, Mussolini declared war on reeling France, and for good measure on Britain as well. *Il Duce* thus dashed any lingering hopes that Italy might yet be detached from its German ally. A week later, on June 17, France asked for an armistice. On June 22, 1940, in the same railway car in which the Germans had been forced to capitulate in 1918, Hitler gleefully accepted the official French surrender. By the terms of the surrender document, Germany occupied all the French Atlantic coastline and the French interior to a demarcation line south of the Loire River. A vassal government, headed by the authoritarian patriarch Marshal Philippe Pétain and installed at the spa town of Vichy, was allowed to preside over the rump French state. "The Battle of France is over," Churchill told a somber House of Commons. "I expect that the Battle of Britain is about to begin." England, Pétain sourly predicted, "will have her neck wrung like a chicken."[22]

The French surrender fundamentally altered the military calculus, whether the equations were plotted in London or Washington. Until the French defeat, British planners had counted on France to absorb the initial shock of a German attack, allowing Britain time to rearm. American strategic doctrine, such as it was, had in turn implicitly rested on the triad of French land power, British sea power, and American industrial power, especially aircraft production for the European democracies. Now France lay prostrate under the Nazi boot. Could Britain, alone and largely disarmed after the Dunkirk debacle, long survive?

Ambassador Bullitt had warned that France would collapse with unseemly haste in the face of German invasion. The events of May and June 1940 had confirmed his worst premonitions. Ambassador Kennedy had been issuing similar warnings about England. In the wake of Dunkirk, a disaster he had accurately foretold, Kennedy repeated his prediction that the Germans, having expelled England from the Continent and conquered her most important ally, would make London a peace offer it could not refuse. Who could now confidently rebut Kennedy's prophecy? And if Britain fell, what then would—or could—America do? If Britain were defeated, Churchill ominously intoned, "then the whole world, including the United States, including all that we have known and cared for, will sink into the abyss of a new Dark Age." Speaking at Charlottesville, Virginia, Roosevelt concurred. The United States could

22. Bullitt, *For the President*, 416; Churchill 2:42, 43, 141; Ickes Diary 3:203; Pétain quoted in Davis 4:560.

not survive as "a lone island in a world dominated by the philosophy of force," Roosevelt said. "Such an island may be the dream of those who still talk and vote as isolationists," but that fatuous and dangerous dream "represents to me," said the president, "the nightmare of a people lodged in prison, handcuffed, hungry, and fed through the bars from day to day by the contemptuous, unpitying masters of other continents. . . . On this tenth day of June 1940, in this University founded by the first great American teacher of democracy, we send forth our prayers and our hopes to those beyond the seas who are maintaining with magnificent valor their battle for freedom."[23]

It was now urgently incumbent on Churchill to vindicate that faith in British valor. He had not only to rally his own countrymen but also to convince the Americans that England had put all the temptations of appeasement behind her. Ultimately, of course, Churchill also hoped to bring the United States into the war at England's side. He made scant secret of those intentions in a famous peroration to a speech at the time of the Dunkirk evacuation, a speech as remarkable for its frank cry for help as for its hypnotic rhetorical flights. South African premier Jan Smuts once remarked of Churchill's speeches that "Every broadcast is a battle."[24] This one, delivered on the floor of the House of Commons on June 4, was at once Churchill's Trafalgar and his Agincourt, a soaring triumph of the orator's art. Speaking in lyrical Elizabethan cadences, Churchill addressed himself as much to Americans as to Britons (though Americans had little idea that it was not Churchill's voice but the recorded voice of his designated impersonator, Norman Shelley, that rumbled into millions of their homes via transatlantic radio):

> We shall go on to the end, we shall fight in France, we shall fight on the seas and oceans, we shall fight with growing confidence and growing strength in the air, we shall defend our island, whatever the cost may be, we shall fight on the beaches, we shall fight on the landing grounds, we shall fight in the fields and in the streets, we shall fight in the hills; we shall never surrender . . . until in God's good time, the new world, with all its power and might, steps forth to the rescue and the liberation of the old.[25]

23. David Cannadine, ed., *Blood, Toil, Tears and Sweat: The Speeches of Winston Churchill* (Boston: Houghton Mifflin, 1989), 177; *PPA* (1940), 261, 263–64.
24. Martin Gilbert, *Churchill: A Life* (New York: Henry Holt, 1991), 690.
25. Cannadine, *Blood, Toil, Tears and Sweat*, 165; for the impersonator's role, see *C&R* 1:42.

With those words, Churchill resoundingly confirmed Sumner Welles's estimate of the British leader's bellicosity and tenacity. "It was a great speech," the usually dour Ickes noted in his diary. Roosevelt thought the speech was "firmness itself." "The President and I," wrote Secretary of State Hull, "believed Mr. Churchill meant what he said. . . . There would be no negotiations between London and Berlin." Like a sorcerer's incantation, Churchill's words literally spoke open the door to American cooperation. "Had we had any doubt of Britain's determination to keep on fighting, we would not have taken the steps we did to get material aid to her," Hull later wrote.[26]

Yet not all Americans swooned so readily under the British leader's spell, nor were all doubts about Britain's prospects for survival so swiftly laid to rest. Churchill had charmed open the door to Anglo-American partnership, but only a crack. The winds of war and anxiety could easily slam it shut again. Churchill's toils, verbal and otherwise, were just beginning.

Winston Spencer Churchill was peculiarly suited to the task of summoning the New World to the salvation of the Old. The son of an English father and an American mother, he was the very incarnation of Anglo-American unity. The mysterious caprices of character and the purgatories of his sixty-four years had combined to gird him by 1939 with an impressive armamenture of mettle, guile, and prowess. Graced as well with superbly honed rhetorical gifts, Churchill was a formidable suitor for the hand of his American cousins. On them, he knew, everything depended. All of his wile and wit Churchill now directed to the task of persuading the Americans to become England's comrades-in-arms.

While he courted the American public over the radio, Churchill also cultivated Franklin Roosevelt by telephone and telegraph. They had met only once, in London in 1918. In the early days of the New Deal, Churchill had sent to the White House a copy of his biography of his ancestor John Churchill, the first duke of Marlborough. He inscribed it "with earnest best wishes for the success of the greatest crusade of modern times." The two men had no further contact until September 11, 1939, just days after Churchill had joined Chamberlain's cabinet as first sea lord, when Roosevelt sent a personal note: "It is because you and I occupied similar positions in the World War [when Churchill had been first lord of the admiralty and Roosevelt assistant secretary of the navy]

26. Ickes Diary 3:202; Lash, *Roosevelt and Churchill*, 150.

that I want you to know how glad I am that you are back in the Admiralty. . . . What I want you and the Prime Minister to know is that I shall at all times welcome it if you will keep me in touch personally with anything you want me to know about." That brief message laid the foundation of a remarkable personal and political relationship.[27]

With Chamberlain's full approval, Churchill had seized the opportunity to open a direct line of communication with the American president. Not the least of the Englishmen's reasons was their desire to offset what they knew were Ambassador Kennedy's increasingly dark assessments of Britain's prospects. Kennedy, one British diplomat observed, was "malevolent and pigeon-livered." Another called the American ambassador "a very foul specimen of double-crosser and defeatist." Given the pessimistic reports that he knew Kennedy to be filing, Churchill shrewdly intuited "that it was a good thing to feed [Roosevelt] at intervals," and to feed him more bracing fare than he was being served by Kennedy.[28]

In Roosevelt, Churchill found a resonant soulmate for his own uncompromising spirit. During the preceding half decade, the president had sometimes been as annoyed with British appeasement as the British had been dismayed with American isolation. "I wish the British would stop this 'we who are about to die, salute thee' attitude," Roosevelt had written exasperatedly to a Harvard historian in early 1939. "What the British need today is a good stiff grog, inducing not only the desire to save civilization but the continued belief that they can do it. In such an event they will have a lot more support from their American cousins." Churchill might well be the man to brew that grog. As for Kennedy, Roosevelt had long since taken his ambassador's measure. "Joe Kennedy . . . has been an appeaser and always will be an appeaser. . . . [H]e's just a pain in the neck to me," Roosevelt exclaimed to Morgenthau in October 1939.[29]

Yet Kennedy's reports could not be so easily dismissed. The messenger may have been a pain in the neck, but his message had a sobering plausibility. Britain might indeed be about to die, or at least to bow subserviently before Hitler's overbearing force, however hearty the drafts of rhetorical grog that poured from Churchill's prodigious oratorical

27. C&R 1:23, 24.
28. Rock, *Chamberlain and Roosevelt*, 277; Lash, *Roosevelt and Churchill*, 138.
29. Freidel, *Rendezvous with Destiny*, 312–13; John Morton Blum, *From the Morgenthau Diaries: Years of Urgency, 1938–1941* (Boston: Houghton Mifflin, 1965), 102.

well. Even Roosevelt thought on at least one occasion in the spring of 1940 that "the English were going to get licked."[30] Just as Kennedy surmised, influential members of the British government, even at this late date, still entertained the idea of reaching an understanding with Hitler, not least because they continued to despair of American assistance. "U.S. looks pretty useless," Alexander Cadogan, senior adviser to Lord Halifax, still the foreign secretary in Churchill's government as he had been in Chamberlain's, noted at the time of the French collapse. "Well, we must die without them," Cadogan concluded.[31] At a secret meeting of the five-member War Cabinet on May 28, 1940, Halifax, prince of appeasers, urged taking up Mussolini's offer to mediate a settlement. Chamberlain, stripped of the premiership but still a political force to be reckoned with, agreed. He admonished his colleagues that they should be "ready to consider decent terms if such were offered to us." These sentiments outraged Churchill, whose overriding goal was to purge them and all their vestiges from the British body politic. Speaking to the full cabinet moments later, the new prime minister administered a potent verbal emetic: "[E]very man of you would rise up and tear me down from my place if I were for one moment to contemplate parley or surrender," Churchill fulminated. "If this long island history of ours is to end at last, let it end only when each one of us lies choking in his own blood upon the ground." Churchill "was quite magnificent," one minister wrote in his diary. He was "the man, and the only man we have for this task."[32]

The new prime minister also proffered a bracing round to Roosevelt on May 15, just five days after assuming office. Coyly styling himself "Former Naval Person," a transparent reference to his previous stints at the admiralty and an uncharacteristically labored attempt to emphasize his common ground with Roosevelt, Churchill penned a chillingly frank overview of the British situation and initiated what would become a cascade of importunings for American help. Through all of Churchill's bravura, Roosevelt could hardly fail to register the prime minister's tone of desperation.

"Although I have changed my office," Churchill ingratiatingly began,

30. Dallek, 220.
31. David Dilks, ed., *The Secret Diaries of Sir Alexander Cadogan* (New York: G. P. Putnam's Sons, 1972) 299.
32. Gilbert, *Churchill A Life*, 651.

"I am sure you would not wish me to discontinue our intimate, private correspondence." Then he quickly got down to cases:

> As you are no doubt aware, the scene has darkened swiftly. The enemy has a marked preponderance in the air. . . . The small countries are simply smashed up one by one, like matchwood. . . . We expect to be attacked here ourselves, both from the air and by parachute and air borne troops in the near future, and are getting ready for them. If necessary, we shall continue the war alone and we are not afraid of that. But I trust you realize, Mr. President, that the voice and force of the United States may count for nothing if they are withheld too long. You may have a completely subjugated, Nazified Europe established with astonishing swiftness, and the weight may be more than we can bear. . . . Immediate needs are: first of all, the loan of forty or fifty of your older destroyers. . . . Secondly, we want several hundred of the latest types of aircraft. . . . Thirdly, anti-aircraft equipment and ammunition. . . . Fourthly, [we need] to purchase steel in the United States. This also applies to other materials. We shall go on paying dollars for as long as we can, but I should like to feel reasonably sure that when we can pay no more, you will give us the stuff all the same. Fifthly . . . , the visit of a United States squadron to Irish ports, which might well be prolonged, would be invaluable. Sixthly, I am looking to you to keep that Japanese dog quiet in the Pacific.

This was an extraordinary communication from one head of government to another. It bordered on the presumptuous in its naked candor and nearly abject pleading. Churchill soon grew more brazen still. Just five days later he wrote to Roosevelt that though he personally intended to fight to the finish, should things go badly, "[m]embers of the present administration would likely go down [and] if members of the present administration were finished and others came in to parley amid the ruins, you must not be blind to the fact that the sole remaining bargaining counter with Germany would be the fleet, and if this country was left by the United States to its fate no one would have the right to blame those then responsible if they made the best terms they could for the surviving inhabitants. Excuse me, Mr. President, putting this nightmare bluntly. Evidently I could not answer for my successors who in utter despair and helplessness might well have to accommodate themselves to the German will." Churchill conjured this dark prospect again on June 15: "I know well, Mr. President, that your eye will have already searched these depths but I feel I have the right to place on record the vital matter in which American interests are at stake in our battle." A pro-German government might come to power in England and turn the British Isles into a "vassal state of the Hitler empire," making a gift of the British fleet to Germany in the process. At that moment, said Churchill, "overwhelming sea power would be in Hitler's hands."[33]

From another man's pen, or in another man's eye, these forebodings could have been taken for blackmail. Indeed, a British Foreign Office memorandum at the time so described them: "blackmail, and not very good blackmail at that."[34] But Roosevelt chose to ignore the uncloaked threat that if America failed to act, appeasement might yet dictate England's fate, with consequences for America that needed little spelling out. Instead, the president immediately assented to almost all of Churchill's requests. The day after receiving the prime minister's list of needs of May 15, Roosevelt replied that he could not transfer destroyers without authorization from Congress (a rationale that would soon evaporate) but that he was doing his utmost on the other items. Aircraft deliveries were being expedited; antiaircraft equipment and ammunition would be sent; so would steel; he would take under advisement the proposed fleet visit to Ireland; and he had already dispatched the main body of the U.S. fleet to Hawaii, as a warning signal to Japan. On the matter of whether the United States would "give us the stuff all the same," when Allied dollar reserves were exhausted, the president was studiously silent. "The best of luck to you," Roosevelt genially concluded.[35]

The same day, Roosevelt made a dramatic appearance before a joint session of Congress to ask for a supplemental defense appropriation of nearly $1.3 billion. The funds were to begin building what was soon dubbed a "two-ocean navy." No less boldly, the president called for a production goal of "at least 50,000 planes a year"—a truly fantastic leap when measured against the niggardly output of military aircraft since Roosevelt's rather ineffective call for "airplanes—and lots of them" in 1938. Finally, in a clear reinforcement of his short-of-war strategy, Roosevelt insisted that the lion's share of that hugely increased aircraft production should be delivered to overseas buyers. "For the permanent record," the president pointedly declared, "I ask the Congress not to take any action which would in any way hamper or delay the delivery of American-made planes to foreign nations." Unknown to the general

33. C&R 1:37–38, 40, 49.
34. Lash, Roosevelt and Churchill, 135.
35. C&R 1:38–39.

public, Roosevelt had already quietly directed that the Allies would have "first call" on the planes then beginning to roll, with painful slowness, off American assembly lines. Just weeks earlier, Britain and France had placed the first substantial orders for aircraft—five thousand airframes and ten thousand engines of the most advanced design.[36]

Roosevelt's ready agreement to Churchill's requests, and his emphasis on producing arms for foreign buyers, pitched the president once again into a bitter confrontation with his own senior diplomatic and military advisers. Ambassador Kennedy cabled on the very day of Churchill's historic supplication that complying with the British demands would "leave the United States holding the bag for a war in which the Allies expected to be beaten. . . . It seems to me," Kennedy concluded, "that if we had to fight to protect our lives, we would do better fighting in our own back yard."[37] Several key American military leaders emphatically seconded Kennedy's opinion. Their ingrained martial habits of prudence combined with their singular commitment to American defense to produce a cast of mind that was deeply, fearfully skeptical of the president's initiatives. They found Roosevelt's key assumption—that Britain would hold out—dubious, to say the least. They saw their supreme obligation as recruiting, training, and fielding an *American* fighting force, which at that moment scarcely existed and which could not be created without arms and equipment. American production, they argued, must flow to American soldiers, sailors, and airmen, not be tossed away across the sea in a vain farewell gesture to the drowning British. George C. Marshall was reminded of the so-called amalgamation controversy in World War I, when General Pershing had resolutely resisted incessant Allied demands to incorporate American troops directly into Allied units, demands that threatened the very existence of an independent American army. Marshall was not about to cave in where Pershing, the most celebrated living American military hero and his own revered mentor, had stood firm. Marshall worried especially that shipping aircraft to England would cripple the American pilot-training program. Air corps head Hap Arnold estimated that the transfer

36. PPA (1940), 202. For Roosevelt's decision to give the Allies "first call" on American production, see Ickes Diary 3:84–85, describing a conversation with Postmaster General Jim Farley in December 1939. What would happen, Farley asked, if England or France wanted airplanes and we wanted them at the same time? "The President said that it was a matter of confidential information, but that, up to a certain number at any rate, we would let England and France have the first call."

37. L&G, *Challenge*, 481–82.

of a hundred aircraft to the Allies would replace only three days' supply at the rate they were then being shot down but would set back the pilot-training schedule in the United States by six months. "It is a drop in the bucket on the other side and it is a very vital necessity on this side, and that is that," Marshall briskly concluded, and he so advised the secretary of war on May 18: "I regret to tell you that I do not think we can afford to submit ourselves to the delay and consequences involved in accommodating the British Government."[38]

Roosevelt himself agonized over the precariousness of his position that maximum possible aid should go to England. "I might guess wrong," he confided to Ickes on June 4, 1940, in a rare revelation of the doubts that must have besieged him, "and it is nothing more than a guess. And if I should guess wrong, the results might be serious. If we should send some destroyers across, they would be of no particular use to the Allies but they might serve further to enrage Hitler. We cannot tell the turn that the war will take, and there is no use endangering ourselves unless we can achieve some results for the Allies." Ickes, appreciating "that the President was in a delicate position," agreed. "If you do send some help with bad consequences to ourselves, the people will blame you just as they will blame you if you don't send the help and the Allies are crushed." Ickes's concurral was cold comfort—but he described with chiseled accuracy the awful dilemma that Roosevelt faced, a dilemma whose perplexities and dangers vastly deepened when France fell.[39]

Through May and June 1940 the president stuck unflinchingly with his risky bet. Sometimes he had to cudgel his subordinates into backing his high-stakes gamble. Three questions were at issue. First, should the Allies have prior claim on new American aircraft production? Second, could the U.S. Army transfer from its own arsenals to Britain sufficient arms to make good the losses at Dunkirk? Third, could the U.S. Navy release the destroyers that Churchill had requested? Roosevelt answered yes to all three and brooked no opposition. When Secretary of War Harry H. Woodring, a Kansas isolationist committed to a "Fortress America" strategy, balked at releasing aircraft for overseas delivery, Roosevelt ordered him either to go along with the program or resign. Informed that Hap Arnold continued to complain about the devastating impact of Roosevelt's priorities on the army air corps, Roosevelt said brusquely, "Well, if Arnold won't conform, maybe we will have to move him out

38. Morgenthau Diary, 318–19.
39. Ickes Diary 3:200.

of town," perhaps to the career burial-ground of Guam. Arnold soon bowed to the presidential will. When Secretary of the Navy Charles Edison reported that the navy's judge advocate general considered any destroyer transfer to be unlawful, Roosevelt denounced the navy's highest legal officer as nothing but a "sea lawyer" and advised Edison to send the troublesome subordinate away on a vacation. "If the man next in line didn't know any more law, he should also be sent on a vacation, and so on down the list." Edison persisted in presenting the Judge Advocate General's case. "[F]orget it and do what I told you to do," the president snapped. Within weeks, Roosevelt shoved both Woodring and Edison out of the Cabinet. A newly potent, decisive Roosevelt was emerging, a different man from the president who had been politically wounded and checkmated through much of his second term. Now he was ready to play the lion, and he appeared to relish the role.[40]

Virtually commanding his military chiefs to declare certain items as "surplus," the key to their legal release, Roosevelt forced some of the arms transfers through. Churchill's question about the destroyers still remained unanswered, but on the night of June 11, New Jersey stevedores began handling some six hundred freight-car loads of Enfield rifles, machine guns, 75mm field guns, and over one hundred million rounds of ammunition onto British ships. The military men who grudgingly expedited the shipments were aghast at the spectacle unfolding on the New Jersey docks. "[I]f we were required to mobilize after having released guns necessary for this mobilization and were found to be short in artillery materiel," one army officer warned, "everyone who was a party to the deal might hope to be found hanging from a lamp post."[41]

Roosevelt could not indefinitely continue stuffing his undefended hunches down the throats of his cabinet secretaries and his senior military and naval commanders. On June 13, 1940, searching for system and consensus, he set down his strategic assumptions on paper. He requested the army and navy chiefs to assess the reasonableness of his premises and to comment on the economic, political, military, and psychological implications of his aid-to-Britain policy. This meager and imperfectly prophetic outline, penned just two days after the forced arms shipments of June 11 and less than a week before the fate of France was finally sealed, set off an even angrier round of controversy that reverberated through the frantic summer of 1940 and beyond.

40. Morgenthau Diary 301–32; Ickes Diary 3:202.
41. Watson, *Chief of Staff*, 312.

Peering with as much confidence as he could muster into the future, Roosevelt laid out his vision of the world six months hence. He ventured six predictions:

1. Time. Fall and winter of 1940.
2. Britain and the British Empire are still intact.
3. France is occupied, but the French Government and the remainder of its forces are still resisting, perhaps in North Africa.
4. The surviving forces of the British and French Navies, in conjunction with U.S. Navy, are holding the Persian Gulf, Red Sea and the Atlantic from Morocco to Greenland. The Allied fleets have probably been driven out of the Eastern Mediterranean, and are maintaining a precarious hold on the Western Mediterranean.
5. Allied land forces are maintaining their present hold in the Near East. Turkey maintains its present political relationship to the Allies.
6. Russia and Japan are inactive, taking no part in the war.
7. The U.S. active in the war, but with naval and air forces only. Plane production is progressing to its maximum. America is providing part of Allied pilots. Morocco and Britain are being used as bases of supplies shipped from the Western Hemisphere. American shipping is transporting supplies to the Allies. The U.S. Navy is providing most of the force for the Atlantic blockade (Morocco to Greenland).[42]

Army Chief of Staff Marshall and his counterpart, Chief of Naval Operations Admiral Harold Stark, took this presidential prognosis under intense advisement for the next several days. At a White House meeting on June 22 they presented Roosevelt with their own considered response. On the crucial point—Britain's survivability—they took strong issue with the president's assumptions. They agreed instead with Ambassador Kennedy that "[t]he actual invasion and overrunning of England by German military forces" appeared to be "within the range of possibility." Consequently, they advised that "to release to Great Britain additional war material now in the hands of the armed forces will seriously weaken our present state of defense and will not materially assist the British forces"—an opinion they had long held and now stated officially. They also took the occasion to criticize Roosevelt's decision to keep substantial portions of the fleet at Pearl Harbor, a move they judged too feeble to deter Japan but belligerent enough to antagonize her, and

42. Maurice Matloff and Edwin M. Snell, *United States Army in World War II: The War Department: Strategic Planning for Coalition Warfare, 1941–1942* (Washington: Department of the Army, 1953), 14.

in any case a deployment that dangerously weakened American naval strength in the far more important Atlantic theater. American unreadiness in all arms was so great, Marshall and Stark counseled, that the United States should carefully husband its own resources and scrupulously avoid provoking any of its potential adversaries. Meanwhile, the administration should look to hemispheric defense by strengthening relations with South America, adopting conscription as a step toward "complete military and naval mobilization" and taking all means to speed up arms production, including putting workers onto seven-day overtime shifts in the major arms plants.[43]

Roosevelt listened respectfully but rejected his chiefs' advice. On their last point, the president vigorously demurred. With unemployment still high, he would tolerate no changes in the standard five-day workweek. So long as the Depression lingered, jobs were more important than expedited arms production, though Roosevelt surely appreciated that increased arms production eventually meant more jobs, and lots of them. Nor did he assent to the recommendation to shift fleet elements to the Atlantic. He accepted the necessity for conscription, though he downgraded the goal of "complete" mobilization to "progressive" mobilization. Most important, Roosevelt mulishly reconfirmed his commitment to keep aid flowing to Britain.

Given the formally declared opposition of his military and naval chiefs, not to mention, in this election year, the preponderantly contrary opinion of the American public, two-thirds of whom believed Britain was about to go down, Roosevelt acted with remarkable boldness — or with wanton recklessness. Former NRA director Hugh Johnson, now an outspoken isolationist and still a fountain of invective, charged that Roosevelt was irresponsibly "shooting craps with destiny."[44]

For their part, the British knew on what rolls of the dice their destiny depended. "The degree to which the U.S.A. will come to our assistance rather than concentrate upon the defence of her own hemisphere," a Foreign Office official observed, "depends in the highest degree upon our ability to prove that we are vigorously prosecuting the war." No one appreciated that logic more acutely than Churchill. Speaking at a secret session of the House of Commons on June 20, he dwelled at length on the attitude of the United States and how Britain might affect it. No

43. Matloff and Snell, *Strategic Planning for Coalition Warfare, 1941–1942*, 14; Watson, *Chief of Staff*, 111.
44. Dallek, 231.

formal record was kept, but his surviving notes capture his themes: "The heroic struggle of England best chance of bringing them in. . . . A tribute to Roosevelt. It depends upon our resolute bearing and holding out until Election issues are settled there."

Churchill soon found a dramatic opportunity to demonstrate British resolution. Elements of the French fleet, nominally under Vichy's control by the terms of the French-German armistice but clearly vulnerable to German seizure, lay at anchor, fully combat-ready and with their French crews still aboard, at the naval base of Mers el-Kebir, near Oran in French Algeria. Taking care to apprise Roosevelt in advance, Churchill ordered a Royal Navy task force to steam for Mers el-Kebir. The British arrived on July 3 and demanded that the French commander either surrender or scuttle his ships. When he refused to do either, the Royal Navy gunners opened fire, sinking several French vessels and killing 1,297 French sailors. The British seamen took little pleasure in this attack on their erstwhile allies. But however distasteful to the men who executed it, the Mers el-Kebir incident gave bloody punctuation to Churchill's belligerent pronouncements. Mers el-Kebir was "the turning point in our fortunes," Churchill later remarked. "[I]t made the world realise that we were in earnest in our intentions to carry on."[45]

Mers el-Kebir ruthlessly displayed Britain's ability to deliver a punch. There soon followed a test of the far more consequential matter of her ability to take one. The Battle of Britain, predicted by Churchill at the time of the French-German armistice, opened on July 10, 1940. Great German aerial flotillas, wave after wave of Heinkel and Junkers bombers accompanied by phalanxes of Messerschmitt fighters, began bombing British coastal installations, preparatory to a cross-Channel invasion. "The Führer has ordered me to crush Britain with my Luftwaffe," German air minister Hermann Goering told his generals. "By means of hard blows I plan to have this enemy . . . down on his knees in the nearest future."[46] But this enemy, uniquely in Hitler's experience to date, declined to genuflect. Against forbidding odds, the Royal Air Force struggled instead to drape a ragged protective curtain of Spitfire and Hurricane fighter planes over the British Isles. Aided by the new technology of radar, which gave advance warning of German bombing runs, and by the cracking of the top-secret German "Enigma" codes, which provided further intelligence about the tactics and targets of the attack-

45. Lash, *Roosevelt and Churchill*, 151, 165; Gilbert, *Churchill: A Life*, 667.
46. John Keegan, *The Second World War* (New York: Viking, 1989), 91.

ers, British Fighter Command managed to keep the Germans at bay through July. Goering shifted his targeting to RAF airfields in August, and then to terror-bombing of London in September—the "Blitz," Londoners soon named this phase of the battle. Americans followed the drama keenly, tuning their radios to Edward R. Murrow's nicotine-lubricated voice reporting from BBC House. "London is burning," Murrow began nightly in his trademark funereal tone, and Americans anxiously awaited the apparently inevitable announcement of Britain's final subjugation.

As the Battle of Britain raged, Churchill dunned Roosevelt anew for aid. On July 16, Enigma cryptanalysts, working in tweedy academic surroundings in the Buckinghamshire village of Bletchley, the priceless value of their top-secret unit implied in their operation's code name— Ultra—furnished him with a copy of Hitler's Führer Directive No. 16: "I have decided to prepare a landing operation [code-named Sealion] against England," Hitler instructed his generals. This intercepted message confirmed Churchill's worst fears. It now "seemed certain," he later recalled, "that the man was going to try." With invasion imminent, Churchill pleaded again for the destroyers he had first requested on May 15. "Mr. President," he cabled to Roosevelt on July 31, "with great respect I must tell you that in the long history of the world, this is a thing to do now. . . . I am sure that with your comprehension of the sea affair, you will not let this crux of the battle go wrong for the want of these destroyers."[47]

The requested destroyers were ostensibly intended to help screen the English Channel against the expected German amphibious assault. But Roosevelt and Churchill alike understood that the American vessels had more psychological and political utility than they had naval value. The ships in question were four-funneled World War I–era heirlooms, barnacled old battlewagons in no condition for modern naval warfare. It would take months to refit them for use by the Royal Navy. If invasion were indeed as imminent as Churchill believed in July, they would never be ready on time and might in any event prove more a liability than an asset on the battle line. But both leaders also knew that morale and perception were scarcely less important than metal and firepower at this pivotal moment. Delivering the destroyers to Britain would bolster British spirits, signal Hitler that the patience of the neutral Americans was wearing thin, and, most significant, help drive home to those same

47. Churchill 2:296, 302; C&R 1:57.

Americans their stake in the struggle against Nazism. For those reasons, at least as much as for his "comprehension of the sea affair," Roosevelt was determined to transfer the vessels.[48]

As Roosevelt well knew, however, even presidential determination is not always dispositive. With the aircraft sales and arms transfers of the preceding weeks, Roosevelt had stretched his constitutional prerogatives to their outermost boundaries. He had also risked his own political neck. Now, in the summer of 1940, his neck was more than ever on the block.

It is a quirk of the American constitutional system that presidential elections come by the calendar, not by the crisis. By awkward coincidence, the quadrennial American political ritual of nomination, campaign, and election fell amidst the abounding crises of the desperate summer and fall months of 1940. Britain's fate hung by what Churchill described as "a slender thread," a makeshift gossamer woven of flimsy planes and a handful of valiant but green pilots. As if persistent isolationism and the uncertain outcome of the Battle of Britain were not enough to vex his calculations in that excruciating moment, Roosevelt also had to reckon with the inevitable electoral season.

Just when Roosevelt decided to seek a third term as president remains a puzzle. He kept his own counsel more closely than usual. Even Eleanor did not know for certain what his intentions were or by what process he eventually shaped them. Custom dictated that he give up the office; no man before him had dared breach George Washington's two-term example. As 1940 opened, Roosevelt gave every appearance that he would follow tradition and retire to his beloved Hyde Park estate. There he was actively supervising the construction of Top Cottage, a snug stone-and-timber hideaway in a remote corner of the sprawling grounds. He seemed already to be looking to his place in history, setting a precedent of his own with the erection at Hyde Park of the nation's first presidential library, a repository for the records of his administration and a place where he could edit his papers and perhaps write his memoirs. He was looking to bolster his personal financial future as well. In January he signed a contract with *Collier's* magazine to produce a series of articles after leaving office, for a fee of seventy-five thousand dollars a year, his presidential salary. "I do not want to run," he confided to Mor-

---

48. Some of the destroyers, it turned out, were scarcely seaworthy, barely able to make the Atlantic crossing. See Lash, *Roosevelt and Churchill*, 272.

genthau at that time, but then added, "unless between now and the convention things get very, very much worse in Europe."[49]

Things got infinitely worse, of course, and, though the particulars of Roosevelt's thinking remain obscure, the European crisis surely provided the ultimate explanation for his eventual decision to try to shatter the two-term tradition. The European scene weighed not only on Roosevelt's mind but also on the strategy of his political adversaries. Had it not been for the collapse of France, the Republican Party might well have nominated for president one of its powerful senatorial barons, such as Ohio's Robert Taft or Michigan's Arthur Vandenberg. But both those midwestern senators were unyielding isolationists. When the Republican convention was gaveled to order in Philadelphia on June 24, just two days after the French surrender, the delegates were in no mood to nominate a candidate as parochial as Taft or as insular as Vandenberg, for all the senators' standing in the Grand Old Party. Instead, in one of the most astonishing surprises in the history of American presidential politics, unmatched for its sheer improbability since the Democratic nomination of Horace Greeley in 1872, the Republicans chose an erstwhile Democrat and rank political amateur, Wendell Willkie.

Open-faced and tousle-haired, the boyish, plain-spoken, forty-eight-year-old Willkie was a rumpled and charismatic Hoosier who had made good as a corporate attorney and utilities executive, prompting Harold Ickes's impish description of him as "a simple barefoot Wall Street lawyer." As head of Commonwealth and Southern Corporation, a public utility holding company with extensive interests in the South, Willkie had dueled with Roosevelt's TVA over the issue of public power. By the late 1930s he had emerged as a leading spokesman for those in the business community who felt themselves aggrieved by the New Deal. Yet Willkie was no old-fashioned conservative. He gave his blessing to most of the New Deal's social legislation and conspicuously refrained from endorsing right-wing Republican preachments about the virtues of unbridled laissez-faire. Instead, he denounced the Democrats as having acquired a vested political interest in the Depression and therefore as having willfully throttled the wealth-making and job-creating potential of private enterprise — the nut of the political case that the Republicans would make against the Democrats for a generation or more to come, and an argument that marked the seismic shift in American politics that the New Deal had wrought. Until just a few years earlier Willkie himself

49. Freidel, *Rendezvous with Destiny*, 328.

had been a registered Democrat. Former Indiana Republican senator James E. Watson, on hearing that the ex-Democrat Willkie was his party's nominee, fumed: "If a whore repented and wanted to join the church I'd personally welcome her and lead her up the aisle to a pew. But, by the Eternal, I'd not ask her to lead the choir the first night."[50]

Most important, Willkie was an unshakeable internationalist. He had publicly criticized Nazi aggression and had spoken out eloquently in favor of repealing the arms embargo and in support of aid to Britain. Just for those reasons he appealed strongly to eastern, Anglophilic Republicans, who saw Willkie as an instrument with which to contain their party's formidable isolationist wing. Backed by internationalist Republicans like the influential and deep-pocketed publishers Henry Luce and Roy Howard, a Willkie-for-president organization had formed as early as 1939. On the sixth ballot at Philadelphia, Willkie won the nomination. In one of the shotgun marriages typical of presidential politics, his running mate was Oregon's Senator Charles McNary, who favored public power projects as fervently as Willkie condemned them.

Enigmatically refraining from any specific statement of his intentions, Roosevelt remained at the White House while the Democrats prepared for their own July convention in Chicago, the sentimental site of Roosevelt's first nomination in 1932 and, more important, a city firmly under the fist of Mayor Edward J. Kelly, the local Democratic boss. Kelly could be counted on to pack the galleries with Roosevelt enthusiasts and to help orchestrate a supposedly spontaneous surge to draft Roosevelt. Sphinx-like, Roosevelt still made no overt move to seek the nomination as the conventioneers poured into Chicago. His precedent-breaking third-term candidacy must have the appearance, at least, of responding to enthusiastic pleading from the delegates. In reality he was by now determined to have the nomination. The delegates, however, threatened to flub their designated roles. They appeared to be going about the chore of nominating Roosevelt, one newspaper observed, with all the gusto of a chain gang. At the critical juncture, as the presiding officer read a statement from Roosevelt that the delegates were free to vote for whomever they pleased, Kelly ordered a pro-Roosevelt demonstration to begin. From the loudspeakers an unidentified voice bellowed, "We want Roosevelt," and the demonstrators mimicked and swelled the cry, chanting it for nearly an hour. Meanwhile, a reporter tracked the mysterious voice

50. Davis 4:582.

to the convention hall's basement, where he found Mayor Kelly's superintendent of sewers seated at a microphone, surrounded by amplification equipment and a detailed script for stimulating the "spontaneous" spectacle on the floor above.

Thanks to the "voice from the sewer," the charade of a "draft" was at least momentarily sustained, and Roosevelt was nominated on the first ballot. In a provocative move, he designated as his running mate Agriculture Secretary Henry Wallace, a former progressive Republican who had first registered as a Democrat only in 1936. Wallace was an unreconstructed liberal reformer and an unflinching New Dealer, qualities that recommended him to Roosevelt. But old-guard Democratic Party regulars deeply distrusted Wallace as an apostate Republican and as a doe-eyed mystic who symbolized all they found objectionable about the hopelessly utopian, market-manipulating, bureaucracy-breeding New Deal. Boos echoed through the Chicago convention hall when Roosevelt's choice of Wallace was announced. The delegates appeared to be on the brink of mutiny. Roosevelt later tried to appease Democratic conservatives by naming RFC director Jesse Jones, an archconservative Texan, as secretary of commerce. But for the moment, it was only after Roosevelt threatened to decline his own nomination if Wallace were not on the ticket, and after a conciliatory speech by Eleanor Roosevelt, the first wife of a nominee ever to address a national political convention, that the delegates grudgingly yielded. Their grumpy acquiescence and the soon-to-be-announced Jones appointment provided yet more proof of the deep ideological divisions in the Democratic Party.

When he named Wallace his vice-presidential partner, Roosevelt flung a farewell bouquet to the old progressive wing of the Republican Party — the wing of George Norris, Hiram Johnson, and Robert La Follette Jr. — with whom he had once hoped to forge a lasting partnership for liberalism. In a far more telling pair of appointments in June, unmistakably signaling that foreign policy, not domestic reform, was now his urgent priority, Roosevelt had extended his hand to an altogether different Republican constituency. In the process, he cut some important political ground out from under Willkie. Remembering the sad fate of his old chief, Woodrow Wilson, whose foreign policies had been unraveled by partisan wrangling, Roosevelt named two prominent Republicans to his cabinet just four days before the GOP gathered in Philadelphia. Frank Knox now became secretary of the navy and Henry L. Stimson secretary of war (to replace the argumentative Charles Edison and the recalcitrant

Harry Woodring, respectively). Knox was a onetime Rough Rider, a well-known Chicago newspaper editor, the Republican vice-presidential nominee in 1936, and a vociferous internationalist.

Stimson was an elder statesman of impeccable personal and political pedigree. Born to wealth, he had been educated at Andover, Yale College, and Harvard Law School. Effortlessly assuming his station in what passed for the American aristocracy of his day, he had served as secretary of war in William Howard Taft's administration and as secretary of state under Herbert Hoover. The arc of Stimson's career traced the breathtaking transformations in American life in the near-century since the Civil War had ended. Born during Reconstruction, Stimson was seventy-three years old in 1940, a man who had lived out his boyhood in the bow-and-arrow era of the Plains Indian wars and was destined to help direct a thoroughly modern world war to its shattering nuclear conclusion. Shaped by the values of the nineteenth century, Stimson was a paragon of probity, both public and private (the Stimsons did not entertain divorced persons). He was also the very model, indeed monument, of internationalist Republicanism, a figure of towering prestige and unflappable self-possession that immunized him against the inevitable accusations that he had betrayed his party by accepting Roosevelt's invitation to join the cabinet. Stimson was, if anything, an even more ardent and outspoken internationalist than Knox. In the months leading up to his appointment, he had grown increasingly uncomfortable with his isolationist associates in the Republican Party. On the very eve of his cabinet appointment, Stimson delivered an earnest radio address urging maximum possible aid to Britain, including U.S. Navy escorts to shepherd the great British merchant convoys bearing munitions across the Atlantic—a position that Roosevelt himself had not dared to take publicly.

The appointments of Knox and Stimson bespoke Roosevelt's high-minded intention to seek bipartisan consensus in a time of grave national crisis. "Not since that titanic conservative, Alexander Hamilton, handed the election of 1800 to his hated rival, the liberal Jefferson, to save and unite the nation in a time of crisis," wrote Dorothy Thompson in the *New York Herald Tribune*, "has a political leader of America made a more magnanimous and wholehearted gesture." The Knox and Stimson appointments had a less edifying partisan logic as well. Roosevelt knew that these two high-profile cabinet nominations would drive a wedge into Republican ranks on the issue of aid to Britain, isolating the isolationists and thereby weakening the hand of whoever was the Republican presidential candidate.[51]

Willkie thus commenced his already curious political career with considerable handicaps. He attempted to overcome them by campaigning with muscular and sometimes madcap eccentricity. An energetic but amateurish speaker, he often ad-libbed witlessly—as when he promised to replace social worker Frances Perkins with a new secretary of labor drawn from labor's own ranks, and then added gratuitously, "and it won't be a woman, either." He frequently grew so animated at the podium that he jittered away from the fixed microphone—a fatal mistake in the radio age.

Yet whatever his crotchets as a campaigner, Willkie shared enough of Roosevelt's own internationalist convictions that his candidacy, along with the Knox and Stimson appointments, helped to neutralize foreign policy as an issue for much of the campaign. Roosevelt, for example, had hesitated to embrace the Burke-Wadsworth selective service bill, a bipartisan proposal then making its way through Congress, though its provisions fitted well with his own declared policies. In defiance of Marshall's and Stark's call for "complete mobilization," and in keeping with Roosevelt's short-of-war thinking, the selective service bill mandated just one year of service for draftees and forbade their deployment outside the Western Hemisphere. The bill would nevertheless impose the first peacetime draft in American history, and its potential electoral fallout chafed on Roosevelt. Even "a limited form of selective draft," he told a correspondent, "may very easily defeat the Democratic National Ticket."[52] But when a reporter advised Willkie that "if you want to win the election you will come out against the proposed draft," Willkie shot back: "I would rather not win the election than do that." Selective service, Willkie declared in a campaign speech, "is the only democratic way in which to assure the trained and competent man-power we need in our national defense."[53] With the backing of both presidential candidates, the bill passed on September 16. One month later, more than sixteen million men between the ages of twenty-one and thirty-five were registered on the draft rolls.

51. *New York Herald Tribune*, October 9, 1940, 25.
52. Dallek, 249.
53. Ellsworth Barnard, *Wendell Willkie, Fighter for Freedom* (Marquette: Northern Michigan University Press, 1966), 204–5.

The vexed and long-delayed destroyer transfer was a different matter. By early August, Roosevelt thought he had hit upon a device for getting the destroyers into Churchill's hands. He proposed to exchange the warships for a gift from Britain to the United States of two naval bases in Newfoundland and Bermuda and ninety-nine year leases on additional bases in the British West Indies. In this form, the destroyers-for-bases deal could be presented as a means of upgrading hemispheric defense, thus shrewdly blunting isolationist criticism and neatly sidestepping a statutory prohibition on the release of equipment deemed essential for national defense.[54] The exchange provisos of the deal also constituted a shaky but arguably supportable legal basis on which to ask Congress for authorization to make the transfer. Would Willkie use his good offices with congressional Republicans to facilitate the transaction? Roosevelt sent his personal emissary, journalist William Allen White, head of the Committee to Defend America by Aiding the Allies, to put the question to Willkie, then campaigning in Colorado. "Willkie ducked," White reported, "for various good reasons. . . . [H]e feels a natural diffidence about assuming Congressional leadership before his ears are dry." But, White told the president, "It's not as bad as it seems." Willkie would not endorse the deal, but neither would he condemn it outright. Bereft of Willkie's help with Congress, Roosevelt brooded that he "might get impeached" if he proceeded with the transfer.[55] But reassured that Willkie would not make the destroyer-bases deal a major campaign issue, Roosevelt eventually bypassed Congress altogether and ordered the exchange on his own executive authority. It was consummated on September 2.

The destroyer-bases deal was a ringing triumph for Churchill. In a speech honoring the airmen waging the Battle of Britain — "Never in the field of human conflict was so much owed by so many to so few," he said, coining the soubriquet ("the Few") by which the RAF pilots

---

54. The National Defense Appropriation Act that Roosevelt had just signed on June 28, 1940, contained a clause that reflected the mounting American concern that Roosevelt was doing to America by policy what Dunkirk had wrought upon Britain by retreat — exhausting the nation's already meager weapons stockpile. The act permitted the transfer only of equipment that had been certified as not essential for national defense. Since the understrength navy had just declared even its aging World War I–vintage ships indispensable for that purpose, the act's language appeared to present an insuperable obstacle to transferring the destroyers to Britain.

55. L&G, *Challenge*, 754; David E. Lilienthal, *The Journals of David E. Lilienthal* (New York: Harper and Row, 1964), 1:209.

would forever be known—Churchill also extravagantly hailed the destroyer-bases agreement. Well he might have. The deal helped bring closer to realization the vision that had guided all Churchill's foreign policy since assuming office. It signified, he said, the deepening of a process whereby "the English-speaking democracies, the British Empire and the United States, will have to be somewhat mixed up together in some of their affairs for mutual and general advantage. For my part, looking out upon the future, I do not view the process with any misgivings. I could not stop it if I wished; no one can stop it. Like the Mississippi," Churchill artfully concluded for the benefit of his American audience, "it just keeps rolling along. Let it roll. Let it roll on full flood, inexorable, irresistible, benignant, to broader lands and better days."[56]

The destroyers themselves did not roll on with comparable inexorability. By the end of the year, only nine of the promised fifty had reached Britain, where the admiralty found them even less seaworthy than expected. In any case, on September 17, just two weeks after the destroyer-bases deal was announced, Enigma decrypts confirmed that Hitler had indefinitely postponed Operation Sealion, the expected invasion against which the destroyers were to have been deployed.[57] It was "the Few," not American ships, that had won the Battle of Britain. But as Churchill understood, the compelling logic for the destroyer-bases exchange had always been more political and psychological than military. The deal's true payoff lay in the future. It was to be measured not in its contribution to the defense of Britain in the summer of 1940 but in its catalytic effect on cementing the Anglo-American alliance—and in edging the United States closer to belligerency.

Willkie confined himself to denouncing the executive order that implemented the destroyer-bases deal as "the most arbitrary and dictatorial action ever taken by any President in the history of the United States"— a sweeping charge, to say the least, but also a hollow and ironic one, since Willkie could have made himself the instrument of congressional involvement had he chosen.[58] In any event, Willkie's criticism was restricted to the method, not the substance, of the destroyers-for-bases swap. The archisolationist *Chicago Tribune*, in contrast, damned the deal as "an act of war." Churchill put the matter more temperately but essentially agreed with that assessment. "The transfer to Great Britain

56. Cannadine, *Blood, Toil, Tears and Sweat*, 192.
57. Ronald Lewin, *Ultra Goes to War*, 95.
58. Freidel, *Rendezvous with Destiny*, 352.

of fifty American warships was a decidedly unneutral Act," he later wrote. "It would, according to all the standards of history, have justified the German Government in declaring war upon [the United States]. . . . [I]t was the first of a long succession of increasingly unneutral acts in the Atlantic which were of the utmost service to us. . . . All the world," Churchill concluded, "understood the significance of the gesture."[59]

In the closing days of the campaign, Willkie's mounting political desperation and the abrasive nagging of isolationist Republicans like Vandenberg temporarily eclipsed the candidate's internationalist convictions, not to mention his poise. Abandoning the civil tone that had informed his early campaign statements, Willkie took to stridently denouncing Roosevelt as a warmonger. "We do not want to send our boys over there again," he said in a speech in St. Louis. "[I]f you elect the third-term candidate, I believe they will be sent."[60] In an increasingly emotional series of speeches on Willkie's behalf, Charles Lindbergh bruited the same theme. So did John L. Lewis, who endorsed Willkie and damned Roosevelt in a nationwide broadcast on October 25. For good measure, Lewis threatened that if the nation's industrial workers repudiated his advice, he would resign as president of the CIO.[61]

The Lindbergh and Lewis endorsements and Roosevelt's clear vulnerability on the warmongering charge unsettled the Roosevelt camp in the campaign's closing days. "This fellow Willkie is about to beat the Boss," presidential adviser Harry Hopkins fretted.[62] Roosevelt remained in the White House for most of the campaign, but at the end of October, appearing presidential and statesmanlike, he at last took to the campaign trail. As with Willkie, the rising political stakes as election day neared clouded Roosevelt's usually careful judgment. At first he contented himself with reminding audiences that Willkie's was also the party of "Martin, Barton, and Fish," three notoriously isolationist congressmen whose names formed a catchy trinomial chant with which Roosevelt worked Democratic crowds into paroxysms of partisan enthusiasm.[63] But as he

---

59. An excellent brief account of the destroyers-for-bases deal is in L&G, *Challenge*, 742–76. Churchill's remarks are in Churchill 2:404. Contrary to much mythology, the destroyers were hardly, as the title of one melodramatic account claims, *Fifty Ships That Saved the World* (by Philip Goodheart; Garden City, N.Y.: Doubleday, 1965).

60. Lash, *Roosevelt and Churchill*, 237.

61. As good as his word, Lewis resigned after the election returned Roosevelt to the White House.

62. Lash, *Roosevelt and Churchill*, 235.

63. Joseph Martin was from Massachusetts; Bruce Barton and Hamilton Fish were from New York. All three were Republicans.

headed for a crucial speech in Boston on October 30, Roosevelt was manifestly worried. Neither for the first time nor the last, he requested from Churchill a gesture that would give him a boost with American voters, a statement, he instructed Morgenthau, "in Churchill's own language — he is a writer — that the president can use to the Boston Irish."[64] But Churchill's word-mill failed him on this occasion. Roosevelt, left to his own devices in Boston, zestfully invoked the now familiar litany of "Martin, Barton, and Fish." He also ventured a reckless promise: "I have said this before, but I shall say it again and again: Your boys are not going to be sent into any foreign wars." Conspicuously, Roosevelt omitted the qualifying phrase that he had used on previous occasions: "except in case of attack."[65]

Listening on the radio, Willkie exploded: "That hypocritical son of a bitch! This is going to beat me."[66] He was half right. Willkie was decisively beaten, to be sure, but it was not Roosevelt's tortuously hedged promises to stay out of foreign wars that carried the president to his unprecedented third-term victory. Public opinion surveys indicated that it was in fact the looming reality of American involvement in armed conflict, not Roosevelt's seductive assurances about peace, that hurt Willkie the most. Asked how they would vote if there were no war, voters favored Willkie by a 5.5 percent margin, reflecting disillusion with the New Deal and disaffection over the third-term issue. But when confronted with the possibility of fighting, they preferred Roosevelt by a far larger percentage. By election day many voters had obviously made their reckoning with the dread prospect of war. They had decided it was no time to exchange the reliable Roosevelt they had known through eight years of depression, reform, and ratcheting international tensions for the edgy Willkie they had seen in the campaign. The Republican candidate prevailed in just ten states — the traditional Republican strongholds of Maine and Vermont and eight more in the isolationist Midwestern heartland. Roosevelt's winning margin was his narrowest yet. Willkie polled five million more votes than Landon had four years earlier, a

64. Warren F. Kimball, *The Most Unsordid Act: Lend-Lease, 1939–1941* (Baltimore: Johns Hopkins Press, 1969), 84.
65. *PPA* (1940), 517. In previous campaign speeches, Roosevelt had added the words "except in case of attack" to his promise not to send Americans into "foreign wars." When an adviser remarked the absence of that qualifier in the Boston speech, Roosevelt testily replied, "If somebody attacks us, then it isn't a foreign war, is it?" — a pettifogging cavil that betrayed the president's uneasiness on this most volatile of all issues. See Freidel, *Rendezvous with Destiny*, 355.
66. Barnard, *Wendell Willkie, Fighter for Freedom*, 258.

telling index of how far Roosevelt's popularity had diminished from the triumphal referendum on the New Deal in 1936. But in the last analysis, Willkie owed his defeat to anxiety about his inexperience—and to the faint signs of returning prosperity.[67]

Roosevelt had in fact devoted most of his speech in Boston not to fatuous promises of peace but to a somewhat callous recitation of the good economic news spawned by the British war orders. "You good people here in Boston know of the enormous increase of productive work in your Boston Navy Yard," he reminded his listeners. At the same time he spoke, through the radio, to the "citizens of Seattle—you have watched the Boeing plant out there grow." Similarly, he addressed listeners in southern California, Buffalo, St. Louis, Hartford, and Paterson, New Jersey—all communities where war orders were terminating a dreary decade of mass unemployment. Roosevelt well understood the cold political logic of rising employment. "These foreign orders mean prosperity in this country and we can't elect a Democratic Party unless we get prosperity and these foreign orders are of the greatest importance," he had said privately some eight months earlier, when the big Allied aircraft contracts were starting to come in.[68] Thanks largely to British weapons purchases, by election day nearly 3.5 million more workers were employed than in the trough of the Roosevelt Recession of 1937–38. Unemployment had shrunk by the end of 1940 to 14.6 percent, its lowest level in ten years, and was swiftly trending lower still.

In Britain, meanwhile, by the time of Roosevelt's reelection more than ten thousand Londoners had perished in the Blitz, six thousand in October alone. Those rising death tolls made a somber contrast with falling American unemployment statistics, a contrast that foretold much about the different destinies that the gods of war had in store for America and for its eventual allies, not to mention the fates that awaited their common enemies. The contrast was hardly lost on Winston Churchill. He grumbled privately that the Americans were "very good in applauding the valiant deeds done by others," but to Roosevelt he was the soul of graciousness. "I prayed for your success," he cabled to Roosevelt after the election. "I am truly thankful for it. . . . Things are afoot which will be remembered as long as the English language is spoken in any quarter of the globe."[69]

67. Dallek, 250.
68. Morgenthau Diary, 302.
69. Gilbert, *Churchill: A Life* 672; C&R 1:81.

15

To the Brink

We must be the great arsenal of democracy.
— Franklin D. Roosevelt, Fireside Chat,
December 29, 1940

The supreme geopolitical fact of the modern era, Prince Bismarck is alleged to have remarked, is that the Americans speak English. Winston Churchill, with his incessant references to the common ideals and interests of the "English-speaking peoples," exploited that theme shamelessly. On it, indeed, he based his strategy for Britain's survival. But for all the apparent inevitability of Anglo-American cooperation against the Nazi threat, in actual practice the transatlantic partnership was devilishly difficult to forge. Churchill's anxieties and often cunning manipulations, as well as Roosevelt's own hesitations and evasions, his wary deference to the isolationists, and his frequently cagey misrepresentations to the American public, all testified to the abundant difficulties that impeded collaboration between Britain and the United States — not to mention the even more formidable obstacles that blocked full-blown American belligerency.

As 1940 drew toward a close, an especially complicated difficulty arose. With flatfooted lack of ceremony, Lord Lothian, the British ambassador to the United States, announced the problem on November 23, upon his return from a brief trip to London. Alighting from his plane at New York's La Guardia Airport, Lothian declared to the waiting reporters: "Well, boys, Britain's broke. It's your money we want."[1]

Lothian's statement surely lacked diplomatic subtlety, but it just as

1. Warren F. Kimball, *The Most Unsordid Act: Lend-Lease, 1939–1941* (Baltimore: Johns Hopkins Press, 1969), 96.

465

surely came as no surprise. The British themselves had long anticipated their impending insolvency. In early 1939, even before the war's out-break, the British treasury had begun to seize control of all gold hold-ings, foreign securities, and dollar balances held by British nationals. Further to conserve precious dollar reserves, and to the annoyance of American business interests, the London government had curtailed cer-tain American imports, including fruit, tobacco, and Hollywood films. But those measures only postponed the inevitable. The day of reckoning was now at hand.

It was no easy thing for Americans accustomed to thinking of Britain as the swaggering master of a global empire now to believe the assertions of British bankruptcy. Many American observers had special difficulty grasping the crucial distinction between Britain's still-formidable sterling reserves and her meager stock of dollars, dwindled by a decade of con-stricted U.S.-British trade. Meeting to analyze the British financial sit-uation on December 3, 1940, at Woodley, Secretary of War Stimson's Washington home, several officials squinted in puzzlement at the figures that Treasury Department specialists scrawled across the blackboard. The inescapable conclusion of the complicated mathematical exercise was that Britain would exhaust its gold and dollar balances within weeks, just to pay for orders already placed. The dollars to pay for future orders were nowhere in sight. At length Secretary of the Navy Knox asked simply, "We are going to pay for the war from now on, are we?" To which Treasury Secretary Morgenthau replied: "Well, what are we going to do, are we going to let them place more orders or not?" On the response to that question hung Roosevelt's short-of-war strategy, which relied on an adequately supplied Britain to carry the battle to Germany. On it, too, depended the reviving health of the American economy, stimulated since mid-1940 by accumulating British war orders. Aware of those facts, Knox and the other leaders in the room did not need long to ponder the implications of Morgenthau's question. "Got to. No choice about it," Knox answered.[2]

There may have been no choice, but neither were there readily ap-parent means for the United States to facilitate further British purchases. The Johnson Act of 1934, prohibiting loans to countries in default on their World War I debts, remained on the books; so did the cash-and-carry provisions of the neutrality legislation of the preceding decade. Legally, not to mention politically, Uncle Sam's hands seemed to be

2. L&G, *Undeclared*, 229.

tied. The only recourse, Morgenthau confided to his diary, was to trust in Franklin Roosevelt's inventive mind. "It gets down to the question of Mr. Churchill putting himself in Mr. Roosevelt's hands with complete confidence," Morgenthau wrote. "Then it is up to Mr. Roosevelt to say what he will do."[3]

On December 9 a navy seaplane feathered down through the balmy Caribbean air to deliver a packet of mail to President Roosevelt, cruising aboard the USS *Tuscaloosa* on a postelection vacation. The mail pouch contained a historic letter from Churchill, one that has been described as "the most carefully drafted and re-drafted message in the entire Churchill-Roosevelt correspondence" and that amounted to what the historian Warren Kimball calls an "epitaph to the British Empire as [Churchill] knew it."[4] Perhaps understandably, Churchill took up several other matters before facing the moment of fiscal truth. "It takes between three and four years to convert the industries of a modern state to war purposes," Churchill began. By that reckoning, the United States would need at least two more years to reach "maximum industrial effort." During that preparatory interval, Britain alone would "hold the front and grapple with Nazi power until the preparations of the United States are complete." But two dangers threatened Britain's ability to persevere. Both of them could be alleviated only by the repeal of the American cash-and-carry provisos. Churchill first elucidated the "carry" problem. There was "mortal danger," Churchill warned, in "the steady and increasing diminution of sea tonnage." If shipping losses continued at their present rate, Churchill predicted, the results would be "fatal," for Britain as well as the United States, because "we may fall by the way and the time needed by the United States to complete her defensive preparations may not be forthcoming." Only American merchant ships, and ultimately armed escorts of merchant convoys by the U.S. Navy, could keep the Atlantic lifeline intact.

The shipping problem was grave, but the second threat was even more urgent. It was the one that Lothian had already advertised and the one that especially galled Churchill to discuss: Britain's lack of cash. The prime minister got to it only in his closing paragraphs: "Last of all I come to the question of finance. The more rapid and abundant the flow of munitions and ships which you are able to send us, the sooner will

3. L&G, *Undeclared*, 231.
4. C&R. 1:88, 111.

our dollar credits be exhausted. . . . The moment approaches when we shall no longer be able to pay cash for shipping and other supplies." Contemplating the liquidation of centuries' accumulation of imperial wealth, the prime minister suggested that it would be wrong if "Great Britain were to be divested of all saleable assets so that after victory was won with our blood, civilization saved and time gained for the United States to be fully armed against all eventualities, we should stand stripped to the bone. . . . We here would be unable after the war to purchase the large balance of imports from the United States. . . . Not only should we in Great Britain suffer cruel privations but widespread unemployment in the United States would follow the curtailment of American exporting power."[5]

Back in Washington a week later, tanned and rested from his Caribbean cruise, Roosevelt gave his answer to Churchill at a press conference. Confirming his view that "the best immediate defense of the United States is the success of Great Britain in defending itself," Roosevelt went straight to the financial question. "I have read a great deal of nonsense in the last few days by people who can only think in what we may call traditional terms about finances," Roosevelt said airily to the reporters crowded around his desk on December 17. "Now, what I am trying to do," Roosevelt continued, is to "get rid of the silly, foolish old dollar sign." The president illustrated his point with what became a famous parable. If a neighbor's house was on fire and he needed your garden hose to put it out, you wouldn't haggle about the price; you would loan him the hose, and he would return it when the blaze was extinguished. By the same token, Roosevelt proposed, the United States would provide Britain whatever supplies she needed, "with the understanding that when the show was over, we would get repaid something in kind, thereby leaving out the dollar mark in the form of a dollar debt and substituting for it a gentleman's obligation to repay in kind. I think you all get it."[6]

Roosevelt drove the point home twelve days later. In one of his most memorable Fireside Chats, on December 29, 1940, he offered his countrymen a basic primer on American national security policy. "If Great Britain goes down," he explained, "the Axis powers will control the continents of Europe, Asia, Africa, Australasia, and the high seas — and they will be in a position to bring enormous military and naval resources

5. C&R 1:102–9.
6. PPA (1940, 604–8.

against this hemisphere. It is no exaggeration to say that all of us, in all the Americas, would be living at the point of a gun." To prevent that result, "we must have more ships, more guns, more planes—more of everything. . . . We must be the great arsenal of democracy." The nations already contending against Hitler, Roosevelt insisted, "do not ask us to do their fighting. They ask us for the implements of war. . . . Emphatically we must get these weapons to them in sufficient volume and quickly enough, so that we and our children will be saved the agony and suffering of war which others have had to endure."[7]

That last statement reflected Roosevelt's continuing public adherence at the end of 1940 to the short-of-war strategy. For the record, he was proposing that America should be an arsenal, not become a combatant. Yet the president's military advisers were already giving him reason to believe that he could not indefinitely adhere to his carefully measured strategy of pro-British nonbelligerency. "We cannot permanently be in the position of toolmakers for other nations which fight," thought Henry Stimson.[8] In the new year that was dawning, events soon threatened to shove the United States to the forwardmost edge of the combat zone, especially in the embattled North Atlantic.

The release of "surplus" military supplies in the summer of 1940 and the destroyer-bases deal in September of that year had been consummated as executive actions. Roosevelt's new proposal to supply Britain without reference to the dollar sign, soon popularly known as "Lend-Lease," would not be—indeed, could not be—an executive action, since Lend-Lease required an initial congressional appropriation of some $7 billion. "We don't want to fool the public; we want to do this thing right out and out," Roosevelt said to Morgenthau.[9] Lend-Lease would now be the subject of a "Great Debate," conducted publicly, noisily, lengthily, and for the most part responsibly, but not always with the unvarnished candor that Roosevelt claimed.

The president inaugurated the debate in his annual message to Congress on January 6, 1941, when he announced that he was sending the Lend-Lease Bill to Congress. He ended with a ringing flourish in which he defined the "four essential human freedoms" that his policies were ultimately aimed at securing: freedom of speech and religion, and freedom from want and from fear. These Four Freedoms, promulgated in

7. *PPA* (1940), 633–44.
8. Kimball, *Most Unsordid Act*, 129.
9. L&G, *Undeclared*, 255.

every then-known medium, including a sentimental painting and poster by the popular artist Norman Rockwell, soon became a sort of shorthand for America's war aims. They could be taken, too, especially the concepts of freedom from want and fear, as a charter for the New Deal itself. At this level of basic principle, there was unmistakable continuity between Roosevelt's domestic policies during the Great Depression and his foreign policies in the world war.

Congressional hearings on the Lend-Lease bill — the House version cleverly numbered H.R. 1776 — opened on January 10, 1941. Beyond the Capitol, in blue-collar bars and paneled clubrooms, in classrooms and church basements and around kitchen tables, over the airwaves and in editorial columns, the bill was ventilated, analyzed, criticized, probed, and praised. Fortunately for the president's purposes, the debate over Lend-Lease took place at a favorable moment. England's apparent victory in the Battle of Britain had fended off the threat of immediate invasion, and Roosevelt's recent electoral victory had freshened his political popularity. As the debate began, public opinion polls showed solid majorities behind the president's Lend-Lease policy.[10]

Leaving nothing to chance, Roosevelt sent both Harry Hopkins and Wendell Willkie to England to coach Churchill on how best to support the Lend-Lease legislation. Hopkins helped to draft one Churchill speech that was both disingenuous and, even by the prime minister's own occasionally mawkish standards, more than a little treacly. Churchill declared: "We do not need the gallant armies which are forming throughout the American Union. We do not need them this year, nor next year; nor any year that I can foresee. But we do need most urgently an immense and continuous supply of war materials and technical apparatus of all kinds. . . . We need a great mass of shipping in 1942, far more than we can build ourselves." Churchill next directly addressed his American listeners with a passage from Longfellow that Roosevelt had copied out in longhand and asked Willkie to deliver:

> Sail On, O Ship of State!
> Sail on, O Union, strong and great!
> Humanity with all its fears,
> With all the hopes of future years,
>   Is hanging breathless on thy fate!

10. Cantril, 409–11, 588.

Then, more than a little misleadingly, Churchill concluded: "Give us the tools, and we will finish the job."[11]

American isolationists were not so easily taken in by this display of Churchillian charm. The prime minister's soothing assurances that Britain needed only American materiel, not men, they branded as transparently counterfeit. They believed that Lend-Lease was not just another measure to aid Britain. By openly committing the United States government to financing the British war effort, America became Britain's co-belligerent in all but name. If Lend-Lease passed, it was only a matter of time until American naval and military forces would be engaged in a shooting war. In all this, events proved the isolationist critics to be quite correct.

Fear of Lend-Lease's eventual consequences even attracted some new adherents to the anti-interventionist cause. Roosevelt's former supporter William Allen White, head of the Committee to Defend America by Aiding the Allies, created a year earlier to promote aid to Britain, resigned from the committee in protest over Lend-Lease, which he thought ran too close a risk of precipitating American belligerency. America's motto, White declared, should be "The Yanks Are Not Coming." Mothers, coated against the January chill, knelt on the Capitol steps to pray histrionically: "Kill Bill 1776, not our sons." Other opponents of Lend-Lease voiced additional criticisms. The America First Committee, organized several months earlier in the wake of the destroyer-bases deal, argued that funneling Lend-Lease resources to Britain would criminally retard America's own rearmament program. Spokesmen for the German-American Bund predictably denounced the bill as wantonly provocative. So did representatives of the Communist

11. David Cannadine, ed., *Blood, Toil, Tears and Sweat: The Speeches of Winston Churchill* (Boston: Houghton Mifflin, 1989), 202–13. Churchill's disingenuousness went further still. He encouraged Hopkins to believe that the Germans might invade any day, going so far as to tell Hopkins that he had already devised the peroration for his speech announcing the German landings: "The hour has come; kill the Hun." Hopkins reported to Roosevelt on January 28: "The most important single observation I have to make is most of the Cabinet and all of the military leaders here believe that invasion is imminent." What neither Churchill nor anyone else told Hopkins was that on January 12 a Bletchley decrypt of a German order shutting down the Continental wireless stations necessary to an invasion had confirmed that Operation Sealion had been canceled. See Robert E. Sherwood, *Roosevelt and Hopkins* (New York: Grosset and Dunlap, 1950), 257, and Martin Gilbert, *Churchill: A Life* (New York: Henry Holt 1991), 688.

Party, still slavishly in thrall to the tortured party line that Nazi Germany, as an ally of Moscow since the Molotov-Ribbentrop Pact, should not be antagonized. One Irish-American congressman from Cleveland, Ohio, gave vent to the Anglophobia that pervaded many American communities by penning a new stanza for "God Bless America:"

> God save America from British rule:
> Stand beside her and guide her
> From the schemers who would make of her a fool.
> From Lexington to Yorktown,
> From blood-stained Valley Forge,
> God Save America
> From a king named George.[12]

In the isolationist capital of Chicago, the ever-pugnacious Robert R. McCormick fulminated against the bill. Along with his cousin Joseph Patterson's New York *Daily News* and his cousin Cissy Patterson's *Washington Times-Herald*, McCormick's two-penny, million-circulation *Tribune* had long numbered among the biggest megaphones for isolationist pronouncements. The internationally minded publisher Henry Luce called the cousins "the Three Furies of Isolation." Roosevelt called them "the McCormick-Patterson Axis." Together the cousins brewed up a gale of complaint against Lend-Lease. The *Daily News* ran cartoons showing a ghoulish figure of World War II as "Uncle Sap's new girlfriend." From McCormick's archconservative *Tribune* (as well as from the Communist *Daily Worker*) came the dark pronouncement that H.R. 1776 was a "Dictator Bill" designed "to destroy the Republic." In testimony before the Senate Foreign Relations Committee, McCormick flatly asserted: "I do not think [Britain] needs anything." When Wendell Willkie testified in favor of Lend-Lease, the *Tribune* took to referring to him as "the Republican Quisling."[13] Some other critics were rougher still. Roosevelt's onetime progressive ally Montana senator Burton Wheeler, now his implacable adversary in foreign policy, charged that the Lend-Lease legislation was the New Deal's "triple-A foreign policy; it will plough

12. Kimball, *Most Unsordid Act*, 186–87.
13. Richard Norton Smith, *The Colonel: The Life and Legend of Robert R. McCormick, Indomitable Editor of the* Chicago Tribune (Boston: Houghton Mifflin, 1997), 403–4. Vidkun Quisling was the Norwegian collaborator who helped the Germans prepare the conquest of Norway and became the premier of Nazi-occupied Norway in 1942.

under every fourth American boy." Roosevelt called that accusation "the rottenest thing that has been said in public life in my generation."[14]

To counter isolationist criticism, Roosevelt reasoned, Britain must be seen to have exhausted all its dollar resources before receiving American aid. The administration made a particular point of requiring Britain to use her remaining dollar reserves to finance the capital costs of the plant expansion necessary to servicing her future war orders. Accordingly, and to Churchill's extreme consternation, Roosevelt seized some British assets and compelled the sale of others. When a U.S. naval vessel showed up in Cape Town to collect some $50 million in British gold reserves, Churchill penned a stinging note protesting that the American action had "the aspect of a sheriff collecting the last assets of a helpless debtor." It was "not fitting that any nation should put itself wholly in the hands of another," the prime minister complained, but on sober second thought he decided that supplication and scolding did not gracefully mix, and refrained from sending the letter.[15] By late January 1941 the British treasury agent in New York, under intense American pressure, was liquidating Britain's American securities holdings at the rate of some $10 million per week. When London protested, Secretary Morgenthau explained: "[W]hat is in the mind of the ordinary citizen is that England yet hasn't gone far enough. . . . It is a matter of—well, convincing the general public of the determination, of just how far the English businessman is ready to go. It is a psychological matter as much as anything else."[16] Psychological indeed. Eventually the Reconstruction Finance Corporation arranged for loans to finance the plant expansion necessary to service the British—and American—war orders, ending the need for Britain to sell off her remaining direct investments in the United States. But the public spectacle of forced British sales in the early months of 1941 helped see the Lend-Lease bill through to congressional passage.

The isolationists were strong enough to attach several amendments to the Lend-Lease bill. By far the most consequential of them anticipated the issue over which administration policymakers were to agonize for much of the remainder of 1941: the question of providing U.S. Navy

14. L&G, Undeclared, 258–59.
15. C&R 1:120; see also Gilbert, Churchill, 687.
16. L&G, Undeclared, 230. Morgenthau had additional motives for promoting the sale of British securities. "The tie-up between the so-called 'City' in London and our own Wall Street is terribly close," he remarked when one important sale was consummated. "I consider this a great New Deal victory." Kimball, Most Unsordid Act, 225.

escorts on the Atlantic to ensure the safe arrival of the convoys carrying Lend-Lease goods to Britain. (In naval parlance, a warship "escorted" a convoy of merchant ships; but among laymen, including the legislators in Congress, the term "convoy" was often used in place of "escort.") "Nothing in this Act," the relevant clause read, "shall be construed to authorize or to permit the authorization of convoying vessels by naval vessels of the United States."[17] The administration accepted that amendment, but here, too, there was an element of evasion. In their congressional testimony, both Secretary Stimson and Secretary Knox publicly acquiesced in the no-convoy clause while maintaining that the president already had the constitutional authority as commander-in-chief to order naval escorting. Whether the president himself believed that he had the constitutional power — and, no less important, the political license — actually to implement escorting remained an open question. At a press conference on January 21, Roosevelt denied that he had even thought about naval escorts. Escorting could lead to shooting, he said, "and shooting comes awfully close to war, doesn't it? That is about the last thing we have in our minds."[18]

In early March Congress passed the amended Lend-Lease bill by substantial majorities: 60–31 in the Senate and 317–71 in the House. Almost all the opposition was Republican, and it was heavily concentrated in the still staunchly isolationist Midwest, the great land-island dominated by Robert McCormick's Chicago. But in the rest of the country, the Great Debate over Lend-Lease had produced a rough consensus of the sort that Roosevelt had long sought. Two-thirds of respondents told polltakers in January 1941 that they approved of the Lend-Lease bill. Before the Lend-Lease debate, the most that Americans would commit themselves to was aid to the democracies short of war. Now, despite Roosevelt's studied reluctance to cross all his *t*'s and dot all his *i*'s, he had edged them closer to a commitment to aid the democracies even at the risk of war.[19]

Roosevelt signed the Lend-Lease bill on March 11. Congress obligingly appropriated $7 billion to fund the first shipments. The *New York Times* hailed Lend-Lease as marking "the day when the United States ended the great retreat which began with the Senate rejection of the

17. Thomas A. Bailey and Paul B. Ryan, *Hitler vs. Roosevelt: The Undeclared Naval War* (New York: Free Press, 1979), 113–14.
18. *The Complete Presidential Press Conferences of Franklin Delano Roosevelt* (New York: Da Capo, 1972), 17:86–87 (January 21, 1941).
19. Cantril, 410.

Treaty of Versailles and the League of Nations. Our effort to find security in isolation has failed. By the final passage of the lend-lease bill we confess its failure."[20] The president quickly established an independent Office of Lend-Lease Administration, briefly headed by Harry Hopkins and later by businessman Edward Stettinius. Lend-Lease mooted the "cash" portion of cash-and-carry. Restrictions remained in force against sending American ships into a designated war zone. Thus it was mostly British vessels that began hauling munitions, foodstuffs, and other supplies away from American ports, the first of nearly $50 billion of American aid, most of it directed to Britain, that would flow from American assembly lines, mills, refineries, and farms during the war. Fittingly enough, given the homely analogy with which Roosevelt had inaugurated the Lend-Lease debate, the first consignment to Britain included nine hundred thousand feet of fire hose.[21]

Lend-Lease effected a kind of "common-law alliance" between Britain and the United States. As in many such unions, attraction and suspicion commingled in sometimes volatile proportions. Churchill told the House of Commons that Lend-Lease was "the most unsordid act in the history of any nation." He telegrammed his thanks to Roosevelt: "Our blessings from the whole of the British Empire go out to you and the American nation for this very present help in time of trouble." More grandiloquently, he capped a radio broadcast on April 27 with yet another paean to American generosity:

> In front the sun climbs slow, how slowly,
> But westward, look, the land is bright.

Yet in private Churchill grumbled that the terms of the legislation, especially the forced sales of British assets that had preceded the bill's passage, meant that "we are not only to be skinned, but flayed to the bone." More calculatingly, he crowed to a British treasury official that after months of angling for American support, he had the Yanks almost where he wanted them: "I would like to get them hooked a little firmer," he said, " but they are pretty on now." Old suspicions died hard, however. Within the Foreign Office, some officials even now doubted that the Americans were safely hooked. Roosevelt's continued fidelity in public to the short-of-war strategy and his manifest reluctance to embrace the manifestly necessary tactic of naval escorts left "many of us here" a

20. *New York Times*, March 12, 1941, 20.
21. Kimball, *Most Unsordid Act*, 229n.

senior Foreign Office official noted, with "an uneasy feeling." America, he speculated, "may in her turn yet rat on us." That decidedly ungrateful attitude had its counterpart on the American side. An Army War Plans Division report in the month following the Lend-Lease Act's signing revealed that American planners, too, had not yet submerged all their anxieties about Britain. The ghost of Neville Chamberlain's sorry ministry still chilled American ardor for embracing the British common-law bride. The danger still loomed, the report warned, of "a material change in the attitude of the British Government directed toward appeasement."[22]

ROOSEVELT HAD COMMITTED the United States to becoming the "great arsenal of democracy." Now it remained to stock that arsenal, a herculean task after years of willful neglect of military preparedness. Time was the most precious of military assets, and America had already squandered much of it. "Dollars cannot buy yesterday," Admiral Harold Stark had said in pleading for the "two-ocean navy" bill in 1940, but 1941 saw a flood of dollars directed toward buying the weapons for a tomorrow that was approaching with hurricane speed.[23] By this date money was no problem. As Senator Henry Cabot Lodge Jr. declared to General Arnold: "[I]t is the general feeling of the Congress, and as far as I can gather, among public opinion throughout the country, to provide all of the money necessary for the National Defense, so all you have to do is ask for it."[24] Ask the administration did: for $7 billion in Lend-Lease authorizations and for $13.7 billion in requisitions for the army and navy before 1941 was over—a mammoth increase over the paltry $2.2 billion appropriated for defense in 1940.[25] That rising tide of military spending began at last to float the wallowing hulk of the economy out of the slough of depression. As nearly one million draftees filed into hastily hammered, green-timbered military training camps,

---

22. Kimball, *Most Unsordid Act*, 236; *C&R* 1:143; Gilbert, *Churchill: A Life*, 692; Frank Freidel, *Roosevelt: A Rendezvous with Destiny* (Boston: Little, Brown, 1990), 362; Joseph P. Lash, *Roosevelt and Churchill: The Partnership That Saved the West* (New York: Norton, 1976), 291; Mark Skinner Watson, *The United States Army in World War II: The War Department: Chief of Staff: Prewar Plans and Operations* (Washington: Department of the Army, 1950), 389.
23. Morison, 30.
24. Watson, *Chief of Staff*, 166.
25. Figures are for calendar, not fiscal, years. They are taken from Harold Vatter, *The U.S. Economy in World War II* (New York: Columbia University Press, 1985), 9.

and as war orders poured into the big industrial centers, unemployment sank below 10 percent for the first time in more than a decade.

But if money was no problem, other obstacles still impeded the stocking of democracy's arsenal. Among them, ironically, was prosperity itself. Contemplating the prospect of their first substantial profits in years, many manufacturers resisted conversion from civilian to military production. "In the beginning most of our industrialists were rather cautious about having their companies undertake war work," RFC head and Secretary of Commerce Jesse H. Jones recalled. "They didn't want to invest a lot of their own funds in equipment to manufacture things they believed would not be in demand after the shooting ceased."[26] The case of the automobile industry exemplified the stiffening competition between civilian and military demands on the economy. Detroit was anticipating sales of some four million cars for 1941, a million more than it had sold in 1939. When United Auto Workers vice-president Walter Reuther proposed utilizing the remaining estimated 50 percent idle capacity in automobile plants by converting them to the manufacture of military aircraft under government contract, the Detroit carmakers flatly refused. Turning a motor vehicle plant to the making of airplanes was not simply a matter of having a different product roll off the end of the assembly line, the automakers insisted. Expensive new investment, the hiring of new designers and engineers, retooling, retraining of workers, and, above all, diversion of resources from that hungrily contemplated four-million-car sales target would all prove necessary. What was more, Reuther's plan would squarely deliver the automobile industry into the clutches of a single powerful customer, the federal government. After years of being badgered by New Deal reformers, the automakers had little desire to clasp the hand of their nemesis and place themselves at the mercy of such an unequal and unpredictable business partner.

A further problem was organizational, or, more precisely, political. Roosevelt could not easily envision any coordinating body powerful enough to organize economic mobilization that would not repeat the distasteful experience of the War Industries Board of World War I, which wrapped private businessmen in the mantle of government authority and effectively licensed them to control the nation's economy. Because those very businessmen, or their successors, had been his stoutest adversaries through the New Deal years, Roosevelt now groped for ways to rationalize economic mobilization without empowering his political

26. Jesse H. Jones, *Fifty Billion Dollars* (New York: Macmillan, 1951), 320.

opponents. (The New Dealers, Hugh Johnson growled, that "pack of semi-communist wolves," did not "intend to let Morgan and Du Pont men run a war.")[27]

Roosevelt began his fumbling effort to wring a measure of order out of the economic chaos of the budding war economy in May 1940, when he revived another World War I–era agency, the National Defense Advisory Commission (NDAC). The NDAC was a weak and ineffective body that was replaced by the only slightly less weak and ineffective Office of Production Management (OPM) in January 1941. OPM had not one director but two: General Motors head William Knudsen and Amalgamated Clothing Workers president Sidney Hillman. Beyond the fact that they were both immigrants — Knudsen from Denmark and Hillman from Lithuania — they had little in common, but their joint appointment signaled the administration's commendable ambition to reconcile the interests of both capital and labor as the job of moving the economy onto a war footing went forward. Roosevelt blithely described OPM's duo as "a single responsible head; his name is Knudsen and Hillman," but the most conspicuous fact about OPM under Knudsen and Hillman was how little responsibility Roosevelt allotted them.[28] Their operational weakness was soon illustrated when Roosevelt supplemented OPM with two additional agencies: the Office of Price Administration and Civilian Supply, under New Deal economist Leon Henderson, as well as the Supply Priorities and Allocation Board, headed by Sears, Roebuck executive Donald Nelson.

This proliferation of mobilization agencies kept economic organization out of the hands of the dreaded businessmen — indeed, effectively out of anyone's hands save possibly Roosevelt's. But it also violated all the rules of sound administrative practice and vastly complicated the task of sorting out all the competing claims on the nation's economy. Confusion as to the country's eventual purpose in the war and the means it might bring to bear to achieve that purpose was by no means new. But as 1941 opened, the continuing irresolution of those questions was becoming painfully acute. It threatened to confirm Nazi foreign minister Joachim Ribbentrop's sneering comment that "American re-armament was the biggest bluff in the world's history."[29] Lend-Lease exacerbated

---

27. Richard Polenberg, *War and Society: The United States, 1941–1945* (Philadelphia: Lippincott, 1972), 7.
28. *PPA* (1940), 684.
29. L&G, *Undeclared*, 495.

TO THE BRINK 479

the confusion. Did the British or the American military have first claim on production? Did the president really believe the short-of-war strategy would work? If so, then for what purpose was the American military and naval buildup intended? What would be the overall scale and duration of American mobilization? Would the United States be called upon to field a ground force or not? If it did, when and where would it be deployed? What would be its size and the composition of its various arms—infantry, armor, artillery? Should the ground, air, or naval services receive priority in development?

AT BOTTOM, the inefficiencies that beset economic mobilization in 1941 were due to the persistent confusion over American strategy. "How much munitions productive capacity does this country need and how rapidly must it become available?" Knudsen had asked as early as June 1940—a businesslike question to which a businesslike answer might have been forthcoming if only politics were as simple as business. Well into 1941 the stubborn fact was that at the highest political levels no firm answers had yet been determined about "the nation's main objective"—or at least none that could be publicly declared and hence made available to shape the mobilization effort.[30]

In the last weeks of 1940 Roosevelt had reviewed one notable attempt to set down a comprehensive strategic vision that might guide future planning. Its basis was a memorandum prepared by Admiral Harold Stark, the chief of naval operations. Stark laid out four options for American military and naval policy but strongly advocated the fourth, listed as item D in Stark's summary, or "Plan Dog," in the signalmen's jargon by which it was ever after known. Plan Dog essentially ratified an older strategic doctrine, code-named Rainbow 5, one of the American military's many contingency plans drafted in the prewar years. Rainbow 5

30. Watson, *Chief of Staff*, 174, 177, 308. Roosevelt frequently seemed oblivious to the fact that short-term needs were directly competitive with long-term plans. When George C. Marshall, for example, asked in December 1940 whether Roosevelt's order allocating half of aircraft production to Britain referred to half of the planes already delivered or half of those scheduled for future delivery, and exhibited a chart illustrating the considerable difference between the two calculations, Roosevelt waved him off, saying, "Don't let me see that chart again." Not for nothing did Stimson remark, "Conferences with the President are difficult matters. His mind does not follow easily a consecutive chain of thought but he is full of stories and incidents and hops about in his discussions from suggestion to suggestion and it is very much like chasing a vagrant beam of sunshine around a vacant room." Stimson Diary, December 18, 1940.

had anticipated waging war simultaneously against two or more enemies, Germany and Japan in particular. It assumed cooperation with Britain and France and envisioned sending American ground forces to Europe. Rainbow 5's premises, revised now to take account of France's defeat and the looming menace that Japan posed in the Pacific, deeply informed Plan Dog and constituted the foundation of all American strategic thinking from this date forward.

Stark began by emphasizing the indispensable importance of Britain's survival—a tacit but generous endorsement of Roosevelt's wager on Britain during the preceding summer, a wager against which Stark himself had then recommended. "[I]f Britain wins decisively against Germany we could win everywhere," Stark reasoned. But "if she loses the problem confronting us would be very great; and while we might not lose everywhere, we might, possibly, not win anywhere." From that simple starting point, weighty conclusions followed. The United States should devote its principal effort to the European theater, remain strictly on the defensive in the Pacific, and take care to avoid open conflict with Japan. For the foreseeable future, all possible aid should flow to Britain. As for longer-term developments in Europe, Stark minced no words: naval blockade and aerial bombardment might weaken Germany, but certain victory could come only "by military successes on shore." Britain was essential not only as a comrade in arms but, no less importantly, as an indispensable piece of real estate, an unsinkable aircraft carrier and a safe marshaling yard "from which successful land action can later be launched." Finally: "For making a successful land offensive, British man power is insufficient. Offensive troops from other nations will be required. I believe that the United States, in addition to sending naval assistance, would also need to send large air and land forces to Europe or Africa, or both, and to participate strongly in this land offensive. The naval task of transporting an army abroad would be large." In those few, spare sentences, Stark accurately foretold much of the story of American military and naval participation in World War II.[31]

Plan Dog had passed under Roosevelt's eyes well before he launched the Lend-Lease debate, but because he remained wary about the degree of candor that public opinion permitted him, he was scrupulously noncommittal about Stark's plan and breathed no syllable about it in public. ("Less than 1% of our people," he confided to Norman Thomas in May 1941, understood the lessons of the war then being fought. "It takes

31. Matloff and Snell, *Strategic Planning for Coalition Warfare, 1941–1942,* 25–27.

several generations," Roosevelt said, "to understand the type of 'facts of life' to which I refer.")[32] But he agreed sufficiently with Stark's prognosis that he authorized a further and momentous step, as Stark had recommended: joint staff talks between British and American military and naval planners.

In mid-January, the British battleship *King George V* hove into the Chesapeake to deliver the new British ambassador, Lord Halifax, to Washington. (He replaced Lothian, who had died unexpectedly a month earlier.) The *King George* also debarked five senior British officers, dressed in mufti and listed on the ship's manifest as "technical advisers" to the British Purchasing Commission. A few days later, Marshall and Stark welcomed the "advisers" in Washington. The Americans stressed the need for secrecy, warning the Britons that public knowledge of their presence "might well be disastrous" for the Lend-Lease bill being debated at that very moment in Congress. With those preliminaries, the American and British officers launched their discussion, known by the code name ABC-1, American-British Conversation Number 1.[33]

Less than a year earlier, wary British officials had refused Sumner Welles's request to visit the British Expeditionary Force in northern France. Now the British planners opened their arms and their briefing books to their American colleagues. Prior to their arrival Roosevelt had outlined his own strategic views in a meeting with his secretaries of war, navy, and state, as well as his two service chiefs, Marshall and Stark. Roosevelt's directions for the American positions in the upcoming talks showed the imprint of Plan Dog: continued aid to Britain; for the moment a defensive posture in the Pacific, with no squandering of scarce resources, not even for naval reinforcement of the Philippines. As for ground forces, the president wished to avoid any commitment "until our strength had developed." Meanwhile, the planners should consider "the possibility of bombing attacks against Japanese cities." When it came to naval escorts in the Atlantic, which Roosevelt was publicly denying even thinking about, the President advised that "the Navy should be prepared to convoy shipping in the Atlantic to England."[34]

Meeting from January 29 to March 29, the Anglo-American planners hammered out substantial agreements along those lines. Most important, they agreed that in the event of a two-front war in both Asia and

32. L&G, *Undeclared*, 441.
33. Matloff and Snell, *Strategic Planning for Coalition Warfare, 1941–1942*, 33.
34. Watson, *Chief of Staff*, 124.

Europe, Germany must be defeated first, even at the risk of serious reverses in the Pacific theater. As Marshall put it: "Collapse in the Atlantic would be fatal; collapse in the Far East would be serious but not fatal."[35] Yet at the conclusion of the talks, three questions remained unresolved: What, in light of Lend-Lease's passage, would be the precise allocation of production between British and American needs? Could the United States in fact undertake to provide naval escorts for the merchant convoys bearing arms to Britain? And how, exactly, might the United States "keep that Japanese dog quiet in the Pacific," as Churchill had earlier put it, without provoking a shooting war with Japan?

Military and economic officials struggled through the spring of 1941 to make headway within these broad and imperfect guidelines. Then, as the summer officially began, Adolf Hitler introduced a new variable that threatened to scramble all of the planners' already labile equations. On June 22, 1941, he launched Operation Barbarossa, an attack on his supposed ally the Soviet Union. With 153 divisions numbering some 3.6 million troops and thousands of aircraft and tanks, Barbarossa was Hitler's boldest military venture to date, and indeed one of the most gigantic military operations in history. As the awesome wave of the *Wehrmacht's* men and machines rumbled eastward toward Moscow, opinion divided sharply in the United States about the implications of this new phase of the war. In many ways, the debate over America's relationship to the now belligerent Soviet Union was a reprise of the long-running controversy over aid to Britain, though further complicated by deep ideological estrangement. Would the Soviets be able to survive the German onslaught, or would they crumple like all of Hitler's previous victims, save only England? If the Russians somehow managed to stay in the field, how could the United States lend them material support—indeed, given the communist character of the Soviet state, *should* the United States make common cause with the Russians? "If we see that Germany is winning we ought to help Russia, and if Russia is winning we ought to help Germany, and that way let them kill as many as possible," said Missouri senator Harry S. Truman, expressing in his own unvarnished, show-me, Missouri idiom the feelings of many of his countrymen. "[A]lthough," Truman added, "I don't want to see Hitler victorious under any circumstances."[36]

35. Watson, *Chief of Staff*, 397.
36. David McCullough, *Truman* (New York: Simon and Schuster, 1992), 262.

From London, Churchill extended the hand of comradeship-in-arms to Stalin. "No one has been a more consistent opponent of Communism than I have for the last twenty-five years," the prime minister declared in a radio broadcast on June 22. "I will unsay no word that I have spoken about it. But all this fades away before the spectacle which is now unfolding. . . . Any man or state who fights on against Naziism will have our aid. . . . [W]e shall give whatever help we can to Russia and the Russian people."[37] American officials, however, were more cautious. Secretary of War Stimson forwarded to Roosevelt the army's estimate that the Russians would last three months at the most and could conceivably collapse within four weeks.[38] Roosevelt's own thinking at first reflected the uncertainty bred by these conflicting appraisals: "Now comes this Russian diversion," he wrote to Ambassador William D. Leahy in Vichy, a description of the events in eastern Europe that suggested the president's agreement with Stimson's and the army's assessment. But, Roosevelt added: "If it is more than just that it will mean the liberation of Europe from Nazi domination."[39]

Like Churchill, Roosevelt had no illusions about the essential nature of the Soviet state. Several months earlier, he had somewhat reluctantly agreed to Eleanor's request that he address a gathering of the Communist-sponsored American Youth Congress. "The Soviet Union," said the president to the young people assembled on the White House lawn, "as everybody who has the courage to face the fact knows, is run by a dictatorship as absolute as any other dictatorship in the world." Boos arose from the crowd of leftist students.[40]

But however ideologically unsavory the Soviets might be, in time of danger, the old saying went, it was permissible to walk with the devil. Just as he had repudiated the counsel of his military chiefs that Britain could not endure, Roosevelt now discounted their pessimistic evaluations of the Russian situation and edged cautiously toward cooperation with Stalin. He may well have reasoned that Operation Barbarossa presented him with a unique, heaven-sent opportunity to clinch the tenuous logic of his short-of-war strategy. Keeping a Russian army in the field would certainly delay, and might even make entirely unnecessary, send-

---

37. Churchill 3:371–72.
38. Sherwood, *Roosevelt and Hopkins*, 303.
39. Elliot Roosevelt, ed., *FDR: His Personal Letters, 1928–1945* (New York, Duell, Sloan and Pearce, 1950), 2:1177.
40. Freidel, *Roosevelt*, 325.

ing American troops to Europe. The suspicion that Roosevelt coldly calculated just that possibility festered in Stalin's mind in the months and years ahead.

Whatever his reasoning in the uncertain summer of 1941, the president invited the Soviet ambassador, Konstantin Oumansky, to draw up a list of items that the United States might supply to the Soviet armed forces. Within a week the Russian diplomat submitted a detailed request. Significantly, it included industrial materials such as machine tools, rolling mills, and petroleum-cracking plants for the manufacture of aviation gasoline. Those items, looking to the long-term support of a mechanized army, strongly indicated the Soviets' intention to fight a lengthy war. That impression was soon emphatically confirmed by Harry Hopkins, who traveled to Moscow as Roosevelt's personal envoy in late July and reported positively on Stalin's resolve, just as Sumner Welles had helped Roosevelt to take the measure of Churchill's will to fight in 1940. Soon Roosevelt was putting even more American eggs in the Russian basket. In early August he ordered the delivery of a hundred fighter planes, even if they had to be taken from the U.S. Army. "Get the planes right off with a bang next week," he instructed an aide. "[U]se a heavy hand and act as a burr under the saddle. . . . Step on it."[41] Even though Churchill warned him candidly in September that British officials negotiating with the Soviets "could not exclude the impression that they might be thinking of separate terms," Roosevelt persuaded Congress the following month to include the Soviets in the Lend-Lease program, opening the door to an eventual total of some $10 billion in aid.[42]

"It is ridiculous," thundered McCormick's reliably outraged *Chicago Tribune*, "that sane men should have the slightest faith that . . . the supreme monster . . . Bloody Joe . . . , who brought on the war by selling out the democracies, will not sell them out again and make another deal with Hitler."[43] More temperately, the *New York Herald Tribune* opined: "A Hitler victory over Russia and Britain means . . . the triumph of totalitarian barbarism throughout the world. A victory of Great Britain, the United States and Communist Russia holds out no such prospect. Even if Communist totalitarianism survives the strain in Russia, the fact that it would only do so in association with victorious democracy

---

41. James MacGregor Burns, *Roosevelt: The Soldier of Freedom* (New York: Harcourt Brace Jovanovich, 1970), 115.
42. *C&R* 1:238
43. L&G, *Undeclared*, 819.

in Britain and the United states would give it no such untrammeled prestige and power as success would bring to Nazi totalitarianism. An essentially democratic world would still be possible."[44] In such an atmosphere of wary suspicion and cynical calculation, and on such a bed of fragile hopes, the "Grand Alliance" was conceived.

Roosevelt's decision to join hands with Stalin raised new logistical nightmares for the beleaguered American planners. They continued to be frustrated by the timidity of civilian manufacturers and were still racked between the pull of their mandate to expand the American armed forces and the tug of the president's insistence on sending Lend-Lease supplies to Britain, and now to Russia as well. Just a few months earlier, thanks to Roosevelt's order to divide B-17 production "fifty-fifty" with Britain, one general had complained: "We have a school at Shreveport, instructors, schedules, students, everything except planes." The slow-downs in the pilot-training program drove even the stolidly professional Marshall to the brink of insubordination. In late 1940 he had instructed his air chief, Hap Arnold, to "see if there is anything more we dare do" in frustrating implementation of the president's "even-Stephen" direc-tive. "What will this do in blocking training of pilots?" Marshall asked rhetorically. "If the British collapse there are certain things of theirs we can seize," said Marshall, "but we can't seize trained pilots. We will be the sole defenders of both the Atlantic and the Pacific. What do we dare do in relation to Britain?" Now Roosevelt's response to the Russian re-quests threatened to make Marshall's job all but impossible. "I think the President should have it clearly pointed out to him," Marshall noted crisply to Stimson, "that Mr. Oumansky will take everything we own." Things were already bad enough, Marshall emphasized: "We have planes on the ground because we cannot repair them." Stimson agreed. He thought that "this Russian munitions business thus far has shown the President at his worst. He has no system. He goes haphazard and he scatters responsibility among a lot of uncoordinated men and con-sequently things are never done." Besides, Stimson personally regarded Oumansky as "nothing but a crook" and "a slick, clever little beast." The secretary therefore readily joined Marshall in yet another supplication to Roosevelt to clarify his overall strategic plan.[45]

On July 9 the president responded. He instructed his war and navy secretaries to undertake a systematic survey of "the overall production

44. L&G, Undeclared, 544.
45. Watson, Chief of Staff, 307, 329; Stimson Diary, August 4, 5, 1941.

requirements required to defeat our potential enemies. . . . From your report we should be able to establish a munitions objective indicating the industrial capacity which this nation will require. . . . I realize," the president wrote, "that this report involves the making of appropriate assumptions as to our probable friends and enemies and to the conceivable theaters of operation which will be required."[46] This was not precisely the concrete strategic directive that Marshall and Stimson wanted, but it was useable enough. The president had now empowered the military to come up with a reasonable estimate of the material and logistical needs of the defense program, based on specified assumptions about allies, adversaries, and likely battlefields. Here at last was a license to think comprehensively about the complex relationship between America's likely commitments and schedule of deployments in the event of war, the probable scale and composition of the American armed forces, and the financial and industrial means required to equip them.

The assignment to draft the plan fell principally on the shoulders of Major Albert Wedemeyer in the army's War Plans Division. "I never worked so hard on anything in my life," Wedemeyer later recalled. "We were spending billions on arms without any clear idea of what we might need or where and when they might be used. I went to every expert in the Army and the Navy to find out the ships, the planes, the artillery, the tanks we would require to defeat our already well-armed enemies."[47] The document Wedemeyer and his team produced, soon known as the "Victory Program," reached the White House in late September. From the planners' perspective, it was still an imperfect work-in-progress, not yet firmly grounded on specific strategic commitments and defined war objectives, and therefore riddled with more uncertainties and contingencies than were comfortable. "The estimate is based upon a more or less nebulous policy," the War Plans Division observed, "in that the extent to which our government intends to commit itself with reference to the defeat of the Axis powers has not as yet been defined."[48] Nevertheless, Wedemeyer's team drew up a remarkably extensive survey, which for better or worse served thereafter as the basic planning matrix for American mobilization. The Victory Program comprised a bulging

46. Watson, *Chief of Staff*, 338–39. On August 30 Roosevelt added further instructions, stipulating that the final plan provide for "all reasonable munitions help" to Russia. Nevertheless, the planners appear not to have weighed Russian requirements heavily in their calculations. Watson, *Chief of Staff*, 348–49.
47. *American Heritage* 38, no. 8 (December 1987):66.
48. Watson, *Chief of Staff*, 341.

sheaf of reports canvassing possible theaters from the Atlantic to the Mediterranean and from western Europe and Siberia to the islands and seas of the far western Pacific. Among the welter of the report's minutiae several items stood out starkly:

- the first major objective of the United States and its associates ought to be the complete military defeat of Germany
- it will be necessary for the United States to enter the war
- only land armies can finally win wars
- July 1, 1943 [is] the earliest date when US armed forces can be mobilized, trained, and equipped for extensive operations.

To accomplish its objectives, the Victory Program report concluded, the U.S. Army would eventually have to field 215 divisions, totaling some 8.7 million men (this estimate assumed that the Russians would no longer be in the war by 1943, the single greatest forecasting error in the entire document). Equipping that force and supplying the Allies in the meantime would require at least doubling current production plans, at the previously unimaginable expense of some $150 billion (this figure also turned out to be far off, as the war's eventual cost approached $300 billion). "Ultimate victory over the Axis powers," one planner wrote presciently, "will place a demand upon industry few have yet conceived."[49]

F.D.R.'S WAR PLANS! screamed the headline of McCormick's *Chicago Tribune* on Thursday, December 4, 1941. GOAL IS TEN MILLION ARMED MEN; HALF TO FIGHT IN AEF. PROPOSES LAND DRIVE BY JULY 1, 1943, TO SMASH NAZIS. PRESIDENT TOLD OF EQUIPMENT SHORTAGE. The following story quoted liberally from the Victory Program report. It even reproduced verbatim the president's letter ordering the preparation of the plan. The German chargé in Washington radioed to Berlin: "Report confirms that full participation of America in war is not to be expected before July 1943. Military measures against Japan are of defensive character."[50]

The *Tribune's* scoop was one of the most sensational and potentially damaging news leaks in the history of American journalism. Whoever

49. Watson, *Chief of Staff*, 350. The excerpts from the Victory Program plan are drawn from several sources: Watson, *Chief of Staff*, 331–66; L&G, *Undeclared*, 739ff.; and Sherwood, *Roosevelt and Hopkins*, 410–18.
50. *Chicago Daily Tribune*, December 4, 1941, 1; William L. Shirer, *The Rise and Fall of the Third Reich: A History of Nazi Germany* (New York: Simon and Schuster, 1960), 894–95n.

leaked the Victory Program to the *Tribune*, Henry Stimson said, was "wanting in loyalty and patriotism." Publication of the report made liars out of those administration spokesmen who had been denying the possibility of sending American troops overseas. Yet however mortifying to some political leaders, the *Tribune* story proved to be the isolationists' last hurrah, a final attempt to sabotage the preparedness effort. By now, most Americans had accepted the necessity of the military buildup and were expressing a willingness to countenance armed intervention. Even in Chicagoland, McCormick's grandstand stunt outraged many readers. Thousands of them took up the anti-McCormick cry of "Millions for defense, but not two cents for the *Tribune*," and canceled their subscriptions. However sensational, the *Tribune*'s effort to spike the mobilization program was also by this date largely irrelevant. Just three days later, the United States was at war.[51]

THE LEND-LEASE ACT also aggravated the controversy over naval escorts on the Atlantic. There was little sense in spending $7 billion for Lend-Lease goods that ended up at the bottom of the ocean. In alarmingly mounting volume, that was just where the munitions and other materiel leaving America's East Coast ports in 1941 were headed. German attacks were sinking British ships at nearly five times the rate that new construction could replace them. At that rate, the British merchant marine, the steel bridge of gray-hulled vessels on which America's strategy and England's very life depended, would soon vanish altogether.

The deadliest marine weapon, responsible for over half the lost tonnage, was the U-boat (from the German word for submarine, *Unterseeboot*). The architect of Germany's U-boat campaign was Erich Raeder, commander-in-chief of the German navy; its resourceful executor was Karl Dönitz, head of the U-boat service. Raeder had long dunned the reluctant ex-soldier Hitler to commit more resources to the naval war. Raeder especially wanted to unleash his U-boats into the three-hundred-mile deep U.S. Neutrality Zone, proclaimed by Roosevelt in October 1939 to keep warships out of North America's offshore waters. After the introduction of the Lend-Lease bill, Raeder redoubled his efforts, with notable success. On 6 February 1941 Hitler directed that Germany's

51. Cantril, 976; *American Heritage* 38, no. 8 (December 1987): 65. Though the FBI investigated the matter, the leaker of the *Tribune* story was never discovered. Some writers have speculated that it might have been the president himself who released the document, as a way of provoking Hitler into a declaration of war. No convincing evidence has been adduced to support that claim.

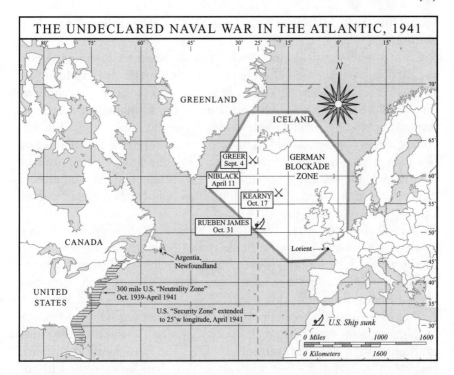

THE UNDECLARED NAVAL WAR IN THE ATLANTIC, 1941

main objective in the war against England would now be to achieve "high losses in merchant shipping inflicted by sea and air warfare."[52] In Churchill's words, the Battle of Britain now gave way to the Battle of the Atlantic. Hitler stopped short of allowing Raeder to penetrate the American Neutrality Zone, but on March 25, 1941, he reacted to the passage of the Lend-Lease bill by extending the German naval combat area far out into the Atlantic, to the eastern coast of Greenland.

From their pens on the Nazi-occupied Atlantic coast of France, Dönitz's U-boats now swarmed into the midocean "gap" south of Greenland where British air reconnaissance was thinnest and little or no escort was available. By early 1941 Germany was producing four new submarines per month, including the long-range type IX boats, with a cruising range of at least 10,500 miles. Armed with a complement of twenty-two torpedoes, they packed nearly twice the firepower of earlier models. Soon Dönitz commanded a fleet of more than two hundred boats, of which he could keep thirty-six at sea, operating routinely as far westward

52. Dan Van der Vat, *The Atlantic Campaign: World War II's Great Struggle at Sea* (New York: Harper and Row, 1988), 177.

as the line of forty degrees west longitude, and occasionally prowling beyond.

Dönitz's growing fleet also allowed him to perfect a new tactic—the so-called wolf-pack attack. Directed by radio from Dönitz's headquarters at Lorient, in Britanny, several U-boats would converge on a convoy. One would fire a torpedo into the flank of the formation of merchant ships, typically a diagonal shot to maximize the chance of a hit. Escorting vessels, if any, would then break away to pursue the attacker or rescue survivors, leaving the disrupted and defenseless merchantmen at the mercy of the several other raiders that had taken up positions athwart the convoy's path. In April 1941 alone these tactics claimed more than 650,000 tons of shipping.

"The decision for 1941 lies upon the seas," Churchill warned Roosevelt. On the outcome of the Battle of the Atlantic "the crunch of the whole war will be found." More ships and better protection for them on the transatlantic passage were absolutely necessary, and "only the United States can supply this need."[53]

Only the United States could not—at least not legally. The vestiges of the neutrality laws still on the books banned American cargo ships from entering a declared war zone. Worse, the Lend-Lease statute unambiguously declared: "Nothing in this Act shall be construed to authorize or to permit the authorization of convoying vessels by naval vessels of the United States." Faced with those obstacles, Roosevelt resisted the advice of "all-outers" like Henry Stimson, Henry Morgenthau, Harold Ickes, and his top naval commanders, who urged him to deploy the newly designated Atlantic Fleet, recently trained in antisubmarine warfare, for escort duty. Failure to do so, argued the all-outers, would mean feeding Lend-Lease aid to the fishes, would render ABC-1 a mere thinking exercise, and might well leave Britain with no choice but to surrender. (As late as September 1941, Harry Hopkins was still worrying that under worsening war conditions "the British appeasers might have some influence on Churchill.")[54] But authorizing armed escorts, Roosevelt fretted, would vitiate both his and Churchill's promises that Lend-Lease was sufficient to guarantee British victory without risking further American involvement. Committing U.S. Navy ships to escorting would confirm the most dire predictions of the isolationists and expose the president to potentially vicious political reprisals. "I realized from the

53. C&R 1:103, 107.
54. Sherwood, Roosevelt and Hopkins, 374.

first," declared Senator Wheeler on April 2, "after the Lend-Lease bill was passed, that the next step would be that the warmongers in this country would cry for convoys, and everyone recognizes that convoys mean war."[55] (Roosevelt himself had said as much in his press conference of January 21.)

Opinion polls reinforced Roosevelt's assessment of his political vulnerability. Bare majorities supported escorting, even at the risk of war, but even stronger majorities continued to oppose entering the war altogether, and 70 percent of respondents felt that the president had already done enough or too much by way of helping Britain.[56] Such ambivalence formed a poor basis for a risky policy initiative like escorting. A further constraint on Roosevelt's ability to deploy American ships in the Atlantic was the need to maintain naval elements in the Pacific as a check on Japanese ambitions. Legally, politically, and operationally, there seemed to be no way that the U.S. Navy could offer protection to the precious Lend-Lease convoys. Admiral Stark, for one, appreciated the president's awful predicament. "The President has on his hands at the present time," Stark wrote in mid-April, "about as difficult a situation as ever confronted any man anywhere in public life."[57]

Roosevelt writhed on the horns of this dilemma through the spring and summer of 1941. Needled by conflicting counsel and buffeted by irreconcilable demands, he flipflopped, dodged, waffled, and dissembled. In early April he approved Hemisphere Defense Plan No. 1. It called for the transfer of three battleships, an aircraft carrier, and several supporting vessels from the Pacific to the Atlantic and for active escorting of England-bound convoys. Scarcely a week later he rescinded those orders, leaving the ships in the Pacific and settling for a policy of "patrolling" rather than escorting. Even this limited policy he embraced gingerly. He explained in a telegram to Churchill on April 11 that he was extending the coastal American security zone into the distant mid-Atlantic — to west longitude twenty-five degrees, which took in virtually all of Greenland and, not insignificantly, overlapped the western third of Hitler's recently expanded German combat zone. But the navy's role in this newly defined American security zone was to be something less than what Churchill and the all-outers wanted. "[I]n great secrecy,"

55. L&G, *Undeclared*, 443.
56. Cantril, 973, 1128; Dallek, 267.
57. Eric Larrabee, *Commander in Chief: Franklin Delano Roosevelt, His Lieutenants, and Their War* (New York: Harper and Row, 1987), 63.

Roosevelt explained to the prime minister, American naval vessels patrolling within the new hemispheric defense belt would notify the British about any enemy ships or aircraft sighted. The implication of "patrolling" was that the U.S. Navy would do no shooting but serve only as a reconnaissance arm for the Royal Navy and Air Force. Moreover, Roosevelt added, "it is important for domestic political reasons . . . that this action be taken by us unilaterally and not after diplomatic conversations between you and us. . . . I believe advisable that when this new policy is adopted here no statement be issued on your end. It is not certain I would make specific announcement. I may decide to issue necessary naval operations orders and let time bring out the existence of the new patrol area." The patrols were "a step forward," Roosevelt somewhat sheepishly explained to the all-outers. "Well, I hope you will keep on walking, Mr. President. Keep on walking," urged Stimson. But for the moment, Roosevelt remained planted where he stood.[58]

Roosevelt did announce on April 10 that the United States was occupying Greenland, an orphaned Danish colony at risk of German seizure now that Denmark itself lay under Nazi occupation. Summarily defining the remote, snow-cloaked Danish colony as part of the Western Hemisphere, and hence subject to the Monroe Doctrine's protection against intervention by a European power, the president waved aside an issue that had stumped generations of cartographers. Two months later, Roosevelt sent a scratch force of some four thousand marine regulars to occupy Iceland, having bent the geographers' logic still further by declaring Iceland to be part of the New World as well, thereby deftly sidestepping the Selective Service Act's prohibition on stationing draftees outside the Western Hemisphere.

In Berlin, Raeder insisted that these new American moves meant war. He pleaded again for authorization to carry the fight directly to the Americans. But Hitler, about to launch Barbarossa against the Russians, wanted no distractions. He was "most anxious to postpone the United States entry into the war for another one or two months," he told Raeder. Naval encounters with the Americans should be avoided "as far as possible."[59]

As Roosevelt anticipated, time soon brought the existence of the expanded Atlantic patrols to the American public's attention. Reporters at

58. C&R 1:166; Stimson Diary, April 25, 1941.
59. *Fuehrer Conferences*, in Rear-Admiral H. G. Thursfield, ed., *Brassey's Naval Annual*, 1948 (London: William Clowes and Sons, 1948), 221.

the president's press conference on April 25 pressed for clarification: "Can you tell us the difference between a patrol and a convoy?" one journalist asked. Just as much difference as between a cow and a horse, Roosevelt opaquely answered. Could the president define the functions of the patrols? "The protection of the American hemisphere," Roosevelt replied, repeating that answer three times, without further elucidation. Exactly how far would the new patrols extend? "As far on the waters of the seven seas as may be necessary for the defense of the American hemisphere," said the president. The reporters persisted: "Mr. President, if this patrol should discover some apparently aggressive ships headed toward the Western hemisphere, what would it do about it?" "Let me know," Roosevelt joked.[60]

In the meantime, Hitler was scoring spectacular gains in the Mediterranean. In April German troops pushed British forces back across the North African desert to the borders of Egypt. Other elements of the *Wehrmacht* swept through Yugoslavia and expelled the British army from Greece. On May 3 Churchill abandoned all restraint and frankly begged Roosevelt for an American declaration of war. Roosevelt demurred. The losses in the Mediterranean were regrettable, he said, but "this struggle is going to be decided in the Atlantic."[61]

Yet in the Atlantic the Americans were still doing no more than conducting reconnoitering patrols. "I am not willing to fire the first shot," Roosevelt told his cabinet.[62] Some of the all-outers were disgusted. "The President is loath to get into this war, and he would rather follow public opinion than lead it," an exasperated Morgenthau noted in mid-May. If the president would not ask for a declaration of war, Morgenthau suggested, "how about doing something internally first?" Two weeks later, seizing upon the news that the German battleship *Bismarck* had got loose on the Atlantic and had sunk the *Hood*, the obsolescent pride of the Royal Navy and the biggest battleship afloat, Roosevelt took up Morgenthau's suggestion and "did something internal." He gave a Fireside Chat that one of its authors described as "calculated to scare the daylights out of everyone" — but, he added, "it did not do much else."[63] Speaking from the White House on May 27 to an estimated audience

---

60. *PPA* (1941), 132ff.
61. *C&R* 1:184.
62. Ickes Diary 3:523.
63. Dallek, 266. The British succeeded in sinking the *Bismarck* a few days later, after she had been sighted from the air by Tuck Smith, an American pilot on loan to the British Coastal Command.

of eighty-five million radio listeners worldwide, Roosevelt declared an "unlimited national emergency." But what did that mean in practice? At a press conference the following day, the president bewildered the reporters by suggesting that it meant very little. He had no intention of asking for neutrality revision, he explained. As for aggressive naval escorts, he breezily opined that they were "outmoded." Stimson fumed that the press conference was "one of his worst and almost undid the effect of his speech. . . . The President shows evidence of waiting for the accidental shot of some irresponsible captain on either side to be the occasion of his going to war."[64]

Other all-outers shared Stimson's dismay. "My own feeling," Harold Ickes wrote in his diary, "is that the President has not aroused the country; has not really sounded the bell . . . , does not furnish the motive power that is required. . . . In his speech [of May 27] the President said that we would do everything necessary to defend our own land [and] he also left the way clear to convoy ships carrying food, merchandise, and arms to England. . . . But we really are in the same *status quo* . . . it seems that he is still waiting for the Germans to create an 'incident.' "[65]

In the spring of 1941, at least two incidents had already gone unused. The U.S. destroyer *Niblack*, steaming five hundred miles southwest of Iceland on April 11, picked up a sonar contact with what it thought was a U-boat and dropped several depth charges. Sometimes labeled the first hostile act of World War II between U.S. and Axis naval forces, the *Niblack*'s depth bombs were proved by postwar investigation to have exploded in an empty sea. No U-boat was in the area. Had Roosevelt seized on this "incident" to wage war against Hitler, he would have egregiously compounded the folly of relying for a *casus belli* on "an accidental shot of some irresponsible captain."[66]

On May 21 a U-boat sank the American freighter *Robin Moor* well outside the declared war zone, midway between the bulge of Brazil and the bight of Africa in the South Atlantic. In violation of international conventions, the U-boat captain cast the freighter's crew adrift in lifeboats with meager rations and without radioing their position to nearby ships that might come to the rescue. When the first survivors were picked up on June 9 and told the story of the *Robin Moor*'s illegal sinking and the abandonment of its crew, the head of the British Pur-

64. Stimson Diary, May 23, 29, 1941.
65. Ickes Diary 3:526–27.
66. See the account in Bailey and Ryan, *Hitler vs. Roosevelt*, 129–32.

chasing Mission in the United States was not alone in praying for some "dividends" from the episode. The American all-outers also urged Roosevelt to seize upon this "incident," far more concrete and outrageous than the *Niblack*'s shadowy encounter of the previous month, to transform the Atlantic reconnaissance patrols into aggressive escorts. Roosevelt once again disappointed such hopes. He used the occasion only to close the remaining German consulates in the United States. Hitler's reaction to the *Robin Moor* incident, expressed on the very eve of Barbarossa, was once more to admonish Raeder "under all circumstances" to "avoid any possibility of incidents with the U.S.A." until the outcome of the Soviet invasion "becomes clearer, i.e., for a few weeks."[67]

As spring passed into summer in 1941, the Nazi juggernaut appeared unstoppable. With stunning successes in the Mediterranean and the Atlantic and with Barbarossa gaining lethal momentum, Hitler seemed about to sweep all before him. His adversaries in the emerging Grand Alliance looked on in dismay. Stalin anguished as the *Wehrmacht* rolled eastward into Russia, gobbling up miles of Soviet territory daily and carving a path of mayhem and destruction unparalleled in the annals of warfare. Churchill brooded over the losses in North Africa and the Balkans and the even more appalling losses of British ships in the Atlantic. He worried if he would ever succeed in coaxing his American cousins to take up arms. Roosevelt fretted over the competing demands of the Pacific and Atlantic theaters and struggled to get a grip on industrial mobilization.

The president also faced a nasty fight in the Congress over the extension of the Selective Service Act. Particularly nettlesome was a clause extending draftees' tour of duty for eighteen additional months beyond the twelve months specified in the original legislation of 1940. The recruits called up under that act a year earlier, chafing under the unfamiliar military discipline, confused about their part in a war that the president was still insisting they would never have to fight, were scrawling OHIO on the walls of their encampments. Had the fledgling troops in fact melted away—either by statutory release from duty, or by mass desertion, as the ubiquitously chalked code for "Over the Hill in October" threatened—the army would have had to start all over again,

67. A good account of the *Robin Moor* episode is in Bailey and Ryan, *Hitler vs. Roosevelt*, 138–47. At about the same time, another near-incident occurred in the North Atlantic, when U203 mistook the U.S. battleship *Texas* for a British warship and shadowed her for 140 miles but failed to get into proper firing position. See Bailey and Ryan, *Hitler vs. Roosevelt*, 148–49.

inflicting catastrophic delays on the Victory Program's timetable. Congress on August 12 approved the extension of service (while retaining the prohibition on deployment outside the Western Hemisphere) by a margin of a single vote in the House. The threatened desertions did not occur, and the army continued to grow, but the perilously thin margin in the House vote provided a sobering reminder of the nation's continuing reluctance to move to a full war footing.

The congressional vote on selective service came just as Churchill and Roosevelt were rendezvousing for their first face-to-face meeting as prime minister and president. On August 9 HMS *Prince of Wales*, bearing Winston Churchill, steamed into Placentia Bay, offshore of Argentia, a defunct Newfoundland silver-mining camp. The British battleship sidled up to the U.S. cruiser *Augusta*, aboard which Roosevelt awaited Churchill's arrival. The two ships rode at their anchors off Argentia for three days as the two leaders engaged in strategy sessions and camaraderie.

The Argentia meeting's most publicized accomplishment was a document that became known as the Atlantic Charter. Initiated by Roosevelt partly as a way of assuaging American anxieties that a war in alliance with Soviet Russia might contaminate democratic ideals, the charter pledged the two Western leaders to seek a postwar world that would honor the principles of self-determination, free trade, nonaggression, and freedom of the seas. The charter made vague reference to "the establishment of a wider and permanent system of general security." The two leaders also sent a message to Stalin pledging their assistance and proposing high-level political and military discussions at an early date.

Almost as soon as they settled into their chairs in the *Augusta*'s wardroom on the first evening of their talks, Churchill again pressed Roosevelt for an American declaration of war. "I would rather have an American declaration of war now and no supplies for six months than double the supplies and no declaration," he said. Roosevelt, certain that Congress would balk, again demurred. The president did agree at last that the U.S. Navy would provide armed escorts as far as Iceland. How he would announce such a bold step to the American public and to Congress remained a problem. As Churchill later explained to his War Cabinet, Roosevelt "said he would wage war, but not declare it, and that he would become more and more provocative. . . . Everything was to be done to force an 'incident.' . . . The President . . . made it clear that he would look for an 'incident' which would justify him in opening hostilities."[68]

68. Dallek, 285.

Soon after the two leaders steamed away from Argentia on August 12, an "incident" presented itself. True to his pledge to Churchill aboard the *Augusta*, Roosevelt quickly grasped it, indeed substantially distorted it, as the occasion for his long-deferred announcement of armed escorts. On September 4 the U.S. destroyer *Greer*, proceeding toward Iceland with mail and supplies for the tiny marine garrison, received a blinker message from a patrolling British aircraft that a U-boat had been sighted ten miles ahead on the *Greer's* course. The destroyer captain, conscious of his standing orders not to shoot but only to trail and report, rang up full speed and zig-zagged toward the U-boat, making sonar contact at a range of two thousand yards. The *Greer* locked on her quarry and assumed a narrow-target, bow-on orientation to the submarine. She held that position for over three hours while continuously reporting the U-boat's position to the British plane circling overhead. When the aircraft, running low on fuel, inquired if the U.S. ship was going to attack and got a negative reply, the pilot released four depth charges and flew away. The U-boat commander, knowing only that he was under attack and that as much of the *Greer's* profile as he could see suggested she was one of the type of ships transferred to the Royal Navy in the destroyer-bases deal, loosed two torpedoes at the *Greer*. Both missed. The *Greer* retaliated with a pattern of eight depth charges, then a second pattern of eleven charges. None was effective, and U-652 eventually slipped away unharmed, as did the *Greer*.

A week went by, ample time for Roosevelt to get the facts of this encounter straight. But on September 11 he took to the radio and announced with studied hyperbole that an American warship had been the innocent victim of a wanton attack. "I tell you the blunt fact that the German submarine fired first upon this American destroyer without warning, and with deliberate design to sink her," the president misleadingly said. "These Nazi submarines and raiders are the rattlesnakes of the Atlantic," he went on, and then announced what was soon called the "shoot-on-sight" policy: "American naval vessels and American planes will no longer wait until Axis submarines, lurking under the water, or Axis raiders on the surface of the sea, strike their deadly blow. . . . From now on, if German or Italian vessels of war enter our waters . . . they do so at their own peril."[69] Six days later, off Newfoundland, Canadian escorts handed over a fifty-ship convoy eastbound from Halifax to five U.S. destroyers, who safely shepherded the merchantmen

69. *PPA* (1941), 384.

across the North Atlantic and into the hands of a Royal Navy squadron waiting just south of Iceland. The North Atlantic, remorselessly transforming with the autumn's waning light into a gloomy, frigid hell of mountainous seas, howling winds, and gathering danger, began slowly to fill with U.S. destroyers, warily flanking the precious merchant convoys.

Roosevelt's prolonged indecision and his ultimate deviousness in implementing the escort policy have exercised generations of critics. With respect to his indecision, it might be said that if statecraft were chemistry, the president's actions between March and September of 1941, and indeed in the periods before and after those dates, could be described as titrating—a series of experiments with various policy reagents to measure the volume and concentration of the isolationist acid that remained in the American body politic. Much polling data supports the argument that in fact Roosevelt took the wrong measurements from those experiments, that a majority of the American people were prepared to accept escorting well before the president's dubious rendition of the *Greer* episode.[70] But Roosevelt was more alchemist than chemist. His tools were the sorcerer's arts of politics, not the deceptively tidy algorithms of science. He was also true to the democratic politician's creed when he worried about the political necessity of creating a consensus among the American people as he brought them to the brink of war. As the historian Robert Dallek persuasively concludes, "it is difficult to fault Roosevelt for building a consensus by devious means. . . . [I]f he had advised the public of the fact that the U-boat had fired in defense and that Hitler did not then seem intent on attacking America's Atlantic traffic . . . he would have risked having to wait for the collapse of Russia and Britain's near demise before gaining broad national support for a resort to arms. . . . [T]hat would have been a failure of his responsibility as Commander in Chief."[71] It is also important to note that whatever Roosevelt's duplicity concerning the *Greer*, he used the incident not to take the country into full-blown war but only to secure the much more limited policy of an armed response to Hitler's U-boats.

As for Hitler, his restraint had all along matched Roosevelt's hesitation, and it lasted longer. Even after the *Greer* speech and Roosevelt's

70. Robert A. Divine, for example, concludes flatly that "Roosevelt could have begun convoys months earlier with solid public support." Divine, *The Reluctant Belligerent* (New York: John Wiley and Sons, 1965), 144.
71. Dallek, 289.

announcement of a state of virtual naval warfare in the Atlantic, *der Führer* continued to reject Raeder's advice to attack American ships. Instead, he ordered his submariners "to avoid any incidents in the war on merchant shipping before about the middle of October"—when he apparently expected the Soviet invasion to be wrapped up.[72]

Incidents nevertheless ensued. U-boat commanders making spot decisions in the sweat of battle were less punctilious than their superiors calmly calibrating policies in the security of headquarters. On October 17 U568 put a torpedo into the bowels of the U.S. destroyer *Kearny*, which limped into Iceland, escorted by the now notorious *Greer*, bearing eleven dead sailors, the first American casualties of the still undeclared war. On October 27, Roosevelt responded with an exceptionally belligerent address. "America has been attacked," he proclaimed. "The U.S.S. *Kearny* is not just a Navy ship. She belongs to every man, woman, and child in this Nation. . . . I say that we do not propose to take this lying down. . . . [W]e Americans have cleared our decks and taken our battle stations." To justify his bellicosity, Roosevelt charged that he had seen a document laying out Hitler's "plan to abolish all existing religions— Catholic, Protestant, Mohammedan, Hindu, Buddhist, and Jewish alike." No less wildly, and with even less basis in fact than his account of the *Greer* attack, Roosevelt alleged that he had in his possession a "secret map" showing the Nazi plan to divide all of South America into "five vassal states."[73] But the president still declined to ask for a declaration of war. Instead, Roosevelt merely asked for the authority to arm American merchant vessels and to allow them to enter combat zones— in effect repealing the "carry" provisions of the neutrality laws. Congress obliged him in early November.

Just three days after Roosevelt's egregiously inflammatory remarks of October 27, six hundred miles west of Ireland, U552 sent a single torpedo into the midship ammunition magazine of the USS *Reuben James*. The American destroyer broke in two and sank almost instantaneously, killing 115 seamen. Despite these escalating provocations from both sides, America still remained officially neutral. The Germans and the Americans faced each other in the North Atlantic through periscope and gunsight in a tense standoff. With Germany absorbed in the east

---

72. *Fuehrer Conferences on Matters Dealing with the German Navy* (Washington: U.S. Office of Naval Intelligence, 1947), 2:33 (September 17, 1941).

73. *PPA* (1941), 438ff. The maps and documents that Roosevelt referred to were almost certainly forgeries. See Bailey and Ryan, *Hitler vs. Roosevelt*, 203.

and with America still largely unarmed, neither side was prepared to take the next step toward a formal declaration of all-out war. So things might have remained indefinitely save for another "incident," replete with drama and consequence, that exploded not in the gray expanse of the wintry Atlantic but in the blue waters of the tropical Pacific.

IF THE TANGLED SKEIN of events that eventually led to war between Japan and the United States could be summed up in a single word, that word would be "China." From the 1890s onward, Japan had cast covetous eyes on China, especially on the fertile, resource-rich region of Manchuria. There Japan longed to pursue its own imperial destiny, in emulation of the Western powers that had already laid claim to much of Asia and threatened the integrity of China itself. Following the Meiji Restoration of 1868, Japan had embarked on an astounding program of modernization, leaping from feudal insularity to advanced industrial status in scarcely more than a generation, and whetting an imperial appetite commensurate with its growing economic heft. In 1905 Japan spectacularly demonstrated both its economic achievements and its surging ambitions by waging a successful war against czarist Russia, Japan's foremost rival for control of Manchuria and, along with Britain, for supremacy in East Asia. The Russo-Japanese War's climactic naval battle at Tsushima Straits also offered a prophetic glimpse of Japan's mastery of naval warfare, then the most technologically sophisticated branch of combat. Victory over Russia made Japan the first non-Western state ever to achieve military success against one of the traditional European "great powers," an exhilarating triumph that further fed Japan's imperial aspirations.

The United States, however, had stepped in as the spoiler of Japanese dreams as early as 1905. Theodore Roosevelt arbitrated a settlement of the Russo-Japanese conflict that denied the Japanese claim for a large indemnity payment from the czar and rejected the full menu of territorial concessions in Manchuria that Tokyo demanded. In Japanese eyes, the pattern was thus early established of inexplicably gratuitous American resistance to Japan's just deserts, as well as American refusal to accept Japan as a legitimate imperial power in Asia—such as the United States itself had recently become, with its annexation of the Philippine Islands in 1898. In the years that followed, again and again Japan watched the United States assume the spoiler's part, the American role often colored with an ugly tincture of racial condescension that exacerbated Japanese resentment. The Americans shut off further immigration from Japan to the United States in the so-called Gentlemen's Agreement of 1908; they declined in 1919 to accept the Japanese proposal for a declaration of racial equality in the Versailles peace treaty, forced unwanted naval limitations on Japan in the Washington Naval Disarmament Conference of 1922, permanently debarred from American citizenship the tiny Japanese immigrant community in the notorious "national origins" immigration law of 1924, and, most provocative of all, refused to extend diplomatic recognition to the Japanese military take-over of Manchuria in 1931.

Japan had a huge stake in Manchuria. Manchuria promised salvation from the ills of the Great Depression, which had closed many traditional markets to Japan and heightened the sense of vulnerability that came from its lack of raw materials and adequate foodstuffs. Tokyo installed a puppet government in Manchuria, renamed the territory the state of Manchukuo, and dispatched half a million Japanese colonists to settle there, including 250,000 farmers to relieve the island kingdom's dependence on foreign food imports. America's response was the Stimson Doctrine, proclaimed in 1932 by Herbert Hoover's secretary of state, the same man who in 1940 became Franklin Roosevelt's secretary of war. Stimson's manifesto declared that the United States would not officially recognize the Manchukuo regime, nor any other arrangements imposed on China by force.

The Stimson Doctrine served as the foundation of American policy regarding China and Japan for the following decade. It provided the political and ideological framework for the unfolding events that eventually led to war. The doctrine irritated and baffled the Japanese, as it did some Americans. It was a statement of high principle but based on no concrete American material stake in China — certainly nothing to match the substantial Japanese investment there, and for that matter nothing to match the scale of America's trade with Japan. Under neither Hoover nor Roosevelt did Washington choose to back the Stimson Doctrine with economic or military muscle. The Stimson Doctrine represented "an attitude rather than a program," the historian Herbert Feis concluded. As events were to prove, mere attitudes were dangerous guides to foreign policy, especially when they were premised on morally charged and uncompromisable principles rather than on negotiable material assets. But for better or worse, the Stimson Doctrine remained the cornerstone of American policy in Asia. And in 1940 the man who had laid that stone once again took his seat in the highest councils of the American government.

Japan's renewed assault on China in 1937 exposed both the hollow-ness and the rigidity of the Stimson Doctrine. "We have large emotional interests in China, small economic interests, and no vital interests," William Bullitt reminded Roosevelt. For those reasons, Bullitt urged the president to take a more conciliatory tone with the Japanese, especially in light of the very tangible American interests that needed attending to in Europe, the historically paramount theater of American concern. Roosevelt instead loudly condemned Japan's action—but he did little more than that. He extended some token aid to Chiang Kai-shek, the head of China's Nationalist, or Kuomintang, government, though Chiang seemed undecided whether his principal foe was the Japanese invader or his Chinese Communist opponents. Simultaneously, Roosevelt continued to allow American exports to flow to Japan, including the steel and petroleum products that fueled the Japanese army's brutal subjugation of China's coastal cities and its occupation of the valleys of the Yangtze and Yellow rivers. The "China Incident," as the Japanese incursion was called, threw into high relief the four-decades-old central paradox of America's Asian diplomacy: the United States wanted to champion Chinese sovereignty and to control developments in Asia, even in the absence of any substantial American interests on the ground; at the same time, Washington resisted the commitment of any appreciable economic, diplomatic, or military resources to the region. Here was a perilous disconnect between American aspirations and American means, a gap between the national wish and the national will. In that dangerously inviting space, Japan dared to seek its advantage.[74]

By 1940 the China Incident was three years old. Its continuation was a burden, even an embarrassment, to the Tokyo regime. Japanese troops, spearheaded by the quasi-independent Manchurian occupational force, the Kwantung Army, had inflicted appalling hardships on the Chinese. The war had also wrung ever-greater sacrifices from the Japanese people themselves, but the army had not yet succeeded in quelling Chinese resistance. Chiang Kai-shek withdrew deep into the Japanese interior, established a new capital at Chunking in Szechwan province, and waited for Tokyo to tire of its costly China adventure. Frustrated by those tactics, Japanese military leaders sought with increasing desperation to resolve the incident once and for all. They groped for ways to insulate China from outside help. They simultaneously sought to liberate island

74. Donald B. Schewe, ed., *Franklin D. Roosevelt and Foreign Affairs* (New York: Clear-water, 1969), 2d ser. 7:349.

Japan from dependence on foreign sources of supply, perhaps by widening the arc of conflict to include Siberian Russia or Southeast Asia. But the Americans, still somewhat incomprehensibly in Japanese minds, continued to oppose Japanese designs. "In particular, after the entry of Stimson into the Government," a Japanese diplomat explained to the German foreign minister in 1940, "Japan had to be very careful in regard to America in order not to provoke that country into taking severe measures against Japan." The Americans had by that time already put themselves on the road to taking severe measures: in January 1940 they abrogated their 1911 commercial treaty with Japan, opening the way at last to the possible imposition of trade embargoes.[75]

The Japanese military's gnawing impatience to find a way to break the stalemate in China brought down Japan's government in July 1940. It was the third Japanese cabinet to fall in less than two years — strong evidence of the tension and uncertainty besetting the Japanese leadership. Prince Fumimaro Konoye, prime minister when the Sino-Japanese war had begun in 1937, and notoriously opposed to any negotiated settlement with Chiang, formed a new cabinet pledged to "expedite the settlement of the China Incident" and "solve the Southern Area problem." A docile aristocrat, Konoye was destined to be Japan's last prewar civilian prime minister.

Konoye's government included General Hideki Tojo as war minister. Tojo was a second-generation professional soldier whose reputation as a ruthless disciplinarian had earned him the nickname "the Razor." As chief of staff of the Kwantung Army in 1937, he had been a major architect of the Chinese incursion. He was among the hardest of Japan's legions of hard-liners. Like Konoye, he opposed any diplomatic compromise with Chiang Kai-shek. He believed that only a crushing application of military force could bring the China Incident to an end. Unlike Konoye, Tojo did not flinch from facing additional enemies, including the Soviet Union, Britain, and the United States, if that would bring success in China, and secure Japanese paramountcy in Asia.[76]

Tojo now wielded fearsome power, not least because of the peculiar role of the Japanese military in the scheme of Japanese civil government. By political convention and, after 1936, by law, the ministers of the army

75. Herbert Feis, *The Road to Pearl Harbor* (Princeton: Princeton University Press, 1950), 77.
76. Scott D. Sagan, "The Origins of the Pacific War," in Robert I. Rotberg and Theodore K. Rabb, *The Origin and Prevention of Major Wars* (Cambridge: Cambridge University Press, 1988), 326.

and navy were chosen not from civilian ranks but from the senior officer corps of the respective services. Thus by refusing to nominate a candidate or by withdrawing its officer from the cabinet, either of the armed services could topple a government. Moreover, the military reserved unto itself "the right of supreme command," by which it could deal directly with the emperor, bypassing the civilian government altogether. Konoye was thus Tojo's hostage, and the Razor quickly bent the pliant, melancholic prime minister to his will.

Until 1940, the Japanese invasion of China had been a regional event. It convulsed Asia, to be sure, and proceeded in worrisome parallel with the quickening pace of aggression in Europe, but it remained essentially an isolated affair, unlinked to the other fateful moves being played out on the great game board of global strategy. But Hitler's *Blitzkrieg* conquest of France and the Netherlands and the onset of the Battle of Britain in the summer of 1940 rearranged that game board and rewrote the geopolitical rules. Tojo and other Japanese imperialists now saw prospects opening before them that they had not earlier dared to dream. Hitler's successes, American ambassador to Tokyo Joseph Grew observed, had "gone to their heads like strong wine."[77]

With the colonial powers under Hitler's guns in Europe, Japan brought pressure to bear on French Indochina and the Dutch East Indies to supply Japan with rice, rubber, oil, and basing rights, as well as on British Burma to close the Burma Road, cutting off Chiang's principal supply route. In one of his rare recorded criticisms of the militarists' policies, Emperor Hirohito likened those initiatives to the actions "of a thief at a fire."[78] Tojo was unmoved. With broad support from both military and civilian leaders, Tojo breathed defiance at the distracted British and the meddlesome but weak and unarmed Americans and began negotiating a formal alliance with Nazi Germany and Fascist Italy. These steps in mid-1940 set events on the pathway to a *world* war.

Washington had two means of restraining Japan: either by bolstering China, as it was bolstering Britain, or by imposing economic sanctions on Japan—a policy instrument all but useless against virtually self-sufficient Germany but potentially highly effective against import-dependent Japan. As for direct aid to China, the simple facts were that China was not Britain, and Chiang Kai-shek was no Churchill. China's

77. Leuchtenburg, 309.
78. Feis, *Road to Pearl Harbor*, 95.

military performance was pitiful and deteriorating, and Chiang's inability to shape an effective government inspired little confidence. Roosevelt did extend modest credits to China. He also allowed American military pilots to resign their commissions and join Colonel Claire Chennault's Flying Tigers, a volunteer combat air squadron that flew for the Chinese. Eventually a trickle of Lend-Lease aid reached Chiang. But Washington's principal tool for restraining Tokyo was economic sanctions against Japan.

By 1940 Japan depended on the United States for a long list of indispensable strategic materials, conspicuously including oil; 80 percent of Japan's fuel supplies came from America. Roosevelt knew that Japanese dependence on American sources of supply gave him a powerful club. He also knew that it was a dangerous weapon to use. "If we once start sanctions against Japan we must see them through to the end," Ambassador Grew warned Roosevelt in the autumn of 1939, "and the end may conceivably be war. . . . [I]f we cut off Japanese supplies of oil . . . [Japan] will in all probability send her fleets down to take the Dutch East Indies."[79]

On July 26, 1940, Roosevelt forged an important link in the chain of events that would lead to war. Seeking to restrain Japanese pressure on the European colonial possessions in Southeast Asia, he declared an embargo on the shipment to Japan of premium grades of scrap iron and steel, as well as high-octane aviation gasoline. That move nettled the Japanese but did not deter them. Tokyo landed troops in northern French Indochina, with the Vichy government's compliant approval, and officially joined the Axis by signing the Tripartite Pact with Germany and Italy in September. By terms of the accord, the signatories pledged "to assist one another with all political, economic and military means when one of the three contracting Parties is attacked by a power at present not involved in the European War or in the Sino-Japanese Conflict."[80] An additional clause specifically exempted the Soviet Union from that last description—making it unmistakably clear that the pact was intended above all to cow the United States into remaining neutral by menacing the Americans with the prospect of a two-ocean war. Wash-

79. Grew quoted in Daniel Yergin, *The Prize: The Epic Quest for Oil, Money, and Power* (New York: Simon and Schuster, 1991), 310.
80. *Documents on German Foreign Policy, 1918–1945* (Washington: USGPO, 1960), Series D (1937–1945), *The War Years,* September 1, 1940–January 31, 1941, 204–205.

ington responded to the Tripartite Pact with a further turn of the economic screw, extending the list of embargoed items to include *all* iron and steel shipments.

Both Japan and the United States by this point had settled into the rhythm that would characterize their relationship for the next year. Each stepped through a series of escalating moves that provoked but failed to restrain the other, all the while lifting the level of confrontation to ever-riskier heights. Tokyo calculated what aggression it could pursue without precipitating open conflict with Washington. The Americans gambled that they could pressure Japan by economic means without driving Tokyo to war. For each side, however, the attitude of the other remained a secondary consideration. Japan's highest priority was still China. America's was Europe.

Conspicuously absent from the expanded American embargo list in September 1940 was the most vital of Japan's needs: oil. Other than aviation gasoline, petroleum products remained unembargoed thanks largely to the influence of Secretary of State Hull. Within the American government, a Great Debate over policy toward Japan raged from the summer of 1940 virtually until the outbreak of open hostilities in December 1941. This debate was much less publicly audible than the discussion of aid to Britain, but no less portentous. Not incidentally, the two struggles to define American policy, in Europe and in Asia, were also virtually synchronous. Many of those who favored all-out assistance to Britain also lined up in favor of strong measures against Japan. They included the quietly aggressive Morgenthau, Ickes, who truculently branded any lesser policy "appeasement," and of course the stiffly principled Stimson. Hull, on the other hand, with the strong backing of the U.S. Navy, as well as the generally consistent support of Ambassador Grew in Tokyo, argued that broader sanctions would simply prod the Japanese into seeking alternative sources of supply, by military force if necessary, in French Indochina, British Burma and Malaya, the Dutch East Indies, and even the Philippines. Those moves the United States would be powerless to prevent, especially given the American commitment, embedded in Plan Dog, ratified at ABC-1, and reaffirmed at Argentia and in the Victory Program, to give priority to the struggle against Hitler. An armed confrontation with Japan, in the view of Hull and the senior military leaders, would be the wrong war, with the wrong enemy, in the wrong place, and at the wrong time. For a long season, Hull's views prevailed, if only partially.

Hull by this date had grown accustomed to partial victories. Born in a log cabin in 1871, he had soldiered his way up through the political ranks in his native Tennessee. He had served first in the state legislature, then for more than two decades as a congressman. His fellow Tennesseans sent him to the U.S. Senate in 1930, but he cut his term short in 1933 to accept appointment as secretary of state. Roosevelt always dominated him and frequently undercut him, most notoriously at the London Economic Conference in 1933. Another man might have resigned after that humiliation, but Hull plowed on, pushing his special interests in the Good Neighbor Policy and in free trade and swallowing the further humiliation of watching his undersecretary, Sumner Welles, enjoy better access to the president than he himself did. Roosevelt did not consult Hull about Welles's mission to Europe in 1940 and excluded Hull from the Argentia Conference, the ABC-1 talks, and the Lend-Lease negotiations. Dogged, conscientious, and dull, Hull was a plodding bureaucrat, a predictable thinker, and a boring public speaker. He worked six full days a week plus Sunday mornings, took a briefcase of papers home every evening, and shunned the capital's social life. His only recreation was an occasional game of croquet on the lawn of Henry Stimson's estate. Washington insiders called him "Parson Hull."

That Hull enjoyed such influence as he did in shaping policy toward Japan indicated how relatively unimportant Roosevelt considered the entire Pacific region to be. When it came to Europe, Roosevelt handled matters himself. To Hull he left the decidedly lesser matter of negotiating with the Japanese. Hull succeeded for a time in dampening the tempo of economic warfare against Japan, but the coil of sanctions was nevertheless tugged progressively tighter. In December 1940 Washington added iron ore and pig iron to the prohibited list; the following month, copper and brass, and additional materials on a regular basis thereafter — but still not oil.

The closing cinch of the American embargo only slightly reined in the Japanese, but it worried them greatly, especially as they contemplated the ever-present threat of its extension to oil. In early 1941 Tokyo sent a new ambassador to Washington, Kichisaburo Nomura, an earnest naval officer and former foreign minister who had some acquaintance with the United States and a serviceable, but halting, command of English. In March he began a series of what would be some fifty meetings with Hull, many of them conducted in the secretary's suite at the Wardman Park Hotel. Nomura labored under heavy handicaps from the outset. Unknown to him, American cryptanalysts had cracked the highest Japanese diplomatic codes. Thanks to Magic — the code name for this intelligence breakthrough—they were able to brief Hull on Nomura's positions even before the Japanese ambassador presented them, and often with greater clarity than Nomura's broken English could manage. (He insisted on working without a translator, a practice that also led to his frequent misunderstanding of what Hull was saying.) Beyond that, Nomura was hobbled by the policies he was compelled, somewhat against his own better judgment, to defend and by his despair over the accelerating momentum for war in Tokyo. He poignantly expressed his discomfort. "I deeply fear lest I should make a miscalculation at this moment, and besides, there is a limit to my ability," he wrote to his superiors in Tokyo. "I am unable to perceive the delicate shades of the policy of the Government, and am quite at a loss what to do."[81]

In reality, Nomura's government's policy was not so much delicately shaded as it was intractable, a disagreeable fact that Nomura struggled to downplay but could not in the end evade. On his side, Hull, too, represented a government that was inflexibly committed to the one thing Nomura could not possibly concede—a Japanese withdrawal from China. Time and again through 1941 Nomura indicated that Japan might be willing to back off from pressuring Southeast Asia if the Americans would stop aiding China and lift the trade sanctions. Time and again Hull replied that Japanese withdrawal from China was the precondition for further negotiations. Throughout their tedious, repetitive conversations, each of the two negotiators did little more than affirm his opinion of the other's intransigence. Through the spring and summer the one goal they shared was to gain time, to postpone the moment of confrontation until, in Nomura's case, cooler and wiser heads might prevail, or, in Hull's case, until the American naval and military buildup might alter the balance of forces in the Pacific.

Hitler stepped forward in June 1941 as the thief of time. Just as it shattered so many other assumptions and plans, Operation Barbarossa broke the temporizing stalemate in Hull's hotel room. In a callous exhibition of his opportunistic attachment to the Tripartite Pact accord, Hitler launched Barbarossa without forewarning his Japanese "ally." His attack on the Soviet Union surprised the Japanese as much as it did the Russians. It also triggered a fateful argument within the Japanese government. "Northerners" who favored joining Hitler's attack on the Soviet Union were pitted against "southerners" who argued that now was the time, while the Soviet-German death struggle secured Japan's Si-

81. L&G, *Undeclared*, 657.

berian flank, to plunge into the rice paddies and rubber plantations of Indochina and Malaya and the coveted oil fields of the Dutch East Indies. The southerners invoked weighty arguments. Seizing Southeast Asia would girdle much of China's periphery with Japanese power, seal Chiang off from outside help, and thereby seal his fate. Moreover, the southerners argued, Japan had only a two-year reserve of oil, eighteen months under war conditions, and the American spigot could be turned off any day. Now was the moment to seize the rich Dutch East Indian oil fields and end Japan's humiliating dependence on the Americans for essential fuel supplies. If Japan were ever to end the China Incident, claim industrial self-sufficiency, and make good on its promise of creating an "Asia for the Asians," cleansed of the Western colonial powers, then the time was now.

The most aggressive of the northerners, Foreign Minister Yosuke Matsuoka, urged Japan to join Hitler's attack on the Soviet Union, thus extinguishing for all time the age-old Russian threat. "He who would search for pearls must dive deep," Matsuoka told the cabinet. "The outbreak of war between Germany and the Soviet Union presents Japan with a golden opportunity such as comes only once in a thousand years," declared another of the northerners, mindful of Japan's historic contest with Russia for hegemony in East Asia.[82] But by this time the northern option looked decidedly unattractive. The Kwantung Army was still smarting from its mortifying defeat by Soviet forces in the summer of 1939 at Nomonhan, a speck of an outpost on the Halha River, which defined the frontier between Soviet Mongolia and Japanese-controlled Manchukuo. Remembering Nomonhan, chastened Japanese army generals refused to take the offensive against a Soviet force unless they enjoyed overwhelming numerical superiority. Stalin's daring decision not to shift his Siberian garrisons to the defense of Moscow, along with evidence of stiffening Soviet resistance against the Germans, robbed the northerners of their "golden opportunity." At a conference in the emperor's presence on July 2, the southerners carried the day. The decision to go south was confirmed. "We will not be deterred by the possibility of being in a war with England and America," the conferees confidently recorded. Before the month was out, Japanese troops, already ensconced in northern Indochina, had moved into southern Indochina, clearly a

82. Hosoya Chihiro, "The Japanese-Soviet Neutrality Pact," in J. W. Morley, ed., *The Fateful Choice: Japan's Advance into Southeast Asia, 1939–1941* (New York: Columbia University Press, 1980), 97, 101.

preparatory move for the leap into British Malaya and the Dutch East Indies.[83]

Thanks to Magic, officials in Washington were able to follow closely these deliberations in Tokyo. "[T]he Japs are having a real drag-down and knock-out fight among themselves," Roosevelt told Harold Ickes, "trying to decide which way they are going to jump—attack Russia, attack the South Seas . . . , or whether they will sit on the fence and be more friendly with us. No one knows what the decision will be but, as you know, it is terribly important for the control of the Atlantic for us to help keep peace in the Pacific." As for what, precisely, to do in the face of this new Japanese threat, Roosevelt was less sure. His preoccupation with "the control of the Atlantic" was a heavy constraint on any show of force against the Japanese. "I simply have not got enough Navy to go round," Roosevelt complained, "and every little episode in the Pacific means fewer ships in the Atlantic."[84]

While Roosevelt tried to devise a response to Japan's southward thrust, the American naval chiefs counseled prudence. An embargo on oil was the obvious step to take, and the American hard-liners were warmly urging such a step. But the War Plans Division of the navy cautioned the president on July 21, 1941, that "an embargo would probably result in a fairly early attack by Japan on Malaya and the Netherlands East Indies, and possibly would involve the United States in early [the implication was "premature"] war in the Pacific. . . . Recommendation: That trade with Japan not be embargoed at this time."[85]

On July 26 Roosevelt announced the American response. He declared an immediate freeze on all Japanese assets in the United States, requiring any further Japanese purchases to be cleared through a government committee that would unblock dollars to pay for the exports. Despite much misunderstanding then and later, this was not a total embargo on trade with Japan. Roosevelt was merely unsheathing that ultimate economic weapon, not yet plunging it into the vitals of his foe. He conceived of the freeze on assets as a temporary and complicating device, one more click of the trade-sanction ratchet, a carefully measured policy consistent with the slowly escalating restrictions that had gone before. The American hard-liners were disappointed. "Notwithstanding that Japan was boldly making this hostile move," a frustrated Ickes noted in

83. Feis, *Road to Pearl Harbor*, 216.
84. Ickes Diary 3:567.
85. Feis, *The Road to Pearl Harbor*, 232.

his diary, "the President . . . was still unwilling to draw the noose tight. . . . [He] indicated that we would still continue to ship oil and gasoline." Over the objections of cabinet members who wanted "a complete job as quickly as possible . . . , [the President] thought that it might be better to slip the noose around Japan's neck and give it a jerk now and then."[86] Freezing Japanese assets was, in the last analysis, intended to be but another instance in Roosevelt's continuing policy of "appeasement" toward Japan that so infuriated Ickes and other hard-liners. They soon found a means to turn the president's latest pronouncement to their own purposes.[87]

The goal of Roosevelt's move was to cultivate maximum uncertainty in Japan about future American intentions. More uncertainty in Tokyo meant more time for American shipyards and aircraft plants, and more apprehension about the future of trade relations with America should breed a greater Japanese willingness to yield something at the negotiating table. Certainly Roosevelt did not envision the freeze as a provocation to war. All to the contrary, America's "chief objective in the Pacific for the time being," Sumner Welles told his British counterpart at the Argentia Conference just days later, "was the avoidance of war with Japan."[88] But in one of those striking vignettes that illustrate the contingent character of history, the freeze was promulgated on the eve of Roosevelt's departure for Argentia, and in his absence poorly instructed and temperamentally aggressive government officials refused to thaw any Japanese assets at all, for any purchases whatever. Roosevelt learned only in early September, after his return from Newfoundland, that his intended temporary freeze had congealed into the glacial hardness ofa total embargo. By then it would have been a sign of weakness to back down. Contrary to the president's original intention, all American trade with Japan was now cut off. "The vicious circle of reprisals and counter reprisals is on," a gloomy Grew recorded in his diary in Tokyo, lapsing into the Latin that came naturally to the Groton-and-Harvard-educated diplomat: "Facilis descensus averni est," the descent into hell is easy.[89]

---

86. Ickes Diary 3:588.
87. See the excellent account of this episode in Waldo Heinrichs, *Threshold of War: Franklin D. Roosevelt and American Entry into World War II* (New York: Oxford University Press, 1988), 133ff.
88. Dallek, 300.
89. Feis, *Road to Pearl Harbor*, 248. Assistant Secretary of State Dean Acheson played a crucial role in transforming what Roosevelt had intended to be a temporary mea-

The Japanese now watched with envy and anger as heavily laden American tankers plowed through La Perouse Strait between Hokkaido and Sakhalin, headed for Vladivostok with oil for the Russians, while the last Japanese tankers churned away high-hulled and empty from the American West Coast. The clock now measured time differently in Tokyo and Washington. The Americans still wanted more of it. The Japanese worried that it was rapidly running out on them. They felt, said one Japanese leader, "like a fish in a pond from which water was gradually being drained away."[90] The Imperial Navy calculated that in the event of war it had an eighteen-month oil reserve and that it would enjoy no more than a two-year period of superiority over the U.S. Navy in the Pacific, given the pace of the naval building program then proceeding in the United States. The window of opportunity was narrow and closing rapidly. The Americans had thrown down the gauntlet. The challenge had to be accepted soon.

On September 6 a Japanese Imperial Conference stipulated that if a reversal of the American policy were not achieved through diplomatic means by early October, Japan should launch the "Southern Operation." Its main strategic objective would be the oil of the Dutch East Indies. As Japanese war games had repeatedly demonstrated, however, for the Southern Operation to be successful Japan must first knock out the huge British naval facility at Singapore, deny the Americans the use of the Philippines as a forward basing area, and venture far out into the Pacific to cripple the main elements of the American Pacific Fleet at Pearl Harbor, Hawaii. The plan was hugely ambitious but not insane. Its slender logic resided largely in the hope that the Americans would be so stunned by Japan's lightning blows that they would lose the will to fight a protracted war and accept a negotiated settlement guaranteeing Japan a free hand in Asia. All the Japanese planners understood that a conventional victory, ending in the complete defeat of the United States, was an impossibility. Admiral Takijiru Onishi was one of the few voices warning that an attack on Pearl Harbor might make the Americans "so insanely mad" that all hope for compromise would go up in flames. If the Americans should choose to fight a war to the finish, all knew, Japan was almost certainly doomed. The emperor, a diminutive figure revered

---

sure into an airtight (and war-breeding) embargo. Acheson later unapologetically defended his behavior: "whether or not we had a policy, we had a state of affairs," he wrote in his memoirs. See Acheson, *Present at the Creation: My Years in the State Department* (New York: Norton, 1969), 26.

90. Satō Kenryō, quoted in Heinrichs, *Threshold of War*, 182.

by his people as the son of God, a taciturn man who usually sat impassively during these ritualized conferences, appreciated the perils ahead. He sharply reminded his military leaders that China's extensive hinterland had cheated Japan of victory on the Asian mainland and that "the Pacific was boundless." To that cryptic utterance he added nothing more, and the plan was approved.[91]

Prime Minister Konoye made one last bid to prevent war. On the evening after the September 6 Imperial Conference he invited Grew to dine, taking elaborate precautions to keep the occasion secret: using a friend's home, removing the license plates from his car, dismissing the servants. Over the sake and rice, Konoye pressed for a personal meeting with Roosevelt, perhaps in Honolulu. Grew vigorously supported the idea, but when it became clear that the Americans still insisted on Japanese abandonment of China as a precondition for such a meeting, the proposal collapsed. On October 16 Konoye was ousted as prime minister. Tojo replaced him.

In both capitals the measured language of diplomacy could no longer muffle the rising beat of the military tatoo. On November 5 another Imperial Conference directed that war plans should go forward, to be confirmed on November 25 if a last diplomatic effort failed. Ironically enough, on that same date of November 5, the American Joint Board of the Army and Navy reaffirmed that the primary objective of the United States "is the defeat of Germany." Therefore, the Joint Board concluded, "[w]ar between the United States and Japan should be avoided." Even further Japanese offensives in China "would not justify intervention by the United States against Japan." In short, American military planners were conceding their inability to affect events in China and were still looking for ways to avoid an Asian distraction when their main concern was Germany.[92]

Well might the question be pondered: Why did the American government not publicly accept the logic of this reasoning? Why not acquiesce, however complainingly, in the Japanese action in China, reopen at least limited trade with Japan, and thereby deflect Tokyo from its course of aggression in Southeast Asia? By the American military planners' own admission, such a policy would have had little immediate bearing on the situation in China, which the United States was all but

91. Gordon W. Prange, At Dawn We Slept: The Untold Story of Pearl Harbor (New York: Penguin, 1981), 261; Feis, Road to Pearl Harbor, 266.
92. Feis, Road to Pearl Harbor, 302.

powerless to influence in any case. More important, it would have de-layed—perhaps postponed indefinitely—a showdown between America and Japan. Delay would have given the Americans more time to arm and more munitions to share with the British and the Russians. Whether under those circumstances a Japanese-American war could have been avoided altogether is among the weightiest of might-have-beens, with implications for the nature and timing of America's struggle against Hit-ler and for the shape of postwar Europe as well as Asia. But it was not to be.

Just days after the November 5 Imperial Conference, Tokyo dis-patched the seasoned diplomatist Saburo Kurusu to assist the hapless Nomura in presenting a final proposal to Washington. On November 20 Nomura and Kurusu described the Japanese offer to Hull: they asked for a free hand in China and an end to American trade restrictions, in return for a Japanese withdrawal from Indochina and a pledge to un-dertake no further armed advances in Southeast Asia. There was little new here. But given the Joint Board's recent recommendation to ac-quiesce in events in China and avoid war with Japan, this Japanese approach held some promise, at which Roosevelt momentarily grasped. Though he remained wary of the Japanese, telling Ickes that "he was not sure whether or not Japan had a gun up its sleeve" (to which Ickes replied that he was sure that before long "Japan would be at our throats"), he drafted notes for a conciliatory reply to this latest Japanese proposal. He envisioned a 6-month *modus vivendi* with Japan and in-cluded a significant concession: he dropped the American insistence on withdrawal from China.[93]

Roosevelt next circulated his draft notes for comment by Churchill, Chiang, and his own cabinet members. Morgenthau, Ickes, and Stimson were outraged. So was Chiang, who predicted the utter demoralization and certain surrender of China if American opposition to Japan's role there were relaxed. Churchill concurred with Chiang and spelled out the strategic implications of China's possible downfall: "What about Chiang Kai-shek? Is he not having a very thin diet? Our anxiety is about China. If they collapse our joint dangers would enormously increase."[94] Despite the Joint Board's recommendation that China be cut adrift, China, Roosevelt now saw, had taken on more significance, not less, after the German invasion of Russia. If Chiang were not sustained in

93. Ickes Diary 3:649.
94. C&R 1:277–78.

the war, Japan would be free to attack the Soviet Union, perhaps precipitating a Soviet collapse and thus nullifying the great gift that Barbarossa had bestowed upon American and British strategists. In any case,
prospects for Japanese acceptance of the proposal looked slim. Reports
were already coming in to Washington of Japanese troop transports heading south past Formosa, toward Southeast Asia. Roosevelt discarded the
modus vivendi. The last flimsy hope of avoiding, or even delaying, war
with Japan thus evaporated.

At a White House meeting on November 25, administration officials
agreed that little room for negotiation remained. War, in some form,
seemed inevitable. "The question," Stimson thought, "was how we
should maneuver them into the position of firing the first shot without
allowing too much danger to ourselves."[95] The second part of Stimson's
observation was at least as important as the first. Despite decades of
investigation, no credible evidence has ever been adduced to support
the charge that Roosevelt deliberately exposed the fleet at Pearl Harbor
to attack in order to precipitate war. Risking the entire Pacific Fleet to
create a *casus belli* surely constituted far "too much danger to ourselves,"
especially in light of Roosevelt's repeated efforts to avoid war in the
Pacific, his unwavering emphasis on the priority of the Atlantic, and his
studied refusal even there to leverage the several naval incidents of 1941
into a request for a declaration of war against Germany.

On November 26 Hull handed Nomura and Kurusu a ten-point statement of the American position. It essentially reiterated the principles to
which American diplomacy had clung for the preceding two years: insistence on Japanese withdrawal from China and abandonment of the
Southeast Asian adventure.

On December 6 Roosevelt tried one last gambit. He sent a personal
message to the Emperor, going so far as to revive some of the promises
contained in the recently discarded *modus vivendi*. He had little hope
of success. "Well," he joked to a dinner guest, "this son of man has just
sent his final message to the Son of God." Later that evening, a navy
courier brought to Roosevelt in his White House study the Magic decrypts of the Japanese reply to Hull's November 26 ten-point statement.
They offered no hope of any further diplomatic discussion. Roosevelt
glanced at them, then turned to Harry Hopkins and said simply: "This
means war."[96]

95. Stimson Diary, November 25, 1941.
96. Sherwood, *Roosevelt and Hopkins*, 426.

16

War in the Pacific

The closest squeak and the greatest victory.
— George C. Marshall Jr. on the Battle of Midway

During the first days of December 1941, Admiral Isoroku Yamamoto, commander-in-chief of Japan's Combined Fleet, fretted in his headquarters aboard the battleship *Nagato* in Hiroshima Bay. On November 26 he had directed a powerful task force under Vice-Admiral Chuichi Nagumo to sortie from Hitokappu Bay in the Kurile Islands, under orders to attack the U.S. Pacific Fleet base at Pearl Harbor, Hawaii. Though Yamamoto had provided that "in the event an agreement is reached in the negotiations with the United States, the Task Force will immediately return to Japan," the negotiations had by now irretrievably collapsed. There would be no turning back.[1]

Other Japanese naval forces were at the same time initiating the massive Southern Operation, slicing southward from Japan to land invasion troops in the Philippines, Malaya, and the great oil-rich prize of the Dutch East Indies. The Hawaii expedition was the pivot of this complex scheme. On the outcome at Pearl Harbor turned the fate of the Southern Operation, which could not imaginably succeed if its eastern flank remained exposed to the firepower of the U.S. Pacific Fleet. Because of the very power of that fleet, concentrated in the midocean anchorage of Hawaii, Nagumo's mission was also the most perilous of the several huge military operations Japan now had under way.

Preparations for the assault on Pearl Harbor had been exhaustive, including repeated mock attacks on a model of the Hawaiian base set

1. Gordon W. Prange, *At Dawn We Slept: The Untold Story of Pearl Harbor* (New York: Penguin, 1982), 387.

up in Japan's Saeki Bay. Sailors and airmen had analyzed knotty problems of resupplying ships at sea, navigating the attack convoy without radio communication, and coordinating the waves of high-level horizontal bombers, dive-bombers, torpedo bombers, and fighter planes that would deliver the blow.[2]

Yet so much could go wrong. The strike force, designated First Air Fleet, had been organized only eight months earlier and had never fought a concerted action. With the six aircraft carriers that composed its fighting core, it embodied the experimental concept of naval air power, long advocated by visionaries like the American Billy Mitchell and First Air Fleet's own air staff officer, Commander Minoru Genda, but still virtually untested in the unforgiving crucible of battle. The very length of the attack route — thirty-five hundred miles, well beyond the Japanese navy's traditional radius of action — necessitated tricky refueling at sea and amplified the chances for detection.

Surprise would enormously enhance the prospect of success, just as surprise had favored Japan when it launched its other great war against a Caucasian power by besieging the Russian fleet at Port Arthur in 1904. So Nagumo's ships plowed methodically eastward from Hitokappu Bay in strict radio silence, enveloping themselves as well in the cloud and mist of an eastering weather front. Yamamoto could trace their putative movements on his charts but would know nothing for certain until radio silence was broken.

Short, deep-chested, swift and sarcastic in argument, bold and ingenious in battle, born in 1884 in the great flowering of the Meiji Restoration, Yamamoto was at the summit of his distinguished naval career in 1941. He had firsthand knowledge of his adversary. He had studied English at Harvard in the 1920s and later served as naval attaché in Washington, where he had earned a reputation as a shrewd poker player. He had also acquired a sober respect for the warmaking potential of the United States. He knew that its vast industrial base and large population would make it a formidable foe if it ever mustered the political will to fight, and probably an invincible foe if the conflict were protracted. Through the tense debates since 1937 about Japan's foreign policies, Yamamoto's had been a voice of moderation. He did not fully trust Japan's Axis allies and repeatedly pleaded for alternatives to war with

2. Ironically, a successful British aerial-torpedo attack on the Italian fleet at Taranto in November 1940 gave the Japanese planners confidence that they could adopt shallow-water torpedo tactics for the assault on Pearl Harbor.

the United States. Yet to Yamamoto had fallen the task of devising the battle plan for that war. A devoted patriot and loyal warrior, Yamamoto had done his duty faithfully—and brilliantly.

The attack on Pearl Harbor fitted Yamamoto's gambler's temperament. It entailed gigantic risks but also held out the promise of extravagant rewards. If fully successful, it might cow the isolationist Americans into acquiescing in Japan's dominance over China and the Pacific. At a minimum, crippling the U.S. Pacific Fleet would buy precious time for the Southern Operation to go forward unmolested and for Japan so to consolidate its hold on Southeast Asia that it could not easily be dislodged.

What was more, success at Pearl Harbor would vindicate the Japanese navy, so long denied a role in the land war in China, yet fiercely proud of the part it had played in the Russo-Japanese War of 1904–5, especially its legendary conquest of the Russian fleet at the Battle of Tsushima Strait in 1905. For the Japanese people, and especially for seamen like Yamamoto, Tsushima represented not only a glorious naval victory but a confirmation and font of racial pride. Tsushima had demonstrated the vulnerability of the haughty Western powers in the face of Japan's rising industrial might and abiding moral superiority. Yamamoto himself had been blooded at Tsushima. His left hand, missing two fingers lost in that battle, daily reminded him of the near-mythical spell that Tsushima still cast for his service and his nation.

At sea on December 4, silent and undetected several hundred miles northwest of Hawaii, Nagumo's sprawling flotilla of nearly three dozen ships pivoted from its easterly course to a southeasterly bearing. On the morning of December 6 Nagumo completed his final refueling. His oilers angled away to take station at the rendezvous point for the return voyage. Freed of the lumbering tankers, at 11:30 Nagumo ordered speed increased to twenty knots and pointed his ships due south, carving a course that would bring them to the launching sector two hundred miles north of Oahu just before dawn the next day. At 11:40 his flagship, the giant carrier *Akagi*, ran up the very Z flag that Admiral Togo had flown at the Battle of Tsushima Strait thirty-six years before. Flushed with patriotic emotion, Japanese sailors and pilots cheered wildly.

With Togo's historic pennant snapping in the wind, Nagumo's arrowhead-shaped armada plunged through heavy seas, bearing relentlessly down on its target. Destroyers patrolled along its flanks, submarines guarded its rear, and an imposing cordon of battleships and cruisers closely jacketed the precious carriers with their lethal cargos at the arrowhead's heart.

Just before 6:00 A.M., Nagumo wheeled due east again, to launch his planes into the wind. Pilots, each wearing a bandana emblazoned with the word *hissho* (certain victory), scrambled into their aircraft. Within minutes, 183 planes had lifted from the decks of the six carriers and were shaping their triangular formations for the first attack wave. Fifty-one dive-bombers made up the high squadron, with forty-nine level bombers below and forty torpedo planes lower still. High overhead ranged forty-three Mitsubishi A6M fighters—the swift and nimble "Zeros" that would soon terrorize American fighting men all over the Pacific. By the time the second attack wave had been launched about an hour later, some 350 aircraft, led by Commander Mitsuo Fuchida, were droning through the leaden dawn southward toward Oahu.

At the very moment that Nagumo ordered his carriers to point their bows into the wind, shortly before noon Washington time, George C. Marshall was returning from a Sunday-morning horseback ride to his War Department office in Washington. There aides presented him with a translation of a freshly decrypted message from Tokyo. It contained a lengthy and final reply to the ten-point American position that Hull had presented to Ambassador Nomura on November 26 and instructed Nomura once and for all to break off negotiations. As Marshall scanned the sterile diplomatic prose, he reached its alarming codicil, ordering Nomura to submit the reply "at 1:00 P.M. on the 7th, your time." To Marshall the highly unusual specification of a precise time, and on a Sunday at that, was ominous. One P.M. was scarcely an hour away. Marshall immediately drafted a message to be sent to army commands in the Philippines, Panama, Hawaii, and San Francisco: "Japanese are presenting at one pm eastern standard time today what amounts to an ultimatum. . . . Just what significance the hour set may have we do not know but be on the alert accordingly. Inform naval authorities of this communication." Within minutes the message was encoded and dispatched by radio to all destinations—except Hawaii. Atmospheric conditions were creating heavy static that temporarily blocked the wireless channel to Honolulu. The War Department signal officer chose the next-fastest communication route: a commercial Western Union teletype. The message left Washington on the Western Union wire at 12:17 P.M. and was relayed by the RCA (Radio Corporation of America) installation near San Francisco to Hawaii. It reached Honolulu sixteen minutes later—7:33 A.M., Hawaii time. A messenger picked up the telegram at RCA's Honolulu office, mounted his motorcycle, and roared away to deliver it to General Walter C. Short at Fort Shafter, several miles away. Fuchida's planes were then twenty minutes north of Oahu. Still en route when the attack commenced, the messenger reached Fort Shafter only several hours after Fuchida's planes had wreaked their destruction.[3]

That communications delay was not the only missed opportunity to spoil the Japanese surprise. As Fuchida's attackers formed up over their carriers, just before 7:00 A.M., an American destroyer patrolling outside Pearl Harbor's mouth sighted and depth-bombed a Japanese midget submarine trying to slip into the anchorage. But the destroyer's report of this contact was discounted as another in a series of frustratingly unconfirmed submarine sightings and set aside for further verification.

Minutes after the submarine contact, an army radar operator on northern Oahu reported an unusually large flight of incoming aircraft. They were, in fact, Fuchida's first wave, still nearly an hour away, but the operator's superior officer irresponsibly intuited that the blips on the screen represented a flight of B-17 Flying Fortresses being ferried in from California to Hickam Field for eventual posting to the Philippines. The officer was brought to this tragic miscalculation at least in part by his recollection that radio station KGMB had been broadcasting all night—a programming schedule that almost invariably meant B-17s were arriving from the mainland, their navigators using the station's beam as a homing signal. In one of the many ironies on this day when irony was in abundant and cruel supply, Fuchida's pilot was meanwhile using that same beam, carrying saccharine Hawaiian tunes, to guide him to Oahu.

When Fuchida sighted land from his lead bomber about 7:30, he gave the order to assume attack positions. Below the warplanes the American ships and aircraft lay serenely unsuspecting and virtually undefended, exactly as described by the espionage reports from Japan's Honolulu consulate. Now certain beyond doubt that complete surprise had been achieved, Fuchida at 7:53 at last broke radio silence and shouted into his mouthpiece, *"Tora! Tora! Tora!"* (Tiger! Tiger! Tiger!)—the coded announcement that Yamamoto's high-stakes gamble was about to pay off in frightful devastation.

For more than an hour, bombs and bullets pelted down on the unmaneuverable American battleships, mostly moored in pairs in "Battle-

3. Prange, *At Dawn We Slept,* 486, 494–95.

PEARL HARBOR, DECEMBER 7, 1941

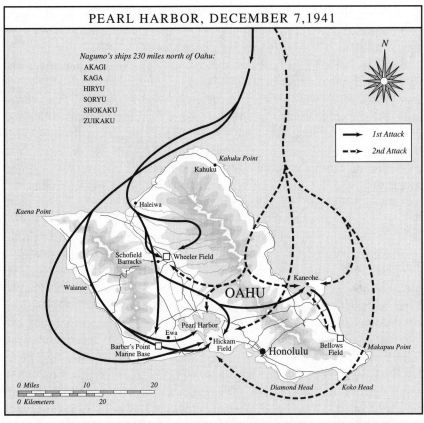

Nagumo's ships 230 miles north of Oahu:
AKAGI
KAGA
HIRYU
SORYU
SHOKAKU
ZUIKAKU

N

→ 1st Attack
⇢ 2nd Attack

Kahuku Point
Kahuku
Haleiwa
Kaena Point
Schofield Barracks — Wheeler Field
Waianae
Kaneohe
OAHU
Ewa — Pearl Harbor
Barber's Point Marine Base
Hickam Field
Honolulu
Bellows Field
Makapuu Point
Diamond Head   Koko Head

0 Miles   10   20
0 Kilometers   20

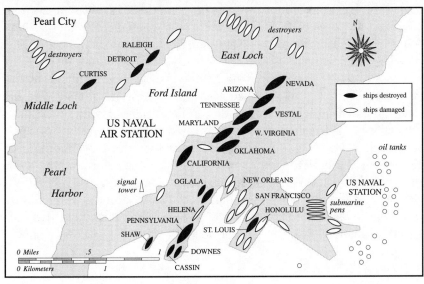

Pearl City
destroyers
RALEIGH
DETROIT
CURTISS
East Loch
destroyers
N

Middle Loch
Ford Island
NEVADA
ARIZONA
TENNESSEE
VESTAL
MARYLAND
W. VIRGINIA
OKLAHOMA
CALIFORNIA

US NAVAL
AIR STATION

● ships destroyed
○ ships damaged

oil tanks

Pearl
Harbor
signal tower
OGLALA
NEW ORLEANS
SAN FRANCISCO
HONOLULU
US NAVAL STATION
submarine pens
HELENA
PENNSYLVANIA
ST. LOUIS
SHAW
DOWNES
CASSIN

0 Miles   .5   1
0 Kilometers   1

ship Row" off Ford Island, and on the unflyable American airplanes, parked wingtip-to-wingtip at Bellows, Wheeler, and Hickam fields so they could be guarded against land-based sabotage. When the last Japanese plane winged away about 10:00 A.M., eighteen U.S. naval vessels, including eight battleships, had been sunk or heavily damaged. More than 180 aircraft were destroyed, and another 120 crippled. Two thousand four hundred and three men were dead — 1,103 of them entombed in the battleship *Arizona*, which sank almost instantaneously when a bomb exploded in its forward magazine. Another 1,178 men were wounded. Columns of smoke obscured Fuchida's final reconnaissance as he departed for the *Akagi*, but he knew beyond question that his airmen had triumphantly accomplished their mission.

OR HAD THEY? Fuchida's fliers had seen to it that not a single battleship remained in action in the U.S. Pacific Fleet. But battleships were the capital weapons of the last war. In the war that was now so bloodily begun, aircraft carriers would be trumps, and no U.S. Pacific Fleet carriers had been at Pearl Harbor on December 7. *Yorktown* had been detached in April for duty in the Atlantic. *Saratoga* was stateside for repairs. *Enterprise* and *Lexington* were at sea near Wake and Midway islands respectively. Fuchida's raiders had also failed to damage Pearl Harbor's repair shops. More important still, they had left intact the enormous fuel-oil tank farm. Loss of that fuel supply, every drop of it laboriously hauled from the American mainland, would probably have forced the U.S. Navy to retreat to its bases on the West Coast, at a stroke sweeping the western Pacific of American ships more cleanly than any other imaginable action. But Nagumo rejected suggestions that he undertake a second strike against the repair and fuel facilities or linger in the area to search for the missing carriers. He seemed paralyzed by the very ease of his victory. He had lost but twenty-nine aircraft, and his fleet remained unsighted. In Gordon Prange's apt phrase, he must have felt "as if he had rushed forward to break down a door just as someone opened it."[4] For Nagumo, what he had achieved on the morning of December 7 was victory enough. Yet his failure to return for the final, definitive kill risked eventual defeat.

Nor were the political consequences of Pearl Harbor unambiguously favorable for Japan. Among the fragile hopes that Yamamoto had harbored as relations with the United States deteriorated was that a knock-

4. Prange, *At Dawn We Slept*, 544.

out blow at the war's outset would set the stage for a negotiated settlement with the Americans. But he had never fully answered, perhaps not even in his own mind, the counterargument that such an attack was by its very nature so provocative as to preclude the possibility of subsequent negotiation. The force of that argument seemed confirmed when the U.S. Congress declared war on Japan on December 8 with but a single dissenting vote, amid ferocious and wrathful outcries for a vengeful war without mercy against the treacherous "Japs." The attack stepped up the voltage of a long-running current of American racial hatred toward the Japanese and threatened to make the Pacific war a singularly bitter clash of cultures, as well as armies.[5]

Even the strategic benefit to Japan of the Pearl Harbor attack was questionable. Yamamoto himself was reported to be deeply depressed in the days after December 7, faced at last with the reality of a war that Japan had such slight prospect of winning. In Chungking, Chiang Kai-shek "was so happy he sang an old opera aria and played Ave Maria all day.... Now China's strategic importance would grow even more. American money and equipment would flow in."[6] Winston Churchill remembered thinking: "So we had won after all . . . ! Hitler's fate was sealed. Mussolini's fate was sealed. As for the Japanese, they would be ground to powder. . . . [T]here was no more doubt about the end. . . . Being saturated and satiated with emotion and sensation, I went to bed and slept the sleep of the saved and thankful." Memory may have distorted Churchill's account. In fact, his first reaction to the news of Pearl Harbor was to make plans for an immediate departure for Washington, to ensure that the clamor for vengeance against Japan did not threaten American supplies for Britain. Britain must be careful, Churchill advised King George, "that our share of munitions and other aid which we are receiving form the United States does not suffer more than is, I fear, inevitable."[7]

5. Fifty representatives and six senators, by contrast, had voted against the resolution taking the United States into World War I in 1917. Jeannette Rankin of Montana, the first woman elected to Congress, has the distinction of being the only person who voted against both war resolutions.
6. Michael Schaller, The U.S. Crusade in China, 1938–1945 (New York: Columbia University Press, 1979), 88.
7. Churchill, 3:606–8; Martin Gilbert, Churchill: A Life (New York: Henry Holt, 1991), 711. If the news of Pearl Harbor worried Churchill, in other ways it emboldened him. When an aide on December 8 urged that at this delicate moment caution was required in dealing with the United States, Churchill replied: "Oh, that is the way we talked to her while we were wooing her; now that she is in the harem, we talk

As for Adolf Hitler, he reportedly exclaimed to his generals: "Now it is impossible for us to lose the war: we now have an ally who has never been vanquished in three thousand years."[8] Though the strict terms of their alliance with Japan did not require it, since Japan had been the attacker, not the attacked, Hitler and Mussolini on December 11 somewhat impetuously declared war on the United States, which then recognized a state of war with Germany and Italy.

Hitler here missed an opportunity to work incalculable mischief with the American commitment to give precedence to the European war. If Hitler had not now obligingly declared war on the United States, Roosevelt, given the apparent willingness of both sides to acquiesce in protracted and undeclared naval war in the Atlantic, would have had undoubted difficulty finding a politically useable occasion for declaring war against Germany. In the absence of such a legal declaration, Roosevelt might well have found it impossible to resist demands to place the maximum American effort in the Pacific, against the formally recognized Japanese enemy, rather than in the Atlantic, in a nondeclared war against the Germans. This was precisely Churchill's worry, and it was not easily laid to rest. Well after the German declaration of war, Roosevelt came under stubborn pressure to give priority to the fight against Japan. Pressure came from the navy, which always took the Pacific war to be its special province, and from public opinion, infected by a legacy of racial animosity toward the Japanese and inflamed by the humiliation of the Pearl Harbor attack.

It was no doubt that same sense of humiliation and wounded racial pride that fueled an almost interminable search for scapegoats for the Pearl Harbor disaster. Conspiracy theories proliferated, as they often do in the face of the improbable. Many Americans instinctively believed that an inferior power like Japan could not possibly have inflicted such damage on the United States unless some individual had failed in his duty, perhaps even behaved treasonably. The most extreme accusations have indicted Roosevelt himself for deliberately putting the Pacific Fleet at risk in order to bait Japan to the attack and thus bring the United States into the war—a thesis that simply will not bear close examination in light of the president's unwavering insistence on the priority of the Atlantic and European theaters and the unambiguous conviction of his

---

to her differently!" See James MacGregor Burns, *Roosevelt: The Soldier of Freedom* (New York: Harcourt Brace, 1970), 172.

8. John Keegan, *The Second World War* (New York: Viking, 1989), 240.

naval and military advisers that not Japan but Germany was the truly dangerous adversary. They all understood that an open conflict with Japan was a distraction, not a back door to war. From that perspective, the question is not who was responsible for Pearl Harbor but who should bear responsibility for failing to pursue a diplomatic settlement with Japan that would have left the United States free to apply its undivided military strength against Hitler. Roosevelt's deepest failure, it might be argued, was his inattentiveness to Asian matters and his unwillingness to be seen as "appeasing" Japan, when in fact a little appeasement—another name for diplomacy—might have yielded rich rewards.

More plausible, but in the end no more convincing, accusations have been leveled at the various military, naval, and civilian intelligence services for failing to predict the Pearl Harbor attack. Exhaustive investigations have turned up numerous "signals" that allegedly should have alerted the authorities to the approach of Nagumo's strike force, including especially an encoded message supposedly intercepted in the early days of December and containing the phrase "east wind rain," code for the announcement of a breakdown in U.S.-Japanese relations. Yet the chief of naval operations had in fact notified all Pacific theater commands on November 27 that "[t]his dispatch is to be considered a war warning" and ordered "appropriate defensive deployment." The War Department sent a similar message the following day, instructing army commanders in the Pacific that "hostile action [is] possible at any moment." It added that "the United States desires that Japan commit the first overt act," while emphasizing the significant qualifier that "this policy should not repeat not be construed as restricting you to a course of action that might jeopardize your defense."[9]

So American forces throughout the Pacific were already on highest alert by the end of November. But Pearl Harbor was only one among many possible places where the first blow might fall, and arguably the least likely. Months, even years, of speculation about Japan's military intentions had focused on China, Soviet Siberia, Malaya, Singapore, Hong Kong, the Dutch East Indies, Thailand, Indochina, and the Philippines as possible Japanese targets—but rarely, if ever, Hawaii. The navy's warning of November 27, for example, plausibly named "the Philippines, Thai or Kra (Malay) Peninsula, or possibly Borneo," as sites for impending hostilities. In the welter of "noise" about the impending

9. Roberta Wohlstetter, *Pearl Harbor: Warning and Decision* (Stanford: University Press, 1962), 44–47.

showdown with Japan that filled the air in the days before Pearl Harbor, scattered and ambiguous warnings about the possibility of action against Hawaii—so distant from Japan, so apparently impregnable—were easy to discount. The American "failure" at Pearl Harbor, if such there was, was not a thing of the moment or of the Hawaiian locale. It was systematic, pervasive, and cumulative, embedded in a tangle of only partially thought-out strategic assumptions and priorities and colored by smug attitudes of racial superiority that had now been violently challenged.

THE SIMPLE FACT is that Pearl Harbor was a masterful, though incomplete, tactical achievement by the Japanese. It would also prove in time to have been a strategic blunder and a political and psychological catastrophe. So much depended on what use Japan would make of its advantage in the immediate aftermath of the Hawaiian attack. Like a judo fighter, Yamamoto had now knocked his larger American opponent off balance. Could he next bring down his foe before the United States shrugged off its post–Pearl Harbor daze and brought all of its prodigious industrial strength to bear? Swift and sharp follow-up jabs were now essential. In a prolonged conflict, Japan would eventually be smothered under an awesome outpouring of metal and flame that would spew from American arsenals. No one knew better than Yamamoto that time was Japan's worst enemy.

That prospect had long haunted him. "If I am told to fight regardless of the consequences," Yamamoto had warned then–prime minister Konoye in September 1940, "I shall run wild for the first six months or a year, but I have utterly no confidence for the second or third year. . . . I hope," he added, that "you will endeavor to avoid a Japanese-American war." But the war had now come. How would Japan use those crucial six months?[10]

At first Yamamoto's slender hope for victory seemed about to be realized. Japanese forces did indeed "run wild" along a gigantic arc that swept from the Aleutians in the north Pacific to Ceylon (Sri Lanka) in the Indian Ocean. Carrier-borne Japanese aircraft sank the British battleships *Repulse* and *Prince of Wales* off the coast of Malaya on December 10. Hong Kong, Guam, and Wake Island all fell to the Japanese within days of Pearl Harbor. In lightning moves, Japanese forces struck from Indochina into Thailand and British Malaya and by mid-January

---

10. *Reports of General MacArthur: Japanese Operations in the Southwest Pacific Area 2*, pt. 1 (Washington: USGPO, 1966), 33 n. 14.

of 1942 were advancing almost unopposed into Burma. The crack Japanese Fifth Division, recently retrained for the unfamiliar task of jungle warfare, brilliantly employed flanking attacks and the terrifying tactics of night-fighting ("The night is one million reinforcements," ran a training slogan) as it made its way down the Malay peninsula toward Singapore. On February 15 that British stronghold, the supposedly unconquerable "Gibraltar of the Pacific," surrendered its garrison of eighty-five thousand troops to a Japanese force half that size, in what is usually regarded as the worst defeat in the history of British arms.

Twelve days later, in the Battle of the Java Sea, a hastily assembled American-British-Dutch-Australian fleet pathetically failed to halt the major Japanese invasion of the Dutch East Indies, whose oil fields constituted the main target and the consuming economic logic of the entire Southern Operation. On March 12 the Allies gave up the East Indies. As happened elsewhere in Asia, though by no means uniformly, the Japanese were welcomed by many Indonesians as liberators who had thrown out the hated Dutch colonials and begun at last to make good on the promise of "Asia for the Asians."

Admiral Nagumo next steamed through the now secure Strait of Malacca and for a week raided at will throughout the Indian Ocean, sinking nearly a hundred thousand tons of British shipping and bombing British bases in Ceylon. The remnants of the British Far Eastern fleet withdrew to East Africa. The Royal Australian Navy retired to its home ports. The U.S. Pacific Fleet had not a single surviving battleship. Yet Japan's armada of eleven battleships, six large and four small carriers, and thirty-eight heavy and light cruisers had not been scratched. From the Bay of Bengal to the Bering Sea, a vast quadrant of the world ocean had become a Japanese lake.

Victory took only a bit longer in the American colony of the Philippines. At his Manila headquarters Douglas MacArthur, commanding general of U.S. forces in the Far East, learned early in the morning of December 8 that Pearl Harbor had been attacked. Incredibly, and unforgivably, he made no use of the next ten hours to mount a counterattack against Japanese positions on Formosa (Taiwan), as his air commander urged, or even to launch or disperse his own aircraft. They were caught bunched on the ground — "On the ground! On the ground!" President Roosevelt exclaimed incredulously — when Japanese bombers and fighters appeared overhead shortly after noon. Within minutes MacArthur's entire force of some three dozen B-17 bombers, on which he had obstreperously premised his claim to be able to defend the Philip-

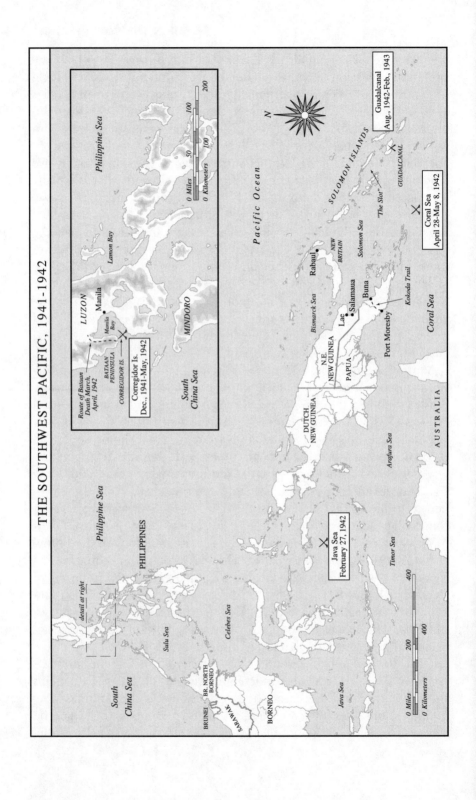

THE SOUTHWEST PACIFIC, 1941-1942

pines indefinitely, was utterly wiped out, along with more than two hundred other aircraft.[11]

When the Japanese began landing troops on the principal Philippine island of Luzon on December 22, MacArthur speedily jettisoned his always dubious scheme to repel the invader on the beaches and on the central Luzon plain and began gathering men and supplies for a retreat into the Bataan peninsula and the island fortress of Corregidor, where he set up his command post. MacArthur, sometimes accused of being a legend in his own mind, soon earned himself the derogatory nickname "Dugout Doug," bestowed on him by his suffering troops on Bataan while he sat in the relative comfort of Corregidor, only once making the brief torpedo-boat run across to the peninsula to hearten his men.

They sorely needed heartening. The swift retreat into the peninsula of some eighty thousand American and Filipino troops and another twenty-five thousand civilian refugees left them all wretchedly undersupplied. Lacking fresh food, medicines, clean drinking water, and sanitary facilities, thousands fell victim to scurvy, beriberi, malaria, and dysentery. The Japanese force, unprepared for a long siege, was in scarcely better condition—a circumstance whose hideous implications were soon to be revealed.

Knowing that the Philippine garrison was doomed, Roosevelt ordered MacArthur to depart for Australia. On the night of March 12 the general and his family and personal staff were evacuated from Corregidor in four PT boats, leaving General Jonathan Wainwright in command. With characteristic self-regard and uncharacteristic lack of orotundity, MacArthur announced: "I shall return." As a face-saving measure—and as a prophylaxis against backlash from the general's many political friends—the president simultaneously conferred upon MacArthur the Congressional Medal of Honor.[12]

The medal was small comfort for the masses of sick soldiers and civilians left behind in the Philippines. Though MacArthur fulminated by radio from his new base in Australia that his troops should break out of Bataan and take to the mountains as guerrillas, Wainwright knew the notion was fatuous. The Bataan contingent surrendered on April 9, and on May 6 an emaciated Wainwright, hopelessly holed up in Corregidor's

11. Eric Larrabee, *Commander in Chief: Franklin Delano Roosevelt, His Lieutenants, and Their War* (New York: Harper and Row, 1987), 316.
12. Burns, *Roosevelt: The Soldier of Freedom*, 209.

putrescent Malinta Tunnel, tortured by the resonant moaning of thousands of ill and wounded men crammed into the dank 826–foot shaft, finally capitulated. In his diary, Dwight Eisenhower took note of these events: "Corregidor surrendered last night. Poor Wainwright! He did the fighting . . . [MacArthur] got such glory as the public could find. . . . MacArthur's tirades, to which TJ [MacArthur's aide, T. J. Davis] and I so often listened in Manila, would now sound as silly to the public as they then did to us. But he's a hero! Yah."[13]

In a war that would grotesquely add to history's already extensive annals of cruelty, one of the cruelest episodes now ensued. The world would learn of it more than a year later, after three American survivors escaped from a prisoner-of-war camp on Mindanao, made their way to Australia, and told the story. There were some extenuating circumstances, but scarcely sufficient to exonerate the Japanese from the indictment that they behaved with wanton barbarity. The Japanese had planned on bagging some forty thousand prisoners of war in the Philippines sometime in the summer of 1942. Instead, they found themselves with nearly seventy thousand captives on their hands in April and May, ten thousand of them Americans, all of them suffering from months of siege and illness, as were the Japanese themselves. These logistical and medical problems only exacerbated a more fundamental clash of cultures.

Japanese military leaders had adopted the ancient samurai ethos of Bushido to develop a military code that engendered what two scholars have described as "a range of mental attitudes that bordered on psychopathy," including the notion of "surrender as the ultimate dishonor, a belief whose corollary was total contempt for the captive."[14] That contempt the Japanese troops now vented savagely on the American and Filipino captives they herded along the route of the "Bataan Death March," a grisly eighty-mile forced trek to crude prisoner-of-war camps near the base of the Bataan peninsula. Japanese guards, along with the already roughly used colonial Korean troops often employed for guard duty, denied water to parched prisoners, clubbed and bayoneted stragglers and subjected all the captives to countless humiliations and petty but excruciating agonies. Some six hundred Americans and as many as ten thousand Filipinos died along the route of the march. Thousands

13. Robert J. Ferrell, ed., *The Eisenhower Diaries* (New York: Norton, 1981), 54.
14. Meirion Harries and Susie Harries, *Soldiers of the Sun: The Rise and Fall of the Imperial Japanese Army* (New York: Random House, 1991), 481.

more perished in the filthy camps. This harrowing episode presaged the pitiless inhumanity that came to possess both sides in the ensuing three and a half years of war in the Pacific.

WITH WAINWRIGHT'S SURRENDER in the Philippines in May, Japan had triumphantly concluded the first phase of the Southern Operation, which envisioned the occupation of territories from Burma through the Dutch East Indies and the subsequent exploitation of their critical natural resources. The second phase called for securing a defensive perimeter, strung like a ribbon from island to atoll across thousands of miles of ocean, against the all but inevitable American counterblow.

Lying vast and menacing on the southernmost rim of that defensive perimeter was Australia. Though the Australians lacked the manpower and material resources effectively to challenge the Japanese, and most of Australia's small but tough fighting forces were in any case at that moment helping to defend the British empire on the sands of North Africa, Australia could serve as a staging area for the expected American counterattack. By establishing bases off Australia's northern coast, Japan could pinch off the supply lines from America, isolating and effectively neutralizing the island continent. Accordingly, Vice-Admiral Shigeyoshi Inoue's South Seas Force had seized Rabaul, on New Britain, in January 1942. He proceeded to transform its magnificent caldera-formed harbor into a major naval and air base, designed to anchor the southern end of Japan's defensive perimeter. Almost immediately, however, Japanese military planners determined to use Rabaul to support the further advance of the ribbon defense into the South Pacific, to Papua, the Solomon Islands, Fiji, New Caledonia, and Samoa—a giddily ambitious extension of the original plan that betrayed the symptoms of overreach and imprudence induced by what came to be called "victory disease."

From Rabaul, Inoue in early May dispatched two invasion forces. One was bound for Port Moresby, facing Australia on the south coast of Papua, on whose northern coast the Japanese had already established beachheads at the villages of Lae and Salamaua. He sent the other force to Tulagi, at the southern end of the Solomon Island chain. Disaster awaited the Port Moresby force, as American intelligence had decrypted the principal Japanese naval code, JN-25, thus knew Inoue's destination, and rushed a task force to intercept the invaders. At the Battle of the Coral Sea, a complex action stretching across hundreds of sea miles and five days, from May 3 to 8, 1942, the two sides made naval history, as all the fighting was conducted by carrier-based aircraft. Separated by

175 miles of ocean, the warships neither directly fired upon nor even actually sighted one another. Indicative of the perils and confusion that attended the still unfamiliar tactics of aerial warfare at sea, six Japanese planes tried to land on the U.S. carrier *Yorktown*, mistaking her for one of their own. Japanese pilots also reported sinking two American carriers, *Yorktown* as well as *Saratoga*, but they were less than half right. What they took to be *Saratoga* was in fact *Lexington*, though she had been so badly hit that she was scuttled on May 8. *Yorktown*, nearly mortally damaged, survived to fight another day.[15]

When the Japanese withdrew on May 8, they took the Port Moresby landing forces with them back to Rabaul, never to return. The struggle for Port Moresby would now be waged not on the landing beaches but on the green-draped ridges of the towering Owen Stanley Range, where Australian troops doggedly held out against the Japanese advance from Lae and Salamaua along the steep, fetid, root-choked Kokoda Trail, until relieved by a reborn Douglas MacArthur some six months later. In this sense, Coral Sea represented an allied victory. But it was dearly bought with the loss of *Lexington* and, as events were to prove, with the success of the unopposed Japanese landing on Tulagi, just a few miles across Savo Sound from the jungle-shrouded island of Guadalcanal.

On the flooding tide of Japanese success in early 1942, Coral Sea was at worst a minor back-eddy, a transient nuisance without apparent strategic moment. Its chaotic inconsequentiality underscored the pitiful weakness of the U.S. position in the Pacific, constricted both by the "Germany first" logic of ABC-1 and by the crippling blow received at Pearl Harbor. With its carrier fleet intact, Japan still held all the high cards and all the power of initiative. The Americans seemed reduced to nothing but reactive spoiling tactics like Coral Sea and to harassing but ineffectual air raids, such as had been conducted against some Japanese-held Central Pacific islands in February. But on April 18 one such raid, on the face of it a hare-brained grandstand stunt, set in motion a chain of events with momentous implications.

THE STRING of relatively costless Japanese victories in the first four months of the war provoked a heated debate among Japanese military planners about what their next step should be. The success and

---

15. Ship misidentification and false claims of sinkings were common on both sides, particularly by pilots who mistook the huge waterspouts thrown up by their near-miss bombs for explosions onboard their targets.

momentum of the Southern Operation seemed to dictate one answer: consolidation and buildup of the bases tenuously established in New Guinea and the Solomons, followed by further advances into New Caledonia, Fiji, and Samoa, perhaps eventually into Australia itself. But Yamamoto put the full weight of his authority behind a contrary plan. Finish the job begun at Pearl Harbor, he urged, by seizing Midway Island, some eleven hundred miles west of Hawaii. Politically, Midway in Japanese hands would menace Hawaii with the threat of invasion, providing a potent bargaining chip with which to force the Americans to a negotiated settlement. Militarily, a Japanese presence on Midway would lure forth the remaining elements of the U.S. Pacific Fleet for the "decisive battle." Toward the waging of that battle all of Yamamoto's career and all the training and preparation of the entire Imperial Japanese Navy had long been consecrated.

The doctrine of decisive battle was distilled from decades of Japanese planning about how to wage war against the United States in the Pacific. That planning derived in turn, ironically enough, from the theories of the American naval strategist Alfred Thayer Mahan. A U.S. naval officer and president of Newport War College (later the Naval War College), Mahan argued in his influential work of 1890, *The Influence of Sea Power upon History*, that command of the sea was the key to success in war and that the way to secure the sea was to engage the enemy's main force in overwhelming strength and destroy it. As Japanese planners adopted this thinking for possible war against the United States, they envisioned the swift capture of the Philippines and Guam, thus forcing the U.S. fleet to battle. As the American navy transited the broad Pacific, Japanese submarines would harass it in the eastern Pacific, and land-based aircraft would strike as it passed through the Marshall and Gilbert islands. When the weakened U.S. fleet approached the Marianas or the Carolines, or perhaps the Philippines, it would confront a fresh, overpowering Japanese naval force and be decisively defeated.

To this basic doctrine the Japanese had by 1941 added some formidable refinements. Like the army, the Imperial Navy was highly trained for night battle, relying on superior optics, special communications systems, distinctive ship markings, and endless drills to turn the cloak of darkness to cunning advantage. In addition, its submarines and surface ships alike were armed with the devastating "Long Lance" torpedo, capable of speeds up to forty-nine knots and with a range of up to twenty-four miles. Nothing comparable existed in the American arsenal. Nor could the Americans in 1942 match the investment the Japanese had made in naval air power. With six large carriers, Japan boasted the largest naval air force in the world. It embarked some five hundred high-performance aircraft flown by magnificently trained pilots and operated as a single, awesomely concentrated strike force in First Air Fleet.

Most important, Yamamoto had argued in 1941 that rather than lie in waiting for the American fleet in the western Pacific, the Japanese navy should employ First Air Fleet to go after it directly in midocean, at its base in Pearl Harbor. That task Japan had only partly accomplished on December 7, Yamamoto insisted. Now was the time to hit the Americans again at a place they would be compelled to defend with their full strength — Midway — and destroy the U.S. Pacific Fleet once and for all. With the Pacific cleansed of American ships, Japan would have an unchallenged defensive perimeter, stretching from the North Pacific through midocean to the South Pacific. The Southern Operation would be impregnably secure. Within its perimeter, Japan would hold Guam and the Philippines as hostages, perhaps Hawaii and Australia as well. Safe behind this barrier, Japan could easily sustain a strategically defensive posture, and sue for a negotiated peace on terms it dictated. These were heady notions. In May 1942 they intoxicated even such a calculating pragmatist as Yamamoto. The faint prospect of victory that had earlier swum mistily at the outermost rim of his imagination, writes John Keegan, now "seemed to lie only one battle away."[16]

American strategic doctrine for war against Japan was virtually the mirror image of this Japanese thinking. Code-named the Orange Plan, it had first been formulated early in the century and also reflected the influence of Mahan. The Orange Plan assumed early Japanese capture of the Philippines and made relief of the Philippines the main American objective. The American garrison there was supposed to hold out for three or four months while the U.S. fleet crossed the Pacific, engaged the main body of the Japanese fleet, destroyed it, and thereby ended the war. Always unrealistic, the plan was revised in 1934 to provide for the capture of the Marshall and Caroline islands as staging areas for the main engagement with the Japanese fleet — a tacit admission that the war would last years, not months, and an admission as well of the cynicism that had always underlain expectations about the sacrificial role of the Philippine garrison. Yet whatever its flaws, the Orange Plan constituted the foundation of the United States' Pacific war strategy in 1942 and would in many ways remain so right down to 1945. In the two

16. Keegan, Second World War, 267.

interwar decades, war games were fought at the Naval War College on these assumptions no fewer than 127 times, deeply planting the Orange Plan premises into the American strategic mind.

In early 1942, however, the United States could not possibly muster a naval force that would even begin to make Orange operational. The only event that had conformed to the plan's predictions was the loss of the Philippines, and it would take not three months but more than three years to retrieve them. As partial and weak substitute for the great fleet action envisioned by Orange, small strike forces engaged in hit-and-run raids on scattered Japanese island outposts.

By far the most daring and consequential of these raids struck not against outlying military stations in the far Pacific but against the Japanese home islands themselves. Probing carefully westward past Midway Island to within 650 miles of Tokyo, USS *Hornet* on April 18 launched sixteen cumbersome B-25 bombers never designed to be flown from a carrier deck. Wobbling up over the violently churning sea, the planes sidled into formation behind their leader, Lieutenant Colonel James H. Doolittle, bombed Tokyo and a handful of other Japanese cities, then, at the extreme limit of their flying range, crash-landed in China. Japanese occupation troops captured some of the airmen. One died in prison and three were executed after facing charges at a show trial that they had bombed civilian buildings and machine-gunned a school. Not incidentally, these events further fed the appetites of both combatants for a war of vengeance.

The Doolittle raid did little material damage. The Japanese government made no official acknowledgment of the attack, even to its own citizens, to whom the scattered and mostly harmless explosions of April 18 remained somewhat mysterious. But Doolittle's B-25s packed a momentous psychological wallop. They vividly demonstrated to Japanese military leaders the vulnerability of their home islands through the Midway slot in Japan's defensive perimeter. To all of Yamamoto's already weighty arguments about the attractions of an attack on Midway, the necessity of sealing that slot was now added. Debate ceased in the Japanese high command about the relative priority of the South or Central Pacific. Both operations would now go forward, straining to the utmost the already tautly stretched resources of the Imperial Navy.

Summoning Nagumo, hero of Pearl Harbor, Yamamoto began to fit First Air Fleet for an offensive operation against Midway Island. Nagumo's orders this time were to land an occupation force on Midway and begin its outfitting as a forward base that would lure the Americans to the decisive battle and might serve in time as a launching ground for the invasion of Hawaii. It was Yamamoto's most ambitious plan ever, overshadowing even the audacity of the December 7 attack, and it demonstrated that even this prudent planner was not immune to the incautious recklessness induced by victory disease.

Nagumo, buoyed by the magnitude of his success at Pearl Harbor, by the effortlessness of his marauding cruise around the Indian Ocean, and by what he understood to be the results of the Battle of the Coral Sea, had reason to be confident. He commanded at that moment the most advanced naval force in the world. At Pearl Harbor he had disabled the entire American Pacific battleship force, whereas his own unscathed battleships were still capable of screening his carriers from enemy attack and of supporting an amphibious landing. He believed that his failure to find the American carriers in port on December 7 had been handsomely redressed at Coral Sea, where Inoue's pilots had (erroneously) reported sinking two American carriers. Though two of his own fleet carriers, *Shokaku* and *Zuikaku*, were sufficiently damaged at Coral Sea that they could not take part in the assault on Midway, First Air Fleet retained *Akagi*, *Kaga*, *Hiryu*, and *Soryu*, a still potent quartet of fleet-class carriers that embarked more than 270 warplanes.

Nagumo trusted, too, in the complicated battle plan for the Midway operation. It called for a diversionary raid on Alaska's Aleutian Island chain, to draw off American naval strength. Nagumo's First Air Fleet and the invasion transports would also be backstopped by a powerful battleship group, with Yamamoto himself in command aboard *Yamato*, the largest battleship afloat. Yamamoto's battlewagons would lurk in Nagumo's rear, ready to pounce, preferably at night, on any American force that might challenge Nagumo's vanguard. And of course Yamamoto and Nagumo both took comfort as well from the reflection that they held again, as they had so triumphantly at Pearl Harbor, the hole card of secrecy. Anticipating the decisive battle that would crown his career and seal his nation's dream of empire, amid lavish pomp and ceremony on May 27, the anniversary of the Battle of Tsushima Strait, Nagumo sortied First Air Fleet through Bungo Strait from Japan's Inland Sea—and into the jaws of a trap.

While Yamamoto and Nagumo gathered the nearly two hundred ships of the Midway strike force from over the far horizons that bounded Japan's immense area of conquest, American cryptanalysts feverishly studied their transcripts of the swelling volume of encoded Japanese radio traffic, trying to determine where Japan would strike next. The collective effort to crack the Japanese codes was known as "Magic," and in the upcoming Battle of Midway, Magic would demonstrate its military value as well as the aptness of its name.

Working without sleep amid spine-cracking tension in a windowless basement room at Pearl Harbor, Commander Joseph Rochefort, chief of the Combat Intelligence Office colloquially known as "Station Hypo," pored repeatedly over the maddeningly fragmentary intercepts piled atop his makeshift worktable of planks and sawhorses. Rochefort had adapted to his mole-like existence in his cellar office by working in slippers and a red smoking jacket. In the spit-and-polish navy, he and his equally unkempt colleagues were regarded as eccentric, even downright weird. But their knowledge of the Japanese language, in a navy that only had about forty officers competent in Japanese, was indispensable. Even more indispensable was their mastery of the arcane mysteries of cryptanalysis—the sorcerer's art of deciphering the enemy's most carefully guarded secret communications codes.

Station Hypo's nemesis and obsession was the Japanese naval code, JN-25. It was an immensely complex cipher, and Rochefort and his colleagues could make sense of only 10 to 15 percent of most intercepts. But in the welter of communications traffic that Hypo was monitoring in the spring of 1942, one term recurred with unsettling frequency: "AF," obviously the name of the next major Japanese target. But where or what was "AF"?

Rochefort had a hunch, and he played it shrewdly. Guessing that "AF" designated Midway, in early May he baited a trap by arranging for the small marine and army air force garrison at Midway to radio in clear that their distillation plant had malfunctioned and they were running short of fresh water. The ruse worked. Within two days, Station Hypo received confirmation of a coded Japanese message signaling that "AF" was low on water. Jackpot! Midway it was, then, and Hypo had proved it. The U.S. Navy would be there, ready and waiting.

Admiral Chester Nimitz wasted no time using Rochefort's information, which proved to be the single most valuable intelligence contribution to the entire Pacific war. A descendant of German colonists who had settled the West Texas Pedernales River country early in the nineteenth century, Nimitz was a quiet, scholarly man, fluent in his ancestral German tongue. He sought relaxation by firing his pistol on a target range. He had arrived in Hawaii to take up the position of CINCPAC (commander-in-chief, Pacific Fleet) on Christmas morning 1941. The whaleboat ferrying him from his seaplane to shore had passed the devastated hulks along Battleship Row and threaded through small craft still retrieving surfacing bodies from the sunken ships. As much as any man in the navy, Nimitz burned to retaliate for December 7. But in what his naval academy class book described as his "calm and steady Dutch way," he was determined to do it methodically, with a minimum of risk and more than a fair chance of success. Rochefort's cryptanlysts had now handed this careful, deliberate man a priceless opportunity.[17]

Nimitz reinforced Midway with planes, troops, and antiaircraft batteries. He ordered Task Force 16, comprising the carriers *Enterprise* and *Hornet*, back to Pearl Harbor from the South Pacific. He issued similar orders to Rear Admiral Frank Jack Fletcher's Task Force 17, left now with only the wounded *Yorktown*, which limped into Pearl Harbor on May 27, trailing a long, glistening oil slick as she nosed into a giant drydock. A hipbooted Nimitz was sloshing about at her keel even before the drydock had fully drained, inspecting the damage. Told that repairs would take weeks, a reasonable estimate, Nimitz curtly announced that he must have the ship made seaworthy in three days. The drydock instantly became a human anthill. Hundreds of workers swarmed over the *Yorktown*, amid showers of sparks and clouds of smoke from the acetylene torches cutting away and replacing her damaged hull-plates. As the ship's band incongruously played "California Here I Come," *Yorktown* refloated on May 29. Accompanied by her support ships in Task Force 17, she headed toward the rendezvous point—hopefully dubbed "Point Luck"—with Task Force 16, commanded by Rear Admiral Raymond A. Spruance. Fletcher, aboard *Yorktown*, was in overall command of the task forces.[18]

While the three American carriers stealthily moved to their stations northeast of Midway, Nagumo approached from the northwest. The Japanese commander had good reason to assume that only *Enterprise* and *Hornet* remained afloat in the U.S. Pacific Fleet, and he believed them still to be in the South Pacific, where they had been spotted on May 15. (To abet this misapprehension, Nimitz ordered a cruiser in the South Pacific to transmit on frequencies usually employed by air groups.) As dawn approached on June 4 Nagumo had no inkling that Fletcher and Spruance awaited him over the eastern horizon. All his

---

17. Larrabee, *Commander in Chief*, 355.
18. Walter Lord, *Incredible Victory: The Battle of Midway* (New York: Harper and Row, 1967), 33–39, provides a colorful account of *Yorktown*'s refitting.

attention focused on Midway, from which B-17s and Catalina flying boats had ineffectually bombed his troop transports during the preceding afternoon and night.

At 4:30 A.M. on June 4 Nagumo flew off several squadrons of bombers to attack Midway, preparatory to the troop landings. They dropped their ordnance, high-explosive fragmentation bombs designed for ground targets, according to plan. But the strike force commander asked for a second attack to finish the reduction of Midway's defenses. His message arrived just as Nagumo's carriers were coming under attack from Midway-based aircraft. Not a single American bomb touched his ships, but the very appearance of the American planes was enough to convince Nagumo to accede to the request for a second strike on Midway. On *Akagi* and *Kaga*, Nagumo had been holding some ninety-three aircraft armed with armor-piercing antiship ordnance, against the possibility that he might engage elements of the American fleet. But at 7:15, increasingly confident that he had little to fear from American ships, he gave the order to rearm those aircraft with fragmentation bombs for a second assault against Midway. The refitting operation would take about an hour.

Even as Nagumo's perspiring sailors set about their task, Spruance was ordering full deck-loads of bombers and torpedo planes to lift off from *Enterprise* and *Hornet* to strike the Japanese carriers. Nagumo still remained unaware of the presence of the American fleet. His seamen toiled about the decks of his giant carriers, shuffling bomb racks and hurriedly stacking torpedoes. Then, in the midst of the complicated rearmament operation, the Japanese cruiser *Tone*'s scout plane reported at 7:28 that ten enemy ships were in sight. Their position was within range of carrier-based aircraft, but the initial report did not identify the types of ships. Nagumo nevertheless decided as a precaution to halt the rearmament process. Meanwhile he desperately implored the reconnaissance plane to ascertain the ship types.

Nagumo's skull must have throbbed with the agonies of decision and command. He was still under attack from Midway-based aircraft, his own returning assault planes were beginning to appear overhead, his decks were stacked with bombs of all types, and an unexpected American fleet had now been spotted. Ominously, the *Tone*'s patrol plane next radioed that the enemy flotilla was turning into the wind, the position from which carriers launch their aircraft. Apprehension gripped the surprised Japanese, only to be allayed moments later by a report that the

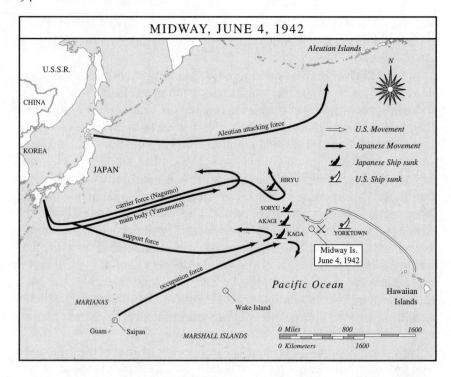

MIDWAY, JUNE 4, 1942

Aleutian Islands

U.S.S.R.

CHINA

Aleutian attacking force

⟹ U.S. Movement

➤ Japanese Movement

Japanese Ship sunk

U.S. Ship sunk

KOREA

JAPAN

carrier force (Nagumo)

main body (Yamamoto)

HIRYU

SORYU

AKAGI

support force

KAGA   YORKTOWN

Midway Is.
June 4, 1942

occupation force

Pacific Ocean

MARIANAS

Wake Island

Hawaiian
Islands

Guam   Saipan

MARSHALL ISLANDS

0 Miles   800   1600

0 Kilometers   1600

enemy flotilla consisted of five cruisers and five destroyers—and then to be revivified yet again by a message minutes afterward that the rising dawn's light had revealed a carrier in the rear of the American formation.

This news was alarming but not catastrophic. Nagumo still believed himself to possess a force far superior in numbers, technology, and skill to anything the Americans could throw against him. Indeed, even while anxiously awaiting word from the *Tone* scout plane, First Air Fleet's ships and fighters had badly mauled the Midway-based attackers, not one of whom had yet managed to score a hit. Mitsuo Fuchida, the Pearl Harbor veteran serving now as *Akagi*'s flight leader, later wrote: "We had by this time undergone every kind of attack by shore-based planes—torpedo, level bombing, dive-bombing—but were still unscathed. Frankly, it is my judgment that the enemy fliers were not displaying a very high level of ability."[19]

Emboldened by such thoughts, the Japanese now saw the American carrier less as a threat and more as an opportunity for inflicting addi-

19. Mitsuo Fuchida and Masatake Okumiya, *Midway: The Battle That Doomed Japan* (Annapolis: U.S. Naval Institute Press, 1955), 163.

tional punishment on the inept Americans. The battle thus far had emphatically confirmed Japanese combat superiority. Apprehension gave way to resolve—and to a fatal relaxation of the sense of urgency. Nagumo, confident he still held the upper hand, calmly waited to recover all his Midway bombers and fighters before magisterially turning to meet the American flotilla, still believing that only a single carrier confronted him. Meanwhile, he reversed his earlier rearmament order and directed his planes to be fitted with antiship weapons once again, adding to the confusion and the piles of explosive ordnance strewn about his flight decks.

Shortly after 9:00 A.M., Nagumo executed his change of course to close with the American fleet, perhaps even to force the "decisive battle" that was the stuff of the Japanese navy's dreams. What followed was decisive, all right, but for Japan and the Imperial Navy it was no dream but a nightmare.

Nagumo's several armament changes and his delay in seizing the initiative contributed powerfully to his undoing, but for the moment his change of course proved advantageous. Many of the American planes launched from *Hornet* and *Enterprise*, as well as those from *Yorktown*, which had put its airmen aloft about 8:30, never found him. Flying at the limits of their operational range, they arrived at the sector where the Japanese were supposed to be, only to look out over empty seas. Many wandering American aircraft fell from the sky for want of fuel. Those who did locate the Japanese fleet tried in vain to penetrate the curtain of antiaircraft fire and the swarming Zeros to reach the Japanese carriers. Shortly after 10:00 A.M. a clutch of Zeros almost completely annihilated a torpedo-bombing squadron from *Yorktown* as it came in low to launch its weapons. By 10:24 A.M. Nagumo appeared to have beaten off the last of the attacks. His proud fleet was still unscratched and was poised to loft a massive counterattack against the Americans. For a brief, breathless moment Japan seemed to have won the Battle of Midway, and perhaps the war.

One American flier scanning the scene from above was on the verge of coming to just that conclusion when suddenly he saw "a beautiful silver waterfall" of Dauntless dive-bombers cascading down on the Japanese carriers.[20] Navigating by guess and by God, Lieutenant Commander Wade McCluskey from *Enterprise* and Lieutenant Commander Maxwell Leslie from *Yorktown* had managed to arrive over the Japanese fleet at the precise moment its combat air patrol of Zeros had been

20. Spector, 174.

drawn down to the deck to repel the *Yorktown's* torpedo bombers, and at the moment of First Air Fleet's maximum vulnerability. With the dread Zeros too low to be effective, the Dauntlesses poured down through the miraculously open sky to unload their bombs on the nakedly exposed Japanese carriers, their flight decks cluttered with confused ranks of recovered and warming-up aircraft, snaking fuel hoses, and stacks of munitions from the various rearmament operations.

In five minutes the dive-bombers, no less miraculously scoring the first American hits of the day, mortally wounded three Japanese carriers. Roaring, gasoline-fed fires raged through all three ships. *Kaga* and *Soryu* sank before sunset. *Akagi* was scuttled during the night. Of First Air Fleet's magnificent flotilla of carriers, only *Hiryu* remained to strike a counterblow against Fletcher's flagship, the battered *Yorktown*, which the sea enveloped at last at dawn on June 7. *Hiryu* herself was overtaken by American fliers in the afternoon of June 4 and sank the next morning. Nagumo had lost four of the six carriers with which he had attacked Pearl Harbor just half a year earlier. Spruance wisely refrained from pursuing the remaining Japanese vessels that were retreating to the west, where he would have collided with Yamamoto's battleships — swift, powerful, nighttrained, and thirsty for vengeance — just as darkness fell.

At Midway the Americans turned the trick of surprise back upon the Japanese and at least partially avenged Pearl Harbor. In time it became apparent that they had done much more than that. They had demonstrated the inefficacy of high-level bombing against moving ships. The vaunted B-17 Flying Fortresses had a flawless record of misses at Midway, against carriers, battleships, cruisers, destroyers, and transports alike. Midway also definitively heralded the new age of naval warfare, in which aircraft carriers, not battleships, were the decisive elements. As at Coral Sea, the opposing surface ships had not come within sight or gun range of one another. The carriers had shown that they could project firepower further over the horizon than any previous device in the history of sea battles and that naval air power, when properly applied, was lethal in attacks on other ships. Midway also confirmed the value of those oddly attired intelligence officers, though the cryptanalysts would never again play so a dramatic a role as they had in this crucial engagement.[21]

21. The priceless asset of Magic was almost lost on June 7, when the *Chicago Tribune* ran a story under the headline NAVY HAD WORD OF JAP PLAN TO STRIKE AT SEA, followed by a remarkably detailed account of Japanese naval dispositions. The author was correspondent Stanley Johnston, to whom a naval officer had indiscreetly shown a copy of a dispatch from Nimitz revealing this information. The navy urged that Johnston be prosecuted for espionage, but the case was eventually dropped.

When the chaos of combat had subsided, the essential truth of Midway stood revealed: in just five minutes of incredible, gratuitous favor from the gods of battle, McCluskey's and Leslie's dive-bombers had done nothing less than turn the tide of the Pacific war. Before Midway the Japanese had six large fleet-class carriers afloat in the Pacific, and the Americans three (four with *Saratoga*, which was returning from repairs on the West Coast at the time of the battle at Midway). With the loss of just one American and four Japanese carriers, including their complements of aircraft and many of their superbly trained fliers, Midway precisely inverted the carrier ratio and put the Imperial Japanese Navy at a disadvantage from which it never recovered.

As a bonus, the Japanese landings on Attu and Kiska in the Aleutians, though successful, yielded a virtually intact crash-landed Zero fighter on Akutan Island. Analyzed thoroughly by Grumman Aircraft's aeronautical engineers, it helped inspire the F6F Hellcat, a carrier-based fighter plane specifically designed to outperform the Zero. The Hellcat climbed faster and higher, flew and dove more swiftly, maneuvered more agilely, and carried heavier armament than its Japanese opponent. By 1943 Hellcats poured forth in profusion from American aircraft plants and helped to establish American air supremacy over the Pacific.

The Hellcat fighter was but one example that the stage was now set for Yamamoto's worst nightmare. His hopes for a short war vanished at Midway, to be replaced by the prolonged agony of a battle of production between the behemoth American economy and the much tinier Japanese industrial plant. Other examples proliferated. In the two years following Midway, Japanese shipyards managed to splash only six additional fleet carriers. The United States in the same period added seventeen, as well as ten medium carriers and eighty-six escort carriers. Those kinds of numbers, to be repeated in myriad categories of war materiel, spelled certain doom for Japan, though it was a doom still a long and harrowing distance in the future.[22]

THE BATTLE OF MIDWAY nudged both Japan and the United States into strategic transition, though neither side fully realized it at the

---

Meanwhile, an irate but slow-witted congressman, Elmer J. Holland, denounced the *Tribune* from the floor of the House, declaring in part that "the Navy had secured and broken the secret code of the Japanese Navy." Incredibly, the Japanese apparently failed to get wind of either of these egregious security breaches. A good brief account of these episodes is in Spector, 451–52.

22. Edmund L. Castillo, *Flat-tops: The Story of Aircraft Carriers* (New York: Random House, 1969), 86.

time. Japan was passing onto the defensive after its string of initial victories, fulfilling almost to the day Yamamoto's prophecy about running wild for six months. The United States, for its part, began groping for a place to begin an offensive. The Americans settled finally on the remote, virtually unheard-of southern Pacific island of Guadalcanal, in the Solomon archipelago.

Midway had dramatically turned back the Japanese advance in the Central Pacific, but Japan was still moving forward in the South Pacific. The Battle of the Coral Sea had failed to prevent Japanese landings on Tulagi, in the Solomons. On June 8, just hours after the clash at Midway, the first elements of Japanese construction battalions sailed across Savo Sound from Tulagi, debarked on the Lunga Plain of Guadalcanal Island, and began building an airstrip. Through Magic intercepts and reports from Australian coastwatchers (clandestine observers scattered through the South Pacific atolls with powerful radio sets), Nimitz and his Washington boss, Commander-in-Chief of the U.S. Fleet (COMINCH) Ernest J. King, learned that the Japanese had landed at Guadalcanal. King was determined to evict them.

King, sixty-three years old in 1942, was as gruff a man as Nimitz was a serene one. Hard-drinking and legendarily ill-tempered, he once confessed that he had not actually uttered the self-descriptive epithet "when they get in trouble they send for the sonsabitches" but that he would have if he had thought of it.[23] Yet King's choleric manner masked an incisive strategic intelligence, possessed of qualities that perfectly fitted him for senior command: the ability to anticipate, the capacity for penetrating analysis of his adversary's predicaments, an unerring grasp of the reach and limits of his own forces, and a pit bull's determination to seize the initiative and attack, attack, attack.

King had grown up alone with his father in an Ohio household from which his chronically ailing mother had been removed. He was ever after a loner, a brusque man who fathered seven children but seemed to love only the navy. After graduation from Annapolis near the top of his class in 1901, he had been posted to the Asiatic Squadron and served as a naval observer during the Russian-Japanese War. He had experience in both surface ships and submarines and at the age of forty-eight, in 1927, had qualified as a naval aviator. Roosevelt had appointed King COMINCH in December 1941, and three months later King also assumed Harold Stark's functions as chief of naval operations (CNO).

23. Larrabee, *Commander in Chief*, 153.

Reflecting his single-minded devotion to duty, he took up residence for the duration of the war aboard the yacht *Dauntless*, moored in the Washington Navy Yard, so that he might work at any hour with a secure communication system at hand.

King had long chafed at the restraints imposed on the navy by Plan Dog, Stark's November 1940 memorandum recommending offensive operations in the Atlantic and a defensive posture in the Pacific. To King, Plan Dog and ABC-1 ignominiously consigned the Pacific, the navy's principal arena, to the status of a subordinate theater. Moreover, as a faithful student of Mahan, King gagged on the idea of defensive naval warfare. The "nation that would rule upon the sea," Mahan had preached, "must attack."[24]

Roosevelt found King's headstrong belligerence attractive, though King's implacable insistence on more resources in the Pacific occasionally threatened to play hob with the grand Hitler-first strategy on which the entire American military effort turned. Indeed, even while King pressed for a license to pursue the navy's post-Midway advantage in the Pacific, preparations were grinding ahead in the summer of 1942 for joint British-American landings in North Africa in the autumn, an operation that grand strategy dictated should have priority. Yet King, invoking the offense-minded logic of the venerable Orange Plan, skillfully wrung from his navy-oriented president a concession. The North African campaign would continue to have first claim on all American resources, but Roosevelt's beloved navy, if it could muster the means, would be allowed to undertake its own, smaller offensive in the Pacific.

Just as the Solomons had not figured in Japanese prewar planning, so did they form no part of the traditional Orange Plan's war-gaming. The U.S. Navy even lacked adequate charts of the region. But the news that Japan was constructing an airstrip on Guadalcanal clinched that island's fate as the target of the American initiative. With air power based at Guadalcanal, the Japanese could control the skies over the crucial shipping lanes to Australia and could support a further military advance to the southeast. Yet in American hands, Guadalcanal and its precious airstrip could provide the essential toehold for a step-by-step advance upon Rabaul, the heavily fortified hub of all Japanese operations in the southwestern Pacific.

On these premises, King launched the Solomons campaign on a shoe-

24. Alfred Thayer Mahan, *The Influence of Sea Power upon History* (New York: Hill and Wang, 1957), 68.

string and in a hurry. It was attended by none of the stately planning and meticulously analyzed game-board exercises that had informed the Orange Plan and been the principal occupation of the peacetime navy. From the outset, it was characterized by makeshift and make-do, even at the level of command structure, which was already distorted by the thespian presence of Douglas MacArthur in the Pacific.

MacArthur was, by any measure, a character to be reckoned with. Born in 1880 into a distinguished military family, he followed in his father's footsteps and beyond. After graduating first in his class at West Point, he was posted to the Philippines, where his father commanded the American military forces. He served later as President Theodore Roosevelt's military aide, as superintendent at West Point, and as army chief of staff under Herbert Hoover, whose orders he had exceeded when he had cleared the Bonus Army from Washington's Anacostia Flats. President Manuel Quezon named him field marshal of the Philippine army in 1936. He retired from the U.S. Army in 1937, only to be recalled to active duty in 1941 as war approached. By age and experience he was by that time senior to virtually every American officer in all services. He was also the military personality best known to the American public, a position he had carefully cultivated, even turning his questionable behavior in the Philippines in late 1941 and early 1942 to his advantage. His crushed hat, aviator glasses, aquiline profile, and corncob pipe all designedly contributed to the image of the gentlemanly general, the squire at war, the scholarly soldier, perhaps the soldier as political savior.

By theatrical gesture and brassy rodomontade, MacArthur, writes Ronald Spector, had by this time manufactured a public persona as "a hero of towering stature, a man who had to be employed in some task commensurate with his supposed greatness."[25] To propitiate the vainglorious MacArthur and placate his legions of admirers, Roosevelt named him commander-in-chief, Southwest Pacific Area, chiefly comprising Australia, the Philippines, New Guinea, and Papua. As supreme *Allied* commander for the Southwest Pacific, MacArthur also controlled the Australian forces in the area, to their frequent dismay. The navy's Nimitz was assigned command of the blue vastness called Pacific Ocean Areas, arcing from the Solomons in the tropical southwestern ocean to the Aleutians in the frigid northeast and subdivided into North, Central, and South Pacific sectors. Nimitz in Hawaii retained direct command of the former two and assigned the third, southernmost sector—and the

25. Spector, 144.

Guadalcanal campaign—to Admiral Robert F. Ghormley, stationed at Noumea in New Caledonia.

The stresses inherent in this bizarre command apparatus, divided both by geography and service, and bereft of an overall theater commander to carry the war against Japan, appeared vividly in the planning for the Solomons campaign. MacArthur at first proposed a direct assault on Rabaul, but the navy refused to relinquish to an army general—especially *this* general—the two-carrier task force that MacArthur demanded to support his landing operations. With only four carriers available in the Pacific after Midway (*Wasp* had now joined the Pacific Fleet), the navy was understandably determined to husband them as carefully as possible, and that meant keeping them out of the confined waters of the Solomon Sea, within range of Japanese airfields. Far better, urged the navy, to proceed methodically and sequentially, first securing airfields for American use before undertaking the final strike at Rabaul.

As finally agreed, the American South Pacific offensive, code-named Watchtower, envisioned three phases: first, the capture of Guadalcanal and the southernmost Solomons; second, the expulsion of the Japanese from Papua and an advance up the Solomon chain toward Rabaul; third, amphibious landings from Papua and the northern Solomons onto New Britain, and the final extinction of Rabaul. The first job fell to the navy. The second and third tasks were to be MacArthur's responsibilities. Like so many war plans, this one bore only a tenuous relation to the eventual reality.

The Japanese had already dislodged, captured, or scattered into the moldy jungle the five hundred or so Europeans who ran the Solomon Islands' few shabby coconut plantations, hacked laboriously by native workers out of the vine-choked tropical rain forest. The Solomons were annually drenched by some of the planet's heaviest rainfalls. The fetid atmosphere buzzed with insects. The damp jungle floor slithered with rodents and reptiles. Above it soared giant hardwood trees with forty-foot-diameter trunks arising from splayed, fin-like bases 150 feet into the virtually opaque canopy. The nearly one hundred thousand Melanesians who had inhabited the islands since time immemorial had already had a taste of Western ways when in 1893 they came under the rule of the British Solomon Islands Protectorate with its rustic and sleepy colonial capital at Tulagi. Now their verdant islands and blue lagoons were about to be convulsed by a spectacle so violently improbable, so murderously fantastic, that their horror and wonder could only be guessed by imagining the citizens of Los Angeles awaking one morning to find flotillas of Eskimos and Mayans, somehow armed with weapons destructive beyond reckoning, descending massively upon the coast of California, there to wage colossal battle.

The improvised character of the Solomons campaign blighted it from the outset, when elements of the First Marine Division, commanded by Major General Archer Vandegrift, steamed into Wellington, New Zealand, in mid-June 1942. Vandegrift had been sent to the South Pacific in what the navy considered an "administrative" move, a preemptive forward positioning of just a part of his division, to await further eventualities. Mostly young recruits who had enlisted in the post–Pearl Harbor rush, Vandegrift's marines were understrength, undertrained, and ill equipped (with WWI-vintage bolt-action rifles). When Vandegrift had sailed from Norfolk in late May, he had no expectation of taking his eager but grass-green troops into combat before 1943. Accordingly, their support ships arrived at Wellington without being "combat loaded"—that is, without their cargo arranged for expeditious unloading in the order necessary to support an amphibious landing. Consequently, when they received their combat orders in New Zealand in late June, and the local longshore unions refused to bend their rules to accelerate the work, the marines' first assignment was to serve as stevedores on the Wellington docks, reloading their own ships. To speed up the task, they downsized everything. They reduced supply stocks from the regulation ninety days to sixty and squeezed personal belongings to a minimum. They cut ammunition to a ten-day reserve.

Escorted by three carrier groups under the command of Frank Jack Fletcher, the transports bearing this skeletally equipped, untested force glided into Savo Sound before dawn on August 7. Under covering fire from naval guns, the marines poured onto the beaches at first light. Despite indescribable snarls and bottlenecks in unloading their supplies, the Guadalcanal landing parties, facing light opposition from construction troops, quickly established their beachhead and seized the nearly completed Japanese airstrip—soon christened Henderson Field in honor of a marine flier killed at Midway. Across Savo Sound on Tulagi, however, where the main Japanese force was well dug in, the marines received their first taste of the Japanese army's tenacious defensive tactics. To the astonishment of the Americans, Japanese defenders in caves and dugouts refused to surrender, even when they witnessed their shrieking comrades being incinerated by gasoline drums lowered into cave mouths on ropes and ignited. Of Tulagi's 350 Japanese defenders, only 3 survived. On the nearby islets of Gavutu and Tanambogo, another five hundred Japanese perished, while only twenty surrendered. One hundred fifteen Americans died during this landing phase, in a curdling preview of the loss ratios of nearly ten to one, Japanese to American, that would characterize the entire Pacific war.

Alerted by the garrison at Tulagi, Vice-Admiral Gunichi Mikawa sortied from Rabaul with a group of five heavy and two light cruisers, plus one destroyer. He intended to race down the "Slot" of the Solomon chain, attack the American transports in Savo Sound, and thereby break up the landings. Given the presence of the American carriers, Mikawa's plan to attack with only a handful of surface ships displayed audacity that verged on bravery. It also benefited, as events soon proved, from American ineptitude that verged on cowardice.

Admiral Fletcher, in command of the carrier escort force comprising *Enterprise*, *Wasp*, and *Saratoga*, had declared during the planning for the Guadalcanal operation that he would hold his carriers on station to cover the landings for only three days. Vandegrift countered that it would take five days to put all his marines ashore and complete the unloading of their already precariously reduced supplies. Fletcher remained adamant. Three days it would be and no more; on August 9 he would withdraw. This was bad news for Vandegrift, but it got worse. On the afternoon of August 8, while the offloading of the transports was proceeding with only slightly diminished confusion, Fletcher received word of Japanese torpedo planes in the area. He peremptorily announced that he was leaving immediately, a day earlier than promised and three days sooner than Vandegrift had wanted. At 6:30 that same evening Fletcher's three carriers commenced their withdrawal to the southeast and out of harm's way.

Fletcher was understandably skittish. *Lexington* had been lost under his command at the Battle of the Coral Sea three months earlier to the day, and *Yorktown* had been virtually blown out from under him at Midway just two months before. The three carriers that he now held off the Solomons represented fully 75 percent of the Pacific carrier fleet. To risk losing them would be to risk reversing the gains of Midway, not to mention clinching Fletcher's reputation as the man who could not keep his capital ships afloat. But whatever allowance he might be granted, the fact remains that Fletcher displayed highly questionable judgment and a conspicuous want of courage. Believing the preservation of the carriers to be more important than protecting the landings, he withdrew the marines' air cover and left Rear Admiral Richard Kelly Turner with a few surface ships to guard the vulnerable beachhead.

Turner considered Fletcher's withdrawal tantamount to desertion. It compelled him to make a tough decision of his own. Late on the muggy night of August 8, Turner called a conference on his flagship to discuss whether Fletcher's departure dictated withdrawing the transports that same night, now that their air cover was gone. Rear Admiral Victor Crutchley, a British officer in the Australian service who commanded the force screening the northern entrances to Savo Sound, pulled his heavy cruiser *Australia* out of the picket line of patrolling ships and steamed twenty miles south to rendezvous with Turner. Crutchley left his American colleague Captain Howard D. Bode, aboard the heavy cruiser *Chicago*, in command of the screening force. Its ships continued their leisurely, box-shaped patrols in the two channels flanking the dimly silhouetted cone of Savo Island. Downsound, off Tulagi and Lunga Point, the American transports undulated at anchor, their holds still crammed with supplies for the marines ashore.

Mikawa, meanwhile, was just miles away, plunging furiously southward across the glassy sea toward Savo Island. The moonless, overcast sky provided ideal cover for the night-fighting at which his sailors ex-

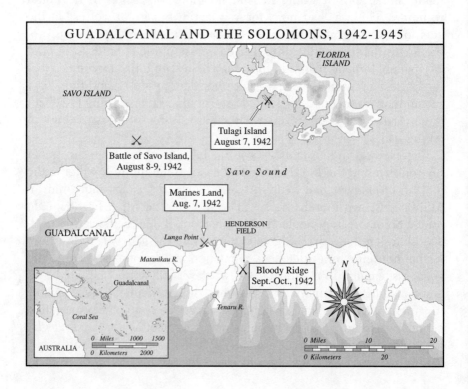

GUADALCANAL AND THE SOLOMONS, 1942-1945

celled. At almost the precise moment that Crutchley stepped aboard Turner's flagship, Mikawa catapulted four float planes for reconnaissance and flare illumination once the battle was joined. Minutes later he changed course and cut speed slightly to dampen wakes that might alert the outermost American picket ship, the destroyer *Blue*, spotted by his sharp-eyed lookouts as it progressed obliviously across the very path of his oncoming ships.

Leaving *Blue* unaware in his rear, Mikawa resumed attack speed, rounded Savo Island, and lunged toward the first group of Allied cruisers, steaming serenely in the west channel. Signaling his ships with hooded blinkers visible only in his own column, he commenced the action at 1:30 by loosing a volley of Long Lance torpedoes at the still unsuspecting Allied vessels. As the torpedoes hissed toward their targets, Mikawa unleashed his gunners. In a devastating demonstration of their prowess, his sailors firing from five separate ships sent twenty-four shells smashing into the Australian cruiser *Canberra* in the space of one minute. Still untouched, Mikawa's force split in two and curled to port, toward the second group of cruisers in the eastern channel.

The sea south of Savo suddenly lit up with aerial flares, searchlights, muzzle blasts, and flames from the doomed *Canberra*. Aboard the Allied ships all was bedlam. A torpedo slamming into *Chicago* awakened Captain Bode, the officer in tactical command in Crutchley's absence. Bode was so rattled by the lightning assault that he neglected to inform his ships in the far channel that they were about to come under attack. He then limped off in futile pursuit of Mikawa's lone destroyer, leaving the much more destructive Japanese cruiser force unscathed as it executed its high-speed turn and bore down on the remaining American vessels.

Harassed but undeflected by groping gunfire from American destroyers, at 1:50 Mikawa's cruisers locked their searchlights on the heavy cruisers *Quincy*, *Astoria*, and *Vincennes* and began firing. Though the battle had now raged for nearly a quarter of an hour, all three American captains were asleep and caught utterly by surprise. Japanese torpedo and gun crews expertly poured salvo after salvo down their light-beams into the U.S. ships. *Quincy* was the first to succumb. Shuddering violently from countless hits, she rolled over and sank within minutes, taking nearly four hundred sailors with her to the bottom of what soon became known as Ironbottom Sound. *Astoria* went down minutes later, with a loss of more than three hundred men. *Vincennes* survived the night, only to slip beneath the water shortly after noon the next day.

Scarcely thirty minutes after he had launched his first torpedoes, Mikawa completed his U-shaped swing around Savo Island, slapped a half-dozen shells into an outlying American destroyer, and steamed away up the Slot. He had inflicted what the official naval historian calls the worst defeat ever suffered on the high seas by the U.S. Navy.[26] His own ships received only trifling damage, while he had demolished one Australian and three U.S. cruisers. Against his own casualty list of about two hundred could be counted nearly two thousand American killed and wounded — a singular reversal of the loss ratios incurred during the landings some forty-eight hours earlier. While Mikawa sped jauntily back to Rabaul, huge human rafts of dazed American seamen, awaiting dawn and rescue, bobbed about amidst the flaming wreckage and the predatory sharks south of Savo Island.

Recriminations soon followed. Much criticism fell upon Fletcher, whose withdrawal had precipitated Turner's conference, removing Crutchley from command and his heavy cruiser from the battle line at a crucial moment. Moreover, Fletcher, fleeing south to safety during the night, was out of range to pursue Mikawa's force up the Slot the next day. Fletcher would fight one more battle, but his controversial departure on the evening of August 8 shadowed his reputation, and by the end of the month he was relieved of command. As for Captain Bode, his despondency over his sorry role on that devastating night may well have contributed to his later decision to take his own life.

Yet for all the ruination that Mikawa's tornado had visited upon the U.S. Navy, he had in fact failed to reach his objective: the still-unloaded transports lying off Guadalcanal and Tulagi. Like Nagumo at Pearl Harbor, his own special case of victory disease inclined him to clasp the prize of his effortless triumph without gathering the final fruits of victory by smashing the supply ships and thus breaking the back of the American invasion.

On the mournful dawn of August 9, as rescue ships plowed about Savo Sound gathering bodies and traumatized survivors, Admiral Turner took stock of his situation. He decided to continue unloading the transports for one more day. But at sunset, unwilling to tarry any longer without air cover, he sailed for Ghormley's South Pacific base at Noumea, nearly a thousand miles south of Guadalcanal. He took with him some eighteen hundred marines who had not managed to get ashore and left the six thousand marines on Tulagi and the eleven thousand on Guadalcanal to their own devices. He also took with him nearly half

26. Morison, 167.

their supplies, already scaled back by the haste of the reloading operation at Wellington.

Under these less than auspicious circumstances the siege of Guadalcanal began. It would constitute one of the longest and most complicated American campaigns of the war, including six separate naval battles and three major clashes on the island of Guadalcanal itself. On its outcome came to depend not only the military balance in the Pacific but the war-morale of the American public. It was, as much as any single engagement could be, a decisive battle. Yet in the annals of the Pacific war it was also an odd, untypical engagement in many ways. In a strange inversion of much of what was to follow, the Americans were defending an island and the Japanese were trying to dislodge them. Nor did the Americans enjoy, at least at the beginning, the overwhelming logistical advantages that prevailed through much of the subsequent war. When Turner's convoy slipped over the horizon, the marines on Guadalcanal were left on a two-meals-per-day regimen and had only four days of ammunition reserves. Soon they were plundering the meager stocks of food and equipment left behind by the fleeing Japanese construction crews and ripping up cattle fencing to jury-rig a defensive perimeter around Henderson Field.

The airfield constituted not only their objective but their greatest tactical asset. Within two weeks of the landings, it was ready to receive its first aircraft, a handful of Dauntless dive-bombers and Wildcat fighters. More planes followed, as the Americans slowly built up the "Cactus Air Force," titled after the code name for Guadalcanal.

The Japanese, meanwhile, badly failed to grasp American intentions at Guadalcanal. Even after the humiliation of Midway, they believed the Americans incapable of a major military initiative until 1943. They had not reckoned with King's impatient bellicosity. Nor did they correctly estimate the American strength on the island. Misjudging the implications of the Battle of Savo and the hasty withdrawal of the American transports, the Japanese concluded that a maximum of ten thousand Americans had been landed, probably even fewer, and that they were in any case demoralized, undersupplied, and abandoned—much as the recently vanquished Philippine garrison had been.

On the basis of those faulty estimates, Colonel Kiyoano Ichiki recklessly landed on Guadalcanal with 917 men on the night of August 18–19 and began slogging across the several watercourses that separated him from the American perimeter. In the predawn darkness of August 21 he collided with a much larger than anticipated marine force, equipped with machine guns and a few light tanks, at the mouth of Alligator Creek, which became the scene of appalling slaughter. Waves of Japanese troops mounting foolhardy frontal attacks fell to marine bullets and mortars or were ground to death under the tank treads. At dawn Ichiki committed ritual suicide, while marines shot his remaining troops as they swam away from the blood-reddened lagoon. When some Japanese wounded tried to kill the approaching American medics, the marines systematically massacred all Japanese survivors. Nearly eight hundred Japanese died. One surrendered. The rest disappeared into the jungle or the sea.

At this moment neither the American nor the Japanese high command seemed to have a clear understanding of Guadalcanal's military worth, nor even of the ultimate purpose of the Solomons campaign that was just aborning. The persistent inability of both the Americans and the Japanese to place a precise value on Guadalcanal engendered hesitation and a constant shifting of priorities, at all levels of command of both countries' forces.

On the American side, that pattern had been dimly evident in the haste and niggardliness of Vandegrift's preparations for the landing and darkly foreshadowed in Fletcher's retreat on the night of August 8. Admiral Ghormley, in overall command in the South Pacific Area, shuttered in humid isolation aboard his command ship at Noumea, rarely going ashore or taking recreation of any kind, vacillated between defensive and offensive conceptions of his assignment in the Solomons. Was his mission to protect the sea lanes to Australia, in which case he had merely to deny the use of Guadalcanal and its airfield to the Japanese? Or was he expected to prepare Guadalcanal as a base from which to carry the war northward to Rabaul, a much more demanding task? Ghormley appeared to be incapable of sorting these questions out and slipped ever more deeply into gloom and despondency. And overshadowing the entire operation was the simultaneous and much larger enterprise in North Africa, which severely constrained Admiral King's ability to reinforce Guadalcanal, especially with critical air power.

Analogous ambiguities and conflicting claims plagued the Japanese. The impetuosity of Ichiki's calamitous raid suggested that Guadalcanal at this stage was but a daub on the palette of Japan's strategic drawing board. Japan's main goal in the southeastern Pacific remained the thrust to Port Moresby in Papua. Beyond that, the Imperial Japanese Army was busily consolidating its grip on occupied Malaya, Indochina, the East Indies, and the Philippines. Japan also had a major initiative under way in Burma, not to mention its enormous continuing commitment in China, always the principal focus of all Japanese strategy. As for the Imperial Navy, it still bled from Midway but had by no means given up the doctrine of decisive battle. Yamamoto in particular could not rid himself of the temptation to see the Solomons not as an objective in their own right but simply as the place where that battle might be made to happen at last.

That prospect tantalizingly presented itself in the Battle of the Eastern Solomons on August 24, the war's third great carrier battle. It pitted one light and two Japanese heavy carriers, commanded by the redoubtable Nagumo, against Fletcher's trio of *Enterprise*, *Wasp*, and *Saratoga*. In an ironic reprise of Fletcher's predicament some two weeks earlier, Nagumo, ostensibly providing air cover for a troop convoy transporting the hapless Ichiki's reinforcements, effectively abandoned the transports in order to give battle to the American carrier force. Once again the re-solving climax of the decisive battle eluded him. Nagumo lost his light carrier while damaging *Enterprise* enough to send her back to Pearl Harbor for repairs. His unshielded transports, meanwhile, never did reach their destination.

Slowly, incrementally, tentatively, both sides now began a months-long process of upping their stakes in Guadalcanal. High-speed Japanese destroyer convoys—dubbed the "Tokyo Express" by the marines—nightly ran contingents of troops down the Slot, depositing them ashore at the far ends of Guadalcanal, miles from the tiny marine foothold at Lunga Point. By early September the jungle rustled with some six thou-sand Japanese soldiers. Vandegrift meanwhile shifted units across from Tulagi in anticipation of another Japanese ground offensive, this time in strength. His marines, plagued by heat, bugs, poor diet, jaundice, dermatitis, and gnawing apprehension, tensed for action. Many of them already verged on being unnerved by jungle warfare. Some began to show signs of "going Asiatic"—the marines' term for symptoms of battle psychosis. The Japanese were "full of tricks," one marine told war cor-respondent John Hersey. "They hide up in the trees like wildcats. Some-times when they attack, they scream like a bunch of terrified cattle in a slaughter house. Other times they come so quiet they wouldn't scare a snake. One of their favorite tricks is to fire their machine guns off to one side. That starts you shooting. Then they start their main fire under the noise of your own shooting. Sometimes they use firecrackers as a diversion. Other times they jabber to cover the noise of their men cut-ting through the underbrush with machetes. You've probably heard about their using white surrender flags to suck us into traps. We're onto that one now."[27]

After an exhausting march through diabolically braided jungle, on the night of September 13 a Japanese force crawled up to the base of a low, knobby ridge that bounded the Lunga River drainage to the south of Henderson Field. Atop the ridge, elite marine raider and parachute battalions, commanded by Lieutenant Colonel Merritt Edson, awaited them. Bolstered by the charismatic and fearless Edson, who roamed up and down the firing line murmuring profane encouragement, the marines repelled repeated charges by screaming Japanese soldiers. In the respites between the enemy lunges they rolled grenades down the grassy slope. Daybreak revealed a ghastly mat of some five hundred Japanese corpses carpeting the ridge's shoulder. The marines were shaken and badly blooded but still held what soon became known as "Bloody Ridge" or "Edson's Ridge."

The clash on Bloody Ridge spurred both sides to accelerate their reinforcements. Four thousand more marines arrived on September 18. Four weeks later the 164th Infantry regiment landed, its three thousand former Dakota National Guardsmen looking like old geezers to the nearly adolescent marines. But the soldiers of the 164th toted the army's standard-issue Garrand M-1 semiautomatic rifles, which provided considerably more firepower than the marines' aged weapons. By October some twenty-seven thousand Americans of all services were ashore on Guadalcanal and Tulagi.

The Cactus Air Force, however, grew only haltingly, as the army air force's General Hap Arnold refused to reassign planes from the North African theater. In any case, the American aircraft available at this point in the war suffered from technological deficiencies relative to their opponents that made them of limited value. The B-17s had by now conclusively demonstrated their inability to inflict damage on ships at sea, and the Wildcat fighters, which furnished the principal air defense for Guadalcanal, could only barely claw up to combat altitude if radar and coastwatchers gave them maximum warning time — thirty-five or forty minutes — of approaching Japanese bombers. In any event, the Zeros that accompanied the bombers still easily outclassed the Wildcats in speed and maneuverability and routinely shooed the marine fliers from the sky.

27. John Hersey, *Into the Valley: A Skirmish of the Marines* (New York: Knopf, 1943), 20.

The Americans undertook a kind of psychological reinforcement as well, aimed at shoring up the home front as much as bracing the fighting line on Guadalcanal. They brought war correspondents like Hanson Baldwin, Richard Tregaskis, and John Hersey to the island. Baldwin's series of articles in the *New York Times* in late September was among the first frontline reports from any theater to reach the home-front public. Americans now began to invest Guadalcanal, the first land action in which the United States had a fighting chance against Japan, with a psychological value no less weighty than its purely military importance. "The shadows of a great conflict lie heavily over the Solomons," the *New York Herald Tribune* editorialized on October 16, reflecting the growing American sense that in this remote and exotic corner of the South Pacific men and machines were gathering for a historic showdown.[28] A fresh sense of resolve gripped President Roosevelt too. He instructed the Joint Chiefs on October 24 to "make sure that every possible weapon gets into that area to hold Guadalcanal"—though not at the expense of the about-to-be-launched North African invasion.[29]

All this was too much for Admiral Ghormley. Stewing at Noumea in the face of these mounting expectations, he wrote to Nimitz on October 15: "My forces [are] totally inadequate to meet [the] situation." Three days later, Nimitz replaced Ghormley with Vice-Admiral William F. "Bull" Halsey, a commander of proved aggressivity who did not suffer from the defeatism that had ground down the bewildered and cloistered Ghormley.

While building up their own ground forces on Guadalcanal, the Japanese continued daily bombing raids on Henderson Field, though the distance from their airbase at Rabaul confined them to brief and predictable appearances at midday. More threatening to the Americans, and deeply injurious to morale, were the almost nightly naval bombardments that accompanied runs of the Tokyo Express. One of the most intensive bombardments occurred on October 13, the night of the 164th Infantry's arrival. It covered the landings of an unusually large Japanese troop contingent, preparatory to a major Japanese offensive.

Three days later some twenty thousand Japanese troops started hacking into the barely penetrable jungle curtain to mount the Imperial Army's

---

28. Richard B. Frank, *Guadalcanal: The Definitive Account of the Landmark Battle* (New York: Random House, 1990), 332. My account draws liberally from Frank's thorough—indeed, "definitive"—study.

29. Frank, *Guadalcanal*, 405.

third assault on Henderson Field. Each soldier shouldered twelve days of rations, a full ammunition pack, and one artillery shell for the thirty-mile trek across the trackless island to the American perimeter at Lunga. Terrain, temperature, vegetation, insects, and fear punished them every step of the way. Vandegrift had in fact counted upon his jungle "ally" in arranging his defensive dispositions. The shrewdness of his calculation was proved when the first Japanese column arrived exhausted and tattered on the western American perimeter along the Matanikau River and was virtually annihilated by devastating marine artillery fire. A second Japanese column was scheduled to attack simultaneously from the south, but its tortuous progression through the jungle brought it to the base of Bloody Ridge in an equally sorry state and a full day late, permitting the marines to shift their forces from the Matanikau. Once again Bloody Ridge confirmed the fitness of its name. Japanese troops, many of them ignorant rural recruits cowed by the Imperial Army's brutal military indoctrination, were on this as on so many occasions badly and profligately used by their commanders. They spent themselves in waves of useless assaults, their screams of *"banzai"* striking terror into the Seventh Marines and 164th Infantrymen on the ridge top, but falling nonetheless under the disciplined fire of the Americans. Perhaps thirty-five hundred Imperial soldiers died in this second battle of Bloody Ridge, which also proved to be Japan's last ground assault against Henderson Field.

Vandegrift spent the next two months enlarging his defense perimeter and stalking the scattered Japanese detachments in the jungle, until his battered First Marine Division was relieved in early December, when he turned over his command to the Army's Lieutenant General Alexander M. Patch. In four months of grueling siege warfare and frenzied jungle fighting, he had lost 650 dead and another thirteen hundred wounded. The jungle, sometimes his military ally but always his medical nemesis, no less than it was for the Japanese, left fully half of his command carrying away from Guadalcanal one or another tropical disease, chiefly malaria.

The battle for Guadalcanal was now turning into a grisly demonstration of the awful logic of American numbers that Yamamoto had feared. With sure and relentless momentum, the Americans steadily built up their ground and air forces on Guadalcanal. They counted some sixty thousand personnel ashore by year's end. But the Japanese succeeded in landing only a few thousand more troops after the big convoy and the disastrous offensive of October, and they were soon outnumbered nearly two to one. Growing American naval power in the region also hampered efforts to supply the Japanese troops already ashore. The Imperial Navy was eventually reduced to shoving drumloads of rice or barley overboard from high-speed destroyers, to be pulled to the beaches by shore parties. Strafing American pilots and PT-boat gunners soon grew adept at sinking the drums before they made it to shore.

Before long frontline Japanese troops were on one-sixth rations. Rear-echelon personnel made do with one-tenth. Of six thousand men in one Japanese division, only 250 were judged fit for combat by mid-December. One Japanese officer calculated a grim formula for predicting the mortality of his troops:

> Those who can stand — 30 days
> Those who can sit up — 3 weeks
> Those who cannot sit up — 1 week
> Those who urinate lying down — 3 days
> Those who have stopped speaking — 2 days
> Those who have stopped blinking — tomorrow

Shortly thereafter a report reached Yamamoto with a description of soldiers so ravaged by undernourishment and dysentery that their hair and nails had stopped growing. Their buttocks had wasted away to an extent that completely exposed their anuses.[30]

Still, the hope lingered in Yamamoto's mind that Guadalcanal might yet prove the bait to draw the Americans to the decisive battle. He moved his command headquarters to Truk to be in closer touch with the southern Pacific campaigns. Confident that one last blow would dislodge the Americans and provide a chance to exterminate the remainder of the U.S. Pacific Fleet, Yamamoto decided to mount another major offensive in early November, with a large convoy of reinforcements and supplies for Guadalcanal to be covered by a powerful battleship and cruiser escort.

Magic, however, again tipped the scales in favor of the Americans. Knowing the Japanese plans in advance, Halsey countered with a strong battleship force of his own and issued emergency orders for *Enterprise* to dash from the Pearl Harbor repair yards to the Solomons. The ensuing battle raged over four days and nights from November 12 to November 15. Despite their forewarning, American ships fared badly in the first encounters, losing among other ships the ill-starred cruiser *Juneau*. Its spectacular explosion claimed 683 lives, including five Sullivan

---

30. Frank, *Guadalcanal*, 527, 588.

brothers whose family tragedy formed one of the war's most poignant tales. As the battle raged on around them, *Juneau*'s unrescued seamen drifted for days under the tropical sun without food or water. About them circled an ever more aggressive pod of sharks that chewed off terrified survivors clinging to the nets on the sides of the life rafts.

Despite these agonies, at battle's end the Americans had won a conclusive victory. With *Enterprise*'s timely arrival they destroyed two Japanese battleships, along with sundry other vessels, and almost completely interdicted the Guadalcanal-bound transports, the last of which desperately ran themselves aground on the island's beaches. American pilots and antiaircraft gunners also took a fearsome toll of Japanese fliers, further eroding Japan's already tenuous air superiority.

This so-called Naval Battle of Guadalcanal clinched a decision that had been slowly gathering momentum in Japanese headquarters. In one of the few retreats executed by the Imperial Army in all the war, it evacuated its forces from Guadalcanal in the first weeks of 1943. Probing into the Japanese encampment in early February, Patch's troops found it deserted. On February 9 Patch radioed to Halsey: "Tokyo Express no longer has terminus on Guadalcanal."[31]

If King had launched the Guadalcanal campaign on a shoestring and somehow bootstrapped it to success, the Japanese operation from the outset had dangled from a slender thread that eventually frayed to the breaking point. The remorseless tipping of the military balance in favor of the Americans at Guadalcanal illustrated in microcosm the central logic of the Pacific war. Given time and a fair opportunity, the weight of growing American manpower and munitions inevitably crushed the steadily wasting Japanese reserves of men and materiel. To be sure, the Japanese had abetted their own defeat at Guadalcanal by violating basic military axioms and throwing themselves piecemeal at their foe, when a single, massed assault, delivered at the right time and place, might conceivably have brought them victory. Contempt for their enemy's fighting prowess, ignorance of American intentions, and confusion about their own conception of Guadalcanal's importance all contributed to the fragmentation and eventual inefficacy of the Japanese campaign. But more than anything else Guadalcanal demonstrated vividly the ravaging implications of victory disease. For Japan, Guadalcanal was an island too far, a prize beyond reasonable reach given the competing claims of so many simultaneous operations. The repeated Japanese deflection of

31. Morison, 214.

resources to Guadalcanal from the parallel campaign in Papua proved the point — but too late to salvage Guadalcanal from the Americans.

For their part, the victors at Guadalcanal had learned much about the fiendish arts of jungle fighting and about the three-dimensional geometry of naval aerial warfare. Yet because the Americans had fought a tactically defensive battle on Guadalcanal, they still had much to learn about amphibious fighting as they took to the offensive in the war of a hundred islands that lay ahead.

WITH THE MILITARY EDUCATION of the Americans came, perhaps inevitably, moral coarsening as well. Atrocities on both sides would grow in wretchedness as the war progressed, but for the Americans at least, Guadalcanal provided an early lesson in the wanton barbarism of warfare between two peoples separated so distantly by culture, religion, and race. "I wish we were fighting against Germans," said one marine on Guadalcanal. "They are human beings, like us. . . . But the Japanese are like animals."[32] Of the inhumanity of the Japanese-American war, however, the American public as yet knew little. The news that reached home from Guadalcanal presented a different image entirely. "[Y]ou felt sorry for the boys," correspondent John Hersey wrote. "The uniforms, the bravado, the air of wearing a knife in the teeth — these were just camouflage. The truth was all over their faces. These were just American boys. They did not want that valley or any part of its jungle. They were ex–grocery clerks, ex–highway laborers, ex–bank clerks, ex–schoolboys, boys with a clean record and maybe a little extra restlessness, but not killers. . . . [T]hey had joined the Marines to see the world, or to get away from a guilt, or most likely to escape the draft, not knowingly to kill or be killed." There was truth in that picture, but the makings of a myth as well.[33]

WITH GUADALCANAL SECURE , it was the Americans' turn to attempt a two-pronged offensive, in the Solomons as well as on Papua. MacArthur had assembled sufficient troops and aircraft by October 1942 to come to the aid of the Australians defending Papua. He made few friends among the Australians, however, when he described their more than six hundred dead along the Kokoda Trail as "extremely light casualties" indicating "no serious effort."[34] MacArthur was no less abusive

32. Hersey, *Into the Valley*, 56.
33. Hersey, *Into the Valley*, 43.
34. Larrabee, *Commander in Chief*, 324.

to his own subordinates. When his troops stalled in front of the heavily fortified Japanese bastion of Buna on Papua's north coast, MacArthur dispatched two senior officers, Robert Eichelberger and Clovis Byers, to assume command in front of Buna. He admonished Eichelberger: "If you don't take Buna I want to hear that you and Byers are buried there."[35] By such hectoring and reckless wastage of his troops, hurled against strong Japanese defenses without adequate air, artillery, or armored support, MacArthur's combined American and Australian force took Buna and the nearby Japanese stronghold of Gona by December 1942, ending the threat to Australia.

Both sides now briefly marked time, preparing for the next round. The Japanese slipped troops surreptitiously to the northwest along the Papuan "tail" of the New Guinea "bird" to strengthen their positions at Lae and Salamaua. They also rushed ahead with construction of new airfields along the Solomon chain, at Buin and other sites on Bougainville and in the New Georgia group at Munda. There Japanese engineers cunningly but unavailingly tried to cloak their work under the jungle canopy, held in place by wires as the giant trees were felled beneath it. The Americans meanwhile reaffirmed the basic goals of Operation Watchtower. They agreed that MacArthur should continue to advance up the Papuan coast, take Lae and Salamaua, and then make the jump across to New Britain. Halsey in the meantime would climb up the Solomon ladder to Bougainville. They would then proceed to close the pincers on Rabaul in a final, coordinated attack. They rechristened their joint undertaking "Operation Cartwheel."

MacArthur forged ahead along the northern New Guinea shore, aided by innovative air tactics devised by General George Kenney, his new air chief. Kenney once and for all put an end to futile high-level bombing of ships by B-17s. Instead he trained his pilots in low-level sweeps by medium bombers carrying fragmentation bombs. These methods proved spectacularly successful in the first week of March, 1943 in a hundred-plane assault in the Bismarck Sea against a Japanese convoy bound for Lae. After Kenney's bombers sank all the transports and four of the escorting destroyers, strafing aircraft and PT boats machine-gunned the Japanese survivors struggling in the water.[36] Given Kenney's triumphantly established air superiority, Japan thereafter could resupply and

35. Clovis Byers Diary, November 30, 1942, Hoover Institution, Stanford University, Stanford, California.
36. Morison, 273.

reinforce Lae only with the utmost difficulty. Lae fell at last to MacArthur in September.

New American aircraft also made their appearance at this time, early tokens of the American production explosion that was about to engulf all the Allied fighting fronts. Especially notable was the P-38 Lightning, a twin-tailed, twin-engined fighter; it could not outmaneuver the Zero in a dogfight, but its greater speed and higher ceiling enabled it to jump enemy air formations from above.

Witnessing the awesome destruction that Kenney's bombers and the new P-38s were wreaking, Yamamoto scraped together every available Japanese aircraft for a series of massive raids on American airfields — particularly Henderson Field — in April 1943. To encourage his fliers, he rashly decided to visit the forward Japanese airbase near Buin on Bougainville on April 18. It was a fatal decision. Nimitz's cryptographers intercepted a message announcing the legendary admiral's arrival and resolved to get him. An ambush might risk revealing the secret of Magic, but Yamamoto was too tempting a target. As his plane and its escort of Zeros approached their landing field on the morning of the eighteenth, a squadron of P-38s dropped from on high like avenging angels, blasting away with 20mm cannon fire. Yamamoto, the survivor of Tsushima, the reluctant foe of America, the dutiful architect of Pearl Harbor, the disappointed mastermind of Midway, the greatest naval strategist in the Imperial Navy, fell to a warrior's death as the flaming wreckage of his plane slammed into the jungle. Perhaps the gods of war had been kind to Yamamoto after all, as death spared him the agony of watching his nation's inexorable, humiliating defeat.

Yamamoto's passing marked but the briefest cadence in the gathering American onslaught rolling up toward Rabaul. While MacArthur pressed toward Lae, Halsey hammered at Munda, where Japanese resistance was fierce. A month of grueling combat finally pried Munda loose from its Japanese defenders in early August, but the Americans absorbed horrendous losses, especially in the poorly prepared Forty-third Infantry Division, mostly composed of New England National Guardsmen. (It was during this engagement, too, that a Japanese destroyer, racing down Blackett Strait on the night of August 1, sliced through Lieutenant John F. Kennedy's PT 109.) Sobered by the spectacle of his ravaged troops, Halsey calculated that a steady, island-by-island progression toward Rabaul would prove inexcusably costly, and, by extension, would take years — perhaps a decade — to reach Japan itself. Halsey therefore decided to bypass the next fortified island up the Solomon chain,

Kolombangara, and strike his next blow instead against lightly defended Vella Lavella, further up the Solomons ladder. The lifesaving purpose of this "island-hopping" or "leapfrogging" strategy was to avoid Japanese strongholds so far as possible and leave isolated Japanese garrisons to wither on the vine, cut off from communication and supply. This thinking would soon reshape the objectives of Operation Cartwheel and, indeed, deeply color the tactics of the war all over the Pacific.

Vella Lavella fell easily to the Americans and their New Zealand allies in August, and Halsey began to prepare it as a forward base for the assault on the last and largest of the Solomons, Bougainville. At Empress Augusta Bay on November 1, Halsey's invasion force quickly established a beachhead on Bougainville, while his ships beat back a Japanese effort to inflict another Savo-like humiliation on the landing operation. The Bougainville landings also occasioned ferocious air battles that further winnowed the steadily deteriorating pool of first-rate Japanese pilots. The next month MacArthur finally made the leap from New Guinea to Cape Gloucester, on the western tip of New Britain. After fierce fighting, Japanese resistance on Bougainville was overcome in March 1944. From secure airfields at both ends of the American pincers, planes now routinely bombed Rabaul.

Yet the prize fruit of Rabaul, the goal of Watchtower and Cartwheel, now within Halsey's and MacArthur's grasp, was not to be harvested. Just as Kolombangara had been bypassed, so too would Rabaul be left to wither on the vine — punished daily by bombing raids but never invaded. Meanwhile, in early 1944, the submerged dreams of the Orange planners resurfaced and beckoned American attention to the horizonless expanses of the Central Pacific.

17

Unready Ally, Uneasy Alliance

*The British are trying to arrange this matter so that the British and the
Americans hold the leg for Stalin to kill the deer and I think that will
be a dangerous business for us at the end of the war. Stalin won't have
much of an opinion of people who have done that and we will not be
able to share much of the postwar world with him.*
— Secretary of War Henry Stimson, May 17, 1943

America's war against Germany, like its war against Japan, began at sea.
The Battle of the Atlantic, already two years old when the United States
entered the war, was a contest for supremacy on the ocean highway
across which all American supplies and troops must flow to Europe.
Everything depended on keeping that highway open. Dwight D. Eisenhower, newly promoted to brigadier general and freshly installed as chief
of the army's War Plans Division, submitted a penetrating assessment of
the importance of the North Atlantic sea lanes to George Marshall on
February 28, 1942. "Maximum safety of these lines of communication
is a 'must' in our military effort, no matter what else we attempt to do,"
Eisenhower emphasized. Shipping, he presciently added, "will remain
the bottleneck of our effective effort," a statement that echoed repeated
pronouncements by both Churchill and Roosevelt that the struggle with
Hitler would be won or lost at sea.[1]

It looked at first more likely to be lost. When he declared war on the
United States shortly after the Pearl Harbor attack, Hitler untethered the
German submarine service from the restraints against which it had long
chafed. Karl Dönitz could now loose his U-boats as far westward as
America's Atlantic shoreline, cutting the Allied supply lines at their

1. *PDDE* 1:150.

source and avenging the insults of the destroyer-bases deal and the Lend-Lease Act. He determined "to strike a blow at the American coast with a *Paukenschlag*," a word usually translated as "drumbeat" but that also, in German, connotes "thunderbolt."[2] German submariners themselves described the campaign against American coastal shipping as the "Happy Time," or even the "American turkey-shoot." By whatever name, the naval *Blitzkrieg* that Dönitz launched in early 1942 threatened to shut down America's war against Hitler almost before it could get started.

As early as mid-January 1942 Dönitz had dispatched five U-boats, each packing between fourteen and twenty-two torpedoes, to the eastern coastal waters of the United States. Up to a dozen additional boats soon followed, their operational range and ability to remain on battle station enhanced by submarine tankers, or *Milchkuhen* (milkcows), that refueled the U-boats at sea. Within just two weeks Dönitz's undersea raiders sank thirty-five ships in the waters between Newfoundland and Bermuda, a loss of more than two hundred thousand tons. The prize targets were tankers lumbering up from Caribbean and Gulf Coast oil ports to northeastern refineries and storage depots. "By attacking the supply traffic—particularly the oil—in the U.S. zone," Dönitz gloated, "I am striking at the root of the evil, for here the sinking of each ship is not only a loss to the enemy but also deals a blow at the source of his shipbuilding and war production. Without shipping the [English] sally-port cannot be used for an attack on Europe."[3]

Still imagining the war to be far away, and fearing to cramp the tourist trade, seaboard cities like New York, Atlantic City, and Miami refused to enforce blackouts. The backdrop of their bright lights, visible up to ten miles from shore, created a neon shooting gallery in which the U-boats nightly lay in wait on the seaward side of the shipping lanes and picked off their sharply silhouetted victims at will. A single U-boat prowling off New York harbor in January sank eight ships, including three tankers, in just twelve hours. On February 28 a German submarine torpedoed and sank the American destroyer *Jacob Jones* in sight of the New Jersey coast. Only 11 of its 136 sailors survived. On the evening of April 10 a surfaced U-boat used its deck gun to scuttle the SS *Gulfamerica* off of Jacksonville Beach, Florida. The flaming tanker went down so close to shore that the departing U-boat captain gazed in fasci-

---

2. Dan Van der Vat, *The Atlantic Campaign: World War II's Great Struggle at Sea* (New York: Harper and Row, 1988), 236.
3. Van der Vat, *Atlantic Campaign*, 266.

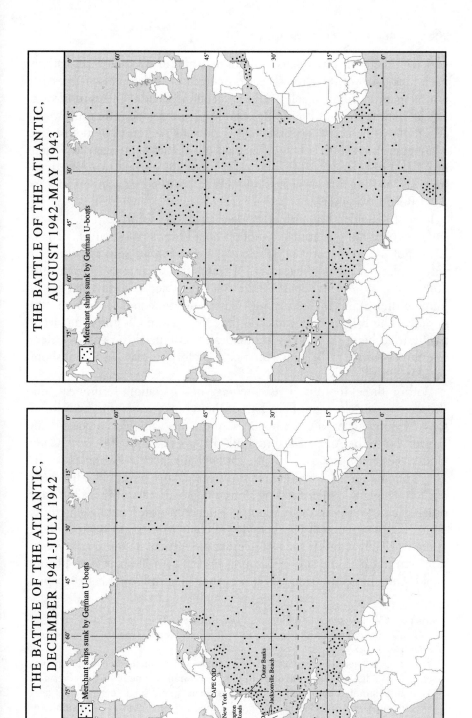

nation through his binoculars as thousands of tourists, their faces bathed in the red glow of the ship's fire, poured out of their hotels and restaurants to gape at the spectacle. "All the vacationers had seen an impressive special performance at Roosevelt's expense," Commander Reinhard Hardegen gleefully recorded in his log. "A burning tanker, artillery fire, the silhouette of a U-boat—how often had all of that been seen in America?"[4] In broad daylight on June 15 a U-boat torpedoed two American freighters within full view of thousands of horrified vacationers at Virginia Beach, Virginia.

In a still bolder but ultimately less successful venture, one U-boat surfaced near Long Island and another off a Florida beach in May 1942. Each put ashore a party of saboteurs, two four-man squads equipped with explosives, detonators, maps of industrial sites, and thousands of dollars in cash. A lone Coast Guardsman stumbled onto the first group burying their uniforms in a Long Island sand dune and took them into custody. The FBI quickly captured the others. All eight infiltrators were swiftly tried before a military tribunal and sentenced to death by electrocution—virtually the only American "victory" to date in the offshore naval war.[5]

Within three months, *Paukenschlag*, or Operation Drumbeat, destroyed 216 vessels, more than half of them tankers. Some 1.25 million tons of shipping capacity, not to mention the valuable cargoes, were forever lost to the Allies. Burning hulks lit American beaches from Cape Cod to Hampton Roads, from the Outer Banks to the Florida Keys. In New York harbor, merchant crews mutinied against sailing into the teeth of such danger. Coastal shipping slowed nearly to a standstill as the navy ordered coastwise vessels to adopt a "bucket brigade" sailing schedule, compelling them to steam only in daylight and to scurry into safe harbors at night. Heady with his success, Dönitz quickened the tempo of Operation Drumbeat in the spring, fanning his refueled U-boats even further afield into the Caribbean. By June 1942 4.7 million tons of Allied

---

4. Michael Gannon, *Operation Drumbeat: The Dramatic True Story of Germany's First U-Boat Attacks along the American Coast in World War II* (New York: Harper and Row, 1990), 363.

5. Two of the saboteurs testified against their comrades, for which one had his sentence reduced to a life term and the other to thirty years imprisonment. In 1948 President Truman commuted both men's remaining sentences, and they were deported back to Germany. See Francis Biddle, *In Brief Authority* (Garden City, N.Y.: Doubleday, 1962), 325ff, and Kai Bird, *The Chairman* (New York: Simon and Schuster, 1992), 163ff.

shipping had gone to the bottom, the majority in American coastal waters, the operational area the navy called the Eastern Sea Frontier.

"The losses by submarines off our Atlantic seaboard and in the Caribbean now threaten our entire war effort," Marshall warned Admiral King on June 19, 1942. The submarines had sunk one-fifth of the bauxite fleet that hauled precious Jamaican aluminum ore, essential for aircraft manufacture, to North American smelters. Tanker sinkings were consuming 3.5 percent of available oil-carrying capacity every month, a rate of loss so ominous that King had recently confined all tankers to port for two weeks. "I am fearful," Marshall concluded, "that another month or two of this will so cripple our means of transport that we will be unable to bring sufficient men and planes to bear against the enemy in critical theaters to exercise a determining influence on the war."[6]

To counter this menace King could at first do little. In Roosevelt's quaint phrase, there was simply a "lack of naval butter to cover the bread."[7] The U.S. Atlantic Fleet was already hard pressed to shoulder its modest share of the burden of escorting North Atlantic convoys, and the sudden flaring of the Pacific war vacuumed up virtually all new naval construction. The entire antisubmarine force available to the Eastern Sea Frontier command when Operation Drumbeat began consisted of three 110-foot wooden sub-chasers, two 173-foot patrol craft, a handful of World War I–vintage picket ships and Coast Guard cutters, and 103 antiquated, short-range aircraft, almost none of them equipped with submarine-seeking radar. For a time this puny fleet was supplemented by the Coastal Picket Patrol, or "Hooligan's Navy," a motley flotilla organized by private yachtsmen (including a pistol and grenade-toting Ernest Hemingway at the helm of his sport-fishing boat *Pilar*). They formed a swashbuckling but decidedly amateurish patrol line some fifty miles offshore, reporting countless false submarine sightings that caused further dissipation of Eastern Sea Frontier's desperately scant resources.[8]

In an ironic reversal of the Lend-Lease help that America had extended to Britain a year earlier, the Royal Navy transferred ten escort vessels and two dozen antisubmarine trawlers to the Americans for coastal defense, as well as two squadrons of aircraft. In a compound irony, the planes had originally been built in the United States. But even as Eastern Sea Frontier began to accumulate the rudiments of an

6. Van der Vat, *Atlantic Campaign*, 267.
7. C&R 1:455.
8. Morison, 110; Van der Vat, *Atlantic Campaign*, 244.

antisubmarine force, King persisted in deploying it badly. Contrary to all the hard-won lessons of the North Atlantic naval war, King clung to the belief that "inadequately escorted convoys are worse than none, because they made for concentrated targets, only thinly protected."[9] In consequence, merchant ships continued to sail independently, making easy prey for single submarines, while the handful of vessels that Eastern Sea Frontier could muster to protect coastal shipping were dispatched together in futile pursuit of frequently phantom sightings. King's stubbornness infuriated his colleagues. King was "the antithesis of cooperation, a deliberately rude person . . . a mental bully," Eisenhower noted in his diary. "One thing that might help win this war," Eisenhower added, "is to get someone to shoot King."[10]

When King finally relented and in May organized a convoy system along the Atlantic coast, the results were dramatic. Just fourteen ships went down in the Eastern Sea Frontier during that month, a sharp decline from the winter's disastrous loss rates. Dönitz's boats continued to prey upon Caribbean shipping for another two months, but by the summer of 1942 the Interlocking Convoy System protected coastwise sailings from Brazil to Newfoundland. On July 19 Dönitz withdrew his last two U-boats from North American waters. *Paukenschlag* was ended. It had dealt a grievous blow to American shipping and measurably slowed American mobilization, not to mention wounding the pride of the U.S. Navy, but it had been stopped short of catastrophe. Though a few daring marauders continued to mount occasional attacks, the Eastern Sea Frontier was secure.

But if Dönitz had retired from the American coastline, it was merely to concentrate his forces in the midocean zone where the Battle of the Atlantic was now most fiercely joined. After reallocating the last of the U-boats from Operation Drumbeat, Dönitz had well over two hundred submarines available for deployment in the broad Atlantic. German boatyards were adding fifteen new submarines to his fleet every month. Against those growing numbers Dönitz tallied his estimates of Allied carrying capacity and replacement rates. If he could sink seven hundred thousand tons of Allied merchant shipping per month, he calculated, victory would be his: Britain would face starvation, Russia defeat, and America permanent isolation on the far side of the Atlantic. By mid-1942 success seemed to be at hand, as worldwide Allied shipping losses exceeded eight hundred thousand tons per month. Despite frantic,

9. Van der Vat, *Atlantic Campaign*, 242, 247, 239.
10. Robert H. Ferrell, ed., *The Eisenhower Diaries* (New York: Norton, 1981), 50.

round-the-clock construction in both British and American shipyards, new Allied shipbuilding could not offset deficits on that scale. For 1942 as a whole, net U.S. and British shipping tonnage shrank by more than a million tons, a cumulative loss that threatened to rob the Allies of their warmaking power if not soon reversed. "The U-boat attack was our worst evil," Churchill later wrote, "the only thing that ever really frightened me during the war."[11]

The lengthening roster of his U-boat fleet was not Dönitz's only advantage. On February 1, 1942, the German navy switched to the new "Triton" code. Simultaneously, the Germans added a fourth wheel to their Enigma machines, multiplying by a factor of twenty-six the difficulty of deciphering encrypted messages. Those steps instantly blinded the Ultra codebreakers at England's Bletchley Park, and they stayed blind for the remainder of the year. Still worse, just weeks later the German naval intelligence service (*Beobachtungdienst*, "Observation Service," or *B-dienst*) salvaged a British code book from a sinking merchantman off the Norwegian coast, allowing the *B-dienst* to eavesdrop on the convoys' radio traffic. The advantage in the intelligence duel now passed decisively to the Germans. Throughout 1941 Bletchley's painstaking translation of encrypted German radio transmissions had betrayed the wolf packs' whereabouts and allowed many a convoy to be routed out of harm's way. But in 1942, the gray cloak of the Atlantic's surface again drawn securely over them, Dönitz's submariners lurked at points of their own choosing along the vital ocean highway.

Cruising in packs of a dozen or more, guided by *B-dienst* signals that remained opaque to the Allies, the U-boats inflicted increasingly costly damage as 1942 unfolded. The Allied convoys were typically composed of ten columns totaling about sixty vessels, mostly American merchantmen carrying mostly American cargoes. They slogged eastward at eight or nine knots, loosely girdled by as many as a dozen warships, almost all of them British or Canadian, weaving warily around their flanks. (The U.S. Navy provided just 2 percent of the escorts in the North Atlantic.) When aided by aerial reconnaissance, the escorts had a fighting chance of harassing the U-boats away from the convoy's path. But once a submerged wolf pack had closed undetected to torpedo range, it could wreak wholesale destruction on convoy and escorts alike.

The U-boats naturally concentrated, therefore, in those ocean areas out of range of Allied aircraft. There they could steam with impunity on the surface, diving only for the final attack. They especially favored

11. Churchill 4:110, 2:598.

two locations: the Norwegian Sea, the far northern passage to the Russian ports of Murmansk and Archangel; and the "air gap" southeast of Greenland, through which all convoys to both Britain and Russia had to pass. One combined surface, undersea, and air attack on the Russia-bound Convoy PQ17 in the Norwegian Sea in July forced the escorting warships to separate from the convoy, then scattered and sank twenty-three of the thirty-four merchantmen, an especially large loss. Only seventy thousand tons of the original two hundred thousand tons of cargo reached its destination. In August and September U-boats attacked seven convoys in the Greenland air gap and sank forty-three ships. In November total Allied losses again topped eight hundred thousand tons, 729,000 tons of which fell to the U-boats.

Nature added to the Allies' woes in the man- and ship-eating North Atlantic. Blast-force winds, towering green seas, snow squalls, and ice storms claimed nearly one hundred ships during the winter of 1942–43. In March 1943 a screaming gale slammed two convoys together, chaotically scrambling their sailing columns and wreaking wild confusion among their escorts. Dönitz capitalized on the disruption by dispatching elements of four wolf packs to feed on the havoc. At a cost of just one U-boat lost, twenty-two merchantmen were sunk out of the ninety that had set sail from New York a few days earlier, along with one of the escort vessels.

At these rates of loss, the Atlantic lifeline might soon be permanently severed. In fact, the disaster of PQ17 contributed to the Western allies' decision to suspend all North Atlantic convoys to the Russians for the remainder of 1942, triggering bitter complaints from Stalin. (The alternative but much lower capacity supply route to Russia, through the Persian Gulf and overland from Iran, remained open.) As for Britain, the sinkings in the Atlantic had by year's end cut its civilian oil reserves to a three-month supply, and imports of all kinds had withered to two-thirds of prewar levels. The Grand Alliance seemed about to be strangled in its cradle. Dönitz meanwhile added steadily to his undersea fleet, which numbered nearly four hundred boats by the beginning of 1943.

DÖNITZ'S MOUNTING SUCCESSES were menace enough. But in the midst of the shipping emergency the Western allies manufactured a new crisis of their own. It further threatened the North Atlantic supply routes, and it put additional strain on relations with Russia. It also threatened to disrupt all of the American military's best-laid plans for carrying the war to Hitler. American military doctrine had long been Doric in its simplicity: bring overwhelming force to bear against the enemy's main strength and decisively destroy his warmaking capacity. This was "the American way of war," a penchant for swift and total victory that came naturally to a nation rich in materiel and manpower and historically averse to the hair-splitting compromises of diplomacy. It was a tradition rooted in Ulysses Grant's Civil War campaigns and drummed into generations of West Point cadets. It applied axiomatically to the circumstances of 1942: gather a huge, awesomely equipped army in the British Isles and hurl it across the English Channel toward the German economic heartland of the Ruhr. The *Wehrmacht*, obliged to marshal all its resources in defense of Germany's industrial core, would be consumed by that irresistibly superior force. The eventual capture of the Ruhr would tear the heart out of the German economy and shut down Hitler's war machine for good.

To the already formidable logic of that approach the situation of the Soviet Union in 1942 added urgent reinforcement. From the outset of Operation Barbarossa, Stalin had pleaded with the Western powers to open a "second front" that would draw away thirty to forty of the German divisions facing the Red Army in the east. Without such support, Stalin hinted darkly, the USSR might soon collapse, freeing Hitler to loose his full fury on Britain and, eventually, on America. American analysts shared that assessment. "*We should not forget*," Eisenhower noted with emphasis in July 1942, "*that the prize we seek is to keep 8,000,000 Russians in the war.*"[12] That indispensable prize required opening the second front at the earliest possible date.

In April 1942 Roosevelt sent Marshall and Hopkins to London to secure British agreement to a crash program to launch a cross-Channel attack. Russia's needs loomed large in Roosevelt's thinking. "What Harry and Geo. Marshall will tell you," Roosevelt cabled Churchill in advance of their arrival, "has my heart and *mind* in it. Your people and mine demand the establishment of a front to draw off pressure on the Russians, and these peoples are wise enough to see that the Russians are today killing more Germans and destroying more equipment than you and I put together."[13] Meeting with Churchill at 10 Downing Street in the afternoon of April 8, the American envoys presented their proposal. It consisted of three parts. The first, transparently code-named Bolero, envisioned an unrelenting buildup of men and munitions in Britain

12. *PDDE* 1:391; italics in original.
13. *C&R* 1:441.

throughout 1942, swelling in the spring of 1943 to the crescendo of a massive cross-Channel invasion, forty-eight divisions strong, to which the code name Roundup was given. A smaller landing, code-named Sledgehammer, would be launched in 1942 in either of two circumstances, the first more likely than the second: if the Russians were on the point of collapse or if the Germans were about to surrender. In Marshall's shrewd mind, Sledgehammer had another purpose as well. It provided a kind of insurance policy that the pace of Bolero would not slacken. Even if Sledgehammer never happened, preparation for it would seal the Allied commitments to continue waging the Battle of the Atlantic and to concentrate troops and supplies in the British Isles, thus protecting the timetable for Roundup in 1943 and guaranteeing that America's grand strategic design would be realized. As events were to prove, Marshall's preemptive effort to guard Roundup against delay or even derailment was not misplaced.

Late in the evening of April 14, 1942, surrounded by members of his War Cabinet and military chiefs of staff, Churchill solemnly delivered his reply to Hopkins and Marshall: "Our two nations are resolved to march forward into Europe together in a noble brotherhood of arms, in a great crusade for the liberation of the tormented peoples."[14] That statement was as disingenuous as it was melodramatic. Churchill in fact had deep reservations about the entire Bolero-Sledgehammer-Roundup plan, but at this moment he calculated that he dare not risk an open disagreement with Roosevelt. "Anything like a serious difference between you and me would break my heart and surely deeply injure both our countries at the height of this terrible struggle," he cabled to Roosevelt on April 12, while declaring in the same message that "I am in entire agreement in principle with all you propose, as so are the Chiefs of Staff."[15] But Marshall and Hopkins had scarcely departed from London when Churchill revealed just how little he and his chiefs were in agreement with the second-front strategy he had feigned to endorse.

Soviet foreign minister Vaycheslav Molotov arrived in London on May 20, accompanied by unsettling news of a renewed German offen-

---

14. Robert E. Sherwood, *Roosevelt and Hopkins* (New York: Grosset and Dunlap, 1950), 535.

15. *C&R* 1:448–49. Churchill's agreement with the American plan in fact carried one big reservation: that he would not undertake any operation that interfered with British efforts to secure India and the Middle East. But his theatrical display of comradely union was so convincing that Marshall and Hopkins scarcely registered that important qualifier.

sive that had overrun the Crimean peninsula. A droll joke circulated in the British capital that the dour Molotov spoke only four words of English: "yes," "no," and "second front."[16] But Churchill swiftly disabused the Russian diplomat of the hope that any such front might soon be opened. In a display of evasion, dissembling, and diversion that soon became familiar, Churchill orated away at the impassive Russian about the shortages of amphibious landing craft necessary to a cross-Channel attack, about the titanic struggle that Britain was waging in North Africa (against eight Italian and three German divisions), and about the fantastic prospect of a ten-day air war that "would lead to the virtual destruction of the enemy's air-power on the Continent"—but conspicuously not about the second front that Molotov wanted. The American plan for a second front was vastly premature, Churchill finally told the Russian, reminding his visitor that "wars are not won by unsuccessful operations."[17]

The discouraged Soviet minister went on to Washington. There he got an altogether different reception. Meeting with Roosevelt, Hopkins, Marshall, and King on May 30, Molotov noted bluntly that he had received no positive response in London on the question of a second front. He demanded a straight answer from the Americans. With Marshall's assent, the president told Molotov "to inform Mr. Stalin that we expect the formation of a second front this year." Roosevelt repeated that promise the following day. He added the unwelcome news that in order to facilitate the buildup in Britain necessary for opening a second front in 1942, Lend-Lease supplies to Russia must be reduced to 60 percent of the originally agreed amounts. Molotov grew agitated. What would happen if Russia agreed to cut its Lend-Lease requirements and then no second front eventuated? The Soviets could not have their cake and eat it too, Roosevelt blithely replied, and promised for a third time that a second front would be established during the current year. Two days later, the Russians and the Americans agreed to the wording of a joint public communiqué declaring that "full understanding was reached with regard to the urgent tasks of creating a Second Front in Europe in 1942." Privately, Roosevelt wired Churchill: "I have a very strong

16. Mark A. Stoler, *The Politics of the Second Front: American Military Planning and Diplomacy in Coalition Warfare, 1941–1943* (Westport, Conn.: Greenwood, 1977), 43.

17. Churchill 4:298; Leo J. Meyer, "The Decision to Invade North Africa (Torch) (1942)," in Kent Roberts Greenfield, ed., *Command Decisions* (New York: Harcourt, Brace, 1959), 136.

feeling that the Russian position is precarious and may grow steadily worse during the coming weeks. Therefore, I am more than ever anxious that BOLERO proceed to definite action beginning in 1942." In a speech at Madison Square Garden several days later, Harry Hopkins flamboyantly proclaimed that General Marshall was not training his troops "to play tiddlywinks. A second front? Yes," Hopkins declared, "and if necessary a third and a fourth front, to pen the German Army in a ring of our offensive steel."[18]

All this was too much for Churchill. Almost immediately after receiving Roosevelt's message, he hastened to Washington, determined to dissuade the president from keeping his promises to Molotov. Memory and anxiety gnawed at Churchill as he flew westward toward the American capital. In World War I, Britain had departed from its historic policy of avoiding major land war in Europe and landed a large body of troops on the continent. The results had been horrendous, notably at the slaughterhouses of the Somme and Passchendaele, as well as at Gallipoli, the failed amphibious attack on Turkey for which Churchill bore especially heavy responsibility. Those nightmares Churchill was resolved never to see repeated. Better to wait, years if necessary, until the Germans were at the point of exhaustion before attempting a hazardous cross-Channel invasion. In the meantime, Britain should pursue its age-old strategy toward Europe: isolate and weaken its Continental enemies by blockade (and aerial bombing), secure the Mediterranean routes to Asia and the oil fields of the Middle East, incite and support popular uprisings within Nazi-occupied Europe, consolidate a defensive ring around the Continent that would both contain further Axis expansion and serve as the launching area for a series of later, small-scale attacks, and stay alert for opportunities to exploit Nazi vulnerabilities with the time-honored tools of diplomacy.

This "peripheral" strategy entailed huge risks, not least the possibility that Hitler would knock the Soviets out of the war and so tighten his grip on Europe that he would be invulnerable to pinpricks around the Continental littoral. But it was a strategy that suited the character of a traditional maritime power and a seasoned diplomatic actor, especially one badly bloodied in World War I and whose army the *Wehrmacht* had thrice ejected from the Continent in the course of the current war (from Norway and France in 1940, and from Greece in 1941). By the same token, the American way of war reflected the capacities and history

18. Sherwood, *Roosevelt and Hopkins*, 558–79, 588; *C&R* 1:503.

of a well-endowed nation impatient with protracted conflict, unpracticed in diplomacy, and eager to get the war won pronto and be done with it. Could those incompatible strategic visions be reconciled?

Huddled with Roosevelt at Hyde Park on June 19, Churchill began his campaign to block a 1942 cross-Channel attack. He played his hand skillfully, and he held a trump card: because America was so militarily unready, most of the troops in any 1942 operation would necessarily be British. Churchill was not about to commit them to a second front in Europe. The right place to attack, he urged the president, was North Africa, key to the Middle East, where the British had been grappling for two years with the Germans and the Italians in an inconsequential seesaw struggle. Two days later, while seated with Roosevelt in the president's White House study, the prime minister received news that the British stronghold at Tobruk in Libya, the gateway to Egypt and the oil-rich region beyond, had fallen to the Axis. Thirty-three thousand British troops had laid down their arms to half that number of the enemy, a sickening reprise of the capitulation of eighty-five thousand British soldiers to a numerically inferior Japanese force at Singapore in February. "I did not attempt to hide from the President the shock I had received," Churchill remembered. "It was a bitter moment. Defeat is one thing; disgrace is another."[19] The shock of defeat and the sting of disgrace combined to redouble Churchill's effort to deflect the Americans from the Channel attack to a landing in North Africa, where they might help to stem the mortifying British reverses. In an impressive feat of political and psychological legerdemain, the prime minister even strove to convince Roosevelt that a North African landing had been the president's idea to begin with. "This has all along been in harmony with your ideas," he said. "In fact it is your commanding idea. Here is the true second front of 1942."[20]

The American military chiefs disagreed vehemently. In their view North Africa was a marginal, inconsequential theater, far from Germany's vitals and unlikely to provide an opportunity to engage more than a token Axis force. Moreover, the logistical and manpower demands of a North African operation would necessarily dampen the tempo of Bolero and might indefinitely postpone the cross-Channel attack. When on the evening of the Tobruk disaster Churchill in Marshall's presence raised the matter of committing American troops to

19. Churchill 4:344.
20. C&R 1:520.

North Africa, the general turned to Roosevelt and declared that such a plan would be "an overthrow of everything they had been planning for." In a rare loss of temper, Marshall then rose and strode red-faced out of the room, saying he refused to discuss the matter further.[21] But, to the dismay of his military advisers, Roosevelt remained susceptible to Churchill's seductive charm.

As Roosevelt inclined ever further to the North African operation, his military chiefs stiffened their opposition to it. Marshall proposed to the Joint Chiefs of Staff that if the British held out for North Africa and refused to go ahead with Sledgehammer, then the Americans should rewrite the fundamentals of their own highest strategy, abandon the Germany-first principle, and "turn to the Pacific for decisive action against Japan." King emphatically agreed, commenting disgustedly that the British would never invade Europe "except behind a Scotch bagpipe band," in a militarily useless ceremonial finale. On July 14 the two American chiefs formally recommended to Roosevelt that in the event of British insistence on "any other operation rather than forceful, unswerving adherence to full Bolero plans," then "we should turn to the Pacific and strike decisively against Japan; in other words, assume a defensive attitude against Germany . . . and use all available means in the Pacific."[22] Marshall may have been bluffing. King almost certainly was not; just days later, he approved plans for the American assault on Guadalcanal, a sharp break from the earlier concept of fighting only a defensive war in the Pacific. In any case, Roosevelt swiftly squelched any thought of shifting American priorities to the Pacific. The chiefs' suggestion was a "red herring," he told them, akin to "taking up your dishes and going away."[23] Instead, he sent Marshall and King, accompanied by Hopkins, to London for one last effort to salvage Sledgehammer. "I am opposed to an American all-out effort in the Pacific," he instructed his emissaries, because "defeat of Japan does not defeat Germany," while "defeat of Germany means defeat of Japan," adding curiously, "probably without firing a shot or losing a life." If Sledgehammer was definitely impossible, Roosevelt said, "I want you to . . . determine upon another place for U.S. Troops to fight in 1942. . . . It is of the highest importance," the president emphasized, "that U.S. ground troops be brought into action against the enemy in 1942."[24]

21. Stimson Diary, June 22, 1942.
22. Stoler, *Politics of the Second Front*, 55.
23. Stimson Diary, July 15, 1942.
24. Sherwood, *Roosevelt and Hopkins*, 605.

Because American production and troop training had still accomplished little, the Americans held a weak hand in London. They encountered a granite wall of opposition to Sledgehammer. On July 22, with little choice and with Roosevelt's blessing, they at last acceded to the British plan for a North African invasion, now code-named Torch. Considerations of domestic morale and politics played no small part in clinching Roosevelt's decision, as did the president's concern to protect the Germany-first strategy. With public opinion howling for vengeance against the Japanese, Roosevelt felt the need to come to grips somewhere with the Germans, if for no other reason than to remind the American public of the United States' strategic priorities. What was more, congressional elections loomed in November, and Roosevelt wanted a victory, or at least a dramatic confrontation with the principal enemy, before his party faced the voters. The tentative date for Torch was October 30. "Please," Roosevelt remarked to Marshall, his hands steepled together prayerfully, "make it before election day."[25]

Only later did Marshall come to appreciate that Roosevelt's militarily dubious decision to invade North Africa did have a defensible political logic. "We failed to see," Marshall reflected, "that the leader in a democracy has to keep the people entertained. . . . The people demand action. We couldn't wait to be completely ready."[26] For the moment, however, Marshall was badly disquieted at the decision for Torch, as were the other members of his delegation. "I feel damn depressed," Hopkins noted, as he contemplated the unraveling of all American strategic planning and the possible cancellation of the cross-Channel attack. Eisenhower wrote that the North African plan was "strategically unsound" and that it "would have no effect on the 1942 campaign in Russia." The day the decision for Torch was made, Eisenhower predicted, would go down as the "blackest day in history," particularly, he added, if Russia were defeated in the meantime, as seemed likely.[27]

If Roosevelt's subordinates were upset, Stalin was livid. The North Atlantic convoys had already been discontinued. As Molotov had feared, the 40 percent shrinkage in Lend-Lease shipments to the Soviets was not to be compensated by a mighty Anglo-American campaign against

25. Forrest C. Pogue, *George C. Marshall: Ordeal and Hope* (New York: Viking, 1966), 402. As it happened, the North African landings came after election day, a quirk of timing that may have contributed to Democratic losses in the 1942 congressional election.

26. Pogue, *George C. Marshall: Ordeal and Hope*, 330.

27. Sherwood, *Roosevelt and Hopkins*, 609; PDDE 1:389; Harry C. Butcher, *My Three Years with Eisenhower* (New York: Simon and Schuster, 1946), 29.

Germany's vital organs but only by an insignificant jab at a largely Italian force in the desert wastes of North Africa. The Western allies were apparently not taking the second-front issue seriously, Stalin wrote acidly to Churchill. "I must state in the most emphatic manner," said the Soviet leader, "that the Soviet Government cannot acquiesce in the postponement of a Second Front in Europe until 1943."[28]

Seeking to mollify Stalin, Churchill traveled to Moscow in August. He brooded as he went "on my mission to this sullen, sinister Bolshevik State I had once tried so hard to strangle at its birth." His mission, he thought, was "like carrying a large lump of ice to the North Pole."[29] Stalin received Churchill in his Kremlin rooms with what an American observer described as "bluntness almost amounting to insult." As Churchill summed it up: "Stalin observed that from our long talk it seemed that all we were going to do was no Sledgehammer, no Roundup, and pay our way by bombing Germany," pathetic recompense for the cancellation of the promised second front. "I decided to get the worst over," Churchill later wrote, and "did not therefore try at once to relieve the gloom."[30]

Peering into that Kremlin gloom in August 1942, some historians have discerned the first shadows of the Cold War, that decades-long legacy of distrust and tension that was among the most bitter and ironic fruits of the wartime Grand Alliance. Certainly the Soviets at this point had ample reason to doubt their Western partners. The North African debate might have rent a tear in the fabric of Anglo-American unity, but it threatened to open a gaping chasm separating the Western allies from their Russian comrades-in-arms. Roosevelt meanwhile could do little more than reassure the Soviet leader that "we are coming as quickly and as powerfully as we possibly can."[31]

But the Western allies were coming to Africa, not Europe, and they were coming neither so powerfully nor so quickly. A dense thicket of logistical and political underbrush remained to be cleared before Torch could take place. The decision to throttle back on Bolero and invade North Africa, Eisenhower later wrote, constituted a "violent shift in target, timing, and the circumstances of attack, [which] necessitated a complete reversal in our thinking and drastic revision in our planning and preparation."[32] The elaborately contrived North Atlantic convoy system

28. Churchill 4:242.
29. Churchill 4:248.
30. Churchill 4:432.
31. Sherwood, *Roosevelt and Hopkins*, 622.
32. Dwight D. Eisenhower, *Crusade in Europe* (New York: Doubleday, 1948), 72.

had to be redesigned and redirected toward the Mediterranean. The precious reserves that Bolero had so laboriously built up in Britain, including three U.S. Army divisions, had to be reloaded and reshipped southward. Troops preparing for a battle in northwest Europe had to be retrained and reoutfitted for desert warfare. Not least, the sudden shift in Allied focus from Europe to Africa plunged the United States into a devil's tangle of utterly unanticipated political challenges.

Torch's strategic architecture was simple enough. A combined Anglo-American force, sixty-five thousand strong, would push the Axis armies from the west, while Bernard Montgomery's British Eighth Army squeezed them from the east. There simplicity ended, as military planning encountered political reality. The zones for the Anglo-American landings lay in French Morocco and Algeria, still under the administrative control of Marshal Henri Phillipe Pétain's collaborationist but nominally independent French government at Vichy. Unlike the British, the Americans had held their noses and maintained diplomatic relations with the Vichy regime. Now Roosevelt hoped to cash in on that unsavory political gamble by persuading Pétain to instruct his troops not to resist the Allied landings in North Africa. In the intricate diplomatic dance that ensued, the Americans stumbled repeatedly.

The first step was to convince the French, still embittered toward the British after the melee at Dunkirk and the Royal Navy's attack at Mers el Kebir, that Torch was primarily an American operation. Though the British contributed nearly half the troops and virtually all the naval strength, not to mention the fact that they had fathered the very concept of a North African operation, an American, Eisenhower, was designated the commander. Americans were to hit the beaches first, followed only at a decent interval by British soldiers, thus protecting British troops from vengeful French reprisals. Despite these concessions, direct appeals to the haughty Pétain to suppress resistance in the Moroccan and Algerian landing areas availed little. Eisenhower then looked for an alternative French leader who might command sufficient respect among the French North African garrisons that he could induce them not to oppose the Allied landings. He quickly ruled out Charles DeGaulle, the favorite of the British. As self-proclaimed leader of the "Free French," DeGaulle had been branded a traitor by the Vichy government and condemned to death in absentia, credentials unlikely to recommend him to the French North African commanders who had thrown in their lot with Pétain. For a time Eisenhower tried to recruit General Henri Giraud, whose recent escape from Nazi imprisonment and studied refusal to break completely with Vichy made him an apparently plausible candi-

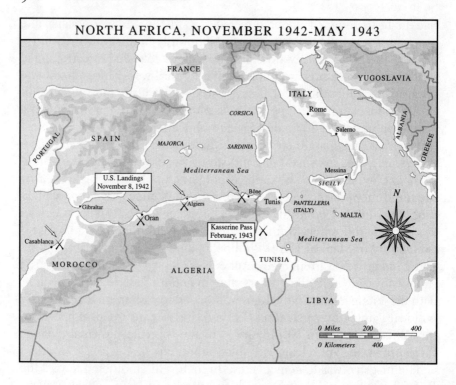

NORTH AFRICA, NOVEMBER 1942-MAY 1943

date. But Giraud insisted on taking over from Eisenhower as supreme commander, an impossible demand, and dithered in Vichy until the landings had already commenced. When the first green American troops went ashore on November 8, to be greeted not with French bouquets but French bullets, Eisenhower cast about desperately for a credible figure who could impose a cease-fire on the French forces. The person he found was Admiral Jean François Darlan, a Nazi sympathizer who had supported the French surrender in 1940 and been rewarded with appointment as commander-in-chief of Vichy's armed forces and anointment as Pétain's designated successor. After forty-eight hours of tense negotiations in Algiers, while hundreds of American soldiers were dying in the landing zones, Darlan at last arranged for a general cease-fire to take effect on November 10, in exchange for Allied recognition of himself as high commissioner for French North Africa.

The "Darlan Deal" saved American lives in North Africa, but it ignited an uproar in the United States. Critics denounced Eisenhower's embrace of the odious Darlan as "sordid" and "squalid," a loathsome repudiation of all that America professed to be fighting for. "If we will make a deal with a Darlan in French territory, then presumably we will make one with a Goering in Germany or with a Matsuoka in Japan," declared one newspaper. Churchill worried that the Allies would suffer "serious political injury . . . throughout Europe, by the feeling that we are ready to make terms with local Quislings [so named after the notorious Nazi collaborator in Norway]."[33] An embittered DeGaulle never forgave Roosevelt for the political and personal affront of being snubbed while the traitorous Darlan was exalted. For his part, Roosevelt concluded that the wrangling among DeGaulle, Giraud, and Darlan foreshadowed chaos, maybe even civil war, in postwar France, a perception that clinched his determination to avoid aligning himself with any French faction for the remainder of the war. Nor did the reverberations from the Darlan Deal stop there. Ignoring Pétain's protests that Darlan had acted without authorization from Vichy, Hitler ordered the immediate occupation of the remainder of France. Italy meanwhile occupied the French Mediterranean island of Corsica. Vichy broke diplomatic relations with the United States and, under extreme duress from Hitler, invited German forces into Tunisia. As for Darlan, a traitor thrice over— to France, to Pétain, and to his German masters—he fell to a French assassin's bullet on Christmas Eve 1942.

The thousands of German troops rapidly pouring into Tunisia were soon joined by hundreds of thousands of German and Italian soldiers streaming westward across Libya after Montgomery's signal victory at El Alamein in early November. Commanded by Erwin Rommel, the Axis forces took up strong defensive positions in the Tunisian mountain ranges and prepared to offer Dwight Eisenhower, a lifelong professional soldier who had never before North Africa heard a shot fired in anger, his first taste of battle. Eisenhower's rickety binational command structure and his unblooded, ill-prepared American troops at first proved no match for Rommel's seasoned staff and battle-hardened veterans. In a series of poorly conceived tank-to-tank duels, the humiliated Americans quickly learned that their vaunted Sherman tanks were easily outgunned by their massively armored and skillfully deployed German adversaries. Tank crews soon dubbed the vulnerable Shermans "Purple Heart Boxes," named for the medal awarded to the wounded.[34] A despondent

---

33. Dallek, 364. As for Stalin, he observed that "the Americans used Darlan not badly" and that "military diplomacy must be able to use for military purposes" not only Darlan but "even the Devil himself and his grandma"—a chill reminder of the cynical calculus with which the wily Soviet leader gauged the ethics of war and diplomacy. C&R 2:51.

34. George F. Howe, *Northwest Africa: Seizing the Initiative in the West* (Washington: Department of the Army, 1957), 480.

Eisenhower wrote to a confidante that "the best way to describe our operations to date is that they have violated every recognized principle of war, are in conflict with all operational and logistic methods laid down in text-books, and will be condemned, in their entirety, by all Leavenworth and War College classes for the next twenty-five years."[35] At Kasserine Pass in late February, muddle in General Lloyd Fredendall's headquarters contributed to a disorganized American rout before the guns of a powerful German panzer division. Eisenhower soon replaced Fredendall with a new commander already fabled for his aggressive instincts, though not yet for his military accomplishments, George Patton.

Slowly the tide of logistics began to turn the battle in the Allies' favor. By the time an ailing Rommel was invalided back to Germany in March, the 157,000 German and 193,000 Italian troops in North Africa no longer enjoyed air superiority. The tourniquet of the British naval blockade interdicted fresh supplies of munitions and gasoline. Before long the Germans had only seventy-six operational tanks and were reduced to running them with fuel distilled from wine. Patton launched a probing attack against the Axis lines on March 7. It did not succeed, but it provided sufficient distraction that Montgomery effected a breakthrough that ended with the surrender of a quarter of a million Axis troops, 125,000 of them Germans, on May 13. In Russia, meanwhile, the Red Army still confronted more than two hundred Axis divisions, even after destroying twenty German divisions and killing some two hundred thousand Germans in the single, epic battle of Stalingrad.

THE SOVIET VICTORY at Stalingrad in February 1943 rewrote the Grand Alliance's fundamental strategic equation. Russia's survival was now all but guaranteed. What was more, the Red Army now passed irreversibly onto the offensive. With painful slowness at first but then with gathering, inexorable momentum, it began to roll the *Wehrmacht* back across the Russian steppes. If the Western allies had worried through 1942 about Russia's staying power, they began to fret in 1943 about the implications of Russia's fighting power. A new anxiety crept into American assessments of the political geometry of the Grand Alliance triangle. As the moment approached for another full-dress conference between Churchill and Roosevelt, attended by their senior military and naval advisers, that anxiety grew acute. "A defeated and prostrate

35. *PDDE* 2:811.

Germany leaving a strong and triumphant Russia dominating Europe," the U.S. Army's Joint Strategic Survey Committee advised Marshall in the first week of the new year, was not in accord with Britain's historic foreign policy of sustaining a balance of power on the Continent. "It would be in strict accord with that policy, however, to delay Germany's defeat until military attrition and civilian famine had materially reduced Russia's potential toward dominance in Europe." Russia's growing military muscle, in short, might give Britain new reasons to postpone the second front and fresh incentives to temporize with further peripheral operations, probably in the Mediterranean. Such a strategy would prolong the war between Germany and the Soviet Union and leave neither power able to command the Continent. But Britain's policy must not be America's, the army planners warned Marshall. The United States "should forego indirect and eccentric concepts and strike hard and straight at Germany."[36]

Those thoughts were much on Marshall's mind at a White House meeting on January 7, 1943, convened to advise the president about his upcoming conference with Churchill in the Moroccan city of Casablanca. There the issue would be sharply joined: did Mediterranean operations represent a temporary diversion or a way of life? Marshall, as usual, set his face sternly against further "periphery-pecking." Continuing to fight in the distant Mediterranean, he warned, would dissipate Anglo-American strength and risk intolerable shipping losses while achieving no significant strategic purpose. Though Marshall acknowledged that a cross-Channel attack would take a heavy toll in human casualties, he chose to underscore instead what was still the greatest single constraint on all American actions. "To state it cruelly," he said, "we could replace troops whereas a heavy loss in shipping . . . might completely destroy any opportunity for successful operations against the enemy in the near future."[37]

Two days later, Roosevelt departed Washington by train for Florida, where he boarded an aircraft for the lengthy transatlantic flight to North Africa — his first presidential foray outside the Americas. Roosevelt relished the occasion. He would be the first president since Lincoln to visit American troops in the field. Like his former chief, Woodrow Wilson, he fancied himself heading abroad to dispose of the destinies of

---

36. Stoler, *Politics of the Second Front*, 73.
37. Forrest C. Pogue, *George C. Marshall: Organizer of Victory, 1943–1945* (New York: Viking Press, 1973), 15.

nations. Even grander historical comparisons swam in his head. "I prefer a comfortable oasis to the raft at Tilsit," he mused about the upcoming seance in Casablanca's winter sunshine. That was a telling allusion to the legendary encounter between the Emperor Napoleon and Czar Alexander I in 1807, when the two potentates had met in a Baltic riverport after defeating another German state (Prussia) and redrawn the map of Europe.[38]

But Casablanca was to be no Tilsit. Parlaying among the palms and bougainvilleas in Morocco, two statesmen still militarily on the defensive, Churchill and Roosevelt commanded only a fraction of the power that the pair of supremely self-assured despots afloat on the Neman River had wielded more than a century earlier. And Roosevelt at this moment perhaps resembled Woodrow Wilson more than he appreciated. Like the hapless Wilson vainly urging a liberal peace settlement on the implacable Georges Clemenceau and David Lloyd George at Paris in 1919, Roosevelt still lacked the means to bend Churchill to his will in the ongoing inter-Allied struggle over the second front. Though British foreign minister Anthony Eden described Roosevelt at this time as the "head of a mighty country which was coming out into the arena," the characterization was not yet quite apt.[39] In early 1943 Churchill remained the senior partner in the Anglo-American alliance. More time must pass before American might had been sufficiently amassed to allow Roosevelt to dominate the strategic debate with Churchill, and more time still before the American leader could aspire to be a geopolitical arbiter on an imperial scale.

Churchill arrived in Casablanca attended by a huge retinue, dozens of military and naval advisers and their staffs, all of them supported by a sophisticated communications ship that kept them in touch with even larger staffs in London. The American delegation was small and, as the British had observed on earlier occasions, neither well prepared by staff work nor fully agreed on its own priorities. Marshall clung to the idea of the cross-Channel attack. King continued to demand more resources for the Pacific. The American air chiefs were beginning to insist that air power alone might bring the *Reich* to its knees, without the need for a costly land invasion. Facing those divided ranks and confidently holding the lion's share of disposable military assets, the British easily prevailed. "We lost our shirts," the U.S. Army planner General Albert Wed-

38. Pogue, *Marshall: Organizer of Victory*, 5.
39. Anthony Eden, *The Reckoning* (Boston: Houghton Mifflin, 1965), 430.

emeyer complained. "One might say we came, we listened, and we were conquered."[40]

The joint communiqué issued by the Casablanca conferees on January 23 announced a bundle of decisions. Taken together, they reflected some compromises between the competing priorities of the two nations and the various service arms, but they also unmistakably signified that Churchill's deepest purposes had in the end been faithfully served. The two allies committed themselves anew to overcoming the U-boat menace in the Atlantic. They promised to fulfill their Lend-Lease commitments to the Russians. And they announced a Combined Bomber Offensive that was to inflict round-the-clock punishment on Germany from the air. In a significant concession to King, they also agreed to allocate 30 percent of their war effort to the Pacific theater, almost double the amount envisioned in earlier Anglo-American plans and a margin that allowed King to remain on the offensive against Japan. Most important, and most galling to the American military chiefs, not to mention the Russians, Churchill and Roosevelt declared that upon termination of the North African campaign they would not immediately undertake the cross-Channel invasion but instead press ahead in the Mediterranean, probably with an invasion of Sicily. Marshall's worst fears were being realized. He warned that the Mediterranean was becoming a "suction pump" that would lead to "interminable" dissipation of effort in that inappropriate theater. Stalin, Churchill predicted, would be "disappointed and furious."[41]

He was. While the British and the Americans had been pretending that North Africa constituted an authentic second front, Germany had transferred thirty-six fresh divisions to the eastern front, six of them armored. An invasion of Sicily, Stalin wrote to Roosevelt, "can by no means replace a Second Front in France. . . . I consider it my duty to state that the early opening of a second front in France is the most important thing. . . . I must give a most emphatic warning . . . of the grave danger with which further delay in opening a second front is fraught."[42]

It is in light of those sentiments that the most notorious fruit of the Casablanca Conference must be understood. Roosevelt made one ad-

40. Stoler, *Politics of the Second Front*, 77.
41. Dallek, 371–72; Stoler, *Politics of the Second Front*, 85.
42. Ministry of Foreign Affairs of the USSR, comp. *Stalin's Correspondence with Roosevelt and Truman, 1941–1945* (New York: Capricorn, 1965), 59.

ditional pronouncement before departing Morocco, not as part of the officially printed joint communiqué but orally, in a press conference on January 24. In an apparently spontaneous but almost certainly well-considered statement, the president called for nothing less than the "unconditional surrender" of Germany, Italy, and Japan. Ostensibly a declaration of bellicose resolve, the unconditional-surrender formula in fact reflected continuing American military and political weakness. Still unable to bring meaningful force to bear against Hitler, unable even to persuade the British to join in delivering on the promise of a cross-Channel attack, fearful that the Darlan affair might nourish Soviet suspicions of his willingness to cut a deal with Rome or Berlin, increasingly worried about Stalin's ultimate intentions in eastern Europe, Roosevelt at this date had little other means with which to reassure his long-suffering Soviet ally. Without the leverage to prise specific agreements about the postwar world out of either the British or the Russians, Roosevelt also seized upon the unconditional-surrender doctrine as a way to defer tough political bargaining until the war's end. When unconditional surrender was announced it was the policy of a militarily unprepared nation with little scope for maneuver. It would survive into an era when America wielded unimaginable power and when the supple Roosevelt was no longer alive to temper its application. By then the unconditional-surrender doctrine would have taken on a life of its own, with consequences not visible in January 1943.[43]

THE TWO WESTERN STATESMEN had received a spectacular reminder of the importance and vulnerability of the Atlantic lifeline even as they had greeted one another in balmy Casablanca. Only days earlier, U-boats off the West African coast had attacked a special convoy ferrying precious oil from Trinidad to support the North African campaign. Just as the Casablanca Conference opened, the convoy's few survivors reached Gibraltar, directly across the mouth of the Mediterranean from Morocco, telling harrowing tales of the shattering losses they had wit-

43. For an excellent account of the background and provenance of Roosevelt's unconditional-surrender pronouncement, see Dallek, 373–76, to which it might be added that, despite Churchill's apparent surprise at Roosevelt's statement, unconditional surrender was also consistent with the policies of no compromise with Hitler enunciated in Neville Chamberlain's last days in office and with such vehemence by Churchill himself in 1940 and 1941, when Britain had few other means of reassuring the Americans, just as Roosevelt in 1943 had few other means of reassuring the Russians.

nessed: seven of nine tankers sunk, fifty-five thousand tons of shipping and more than a hundred thousand tons of fuel gone, one of the most devastating U-boat attacks of the war. That sorry spectacle surely reinforced Churchill's and Roosevelt's determination to gain the upper hand in the Atlantic.

But though even greater losses lay ahead, in fact the Battle of the Atlantic was already turning in the Allies' favor, and with astonishing swiftness. The scientists at Bletchley had in December 1942 finally broken the Triton cipher and puzzled through the vexations presented by Enigma's fourth wheel. Most important, the arrival from American shipyards of more abundant escort vessels, particularly the new "escort carriers," or "baby flat-tops," each carrying up to two dozen aircraft, at last gave the Allies an insuperable advantage, one that probably weighed more heavily in the scales than did Bletchley's restored electronic eyes and ears.

The U-boats of this era were in fact not true submarines at all but submersible torpedo boats that could dive for brief periods before, during, and after an attack. They were unable to remain submerged for long and were not designed for high-speed running under water. To reach their attack stations, to overtake a prey, and to replenish their air supply, they were obliged to steam on the surface, where they were especially vulnerable to sighting and assault from the air.[44] When Roosevelt in March 1943 compelled King to transfer sixty Very Long Range B-24 Liberator aircraft from the Pacific to the Atlantic, the Allies at last closed the midocean air gap in which Dönitz's submarines had done their worst damage.

After years of terrorizing Allied sailors in the North Atlantic, now it was the German submariners' turn to quail. Aided by aerial reconnaissance as well as by improved shipborne radar and sonar, the naval escorts began to scour the submarines from the sea. Forty-three of the fragile undersea craft died in May 1943 alone, more than twice the rate at which they could be replaced. As Dönitz radioed to one U-boat commander after another, "Report position and situation," he more and more often waited in vain for a reply, while the listeners at Bletchley

44. Later in the war the Germans developed the *Schnorkel* type of U-boat, a true submarine whose diesel engines could breath air through a retractable tube, making the boat fully operational underwater for long periods of time. Had it been available in early 1943 it would have instantly negated almost all the advances in Allied anti–submarine warfare tactics. But the *Schnorkel* boats appeared too late in the war, and in insufficient numbers, to turn the tide in the Battle of the Atlantic.

eavesdropped on the ominous silences. In the "Happy Time" of 1942, a U-boat had enjoyed an operational life of more than a year. Now the average U-boat survived less than three months. Dönitz's orders to sail had become virtual death sentences. Overall the German submarine service lost more than twenty-five thousand crew to death and another five thousand to capture, a 75 percent casualty rate that exceeded the losses of any other service arm in any nation. Faced with such relentless winnowing of his ranks, Dönitz ordered all but a handful of his U-boats out of the North Atlantic on May 24, 1943. "We had lost the Battle of the Atlantic," he later wrote. In the next four months, sixty-two convoys comprising 3,546 merchant vessels crossed the Atlantic, without the loss of a single ship.[45]

Stalin had every reason to expect that victory over the U-boats in the Atlantic would mean full resumption of Lend-Lease shipments to the Soviets, as promised at Casablanca. Four convoys did manage to reach Murmansk in the first few weeks of 1943, paltry recompense, in Stalin's eyes, for the military agonies and the punishing supply famine that the Soviets had been enduring for the preceding six months. "We've lost millions of people, and they want us to crawl on our knees because they send us Spam," one Russian groused about the Americans.[46] But just as Torch had required that shipping be redirected from the North Atlantic to North Africa in mid-1942, now the decision at Casablanca to invade Sicily once again dictated that scarce shipping resources be pulled off the Russian supply routes. Stalin greeted the news curtly: "I understand this unexpected action as a catastrophic diminution of supplies of arms and military raw materials," he wrote to his Western comrades-in-arms. "You realize of course that the circumstances cannot fail to affect the position of the Soviet troops"—a statement sufficiently susceptible to being read as a threat to conclude a separate peace that Churchill felt the need to reassure Roosevelt that it was not. Yet even Churchill shared with Hopkins his anxiety "that in April, May and June, not a single American or British soldier will be killing a single German or Italian soldier while the Russians are chasing 185 divisions around." The Americans meanwhile had moved but eight divisions into the European theater, well short of Bolero's schedule of twenty-seven by this date. Only one of them was in England, the staging ground for the cross-Channel attack.[47]

In February 1943 Stalin broadcast a message to the Soviet armed forces in which he made no reference to British or American aid and claimed, not without reason, that the Red Army was fighting the war alone. The Soviet armed forces faced four million Axis troops on a two-thousand-mile front, Stalin told Roosevelt's special emissary, Joseph Davies, in May. "The Red Army is fighting on their front alone, and suffering under the occupation of a large part of our territory by a cruel enemy. We are waiting for a real offensive in the west to take some of the load off our backs. We need more fighting planes, more locomotives, more equipment, more rails, more food, more grain."[48]

BUT RATHER THAN UNDERTAKING the "real offensive" that Stalin had in mind—the long-sought invasion of northwest France in overwhelming strength—the Anglo-Americans instead proceeded with their considerably less consequential offensive against the Italian island-province of Sicily. In a remarkable address on the eve of their embarkation from Tunisia, General George S. Patton Jr. sought to embolden his invading troops by playing on all the resonances of American immigrant myths as well as venerable stereotypes about the relation of the New World to the Old:

> When we land, we will meet German and Italian soldiers whom it is our honor and privilege to attack and destroy. Many of you have in your veins German and Italian blood, but remember that these ancestors of yours so loved freedom that they gave up home and country to cross the ocean in search of liberty. The ancestors of the people we shall kill lacked the courage to make such a sacrifice and remained as slaves.[49]

The speech was vintage Patton. He was the grandson of a Confederate colonel who had been killed in action, and war was in his blood. Born in 1885, Patton had grown up in a well-to-do family in then bucolic Pasadena, California, riding his horse through the San Gabriel mountains as a boy, taking no formal schooling until he was twelve years old.

47. C&R 2:179–80; Dallek, 380; Maurice Matloff and Edwin M. Snell, *United States Army in World War II: Strategic Planning for Coalition Warfare, 1941–1942* (Washington: Department of the Army, 1953), 390.
48. Dunn, *Caught between Roosevelt and Stalin,* 186.
49. Harry H. Semmes, *Portrait of Patton* (New York: Paperback Library, 1955), 155.

He arrived at West Point after a year at Virginia Military Institute and immediately established a reputation as a gifted, dedicated athlete, though only a middling student. In 1912 he competed in the military pentathlon in the Stockholm Olympic Games, placing fifth in the event, which comprised a steeplechase, pistol shooting, fencing, swimming, and a five-thousand-meter run. As an aide to John J. Pershing in Mexico in 1916, he had killed three of Pancho Villa's bodyguards in a gunfight, and as a general he toted twin pearl-handled revolvers as a token of his skill with a six-gun. He led a tank brigade at the Meuse-Argonne in 1918 and in the interwar years became a leading proponent of armored warfare. Religious and profane, irascible and sentimental, Patton was one of the most combative and colorful characters in the American or any other army, a man whose swaggering, self-assured manner and edgy pugnacity gave him the aura of having just dismounted from a foam-flecked horse.

On July 10 soldiers from one Canadian, four British, and three American divisions added themselves to the millennia-old roster of armies, from the Phoenicians and the Greeks to the Saracens and the Normans, that had essayed the conquest of polyglot Sicily. British commander Harold Alexander, underwhelmed with the performance of American troops in North Africa, designated his countryman Bernard Montgomery to wield the offensive sword of the attack along Sicily's east coast, with the goal of sealing the island exit across the Strait of Messina to mainland Italy. Patton was given the lesser role of holding a defensive shield to protect Montgomery's left flank on the west. A notable breakdown in the ramshackle Allied communications system caused several of the invasion fleet's antiaircraft crews to open fire on their own transport aircraft, which were towing gliders filled with American paratroopers. Nearly half the gliders were shot down or crash-landed into the sea in the ensuing confusion, drowning hundreds of paratroopers. Only 12 of the 147 gliders launched managed to land on their assigned landing zones.[50]

On the beaches, however, the war's largest amphibious operation to date unfolded fairly smoothly. A wild ruse had helped achieve a measure of surprise. Three months earlier, British agents had planted a corpse, dressed in the uniform of a Royal Marine officer, on a Spanish beach. Falsified papers in a despatch case chained to the body's waist were intended to convince the Axis that the next Allied blow would fall on

---

50. Carlo D'Este, *Bitter Victory: The Battle for Sicily, 1943* (New York: Dutton, 1988), 227–37.

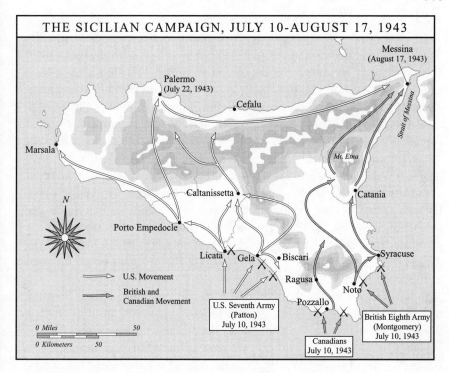

THE SICILIAN CAMPAIGN, JULY 10-AUGUST 17, 1943

Messina
(August 17, 1943)

Palermo
(July 22, 1943)

Cefalu

Strait of Messina

Marsala

Mt. Etna

Caltanissetta

Catania

N

Porto Empedocle

Licata   Gela   Biscari   Syracuse

U.S. Movement

British and
Canadian Movement

Ragusa

Noto

U.S. Seventh Army
(Patton)
July 10, 1943

Pozzallo

British Eighth Army
(Montgomery)
July 10, 1943

0 Miles   50

0 Kilometers   50

Canadians
July 10, 1943

Sardinia. The Germans and Italians took the bait and concentrated most of their defensive effort in the large island to Sicily's north.

Though the Americans encountered stiff resistance near Gela, on Sicily's southern coast, in other areas the landings were virtually unopposed. Some Sicilians even helped unload the invaders' landing craft. Inland, Montgomery met two German divisions that notably slowed his progress toward Messina. Patton thereupon seized the initiative. Declaring that "if I succeed Attila will have to take a back seat," he mounted a memorable demonstration of the mobility and aggression soon recognized as his trademarks. Slicing rapidly through weak Italian opposition across western Sicily, he entered Palermo on July 22 while huge crowds cheered, "Down with Mussolini!" and "Long Live America!"[51] Scarcely pausing for breath, Patton's troops then plunged along the island's north coast to Messina. By this circuitous route Patton beat Montgomery to the shores of Messina Strait on August 17. Both generals arrived too late, however, to prevent the successful evacuation of sixty-

51. D'Este, *Bitter Victory*, 412, 423.

two thousand Italian and forty thousand German troops, who survived to fight another day. Patton's performance had been characteristically flamboyant and fast-moving. It had also been costly for his inexperienced and profligately deployed troops, one in eight of whom was a casualty.[52]

The campaign proved personally costly for Patton too. In two separate incidents, soldiers under his command massacred seventy-three unarmed Italian and three German prisoners of war near the airfield at Biscari. Patton tried to cover the matter up—"it would make a stink in the press and also would make the civilians mad," he told a subordinate—but the facts came out, and a sergeant and a captain were charged with murder. Both pleaded that they believed themselves to be following Patton's orders in an inflammatory preinvasion speech, when he admonished his men to beware of enemy troops who might be feigning surrender in order to bait a trap. In case of doubt, Patton had said, "Kill the s.o.b.'s." The captain was acquitted, but the sergeant was sentenced to life imprisonment, later commuted.

In two further incidents, Patton verbally abused and physically struck two soldiers recovering from "battle fatigue" in field hospitals. Patton thought the men were malingerers. "You yellow son of a bitch," he yelled at one of them, brandishing one of his twin pearl-handled revolvers. "I won't have these brave men here who have been shot seeing a yellow bastard sitting here crying. . . . You ought to be lined up against a wall and shot. In fact, I ought to shoot you myself right now, God damn you!" Patton then slapped the man repeatedly. For these actions Eisenhower ordered Patton to apologize publicly to his troops and temporarily removed Patton from command.[53]

In the midst of the whirlwind battle for Sicily, Italy's King Victor Emmanuel III summoned Benito Mussolini to the royal palace, forced his resignation as prime minister, and ordered the humbled dictator arrested and imprisoned. Mussolini's successor was Marshal Pietro Badoglio, former chief of the Italian Supreme General Staff and a longtime Fascist. Though not as unpalatable a specimen as the malodorous Darlan, Badoglio soon proved to have comparably elastic loyalties. While

---

52. George F. Botjer, *Sideshow War: The Italian Campaign, 1943–1945* (College Station: Texas A&M University Press, 1996), 25–26.

53. D'Este, *Bitter Victory,* 317–29, 483–96. By one accounting, if Patton had been held to the standard applied after the war to the German perpetrators of the Malmédy massacre of American soldiers in December 1944, he would have received a sentence of life imprisonment for the murders at Biscari. See I.C.B. Dear, ed., *The Oxford Companion to the Second World War* (New York: Oxford University Press, 1995), 132.

earnestly reassuring Hitler that Italy would continue to fight by his side, Badoglio opened secret negotiations with Allied representatives to arrange a surrender. Roosevelt responded with his own display of diplomatic dexterity. He declared in a Fireside Chat on July 28 that "our terms to Italy are still the same as our terms to Germany and Japan — 'unconditional surrender.' We will have no truck with Fascism in any way, in any shape, or manner. We will permit no vestige of Fascism to remain." At the same time, he conceded to Churchill that he would settle merely for coming "as close as possible to unconditional surrender" in Italy, opening the possibility that the dubious Badoglio might be allowed to retain power.[54] Separating Italy from its Axis partner had been a goal of British diplomacy for nearly a decade. As the Hoare-Laval deal in 1935 had notoriously illustrated, London had long since shown its willingness to bend principle to that end. After aggravatingly lengthy negotiations with the Italians, Eisenhower was eventually instructed to accept a complicated surrender formula. It not only allowed Badoglio to stay in office but also recognized Italy as a co-belligerent in the war against Hitler. In its first test, the unconditional-surrender doctrine had hardly proved to be the terrible swift sword brandished so belligerently at Casablanca. Nor had the terms of the Italian surrender, entailing the embrace of a barely fumigated Fascist as a comrade-in-arms, done much to reassure the Soviets. "To date it has been like this," Stalin wrote to Roosevelt: "the U.S.A. and Britain reach agreement between themselves while the U.S.S.R. is informed of the agreement between the two Powers as a third party looking passively on. I must say that this situation cannot be tolerated any longer."[55]

The prospect of Italy's capitulation had opened another round in the still-smoldering Allied debate over strategy. At Casablanca the reluctant Americans had agreed only to the Sicilian invasion, hoping that would write finis to the Mediterranean chapter of the war. But at a follow-up Anglo-American planning conference in Washington in May 1943 (code-named Trident), Churchill urged pressing on to the Italian mainland. Knocking Italy out of the war was now the "great prize" to be gained in the Mediterranean, Churchill declaimed. Italy's loss would "cause a chill of loneliness over the German people, and might be the beginning of their doom."[56] That extravagant claim did not much im-

54. *PPA* (1943), 327; *FRUS* (1943) 2:332.
55. *Stalin's Correspondence with Roosevelt and Truman*, 84.
56. Stoler, *Politics of the Second Front*, 92.

press the Americans, but another of Churchill's arguments did. The repeated slowing of Bolero to date had now compelled the postponement of the cross-Channel attack to the spring of 1944, a conclusion to which the Americans were grudgingly driven at the Trident Conference. Thus the only force-in-being capable of taking action in the European theater for the next twelve months was Eisenhower's Mediterranean command. Eisenhower's troops "could not possibly stand idle" for a year, Churchill insisted. "So long a period of inaction," he said, "would have a serious effect on relations with Russia, who was bearing such a disproportionate weight."[57] Roosevelt was forced to agree, but with qualifications. He first insisted on a British commitment to May 1, 1944, as the target date for the cross-Channel invasion. That agreement signaled the beginning of Roosevelt's ascendance over Churchill in the scales of geopolitical influence and cheered the president's advisers. At long last, Hopkins believed, his boss could "be safely left alone with the Prime Minister."[58] To ensure that Churchill did not again disrupt Bolero with still more Mediterranean distractions, Roosevelt further insisted that Eisenhower should proceed to the Italian mainland with only "the resources already available." All fresh troops and new equipment coming from America would be directed toward the buildup in Britain.[59]

The Italian campaign thus began with weighty liabilities. It had formed no part of earlier planning exercises, was decided on short notice and for opportunistic reasons, and was required to go forward with severely restricted resources. Most important, it had no compelling strategic goal. Its thin rationale of keeping at least some Western forces engaged against the enemy through the remainder of 1943 seemed plausible so long as the Italian surrender negotiations gave promise of an easy victory. But while the two-faced Badoglio was haggling over surrender terms, Hitler poured sixteen divisions into the boot-shaped peninsula. Overnight, Italy went from German ally to German-occupied country. Now it was about to become a battleground in a grinding war of attrition whose costs were justified by no defensible military or political purpose.

On September 8, 1943, three British and four American divisions commanded by the American General Mark Clark glided shoreward in their landing craft across the glassy predawn waters of the Gulf of

57. Dallek, 394.
58. Stoler, *Politics of the Second Front*, 93.
59. Morison, 349.

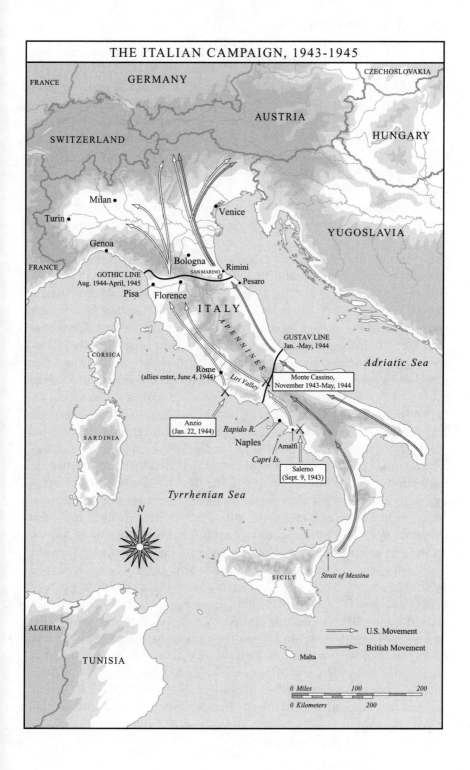

THE ITALIAN CAMPAIGN, 1943-1945

FRANCE

GERMANY

CZECHOSLOVAKIA

AUSTRIA

HUNGARY

SWITZERLAND

Milan

Turin

Venice

YUGOSLAVIA

Genoa

FRANCE

Bologna

SAN MARINO

Rimini

GOTHIC LINE
Aug. 1944-April, 1945

Pisa

Florence

Pesaro

ITALY

APENNINES

CORSICA

GUSTAV LINE
Jan. -May, 1944

Adriatic Sea

Rome
(allies enter, June 4, 1944)

Liri Valley

Monte Cassino,
November 1943-May, 1944

Anzio
(Jan. 22, 1944)

Rapido R.

SARDINIA

Naples

Amalfi

Capri Is.

Salerno
(Sept. 9, 1943)

Tyrrhenian Sea

N

SICILY

Strait of Messina

ALGERIA

U.S. Movement

British Movement

TUNISIA

Malta

0 Miles   100   200

0 Kilometers   200

Salerno. As the boats churned ahead, the huddled American troops pointed out to one another the jagged silhouette of the Isle of Capri to their north, in the mouth of Naples harbor, from which many of their forebears had sailed to the United States. They could see the gently bobbing lights of fishing boats beneath the terraced cliffs of the Amalfi coast. They knew that Montgomery had landed unopposed on the toe of the Italian boot just days earlier. Adding to their sense of complacency, at first light Eisenhower's voice came over the radio, announcing a preliminary Italian armistice.

If the landing forces expected that a tourist idyll awaited them on the beaches of Salerno, they were soon disillusioned. Ignoring all the lessons that the Pacific war was teaching about amphibious attack, Clark, a vainglorious third-generation professional soldier and one of the few American senior officers who had seen combat in World War I, chose to forego preliminary bombardment in the hope of achieving tactical surprise. But it was Clark who got the surprise. Awaiting him ashore were some of the same Germans who had recently eluded Patton and Montgomery in Sicily. They counterattacked with such force that Clark prepared to evacuate the beachhead and accept defeat on September 12. He was saved only by aggressive, close-in naval fire support, poured ashore from ships that ran their keels to within inches of the sand.

The near disaster at Salerno was but the prelude to a year-and-a-half-long ordeal in the elongated Italian cul-de-sac. German field marshal Albert Kesselring took ingenious advantage of the Italian peninsula's mountainous spine, seamed by rivers and wrinkled by narrow defiles, to bottle up the Allies without having to transfer additional German troops from other fronts. After effecting an orderly withdrawal from the narrow plain behind Salerno, Kesselring fortified a line (the "Gustav Line") that stretched from the Tyrrhenian Sea to the Adriatic just north of Naples. Its western end was anchored on the Appenine peak of Monte Cassino, overlooking the confluence of the Rapido and Liri rivers and crowned by a magnificent monastery founded by Benedict in the sixth century, one of the jewels of European piety, learning, and art. Repeatedly destroyed by invading Lombards and Arabs, restored most recently in the seventeenth century, Monte Cassino now once again attracted the wrath of the gods of war, who cared little for the Christian god of peace to whom the monastery's gentle monks chanted their nightly vespers. Monte Cassino dominated the entrance to the valley of the Liri, one of the few north-south watersheds in the Appenine range, and for that reason an ancient route to Rome and a coveted military objective.

Repeated attempts by a multinational Allied force to get past Cassino into the Liri Valley all broke against the obstacles of rock, rivers, and German doggedness, abetted by atrocious weather that buried vehicles in axle-deep mud and frequently closed the skies to aircraft. The U.S. Thirty-sixth Division, a National Guard outfit from Texas, suffered especially appalling losses in an abortive attempt to cross the swollen and frigid Rapido River in January. In one of the war's most lamentably destructive actions, Allied bombers pounded the ancient monastery to rubble in February 1944, only to learn that it had held no German troops but that its ruins made for superior defensive emplacements.

Desperate for an exit from the wintry deadlock at Monte Cassino, Churchill championed the bold move of a "cat's-claw" or "end-run" — a second amphibious landing, this time behind the enemy line at Anzio, just south of Rome. Predictably, the Americans took scant interest in this suggestion of a fresh initiative in what they had from the outset regarded as a secondary theater. They had already begun in late 1943 to transfer men and materiel to England preparatory to the cross-Channel attack. "Here the American clear-cut, logical, large-scale, mass production style of thought was formidable," said Churchill, marking his frustration with the increasingly evident fact of American dominance in Allied councils, a dominance symbolized by the accumulating stockpiles of American economic output.[60] But at last, in a direct appeal to Roosevelt, the prime minister succeeded in persuading the president to order a delay in the transfer of landing craft to England from the Mediterranean, in order that the amphibious assault on Anzio, code-named Shingle, might be launched. Marshall had his usual misgivings. "I was furious," he said, that at this late date the Prime Minister still "wanted to push us further in the Mediterranean."[61] The American commander ordered to undertake the Anzio landing, General John P. Lucas, shared Marshall's apprehension. Lucas gave vent to feelings that might have been thinkable but surely inexpressible at Casablanca a year earlier. In a stormy meeting with his British superior, he likened Shingle to Churchill's disastrous World War I brainchild, Gallipoli, acerbically adding, "with the same amateur on the coach's bench."[62]

On January 22, 1944, amphibious trucks, driven by black troops rele-

60. Churchill 5:377.
61. Pogue, *Marshall: Organizer of Victory*, 331.
62. Lucas quoted in David Eisenhower, *Eisenhower at War, 1943–1945* (New York: Vintage, 1987), 124.

gated to noncombat service, began ferrying an Anglo-American force, fifty thousand strong, to the Anzio beaches. The assault troops splashed ashore against mercifully light resistance. But in yet another violation of the principles of amphibious warfare, Lucas failed to exploit his good fortune on the beaches by advancing swiftly inland. He contented himself instead with stabilizing and securing his landing zone. Hitler soon ordered a powerful counterattack, determined to demonstrate that he still had the capacity to hurl an amphibious landing into the sea. As at Salerno, he nearly succeeded. He did seal Lucas's troops inside their besieged beachhead, where they huddled, paralyzed and despondent, for the next four months. One soldier captured the agony of Anzio in verse:

> Praise be to God for this captured sod that rich with blood does seep;
> With yours and mine, like butchered swine's; and hell is six feet deep.
> That death awaits there's no debate; no triumph will we reap.
> The crosses grow on Anzio, where hell is six feet deep.[63]

Landed to rescue the deadlocked force at Monte Cassino, the men on the beaches of Anzio now cowered under the Alban Hills and awaited their own rescue until French Moroccan and Polish divisions finally cracked the Monte Cassino defenses in May and broke through into the Liri Valley. Even then, Clark muffed the opportunity to bag Kesselring's retreating forces. Instead of cinching the noose around them by joining with the British army heading northward from Monte Cassino, he directed his troops to strike for the political prize of Rome, a histrionic gesture that availed little. The Germans swiftly abandoned the city and retreated further to the north. As they passed through the great Renaissance city of Florence, they blew up all the bridges across the River Arno save the famed Ponte Vecchio, deemed too fragile to bear the weight of tanks and hence of little military value. Just north of Florence, Kesselring set up a new defensive line (the "Gothic Line") along the Appenine crest between Pisa and Rimini. His troops held there, unbudgeable, until virtually the last weeks of the war.

The Italian campaign was a needlessly costly sideshow. It wantonly inflicted 188,000 American casualties, as well as 123,000 British, while Kesselring held the peninsula to the end with fewer than twenty divisions, virtually none of them transferred from the eastern front. There in the east, even as Eisenhower had been dickering with Badoglio and

63. Audie Murphy, *To Hell and Back* (New York: Henry Holt, 1949), 125.

while Clark's seven divisions had been preparing to go ashore at Salerno in the summer of 1943, the Red Army had conclusively extinguished the *Wehrmacht's* offensive capability in the cataclysmic battle of Kursk, a colossal clash of four thousand aircraft, six thousand tanks, and two million men.

Stalin's aggravation with his dilatory Western partners was growing ever more pronounced. Roosevelt and Churchill wrestled for days at the Trident Conference over the language of a message that would inform their Soviet ally of their decision to go ahead in Italy and delay the cross-Channel attack until 1944. Stalin responded with cold fury. "Your decision creates exceptional difficulties for the Soviet Union," Stalin wrote to Roosevelt. This latest delay, he said, "leaves the Soviet Army, which is fighting not only for its country, but also for its Allies, to do the job alone, almost single-handed." When, he wondered, would the promised second front ever materialize? "Need I speak of the dishearteningly negative impression that this fresh postponement of the second front and the withholding from our Army, which has sacrificed so much, of the anticipated substantial support by the Anglo-American armies, will produce in the Soviet Union—both among the people and in the Army?"[64]

NORTH AFRICA had been no kind of second front adequate to Stalin's needs. Neither was the brief expedition into Sicily, and surely not the deliberately limited campaign that ground to such a frustrating stalemate in Italy. But at Casablanca the Western allies had also conjured the prospect of another kind of second front altogether—in the air. The Combined Bomber Offensive that Churchill and Roosevelt announced in Morocco was invested with extravagant hopes. Its architects nursed the dream that the novel technology of flying machines had at last brought within their grasp the military equivalent of the Holy Grail: an ultimate weapon, one that would not only win this war but revolutionize the nature of warfare itself.

"Generals always fight the last war," the old adage has it, but the infatuation with air power in World War II gave the lie to that conventional wisdom. The pursuit of winged victory stemmed above all from a conscious determination *not* to refight World War I, a nightmarish, static war of attrition that had annihilated men by the millions. The fascination with air power infected virtually every nation that had been

64. *Stalin's Correspondence with Roosevelt and Truman*, 70–71.

sucked into that earlier conflict. It was driven everywhere by the desperate quest for some means to restore the power of the offensive and foreshorten war's duration. The same quest had propelled innovators in ground combat like Guderian in Germany, Liddell Hart in Britain, DeGaulle in France, and Patton in America to emphasize a mechanized, armored war of mobility, or *Blitzkrieg*. But aerial warfare in particular peculiarly suited the distinctive political, strategic, and economic circumstances of the United States. An unwarlike people living at a great distance from the major theaters of conflict and commanding awesome productive potential took naturally to the idea of a weapon that could be deployed far from American shores, put relatively few Americans in harm's way, and make maximum use of American industrial might and technological know-how.

The principal theorist of war in the air was the Italian Giulio Douhet. His 1921 treatise, *The Command of the Air*, was to the emerging science of combat aloft what Alfred Thayer Mahan's works had been to naval doctrine a generation earlier. Douhet argued that the deadlock on the Italian-Austrian front in World War I could have been broken most efficiently not by applying more force at the points of contact between the two armies along the Isonzo and Piave rivers but by destroying with air attacks the enemy's sources of supply—the arms factories deep inside the Czech provinces of the Austro-Hungarian Empire. Douhet endorsed without scruple the concept that modern warfare was not merely a conflict between uniformed combatants but a total war between entire peoples, in which "the woman loading shells in a factory, the farmer growing wheat, the scientist experimenting in his laboratory" were targets just as legitimate as "the soldier carrying his gun." Douhet envisioned that aerial warfare could be directed against something more than just the physical destruction of the enemy's economic assets. It would prove far easier, he argued, for air power to shatter the morale of civilians at home than of trained troops in the field. Douhet thus helped foster the concept of a "home front," a telling neologism that testifies to the totalizing, all-engulfing implications of warfare in the modern era. "How could a country go on living and working," he asked, "oppressed by the nightmare of imminent destruction and death?"[65]

65. Giulio Douhet, *The Command of the Air*, trans. Dino Ferrari (New York: Coward-McCann, 1942), 196, 22. Douhet more than hinted that the "soldier carrying his gun" was an even *less* legitimate target than civilians. Compared to "a few women and children killed in an air raid," he wrote, "a soldier, a robust young man, should

At the U.S. Army's Air Corps Tactical School in the post–World War I years, Douhet's texts had been required reading. So were the writings of his American counterpart, General Billy Mitchell, whose *Our Air Force* appeared in the same year as *The Command of the Air*. The American air enthusiasts evolved their own version of the doctrine of aerial warfare. Like Douhet, they called for the establishment of an independent air arm, and they championed the idea that air power alone offered the key to military success. In a significant revision of Douhet's thinking, however, they resisted the idea of wholesale assaults on civilian populations, emphasizing instead precision attacks on high-value economic targets like transportation networks, electric power plants, oil supplies, and arms factories. Yet from the outset Douhet's thoughts about the intimidating effects of air attacks on civilian morale shadowed American thinking about aerial war. A 1926 training manual spoke of air power as "a method of imposing will by terrorizing the whole population." A 1930 manual acknowledged the importance of attacks "on civilian populations in the back areas of the hostile country," though it cautioned that such strikes had to be weighed against "the effect upon public opinion," a large consideration in light of the airmen's aspiration to win the public and political approval necessary to establishment as an independent service arm.[66]

Those two very different conceptions of the targeting choices of aerial warfare — economic assets or civilian populations — continued to reside uncomfortably together in AWPD-1, drafted in the context of the Victory Program discussions in late 1941. AWPD-1, the founding document that guided America's air war, declared that the air arm's first objective was the German economy. But "as German morale begins to crack," the document allowed, terror raids on civilians might speed the final collapse. Specifically, AWPD-1 urged that it might be "highly profitable to deliver a large-scale, all-out attack on the civil population of Berlin."[67]

In 1933 the U.S. Army, of which the air arm was then and would through the war be a part, sponsored a design competition to develop the technological means by which the airmen's large ambitions might be realized. The winner was Boeing Model 299. By 1937 Boeing's plane was in production as the B-17, the United States' first weapon designed

---

be considered to have the maximum individual value in the general economy of humanity" (195). The discussion that follows is heavily indebted to Ronald Schaffer's superb study, *Wings of Judgment* (New York: Oxford University Press, 1985).
66. Schaffer, *Wings of Judgment*, 27–28.
67. Schaffer, *Wings of Judgment*, 32–33.

to accomplish a "strategic" mission. Popularly known as the "Flying Fortress," the B-17 lived up to its nickname. Designed to be self-defending, it was heavily armed and armored. The models being produced by the time the United States entered the war bristled with thirteen machine guns. They were intended to be flown in tight formations of a hundred aircraft and more, whose combined firepower could spew out up to thirty tons of .50-caliber machine gun slugs per minute. That deadly curtain of defensive fire was thought sufficient to ward off fighter attacks, while heavy steel plating and bulletproof Plexiglas windows would supposedly protect against antiaircraft fire from the ground. Though the B-17s sacrificed bomb-carrying space to all that defensive capacity, the United States Army Air Forces (USAAF) counted on the "Forts" to penetrate deep into enemy territory, precisely lay down their destructive loads, and fight their way home to bomb again another day.

By the time the Americans entered the war, rough experience had already taught the British that "precision bombing" was extraordinarily difficult and intolerably costly to accomplish. Heavy losses early in the war drove the Royal Air Force to bomb only under the cape of darkness, which badly compromised accuracy. A study in the summer of 1941 concluded that just one in three British bombers managed to get within five miles of its target; in the heavily defended Ruhr, only one in ten. In February 1942, therefore, the Imperial Air Staff directed that British Bomber Command should henceforth focus on destroying "the morale of the enemy civil population and in particular of the industrial workers." The British euphemistically called this new practice "area bombing," but the bald truth was that terror bombing, not precision targeting, was now Britain's official policy.

When the first elements of the USAAF appeared in Britain in the spring of 1942, they shunned the British approach, less for moral reasons than for military and political ones. They believed that scarce resources were best used against high-value targets and that in any case "area bombing" would have a disastrous impact on American public opinion, crippling the airmen's campaign to be recognized as an independent service. USAAF head General Hap Arnold therefore welcomed the Casablanca commitment to "round-the-clock" aerial attacks, with the British continuing area bombing by night and the Americans precision bombing by day. Casablanca was "a major victory," said Arnold, "for we would bomb in accordance with American principles using methods for which our planes were designed."[68]

68. Schaffer, *Wings of Judgment*, 38.

Organized as the Eighth Air Force under General Ira C. Eaker, American heavy bombers flew their first mission of the European war in August 1942.[69] A dozen B-17s, shielded by a swarm of RAF Spitfire fighters, took off from England, bombed railroad marshaling yards near Rouen in France, and returned to base without the loss of a single Fortress. For the remainder of 1942, the handful of American bombers available to Eaker hit targets in France and the Low Countries, rarely venturing beyond the 175-mile combat radius of the protecting Spitfires. By the time of the Casablanca Conference in January 1943, not a single USAAF bomber had yet penetrated German airspace. But by then Eaker had five hundred planes in England. He was eager to carry the attack directly to the *Reich* and to demonstrate that the "self-defending" Flying Fortresses could do the job they were designed to do. On January 27, 1943, just days after the conferees had departed from the subtropical warmth of Casablanca, ninety B-17s lifted off their airfields in the south of England to strike their first blow against Germany. Their target was the submarine construction yards in Vegesack, on the Weser River near Bremen. Bad weather, however, forced their diversion to the less important objective of the North Sea port of Wilhelmshaven. Only fifty-five planes managed to find it. Three did not return. It was scarcely an auspicious beginning.

The theorists of air war had reckoned little with the human factor in their strategic equations. They had also underestimated the cunning of their adversaries. Men went aloft in bulky flying suits that poorly insulated them from temperatures that could fall to fifty below zero at cruising altitudes. Fliers frequently suffered from frostbite and went woozy or even passed out from hypoxia when moisture froze in the tubes of their oxygen masks or when airsickness or fear caused them to vomit into their mouthpieces. Crews often returned with uniforms befouled from long missions that precluded any chance to urinate or defecate. Fear was the aircrew's companion from the moment of takeoff. The difficulty of flying off hundreds of aircraft within minutes of one another, then assembling them in the sky into their huge formations—high, middle, and low squadrons of up to sixteen planes each, endless streams of fully laden bombers laboriously circling upward for nearly three-quarters of an hour to operational altitude—resulted in frequent midair collisions

69. The first American air action in Europe was a joint USAAF-RAF raid on July 4, 1942, against enemy airfields in Holland. The six American crews flew only light bombers, however, and only two of them managed to drop their bombs on the target. The Rouen raid was the first *heavy* bomber attack by the Americans. See Craven and Cate 1:658.

even before the big sky convoys headed across the Channel. Accidents claimed nearly as many airmen's lives (approximately thirty-six thousand) as did combat (approximately forty-nine thousand).[70]

Despite the B-17's legendary defensive power, the Fortresses proved highly vulnerable once they flew beyond the range of fighter escort. Though the sturdy bombers could absorb up to twenty hits from 20mm cannon fire and still keep flying, they were not indestructible. German interceptors soon learned that the bombers' forward turret guns could not be depressed to an angle that adequately covered a head-on attack. Luftwaffe pilots adopted the harrowing tactic of flying a parallel course to the bomber stream, in sight of the traumatized B-17 crews but out of range of their guns. At a point about two miles ahead of the lead planes, the fighters U-turned into the path of the bombers and opened fire at a closing rate of up to six hundred miles per hour. The planes that survived the fighter attacks had ultimately to fly through a preset "box barrage," a flak-saturated section of sky athwart the final approach to the target. The Eighth Air Force in 1943 lost on average 5 percent of its aircraft per mission to accident, destruction in combat, or irreparable damage. Two-thirds of all American airmen in that year did not finish their required tour of twenty-five missions.

In March 1943, pursuant to the dictates of prewar strategic doctrine, USAAF drew up a list of precisely sixty specific targets. Their destruction, the airmen claimed, would "gravely impair and might paralyze the Western Axis war effort."[71] These "strategic" objectives, the supposed Douhetian vital points in the German production machine, conspicuously included oil refineries and ball-bearing plants. To knock them out, USAAF estimated, would require a force of 2,702 heavy bombers and 800 medium bombers. USAAF at the time disposed of fewer than half that many aircraft, but Hap Arnold was determined to get started. Here was the opportunity to deliver on the second-front promise, and not incidentally to vindicate the war-winning claims of the air barons.

In the recently recaptured Libyan desert, squadrons of the Ninth USAAF's B-24 Liberator bombers, the B-17s' longer-range but more balky and less technologically sophisticated teammates, began in the summer

70. *United States Strategic Bombing Survey: Over-All Report, European War* (Washington: USGPO, 1945); Michael Clodfelter, *Warfare and Armed Conflicts: A Statistical Reference to Casualty and Other Figures, 1618–1991* (Jefferson, N.C.: McFarland, 1992), 960.

71. Alan J. Levine, *The Strategic Bombing of Germany, 1940–1945* (Westport, Conn.: Praeger, 1992), 85.

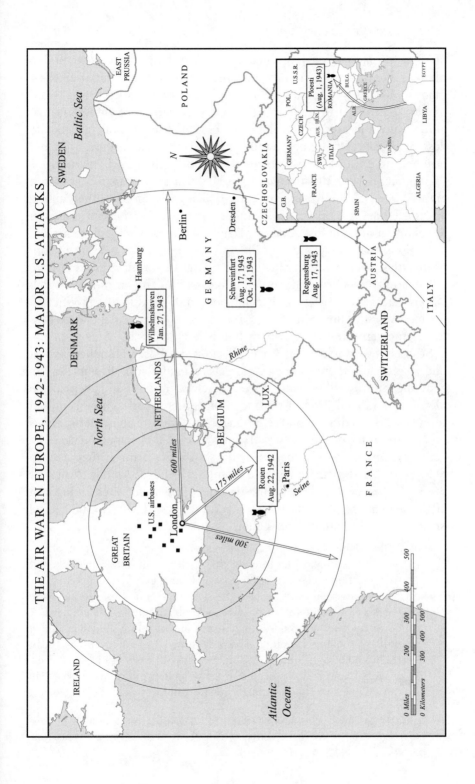

THE AIR WAR IN EUROPE, 1942-1943: MAJOR U.S. ATTACKS

SWEDEN

Baltic Sea

EAST PRUSSIA

POLAND

N

CZECHOSLOVAKIA

Berlin

Dresden

GERMANY

Hamburg

Schweinfurt
Aug. 17, 1943
Oct. 14, 1943

Regensburg
Aug. 17, 1943

Wilhelmshaven
Jan. 27, 1943

DENMARK

AUSTRIA

ITALY

Rhine

SWITZERLAND

NETHERLANDS

North Sea

BELGIUM

LUX.

600 miles

175 miles

Rouen
Aug. 22, 1942

Paris

Seine

U.S. airbases

London

GREAT
BRITAIN

300 miles

FRANCE

IRELAND

Atlantic
Ocean

0 Miles   200   300   400   500
0 Kilometers   300   400   500

Ploesti
(Aug. 1, 1943)

U.S.S.R.

POL.

CZECH.

GERMANY

AUS. HUN.

BULG.

GREECE

ALB.

ROMANIA

EGYPT

G.B.

FRANCE

SWI.

ITALY

SPAIN

TUNISIA

LIBYA

ALGERIA

of 1942 to practice low-level attacks on a mock-up of the great Ruma-
nian refinery complex at Ploesti, which processed a quarter of Germany's oil supply. On August 1, 1943, 177 bomb-laden B-24s, even
trickier than usual to fly because they were overloaded with extra machine guns and auxiliary fuel tanks, took off from Libyan airbases to
destroy Ploesti. No fighters could accompany them on the thirteen-
hundred-mile run. Surprise and mass would be their best defenses.

Approaching the Albanian coast, the lead plane went out of control and
crashed. Dense cloud banks over the Balkans enveloped the remaining
aircraft. Under strict orders to maintain radio silence, the five groups in
the giant air armada lost contact with one another. The badly disrupted
formations finally emerged over Ploesti into a hell-in-the-heavens of confusion, flak, and fighters. Fifty-four B-24s went down, 310 fliers were
killed, and another 150 parachuted into captivity. The burning oil installations that the returning bombers left behind slowed Ploesti's production
for a few months, but by drawing on reserves and forcing slave workers to
make emergency repairs, Germany hardly felt the pinch.

Scarcely two weeks later, Eaker's Eighth Air Force launched a dual
raid against two more "strategic" targets: a fighter-aircraft plant in Regensburg and a ball-bearing works at Schweinfurt—both deep inside
Germany and well beyond the range of fighter escort. Three hundred
seventy-six B-17s droned off the tarmac from various English aerodromes
on the morning of August 17. Twenty-four of the planes on the Regensburg run never returned, nor did thirty-six of those that flew to
Schweinfurt, a 16 percent loss rate. Some six hundred American aircrew
were killed or captured. One flier described the scene after a squadron
of the feared Messerschmitt 109s made their usual U-turn and closed
on the advancing bomber formation:

> [T]he plane shook with the chatter of our guns. . . . As other planes
> were hit, we had to fly through their debris. I instinctively ducked as
> we almost hit an escape hatch from a plane ahead. When a plane blew
> up, we saw their parts all over the sky. We smashed into some of the
> pieces. One plane hit a body which tumbled out of a plane ahead. A
> crewman went out the front hatch of a plane and hit the tail assembly
> of his own plane. No chute. His body turned over and over like a bean
> bag tossed into the air. . . . A German pilot came out of his plane, drew
> his legs into a ball, his head down. Papers flew out of his pockets. He
> did a triple somersault through our formation. No chute.[72]

72. Harry H. Crosby, *A Wing and a Prayer: The "Bloody 100th" Bomb Group of the
    U.S. Eighth Air Force in Action over Europe in World War II* (New York:
    HarperCollins, 1993), 94–95.

Neither raid had achieved success remotely commensurate with the price paid in machines and men. Surviving crews were demoralized by the losses. When they learned at their morning briefing of October 14 that Eaker was sending them back to Schweinfurt, many were gripped by icy dread. Like Ulysses Grant's troops at Cold Harbor, who advanced to all but certain death with papers pinned to their jackets bearing their names and addresses, some fliers returned to their barracks to scrawl a last letter and to don additional clothing, suitable for surviving capture — or for burial. Others piled aboard so much extra .50-caliber ammunition that officers had to order it offloaded to remain within operational weight limits. Three hundred eighty-three Fortresses and a handful of Liberators took off. Too few B-24s made it into the air to compose a formation, so the remainder flew a diversion over the North Sea. Fright, confusion, and chaos thinned the bomber stream to just 291 Fortresses even before the Channel was reached. Two hundred twenty-eight reached Schweinfurt, where they inflicted only minimal damage. There and back, the Germans unleashed a savagely effective combination of antiaircraft fire and fighter attacks, including time-fused bombs dropped from above on the bomber formations. The B-17s vibrated wildly from the firing of their heavy machine guns and bucked when hit by enemy 20mm cannon fire. Sixty Fortresses never made it back, nor did more than six hundred airmen who were killed or captured. Some men too badly wounded to make it home were shoved out in their parachutes, desperately consigned to the mercies of enemy medical personnel. Several shot-up B-17s lowered their wheels, the sign of surrender, as their pilots struggled to get the disabled planes onto the ground, where the crews, if they were lucky, might hope for internment.

Ploesti, Regensburg, and the two Schweinfurt raids consumed nearly two hundred heavy bombers and well over a thousand airmen in a matter of weeks. Faced with such horrendous losses, Eaker grudgingly accepted that his supposedly self-defending bombers fared little better than slow-flying ducks when they ventured into well-defended enemy airspace without fighter escort. He yielded to the inevitable and suspended further deep-penetration raids. For the time being, the American strategic revolution in the air was grounded. And the second front whose promise it held still lay well over the horizon of the future.

ONLY IN THE PACIFIC could Americans seek some consolation at the close of their second year at war, and chill comfort it was. King had succeeded at Casablanca in securing an agreement to allocate 30 percent of the American war effort to the struggle against Japan. In the ensuing weeks he hurried to launch a new offensive campaign in the Central Pacific, not least, as he explained to Nimitz, "so that the British would not back down on their agreements and commitments. We must be so committed in the Central Pacific," he said, "that the British cannot hedge."[73] King had never counted on much from the campaign in the Southwest Pacific, other than to block Japan's advance while awaiting some opportunity to shape an offensive along the lines of the old Orange plans. But by the end of 1943 the outlines of a plan for the defeat of Japan had begun to emerge. It envisioned a powerful thrust into the Central Pacific area, first cracking the outer ring of Japan's far-flung oceanic defensive perimeter in the Gilbert and Marshall islands, then puncturing the inner ring of the Carolines and Marianas. Meanwhile, MacArthur would continue his drive along the north coast of New Guinea toward the Philippines, a stepping-stone to the Chinese coast and Formosa, from which air attacks on the Japanese home islands could be launched.

The first objectives in the Central Pacific campaign were the tiny atolls of Makin and Tarawa in the Gilbert archipelago, necessary as bases to support further jumps into the Marshalls. Tarawa, a three-square-mile dot on the map, about the size of New York City's Central Park, proved an especially bloody affair. Garrisoned by some five thousand Japanese soldiers, Tarawa was encircled by a coral reef, a hazard that landing craft could clear only at high tide. A twenty-minute interval between an ineffectually brief naval bombardment and the first wave of landing ships allowed the Japanese defenders to man their guns just as the assault craft began to hang up on the reef. At least twenty landing vessels crammed with dead and dying marines perched helplessly on the coral outcropping while the gunners ashore raked them with deadly accurate fire. Photographs of dead marines floating in the tide and half-buried in the beaches shocked the American public. But at a cost of some one thousand dead and two thousand wounded, Tarawa was taken, as was Makin. King was at last positioned to push his advance through the Pacific island chains toward Japan: to Kwajelein and Eniwetok in the Marshalls, Truk in the Carolines, then on to the great prize of the Marianas, only two thousand miles from Japan.

Success in the Pacific, however, was small comfort to Stalin. He pointedly reminded Roosevelt that "in the Far East . . . the U.S.S.R. is not in a state of war."[74] In a bitter tirade addressed to Churchill in mid-

73. Spector, 260.
74. *Stalin's Correspondence with Roosevelt and Truman,* 50.

1943, Stalin gave full vent to his accumulated frustrations. Even the woodenness of Soviet diplomatic prose could not mask the old Bolshevik's anger. From the war's outset, he complained, he had been given nothing but a beggar's diet of broken pledges. He rehearsed in detail the long and lamentable record: the empty assurances to Molotov of a second front in 1942; the repeatedly canceled North Atlantic convoys; the several diversions into North Africa, then Sicily, then Italy; Casablanca's hollow promise of a second front in the air; the persistent infatuation of the British with the Mediterranean; and the unceasing attraction of the Americans to their own version of the Mediterranean, in the Pacific. "The point here," Stalin concluded, "is the preservation of [Soviet] confidence in its Allies, a confidence which is being subject to severe stress." The Red Army had sustained millions of casualties, Stalin reminded Churchill, "compared with which the sacrifices of the Anglo-American armies are insignificant." Churchill found the message "very unpleasant" and replied in kind.[75] He worried that the acerbic exchange might terminate his relation with Stalin.

Roosevelt, meanwhile, was casting about on his own for some means to retain what was left of Stalin's rapidly waning confidence. A way had to be found, Secretary of State Cordell Hull said, "to talk Mr. Stalin out of his shell, so to speak, away from his aloofness, secretiveness, and suspiciousness."[76] Roosevelt characteristically sought a face-to-face meeting, a setting in which he could work his legendary charm, man to man. In May 1943 he entrusted his former ambassador to the Soviet Union, Joseph E. Davies, with a personal message to be hand-delivered to Stalin in the Kremlin. It proposed "an informal and completely simple visit for a few days between you and me." No staff should attend, Roosevelt suggested; he would bring only Harry Hopkins, already known to Stalin, as well as an interpreter and a single stenographer. Where to meet? Iceland was approximately equidistant from Moscow and Washington, but Roosevelt wanted to see Stalin alone, and meeting in Iceland "would make it, quite frankly, difficult not to invite Prime Minister Churchill at the same time." One or another side of the Bering Strait seemed the best solution, the president concluded, repeating his hope "that you and I would talk very informally and get what we call "a meeting of the minds.""[77]

Churchill was understandably nervous when he got wind of a possible

75. *Stalin's Correspondence with Roosevelt and Truman*, 74–76; *C&R* 2:285.
76. Cordell Hull, *The Memoirs of Cordell Hull* (New York: Macmillan 1948), 2:1248.
77. *Stalin's Correspondence with Roosevelt and Truman*, 63.

Roosevelt-Stalin meeting from which he would be excluded. Roosevelt awkwardly tried to reassure him with the outright lie that such a meeting had been "Uncle Joe's" idea. Stalin meanwhile refused to travel so far as the Bering Sea. Eventually all three leaders agreed to meet in December in Teheran, the Iranian capital, just beyond the Soviet Union's southern frontier. A preliminary October meeting of foreign ministers in Moscow would help prepare the agenda.

As preparations for the historic encounter at Teheran went forward in the last weeks of 1943, the stresses in the Grand Alliance grew more, not less, pronounced. At another full-dress joint Anglo-American staff conference in Quebec in August 1943, the British nominally reaffirmed their promise to open a second front in France in 1944, but the Americans still had reason to doubt the firmness of Churchill's commitment. On the eve of the Quebec Conference, Henry Stimson had an angry exchange with Churchill in which the prime minister conjured a "Channel full of corpses" if the invasion plans went ahead. Even after Quebec, Harry Hopkins worried out loud to the prime minister's physician and confidante, Lord Moran, about Churchill's steadfastness: "I don't believe he is really converted," Hopkins opined.[78] On the eve of Teheran, at a preliminary British-American gathering in Cairo, Churchill justified Hopkins's skepticism when he once again proposed a still further operation in the Mediterranean, this time to dislodge the Germans from the island of Rhodes. "His Majesty's Government can't have its troops standing idle," Churchill said. "Muskets must flame." An exasperated George Marshall could take no more: "Not one American soldier is going to die on [that] goddamned beach," he replied, with apparent finality. But as events soon revealed, Churchill was not yet done with the Mediterranean.

Even larger anxieties proliferated about Soviet intentions. In midsummer Stalin had withdrawn his ambassadors from both London and Washington. In September came rumors that the Germans had extended a peace feeler to Moscow through Japan, stimulating anew the fear of a separate settlement in eastern Europe before a second front had even opened in the west. One observer detected "an atmosphere alarmingly reminiscent of that which had preceded the Molotov-Ribbentrop Pact of August, 1939."[79] Then, at the Moscow foreign min-

78. Stimson Diary, August 4, 1943; Lord Moran, *Churchill: Taken from the Diaries of Lord Moran: The Struggle for Survival, 1940–1965* (Boston: Houghton Mifflin, 1966), 117.
79. *FRUS* (1943) 3:697; Sherwood, *Roosevelt and Hopkins*, 734.

isters' meeting in October, the Russians baffled and worried the American delegates with their own endorsement of possible further action in the Mediterranean theater, directed at a heavier investment in Italy, or maybe even the Balkans. In early November the U.S. military attaché at the Moscow embassy sent a message to the War Department that Stimson described as "throwing disquiet into our ranks by suggesting that the Russians were not quite so keen about Overlord [the new code name for the cross-Channel attack] as they had been."[80] Perhaps Stalin had at last arrived at the point that many American analysts had anticipated and dreaded, where he no longer needed Western help and in fact preferred that the British and the Americans stay out of Europe altogether. "If Germany collapses before the democracies have been able to make an important military contribution on the continent of Europe," a State Department assessment had warned, "the peoples of Europe will with reason believe that the war was won by the Russians alone. Under such conditions the prestige of the Soviet Union will be so great that it will be difficult for Great Britain and the United States to oppose successfully any line of policy which the Kremlin may choose to adopt."[81]

What might that line of policy be? Unknown to his Allies, Stalin confided something of his intentions to the Yugoslav Communist Josip Broz Tito: "This war is not as in the past," Stalin said. "Whoever occupies a territory also imposes his own social system. Everyone imposes his own system as far as his army can reach. It cannot be otherwise."[82] Successful at Stalingrad and victorious at Kursk, as 1943 ended Stalin's Red Army was about to evict the *Wehrmacht* from the Soviet Union once and for all and was poised to cross the Soviet frontier and enter Europe. William Bullitt had warned Roosevelt some months earlier that Stalin intended to reach "as far west as the Rhine, perhaps even beyond."[83] America's unreadiness, the halting pace of mobilization in the United States, Roosevelt's repeated submission to Churchill's importunings to delay the second front, the distractions of the Mediterranean and the Pacific—all might in the end mean that much of Europe would be lost to the Soviets even before the British and the Americans had a fighting chance to win it back from the Germans.

80. Stimson Diary, November 11, 1943.
81. Stoler, *Politics of the Second Front*, 88.
82. Milovan Djilas, *Conversations with Stalin* (New York: Harcourt, Brace and World, 1962), 114.
83. Stoler, *Politics of the Second Front*, 88.

At Teheran, Roosevelt would at last have his chance to take the measure of the man who seemed on the verge of locking all of Europe within his grasp. Even before America had fully entered the war, the American president would have to begin the process of preparing for the postwar world that was already aborning.

18

The War of Machines

The most important things in this war are machines. . . . The United States . . . is a country of machines.

         —Josef Stalin, Teheran Conference, 1943

"I don't see much future for the Americans," Adolf Hitler crowed to his cronies in the aftermath of the Pearl Harbor attack. "It's a decayed country. And they have their racial problem, and the problem of social inequalities. . . . American society [is] half Judaized, and the other half Negrified. How can one expect a State like that to hold together—a country where everything is built on the dollar." Hitler's foreign minister, Joachim von Ribbentrop, took a more sober view of the possible consequences of American belligerency. He warned Hitler in December 1941: "We have just one year to cut off Russia from her American supplies. . . . If we don't succeed and the munitions potential of the United States joins up with the manpower potential of the Russians, the war will enter a phase in which we shall only be able to win it with difficulty." More than a year earlier Admiral Yamamoto had made the same point to Fumimaro Konoye when he had predicted that Japanese forces would run wild for six months but that he had "utterly no confidence for the second or third year."[1]

Between them, Ribbentrop and Yamamoto illuminated the three fundamental determinants of the war's eventual outcome and hinted at their complex interaction: time, men, and materiel. Time was the Axis

---

1. William L. Shirer, *The Rise and Fall of the Third Reich* (New York: Simon and Schuster, 1960), 895n.; David Irving, *Hitler's War* (New York: Viking, 1977), 354; *Reports of General MacArthur: Japanese Operations in the Southwest Pacific Area* 2, pt. 1 (Washington: USGPO, 1966), 33, n. 14.

powers' most threatening enemy. By the same token, time was the fourth and most potent partner in the Grand Alliance. Germany and Japan alike pinned their hopes for victory on a short war. Both powers had formulated their strategies and composed their force structures on that premise. Hitler built the *Wehrmacht*'s highly mechanized but relatively small panzer force for *Blitzkrieg* warfare, a concept whose essential logic was to rob the enemy of time, to win quick victories before his adversaries could marshal their resources, before they could force the painful burdens of full economic mobilization upon Germany and turn the war into the kind of prolonged battle of attrition that had ground down the kaiser's regime in 1918. Japan, because it was far less well economically endowed than Germany, had for similar but even more compelling reasons starved its other services in the 1930s to assemble a sophisticated naval air spearhead that it counted upon to deliver a one-punch knockout blow, as it had tried to do at Pearl Harbor. If that first strike failed to fell the Americans in the war's opening round, disaster loomed. Japan was even less prepared than Germany to endure sustained counterpunching from an enemy with practically boundless industrial potential.

Hence the crucial role of men — especially Russians, the hard-used masses of Soviet soldiery that stopped the *Wehrmacht* in front of Moscow in late 1941 and snuffed out the German offensive at the cruel pivot of Stalingrad a year later. The staggering Soviet sacrifices of men — more than three million lost to wounds, death, or capture in 1941 alone — bought in turn the precious, crucial asset of time, time for the Americans to amass the arms and machines that could clinch Allied victory. With the Russians battered but still holding the field, Allied hopes now squarely rested, said Britain's Lord Beaverbrook, on "the immense possibilities of American industry."[2] Yet as 1942 opened, those possibilities were not yet realities. Could the Americans grasp the opportunity that the Russians had given them? And could they do it in time to make a difference?

Even in its weakened Depression state, the American economy was a fearsome, if slumbering, behemoth. In 1938, the last full peacetime year and a year in which the pinch of the Roosevelt Recession especially dampened American production, national income in the United States was nevertheless nearly double the combined national incomes of Germany, Japan, and Italy. In that same Depression year, American steel

2. Richard Polenberg, *War and Society: The United States, 1941–1945* (Philadelphia: Lippincott, 1972), 221.

output dwarfed Germany's, and American coal miners hauled up out of the earth almost twice the tonnage of their German counterparts. Automobile manufacturing, the characteristic twentieth-century high-mass-production industry and a crucial contributor to military success in the age of mechanized warfare, spectacularly illustrated the wildly asymmetric advantage in economic resources that America wielded. American carmakers turned out 4.8 million automobiles in 1937; in the same year Germany produced 331,000 cars; Japan, just 26,000.[3]

America enjoyed other advantages too. Somewhat paradoxically, the Great Depression itself was one of them, as comparison with the First World War suggests. The United States had entered that earlier war in 1917 with a fully employed civilian economy. Raising an army from the ranks of already employed workers and converting factories and forges from civilian to military production were consequently slow and tortured processes that never did come to complete fruition. The United States mustered only a two-million-man American Expeditionary Force and managed to field it in France only at the very end of 1918; the British and the French meanwhile supplied the great bulk of the its ships, planes, and artillery. But in 1940, after more than a decade of depression, the situation was different. Nearly nine million workers were out of work at the time of the fall of France, and even as late as the Pearl Harbor attack three million were still unemployed. Vast reservoirs of physical productive capacity also lay unused, including factories, heavy construction equipment, machine-tool stocks, electrical generating plants, trucks, locomotives, and railcars. Average plant utilization was about forty hours a week. As much as 50 percent of capacity stood idle in automobile manufacturing plants alone. As the war crisis now snapped the drooping American economy to attention, all those dormant resources could be swiftly directed to martial purposes with minimal disruption to the fabric of peacetime life. In that sense, not only did the war rescue the American economy from the Depression; no less significant, the Depression had in turn poised the economy for phenomenally rapid conversion to war production. What was more, the United States commanded a virtually self-sufficient continental economy, and the huge American industrial heartland rested safely distant from the threat

3. Harold G. Vatter, *The U.S. Economy in World War II* (New York: Columbia University Press, 1985), 15; Alan S. Milward, *War, Economy, and Society, 1939–1945* (Berkeley: University of California Press, 1979), 49; Richard Overy, *Why the Allies Won* (New York: Norton, 1995), 224.

of invasion or bombing. Alone among the belligerent states, the United States was an abundantly endowed and uniquely privileged sanctuary where economic mobilization could proceed free from most supply problems, safe from enemy harassment, and therefore with maximum efficiency. The country where Hitler thought everything was built on the dollar was thus capable, at least in theory, of an astonishing demonstration of just how many weapons the dollar could build, and how swiftly. Could the Americans pull it off?

"It will not be sufficient for us and the other United Nations to produce a slightly superior supply of munitions to that of Germany, Japan, Italy," Roosevelt told Congress in January 1942. "The superiority of the United Nations in munitions and ships must be overwhelming ... a crushing superiority of equipment in any theater of the world war." Roosevelt went on to set breathtakingly ambitious production goals: 60,000 aircraft in 1942 and 125,000 more in 1943; 120,000 tanks in the same period; 55,000 antiaircraft guns; 16 million deadweight tons of merchant shipping. At the same time, he warned that at some point civilian consumption might have to yield to the need for military production. That moment might be closer than many people realized. "I was a bit appalled," he told reporters as 1942 opened, to learn "that so much of our production was still going into civilian use."[4]

Donald Nelson, head of one of the principal mobilization agencies, was not the only person who was "startled and alarmed" when he heard Roosevelt's numbers. "He staggered us," Nelson recalled. "None of our production people thought that this volume was possible.... We thought that the goals set by the President were out of the question." Nelson was especially anxious about the threat the military program posed to civilian standards of living. Yet there was a deep strategic logic in what Nelson thought were Roosevelt's "awesome" plans for military production. Part of that logic lay in the realm of psychological warfare. "I believe these figures will tell our enemies what they are up against," Roosevelt said. The Germans and the Japanese would be intimidated by a truly monstrous vision of the nightmarish war of economies that they most feared. Just for that reason, the president explained to a skeptical Nelson, "I want to make the figures public."[5]

4. *PPA* (1942), 7, 36–37, 22. I have combined remarks from Roosevelt's annual budget message of January 5, his State of the Union address on the following day, and his press conference of the same date.
5. Donald M. Nelson, *Arsenal of Democracy: The Story of American War Production* (New York: Harcourt, Brace, 1946), 185–87.

The president's call for "crushing superiority of equipment" had a deeper rationale still, one that stemmed from a shrewd calculation of America's comparative advantage in modern warfare and of the political dangers and economic opportunities that American belligerency posed on the home front. Thanks to the dispensations of timing and geography, the United States could choose to fight a war of machines rather than men. Substituting material production and technology for manpower had been the essence of the "arsenal of democracy" or short-of-war strategy during the neutrality period. That same strategic doctrine continued to resonate vibrantly in American planning even after Pearl Harbor. Expending motors and metal rather than flesh and blood was the least-cost pathway that the Americans could take toward victory. It was the route that would claim the smallest toll in American lives, by leaving most of the battlefield fighting to others while Americans toiled on the production lines. It would run the lowest risk of alienating public commitment to the war effort. It was a pathway that opened naturally in front of a president who had struggled for years to convince a skeptical public of its stake in the international order and who worried even now that if he asked his countrymen to bear too great a burden of sacrifice he might trigger a sharp isolationist backlash. The strategy of "overwhelming" material superiority also opened a road that led beyond military victory to other especially alluring destinations: an end to the Depression, the revitalization of the American economy, and the positioning of the United States for the exercise of unprecedented international economic power at the war's conclusion. That vision may not have been fully formed in Roosevelt's mind in early 1942, but it was consistent with his policies in the neutrality period, and its possibilities were latent both in the military strategy he adopted and in the mobilization program he outlined. In time the full implications of this peculiarly American way of war would be much more clearly visible. Nineteen forty-two was thus a year that swung like a gate to the future. The choices made then would deeply affect the course of the fighting, the shape of American society both during and after the war, and the fate of the wider postwar world.

JUST AS THE NEW DEAL had to invent the apparatus of the modern American state in the midst of the Depression crisis, so Roosevelt now had to cobble a war administration out of the patchwork mobilization machinery slapped together during the period of American neutrality. The pathetic inadequacy of the Office of Production Management for orchestrating the kind of robust military economy that Roosevelt envisioned was vividly illustrated on January 5, 1942, when OPM head William Knudsen gathered a roomful of businessmen, recited a list of needed military items, and asked for volunteers to produce them.[6] Yet even now the daunting logistical complexities of mobilizing a multibillion-dollar economy, the ticklish political difficulties of reconciling all the interested parties, and Roosevelt's penchant for administrative profligacy all contributed to the creation of a notably ramshackle, poorly articulated array of mobilization agencies with overlapping and sometimes conflicting missions. Mimicking the administrative proliferation of the New Deal, a bewildering host of new war bureaucracies sprang into being. The National War Labor Board (NWLB), with power to impose binding arbitration and even to request federal seizure of struck plants, replaced the National Defense Mediation Board in January 1942. The War Manpower Commission appeared in April 1942, a new agency charged with allocating workers between civilian and military demands but effectively denied any voice either in labor relations, the province of the NWLB, or in occupational deferments, whose assignment remained the prerogative of the semiautonomous Selective Service System. The Supply Priorities and Allocation Board, as well as the hapless Office of Production Management, disappeared into the War Production Board (WPB), created in January 1942 and headed by former Sears, Roebuck executive Donald Nelson.

Nelson was amiable, slow-moving, and conciliatory. He had worked at Sears for thirty years, rising to the chairmanship of the giant retailer's executive committee. He liked to brag to reporters that in his day he had edited the largest-circulation publication in America—the Sears, Roebuck catalogue. He was also a dedicated public servant and a favorite of the New Dealers, "the one leading businessman," said the journalist I. F. Stone, "prepared to uphold the rights of labor . . . bargaining as firmly in buying for his country as he would have in buying for his company."[7]

In theory the WPB was to be a commanding superagency, loosely modeled on the War Industries Board of World War I. But in practice Nelson's powers were far less formidable than they appeared on paper (as had in fact been the case with the WIB in the earlier war). His mandate did not extend to labor and manpower issues. The Office of

6. Alan Clive, *State of War: Michigan in World War II* (Ann Arbor: University of Michigan Press, 1979), 25.

7. David Brinkley, *Washington Goes to War* (New York: Knopf, 1988), 68.

Price Administration (OPA) retained authority over prices. Most telling, the old military and naval purchasing bureaus—the Army Service Forces, the Army Air Forces, the U.S. Maritime Commission (which contracted for cargo ships), and several navy agencies under the Office of Procurement and Material—refused to relinquish the power to place contracts.

These jerry-built arrangements had far-reaching consequences. The WPB was supposedly a civilian agency, and Nelson fancied himself the civilians' advocate, a friend of the consumers he had long served at Sears and a patron of both labor and small business. But the retention of final contracting authority by the army and navy naturally left preponderant power in the hands of the military. The mild-mannered Nelson proved no match for the single-minded warriors devoted to brassing through the military's production program. Army Undersecretary Robert Patterson sported a belt stripped from the body of a German soldier he had killed in 1918. He took his leisure on a seventy-acre farm directly across the Hudson River from West Point, where he was a frequent and reverential visitor. Patterson was not the sort of man who was likely to knuckle under to the pipe-smoking, pencil-pushing, former mail-order salesman at the WPB. Lieutenant General Brehon B. Somervell, the no-nonsense, spit-and-polish professional soldier who ran the Army Service Forces, was cut from the same cloth as Patterson. A decorated hero of the Battle of the Meuse-Argonne in 1918, he was a man in whom organizational genius and Olympian arrogance were mixed in equal measure. In Somervell's view, all the civilian war agencies amounted to nothing more nor less than an effort by "Henry Wallace and the leftists to take over the country."[8]

Military procurement officers understandably preferred to deal with familiar, reliable large manufacturers. A pattern quickly emerged whereby the very largest corporations, including Ford, U.S. Steel, General Electric, and DuPont, garnered the lion's share of military contracts. General Motors alone supplied one-tenth of all American war production. More than two-thirds of prime military contracts went to just one hundred firms. The thirty-three largest corporations accounted for half of all military contracting.[9] In June 1942 Congress tried to buck that trend by establishing the Small War Plants Corporation (SWPC) to

8. Polenberg, *War and Society*, 220.
9. R. Elberton Smith, *The Army and Economic Mobilization* (Washington: Department of the Army, 1959), passim; see also Vatter, *U.S. Economy in World War II*, 60, and Polenberg, *War and Society*, 219.

provide working capital to small businesses and otherwise facilitate their efforts to land military contracts. But the SWPC made little headway in the face of Somervell's adamant insistence that "all the small plants of the country could not turn out one day's requirements of ammunition." The war thus made the nation's biggest corporations bigger, and considerably richer as well. The pattern of military contracting intensified the tendency toward oligopoly in large sectors of American industry. Firms with fewer than one hundred employees accounted for 26 percent of total manufacturing employment in 1939 but only 19 percent by the war's end. After-tax corporate profits fattened — from $6.4 billion in 1940 to nearly $11 billion in 1944. None of this troubled the military authorities. "If you are going to try to go to war, or to prepare for war, in a capitalist country," Henry Stimson reflected, "you have got to let business make money out of the process or business won't work." Robert Patterson brushed aside criticism of the War Department's pro–big business policies with the bland statement that "we had to take industrial America as we found it." The historian Richard Polenberg wryly observes that "he might have added that they by no means left industrial America as they found it." At war's end, when some $17 billion of government-financed plant and equipment was sold at distress prices, two-thirds of it ended up in the hands of just eighty-seven companies.[10]

After months of trial and error, by the end of 1942 the government had hammered out a set of policies to lever the economy onto a war footing. There were elements of command and coercion in the methods used, and occasional examples of outright government fiat, but for the most part the administration tried when it could to brandish the carrot, not the stick — to rely on voluntary methods, on tax inducements, financial enticements, and market mechanisms rather than on the naked fist of government power. When that fist had to be bared, it was usually as far "upstream" in the production process as possible — by creating incentives in the tax codes and setting raw materials allocations and transportation priorities, for example, rather than commandeering shops or railroads. On occasion the government did resort to outright seizure of industrial and transportation facilities, but always temporarily and only when driven by extreme emergencies. In this, war mobilization resembled the New Deal itself, which despite its occasional *diktats* preferred whenever possible to work by indirection and by artful tinkering, by

10. Vatter, *U.S. Economy in World War II*, 59, 61, 65; Stimson Diary, August 26, 1940; Polenberg, *War and Society*, 13, 219.

ingenious commingling of the private and public realms rather than by roughly closing the hand of state power over the free market.

There was, however, one enormous difference between the economic policies of the New Deal and those of the war administration. The highest objectives of the former had been economic security and social equity—stability, not expansion. The overriding goals of the latter were production and more production—expansion, not stability. The result was far more direct government intrusion in the marketplace in wartime than the New Deal had ever attempted, but also the creation of a business-friendly economic climate unimaginable in the confrontational days of the 1930s. To many veteran New Dealers, such as Harold Ickes, Leon Henderson, and Eleanor Roosevelt, it seemed that the Depression decade's reform spirit was among the first casualties of the war.

Tax legislation passed in 1940, for example, began to fuel the engines of the war economy and provided a kind of template for wartime policies by relying on incentives, not compulsion, to nudge the nation's industries onto a war basis. The law aimed to stimulate industrial retooling for military production by allowing the full amortization of investment in war-related plant and equipment over just five years, a provision that sheltered otherwise taxable profits. To some observers that simple but powerful device seemed unconscionably generous to business. "This is abandoning advanced New Deal ground with a vengeance," Harold Ickes railed to his diary. "It seems to me intolerable to allow private people to use public capital in order to make a guaranteed profit for themselves."[11] If the new tax law offended New Deal sensibilities, worse was yet to come. When tax-advantaged private capital was not forthcoming, the Reconstruction Finance Corporation stood ready to provide government loans for needed plant expansion. As a further emolument, Roosevelt ordered the Justice Department to relax antitrust prosecutions. In perhaps the sweetest deal of all, military procurement agencies let contracts on a cost-plus basis, providing iron-clad guarantees of profits beyond the most avaricious monopolist's dreams.

Money for defense was no problem. If anything, the government's principal worry in wartime was not too little money but too much. Fighting inflation, not finding funds, became the principal task. One obvious way to close the so-called inflationary gap in World War II was to ration certain commodities and to impose a legal limit on both wage and price increases, but that was predictably a messy business, fraught with politi-

11. Ickes Diary 3:295, 210.

cal and administrative difficulties. Another and much simpler method, though not without its own political liabilities, was to confiscate excess personal income through taxation or to sterilize it for the duration of the war through a forced-saving program. The Roosevelt administration employed a mix of all those methods, but it adopted voluntary means when possible and tried to the extent it could to take the sting out of those unavoidably coercive measures that it was compelled to adopt, such as stiffer taxation policies.

The Revenue Act of 1942 provided for some $7 billion in new individual income taxes, a near doubling of the federal tax burden. The act filled the treasury's vaults and soaked up at least some potentially inflationary purchasing power. It also permanently revolutionized the American tax system. Up to the eve of the war no more than four million Americans had been required to file tax returns. All those with incomes below the basic exemption level of fifteen hundred dollars (a heavy majority of wage-earners, as median wage income was only $1,231 in 1939) had paid nothing. Depending on marital and family status, those with incomes up to four thousand dollars (some 70 percent of all households fell below that level in the 1930s) had been liable to federal income taxation, but at a rate no higher than 4 percent. Despite the alleged fiscal promiscuity of the New Deal, to all but a plutocratic few Americans the prewar federal tax system was an utter irrelevancy, or at most a decidedly minor nuisance. All that now changed, forever. By lowering the personal exemption to $624, the 1942 law immediately brought thirteen million new taxpayers into the system. Mushrooming employment rolls and rising incomes soon caught millions more in the tax net. By war's end, 42.6 million Americans paid personal income taxes, at rates ranging from 6 to 94 percent. In the aggregate, individuals for the first time now paid more in income taxes than did corporations, a pattern that held and even deepened in the postwar years. And as of 1943 they paid at work, thanks to a new withholding system whereby employers became tax collectors and deducted taxes from paychecks—another feature of the wartime tax regime that became a permanent part of America's remarkably compliant "taxpayer culture."[12]

12. The discussion of the Revenue Act of 1942 is based primarily on W. Elliot Brownlee, "Tax Regimes, National Crisis, and State-building in America," and Carolyn C. Jones, "Mass-Based Income Taxation: Creating a Taxpayer Culture, 1940–1952," both in Brownlee, ed., *Funding the Modern American State* (New York: Woodrow Wilson Center and Cambridge University Press, 1996), 37–104 and 107–147 respectively; on Sidney Ratner, *Taxation and Democracy in America*, rev. ed. (New York: Science Edi-

The administration took several steps to ease the pain of these un-accustomed levies. To avoid a double tax bite when the new withholding system went into effect in 1943, it forgave most taxes due for 1942.[13] It appealed to patriotism with a specially commissioned Irving Berlin jin-gle, "I Paid My Income Tax Today," broadcast endlessly from hundreds of radio stations:

> You see those bombers in the sky
> Rockefeller helped build them and so did I
> I paid my income tax today.[14]

Despite such patriotic emotion, and despite the unimpeachable soundness of the principle of paying for as much of the war as possible out of current taxation, the country stoutly resisted any further tax in-creases. When Roosevelt sought $10.5 billion in additional tax revenues in 1943, Congress presented him with legislation that raised only $2 billion. The Revenue Act of 1943 also contained so many benefits tar-geted on special interests that Roosevelt issued a stinging veto. He con-demned the bill as "not a tax bill but a tax relief bill, providing relief not for the needy but for the greedy."[15] Congress passed the bill over the president's veto—the first time in American history that a revenue law was enacted without presidential approval, and one of several times in the war that Congress overrode the president's will.

In the end, the United States covered about 45 percent of the $304 billion cost of the war out of current taxation. That was a far higher percentage than in either the Civil War or World War I but markedly lower than the comparable figures in England (53 percent), Canada (55 percent), or Germany (48 percent).[16] Borrowing paid the remainder of

---

tions, 1967); John R. Craf, A Survey of the American Economy, 1940–1946 (New York: North River, 1947); and on HSUS, 303, 1107.

13. The new withholding system created a problem; through 1942 the handful of federal taxpayers were always one year in arrears in their tax obligation—paying in 1942, for example, the taxes due on their 1941 incomes. Withholding would keep tax payments current and smooth the flow of revenues into the treasury, but it meant that when the new payroll-deduction system was first implemented in 1943 taxpayers would be simultaneously liable for their new and higher 1943 taxes as well as their 1942 obligation. The solution was a onetime forgiveness of all 1942 taxes under fifty dollars and of 75 percent of any amount over that. That ingenious scheme's prin-cipal architect, New York financier Beardsley Ruml, said that his plan would simply move the tax clock forward, with no fiscal consequence "until the day of Judgment, and at that date no one will give a damn." Polenberg, War and Society, 28.

14. Jones, "Mass-Based Income Taxation," 122.

15. PPA (1944–45), 80.

16. Milward, War, Economy, and Society, 107.

the war bill. Some government officials, remembering the hysteria and intimidation that accompanied World War I–era bond sales campaigns, favored a forced-saving plan through compulsory bond purchases, but Roosevelt and Treasury Secretary Morgenthau characteristically preferred a voluntary program. Morgenthau especially favored small-denomination Series E bonds, registered in the bearer's name and therefore replaceable if lost (an important feature in the frantically mobile society that was wartime America). Like taxes, bond sales both provided the treasury with revenue and soaked up purchasing power, helping to keep inflation in check. Morgenthau saw still further virtues in bonds. There were to be "no quotas . . . no hysteria . . . no appeal to hate or fear," Morgenthau directed, but he nevertheless insisted that selling bonds could be used "to sell the war, rather than vice-versa." He envisioned mass bond-sales campaigns as "the spearhead for getting people interested in the war," occasions for patriotic displays that would stamp out isolationist indifference and "make the country war-minded." Artists and entertainers from the concert violinist Yehudi Menuhin to the movie star Betty Grable pitched in to peddle bonds and in the process peddle the war. From a strictly financial point of view, the results were mixed. Wartime government borrowing added up to nearly $200 billion, but only about a quarter of that came out of the pockets of individual bond buyers. The rest came from the vaults of banks and other financial institutions, which held billions of dollars' worth of monetizable government paper at war's end, helping to set the stage for an explosive postwar increase in the money supply. Commercial banks alone increased their holdings of Treasuries from less than $1 billion in 1941 to more than $24 billion in 1945.[17]

As MONEY BEGAN to pour into the treasury, contracts began to flood out of the military purchasing bureaus — over $100 billion worth in the first six months of 1942, a stupefying sum that exceeded the value of the entire nation's output in 1941. Straining to meet the ambitious goals the president had set, procurement officers loosed their imaginations, abandoned any vestige of managerial discipline, and lost all sight of the larger context within which they were operating. Military purchase orders became hunting licenses, unleashing a jostling frenzy of

17. John Morton Blum, V Was for Victory: Politics and American Culture during World War II (New York: Harcourt Brace Jovanovich, 1976), 16–21; Vatter, U.S. Economy in World War II, 107–9.

competition for materials and labor in the jungle of the marketplace. Contractors ran riot in a cutthroat scramble for scarce resources. Makers of cargo vessels gobbled up steel supplies, snarling the construction of warships. Naval purchasing agents robbed aircraft assembly plants of aluminum. Locomotive foundries converted to tank production when locomotives were far more urgently needed. When construction was not stalled outright, it could end up uselessly squandered. A manufacturer who contracted to make a hundred thousand trucks, for example, might be able to deliver twenty-five thousand completed vehicles, but because aircraft and tank plants expropriated tires and spark plugs, the remaining seventy-five thousand trucks sat unfinished and unuseable, having meanwhile wastefully consumed and criminally idled millions of tons of steel that could have built dozens of cargo ships or made billions of bullets. At the same time, troops in training were throwing rocks in the grenade course and using firecrackers to simulate the scarce live ammunition that had to be carefully husbanded for the battlefield.[18]

Economists working under Simon Kuznets at the WPB labored over the summer of 1942 to breathe some realism into the helter-skelter armament program. Kuznets's 140-page report, recommending significant cutbacks and slowdowns in military purchases, landed on General Somervell's desk late on the Saturday afternoon of September 8, 1942, igniting the so-called Feasibility Dispute. His predictable wrath no doubt exacerbated by the hour and day of the report's arrival, Somervell erupted in rage. In a handwritten response to the WPB, he sneered that the economists' analysis was nothing but "an inchoate mass of words" that should be "carefully hidden from the eyes of thoughtful men." Kuznets fired back that Somervell was "adopting an ostrich-like attitude when goals are established that are above probability of achievement." Portions of Kuznets's letter became public when the columnist Drew Pearson began to bruit the confrontation as a fight to the finish between civilian and military officials. There was no denying the menace that a runaway military procurement program posed to civilian standards of living. The army alone was placing orders for a quarter-billion pairs of trousers, 250 million pairs of underwear, and half a billion socks. By one estimate, fulfilling all the army and navy orders would cut civilian

18. John E. Brigante, *The Feasibility Dispute: Determination of War Production Objectives for 1942 and 1943* (Washington: Committee on Public Administration Cases, 1950), 35. See also Bureau of the Budget, *The United States at War* (Washington: USGPO, 1946), 113–14, and Eliot Janeway, *The Struggle for Survival* (New Haven: Yale University Press, 1951), 308–9.

consumption to 60 percent of its level in 1932, the darkest year of the Depression. Vice-President Henry Wallace was not alone in wondering if "the public could be brought to accept such a reduction."[19]

The showdown came in Nelson's office on October 6, 1942. Wallace and OPA chief Leon Henderson squared off for the civilians against Patterson and Somervell for the military. Tempers flared and bitter words flew. "If we can't wage war on 90 billions," Henderson snapped, "we ought to get rid of our present Joint Chiefs, and find some who can." In the end, it was Henderson who got the sack. He resigned in December, to the acute distress of the New Deal faithful, the victim both of his clash with the generals and of the inevitable unpopularity he accrued as director of the price-control program. I. F. Stone lamented that Henderson's departure marked "the second phase of the New Deal retreat, as the alliance with big business in May 1940 marked the first."[20] But if the WPB civilians lost one of their paladins, they nevertheless won some kind of victory. At the end of 1942 the Joint Chiefs agreed to shrink their purchasing program by $13 billion and to extend production schedules for many items. The ground forces bore most of the reduction. Their projected numbers were cut by three hundred thousand, and their scheduled shift to full live-ammunition training was delayed.[21]

The Feasibility Dispute defined a major turning point in the war mobilization program. Eventually, it also helped to underwrite a redefinition of American military strategy. The controversy had forced recognition of the fact that even the enormous American economy was not exempt from the laws of scarcity and the iron necessity of choice. The dispute's resolution fostered a new mechanism for allotting scarce raw materials: the Controlled Materials Plan, announced in November 1942. Instead of allowing each individual contractor to shop willy-nilly for critical materials, bidding up prices and creating production logjams, the new plan gave the major government contracting agencies the power to allocate the key metals of copper, aluminum, and steel to their suppliers. The WPB itself was to arbitrate competing claims among those major purchasing agencies. This new scheme brought a measure of order to economic mobilization. It also further advantaged the largest contractors, the favorites of the military and naval bureaus, by making

19. Brigante, *Feasibility Dispute*, 83–86; Polenberg, *War and Society*, 223.
20. Doris Kearns Goodwin, *No Ordinary Time: Franklin and Eleanor Roosevelt: The Home Front in World War II* (New York: Simon and Schuster, 1994), 395.
21. Brigante, *Feasibility Dispute*, 83–86, 105; Smith, *Army and Economic Mobilization*, 156.

it more difficult than ever for small producers to gain access to needed materials in the open market. The Controlled Materials Plan also concentrated the tough questions about trade-offs at the highest political level, where they could be dealt with more expeditiously and efficiently, though scarcely less urgently, than in the hugger-mugger of the marketplace. Just for that reason, the WPB found itself under excruciating pressure as the cockpit where all the controversies between the various services, between the services and the civilians, and between competing economic sectors, were bitterly contested.

Roosevelt characteristically reacted to the rising pressure on the WPB in October 1942 by creating yet another mobilization body, the Office of Economic Stabilization, which officially metamorphosed into the Office of War Mobilization (OWM) in May 1943. Each was headed in its turn by former South Carolina senator and Supreme Court justice James Byrnes. In a blunt demonstration of the president's sometimes callous administrative techniques, Nelson learned of Byrnes's initial appointment from the news ticker in his WPB office and assumed he was being fired. Nelson in fact lingered on at the WPB until the summer of 1944, when he went down at last in yet another confrontation with the generals, this time over the scheduling of reconversion to civilian production.

With the appointment of Byrnes, Roosevelt openly acknowledged the political dimension of economic mobilization. The crooked timber of humanity, not scarce critical materials, was now recognized as the principal obstacle to efficient production. Byrnes was no businessman. He had neither executive experience nor technical expertise. But he was a consummate political operator. He had begun his long Washington career as a protégé of Pitchfork Ben Tillman, South Carolina's infamously racist baron, and he enjoyed the lavish patronage of his sometime fellow South Carolinian, Bernard Baruch, the Democratic Party's multimillionaire gray eminence. Elected to the House in 1910 and the Senate in 1930, Byrnes had fully mastered the ways of the capital by the time of Roosevelt's assumption of the presidency and had made himself into an indispensable lieutenant for Roosevelt's New Deal. A man of slight build and cool blue-gray eyes, he dominated other men with his hypnotically penetrating gaze. Cocking his head birdlike to one side when he spoke, he had for nearly a decade worked the corridors and offices of the Senate on Roosevelt's behalf, skillfully ringmastering his skeptical southern colleagues in support of the president's reform program. His reward was appointment to the Supreme Court in 1941, but after little more than a year in what the restless Byrnes regarded as the "marble mausoleum" atop Capitol Hill he now left the bench and set up shop as the supreme war mobilizer in the new east wing of the White House. The location of his office served as a potent reminder, in the words of a biographer, "that he was in the presidential, rather than the bureaucratic, business." "Your decision is my decision," Roosevelt told him. "[T]here is no appeal. For all practical purposes you will be assistant president" — a soubriquet by which Byrnes was soon familiarly known.[22] Though the WPB endured, its influence waned as Byrnes turned his east-wing office into the real command center of the mobilization effort. By mid-1943 Byrnes had his hands securely on the big levers of economic and political power. Nearly four years after the German invasion of Poland, and a year and a half after Pearl Harbor, America's mobilization machinery was at last complete.

The Feasibility Dispute that brought Byrnes to the pinnacle of power along the Potomac converged with two other developments in late 1942, one along the Seine in northern France and the other on the frozen banks of the Volga, deep within the Soviet Union. Together these events changed the very nature of the mobilization program over which "assistant president" Byrnes now presided. On August 17, 1942, the U.S. Army's Eighth Air Force carried out its first heavy bomber raid on continental Europe. A squadron of a dozen B-17s attacked railroad marshaling yards near Rouen on the lower Seine River. Their bombs caused minimal damage, but the very appearance of American planes in the air over Nazi-held Europe further fed the already ravening ambitions of the advocates of aerial warfare. The second development, far more immediately consequential, was the Battle of Stalingrad, a savage four-month ordeal that slaughtered tens of thousands of German and Soviet troops before the exhausted Germans surrendered at last in February 1943. As much as any single battle could be, Stalingrad was the turning point of Hitler's war. It broke the back of the *Wehrmacht*'s eighteen-month-old Russian offensive and allowed the Soviets to seize the initiative. Stalingrad did not allay all anxieties about Russia's ultimate military and political goals, but it forever laid to rest doubts about Russia's ability to survive. In the highest reaches of the American government, Stalingrad also helped to clinch a crucial strategic decision.

Driving the maniacal frenzy of the first year's mobilization effort were

22. David Robertson, *Sly and Able: A Political Biography of James F. Byrnes* (New York: Norton, 1994), 323.

THE WAR OF MACHINES

the assumptions of the Victory Program of 1941. It had envisioned a Russian collapse and the consequent need to build a mammoth American ground force of 215 divisions. The practical limits on American production that the Feasibility Dispute laid bare, combined with Rouen's fragile promise of a successful air war and Stalingrad's convincing demonstration of Russian staying power, now prompted a thorough rethinking of the Victory Program's premises. Army planners in late 1942 began to scale back their estimates of future troop needs—first to one hundred divisions, then to ninety, a number that by the summer of 1943 was firmly ratified as the uppermost limit of the army's needs. "The strategic basis for this conclusion," writes official army historian Maurice Matloff, "was in part the demonstration by the Soviet armies of their ability to check the German advance. Another significant factor brightening the strategic picture was the improving prospect of gaining air superiority over the Continent. These developments finally made obsolete the initial Victory Program estimates of 1941." The economic basis for that conclusion was the sense of economic limits that the Feasibility Dispute had imposed. With the so-called Ninety-Division Gamble the logic of Roosevelt's "arsenal of democracy" strategy had fully matured. American military planners now irrevocably embraced the concept of a war of machines rather than men. As Matloff writes, the Ninety-Division Gamble cemented into place the core American strategic principle that until the end of 1942 had been hopefully but still somewhat tentatively held: "that the single greatest tangible asset the United States brought to the coalition in World War II was the productive capacity of its industry." The United States now aimed not to field a numerically overwhelming land force but a relatively small one. That force would count for its battle weight not on masses of manpower but on maximum possible mechanization and mobility. Building a smaller army would be compensated by the construction of a gigantic, heavy-fisted air arm: bombers in fantastic numbers that would ultimately carry bombs of unimaginable destructive power.[23]

THE NINETY-DIVISION DECISION, though it settled the key question of the size of the military establishment the nation was building, brought only partial resolution to the conundrum of manpower policy. The gods of war demanded men—but exactly which ones were most

23. Maurice Matloff, "The 90-Division Gamble," in Kent Roberts Greenfield, ed., *Command Decisions* (Washington: Department of the Army, 1960), 373.

needed where and when, in precisely what numbers and, most puzzling of all, whether in uniform or overalls, toting a rifle or tending a machine tool, were questions that had defied easy answers in the war's first year. So, too, and for even longer, did the related question of the degree to which womanpower might take the place of manpower, either in the armed forces or on the factory floor. The riddle of manpower mirrored the perplexities of materials allocation, but a solution like the Controlled Materials Plan was not as easily imposed on human beings as it was on critical metals. The division of responsibilities between the War Manpower Commission (WMC) and the Selective Service System further complicated matters.

The original Selective Service Act of 1940 had registered some sixteen million men between the ages of twenty-one and thirty-six. Amendments in the following two years extended the age limits from eighteen to sixty-five, yielding some forty-three million registrants by the end of 1942. That was by any standard a huge manpower pool, rivaled among the major belligerents only by the Russians. But the military wanted no men over forty-five and strongly preferred to take only those under the age of twenty-six. Those considerations instantly shrank the pool of military eligibles to fewer than thirty million, a number that contracted still further when the needs of the civilian work force, family status, and physical, mental, and educational disqualifications were taken into account. Confusion and compromise beset all efforts to sort out those competing demands in the war's early months. The programs for both military induction and industrial employment were conspicuously deficient in coordination, efficiency, and, most telling, in fairness.

The Selective Service System established guidelines for classifying registrants: Category I for those judged fit for military service, II for those exempted by reason of critical occupation, III for those deferred because they had dependents, and IV for men deemed physically or mentally unqualified. Effective authority over classification and deferment decisions rested with the 6,443 local draft boards. As in World War I, this system was deliberately designed to sustain the illusion of local control and democratic participation and, not least, to diffuse accountability. In case of controversy, Selective Service director Lewis B. Hershey explained, "6,443 local centers absorb the shock."[24]

24. George Q. Flynn, *Lewis B. Hershey, Mr. Selective Service* (Chapel Hill: University of North Carolina Press, 1985), 77.

There was controversy aplenty. Local volunteers composed the boards, prominent men of substance and standing, often veterans of World War I, who were supposed to embody their community's standards of deference and hierarchy and thus legitimate the boards' authority. They could also reflect their community's prejudices: just three southern states, for example (Virginia, North Carolina, and Kentucky), allowed blacks to sit on local boards, and only 250 blacks served nationwide.[25]

A local board's most important and ticklish function was to grant deferments from military service. Contrary to much later mythology, the nation's young men did not step forward in unison to answer the trumpet's call, neither before nor after Pearl Harbor. Deferments were coveted, and their distribution traced a rough profile of the patterns of political power, racial prejudice, and cultural values in wartime America.

No deferments proved more controversial than those claimed by conscientious objectors. In World War I only members of the traditional peace churches (Quakers, Brethren, and Mennonites) had been exempted for military service by reason of conscience. The Selective Service Act of 1940 defined considerably broader grounds for exemption; it released from the obligation to serve any person "who, by reason of religious training and belief, is conscientiously opposed to participation in war in any form." Hershey, who came from Mennonite stock but was not a practicing churchgoer, defined permissive guidelines for conscientious objection: the applicant need not prove membership in a traditional peace church, only that his objection was based on "religious training and belief." More than seventy-thousand young men so described themselves. The Selective Service System honored more than half of those claims and consigned about twenty-five thousand to noncombat military duty and another twelve thousand to "alternative service" in CCC-like Public Service Camps, where they worked without pay on forestry projects, on road building, and in mental hospitals. Jehovah's Witnesses, whose theology led them to oppose this particular war but not violence in general, posed particularly thorny problems for Hershey's boards, and some five thousand Witnesses ended up in jail.[26]

Congress imposed the most egregious of the blanket deferments when

25. Flynn, *Lewis B. Hershey*, 121.
26. *Selective Service System: Conscientious Objection: Special Monograph No. 11* (Washington: USGPO, 1950), 327–28; Mulford Q. Sibley and Philip E. Jacob, *Conscription of Conscience: The American State and the Conscientious Objector, 1940–1947* (Ithaca: Cornell University Press, 1952), 83–84.

it succumbed to pressure from the still potent Farm Bloc and passed the Tydings Amendment in November 1942, effectively exempting all agricultural workers from the draft. Nearly two million farm laborers thus hoed and shoveled beyond General Hershey's reach. They made up three times the proportion of the under-twenty-six-year-olds who were deferred for industrial work, though as the sheltering power of occupational exemption became clear, over four million men of all ages sought and received industrial occupational deferments. "Essential occupation lists mushroomed," one authority concludes, with thirty-four "essential" occupations listed in the repair and trade services alone.[27]

The situation of black Americans posed compound problems of equity. At the insistence of black leaders, the Selective Service Act stipulated that "there shall be no discrimination against any person on account of race or color." But because the army remained committed to segregated units, Hershey issued draft calls on a racial basis, reaching into the black community only when it was necessary to bring an all-black outfit up to strength. That practice stretched the outermost boundaries of the law. Furthermore, because the army also remained skeptical about sending blacks into combat, relatively few black units were formed in the first place. (The marines at first refused all black enlistments; the navy took only a few as messmen.) The result was that though blacks represented 10.6 percent of the population, they constituted less than 6 percent of the armed forces at the beginning of 1943. While some three hundred thousand single black men in the prime eligibility pool, I-A, went undrafted, many southern draft boards were eventually compelled to send up married white men for induction, a disparity that provoked bitter resentment in southern black and white communities alike. In his state, Mississippi senator Theodore Bilbo complained to Hershey in the fall of 1942, "with a population of one half Negro and one half white . . . the system that you are now using has resulted in taking all the whites to meet the quota and leaving the great majority of Negroes at home."[28]

Married men had enjoyed exemption from the first draft calls—a provision that by one estimate prompted 40 percent of the twenty-one-year-olds caught in the first registration in late 1940 to marry within six weeks. Hershey declared in February 1942 that he would act on "the presumption that most of the recent marriages . . . might have been for

---

27. Flynn, *Lewis B. Hershey*, 108.
28. Flynn, *Lewis B. Hershey*, 119–26; Paula S. Fass, *Outside In: Minorities and the Transformation of American Education* (New York: Oxford University Press, 1989), 144.

the purpose of evading the draft." Fathers proved even more untouchable, especially those with children born before Pearl Harbor. Down to early 1944 only 161,000 pre–Pearl Harbor fathers were conscripted. A story circulated about a young couple who named their baby "Weatherstrip" because he kept his father out of the draft. Only late in the war did Hershey finally abolish the exemption for fathers, and in 1944 and 1945 nearly a million fathers were drafted. By war's end one out of every five fathers between the ages of eighteen and thirty-seven was on active duty.[29]

Many youngsters—flushed with patriotic fervor or driven by youthful passion for adventure, or simply motivated by the wish to "choose while you can," as the navy's recruitment slogan put it—did indeed volunteer (the navy and marine corps relied exclusively on volunteers until the end of 1942). But they stepped forward in such unpredictable numbers and in such haphazard patterns that volunteering raised hob with the concept of efficient manpower utilization. Army and navy recruiters pulled in men from all walks of life and sometimes "parked" them in cadet training programs, as a reserve against an uncertain future. The army's Special Training Program absorbed 140,000 young men at its height. The navy's V-12 program signed up seventeen-year-olds and sent them to college for as long as two years, rendering them draftproof when they reached eligibility on their eighteenth birthday. The air force cadet program by war's end held some two hundred thousand young men who never left home. Those practices indiscriminately depleted the industrial labor pool, complicated military staffing, and raised rankling questions about fairness. One Selective Service official recalled the tense situation in his New England community "when fathers in their middle thirties were being inducted from their stores, garages, and other businesses. The presence of several hundred able-bodied students in uniform in that community created a situation difficult to describe."[30]

All these chronic ineffiencies and inequities were begging for remediation by the end of 1942. In the wake of the Feasibility Dispute and in the context of firming up the ninety-division decision, Roosevelt ordered an end to all voluntary enlistments and repealed the marital exemption. On December 5 he placed the Selective Service System under the direct control of Paul McNutt's War Manpower Commission, an

29. Flynn, *Lewis B. Hershey*, 108; William M. Tuttle Jr., *Daddy's Gone to War: The Second World War in the Lives of America's Children* (New York: Oxford University Press, 1993), 20, 31; Lee Kennett, *G.I.: The American Soldier in World War II* (New York: Charles Scribner's Sons, 1987), 5.

30. Kennett, *G.I.*, 21–22.

obvious step toward a single, coordinated civil-military manpower policy, but one that alarmed Hershey and the military authorities. By delivering both the carrot of deferment and the stick of induction into one pair of hands, Roosevelt hoped to enable McNutt to channel manpower where it could best be utilized. To that end McNutt in early 1943 announced a draconian "work-or-fight" order. Most startling, he ended blanket deferments for fathers. He invoked the quite defensible rationale that occupational status should be a stronger determinant of manpower disposition than family status.

But McNutt's sweeping directive staked out a policy position well beyond the boundaries of what organized labor, General Hershey, or the Congress would tolerate. His work-or-fight order was virtually dead on arrival. Hershey administered the coup de grace. McNutt's order had set the stage for a confrontation between the WMC and the Selective Service System that paralleled the clash between the military and the WPB. Hershey, a career army officer who affected the manner of a village rustic, was in fact an exceptionally wily political infighter. In wartime Washington he first displayed the skills that would sustain him as director of the Selective Service System for three decades, well into the Vietnam era—a tenure in office by a senior political appointee probably exceeded only by J. Edgar Hoover's forty-eight-year stint as director of the FBI, and one that surely touched far more lives. Hershey now flexed his bureaucratic muscle to frustrate McNutt's effort to elevate the WMC over the military's own Selective Service System. He flatly informed McNutt that "I will not transmit any order from you for classification," thus nullifying the WMC's fathers-must-fight announcement. Though he himself had earlier proposed drafting fathers, and would eventually take a million of them, Hershey cunningly lent his support to a congressional bill, passed in December 1943, explicitly protecting them from military service, because the bill also contained provisions preserving Hershey's paramount authority over the military draft. Hershey had fought McNutt to a messy draw. Manpower policy remained divided between civil and military authorities.

Hershey proceeded in 1943 to draft men in accord with the lesser levels and the recomposed configurations targeted in the ninety-division scheme: 7,700,000 for the army, of whom 2 million were now slated for the army air forces; 3,600,000 for the navy, almost 500,000 of them marines. Before 1943 was out he was nearly there: 7,500,000 in the army, 2,800,000 in the navy and marines. Almost one family in five— 18.1 percent—contributed at least one member to the armed forces. All told, more than 16 million men and women served in uniform during the war. A revision to the Selective Service law passed in the week after Pearl Harbor made them liable to service for "the duration of the war," and they served, on average, for nearly three years. For many of them, those war years were the pivot of their lives, a defining moment whose importance advancing age could not diminish, nor whose details could memory dim.[31]

Yet even at those levels, the U.S. Army, especially as a fraction of the U.S. manpower pool, would scarcely be a mighty host: somewhat larger than the Japanese army (5.5 million at war's end), somewhat smaller than the *Wehrmacht* (6.1 million), and less than half the size of the Red Army (which the Germans estimated at more than 12 million by 1945).[32]

WHILE HERSHEY was imposing at least a measure of order on the military side of the manpower equation, something approaching chaos continued to reign on the civilian side. As the remaining pools of unemployed workers swiftly evaporated in 1942, labor markets tightened severely. Competitive bidding for increasingly scarce labor sucked women from their homes and farmers from the countryside into the roaring maw of the booming industrial economy. Labor shortages drove workers from plant to plant, from city to city, even from region to region, in search of fatter paychecks. Their restless mobility wreaked havoc with production schedules, and their giddily levitating wages threatened to kick off a cyclonic inflationary spiral. The administration consequently groped for ways both to reduce labor turnover and to control wages as well as prices.

McNutt's abortive work-or-fight order in 1943 had given brief public display to one scheme for regulating labor that had lurked beneath the surface ever since Pearl Harbor: a comprehensive national service policy that would lay the government's hand upon all citizens and push them into whatever employment was deemed necessary. Other countries adopted such forced-labor drafts in wartime, and the United States itself had experimented with a feeble version of such a policy in World War I. But coercing labor cut deeply against the American grain, and in any case the Depression years had helped the organized union

31. *HSUS*, 1140; Tuttle, *Daddy's Gone to War*, 31; Flynn, *Lewis B. Hershey*, 85, 100.
32. John Ellis, *World War II: A Statistical Survey* (New York: Facts on File, 1993), 227–28; I.C.B. Dear, ed., *The Oxford Companion to the Second World War* (New York: Oxford University Press, 1995), 1235.

movement to acquire the kind of political clout that made such a drastic measure difficult to impose. Union leaders and the Roosevelt administration alike strongly preferred less heavy-handed techniques. The West Coast Manpower Plan, devised in the fall of 1943 and generalized elsewhere, brought some reduction in turnover rates by letting contracts only where labor was certified to be available and by regulating job-shifting through a central employment referral service. But the problems of wages and prices, and the exceptionally thorny issues of union prerogatives and union integrity, eluded tidy solution.

All the major union leaders dutifully announced "no-strike" pledges in the days after the Pearl Harbor attack, evincing their desire to play statesmanlike roles in the war crisis, as well as their wariness about their own members' attitudes and their fear of a government clamp-down if they did not put their own house in order. Labor was restless on the eve of the war. Just as in 1937, when the first flush of genuine economic recovery had triggered the massive organizing campaigns in steel and autos, so in 1941 war-borne prosperity had sparked campaigns to complete the union movement's unfinished business. Some two million workers staged more than four thousand strikes in 1941, many of them over organizational issues. Ford recognized the UAW at last in April; the steelworkers unionized Bethlehem Steel; International Harvester, Weyerhauser, and Allis-Chalmers all capitulated to the CIO in the course of that last peacetime year.

Several of those industrial actions in 1941 gave warning about the dangers that lay ahead. Workers walked out of the Allis-Chalmers plant in Milwaukee in the winter of 1940–41 just as the company was gearing up to fulfill a $40 million contract to build turbines for navy destroyers—a chilling display of the capacity of labor disturbances to cripple the rearmament program. Equally ominous, and even more dramatic in its outcome, was a strike in June against North American Aviation's plant in Inglewood, California. The situation at North American was tangled, a jumble of jurisdictional disputes between CIO and AFL organizers trying to come to terms with the thousands of new workers streaming into the aviation industry, with wage and workplace grievances, and with Communist intrigue.[33] But a work stoppage that threatened to shut down

33. The Communist Party USA still toed the official Moscow line that Germany was a Soviet ally and should be protected from British and American imperialist harassment; ironically, the Germans invaded Russia virtually in the midst of the North American strike, prompting an instantaneous reversal of Moscow's position. Thereafter the CPUSA became among the most impassioned advocates of peaceable labor relations and maximum production.

25 percent of all fighter aircraft production was intolerable to the government, whatever the grounds. At the urging of Secretary Stimson, the administration made an example of the North American strikers. Hershey canceled their occupational deferments and threatened them with immediate induction into the armed services. On June 9, 1941, twenty-five hundred soldiers with fixed bayonets seized the North American plant. The cowed workers soon returned to their lathes and drill presses. But the prospect of having repeatedly to crush labor under the army's mailed fist was not pleasant to contemplate. Neither were the renewed antics of John L. Lewis. He demonstrated his continuing capacity for mischief in 1941 when he called his United Mine Workers out on a nationwide strike to secure the union shop in the so-called captive mines, owned by the steel companies and excluded from the coal settlements of the 1930s. After a long, acrimonious standoff, amid mounting wintertime coal shortages and bitter denunciations of Lewis as a traitor and saboteur, the miners finally went back to work—on December 7, 1941.

Labor had two great fears in wartime: that prices would rise while workers' ability to negotiate wage increases would be curtailed; and that the great industrial unions born in the 1930s would decompose under the triple burden of management pressure, public hostility, and worker indifference. The isolationism of many union leaders, including conspicuously Lewis, was due in large part to their memories of labor's setbacks in the World War I era, when inflation more than ate up all of workers' wage gains and a mood of hyperpatriotism helped management to crush the AFL's great membership drives, notably in steel.

The CIO in particular was an immature, unstable institution in 1941. The very rapidity of its growth left it an organizational hollow shell. Its headquarters had but the thinnest apparatus for managing a far-flung and now highly mobile membership, and in many localities it could field only a skeletal staff. How could this young, untried union cope with the vast demographic surges that were washing over the nation's wartime workplaces? CIO leaders were rightly apprehensive that the millions of new workers crowding through the factory gates into the throbbing war plants lacked the kind of commitment to unionism that had made possible the historic gains of the 1930s. North American Aviation employed so many green, first-time industrial workers at its troubled Inglewood, California, plant that shift change was said to resemble a high school dismissal. To the teenagers, women, blacks, Dust Bowl refugees, and other rural migrants who now thronged into their first-ever industrial jobs, the concepts of worker solidarity, wage guarantees, seniority rules, pay differentials, collective bargaining, jurisdictional boundaries, shop stewards, grievance procedures, and union-consciousness—the very stuff of trade union life and the union movement's reasons for being—were alien and irrelevant. In the let-'er-rip, booming, steady-work, high-wage environment in which these new workers found themselves, who needed a union?

Against this backdrop the administration took three significant policy steps affecting labor in the first months of 1942. Faced with evidence of mounting price inflation, Leon Henderson's OPA announced its General Maximum Price Regulation in April, soon ubiquitously though not always fondly referred to as "General Max." It capped prices as of March. In a companion initiative, the National War Labor Board in July settled a wage dispute with the lesser steelmakers—Bethlehem, Republic, Youngstown, and Inland—by imposing a settlement limiting wage increases to the rise in the cost of living between January 1941 and May 1942: about 15 percent, a number soon generalized to all wage settlements. The intended effect of these twin measures, General Max and the Little Steel Formula, was to preserve workers' standards of living for the duration of the conflict. Whether that preservation was better described as a "freeze" or as "stabilization" was a matter of dispute. However it was described, the administration's wage-and-price control policies represented a significant departure from the mildly redistributive thrust of the New Deal, which had sought to redress imbalances among various social and economic sectors, not hold their economic relationships constant.

These wage-and-price policies soon ran afoul of the usual difficulties, including hard-to-monitor evasions and political interference, that beset all command economies. Though General Max put a fairly effective lid on some commodity prices, it was easily frustrated in many product lines by model changes or relabeling. Congress dealt pricing policy one of its first and most damaging blows when it once again truckled to the Farm Bloc in early 1942 and legislated ceilings on farm prices that had no relation to the General Max directive. Taking the farmers' exceptionally prosperous years 1910–14 as the baseline for defining the parity ratio between agricultural and industrial prices, the legislators mandated crop price ceilings at 110 percent of parity. Only extensive government subsidies kept something of a damper on food bills in neighborhood markets, as the administration bought crops at parity prices and sold them to retailers at a loss. Consumers thus paid less at the grocer's but more in taxes, while farmers waxed fat. As for wages, job reclassification, premium pay for specified shifts, and overtime payments were all ways to end-run the nominal wage freeze.

Seeking to contain these various evasive maneuvers, Roosevelt tried to bring the farmers to heel and stiffen the spines of his price and wage regulators with a "hold-the-line" wage-and-price order in April 1943. Yet by war's end farm prices had risen nearly 50 percent. The overall inflation rate was 28 percent, a much better performance than World War I's 100 percent rate, but still well short of the regulators' ambitions. Average weekly earnings, thanks more to overtime than to wage gains, went up 65 percent; adjusted for inflation, manufacturing workers enjoyed about 27 percent more real income in 1945 than they had in 1940. Corporate profits, meanwhile, nearly doubled.[34]

With the no-strike pledge, unions had denied themselves their historically most powerful weapon. With the Little Steel Formula, the government had sharply confined their power to influence wages, the item that most interested their members. CIO chief Philip Murray damned the Little Steel agreement less because of its strictly economic restrictions than because it threatened to enfeeble the unions by leaving them no legitimate role to play. Wage controls, he warned, conjuring the unsettling prospect that John L. Lewis's fallen star might rise again, "would decrease the prestige of those labor leaders who have supported the President," and would "leave the field wide open for the isolationists in the union movement and result in chaotic labor conditions."[35]

But in June 1942 the labor movement received a notable consolation prize for these debilitating restrictions. In the third and most cunning of the government's major labor policy pronouncements, the National War Labor Board promulgated its supremely important "maintenance-of-membership" rule. That regulation provided that in any place of employment already covered by a union contract, all new employees would be automatically enrolled in the union unless they explicitly requested otherwise in the first fifteen days on the job. The maintenance-of-membership ruling was a fabulous boon for organized labor. Employers had long hated the concept of mandatory union membership — the so-called closed shop. Now the NWLB required not only that employers live with the closed shop but that they play the role of enforcers, collecting union dues and firing workers who fell behind in their payments.

34. *HSUS*, 210–11; Nelson Lichtenstein, *Labor's War at Home: The CIO in World War II* (Cambridge: Cambridge University Press, 1982), 111.

35. Lichtenstein, *Labor's War at Home*, 77.

At a stroke, the government's maintenance-of-membership rule not only provided powerful protections against union disintegration; it also allowed the unions easily to capture all those new workers freshly recruited for war production. At the same time, maintenance-of-membership became the principal mechanism by which labor was kept in line. What government gave, government could take away. Fear of losing the maintenance-of-membership guarantee worked powerfully to restrain the militancy of labor leaders.

The Roosevelt administration offered labor dramatically impressive evidence that it would honor the maintenance-of-membership rule when the Montgomery Ward Company tried to repudiate its provisions. Leading a contingent of steel-helmeted U.S. soldiers, Attorney General Francis Biddle personally entered the Chicago office of Montgomery Ward president Sewell L. Avery on April 27, 1944. He ordered the troops to eject Avery and seized control of the company in the name of the government. "To hell with the government," the fuming Avery shouted as he was being toted out the door of his office. Glaring at Biddle, he summoned the most contemptuous words he could think of: "You— New Dealer!" he spat. A widely published photograph of the slight, elderly Avery being carted away by uniformed troops brought down a torrent of abuse on Biddle from conservatives. The *Chicago Tribune* caricatured him as a black-capped executioner. But Biddle's flamboyant assertion of federal supremacy had potently demonstrated to labor the indispensable importance of its wartime partnership with government.[36] Under the WLB's benign patronage, union membership vaulted upward, from fewer than ten million to nearly fifteen million over the course of the war.

For all of its efficacy in calming labor and promoting union growth, the maintenance-of-membership rule was a devil's bargain, and labor leaders knew it. The unions gave up effective power in wartime in exchange for mushrooming membership rolls and the prospect of enhanced influence later. As historian Alan Brinkley concludes, "the labor movement had become, in effect, a ward of the state."[37] One labor leader, John L. Lewis, would have none of it. Lewis's United Mine Workers in fact reaped no benefit from the rule, since they already enjoyed the privilege of a closed shop. Unconstrained by the fear of

36. Francis Biddle, *In Brief Authority* (Garden City, N.Y.: Doubleday, 1962), 314–18.
37. Alan Brinkley, *The End of Reform: New Deal Liberalism in Depression and War* (New York: Knopf, 1995), 200.

being stripped of the government guarantee, Lewis had little to lose. In 1943, openly scorning both the Little Steel Formula and the hold-the-line order, he demanded a two-dollar-a-day wage increase for his coal miners. He sought as much to loosen the NWLB's stranglehold over labor relations as to put more money in miners' pockets. When the coal operators refused to cave in, he hurled defiance in their face, and in the NWLB's too. Lewis ordered his half-million UMW members out of the pits. The government seized the mines and blustered about drafting the miners. As coal stocks dwindled, steel mills banked their blast furnaces and railroads cut back their schedules. Newspapers condemned the miners as traitors and heaped vilification on Lewis. An air force pilot reportedly said: "I'd just as soon shoot down one of those strikers as shoot down Japs—they're doing just as much to lose the war for us." *Stars and Stripes*, the army's official newspaper, editorialized: "John L. Lewis, damn your coal-black soul."[38] Some members of Congress demanded his indictment for treason. Polls confirmed that he was the most unpopular man in America. (Eighty-seven percent of respondents had an "unfavorable opinion" of him in June 1943.)[39] In the end, after a messy struggle that dragged on into 1944, Lewis won the wage concessions for his miners. But it was a Pyrrhic victory; the losses in public confidence and political support for labor were immeasurable. When Lewis's defiant example helped to trigger more labor disturbances, including a railroad strike that led to federal seizure of the roads in December 1943, President Roosevelt despaired of his self-absorbed countrymen's commitment to the war effort. "One of the best things that could happen," he remarked darkly to his presumably astonished cabinet, "would be to have a few German bombs fall here to wake us up."[40]

By mid-1943 the country had had a bellyful of John L. Lewis. Egged on by the rising tide of public anger over the coal strike, a wrathful Congress passed the Smith-Connally War Labor Disputes Act in June. Ostensibly a war measure, it actually dealt the labor movement a blow that conservatives had been itching to land since the passage of the Wagner Act in 1935. Capitalizing on Lewis's plummeting reputation, they took their revenge for nearly a decade's worth of labor gains. The

38. William L. O'Neill, *A Democracy at War: America's Fight at Home and Abroad in World War II* (New York: Free Press, 1993), 210–11. Harry S. Truman later opined that "Lewis ought to have been shot in 1942, but Franklin didn't have the guts to do it" (213).

39. Cantril, 397.

40. Frank Freidel, *Franklin D. Roosevelt: Rendezvous with Destiny* (Boston: Little, Brown, 1990), 496.

Act broadened presidential authority to seize struck war plants, imposed a thirty-day "cooling-off" period for strikes, established criminal penalties for strike leaders, required majority approval of a union's membership before a strike, and, for good measure, forbade union contributions to political campaigns in wartime. Not least because of that last provision, a transparent effort to slap at Roosevelt and stem the growth in labor's political influence that the New Deal had fostered, the president vetoed the bill. Congress speedily repassed it, in another pointed reminder of Roosevelt's loss of control over the Congress and the antilabor swing in public sentiment since the reforming heyday of the Depression years. "I think," Roosevelt remarked glumly to Eleanor, "the country has forgotten we ever lived through the 1930s."[41]

FOR MANY AMERICANS on the home front, the Depression years did seem but a distant, if painful, memory. The war did not merely banish the decade-long scourge of unemployment. It also provided jobs for the 3.25 million new job-seekers who reached employable age during the conflict, as well as to another 7.3 million workers, half of them women, who would not normally have sought work even in a full-employment peacetime economy. Thanks to the government's cost-plus contracting practices and the ubiquitous availability of overtime, wartime jobs paid fabulously well, especially for Americans who had suffered through the cramped years of the 1930s. Even more than the purpose-built programs of the New Deal, this economic sea-change bestowed an unprecedented sense of security on men and women who had long made do without it. "Going to work in the navy yard," one shipyard laborer in Portsmouth, Virginia, recalled, "I felt like something had come down from heaven. I went from forty cents an hour to a dollar an hour. . . . At the end of the war I was making two seventy-five an hour. . . . I couldn't believe my good fortune. . . . I was able to buy some working clothes for a change, buy a suit. . . . It just made a different man out of me. . . . After all the hardships of the Depression, the war completely turned my life around." Another man, recollecting his wartime boyhood in Portland, Oregon, remembered that "for the first time we began to have money. . . . You started to think you could do things. We used to go out to a restaurant now and then, where we would never do that before the war. We hardly ever went to picture shows during the Depression; now I did all the time. . . . My mother saved

41. Goodwin, No Ordinary Time, 443.

enough money to buy a modest home. That was the first home we ever bought."[42]

Rationing curbed the purchase of a few items—notably meat, butter, coffee, tires, and gasoline—forcing some changes in menus and life habits. Regulations aimed at conserving scarce materials also wrought some conspicuous changes in fashion. To save scarce fabrics, the War Production Board banned double-breasted suits, vests, trouser cuffs, and patch pockets for men; pleated skirts disappeared, hemlines went up, and women's bathing costumes got skimpier, promoting the widespread adoption of the previously rare two-piece swimming suit. Some items disappeared altogether. The WPB sharply restricted new private home construction in 1942 and prohibited the manufacture of automobiles for private use. Autoworkers organized little ceremonies as the last motorcar chassis moved down the assembly lines on February 10, 1942, then proceeded to rip out the old dies and stamping presses and prepare for weapons production.

Even with a handful of such restrictions, the war created a glittering consumer's paradise. Though Roosevelt had warned that the nation could not afford to build a war economy on top of a consumer economy, in fact the United States managed to do exactly that—mounting a robustly expanding military production machine atop a steadily rising curve of civilian output. Three developments underwrote the war's fantastic explosion of goods: full resource utilization, including both unemployed workers and idle plants; the diversion of resources, especially underutilized agricultural labor, from lower- to higher-productivity employments; and notable gains in productivity, fueled by burgeoning investment in more efficient plant and equipment, increased reliance on electrical power, and technological improvements. By one estimate American output per worker hour was double that in Germany, five times that in Japan.

Despite the occasionally bitter tension between the administrators who oversaw them, the civilian and the military sectors alike benefited from these economic improvements, even if disproportionately. War spending skyrocketed from $3.6 billion in 1940, about 2 percent of national product, to a peak of $93.4 billion in 1944, by which date roughly half of the nation's productive energy was flowing to military uses. Yet

42. Mark Jonathan Harris et al., *The Homefront: America during World War II* (New York: G. P. Putnam's Sons, 1984), William Pefley interview, 39–40, 241; James Covert interview, 240.

in that same span of time, civilian purchases of goods and services managed to grow by 12 percent.[43] Most Americans had never had it so good. They started half a million new businesses. They went to movies and restaurants with unhabitual frequency. They bought books, recordings, cosmetics, pharmaceuticals, jewelry, and liquor in record volumes. Racing fans wagered two and a half times more on the horses in 1944 than they had in 1940. Housewives shopped at well-stocked supermarkets, eleven thousand of them newly built during the war. The war even narrowed the gap between rural and urban living standards that had been widening for nearly half a century. "As farm prices got better and better," a young woman from Idaho remembered, "the farmers suddenly became the wealth of the community. . . . Farm times became good times. . . . We and most other farmers went from a tarpaper shack to a new frame house with indoor plumbing. Now we had an electric stove instead of a woodburning one, and running water at the sink where we could do the dishes; and a hot water heater; and nice linoleum. . . . We bought a vacuum cleaner too. . . . [It] had a little gadget with a jar on it that sprayed floor wax, and, oh, God that was really wonderful. It was just so modern we couldn't stand it."[44] Retail sales ascended to a record high in 1943 and then went higher still in 1944. On a poignantly symbolic date, December 7, 1944, the third anniversary of Pearl Harbor, the thousands of cash registers in the Macy's department store chain rang up the highest volume of sales in the giant retailer's history.[45]

That civilian consumption increased at all in the United States was a singularly American achievement. In Britain personal consumption shrank by 22 percent. In the Soviet Union, the third Grand Alliance partner, the home-front experience was nearly the opposite of that in the United States—massive invasion, followed by a crash mobilization program characterized by harshly regulated scarcity rather than the Americans' loosely supervised abundance. While the Americans fought the war from an ever-expanding economic base, the Russians were the

43. Bureau of the Budget, *The United States at War* (Washington: USGPO, 1946); Mark Harrison, "Resource Mobilization for World War II: The U.S.A., U.K., U.S.S.R., and Germany," *Economic History Review* 2d ser. 16 (1988): 171–92; Milward, *War, Economy, and Society*, especially 63ff.; and Smith, *Army and Economic Mobilization*. The WPB estimated that labor productivity in the United States increased by 25 percent during the four war years, a remarkable gain, accounting for a third of the total increase in output; see Milward, 230.

44. Harris et al., *Homefront*, Laura Briggs interview, 164.

45. Blum, *V Was for Victory*, 98.

only people forced to fight the war on a steadily diminishing one, a circumstance that inflicted large and punishing transfers from the civilian to the military sector. As German armies advanced over the Soviet agricultural heartland, Russian food output fell by two-thirds. Even in areas the *Wehrmacht* did not reach, Russians by the millions slid into agonies of squalor and deprivation; many starved.[46] In Germany and Japan as well the demands of war production, not to mention Allied bombers and submarines, inevitably encroached upon civilian production, sharply degrading standards of living. Both the Axis powers devoted well over half of their productive capacity to the war effort by war's end. Over the course of the war, civilian consumption fell by nearly 20 percent in Germany and 26 percent in Japan.[47] Only in America was it different. The United States, alone among all the combatant societies, enjoyed guns and butter too—and both of them in unrivaled quantities.

NATIONAL ECONOMIES, like people, have their own distinctive personalities. America's singular economic character in World War II was defined first of all by its matchless plenty, by the prodigious quantity of resources it could command and the avalanche of goods it could pour out. From that central fact flowed the credibility of Roosevelt's strategy of "overwhelming" superiority in the implements of war, as well as the unique achievement of expanding both the civilian and military sectors in wartime. So plentiful were American resources that what the American economy lacked in physical materials it simply created. Entirely new industries came into being, notably synthetic rubber. When Japan seized Malaya and the Dutch East Indies, cutting the United States off from virtually all its usual sources of natural rubber, the government invested some $700 million in fifty-one spanking-new synthetic plants, enough to replace the annual harvest from millions upon millions of rubber trees. The Farm Bloc managed to compromise the efficiency of the synthetic rubber program by insisting that some portion of the essential ingredient of butadiene be derived from alcohol rather than the more sensible chemical base of petroleum. Even with that politically imposed encumbrance, American rubber companies more than made up for the lost imports. By 1944 they were producing some eight hundred thousand tons of the synthetic material; one sprawling,

46. Richard Overy, *Why the Allies Won* (New York: Norton, 1995), 206; Milward, *War, Economy, and Society*, 92ff.
47. Bureau of the Budget, *United States at War*, 509.

seventy-seven-acre West Virginia facility alone accounted for more than 10 percent of the total.

But the American "production miracle" owed to more than just a plethora of resources. Precisely how those resources were used made a difference too. The German armaments minister, Albert Speer, shrewdly assessed the peculiar nature of the American economy in a memorandum to Hitler in 1944. The war, he said, was a "contest between two systems of organization." The Americans, he insisted, "knew how to act with organizationally simple methods and therefore achieved greater results, whereas we were hampered by superannuated forms of organization and therefore could not match the others' feats. . . . If we did not arrive at a different system of organization . . . it would be evident to posterity that our outmoded, tradition-bound, and arthritic organizational system had lost the struggle."[48]

Speer took accurate measure of his adversary's economic system, as well as of his own. It was universally understood, as the economic historian Alan Milward has explained, "that the gain in output was far greater than 10 percent if an armament was produced to only 90 percent rather than to 100 percent, of the specifications."[49] In the inescapable trade-off between quality and quantity, the Germans characteristically chose the former, the Americans the latter. The *Wehrmacht* counted for its margin of victory on "qualitative superiority," on precision-made, flawlessly performing, high-standard weapons. It encouraged special ordering and custom designing that frustrated long production runs and thereby prevented optimal resource utilization. Until Speer brought a modicum of efficiency to the German production effort late in the war, the Germans were making 425 different kinds of aircraft, 151 types of trucks, and 150 different motorcycles.[50] The Americans, in contrast, consciously eschewed variety and willingly sacrificed some measure of quality in order to achieve higher production numbers: "quantitative superiority." Given their national "style" of production, the Germans typically excelled at performance-enhancing improvements in machine-tool technology and metallurgy. Though the Americans also ultimately proved capable of some epochal scientific and technical breakthroughs, they innovated most characteristically and most tellingly in plant layout, production organization, economies of scale, and process engineering.

48. Albert Speer, *Inside the Third Reich* (New York: Macmillan, 1970), 213.
49. Milward, *War, Economy, and Society*, 186.
50. Overy, *Why the Allies Won*, 201.

If Germany aimed at the perfection of many things, America aspired to the commodification of virtually everything.

In part, the Americans made a virtue of necessity. Their wartime preference for generic, high-volume output over specially engineered, high-performance armaments flowed in significant measure from the historical nature of the American work force, disproportionately composed of ill-educated immigrants with scant industrial skills. From the dawn of the industrial revolution in the United States, the characteristics of America's working class had placed a premium on organizing production around simple repetitive tasks that did not demand technical adeptness or extensive training. Henry Ford's clattering automobile assembly line, tended by gangs of often unlettered Polish and Italian immigrants, Appalachian whites, and transplanted southern black sharecroppers, was the archetypal example of America's peculiar industrial style. From its introduction in 1908 through the 1920s, Ford's Model T ascended to a near-mythological status as the characteristic American product. Ford manufactured some fifteen million Model T's and made the United States into the most motorized society in the world by perfecting his assembly-line methods, steadily lowering his production costs and his selling price, and putting his simple car within the average workingman's financial reach. Frederick Winslow Taylor and other "efficiency experts" had tried to give Ford's production practices a systematic rationale and mantle them with the dignity of management theory. Fordism was in many ways a dehumanizing, impersonal production method, long vilified in books like Aldous Huxley's *Brave New World,* caricatured in films like Charlie Chaplin's *Modern Times*—and bitterly contested by the craft unions affiliated with the American Federation of Labor. But for better or worse, it was a system that had taken deeper root in America than in any other industrialized country, and it had proved its capacity to deliver the goods. Now, in the heat of war, the distinctive national genius for that way of working, already an American signature, spectacularly blossomed.

No wartime product better exemplified the American talent for mass production than the Liberty Ship. In a perfectly apt tribute, Donald Nelson called it "the Model T of the seas." Others, including naval aficionado Franklin Roosevelt, called it an ugly duckling. By whatever name, the Liberty Ship was the workhorse of both the British and the American merchant fleets: a 440-foot-long vessel that could steam at a sluggish ten knots and into whose five holds a skilled cargo master could pack 300 freight cars, 2,840 jeeps, 440 tanks, 230 million rounds of rifle ammunition, or 3.4 million servings of C-rations. Swinging the traditional bottle of champagne, Mrs. Henry A. Wallace, wife of the vice-president, christened the first Liberty Ship, appropriately named the *Patrick Henry*, in Baltimore's Bethlehem-Fairfield shipyard on December 30, 1941. It was one of sixty vessels ordered by Britain to make up for losses in the Battle of the Atlantic. To assemble its 3,425-ton steel hull, 2,725 tons of plate, and 50,000 castings, the many men and the handful of women who made the *Patrick Henry* had toiled for 355 days.

Just six months later, in mid-1942, shipyard gangs could take a Liberty Ship from keel-laying to launch in less than a third of that time, 105 days. By 1943 construction crews were splashing Liberty Ships from scratch in forty-one days. In November 1942 workers in Henry Kaiser's mammoth Richmond, California, shipyard put together one ship, the *Robert E. Peary*, complete with life jackets and coat hangers aboard, in exactly four days, fifteen hours, and twenty-six minutes. The *Peary* was a publicity stunt, but it augured a further reduction in average construction time at the extraordinarily productive Richmond yard to just seventeen days.[51]

Admirers dubbed Kaiser "Sir Launchalot" for his prodigies of ship construction, and in many ways Kaiser was the very model of the modern manufacturer, a quintessentially American big-time operator for whom the era of the Depression and the war—and the emergence of big government—opened dazzling opportunities. Kaiser became a wartime symbol of entrepreneurial energy and the glories of the free enterprise system, but he was also a creature of government, the living embodiment of what later came to be known as the military-industrial complex. Well before Pearl Harbor triggered the flood of government war orders, Kaiser had erected a business empire on government contracts. His was one of the fabled Six Companies that built Boulder (later Hoover) Dam, the biggest public works project to date in American history and a venture that yielded Kaiser some $10 million in after-tax profits. In the New Deal years, government paid Kaiser and the Six Companies more millions to build Bonneville and Grand Coulee dams on the Columbia River, Shasta Dam on the Sacramento, and the great bridges across San Francisco Bay. From his suite in Washington's Shoreham Hotel, Kaiser built bridges of his own to the federal officers who signed the big contracts. When the war came, few businessmen were

51. Marilynn S. Johnson, *The Second Gold Rush: Oakland and the East Bay in World War II* (Berkeley: University of California Press, 1993), 66.

better placed than Kaiser to exploit its rich possibilities for gain. With astonishing speed and with the government's money, he threw up sprawling shipyards at Portland and Vancouver along the Columbia and at Richmond on San Francisco Bay. An RFC loan helped him to erect a gigantic new steel mill at Fontana, in southern California, to keep the yards supplied with steel.

The Richmond shipyard was a monument to Kaiser's all-American production techniques, and Richmond itself became a prototypical example of the boom towns that pulsed to life in the months after Pearl Harbor. Abandoning the traditional method of building a ship from the keel upward, rib by rib, plate by plate, and rivet by rivet, Kaiser adopted techniques developed in his prewar dam-construction ventures, especially prefabrication. He laid out the huge Richmond facility on the grid pattern distinctive to American cities, especially those in the West, with numbered and lettered streets. Behind the several shipyards at the water's edge, streets and rail lines rayed back as far as a mile from shore to great assembly sheds. There the huge superstructures of several ships at a time inched forward along assembly lines, parts and components fed into the sheds by overhead conveyors from still more subassembly plants beyond. Giant cranes eventually lifted completed superstructure sections and bulkheads, already plumbed, wired, and finished, onto the hull, which was not riveted together but welded—a highly innovative technique whose merits were hotly contested by many naval architects. The enormous Richmond complex crawled with tens of thousands of workers, many of them first-time industrial employees—men as well as women, young and old, black and white, including the Oakies, Arkies, and Texies who had drifted into California in the Depression years or rushed to the coast in search of wartime jobs. A woman shipyard worker from Iowa described the Richmond yard as "such a huge place, something I had never been in. People from all walks of life, all coming and going and working, and the noise. The whole atmosphere was overwhelming to me."[52]

The history of the Kaiser shipyard at Richmond recapitulated in the compressed compass of the war's several months the saga of mass industrial production, with all its possibilities and problems, that had taken decades to unfold at Ford. Assembly-line prefabrication fractured the ancient art of shipbuilding into a series of discrete processes. An individual worker performed only a few basic tasks, a construction method

52. Johnson, *Second Gold Rush*, 63.

that deskilled many occupations but optimally used the novice workers who thronged into the shipyard's employment office. Seasoned journeyman electricians, for example, might once have strung together an entire vessel's wiring system. Now neophyte workers were given brief electrical training courses and assigned to a single specific job, like cabin lighting or control panels. Replacing riveting with the much less technically demanding technique of welding opened up a whole new category of employment for women, who constituted 40 percent of the welders at Richmond.

Predictably, the American Federation of Labor's affiliated unions resented Kaiser shipyards' wholesale assault on traditional craft specializations, just as the International Association of Machinists (IAM) had at North American Aviation. As the IAM had done at North American, the Boilermakers Union at Kaiser took advantage of the maintenance-of-membership rule and enrolled all those thousands of new workers. But at Richmond as at Inglewood, the AFL affiliates stuck those new members, particularly if they were female or black, into auxiliaries where they had little voice in the union's affairs. Their membership dues amounted to little more than a fee they paid for the right to work. Kaiser, meanwhile, tried to dampen labor turnover by extending unprecedented benefits to his workers, especially health care — the origins of the postwar era's most noted health maintenance organization, a war-born creation destined to outlive Kaiser's industrial empire, the Kaiser Permanente Health Plan. The combined effect of the AFL's hostility and Kaiser's paternalistic solicitude toward workers, as historian Marilynn Johnson concludes, heightened workers' distrust of unions and encouraged many employees, especially if they were blacks or women, "to see employers — rather than unions — as the true guardians of their interests." Those attitudes did not bode well for organized labor in the postwar era, but they did open the door to a "benefits revolution," a new era of corporate welfare in which perquisites like Kaiser's health plan became standard employment practices — and something in the gift of employers, not of unions, nor of the government.[53]

Kaiser's shipbuilding techniques did not always make for seaworthy ships; at least one foundered at the pier before sailing, and seamen lived in dread that the welded hulls would split open in heavy seas, as some tragically did. But what they lacked in artful design and elegant construction the Liberty Ships more than made up in the poetry of num-

53. Johnson, *Second Gold Rush*, 82.

The Nazi juggernaut. Hitler seemed unstoppable as he swallowed up Austria and part of Czechoslovakia in 1938. The other European countries looked on helplessly, while the isolationist Americans remained aloof and unarmed. (FITZPATRICK COLLECTION, STATE HISTORICAL SOCIETY OF MISSOURI, COLUMBIA)

"Expecting us to untie 'em again?" Sour memories of America's apparently futile sacrifices in World War I powerfully reinforced isolationist sentiment in the 1930s—particularly in the pages of the stridently anti-internationalist *Chicago Tribune*, which regularly published opinions like this cartoon from February 28, 1940. (© COPYRIGHTED CHICAGO TRIBUNE COMPANY)

The Four Freedoms. Popular artist Norman Rockwell here rendered artistically a notable passage from Franklin Roosevelt's address of January 6, 1941, when he spoke of the "four freedoms" that were threatened by German and Japanese aggression. (NATIONAL ARCHIVES 208-PMP-43, 208-PMP-44, 208-PMP-45, 208-PMP-46)

War in the Pacific

The USS Arizona at Pearl Harbor, December 10, 1941. More than 1100 sailors went down with the battleship on December 7, 1941, when a Japanese bomb exploded in its forward magazine. (NATIONAL ARCHIVES PACIFIC REGION, SAN FRANCISCO, NRHS-181-GENCORFC-L[11]1[BB3]2-8)

War at sea. This Japanese hit on the flight deck of the USS *Enterprise* in August 1942 killed the photographer who took the picture. (NATIONAL ARCHIVES W&C 976)

The jungle war. The Pacific War was a war of islands, involving dangerous amphibious landings like this one on Cebu Island, in the Philippines, in 1945. (LIBRARY OF CONGRESS LC-USZ62-99499)

Tarawa, November 1943. As yet unskilled in amphibious warfare, American forces suffered heavy casualties at Tarawa. The War and Navy Departments did not at first allow photographs like this to be shown to the American public. (NATIONAL ARCHIVES W&C 1342)

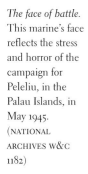

The face of battle. This marine's face reflects the stress and horror of the campaign for Peleliu, in the Palau Islands, in May 1945. (NATIONAL ARCHIVES W&C 1182)

War without mercy. A flamethrower, one of the war's most hideous weapons, in action on Kwajelien, February 1944. (NATIONAL ARCHIVES W&C1187)

The Grand Alliance

Roosevelt and Churchill at Casablanca, January 1943. At this fateful meeting, the two western leaders declared the "unconditional surrender" formula. They also announced the Combined Bomber Offensive, a coordinated plan of Anglo-American night-and-day bombing of Germany. Both measures were designed in part to compensate the Soviets for the western allies' failure to open a second front in 1943. (NATIONAL ARCHIVES [AMERICAN IMAGE 158])

Peril in the air. This U.S. bomber over Germany has apparently just had its rear wing sheared off by bombs falling from above. Yet another bomb appears to be about to hit the fuselage. (FRANKLIN D. ROOSEVELT LIBRARY 74201301)

Teheran, November 1943. Roosevelt and Stalin meet at last, the first of two occasions (the second would be at Yalta in February 1945). The President tried to win the confidence of the Soviet dictator, with mixed results. Tensions in the alliance persisted to the end of the war, laying the groundwork for the half-century of Cold War that followed. (LIBRARY OF CONGRESS LC-USZ62-122309)

The Production Miracle

"The Run." The American economy rebounded from the greatest depression in memory to unprecedented outputs of war materiel. Here B-24 bombers pour off the assembly line at Ford's Willow Run plant, which at its peak produced one aircraft every sixty-three minutes. (FRANKLIN D. ROOSEVELT LIBRARY 66129 [31])

The war of motors. Men and women alike assembled these Dauntless dive bomber engines at the Douglas Aircraft plant in El Segundo, California. (NATIONAL ARCHIVES RG 80G-412712)

The night shift. Wartime factories and shipyards worked round the clock to make up for a decade of unpreparedness and to field a fighting force in time to win the war. Even with this crash effort, it took more than two years after the attack on Pearl Harbor to open a second front that engaged major elements of the German army in western Europe. (NATIONAL ARCHIVES RG 208 PP-252-2, BOX 23)

Women at war. The government mounted a vigorous propaganda campaign to lure women into the wartime work force. Contrary to legend, most chose to stay at home. (NATIONAL ARCHIVES W&C 823)

D-Day: A Second Front at Last

The fruits of production. By mid-1944, crammed equipment parks like this one were to be found throughout southern England, in preparation for the long-awaited cross-Channel attack. (FRANKLIN D. ROOSEVELT LIBRARY 65592[28])

A final briefing. Supreme Allied Commander General Dwight D. Eisenhower talks to paratroopers on June 5, 1944, the eve of the D-Day invasion. The encounter weighed heavily on Eisenhower, who feared that he was sending most of these men to their deaths. (NATIONAL ARCHIVES W&C 1040)

D-day, June 6, 1944. History's largest naval armada disgorged an enormous weight of men, materiel, and fire-power onto the Normandy beaches, beginning the Battle for Northwest Europe. (NATIONAL ARCHIVES RG26-G-2517, BOX 37)

The price of victory. The landing craft carrying these men ashore on D-Day was sunk before it reached the beach. They were lucky to have survived. (NATIONAL ARCHIVES W&C 1042)

The Battle of the Bulge. In a last desperate lunge, Hitler threw much of his remaining army at the Allies in the Ardennes Forest in December, 1944, pushing a large "bulge" into the Anglo-American line. The advancing Germans had stripped these dead G.I.s of much of their equipment, including their shoes. (NATIONAL ARCHIVES W&C 1339)

Confronting the Holocaust. Kentucky Senator Alben Barkley at the Nazi death-camp of Buchenwald, April 24, 1945. The enormity of the Holocaust struck much of the world as simply incomprehensible. (NATIONAL ARCHIVES RG-111-SC-204745, BOX 63)

Evacuation of Japanese and Japanese-Americans from the West Coast. In March 1942, the U.S. Army's Western Defense Command ordered the forced evacuation of all Japanese living on the Pacific Coast, including American-born citizens. Most spent much of the remainder of the war in "relocation centers" in the western interior. A divided U.S. Supreme Court eventually upheld the constitutionality of the deportations, in a case that has remained controversial ever since. (LIBRARY OF CONGRESS LC-USF34-72313-2)

The war of cultures. The Japanese-American war was to an unusual degree a race war, characterized by racial stereotyping, the demonization of the adversary, hatred, and atrocities—on both sides. (NATIONAL ARCHIVES NWDNS-208-COM-132)

Women welders, New Britain, Connecticut, 1943. Employment opportunities in defense industries drew millions of African-Americans out of the South in wartime, changing America's racial demography and opening the door to the civil rights revolution of the post-war era. (LIBRARY OF CONGRESS LCUSW3-34282-C)

Waging Total War

Tokyo, August 1945. Firebomb raids on Tokyo and other Japanese cities killed far more people than the two atomic blasts at Hiroshima and Nagasaki. A single attack on Tokyo on the night of March 9, 1945, killed 90,000 Japanese and left another million homeless. (NATIONAL ARCHIVES 80-G-490421)

J. Robert Oppenheimer and Leslie Groves. The scientist and the administrator who brought the Manhattan Project to completion in time to help end the war against Japan. They are pictured here at the Alamogordo, New Mexico, test site where the first device was exploded. (ENERGY TECHNOLOGY VISUALS COLLECTION, U.S. DEPARTMENT OF ENERGY)

"Little Boy." The dark herald of the nuclear age: the uranium-fueled atomic bomb dropped on Hiroshima on August 6, 1945. The plutonium-fueled bomb dropped on Nagasaki 3 days later was code-named "Fat Man." (NATIONAL ARCHIVES RG-77-BT-115)

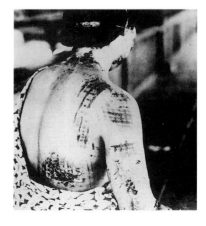

Atomic wounds. The pattern of this Hiroshima survivor's kimono was burned into her skin by the nuclear explosion. (NATIONAL ARCHIVES W&C 1244)

General George C. Marshall, "the organizer of victory." Pictured at the Cairo Conference in 1943, en route to the fateful meeting of the Big Three at Teheran. (NATIONAL ARCHIVES RG-306-NT-320D-2)

General George S. Patton Jr. in Sicily in 1943. He was among the most able and controversial of all the American military leaders. (NATIONAL ARCHIVES W&C 1024)

Pacific War Conference, Hawaii, July 1944. From the left,
General Douglas MacArthur, Roosevelt, Admiral William
D. Leahy, and Admiral Chester Nimitz. Roosevelt summoned the conference largely for political purposes related
to his 1944 presidential re-election campaign. When the
President refused to choose between MacArthur's Southwest
Pacific drive and Nimitz's Central Pacific campaign, both
campaigns went forward, possibly delaying the final assault
on the Japanese home islands. (NATIONAL ARCHIVES W&C
749)

"I have returned." Douglas MacArthur returns to the Philippines at Leyte, October 20, 1944. With
characteristic self-dramatization, he announced: "People of the Philippines…. The hour of your
redemption is here…. Rally to me." (NATIONAL ARCHIVES W&C 1207)

Victory

The victors. Churchill, Truman, and Stalin at Potsdam, July 25, 1945. Roosevelt had been dead since April; an election replaced Churchill before the Potsdam Conference ended. Of the great Allied wartime leaders, Stalin alone remained. At Potsdam unresolved issues about the nature of the post-war world boiled menacingly to the surface. The new American president soon had to grapple with a new kind of conflict, the Cold War. (NATIONAL ARCHIVES CENTRAL PLAINS REGION NRE-338-FTL[EF]-7215[5])

bers. Some twenty-seven hundred Liberty Ships slipped down the ways in the four years after Mrs. Wallace wetted the bow of the *Patrick Henry*, almost a third of them from Kaiser's yards. They carried guns to the marines in the Pacific, planes and medical supplies to the army in Europe, trucks to the Russians, food and tanks to the British. Some were pressed into service as hospital ships and freshwater distilling plants. Other shipyards, adopting their own versions of the techniques that Kaiser had perfected and employing nearly two million workers by war's end, turned out another three thousand ships of all types, including no fewer than 1,556 naval vessels.

Not to be outdone by the upstart Kaiser, Henry Ford himself, seventy-eight years old as the war began and a crusty icon of industrialized America, erected a gargantuan war installation of his own some thirty-five miles southwest of Detroit along a meandering creek named Willow Run. Like Richmond, "The Run" was an instant facility. The foundations of its L-shaped sixty-seven-acre main building sprouted almost overnight out of bucolic Washtenaw County's prairie farmland in March 1941. Eight months later, the first of the plant's eighty-five hundred B-24 bombers rolled off the end of the mile-long assembly line. Like Richmond, too, The Run was huge, a monument to American mass, muscle, and know-how. Its surreal scale inspired countless wartime ovations to the American production miracle. One awed visitor found it "impossible in words to convey the feel and smell and tension of Willow Run under full headway. . . . The roar of the machinery, the special din of the riveting gun absolutely deafening nearby, the throbbing crash of the giant metal presses . . . the far-reaching line of half-born skyships growing wings under swarms of workers, and the restless cranes swooping overhead." Novelist Glendon Swarthout evoked The Run's "immensity, insane, overpowering immensity." Famed aviator Charles Lindbergh called it "a sort of Grand Canyon of the mechanized world." "Bring the Germans and Japs in to see it," boasted Ford's production chief, Charles Sorenson. "Hell, they'll blow their brains out."[54]

The Run vacuumed up workers from the midwestern industrial heartland and from the gutted hollows of Appalachia, though Ford's indifference to providing amenities like adequate housing badly exacerbated problems of labor turnover and kept production runs beneath predictions. Ford put them to work making airplanes the way he made cars and the way Kaiser made ships, by dividing and subdividing the man-

54. Clive, *State of War*, 30–31; Goodwin, *No Ordinary Time*, 363.

ufacturing and assembly processes into hundreds of repetitive tasks. At peak operation more than forty thousand men and women toiled at The Run, including midgets specially recruited to work in the cramped wing spaces. By 1944 Willow Run's crews were rolling a B-24 through the main assembly shed's gaping exit and out on to the airfield every sixty-three minutes.

What the Liberty Ship was to the sea, the B-24 was to the air. Produced in greater quantity than any other American aircraft, it was the main battlewagon of the army air forces' bomber fleet. And like the Liberty Ship, the B-24 traded numbers for performance. Charles Lindbergh labeled an early production model "the worst piece of metal aircraft construction I have ever seen."[55] With a combat range of three thousand miles and an operational ceiling above thirty-five thousand feet, the B-24's specifications ostensibly exceeded those of its stablemate, the B-17. But though it could supposedly fly higher and further, it lacked the armament and handling characteristics of the Flying Fortress, which most American pilots preferred to fly.

All told, American war plants delivered some 18,000 B-24s, almost half of them from Willow Run, while building 12,692 B-17s and 3,763 B-29s, which went into production only late in the war. The soaring demands of the air war, especially after the decision at Casablanca to mount the round-the-clock Combined Bomber Offensive, drew more than two million workers into the aircraft industry. At plants in Seattle, San Diego, and Wichita, as well as at Willow Run, they produced 299,293 airplanes between 1940 and 1945, at a cost of some $45 billion dollars, nearly a quarter of the war's $183 billion munitions bill. At maximum output in 1944, the 96,318 military and naval aircraft that poured out of American factories exceeded the combined production in that year of Germany and Japan, as well as Britain.[56]

American armaments output surged passed that of Britain in the summer of 1942. By 1944 it was six times greater. The United States was then producing 60 percent of the Allies' munitions and 40 percent of all the world's arms. More than a quarter of all Britain's implements of war were coming from the United States. By war's end the Americans supplied as much as 10 percent of Russia's military needs, including

55. *The Wartime Journals of Charles A. Lindbergh* (New York: Harcourt Brace Jovanovich, 1970), 645.
56. Craven and Cate 6:331, 350.

1,966 locomotives, 7,669 miles of track, 350,000 trucks, 77,900 jeeps, and 956,000 miles of telephone cable.[57]

By 1943 the United States had completed its administrative apparatus for managing economic mobilization, revised its strategic plan and estimates of force requirements, stabilized its manpower and labor problems, and erected the factories and recruited the workers necessary to pour out the greatest arsenal of weaponry the world had ever seen. The military production machine was running in such high gear by mid-1943 that Donald Nelson tried to slow it down. He began to plan for "reconversion," the transition back to a peacetime economy. Military authorities resisted vigorously. Brehon Somervell contemptuously dismissed the civilians who in his eyes were prematurely dreaming of peace. "They have never been bombed," Somervell said, accurately enough. "They have little appreciation of the horrors of war and only in a small percentage of instances do they have enough hate."[58] In the face of sentiments like those, stoutly seconded by Henry Stimson and all the military and naval chiefs, Nelson's tentative effort to begin reconversion flopped. The engines of the military economy roared on, pounding out by the war's end a fantastic statistical litany: 5,777 merchant ships, 1,556 naval vessels, 299,293 aircraft, 634,569 jeeps, 88,410 tanks, 11,000 chain saws, 2,383,311 trucks, 6.5 million rifles, 40 billion bullets. By comparison, Germany made 44,857 tanks and 111,767 aircraft; Japan a handful of tanks and 69,910 planes; Britain, over the much longer period of 1934 to 1945, just 123,819 military aircraft.[59]

IN ALL THAT STUPENDOUS NIAGARA of numbers, the figure that in the end weighed most heavily in the scales of war and still leaps dramatically from the pages of history's ledger book is, simply, two — the two atomic bombs that brought the fighting to its awful crescendo at Hiroshima and Nagasaki in August 1945. The bombs were the singular achievement of the age. It was no accident that they were made in

---

57. Milward, *War, Economy, and Society,* 67–74.
58. Polenberg, *War and Society,* 229–30.
59. Smith, *Army and Economic Mobilization,* 9–22; Craven and Cate 6:352; Frederic C. Lane, *Ships for Victory: A History of Shipbuilding under the U.S. Maritime Commission in World War II* (Baltimore: Johns Hopkins University Press, 1951), 4; F. G. Fassett Jr., *The Shipbuilding Business in the United States of America* (New York: Society of Naval Architects and Marine Engineers, 1948), 120; Milward, *War, Economy, and Society,* 74.

America, and only in America. Indeed, the tale of the bombs' making braids together into one plot so many strands of the era's history that it might be taken as the greatest war story of them all, the single most instructive summary account of how and perhaps even why the conflict was fought and the way the Americans won it.[60]

With the discovery in the 1890s of radioactivity—the spontaneous decay of the nuclei of certain elements by the emission of particles— scientists had begun to speculate on the powerful forces locked within the atom. They wondered if man might somehow accelerate the schedule of nuclear disintegration, forcing the atom to pump out in mighty bursts the energy that niggardly nature took millions of years to release in infinitesimal emanations. The quantity of energy involved was clearly enormous. One physicist, applying Albert Einstein's famous equation defining the equivalence of mass and energy ($E = mc^2$), estimated that changing the hydrogen atoms in a single glass of water into helium "would release enough energy to drive the 'Queen Mary' across the Atlantic and back at full speed."[61] As the twentieth century opened, the quest to understand the nature of the atom and tap into nature's atomic powerhouse drove one of the most feverish inquiries in the history of science. The possibility of a military application of the atom's awesome power stalked that inquiry from the start. As early as 1904 the British physicist Frederick Soddy warned that "the man who put his hand on the lever by which a parsimonious nature regulates so jealously the output of this store of energy would possess a weapon by which he could destroy the earth if he chose."[62]

When James Chadwick discovered the neutron in 1932, the scientists' knowledge-fever spiked. Breakthroughs in understanding came at an accelerating pace, heralding a golden age for physics. Neutrons had mass but no electrical charge. They could thus pass through the electrical barrier of the nucleus and probe the astonishingly strong forces that

60. The story has been magnificently well told by Richard Rhodes in The Making of the Atomic Bomb (New York: Simon and Schuster, 1986), a superb book on which the account here liberally draws, as it does also on Richard B. Hewlett and Oscar E. Anderson Jr., The New World, 1939–1946 (University Park: Pennsylvania State University Press, 1962), vol. 1 of A History of the United States Atomic Energy Commission, and on David Holloway, Stalin and the Bomb: The Soviet Union and Atomic Energy, 1939–1946 (New Haven: Yale University Press, 1994).
61. Rhodes, Making of the Atomic Bomb, 140.
62. Rhodes, Making of the Atomic Bomb, 44.

somehow bound its particles together. Neutron bombardment could force the nucleus to give up its secrets — and possibly some of its power.

Thinking about neutrons while waiting for a London traffic light in late 1933, the peripatetic physicist Leo Szilard had a key insight. Neutron penetration might so perturb the atomic nucleus, Szilard reasoned, that more energy would be released than the neutron itself supplied. "As the light changed to green and I crossed the street," he recalled, "it . . . suddenly occurred to me that if we could find an element which is split by neutrons and which would emit *two* neutrons when it absorbs *one* neutron, such an element, if assembled in sufficiently large mass, could sustain a nuclear chain reaction. . . . If the [mass] is larger than the critical value," he concluded, "I can produce an explosion."[63]

Szilard was an intense, eccentric Hungarian who had studied physics with Einstein in the 1920s and taken up an academic career at the University of Berlin. He was also a Jew, which is why in 1933 he found himself in London, not Berlin. When the Nazis promulgated their first anti-Jewish ordinance on April 7, 1933, forcing the retirement of all "non-Aryan" civil servants, Szilard and hundreds of other Jewish university professors lost their jobs, including a quarter of all the physicists in Germany, eleven of whom were already or would become Nobel Prize winners. Like Szilard, many emigrated. Einstein himself, long harassed for the compound crime of being both a Jew and a pacifist, had already departed for the new Institute for Advanced Study in Princeton, New Jersey (which he found to be "a quaint and ceremonious village of puny demi-gods on stilts"). So had Einstein's fellow physicist and eventual Nobel Prize winner Eugene Wigner and the distinguished mathematician John von Neumann.[64] Helped by Columbia University philosopher John Dewey, scores of other scholars fled their German university posts for America. Their ranks included Hans Bethe, who moved from Tübingen to Cornell, and Edward Teller, who left Göttingen for George Washington University, both of them destined to win the Nobel Prize. Szilard himself eventually moved on to America from England. Scientist-refugees came from Italy, too, following Benito Mussolini's announcement in July 1938 that "Jews do not belong to the Italian race" and the commencement of Rome's own anti-Semitic campaign. Future Nobelist Emilio Segré left Palermo for the University of

63. Rhodes, *Making of the Atomic Bomb*, 28, 214.
64. Rhodes, *Making of the Atomic Bomb*, 196.

California at Berkeley. Listening to his radio in Rome, Enrico Fermi heard the announcement of his own Nobel Prize during the same news broadcast, on November 10, 1938, that reported the horrors of *Kristallnacht*, the murderous pogrom that had swept Germany the night before. Fermi used his Nobel Prize money to emigrate to New York, evading Italian financial restrictions on emigrants and sheltering his Jewish wife from Mussolini's clutches. Thirty Jewish scientists and other scholars came to America from Europe in 1933, thirty-two in 1934, nearly one hundred physicists over the course of the decade. They came not to make war but to seek refuge. They came for the same reasons that had propelled so many of their immigrant predecessors across the Atlantic. "America," wrote Segré, "looked like the land of the future, separated by an ocean from the misfortunes, follies, and crimes of Europe" — a sentiment that isolationist Americans broadly shared in the 1930s.[65] But by the time the European war erupted and engulfed America too, Hitler's and Mussolini's racialist policies had bestowed a priceless intellectual endowment on the United States.

While other Germans were smashing glass in Jewish stores and synagogues, two German scientists, Otto Hahn and Fritz Strassmann, were trying to smash atoms at Berlin's Kaiser Wilhelm Institute for Chemistry. In the month after *Kristallnacht* they succeeded, splitting uranium into two other elements and releasing an astonishing two hundred million electron volts of energy. In the first week of the year that would bring the war, they published their results in *Die Naturwissenschaften*. A new word flashed into the scientific lexicon: fission. News of the Hahn-Strassmann experiment raced like lightning through the international physics community. Within a year scientists in several countries published more than one hundred papers on fission. The basic understanding of what it would take to build an atomic weapon was swiftly and widely diffused. In his office overlooking San Francisco Bay at the University of California at Berkeley, the physicist Robert Oppenheimer was chalking a crude diagram of a bomb on his blackboard within a week of hearing of the Hahn-Strassmann results. In Germany a young physicist described to the War Office in April "the newest development in nuclear physics, which . . . will probably make it possible to produce an explosive many orders of magnitude more powerful than the conventional ones. . . . That country which first makes use of it has an unsurpassable advantage over the others." At a secret conference in Berlin on

65. Rhodes, *Making of the Atomic Bomb*, 241.

April 29, 1939, it was agreed to pursue research on a possible nuclear weapon. The War Office took over the Kaiser Wilhelm Institute. German agents hurried to the synthetic ammonia plant at Vermork, Norway, to buy its tiny but precious stocks of deuterium oxide ("heavy water"), a by-product of ammonia manufacture and one of the few known neutron moderators that might make a chain reaction possible. All exports of uranium from the Joachimsthal mines in Nazi-controlled Czechoslovakia, one of the world's few sources of the newly precious metal, were banned. Other governments stirred themselves as well. Nuclear weapons research commenced in Britain in the summer of 1940. The Japanese Imperial Army Air Force authorized an atomic bomb project in April 1941. Stalin launched a Russian research program a year later.[66]

Fittingly, it was the refugees who alerted the American government to the menace of nuclear weaponry. Fermi was the first to try. On March 17, 1939, he went to the Navy Department to brief officers from the army's Bureau of Ordnance and the Naval Research Laboratory on the recent developments in atomic physics. He carried a letter of introduction from a Columbia University colleague, who noted "the possibility that uranium might be used as an explosive. . . . My own feeling," the colleague added, "is that the probabilities are against this." Introduced with such skepticism, Fermi hit a wall of ignorance and doubt at the Navy Building. "There's a wop outside," Fermi heard the receptionist say by way of announcing him, rudely foreshadowing the puzzled indifference of the officers he addressed. A few months later, the refugee scientists tried again. Szilard, Wigner, and Teller—the so-called Hungarian Conspiracy—visited Einstein at his vacation home on Long Island in the summer of 1939. Together they drafted a letter for Einstein's signature. Alexander Sachs, an economist with access to the White House, agreed to carry Einstein's message to Franklin Roosevelt.

On October 11 Sachs finally got his appointment with the president. Reminding Roosevelt that Napoleon had muffed the chance to exploit the greatest technological marvel of his day when he foolishly rejected the young Robert Fulton's offer to build a fleet of steamships, Sachs tendered Einstein's letter and proceeded to explain the military potentialities of nuclear energy. Einstein had closed his appeal to the president with a warning that the *Reich* had stopped the sale of uranium from the Czech mines, a sure tipoff that the Germans were already at

66. Rhodes, *Making of the Atomic Bomb*, 296, 346; Holloway, *Stalin and the Bomb*, 84.

work on a nuclear weapon. The president quickly grasped the point. "Alex," he said, "what you are after is to see that the Nazis don't blow us up." The president called in an aide. "This requires action," he said. Thus was born the Advisory Committee on Uranium, which met for the first time at the Bureau of Standards on October 21 to explore an American nuclear weapons program. The committee continued to meet sporadically for more than two years, but the scientific novelty of nuclear physics and the daunting engineering challenges of actually fabricating a bomb made it difficult to arrive at firm recommendations.[67]

The scientific principles that pointed to the ultimate promise of a nuclear weapon were clear enough. Far less clear was the technical feasibility of constructing a deliverable weapon in time to be useful. Three questions overshadowed all others. How could a sufficient amount of radioactive material be collected? What quantity of such material might constitute the critical mass that would sustain a chain reaction? And how could the material be assembled rapidly enough so that it exploded, rather than simply fizzled like a pile of gunpowder?

The near-maniacal nuclear research frenzy of 1939 established that the energy Hahn and Strassmann had released came from the relatively rare isotope U-235, which occurred in natural uranium, U-238, in the ratio of one part in 140. Plutonium, a man-made radioactive element first created from uranium in experiments at Berkeley in 1940, soon emerged as a second possible energy source. But isolating enough U-235 or fabricating enough plutonium to make a weapon struck many scientists as next to impossible. "It would take the entire efforts of a country to make a bomb," said the eminent Danish physicist Niels Bohr. "[I]t can never be done unless you turn the United States into one huge factory."[68] What was more, early estimates of the critical mass necessary to sustain a nuclear chain reaction ran to many tons, far too big and unwieldy a radioactive lump for a practical, deliverable weapon, with the possible but highly implausible exception of a device that could be carried into an enemy port aboard a ship.

Roosevelt's Uranium Committee shared those doubts. The expense of isotope separation and the uncertainty about whether a controlled chain reaction was even possible seemed like insurmountable obstacles. Assessing those difficulties, the committee easily fell into a mind-set that

---

67. Hewlett and Anderson, *New World*, 16–20; Rhodes, *Making of the Atomic Bomb*, 304–15.
68. Holloway, *Stalin and the Bomb*, 51; Rhodes, *Making of the Atomic Bomb*, 294.

was much more interested in proving that no one, the Germans in particular, could build a bomb than in committing the United States to a bomb-making program. "This uranium business is a headache!" wrote Vannevar Bush, director of the Office of Scientific Research and Development, in mid-1941.

Bush, an engineer trained at Harvard and MIT, enjoyed a reputation as an innovator. He was a pioneer in the emerging field of electronic calculating who had helped build a hundred-ton analog computer that could solve differential equations with up to eighteen variables. In the ferment following the German scientists' achievement of nuclear fission in 1939, Bush, then head of the Carnegie Institution in Washington, pushed for the creation of the National Defense Research Council (NDRC), a body of scientists committed to lending their expertise to war work. In May 1941 the Roosevelt administration subsumed the NDRC in the newly created Office of Scientific Research and Development (OSRD), which it named Bush to head. Under his leadership, the government began to move weapons research out of government-run arsenals and into corporations and, significantly, into universities. The OSRD forged a lasting relationship between government-funded scientific research and American higher education that was institutionalized after the war with the creation of the National Science Foundation in 1950.

Yet for the moment even a man as temperamentally inclined to innovation as Bush remained skeptical about the prospects for a nuclear weapon. "Even if the physicists get all that they expect," he wrote, "I believe that there is a very long period of engineering work of the most difficult nature before anything practical can come out of the matter, unless there is an explosive involved, which I very much doubt."[69] Then, in the summer of 1941, British scientists produced credible estimates that only a few kilograms of U-235 might be enough to manufacture a highly explosive weapon, a key conclusion that began to bring the prospect of a deliverable weapon into the circle of the possible. This so-called Maud Committee report made a believer of Bush. The fact of American belligerency made a gambler out of Roosevelt. Armed with the Maud Committee's findings, Bush recommended a full-scale American effort to the White House. It would be a serious and costly undertaking, Bush warned. Seeking to impress upon the president the scale of the effort required, Bush opined that "a vast industrial plant costing

69. Rhodes, *Making of the Atomic Bomb*, 362, 366.

many times as much as a major oil refinery would be necessary to separate the U235"—an estimate that proved orders of magnitude too modest. On January 19, 1942, Roosevelt penned a terse reply: "O.K.—returned—I think you had best keep this in your own safe."[70]

Roosevelt's simple "OK" proved galvanic. In Washington, the president created a Top Policy Group to oversee the bomb program. It consisted of Vice-President Wallace, Secretary of War Stimson, Army Chief of Staff Marshall, Bush, and James Bryant Conant, Harvard president and, for the duration, head of the National Defense Research Council. In Chicago, where Fermi had moved after burying some cash in the coal bin of his New Jersey house as a precaution against the prospect that as an "enemy alien" his assets would be confiscated, the Italian scientist began to put together a "pile" of radioactive materials. It "went critical"—attained a sustained chain reaction—in December 1942, a crucial breakthrough that established the reality of what had theretofore been only a theoretical prospect. Fermi celebrated with a straw-covered fiasco of Chianti. In Berkeley, Robert Oppenheimer gathered a group of physicists to work on bomb design. For security reasons they and others would soon remove to a remote mesa at Los Alamos, in the New Mexican desert.

At Los Alamos, behind a high steel fence topped with a triple course of barbed wire, Oppenheimer's scientists grappled with the myriad scientific and ordnance problems of bomb design. "The object of the project," the scientists heard on arrival, "is to produce a practical military weapon in the form of a bomb in which the energy is released by a fast neutron chain reaction in one or more of the materials known to show nuclear fission."[71] The question of assembly posed an especially stubborn puzzle. A difference of just a few microseconds in pushing subcritical quantities of fissile material together into a "critical mass" made the difference between a spectacular but militarily useless radioactive splutter or a large-scale explosion. A gun-type mechanism, in which a cannon fired a subcritical slug into a subcritical core, eventually proved a useable design for a bomb made from U-235. But neutron flux in plutonium happened at such a rate and in such quantities that even a cannon-fired assembly was too slow. The plutonium-based bomb required the devilishly tricky design of an assembly mechanism that would

70. Rhodes, *Making of the Atomic Bomb*, 377, 388.
71. Rhodes, *Making of the Atomic Bomb*, 460–61.

symmetrically implode a plutonium sphere in upon itself, instantaneously assembling a critical mass.

Over such matters as these the scientists labored. Their ranks included refugees and native-born Americans alike, an assemblage of scientific brains and intellectual prima donnas the likes of which had never been gathered before. Yet among their remarkable characteristics was the fact that for all their density of numbers and ability, they represented only a fraction of wartime America's scientific talent. Hundreds of other scientists continued to work on other projects, including radar and aircraft design. Some chose to work elsewhere for moral reasons. The physicist I. I. Rabi, for example, turned down Oppenheimer's invitation to be the associate director at Los Alamos because he could not stomach the idea that making a weapon of mass destruction represented "the culmination of three centuries of physics."[72]

Oppenheimer, a cadaverously thin theorist widely acknowledged to have a preternaturally swift and absorptive mind, occasionally shared some of Rabi's moral anxieties. Oppenheimer would in later years come to symbolize the dilemmas of an era when the growth of scientific knowledge seemed to have outraced the evolution of moral wisdom. A second-generation German-Jewish American, he had been raised in privilege on New York's Upper West Side, graduated summa cum laude from Harvard in just three years, went off to study physics in Europe, and returned to a notable scholarly career—and a flirtation with left-wing politics—in Depression-era California. As a young man he had hiked through the Joachimsthal Valley. As a graduate student in Germany in the 1920s he had made the acquaintance of many of the scientists who were now working on Hitler's atomic project.

Besides the Top Policy Committee in Washington and the scientists at Los Alamos, few others shared in the deep secret of the bomb project. One who did was General Leslie Groves. In September 1942 Groves took charge of the bomb project, now placed under the War Department's control and code-named the Manhattan Engineering District. Groves was then a forty-six-year-old second-generation career army officer. He had grown up as an itinerant service brat in Cuba, the Philip-

---

72. Rhodes, *Making of the Atomic Bomb*, 452. In yet another indication of the surplus of scientific talent in wartime America, even some of the scientists at Los Alamos, notably Edward Teller, did not work exclusively on the atomic bomb project but also found time to explore the even more distant possibility of a "super" or hydrogen bomb based on fusion.

pines, and the western United States. Following in his father's footsteps, he had attended West Point, where he placed fourth in his class. He took graduate degrees in engineering and joined the Army Corps of Engineers. In 1942 he had just finished building the Pentagon, then the world's largest office building. He was big, bluff, all-army and can-do, an overstuffed man with a brusque front and no apologies. "I hated his guts," his chief aide once remarked, "and so did everybody else." In one of his first meetings with the scientists who were now nominally his underlings, Groves noticed an equation that had been improperly cop-ied and thought the learned professors were trying to trick him. He pointed out the error and put them on notice that his engineering work was worth two of their Ph.D.'s. "They didn't fool me," he later reflected. "There were a few Nobel Prizewinners among them. But I showed them. . . . They never forgave me for that."[73]

It is easy to see Professor Oppenheimer and General Groves as foils for one another—the gaunt, soul-tortured scientist, melancholic child of the Jewish diaspora, sensitive reader of Sanskrit epics and T. S. Eliot's poetry, the brooding genius who orchestrated all the exotic savants gath-ered at Los Alamos, playing the tragic hero opposite Grove's corpulent Rotarian Babbitt, West Point engineer, career soldier, gruff maker of buildings and bombs and a man without scruple, delicacy, or con-science. But if Oppenheimer and his scientists at Los Alamos constituted a crucial American asset in the race to build the bomb, Groves also embodied a kind of genius—the peculiarly American genius for orga-nization and management and for thinking in terms of stunningly vast enterprises.

Oppenheimer managed mathematical formulae and the art of or-chestrating the often idiosyncratic men who generated them. Groves managed the much more prosaic but no less indispensable arithmetic of budgets and the engineer's arts of sheer prodigiousness. Confronted with choices among five different methods of isotope separation and seven different techniques for plutonium extraction, for example, Groves's Manhattan Project went to work on all of them. "This Napo-leonic approach," Conant thought, "would require the commitment of perhaps $500,000,000 and quite a mess of machinery."[74] That proved an understatement. Before it was over, the Manhattan Project consumed

73. *Dictionary of American Biography* (New York: Charles Scribner's Sons, supp. 8, 1988), 231, 229.
74. Rhodes, *Making of the Atomic Bomb*, 407.

more than $2 billion, employed 150,000 people, and required a mess of machinery, plant, and other resources that were available nowhere but in America. In places, the bomb project changed the very face of the continent. On a fifty-nine-thousand-acre site near Oak Ridge, Tennessee, squarely in the midst of the vast power grid that the TVA had been building for nearly a decade, twenty thousand construction workers laid down fifty miles of railroad and three hundred miles of paved roads and streets and built several gaseous diffusion and electromagnetic installations for the extraction of U-235. The precious isotope offered itself in minuscule quantities at first. Yields were so low from the tons of ore being processed that workers plucked mere specks from their overalls with tweezers.

Along the banks of the Columbia River, whose pristine waters Lewis and Clark had paddled a century and a half before, thousands of other workers erected a brand-new town at Hanford, the site of an old ferry crossing in the nearly vacant interior of Washington State. The Hanford plant used the river's water for coolant and the river's energy — transformed into electricity by the New Deal's Bonneville and Grand Coulee dams — to drive its three atomic piles and four chemical separation plants. In those gargantuan facilities rising improbably from the sere tableland of the Columbia bench, workers tortuously squeezed out plutonium from grudging nature, a dime-size radioactive pellet from every two tons of uranium.

At both plants, forbidding technical problems repeatedly threatened to sink or fatally delay the project. Groves coped imperiously with them all. When boron contamination in graphite control rods threatened the operation of Fermi's uranium piles, he badgered manufacturers to make graphite to standards of purity once considered impossible. Building the Oak Ridge gaseous-diffusion plant was in itself a herculean assignment, even for a man who had erected the Pentagon. When completed, at a cost of $100 million, it was a forty-two-acre building housing thousands of diffusion tanks and flanked by a 2.9-million-square-foot machine shop and other buildings covering some fifty additional acres. When copper shortages threatened to scuttle Oak Ridge's electromagnetic separation facility, Groves contracted for more than thirteen thousand tons of silver from the federal depository at West Point with which to wind the separator's two thousand giant magnets. When some of the magnets proved defective, Groves ordered Allis-Chalmers to remake them. When output at Oak Ridge proved too slow, Groves directed an engineering firm to build an additional twenty-one-hundred-column diffusion plant to enrich the ore being fed to the electromagnetic separators, and he ordered it to be done in ninety days or less, a schedule that was met.

Under these engineering hammer-blows, nature began at last to yield useable quantities of fissionable material. By early 1945 Oak Ridge was giving up some seven ounces a day of 80 percent enriched U-235, enough to make one bomb by midyear and a bomb every six weeks thereafter. Hanford's giant piles went reliably critical in December 1944, prompting Groves to predict to George Marshall that he could have about eighteen five-kilogram plutonium bombs ready by the second half of 1945. In the space of three years, Groves had erected out of nothing a vast industrial complex, as large in scale as the entire prewar automobile industry. "You see," said Bohr on a later visit to the United States, "I told you it couldn't be done without turning the whole country into a factory. You have done just that."[75]

Fear of Germany had spurred the American atomic project. "We may be engaged in a race toward realization," Bush advised Roosevelt in early 1942. Conant worried about the same time that "there are still plenty of competent scientists left in Germany. They may be ahead of us by as much as a year."[76] Ironically, at virtually the same time the Americans were expressing these anxieties, and unbeknownst to them, the Germans were canceling their own bomb project. The reasons are instructive. In June 1942 German armaments minister Albert Speer summoned German scientists, including Otto Hahn and the brilliant Werner Heisenberg, to brief him about the possibilities of nuclear weapons. Heisenberg answered vaguely. It would take at least two years, he said, and would require enormous and unstinting economic and technological support. Speer considered the matter carefully, discussed it with Hitler, and made his decision. By the autumn of 1942, he later wrote, "[we] scuttled the project to develop an atom bomb. . . . Perhaps," Speer reflected in his memoirs, "it would have proved possible to have the atom bomb ready for employment in 1945. But it would have meant mobilizing all our technical and financial resources to that end, as well as our scientific talent. It would have meant giving up all other projects. . . . [I]t would have been impossible—given the strain on our economic resources—to have provided the materials, priorities, and technical workers corresponding to such an investment." Finally, Speer added, "our failure to pursue the possibilities of atomic warfare can be partly

75. Rhodes, *Making of the Atomic Bomb*, 500.
76. Rhodes, *Making of the Atomic Bomb*, 405–6.

traced to ideological reasons. . . . To his table companions Hitler occasionally referred to nuclear physics as 'Jewish physics.' "[77]

Similarly, Japanese officials estimated in 1942 that U-235 separation would consume one-tenth of Japan's electrical capacity as well as half its copper output and would in any case take ten years to produce results, a prospective schedule that ruled out any serious commitment to atomic weapons development. Japanese scientists further advised their government that neither the Germans nor the Americans could possibly deflect enough of their productive resources to a bomb project to have a weapon useable in the current war—a judgment in which they were half right. Some atomic work went ahead in wartime Japan, but the results were exceedingly sparse. By the summer of 1944 Japan had manufactured a total of 170 grams of uranium hexafluoride, a crucial element in the isotope-separation process. The American plants by then measured their production of uranium hexafluoride in tons. A fire raid on Tokyo in April 1945 definitively ended Japan's feeble atomic effort when it burned Japan's one tiny nuclear research laboratory to the ground. Britain, under the shadow of the Luftwaffe and unable to keep up even in conventional armaments without American aid, had long since abandoned its own atomic project. Most British nuclear scientists had transferred to the United States and been folded into the American project. As for the Russians, they lurched ahead with atomic research during the war, fed periodic and incomplete espionage reports on the American effort by a wary Stalin but making little progress.[78]

World enough and time, the poet sang, and when it came to atomic weapons development the United States was the one country that enjoyed amplitudes of both. The United States had a world of resources, physical as well as intellectual, a pool of things and talent so vast and deep that the Americans could build the first atom bombs while simultaneously pursuing advanced scientific research on other wizardly war technologies, including sonar, radar, the proximity fuse, the bazooka, amphibious vehicles, and steady improvements in the range, speed, and performance of combat aircraft, culminating in the B-29 "Superfortresses" that eventually delivered the two atomic bombs. Thanks to the pugnacity of the British in 1940 and the tenacity of the Russians since

77. Speer, *Inside the Third Reich*, 225–29. Einstein later commented, "If I had known that the Germans would not succeed in constructing the atom bomb, I would never have lifted a finger." Quoted in Michael Walzer, *Just and Unjust Wars* (New York: Basic, 1977), 263.

78. Rhodes, *Making of the Atomic Bomb*, 458, 581.

1941, the United States had been granted the time to do all those things, and more. The Manhattan Project thus stands as the single best illustration of the American way of war—not so much for the technological novelty of the bombs, or the moral issues they inevitably raised, but because only the Americans had the margins of money, material, and manpower, as well as the undisturbed space and time, to bring an enterprise on the scale of the Manhattan Project to successful completion. They did it while making good on the promise that they would build an arsenal of democracy with a crushing superiority in munitions. And they did it while equipping their allies abroad, lifting civilian living standards at home, and raising, training, and equipping a triphibious force of their own that was the best equipped and most mechanized in the world.

By the end of 1943 the Americans had stockpiled an arsenal that would give them a three-to-one munitions advantage over their foes when they finally took the field in force. In the Pacific the disparities were especially dramatic. Every American combatant in the last year and a half of war in the Pacific islands could draw on four tons of supplies; his Japanese opponent, just two pounds. So far, American forces had fought only scratch actions in the Mediterranean, mounted a few foolhardy forays in the skies over Europe, and struggled to some brave but still inconclusive victories in the Pacific. But as 1943 drew toward its close, the Americans and their overwhelming array of machines were nearly ready to swing into action, with all the energy of an exuberant economy and all the craft of modern science breathing power unimaginable behind them. After years of indifference, muddle, and make-do, the United States was at last prepared to fight its kind of war. It remained actually to fight it.

19

The Struggle for a Second Front

The year 1944 is loaded with danger.
— Winston Churchill to Franklin Roosevelt, October 27, 1943

Late on the evening of Armistice Day, November 11, 1943, Roosevelt and a handful of aides stole away from the White House and boarded the presidential yacht *Potomac*. At dawn the president's little craft lay alongside the massive battleship *Iowa*, anchored in Chesapeake Bay. A special rig hoisted the commander-in-chief up onto the *Iowa's* main deck. The dreadnought weighed anchor and headed out to the open sea. Eight days later the presidential party disembarked at Oran, in French North Africa. Roosevelt transferred to a specially fitted Army Air Corps Douglas C-54 transport plane, whimsically named "the Sacred Cow." His ultimate destination was Teheran and his first-ever meeting with Stalin. But the Sacred Cow first touched down at Cairo. It was not a stop that the president had originally wanted, and not one he anticipated with relish.

Just weeks earlier Churchill had warned Roosevelt that in the new phase of the war then emerging, when American might was at last beginning to weigh heavily in the scales, "[g]reat differences may develop between us." The first such difference had been over whether Roosevelt should meet Stalin alone, as the president wished. Churchill had muscled in and claimed a chair at the Teheran conference table. The prime minister then went further and insisted on a preliminary meeting between the two Western allies at Cairo before they confronted the Soviets at Teheran. Roosevelt had countered by suggesting that Soviet representatives as well as Chinese generalissimo Chiang Kai-shek should attend the preparatory talks. But the Soviets, still at peace with Japan, refused to parlay with Chiang for fear of provoking Tokyo. Thus it was just Churchill, Roosevelt, and Chiang who sat down for dinner at Ambassador Alexander C. Kirk's Nile-delta villa on the evening of November 22 to initiate the Cairo Conference.[1]

Perhaps to repay his annoyance with Churchill, Roosevelt spent most of his time over the next four days with Chiang, and the president saw to it that whatever discussion there was among all three leaders focused principally on the war in Asia. In that theater the differences between Churchill and Roosevelt were especially great and potentially explosive. Unlike the conflict in Europe, the war in Asia was in no small part a war about colonies. Britain was determined to hold on to India and to reclaim its other Asian possessions, lost to Japan in the first weeks of the war. France and the Netherlands, though for the moment under the Nazi heel, had similar plans to recapture their Japanese-occupied Asian colonies as soon as the war was over. The Americans, on the other hand, had long since pledged themselves to grant independence to the Philippines, and Roosevelt frequently badgered Churchill to do the same for India, Burma, Malaya, and Hong Kong.

In Roosevelt's mind, China would serve as a counterweight to Britain and the other European powers in postwar Asia, thus helping to secure permanent decolonization. A strong China would also help protect against a resurgent Japan and would check Soviet ambitions in the region as well. Churchill considered Roosevelt's concept of China as an eventual great power nothing less than ludicrous. "To the President, China means four hundred million people who are going to count in the world of tomorrow," Churchill's physician noted in his diary. "But Winston thinks only of the colour of their skin; it is when he talks of India or China that you remember he is a Victorian." At Cairo, Churchill tried in vain to send the irrelevant and pestiferous Chiang off sightseeing to the Pyramids. Instead, Churchill recalled drily, "the talks of the British and American staffs were sadly distracted by the Chinese story, which was lengthy, complicated, and minor."[2]

America's part in the Chinese story began well before Pearl Harbor. Indeed, it was America's stubborn commitment to China that had set the stage for Pearl Harbor. Early in 1941 the retired U.S. Army Air Corps colonel Clair Chennault had begun recruiting American pilots to fly under Chinese command in the American Volunteer Group, which

1. C&R 2:565.
2. Lord Moran, *Churchill: Taken from the Diaries of Lord Moran: The Struggle for Survival, 1940–1965* (Boston: Houghton Mifflin, 1966), 140; Churchill 5:289

journalists soon inappropriately labeled the "Flying Tigers" because of the sharks' teeth painted on the noses of their aircraft. Chennault entertained extravagant dreams of bringing Japan to its knees by flying from Chinese airbases to interdict Japanese merchant shipping and to inflict incendiary raids on Japanese cities. All he needed to accomplish this, he said, were thirty medium and twelve heavy bombers!

Few people, least of all George Marshall, took Chennault's wild claims seriously. Marshall instead looked for ways to help Chiang wage a more effective ground war against the one million Japanese troops in China and Southeast Asia. In early 1942 he sent Lieutenant General Joseph W. Stilwell to Chunking. Stilwell wore many hats in Chiang's capital: commander of all the American forces in China, Burma, and India (designated the CBI theater); Roosevelt's personal military representative to Chiang; Lend-Lease administrator for China; and, at least nominally, Chiang's chief of staff. Stilwell was a peppery, profane combat veteran of World War I and a seasoned infantry commander. He had done four tours of duty in China in the interwar years and spoke fluent Chinese. On paper, he seemed a perfect choice for the assignment.

But Stilwell's troubles began as soon as he arrived in Chunking in March 1942. At that moment Japanese forces were driving the remnants of the British army from Burma. Stilwell took personal command of a Chinese force and raced to Burma to prop up the British. Instead, the British-Chinese lines collapsed, and Stilwell had to execute a 140-mile retreat through rugged mountains to India. The Japanese victory closed the last overland supply route to China, the "Burma Road," a sinuous track that ran from the Irrawaddy River north of the Burmese port of Rangoon easterly into China's Yunan province. All Lend-Lease supplies for China now had to be laboriously airlifted from India over a series of towering Himalayan ranges known as "the Hump." Stilwell began immediately to plan a campaign to retake Burma and meanwhile started construction on the Ledo Road, a gargantuan engineering undertaking to build a new land route from Ledo in India, across northern Burma to Myitkyina, and thence into China. His inaugural defeat stung. "We got a hell of a beating," Stilwell told reporters. "We got run out of Burma and it's humiliating as hell."[3]

It was more than humiliating. Stilwell discovered during the brief and disastrous Burma campaign that the Chinese officers allegedly under his

---

3. Spector, 332.

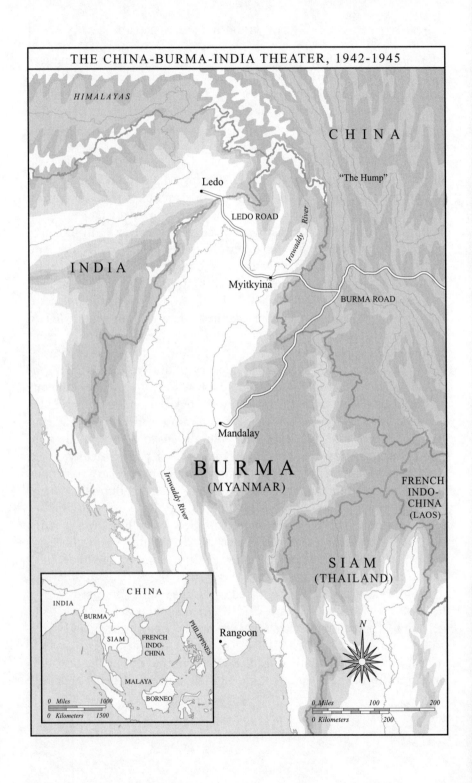

THE CHINA-BURMA-INDIA THEATER, 1942-1945

HIMALAYAS

CHINA

"The Hump"

Ledo

LEDO ROAD

Irawaddy River

INDIA

Myitkyina

BURMA ROAD

Mandalay

BURMA
(MYANMAR)

Irawaddy River

FRENCH
INDO-
CHINA
(LAOS)

SIAM
(THAILAND)

N

CHINA

INDIA

BURMA

FRENCH
INDO-
CHINA

PHILIPPINES

SIAM

Rangoon

MALAYA

BORNEO

0 Miles   1000
0 Kilometers   1500

0 Miles   100   200
0 Kilometers   200

command were in fact taking their instructions from Chiang, who frequently countermanded Stilwell's orders. The Burma episode sowed the seed of Stilwell's frustration with the evasive, scheming Chiang. Stilwell soon concluded that the Chinese leader was content to leave the job of defeating Japan to the Americans in the Pacific, while in China Chiang intended to wait out the war, accumulate reserves of American money and materiel, and prepare for an eventual showdown with Mao Tse-tung's Communists, against whom he had been waging a civil war since 1927. The Japanese, Chiang reportedly said, were merely "a disease of the skin," while the Communists were a "disease of the heart." By the time of the Cairo Conference, Stilwell had been struggling for nearly two years with the several Sisyphean tasks of reconciling Chiang and Mao, forging the corrupt and undisciplined Chinese army into an effective fighting force, and inducing it to fight. Stilwell's cantankerous temperament had earned him the nickname "Vinegar Joe" even before he arrived in China. Trying to grapple with the mercurial Chiang soured him still further. His aggravation with Chiang grew into scarcely concealed contempt. He took to calling Chiang, a compact man with a clean-shaven head, "the peanut."[4]

The peanut now sat across the table from FDR, while Vinegar Joe stewed in the wings at Ambassador Kirk's suburban Cairo villa. Roosevelt began to take his own measure of the generalissimo and found him grasping, weak, and indecisive. Nevertheless, wanting to keep China in the war and to retain Chinese friendship, Roosevelt gave Chiang several assurances: continued backing for Chennault's airmen; stepped-up Lend-Lease supplies over the Hump; resources for a simultaneous land offensive in northern Burma and an amphibious assault on the Andaman Islands, off the Burmese coast; and support for the newly created inter-Allied Southeast Asia Command (SEAC) under the British vice-admiral Lord Louis Mountbatten. Stilwell objected in vain that these several piecemeal efforts dissipated his scant resources and amounted to no strategy at all. His staff cracked that "SEAC" stood for "Save England's Asiatic Colonies." The several thousand mostly air and engineering troops under Stilwell's command in Ledo meanwhile quipped that "CBI" described them all too well: "Confused Bastards in India."

In fact, developments in late 1943 and 1944 were rapidly diminishing China's military significance. Stilwell would eventually reach Myitkyina

4. Michael Schaller, *The U.S. Crusade in China, 1939–1945* (New York: Columbia University Press, 1979), 39

in August 1944 and begin pushing the Ledo Road eastward into China. But the Japanese Ichi-go offensive at the same time captured all the Chinese airbases from which the bombing of Japan was to be conducted. And even while the statesmen were talking in Cairo, U.S. marines were taking the Gilbert Island atoll of Tarawa, opening the door for an American advance into the Central Pacific and the even more useful airfields of the Mariana Islands, just two thousand miles south of Japan. Chiang at last forced Stilwell's removal in October 1944, though he had the grace to rename the Ledo Road in Stilwells' honor on its completion in January 1945. By that time, China was a hopeless mess of renewed civil war and had ironically become all but irrelevant to the defeat of Japan.

THE "CHINESE BUSINESS occupied first instead of last place at Cairo," Churchill fumed. He and Roosevelt alike itched to put first things first at Teheran—above all, Overlord. As the sun touched the tops of the Giza pyramids on November 27, 1943, the Sacred Cow lifted off from Cairo West airport, bearing Roosevelt toward his long-anticipated encounter with Josef Stalin. The president's plane winged over Suez, swooped low for sight-seeing over the Holy Land, droned on across the Syrian desert to the green valleys of the Tigris and Euphrates, and finally topped the mountainous shoulder of western Iran. Looking out his window at the landscape passing below, Admiral William Leahy, Roosevelt's chief of staff, reflected on this flight "over territory rich in history that dated back to the earliest days of our civilization." The meeting of the "Big Three" that lay ahead in Teheran, representing what Churchill called "the greatest concentration of worldly power that had ever been seen in the history of mankind," promised to take its own prominent place in this ancient tapestry of historical significance.[5]

Roosevelt's continuing anxiety about Soviet intentions had been exacerbated not three weeks earlier when Major General John R. Deane, chief of the American military mission in Moscow, had cabled to Washington his alarming impression that now, as the Red Army rolled toward the Polish frontier, the Russians might be losing interest in Overlord. In the upcoming meetings at Teheran, Deane warned, the Soviets might well present demands for increased pressure in Italy and the Balkans,

5. William D. Leahy, *I Was There: The Personal Story of the Chief of Staff to Presidents Roosevelt and Truman Based on His Notes and Diaries Made at the Time* (New York: McGraw-Hill, 1950), 202–3; Churchill 5:290, 307.

coupled with a request that Overlord be postponed. Whether long-term political considerations—a desire to keep the Anglo-Americans out of the European heartland, or possibly even a plan to negotiate a separate peace with Germany—underlay this Russian line of thinking was impossible to say. But the prospect that Stalin, for whatever reason, might at Teheran buttress Churchill's familiar reservations about Overlord deeply disturbed American planners. For them, the cross-Channel invasion remained the supreme and jealously guarded foundation stone of anti-German strategy.

In midafternoon on the twenty-seventh, the presidential aircraft slipped through a pass in the mountains and descended into the horseshoe-shaped valley that cradled Teheran, a picturesque city surrounded by earthen ramparts and a moat, its historic center reached by twelve arched gates. To mollify Stalin and facilitate their exchanges, Roosevelt agreed to stay in the Russian compound. Stalin offered to call on the president the following day.

The man Roosevelt had flown halfway around the earth to meet remained an enigma, a shadowy figure even after nearly two decades at the pinnacle of power in the world's only Communist state. The menacing persona that constituted his image in the West reflected his own brooding, furtive temperament and testified as well to the character of the suspicion-saturated society over which he presided. Churchill had dreaded his own first encounter with the leader of the "sullen, sinister Bolshevik State I had once tried so hard to strangle at its birth." But at their initial meeting, in Moscow in August 1942, the prime minister had found Stalin to be remarkably astute, with a startling capacity for "swift and complete mastery of a problem hitherto novel to him."[6] Less generously, Lord Moran, Churchill's physician and confidant, called Stalin a "hard-boiled Asiatic."[7] Averell Harriman, the American ambassador to Moscow since October 1943, considered Stalin "the most inscrutable and contradictory character I have ever known," a baffling man of "high intelligence [and] fantastic grasp of detail," possessed of both "shrewdness" and "surprising human sensitivity." In Harriman's judgment, Stalin was "better informed than Roosevelt, more realistic than Churchill, in some ways the most effective of the war leaders. At the same time he was, of course, a murderous tyrant."[8] George Marshall

6. Churchill 4:428, 434
7. Moran, *Churchill*, 146.
8. W. Averell Harriman and Elie Abel, *Special Envoy to Churchill and Stalin, 1941–1946* (New York: Random House, 1975), 536.

thought Stalin simply "a rough SOB who made his way by murder."[9] Admiral Leahy, who observed Stalin closely throughout the meetings that were about to begin, came to Teheran expecting to meet "a bandit leader who had pushed himself up to the top of his government" but later confessed that "that impression was wrong. . . . [W]e were dealing with a highly intelligent man who spoke well . . . quietly, without gestures."[10] Hopkins, Roosevelt's personal emissary to Moscow in 1942, had reported that in his conversations with Stalin "not once did he repeat himself. . . . There was no waste of word, gesture, nor mannerism. It was like talking to a perfectly co-ordinated machine, an intelligent machine. . . . What he says is all the accent and inflection his words need."[11]

Into Roosevelt's quarters in the Soviet compound Stalin strode self-confidently at 3:15 on the twenty-eighth. This was the moment Roosevelt had so long awaited, when his personal charm and political skill could be directed full force at the taciturn Russian. Roosevelt had "come to Teheran determined . . . to come to terms with Stalin," Harry Hopkins told Lord Moran, "and he is not going to allow anything to interfere with that purpose. . . . After all," Hopkins said, "he had spent his life managing men, and Stalin at bottom could not be so very different from other people."[12]

"I am glad to see you," Roosevelt began ingratiatingly. "I have tried for a long time to bring this about." Stalin, his chunky frame draped in a simple khaki tunic, extended his hand. He accepted the blame for the delay in this meeting—and pointedly added that "he had been very preoccupied because of military matters."[13]

Seeing an opening, Roosevelt inquired as to the situation on the eastern front. Stalin said that while his forces held the initiative around Kiev, the Germans were still able to bring in reinforcements from the west and were counterattacking. Roosevelt replied that he had, of course, come to Teheran to discuss the Anglo-American plan to draw off thirty to forty German divisions from the eastern front. Stalin responded tersely that this would be "of great value." Roosevelt then tendered the surprisingly generous suggestion that after the war British and American

9. Forrest C. Pogue, *George C. Marshall: Organizer of Victory, 1943–1945* (New York: Viking Press, 1973), 313.
10. Leahy, *I Was There*, 205, 204.
11. Robert E. Sherwood, *Roosevelt and Hopkins: An Intimate History* (New York: Grosset and Dunlap, 1948, 1950), 343–44.
12. Moran, *Churchill*, 143.
13. *FRUS: The Conferences at Cairo and Teheran*, 1943, 483.

merchant ships might be turned over to the Soviets. This too, Stalin said laconically, would be "of great value." The conversation turned briefly to the Asian theater. Stalin declared that "the Chinese have fought very badly." He went on to speak scornfully about the shameful collaboration of the French with their Nazi masters and the need to punish France after the war, including stripping her of her colonies in Indochina. Roosevelt said he was "100% in agreement." After forty-five minutes of talk, much of it consumed by the awkward business of translation, the two leaders adjourned to join Churchill and the senior military planners for the first plenary session of the conference.[14]

Roosevelt, the master charmer, felt frustrated. "I couldn't get any personal connection with Stalin," he later reflected. "He was correct, stiff, solemn, not smiling, nothing human to get ahold of. . . . I had come there to accommodate Stalin. I felt pretty discouraged because I thought I was making no personal headway. . . . I had to cut through this icy surface."[15]

In a large Soviet Embassy conference room, seated at a round table with a green baize cover, the Big Three opened the first formal session of the Teheran Conference. Roosevelt and Churchill began with introductory badinage. Stalin sat silently through these ceremonial preliminaries, then simply announced: "Now let us get down to business."[16]

There was much business at hand. For four days discussion among the heads of state and their military advisers ranged over the globe and reached out toward the uncertain future of the war's next stages and the even more unknowable contours of the postwar world. The three leaders probed the sensitive issue of Poland's postwar boundaries. They opened the volatile subject of what to do with defeated Germany. They talked about the war in Asia. They sketched a tentative accord on a successor organization to the League of Nations, without defining its exact structure. Most important, they talked about Overlord.

With respect to Poland, Roosevelt acquiesced in Stalin's proposal to move the entire Polish state westward by setting the eastern Polish frontier at the World War I–era "Curzon Line" and the western frontier at the Oder River. In a remarkable one-on-one session with Stalin, Roosevelt spoke frankly as one politician to another. He explained "that

14. The Roosevelt-Stalin exchange is described in FRUS: Cairo and Teheran, 483–86. The same volume is the principal source of the account that follows.
15. Frances Perkins, The Roosevelt I Knew (New York: Viking Press, 1946), 83–84.
16. Moran, Churchill, 145. Other accounts of this meeting are in FRUS: Cairo and Teheran, 487ff.; Pogue, Marshall: Organizer of Victory, 310ff.; and Dallek, 431ff.

there were in the United States from six to seven million Americans of Polish extraction, and, as a practical man, he did not wish to lose their vote." (Roosevelt here foreshadowed his intention to run for a fourth term in 1944.) He hoped, therefore, that Stalin would understand that "he could not publicly take part in any such arrangement [to redefine Poland's frontiers] at the present time." By the same token, Roosevelt "went on to say that there were a number of persons of Lithuanian, Latvian, and Estonian origin" in the United States. He joked that "when the Soviet armies re-occupied these areas, he did not intend to go to war with the Soviet Union on this point," but pointed out to Stalin that he could use some political cover with the American electorate. "[I]t would be helpful for him personally," the president pleaded, "if some public declaration in regard to . . . future elections [in eastern Europe] could be made."[17]

Stalin would thus leave Teheran confident that the Western allies had no stomach for interfering with his intention to close the hand of Soviet power over eastern Europe. Roosevelt had conceded as much even before leaving for Teheran. To an American Catholic prelate, New York's Archbishop Francis Spellman, he had confided that eastern Poland, the Baltic States, Bessarabia, and Finland were already lost to the Soviets. "So better give them gracefully," he told Spellman. "What can we do about it?" Roosevelt rhetorically questioned the Polish ambassador in Washington: "[Do] you expect us and Great Britain to declare war on Joe Stalin if they cross your previous frontier? Even if we wanted to, Russia can still field an army twice our combined strength, and we would just have no say in the matter at all."[18]

Though Roosevelt remained diffident about publicly acknowledging such distasteful realities, they were the inevitable precipitate of the war's military chemistry. Soviet power would stand supreme in the east, in all those territories overrun by the Red Army. The Western allies would dominate such areas as they could manage to liberate from Axis control — Italy, for example, and whatever other zones the eventual second front might allow them to penetrate. Stalin himself had said as much when he told the Yugoslav Communist Josef Tito that "whoever occupies a territory also imposes his own social system. Everyone imposes his own system as far as his army can reach. It cannot be otherwise."

17. FRUS: Cairo and Teheran, 594–95.
18. Frank Freidel, Franklin D. Roosevelt: A Rendezvous with Destiny (Boston: Little, Brown, 1990), 479; Dallek, 436.

Here was darkly foreshadowed the division of Europe in the half-century-long Cold War.[19]

As for Germany, Stalin made it clear that he intended to deal harshly, even cruelly, with his Nazi foes. He spoke bitterly about the political docility and submissiveness of the German people. He recalled an old story about a band of several hundred German workers who failed to reach a political rally in Leipzig because they meekly declined to leave a railway station at which there was no controller to punch their tickets. Time and again he insisted that Germany must be reduced to several smaller states, else it would recover within a generation and once again plunge the world into the maelstrom. At dinner on the twenty-ninth Stalin proposed that fifty thousand German officers be "physically liquidated." The statement brought Churchill indignantly to his feet, saying: "I will not be a party to any butchery in cold blood. . . . I would rather be taken out now and shot than so disgrace my country." Roosevelt, ever eager to play the conciliator, interjected: "I have a compromise to propose. Not fifty thousand, but only forty-nine thousand should be shot."[20] The discussion ended with general but unspecified agreement on the postwar dismemberment of Germany, which, Roosevelt remarked, "had been less dangerous to civilization when in 107 provinces," before Bismarck's day.[21]

Yet the president, mindful as ever of the hesitant and unreliable commitment of his countrymen to international involvement, stopped well short of accepting Stalin's suggestion that American ground forces participate in the long-term occupation of a splintered Germany. By way of explaining to Churchill and Stalin the persistent strength of American isolationism, Roosevelt observed that "if the Japanese had not attacked the United States he doubted very much if it would have been possible to send any American forces to Europe."[22]

Roosevelt's repeated references to the tenuousness of American internationalism cannot have failed to make a deep impression on Stalin's calculations about the correlation of forces that would shape the postwar international order. The Americans, Stalin had every reason to conclude, would in all likelihood retire from the international scene at war's end, just as they had after World War I. Whatever the ambitions of

19. Milovan Djilas, *Conversations with Stalin* (New York: Harcourt, Brace and World, 1962), 114–15.
20. Moran, *Churchill*, 152. Another account is in *FRUS: Cairo and Teheran*, 553–54.
21. *FRUS: Cairo and Teheran*, 603.
22. *FRUS: Cairo and Teheran*, 531.

American leaders, including the obviously internationalist Roosevelt, public opinion would compel a return to the historic American policy of isolation. Churchill, indeed, never wasted an opportunity to sermonize his American audiences about the dangers of such a regression, as he had in a speech at Harvard the preceding September. ("There was no use saying . . . 'our forebears left Europe to avoid those quarrels; we have founded a new world which has no contact with the old,' " Churchill had preached. "The price of greatness is responsibility. . . . The people of the United States cannot escape world responsibility.")[23] But Churchill's nightmare was Stalin's dream. With Germany broken, Britain enfeebled, and America withdrawn across the sea, Europe at war's end would lie prostrate and helpless before Soviet power.

Even as these contrasting visions of the postwar world swam in the heads of Churchill, Roosevelt, and Stalin at Teheran, more immediate questions clamored for answers. None was more urgent than Overlord. "The second front decision," Admiral Leahy wrote, "overshadowed all other accomplishments of the Teheran meeting."[24] In the first plenary session, Roosevelt forthrightly opened the subject. Stalin sat inscrutable and silent, his eyes downcast. He chain-smoked mechanically and doodled wolf heads with a red pencil. For more than a year, Roosevelt explained, the British and American military staffs had been addressing the question of relieving German pressure on the Soviet front. At Quebec the previous August the decision had been taken to launch Overlord, an attack across the English Channel onto the French coast, at the earliest feasible date. Because the Channel was such "a disagreeable body of water," Roosevelt went on, the invasion could not begin before May 1944. (The British, Churchill interjected, had much reason to be thankful for the disagreeableness of the Channel.)

Then, to the astonishment of his entire entourage, Roosevelt veered away from the Channel altogether. Before Overlord could be launched in the spring of 1944, he mused, what use might be made of the British and American forces already deployed in the Mediterranean? At the risk of delaying Overlord by as much as three months, he said, those forces could be employed to intensify the offensive in Italy, or perhaps to undertake new offensives in the Adriatic or Aegean Sea. What did Stalin think?

23. "The Ceremonies in Honor of the Right Honorable Winston Spencer Churchill" (Cambridge: Harvard University, September 6, 1943), 11.
24. Leahy, I Was There, 209.

It was a tense moment. These various Mediterranean schemes, Roosevelt knew, were anathema to his own military chiefs. Marshall later remarked that he was "always fearful that Roosevelt might lightly commit them to operations in the Balkans. 'When President Roosevelt began waving his cigarette holder,'" Marshall told an interviewer, "'you never knew where you were going'"[25] Yet these same Mediterranean strategies were dear to Churchill, and General Deane had warned just days earlier that Stalin seemed to be favoring them. So just what, Roosevelt now asked, was Stalin's opinion?

Stalin replied in barely audible Russian. No hint of animation or emphasis gave his Anglophone listeners any clue to the drift of his remarks. Roosevelt, Churchill, and their military chiefs impatiently waited for the interpreter. At last they heard that Stalin was confirming the Soviet Union's commitment to enter the war against Japan after Germany was finally defeated. This was a matter of no small consequence. The war in Asia showed little prospect at this date of being won soon or easily. Chinese forces, corrupt, divided, and inefficient, proved hopelessly unable to inflict serious damage on the Imperial Japanese Army on the mainland. In the broad Pacific, American ground forces were still only inching forward against stiff Japanese resistance in the Solomons and New Guinea. The navy's Central Pacific thrust was just beginning to crack the outermost shell of Japan's many-layered defensive perimeter in the Gilbert Islands. To reach Japan from the Gilberts, the Americans still had to cross more than four thousand miles of an ocean studded with fortified islands. It seemed axiomatic at this point in the war—and for a long time thereafter—that to avoid a protracted bloodbath in the fight against Japan, Russian help was desperately needed. The Russian's pledge to declare war on Japan had still further strategic implications: it drastically reduced the importance of China as a base from which to attack Japan, and it reduced the threat that the Soviets would expand beyond the agreed armistice lines at the end of the fighting in Europe while the British and Americans were busy finishing the war in Asia.

Following this brief but important statement about Asia, Stalin addressed himself directly to Roosevelt's question about Europe. He reminded his allies that 210 German and fifty satellite divisions were now battling the Soviet armies in the scorched and devastated Russian heartland. Italy, effectively sealed off from the rest of Europe by the Alps, he

25. Pogue, *Marshall: Organizer of Victory*, 641, n. 35.

said, was hardly a proper place from which to attack the Germans. Likewise, he continued, the Balkans were far from the heart of Germany. Northern France, he declared unequivocally, was still the best place to open the second front.

Churchill conceded that the North African and Italian offensives had never amounted to the kind of second front that the Soviets had been promised since 1942. Overlord, he said, continued to have the highest claim on British and American resources. But he then plunged into an exposition of the advantages to be gained by continued operations in the Mediterranean theater.

Roosevelt, perhaps intending to placate Churchill, whom he had been snubbing since Cairo, interjected with a suggestion of a drive from Italy across the Adriatic into the Balkans. The other Americans present were flabbergasted. "Who's promoting that Adriatic business?" a startled Harry Hopkins scribbled to Admiral King, who was as mystified and worried as Hopkins.[26] Stalin, however, peremptorily discounted Churchill's assurance that continued Italian operations would not compromise the buildup for Overlord. He declared that scattering Allied forces in uncoordinated attacks was unwise. Overlord must be the priority, Stalin repeated. Along with a closely coordinated attack from the south of France, Overlord would enclose the German armies in the west within the arms of a giant pincer movement.

Churchill, upset that "the President was in private contact with Marshal Stalin and dwelling at the Soviet Embassy, and that he had avoided ever seeing me alone since we left Cairo," returned to the subject at the next day's plenary session.[27] Roosevelt's musings on the preceding day seemed to offer him an opening. Now the prime minister, according to Hopkins's biographer, "employed all the debater's arts, the brilliant locutions and circumlocutions of which he was a master."[28] He again went on at length about Italy, Yugoslavia, Turkey, the island of Rhodes. Stalin at last, fed up with "all the dodges and feints of his practiced adversary," said that he wished to ask an "indiscreet question": "[D]o the British really believe in Overlord or are they only saying so to reassure the Russians?"[29]

Churchill countered with a proposal for further study of the political

26. Sherwood, *Roosevelt and Hopkins*, 780.
27. Churchill 5:331.
28. Sherwood, *Roosevelt and Hopkins*, 789.
29. Sherwood, *Roosevelt and Hopkins*, 789; FRUS: *Cairo and Teheran*, 539.

implications of his Mediterranean proposals. "Why do that?" Stalin exploded in a rare burst of animation. "We are the chiefs of government. We know what we want to do. Why turn the matter over to some subordinates to advise us?"[30] The Mediterranean proposals were nothing more than "diversions," said Stalin. He had no interest in them. "Who will command Overlord?" he demanded. Told that the matter of command was not yet decided, he growled: "Then nothing will come out of these operations." He insisted on knowing the precise date of the invasion. "If we are here to discuss military matters," Stalin declared summarily, "then Russia is only interested in Overlord."[31]

Roosevelt now said, finally and firmly, that the target date ("D-Day") for Overlord was May 1, 1944. Nothing, he added emphatically, would be allowed to alter that date. "[T]here was no God-damn alternative left," Hopkins gloated later to Lord Moran. Stalin looked triumphantly at Churchill, according to Hopkins, as if to say, "Well, what about that?"[32] Then, in his conciliatory way, the president observed "that in an hour a very good dinner would be awaiting," and the session adjourned.[33]

The following day all three leaders formally approved the Overlord plan. It called for a massive attack across the Channel in May 1944, supported by landings in the south of France and coordinated with a Russian offensive in the east. They further agreed to implement a "cover plan" to mystify and deceive the enemy as to the site and timing of the invasion. "The truth," said Churchill in one of his inimitable flourishes, "deserves a bodyguard of lies."[34]

"I thank the Lord Stalin was there," said Stimson upon hearing the reports of the Teheran Conference. "[H]e saved the day. He was direct and strong and he brushed away the diversionary attempts of the Prime Minister with a vigor which rejoiced my soul."[35] The prime minister meanwhile moped, gripped by what his physician called a "black depression." His ability to guide Roosevelt had clearly waned. No longer was Britain the dominant partner in the Anglo-American alliance, as it had been at least through the Casablanca Conference at the beginning of 1943. Indeed, Churchill's dogged insistence on his Mediterranean

30. Leahy, *I Was There*, 207.
31. Moran, *Churchill*, 147.
32. Moran, *Churchill*, 147.
33. *FRUS: Cairo and Teheran*, 552.
34. *FRUS: Cairo and Teheran*, 578.
35. Stimson Diary, December 5, 1943.

proposals may have stemmed in part from what British historian Michael Howard calls his "sheer chauvinism," his "chagrin at the increasing preponderance of American forces in the European war," and his "desire to form a purely British theater where the laurels would be all ours."[36]

"I could have gained Stalin," Churchill later reflected, "but the President was oppressed by the prejudices of his military advisers and drifted to and fro in the argument. . . . I regard the failure to use otherwise unemployable forces to bring Turkey into the war and dominate the Aegean as an error in war direction which cannot be excused by the fact that in spite of it victory was won."[37] Stalin, Churchill brooded, "will be able to do as he pleases. Will he become a menace to the free world, another Hitler?" Roosevelt had behaved ineptly, in Churchill's view; he "was asked a lot of questions and gave the wrong answers. . . . Stupendous issues are unfolding before our eyes," Churchill told Lord Moran, warming grandiloquently to his subject, "and we are only specks of dust, that have settled in the night on the map of the world. . . . We've got to do something with these bloody Russians."[38]

Roosevelt's translator at Teheran, Foreign Service officer Charles E. Bohlen, shared many of Churchill's forebodings. The Big Three had left "all political questions, except for the British-Soviet accord on Poland's eastern border . . . , completely up in the air," Bohlen reflected. Germany was apparently to be broken up, France stripped of her colonies, and Poland relocated to the west, but, he noted, "these ideas were so inchoate and informal that they did not constitute decisions. . . . Viewed in retrospect, there were many forerunners of Yalta [the second

---

36. Michael Howard, *The Mediterranean Strategy in the Second World War* (New York: Praeger, 1968), 57.
37. Churchill 5:305–6.
38. Moran, *Churchill*, 149–55. Churchill's despondency was due ostensibly to his anxiety about Russian expansion into eastern Europe, the Balkans, and the eastern Mediterranean. But Churchill's memoirs record an intriguing private conversation that he held with Stalin on the morning of November 30 at Teheran, in which Stalin raised the specter of another kind of danger in the east—Russian withdrawal from the war. "Stalin said he must warn me," Churchill wrote, "that the Red Army was depending on the success of our invasion of Northern France. If there were no operations in May 1944 then the Red Army would think that there would be no operations at all that year. . . . If there was no big change in the European war in 1944 it would be very difficult for the Russians to carry on. They were war-weary." Churchill 5:335.

and endlessly controversial meeting of the Big Three, in February 1945] at Teheran." It seemed to Bohlen entirely possible that at war's end "the Soviet Union would be the only important military and political force on the continent of Europe. The rest of Europe would be reduced to military and political impotence." The only definite consequence of the Teheran meeting, Bohlen concluded, was "that we had reached a solid military agreement."[39]

Roosevelt, too, left Teheran harboring some doubts about Russian intentions. Would Stalin actually deliver on his promise to declare war on Japan? Would the Russians in fact join a postwar international league? These questions worried the president in private. In public, concerned as ever to wean his countrymen from their isolationist ways, he insisted that the Teheran Conference had cemented the basis for great-power cooperation and established a close personal relationship between himself and Stalin. The Soviet premier was a "realist," he told a journalist, "something like me." "I got along fine with Marshal Stalin," he reported in a Christmas Eve Fireside Chat to the American people. "I believe that we are going to get along very well with him and the Russian people—very well indeed."[40] There was some dissembling in those remarks, though as in so much of Roosevelt's prewar struggle against isolationist opinion, it was a dissembling born of necessity and hope—the necessity now of nurturing the Soviet alliance and the hope that American influence might be brought to bear in the postwar world.

Yet Roosevelt the realist remained capable of more dissembling still. Despite his eagerness to win Stalin's confidence, he had conspicuously declined at Teheran to share with the Soviet leader the secret of Ultra and the infinitely more consequential secret of the Manhattan Project. As for the political commitments he had signaled at Teheran, Roosevelt disingenuously replied to an inquiring congressman in March 1944 that "there were no secret commitments made by me at Teheran. . . . This, of course, does not include military plans which, however, had nothing to do with Poland."[41] Left unmentioned was Roosevelt's effective acquiescence in a Soviet sphere of influence in Poland and the Baltic States. With these silences, the president laid up trouble for the future— trouble with his wartime ally and trouble with his own people, who

39. Charles E. Bohlen, *Witness to History, 1929–1969* (New York: Norton, 1973), 153.
40. Dallek, 439.
41. *FRUS: Cairo and Teheran*, 877

would one day have to divest themselves of the idealistic illusions spun by their calculating leader and try to face the world the war was making with as much realism of their own as they could muster.

"WHO WILL COMMAND OVERLORD ?" Stalin had demanded at Teheran. Stopping again in North Africa on his way home, Roosevelt gave Stalin his answer, though it was not one easily arrived at. At Quebec in August 1943 Churchill had conceded that the command of Overlord should go to an American, since the Americans would contribute the bulk of the materiel and the manpower. It had been widely assumed that the American would be George Marshall. In anticipation of her husband's new assignment, Mrs. Marshall had even begun to move the family belongings out of the chief of staff's residence at Fort Myer, in northern Virginia. Marshall, it was thought, was the only American with sufficient prestige and resolve to pull off Overlord in the face of all kinds of British blandishments to engage in delay and "scatterization." "[T]he one prayer I make for the Commander-in-Chief is steadfastness," Stimson wrote on the eve of the Teheran meetings. "Marshall's command of Overlord is imperative for its success," Stimson continued. "Marshall's presence in London will strongly tend to prevent any interference with Overlord."[42]

The prospect of Marshall's appointment provoked a controversy that festered through the autumn of 1943 and was not yet resolved when Roosevelt arrived at the conference table in Teheran. In his usual fashion, the president listened to many voices and kept his own counsel. When World War I icon General John J. Pershing protested to Roosevelt that Marshall's value as chairman of the Combined Chiefs of Staff far outweighed his possible contribution as a field commander, the president had disarmingly replied: "I think it is only a fair thing to give George a chance in the field. . . . I want George to be the Pershing of the Second World War—and he cannot be that if we keep him here."[43] On his way to the Cairo and Teheran meetings, the president had expanded on this theme in a conversation with General Eisenhower—the most frequently mentioned alternative to Marshall as Overlord commander. "Ike," said Roosevelt, "you and I know who was the Chief of Staff during the last years of the Civil War [it was Major General Henry W. Halleck, a feckless gossip deservedly swallowed by obscurity] but

42. Sherwood, Roosevelt and Hopkins, 766.
43. Sherwood, Roosevelt and Hopkins, 770.

practically no one else knows, although the names of the field generals — Grant, of course, and Lee, and Jackson, Sherman, Sheridan and the others — every schoolboy knows them. I hate to think that 50 years from now practically nobody will know who George Marshall was. That is one of the reasons I want George to have the big command — he is entitled to his place in history as a great General."[44] Hopkins and Stimson, Roosevelt knew, strongly supported this reasoning. So too, he had every reason to believe, did Churchill and Stalin.

Yet the president's military advisers voiced powerful reservations. Admiral Leahy, along with Marshall's colleagues on the Chiefs of Staff, Admiral King and General Arnold, agreed with Pershing. They wanted Marshall to remain in Washington. There his towering intelligence and monumental integrity made him a uniquely effective leader in the ceaseless clamor of argument over the competing claims of different services, widely separated theaters of war, and fractious allies. Marshall himself scrupulously determined not to embarrass the president by expressing his own preference, though surely, his biographer notes, command of Overlord was "the climax to which all his career had been directed."[45]

Roosevelt in the end acceded to the arguments of his military advisers. He may have been influenced as well by the consideration that, with Stalin's strong advocacy of Overlord now assured, there was less need for a figure of Marshall's stature to stand up to the British in London. On December 5 Roosevelt summoned Marshall to his villa in Cairo and told him, "I didn't feel I could sleep at ease if you were out of Washington."[46] Betraying no sign of disappointment, Marshall graciously drafted for the president's signature a note informing Stalin that "the immediate appointment of General Eisenhower to Command of Overlord operation has been decided upon." If Stalin harbored any thought that the appointment of Eisenhower rather than Marshall signaled some downgrading of the Overlord operation, the record does not reveal it.

The president then flew on to Tunis. Eisenhower, a balding, middle-aged man of average height, his open face brightened by a luminous grin, a warm, popular, plain-spoken officer known affectionately to his associates as "Ike," awaited him at the airport. Roosevelt "was scarcely seated in the automobile," Eisenhower later recalled, when he said,

44. Sherwood, *Roosevelt and Hopkins*, 770.
45. Pogue, *Marshall: Organizer of Victory*, 320.
46. Pogue, *Marshall: Organizer of Victory*, 321.

"Well, Ike, you are going to command Overlord." It was December 7, 1943, two years to the day since the Pearl Harbor attack.[47]

So it would not be Marshall but Eisenhower whose name, like Grant's, would be inscribed in the schoolbooks as the man who held the "big command." Like Grant, too, another renownless midwestern career military officer plucked from obscurity by the caprice of war, Eisenhower would later ascend to the presidency—the first general since Grant, in fact, to be so honored. The prospect that command of Overlord might well clear a pathway to the White House cannot have escaped Roosevelt and had doubtless contributed to his anguish over withholding the prize from Marshall.

Dwight David Eisenhower, like nearly all the senior American commanders in the war, was a man of the nineteenth century. Born in Texas in 1890 and reared in Abilene, Kansas, he was an army "lifer," approaching twenty-five years of service when World War II broke out. He had scant hope, before the war changed everything, for promotion beyond the rank of colonel, which he attained only in March 1941. In common with many officers in the interwar army, he had never seen combat. He had spent World War I training tank troops in a stateside camp and had languished through the postwar years in a series of humdrum assignments, including service in France writing a guidebook to American battlefields. Though only a middling student at West Point, he shone during a stint at the army's Command and General Staff School at Fort Leavenworth in 1926, placing first in his class of 275 officers. He had served on Douglas MacArthur's staff in Washington in 1933 and accompanied MacArthur to the Philippines in 1935. MacArthur called him "the best officer in the Army. When the next war comes," MacArthur advised, "he should go right to the top."[48]

He did. Marshall summoned him to Washington in December 1941 to head the Pacific and Far Eastern Section of the War Department's War Plans Division. Amidst the chaos of war-girding Washington, Marshall needed assistants who would shoulder heavy responsibilities and act decisively without coming to him for consultation. Eisenhower did not disappoint. He quickly distinguished himself for the thoroughness of his analyses and the lucidity of his reports. Literally within hours of his arrival in Washington, Eisenhower had drafted a plan to use Australia

47. Dwight D. Eisenhower, *Crusade in Europe* (New York: Doubleday, 1948), 207–8.
48. Stephen E. Ambrose, *Eisenhower: Soldier, General of the Army, President-Elect, 1890–1952* (New York: Simon and Schuster, 1983), 93.

as a base of operations against the beleaguered Philippines. Sounding what would become a characteristic note, he justified his proposal for swift and heavy military effort with an appeal to considerations of morale: "The people of China, of the Philippines, of the Dutch East Indies will be watching us. They may excuse failure but they will not excuse abandonment."[49] Marshall was impressed. He selected Eisenhower in June 1942 over 366 senior officers to command all American forces in the European theater. Promoted to lieutenant general the following month, Eisenhower then assumed command of the Allied armies that cleared North Africa and invaded Italy.

A careful student of war, Eisenhower was a still more careful student of human psychology—especially of those elements that made up the mysterious compound of effective leadership. "The one quality that can be developed by studious reflection and practice is the leadership of men," he wrote to his son in 1943. "The idea is to get people working together . . . because they instinctively want to do it for you. . . . [E]ssentially, you must be devoted to duty, sincere, fair and cheerful."[50] Conspicuously absent from this list of a military leader's qualities was any mention of the need for aggression or for the bravura posturing associated with the likes of Douglas MacArthur or George Patton. Eisenhower, clearly, was no ordinary soldier.

As the head of the combined-service, inter-Allied forces in the North African and Italian campaigns, Eisenhower had amply demonstrated his capacity for leadership in the uniquely collaborative circumstances of the Anglo-American military partnership. "The seeds for discord between ourselves and our British allies were sown," he wrote to Marshall in April 1943, "as far back as when we read our little red history school books. My method is to drag all those matters squarely into the open, discuss them frankly, and insist upon positive rather than negative action in furthering the purpose of Allied unity."[51] Unity in allied command, he advised Lord Louis Mountbatten, "involves the human equation. . . . Patience, tolerance, frankness, absolute honesty in all dealings, particularly with all persons of the opposite nationality, and firmness, are absolutely essential."[52]

In the Mediterranean campaigns Eisenhower had proved his ability

49. Stephen E. Ambrose, *The Supreme Commander: The War Years of General Dwight D. Eisenhower* (Garden City, N.Y.: Doubleday, 1970), 6.
50. *PDDE* 2:1198.
51. *PDDE* 2:1071.
52. *PDDE* 3:1420–23.

to fathom and manipulate "the human equation." He had established his reputation as a sunny personality, fair and upstanding in his dealings with all, unflappable in crisis. Yet even Eisenhower's geniality contained elements of his purposeful artifice. No matter how wearing his duties or how grim the military outlook, Eisenhower by act of will "firmly determined that my mannerisms and speech in public would always reflect the cheerful certainty of victory."[53] This stratagem worked, to marvelous effect. Even his sometimes bitter critic Bernard Montgomery conceded that Ike's "real strength lies in his human qualities. . . . He has the power of drawing the hearts of men towards him as a magnet attracts the bits of metal. He merely has to smile at you, and you trust him at once. He is the very incarnation of sincerity." His colleague General Omar Bradley said simply that Ike's smile was worth twenty divisions.[54]

Eisenhower's studied geniality found an appreciative admirer in Franklin Roosevelt, himself an adept scholar of the human psyche and a virtuoso practitioner of the recondite craft of leadership. Now, flying from Tunis to Sicily for an inspection tour of American troops, Roosevelt the accomplished master instructed Eisenhower the sedulous apprentice in the arts that he must summon and hone in his new assignment. Huddling in a seat alongside the general as their aircraft droned over the Mediterranean, the president dwelt on the teeming difficulties that awaited Eisenhower in London. There he would confront head-on, day in and day out, the full majesty of the British Government and the seductive personality of Winston Churchill. Churchill still believed, Roosevelt warned, that a failed Channel attack could cost the Allies the war—and that the risk of failure was large. Despite his assurances at Quebec and his submission at Teheran, Churchill had not laid to rest his gnawing anxieties about Overlord. It would take all of Eisenhower's skill and resolution, Roosevelt advised, to keep Overlord on schedule.

Eisenhower listened carefully. Occasionally he gazed pensively at the blue waters beneath as the aircraft approached the Sicilian coast. To him now fell not only the task of managing the inevitable tensions that beset the British-American alliance. He also faced the colossal responsibilities of organizing a vast command that embraced land, sea, and air arms, orchestrating the tendentious wills of countless admirals, generals,

53. Unpublished introduction to Eisenhower's *Crusade in Europe*, quoted in Fred I. Greenstein, *The Hidden-Hand Presidency: Eisenhower as Leader* (New York: Basic, 1982), 37.

54. Ambrose, *Supreme Commander*, 325; Omar N. Bradley and Clay Blair, *A General's Life* (New York: Simon and Schuster, 1983), 240–41.

and statesmen, and meshing the million upon million gears, the prodigious material tonnage and the precious human flesh, that would constitute the largest, most complex military operation in history.

PLANNING FOR OVERLORD had already begun — on both sides.
Even as the final preparations for the Teheran Conference were being
made, Hitler had issued Führer Directive 51 on November 3, 1943.
"The threat from the East remains," Hitler proclaimed,

> but an even greater danger looms in the West: the Anglo-American
> landing! In the East, the vastness of space will, as a last resort, permit
> a loss of territory even on a major scale, without suffering a mortal
> blow to Germany's chance for survival.
>
> Not so in the West! If the enemy here succeeds in penetrating our
> defenses on a wide front, consequences of staggering proportions will
> follow within a short time. All signs point to an offensive against the
> Western Front of Europe no later than spring, and perhaps earlier....
> I have therefore decided to strengthen the defenses in the West, par-
> ticularly at places from which we shall launch our long-range war
> against England. [Hitler here referred to the pilotless V-1 flying bombs
> and the later V-2 rocket bombs then under development in the Baltic
> village of Peenemunde.] For those are the very points at which the
> enemy must and will attack; there — unless all indications are mislead-
> ing — will be fought the decisive invasion battle.[55]

Hitler had much to worry about. Where would the eventual blow
fall? The "West" as Führer Directive 51 defined it stretched from the
Bay of Biscay to Denmark, even to Norway, where *der Führer* insisted
on keeping eleven divisions in readiness to repel an invasion. To the
urgent task of fortifying that vast perimeter, a task that necessarily implied guessing at the most likely landing zone, Hitler assigned one of
his most senior commanders, the seasoned "Desert Fox" of the North
African campaigns, Field Marshal Erwin Rommel. His nominal superior
but effective co-equal in command was Field Marshal Gerd von Rundstedt, an elderly, aristocratic veteran who had distinguished himself in
Poland, the Low Countries, and Russia in the early phases of the war
before reaching retirement age in late 1941. Rundstedt had been called
back to active duty in July 1942 and appointed commander-in-chief for
the west, responsible for anti-invasion preparations. Two field marshals,
Rommel and Rundstedt, now essentially held the same assignment, with

55. Gordon A. Harrison, *Cross-Channel Attack* (Washington: Department of the Army,
    1951), 455.

telling consequences for the inefficiency of the German command structure in the west.

After a brief inspection of defensive preparations in Denmark, Rommel arrived in December 1943 in France. Its northern coast, he rightly calculated, was the overwhelmingly probable site of the anticipated invasion. But without knowing precisely where his enemy would strike on that still expansive terrain, Rommel still faced a daunting challenge.

Even as Eisenhower was heading toward his new headquarters in England, directly across the English Channel Rommel was commandeering his own command post on the upper reaches of the Seine River, in the Château La Roche-Guyon, where Thomas Jefferson had once been a guest. Before Rommel's arrival, France had been a kind of convalescent hospital for German troops recovering from the ghastly slaughter in the east. From his sumptuous headquarters in the Hotel George V in Paris, Rundstedt presided serenely over his mercifully placid sector. Far from battle, members of an occupying army to be sure, but one rarely put on its mettle by the mostly subdued French population, Rundstedt's soldiers ate well, idled much, slept soundly, gave thanks for their agreeable billeting, and prayed that their good fortune would last.

Rommel changed all that. Within weeks of his arrival, toiling at obsessive pace under his swinging field marshal's baton, the Germans cobbled together an "Atlantic Wall" along the northern French coast, designed with desperate cunning to repel the Allied invasion before it ever got off the tidal flats. They beavered up half a million bristling steel and concrete antitank obstacles on the beaches from Brest to Calais, emplaced and registered gun batteries, built and armed pillboxes, laid four million mines, flooded lowlands, and planted countless inland fields with "Rommel's asparagus," cruel spikes rising eight to twelve feet out of the earth, festooned with barbed wire and booby traps and intended to impale descending parachutists or blow up landing aircraft. By early May Rommel would survey his work with satisfaction. "If the British give us just two more weeks," he said on May 5, "I won't have any more doubt of it."[56]

On their side, the British and the Americans had set the ponderous machinery of planning in motion in the spring of 1943, even before the Teheran Conference. An Anglo-American team working in London under British General Frederick Morgan, designated COSSAC (chief of

56. Rommel quoted in John Keegan, *The Second World War* (New York: Viking, 1990), 372.

staff to the supreme Allied commander, who was of course not yet named), had first wrestled with the same question that confounded the Germans: where, exactly, should the blow be struck? Because the planners deemed air superiority over the landing zone to be essential, the site must necessarily lie within an arc defined by the 175–mile radius of action of the British Spitfire—still, as planning began in 1943, the principal fighter aircraft in the Allied arsenal. That simple calculus immediately eliminated Denmark and Norway, as well as Brittany, a sentimental favorite with the Americans, who had landed the American Expeditionary Force through the Breton ports of Brest and St. Nazaire in the First World War. From their bases in the south of England, Spitfires could cover a zone stretching from Holland in the north to France's Cotentin peninsula in the south. The Netherlands' watery lowlands lacked sufficiently hard beaches or solid interior plains across which to transport large numbers of men and machines. The Cotentin peninsula could be easily sealed at its base, marooning an invasion force.

By process of elimination, therefore, the choice reduced to two sites: the Pas de Calais, a short hop across the English Channel from Dover; or the bucolic region to the west of the Seine's mouth, Normandy's Calvados Coast, so called from the apple-based drink typical of the region. Calais had conspicuous attractions, especially the shortness of the sea voyage from Dover and its proximity to the great German industrial plexus of the Ruhr—the Allies' ultimate and highest strategic objective. But the very conspicuousness of those considerations meant that the Germans would expect an attack there and mount a fierce defense.

Normandy was farther from Germany, and from England, too, for that matter, but it had irresistible advantages. Its broad, hard beaches could accommodate the hundreds of thousands of troops and the tens of thousands of vehicles that must come ashore, until such time as proper ports—at Cherbourg, Brest, and eventually Antwerp—could be secured and fitted to supply the expeditionary force. In the meantime, two artificial harbors, known as "Mulberries," would be towed across the Channel to the Normandy shore.

Normandy had a further and invaluable advantage, one that compounded the returns on the deception scheme agreed upon at Teheran. Code-named Fortitude, that scheme enfolded the secret of secrets—the location of the Overlord landing—deep within the fraudulent embrace of Churchill's "bodyguard of lies." Fortitude constituted perhaps the war's most extravagant demonstration of the wonderful wages of untruth. The lie that Fortitude fed to the Germans was simple enough: that the cross-Channel invasion would be aimed at Calais (or even, possibly, at Norway).[57] To render this already plausible fiction credible, a real general, George Patton, was named to command a wholly imaginary body, First U.S. Army Group. The illusion of First U.S. Army Group's existence, some fifty fictive divisions strong, was sustained by generating radio traffic, sure to be overheard on the Continent, among Patton's notional units and by sprinkling the countryside and waterways of Kent and Sussex, opposite Calais, with dummy aircraft, tanks, trucks, and landing craft, all to fool aerial reconnaissance. Perhaps most consequentially, the shadowy "Twenty Committee," cryptically taking its name from the Latin signification of the "double cross" (XX), cashed in on the elaborately cultivated plot by means of which it had turned every single German informant in England into an Allied agent. Through these sources word passed to German headquarters that Patton's army was real and that Calais was almost certainly the place.

Diverting German attention to Calais held out the prospect of rich rewards. Achieving surprise, to be sure, would enormously facilitate the initial landings, but even more important than achieving surprise at the battle's outset was inducing lingering indecision once the battle was joined. Establishing the beachhead was the relatively easy part of Overlord, Morgan's planners reasoned. The race of the buildup, which would wager the Allies' capacity to reinforce against the enemy's ability to counterattack, would ultimately determine the success or failure of Overlord.[58] Thus the Germans might at first consider the Normandy landings a feint—something they would never presume in the case of a direct assault on Calais—and so hesitate to commit the full force of their mobile reserves. He who hesitates is lost, the old maxim goes, and the hope of producing a fatal tentativeness in the German response to the cross-Channel attack was the greatest prize for which Fortitude aimed.

As it happened, the confusion that Fortitude sought to sow exacerbated one of the knottiest problems that the Germans faced as they

---

57. "Fortitude" actually consisted of two lies—one that the invasion would fall at Calais (Fortitude South) and the other that it would fall on Norway (Fortitude North). Fortitude South, however, was far the more elaborate and consequential deception. See Charles Cruickshank, *Deception in World War II* (New York: Oxford University Press, 1979); and J. C. Masterman, *The Double-Cross System in the War of 1939 to 1945* (New Haven: Yale University Press, 1972).

58. As Churchill had told Stalin at Teheran: "I was not afraid of going on shore, but of what would happen on the thirtieth, fortieth, or fiftieth day." Churchill 5:335.

attempted to implement Führer Directive 51: what mix of static and mobile forces, deployed in what dispositions, offered the best possibility of repelling the Allied invaders? From the moment that Rommel had arrived in France, he and Rundstedt had disagreed over this issue. Rundstedt, despairing of adequately defending his entire coastal sector and wary of a feint, proposed to let the invaders come ashore and then massively counterattack. Once the main enemy force was clearly identified, he would choose his own battleground and unleash armored panzer divisions held in reserve well behind the beaches. Rommel, on the other hand, like Yamamoto in the Pacific, feared "the numerical and material superiority of the enemy striking-forces" and wanted to give his enemy no opportunity to put ashore in France even a part of the stupendous weight of flesh and firepower he knew to be accumulating in England. More immediately, unlike Rundstedt, who had never fought a major battle in which the enemy enjoyed air superiority, Rommel in Africa had firsthand experience of the difficulty of shifting even fast-moving mechanized formations under the wrathful eye of Allied air power. "British and American superiority in the air alone has again and again been so effective," he wrote, "that all movement of major formations has been rendered completely impossible, both at the front and behind it, by day and by night." From this analysis it followed axiomatically, in Rommel's view, that the *Wehrmacht* must be committed to "beat off the enemy landing *on the coast* and to fight the battle in the more or less strongly fortified coastal strip."[59] Rommel proposed, therefore, to pre-position the panzer divisions as near to the beaches as possible. As his old desert foe Montgomery worriedly described it on the eve of D-Day:

> Rommel is an energetic and determined commander; he has made a world of difference since he took over. He is best at the spoiling attack; his forte is disruption; he is too impulsive for the set-piece battle. He will do his level best to "Dunkirk" us — not to fight the armoured battle on ground of his own choosing but to avoid it altogether and prevent our tanks landing by using his own tanks well forward.[60]

Yet for all that he worried Montgomery, Rommel could never adequately answer Rundstedt's practical objections to his theoretically

---

59. Rommel quoted in Carlo D'Este, *Decision in Normandy* (New York: HarperCollins, 1994), 116–17; emphasis added.
60. Montgomery quoted in Keegan, *Second World War*, 374, and more fully in D'Este, *Decision in Normandy*, 85.

sound doctrine: well forward *where*, near to *which* beaches, exactly, in Normandy or the Pas de Calais? The result was a compromise by which some panzer divisions were assigned to Rommel and some to Rundstedt, with Hitler himself thickening the viscosity of this already awkwardly divided command by retaining final authority over release of the reserve units. This poorly resolved dispute over defensive doctrine—aggravated by the poorly articulated German command structure in the west— Fortitude had helped to foster and would artfully exploit.

Despite the problems that plagued the German defense, Rundstedt and Rommel still had a formidable fighting machine at their disposal. To be sure, the principal theater of war was still in the east, where 165 German divisions continued to bleed before the relentless advance of the Red Army. But through the winter of 1944 Germany deployed some sixty German divisions, eleven of them panzers, all superbly equipped and many of them combat-hardened, in France and the Low Countries. Most of that force was gathered north of the Loire River. The Seventh Army stood in Normandy, the Fifteenth Army at Calais; the panzer reserves waited near Paris. All knew that with the spring the war would come to the west. As the days lengthened, they drilled and dug, watched and prayed.

Across the Channel, meanwhile, Eisenhower struggled to assemble his invasion force. His command structure reflected the combined-arms, inter-Allied complexities of Overlord. Eisenhower's deputy supreme commander, Air Marshal Sir Arthur Tedder, and all three subordinate commanders, were British: Sir Trafford Leigh-Mallory for air, Sir Bertram Ramsey for sea, and Sir Bernard Montgomery for land. In the first phase of the battle, Montgomery's Twenty-first Army Group would include both British and American ground forces, the latter under the command of General Omar N. Bradley. When American troop strength had built to sufficient size—it would eventually greatly outnumber the British—Bradley would assume command of Twelfth U.S. Army Group and report thereafter directly to Eisenhower. At a later stage of the battle, Eisenhower himself would move his headquarters to the Continent and assume direct control of the land battle.

Eisenhower had much confidence in Tedder, and affection for him as well. Ramsey and Leigh-Mallory, on the other hand, especially the latter, he regarded as "ritualistic" in outlook. And in Montgomery, Eisenhower found himself again at close quarters, as he had been in Africa and Italy, with one of the most colorful and controversial personalities of the war. A compact man, jittery in public, solitary and reclusive by nature, Montgomery was in demeanor and temperament the gregarious Eisenhower's opposite. At El Alamein, Montgomery had stopped the German advance in North Africa, giving Britain its first major victory of the war and earning a hero's laurels for himself. But the victory he wanted most was not in Africa, or even in Italy, but in France. Montgomery seethed to avenge the humiliation of Dunkirk, where he had been evacuated along with the rest of the British army in 1940.

Grievously wounded and taken for dead in the First World War, "Monty" bore with him for the rest of his life not only the battle scars on his body but a deep horror of the futile, homicidal wastage of troops he had witnessed in trench warfare. This dread Churchill shared, as indeed did all the British leaders. With methodical application, Montgomery devoted himself to sustaining the morale of troops under his command. He cultivated eccentricities, including his trademark beret, in order to facilitate his recognition by his men and their identification with him; his beret, he once said, was worth two divisions in bolstered morale. Montgomery also laboriously trained his troops to a knife-edge sharpness and committed them to action only after the most careful deliberation. As with General George McClellan in the American Civil War, these characteristics made him fabulously popular with his soldiers. But his notorious reluctance to move until his army was prepared to the last button also frequently aggravated his allies and even his own superiors. Montgomery's caution on the Normandy battlefield would cause Eisenhower and Churchill alike many headaches. Yet in defense of Montgomery's record in Overlord, it might be added that no one knew better than he that the British forces he led were a wasting asset. Unlike the Americans, with their huge potential reserves of manpower, the British army by 1944 had been severely winnowed by battle. The army Britain fielded in Normandy would be the last force it could throw into the war. Its losses could not be made good by reinforcements. It must, therefore, be used wisely and sparingly.

Omar Bradley, on the other hand, would assume a command position in Overlord whose growing responsibilities would reflect the growing preponderance of American strength on the ground, just as Montgomery's role would shrink in proportion to the relative role of the British army. A steady, self-effacing Missourian, Bradley was as loyal a subordinate as Montgomery was an aggravating one. Like his West Point classmate Eisenhower, Bradley had never seen combat until he arrived in North Africa in 1942. But he had by 1944 already acquired a reputation, nourished by the worshipful dispatches of war correspondent Ernie

Pyle, as "the GI's general"—a persona reflected in the title of his postwar memoir, *A Soldier's Story*.

BY THE EVE OF D-DAY southern England teemed with twenty American divisions, fourteen British, three Canadian, one Polish, and one French. Those numbers did not add up to the three-to-two attacker-to-defender ratio that conventional military wisdom held to be minimally necessary for a successful offensive, but the Allied plan hoped to improve upon that classical arithmetic with deception, air power, and time. Deception would divide and delay the enemy's forces, reducing his effective strength at the point of attack. Air power would isolate the battlefield, interdicting Rommel's and Rundstedt's ability to reinforce and resupply. If the initial landing could thus buy sufficient time, a lodgement area would be secured into which an additional million Allied troops, most of them American, could eventually be poured. Then the full logic of what Rommel called the Americans' "numerical and material superiority" would play itself out in a relentless war of attrition, pitting the exhausted Germans against wave after wave of fresh manpower and the lavish output of American factories. This, reduced to its bare essentials, was the Overlord plan.

Yet there were limits even upon the Americans' apparently prodigious supplies of men and machines—especially machines. When he first saw the COSSAC plan in October 1943, even before his appointment to head the Supreme Headquarters Allied Expeditionary Forces (SHAEF), Eisenhower instantly concluded that it projected too puny a force for the initial landing. Among his first decisions as supreme Allied commander was to increase the D-Day assault from three attacking infantry divisions to five, with additional divisions to land by the end of the first day. That decision raised anew a maddeningly familiar problem: Where would the landing craft come from to carry the additional divisions across the Channel on D-Day? The debate over this issue, tortuously protracted and inordinately wearing on Eisenhower, illustrated once again the shaping role of industrial production on military strategy, as well as the bitter competition among various theaters for the inevitably finite material resources on which modern warfare depended.

Those lessons had been borne in upon President Roosevelt within hours of parting from Stalin at Teheran. On his return to Cairo after the Big Three meeting, Roosevelt reneged on his promise to Chiang Kai-shek, scarcely a week old, to support an amphibious operation in connection with Stilwell's offensive in northern Burma. Roosevelt explained his reasoning to Chiang, pleading the finitude of American re-sources but avoiding any mention of China's diminished strategic im-portance now that Stalin had agreed to enter the war against Japan. The commitment made to Stalin to launch the cross-Channel attack in May, said Roosevelt, imposed "so large a requirement of heavy landing craft as to make it impracticable to devote a sufficient number to the am-phibious operation in the Bay of Bengal." Chiang received a consolation prize of sorts in the form of the Cairo Declaration, reiterating the unconditional-surrender formula and applying it to Japan in particular.[61]

Now Eisenhower had complicated the logistical equation still further by doubling the projected size of the D-Day landing force. The practical result of that decision soon became apparent. The specific items re-quired, their numbers starkly modest yet irreducible in their concrete-ness, were 72 LCIs, 47 LSTs, and 144 LCTs.[62] "The destinies of two great empires," Churchill grumbled, "seem to be tied up in some God-damned things called LSTs."[63] Eisenhower determined that half of this added "lift" necessary to an expanded Normandy assault would be found by scaling back the projected simultaneous landing in southern France, code-named Anvil, and transferring some of its ships to Overlord. The remaining vessels would be provided by postponing D-Day to a new target date of June 5, in order to secure an additional month of factory production.

Thus, almost from the moment of assuming command, Eisenhower had been compelled to take decisions that delayed Overlord and re-duced and reconfigured the Anvil supporting operation. Those devel-opments directly contradicted assurances that Roosevelt had made to Stalin about both the timing and the shape of the second front. By the same token, delay of the cross-Channel attack and deemphasis on south-ern France suited the British just fine.

Back in Washington, Marshall watched these developments with mounting concern. Anvil in fact was destined to persist as an item of contention between the British and Americans for the next eight months. It was in the end as much a test of wills among the Allied

61. Sherwood, *Roosevelt and Hopkins*, 802.
62. Respectively, Landing Craft, Infantry; Landing Ship, Tank; and Landing Craft, Tank.
63. Harrison, *Cross-Channel Attack*, 64. Churchill also wrote to George Marshall on April 16, 1944: "How it is that the plans of two great empires like Britain and the United States should be so much hamstrung and limited by a hundred or two of these particular vessels will never be understood by history." Churchill 5:454.

leaders as it was a military or strategic issue. The British had never wanted Anvil. Churchill repeatedly insisted that Anvil and Overlord bore no strategic relation to one another, given the huge distance (some five hundred miles) between them. He also, no doubt, resented Anvil because it oriented Allied resources in the Mediterranean northwestward, out of Italy and the east, the regions of his own nearly obsessive strategic preoccupation. The Americans, on the other hand, Marshall in particular, saw Anvil and Overlord as parts of a single operation, not in competition with one another but mutually supportive. Besides, the Americans had promised Stalin at Teheran that they would undertake Anvil as an integral part of the Overlord plan.

Behind Marshall's thinking lay both military and political considerations. Marshall the soldier worried that a diminished Anvil would preclude the envelopment of the German forces in France in the pincer movement Stalin had touted at Teheran, require the Allies to secure a long, vulnerable flank along the Loire River to forestall the Germans from shifting troops from southern France to the Normandy front, and delay the Allied acquisition of desperately needed port facilities at Marseilles.

Marshall the statesman worried, as did Roosevelt, that a smaller Anvil would break faith with Stalin. Equally worrisome, marooning in Italy a sizeable body of troops previously intended for Anvil threatened to reopen the eternally vexed Mediterranean question. For the Americans, Anvil was a prophylaxis against further British "periphery-pecking" in Italy and to the east. It would supplant the dead-end Italian campaign and in the process ensure that whatever Allied effort was to be made in the Mediterranean would be oriented northwestward, toward Germany, away from the Adriatic and the Balkans, a region the Americans regarded with a blend of ignorance and dread. Eisenhower's retreat from Anvil put all those benefits at risk. It seemed to return the Anglo-American strategic dialogue to its unresolved status of pre-Teheran days. In the words of Marshall's biographer: "All the Churchillian predilections for an overall strategy of bleeding Hitler's Reich to death by a lengthy nibbling at the fringes rather than risking dwindling British manpower in a now-or-never assault, apparently buried at Teheran, now were resuscitated."[64] Marshall fretted that Eisenhower was perhaps showing insufficient spine, succumbing to the very Churchillian blandishments about which Roosevelt had cautioned him at the time of his appointment

64. Pogue, *Marshall: Organizer of Victory*, 337–38.

to SHAEF. In a pointed warning, Marshall admonished Eisenhower in early February "to be certain that localitis is not developing and that pressures on you have not warped your judgment."[65]

Events in Italy reinforced Churchill's anxieties and compounded Eisenhower's difficulties. The Anzio landing, undertaken in January 1944, was still stalled as winter passed into spring. If the Anzio beachhead were not to be written off as a failure, it might have to be reinforced with a second amphibious attack. Did a similar—or a worse—fate await the landings in Normandy, where the enemy was prepared and watchful? The Italian stalemate stirred Churchill's darkest memories of the First World War. "I was not convinced," Churchill later reflected, that "a direct assault across the Channel on the German sea-front in France . . . was the only way of winning the war, and I knew that it would be a very heavy and hazardous adventure. The fearful price we had had to pay in human life and blood for the great offensives of the First World War was graven in my mind. Memories of the Somme and Passchendaele and many lesser frontal attacks upon the Germans were not to be blotted out by time and reflection."[66]

The difficulties at Anzio quickened long-standing British fears and had a more immediate consequence as well: not merely the reduction of Anvil, but its postponement. Landing craft scheduled for release from Italy to the Anvil landing must now be held in reserve for further possible operations to break the Italian deadlock. Consequently, Eisenhower noted in his diary on February 7, 1944: "It looks like Anvil is doomed. . . . I hate this."[67] In the weeks that followed, Eisenhower formally agreed to postpone Anvil—until August, as it eventually turned out. Though the Allies did proceed to transfer troops from Italy to England, the fighting in the Mediterranean peninsula ground on, to D-Day and beyond. Bit by bit, the promises made at Teheran to quit the Mediterranean and give unassailable priority to Overlord were being eroded.

THE ITALIAN FIASCO, with its claim to retention of landing-craft in the Mediterranean, threatened Anvil-Overlord from the sea. Another no less formidable threat loomed in the air. Eisenhower was nominally the supreme Allied commander, yet his apparently sweeping authority

65. Pogue, *Marshall: Organizer of Victory*, 331, 335.
66. Churchill 5:514.
67. Robert H. Ferrell, ed., *The Eisenhower Diaries* (New York: Norton, 1981), 110–11.

did not at first extend to the air forces. Though SHAEF did control something called the Allied Expeditionary Air Force (AEAF), ostensibly committed to tactical support for Overlord, AEAF remained an under-nourished organization, headed by the widely distrusted British officer Leigh-Mallory. The huge "strategic" air arms—British Bomber Command under the single-minded Arthur Harris, and the United States Strategic Air Forces in Europe (USSTAF), now commanded by the calculating Carl Spaatz, who in January 1944 had become commander-in-chief of the U.S. strategic air arm in Europe—remained anomalously beyond the reach of Eisenhower's authority. Bringing their fearful power to bear on the success of Overlord proved to be one of Eisenhower's most daunting challenges.

The big bombers had been shouldering the main burden of the Allied war effort against Germany for years—since 1940 in the British case and 1942 in the American. Whatever their national differences, the airmen, British and American alike, nursed a passionate ambition to demonstrate once and for all the truth of the Douhetian doctrine that strategic bomb-ing was the ultimate war-winning weapon. They resisted any surrender of the independent role necessary to clinching their alluring—and self-justifying—thesis. They resisted with special obduracy now, in the early months of 1944, when the promise of air power's singular capacity to change the very nature of warfare seemed to hover tantalizingly within their reach.

After the disastrous raids on Schweinfurt and Regensburg in 1943, the Americans had been forced to curtail the deep-penetration missions that held the promise of extinguishing German industrial production and thus starving the *Wehrmacht* into submission. But as he arrived in Europe to assume command of the air arm in early 1944, Spaatz be-lieved a new weapon had brought America's bomber force to the brink of success at last, to the exciting edge of nothing less than a strategic revolution. The development that invigorated Spaatz was the advent of a new aircraft, the P-51 Mustang fighter. Able to stay aloft for more than seven hours, with a range of eight hundred miles and beyond, faster, nimbler, and with a higher operational ceiling than its German coun-terparts, the P-51 could now protect bomber streams flying to the farthest reaches of the *Reich*. Like the F6F Hellcat in the Pacific, the Mustang dramatically altered the combat equation in the skies over Europe. The Luftwaffe acknowledged as much when it rewrote the rules of engage-ment for its own Me109s and Focke-Wulf 190s in early 1944. Hence-forward, German fighters were instructed to continue attacking P-38s anywhere, to engage P-47s below twenty thousand feet, but to break off and dive away on contact with P-51s.[68]

Exulting in the promise of this new weapon, and sensing the imminent vindication of the airmen's cherished strategic doctrine, Spaatz, joined by Harris, returned with a vengeance in February 1944 to the implementation of one of the Combined Bomber Offensive's priority missions: suppression of the Luftwaffe by destroying German aircraft production facilities. During "Big Week," February 19–26, 1944, British and American bombers flew more than six thousand sorties and dropped some eighteen thousand tons of bombs on German airframe and ball-bearing factories. As Midway had avenged Pearl Harbor, Big Week avenged the Schweinfurt debacles of August and October 1943. American bomber losses for Big Week were less than 6 percent. Even more telling, fighter losses were only 1 percent. The Luftwaffe, on the other hand, lost over one-third of its strength in that single week. Through dispersal and improvisation, Germany managed to resume and even increase aircraft production for another several months, but the German pilots who had plummeted from the heavens during the murderous raids of Big Week proved irreplaceable.

Big Week was a pivot, and the airmen knew it. While the Luftwaffe shriveled as a fighting force, spanking new P-51s and fresh, well-trained American pilots poured in swelling numbers into the British airdromes. With even more dramatic suddenness than the turnaround in the Atlantic sea battle in the spring of 1943, Big Week decisively marked the Allies' ascendancy in the European air war.

Confident of his new superiority, Spaatz shifted tactics at the end of February. The new objective would be not simply to crush the Luftwaffe on the ground, by pouring bombs on airfields and factories, but to capitalize on the technical and numerical superiority of the P-51s by engaging and destroying enemy aircraft in the sky. The new mission was graphically defined when the head of the Eighth Air Force Fighter Command changed the sign on his office wall. It had previously read: "The first duty of the Eighth Air Force fighters is to bring the bombers back alive." Now it stated: "The first duty of the Eighth Air Force fighters is to destroy German fighters."[69] The "little friends" in their sleek

---

68. Stephen L. McFarland and Wesley Phillips Newton, *To Command the Sky: The Battle for Air Superiority over Germany, 1942–1944* (Washington: Smithsonian Institution, 1991), 56.

69. McFarland and Newton, *To Command the Sky*, 160.

new P-51s were to be freed of the bomber formations, encouraged to pursue enemy interceptors and leave the lumbering "big friends" to fend for themselves. The chilling realization dawned on the bomber crews that the amply discredited notion of the B-17s as self-defending Flying Fortresses was being resurrected—ironically enough, just at the moment when the arrival of the P-51s had promised a new level of safety for the bomber formations. One B-17 pilot recollected bitterly that "morale was declining" as the realization sank in that "we were expendable . . . we were bait."[70]

In the first week of March, Spaatz aggressively implemented this new approach of baiting the Germans to the attack. The strategy required selecting a target so precious that German fighters would be obliged to rise in swarms to defend it. That thinking led directly to Berlin. British Bomber Command had been targeting Berlin heavily since November and imploring Spaatz to join in the attack. Now Spaatz agreed. In the process he edged uncomfortably close to mimicking Harris's practice of bombing "area targets."[71] In a directive explaining that pre-D-Day bombing targets in France had been selected with an eye to minimizing civilian casualties, Spaatz added: "This consideration does not apply in Germany."[72] Huge airfleets of Fortresses and Liberators began dumping their deadly tonnage on Berlin, their crews less concerned now about the accuracy of their bomb drops than about their ability to attract and annihilate Luftwaffe fighters.

Spaatz and the American airmen had now narrowed the moral ground that they had proudly insisted separated them from the indiscriminate terror tactics of the British Bomber Command. To be sure, Harris and Spaatz had different motives—the former to "dehouse" workers and break the back of civilian morale, the latter to lure the Luftwaffe into the sky—but to the dying civilians on the ground below that was a distinction without a difference. The British pacifist Vera Brittain made just that point when she published a stinging condemnation of area bombing in a religious journal in March 1944. She sparked an intense but brief flurry of commentary in the United States, where the destruction by bombing of Monte Cassino had already provoked a similar controversy. These scattered protests registered the first faint stirrings

70. McFarland and Newton, *To Command the Sky*, 163–64, 215.
71. Spaatz used the phrase in a memo to his chief, General H. H. Arnold, on January 23, 1944, quoted in McFarland and Newton, *To Command the Sky*, 194.
72. Ronald Schaffer, *Wings of Judgment: American Bombing in World War II* (New York: Oxford University Press, 1985), 68.

of the American conscience about the ghastly havoc that Yankee technological ingenuity was now able to wreak on civilians as well as soldiers.

Aglow with renewed ambition in the wake of their triumphs of February and March, both Spaatz and Harris were emboldened to assert the classic Douhetian dogma with new vigor. More loudly than ever they claimed that air power alone could win the war. Overlord, they trumpeted, with its huge risks and inevitable carnage, was unnecessary. Harris had already claimed that if he were allowed to continue full force with his saturation bombing of German cities he could achieve "a state of devastation in which surrender is inevitable" by April 1, 1944.[73] April came and that claim proved to be inflated, as had so many of the airmen's promises. Yet Spaatz could still declare in that same month that "it is of paramount importance the Combined Bomber Offensive continue without interruption. . . . If this were done, the highly dangerous Overlord operation could be eliminated."[74]

Churchill predictably seized upon these enthusiasms as providing yet another possible alternative to the dreaded cross-Channel attack. In a meeting with Eisenhower that dragged late into the night of February 28, he heatedly refused to release Bomber Command to the supreme commander's control. The huge Lancasters, he said, were like the historic British "Home Fleet," indispensable symbols of British prestige and independence. Eisenhower replied that without full control of all the air arms of both nations he might "have to pack and go home."[75]

Against this backbeat of renewed confidence among the airmen and renewed intransigence on Churchill's part, Eisenhower convened a tense meeting at his suburban London headquarters on March 25. "If a satisfactory answer is not reached," Eisenhower wrote in his diary on the eve of the meeting, "I will request relief from this command."[76] At issue were Spaatz's proposal to accelerate the momentum of recent airwar successes by attacking German oil refineries and a competing scheme to employ the heavy bombers against French transportation facilities in the Normandy hinterland in order to isolate the invasion beachhead and allow the buildup to go forward with minimum disruption. Both plans had their advocates.

Oil was the lifeblood of German industry, Spaatz argued, and, not

73. Hastings, *Overlord*, 48.
74. Hastings, *Overlord*, 49.
75. Accounts of the Churchill-Eisenhower meeting on February 28 are found in David Eisenhower, *Eisenhower*, 152, and in *PDDE* 3:1755–60.
76. Ferrell, *Eisenhower Diaries*, 115.

incidentally, of the feared panzer divisions as well. Deprive Germany of oil, and its economy and army alike would grind to a halt. As a bonus, Spaatz added, the Luftwaffe would have no choice but to raise whatever fighter strength it had left in defense of the refineries, thus bringing to a triumphant climax the ongoing elimination of the German air arm as an effective fighting force. Whatever its promised benefits, the "oil plan" was also, Eisenhower recognized, a scheme to maintain the independence of the bomber forces so that they might continue to pursue the elusive dream of winning the war through air power alone. It would also leave the Normandy beaches dangerously exposed to the threat of German counterattack.

Eisenhower's deputy supreme commander, Air Chief Marshal Sir Arthur Tedder, presented the alternative "transportation plan." It was premised on the assumption that the ground invasion—Overlord—not the air war, had the highest priority. Accordingly, it envisioned using air power primarily to isolate the Normandy battlefield by knocking out bridges along the Seine River and creating a "railway desert" in the French interior through concerted and repeated attacks on carefully selected marshaling yards and switching points. To achieve those goals, Tedder argued, Bomber Command and USSTAF must come under SHAEF's direction.

Eisenhower weighed these arguments carefully. The oil plan had merit, he knew, but it also had a formidable defect: it would take time to work its effects. "[N]o one who does not have to bear the specific and direct responsibility of making the final decision . . . can understand the intensity of these burdens," he complained to his diary a few weeks later. "The supreme commander, much more than any of his subordinates," he reflected, must assess "the political issues involved, particularly," he emphasized, "the anticipated effect of delay upon the Russians."[77] Adopting the oil plan almost certainly implied another delay in Overlord. Eisenhower therefore declared in favor of the transportation plan. That should have settled things. But the issue was not yet resolved.

Churchill fought a further delaying action to avoid implementing the March 25 decision. Showing a solicitude for French civilian casualties that formed no part of his thinking when it came to Germans, he appealed to Roosevelt in May to reconsider whether the transportation plan was "the best way to use our Air Forces," particularly in view of the "French slaughters" that it entailed. In yet another reminder of who was

77. Ferrell, *Eisenhower Diaries*, 119–20.

now the senior partner in the alliance, Roosevelt brusquely replied that the decision had been Eisenhower's and he would not second-guess it.[78]

Spaatz succeeded in retaining sufficient independence to continue bombing at least some of his oil targets, but Eisenhower had won his own "air war" against the strategic bombing enthusiasts. On April 14 the strategic air wings passed under Eisenhower's control. They were to remain there until such time as the invasion force was considered to be safely ashore. Systematic attacks now began against the Seine crossings and the railways of northern France—attacks deliberately spread over a considerably wider area than the intended landing zone, for purposes of sustaining the Fortitude deception.

Having won these battles to secure Overlord against threats from sea and air, Eisenhower in the spring of 1944 fought a final battle for Overlord on the ground—or, rather, a battle over who would control the ground of France once it was liberated. This one he lost. Two considerations drove the supreme commander's thinking. First, he wanted the cooperation of the French resistance forces, modest though they were in scale and influence, during the landings and thereafter. Second, and far more important, he wanted a civil authority to govern liberated France, freeing the Allies of the burden of deploying an occupying army for administrative purposes.

The obvious candidate to constitute such a civil authority was Charles DeGaulle. His French Committee of National Liberation (FCNL) had joined hands with the Allies in North Africa, had fighting divisions to offer (especially General Jacques Phillipe LeClerc's Second Armored Division), and had clearly positioned itself as a government-in-exile, awaiting only liberation to establish its legitimate rule over France. To Eisenhower all this seemed self-evident. He had in fact as early as December 1943 assured DeGaulle at a meeting in Algiers that his forces would play a role in Overlord, including the liberation of Paris. But the supreme commander here ran afoul of his own president, whose obstinacy on the question of DeGaulle rivaled or exceeded Churchill's tenacity on all matters touching on the Mediterranean.

Roosevelt's policy toward France was a tangled skein of contradictions, shot through with an unreasoning disdain for DeGaulle whose ultimate sources are not easily located. Washington had made an uneasy and unholy peace with Vichy and had cut a controversial deal with General Darlan to facilitate the invasion of North Africa. Yet Roosevelt had

78. C&R 3:122–23, 127.

uttered no dissent from Stalin's vindictive tirade against the French at Teheran, nor had he shown the slightest interest in supporting DeGaulle, transparently the chief challenger to Vichy's authority and the towering symbol of French resistance to Nazi rule. Roosevelt insisted, rather, that embracing DeGaulle would amount to foisting an unwanted ruler on the French by force of arms and would likely precipitate a civil war. To DeGaulle, Roosevelt's attitude "seemed to me on the same order as Alice's Adventures in Wonderland," a judgment from which it is frankly difficult to dissent. Eisenhower patiently explained to his president that "there exists in France today only two major groups, of which one is the Vichy gang, and the other characterized by unreasoning admiration for DeGaulle." But Roosevelt would not relent. He refused to recognize the FCNL as the legitimate or even provisional government of France, and he would not extend the hand of friendship to DeGaulle. Under those circumstances, the haughty DeGaulle flatly refused to make an invasion-eve broadcast in support of Overlord. "To hell with him," said Eisenhower, "if he doesn't come through we'll deal with someone else." It was a hollow threat, as there was no someone else.[79] DeGaulle would have the last word. He gave his own broadcast on D-Day itself, unapologetically claiming for the FCNL the title of "the French government." And when Paris was liberated, he, and LeClerc, would be there.

79. This account relies heavily on Ambrose, *Supreme Commander*, 377–91.

20

The Battle for Northwest Europe

Almighty God: Our sons, pride of our Nation, this day have set upon a mighty endeavor. . . . These men are lately drawn from the ways of peace. . . . They yearn but for the end of battle, for their return to the haven of home.

— Franklin Roosevelt, D-Day prayer, June 6, 1944

As spring began to unroll its green carpet across the south of England in 1944, American GIs drilled on the softly undulating fields, staged mock attacks on the shingle beaches and in the leafing copses, rumbled in trucks and tanks along stone-hedged roads, snickered at the quaint ways of the tea- and warm-beer-drinking British, and oiled and sighted their gleaming new weapons. Occasionally they relieved their boredom by setting fire to haystacks with tracer bullets. The teeming Yanks, arriving at a rate of 150,000 per month since late 1943, were "overpaid, oversexed, and over here," the British quipped. (To which the Yanks replied that their British comrades-in-arms were underpaid, undersexed, and under Eisenhower.) Yanks and Britons alike joked that only the thousands of barrage balloons tethered to southern England kept the island afloat under the stupendous weight of materiel stockpiled for the invasion: some five million tons of munitions and supplies, including more than a hundred thousand vehicles. Offshore, an armada of more than six thousand ships was assembling to move that horde of apprehensive men and those mountains of weapons, food, and equipment across the Channel.

The nearly two million American ground troops and the almost equal number of U.S. Army Air Forces personnel in Britain represented the bulk of the more than seven million men the U.S. Army then had under arms. That huge force, mass-produced in short order like so much else in the American arsenal, had mushroomed from the skeletal prewar regular army of fewer than two hundred thousand men in 1940. Over the course of the war, almost sixteen million men, most of them conscripted, as well as half a million women, all of them volunteers, would serve in the U.S. armed forces. Young men had begun pouring into the Selective Service System's induction centers for physical and psychological examinations in the last weeks of 1940. Eventually nearly eighteen million were examined, and their records provided a remarkable composite portrait of a generation's physical and mental makeup. Most were judged fit for service, though almost two million men were rejected for neuropsychiatric reasons (conspicuously including homosexuality, though many homosexuals in fact served in all service arms), and four million more for various medical and educational deficiencies, such as rotten teeth, poor eyesight, and illiteracy. To meet its manpower needs, the army eventually undertook remedial work with draftees. Some twenty-five thousand army dentists pulled fifteen million teeth and fitted 2.5 million sets of dentures; army optometrists fitted 2.25 million pairs of eyeglasses; and special army schools bestowed the gift of literacy on almost a million recruits.

The average GI was nearly twenty-six years old in 1944, born in the year the war to end wars had ended (sailors and marines were somewhat younger). He stood five feet eight inches and weighed 144 pounds, an inch taller and eight pounds heavier than the typical recruit in World War I. Four out of ten white but fewer than two out of ten black draftees had finished high school. Almost a third of the whites and more than half the black recruits had no education beyond grade school. Overall, the statistically average GI had completed one year of high school — three full years more education than the average "Doughboy" of 1917.[1]

Those judged fit to serve at the induction center were fingerprinted and then given a perfunctory interview in which they could indicate

---

1. Lee Kennett, *G.I.: The American Soldier in World War II* (New York: Charles Scribner's Sons, 1987), passim. Much of the following discussion relies on Kennett's work and on Geoffrey Perret, *There's a War to Be Won: The United States Army in World War II* (New York: Random House, 1991). See also Samuel A. Stouffer's classic study, *The American Soldier* (Princeton: Princeton University Press, 1949); and the relevant volumes in the official *U.S. Army in World War II* series: *The Organization of Ground Combat Troops, The Procurement and Training of Ground Combat Troops,* and *The Employment of Negro Troops* (Washington: Department of the Army, 1947, 1948, 1966, respectively); and *Selective Service and Victory: The 4th Report of the Director of Selective Service* (Washington: USGPO, 1948).

their choice of service. Until the end of 1942, the period when most men were inducted and when the navy and marines took only volunteers, draftees had just three choices: the Army Ground Forces, the Army Services of Supply, or the Army Air Forces. The last was the most popular, but individual choice yielded to the army's estimation of its own needs. The air forces skimmed off the best performers on the Army General Classification Test, a 150-question, forty-minute aptitude test administered to every recruit. (Sample question: "Mike had 12 cigars. He bought 3 more and then smoked 6. How many did he have left?") A disproportionate share of low-scorers on the AGCT ended up in the infantry. Interestingly, the typical combat infantryman was also shorter and weighed less than his counterparts in the Services of Supply or the air forces. The infantry's fighting echelons were almost entirely white. Ignoring the performance of Negro troops in the Civil War, the World War II army considered blacks unfit for combat duty and consigned the great majority of them to service units.

During 1941 and 1942 millions of draftees flowed into the hastily erected training camps, 242 of them in all, concentrated in the South, where the requirements for camp siting were most easily met. A divisional training camp ideally needed at least forty thousand acres of varied terrain for weapons practice and maneuvers, a reliable water source, adequate roads, access to rail transport, proximity to an urban center for recreation and supply, and good weather. Fort Lewis in Washington State was among the few large training facilities outside the South that fitted those specifications. Among the biggest camps were Fort Benning, Georgia, which could handle almost one hundred thousand trainees; Fort Shelby, Mississippi (eighty-six thousand); Fort Bragg, North Carolina (seventy-six thousand); and Fort Jackson, South Carolina (sixty-five thousand).

Reveille woke the inductees at 6:05 A.M. They ate breakfast, cleaned their barracks, trained from 8:00 to 5:30, took evening mess, were back in barracks at 7:00, and observed "lights out" at 9:45. They passed first through "basic" or "branch-immaterial" training, including close-order drill, military protocol, and physical conditioning. They also underwent seven hours of indoctrination about their country's war aims, much of it conveyed in a series of films, *Why We Fight*, made by the renowned Hollywood director Frank Capra. They then passed to a second phase of instruction in small-arms firing and weapons maintenance and proceeded to specialized training in skills such as radio communications and heavy weapons deployment. Next came combined-arms training, in which infantry, armor, artillery, and tactical air units worked together, forty-four weeks in all, followed by eight weeks of exercises and maneuvers at divisional strength, and capped by a twenty-five-mile road march with full thirty-pound pack. At all levels of training, the army's basic instructional technique was the same: demonstration, explanation, performance.

A handful of National Guard divisions retained a regional identity, and blacks were rigidly segregated both in the camps and in the field, but the army tossed the remaining millions of men into the mother and father of all melting pots. The dozens of conscript divisions were all-American mixtures recruited from north, south, east, and west. They jumbled together farm boys and factory hands, old-stock Yankees and new immigrants, rich as well as poor, Protestants, Catholics, and Jews. Many young men who had never left their rural county or urban neighborhood confronted in the army more social, ethnic, and religious diversity than they had ever encountered, perhaps ever imagined. In the year that it took to train a division, and in the months of service that followed—most men remained in uniform "for the duration," usually a term of thirty-three months, half of it overseas—human barriers were often breached and long-lived bonds between men created. Old stereotypes withered and once-improbable friendships flowered. Because no new divisions were formed after the ninety-division program was completed in late 1943, individuals were trained thereafter as replacements in cycles of eight to seventeen weeks. They were destined to be slotted into the line as needed and had less chance to form close ties with their comrades-in-arms than the original trainees did.

For millions of men born during and just after the Great War of 1914–18, their experience as GIs defined their generational identity as nothing else could, not even their long boyhood agony during the Great Depression. World War II took them away from home, taught them lessons both dreadful and useful, formed their friendships, and, if it did not end them, shaped the arc of their lives ever after. For those who survived, the war laid up a store of memories that time could not corrode —indeed, memories often embroidered by time's indulgent hand. Benjamin Bradlee, later the editor of the *Washington Post*, spoke for many veterans when he remembered the war as "more exciting, more meaningful than anything I'd ever done. This is why I had such a wonderful time in the war. I just plain loved it. Loved the excitement, even loved being a little bit scared. Loved the sense of achievement, even if it was only getting from Point A to Point B; loved the camaraderie . . . the responsibility. . . . The first time a man goes into battle," Bradlee added, "is strangely like the first time a man makes love to a woman. The anticipation is overpowering; the ignorance is obstructive; the fear of disgrace is consuming; and survival is triumphant." And if the war made its mark on these men, they left their mark too — not only on the women they wooed and in the battles they fought but also on every flat surface from Fort Benning to Normandy and Okinawa, their own ubiquitous inscription, probably the single most famous sentence of the war: "Kilroy was here."[2]

The army improved the standard of living of many recruits. Not only did they receive proper medical attention, some for the first time in their lives, but at the garrison food ration of 4,300 calories per day, many ate better than they ever had before. Even the standard field provender, the C-ration and the K-ration, contained about 3,400 calories, as well as a stick of chewing gum and four cigarettes. Training typically expanded a man's chest measurement by an inch and added six pounds to his weight. Privates, many ladled from the vast pool of the unemployed, earned fifty dollars a month after mid-1942, and every soldier was covered by a ten-thousand-dollar life insurance policy.

The American bases in wartime England were oases of abundance that were the wonder and envy of the British. Liberty Ships disgorged tons of commodities that had all but disappeared from British civilian life. Hungry Britons, whose standard of living declined by more than 20 percent after the war's outbreak, counted themselves lucky to befriend American servicemen. Then they might feast on the cocoa, canned meat ("Spam"), orange juice, tinned and even fresh fruit, soft drinks, candy bars, chewing gum, and tobacco that GIs obligingly liberated from their overstuffed military warehouses. The Americans had more of everything: more men, more food, more trucks, more guns — even more toilet paper. The allotment in the British army's bathrooms was 3 sheets per man per day; the American ration was 22.5 sheets.[3]

The U.S. Army's tail-to-teeth ratio, the relation of its service to its combat arms, was the highest of any army in the war. In the *Wehrmacht's* order of battle, one noncombatant provided for every two frontline soldiers. The Americans reversed the ratio: two service personnel

---

2. Ben Bradlee, *A Good Life: Newspapering and Other Adventures* (New York: Simon and Schuster, 1995), 76, 65; Samuel Hynes, "So Many Men, So Many Wars: 50 years of Remembering World War II," *New York Times Book Review*, April 30, 1995, 12.
3. Kennett, *G.I.*, 96.

stood behind every combatant in the field. Every GI landed in Europe would be supported with forty-five pounds per day of supplies, a quarter of it petroleum and petroleum products, contrasted with twenty pounds for a British soldier and a German quota that sometimes fell to four pounds. Much of that fabulous wealth of material, especially the fuel, was necessary for the war of movement that the Americans had come to fight. But some British observers grumbled that the shipping shortages that had bedeviled the planning for Overlord might have been avoided if the Americans were less committed to maintaining troops in training and even in combat at the standard of living to which they were accustomed in civilian life.[4]

The GIs' army was designed by George Marshall. Well before the war began, Marshall had led an effort to replace the old four-regiment "square" divisions that had fought in France in World War I with a new three-regiment "triangular" formation. The triangular structure informed the army's table of organization from top to bottom. Three twelve-man squads, led by noncommissioned officers, made up a platoon. Three platoons, each led by a lieutenant, composed a company. Three companies, each commanded by a captain, made a battalion. Three battalions, each under a major or lieutenant colonel, formed a regiment. Three regiments, each commanded by a colonel, made up a division, which was led by a general. The battalion was the smallest unit to have a staff, or headquarters company. It also comprised a heavy weapons company, wielding antitank guns, mortars, and .50-caliber machine guns. Under divisional command was a two-thousand-man field artillery unit, equipped with 75mm, 105mm, and 155mm howitzers. Division also controlled a medical detachment, five hundred strong, as well as another two thousand men in various service and auxiliary units, such as engineers and military police. Marshall also organized several independent tank battalions that could be assigned as needed, as well as five airborne and sixteen armored divisions, the latter composed of two tank regiments with a total of 375 tanks, an armored infantry regiment mounted on half-tracks, and an attached self-propelled artillery regiment. The infantryman's standard weapon was the .30-caliber M-1 Garrand rifle, which could be field-stripped and reassembled using only

4. Richard Overy, *Why the Allies Won* (New York: Norton, 1995), 319; Max Hastings, *Overlord: D-Day and the Battle for Normandy, 1944* (London: Pan, 1985), 234; Richard M. Leighton and Robert W. Coakley, *United States Army in World War II: Global Logistics and Strategy, 1940–1943* (Washington: Department of the Army, 1955), 723.

a bullet's nose and firing rim as a tool. An average rifleman could fire forty rounds per minute, an expert up to one hundred. All told, the fifteen-thousand-man triangular division packed twice the firepower of the twenty-four-thousand-man square division of World War I.

The U.S. Army had also modernized in other ways since that earlier conflict, though in some cases belatedly. Only in 1940 did West Point abandon the genteel requirement that cadets devote six hours a week to horsemanship, to be replaced by the same basic training that the millions of conscripts were receiving. But at the army's Command and General Staff School at Fort Leavenworth, Kansas, senior officers had for almost two decades before 1941 passed through a challenging curriculum of 124 map problems and terrain exercises. The program at Leavenworth emphasized speed and skill in deploying mobile formations. It was there that future generals learned how to handle multidivisional corps, armies, and army groups. And it was there that they came to appreciate the value of a war of movement and the fluid genius of the triangular scheme, which put a premium on swift decisiveness at the highest levels of command.

The triangular organizational device was meant above all to maximize mobility. Movement was everything in American military planning: movement in amphibious vehicles onto the landing beaches, movement of men and guns on the ground, movement by tank and half-track and truck, and movement in the air as well. All American divisions were motorized, and the armored divisions' half-track troop transport and supply vehicles meant that they were not confined to the road. By some estimates, the GIs' army could move ten times faster and farther than the American Expeditionary Force in World War I. Mobility was the Americans' trump card on the battlefield, at all levels of engagement. The operational doctrine for the triangular force, whatever its size, was the "holding attack": one unit, whether platoon, battalion, or regiment, engaged the enemy's front; a second tried to turn his flank; a third was held in reserve, ready to move swiftly to the point of maximum advantage. George Patton, perhaps the premier tactician of mobile warfare, reportedly summarized the logic of the holding attack as "grab the enemy by the nose, then kick him in the seat of the pants." The ultimate application of the holding attack, at divisional level and above, was the "wide envelopment," in which a nose-held enemy would be encircled by a lightning run to his rear. In the battle that was about to be joined, the wide envelopment of the German forces in Normandy by Patton's high-speed armored divisions would hold the key to victory.

These were the men, and this was the army, whose job it now was to turn the pronouncements of the statesmen and the diagrams of the planners into reality. One disaster marred the preinvasion training exercises in Britain: German torpedo boats chanced upon troop-laden landing craft rehearsing an amphibious landing at Slapton Sands near the Devonshire village of Dartmouth on April 28, 1944, drowning some seven hundred Americans. But to a remarkable degree, the assemblage and training of the Overlord invasion force went forward methodically. Steadily the British equipment parks filled with rank upon rank of jeeps, Dodge trucks, Sherman tanks, half-tracks, howitzers, self-propelled guns, ambulances, bulldozers, towering stacks of artillery shells, cartons of grenades, cartridges, bazookas, K-rations, C-rations—and medical supplies.

Of the 5.4 million Americans who would eventually fight in the Battle for Northwest Europe, 135,576 GIs and airmen would die. In all theaters, and in all service arms, 291,557 Americans were killed in action, another 113,842 succumbed to accident or disease, and nearly a million more were wounded. Wounded American servicemen benefited from dramatic advances in medical science, especially whole-blood transfusions and penicillin, the first effective antibiotic, developed in England in 1941 and available in significant quantities by late 1944, just as the major American offensives began. Only 4.5 percent of wounds proved mortal in the army and 3.2 percent in the navy, where a stricken sailor could swiftly reach onboard hospital facilities. An American's chance of dying in battle in World War II was about one in one hundred, one-third the rate of World War I and one-tenth the rate of the Civil War.[5]

In the last days of May endless columns of troops, trucks, and tanks began to snake down the narrow roads of southern England, squeezing into the "sausages," the assembly areas that bulged on the planners' maps behind the loading ports from Cornwall to Dorset. After months of argument and planning, of agonies political, psychological, and logistical, "the mighty host," wrote Eisenhower, "was tense as a coiled spring... coiled for the moment when its energy should be released and it would vault the English Channel in the greatest amphibious assault ever attempted."[6]

5. Kennett, G.I., 173–78; HSUS, 1140; Charles B. MacDonald, United States Army in World War II: The European Theater of Operations, the Last Offensive (Washington: Department of the Army, 1973), 478; Michael Clodfelter, Warfare and Armed Conflicts: A Statistical Reference to Casualty and Other Figures, 1618–1991 (Jefferson, N.C.: McFarland, 1992), 962–63.
6. Dwight D. Eisenhower, Crusade in Europe (New York: Doubleday, 1948), 249.

At SHAEF's new forward headquarters at Southwick House in Portsmouth, one last ordeal tortured Eisenhower: the weather. The success of the amphibious attack depended on a peculiar constellation of moon, sun, and tide. The airborne troops to be dropped before dawn on D-Day needed at least a half-moon to illuminate their landing zones. The engineers needed a low tide at first light to expose Rommel's beach obstacles and allow maximum time for demolition. The necessary conjunction of tide and light occurred on only three days in early June — the fifth, sixth, and seventh. The next available date was June 19, a fortnight that might as well have been an eternity when the effects on troop morale, logistical revision, and Russian impatience were taken into account.[7]

By June 3 all troops were aboard their ships along the coast of southern England. Some elements of the American fleet, harbored in more distant ports in the Bristol Channel and beyond, had already put to sea, in order to arrive off the Normandy beaches on schedule on the morning of June 5. Then, early in the morning of June 4, Eisenhower received word from his meteorologists that a rising Atlantic storm headed for the Channel spelled disaster. Blanketing cloud layers, heavy rain, and heaving seas would deprive the assault forces of air cover, jeopardize small craft, and rob supporting naval gunfire of accuracy. Eisenhower recalled the ships already at sea and ordered a twenty-four-hour postponement, to June 6.

At 3:30 the next morning, June 5, Eisenhower awoke to violent confirmation of his meteorologists' forecast. A gale-force wind keened through the steel cables anchoring the barrage balloons to the ships in Portsmouth harbor. Rain pelted in sheets against the windshield of Eisenhower's car as he made his way through the glowering darkness to the elegant white Georgian mansion of Southwick House. In theory, he still had the option of postponing one more day, to June 7. In fact, the difficulty of refueling the convoys already once recalled meant that any further postponement must be to June 19 — a prospect whose consequences, Eisenhower recalled, "were almost too bitter to contemplate."[8]

7. Unforeseeable at this time was the fact that June 19 would also witness the most severe summer storm in the Channel in forty years. The storm destroyed the American "Mulberry" artificial harbor off Omaha Beach and rendered any Channel crossing of the invasion force on that date impossible. Thus a postponement beyond June 6 would, as events turned out, have delayed the invasion by at least another month.

8. Eisenhower, *Crusade in Europe*, 250.

Far to the east in Moscow, General Deane suffered similar agonies at the American military mission. "Each time I announced a postponement," he recalled, "my stock reached a new low. The [Russian] General Staff had never been convinced that the May date agreed upon in Teheran was not part of a deception plan that the western powers were using against their Russian ally."[9]

At Southwick House in the predawn gloom of June 5, Eisenhower and his military chieftains sipped coffee around the fireplace in the high-ceilinged conference room, awaiting the latest weather reports. The weather officer arrived. "I think we have found a gleam of hope for you, sir," he said. A break in the storm front was developing. A thirty-six-hour window of relatively clear weather would open on the morning of June 6. When it closed again the following day it might wreak havoc on the follow-up forces scheduled to land after the initial waves had gone ashore. But at least it was an opening. Eisenhower asked for the opinions of his assembled colleagues. "I would say—Go!" Montgomery replied. The others agreed. Eisenhower sat on a sofa in silence, weighing his choices. The rain wept at the windows. Finally he looked up and said: "Well, we'll go."[10]

ON THE FAR NORMANDY SHORE, the same storm convinced the Germans that no landing was imminent. Rommel took advantage of the respite provided by the ugly weather to motor to his hometown of Ulm for a family visit. In the early hours of June 6, Rundstedt slept in the suburbs of Paris. Hitler, in his Bavarian mountain stronghold at

9. John R. Deane, *The Strange Alliance: The Story of Our Efforts at Wartime Cooperation with Russia* (New York: Viking, 1947), 150.

10. Montgomery quoted in Gordon A. Harrison, *Cross-Channel Attack* (Washington: Department of the Army, 1951), 274. Eisenhower quoted in Walter Bedell Smith, *Eisenhower's Six Great Decisions* (New York: Longman's, 1956), 55. Different accounts of this meeting place slightly different words in Eisenhower's mouth. See Stephen E. Ambrose, *The Supreme Commander: The War Years of General Dwight D. Eisenhower* (Garden City, N.Y.: Doubleday, 1970), 417n. In Eisenhower's pocket as he made this decision was a handwritten note that he had prepared in the event the landings failed: "Our landings in the Cherbourg-Havre area have failed to gain a satisfactory foothold and I have withdrawn the troops. [In his first draft Eisenhower had written: "and the troops have been withdrawn."] My decision to attack at this time and place [the first draft read "This particular operation"] was based upon the best information available. The troops, the air and the Navy did all that bravery and devotion to duty could do. If any blame or fault attaches to the attempt it is mine alone." See *PDDE* 3:1908.

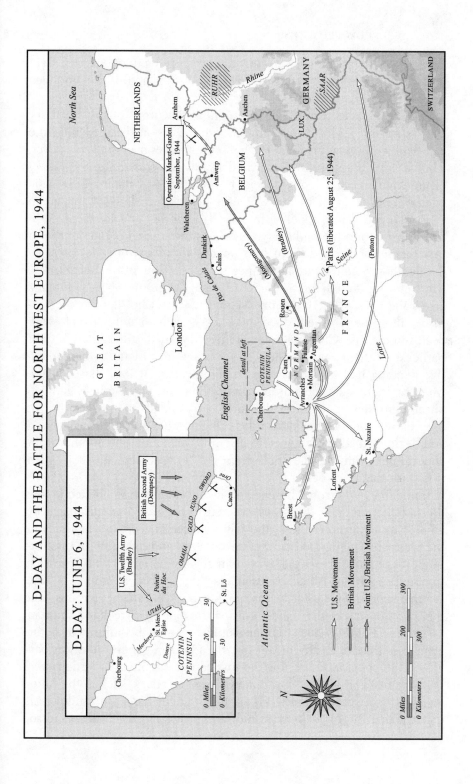

D-DAY AND THE BATTLE FOR NORTHWEST EUROPE, 1944

D-DAY: JUNE 6, 1944

U.S. Twelfth Army (Bradley)

British Second Army (Dempsey)

Cherbourg

COTENIN PENINSULA

Merderet

St. Mère Eglise

UTAH

Douve

St. Lô

Pointe du Hoc

OMAHA

GOLD JUNO SWORD

Caen

Orne

0 Miles 30

0 Kilometers 30

Atlantic Ocean

N

U.S. Movement

British Movement

Joint U.S./British Movement

0 Miles 200

0 Kilometers 300

North Sea

NETHERLANDS

Arnhem

Operation Market-Garden September, 1944

Walcheren

Antwerp

RUHR

Rhine

GERMANY

Aachen

LUX.

SAAR

SWITZERLAND

BELGIUM

Dunkirk

Calais

Pas de Calais

(Montgomery)

(Bradley)

Paris (liberated August 25, 1944)

Seine

Rouen

GREAT BRITAIN

London

English Channel

detail at left

COTENIN PENINSULA

Cherbourg

Caen

NORMANDY

Falaise

Mortain Argentan

Avranches

(Patton)

FRANCE

Loire

St. Nazaire

Lorient

Brest

Berchtesgaden, prepared to take his nightly sleeping draft. His staff were under strict orders not to disturb his few hours of fretful, drug-induced repose.

Parachutes, meanwhile, began soughing down out of the night sky over Normandy. The British 6th Airborne Division dropped onto the east flank of the landing area, to secure the bridges over the Orne River. The U.S. 82nd and 101st Airborne divisions descended into the valleys of the Merderet and Douve rivers, to hold the west flank and impede enemy reinforcement of the Cotentin peninsula. Many of the green C-47 transport pilots, spooked by flak, flew too fast and too high. Men had to jump into the darkness at airspeeds that ripped equipment from their bodies and jolted them into unconsciousness from the too-rapid deceleration when their static lines tore the cover from their chutes. The pilots scattered their "sticks" of eighteen paratroopers per plane across the neck of the Cotentin. Many C-47s overshot the narrow peninsula altogether and jettisoned their heavily laden paratroopers to swift deaths in the inky Channel waters. Others drowned, still snarled in their harnesses, in the swampy valleys of the Cotentin, which German defensive flooding had turned into vast shallow lakes. At the village of Ste. Mere Eglise, paratroopers dropped into the midst of a German garrison already aroused by a fire in the town square, and many were shot in their chutes even as they descended. Once on the ground the dispersed and decimated sticks struggled to assemble, signaling one another from concealment with double clicks from the "cricket" toys they had been issued for that purpose.

Ironically, the chaotic dispersal of the airborne troops, abetted by the drop of thousands of dummies, worked to the invaders' advantage by amplifying confusion among the German defenders. The liabilities of the Germans' fragmented command structure and the value of the Fortitude deception plan were now dramatically demonstrated. The first jumbled reports of Allied paratroopers prompted pleas from frontline German commanders for release of the reserve panzer divisions, but that decision lay in the hands of a man tossing in narcotized slumber in faraway Berchtesgaden. Hitler would not even be informed of the attack until noon. In the meantime, the German general staff was paralyzed by indecision: was this *the* invasion or simply *an* invasion, perhaps the first and fainter blow of a two-pronged attack, such as the Allies had just successfully pulled off in Italy? Logic—and Fortitude—still dictated that the main blow would land at the Pas de Calais. And so, for fateful hours, while the Allies poured soldiers and weapons ashore, the panzer reserves did not move.

In the Channel, still furrowed by foam-rows from the unspent storm, the colossal armada of 6,483 vessels churned toward the Normandy coast in the gray dawn. Overhead swarms of aircraft roared southward to bomb and strafe German installations. So thoroughly had the earlier air war suppressed the Luftwaffe that the Germans could mount only 319 ineffective sorties on D-Day, against some fifteen thousand by the Allies. Warships, some of them running in as close as eight hundred yards from the shore, blasted the coastal defenses with their big guns. In the bucketing assault boats, frightened men huddled together, cold and seasick, bent by their sixty-eight-pound battle packs, as the boats yawed and slewed through the choppy water toward the beaches.

In the eastern landing zones, code-named Sword, Juno, and Gold, one Canadian and two British divisions splashed ashore against moderate resistance and linked up with the airborne troops on the Orne. By late afternoon they awaited only the arrival of their inexplicably delayed armored brigades to push inland toward their immediate objective, the old Norman capital of Caen, some eight miles inland up the Orne. Safely ensconced on the beaches, their purgatory was soon to come.

To the westward, the U.S. 4th Division, though pushed by an erratic current some two thousand yards south of its targeted landing zone, code-named Utah, otherwise enjoyed almost unimaginable good fortune. It overwhelmed the poor-quality German 709th Division waiting in the low dunes behind the waterline, quickly secured several exits from the beach lodgement, and joined hands with the airborne units raggedly reassembling inland. With casualties of only 197 out of some twenty-three thousand put ashore, the 4th was the most lightly scarred of all the invasion forces.

The veteran 1st Division at Omaha Beach was less lucky. It confronted the excellent 352nd German Division, well dug into the brow of towering cliffs from which their precisely registered gun batteries raked the shoreline with deadly artillery and machine-gun fire. Invasion planners had hoped that "swimming" Sherman tanks, fitted with duplex-drive propellers and waterproof canvas skirts, would shoot their way ashore in the first wave, providing a screen for the infantry to follow. At Omaha those hopes sank along with the tanks themselves, many of which foundered in deep water far from the beaches. Unprotected infantrymen, clothes and equipment crusted with salt, throats clogged with terror and vomit, emerged dazed and unprotected from the pitching landing craft into a fearsome curtain of fire. Those that survived the first murderous seconds cringed for shelter behind the beach obstacles, hampering the engineers' efforts to destroy them. When the follow-up wave of troops from the 29th Division landed on the day's second low tide later in the afternoon, they stumbled across a shoreline awash in a chaos of floating bodies, beached ships, and wrecked equipment. So appalling was the slaughter that the Allied commanders offshore briefly considered abandoning Omaha and directing all further landings eastward, to the British beaches. At day's end Omaha claimed more than two thousand casualties, the highest of any of the landing beaches and a number that, had it been matched elsewhere, would have confirmed Churchill's most sanguinary nightmares of the costs of the cross-Channel attack. Yet somehow the sheer weight of newly arriving troops seemed to push the soldiers already on the beach out of their cowering paralysis. To this "thin wet line of khaki that dragged itself ashore," Bradley reflected, the battle now belonged.[11]

Among the first units to move inland were the specialized Ranger companies assigned to scale the promontory of Pointe du Hoc and to spike its 155mm guns dominating Omaha Beach. With grappling irons and climbing ropes, suffering horrendous losses, the Rangers emerged on the bomb-cratered clifftop only to find the gun emplacements empty. On a day that tested men's courage and sported war's caprice like no other, theirs was among the most brave—and futile—of acts.

By nightfall the three airborne and five assault infantry divisions, plus elements of the follow-up 29th Division, were ashore—more than a hundred thousand men in all. D-Day, the long-awaited mother of battles and perhaps history's most prolific womb of war stories, was over. But the real test—the battle of the buildup and breakout—was to come. The catastrophe at Anzio had shown the danger of allowing an amphibious attack to "congeal" or "stabilize" on the beachhead. "We must blast our way ashore and get a good lodgement before the enemy can bring sufficient reserves up to turn us out," Montgomery had said at the last high-level preinvasion briefing. "Armoured columns must penetrate deep inland, and quickly on D-Day. . . . We must gain space rapidly and peg out claims well inland."[12]

The most important of those claims was the city of Caen, a road and

11. Omar N. Bradley, *A Soldier's Story* (New York: Henry Holt, 1951), 219.
12. Carlo D'Este, *Decision in Normandy* (New York: HarperCollins, 1994), 86.

rail hub and the gateway to the open country to the south, toward Falaise. There tanks could be brought to bear and the American tactics of mobile warfare fully employed. The master plan for Overlord called for Montgomery to reach Caen on D-Day itself, June 6, and Falaise just days later. The bulk of the British and American force would then "break out" of the beachhead and execute a great left wheel eastward to the line of the Seine River, where the Germans could be expected to take up a strong defensive position. Closest to the pivot of Caen, the British armies would break out first, swinging the inner hub of the wheel toward the lower Seine. The Americans would form the wheel's outer rim—the classic wide envelopment—by sweeping far southward and then up the Loire River to the upper Seine. In the meantime, a portion of the American forces was to veer westward to secure vital ports, necessary to supply the buildup of the invasion force: first Cherbourg on the Cotentin, then the Brittany ports at Brest, Lorient, and St. Nazaire.

By the afternoon of June 6, as Rommel was racing by motorcar back from Germany to take direct command of the battle, his troops were already wreaking havoc on this tidy Allied plan. At 4:30 P.M. 21st Panzer Division, the German armored unit positioned closest to the beaches, launched a savage counterattack, with orders to throw the British into the sea. In that it failed, but 21st Panzer, soon joined by 12th SS Panzer, succeeded spectacularly in checking the British advance on Caen—not just on June 6, but for a full month to follow. Repeatedly Montgomery tried to take Caen, and repeatedly he failed. The British front congealed much as the beachhead at Anzio had done, much as the assault on Gallipoli had done, with colossal traffic jams on the beaches and no room to maneuver in the straitened strip of the lodgement. Churchill hounded Montgomery to move. The prime minister murmured darkly to Eisenhower about his fears of another Anzio.[13] By early July, Omar Bradley later wrote, "we faced a real danger of a World War I–type stalemate in Normandy."[14]

At the American end of the front, the battle at first went little better. A great Channel storm on June 19 demolished the American artificial Mulberry harbor at Omaha Beach, seriously constricting the flow of supplies to the American beachhead and delaying Bradley's advance on Cherbourg—whose port facilities were now all the more urgently needed. When at last the Americans entered Cherbourg on June 27,

13. D'Este, *Decision in Normandy*, 302.
14. Omar N. Bradley, A *General's Life* (New York: Simon and Schuster, 1983), 272.

they found its harbor so systematically devastated by the Germans as to be useless for at least another month.

By the end of June the Americans had secured the entire Cotentin peninsula to the west of the landing beaches, but they proved scarcely more able than the British to advance southward, through the marshy hinterland behind Utah and the unexpectedly treacherous terrain of the *bocage* country that belted the Norman interior. Over the centuries the methodical Norman farmers had turned their land into a quilt of pastures and meadows, their boundaries demarcated by densely planted berms called hedgerows. Seamed and cross-hatched by those ancient barriers — up to five feet high and ten feet wide, the earth thickly braided with the roots of trees planted over innumerable generations — the *bocage* was a countryside as ill suited to offensive warfare as it was picturesque to the eye. Every field became a tiny natural fortress bounded by hedgerows that served as deadly tank obstacles and provided superb concealment for machine guns whose fire swept every line of approach at ground level. The hedgerows, Eisenhower later wrote, afforded "almost the ultimate in battle-field protection and natural camouflage." The tremendous advantage that this terrain offered to the defense was one item that had escaped even COSSAC's meticulous planners. "Although there had been some talk in the U.K. before D-Day about the hedgerows," one American general wrote, "none of us had really appreciated how difficult they would turn out to be."[15]

On June 17 Hitler came to Soissons, fifty miles northeast of Paris and as close as he ever got to the Normandy battlefield, to confer with Rundstedt and Rommel. Still expecting that the main attack was yet to come across the Strait of Dover, Hitler continued to reject all suggestions that the German Fifteenth Army at Calais be released for action in Normandy. Hitler's reasoning proceeded in part from the fact that the Calais area harbored the launching sites for the *Vergeltungswaffe* (reprisal weapons), the pilotless flying bombs or V-1s. They were Hitler's response to Bomber Command's terror attacks, devices that conjured for him, as the manned bombers did for Arthur Harris, the dream of an ultimate war-winning weapon. On June 13 the first V-1s, powered by crude jet

15. Eisenhower, *Crusade in Europe*, 268. The American general was James M. Gavin, in his *On to Berlin: Battles of an Airborne Commander, 1943–1946* (New York: Viking Press, 1978), 121. Eventually an American sergeant, Curtis G. Culin, devised a "hedgehog" for fitting on the front of tanks. It consisted of a two-bladed steel prow that sliced through the hedgerows and helped to restore mobility to the American advance.

engines and carrying thousand-pound bombs, had begun to rain upon London. Hitler calculated that their fearful effect would compel the Allies to throw the main weight of their invasion force against the launching sites, where Fifteenth Army waited to crush the attackers. At Soissons *der Führer* also heard and rejected his generals' proposal to execute a limited withdrawal in Normandy and mass their armored forces for a concerted counterattack. "[T]here must be no withdrawal— You must stay where you are," Hitler ordered. Rundstedt demurred, and was soon relieved of command, to be replaced by Field Marshal Gunther Hans von Kluge, a weathered veteran of the eastern front. "What shall we do?" the retiring Rundstedt's military superiors asked him. "End the war!" he replied. "What else can you do?"[16]

Hitler's refusal to countenance either significant reinforcement or withdrawal—not to mention peace—condemned Rommel's Seventh Army to fight a piecemeal battle of delay. For the next several weeks, Normandy became the stage for a patternless series of small-unit clashes, savage encounters among men rendered steadily more callous by the dehumanizing slaughter of face-to-face combat. Yet even without Hitler's interference, Rommel would have had enormous difficulty mounting an organized counterattack in force. Allied aircraft, roaming by the thousands at will over northern France, had already snarled his transportation system and harassed every movement of his troops and tanks in daylight. But *der Führer's* obstinacy sealed Seventh Army's fate.

Despite the handicaps imposed on them by Hitler's rigidity and Allied air supremacy, Rommel's troops sustained a remarkably effective defense. To the advantages of terrain they added the astonishing ferocity of their own fighting spirit and the undisputed superiority of their weaponry, especially their tanks. Nothing in the Allied armory could match the solidity and the slugging power of the German heavy tanks, the Mark V Panther and the still more formidable Mark VI Tiger. A fifty-six-ton behemoth, the Tiger had only to rumble onto the battlefield to strike terror into the hearts of its opponents. It outweighed the American Sherman tank by twenty-three tons and mounted a tank-adapted version of the infamously deadly 88mm gun. Against the Panthers, and especially against the ponderous Tigers, the vulnerable and undergunned Shermans had scant chance. The Shermans were designed for speed and mobility, for infantry support, pursuit, and exploitation, but not for tank-

16. B. H. Liddell Hart, *The German Generals Talk* (1948; New York: Quill, 1979), 244–45.

to-tank duels. Dubbed "Ronsons" after the ubiquitous GI cigarette lighters because of their propensity to burn when hit—or "brew up," as the tankers said—the Shermans could not throw a shell from any range that would pierce the Tiger's hundred-millimeter-thick frontal armor. The Tigers, in contrast, could penetrate the thin skin of the Shermans at a range of four thousand yards. But the Shermans did have, in addition to their speed and simplicity of operation, the advantage of numbers. Some eighty-eight thousand Shermans rolled out of American factories by the end of 1944, against some twenty-five thousand tanks produced by the Germans—another example of the fabulous industrial preponderance that constituted the key element in the American way of war. The sheer abundance of the Shermans could in some cases make up for their individual deficiencies. Under certain conditions, attacking in a pack from front and sides, the Shermans could stand up to their German foes. The rule of thumb was that it took five Shermans to knock out one Panther. The Tigers usually took more.

Stalled before Caen and in the *bocage*, the Allied armies came under growing pressure to advance, and Montgomery bore the brunt of the criticism. American newspapers began to draw stinging contrasts between the slowdown in Normandy and the spectacularly successful Russian offensive that began on June 22 (the third anniversary of Barbarossa). In keeping with his promise at Teheran, Stalin launched a broad frontal assault on German Army Group Center north of the Pripet Marshes. It crunched forward hundreds of miles in weeks, with a bag of 350,000 *Wehrmacht* troops killed, wounded, or captured. Churchill, his anxieties about stalemate in Normandy exacerbated by the V-1s falling upon London, grew increasingly impatient for movement. Eisenhower griped to Montgomery that American journalists were asking why British casualties were so much lower than American. The supreme commander made the same point to Churchill, imploring the prime minister "to persuade Monty to get on his bicycle and start moving."[17]

Montgomery responded in early July by pushing his troops forward along a "carpet" of destruction prepared by the heavy bombers—one of the first uses of the "heavies" in direct tactical support of a ground action. He took Caen at last on July 10, more than a month behind schedule. But in Operation Goodwood, a follow-up action several days

---

17. Arthur Bryant, *Triumph in the West, 1943–1946: Based on the Diaries and Autobiographical Notes of Field Marshal the Viscount Alanbrooke* (London: Collins, 1959), 241, 243.

later, again preceded by heavy bombing, Montgomery failed once more to reach the open ground of the Falaise plain. Eisenhower worried that Goodwood had gained only seven miles at a cost of seven thousand tons of bombs and wondered if even the Allies' well-stocked arsenal could afford a thousand tons of bombs per mile of advance.[18]

Yet Goodwood had in fact served a crucial purpose. It drew several panzer divisions to the British front just as the Americans were about to uncoil their own offensive, code-named Cobra, near St. Lô, a key cross-roads village they had taken on July 18. Allied strategy now shifted. The British sector, instead of being the first-turning inner hub of the great wheel envisioned in Overlord planning, was to become a solid, stationary anvil against which Montgomery held the bulk of the panzer divisions while the heavy American hammer smashed through on the western end of the front.

Operation Cobra opened on the night of July 24–25 with another mammoth carpet bombing of the German positions facing the Americans west of St. Lô. Waves of fighter-bombers, fifty at a time, laid high explosives and incendiaries along the German line. Next came four hundred medium bombers with five-hundred-pound fragmentation bombs, followed by fifteen hundred heavy bombers and then three hundred additional fighters with more high explosives and incendiaries. The bombardment annihilated half the German defenders. "Short" bomb drops also fell into the American lines, killing hundreds of GIs as well as Lieutenant General Lesley J. McNair. (The GIs dubbed the inexperienced U.S. tactical air units "the American Luftwaffe.") Despite these tragedies, the overwhelming weight of the American bombing succeeded at last in cracking the defensive ring that the Germans had so desperately tightened around the Normandy beachhead. In a manner unforeseen, with consequences unanticipated, the breakout had finally happened. It soon developed into a virtually all-American show.

Once unleashed, the Americans moved with astonishing speed. Within five days they were at Avranches, at the far southwestern extremity of Normandy. General Patton, the master of mobile warfare and the phantom of the Fortitude deception, arrived to take command of a very real U.S. Third Army. Patton's infantry and armor poured through the narrow Avranches corridor, turned the corner into Brittany, and spilled out toward the Atlantic ports. Patton's mechanized columns plunged

---

18. Harry C. Butcher, *Three Years with Eisenhower* (New York: Simon and Schuster, 1946), 617.

exuberantly through a region that had been virtually denuded of German troops for the defense of Normandy. In what has variously been called an "armored parade" and a "road march," Third Army raced virtually unopposed across Brittany to the west and toward the Loire to the south. They reached Brest by August 7, though it remained in German hands until September and then was so thoroughly demolished as to be useless. At Lorient and St. Lazaire the German garrisons held out until the end of the war. This denial of the French Atlantic ports to the Allies, along with the stubborn German defense of the Channel ports at Le Havre, Boulogne, Calais, and Dunkirk, with all the complications thus entailed for Allied supply operations, had telling consequences later in the war.

Gasping at the speed of the American breakout and stupefied by the fantastic "wealth of material" that the Anglo-Americans brought to the battlefield, Kluge concluded that "whether the enemy can still be stopped at this point is questionable. The enemy air superiority is terrific, and smothers almost every one of our movements. . . . Losses in men and equipment are extraordinary." His superiors on the German general staff agreed. They advised Hitler that the *Wehrmacht* should execute an orderly withdrawal from France. The recommendation rested upon sound military logic. But logic proved a weak instrument in the face of *der Führer*'s wrath.[19]

In one among the abundant ironies of war, all the horrendous tonnage of the bombs dropped in Normandy counted for less in shaping the next phase of the battle than did a single explosion in East Prussia on July 20. Shortly after noon on that day, Colonel Claus von Stauffenberg, a handsome, debonair German officer, his gait stiffened by wounds suffered in North Africa, walked into Hitler's headquarters and placed a bomb under the conference table. He reached down and broke a tiny vial of acid that would disintegrate a wire restraining the firing pin, then excused himself. Ten minutes later the acid had done its work, releasing a blast that killed four men in the room. Hitler, protected by the heavy tabletop over which he was leaning, was not one of them.

The attempt on his life invested Hitler's chronic suspicion of his generals with a ghastly and diabolical fury. Stauffenberg was summarily shot in Berlin. Other conspirators were hanged in front of movie cameras, so that Hitler might watch the filmed record of their death throes. The fear of further bloody reprisals swept through the German officer corps

19. D'Este, *Decision in Normandy*, 459; Hastings, *Overlord*, 325.

like an Arctic wind, withering whatever faint will remained to stand up to *der Führer*'s increasingly deranged military dicta. Unquestioning obedience to Hitler's orders, without demurral or commentary, was now the test of loyalty, and perhaps the price of life itself.

To Kluge Hitler now issued the command to counterattack. The blow was to be aimed at the village of Mortain at the narrow neck of the Avranches corridor, in the hope of severing the American columns that had already passed through Avranches from their sources of supply. It was a hopeless scheme. The divisions still left to Kluge in Normandy had been mercilessly shredded in two months of constant bombing and grinding battles of attrition. What was more, Hitler was choosing to make battle at the farthest end of the Normandy battlefield. Kluge's weakened forces would have to stretch westward between the enlarging Allied beachhead to their north, anchored on the firm British shoulder at Caen, and the growing strength of Patton's Third Army to the south, already building along the Loire in anticipation of executing a wide envelopment of the German forces west of the Seine. The Mortain counteroffensive, in short, was launched into the jaws of an immense trap. Kluge recognized the hollow futility of what he was about to do but after the events of July 20 was powerless to resist *der Führer*'s command. "If, as I foresee, this plan does not succeed," Kluge noted with resignation, "catastrophe is inevitable."[20]

Ultra helped spring the trap. Bradley received word from the code-breakers on the night of August 6 that the Germans would strike in the morning. Deprived even of the advantage of surprise, the four tattered panzer divisions that Kluge was able to cobble together were decisively checked at Mortain. Now a matchless opportunity presented itself. Instead of the long envelopment for which Patton was positioning his troops, a short envelopment, enclosing virtually all the remaining German forces in Normandy, might be executed by drawing the noose taut between Falaise and Argentan at the eastern edge of the elongated Normandy battlefield. All that was needed was more time for Patton to swing around the enemy's flank. "This is an opportunity that comes to a commander not more than once in a century," Bradley exulted to visiting Treasury Secretary Henry Morgenthau on August 9. "If the other fellow will only press his attack here at Mortain for another 48 hours, he'll give us time to close at Argentan and there completely destroy him. And when he loses his Seventh Army in this bag," Bradley tantalizingly

20. D'Este, *Decision in Normandy*, 415.

predicted, "he'll have nothing left with which to oppose us. We'll go all the way from here to the German border."[21]

Kluge obligingly pressed his attack for more than the requisite forty-eight hours before ordering a full-scale retreat on August 16. It was the last order he ever gave. Pinned down in a ditch by Allied aircraft on August 15, Kluge lost contact with his forces for nearly twelve hours, nourishing Hitler's suspicion that his incommunicado commander was trying to arrange a surrender to the Western allies. Kluge was relieved of command on the seventeenth, to be replaced by Field Marshal Walter Model. Ordered back to Germany for an accounting, including an explanation of rumors linking him to the July 20 assassination attempt, Kluge swallowed a capsule of poison. Under a similar cloud of suspicion, Erwin Rommel joined Kluge in suicide some two months later.

By the evening of August 12 the first elements of Patton's armored units were nosing into Argentan. To cinch the noose around Seventh Army, it only remained to close the "Falaise Gap" that separated the Americans entering Argentan from the British and Canadians, stalled some fifteen miles northward at Falaise. Ravening to plunge ahead, scornful as ever of Montgomery's alleged timidity, Patton hectored Bradley for permission to push on: "Let me go on to Falaise and we'll drive the British back into the sea for another Dunkirk," Patton blustered. But at this crucial juncture Bradley, in one of the campaign's most controversial decisions, held back. "Nothing doing," he told Patton. Nineteen German divisions were now stampeding eastward to escape the trap sprung at Mortain, Bradley reasoned. Their headlong retreat might easily smash through the thin line Patton was then able to stretch across the Falaise Gap. Better to pound the Germans in their shrinking pocket than attempt to draw it shut altogether, Bradley prudently concluded. As he said later: "I much preferred a solid shoulder at Argentan to the possibility of a broken neck at Falaise."[22]

The Allies hesitated just long enough over the prospect of the short envelopment at Falaise to frustrate the full achievement of the long envelopment at the Seine. But it scarcely mattered. While 12th SS Panzer Division fought tenaciously to hold the narrow neck of the Falaise pocket open, some twenty thousand Germans braved the gauntlet of Allied artillery and aircraft fire to escape across the Seine, taking with them thousands of trucks but only a few dozen tanks and artillery pieces.

21. Bradley, Soldier's Story, 304.
22. Bradley, Soldier's Story, 304–5.

Left behind on the hellish escape corridor around Falaise were piles of wrecked guns and charred tanks, as well as fifty thousand prisoners and ten thousand dead, putrefying in the summer sun. The sheer weight of American ordnance and firepower had simply overwhelmed the Germans. "If I did not see it with my own eyes," one German commander wrote of the American onslaught, "I would say it is impossible to give this kind of support to front-line troops so far from their bases." American resources seemed inexhaustible. "I cannot understand these Americans," wrote another overawed German officer. "Each night we know that we have cut them to pieces, inflicted heavy casualties, mowed down their transport. But—in the morning, we are suddenly faced with fresh battalions, with complete replacements of men, machines, food, tools, and weapons. This happens day after day."[23] Eisenhower wrote:

> The battlefield at Falaise was unquestionably one of the greatest "killing grounds" of any of the war areas. Roads, highways, and fields were so choked with destroyed equipment and with dead men and animals that passage through the area was extremely difficult. Forty-eight hours after the closing of the gap I was conducted through it on foot, to encounter scenes that could be described only by Dante. It was literally possible to walk for hundreds of yards at a time, stepping on nothing but dead and decaying flesh.[24]

Falaise marked the ghoulish finale of the battle for Normandy. In the meantime, finally fulfilling the Anvil plan—now renamed Dragoon in peevish recognition of Churchill's continuing resistance to it—additional Allied forces had landed in the south of France on August 15. They rushed virtually unopposed up the Rhone Valley. By the end of August the "thin wet line of khaki" that had stumbled ashore on June 6 had swelled to twenty American divisions, twelve British, three Canadian, one French, and one Polish, and was still growing.[25] And while Allied strength in France grew, Germany's collapsed. The *Wehrmacht* had sacrificed nearly 450,000 men in Normandy, half of them killed or wounded, the rest taken prisoner. Fifteen hundred tanks and over twenty thousand other vehicles were destroyed. More than forty German divisions had been utterly annihilated. The gaunt men who escaped were reduced to scattered and fugitive remnants, shorn of both weapons and elan. Their pell-mell retreat carried them beyond the Seine to a hastily

23. Overy, *Why the Allies Won*, 227, 319.
24. Eisenhower, *Crusade in Europe*, 279.
25. Eisenhower, *Crusade in Europe*, 289.

organized defensive line along the Meuse and Scheldt rivers in eastern France and Belgium.

Scarcely pausing for breath, the Allied forces harried the Germans across the north of France at breakneck speed. Paris, which Eisenhower originally intended to bypass lest his already stretched supply operation be saddled with the requirement of provisioning two million Parisians, was liberated on August 25. The surging throngs that flanked the Champs Elyseés to greet Charles DeGaulle on August 26 gave the lie to Roosevelt's dogged refusal to recognize the legitimacy of DeGaulle's leadership.

Within another week the British raced past Paris and entered the valley of the Somme. The Americans rolled up to the banks of the Meuse. These were the old battlegrounds of the First World War, when movement had been measured in yards, not the scores of miles that these modern mechanized armies gobbled daily.

The dizzying pace of the pursuit, perhaps accelerated by refreshed memories of the earlier war's stalemate, induced a kind of euphoria in the pursuers. It affected their superiors at home as well. From the Combined Allied Intelligence Committee in London came the prediction that "organized resistance . . . is unlikely to continue beyond December 1, 1944, and . . . may end even sooner."[26] On August 26 the SHAEF intelligence summary exulted that "two and a half months of bitter fighting, culminating for the Germans in a blood-bath big enough even for their extravagant tastes, have brought the end of the war in Europe within sight, almost within reach. The strength of the German Armies in the West has been shattered, Paris belongs to France again, and the Allied Armies are streaming towards the frontiers of the Reich."[27] Less than three weeks later George Marshall notified his senior commanders that redeployment of American forces from the European to the Pacific theater was imminent. "[C]essation of hostilities in the war against Germany may occur at any time," Marshall explained, predicting that the end would come "between September 1 and November 1, 1944."[28]

Eisenhower was more cautious. He wrote to Marshall on September 4: "We have advanced so rapidly that further movement in large parts of the front even against very weak opposition is almost impossible."[29]

26. Cornelius Ryan, A Bridge Too Far (New York: Fawcett Popular Library, 1975), 67.
27. Chester Wilmot, The Struggle for Europe (London: Collins, 1952), 458.
28. PDDE 4:2117.
29. PDDE 4:2118.

Yet even the supreme commander was not immune to the familiar virus of victory disease, the infectious military malady that deluded even prudent commanders, in their heady moments of triumph, into believing that anything was possible. Though abundant evidence indicated otherwise, Eisenhower could not entirely divest himself of the delusion that with just one more push the reeling *Reich* would finally collapse.

That alluring prospect soon confronted some hard realities as the thrill of the chase gave way to the mundane arithmetic of logistics. The original Overlord plan had envisioned an offensive consolidation along the line of the Seine, a manageable distance from the Allies' principal supply points in Normandy, about ninety days after June 6 (D+90). But the dash eastward had carried the Anglo-Americans a hundred miles and more beyond the Seine by D+90 (September 4) and had added the provisionment of Paris to the Allied logistical burden. A week later, D+98, Allied soldiers were crowding up against the frontiers of Germany, defended by the "Siegfried Line" (also known as the "West Wall"), a chain of fortifications hastily refurbished to halt the Allied advance. The Overlord forecasters had assumed that line would be reached at D+350. The British and the Americans had outdone themselves; they were some eight months ahead of schedule. Those numbers registered the sweet fruits of military success. They also contained the seeds of a logistical nightmare.

An American division in active combat consumed six to seven hundred tons of supplies every day. With some forty divisions in France by early September, and more arriving weekly, the Allies required that at least twenty thousand tons of materiel move to the front daily from the Channel beaches and their solitary functioning port at Cherbourg. The difficulty lay not with the availability of goods. Stocks were still piled high in England, and American farms and factories continued to pour out a deluge of food, guns, and munitions. The problem, rather, was transport. Despite monuments of engineering ingenuity like the sole surviving Mulberry and eventually an ingenious cross-Channel oil delivery pipeline (PLUTO—Pipe Line Under the Ocean), many supplies still had to be cumbersomely manhandled across the beaches. Worse, given the havoc wreaked by the transportation plan on the French rail system, the bulk of those goods, including all the army's precious gasoline, then had to be hauled across northern France by truck. The Red Ball Express, a jury-rigged road transport system patched together with herculean effort and named for the railroaders' expression for a fast freight, began on August 25 to shuttle its trucks between the Calvados coast and the fighting front. But relentlessly, as the Allied divisions accelerated eastward, the thinning stream of supplies that reached them raised the old question that had bedeviled planners earlier in the war. Though for a brief season in 1944 it had seemed possible to do this *and* that, now Eisenhower was confronted with the hard choice between this *or* that.

Eisenhower's dilemma consisted in the "this" of Montgomery's clamor to be unleashed with full force toward the Ruhr on the northern end of the eastering front and the "that" of Patton's demand to be allowed to penetrate the Saar region — Germany's other great industrial center — on the southern end. The iron constraints of the supply famine and the gasoline drought that beset the Allied armies at the end of August precluded doing both. Eisenhower compromised. He insisted that both allies should advance shoulder by shoulder on a broad front, as fuel and other supplies permitted. In this the supreme commander was doubtless influenced by political considerations of national prestige as much as by logistical limits and military logic. Neither ally, he reasoned, should be allowed to claim all the glory for the eventual defeat of Germany. Even more compellingly, Eisenhower knew that the American people, not to mention his own American military subordinates, would never tolerate idling the U.S. Army and leaving the triumphal endgame to Montgomery, as the British commander repeatedly demanded.

Yet Montgomery's insistence that his army should have priority made much sense. On his front, along the Channel coast, lay the great port of Antwerp, Europe's largest, sorely needed to relieve the logistics bottleneck by shortening the Allies' lines of supply. Near Antwerp, too, were the remaining V-weapon sites, from which, after September 8, V-2s as well as V-1s were soaring against London.[30] The northern route was also the shortest to the Ruhr, the industrial heart of Germany that had always been Overlord's prime objective. For all these reasons, though he continued to insist on the "broad front" advance, Eisenhower leaned toward Montgomery and the north.

On September 4 Montgomery formally proposed to Eisenhower that he be given all the resources he needed to launch "a powerful and full

---

30. The V-2 was a far more sophisticated weapon than the V-1, a true rocket powered by a liquid-oxygen-fueled jet engine that lofted the missile to an altitude of sixty miles and aimed it earthward in a free-fall of twenty-two hundred miles per hour. The V-2 outran its own sound waves, exploding without any warning of its arrival. At that speed, it was incapable of interception by antiaircraft or fighter interceptors.

blooded thrust toward Berlin" that would end the German war.[31] Patton, meanwhile, thundered that "if Ike stops holding Monty's hand and gives me the supplies, I'll go through the Siegfried Line like shit through a goose."[32] Eisenhower again temporized. He told Montgomery on September 5 that both the Saar and Ruhr, as well as the port of Antwerp, remained his principal objectives and pointedly reminded Montgomery that "no re-allocation of our present resources would be adequate to sustain a thrust to Berlin."[33] Montgomery exploded, haranguing Eisenhower so relentlessly at a meeting aboard the supreme commander's aircraft at Brussels airport on September 10 that Eisenhower put his hand on Montgomery's knee and said: "Steady Monty! You can't speak to me like that. I'm your boss."[34]

But Eisenhower at last relented, at least in part. While Patton continued to badger forward as he could, capturing and cadging gasoline from any available source, Montgomery secured Eisenhower's approval for a major thrust on the northern end of the front. Code-named Market-Garden, it was an uncharacteristically bold plan for the methodical Montgomery. "Had the pious and teetotaling Montgomery wobbled into SHAEF with a hangover," Omar Bradley later wrote, "I could not have been more astonished than I was by the daring adventure he proposed."[35]

Hardly a "full-blooded thrust toward Berlin," Market-Garden was nevertheless to be mounted on such a scale as to preclude, for a brief but crucial period, virtually all other initiatives. Constrained by the continuing supply famine, Eisenhower dismounted three freshly arrived American divisions in Normandy, stripping them of all their vehicles in order to feed Montgomery's demand for forty-seven hundred aircraft, thirty-five thousand airborne troops, and a massive concentration of armor. Market-Garden envisioned a two-phase assault. "Market" called for three airborne divisions, two American and one British, to secure the river crossings along a sixty-mile-long corridor stretching from the Belgian-Dutch border to Arnhem, a river port on the lower Rhine and a gateway into the Ruhr. "Garden" would send British armored units dashing up the corridor to consolidate the paratroopers' "air-heads" and to clear the path for a massive follow-up invasion of the German industrial heart-

31. *PDDE* 4:2120.
32. Ryan, *Bridge Too Far*, 71n.
33. *PDDE* 4:2120.
34. Ambrose, *Supreme Commander*, 515.
35. Bradley, *Soldier's Story*, 335.

land, home to fully half of the enemy's coal and steel production. Deprived of those critical materials, the *Wehrmacht* would be left essentially weaponless and immobilized in the field and must sue for peace. The bridges were the key. Success depended, said one British officer, on "threading seven needles with one piece of cotton and we only have to miss one to be in trouble."[36]

Market-Garden, launched on September 17, 1944, was a breathless gamble, embraced by men intoxicated by the bloodshed at Falaise and the swiftness of the race to the German frontier. As it actually unfolded, it was, in a sense, the anticlimactic coda following the crescendo of victory in Normandy, featuring many of the same players, and recalling many of the earlier battle's scenarios. It marked the end of Overlord, not with a bang but with a whimper.

Normandy veterans of the 101st Airborne Division failed to secure one of their assigned bridges at Eindhoven. That unthreaded needle delayed the advance of the ground forces. The armored units were in any case forced to move up narrow roads single file, in "one-tank fronts," through tightly jacketed valleys that were easily defended. Further up the road, paratroopers in the 82nd Airborne Division, mindful of the slaughter of their comrades descending onto the Cotentin on the night of June 5–6, jumped over Nijmegen shouting, "Remember Ste. Mere Eglise," and with guns blazing. But at the far end of the invasion corridor, the British 1st Airborne Division played out the most ironic reprise of the battle for Normandy. The British found the Arnhem bridges defended by elements of their old foes, 9th and 10th SS Panzer divisions, licking their wounds from Normandy but still packing enough firepower to contain an outgunned and underarmored airborne unit. After a desperate and costly week of trying to take the "bridge too far," the 1st Airborne Division received orders to withdraw, and Operation Market-Garden was declared a failure. With its collapse, the momentum of Overlord sputtered out and dreams of a German surrender in 1944 began to fade.

THE PRICE FOR MARKET-GARDEN was to be reckoned not only in lost lives but in the lost opportunity to relieve the supply famine by quickly securing the immense port of Antwerp. "If we can only get to using Antwerp," Eisenhower told Marshall, "it will have the effect of a blood transfusion."[37] The British had taken the port itself, with its long-

36. Ryan, *Bridge Too Far*, 142.
37. *PDDE* 4:2168.

shore facilities intact, on September 4, but Montgomery's impatience to penetrate the Ruhr deflected the Allies away from the port at a critical moment. Even Montgomery's customary champion, chief of the British Imperial General Staff General Alan Brooke, felt that "Monty's strategy for once is at fault. Instead of carrying out the advance on Arnhem he ought to have made certain of Antwerp in the first place. . . . Ike nobly took all blame on himself as he had approved Monty's suggestion to operate on Arnhem."[38]

The distraction of Market-Garden allowed the Germans to consolidate their hold on the approaches to Antwerp along the fifty-four miles of the Scheldt River estuary that separated the city from the open North Sea, notably on Walcheren Island at the Scheldt's mouth. Efforts to dislodge the Germans commenced on October 2 and took more than a month to complete. The first supply ship finally steamed up the Scheldt only on November 28. In the meantime, the first U.S. Army infantry units nosed into the *Reich*. On October 21 they captured Aachen, a German city west of the Rhine. But they proved unable to breach the West Wall, which ran just to the south of the city, much less to cross the Rhine itself, Germany's last line of defense in the west. The regrouped Germans demonstrated their still formidable capacity for destruction in the Battle of Huertgen Forest near Aachen, where they inflicted some twenty thousand casualties on the Americans and held their ground for more than two months. Hitler meanwhile continued to stuff the Siegfried Line with whatever reserves he could scrape together. Incredibly, he even began to lay plans for one last offensive in the west, through the Ardennes Forest.

In a bravura gesture reflecting the victory disease that still infected many men on the Allied front, some of Bradley's subordinates sent him on September 28 a captured bronze bust of Hitler and boasted: "With seven units of fire [i.e., seven days' supply of ammunition] and one additional division, First U.S. Army will deliver the original in thirty days." But before that thirty-day period ended, Bradley ruefully recollected, "Hitler had briefed his senior commanders on plans for the Ardennes counterattack."[39]

In the weeks that followed Arnhem, Eisenhower despaired that "German morale on this front shows no sign of cracking." He suggested to Marshall that the unconditional-surrender formula might be revised as a way to induce the Germans to lay down their arms.[40] Roosevelt

38. Byrant, *Triumph in the West*, 291.
39. Bradley, *Soldier's Story*, 343.
40. *PDDE* 4:2312.

explored the idea with Churchill, who seized the opportunity to remind the president that "I remain set where you put me on unconditional surrender." Political considerations weighed heavily in Churchill's mind. He explained to Roosevelt that "we can, it seems to me, speak no words of which the Russians, who are still holding on their front double the number of divisions opposite us, are not parties." To drive his point home, Churchill cited a bit of American history: "I do not see any alternative," he said, "to the General Grant attitude 'To fight it out on this line, if it takes all summer.' "[41]

The summer was still a long way off, and a winter of savage fighting remained in front of the West Wall. An even more wretched season loomed in the east. As the Western allies were sprinting across France, the Red Army had been grinding steadily into Poland. In August it reached the suburbs of Warsaw. The ragtag Polish Home Army then did its best to match DeGaulle's achievement in liberating his national capital by mounting an uprising, but the hapless Poles got no help from Stalin. The German occupiers brutally suppressed the Warsaw rising, even while the Red Army idled within earshot, cynically content to let its hated adversary exterminate any threat to Soviet hegemony in postwar Poland. Here were starkly revealed the chilling implications of the free hand in eastern Europe that Roosevelt had conceded to Stalin at Teheran. "Good God," exclaimed Churchill, "the Russians are spreading across Europe like a tide."[42] Yet the Anglo-Americans were still trying to placate their Russian ally. As winter began to settle over the western front, the British and the Americans continued to chip at the Germans as best they could, for political reasons as well as military. Any other course of action, Bradley observed, "would surely have precipitated an angry protest from our allies in the Kremlin."[43]

George C. Marshall, accompanied by War Mobilization director James Byrnes, landed at Verdun on October 7 for an inspection tour of

---

41. *C&R* 3:409. Churchill was referring to a famous communiqué that Grant issued on May 11, 1864, during the Battle of Spotsylvania: "I intend to fight it out on this line if it takes all summer."

42. Lord Moran, *Churchill: Taken from the Diaries of Lord Moran: The Struggle for Survival, 1940–1965* (Boston: Houghton Mifflin, 1966), 173. "Winston never talks of Hitler these days," Moran recorded on August 21. "[H]e is always harping on the dangers of Communism. He dreams of the Red Army spreading like a cancer from one country to another. It has become an obsession, and he seems to think of little else" (185).

43. Bradley, *Soldier's Story*, 350.

the American front. Roosevelt had loaned them the Sacred Cow, the same plane that had borne the president to Cairo and Teheran almost a year earlier. As Bradley recalled, "It was apparent from the Chief of Staff's opening conversations that the chill which had caused us to revise our rosy September estimates on the end of the war had not yet filtered through to Washington and the War Department. While we were now resigned to a bitter-end campaign, he spoke with the cheery optimism we had discarded three weeks before."[44] But after a week at the front, Marshall was fully divested of his illusions. When the Sacred Cow lifted off from Paris on the evening of October 13, the day's last light was just evaporating from the top of the Eiffel Tower. The sun was setting, too, on hopes for an end to the war in 1944.

Hitler, meanwhile, was gathering what strength he could for a last desperate roll of the dice. Antwerp, already under constant V-2 bombardment, was the prize. With the great port again in German hands, the Allied supply famine would starve the Allies to a halt in the west. A full-scale V-weapon blitz could then be loosed against England, and the Anglo-Americans might yet be forced into a negotiated peace, freeing the *Wehrmacht* for a last-ditch defense against the relentlessly oncoming Russians. It was a mad scheme, but reason by now held small purchase in Hitler's mind.

Winter was to be the *Wehrmacht*'s cloak and comrade. The lowering weather would provide respite from the merciless air bombardment that Harris and Spaatz had resumed with a fury after the Normandy breakout. The shortening days would shroud the panzers moving into attack position in the Eiffel Mountains opposite the Ardennes Forest along the Belgian-German frontier. "Fog, night and snow," Hitler told his skeptical but submissive generals, would give them their "great opportunity."[45] In the snowy woods of the Eiffel, the *Wehrmacht* gathered itself up for one final battle.

Eisenhower had deployed his ever-growing army in two great concentrations—the British to the north and the Americans to the south, trying to slug their ways respectively into the Ruhr and the Saar. At the hinge between the British and American armies spread the heavily timbered and hilly Ardennes Forest, launching site for Hitler's great *Blitzkrieg* attack on France in 1940. As if he had forgotten that history, Eisenhower decided the Ardennes was too thickly wooded and confined for a massive

44. Bradley, *Soldier's Story*, 345.
45. Wilmot, *Struggle for Europe*, 478.

Allied attack—or for a German counterattack. He therefore placed just four U.S. divisions to hold his front facing the Ardennes.

At 5:30 A.M. on December 16, just as German forces had done in 1940, one *Panzergrenadier* and eight panzer divisions roared out of the Ardennes, their way forward through the bitterly cold morning air illuminated by searchlight beams reflecting off low-hanging clouds. They had achieved complete tactical surprise. Many American units, totaling some ten thousand men, surrendered almost immediately—a number exceeded in the army's history only by the disaster in the Philippines in 1942. Panic coursed through the Allied ranks, fed by rumors of German infiltrators in American uniforms and reports that near the Belgian village of Malmédy German troops had massacred nearly a hundred unarmed American prisoners of war, as well as a number of civilians. Soon the spearhead of the German attack was approaching the banks of the Meuse. In the southern sector of the salient the attackers surrounded the American garrison in the village of Bastogne, key to a vital road network. Presented with a demand to surrender his troops or risk their annihilation and Bastogne's, Brigadier General Anthony C. McAuliffe gave a reply des-

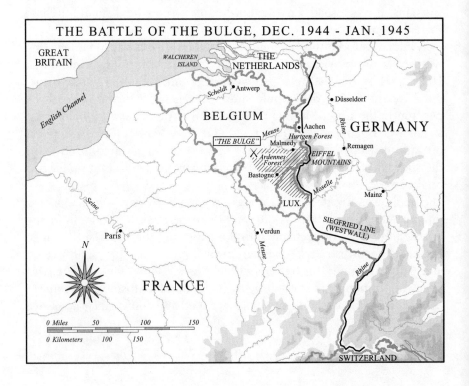

THE BATTLE OF THE BULGE, DEC. 1944 - JAN. 1945

tined to be celebrated in American folklore: "Nuts!" When the English-speaking German lieutenant who received McCauliffe's reply allowed as how he did not understand the term, McAuliffe's aide explained that "in plain English it is the same thing as 'Go to Hell!' "[46]

Eisenhower meanwhile pondered the Germans' strategic intentions. Was this merely a local spoiling attack? A feint? An attempt to drive a wedge between the British and American ground forces? A thrust to recapture Antwerp? As the battle lengthened and more German units swarmed into the swelling "bulge" in the Allied line — the configuration that gave the battle its name — it became clear that the Germans had somehow mustered the wherewithal for a major counterattack and that Antwerp was the objective.

Eisenhower rushed from his headquarters to a meeting at Verdun with his senior commanders on the morning of December 19. Characteristically, he announced that "there will be only cheerful faces at this conference table." The Germans, Ike said, had forsaken their fixed defenses to make battle in the open, presenting the Allies with an "opportunity," not a "disaster." With characteristic bombast, Patton proposed "to let the sons of bitches go all the way to Paris. Then we'll really cut 'em off and chew 'em up." More soberly, Eisenhower asked Patton if he could take three of his divisions facing eastward along the Moselle and pivot them northward to drive into the flank of the German salient. Patton was prepared for the question. Yes, he replied, and what was more, he could do it within forty-eight hours — an astonishing feat of logistical and tactical reorientation.[47]

Patton was as good as his word. In an impressive demonstration of his own genius for war and of the American capacity for battlefield mobility, he swung his columns ninety degrees and relieved the garrison at Bastogne. On December 22 the skies cleared, and Allied air power once again came into play. The Russians meanwhile bestirred themselves from the banks of the Vistula and mounted a massive assault that carried them by the end of January to the banks of the Oder, within miles of Berlin. Hitler at last allowed his tattered forces left in the now-shrinking Ardennes pocket to withdraw. By the second week in January, the Battle of the Bulge was over. It had claimed more than seventy thousand Allied casualties and more than a hundred thousand German. Measured by the numbers

46. Trevor N. Dupuy et al., *Hitler's Last Gamble: The Battle of the Bulge, December 1944–January 1945* (New York: HarperCollins, 1994), 194.

47. Eisenhower, *Crusade in Europe*, 350.

of dead and wounded, it was the single most costly American battle of the war. It had also eaten up Hitler's last reserves of men, armor, and aircraft.

AFTER THE NORMANDY BEACHHEAD had been secured, General Carl Spaatz's U.S. Strategic Air Forces, along with British Bomber Command, had recommenced the air war against Germany in earnest and with a vengeance. With the huge airfleets now at their command, the Eighth and Fifteenth U.S. Air Forces, based respectively in Britain and in the Mediterranean, dropped the majority of their bombs in the eleven months of war after D-Day (72 percent in the case of Eighth Air Force). Most of them fell on the oil and transportation targets whose destruction had always held the promise of a "strategic" constriction of the German economy. By the end of 1944 the bombers had wreaked immense devastation. German synthetic oil production fell to less than 7 percent of pre-D-Day levels, and aviation gasoline output to less than 3 percent. Though German aircraft fabrication actually increased through July 1944, the Luftwaffe's planes sat on the ground for want of fuel to fly them. With the skies thus cleansed of German aircraft, Spaatz's bombers ranged freely over the *Reich*. They cut the traffic on Germany's rail, road, and water transport systems by more than 50 percent, effectively dismembering the German economy into several isolated regions that survived only by consuming their accumulated stores of food and fuel. Some 4.5 million workers, 20 percent of the industrial labor force, had to be committed to debris removal and the production and manning of antiaircraft weapons. For 1944 as a whole, bombing deprived Germany of 35 percent of its anticipated tank production and 31 percent of its expected output of aircraft. Overall economic output fell by 10 percent and munitions production by 15 percent. In January 1945, while Eisenhower's armies were still stalled west of the Rhine, German munitions minister Albert Speer notified Hitler that "the war was over in the area of heavy industry and armaments." On March 15, when coal and steel production, electrical generation, and freight-car loadings had all been reduced to about 15 percent of normal, Speer reported that "the German economy is heading for an inevitable collapse within 4–8 weeks."[48]

Beneath the economy-strangling logic of "strategic" aerial warfare,

---

48. Overy, *Why the Allies Won*, 125–33; *United States Strategic Bombing Survey Summary Report* (Washington: USGPO, 1945); Albert Speer, *Inside the Third Reich* (New York: Macmillan, 1970), 424.

another idea about the role of bombing had long slumbered in the minds of some American air strategists. In the war's final weeks it stirred uneasily to life: that bombardment might not only inflict physical damage but could break the enemy's spirit as well, by so terrorizing civilian populations that they would compel their governments to beg for peace. Though the Americans had somewhat sanctimoniously distanced themselves from the Royal Air Force's "area" attacks on civilian targets, terror bombing had intrigued the American air planners from the outset. AWPD/1, the Army Air Forces' original planning document drafted as part of the Victory Program in 1941, had qualified its acceptance of the tactic but hardly repudiated it outright. "Timeliness of attack is most important in the conduct of air operations directly against civilian morale," it noted. "If the morale of the people is already low because of sustained suffering and deprivation . . . then heavy and sustained bombing of cities may crush that morale entirely. . . . As German morale begins to crack," the document concluded, it might be "highly profitable to deliver a large-scale, all-out attack on the civil population of Berlin." At the Casablanca Conference in 1943, the Allied leaders had affirmed that though the primary objective of the Combined Bomber Offensive was "destruction and dislocation of the German military, industrial, and economic system," a secondary mission was "the undermining of the morale of the German people to a point where their capacity for armed resistance is fatally weakened." Doctrine aside, many American bomber groups regularly took to the air when weather conditions made "precision" bombing next to impossible. The air crews referred to such missions as "women's and children's days."[49]

In the summer of 1944, the British brought to the Americans a proposal aimed explicitly at shattering German civilian morale. Codenamed Thunderclap, it envisioned a combined Anglo-American attack on Berlin in overpowering strength, enough to kill or seriously injure some 275,000 people. Many of the American airmen recoiled. One senior officer called it another of the British "baby killing schemes," and he warned that "this would be a blot on the history of the Air forces and of the U.S. . . . It gives full reign [sic] to the baser elements of our

49. Conrad Crane, Bombs, Cities, and Civilians: American Airpower Strategy in World War II (Lawrence: University Press of Kansas, 1993), 93; Ronald Schaffer, Wings of Judgment: American Bombing in World War II (New York: Oxford University Press, 1985), 33; United States Strategic Bombing Survey Summary Report, 2; Alan J. Levine, The Strategic Bombing of Germany, 1940–1945 (Westport, Conn.: Praeger, 1992), 103.

people." Spaatz advised Eisenhower that Thunderclap was an attempt by the RAF "to have the U.S. tarred with the morale bombing aftermath which we feel will be terrific." Eisenhower's reply was alarming. He had consistently favored precision bombing, said the supreme Allied commander, but "I am always prepared to take part in anything that gives real promise to ending the war quickly."[50]

The result was an Anglo-American attack on Berlin on February 3 that killed twenty-five thousand civilians. A second combined assault on Dresden ten days later ignited a firestorm that killed thirty-five thousand people by both flames and suffocation—a horror described by Kurt Vonnegut Jr., an American POW in Dresden, in his postwar novel *Slaughterhouse-Five*. Though the Americans maintained that their role in these raids was to strike at military targets only, both attacks, especially that on Dresden, became instantly notorious as confirming proof that the USSTAF had now slid across the same moral threshold that the RAF had crossed in 1942. As the *St. Louis Post-Dispatch* described it: "Allied air bosses have made the long-awaited decision to adopt deliberate terror bombing of the great German population centers as a ruthless expedient to hasten Hitler's doom."[51]

In the wake of the invading American ground armies, teams of economists and psychologists swarmed into Germany to analyze the effects of the bombing and to assess the air strategists' claims that air power was decisive in Germany's defeat—lessons that could then be applied in Japan. In its 208 separate studies, the United States Strategic Bombing Survey concluded that bombing had contributed significantly to Allied victory but had not by itself been decisive. German economic output had actually trebled between 1941 and 1944, despite heavy bombing. Only when air attacks were concentrated on oil and transportation did they produce dramatic results, and because that targeting scheme was introduced only late in the war, its effects were difficult to separate from the impact of ground invasion. As for morale, the USSBS psychologists reached even more qualified conclusions. Bombing surely depressed *morale*, they found, but had markedly less effect on *behavior*. Personal habits, police-state discipline, and propaganda all kept workers on their jobs and protected the Nazi regime from overthrow even under the cruelest bombardment.

For the airmen, the USSBS results in Germany were disappointing.

50. Schaffer, *Wings of Judgment*, 83–84; Crane, *Bombs, Cities, and Civilians*, 106.
51. Schaffer, *Wings of Judgment*, 99.

Their claim that air power was not simply one weapon among many but was *the* decisive war-winning weapon remained unproved. They would have one more chance to make their case in the war against Japan. "It seems to me we ought to be shot if we don't have more [air power] than we can deploy in the Pacific," Assistant Secretary of War Robert Lovett wrote to Spaatz in November 1944. The war against Japan held out "the possibility of exerting such overwhelming air power on the enemy as to give us a chance to find out whether air power can bring a nation to its knees or not. I don't see how we can make a bear rug until we have killed the bear."[52]

Eisenhower meanwhile restored his front in mid-January and continued to claw at the West Wall. Pummeled on the ground and from the air, the Germans began slowly to withdraw to the eastward. They executed an orderly retreat, demolishing the Rhine River bridges as they crossed over them into the heartland of the *Reich*. But on March 7 advance units of the U.S. 9th Armored Division probing as far as the Rhine found a railway bridge at Remagen miraculously intact. Bradley poured troops across it into central Germany. Patton meanwhile crossed the upper river near Mainz, and Montgomery leapt the lower Rhine below Düsseldorf. By the first of April the Allies had overrun the Saar and encircled the Ruhr. On April 11 the first American units reached the banks of the Elbe River, the already agreed boundary between the Soviet and Western zones of occupation. There Eisenhower stopped, while the Red Army proceeded to take Berlin in ferocious street fighting that claimed tens of thousands of lives. The Battle for Northwest Europe was all but over. The climactic battle against Japan remained to be fought. The battle for advantage in the postwar world was just beginning.

52. Lovett quoted in Crane, *Bombs, Cities, and Civilians*, 119. For a comprehensive discussion of the USSBS results, see Bernard Brodie, "Strategic Bombing in World War II," chap. 4 in his *Strategy in the Missile Age* (Princeton: Princeton University Press, 1959).

21

The Cauldron of the Home Front

The Second World War is bound to change all trends.... [N]ot since Reconstruction has there been more reason to anticipate fundamental changes in American race relations, changes that will involve a development toward the American ideals.
— Gunnar Myrdal, An American Dilemma, 1944

On September 9, 1942, shortly before the sun peeped over the North American continent's western edge and drove the night from the sea, Japanese submarine I-25 porpoised to the surface of the Pacific Ocean a few miles off the Oregon coast. Moving with practiced efficiency in the darkness, its crew assembled a fragile, single-engine float plane on the boat's deck, slung two 168-pound incendiary bombs under its wings, and pitched it skyward with a catapult. Guided by the beam from the Cape Blanco lighthouse, Warrant Officer Nobuo Fujita piloted his little aircraft over the coastal cliffs and into American airspace. As dawn was breaking, he released his two bombs into the dense pine and fir woods near the logging town of Brookings, wheeled oceanward again, and rendezvoused with his mother ship. Submarine, pilot, and airplane, swiftly restowed with folded wings into the boat's minuscule cargo hold, dove to safety.

Three weeks later, Fujita flew an almost identical mission, dropping two more incendiary devices into the coastal-range evergreen forest. With Fujita's second sortie, Japan's bombing campaign against the continental United States ended. His four bombs were the only ones ever to fall from an enemy aircraft onto any of the forty-eight American states in World War II. None did any serious damage.[1]

1. *New York Times*, October 3, 1997, C20.

746

The puny impact of Fujita's raids, quixotically intended to ignite vast forest fires and compel the diversion of American resources from the Pacific war to firefighting and coastal defense, underscored a fundamental fact about America's unique situation in the war. Despite Franklin Roosevelt's repeated insistence that the ocean barriers no longer shielded the United States from enemy assault, in reality they did. Alone among all the belligerent peoples, Americans went about their daily wartime lives in a mercifully unscarred homeland that lay safely beyond the enemy's reach.

But if Americans were spared from the threat of attack, they were not exempt from the upheavals that the waging of total war everywhere inflicted. Indeed, America's very distance from the battlefields in some ways opened opportunities for more quarrelsome political clashes and perhaps even for more consequential social changes than occurred elsewhere. Most other wartime governments, including Winston Churchill's, suspended elections for the duration of the war, but in the United States the constitutionally mandated rhythms of the political cycle beat on unperturbed. Congressional elections pitted Democrats against Republicans on schedule in 1942. Two years later, the quadrennial presidential campaign unfolded even as the fighting in Europe and the Pacific was reaching a crescendo. Those familiarly contentious rituals reminded Americans that in the political realm, in war as in peace, much in their lives remained the same. Yet in countless other domains of wartime American life things changed, often dramatically. The winds of war lifted up a people dazed and inert after a decade of paralyzingly hard times. As a thunder squall ionizes the sultry summer air, World War II left the American people energized, freshened, and invigorated. Depression America had been a place of resignation, fear, and torpor. America at war was quickened by confidence, hope, and above all by movement.

Not since the great surge of pioneers across the Appalachian crest in the early years of the Republic had so many Americans been on the move. Fifteen million men and several hundred thousand women—one in nine Americans—left home for military training camps. Three-quarters of them eventually ended up overseas, six times the number that had gone to France with the American Expeditionary Force in 1917–18. Another fifteen million persons—one out of every eight civilians—changed their county of residence in the three and a half years after Pearl Harbor. By war's end, one in every five Americans had been swept up in the great wartime migration. Eight million of them moved permanently to different states, half of those to different regions. One great migratory stream carried people from south to north. A second and larger stream flowed from east to west. As if the entire continent had been tilted westward, people spilled out of the South and the Great Plains into the Pacific coastal states, especially California. The populations of Washington, Oregon, and California mushroomed by more than one-third between 1941 and 1945. As the momentum of the wartime migration continued even after the war's end, California was home to 72 percent more people in 1950 than it had been in 1940. Endless rivers of workers poured into the great metropolitan centers of defense production—Detroit, Pittsburgh, Chicago, San Diego, Los Angeles, Oakland, Portland, and Seattle. In a harbinger of postwar social geography they settled disproportionately not in the central cities but in the newly burgeoning suburbs, which grew at nearly three times the rate of the traditional urban cores. By the end of the war decade, the long-depressed farmlands of the South and the Midwest held fewer souls than they had in 1940, while some eight million Americans had lifted their heels for the Pacific Coast. In the long history of the westward movement, this was its most dramatic chapter.[2]

NOT ALL OF THE MOVEMENT in this churning demographic cauldron was voluntary, especially in the case of Warrant Officer Fujita's kinsmen resident in the United States. Some two hundred thousand Japanese immigrants and Japanese-Americans lived in the Territory of Hawaii in 1941. Another 120,000 resided on the American mainland, mostly in the Pacific Coast states, California in particular. For them, geography was destiny.

Following the attack on Pearl Harbor, Hawaii passed under martial law, the writ of habeas corpus was suspended, and the military police took several hundred suspected spies and saboteurs of Japanese extraction into custody. But the very size of the Japanese community in Hawaii (nearly half the territory's population), and its vital importance to the islands' economy, foreclosed any thought of wholesale evacuation. The mainland community, however, was proportionately much smaller (in

2. Henry S. Shryock Jr. and Hope Tisdale Eldridge, "Internal Migration in Peace and War," *American Sociological Review* 12, no. 1 (February 1947): 27–39; Shryock, "Redistribution of Population," *Journal of the American Statistical Association* 46, no. 256 (December 1951), 417–37; Richard White, *It's Your Misfortune and None of My Own: A New History of the American West* (Norman: University of Oklahoma Press, 1991), 496–504.

California, barely 1 percent of the population), more economically marginal and socially isolated, and long buffeted by racist pressures. The
mainland Japanese for the most part kept warily to themselves, many of
them toiling with exemplary efficiency on their family fruit and vegetable farms. Insular and quiescent, they were also internally riven by age
and legal status. Their elders, the forty thousand first-generation immigrant Japanese, or Issei, were generally over the age of fifty and debarred
from citizenship by the Immigration Restriction Act of 1924, a statutory
impediment that perversely exposed them to the accusation that as non-
citizens they were poorly assimilated into American society. A majority
of their children, the eighty thousand second-generation Nisei, were
under the age of eighteen. Born in the United States, they were also
citizens. Alien and citizen alike, the peculiarly vulnerable Pacific Coast
Japanese community was about to feel the full wrath of war-fueled hysteria.

Curiously, no clamor for wholesale reprisals against the mainland Japanese arose in the immediate aftermath of the Pearl Harbor attack. The
Los Angeles Times soberly editorialized on December 8 that most of the
Japanese on the Coast were "good Americans, born and educated as
such," and serenely foresaw that there would be "no riots, no mob law."
General John L. DeWitt, chief of the army's Western Defense Command, at first dismissed loose talk of mass evacuations as "damned nonsense." He condemned any broadside assaults on the rights of the
American-born Nisei. "An American citizen, after all, is an American
citizen," he declared.[3] Individual arrests were another matter. Government surveillance, ongoing since 1935, had identified some two thousand potentially subversive persons in the Japanese community. Along
with fourteen thousand German and Italian security risks nationwide,
they were quietly rounded up in the last days of 1941. But those individual detentions stopped well short of wholesale incarcerations. "I was
determined," Attorney General Francis Biddle wrote, "to avoid mass
internment, and the persecution of aliens that had characterized the
First World War."[4]

---

3. Peter Irons, *Justice at War: The Story of the Japanese Internment Cases* (Berkeley:
University of California Press, 1983), 6, 30; Francis Biddle, *In Brief Authority* (Garden
City, N.Y.: Doubleday, 1962), 215.
4. Biddle, *In Brief Authority*, 207. Biddle also took heed from the embarrassing example
of Britain, where a panicky government in 1940 had briefly impounded some seventy-
four thousand enemy aliens, only to realize that most of them were German and
Austrian Jewish refugees, hardly fifth columnists for the *Reich*. In the United States

In fact, the immigrants whose loyalty had been questioned during World War I had then been freshly arrived and seemed to many observers unarguably alien. But by 1941 those older European groups were settled communities, well assimilated, their patriotism as well as their political loyalty actively cultivated by Roosevelt's New Deal. Though a surprising six hundred thousand Italians—more than 10 percent of the entire Italian-American community—remained Italian citizens and were automatically labeled "enemy aliens" after Mussolini's declaration of war, Roosevelt instructed Biddle to cancel that designation in a joyfully received announcement at Carnegie Hall, shrewdly delivered on Columbus Day 1942, just weeks before the congressional elections.

The Japanese were not so fortunate. As war rumors took wing in the weeks following Pearl Harbor, sobriety gave way to anxiety, then to a rising cry for draconian action against the Japanese on the West Coast. Inflammatory and invariably false reports of Japanese attacks on the American mainland flashed through coastal communities.[5] Eleanor Roosevelt's airplane, en route to Los Angeles on the evening of the Pearl Harbor attack, was grounded in the Midwest while the first lady telephoned Washington to check a radio message that San Francisco was under bombardment. Painters at Stanford University blacked out the skylight of the library's main reading room so that it could not serve as a beacon to enemy pilots. Carpenters hammered up dummy aircraft plants in Los Angeles to decoy Japanese bombers away from the real factories. Athletic officials moved the traditional New Year's Day football classic from the Rose Bowl in Pasadena, California; the game was played instead in North Carolina, presumably safe from Japanese attack. Japan's astonishing string of victories in the Pacific further unsettled American public opinion. Hong Kong fell on December 2, Manila on January 2, Singapore on January 25.

The release at the end of January of a government investigation of

---

in World War II some five thousand Germans and Italians, both citizens and "enemy aliens," were eventually interned, principally in camps at Bismarck, North Dakota, and Missoula, Montana. See Biddle, 204–11; and Rose Schierini, "Executive Order 9066 and Italian Americans: The San Francisco Story," *California History* 70, no. 4 (Winter 1991–92): 367–77.

5. The only authenticated Japanese attacks on the American mainland, other than Fujita's two raids, were the shelling of an oil refinery near Santa Barbara on February 23, 1942, which damaged a pump-house, and of the Oregon coast near Fort Stevens on June 21, which damaged a baseball-diamond backstop. Both incidents involved ineffective fire from a submarine's deck gun, and both happened *after* the presidential evacuation order was signed on February 19.

the Pearl Harbor attack proved the decisive blow. The report, prepared by Supreme Court Justice Owen J. Roberts, alleged without documentation that Hawaii-based espionage agents, including Japanese-American citizens, had abetted Nagumo's strike force. Two days later, DeWitt reported "a tremendous volume of public opinion now developing against the Japanese of all classes, that is aliens and non-aliens." DeWitt himself, described by Biddle as having a "tendency to reflect the views of the last man to whom he talked," soon succumbed to Rumor's siren. He wildly declared to an incredulous Justice Department official that every ship sailing out of the Columbia had been attacked by submarines guided by clandestine radio operators near the river's mouth. When evidence of actual attacks failed to materialize, DeWitt invoked the tortured logic that the very absence of any sabotage activity on the West Coast proved the existence of an organized, disciplined conspiracy in the Japanese community, cunningly withholding its blow until it could be struck with lethal effect. In February the respected columnist Walter Lippmann alleged that military authorities had evidence of radio communications between "the enemy at sea and enemy agents on land" — a charge that FBI director J. Edgar Hoover had already advised Biddle was utterly without foundation. A radio technician from the Federal Communications Commission reviewed DeWitt's "evidence" of electronic signals and declared it hogwash. All 760 of DeWitt's suspicious radio transmissions could be accounted for, and not one involved espionage. "Frankly," the technician concluded, "I have never seen an organization [the U.S. Army's Western Defense Command] that was so hopeless to cope with radio intelligence requirements. The personnel is unskilled and untrained. Most are privates who can read only ten words a minute. . . . It's pathetic to say the least."

But by this time facts were no protection against the building gale of fear and prejudice. "Nobody's constitutional rights," Lippmann magisterially intoned, "include the right to reside and do business on a battlefield." Lippmann's colleague Westbrook Pegler echoed him less elegantly a few days later: "The Japanese in California should be under armed guard to the last man and woman right now," Pegler wrote in his widely read column, "and to hell with habeas corpus until the danger is over." Unapologetically racist voices also joined the chorus. "We're charged with wanting to get rid of the Japs for selfish reasons," a leader of California's Grower-Shipper Vegetable Association declared. "We might as well be honest. We do. It's a question of whether the white man lives on the Pacific Coast or the brown man." Prodded by such sentiments, in early February 1942 DeWitt officially requested authority to remove all Japanese from the West Coast. It was impossible, he claimed, to distinguish the loyal from the disloyal in the peculiarly alien and inscrutable Japanese community. The only remedy was wholesale evacuation. The same man who had said a month earlier, "An American citizen, after all, is an American citizen," now announced, "A Jap's a Jap. . . . It makes no difference whether he is an American citizen or not. . . . I don't want any of them."[6]

At the Justice Department several officials, including conspicuously Edward J. Ennis, director of the Alien Enemy Control Unit, as well as Biddle's assistant James H. Rowe, struggled to quell this irrationally mounting fury. Rowe denounced Lippmann and Pegler as "Armchair Strategists and Junior G-Men" whose reckless charges came "close to shouting FIRE! in the theater; and if race riots occur, these writers will bear a heavy responsibility." Attorney General Biddle informed Secretary of War Stimson "that the Department of Justice would not under any circumstances evacuate American citizens." But at a fateful meeting in the living room of the attorney general's Washington home on the evening of February 17, the gentle and scholarly Biddle buckled. Facing off against Assistant Secretary of War John J. McCloy and two army officers, Ennis and Rowe argued heatedly that DeWitt's request for evacuation orders should be denied. Unknown to his two subordinates, however, Biddle, new to the cabinet, unsure of his standing with Roosevelt, and overawed by the Olympian figure of Stimson, had told the secretary of war by telephone earlier in the day that he would not oppose DeWitt's recommendation. When this became clear, Rowe remembered, "I was so mad that I could not speak. . . . Ennis almost wept." Even Stimson had grave misgivings. "The second generation Japanese can only be evacuated," he wrote in his diary, "either as part of a total evacuation, giving access to the areas only by permits, or by frankly trying to put them out on the ground that their racial characteristics are such that we cannot understand or even trust the citizen Japanese. This latter is the fact but I am afraid it will make a tremendous hole in our constitutional system to apply it." Despite his own reservations and the sput-

6. Eleanor Roosevelt, *This I Remember* (New York: Harper and Brothers, 1949), 236; John Morton Blum, *V Was for Victory: Politics and American Culture during World War II* (New York: Harcourt Brace Jovanovich, 1976), 159; Biddle, *In Brief Authority*, 215; Irons, *Justice at War*, 39–40, 41, 60–61, 283.

tering opposition of the Justice Department officials, Stimson advised the president that DeWitt should be authorized to proceed. The cabinet devoted only a desultory discussion to the matter. On February 19 Roosevelt signed Executive Order 9066. It directed the War Department to "prescribe military areas . . . from which any and all persons may be excluded." No explicit reference to the Japanese was necessary. When Biddle feebly objected that the order was "ill-advised, unnecessary, and unnecessarily cruel," Roosevelt silenced him with the rejoinder: "[T]his must be a military decision."[7]

The original order neither prescribed what should happen to the evacuees nor precluded voluntary withdrawal. Some fifteen thousand Japanese took it upon themselves to leave the prohibited Pacific coastal zone in February and early March 1942, moving in with relatives or friends in the Midwest or East. (Japanese residing outside the Western Defense Command were never subject to detention.) To facilitate this kind of voluntary resettlement, Roosevelt created the War Relocation Authority and named Milton S. Eisenhower, brother of Dwight D. Eisenhower, its director. But many states in the nation's interior made it clear that Japanese migration eastward spelled trouble. "There would be Japs hanging from every pine tree," the governor of Wyoming predicted, if his state became their destination. "We want to keep this a white man's country," said the attorney general of Idaho, urging that "all Japanese should be put in concentration camps."[8]

On March 27 DeWitt put a stop to voluntary withdrawal. He issued a "freeze order," prohibiting the remaining Japanese from leaving the Pacific Coast military zone without permission. Further orders soon followed to report to "assembly centers," makeshift facilities that included southern California's Santa Anita racetrack, where detainees were jammed into hastily converted horse stalls until they could be transferred to permanent "relocation centers." Yamato Ichihashi, a sixty-four-year-old Japanese-born Stanford professor of history swept up in the forced evacuation, described Santa Anita as "mentally and morally depressive," a place where "thousands are housed in stables which retain smells of animals. A stable which housed a horse now houses 5 to 6 humans. . . .

---

7. Irons, *Justice at War*, 61–62; Biddle, *In Brief Authority* 213, 218, 219; Stimson Diary, February 10, 1942; Kai Bird, *The Chairman: John J. McCloy and the Making of the American Establishment* (New York: Simon and Schuster, 1992), 153–54.

8. Irons, *Justice at War*, 72

There is no privacy of any kind. In short the general conditions are bad without any exaggeration; we are fast being converted into veritable Okies."[9]

Like the itinerant Okies, the Japanese were soon on the move again, headed for ten relocation camps, one in Arkansas and the others scattered through the arid western interior. Deeply troubled by this turn of events, Eisenhower resigned as director of the War Relocation Authority. He advised his successor, Dillon S. Meyer, to take the job only if his conscience would allow him to sleep at night. His own, Eisenhower explained, did not. Within weeks, more than a hundred thousand Japanese were uprooted from their homes and livelihoods. In the haste of departure, scant provision could be made for protecting houses, farms, businesses, and other assets. The evacuees' property losses alone would eventually total in the millions of dollars, to say nothing of spiritual stagnation and lost wages as they languished in the camps, odd oases of enforced idleness in the midst of the wartime boom.

The camp at Manzanar, on the barren flats of a dried-up lake bed in California's Inyo County, received the first evacuees in June 1942. Though an improvement on the transient assembly centers, Manzanar, like all the other camps, greeted the new arrivals with stark reminders of their predicament. Barbed wire fencing girdled the six-thousand-acre site. A second range of fence further enclosed the 560-acre residential area. Guard towers, searchlights, and machine-gun installations punctuated the compound's perimeter at regular intervals. The summer's heat made the twenty-by-twenty-foot uninsulated cabins virtually uninhabitable, and the winter's wind drove desert sand into everything. Still, as Ichihashi reported, the sanitary facilities were adequate and the food was good, at least compared with Santa Anita.

The camps soon became little cities, complete with the kinds of tensions endemic to real cities. A riot at Manzanar in late 1942, precipitated by anger over the government's use of "stool pigeons" to keep tabs on dissidents, left two internees dead and eight seriously wounded. "You can't imagine how close we came to machine-gunning the whole bunch of them," one official told a San Francisco reporter. "The only thing that stopped us, I guess, were the effects such a shooting would have had on the Japs holding our boys in Manila and China."[10] But for the

9. Gordon Chang, ed., *Morning Glory, Evening Shadow: Yamato Ichihashi and His Internment Writings, 1942–1945* (Stanford: Stanford University Press, 1997), 104, 108.
10. Bird, *Chairman*, 683, n. 99.

most part, the residents tried to establish as normal a life as they could. They organized newspapers, markets, schools, and police and fire departments. Farmers daily passed through gates in the first fence to tend their plots. Inmates willing to submit to a humiliating process of interrogation to establish their loyalty to the United States could be furloughed for work beyond the second fence.

When Meyer in early 1943 made the loyalty-interrogation process compulsory for all internees, many of them bristled. Asked if they would foreswear allegiance to the Japanese emperor and if they were willing to serve in the armed forces of the United States, several thousand camp inmates, offended at the implication that their presumptive loyalty was to Japan and suspicious that they were being recruited for suicide missions, answered no to both questions. The eighty-five hundred internees in this "No-No" group, mostly Nisei young men, were then labeled disloyal and dispatched to a camp at Tule Lake, California. Among those whose loyalty was confirmed, some three thousand were recruited into the 442nd Regimental Combat Team, an all-Japanese (segregated) unit that distinguished itself fighting in Italy. Slowly, other certifiably loyal internees began to be released. By mid-1944 as many as twenty-five thousand had departed the camps.[11]

The policy of segregating the loyal from the allegedly disloyal Japanese detainees highlighted some of the most painful contradictions in the entire relocation scheme and exposed it to especially potent legal challenge. "When the segregation is effected," Ichihashi shrewdly queried a Stanford colleague in mid-1943, "how could the American government continue to justify the present policy of keeping the loyal citizens and aliens in the relocation centers? It conflicts with the fundamental reason given for the wholesale evacuation."[12]

Ichihashi's question already hung heavily over the minds of many in Washington. Biddle's unquiet conscience continued to trouble him, and he pressed for accelerated releases from the camps. Anything else, he told Roosevelt at the end of 1943, "is dangerous and repugnant to the principles of our government." Secretary of the Interior Harold Ickes advised the president in June 1944 that "the continued retention of these innocent people in the relocation centers would be a blot upon the

11. Jacobus tenBroeck et al., *Prejudice, War, and the Constitution* (Berkeley and Los Angeles: University of California Press, 1970), 150–51; U.S. Department of Interior, War Location Authority, *Impounded People: Japanese Americans in the Relocation Centers* (Washington: USGPO, 1946), 112–33.
12. Chang, *Morning Glory,* 244.

history of this country." Even Stimson favored "freeing those who had been screened and found loyal," but in a significant qualification Stimson added that he "doubted the wisdom of doing it . . . before the [1944 presidential] election." Roosevelt agreed. He feared the ruckus that the returning Japanese might stir up, especially in electorally weighty California. For the time being, releases would continue only at a deliberately controlled snail's pace.[13]

War Department officials watched anxiously as several lawsuits challenging the constitutionality of the relocation scheme made their way through the courts. On June 21, 1943, the Supreme Court ruled unanimously in the government's favor in the first two cases, though both turned on technicalities that allowed the Court to evade a decision on the central issues of coerced evacuation and compulsory internment. In one of those cases, *Hirabayashi v. United States*, Justice Frank Murphy's concurring opinion sounded an ominous warning. The relocation program, he admonished, ventured perilously close "to the very brink of constitutional power." For the first time in history, Murphy wrote, the Court had "sustained a substantial restriction of the personal liberty of citizens of the United States based upon the accident of race or ancestry." The government's policy, he darkly concluded, bore "a melancholy resemblance to the treatment accorded to members of the Jewish race in Germany and in other parts of Europe."[14]

Of the remaining suits, Fred Korematsu's held the greatest threat to the constitutionality of the relocation program. Korematsu was an unlikely paragon of his sorely abused people. A twenty-three-year-old American-born Nisei living in the San Francisco Bay area in the spring of 1942, he had a good welding job and an Italian-American fiancée, and no wish to leave either. When DeWitt issued his evacuation order, Korematsu forged his identity papers, underwent plastic surgery to change his facial appearance, and prepared to wait out the war as a "Spanish-Hawaiian" named "Clyde Sarah." The subterfuge came to an inglorious end on the afternoon of May 30, 1942, when police acting on a tip arrested Korematsu as he was strolling down a street with his girlfriend in San Leandro, California. An American Civil Liberties Union lawyer read of the arrest in the newspaper, visited Korematsu in jail, and asked if he would allow his case to be used as a test of the evacuation decree. Somewhat surprisingly, Korematsu agreed.

13. Irons, *Justice at War*, 271–73.
14. *Hirabayashi v. United States*, 320 U.S. 81 (1943), 62–63.

While Korematsu's case began its slow journey through the legal system, DeWitt's deputy Colonel Karl R. Bendetsen was drafting a document for DeWitt's signature entitled *Final Report, Japanese Evacuation from the West Coast, 1942*. Ten months in preparation, 618 pages long, it offered DeWitt's official explanation for what he had done: "military necessity." Justice Department lawyers first saw the report in January 1944, as they were preparing their briefs in the Korematsu case. What they read stunned them. The *Final Report* ignited an uproar that raged for eight months, a donnybrook between the Justice and War departments that ended with a pathetic but constitutionally fateful whimper in a last-ditch skirmish over a three-sentence footnote.

To buttress the argument that forced evacuation was a matter of military necessity, Bendetsen had laced the *Final Report* with hundreds of examples of subversive activities on the West Coast in the winter and spring of 1942. That evidence was the indispensable basis for the government's claim that its relocation program lay within constitutional bounds. But the Justice Department lawyers quickly saw that Bendetsen had cooked his facts. His statement that an FBI raid had turned up "more than 60,000 rounds of ammunition and many rifles, shotguns and maps," for example, failed to mention that those items had come from a sporting-goods store. Worse, when Biddle asked the FBI and the Federal Communications Commission (FCC) to review the report's charges, the responses were unequivocal. Hoover replied that "there is no information in the possession of this Bureau" that supported Bendetsen's claims about espionage. The FCC's response was even more damning. Citing its own 1942 study that had shown DeWitt's claims about supposedly illicit radio transmissions to be false, the FCC expressed its outrage that the allegations had resurfaced in the report. "There wasn't a single illicit station and DeWitt knew it," an FCC technician said.[15]

Armed with these findings, Justice Department attorneys determined to disavow the *Final Report* in their presentation of the *Korematsu* case. Excluding the evidence in the report—in legal language, instructing the Court to take no judicial notice of it—would fatally undermine the factual basis for the argument that military necessity justified the violation of Fred Koremastu's constitutional right to live where he pleased. To that end, the department's drafting team carefully tamped a high-explosive footnote into its brief:

15. Biddle, *In Brief Authority*, 221; Irons, *Justice at War*, 281, 284.

The Final Report of General DeWitt is relied on in this brief for statistics and other details concerning the actual evacuation and the events that took place subsequent thereto. The recital of the circumstances justifying the evacuation as a matter of military necessity, however, is in several respects, particularly with reference to the use of illegal radio transmitters and to shore-to-ship signaling by persons of Japanese ancestry, in conflict with information in the possession of the Department of Justice. In view of the contrariety of the reports on this matter we do not ask the Court to take judicial notice of the recital of those facts contained in the Report.

Privately, the lawyers used less measured language. The report's allegations of espionage, sabotage, and treason, they said, were "lies." Propagating these intentional falsehoods was "highly unfair to this racial minority." Left uncorrected, the report would mean that "the whole historical record of this matter will be as the military choose to state it."[16]

The footnote detonated in Assistant Secretary of War McCloy's hands when he read a draft of the Justice Department's brief on Saturday morning, September 30, 1944. McCloy reflexively understood that its effect would be to explode the shaky consensus the Court had patched together in the *Hirabayashi* case, and probably to induce a judgment that the entire relocation program was unconstitutional. He insisted that the damning footnote be amended. After two days of frantic argument, the top officials at the Justice Department once again buckled under McCloy's pressure and deleted the offending footnote. Ignorant of this dispute, the Supreme Court justices proceeded to deliberate on the *Korematsu* case deprived of a basis on which to challenge the factual assertions of the *Final Report*.

Even so, the Court was clearly queasy about the *Korematsu* case. Justice Hugo Black's majority opinion upheld Fred Korematsu's original conviction for violating the evacuation decree while carefully avoiding any pronouncement on the legality of his subsequent internment. "All legal restrictions which curtail the civil rights of a single racial group are immediately suspect," Black cautioned, and must be subjected to the strictest scrutiny. But military necessity, Black concluded, provided sufficient grounds to believe that the government's actions passed the strict scrutiny test in Korematsu's case. Justices Roberts, Murphy, and Jackson dissented. Jackson objected that the Court had "validated the

16. Irons, *Justice at War*, 286, 288.

principle of racial discrimination." If McCloy had not succeeded in expunging the footnote that called DeWitt's *Final Report* into question, a majority of the Court would quite possibly have found in Korematsu's favor. As it was, though no racially restrictive law has ever since passed the strict scrutiny test, the *Korematsu* precedent, in Jackson's phrase, "lies about like a loaded weapon ready for the hand of any authority that can bring forward a plausible claim to an urgent need."[17]

When the Court pronounced on the *Korematsu* case on December 18, 1944, safely after the November presidential election, the camps had already begun to empty. Just the day before the Court's decision was announced, the government had declared that the period of "military necessity" was ended. West Coast military authorities rescinded DeWitt's original evacuation order and restored to the remaining camp residents "their full rights to enter and remain in the military areas of the Western Defense Command."[18]

The sorry history of Korematsu's bowdlerized brief condemns the Court's ruling as a judicial travesty. For the Japanese internees, the entire episode had been a cruel torment. By one estimate they suffered some $400 million in property losses as a result of evacuation. Congress in 1948 provided a paltry $37 million in reparations. In another spasm of conscience forty years later, Congress awarded $20,000 to each surviving detainee. President Bill Clinton rendered further atonement in 1998 when he bestowed the nation's highest civilian honor, the Presidential Medal of Freedom, on that implausible paladin, Fred Korematsu.[19]

Yet for the Nisei generation, the ordeal of the camps yielded at least some inadvertently compensatory fruit. The detention experience cracked the thick cake of custom that had encrusted the prewar Japanese community. It undermined the cultural authority of the elderly Issei, liberated their children from hidebound tradition and cultural isolation, and dramatically catalyzed the Nisei's assimilation into the larger society. However painful and unintentional the process, internment allowed younger Japanese-Americans to break out of their defensive ethnic enclaves during the war and rapidly ascend the ladder of social mobility thereafter. Within three decades of the war's end, the Nisei were among

17. *Korematsu v. United States*, 323 U.S. 214 (1944), 216, 245–46.
18. Irons, *Justice at War*, 276.
19. In 1984 a federal court voided Korematsu's 1944 conviction on a writ of coram nobis—a judicial ruling that the original verdict had been tainted by official misconduct. See *Korematsu v. U.S.*, 584 F. Supp. 1406 (N.D. Cal. 1984).

the best-educated Americans and enjoyed incomes more than a third above the national average (ranking second among American ethnic groups only to Jews). Their improbable destiny mirrored the experience of millions of other Americans whose lives were touched by the war.[20]

THE JAPANESE INTERNMENT affronted American ideals of justice. Yet in a sense the harsh treatment of the Japanese may have been no less an anomaly than Fujita's two bombing raids, and the Nisei's eventual fate might be taken as more typical of the war's impact on many Americans. The chronic discomfort of government officials with their own policy, and the obvious caution and even distaste with which the Supreme Court handled the evacuation cases, bore witness to the singular awkwardness with which American culture tried to come to terms with the internment episode. What happened to the Japanese was especially disquieting in wartime America precisely because it so loudly mocked the nation's best image of itself as a tolerantly inclusive, fairminded, "melting pot" society—an image long nurtured in national mythology, and one powerfully reinforced by the conspicuously racialized conflict that was World War II.

The deliberate burnishing of that image had begun well before Pearl Harbor. Citing the contrasting example of Hitler's campaign against the Jews, Franklin Roosevelt throughout the 1930s had purposely invoked religious toleration as a distinguishing American trait, one that spelled the difference between Americans and their adversaries and defined the very essence of the American character. He struck that note with special eloquence when he listed "the freedom of every person to worship God in his own way" as one of the "essential human freedoms" in his famous "Four Freedoms" address in January 1941. He expanded upon that theme time and again in the weeks after Pearl Harbor. "Remember the Nazi technique: 'Pit race against race, religion against religion, prejudice against prejudice. Divide and conquer!' We must not let that happen here," he declared in January 1942. In his State of the Union address in the same month he warned: "We must be particularly vigilant against racial discrimination in any of its ugly forms. Hitler will try again to breed mistrust and suspicion between one individual and another, one group and another, one race and another."[21]

Those sentiments were not simply the ritual incantations of a prag-

20. Thomas Sowell, *Ethnic America* (New York: Basic 1981), 5, 171–79.
21. PPA (1940), 672; (1942), 6, 39.

matic wartime leader presiding over a notoriously plural people. Count-less Americans shared them, and many made a point of saying so pub-licly. Several interfaith and interracial groups sprang up in wartime. In June 1940 more than one hundred prominent social scientists formed the Committee for National Morale to promote the idea, as the historian Henry Steele Commager said, "that the American people is a nation." Visitors to the New York World's Fair in 1940 flocked to "the American Common," a pavilion vacated by the Soviet Union after the Nazi-Soviet Pact and reoutfitted to display what a press release called the "mingled traditions" of the American folk, a modern idiom for an old idea: *e pluribus unum*. The ubiquity of that sentiment on the eve of the war was illustrated by the saga of "Ballad for Americans," a sentimentally patriotic eleven-minute cantata originally composed for a leftish Federal Theater Project revue in 1937 and eventually used to open the Repub-lican presidential nominating convention in 1940.

"Am I an American?" the song asked.

> I'm just an Irish, Negro, Jewish, Italian, French and English, Spanish, Russian, Chinese, Polish, Scotch, Hungarian, Litvak, Swedish, Finnish, Canadian, Greek and Turk, and Czech and double Czech American.
> And that ain't all, I was baptized Baptist, Methodist, Congregationalist, Lutheran, Atheist, Roman Catholic, Orthodox Jewish, Presbyterian, Seventh Day Adventist, Mormon, Quaker, Christian Scientist and lots more.

When the great Negro bass-baritone Paul Robeson sang the "Ballad" on the radio in 1939, the CBS studio audience stamped, shouted, and bra-voed for nearly twenty minutes. Appreciative callers jammed the net-work's switchboard for two hours.

Hollywood, encouraged by the Office of War Information's Bureau of Motion Pictures, gave wartime Americans countless film portraits of themselves as a people both diverse and unified — a message that became a cliché in the image of the legendary World War II infantry rifle squad, invariably portrayed as the cheery nursery of comradely gusto, its roll call announcing an outlandishly diverse roster of exotic ethnic surnames.[22]

Nothing better demonstrated the peculiar wartime intensity of those

22. *New York Times Magazine*, November 10, 1940, 3; Robert W. Rydell, *World of Fairs: The Century-of-Progress Expositions* (Chicago: University of Chicago Press, 1993), 185; *Time*, November 20, 1939, 58–59; "Ballad for Americans," Robbins Music Cor-poration, copyright 1940. I am indebted to Wendy Wall for these references.

inclusionary sentiments than the publication of a remarkable book in the very year that the *Korematsu* case was decided: Gunnar Myrdal's *An American Dilemma: The Negro Problem and Modern Democracy.* Myrdal was a brilliant young Swedish economist commissioned by the Carnegie Corporation to undertake a comprehensive study of the status of American Negroes. He had begun his researches in 1938 by motoring through the South in a big Buick with his black American colleague, Ralph Bunche. (To avoid trouble, Bunche posed as Myrdal's chauffeur.) The onset of war had slowed but not stopped his investigation. More impressive, neither Myrdal nor the Carnegie Corporation flinched from publication when the project was completed while the fighting still raged in 1944. The book's release in that year reflected their confidence that even in the midst of a global war, perhaps precisely *because* of the war, the American people were prepared to hear a probing report about their country's most enduringly painful social issue: race. "[T]he book was published during the most anxious months of the war. I know of no other country where such a thing could have happened," Myrdal recalled. *An American Dilemma* swiftly became a best-seller, confirming Myrdal's and his sponsors' intuitions.[23]

Myrdal's book was in essence a secular sermon. He spared few details in his two-volume, fifteen-hundred-page description of the regime of segregation that still held the majority of black Americans in its malevolent grip. He aimed not only to make his white American readers see the enormity of their racial system but also to prompt them to change it, and he assumed that by accomplishing the first objective he would automatically realize the second. Here, despite his foreignness, Myrdal adopted a strategy with roots in American political culture that reached back to Abraham Lincoln and beyond: it consisted in the simple belief that a factual appeal to the better angels of their nature would induce Americans to do the right thing.

All Americans, Myrdal asserted, "even a poor and uneducated white person in some isolated and backward rural region in the Deep South," carried within them a commitment to what he called "the American Creed," a set of values embracing "liberty, equality, justice, and fair opportunity for everybody." But unreasoning prejudice, he argued, had corrupted the white mind, making a mockery of those ideals. The resulting tension between good values and bad behavior constituted "the

23. Gunnar Myrdal, *An American Dilemma: The Negro Problem and Modern Democracy* (1944; New York: Harper and Row, Twentieth Anniversary Edition, 1962), xxv.

American dilemma." Myrdal believed that such tension was inherently unstable and must inevitably be resolved as Americans brought their attitudes and practices into conformity with the praiseworthy tenets of the American Creed. *An American Dilemma* held out the prospect of a virtually painless exit from the nation's racist history. The book thus complimented and comforted Americans even as it criticized them. In the patriotic glow of wartime, blacks and whites alike greeted Myrdal's message with extravagant hosannas of praise, hymned gratefully by a nation more flattered than shamed by his exposé and obviously hungry for the counsels of hope about race.[24]

In Myrdal's view discrimination by whites was the single most powerful determinant of the baleful condition of American blacks. The mechanism of oppression worked according to what he called the "principle of cumulation": discrimination forced blacks into lowly social positions, which, in turn, confirmed the bigoted belief in black inferiority and thereby reinforced the barriers to change. But this self-reinforcing cycle of perception, behavior, and discrimination could work two ways, he argued: an objective improvement in the social standing of blacks would diminish white prejudice, opening opportunities for further gain. The trick was to find a way to crack open ancient habits of behavior and belief, black as well as white. In the cauldron of war, the principle of cumulation was about to be reforged into a powerful tool for black advancement.

One black leader had already eagerly grasped that instrument. Asa Philip Randolph was the head of the Brotherhood of Sleeping Car Porters, an all-black union of railroad workers. Randolph was a courtly man whose early training as a Shakespearean actor endowed him with a deep, resonant voice. He had come to New York from his native Florida when the Harlem Renaissance was flourishing. The city's intellectual and social ferment nourished him. He became a skilled street-corner orator, writer, editor, and associate of the black nationalist Marcus Garvey. In 1917 Randolph helped to found the *Messenger*, which took outspoken stands against racial discrimination as well as against American participation in World War I. His opposition to that war got him arrested, though the charges were eventually dropped. Attorney General A. Mitchell Palmer had called him "the most dangerous Negro in America." In 1925 he accepted an invitation from a group of Pullman Company porters to lead the new Brotherhood of Sleeping Car Porters; be-

24. Myrdal, *American Dilemma*, lxxii.

cause he was not a porter himself, the Pullman Company could not fire him. Significantly, the Brotherhood was one of the few Negro organizations of any type with a solid foothold in the national industrial economy, and Randolph was one of the rare black leaders with a constituency and a vision that extended beyond Dixie. He also had a remarkable talent for shaping and wielding public opinion, which he called "the most powerful weapon in America."[25]

As Congress was passing the Burke-Wadsworth Selective Service Act in mid-September 1940, the Brotherhood met in its annual convention at the Harlem YMCA. At Randolph's urging, the delegates passed a resolution urging the government to avoid discrimination against blacks in the armed forces. Among the guest speakers at the gathering was Eleanor Roosevelt, here as so often serving as her husband's ambassador to black America. With her help, Randolph arranged a meeting to present the Brotherhood's resolution to the president in person.

Two weeks later, Randolph and a delegation of African-American leaders, including Walter White, executive secretary of the National Association for the Advancement of Colored People (NAACP), arrived at the White House. Randolph and White were veterans of many such Oval Office meetings, in which deferential Negro spokesmen reenacted a tableau from slavery days by humbly supplicating the Boss-man in the Big House for whatever favors he might see fit to dispense. Randolph had been present at one unforgettable encounter in 1925, when Calvin Coolidge sat stonily through a speech by William Monroe Trotter on the evils of lynching, then impassively bade his visitors good day, whereupon Trotter and the other Negroes meekly departed. Franklin Roosevelt was more cordial than the notoriously taciturn Coolidge, but in fact in his first two terms he had done little to change the essential character of these hollow ceremonies, and precious little indeed to improve the lot of black Americans. Though Eleanor had reached out to black America, and though prominent New Dealers like Harold Ickes and Harry Hopkins had made gestures toward racial equality, Roosevelt, like all presidents since Reconstruction, had not meaningfully bestirred himself on behalf of blacks.

Most African-Americans on the eve of World War II lived lives scarcely different from those to which their freedmen forebears had been consigned after the Civil War. In an urban age, black Americans re-

25. Kenneth T. Jackson, ed., *Dictionary of American Biography* (New York: Charles Scribner's Sons, 1995), Supp. 10, 658–61.

mained a rural people. Three of every four Negroes still dwelled in the South, the poorest inhabitants of the nation's poorest region. Jim Crow bound them to make their way warily through the shabby interstices of southern white society, well out of America's mainstream. Three-quarters of adult blacks had not finished high school. One in ten had no schooling whatever, and many more were functionally illiterate. Blacks led shorter and unhealthier lives than whites and worked at tougher and far less lucrative jobs. They earned, on the average, 39 percent of what whites made. Almost nine of ten black families eked out a living on incomes below the federal poverty threshold. Most employed black men were marooned in unskilled occupations. One-third were sharecroppers or tenant farmers. A far higher percentage of black women than white worked for wages, a majority as domestic servants or farmhands. Negroes were politically voiceless throughout the South; fewer than 5 percent of eligible blacks in the states of the old Confederacy could exercise democracy's most fundamental right, the right to vote.[26]

The continued isolation of black Americans was made achingly obvious as war mobilization began to lift the pall of the Depression. Management and labor joined arms to exclude black workers from the benefits of the war boom. "We will not employ Negroes," the president of North American Aviation flatly declared. "It is against company policy." Kansas City's Standard Steel Corporation announced: "We have not had a Negro worker in twenty-five years, and do not plan to start now." In Seattle the district organizer of the International Association of Machinists put the Boeing Aircraft Company on notice that "labor has been asked to make many sacrifices in this war," but the "sacrifice" of allowing blacks into union membership "is too great." As for the armed forces, the army deliberately replicated the patterns of civilian society by confining black troops to segregated units and assigning the bulk of them to noncombat service and construction duty. The regular army in 1940 had just five black officers, three of them chaplains. The navy accepted blacks only as messmen, cooks, and stewards; not one black man had ever attended lily-white Annapolis. The elite services of the air corps and the marines refused any black enlistments whatsoever.[27]

26. Gerald David Jaynes and Robin M. Williams Jr., A Common Destiny: Blacks and American Society (Washington: National Academy Press, 1989), 35–42, 271–73.
27. Jervis Anderson, A. Philip Randolph: A Biographical Portrait (New York: Harcourt Brace Jovanovich, 1973), 241–42.

When Randolph and his colleagues rehearsed these matters for the president at their meeting on September 27, the president worked his customary charm, and the little delegation departed aglow with a sense of satisfaction. But just two weeks later a Roosevelt aide announced that "the policy of the War Department is not to intermingle colored and white enlisted personnel in the same regimental organizations."[28]

Randolph was stunned. It was expressly to put an end to segregation in the military that he had gone to the White House, and he thought Roosevelt had given him a sympathetic hearing. Betrayed and angry, Randolph made a historic decision. "[C]alling on the President and holding those conferences are not going to get us anywhere," he told an associate. Instead, it was time to take the campaign for Negro rights into the streets. The goal would be not simply desegregation in the military but now, even more important, jobs in defense industries. "I think we ought to get 10,000 Negroes to march on Washington in protest, march down Pennsylvania Avenue," he told an aide. This was an incendiary suggestion. Randolph was proposing to have done with the tactics of entreaty and petition and to force the government's hand with a massive public display of Negro strength. He was less concerned with formal legal rights in the South, the traditional agenda of black leaders, than with opportunities for employment in the reviving industrial economy. What was more, Randolph envisioned an all-black demonstration. "We shall not call upon our white friends to march with us," he announced. "There are some things Negroes must do alone." Randolph's strategy and objectives foreshadowed as well as inspired the civil rights movement of the postwar era, but the rich promise of that future was still veiled in 1941, and the brazen novelty of Randolph's idea rattled other Negro leaders. "It scared everybody to death," one recalled. The *Pittsburgh Courier*, the largest-circulation Negro newspaper, branded it "a crackpot proposal." White's NAACP gave only lukewarm support. But Randolph pushed on, and thousands of black men and women responded with enthusiasm. As the idea of the march caught fire in the black community, Randolph raised his sights. By the end of May his March on Washington Movement was summoning a hundred thousand Negroes to descend on the capital on July 1. "I call on Negroes everywhere," he proclaimed, "to gird for an epoch-making march."[29]

28. Ulysses Lee, *United States Army in World War II Special Studies: The Employment of Negro Troops* (Washington: Department of the Army, 1963), 76.

29. Anderson, *Randolph*, 247–53.

The prospect of one hundred thousand Negroes in the streets of the capital rattled Franklin Roosevelt as well. He induced Eleanor to write a letter warning Randolph that "your group is making a very grave mistake." On June 13 the president called in National Youth Administration chief Aubrey Williams, a liberal southerner with good ties to the black community, and told him to "go to New York and try to talk Randolph and White out of this march. Get the missus and Fiorello [La Guardia, mayor of New York] and Anna [Rosenberg, a member of the Social Security Board], and get it stopped." Williams failed in his mission, but out of it came another meeting between Randolph and the president at the White House on June 18. Less than two weeks remained before the marchers were scheduled to throng Pennsylvania Avenue.[30]

Roosevelt opened the session with his customary persiflage, irrelevantly inquiring which Harvard class Randolph was in. "I never went to Harvard, Mr. President," Randolph coolly replied. "Well, Phil, what do you want me to do?" Roosevelt asked at last. Issue an executive order prohibiting discrimination in the defense plants, answered Randolph. "You know I can't do that," said Roosevelt. "In any event, I couldn't do anything unless you called off this march of yours. Questions like this can't be settled with a sledge hammer." He was sorry, said Randolph, but without an executive order the march would take place as scheduled. It was not the policy of the president of the United States to be ruled with a gun at his head, Roosevelt declared. "Call it off," he said curtly, "and we'll talk again." But Randolph was no Trotter, and he calmly stood his ground. Fiorello La Guardia finally broke the impasse. "Gentlemen," he said, "it is clear that Mr. Randolph is not going to call off the march, and I suggest we all begin to seek a formula."[31]

The formula took the shape of Executive Order 8802, issued on June 25, 1941. "There shall be no discrimination in the employment of workers in defense industries or government because of race, creed, color, or national origin," it declared, adding that both employers and labor unions had a positive duty "to provide for the full and equitable participation of all workers in defense industries." A newly established Fair Employment Practices Committee (FEPC) was empowered to investigate complaints and take remedial action. Ironically, there was no mention of segregation in the armed forces, the issue that had been Randolph's original concern. Yet the order represented a spectacular victory

30. Anderson, *Randolph*, 255.
31. Anderson, *Randolph*, 257–58.

for Randolph and defined a crucial pivot in the history of African-Americans. As one Negro newspaper noted, it "demonstrated to the Doubting Thomases among us that only mass action can pry open the doors that have been erected against America's black minority." A rising mood of militancy took hold in the black community. The former Doubting Thomases at the *Pittsburgh Courier* now called for a "Double V" campaign — "victory over our enemies at home and victory over our enemies on the battlefields abroad." The war crisis presented a matchless opportunity, said the *Courier*, "to persuade, embarrass, compel and shame our government and our nation . . . into a more enlightened attitude toward a tenth of its people." The NAACP grew nearly tenfold during the war, to some half a million members. The more militant Committee (later Congress) of Racial Equality (CORE) began in 1942 to mount interracial demonstrations to force the desegregation of restaurants, theaters, and municipal bus lines. Tellingly, picketers outside a Washington, D.C., restaurant in 1944 carried placards that read: "Are you for Hitler's Way or the American Way?" and "We Die Together. Let's Eat Together."[32]

It would be too much to say that Executive Order 8802 was a second Emancipation Proclamation. Yet, however grudgingly, Franklin Roosevelt had set the nation back on the freedom road that Abraham Lincoln had opened in the midst of another war three-quarters of a century earlier. For seven decades it had remained the road not taken. Now, for the first time since Reconstruction, the federal government had openly committed itself to making good on at least some of the promises of American life for black citizens. Coming at a moment that was kindled with opportunities for economic betterment and social mobility, Executive Order 8802 fanned the rising flame of black militancy and initiated a chain of events that would eventually end segregation once and for all and open a new era for African-Americans.

The lure of defense-industry jobs and the assurance of at least a measure of federal protection triggered an enormous black exodus from the South, one that eventually rivaled in size the huge European migrations earlier in the century. Some seven hundred thousand black civilians left the region during the war years. In every month of 1943 ten thousand Negroes, mostly from Texas and Louisiana, streamed into Los Angeles alone. Millions more abandoned the South in the two postwar decades,

32. Anderson, *Randolph*, 259, 260; Blum, *V Was for Victory*, 208, 217–18; Jaynes and Williams, *Common Destiny*, 63.

free at last from the stifling grip of King Cotton and keen to participate in the industrial economy. Within three decades of Pearl Harbor, a majority of blacks lived outside the states of the old Confederacy, and they no longer worked in the agricultural and domestic service sectors.[33]

The war gave Myrdal's principle of cumulation a wide new field on which to work its positive effects. The experience of Sybil Lewis was typical. When defense production began to gear up, Lewis left her position as a $3.50-per-week housemaid in Sapulpa, Oklahoma, and headed for Los Angeles, where she found employment as a $48-per-week riveter at Lockheed Aircraft. "When I got my first paycheck, I'd never seen that much money before," she remembered, "not even in the bank, because I'd never been in a bank too much." On the Lockheed assembly floor she was teamed with a "big strong white girl from a cotton farm in Arkansas." Like many of the white women in the plant, for her workmate "to say 'nigger' was just a way of life. Many of them had never been near, let alone touched a Negro." But shared work meant that "both of us [had] to relate to each other in ways that we never experienced before. Although we had our differences we both learned to work together and talk together." Repeated in thousands upon thousands of wartime workplaces, mundane encounters like Sybil Lewis's with her Arkansas co-worker began to sand away the stereotypes that had ossified under segregation. "We learned that despite our hostilities and resentments we could open up to each other and get along. . . . She learned that Negroes were people, too, and I saw her as a person also, and we both gained from it." Looking back years later, Lewis also recalled that she "saw in California that black women were working in many jobs that I had never seen in the South. . . . I saw black people accepted in the school system and accepted in other kinds of jobs that they had not been accepted in before. . . . Had it not been for the war I don't think blacks would be in the position they are in now," she concluded. "[S]ome people would never have left the South. They would have had nothing to move for." Lewis went on to college, became a civil servant, and entered the middle class. "The war," she said, "changed my life."[34]

Not every story ended as happily as Lewis's. The great black hegira, commingling with the wartime flood of white migrants, sometimes ex-

---

33. The postwar advent of the mechanical cotton picker, which could do the work of fifty field hands, accelerated the displacement of southern blacks.

34. Mark Jonathan Harris et al., *The Home Front: America during World War II* (New York: G. P. Putnam's Sons, 1984), 37–39, 118–21, 251–52.

ploded into violent turbulence. In the roaring, overcrowded war-production centers, petty frictions between people who had little more in common than their shared status as war-borne nomads could erupt into ugly confrontations. Competition for scarce housing in Detroit in 1942 led a white mob, brandishing stones and clubs, to prevent three black families from moving into the Sojourner Truth Homes — a tense rehearsal for a far bloodier confrontation in Detroit a year later. "Hate strikes" were common in the defense plants, as when white women employees shut down a Western Electric factory in Baltimore rather than share a rest room with their black co-workers. In Mobile, Alabama, swollen by an influx of some forty-five thousand war-job seekers, white shipyard workers rioted in 1943 over the promotion of black welders, seriously injuring eleven Negroes. In Beaumont, Texas, plagued by shortages of housing and schools, whites rampaged through the black neighborhoods, murdering two Negroes and wounding dozens of others. Not all such outbursts were directed at blacks. Gangs of soldiers and sailors roamed the streets of Los Angeles in June 1943 attacking Mexican-American youths wearing the outsize outfits known as "zoot suits."

By the summer of 1943 Detroit thundered with war production and throbbed with racial tensions. In the preceding three years, more than fifty thousand blacks had moved into the Detroit metropolitan area, along with some two hundred thousand whites, many of them Appalachian "hillbillies" who brought their undiluted racial prejudices with them. On Sunday, June 20, more than one hundred thousand people, most of them black, sought refuge from the cauterizing summer heat on Belle Isle, a riverfront municipal park. Scuffles broke out between black and white teenagers. By late evening a rumor pulsed through the black neighborhoods that whites had killed three Negroes. Blacks swarmed into the streets, pulled white passengers from streetcars, and beat them savagely. White mobs soon counterattacked, and wide-open racial warfare raged through the night. By the time federal troops quelled the riot at midday on the twenty-first, twenty-five blacks and nine whites were dead, including a milkman murdered while making his rounds and a doctor beaten to death on his way to a house call. Just weeks later, New York's Harlem also exploded in a riot that claimed six black lives. The carnage in Detroit even echoed in faraway England, helping to spark a vicious racial brawl among American troops encamped at Bamber Bridge, in Lancashire.[35]

35. Alan Clive, *State of War: Michigan in World War II* (Ann Arbor: University of Michigan Press, 1979), 94, 133, 156–62.

Some of the worst racial clashes took place in army and navy training centers, where even military discipline could not always keep taut young black and white men from each other's throats. Racial fights and even lynchings occurred at several camps, as well as overseas; one squabble on Guam between Negro seamen and white marines ended in fatalities. At the army's request, the famed director Frank Capra put together a sensitively crafted film, *The Negro Soldier*, intended to alleviate racial tensions in the camps by educating blacks and whites alike about the Negro's military role, but it would take more than Capra's art to overcome racial problems in the military. Northern blacks especially resented their first encounters with formal segregation in the South. All blacks chafed at the gratuitous humiliations that military life inflicted on them—from lack of access to recreational facilities to segregated blood plasma supplies to the galling spectacle of German prisoners of war seated at southern lunch counters that refused to serve Negro soldiers. Worst of all, the army persisted in ghettoizing Negro recruits in all-black outfits and assigning them almost exclusively to noncombat roles.

Negro leaders hammered at the War and Navy departments to end segregation and train blacks for combat, but military authorities took only a few halting steps to mollify them. In 1940 Stimson appointed William Hastie, dean of Howard University's law school, as his civilian aide on Negro affairs and promoted the army's senior black officer, Colonel Benjamin O. Davis, to brigadier general. But when Hastie urged in late 1941 that a start be made toward banishing Jim Crow from the armed forces, General Marshall turned him down cold. Hastie was proposing, said Marshall, that the U.S. Army should solve "a social problem that has perplexed the American people throughout the history of this nation. . . . The Army is not a sociological laboratory."[36]

The army may not have been a sociological laboratory, but it soon generated sociological data that starkly exposed the wretched plight of black America. The Selective Service System rejected 46 percent of black registrants as unfit for service, compared with a 30.3 percent rejection rate for whites. Fully one-quarter of black inductees were infected with syphilis, a disqualification for service that ultimately was removed after treatment with sulfa drugs. Less easily remediable were educational deficiencies. In some units a third or more of black troops were illiterate. Ill-educated southern blacks scored especially poorly on the Army General Classification Test. The AGCT, often misunderstood

36. Lee, *Employment of Negro Troops*, 140–41.

as a general intelligence test, was instead an aptitude test designed to sort recruits into categories according to their suitability for different kinds of duty. As the army's chief psychologist carefully explained, the AGCT "reflects very definitely the educational opportunities the individual has had." Recruits who placed in Grades I, II, and III were tracked to become airmen, officers, specialists, and technicians. Those scoring in Grades IV or V were thought fit mainly for infantry duty or for common pick-and-shovel or dishwashing labor. In a disheartening demonstration of the deficiencies of the South's segregated educational system, 84 percent of blacks scored in the bottom two categories, compared to one-third of whites; almost half of blacks fell into the lowest category, Grade V, six times the rate for whites. Despite Marshall's determination not to turn the military into a social reform agency, the army was soon obliged to offer remedial instruction. By war's end it had taught more than 150,000 black recruits to read and had trained others in valuable work skills.[37]

The poor qualifications of so many black soldiers reinforced the army's already considerable reluctance to send them into combat. Only two black divisions were combat-rated, and the army considered neither fully reliable. The 93rd Division faced enemy fire in the Pacific theater, but mostly in rearguard and "mopping up" operations. The ill-starred 92nd Division, its black bison insignia proudly evoking memories of the Negro "buffalo soldiers" of Indian warfare days, had been removed from the line in disgrace in World War I and continued to suffer from deep distrust between its resentful black troops and condescending white officers. In one incident, enlisted men stoned a car in which white officers were riding. Wracked by such tensions, the 92nd turned in another mixed performance in Italy. It was ultimately reconfigured to include one black and one white regiment, as well as the Japanese-American 442nd Regimental Combat Team—a dubious concession to the principle of desegregation, and one that blacks protested. A handful of other black units saw combat, including the 761st Tank Battalion, sent into battle in Normandy by George Patton with the admonition: "I don't care what color you are, so long as you go up there and kill those Kraut sonsabitches."[38]

37. Lee Kennett, G.I.: The American Soldier in World War II (New York: Charles Scribner's Sons), 34–35: Lee, Employment of Negro Troops, 242–44; Stephan Thernstrom and Abigail Thernstrom, America in Black and White (New York: Simon and Schuster, 1997), 74. See also Samuel Stouffer et al., The American Soldier (Princeton: Princeton University Press, 1949); and Paula S. Fass, Outside In: Minorities and the Transformation of American Education (New York: Oxford University Press, 1989).
38. Lee, Employment of Negro Troops, 661.

Only in the acute manpower crisis of the Battle of the Bulge at the end of 1944 did the army form several dozen black rifle platoons to serve alongside white soldiers in integrated companies. For the most part, the two thousand black service troops who volunteered for this reassignment to combat duty performed admirably, earning the respect and gratitude of their white comrades. In 1948 President Truman at last ordered full desegregation of the armed forces.

The Army Air Corps eventually consented to take a handful of black fliers, including the 99th Pursuit Squadron, trained at the famed Tuskegee Institute founded by Booker T. Washington and known colloquially as the Tuskegee Airmen. When Eleanor Roosevelt visited the trainees in 1941 and went for a flight with Chief Alfred Anderson in a Piper Cub, the photographs were a sensation, in both the white and black press. The 99th distinguished itself in North Africa and Italy and later over Germany, though in 1943 Hastie resigned in protest over the isolation of the "Lonely Eagles" in an all-black, segregated unit. The Marine Corps began training men for its first all-Negro battalion in the summer of 1942, but they would not serve under black officers. The first Negro marine lieutenant was commissioned only after the end of the war.

As for the navy, manpower needs prompted it to step up black inductions in 1943. Most black sailors were indifferently trained and destined for unglamorous and backbreaking shore duty. The navy assigned several gangs of black stevedores to loading ammunition at its sprawling munitions depot at Port Chicago, California. Like all naval facilities, Port Chicago was rigidly segregated. Black sailors waited for white sailors to finish eating before entering the mess hall. Only black crews did the nerve-grating work of wrestling grease-slathered bombs down planks into the holds of the Liberty Ships. They were given no safety manuals or training in the handling of high explosives. "We were just shown a boxcar full of ammunition, wire nets spread out on the docks and the hold in the ship and told to load," one black winch operator remembered. White officers wagered on which crew could load the most tonnage on a shift, a practice known as "racing."

On July 17, 1944, black sailors raced through the afternoon and into the night to finish packing some forty-six hundred tons of explosives into the E.A. Bryan, and to rig its sister ship, the Quinalt Victory, to begin loading the next day. At 10:18 in the evening, a terrific blast obliterated both vessels, hurling debris thousands of feet into the air and shattering windows in San Francisco, thirty-five miles to the west. It was the worst war-related disaster in the continental United States. Flying glass and metal killed 320 men and maimed hundreds more. Of the dead, 202 were black. When the unnerved Negro survivors were ordered back to work three weeks later, fifty refused; they were court-martialed and sentenced to fifteen years hard labor and dishonorable discharge. Thurgood Marshall, chief counsel for the NAACP, declared: "This is not 50 men on trial for mutiny. This is the Navy on trial for its whole vicious policy toward Negroes. Negroes in the Navy don't mind loading ammunition. They just want to know why they are the only ones doing the loading! They want to know why they are segregated; why they don't get promoted, [and] why the Navy disregarded official warnings by the San Francisco waterfront unions . . . that an explosion was inevitable if they persisted in using untrained seamen in the loading of ammunition."

Partly as a result of the Port Chicago catastrophe, the navy tiptoed toward integration in August 1944. It assigned some five hundred black seamen to twenty-five auxiliary vessels. Negroes were not allowed to compose more than 10 percent of a ship's crew—roughly their percentage in the general population—and the experiment went forward without incident. In December 1945 the navy ended segregation altogether, and in 1949 the first black officer graduated from the Naval Academy at Annapolis.[39]

From much of this turmoil Franklin Roosevelt remained studiously aloof. Despite his wife's evident sympathies, and whatever might have been his personal predilections, political considerations continued to stay his hand from bold racial initiatives, as they had in the New Deal years. In 1942 Eugene "Bull" Connor, the commissioner of public safety in Birmingham, Alabama, and a man destined to play a violently repressive role in the civil rights struggles two decades later, presciently warned the president that further federal pressure on the South's segregationist regime would lead to "the Annihilation of the Democratic Party in this section of the Nation." When the Supreme Court ruled in *Smith v. Allwright* in 1944 that the Democratic Party's all-white primary in Texas was unconstitutional, Attorney General Biddle wanted to go forward with a similar suit in Alabama. But an aide who sounded out southern opinion cautioned the President that Biddle's proposal "would translate impotent rumblings against the New Deal into an actual revolt

---

39. John Boudreau, "Blown Away," *Washington Post*, July 17, 1994, sec. F, 1; Robert L. Allen, *The Port Chicago Mutiny* (New York: Warner 1989), 119–20. In 1946 the Port Chicago sailors were quietly released from prison and given less than dishonorable discharges.

at the polls. I am sure that any such action would be a very dangerous mistake." Even Eleanor Roosevelt shared her husband's wariness about the political volatility of racial issues. Responding to a young black woman's complaint that Wendell Willkie professed more advanced racial views than did the president, Eleanor wrote that Willkie enjoyed the luxury of not having to govern. "If he were to be elected President," Eleanor explained, "on that day, he would have to take into consideration the people who are heads of important committees in Congress . . . people on whom he must depend to pass vital legislation for the nation as a whole." Most of those people were southerners, and for them segregation was still a sacrosanct way of life.[40]

But however politically straitjacketed, the president found some room for maneuver on race. When it became apparent that some employers were violating the spirit of Executive Order 8802 by employing blacks only in the most menial jobs and denying them access to the kinds of training necessary for advancement, the president significantly strengthened the FEPC. In 1943 he increased its budget to half a million dollars. He replaced its part-time appointees working out of make-shift Washington quarters with a professional staff distributed through a dozen regional offices. When he learned that unions were shunting blacks into powerless "auxiliaries," he encouraged the National Labor Relations Board to decertify unions that practiced discrimination. He sent in federal troops to break a strike on the Philadelphia transit system in 1944, compelling the hiring of black trolley drivers. By war's end, blacks held some 8 percent of defense-industry jobs, a proportion that approached their presence in the population, and a major advance from the 3 percent they held in 1942. The number of African-American civilians in the federal employ more than tripled, to two hundred thousand. Among whites, meanwhile, the principle of cumulation was slowly working its effects. In 1942 three-fifths of whites told pollsters that they imagined blacks were contented with their lot. Two years later, only a quarter of whites thought that blacks were being treated fairly.[41]

The NAACP's Walter White returned from a tour of the fighting fronts at the war's end to publish a prophetic book: A Rising Wind. Echoing Myrdal, he wrote: "World War II has immeasurably magnified

40. Blum, V Was for Victory, 193, 212; Doris Kearns Goodwin, No Ordinary Time: Franklin and Eleanor Roosevelt: The Homefront in World War II (New York: Simon and Schuster, 1994), 353.
41. Cantril, 988–89.

the Negro's awareness of the disparity between the American profession and practice of democracy." Black soldiers and sailors, he predicted, "will return home convinced that whatever betterment of their lot is achieved must come largely from their own efforts. They will return determined to use those efforts to the utmost." Jim Crow was far from dead in 1945, but he was beginning to weaken.[42]

IF THE WAR HAD BEGUN to usher Jim Crow off the stage of American history, it was ushering another mythical character onto it: Rosie the Riveter. Unlike Jim Crow, born in antebellum Dixie and destined to survive for more than a century, Rosie was a war baby with an uncertain future. She owed her very name not to spontaneous folk usage but to War Manpower Commission propaganda campaigns to entice women to work in war plants. "Rosie's got a boyfriend, Charlie; Charlie, he's a marine," ran a wartime jingle:

> Rosie is protecting Charlie
> Working overtime on the riveting machine.[43]

Like Jim Crow, Rosie was a fictional symbol for a complex social reality that eluded tidy description. Rosie's denim-clad, tool-wielding, can-do figure was meant to personify the nearly nineteen million women who worked for wages at one time or another during the war. In fact, she typified very few of them. She was certainly an imperfect emblem for the 350,000 women who donned uniforms in the Women's Auxiliary Army Corps (WAACs—or WACs after the "Auxiliary" was dropped in 1943), the navy's Women Accepted for Voluntary Emergency Service (WAVES), the air corps' Women's Auxiliary Service Pilots (WASPS), the Coast Guard's SPARS (from the service's Latin motto, Semper Paratus), or the singularly unnicknamed women's branch of the marines. Nor did Rosie make a very good poster girl for the many millions of women who worked not for wages but as volunteers in war-related programs—packing Red Cross surgical dressings, entertaining troops at reception centers, or serving as OPA price monitors. Even for the decided minority of American women who received paychecks in the wartime civilian economy, Rosie was a misleading symbol, though one whose heroically iconic stature powerfully molded memories of the war.

42. Walter White, A Rising Wind (Garden City, N.Y.: Doubleday, Doran, 1945), 142, 144.
43. Alice Kessler-Harris, Out to Work: A History of Wage-Earning Women in the United States (New York: Oxford University Press, 1982), 276.

Nearly twelve million women had been employed on the eve of Pearl Harbor, most of them the victims—or beneficiaries—of traditional occupational segregation along gender and racial lines. Ninety percent of all women workers in 1940 fell into just ten employment categories. If they were black or Hispanic, they were probably domestic servants, living threadbare lives in a spare back room, precariously beholden to the goodwill of their employer. White women who worked were likely to hold jobs in teaching, nursing, social work, and the civil service—largely Depression-proof occupations that had afforded an unusual measure of job security in the 1930s. Minority or white, these prewar women workers were usually single. Following customs unchanged since the nineteenth century, young women typically worked for a few years, then left their jobs when they married, as most eventually did. Almost half of all single women were gainfully employed in 1940, but only 15 percent of the much larger number of married women, and a scant 9 percent of mothers with children under the age of six. Those numbers measured some surprisingly stubborn conceptions of sexual roles that the war crisis only slightly dislodged.

As early as 1942 it became obvious that even the scaled-back draft calls of the ninety-division mobilization would leave the industrial economy short of labor. New workers had to be found. Some came from beyond the nation's borders. In July the United States and Mexico reached an accord, patterned on a similar World War I arrangement. It took its name from the Spanish word for manual laborer, *bracero*. The bracero program licensed over two hundred thousand Mexicans as temporary contract laborers. They maintained railroad tracks in the Southwest and harvested potatoes in Idaho; fruit, sugar beets, tomatoes, and lettuce in California; and apples and wheat in Washington. (Sour memories of the mistreatment of Mexican workers in World War I produced the "Texas Proviso," which for a time excluded Texas from the bracero program.)

But immigrant workers were only a partial solution. Idle pools of domestic labor also had to be tapped. "In some communities," the president said in his 1942 Columbus Day Fireside Chat, "employers dislike to employ women. In others they are reluctant to hire Negroes. . . . We can no longer afford to indulge such prejudices or practices." He might have added that many women themselves, especially married women, apparently disliked to be employed. Fully three-quarters of all women of working age were "at home" as the war began. The overwhelming majority of them were still there when the war ended. In both Britain and the Soviet Union, by contrast, those proportions were almost precisely reversed. There more than 70 percent of women toiled outside their homes during the war, many of them involuntarily drafted into the work force.[44]

Many voices, including that of *Fortune* magazine, advocated conscripting stay-at-home American women into industrial service. But here, as in so many areas of wartime life, America was spared such coercive measures. Instead, government and industry orchestrated advertising campaigns, invoking Rosie's strapping but stylish image, to persuade women willingly to leave kitchen and sewing table for the factory floor. More than six million women responded. By war's end almost nineteen million women were working, more than at any previous time in American history. Yet even that surge looks less dramatic on close inspection. About half of those six million new entrants were young women school-leavers who would have entered the labor force in any case. The number who answered the trumpet's call and entered the war economy over and above the "normal" increase attributable to population growth and maturation has been estimated between 2.7 and 3.5 million.[45]

Nearly two million women—never more than 10 percent of female workers in wartime—did indeed labor in defense plants. Almost half a million worked in the aircraft industry. In some West Coast airframe factories they made up nearly 50 percent of the labor force. Another 225,000 worked in shipbuilding. Following the patriotic example of famously long-locked film star Veronica Lake, women bobbed their hair to keep it out of the machinery, swapped their dresses for slacks, toted their lunches in paper bags (tin lunch pails were deemed unfeminine), ran cranes and tractors, blushed and seethed at their male co-workers' catcalls and wolf whistles—and helped build thousands of ships, tanks, and airplanes. Few, however, drilled rivets, a relatively high-skill task for which employers were unwilling to train workers whom they considered as transient, short-term employees. Instead, defense plant supervisors usually employed women as American management had traditionally

44. *PPA* (1942), 422. Seven out of eight women in the "at home" category in 1941 remained "at home" in 1944. See D'Ann Campbell, *Women at War with America: Private Lives in a Patriotic Era* (Cambridge: Harvard University Press, 1984), 77. See also Claudia D. Goldin, "The Role of World War II in the Rise of Women's Employment," *American Economic Review* 81, no. 4 (September 1991): 741–56.
45. See the slightly divergent estimates in Campbell, *Women at War with America*, 73, and Kessler-Harris, *Out to Work*, 276–77.

used unseasoned laborers—by "Taylorizing" production routines into separate and repetitive functions that required little skill and minimum training. That practice was notorious in the shipyards, where low-skill welding became the typical woman's job. Faced with such work conditions, it was small wonder that a majority of women in a 1943 poll said they would not take a job in a war plant, or that turnover and absenteeism among female defense workers occurred at twice the rate for men. Women held just 4.4 percent of war jobs classified as skilled and a far smaller percentage of management positions. A solitary woman engineer at Lockheed Aircraft remembered her difficulty in winning her male colleagues' respect. "If I say we ought to do it this way, they don't hear me." Only "if I say 'God damn . . . ' then they pay attention."[46]

Rosie the Riveter might therefore have been more appropriately named Wendy the Welder, or more appropriately still Sally the Secretary, or even, as events were to prove, Molly the Mom. Despite the surge of women into heavy industry, markedly larger numbers of new women entrants into the wartime work force took up clerical and service jobs, in line with historical trends, and there women's gains proved far more durable. The number of women factory operatives plummeted at war's end. Shipbuilding effectively ceased, laying off hundreds of thousands of women (as well as blacks, cruelly cutting short their first foray into the industrial workplace). Women left the aircraft and automobile industries in droves. One in four autoworkers was a woman in wartime; only one in twelve in 1946. By 1947 the proportion of working women in blue-collar occupations was actually smaller than it had been at the war's outset—24.6 percent as against 26.2 percent in 1940. The future of women's work lay not in the wartime heavy industries, destined to fade in relative importance in the postwar economy, but in the burgeoning service occupations, which within a decade of the war's conclusion eclipsed factory work as the nation's principal source of employment. Banking, for example, an all-male bastion before the war, employed more women than men by 1950, including most tellers and 15 percent of middle managers.[47]

Women's labor-force participation rate, slowly rising through the century to 26 percent in 1940, spiked to 36 percent in 1944, then swiftly

46. Cantril, 1046; Rosalind Rosenberg, *Divided Lives: American Women in the Twentieth Century* (New York: Hill and Wang, 1992), 132; Campbell, *Women at War with America*, 116.
47. Campbell, *Women at War with America*, 239, 111.

receded to 28 percent in 1947, back in line with longtime historical trends. In a significant harbinger of what the future held, by 1944 married women for the first time made up a majority of female workers. Typically they were women over the age of thirty-five who had already discharged their child-rearing responsibilities. Many women wanted to continue working at the war's end, and some did. But many were also fired, pressured by employers and unions to cede their place at the workbench to returning veterans. Strikingly, a far larger number quit voluntarily, and their reasons proved instructive about the nation's wartime and postwar mood. Among former women war workers polled in a Census Bureau survey in 1951, half cited "family responsibilities" as their principal motive for leaving the work force. In-depth interviews with a sample of women who gave birth in 1946 were even more revealing. Only 8 percent considered it a sacrifice to give up their war jobs; 16 percent had mixed feelings; but an overwhelming 76 percent positively welcomed the transition from employment to motherhood.

Those kinds of attitudes had manifested themselves in wartime as well. Recruitment drives emphasized that women were being hired only "for the duration." Wartime polls repeatedly showed that majorities of women as well as men disapproved of working wives and even more heavily censured working mothers. Alarmists claimed that hordes of "latchkey" children, left to their own devices by employed mothers, were growing up psychologically stunted and even criminally inclined. But talk of wartime juvenile delinquency, and even, as it turned out, of long-term characterological damage to the children of working mothers, was greatly exaggerated—not least because relatively few mothers of young children worked at all during the war. In a striking demonstration of the persistence of traditional cultural norms, the percentage of working mothers with children under the age of six barely inched up in wartime, from 9 percent in 1940 to 12 percent in 1944. The thirty-one hundred day-care centers that the government built to accommodate working mothers operated at one-quarter capacity, serving only 130,000 children. As for the long-term psychological effects on Rosie's children, one postwar study concluded that there was "no evidence that maternal employment affected the personality development of children in unfortunate ways."[48]

48. Campbell, *Women at War with America*, 86–87, 82; Susan M. Hartmann, *The Home Front and Beyond: American Women in the 1940s* (Boston: Twayne, 1982), 84;

"Did deep societal values change [in World War II]?" historian D'Ann Campbell asks. So far as women are concerned, she gives an ironic but unimpeachable answer. "Yes. Americans emphasized more strongly the primacy of family and children in their lives than in previous eras." As the *Ladies' Home Journal* proclaimed in 1944, "Motherhood's Back in Style." The marriage rate, which had dipped in the Depression years, rose rapidly in the war decade. In 1942 it reached the highest level since 1920. By war's end a higher proportion of American women were married than at any time in the century, and women's median age at marriage had dipped to a historic low. Births shot up as well. In 1943 more babies were born than in any previous year in the century, marking the highest birth rate (babies per thousand women of child-bearing age) since the pre-Depression year of 1927. In the immediate postwar years, the average number of children per household climbed from two to three, as Rosie and her sisters abandoned war work to become the mothers of the fabled baby-boom generation, whose statistical origin actually dates from 1940. Ironically, a vigorous resurgence of natalism and what Betty Friedan was later to call the feminine mystique of domesticity and motherhood were the war's immediate legacies to American women.[49]

Jim Crow's days were numbered by 1945 because the war threw into high relief the contradiction between America's professed values and its actual behavior. In contrast, Rosie's day still lay in the future at war's end because her wartime behavior was not yet sanctioned by a shift in social values — and values proved far less mutable than behavior. Yet Rosie had given birth to a mystique of her own. Her strong, capable, tool-toting image lingered in the nation's collective memory. It helped inspire a later generation of women to challenge sexual stereotypes and to demand what Rosie never had: economic freedom as well as family security, a child *and* a paycheck, a place of work and place to call home, too, not one or the other. Rosie thus went on doing her cultural work well after she laid down

---

Kessler-Harris, *Out to Work*, 294. William M. Tuttle Jr., *Daddy's Gone to War: The Second World War in the Lives of America's Children* (New York: Oxford University Press, 1993), 89. The Lanham Act centers were poorly administered; some private centers, notably those at the Kaiser shipyards, were much more heavily utilized. See Susan E. Riley, "Caring for Rosie's Children: Federal Child Care Policies in the World War II Era," *Polity* 26, no. 4 (Summer 1994): 655–75.

49. Campbell, *Women at War with America*, 99–100; Tuttle, *Daddy's Gone to War*, 27; *HSUS*, 49, 64.

her rivet gun. The reverberations that she set off in American culture provided but one example among many of how the war's echoes would ring down the years long after the shooting stopped.

ON ELECTION DAY, November 3, 1942, the fighting on distant Guadalcanal was locked in stalemate. The transports bearing American troops to North Africa were still at sea. At home, all was bustle and confusion, the inevitable effects of a crash mobilization program that had uprooted millions of people but had so far produced more aggravation and griping than tanks and bullets. Frustration and mobility conspired to keep many voters away from the polls. Only twenty-eight million cast their ballots, seven million fewer than in the last off-year election in 1938 and twenty-two million fewer than in 1940. Democrats took a shellacking. Republicans gained forty-seven seats in the House and seven in the Senate, as well as the governorships of several key states, including the electoral colossus of New York, where the youthful Thomas E. Dewey emerged victorious. Post-election analysis attributed the GOP's gains to the low turnout, as well as to smoldering resentment — resentment of mushrooming government bureaucracy, particularly the nettlesome Office of Price Administration, and especially bitter resentment of Uncle Sam's continuing inability to land a glove on his enemies. If "the African campaign had preceded rather than followed the elections," the secretary of the Democratic National Committee opined, "the results would have been different."[50]

The election yielded the most conservative Congress in a decade, filled with what *Fortune* magazine called "normalcy men." Old-guard southern Democrats joined with Republicans to form a substantial majority that was anti-Roosevelt, anti–New Deal, and unreliably internationalist. Of 115 identifiable isolationists, all but five were reelected. Some southerners were reported to be privately hoping for a Democratic defeat in 1944, because it would give them four years to purge the New Dealers once and for all from the party. *Time* magazine saw a parallel with the election of 1918, which had seated the anti-Wilson Congress that thwarted America's entry into the League of Nations. "It is by no means certain," said the *Economist*, that at war's end the Americans would not once again "return to Hardingism."[51]

50. Blum, V Was for Victory, 233.
51. Blum, V Was for Victory, 232; Frank Freidel, *Franklin D. Roosevelt: A Rendezvous with Destiny* (Boston: Little, Brown, 1990), 494; *Time*, November 16, 1942, 16; *Economist*, November 7, 1942, 572.

The New Deal had been a walking corpse since at least 1938, a political casualty well before it became a casualty of war. The new Seventy-eighth Congress moved swiftly to lay the New Deal finally in its grave, and then to drive a stake through its heart. By the end of 1943 congressional conservatives had extinguished many of the signature New Deal agencies. The Civilian Conservation Corps, the Works Progress Administration, and the National Youth Administration—deemed unnecessary in the full-employment wartime economy—were all gone. The National Resources Planning Board, a planning body much favored by the president and headed by his uncle Frederic Delano, was legislated out of existence in the same year. The Farm Security Administration and the Rural Electrification Administration, which had done so much to change the face of the American countryside, were defunded down to skeletal operations. For good measure, Congress also terminated the domestic arm of the Office of War Information, which it accused of being a liberal propaganda organ and Roosevelt's private political tool. Yet significantly, conservatives raised no hand against the New Deal's core achievements: Social Security, farm price supports, child labor and minimum wage legislation, and banking and securities regulation. Those reforms were already firmly in place as untouchable pillars of the new social and economic order that Roosevelt had wrought out of the Depression crisis.

Roosevelt, freshly returned from Teheran and his mind fastened on diplomacy, not domestic reform, appeared to deliver his own ungainly requiem for the New Deal at a rambling press conference on December 28, 1943. "How did the New Deal come into existence?" he asked. "It was because there was an awfully sick patient called the United States of America, and it was suffering from a grave internal disorder. . . . And they sent for the doctor." "Dr. New Deal" had saved the banks and rescued farmers, cleaned up the securities markets, put the idle back to work, built dams and bridges, and prescribed old-age and unemployment insurance. But now, said the president, "[w]e have done nearly all of that," and it was time for "Dr. Win-the-War" to take over.

Roosevelt summoned Dr. Win-the-War into being partly to refocus the nation's evidently flagging attention on the great martial enterprise that had not yet reached its climax. America's major battles against Germany and Japan remained unfought at the end of 1943, yet strikes continued to interrupt military production. He felt "let down" on his return from Teheran, Roosevelt confessed, as he saw so many of his countrymen "laboring under the delusion that the time is past when we must make prodigious sacrifices—that the war is already won and we can begin to slacken off." Some voices were already calling for "reconversion" of war industries to satisfy consumer demand. In a further effort to concentrate the country's energies, the president would soon ask, in vain, for a national service law to "make available for war production . . . every able-bodied adult in this Nation." But if conservatives imagined that Roosevelt had abandoned Dr. New Deal altogether, he quickly proved them mistaken.[52]

In 1935 Roosevelt had briefly placated the right with promises of a "breathing spell," only to launch an exceptionally combative presidential campaign the following year. This time Roosevelt had scarcely dismissed Dr. New Deal before he tried to reinstate him less than two weeks later. The occasion was his annual State of the Union address. Too ill to make his customary personal appearance before Congress, he broadcast his speech over the air from his White House office. As millions of Americans gathered around their radios on the evening of January 11, 1944, they heard the president call for "a second Bill of Rights . . . an economic bill of rights" that would guarantee every citizen a job, a living wage, decent housing, adequate medical care, education, and "protection from the economic fears of old age, sickness, accident, and unemployment." Roosevelt concluded with a ringing reaffirmation of the New Deal's animating philosophy. "All of these rights," he said, "spell security." The speech has been called the most radical of his life, and so it was if advocacy of government-sponsored social provision was the test of radicalism. In 1944, however, much of the country was in no mood to hear it. The president's remarks, notes one biographer, "fell with a dull thud into the half-empty chambers of the United States Congress."[53]

Roosevelt's proposals had their origin in two reports that his uncle's National Resource Planning Board (NRPB) had submitted before its demise: *Post-War Planning* and *Security, Work, and Relief Policies*. Their provenance from a defunct agency offered a clue to the political reception they received. More telling, the clash of the reports' dreary Depression-era premises with the lusty realities of wartime America revealed just how obsolete much of the New Deal was becoming.

52. *PPA* (1943), 569–75; (1944), 34, 36, 37.
53. *PPA* (1944), 32–42. On the radicalism of Roosevelt's speech, and its reception, see James MacGregor Burns, *Roosevelt: The Soldier of Freedom, 1940–1945* (New York: Harcourt Brace Jovanovich, 1970), 424–26.

"The need for socially provided income," said the authors of *Security, Work, and Relief Policies*, in language as lifeless as the ideas it expressed, "is in large measure a consequence of the imperfections in the operation our economy. . . . [F]ull employment of all our resources, including labor, is a condition which cannot as yet be regarded as a normal characteristic of our economy." The problem "antedates the depression" and would continue into the indefinite future: "[I]t is problematical whether private demand for investment will be sufficient, upon termination of the war." Therefore, the planners concluded, "even if spending for war should raise the level of national income to its practical maximum . . . the public-aid problem is likely to be both large and persistent for some time to come." Elsewhere, the planners specified $100 billion as the target "practical maximum" of national income that policy should try to achieve, just $14 billion more than in the less populous America of 1929. "Our recommendation," they concluded, "envisages the attribution to government of a more active role in the economic life of the country."[54]

Those assumptions, fixed on the inadequacy of the economy rather than its promise, lay at the foundations of the reform edifice that the New Dealers had erected in the Depression decade. But in 1942, the year the planners published their reports, national income had already reached $137 billion. In 1944, the year of Roosevelt's "radical" speech, it topped $180 billion. Contrary to the expectations of the NRPB planers, national income did not drop at war's end but ascended to $241 billion in 1950. In the following two fabulously prosperous decades it more than tripled again, to $800 billion in 1970.[55]

No one could have imagined such economic growth in the 1930s, and only a few even remotely sensed its possibility in wartime. The Great Depression had seemed to many to demonstrate that the American economy had "matured," that the age of economic expansion had ended and "secular stagnation" had irrevocably set in. That premise, echoing Frederick Jackson Turner's fin-de-siècle threnody for the closing of the frontier era in 1890, had informed Franklin Roosevelt's thinking from the time of his first presidential campaign in 1932. It was the intellectual bedrock on which the great New Deal reforms had been

54. National Resources Planning Board, *Security, Work, and Relief Policies* (Washington: USGPO, 1942), 445, 487, 490, and *Post-War Planning* (n.p., n.d. [September 1942]), 1, 25.
55. *HSUS*, 224.

built. It had animated John Maynard Keynes's insistence that compensatory public spending was permanently required to stabilize modern economies at high levels of employment, a new policy gospel embraced by a rising generation of economists in the 1930s. The most influential American Keynesian, Harvard's Alvin H. Hansen, had argued in his 1938 tract, *Full Recovery or Stagnation*, that only massive government deficits could maintain full employment. The war, however, was shattering the economists' theories of secular stagnation. Hansen saw the implications of the economy's wartime performance more clearly than many others. He still clung to a preference for public spending over private, but he could not help but be impressed at the economic vitality the war had stimulated. "We know now," he wrote in 1944, "as a result of the war experience, that we have reached a stage in technique and productivity which a few years ago no one believed possible. All of us had our sights too low. . . . We have suddenly realized this enormous advance in productive capacity. We did not know we had it in 1940."[56]

Ordinary Americans shared Hansen's sense of amazement. They had never had it so good, and they wanted it better. Corporate advertisers, with little to sell in wartime but keen to build a reservoir of pent-up demand that could be released later, fed the public's dreams of affluence with seductive images of the consumers' paradise that waited at the war's end. The war was thus opening the window to a future in which building structural reforms would give way to fueling the engines of economic growth, when the politics of equality would yield to the politics of expansion. If the New Deal had stabilized America, the war energized the country in ways inconceivable just years earlier. The goal of the New Deal had been to achieve a measure of security for all Americans in a presumably static economy. The goal, even the obsession, of Americans in the postwar years would be the pursuit of individual prosperity in the midst of apparently endless economic growth.

In those circumstances, the only result of Roosevelt's call for a universal bill of economic rights was another bill of rights altogether, one much more limited in scope but packing powerful implications for those whose lives it touched. Prodded by the American Legion and prompted in part by lingering worries about the postwar economy's ability to absorb demobilized soldiers, Congress unanimously passed the famed GI Bill of Rights, and Roosevelt signed it in June 1944. The bill aimed to regulate the flow of returning veterans into the job market by offering

56. Alvin H. Hansen, "Planning Full Employment," *Nation*, October 21, 1944, 492.

them vocational training and higher education, as well as housing and medical benefits while in school and low-interest loans thereafter for buying homes and starting businesses. Ironically, the only significant opposition to the bill came from educators. "Education is not a device for coping with mass unemployment," University of Chicago president Robert Maynard Hutchins warned, adding snootily that "colleges and universities will find themselves converted into educational hobo jungles. And veterans . . . will find themselves educational hobos."[57]

Events proved Hutchins spectacularly wrong. More than a million eager veterans attended the nation's universities at Uncle Sam's expense in the immediate postwar years. Within a decade some eight million had taken advantage of the bill's educational programs. They were hardly hobos. On the contrary, they were highly motivated students who helped to transform American universities from sleepy citadels of privilege into vibrant educational centers. Fewer than 10 percent of young people attended college in the prewar years; almost 15 percent did in 1948, and double that proportion, nearly a third of young Americans, just two decades later.[58] GI Bill beneficiaries changed the face of higher education, dramatically raised the educational level and hence the productivity of the work force, and in the process unimaginably altered their own lives. The GI Bill thus stood out as the most emblematic of all World War II–era political accomplishments. It aimed not at restructuring the economy but at empowering individuals. It roared on after 1945 as a kind of afterburner to the engines of social change and upward mobility that the war had ignited, propelling an entire generation along an ascending curve of achievement and affluence that their parents could not have dreamed.

Roosevelt's 1944 State of the Union address had been an effort to ring one last hurrah out of the old New Deal record. Congress greeted all its proposals as dead on arrival, as Roosevelt knew they would, but he calculated that impossible policies would make for good politics in an election year. Looking ahead to November, Roosevelt also wooed the soldier vote in 1944, not only with his warm endorsement of the GI Bill but also with his support for the so-called federal ballot. Regretting the low turnout of 1942 and remembering the crucial margin that Union soldiers had provided for Lincoln over McClellan in 1864, Roosevelt

57. Keith Olson, *The G.I. Bill, the Veterans, and the Colleges* (Lexington: University of Kentucky Press, 1974), 25.
58. *HSUS*, 383.

proposed that the federal government should issue special absentee ballots to the eleven million servicemen and women away from home in 1944. Traditional states'-rights advocates, already nervous at federal court encroachments on the white primary, were apoplectic at the prospect of this further intrusion of federal power into the political process. "Who is behind this bill?" Mississippi's John Rankin rhetorically asked on the House floor. The Communists, he viciously responded, and he extended his indictment to include the radio broadcaster Walter Winchell, "the little kike . . . who called this body the 'House of Reprehensibles' " (because it had opposed virtually every reform measure Roosevelt had proposed in wartime). In the end, Congress so emasculated the soldier-vote bill that only 112,000 federal ballots were issued.[59]

Unlike in 1940, Roosevelt made no secret of his intentions to run for reelection in 1944. The real question was who would be his running mate, a matter of more than usual gravity because Roosevelt was not a well man. A secretary remarked that Roosevelt now routinely replied "rotten" or "like hell" when asked how he was. A physical examination in March 1944 disclosed high blood pressure and serious heart disease. Even after a full month's rest at Bernard Baruch's South Carolina estate in April, his associates thought he looked ghastly. He had dark patches under his eyes, his hands noticeably trembled, and his shirt collar hung loosely around his neck. One close friend thought "that he would never survive his term." Should that occur, Vice-President Henry Wallace would become president. That prospect struck fear and loathing into the breasts of the Democratic Party bosses. Roosevelt had shoved the unapologetically liberal and unpredictably loony Wallace down the throat of his party in 1940; the Democratic barons had been gagging on him ever since. Whatever else happened in 1944, they were determined to get Wallace off the ticket.[60]

The Republicans unceremoniously repudiated their 1940 candidate, Wendell Willkie (who as it turned out was dead of a heart attack before election day). Some conservatives, including Robert McCormick of the *Chicago Tribune*, beseeched General MacArthur to run, promising that this time they could stage a victorious replay of General McClellan's unsuccessful challenge to Lincoln in the midst of the Civil War. But when publication of the general's impolitic letters to a supporter re-

59. Burns, *Soldier of Freedom*, 431; Polenberg, *War and Society*, 197.
60. Freidel, *Franklin D. Roosevelt*, 507; Edward J. Flynn, *You're the Boss* (New York: Viking, 1947), 179.

vealed him to be vain and possibly insubordinate, MacArthur's candidacy ignominiously collapsed.

Meanwhile, the star of Thomas E. Dewey steadily rose. A former hard-hitting Manhattan prosecutor, the forty-year-old Dewey had felt cheated out of the 1940 nomination by the surprising Willkie boom. In the Republican resurgence of 1942 he was elected governor of the traditionally Democratic stronghold of New York. Like Willkie, he was an internationalist. Unlike Willkie, he was methodical and dapper. He was also the kind of man who would say to a friend with a hangover, "I told you so." From a thermos on his desk he poured himself ice water at regular intervals. Some thought it flowed in his veins. His critics mocked him as a comically prim figure who was capable of strutting while sitting down. Dewey was so stiff, wrote one journalist, that when he took the stage to speak, "he comes out like a man who has been mounted on casters and given a tremendous shove from behind." Dewey enjoyed the advantages of a strong political base in Roosevelt's own home state, rich in votes and money. But neither he nor any other Republican could hope to mount much of a challenge to a war-winning president whose popularity had been enhanced by war-borne prosperity. Dewey showed himself a man of principle when he chose to remain silent about the potentially explosive information, suggested to him by Republican congressmen and confirmed in strictest confidence by George Marshall, that the government had broken Japanese codes before the Pearl Harbor attack. But in the end Dewey was reduced to campaigning on just two issues: Roosevelt's health and the alleged influence of Communists in the Roosevelt administration.[61]

All the preelection drama revolved around the Democratic vice-presidential nomination. Roosevelt at various times tendered his support to Wallace as well as to Office of War Mobilization chief James Byrnes, though Byrnes was as objectionable to liberals as Wallace was to conservatives. As a lapsed and twice-married Catholic, Byrnes also carried big liabilities with many of the ethnic constituencies that were the heart of the New Deal coalition. The attempt to put either Wallace or Byrnes on the ticket would ignite a raucous political donnybrook and might even fracture the Democratic coalition so painstakingly put together in the New Deal years. Seeking some acceptable middle ground, the party's political operatives pressed Roosevelt to embrace the candidacy of Missouri senator Harry S. Truman.

61. Richard Norton Smith, *Thomas E. Dewey and His Times* (New York: Simon and Schuster, 1982), 509.

Truman was surely a man of the middle. He was a son of the Middle Border, blunt-spoken, plain-living, and proud of his ordinariness. Standing five feet, eight inches tall, he had the taut little body of a jockey and the manner of a country boy who had made good but never forgot his origins. He was as straightforward as a sentence without commas. He had spent his earliest boyhood on a six-hundred-acre farm near Grandview in Jackson County, Missouri. When Harry was six his family moved to the town of Independence. He graduated from high school there in 1901, and that was the end of his formal education. In any case, "[i]t was on the farm that Harry got his common sense," his mother once said. "He didn't get it in town." He was employed briefly as a bank clerk in Kansas City, then returned to Grandview to work the family farm for a time, without much success. World War I offered him an exit. He joined a Missouri National Guard unit, and his comrades, many of them Catholics from Kansas City, elected him a first lieutenant. He commanded an artillery battery at the Battle of the Meuse-Argonne in 1918 and ended the war as a captain. Many of his troops regarded their no-nonsense, bespectacled captain with respect and even affection. Eventually, they became the nucleus of his own modest political machine.

Captain Truman came home in 1919, started a men's clothing store in Kansas City, and went broke in the recession of 1921. Having flopped as a farmer and failed as a haberdasher, he went into politics. He got help from a wartime acquaintance who was a nephew of Thomas J. Pendergast, boss of the Kansas City Democratic machine. Pendergast endorsed Truman for the position of "county judge" — the local description for a county supervisor. With the support of Pendergast and his fellow veterans, he was elected in 1922 and held the position for the next twelve years, punctuated only when he lost an election in 1924 and spent two years selling memberships in a Kansas City automobile club. Pendergast held power by engaging in every known form of political corruption. He eventually fattened on New Deal relief money and construction projects, some of which Judge Truman supervised. "Boss Tom" was convicted in 1939 of tax evasion and served time in federal prison. Through all this Truman kept his hands clean. "Looks like everybody got rich in Jackson County but me," Truman commented to his wife when Pendergast was indicted.[62]

In 1934 the Pendergast machine ran Judge Truman for the U.S. Senate, and he won easily. His colleagues at first dismissed him as the

62. David McCullough, *Truman* (New York: Simon and Schuster, 1992), 240.

"senator from Pendergast," but in fact Truman had not shared in Pendergast's spoils. His own financial circumstances were so modest that Senator Truman took the bus to work on Capitol Hill and had his teeth fixed by a public health dentist. He became known in the Senate as "go-along, get-along Harry," a well-liked and decent legislator who could be counted on to make no waves. He voted the straight New Deal line, breaking ranks only to override FDR's veto of the bonus-bill payments to his World War I comrades-in-arms in 1936. He privately opposed Roosevelt's Court-packing plan but kept mum in public.[63]

Truman won reelection to the Senate in 1940, notwithstanding the fact that Pendergast's fall from grace in the previous year had led to the removal of some fifty thousand "ghost voters" from the Missouri election rolls. In his second term, perhaps because he was now fully free of Pendergast's leading-strings, Truman began to forge a political identity of his own. In February 1941, after checking with Roosevelt, he called for the creation of a Special Senate Committee to Investigate the National Defense Program. Truman and FDR alike feared that Congress might move to replicate the Joint Committee on the Conduct of the War that had so bedeviled Abraham Lincoln. General Brehon B. Somerville, head of the Services of Supply, sneered that Truman's proposal was "formed in iniquity for political purposes." But Roosevelt appreciated that a committee headed by the safe and reliable Truman would preempt the creation of a more troublesome body. The president therefore gave the senator, whom he scarcely knew, his blessing.

The Truman Committee proceeded to expose profiteering and mismanagement in the construction of army camps, abuses of cost-plus contracting, and the delivery of substandard materials to the armed forces — notably the faulty steel plating that caused at least one Liberty Ship to crack in two. In the process, Truman burnished his reputation for honesty and square-dealing. By one estimate, his investigations saved the taxpayers as much as $15 billion. And by tempering his criticisms of the administration and thereby avoiding the kind of wholesale congressional onslaught that Lincoln had been forced to endure, he also earned Roosevelt's gratitude — though not Roosevelt's full confidence. In common with all but a handful of legislators, Truman remained uninformed about the greatest military secret of them all, the Manhattan Project.[64]

Over dinner at the White House on July 11, Roosevelt therefore

63. McCullough, *Truman*, 220.
64. McCullough, *Truman*, 262, 288–91.

agreed to take Truman. The senator was the man who would hurt the ticket the least. Truman, one of them recalled, "just dropped into the slot," a one-man "Missouri Compromise" who might not add much but was unobjectionable to Roosevelt and would do no political harm.

It remained to convince Truman, who had recently remarked to a friend that "the Vice President simply presides over the Senate and sits around hoping for a funeral. . . . I don't have any ambition to hold an office like that." Truman himself favored Byrnes and agreed to put the South Carolinian's name in nomination at the Chicago convention. But on July 19 Roosevelt telephoned Truman in his room in Chicago's Blackstone hotel. An aide took the call. The president's voice was so loud that Truman could hear every word. "Have you got that fellow lined up yet?" Roosevelt asked. No, said the aide, "he is the contrariest goddamn mule from Missouri I ever dealt with." "Well you tell the Senator that if he wants to break up the Democratic party in the middle of the war, that's his responsibility." A faithful party soldier, Truman reluctantly accepted the nomination.

The following day, as the convention formally ratified the ticket, Roosevelt had a seizure in San Diego while preparing to watch a marine amphibious-landing exercise at Camp Pendleton. No one outside the president's inner circle was told. Roosevelt recovered, delivered his acceptance speech over the radio, and boarded a navy vessel for a rendezvous with MacArthur and Nimitz in Hawaii to discuss the endgame strategy of the Pacific war. When Truman joined his running mate for lunch on the White House south lawn a month later, he noticed that Roosevelt's hand shook so badly he could not pour cream into his coffee. But in a rollicking speech on September 23, the old master campaigner roused a nationwide radio audience with a spirited defense of the New Deal and a good-humored rebuttal of Republican charges that he had left his dog, Fala, on an Aleutian island and dispatched a navy destroyer to retrieve him. Fala, said the president, was a Scottie, and "his Scotch soul was furious" at such baseless Republican calumnies. "He has not been the same dog since," said Roosevelt with mock seriousness. "I am accustomed to hearing malicious falsehoods about myself," he said. "But I think I have right to resent, to object to libelous statements about my dog." With that deft stroke Roosevelt suppressed much of the whispering campaign that he had lost his physical and mental vigor and his political touch.[65]

65. Arthur M. Schlesinger Jr., *The History of American Presidential Elections* (New York: McGraw-Hill, 1971), 4:3025; McCullough, *Truman*, 298–99, 314, 323–27; *PPA* (1944–45), 290.

In November, for the third time in history, an American presidential election took place in wartime. As in 1812 and again in 1864, the voters reelected the commander-in-chief, though Roosevelt's victory margin was his smallest ever, 25.6 million votes to Dewey's 22 million, 432 to 99 in the Electoral College. The Democrats gained just twenty seats in the House and maintained their 56–38 majority in the Senate. To Roosevelt's delight, several isolationists went down to defeat, including his own congressman, Hamilton Fish. Yet domestic issues had dominated the campaign. Roosevelt won because he convincingly conjured the prosperous future that the war had licensed Americans to covet, a future full of jobs and houses and cars and all the other fruits of affluence. "He promised what wartime advertising had displayed," writes historian John Morton Blum. "He promised what the polls said the people wanted. He promised the kind of society to which the GIs wanted to return."

Stretched out on a bed in a Kansas City hotel room, Truman listened to the election returns, thought of the future, and confided in a friend. "He knew," the friend recalled, "that he was going to be President of the United States, and I think it just scared the very devil out of him."[66]

THE ROOSEVELT-TRUMAN TICKET had clearly profited from wartime prosperity. It had also been the beneficiary of favorable news from the fighting fronts. Shortly before election day, the navy defeated the Japanese in the war's last great sea duel at Leyte Gulf, MacArthur histrionically waded ashore in the Philippines, and the first U.S. troops entered Germany. Americans prayed for their sons and sweethearts and took pride in their victories, but distance and censorship had conspired to shield Americans on the home front from ever having to stare into the face of battle. The navy had waited a year to release photographs of the destruction at Pearl Harbor, and the pictures showed only smoking wreckage, not human carnage. Not until September 1943, when it was worried about waning civilian war-spirit, did the War Department permit *Life*, the most popular American photo-essay magazine, to run the first photographs of dead GIs. "Here lie three Americans," read the caption alongside a striking image of the dead, strewn limply on the sand of Buna beach in New Guinea.[67] But for the most part Americans at home saw photos and films of the

66. Blum, *V Was for Victory*, 298–99; McCullough, *Truman*, 332.
67. *Life*, September 20, 1943, 34.

GIs as jaunty heroes or gaunt but unbowed warriors. They read in the dispatches of war correspondents like Ernie Pyle, John Steinbeck, or John Hersey about young men who were wholesome, all-American boys, soft-hearted suckers for needy kids, summer soldiers who wanted nothing more than to come home, as one of them famously told Hersey, "for a piece of blueberry pie." But the truth could be quite different. "It is in the things not mentioned," Steinbeck later reflected, "that the untruth lies."[68] "What kind of war do civilians suppose we fought, anyway?" asked one correspondent after the war. "We shot prisoners in cold blood, wiped out hospitals, strafed lifeboats, killed or mistreated enemy civilians, finished off the enemy wounded, tossed the dying into a hole with the dead, and in the Pacific boiled the flesh off enemy skulls to make table ornaments for sweethearts, or carved their bones into letter openers."[69]

Of the war's single greatest horror, Hitler's campaign of genocide against Europe's Jews, Americans also comprehended little. They knew some facts, but facts did not necessarily mean understanding, especially for a people so mercifully sheltered from the war's harshest suffering. In August 1942 Gerhart Riegner, a representative of the World Jewish Congress, informed American officials in Switzerland that Germany had begun mass exterminations of Jews in the areas under Nazi control. The Americans were skeptical, remembering the atrocity stories that British propagandists had manufactured in World War I. They nevertheless forwarded Riegner's report to Washington, with the notation that it had the "earmarks of a war rumor inspired by fear." But further evidence soon came in, and on December 8, 1942, Roosevelt summoned American Jewish leaders to the White House and somberly informed them that the government now had "proof that confirms the horrors discussed by you." No one as yet grasped the degree to which the killing was going on systematically in purpose-built death camps. But it was now clear that the question facing Washington was not a matter of providing asylum to refugees but of rescuing prisoners trapped in a death-machine. How to effect a rescue? For a country that had not yet landed a single soldier on the continent of Europe, the options were few. Roosevelt did induce Churchill and Stalin to join him in a declaration on December 17, 1942, that the allies intended to try "war criminals" in formal courts

---

68. John Hersey, *Into the Valley: A Skirmish of the Marines* (New York: Knopf, 1943), 137; John Steinbeck, *Once There Was a War* (New York: Viking, 1958), xiii.

69. Edgar Jones, "One War Is Enough," *Atlantic Monthly*, February 1946, 49.

of law when the war was over—the origins of the postwar tribunals that convened at Nuremberg and Tokyo.[70]

American Jewish groups publicized what they knew, and the mainstream press reported what scant news of the Holocaust it had. The government meanwhile cast about for an effective policy. Roosevelt called for a Conference on Refugees to meet in Bermuda in April 1943, but it foundered on Britain's refusal even to discuss Palestine as a destination for whatever Jews might somehow be liberated from the Nazis' grasp. A few months later, the uneasy German satellite of Romania tentatively revived a scheme to allow some seventy thousand Romanian Jews to be ransomed, but because their presumed destination would be Palestine, the State Department deferred to British wishes and quietly buried the Romanian proposal. When treasury officials learned at last of the State Department's apparently willful obstruction, they drafted a report for their chief, the cabinet's only Jew, Henry Morgenthau. Its title screamed its outrage: "Report to the Secretary on the Acquiescence by This Government in the Murder of the Jews." It was dated January 10, 1944. By then millions of European Jews had already perished.

At Morgenthau's insistence, Roosevelt established the War Refugee Board (WRB) on January 22, with instructions to do what it could but little hope that it could do much. Eight months later, the board brought 982 refugees, most of them Jews who had managed to make their way into occupied Italy, to a refugee camp near Oswego, New York. The journalist I. F. Stone called it "a kind of token payment to decency, a bargain-counter flourish in humanitarianism."[71]

Opportunities for bigger flourishes soon presented themselves. In March 1944 Hitler occupied Hungary, another satellite growing restless as the tide of war turned against its German ally, and home to the largest intact Jewish community in Europe, some 750,000 souls. SS Obersturmbannführer Adolf Eichmann soon arrived in Budapest to impose the Final Solution on Hungary's Jews. As Eichmann ordered mass deportations to Auschwitz to begin, the WRB sent Raoul Wallenberg to Hungary under Swedish diplomatic cover. With bribery and bravura, he saved thousands of Jews. The WRB also arranged for air-leaflet drops renewing the threat of war-crime prosecutions against Eichmann and his accomplices and induced New York's Francis Cardinal Spellman to

---

70. David S. Wyman, *The Abandonment of the Jews: America and the Holocaust, 1941–1945* (New York: Pantheon, 1984), 42, 72.
71. Wyman, *Abandonment of the Jews*, 187, 266.

record a radio broadcast reminding Catholic Hungarians that persecution of the Jews was "in direct contradiction" to Church doctrine. Eichmann offered to halt the deportations and exchange up to one hundred thousand Jews for ten thousand trucks that he promised would be used only on the eastern front. The Soviets suspected, probably correctly, that this was an eleventh-hour ploy to split the Grand Alliance and prepare the way for a separate peace in the west. The deal collapsed, but in all, the WRB's initiatives in Hungary may have spared some two hundred thousand Jews from the gas chambers.

In the midst of the Hungarian deportations, two inmates miraculously escaped from Auschwitz and brought to the west one of the first accounts revealing the stupefying scale and cold-blooded efficiency of the Holocaust. Even with this evidence, its dimensions defied belief. The WRB nevertheless submitted a recommendation to Assistant Secretary of War McCloy that the Auschwitz death camp should be bombed out of commission, even if the bombs would kill some of the Jewish inmates. McCloy rejected the idea. An attack on Auschwitz, he told the WRB, "could be executed only by the diversion of considerable air support essential to the success of our forces now engaged in decisive operations elsewhere." In a later message McCloy misleadingly added that "the target is beyond the maximum range of medium bombardment, dive bombers and fighter bombers located in UK, France or Italy. Use of heavy bombardment from UK bases would necessitate a round trip flight unescorted of approximately 2000 miles over enemy territory."[72]

In fact, American heavy bombers, escorted by long-range P-51 Mustangs, had already attacked several times in the vicinity of Auschwitz. Two considerations may help to explain McCloy's apparently callous decision. First, the WRB request arrived just as the breakout at Normandy was holding out the alluring prospect that the war would be over in months, perhaps weeks. McCloy may well have concluded that rescue through victory was more likely than rescue through a singular action deep inside Poland.

But a second factor may have figured just as large: McCloy's inability, shared by many of his comfortable countrymen, to imagine the full enormity of the Holocaust. In December 1944 McCloy said to A. Leon Kobowitzki, a World Jewish Congress official, "We are alone. Tell me the truth. Do you really believe that all those horrible things happened?"

72. Wyman, *Abandonment of the Jews*, 296–97.

Even then, Kobowitzki recalled, "he could not grasp the terrible destruction."[73]

Nor could others. In the summer of 1943 Supreme Court Justice Felix Frankfurter, probably the most eminent American Jew and a devoted Zionist, went to the Polish embassy in Washington to meet the Polish socialist Jan Karski, another death-camp escapee. When Karski finished describing what he had seen at Belzec, Frankfurter paced in somber silence for ten minutes. "I am unable to believe you," he said to Karski at last. "Felix, you cannot tell this man to his face that he is lying," the Polish ambassador interjected. "I did not say that this young man is lying," Frankfurter replied. "I said that I am unable to believe him. There is a difference." Frankfurter extended both arms and waved his hands. "No, no," he said, and walked out.[74]

Americans had been fortunate in the war, singularly fortunate in a world that inflicted unspeakable punishments on so many millions of others. But good fortune could be the father of innocence, and the world the war was making would be no place for the innocent, no matter how very much of it they seemed poised to inherit.

73. Bird, *Chairman*, 206.
74. Bird, *Chairman*, 206.

22

Endgame

I . . . have concluded that continuing the war can only mean destruction for the nation.

—Japanese emperor Hirohito, August 9, 1945

On the morning of January 20, 1945, Franklin Roosevelt fitted his wasted legs into his heavy steel braces for the first time in four months. He was wheeled to the south portico of the White House, rose laboriously from his chair with the help of his son James, and gripped a lectern to deliver his fourth inaugural address, the briefest in American history, just 573 words. "We have learned that we must live as men and not as ostriches," he said. "We can gain no lasting peace if we approach it with suspicion and mistrust—or with fear." The perfunctory ceremony was over in minutes. As the president withdrew, observers murmured about his pallor and gauntness. He had lost almost twenty-five pounds since the preceding summer. James told him frankly that he looked like hell. When the presidential party went back inside the White House, FDR sat his son down to talk about his will and about the funeral instructions he had deposited in the White House safe. He did not disclose that ten months earlier the cardiologist Howard G. Bruenn had diagnosed him with hypertension, hypertensive heart disease, and failure of the left ventricular chamber. In plain language, Bruenn described the president's health as "God-awful." But as he had done for years with his paralysis, Roosevelt did his best willfully to ignore his cardiovascular illness. Though Bruenn prevailed upon him to cut his working day back to just a few hours, the president concealed the severity of his condition from others, asked no questions of his physician, and tried to carry on in public as if nothing in his life had changed.[1]

1. *PPA* (1944–45), 524; Howard G. Bruenn, M.D., "Clinical Notes on the Illness and Death of President Franklin D. Roosevelt," *Annals of Internal Medicine* 75: 579–91

Two days after the inauguration, Roosevelt went to the basement of the Bureau of Engraving and Printing, just a few blocks from the White House. On an underground spur line, built to allow the bureau to ship newly printed money in secret, waited the president's specially fitted railroad car, the *Ferdinand Magellan*, a 140-ton armor-plated Pullman coach, equipped with three-inch bulletproof-glass windows, watertight doors, and three emergency escape hatches adapted from submarines. The *Ferdinand Magellan* rumbled away, bearing the president to Norfolk, Virginia. There he boarded the heavy cruiser *USS Quincy* and made course for the Mediterranean island of Malta, where he rendezvoused with Churchill on February 2. The two leaders still faced a seven-hour flight to Yalta, in the Soviet Crimea, where Stalin awaited them. He had slept ten hours a night on the sea voyage, Roosevelt said, but still did not feel rested.

Malta was no Cairo, which had been a full-dress Anglo-American staging ground for the historic three-power meeting that followed at Teheran. Roosevelt remained on the island for less than twenty-four hours, did some sight-seeing, and spent little time with Churchill. The lack of preparation for the upcoming meeting with Stalin made British foreign secretary Anthony Eden uneasy. "[W]e are going into a decisive conference," he complained to Harry Hopkins at Malta, "and had so far neither agreed what we would discuss nor how to handle matters with a Bear who would certainly know his own mind."[2]

On February 2, escorted by fighter planes, the same "Sacred Cow" that had carried the president to Teheran bore FDR from Malta to the airfield at Saki, in the Black Sea's Crimean peninsula. Under three tents at the edge of the landing area the Russians had laid out a welcoming luncheon of hot tea, smoked sturgeon, caviar, and black bread. Roosevelt transferred to an automobile; five hours and eighty miles of wretched road later, he finally reached the moldering czarist resort of Livadia Palace, near the city of Yalta, for the second, and last, wartime meeting of the Big Three Grand Alliance partners. Lord Moran, Churchill's

---

(1970); Robert H. Ferrell, *The Dying President: Franklin D. Roosevelt, 1944–1945* (Columbia: University of Missouri Press, 1998), 101–2, 37. After Dr. Bruenn's diagnosis in March 1944, Roosevelt did alter some of his dietary habits, cut back on his use of both alcohol and tobacco, and take medications. But he apparently never entertained the idea that his health might impede his performance as president or considered not running for a fourth term.

2. Anthony Eden, *The Reckoning: The Memoirs of Anthony Eden* (Boston: Houghton Mifflin, 1965), 592.

physician, was observing Roosevelt keenly. "To a doctor's eye," Moran noted, "the President appears a very sick man. . . . I give him only a few months to live."[3]

Four issues dominated the agenda at Yalta: the voting procedures and membership rules for the United Nations Organization, a new international body approved in outline form at Dumbarton Oaks, in Washington, D.C., in the fall of 1944; the fate of eastern Europe, Poland in particular; the treatment of defeated Germany; and Soviet participation in the war against Japan. The Big Three had touched on all of these matters at Teheran, scarcely more than a year earlier. Then the discussion had been mostly about military matters. At Yalta, with the partial exception of Soviet entry into the Asian war, the discussion would be mainly about political issues. If Teheran was in many ways a rehearsal for Yalta, then Yalta in turn set the stage for the dawning international regime that came to be known as the Cold War.

Roosevelt began at Yalta as he had at Teheran, meeting with Stalin for a private conversation before the conference's first plenary session on February 4. Still hoping to win Stalin's confidence and coax the Soviet Union into playing a cooperative role in the postwar world, he once again strained to be ingratiating to the Soviet dictator. As on the earlier occasion, that gambit prompted the president to say some astonishing things; yet it proved insufficient motive for him to speak about some other things, notably the Manhattan Project.

During the drive from the airfield at Saki, Roosevelt remarked, he had been struck by the devastation the Germans had wrought in the Crimea. Seeing that destruction had made him "more bloodthirsty in regard to the Germans than he had been a year ago," Roosevelt announced. He "hoped that Marshal Stalin would again propose a toast to the execution of 50,000 officers of the German Army."[4] Stalin replied that the ruination in the Ukraine was even worse. There followed, as there had at Teheran, an exchange about the fecklessness of the French and the self-aggrandizing delusions of DeGaulle. Roosevelt gratuitously added a few jibes at the British—"a peculiar people," he called them. Then it was time to proceed to the main conference room. Roosevelt had not mentioned the atomic bomb project to Stalin, nor would he ever.

3. Lord Moran, *Churchill: Taken from the Diaries of Lord Moran: The Struggle for Survival, 1940–1965* (Boston: Houghton Mifflin, 1966), 242.
4. *FRUS: The Conferences at Malta and Yalta, 1945,* 571.

Stalin immediately set the tone for the week's discussions. He was self-confident, assertive, demanding, sarcastic. Sometimes he paced impatiently behind his chair as he talked. As for Roosevelt, Eden found him "vague and loose and ineffective."[5] Militarily, Stalin held all the high cards. The Red Army had overrun Romania, Bulgaria, Hungary, Poland, and East Prussia and had battled to within miles of Berlin. The Western allies, meanwhile, had not yet crossed the Rhine. They had barely recovered from the Ardennes counterattack—and only with the help, Stalin noted pointedly, of an accelerated Soviet winter offensive that prevented Hitler from reinforcing his troops in the "Bulge."

Stalin now moved to translate his hard-won military advantage into permanent political gains. Here, as throughout the war, Bernard Montgomery later reflected, "Stalin made almost no mistakes; he had a clear-cut political strategy and he pursued it relentlessly."[6]

The subject of the United Nations was the least difficult of the topics on the table at Yalta, though not without its vexations. Stalin held out for a single-power veto in the United Nations Security Council, a reasonable demand, and for two extra Soviet votes in the General Assembly, for the Soviet republics of Ukraine and White Russia, respectively—a transparently unreasonable attempt to pack the assembly in favor of the USSR. Eager to please, Roosevelt acceded readily to the first Soviet request, though only grudgingly to the second.

About Poland Stalin was adamant. At Teheran Roosevelt had indicated that he had no objection to shifting the Polish state westward by ceding much of eastern Poland to the Soviet Union and moving Poland's western frontier to the line of the Oder and Neisse rivers. But now Stalin wanted more—not more territory but more iron-fisted political control over the postwar Polish government. For the Russians, Stalin said, Poland "was a question of both honor and security," even "one of life and death."

Since the summer of 1944, the Russians had sponsored a provisional Polish government dominated by Communists and temporarily seated in the eastern Polish city of Lublin. The "Lublin Poles" contended for recognition as the legitimate government of liberated Poland against the "London Poles," a rival government-in-exile resident in the British capital and favored, even if lukewarmly, by the British and the Americans. It was to extinguish elements aligned with the London Poles that Stalin

5. Eden, *Reckoning*, 593.
6. Bernard Montgomery, *A History of Warfare* (Cleveland: World Publishing, 1968) 544.

in 1940 had ordered the massacre of thousands of captured Polish army officers in the Soviet-occupied Katyn Forest near Smolensk, and then in 1944 had instructed the Red Army to stall on the banks of the Vistula so that the Germans might bloodily suppress the Warsaw Rising. Now the Lublin Poles, said Stalin, were sustaining an orderly civil government in Poland, while the London Poles fomented armed resistance to the Red Army. Partisans backed by the London Poles, he charged, had murdered more than two hundred Soviet soldiers. "We want tranquility in our rear," Stalin said. "We will support the government which gives us peace in the rear. . . . When I compare what the agents of the Lublin government have done and what the agents of the London government have done I see the first are good and the second bad."[7]

As at Teheran, Roosevelt had neither the will nor the means to challenge Soviet hegemony in eastern Europe, but he needed political cover for his acquiescence in the Soviet fait accompli. The United States was "farther away from Poland than anyone else here," FDR said. Nevertheless, Roosevelt went on, the Poles were "quarrelsome people" wherever they might be, and therefore he "felt it was very important for him in the United States that there be some gesture made for the six million Poles there indicating that the United States was in some way involved with the question of freedom of elections" to determine the permanent government of Poland. He emphasized, however, "that it was only a matter of words and details." In a personal note he assured Stalin that "the United States will never lend its support in any way to any provisional government in Poland that would be inimical to your interests." The result was the Declaration on Liberated Europe. It pledged the signatories "to arrange and conduct free elections" in liberated countries looking to the creation of governments that were "broadly representative of all democratic elements." These were hollow words, as Roosevelt well knew. "Mr. President, this is so elastic that the Russians can stretch it all the way from Yalta to Washington without ever technically breaking it," said Roosevelt's chief of staff, Admiral William Leahy, when he saw the draft of the declaration. "I know, Bill — I know it," said FDR. "But it's the best I can do for Poland at this time." And it was — unless Roosevelt was prepared to order Eisenhower to fight his way across the breadth of Germany, take on the Red Army, and drive it out of Poland at gunpoint. At this stage of the war in Europe, political

7. *FRUS: Malta and Yalta,* 669–70.

decisions could do little more than ratify military realities. On this point in particular, Yalta was only a postscript to Teheran.[8]

The Big Three next turned to the question of Germany. Stalin wanted to know "whether the President or Prime Minister still adhered to the principle of dismemberment," as they had indicated at Teheran. He also wished to discuss reparations. Unknown to Stalin, these matters had for months been the subject of contentious and unresolved debate within Roosevelt's government and between the British and the Americans.

In September 1944 Treasury Secretary Morgenthau had brought to the Anglo-American conference at Quebec a radical plan to deindustrialize the Ruhr and the Saar and partition Germany into two or more pastoral states. Secretary of State Hull was aghast at this "plan of blind vengeance." Wrecking the German economy, Hull believed, would ruin the economy of all Europe. He considered the Morgenthau Plan "cataclysmic," "a tragedy for all concerned," precisely the kind of Carthaginian peace that had ravaged the interwar international economy and bred the German lust for revenge that Hitler had exploited. Henry Stimson warned Roosevelt, "It is not within the realm of possibility that a whole nation of seventy million people . . . can by force be required to abandon all their previous methods of life, be reduced to a peasant level with virtually complete control of industry and science left to other peoples." Churchill at first agreed with that assessment. When Morgenthau unveiled his plan at Quebec, Churchill unleashed "the full flood of his rhetoric, sarcasm, and violence." An economically moribund Germany would drag down all of Europe, he said. He had not come to Quebec, Churchill declaimed, to discuss chaining England to the body of a dead German. But over Anthony Eden's strenuous objections, the prime minister relented, perhaps mollified by the treasury secretary's intimations that only British agreement to the Morgenthau Plan would secure the treasury's approval of postwar credits for Britain. On September 15, seated at a table in the Citadel in Quebec, Roosevelt and Churchill put their initials to an agreement "for eliminating the war-making industries in the Ruhr and in the Saar" and "converting Germany into a country primarily agricultural and pastoral in its character."

8. *FRUS: Malta and Yalta*, 727, 846–48, 861; William D. Leahy, *I Was There: The Personal Story of the Chief of Staff to Presidents Roosevelt and Truman Based on His Notes and Diaries Made at the Time* (New York: Whittlesey House, 1950), 315–16.

Back in Washington after the Quebec conference, however, Hull and Stimson refused to accept the Morgenthau Plan as settled policy. They bombarded Roosevelt with dissenting memoranda. Hull soon concluded that Roosevelt "had not realized the extent to which . . . he had committed himself at Quebec." When Stimson carefully read the Quebec agreement aloud to the president at lunch on October 3, Roosevelt "was frankly staggered by this and said he had no idea how he could have initialed this; that he had evidently done it without much thought." The president thereupon backed away from the Morgenthau Plan. He now declared, "I dislike making detailed plans for a country which we do not yet occupy." He thus arrived at Yalta with no American plan to present.[9]

Stalin suffered from no such divided counsel, confusion, or apparent mental distraction. The Germans would recover, he said, unless drastic action was taken to contain them. "Give them twelve to fifteen years and they'll be on their feet again," he had predicted to Marshal Tito. Accordingly, Stalin wanted not only to dismember Germany but also to exact heavy reparations from the conquered *Reich*. He proposed to strip Germany of at least $10 billion worth of industrial equipment for shipment to the Soviet Union, with a like amount to be allotted to other victims of Nazi aggression. The Western allies demurred. Churchill called the Soviet demands unrealistic. Though Roosevelt "thought the division of Germany into five states or seven states was a good idea," he tried to deflect the conversation to the topic of zones of occupation, a matter well short of permanent partition. At times he tried to deflect the conversation further still, at one point telling a rambling and perplexing story about a Jew and an Italian who were members of the Ku Klux Klan in a small southern town but "were considered all right since everyone in the community knew them." In the end, these tactics buried the topic of permanent partition. As for reparations, though the Americans agreed in principle to the Soviet proposal for $10 billion in industrial transfers, the fact remained that it would be the British and the Americans who would control the industrial heartland of western Germany and could later grant or withhold reparations as they pleased. Stalin emphasized "the unsatisfactory nature of the reparations question at the conference," but for the time being there the matter rested. Roo-

9. *FRUS: Malta and Yalta*, 612; Cordell Hull, *The Memoirs of Cordell Hull* (New York: Macmillan, 1948), 2:1606, 1611–12, 1619, 1621; *FRUS: The Conference at Quebec, 1944*, 483, 467; Stimson Diary, October 3, 1944.

sevelt did say that "he did not believe that American troops would stay in Europe for much more than two years," encouraging Stalin to believe that he need only bide his time to manage events in postwar Europe as he wished.[10]

The most concrete — and among the most controversial — agreements reached at Yalta concerned Soviet entry into the war against Japan. Roosevelt told Stalin that he "hoped that it would not be necessary actually to invade the Japanese islands." To avoid that bloody business, he needed Soviet help. A Soviet declaration of war against Japan would shock the Japanese into recognizing the hopelessness of their case, enable the Red Army to tie down the large Japanese force in Manchuria, make Siberian bases available to the United States for bombing Japan — and, Roosevelt privately calculated, keep the Russians from working more mischief in Europe while the Americans waged the finish-fight in Asia.

Stalin replied that "it would be difficult for him . . . to explain to the Soviet people why Russia was entering the war against Japan . . . a country with which they had no great trouble." But, he added unctuously, if certain "political conditions were met, the people would understand . . . and it would be very much easier to explain the decision." Specifically, he wanted to annex the Kurile Islands, asked for guarantees that the postwar settlement would not disturb the status of the pro-Soviet Mongolian People's Republic, and demanded restoration of Russia's losses to Japan in the war of 1904 — southern Sakhalin Island, the ports of Dairen and Port Arthur, and control over the Chinese-Eastern and South-Manchurian railroads, "on the understanding that China should continue to possess full sovereignty in Manchuria."

These were considerable demands, and they came largely at China's expense. Roosevelt agreed to all, revealing how much he had come to regard China as America's client state. In return for Stalin's promise to declare war on Japan within two or three months of Germany's surrender, Roosevelt undertook to "inform" Chiang of these arrangements at the appropriate time. When that might be was left unresolved. It would not be soon. The promised movement of twenty-five Soviet divisions into eastern Siberia must be undertaken in secret, and "one of the difficulties in speaking to the Chinese," Roosevelt told Stalin, "was that anything said to them was known to the whole world in twenty-four

---

10. Milovan Djilas, *Conversations with Stalin* (New York: Harcourt, Brace and World, 1962), 114; FRUS: *Malta and Yalta*, 614, 617, 921–22.

hours." Nor did Roosevelt immediately inform Churchill of the terms of this agreement.[11]

Roosevelt left Yalta on February 11. In a fitting postscript to the inconclusive bickering among the Big Three, and a fitting reminder of the global convulsions the war had wrought, Roosevelt returned to the *Quincy*, moored at Great Bitter Lake in the Suez Canal, for brief talks with three kings: Ibn Saud of Saudi Arabia, Farouk of Egypt, and Haile Selassie of Ethiopia. Churchill had been flabbergasted at Roosevelt's surprise announcement on the last day of the Yalta Conference that he was about to insert himself into the complex tangle of Middle Eastern affairs, traditionally a British preserve. In the event, Roosevelt's royal visitations at Suez proved no more conclusive than the talks in the Crimea. The conversation with Ibn Saud, Harry Hopkins recorded, "was short and to the point." Would Ibn Saud allow more Jewish refugees to enter Palestine, Roosevelt asked? "No," Ibn Saud replied, and added that the Arabs would take up arms to prevent further Jewish immigration to Palestine.[12]

On March 1 Roosevelt appeared before a joint session of Congress to report on the Yalta parley. In a highly unusual reference to his disability, he began by asking his listeners' pardon for addressing them from a sitting position. "[I]t makes it a lot easier for me not to have to carry about ten pounds of steel around on the bottom of my legs," the president explained. He then delivered a patchy, inchoate speech laced with ad-lib remarks that one close associate described as "wholly irrelevant, and some of them almost bordered on the ridiculous." He occasionally slurred his words, and his hands trembled. He made much of the prospects for free elections in Poland and of the Declaration on Liberated Europe. He touted the agreements on the United Nations, scheduled to convene for the first time in San Francisco on April 25. He made no reference to his deal with Stalin about Soviet entry into the war against Japan. Nor did he mention his acquiescence in Stalin's demand for the two extra Soviet votes in the U.N. General Assembly. Word of that odd concession nevertheless quickly leaked, lending credibility to the soon-rampant suspicion that Roosevelt had brought back from the Crimea a Pandora's box full of "Yalta Secrets" that compromised the interests of the United States.[13]

11. *FRUS: Malta and Yalta*, 766, 769, 896.
12. Robert E. Sherwood, *Roosevelt and Hopkins* (New York: Grosset and Dunlap, 1950), 872.
13. *PPA* (1944–45), 570–86; Samuel I. Rosenman, *Working with Roosevelt* (New York: Harper and Brothers, 1952), 527.

Controversy over the Yalta Conference reverberated well into the post-war years, when it was alleged that Roosevelt, sick and mentally enfee-bled, possibly misguided by scheming pro-Communist advisers, had wit-lessly kowtowed to Stalin, cut backroom deals, betrayed Poland, delivered eastern Europe into Soviet hands, and sold out Chiang Kai-Shek, opening the door to the eventual Communist takeover in China. All of those charges were vastly overdrawn. If Yalta represented an Amer-ican diplomatic failure, it was attributable not to the frailties of Franklin Roosevelt's mind and body in February 1945, and surely not to the machinations of supposedly subversive aides, but to the pattern of more than five years of war that left the American president with few options. "I didn't say the result was good," Roosevelt conceded to an associate, "I said it was the best I could do."[14]

The president was unquestionably ill at Yalta, but he did little there that he had not signaled his willingness to do at Teheran, when he was in full possession of his faculties, and did little differently than any Amer-ican leader could have done at this juncture. His concealment about the United Nations votes was regrettable but humanly understandable in view of his embarrassment about the matter, and in any case sub-stantively unimportant. He perhaps misjudged his ability to speak can-didly to the American people about Soviet dominance in eastern Europe but surely judged rightly that the United States could not do much about it. With reference to Germany, his obfuscation managed to head off formal partition and deferred the reparations question for discussion on another and presumably more auspicious day. In China, Chiang's regime was already so rotten as to be beyond salvation. Nothing prom-ised at Yalta appreciably contributed to its eventual collapse.

As for Soviet entry into the war against Japan, Roosevelt had two aims in mind. He wanted to tie the Russians' hands in Europe by deflecting at least part of their attention to Asia in the immediate aftermath of the German surrender. With respect to Asia itself, the commander-in-chief followed the best counsel of his senior military advisers, eager for any means to spare American troops from further bloodletting in the in-creasingly vicious Pacific war. The Joint Chiefs estimated that the Soviet declaration of war might shorten the fighting by a year or more and thereby preclude the dreaded invasion of Japan itself. The atomic bomb, still untested — still unmade — its possible tactical effects unknowable

14. Beatrice Bishop Berle and Travis Beal Jacobs, eds., *Navigating the Rapids, 1918–1971: From the Papers of Adolf A. Berle* (New York: Harcourt Brace Jovanovich, 1973), 477.

and its potential strategic impact still conjectural, figured scarcely at all in these calculations.[15]

On March 20 Roosevelt held his last White House press conference. He seemed mentally alert, but to steady his hand sufficiently to light a cigarette, he had to wedge his elbow into a partially closed desk drawer. Visitors in the last days of March noticed that he was repeating himself, unwittingly recounting the same lengthy anecdotes to the same listeners on the same occasion. Dr. Bruenn advised a period of total rest. On March 29 the *Ferdinand Magellan* carried Roosevelt to his retreat at Warm Springs, Georgia. He was deadweight limp when the Secret Service men transferred him to an automobile at the railroad siding in Warm Springs, and observers gasped when the president's head lolled strangely. On April 12 Roosevelt awoke complaining of a headache but proceeded to work at his makeshift desk in the Warm Springs "Little White House." Shortly after one o'clock, he passed his hand jerkily over his forehead and slumped forward, unconscious. At 3:35 P.M., Dr. Bruenn pronounced him dead of a cerebral hemorrhage. By his death-bed was Lucy Mercer, the lover he had promised to forsake twenty-seven years earlier.

Less than four hours later, standing in the White House Cabinet Room under a portrait of Woodrow Wilson, Harry S. Truman put his hand on an inexpensive Gideon Bible and swore the presidential oath. "There have been few men in all history the equal of the man into whose shoes I am stepping," he said the next day. "I pray God I can measure up to the task." In Grandview, Missouri, Truman's mother told reporters: "Harry will get along all right."[16]

While Americans were mourning their fallen leader, Italian partisans shot Benito Mussolini on April 28 and dumped his body in Piazza Loreto in Milano. After several women had squatted over the dead *Duce* and lifted their skirts to urinate in his face, the mob hanged him by his heels. The next day German forces in Italy surrendered, following se-

15. Groves had informed Marshall on December 30, 1944, that a single U-235 bomb (the type ultimately used against Hiroshima), with a predicted explosive power of ten thousand tons of TNT, "should be ready about August 1, 1945," with a second such weapon available "by the end of the year." The first plutonium bomb (the type dropped on Nagasaki) Groves had expected to be ready in the late spring, but "scientific difficulties" had postponed its development until "sometime in the latter part of July." It was expected to have an explosive yield of about five hundred tons of TNT. *FRUS: Malta and Yalta*, 383–84.
16. Ferrell, *Dying President*, 111–119; Bruenn, "Clinical Notes," 590; David McCullough, *Truman* (New York: Simon and Schuster, 1992), 347–52.

cretive negotiations from which the Soviets had been excluded. This had triggered a bitter exchange between Stalin and the dying Roosevelt. "The Germans on the Western front have in fact ceased the war against Britain and America," Stalin had written. "At the same time they continue the war against Russia, the Ally of Britain and the U.S.A." For his part, in what was to be his penultimate communication with Stalin, Roosevelt had replied that he felt "bitter resentment toward your informers, whoever they are, for such vile misrepresentation of my actions" in the Italian surrender negotiations, though he did not offer a convincing explanation for having excluded the Soviets. "It would be one of the great tragedies of history," Roosevelt had concluded, "if at the very moment of victory . . . such lack of faith should prejudice the entire undertaking after the colossal losses of life, material and treasure involved."[17]

Two days after Mussolini's death, in his bunker fifty-five feet below central Berlin, Adolf Hitler pressed a pistol to his head and squeezed the trigger. Red Army troops meanwhile clambered through the charred ruins above, fighting a hellish street-by-street battle for the Nazi capital. Just one week after *der Führer's* suicide, Admiral Karl Dönitz, Hitler's hand-picked successor as head of the thousand-year *Reich*, the wily seaman who had nearly won the Battle of the Atlantic in 1942, tendered Germany's unconditional surrender. On May 7, 1945, Dönitz ordered all German units to cease operations at 11:01 P.M. on the following day. The war in Europe was over.

The war in the Pacific was not.

THE PACIFIC WAR was a parallel war, fought simultaneously with the conflict in Europe but almost never touching it directly. This was as true for the Axis as it was for the Allies. Germany and Japan undertook no joint diplomatic initiatives after 1941, made not the slightest gesture toward economic cooperation, and neither executed nor even discussed a single combined military or naval operation. On the Allied side the war in the Pacific was almost exclusively an American affair, prosecuted from Washington with scant reference to London or Moscow. And as far as Washington was concerned, its war against Japan was "the other war," one that more artful diplomacy in 1940–41 might have postponed or even avoided and that was always subordinate to the premier objective

17. Robert Leckie, *Deliver Us from Evil: The Saga of World War II* (New York: Harper and Row, 1987), 835; Ministry of Foreign Affairs of the USSR, Comp., *Stalin's Correspondence with Roosevelt and Truman, 1941–1945* (New York: Capricorn, 1965), 206, 208.

of defeating Hitler. Prewar American planning had contemplated only defensive action in the Pacific. But the inflammatory insult of the Pearl Harbor attack, followed by fabulous luck at Midway and hard-won success at Guadalcanal, not to mention the prodigious flow of guns and ships from American factories, eventually shaped a pivot on which Admiral King had swung from the anticipated holding action against Japan and gone on the offensive.

The Americans had cracked Japan's outermost defensive shell with the attack on Tarawa in the Gilbert Islands at the end of 1943. They had widened the crack in February 1944 with the capture of Kwajelein and Eniwetok, both in the Marshall Islands, and the destruction by aerial bombardment of the major Japanese base at Truk, in the Carolines. As more machines of war poured off American assembly lines and more men marched out of the training camps, the United States was poised as 1944 began not only to launch Overlord in Europe but at the same time to undertake two distinct offensive operations across the immense reaches of the Pacific.

The Pacific war was a war of distances, distances measured culturally as well as geographically. Each combatant, Japan and the United States alike, saw its adversary through a distorting lens laminated from historically accumulated layers of ignorance, arrogance, prejudice, and loathing. To a degree that had no equivalent in the western European theater, that for the ferocity it spawned compared only with the savage encounter between "Aryans" and Slavs on Hitler's eastern front, the Japanese-American war was a race war, and just for that reason, in the historian John Dower's phrase, a "war without mercy." Japan's desperate gamble at Pearl Harbor had rested on the derisive and fatally erroneous assumption that the supposedly decadent, self-indulgent Americans had no stomach for war's hardship and would be so traumatized by the attack that they would quickly sue for peace. Like so many stereotypes, the Japanese image of the Americans reversed the self-image of the beholder. The Japanese prided themselves on being genetically pure, the "Yamato Race," uncontaminated by immigration, rooted for more than two millennia in their island realm, a single people bound together by blood and history. They were the "One Hundred Million," Japanese propaganda repeatedly reminded them, who lived, worked, and fought as one. They considered the Americans, in contrast, to be a contemptibly polyglot and divided people, historically unanchored, riven by ethnic and racial conflict, labor violence, and political strife, incapable of self-sacrifice or submission to the common weal. Japanese pupils read in their schoolbook *Cardinal Principles of the National Polity* that they were "intrinsically quite different from the so-called citizens of Occidental countries" and that the biggest difference was their immunity to the detestable western virus of individualism.[18]

The Americans reciprocated with depictions of the Japanese as servile automatons devoid of individual identity. Frank Capra strikingly invoked that imagery in an indoctrination film devoted to the Pacific War in his *Why We Fight* series: *Know Your Enemy—Japan*. Viewers saw repeated hammer-blows to a steel bar while the narrator told them that the Japanese were like "photographic prints off the same negative." That dehumanizing motif was reinforced by ideas that had long pedigrees in Western culture. Wartime cartoons and posters routinely depicted the Japanese as murderous savages, immature children, wild beasts, or bucktoothed, bespectacled lunatics. All those images were appropriated from a cultural storehouse built millennia earlier, when the Greeks first distinguished between themselves and "barbarians," and abundantly stocked over the centuries of European expansion into the New World, Africa, and Asia. The long record of Western racialist disdain made it easy to demonize the Japanese. From the war's outset, American officials and the organs of popular culture conspired to breed virulent hatred of the Asian adversary. Admiral William F. "Bull" Halsey notoriously defined his mission as "Kill Japs, kill Japs, kill more Japs" and vowed that at war's end Japanese would be spoken only in hell. Wartime Hollywood films like *The Purple Heart*, about the Doolittle air raid on Tokyo in 1942, depicted Japanese captors torturing downed American fliers, scenes that incited audiences to cold fury. In late 1943, about the time the Tarawa casualty reports were coming in, the War Department released the diary of a Japanese soldier that described the beheading of a captured American airman, and in early 1944, just as the major American offensives in the Pacific were getting under way, the government published grisly accounts of the Bataan Death March. All these were calculated to magnify the American public's already ample animosity toward Japan.[19]

On its side, the Imperial Japanese Army indoctrinated its troops according to the code of Bushido—the Way of the Warrior—an ancient

18. John W. Dower, *War without Mercy: Race and Power in the Pacific War* (New York: Pantheon, 1986), 221. This discussion relies heavily on Dower's excellent study.
19. In another sign of the subordinate status of the Pacific war, *Know Your Enemy— Japan* was the last film to be made in Capra's series. It was released only in August 1945 and was withdrawn after less than three weeks.

samurai ethos that emphasized loyalty, austerity, self-denial, and indifference to pain. "Loyalty is heavier than a mountain, and our life is lighter than a feather," Japanese soldiers were taught. The lesson was rammed home with harsh discipline. All superiors, of whatever rank, regularly kicked, punched, and slapped their subordinates. Brutal treatment made for brutal soldiers and for an ugly war, not only against the Americans in the Pacific but against the Chinese and other Asians as well, as the Rape of Nanking in 1937 and the Bataan Death March in 1942 had grotesquely demonstrated. "If my life was not important," a Japanese soldier recalled, "an enemy's life became inevitably much less important. . . . This philosophy led us to look down on the enemy."[20]

The Japanese army's *Field Service Code*, promulgated by then–war minister Hideki Tojo in 1941, laid out one consequential implication of this severe martial doctrine: "Never give up a position but rather die." The *Field Service Code* contained no instructions on how to surrender, offered no guidance about what to do if captured, made no mention of the Geneva Convention for treatment of prisoners of war. To surrender was to be disgraced. Reciprocally, enemies who surrendered were regarded as craven cowards shorn of dignity and respect. Those few Japanese soldiers who did fall into American hands frequently gave false names (often that of a famous Kabuki actor, Kazuo Hasegawa) or begged that notification of their capture not be sent to their homeland, for fear of reprisals against their families. More immediately, fear of the Americans reinforced Japanese reluctance to raise the white flag. Eighty-four percent of Japanese prisoners interrogated in one study stated that they had expected to be tortured or killed if captured. Rumors circulated among Japanese troops that young Americans qualified for the marine corps by murdering their parents and that raping civilians was standard American military practice.

Those accounts were fanciful, but others were not. American servicemen strafed lifeboats, shot prisoners, mutilated the dead, slashed open the cheeks of the wounded to gouge out gold teeth, made necklaces of severed Japanese ears, decorated vehicles with Japanese skulls, and fashioned letter openers from Japanese bones (one was sent to Franklin Roosevelt, who refused it). The *Baltimore Sun* ran a story in 1943 about a mother whose son had cut off a Japanese ear that she wished to nail to her front door. "It is virtually inconceivable," writes Dower, "that

20. Iris Chang, *The Rape of Nanking: The Forgotten Holocaust of World War II* (New York: Basic Books, 1997), 58.

teeth, ears, and skulls could have been collected from German or Italian war dead and publicized in the Anglo-American countries without provoking an uproar; and in this we have yet another inkling of the racial dimensions of the war."[21]

Beginning with the treacherous ambush of some two dozen marines on Guadalcanal by Japanese soldiers purporting to surrender, both sides fell into the practice of taking few prisoners, though it was the outgunned and overwhelmed Japanese who most frequently were driven to fight to the death. Fear of mistreatment at the hands of the enemy inspired American troops to sometimes superhuman efforts to rescue wounded buddies, as Norman Mailer described in one of the most gripping of all World War II novels, *The Naked and the Dead*. Most of the twenty-five thousand Americans taken prisoner in the Pacific had surrendered in the Philippines in 1942. Their captors accorded them no better treatment than they themselves would have expected in such a fallen state. The Japanese frequently consigned guard duty to Formosans or Koreans, themselves cruelly mistreated by their imperial masters and inclined to mistreat their captives in turn. Ninety percent of American prisoners of war in the Pacific reported being beaten. More than a third died. Those who survived spent thirty-eight months in captivity on average and lost sixty-one pounds. In Europe, by contrast, the average American POW spent ten months in captivity and lost thirty-eight pounds. Virtually all the Americans who fell into German hands—99 percent—survived.[22]

There were other differences from Europe. The Pacific was a peculiarly alien place for American servicemen, and an achingly lonely one too. Most of the fighting took place in the tropics, home to exotic diseases like dengue fever and filariasis, a lymphatic infection. Malaria was so endemic throughout the Pacific islands that troops on the ground were put on a compulsory regimen of Atabrine, a drug of dubious efficacy which the men resisted because it jaundiced the skin and was rumored to cause insanity and impotence. For the moment, impotence was in any case a small worry, since there were few available women, as evidenced by the fact that servicemen in the Pacific had markedly lower rates of venereal disease, the traditional soldier's scourge, than did those in Europe. AWOL (Absent Without Leave) rates were also lower in the Pacific, because there was no place to go. So was the incidence

---

21. Dower, *War without Mercy*, 26n., 68, 66.
22. Lee Kennett, *G.I.: The American Soldier in World War II* (New York: Charles Scribner's Sons, 1987), 184–87.

of death and wounding, since most casualties were inflicted by artillery and mortar shelling, for which the Japanese were not well equipped. The standard Japanese infantry rifle was also of such inferior design that it forced Japanese soldiers into close-quarters fighting, for which they kept their bayonets fixed at all times. Unlike their comrades in Europe, who typically fought long campaigns against modern, mechanized German adversaries, fighting usually at rifle-shot-length and beyond, the American soldiers and marines in the Pacific experienced a war of isolation, boredom, and disease, punctuated by long ocean crossings and brief bursts of combat, much of it in harrowing hand-to-hand struggle with poorly outfitted but ferociously motivated Japanese Imperial soldiers.

THE PACIFIC was also physically vast. More than three thousand miles of ocean separated San Diego from Honolulu; five thousand miles lay between Hawaii and the Philippines; twenty-five hundred between Tarawa and the Marianas; two thousand between the Mariana islet of Tinian and Hiroshima. Those distances dictated Japan's war plan, which was to fight a strategic defense-in-depth behind a series of concentric lines defined by the far-flung island chains that ringed the Japanese homeland: the Gilberts and the Marshalls in midocean Micronesia; the Philippines, Formosa, and the Ryukyus in the China Sea; and the Carolines and Marianas to Japan's south.

To reach and penetrate those widely separated fortifications, the U.S. Navy built a stupendous flotilla, organized around the novel technology of naval air power. Its fighting heart was an immense "Task Force," somewhat confusingly designated Task Force 38, or Third Fleet, when commanded by the impulsive, charismatic Admiral Halsey, and Task Force 58, or Fifth Fleet, when commanded by the methodical, self-effacing Admiral Raymond A. Spruance. The fourteen or more Essex-class carriers at the Task Force's core—888-foot-long floating airfields with three-thousand-man crews—could each embark up to one hundred aircraft. Supported by enormous "fleet trains" of oilers, ammunition ships, tenders, repair vessels, lighters, escort carriers, seagoing tugs, hospital ships, and a screen of battleships, cruisers, and destroyers, Halsey and Spruance could keep their long-legged carriers at sea for indefinite periods and could range over virtually the entire Pacific. From the bridges of their flagships in TF 38/58, they commanded several times the striking power of Nagumo's force that attacked Pearl Harbor.

Not until the end of 1943 was a plan agreed upon for waging offensive

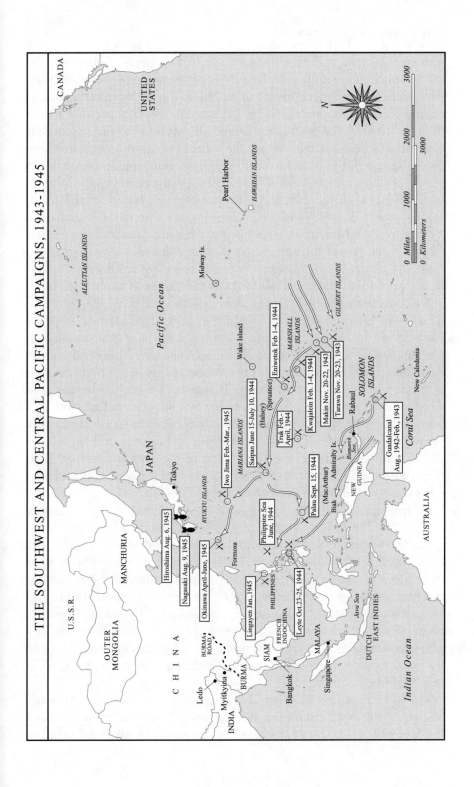

THE SOUTHWEST AND CENTRAL PACIFIC CAMPAIGNS, 1943-1945

CANADA

UNITED STATES

Pearl Harbor

HAWAIIAN ISLANDS

ALEUTIAN ISLANDS

Pacific Ocean

Midway Is.

Wake Island

Eniwetok Feb 1-4, 1944

MARSHALL ISLANDS

Kwajalein Feb. 1-4, 1944

Makin Nov. 20-22, 1943

Tarawa Nov. 20-23, 1943

GILBERT ISLANDS

N

3000

0   1000   2000   3000
Miles
0   Kilometers   3000

U.S.S.R.

OUTER MONGOLIA

MANCHURIA

C H I N A

JAPAN

Tokyo

Hiroshima Aug. 6, 1945

Nagasaki Aug. 9, 1945

RYUKYU ISLANDS

Okinawa April-June, 1945

Formosa

Iwo Jima Feb.-Mar., 1945

MARIANA ISLANDS

Saipan June 15-July 10, 1944

(Halsey)

(Spruance)

Truk Feb.-April, 1944

Ledo

Myitkyina

INDIA

BURMA

BURMA ROAD

Bangkok

SIAM

FRENCH INDOCHINA

MALAYA

Singapore

DUTCH EAST INDIES

Java Sea

Indian Ocean

Lingayen Jan., 1945

PHILIPPINES

Leyte Oct.23-25, 1944

Philippine Sea June, 1944

Palau Sept. 15, 1944

(MacArthur)

Biak

Admiralty Is.

NEW GUINEA

Bismarck Sea

Rabaul

SOLOMON ISLANDS

Guadalcanal Aug., 1942-Feb., 1943

Coral Sea

New Caledonia

AUSTRALIA

war against Japan, and even then it contained elements of opportunism, compromise, and willful indecision. The desire to placate Douglas Mac-Arthur, the political need to appear faithful to the dispossessed American colony of the Philippines, and the investment already somewhat adventitiously made in the Southwest Pacific all conspired to the approval of MacArthur's demand that he be allowed to continue up the northern New Guinea shore, liberate the Philippines, and prepare for a further assault on Formosa and the China Coast. At the same time, the navy would wage a second campaign, thrusting across the Central Pacific, through the Gilberts, Marshalls, Carolines, and Marianas, to converge eventually with MacArthur's anticipated offensive against Formosa and China. Japan would thus be cut off from its sources of supply in South Asia, and China-based American bombers as well as amphibious assault forces would lie within striking range of the Japanese home islands.

Underlying the Central Pacific drive was the navy's old Orange Plan, which had envisioned a "decisive battle" with the Japanese Imperial Navy in the broad waters of the western Pacific. For that reason, the navy tended to favor the Central Pacific advance over MacArthur's effort in the Southwest Pacific, but for the time being the Joint Chiefs assigned no clear priority to either campaign. Before 1944 was out, however, two developments would significantly modify this two-pronged scheme: Japanese successes against Chiang in the Ichi-go Campaign effectively precluded the use of Chinese airbases, robbing Formosa and the China coast of strategic value; and the advent of the new, long-range B-29 Superfortress bomber made it possible to mount aerial attacks on Japan from bases in the Marianas, notably from Tinian.

In June 1944, virtually at the same moment that the huge D-Day armada was churning across the English Channel, Admiral Nimitz launched Spruance and Task Force 58 against the Marianas. After the costly lessons of Tarawa and Anzio, the Americans had refined their techniques of amphibious warfare. They had improved their communication systems, had rehearsed better coordination of naval gunfire and tactical air support for the assault troops, and now defined the landing phase of the attack not as a discrete operation but as part of an "amphibious blitzkrieg," making maximum use of firepower and motorized transport to sweep across the beaches and as far inland as possible in one continuous thrust.

On June 13 a line of seven battleships began raining shellfire onto Saipan, at the northern end of the Mariana chain. On the morning of the fifteenth, ringed by a huge protective cordon of battleships, cruisers, carriers, and support vessels and covered by air strikes along the green fringe of shore, transports began disgorging armored amphibian craft. Their 75mm cannon and machine guns blasted away at the beach, clearing the way for the assault troops in hundreds of amphibious tractors ("amphtracs"), wave after wave of them, ninety-six abreast in every wave. Each amphtrac carried a dozen terrified young men over the island's coral reef, across the lagoon it enclosed, and onto the beaches. Mortar and artillery shell-bursts pocked the water all around them while shrapnel and machine-gun rounds thudded and rattled against the sides of the little landing craft. The offshore breeze assaulted their nostrils with the stench of night soil–covered fields. Many trembling men in the amphtracs vomited; others fouled themselves. Within twenty minutes eight thousand troops were ashore; by nightfall, twenty thousand; within days, nearly a hundred thousand—one army and three marine divisions, as well as numerous service and construction battalions (CBs, or, more colloquially, Seabees).

Despite the Americans' heavy firepower, swift movement, and concentrated force, the Japanese garrison, thirty-two thousand strong, fought back fiercely. The defenders pushed a large bulge into the center of the American line, held by the Army's 27th Division, a New York National Guard unit whose commander was relieved of his post—by the *marine* general in overall command, igniting an interservice squabble that echoed long thereafter.

With continuing support from naval gunfire, the Americans pressed steadily inland. Segregated Negro units performed especially well. Marine Corps Commandant Archer Vandegrift announced that with the Battle of Saipan, "[t]he Negro Marines are no longer on trial. They are Marines, period."[23] The Japanese made the Americans pay for every yard of advance. On July 7 three thousand desperate Japanese troops, some wielding no weapon other than a knife tied to a bamboo pole, rushed the American line, screaming the Japanese battle cry, "Banzai!" (literally, ten thousand years). They inflicted heavy casualties but were themselves annihilated virtually to a man.

Meanwhile, at Marpi Point at Saipan's northern tip, thousands of Japanese civilians, mostly women and children, scuttled frantically to the lip of the two-hundred-foot cliffs at the sea's edge, evidently preferring suicide to capture by the Americans. Interpreters and a few captured Japanese soldiers, shouting through bullhorns from boats below, begged

23. Spector, 390.

them not to jump, but as many as a thousand people leapt to their deaths on the rocks and in the surf below or blew themselves up with hand grenades. The Americans gaped at the spectacle in horrified astonishment. When one couple hesitated at the cliff's edge, a Japanese sniper shot them both, then walked defiantly out of his hiding place and crumpled under a hail of American bullets. "What did all this self-destruction mean?" asked war correspondent Robert Sherrod in *Time* magazine. "Did it mean that the Japanese on Saipan believed their own propaganda which told them that Americans are beasts and would murder them all . . . ? Do the suicides of Saipan mean that the whole Japanese race will choose death before surrender?" The civilian deaths on Saipan, their numbers exaggerated both in American press accounts and in Japanese propaganda, reinforced the conviction of both adversaries that the finish-fight would be bloodiest of struggles. At battle's end on July 9, the Americans on Saipan had suffered some fourteen thousand casualties, including 3,426 killed. Almost the entire Japanese garrison had perished, along with thousands of civilians. Within another month, American forces secured the neighboring island of Tinian, as well as Guam, the first scrap of conquered American territory retaken from Japan.[24]

As the battle for Saipan was raging on the night of July 15, Spruance received word that a large Japanese naval force was bearing down on the Marianas, with the apparent intention of giving battle to Spruance's Task Force 58 — or maybe of disrupting the Saipan landings. The news confronted Spruance with a painful decision: should he continue to protect the landing operation at Saipan, his assigned mission, or break away to intercept and engage the Japanese fleet? His blood raced at the thought that with just a few hours steaming he might at last be in a position to fight the Orange Plan's "decisive battle" and achieve the war's ultimate naval victory. He had fifteen carriers on station, embarking nearly a thousand aircraft, a mighty force. He ravened to go. When Nimitz radioed him that "we count on you to make the victory decisive," go he did. Leaving several surface ships behind to screen Saipan, Spruance gathered up his carriers and plunged away from the Marianas into the open waters of the Philippine Sea.

As Spruance probed southwestward in pursuit of his adversary, Vice-

24. Robert Sherrod, *On to Westward* (New York: Duell, Sloan and Pearce, 1945), 146; *Time*, August 7, 1944, 27; Haruko Taya Cook, "The Myth of the Saipan Suicides," *MHQ* (Spring 1995): 12–19.

Admiral Jisaburo Ozawa pushed his nine carriers northeastward to find Spruance. Despite the greater size of the American fleet, Ozawa held some formidable assets. Japan still possessed numerous island-airfields in the Philippine Sea, from which land-based aircraft could join in the battle and to which his own carrier-based planes could fly in one-way "shuttle" attacks that substantially increased their operational range. The lighter Japanese carrier planes in any case had a greater combat radius than their more heavily armed and armored American counterparts, a difference of some 560 miles to 350 miles. In this oceanic region, too, the easterly tradewinds favored Ozawa with the lee gauge, so that he could launch and recover his aircraft while steaming into the wind and simultaneously closing with his enemy. Spruance, in contrast, had to turn his ships to windward, back toward the Marianas and away from Ozawa, to conduct flight operations. What was more, Spruance could not put out of mind his commitments at Saipan. He well knew what had happened on the night of August 8, 1942, when Frank Jack Fletcher had pulled his carriers away from Savo Sound, contributing to the U.S. Navy's worst-ever defeat at sea and nearly scuttling the Guadalcanal landing. So when he had still not found Ozawa by the night of June 18, Spruance ordered his ships to backtrack toward Saipan, while still flying off search planes to look for the Japanese fleet.

As the two naval forces groped for each other across the waters of the Philippine Sea, both commanders itching for the decisive battle, one of Ozawa's scout planes at last spotted TF 58 on the morning of June 19. Ozawa immediately flew off four waves of attacking aircraft. They had the advantage of surprise, but not for long. Radar operators on the battleship screen to the west of Spruance's carriers picked up Ozawa's lead planes, and within minutes hundreds of aircraft lifted off the decks of the American ships. Deep within the bowels of the carrier *Lexington*, fighter-direction teams made further use of radar to calculate the enemy's direction, level, and speed of approach, environing conditions of cloud cover and sun angles, and relative force sizes and dispositions. Swiftly computing the mix of these complex variables, they vectored American pilots into optimal positions for attack.

The Americans had yet another telling advantage. U.S. naval aviators had at least two years of flight training and over three hundred hours in the air before facing combat. Battle-tested pilots were rotated home to help school the next generation of aviators, so that the entire American air contingent by 1944 represented an accumulation of training and experience that had no equal among its enemies. Japanese pilots flew until they died. Japan had long since lost most of the highly skilled fliers with whom it started the war and had made poor provision for training replacements. Most of Ozawa's pilots had no more than six months of training, and some as little as two. Fuel shortages had by this time become so acute in Japan that student pilots got much of their instruction on the ground, watching films shot by a boom-mounted camera simulating different approaches to six-foot models of American warships in an artificial lake.

The result on June 19 was an immense aerial slaughter. By the end of the day, American pilots had shot down more than three hundred Japanese planes while losing fewer than thirty of their own. U.S. submarines meanwhile sank two Japanese carriers. In a desperate last pursuit of Ozawa's fleet in the twilight hours of June 20, American pilots operating at and beyond the limits of their flying range sent a third Japanese carrier to the bottom. In the darkness that followed, though Spruance defied caution and lit up all his ships to facilitate recovery, dozens of American aircraft were wrecked attempting night landings, for which they were not trained, or were forced to ditch in the inky sea.

In the typically heedless vernacular of the victors, U.S. aviators called the Battle of the Philippine Sea "the Great Marianas Turkey Shoot." It was, by any standard, an overwhelming victory, the greatest carrier battle of the war and one that effectively extinguished the Japanese navy's capacity to give battle in the air. The Imperial Navy had lost three fleet carriers and some 480 aircraft all told, and its pool of already ill-trained pilots had dwindled to the vanishing point. "It will be extremely difficult," a Japanese admiral wrote, "to recover from this disaster and rise again."[25]

Yet some senior U.S. Navy commanders criticized Spruance for letting Ozawa escape with as many ships as he did. Because he had hung back to protect Saipan and had not more aggressively pursued Ozawa, the Battle of the Philippine Sea did not shape up as the "decisive fleet action" for which both American and Japanese sailors still hungered. The unsated yearning of both navies to fight that battle would have telling consequences just sixteen weeks later, in the next battle to be fought in the Philippine Sea, at Leyte Gulf.

NEWS OF SAIPAN'S LOSS brought down the government of General Hideki Tojo on July 18. A few senior Japanese statesmen thought

25. Thomas J. Cutler, *The Battle of Leyte Gulf* (New York: HarperCollins, 1994), 47.

that the time had come for a civilian premier who might put Japan on the road to liquidating its disastrous military adventure, but their faint voices went unheeded. The generals and the admirals still held the upper hand. Kuniaki Koiso, another general, succeeded Tojo as Japan's premier. The men who started the war were still in power and showed no sign of wanting to end it. Though Japan's defeat was now all but certain, its surrender was not. The conflict seemed to have generated its own momentum, with no stopping point in sight.

There was inertia on the American side too. While Tojo's government was falling in the last days of July 1944, Franklin Roosevelt had traveled to Hawaii to confer with his Pacific commanders, Nimitz and MacArthur, about the next phase of the Pacific war. Now that the Marianas were securely in American hands, their ostensible agenda was to decide whether MacArthur's Southwest Pacific or Nimitz's Central Pacific campaign should have priority. Nimitz and some strategists in Washington were advocating that the Philippines be bypassed in favor of an assault on Formosa or the Ryukyus, or even a direct attack on Japan from the Marianas. MacArthur predictably insisted that he should press on to the liberation of the Philippines. If their Filipino "wards" were left to languish, MacArthur reportedly warned Roosevelt, "I dare say that the American people would be so aroused that they would register most complete resentment against you at the polls this fall"—an astonishingly audacious and thinly veiled political threat, unimaginable from any American commander save MacArthur.

Political considerations may in any case have had more to do with Roosevelt's trip than strategic ones. He and MacArthur struck a deal, at least implicitly: the general could go on to Manila, and the president would profit from MacArthur's favorable news reports about the progress of the Pacific war and from the general's flattering comments about FDR's strategic acuity. After a scant three hours of talk on July 28 in an airy mansion on Honolulu's Waikiki Beach, a parody of a strategic discussion, the conferees reached their mutually beneficial nondecision: both campaigns, to the Philippines and through the Central Pacific, would continue.[26]

On August 26, 1944, as scheduled, Fifth Fleet passed from Spruance's hands to Halsey's and once again became Third Fleet. In an exceedingly bloody action, Halsey proceeded to seize the Palau Islands, considered

26. James MacGregor Burns, *Roosevelt: The Soldier of Freedom* (New York: Harcourt Brace Jovanovich, 1970), 489.

necessary to secure the invasion route to the Philippines. He also raided the Japanese airfields on Formosa, destroying more than five hundred of Japan's rapidly disappearing stock of combat aircraft. In the course of air attacks on the Philippines in September, an American flier shot down over Leyte managed to get back to his ship and report that there were virtually no Japanese on the island. That discovery changed the destination for the Philippine invasion and accelerated its timetable. Now the attacking troops would go ashore not on Mindanao, as originally planned, but on the more northerly island of Leyte, in the gulf of the same name on the island's southeastern coast. Halsey's Third Fleet would cover the landings, as Spruance had been charged to do at Saipan. But Nimitz's orders to Halsey contained an unmistakable echo of both men's frustration that Spruance had missed the decisive battle with Ozawa in the Philippine Sea: "In case opportunity for destruction of major portion of the enemy fleet offers or can be created, such destruction becomes the primary task."[27]

On October 20, 1944, the invasion convoys began unloading on the lightly defended beach at Leyte Gulf. In a carefully arranged ritual, MacArthur walked down the ramp of a landing craft and waded ashore through the shallow surf, a moment captured in one of the war's most famous photographs. "People of the Philippines," MacArthur intoned into a waiting microphone, "I have returned. . . . The hour of your redemption is here. . . . Rally to me."[28]

American submarines had by now cut Japan's oil supplies to a trickle. What little there was reached Japan from the Dutch East Indies behind a screen of islands that ran from the Philippines through Formosa and the Ryukyus. Japan had to defend the Philippines or risk seeing its lifeline to the south completely severed.[29]

To conserve precious fuel, the Imperial Navy had been forced to base

27. Cutler, *Battle of Leyte Gulf*, 60.
28. Douglas MacArthur, *Reminiscences* (New York: McGraw-Hill, 1964), 216–17.
29. U.S. submarines largely succeeded in doing to Japan what German submarines had failed to do to Britain: interdicting the island nation's merchant marine and choking off its supplies of food, fuel, and raw materials. Inexplicably, Japan never prepared for antisubmarine warfare and deployed its own submarines almost exclusively against enemy warships or in resupply operations to isolated garrisons. American submarines, in contrast, concentrated on the Japanese merchant marine, which by war's end had been reduced to about one-third of its size in 1941 and consisted mostly of small wooden vessels in the Inland Sea. U.S. submarines accounted for 201 of the 686 Japanese warships sunk during the war but sank more than 1,200 Japanese merchantmen, 60 percent of the total destroyed. Morison, 511.

THE BATTLE OF LEYTE GULF, OCT. 23-25, 1944, AND THE PHILIPPINE CAMPAIGN

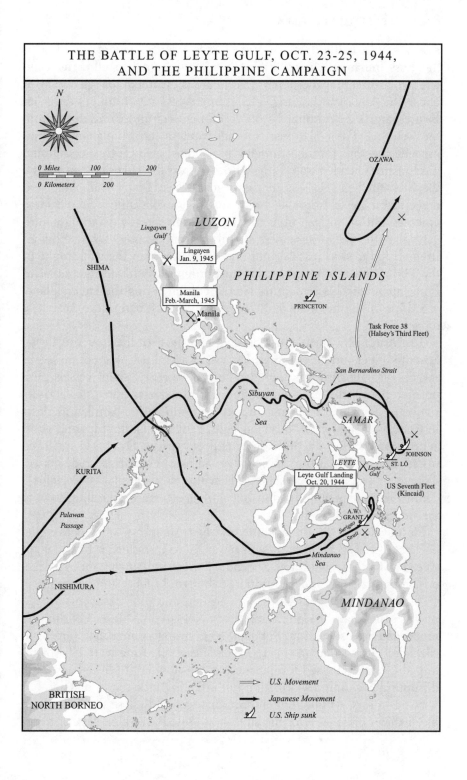

N

0 Miles 100 200
0 Kilometers 200

OZAWA

LUZON

Lingayen Gulf

Lingayen
Jan. 9, 1945

SHIMA

PHILIPPINE ISLANDS

Manila
Feb.-March, 1945

PRINCETON

Manila

Task Force 38
(Halsey's Third Fleet)

San Bernardino Strait

Sibuyan

Sea

SAMAR

JOHNSON
ST. LÔ

KURITA

LEYTE

Leyte Gulf Landing
Oct. 20, 1944

Leyte
Gulf

US Seventh Fleet
(Kincaid)

Palawan Passage

A.W.
GRANT

Surigao Strait

Mindanao Sea

NISHIMURA

MINDANAO

⟹ U.S. Movement

➡ Japanese Movement

⚓ U.S. Ship sunk

BRITISH
NORTH BORNEO

nearly half its battle fleet at Lingga Roads, near Singapore and close to the East Indian oil fields. From there, and from two other fleet anchorages, three Japanese naval formations steamed toward Leyte to check the American landing. Vice-Admiral Shoji Nishimura's force left Brunei, and Vice-Admiral Kiyohide Shima's column came down from the Ryukyus. Their plan was to rendezvous in the Mindanao Sea and proceed together through Surigao Strait into Leyte Gulf. Vice-Admiral Takeo Kurita headed from Lingga Roads across the Palawan Passage and the Sibuyan Sea. He was to pass through San Bernardino Strait and descend on Leyte from the north just as the Nishimura-Shima force emerged out of Surigao from the west. To this already dauntingly intricate plan the Japanese added a further complication: Ozawa, his air strength reduced to just a handful of warplanes after the catastrophe in the Philippine Sea and the raids on Formosa, would steam southward from Japan with his remaining aircraft carriers, using the largely planeless ships as sacrificial decoys to lure away at least part of the American force.

The Americans meanwhile brought two fleets of their own to Leyte. Seventh Fleet, under Admiral Thomas C. Kinkaid, was composed of several big gunships and eighteen "escort carriers," small vessels built on merchant hulls, each embarking just two dozen warplanes and designed principally for ferrying aircraft, anti–submarine patrol, and close-in tactical air support for beach assaults. Kinkaid's battle ships and cruisers took up station off the eastern end of Surigao Strait. He deployed his escort carriers in three six-ship squadrons, respectively code-named Taffy 1, 2, and 3, off Samar Island on the east side of Leyte. Halsey's Third Fleet meanwhile held its big carriers off San Bernardino Strait to the north.

Six naval forces, four Japanese and two American, were converging on Leyte Gulf to fight the largest naval battle in history, a titanic clash spread over three days and a hundred thousand square miles of sea, engaging 282 ships and two hundred thousand sailors and airmen.

Nishimura's two battleships, one cruiser, and four destroyers arrived in the Mindanao Sea on October 24. Not finding Shima, Nishimura proceeded on his own into Surigao Strait, through waters that Ferdinand Magellan had sailed in 1521. As darkness fell, American PT (patrol torpedo) boats harassed the Japanese column while it plowed eastward, disrupting Nishimura's formation but inflicting little damage. Then five U.S. destroyers, withholding gunfire that would disclose their positions, raced down either side of the strait and loosed several volleys of torpedoes that knocked out one of the battleships and three of the destroyers. There followed a maneuver whose classic naval geometry Magellan himself would have appreciated. Arrayed in a battle line across the neck of the strait were Kinkaid's six battleships, five of them survivors of Pearl Harbor, together with four heavy and four light cruisers. Kinkaid had effortlessly "crossed the T," the dream of every sea commander since the dawn of gun-bearing ships. Perpendicular to Kinkaid's six-, eight-, fourteen-, and sixteen-inch guns, Nishimura's truncated column lay all but naked under round after round of thundering American broadsides. Firing by radar direction from a range of more than twenty miles, the American battle line laid down a fearsome barrage. The Japanese formation disintegrated. The second battleship went down, the cruiser was crippled, and the lone surviving destroyer reversed course and withdrew. When the late-arriving Shima sailed into this chaotic melee and collided with Nashimura's wallowing cruiser, he too decided to withdraw, but pursuing American warships and planes sank three of his ships. All told, the Battle of Surigao Strait cost the Imperial Japanese Navy two battleships, three cruisers, and four destroyers. The Americans lost one PT boat, as well as 39 sailors killed and 114 wounded, most of them on the U.S. destroyer *Albert W. Grant*, which was caught in a murderous crossfire from both Japanese and American guns during the bedlam of the night battle.

In the pewter morning light, U.S. rescue vessels crept into the strait to pick up the thousands of Japanese survivors. Most of the swimmers submerged themselves below the oil-stained surface as the Americans approached, choosing death by drowning over the shame of capture.

To the north, meanwhile, U.S. submarines had intercepted Kurita's formidable group of three battleships, twelve cruisers, and thirteen destroyers as they made their way across Palawan Passage on October 23. Several well-placed torpedo volleys damaged one cruiser and sank two others, including Kurita's flagship. Fished from the sea, Kurita transferred his flag to the *Yamato*. The *Yamato* and its sister ship *Musashi* were the two biggest battleships afloat, mounting eighteen-inch guns that fired one-and-a-half ton projectiles, larger than any gun in the U.S. Navy could throw. Halsey's fliers caught Kurita again in the Sibuyan Sea on the following day and sank another cruiser as well as the supposedly impregnable *Musashi*. Land-based Japanese aircraft meanwhile attacked Third Fleet and sent the carrier *Princeton* to the bottom.

Halsey's airmen reported that Kurita's force had no train or transports, a sure sign that the Japanese flotilla had sortied only to give battle at sea, not to land reinforcements on Leyte. Halsey was spoiling for a fight. He drafted a contingency battle plan, signaling to Nimitz at Pearl Harbor that he intended to detach several ships to form a new "Task Force 34" that would stop Kurita at the mouth of San Bernardino Strait. But there was one thing wrong: Kurita's force was composed entirely of surface gunships. Where were the Japanese carriers, the great prize for which Halsey thirsted?

The answer was that they were to Halsey's north, doing their best to be discovered and tempt Halsey away from San Bernardino. When some of Third Fleet's fliers reported at midday on the twenty-fourth that they had engaged planes with tail-hooks, unmistakably identifying them as carrier-based aircraft, Halsey was off like a greyhound after a hare. Faced with the choice of protection or pursuit, and believing erroneously that he had already inflicted enough damage on Kurita to stop him, Halsey scarcely hesitated. He scrapped the plan to create Task Force 34 and steamed away with his entire fleet to chase the Japanese carriers. Like George Armstrong Custer in search of the Sioux on the high plains in 1876, Halsey worried that the Japanese would cut and run before he could wage the decisive battle, as Ozawa had managed to do to Spruance in the Philippine Sea. Emulating Custer in that perilously exhilarating moment atop Medicine Tail Coulee, now that Halsey had spotted his adversary he lunged reflexively after him. He took Ozawa's bait, leaving the door of San Bernardino Strait wide open for Kurita.

Through San Bernardino Kurita steamed unopposed shortly after midnight on October 25. His badly mauled but still powerful force bore down on the most northerly of Kinkaid's escort-carrier squadrons, Taffy 3. A colossal mismatch ensued — the *Yamato* and several heavy and light cruisers against a handful of destroyers and six escort carriers never designed for full-scale battle at sea. Slow, thinly armored, undergunned, and mostly munitioned with ordnance for tactical air support, the "baby flat-tops" were sitting ducks. Great green, purple, and yellow geysers erupted among them as Japanese shells, with their telltale dye-marked bursts, scattered the surprised American ships. Taffy 3's little carriers made smoke and dove into a rain squall for further concealment, while the U.S. destroyers brazenly charged the larger and more numerous Japanese ships. The destroyer *Johnston* took so many hits from the huge Japanese gun batteries that one crewman compared it to "a puppy being smacked by a truck." Eventually, he said, "we were in a position where all the gallantry and guts in the world could not save us," and Abandon

Ship was ordered. A swimming survivor saw a Japanese officer salute as the *Johnston* slipped beneath the surface.[30]

Kinkaid and Nimitz meanwhile were frantically signaling to Halsey for help. At 10:00 A.M. on the twenty-fifth, a signalman handed Halsey a message from Nimitz that was destined to become notorious: "Where is, Repeat, Where is Task Force 34, The World Wonders?" The last phrase, "The World Wonders," was "padding," the kind of verbiage, frequently nonsensical, that was routinely inserted in encrypted messages to foil enemy cryptographers. (Nimitz's full message read: "Turkey Trots to Water RR Where Is Rpt Where Is Task Force Thirty Four RR The World Wonders?," with the double capital letters setting off the real message.) But the decoding officer on Halsey's flagship apparently believed the end-padding in Nimitz's signal was part of the message. He typed it onto the page that was handed to the admiral. The presumed insult unnerved Halsey. He threw his hat to the deck and began to sob. An aide shook him by the shoulders. "What the hell's the matter with you? Pull yourself together!"[31]

Third Fleet's carriers continued to press the attack on Ozawa, all four of whose carriers eventually went down, including *Zuikaku*, the last survivor from the force that had lofted the planes that opened the war at Pearl Harbor. Halsey, however, headed back to Samar with his battleship group. He was too late to relieve Kinkaid, but it scarcely mattered. Kurita, perhaps rattled by his unplanned swim in Palawan Passage, had incredibly concluded that the little scratch force of baby flat-tops desperately trying to evade him off Samar was Halsey's powerful, big-carrier TF 38. Ironically, at about the moment Halsey was reading Nimitz's radiogram, Kurita decided to break off the attack and head back to Lingga Roads.

The epic battle of Leyte Gulf was not quite over. Even as Kurita was withdrawing, the Japanese launched a fearsome new weapon against the Taffy groups: suicide attacks by land-based kamikaze warplanes. *Kamikaze* means "divine wind," a reference to the typhoon that scattered Kublai Khan's invasion fleet headed for Japan in the thirteenth century. Kamikaze pilots prepared for their missions with elaborate ceremonials, including ritual prayer, the composition of farewell poems, and the presentation to each flier of a "thousand-stitch belt," a strip of cloth into

30. Morison, 457–58.
31. Spector, 438; Cutler, *Battle of Leyte Gulf*, 250–51.

which one thousand women had each sewn a stitch, symbolically uniting themselves with the pilot's ultimate sacrifice. Late in the morning of October 25, the first wave of kamikazes lashed out of the sky over Taffy 3. One headed straight for the escort carrier *St. Lô*. Disbelieving antiaircraft gunners tried desperately to knock it down, to no avail. The plane crashed into the *St. Lô*'s flight deck and disgorged a bomb deep into the ship's interior. As sailors on nearby ships watched in horrified fascination, the *St. Lô* exploded, heeled over on her side, and sank with 114 men aboard. It was a grisly demonstration of the kind of resistance Japan was still prepared to offer.

The Battle of Leyte Gulf ended an era, but it did not end the war. The encounters at Surigao and at Samar were the last of their kind. They closed an epoch of ship-to-ship gunnery duels, the standard form of naval warfare for centuries before 1944. No nation would ever again build a battleship; aircraft carriers had proved themselves as the final arbiters of battle at sea. The Imperial Japanese Navy had suffered a crushing defeat, losing four carriers, three battleships, nine cruisers, a dozen destroyers, hundreds of aircraft and thousands of sailors and pilots. But as the kamikaze raids spectacularly illustrated, Japan had not lost its will to fight.

The Japanese army rapidly reinforced Leyte, which MacArthur did not manage to secure until December, when it became the staging area for his next assault on the main Philippine island of Luzon. Renewed and even more deadly kamikaze attacks shredded the American invasion convoys on their way to Luzon's Lingayen Gulf on January 9, 1945. MacArthur landed more than ten divisions at Lingayen, the largest assault force to date in the Pacific war, but General Tomoyuki Yamashita denied it easy victory with a shrewdly executed defensive campaign. Fighting a war of attrition in mountainous, Italian-like terrain that favored the defenders, Yamashita held out for months. Other Japanese units resisted still longer in the outlying Philippine Islands, a few diehards even beyond the formal end of the war. On Palawan Island, the Japanese herded 140 American and Filipino POWs into a trench, doused them with gasoline, and burned them alive. Reports of that and other atrocities spurred MacArthur to intensify his campaign to liberate Philippine territory, a costly operation that had little direct bearing by this time on Japan's ultimate defeat. The Battle of Manila in February and March, a vicious street-by-street affair that resembled some of the cruelest fighting in Berlin or Warsaw, took the lives of a hundred thousand Filipino civilians and thousands of American soldiers. Yamashita's tactics of delay, his soldiers' willingness to fight to the last breath, and the mounting savagery of combat provided a bitter foretaste of what awaited the Americans to the north, on Iwo Jima and Okinawa.

WITH THE PHILIPPINES substantially secure by the end of March and the Formosa-China objective now definitely ruled out, Nimitz focused all his resources on the Central Pacific and on reaching Japan itself. In November 1944 new long-range B-29 Superfortresses had begun bombing Japanese cities from bases in the Marianas. Midway between Saipan and Tokyo lay Iwo Jima, literally "Sulfur Island," a diabolically forbidding 4.5-mile-long and 2.5-mile-wide chunk of rock reeking of sulfur from the dormant volcano of Mt. Suribachi at its south end and covered by a thick layer of fine black volcanic emissions. Nimitz wanted Iwo because its airfields and radar station forced the B-29s to fly a lengthy dogleg course from the Marianas to Japan. The Japanese were determined to hold it, one of their last outer defenses shielding the home islands.

The twenty-one-thousand-man Japanese garrison had honeycombed Iwo's basaltic ridges and Suribachi's ashen flanks with reinforced concrete-and-steel bunkers and stuffed them with artillery, antiaircraft guns, mortars, and machine guns. They were so well and deeply entrenched that seventy-two days of aerial bombing and three days of naval shelling barely scratched them. At first light on February 19 two divisions of marines, each man carrying up to a hundred pounds of gear, stepped from their amphtracs onto Iwo's beaches and sank to their boottops in the powdery mixture of sand and volcanic ash. Vehicles, including tanks and half-tracks, soon bogged down in the quicksand-like topping of pumice and cinder that blanketed the island. From the Japanese bunkers and pillboxes a hellish rain of shells and bullets pelted the beaches, where the marines seemed to be moving in slow motion through the sucking sand.

As they had done in preceding Pacific battles, Navaho "code-talkers" relayed messages among the marine units. The Navaho language, a branch of Athabaskan with no alphabet and highly irregular syntax, was known to fewer than three dozen non-Navahos in the world, none of them Japanese. Many Navahos thus volunteered for duty in the marine signal corps, and their native language was their own very special code. Though Navaho lacked words for many modern military terms, the

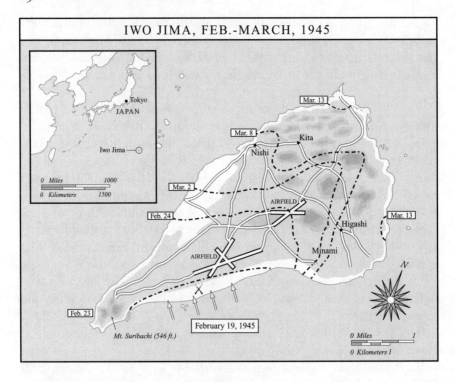

IWO JIMA, FEB.-MARCH, 1945

Tokyo
JAPAN

Iwo Jima —O

0 Miles   1000
0 Kilometers   1500

Mar. 13

Mar. 8
Kita
Nishi

Mar. 2

AIRFIELD

Feb. 24

Higashi   Mar. 13

Minami

AIRFIELD

X

Feb. 23

February 19, 1945

Mt. Suribachi (546 ft.)

N

0 Miles   1
0 Kilometers 1

code-talkers improvised: *chay-da-gahi*, turtle, for example, became their word for tank. Certain that no Japanese eavesdropper could understand them, the code-talkers spoke freely over their radios and walkie-talkies, creating one of the war's most secure communications systems.

On February 22 a Navaho code-talker notified the Pacific high command that the marines had planted an American flag on Mount *'dibeh* (Sheep), *no-dah-ih* (Ute), *gah* (Rabbit), *tkin* (Ice), *shush* (Bear), *wol-la-chee* (Ant), *moasi* (Cat), *lin* (Horse), *yeh-hes* (Itch): S-U-R-I-B-A-C-H-I. Working in a different medium altogether, Associated Press photographer Joe Rosenthal climbed up on some rocks and snapped a photograph of the Suribachi flag-raising that was destined to become one of the most famous images of the war and the inspiration for the Marine Corps monument near Arlington National Cemetery.[32]

Taking Suribachi did not end the fighting on Iwo Jima. The battle ground on for another month, with unmatched barbarity. Japanese soldiers stubbornly refused to surrender. Many died the most hideous of

32. *New York Times*, February 1, 1998, 21.

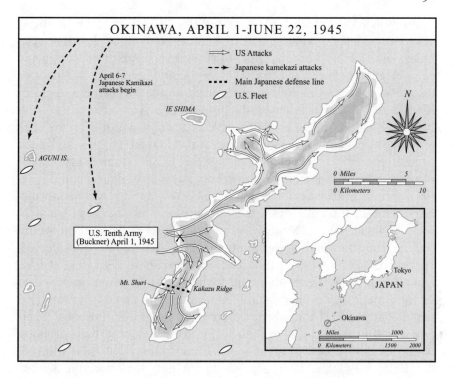

OKINAWA, APRIL 1-JUNE 22, 1945

deaths, incinerated by flamethrowers that jetted burning gasoline into their bunkers. When the fighting ended at last in late March, only a few hundred Japanese, mostly wounded, had allowed themselves to be taken prisoner. More than twenty thousand had perished, along with nearly six thousand U.S. marines. Another seventeen thousand marines had been wounded. Courage in battle, it has been said, consists in the desire to show other men that one has it. On Iwo Jima, many Americans showed courage above and beyond the call of duty. On a single day, five marines in the 5th Marine Division earned the Congressional Medal of Honor. "Among the Americans who served on Iwo Island," Nimitz wrote, "uncommon valor was a common virtue."[33]

More uncommon valor was needed just a month later, on the island of Okinawa, the largest in the Ryukyu chain. Commodore Matthew C. Perry had visited Okinawa in 1853, during the course of his historic voyage that ended two centuries of Japan's studied isolation from the rest of the world. Okinawa had been a Japanese prefecture since 1879.

33. Spector, 503.

Though its indigenous people were racially distinct from the Japanese, Tokyo considered Okinawa part of its heartland. It lay less than 350 miles south of the home islands. In American hands it could provide close-in airbases for attacks on Japan and could serve as a staging area for the massive amphibious assault on the southern Japanese island of Kyushu that was scheduled for the autumn of 1945.

On the Easter Sunday morning of April 1, 1945, standing on the crest of Mt. Shuri at Okinawa's southern end, Colonel Hiromichi Yahara peered through his binoculars across the island's rolling green hills planted to sweet potatoes and sugarcane. Far below him he could see a thousand American landing craft disembarking two army and two marine divisions. It seemed "as if the sea itself were advancing with a great roar," thought Yahara. Scarcely a single Japanese bullet greeted the invaders. "He who wields power is unperturbed," Yahara serenely reflected. He and the seventy-seven thousand other Japanese defenders of Okinawa, along with twenty thousand Okinawan militiamen, intended to let the Americans advance inland, then wear them down in a prolonged battle of attrition, as Yamashita had done to MacArthur on Luzon. Their power was in their spirit, in their fealty to Bushido and their devotion to the emperor. The Japanese on Okinawa knew that their ultimate defeat was inevitable. Their goal was to buy time to prepare the defense of the home islands and to inflict the kind of damage that might even yet induce the United States to sue for a compromise peace. They had built elaborate fortifications into the limestone ridges and rocky escarpments that belted the island's southern end. In that bristling redoubt they would fight to the last cartridge, and then die. They had limited munitions, no hope for reinforcements, and no effective long-range weapons against the Americans' terrifying tank-mounted flamethrowers. But they had volunteers who would serve as human bazookas, strapping twenty-two-pound satchel charges to their bodies and throwing themselves on a tank's hull or under its treads.[34]

As Yahara watched, the Americans kept coming, fifty thousand strong by evening, with nearly three times that number to follow in the succeeding days. General Simon Bolivar Buckner's invasion force rivaled Eisenhower's at Normandy in size. As the American troops felt their way forward and still met no resistance, Admiral Turner radioed to Nimitz:

34. Hiromichi Yahara, The Battle for Okinawa (New York: John Wiley and Sons, 1995), xi, xii, 12–13.

"I may be crazy but it looks like the Japanese have quit the war, at least in this sector." Nimitz replied: "Delete all after 'crazy.'"[35]

Nimitz was right. Five days after the virtually unopposed landing, the Americans ran up against Kakazu Ridge, the first of the Japanese defensive lines. As the marines and GIs tried to claw their way up the near-vertical 250-foot-cliffs, the defenders fought back with whatever they had. They dropped buckets of human excrement on the attackers clinging to the rock faces below them and grappled with the Americans in hand-to-hand combat. On the same day, Japanese fliers launched an enormous kamikaze attack on the U.S. fleet offshore. For weeks, waves of suicide planes in squadrons of up to three hundred aircraft, some three thousand sorties in all, defied steel blizzards of antiaircraft fire to zero in on the American ships. They sank 36, damaged 368 others, killed 4,900 sailors, wounded 4,824 more. Aboard the ships anchored off Okinawa, a correspondent wrote, the terror of the kamikaze onslaught "sent some men into hysteria, insanity, breakdown." In an equally desperate act, the Japanese Imperial Navy sortied the pride of its fleet, the great battleship *Yamato*, with only enough fuel in its bunkers for a one-way trip to Okinawa. Its mission was to disrupt the American fleet, then beach itself and employ its huge 18-inch-guns as a shore battery. But the *Yamato* had scarcely exited the Inland Sea when it was chased down by American planes and sunk on April 7.[36]

On April 12 the Japanese garrison on Okinawa briefly rejoiced at the news of Franklin Roosevelt's death. Their celebration was short-lived. The sheer weight of American men and firepower was taking a gruesome toll. The Americans improvised what the Japanese called "horse-mounting" attacks, placing themselves above and astride the mouth of a fortified cave, dropping drums of napalm into the cave entrance, igniting them with grenades or tracer bullets, then shooting all who fled to escape death by fire or suffocation. To avoid those fates, Japanese soldiers by the thousands retreated deep into the limestone caverns and killed themselves with grenades and cyanide injections. Piles of dead bodies putrefied in the dank caves. "Even the demons of the world would mourn at this sight," Yahara wrote.

Japanese staff officers, sometimes standing in waist-high water from underground flooding, took stock of the dwindling stores in their fetid

---

35. Spector, 534.
36. Spector, 539.

labyrinths with the help of the most ancient of calculators, an abacus. The Americans meanwhile deployed the most modern of technologies and the most abundant of arsenals against them. Radar-directed U.S. naval gunfire and aerial bombardment shook the very mountains, while flamethrowing tanks spewed burning tongues of jellied gasoline into the Japanese fortifications. In early June what was left of the Japanese garrison tried to mount a counterattack. Some six thousand men, armed only with sidearms and bamboo spears, *banzai*ed forward. They encountered "millions of shells from the enemy's formidable fleet, planes, and tanks," Yahara recorded. "All vanished like the morning dew."[37]

Late in June the Japanese commander on Okinawa, General Mitsuru Ushijima, ordered an assistant to behead him after he had thrust the ritual hara-kiri dagger into his own abdomen. Before the general died, one of his staff officers took up a writing brush, dipped it in red ink, and formed the Kanji characters that composed Ushijima's last directive to his few surviving soldiers: "Every man in these fortifications will follow his superior officer's order and fight to the end for the sake of the motherland. . . . Do not suffer the shame of being taken prisoner."[38]

Few did. When the battle officially ended on June 22, only some 7,000 Japanese of the original complement of 77,000 remained alive. The fighting had also killed over 100,000 Okinawan civilians. The Americans suffered 7,613 killed or missing, 31,807 wounded, and 26,211 non-battle casualties on the island, a nearly 35 percent casualty rate, in addition to the nearly 5,000 who died and 4,824 who were wounded at sea. Among the dead were Buckner, his chest sundered by a Japanese shell fragment, as well as the celebrated war correspondent Ernie Pyle, felled by a sniper's bullet. The awful carnage on Okinawa, like that on Iwo Jima, weighed heavily on the minds of American policymakers as they now contemplated the war's endgame.

President Truman met with the Joint Chiefs of Staff on June 18 to discuss the landing on Kyushu scheduled for November, code-named Olympic. Every man in the room expected the Japanese to fight with unyielding ferocity to defend their home islands. Truman pressed the chiefs for an estimate of just how bloody the last battle would be. The record is confused as to precisely what they answered. According to one account, Marshall projected losses that "should not exceed the price we have paid for Luzon"—some 31,000 casualties. Other sources claim that

37. Yahara, *Battle for Okinawa*, 96, 130, 135.
38. Yahara, *Battle for Okinawa*, 134.

Marshall estimated "more than 63,000." Extrapolating from Okinawa's 35 percent casualty rate, Leahy figured that as many as 268,000 Americans would end up dead or injured in the projected invasion force of some 766,000. Leahy also expressed his "fear . . . that our insistence on unconditional surrender would result only in making the Japanese desperate and thereby increase our casualty lists. He did not think that this was at all necessary." Assistant Secretary of War John J. McCloy seconded that idea. "We ought to have our heads examined," he said, "if we don't explore some other method by which we can terminate this war than just by another conventional attack and landing." McCloy named two specific "other methods": modifying the unconditional-surrender formula and/or giving the Japanese a warning about the atomic bomb. The military chiefs swiftly scotched the latter proposal, arguing that the bomb was as yet untested. But McCloy had raised some intriguing possibilities: that the bomb, if successful, might make invasion unnecessary; and that a change in the unconditional-surrender doctrine might make the bomb unnecessary. Both ideas remained for the moment ill-defined and unsupported by the critical decision makers. Truman gave his approval to Olympic. But he hoped, said the president, "that there was a possibility of preventing an Okinawa from one end of Japan to the other."[39]

ON OKINAWA, three Japanese divisions had stood up to an American force twice that size for nearly a hundred days. As many as fourteen Japanese divisions waited on Kyushu, more than 350,000 soldiers. Japan had well over two million men under arms throughout its home islands, plus up to four million reservists, and had husbanded more than five thousand kamikaze aircraft for a last-ditch defense. If Olympic came to pass, the butcher's bill would surely be high. The bill for Coronet, the code name for the still larger invasion of the main Japanese island of Honshu contemplated for the spring of 1946, threatened to be higher still. Yet some leaders in Tokyo, like Truman in Washington, were also hoping to avoid an American invasion.

When MacArthur had landed on Luzon in January 1945, the Marquis Koichi Kido, lord keeper of the privy seal, Emperor Hirohito's confidant and a powerful insider in the tensely muted world of Japanese

39. Spector, 543; FRUS: The Conference of Berlin (The Potsdam Conference), 1945 1: 903–10; Leahy, I Was There, 384; Kai Bird, The Chairman: John J. McCloy and the Making of the American Establishment (New York: Simon and Schuster, 1992), 246.

politics, had concluded that Japan's defeat was inevitable. Japan's *surrender*, however, was another matter. It remained scarcely thinkable and absolutely unutterable. In his pursuit of peace, Kido dared not act openly. Kuniaki Koiso, an army general, was still premier. The war and navy ministers continued to hold any imaginable Japanese cabinet hostage to their oft-proclaimed pledge to fight to the last corpuscle of blood. Kido therefore quietly organized a series of discreet visitations to the Imperial Palace in January and February by several like-minded *jushin*, or senior statesmen, former premiers who served as informal advisers to the emperor. Tentatively, obliquely, clandestinely, they began to explore with Emperor Hirohito the possibility of ending the war by means of negotiation.

The American landings on Okinawa brought down Koiso's government on April 5. That same day, the entire group of *jushin*, including Tojo, "the Razor," convened in the imperial audience chamber to select a new premier, presumably one who would somehow bring the war to a conclusion. But how? By a bloody Armageddon that would extinguish the twenty-six-hundred-year-old Japanese nation in a homicidal finale? By a ferocious finish-fight to wrest some last concessions from the Americans? By submitting to unconditional surrender? The army and navy leaders still wielded formidable power, and they inclined to one or the other of the first two options. Incredibly, Tojo had even exclaimed to the emperor just weeks earlier—after Saipan, after the Battle of the Philippine Sea, after Leyte Gulf and MacArthur's invasion of the Philippines, after Iwo Jima—that "with determination, we can win!" Now he reminded the senior statesmen that the army could still "look the other way," thereby breaking any cabinet it did not control.[40]

The *jushin* finally settled on seventy-seven-year-old Admiral Baron Kantaro Suzuki. He was no stranger to intrigue, nor to the wrath of the militarists. He walked with a limp from the four bullets that ultranationalist army officers had pumped into his body during an attempted coup in 1936. Suzuki selected Shigenori Togo, foreign minister at the war's outbreak, a man who had been skeptical about the Pearl Harbor attack and who had had the courage to resign in protest from Tojo's cabinet, to return to his old post. Kido, Suzuki, and Togo, with the quiet approval of Hirohito (constrained by his status as constitutional monarch from playing an overtly directive role), set out to explore various roads

40. Robert J. C. Butow, *Japan's Decision to Surrender* (Stanford: Stanford University Press, 1954), 47, 61.

toward peace. The chief obstacle they faced, writes historian Robert J. C. Butow, was "the crushing control exerted by the militarists over all forms of national life and thought."[41]

On June 8, while the fighting still raged on Okinawa, the military demonstrated once again their ability to dictate Japan's course. In the presence of the emperor, who characteristically said not a word, senior government officials formally affirmed their "Fundamental Policy": "[W]e shall . . . prosecute the war to the bitter end in order to uphold the national polity (Kokutai), protect the imperial land, and accomplish the objectives for which we went to war." This was a decision to commit national suicide, paralleling the mass suicides at Saipan's Marpi Point and in the caves on Okinawa.[42]

On June 22, the day the Okinawa campaign officially ended, Hirohito, at Kido's urging, took the unusual step of summoning his government leaders back to the Imperial Palace. Although the decision of June 8 had committed Japan "to the bitter end," said the diffident monarch, choosing his words carefully, had the government given any thought to other methods of ending the war? Yes, said Togo, there was a possibility that Japan might approach the Soviet Union to use its good offices to negotiate a cease-fire. Togo suggested that Fumimaro Konoye, Japan's last civilian prime minister, the man who had tried in vain to meet with Franklin Roosevelt to work out a *modus vivendi* in late 1941, be sent to Moscow to open negotiations. Togo emphasized that Konoye's instructions would preclude any offer of *unconditional* surrender. Any formula for capitulation must include guarantees that the person and institution of the emperor would be preserved and that the precious, millenia-old *Kokutai* would be left undisturbed. With luck, Japan might hold out for other conditions as well: no military occupation of the homeland, no international trials of alleged war criminals, and retention of some of its conquered territories.

In Washington, Truman was meanwhile preparing for his own discussions with the Russians. Ten days after addressing the closing session of the first United Nations conference in San Francisco's Opera House on June 26, he boarded the cruiser *Augusta*, bound for two weeks of talks with British and Soviet leaders in the miraculously undamaged Berlin suburb of Potsdam. Late in the morning of July 16, Churchill came to Truman's lakeside residence near Potsdam to meet the new

41. Butow, *Japan's Decision*, 80.
42. Butow, *Japan's Decision*, 99–100, n. 69.

president for the first time. "He gave me a lot of hooey about how great my country is and how he loved Roosevelt and how he intended to love me etc. etc.," Truman wrote in his diary. "I am sure we can get along if he doesn't try to give me too much soft soap." The question was soon moot. In the midst of the Potsdam Conference, Churchill received word that the British elections had turned him out of office. On July 28 Clement Atlee took the British prime minister's seat at the conference table.

In the afternoon of July 16, Truman drove by car through Berlin. He had never seen such devastation. The Nazi capital's "absolute ruin" put him in mind of other conquered cities and other conquerors. "I thought of Carthage, Baalbek, Jerusalem, Rome," he noted in his diary, and of "Scipio . . . Sherman, Jenghis Khan, Alexander, Darius the Great." Even as he wrote those words, science was about to bestow upon Truman himself a destructive power that would dwarf all of theirs combined.[43]

Back in his lakeside mansion on the evening of July 16, Truman received a top-secret telegram from Washington: "Operated on this morning. Diagnosis not yet complete but results seem satisfactory and already exceed expectations." The president understood: hours earlier, scientists in the remote Sonoran desert near Alamogordo, New Mexico, had imploded a plutonium sphere the size of an orange and successfully detonated history's first nuclear explosion.[44]

Stimson and General Leslie Groves had given Truman his first extensive briefing about the Manhattan Project just a dozen weeks earlier, on April 25. "Within four months we shall in all probability have completed the most terrifying weapon ever known in human history," Stimson had read from a carefully prepared memorandum, "one bomb of which could destroy a whole city." The conversation lasted just forty-five minutes. None of the three men expressed any doubt that the bomb should be used as soon as it was ready.

In the weeks thereafter, various groups of Washington policymakers and atomic scientists discussed the implications of the Manhattan Project's imminent success. Given the bomb's momentous implications, and in light of all the subsequent controversy about its use, it is striking how few of those men, and virtually none in the inner circle of decision-making, seriously contemplated not dropping it.

Seated amidst the brilliant foliage of a Hyde Park autumn, Roosevelt

43. Robert H. Ferrell, ed., *Off the Record: The Private Papers of Harry S. Truman* (New York: Harper and Row, 1980), 51, 52.
44. *FRUS: Berlin (Potsdam)* 2:1360.

and Churchill had agreed on September 19, 1944, that the new atomic weapon, if available in time, "might perhaps, *after mature consideration*, be used against the Japanese, who should be warned that this bombardment will be repeated until they surrender." (In the same agreement, Churchill and Roosevelt took steps to continue to keep the Manhattan Project a secret from their Soviet ally. There must be "no leakage of information," they ordered, "particularly to the Russians.") But the deliberate mood of that now distant autumn had long since given way to the frantic tempo of the war's last spring. Amidst the gathering clamor to end the bloodshed, and in the chaotic circumstances of Truman's sudden ascension to the presidency, "mature consideration" proved chimerical. History had its own momentum, and it tolerated no delay.[45]

On May 1 Stimson named an Interim Committee of eight civilian officials, supplemented by a four-member Scientific Panel, to advise him about the bomb. Though Stimson later described the Interim Committee as having "carefully considered such alternatives as a detailed advance warning or a demonstration in some uninhabited area," in fact the committee did no such thing during its brief lifetime. To a degree that later generations would find remarkable, the advent of the nuclear age was heralded by little fanfare and even less formal deliberation. Events were in the saddle, and they rode men hard.[46]

Significantly, Truman at first neglected to appoint his own personal representative to the Interim Committee, an assignment that eventually fell, more or less by default, to James F. Byrnes, soon to become secretary of state. Even more telling, Stimson's charge to the Committee asked principally for advice about postwar controls on nuclear weaponry, and in that connection about *how*, but not *whether*, the bomb should be employed against Japan. "It seemed to be a foregone conclusion,"

45. Richard Rhodes, *The Making of the Atomic Bomb* (New York: Simon and Schuster, 1986), 624; *FRUS: Quebec*, 492–93 (emphasis added).
46. Stimson's co-author, McGeorge Bundy, later wrote: "After the war Colonel Stimson, with the fervor of a great advocate and with me as his scribe, wrote an article [Stimson's famous piece, "The Decision to Use the Bomb," in the February 1947 edition of *Harper's*] intended to demonstrate that the bomb was not used without a searching consideration of alternatives. That some effort was made, and that Stimson was its linchpin, is clear. That it was as long or wide or deep as the subject deserved now seems to me most doubtful." Bundy, *Danger and Survival: Choices about the Bomb in the First Fifty Years* (New York: Random House, 1988), 92–93. Indeed, Bundy's account calls into question whether it is even proper to use the word "decision" in explaining the sequence of events that led to Hiroshima and Nagasaki.

one Scientific Panel member later wrote, "that the bomb would be used." Only briefly and informally, during a lunch break in the Pentagon dining room at their meeting on May 31, did several members of the Interim Committee discuss "some striking but harmless demonstration of the bomb's power before using it in a manner that would cause great loss of life." As the official historians describe it:

> For perhaps ten minutes, the proposition was the subject of general discussion. Oppenheimer could think of no demonstration sufficiently spectacular to convince the Japanese that further resistance was futile. Other objections came to mind. The bomb might be a dud. The Japanese might shoot down the delivery plane or bring American prisoners into the test area. If the demonstration failed to bring surrender, the chance of administering the maximum surprise shock would be lost. Besides, would the bomb cause any greater loss of life than the fire raids that had burned out Tokyo?

So much for Stimson's "careful consideration." The following day, the Interim Committee made its formal recommendation: "that the bomb should be used against Japan as soon as possible; that it be used on a war plant surrounded by workers' homes; and that it be used without prior warning."[47]

Some of the scientists at work on the Manhattan Project, particularly those in Chicago, tried to reopen the question of a demonstration on June 12. They submitted to Stimson's deputy, George L. Harrison, a document authored mainly by Leo Szilard but named for the emigré physicist James Franck. Harrison referred the Franck Report to the Scientific Panel. Truman never saw it. The panel's scientists reported back four days later that "we can propose no technical demonstration likely to bring an end to the war; we see no acceptable alternative to direct military use."[48]

That essentially settled the matter. The "decision" to use the bomb might better be described as a series of decisions not to disturb the momentum of a process that was more than three years old by the spring of 1945 and was rapidly building toward its all but inevitable climax. In a profound sense, the determination to use the bomb at the earliest

47. Richard G. Hewlett and Oscar E. Anderson Jr., *The New World, 1939–1946* (University Park: Pennsylvania University Press, 1962), 358; Martin J. Sherwin, *A World Destroyed: The Atomic Bomb and the Grand Alliance* (New York: Knopf, 1975), 207, 209.
48. Sherwin, *World Destroyed*, app. M, 305.

possible date had been implicit in the original decision to build it at the fastest possible speed. "Let there be no mistake about it," Truman later wrote. "I regarded the bomb as a military weapon and never had any doubt that it should be used." Winston Churchill put it this way: "The historic fact remains, and must be judged in the after-time, that the decision whether or not to use the atomic bomb to compel the surrender of Japan was never even an issue. There was unanimous, automatic, unquestioned agreement around our table; nor did I ever hear the slightest suggestion that we should do otherwise."[49]

As Truman prepared to depart for the Potsdam Conference, two questions remained unresolved: what, if anything, to tell the Russians about the atomic project, and whether there should be any modification of the unconditional-surrender formula with respect to Japan. To the latter question, many American policymakers gave an affirmative answer. Leahy and McCloy had so recommended in the fateful White House meeting of June 18. Former ambassador to Japan Joseph Grew was also urging Truman to offer the Japanese assurances about the future of the emperor. Stimson was edging close to a similar recommendation. He summed up his thinking in a detailed memorandum to Truman on July 2. Contrary to much popular misconception, Stimson argued, "I believe Japan *is* susceptible to reason. . . . Japan is not a nation composed wholly of mad fanatics of an entirely different mentality from ours." The shock of an atomic attack, Stimson reasoned, would "carry convincing proof of our power to destroy the Empire," thereby allowing the "liberal leaders" in Japan to overcome the militarists and bid for peace. The new nuclear weapon thus offered Truman a possible alternative to the dreaded invasion that would confront "a last ditch defense such as has been made on Iwo Jima and Okinawa." And to maximize the possibility that the shock of the bomb might induce the Japanese to surrender, Stimson recommended that "we should add [to the peace terms] that we do not exclude a constitutional monarchy under her present dynasty." Such a guarantee might compromise the unconditional-surrender principle but "would substantially add to the chances of acceptance." Looking to the shape of the postwar world, Stimson also overruled Groves and struck the ancient capital of Kyoto, a shrine of Japanese art and culture, from the roster of proposed targets. The "bitterness which would be caused by such a wanton act might make it

49. Harry S. Truman, *Memoirs: Year of Decisions* (Garden City, N.Y.: Doubleday, 1955), 419; Churchill 6:553.

impossible during the long postwar period to reconcile the Japanese to us in that area rather than to the Russians," Stimson explained. Four other cities—Kokura, Niigata, Hiroshima, and Nagasaki—stayed on the list.[50]

At Potsdam on July 17 Truman met Josef Stalin for the first time. The diminutive president was delighted to discover that the legendary Stalin was just "a little bit of a squirt." For the next several days, discussion among the Big Three rambled tediously, at times rancorously, over issues that had been intractable at Yalta and proved no more tractable now, especially reparations from Germany and the composition of the Polish government. It was the new president's diplomatic baptism. He was understandably edgy, unsure of himself, and not a little frustrated. "I was so scared I didn't know whether things were going according to Hoyle or not," Truman wrote to his wife. "I'm not going to stay around this terrible place all summer just to listen to speeches. I'll go home to the Senate for that," he complained to his diary. Truman wanted to appear resolute, in command, a worthy and credible successor to the fallen Roosevelt. "I don't want just to discuss, I want to decide," he announced at the first plenary session on July 17. "You want something in the bag each day," Churchill responded.[51]

Truman got little decided at Potsdam, even though he had what he called "some dynamite" in his bag—his knowledge of the successful test at Alamogordo. Franklin Roosevelt, diplomatic virtuoso that he was, may have had some fine scheme deep within his mind for laying his nuclear trump card on the table when the moment came for a showdown with Stalin. But as with so much in the life of that enigmatic president, the record does not reveal precisely what his scheme was. He surely never shared it with his last vice-president. As a consequence, Truman at Potsdam appeared uncertain about how to make diplomatic use of America's new atomic asset, or even what precise valuation to put on it. At first he seemed to have scant conception that the bomb might render unnecessary a Soviet declaration of war against Japan—the prize for which Roosevelt had been willing to pay so much, in Chinese coin, at Yalta. When Stalin reiterated to Truman his promise to "be in the Jap War on August 15th," Truman exulted to his diary in the argot he had

50. Henry L. Stimson, "The Decision to Drop the Bomb," *Harper's Magazine*, February 1947, 97–107; and Stimson and McGeorge Bundy, *On Active Service in Peace and War* (New York: Harper and Brothers, 1948), 617; Stimson Diary, July 24, 1945.
51. McCullough, *Truman*, 417, 424; Ferrell, *Off the Record*, 54; FRUS: Berlin (Potsdam) 2:63.

learned as a Doughboy: "Fini Japs when that comes about." "I've gotten what I came for," he wrote to his wife; "Stalin goes to war August 15 with no strings on it. . . . [W]e'll end the war a year sooner now, and think of the kids who won't be killed!" Yet the following day he wrote: "Believe Japs will fold up before Russia comes in. I am sure they will when Manhattan appears over their homeland. I shall inform Stalin about it at an opportune time."[52]

The opportune time, such as it was, soon arrived. As another contentious session was ending late in the afternoon of July 24, Truman nonchalantly walked up to Stalin and his interpreter. "I casually mentioned to Stalin that we had a new weapon of unusual destructive force," Truman recalled. "The Russian premier showed no special interest. All he said was that he was glad to hear it and hoped we would make 'good use of it against the Japanese.'" It was a singularly undramatic moment.

52. McCullough, *Truman*, 424; Ferrell, *Off the Record*, 53, 54. Some historians, notably Gar Alperovitz in *The Decision to Use the Atomic Bomb and the Architecture of an American Myth* (New York: Knopf, 1995) have suggested that Truman's swelling confidence about the bomb led him to try to delay or prevent Russian entry into the war. It was this anti-Soviet strategy, so the argument goes, that precluded the consideration of time-consuming alternative methods of ending the war. The evidence does suggest that Byrnes did some thinking along these lines. Churchill recorded at Potsdam: "It is quite clear that the United States do not at the present time desire Russian participation in the war against Japan." *FRUS Berlin (Potsdam)* 2:276. But a loss of American interest in the Soviet declaration of war scarcely amounts to a calculated strategy for using the bomb as an instrument of diplomacy against the Soviets or for accelerating the scheduled drops on Hiroshima and Nagasaki. American policy regarding the relation of the bomb to the Russian presence in Asia remained uncoordinated and episodic. Byrnes himself said that he "had hoped that we could finish up with the Japanese *without* participation by the Russians, but the atmosphere of the conference, and the attitude of the Russians made it *inevitable* that Russia come in." David Robertson, *Sly and Able: A Political Biography of James F. Byrnes* (New York: Norton, 1994), 427, emphasis added. In McGeorge Bundy's trenchant conclusion, "The assertion [that a desire to impress the Russians with the power of the bomb was a major factor in the decision to use it] is false, and the evidence to support it rests on inferences so stretched as to be a discredit both to the judgment of those who have argued in this fashion and the credulity of those who have accepted such arguments . . . assuming conspiracy when the reality is only confusion." Bundy, *Danger and Survival*, 88, 651; see also Barton J. Bernstein, "The Atomic Bomb and American Foreign Policy, 1941–1945: An Historiographical Controversy," *Peace and Change* 2 (Spring 1974): 1–16; and Bernstein, "The Atomic Bomb and American Foreign Policy: The Route to Hiroshima," in Bernstein, ed., *The Atomic Bomb: The Critical Issues* (Boston: Little, Brown, 1976), 94–120.

Neither man gave any sign that he appreciated the potential of the "new weapon" to alter the course of history.[53]

It remained to decide what to say to the Japanese, especially about the role of the emperor, as Stimson and others were urging. The Americans knew that at least some Japanese officials were trying to arrange a cease-fire. Rumors of Japanese peace initiatives had been flying for a month. They had been discussed on the floor of the U.S. Senate and in the pages of American newspapers. Stalin told Truman on July 28 what the American president already knew from intercepted Japanese cables—that Konoye was asking to come to Moscow. (His answer to the Japanese would be negative, Stalin said, and Konoye never did get to Moscow.) But the Japanese feelers thus far were neither unambiguously official nor signs of willingness to submit to unconditional surrender. Konoye was not a member of the Suzuki cabinet. Who could be sure whether he represented the Tokyo government or merely some Japanese political faction? What was more, Byrnes read an intercepted cable concerning the Konoye mission that declared: "With regard to unconditional surrender, we are unable to consent to it under any circumstances whatsoever."

Byrnes, a southerner, understood the difference between defeat and surrender. He knew that almost two years had elapsed between Gettysburg and Appomattox. He may well have remembered the futility of Lincoln's parley with Confederate negotiators at Hampton Roads in February 1865, when armistice negotiations foundered on the Confederacy's demand to be recognized as an independent state. Now was no time to prolong the killing while the diplomats niggled, nor was it a time to appear weak by modifying America's peace terms. Unconditional surrender had been promulgated by Roosevelt at Casablanca in January 1943 and reaffirmed at Cairo almost a year later, with special reference to Japan. The phrase had long since taken on the character of a political shibboleth, a test of toughness and resolve. When Truman had given his first address as president to Congress on April 16, the packed chamber rose thunderously to its feet when he uttered the words "unconditional surrender." The president would be "crucified," said Byrnes, if he backed off from that commitment now. Cordell Hull advised Byrnes that "terrible political repercussions would follow in the U.S." if the unconditional-surrender formula were abandoned at this climactic moment. Anything less than unconditional surrender would be branded

<hr>

53. Truman, *Year of Decision*, 416.

with that vilest of epithets, "appeasement." Byrnes accordingly repudiated the suggestions of Leahy, McCloy, Grew, and Stimson. He deleted all references to preserving the emperor from the draft of what was soon to be known as the Potsdam Proclamation. Truman offered no dissent. As finally issued on July 26 over the signatures of Truman, Churchill, and Chiang, who wired his concurrence, the proclamation called for "the unconditional surrender of all the Japanese armed forces" and warned: "The alternative for Japan is prompt and utter destruction."

In Tokyo, Suzuki and Togo sought desperately for a response that would reconcile their own inclination to accept the terms of the proclamation and the cry of the militarists to dismiss it out of hand. The compromise term they finally chose was *mokusatsu*, a picturesque word that meant "to ignore" or "to withhold comment" but could also be construed as "kill with contempt." The Americans interpreted *mokusatsu* as outright rejection, tinged with brazen defiance. The nuclear clock now ticked off its last few beats.[54]

THE POTSDAM PROCLAMATION was about to carry the United States across a forbidding military threshold, one that marked the opening of a new chapter in the history of warfare and diplomacy. But by August 1945 the atomic bombs hardly represented a moral novelty. The moral rules that had once stayed men's hands from taking up weapons of mass destruction against noncombatants had long since been violently breached in World War II, first in the aerial attacks on European cities, then even more wantonly in the systematic firebombing of Japan.

On January 7, 1945, Air Force General Curtis LeMay had arrived on Guam to take command of the 21st Bomber Command. He was a gruff, stocky man, one of the youngest generals in the army. He chewed perpetually on a cigar butt to mask his Bell's palsy, a nerve disorder that made the right corner of his mouth droop, the result of flying so many high-altitude bombing missions over Europe in unheated and unpressurized B-17s. LeMay had led the disastrous raid against Regensburg in 1943 but had long since abandoned the idea of "precision" bombing in favor of terror attacks on civilians. "I'll tell you what war is about," he once said, "You've got to kill people, and when you've killed enough they stop fighting." Cheated out of a conclusive demonstration of the war-winning power of aerial bombardment in Europe, LeMay was de-

54. Robertson, *Sly and Able*, 431; *FRUS: Berlin (Potsdam)*, 2:1267, 1476; Butow, *Japan's Decision*, 147.

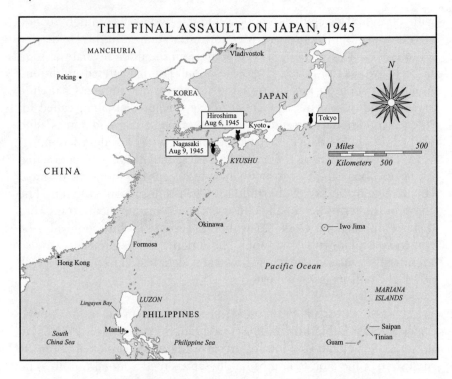

THE FINAL ASSAULT ON JAPAN, 1945

termined to vindicate his service, and the Douhetian doctrine of "strategic" warfare, in the fight against Japan.[55]

LeMay deployed two intimidating new technologies against Japan's highly flammable cities, where most people lived in wooden houses. The first was a fiendishly efficient six-pound incendiary bomblet developed by Standard Oil chemists—the M-69 projectile, which spewed burning gelatinized gasoline that stuck to its targets and was virtually inextinguishable by conventional means. The second was the B-29 Superfortress, an awesome specimen of American engineering prowess and mass-production techniques. The Boeing Corporation had won the army air force design competition for a long-range, intercontinental bomber in 1940, and the first production model B-29s were flying by 1943. LeMay had some 350 B-29s in the Marianas in January 1945 and more arriving constantly. They were nearly one hundred feet in length, with a 141-foot wingspan and a three-story-high tail section. They were powered by four twenty-two-hundred-horsepower Wright eighteen-

55. Richard Rhodes, "The General and World War II," *New Yorker*, June 19, 1995, 47ff.

cylinder radial air-cooled magnesium alloy engines, each fitted with two General Electric exhaust-driven turbo-superchargers. The B-29 carried a crew of eleven in its pressurized cabin and a bomb load of up to twenty thousand pounds. It had an operational ceiling over thirty-five thousand feet and a combat range of more than four thousand miles. An onboard computerized central control system allowed for remote firing from its five defensive gun turrets.

LeMay set out at once to perfect the 21st Bomber Command's fire-bombing techniques. To enlarge bomb loads, he stripped all but the tail-turret guns from his B-29s. To avoid the recently discovered jet stream, which foiled some of his earliest raids on Japan, he trained his pilots in low-altitude attacks. He experimented with bombing patterns and with mixes of explosive and incendiary bomb loads. His goal was to create firestorms, like the ones that had consumed Hamburg and Dresden — conflagrations so vast and intense that nothing could survive them, not mere fires but thermal hurricanes that killed by suffocation as well as by heat, as the flames sucked all available oxygen out of the surrounding atmosphere.

After practice runs on Kobe and on a section of Tokyo in February, Lemay launched 334 Superfortresses from the Marianas on the night of March 9. A few minutes after midnight, they began to lay their clusters of M-69s over Tokyo, methodically criss-crossing the target zone to create concentric rings of fire that soon merged into a sea of flame. Rising thermal currents buffeted the mile-high B-29s and knocked them about like paper airplanes. When the raiders flew away shortly before 4:00 A.M., they left behind them one million homeless Japanese and nearly ninety thousand dead. The victims died from fire, asphyxiation, and falling buildings. Some boiled to death in super-heated canals and ponds where they had sought refuge from the flames. In the next five months, LeMay's bombers attacked sixty-six of Japan's largest cities, destroying 43 percent of their built-up areas. They dehoused more than 8 million people, killed as many as 900,000, and injured up to 1.3 million more. Hiroshima and Nagasaki survived to be atomic-bombed only because LeMay's superiors removed them from his target list.[56]

Japan meanwhile was attempting fire raids of its own against its American enemy. Using the same jet stream that had at first frustrated LeMay,

56. Ronald Schaffer, *Wings of Judgment: American Bombing in World War II* (New York: Oxford University Press, 1985), 128ff.; Craven and Cate 5:614.

Japanese technicians had begun in November 1944 to loft high-altitude balloons designed to carry small incendiary bombs across the broad Pacific and drop them on the western United States. Japanese schoolgirls assembled the balloons in large indoor spaces like sumo wrestling arenas, theaters, and music halls. They painstakingly laminated the four-ply rice paper that formed the balloons' skin, and sealed the seams of each balloon's six hundred joined panels with a potato-flour paste that many of the hungry children surreptitiously stole and ate. Beneath the balloon's thirty-two-foot-diameter inflated sphere, technicians suspended a small gondola basket containing the incendiary device and ringed by thirty-two sandbags. With the help of a simple altimeter, a battery-powered mechanism released hydrogen from the balloon at thirty-eight thousand feet and detonated a small explosive to jettison two counter-balanced sandbags at thirty thousand feet, keeping the balloon stable within the jet stream's vertical envelope through sixteen precisely calculated transpacific up-and-down cycles. When the last sandbag fell, a demolition charge ignited and detached the incendiary device, presumably over the United States.

While LeMay's B-29s were torching the cities of Japan in the winter of 1945, ninety-three hundred Japanese balloons were drifting mutely eastward in the jet stream's embrace. Those that made it across the Pacific dropped their fiery loads to earth all across North America, from the Yukon Territory to Baja California, though most landed in the northwestern corner of the United States. Some alarmed American officials worried that the balloons might be instruments of germ warfare. But though Japan had once tried such a tactic against Russian troops, and the Imperial Army's infamous Unit 731 conducted sadistic biological warfare experiments at a secret station in Manchuria, these balloons were designed to spread fire, not contagion. They ignited some minor forest fires, many of them promptly extinguished by the "Triple Nickels," the 555th Negro Parachute Infantry Battalion, consigned to duty as smoke-jumpers. A voluntary American news blackout denied the Japanese any confirmation that the balloons had actually completed their journey. As Japan's hydrogen stocks dwindled, the last balloons were launched in April 1945. A month later, on May 5, the Reverend Archie Mitchell and his wife, Elsie, were leading a Sunday school outing in the woods near Bly, Oregon. While Reverend Mitchell was moving his car, Mrs. Mitchell and five children tugged at a strange object they had found in the underbrush. The balloon bomb exploded, killing her and all the children. The six victims were the only mainland American casualties of the war.[57]

The Japanese fire raids were no match for what the Americans could do. While the schoolgirls of Japan had been gluing their rice-paper panels together in sumo arenas, the women of Omaha, Nebraska, were riveting together the fuselages of B-29s on the assembly line of the Glenn L. Martin aircraft plant. While Japanese technicians were rigging up the first balloon gondolas on Ninety-nine League Beach east of Tokyo, Air Force Colonel Paul Tibbets went to Omaha to handpick B-29 Number 82 off the Martin production line. He soon renamed it after his mother, *Enola Gay*. As the spent Japanese balloons were soughing down into the western American fir forests, Tibbets was leading his specially selected 509th Composite Group in dummy bomb drops onto the dry bed of prehistoric Lake Bonneville at Wendover Field, Utah, practicing an unorthodox 155-degree diving turn after bomb release. Not long after Elsie Mitchell's funeral in Oregon, two sailors at Hunter's Point in San Francisco Bay shouldered a crowbar from which was suspended a lead bucket holding the U-235 bullet for the first combat atomic bomb. They carried it aboard the USS *Indianapolis*, and the heavy cruiser weighed anchor for Tinian, in the Marianas. On August 6, 1945, while thousands of dud balloon-bombs were rotting away harmlessly on the densely wooded slopes of the Oregon and Washington Cascade Range, Tibbets throttled the *Enola Gay* off the runway from Tinian. Its four twenty-two-hundred-horsepower Wright eighteen-cylinder radial air-cooled magnesium alloy engines, each fitted with two General Electric exhaust-driven turbo-superchargers, barely strained under the load of its single bomb.

TRUMAN WAS AT SEA on August 6, returning from Potsdam. When the news from Tinian came over the *Augusta*'s radio, the White House released a prearranged statement: "Sixteen hours ago an American airplane dropped one bomb on Hiroshima. . . . It is an atomic bomb. It is a harnessing of the basic power of the universe." Some Japanese leaders refused to believe what had happened — nearly forty thousand people killed in an instant, a hundred thousand additional

---

57. Robert C. Mikesh, *Japan's World War II Balloon Bomb Attacks on North America* (Washington: Smithsonian Institution, 1973); John McPhee, "Balloons of War," *New Yorker*, January 29, 1996, 52–60.

dead within days from burns and radiation. Mirroring the astonishment of many Americans at Pearl Harbor, several Japanese scientists thought it was impossible for the United States to have tamed the atom and transported such an unstable explosive all the way across the Pacific. Even if it had, they argued, the Americans could not imaginably have produced enough radioactive material to permit additional atomic bombings, an argument apparently supported by the fact that "conventional" fire raids were meanwhile continuing. Only on August 10, a day after a second nuclear explosion had devastated Nagasaki, eventually killing another seventy thousand people, did Japanese experts agree that their country was under atomic attack and that it might be sustained. By then Suzuki's government had already tendered a surrender offer. It remained to be seen if it would be accepted.[58]

Debate had raged among Japanese officials since the first news reports had come in from Hiroshima. Shortly before midnight on August 8, the Soviet Union declared war on Japan, adding a second shock to the calamity of the atomic bomb. That morning, the Supreme Council for the Direction of the War, the "Big Six," met to discuss the twin crises. They quickly deadlocked. Suzuki, Togo, and the navy minister advocated accepting the Potsdam Declaration, with the sole reservation that the imperial system be maintained. The war minister and the army and navy chiefs of staff held out for three additional conditions: there should be no military occupation of Japan, Japanese armed forces should be allowed to disarm themselves, and any trials of war criminals were to be conducted by Japanese courts. The army chief went so far as to insist that Japan was not yet defeated. "We will be able to destroy the major part of an invading army," he said. The Japanese people would surely fight. Posters were going up all over Tokyo denouncing Kido and the "peace faction" as traitors who should be shot on sight.

As the stalemate continued, word of the Nagasaki bomb arrived. The Big Six adjourned, nothing resolved. The cabinet deadlocked similarly later in the day. Just before midnight, the cabinet and the Supreme Council together entered the air raid shelter under the Imperial Palace grounds for an unprecedented event: a meeting in the emperor's presence at which they were not able to present a unanimous decision. Prime Minister Suzuki apologized to Emperor Hirohito for the embarrassment. The various officials argued their positions. At last Hirohito arose from

58. *Public Papers of the Presidents of the United States: Harry S. Truman, April 12 to December 31, 1945* (Washington: USGPO, 1961), 93; Butow, *Japan's Decision*, 151.

his chair and spoke: "I swallow my own tears and give my sanction to the proposal to accept the Allied proclamation." There would be not four conditions but only one: preservation of the Imperial House.[59]

Palace officials prepared an imperial rescript to announce the decision to the Japanese people. In another unprecedented step, the emperor recorded his surrender announcement for broadcast over the radio. Most Japanese had never heard his voice.

The Japanese surrender offer, relayed through the Swiss government, arrived in Washington on the morning of August 10. Its proviso that "the prerogatives of His Majesty as a Sovereign Ruler" were to remain intact was a sticking point. Byrnes objected that "I cannot understand why now we should go further than we were willing to go at Potsdam when we had no atomic bomb, and Russia was not in the war." Stimson countered that "use of the Emperor must be made in order to save us from a score of bloody Iwo Jimas and Okinawas." A compromise was reached, stating that "the authority of the Emperor and the Japanese Government to rule the state shall be subject to the Supreme Commander of the Allied Powers."[60]

The American response was sufficiently ambiguous that some Japanese officials did not want to accept it. In a second highly unorthodox display of imperial command, Hirohito overruled them on the morning of August 14. That night, some die-hard military officers stormed the Imperial Palace to seize the recording of the surrender announcement, scheduled for broadcast the next day. Others attacked the residences of Suzuki and Kido. All failed. At noon on August 15, the emperor's unfamiliar voice, speaking over the radio in a courtly, archaic Japanese that most of his listeners could scarcely understand, declared Japan's war at an end.

Among the American troops on Okinawa, unconditional jubilation broke out. They fired every available weapon skyward. The subsequent rain of shell fragments killed seven men. Halfway around the world, near Rheims, France, GIs in the 45th Infantry Division, awaiting transfer to the Pacific for the invasion of Honshu, wept with joy. Now they would be going home. "The killing was all going to be over," one of them reflected. "We were going to grow to adulthood after all."[61]

59. Butow, *Japan's Decision*, 163, 176,198–99.
60. Robertson, *Sly and Able*, 434; Stimson Diary, August 10, 1945; Truman, *Year of Decisions*, 429.
61. Kennett, *G.I.*, 225; Paul Fussell, "Thank God for the Atom Bomb," *Guardian*, February 5, 1989, 10.

Epilogue: The World the War Made

We cannot get away from the results of the war.

— Josef Stalin, Potsdam, July 1945

Of the men who had survived the Great War of 1914–18 to lead the major powers into World War II, only one still stood on history's stage by the end of 1945. Roosevelt was dead of natural causes, Hitler and Konoye by their own hands. Churchill had been shunted out of office by a people more weary of sacrifice than warmed by gratitude. Still unsated, Stalin alone remained.[1]

The war with Japan formally concluded on September 2, 1945. Days earlier, the battleship *Missouri* had glided into Tokyo Bay and anchored within cannon-shot of Commodore Matthew C. Perry's moorage of 1853. At dawn on Sunday the second, crewmen set up a table on the *Missouri's* deck and laid out the surrender documents. On a bulkhead above, they displayed the thirty-one-star flag that Perry's flagship, the sidewheeler steam frigate *Mississippi*, had carried into Tokyo Bay nearly a century earlier. High atop the big battleship's flagstaff luffed the forty-eight-star flag that had flown above the Capitol dome in Washington on December 7, 1941.

Shortly before 9:00 A.M., the Japanese delegates arrived, the civilian officials in formal morning clothes, the naval and military officers in dress uniform. A few minutes later General MacArthur and Admirals Nimitz and Halsey stepped onto the deck, dressed simply in open-collar khaki shirts. MacArthur gave a brief speech. He expressed the hope "that from this solemn occasion a better world shall emerge . . . a world founded on faith and understanding." The Japanese officials came for-

1. Rather than face trial as a war criminal, Konoye took cyanide at his Tokyo home on December 16, 1945.

ward under the shadow of the *Missouri*'s sixteen-inch guns and put their signatures to the surrender instruments. MacArthur and Nimitz signed for the Americans. One onlooking Japanese diplomat wondered "whether it would have been possible for us, had we been victorious, to embrace the vanquished with a similar magnanimity. Clearly, it would have been different."[2]

America was officially at peace, and so was Japan. Elsewhere in Asia peace remained elusive. The war in that region had been more than a struggle between the United States and Japan, or even between China and Japan. The conflict also marked the penultimate chapter in the history of Western colonialism in Asia that had lasted since the fifteenth century. "It almost seems that the Japs were a necessary evil in order to break down the old colonial system," Franklin Roosevelt had told a journalist in 1942.[3] From that perspective, it might be said that Japan had won the war after all, finishing the work begun with Admiral Togo's victory over the Russians at Tsushima Strait in 1905, a victory that Nagumo had so vividly memorialized when his aircraft carriers descended on Pearl Harbor flying Togo's old battle flag. If a major Japanese war aim had been to evict the Westerners and build "Asia for the Asians," that aim had been accomplished as early as 1942 and was never effectively reversed. The Philippines proceeded on schedule toward independence on July 4, 1946. India wrested its nationhood from Britain in 1947; Ceylon (Sri Lanka) and Burma (Myanmar), in 1948. In other countries, where the old colonial powers tried to reassert their authority, the final chapter of the struggle to rid Asia of Western dominance took longer to write and was often written in blood, but written it was. Rebellion against the reimposition of Dutch rule went on for four years in the East Indies after 1945, until Indonesia established its independence at last in 1949. Malaya slipped the British harness only in 1957. Japan's former colony of Korea remained divided for the remainder of the century, sucking the United States into a second Asian war within half a decade of the ceremony on the *Missouri*'s deck. The French waged a futile struggle to recolonize Indochina until they gave up in 1954, leav-

---

2. Morison, 574–77; Toshikazu Kase, *Journey to the Missouri* (New Haven: Yale University Press, 1950), 13. Halsey's apparent magnanimity was strained. After the ceremony he told reporters that he would "like to have kicked each Jap delegate in the face." James T. Patterson, *Grand Expectations: Postwar America, 1945–1974* (New York: Oxford University Press, 1996), 7.

3. Christopher Thorne, *Allies of a Kind: The United States, Britain, and the War against Japan, 1941–1945* (New York: Oxford University Press, 1978), 728n.

ing a messy legacy that eventually precipitated America's third twentieth-century Asian war in Vietnam.

As for China, whose friendship had been the great goal of American diplomacy before 1941, a friendship deemed so valuable as to set the United States on the collision course with Japan that led to Pearl Harbor, there the results were peculiarly ironic, and not a little bitter. Mao Tse-tung finally defeated Chiang Kai-shek in 1949. The new Communist regime openly declared its hostility to the United States and committed itself to force-marching China into the modern era. Everywhere in Asia it was clear by century's end that World War II had set the stage for the definitive finale of a five-century saga of Western imperial hegemony.

In Europe the end of World War II almost instantly introduced a new era of conflict with a martial name of its own, the Cold War. Of the traditional great European powers, France was humbled, Britain exhausted, Germany demolished and divided. Hitler had brewed a catastrophe so vast that for his own people it seemed to sunder the web of time itself. Germans would call the moment of their surrender on May 8, 1945, *Stunde null*—zero hour, when history's clock must be made to start anew. Stalin closed his fist over eastern Europe and dared the Western powers to break his grip. Counting on the resurgence of traditional American isolationism, he anticipated having a free hand with which to harvest the fruits of victory in the vast domain he had conquered at the price of more than twenty million Soviet dead.

The Americans surprised him, and perhaps themselves, by taking up Stalin's challenge, inaugurating the four and a half decades of Soviet-American confrontation known as the Cold War, the unwanted war baby conceived in the fragile marriage of convenience that was the Grand Alliance. Who could have predicted that the nation that had repudiated the League of Nations in 1920 would emerge as the foremost champion of the United Nations a generation later? That the Congress that had passed five neutrality statutes in the 1930s would vote overwhelmingly to make the United States a charter member of the North Atlantic Treaty Organization in 1949? That the country that had so reluctantly armed itself in 1941 would become a virtual garrison state in the postwar decades? Or that the people who had refused asylum to Europe's Jews in their hour of greatest peril would welcome some seven hundred thousand refugees in the decade and a half after 1945?[4]

4. David M. Reimers, *Still the Golden Door: The Third World Comes to America* (New York: Columbia University Press, 1985), 26.

World War II led directly to the Cold War and ended a century and a half of American isolationism. Yet future historians may well conclude that the Cold War that came to an end in 1989 was neither the most surprising nor the most important or durable of the war's legacies for American diplomacy. In the long sweep of time, America's half-century-long ideological, political, and military face-off with the Soviet Union may appear far less consequential than America's leadership in inaugurating an era of global economic interdependence. In this dimension, too, there was much that was surprising. Who could have foretold that the nation that had flintily refused to cancel the Europeans' war debts in the 1920s would establish the World Bank in 1945 and commit $17 billion to the Marshall Plan in 1948? That the country that had embraced the Fordney-McCumber and Smoot-Hawley tariffs would take the lead in establishing the General Agreement on Tariffs and Trade, and later the World Trade Organization? That the government that had torpedoed the London Economic Conference in 1933 would create the International Monetary Fund in 1944? That isolationist America would step forward to midwife the European Union, another war baby whose maturation muted centuries of old-world rivalries and symbolized the international regime that by century's end came to be called "globalization"? And who could deny that globalization—the explosion in world trade, investment, and cultural mingling—was the signature and lasting international achievement of the postwar era, one likely to overshadow the Cold War in its long-term historical consequences?

Americans could not see that future clearly in 1945, but they could look back over the war they had just waged. They might have reflected with some discomfort on how slowly they had awakened to the menace of Hitlerism in the isolationist 1930s; on how callously they had barred the door to those seeking to flee from Hitler's Europe; on how heedlessly they had provoked Japan into a probably avoidable war in a region where few American interests were at stake; on how they had largely fought with America's money and machines and with Russia's men, had fought in Europe only late in the day, against a foe mortally weakened by three years of brutal warfare in the east, had fought in the Pacific with a bestiality they did not care to admit; on how they had profaned their constitution by interning tens of thousands of citizens largely because of their race; on how they had denied most black Americans a chance to fight for their country; on how they had sullied their nation's moral standards with terror bombing in the closing months of the war; on how their leaders' stubborn insistence on unconditional surrender had led to the incineration of hundreds of thousands of already defeated Japanese, first by fire raids, then by nuclear blast; on how poorly Franklin Roosevelt had prepared for the postwar era, how foolishly he had banked on goodwill and personal charm to compose the conflicting interests of nations, how little he had taken his countrymen into his confidence, even misled them, about the nature of the peace that was to come; on how they had abandoned the reforming agenda of the New Deal years to chase in wartime after the sirens of consumerism; on how they alone among warring peoples had prospered, emerging unscathed at home while 405,399 American soldiers, sailors, marines, and airmen had died. Those men were dignified in death by their service, but they represented proportionately fewer military casualties than in any other major belligerent country. Beyond the war's dead and wounded and their families, few Americans had been touched by the staggering sacrifices and unspeakable anguish that the war had visited upon millions of other people around the globe.

That would have been a reasonably accurate account of America's role in World War II, but it did not describe the war that Americans remembered. In the mysterious zone where history mixes with memory to breed national myths, Americans after 1945 enshrined another war altogether. It was the "good war," maybe the last good war, maybe, given the advent of nuclear weapons, the last war that would ever be fought by huge armies and fully mobilized industrial economies in a protracted contest of attrition. The future of warfare, if there was one, lay not on the traditional battlefield but in cities held hostage by weapons of mass destruction that the war had spurred American science to create.

Americans remembered World War II as a just war waged by a peaceful people aroused to anger only after intolerable provocation, a war stoically endured by those at home and fought in far-away places by brave and wholesome young men with dedicated women standing behind them on the production lines, a war whose justice and necessity were clinched by the public revelations of Nazi genocide in 1945, a war fought for democracy and freedom and, let the world beware, fought with unstinting industrial might and unequaled technological prowess— an effort equivalent, one journalist wrote at war's end, to "building two Panama Canals every month, with a fat surplus to boot."[5]

The dimensions of the surpluses that rested in America's hands at war's end were staggering. "The United States," said Winston Churchill in 1945, "stand at this moment at the summit of the world." Americans

5. Bruce Catton, *The Warlords of Washington* (New York: Harcourt Brace, 1948), 306.

commanded fully half of the entire planet's manufacturing capacity and generated more than half of the world's electricity. America owned two-thirds of the world's gold stocks and half of all its monetary reserves. The United States produced two times more petroleum than the rest of the world combined; it had the world's largest merchant fleet, a near monopoly on the emerging growth industries of aerospace and electronics, and, for a season at least, an absolute monopoly on the disquieting new technology of atomic power.[6]

The war had shaken the American people loose and shaken them up, freed them from a decade of economic and social paralysis and flung them around their country into new regions and new ways of life. It was a war that so richly delivered on all the promises of the wartime advertisers and politicians that it nearly banished the memory of the Depression. At the end of the Depression decade, nearly half of all white families and almost 90 percent of black families had still lived in poverty. One in seven workers remained unemployed. By war's end unemployment was negligible. In the ensuing quarter century the American economy would create some twenty million new jobs, more than half of them filled by women. Within less than a generation of the war's end, the middle class, defined as families with annual incomes between three and ten thousand dollars, more than doubled. By 1960 the middle class included almost two-thirds of all Americans, most of whom owned their own homes, unprecedented achievements for any modern society. The birth dearth of the Depression years gave way to the baby boom, as young couples confident about their futures filled the Republic's empty cradles with some fifty million bawling babies in the decade and a half after the war. The social and economic upheavals of wartime laid the groundwork for the civil rights movement as well as for an eventual revolution in women's status.

Small wonder that Americans chose to think of it as the good war. It was a war that had brought them as far as imagination could reach, and beyond, from the ordeal of the Great Depression and had opened apparently infinite vistas to the future. The huge expenditures for weaponry clinched the Keynesian doctrine that government spending could underwrite prosperity and inaugurated a quarter century of the most robust economic growth in the nation's history—an era of the very grandest expectations.

6. David Cannadine, ed., *Blood, Toil, Tears and Sweat: The Speeches of Winston Churchill* (Boston: Houghton Mifflin, 1989), 282.

The young Americans who went off to war in the twilight years of the New Deal came home to a different country. By 1950, for the first time in history, a majority of Americans were women, thanks to battle deaths, improvements in maternal health care, and the paucity of immigrants in the preceding generation. Because of the birth slump in the prewar decade, the statistically typical thirty-year-old American woman in 1950 was four years older than her statistically abstracted male counterpart on the eve of the Depression. She had been born in the aftermath of the Great War, spent her childhood in the prosperous twenties, and became a teenager in the year Franklin Roosevelt became president. The Depression had blighted her youth, but as she entered adulthood the country was mobilizing for war and she had found a good job, not in a defense plant but in a clerical position that she had left at war's end and intended one day to take up again. She had married a veteran, a young man who had gone to war believing it was just and necessary and came back still believing so. The GI Bill had sent him to college, and he was on his way up. On his income of almost $3,445 a year they were flush beyond their parents' dreams, or their own Depression-era dreams either, for that matter. They bought a freshly built suburban tract home with room enough for their three children. Their parents talked about the days of outhouses and kerosene lanterns, but their place was plumbed and wired and fitted out with every kind of modern appliance: telephone, radio, refrigerator, washing machine, and the newest gadget of all, television.[7]

They had cast their first presidential ballot for Franklin Roosevelt, in 1944, and their second for his scrappy little successor, Harry Truman, in 1948, though they were uneasy that Truman's party was promising at last to secure full civil rights for Negroes. The Russians had just exploded their own atomic bomb, and the Communists had recently taken power in China. Somehow the good war had not settled things to the degree that Roosevelt had promised. They had inherited a new world, and a brave one too. Like all worlds, it held its share of peril as well as promise.

7. This composite portrait is drawn from data in *HSUS*.

Bibliographical Essay

The literature concerning the major subjects of this book—the Great Depression, the New Deal, and World War II—is enormous. What follows is not an exhaustive bibliography, but a highly selective one, intended as a guide for further reading.

World War I and its immediate aftermath are the subjects of David M. Kennedy, *Over Here: The First World War and American Society* (New York: Oxford University Press, 1980); Thomas A. Bailey, *Woodrow Wilson and the Lost Peace* (New York: Macmillan, 1944), and the same author's *Woodrow Wilson and the Great Betrayal* (New York: Macmillan, 1945). Indispensable to an understanding of the war's economic sequelae are John Maynard Keynes, *The Economic Consequences of the Peace* (New York: Harcourt, Brace and Howe, 1920); Charles Kindleberger, *The World in Depression* (Berkeley: University of California Press, 1973); and Peter Temin, *Lessons from the Great Depression* (Cambridge: MIT Press, 1989).

Frederick Lewis Allen's *Only Yesterday* (New York: Harper and Brothers, 1931) fixed the historical image of the 1920s in the minds of several generations of readers. Its many deficiencies can be offset by reading Preston Slosson, *The Great Crusade and After* (New York: Macmillan, 1930); William E. Leuchtenburg, *The Perils of Prosperity* (Chicago: University of Chicago Press, 1958); Lizabeth Cohen, *Making a New Deal* (New York: Cambridge University Press, 1990); Thomas J. Archdeacon, *Becoming American* (New York: Free Press, 1983); Harvey Green, *The Uncertainty of Everyday Life* (New York: HarperCollins, 1992); Oscar Handlin, *Al Smith and His America* (Boston: Little, Brown, 1958); David Burner, *The Politics of Provincialism* (New York: Knopf: 1968); Allan J. Lichtman, *Prejudice and the Old Politics* (Chapel Hill: University of North Carolina Press, 1979); and Samuel Lubell, *The Future of American Politics* (New York: Harper and Row, 1952). Two exceptionally rich contemporary sources are Robert and Helen Merrell Lynd, *Middletown: A Study in Modern American Culture* (New York: Harcourt, Brace and World, 1929), a classic of sociological investigation; and The President's

Research Committee on Recent Social Trends, *Recent Social Trends in the United States* (Westport, Conn.: Greenwood, 1970; originally published 1933).

John Kenneth Galbraith, *The Great Crash* (Boston: Houghton Mifflin, 1955) is a popular history of the stock market debacle of 1929. Like Allen's *Only Yesterday*, it is more charming than analytical, and should be supplemented by Robert Sobel, *The Great Bull Market* (New York: Norton, 1968), and the same author's *Panic on Wall Street* (New York: Macmillan, 1968). See also the relevant portions of Milton Friedman and Anna Jacobson Schwartz, *A Monetary History of the United States* (Princeton: Princeton University Press, 1963), which in turn should be supplemented by Peter Temin, *Did Monetary Forces Cause the Great Depression?* (New York: Norton, 1976). Herbert Stein, *The Fiscal Revolution in America* (Chicago: University of Chicago Press, 1969) does an especially good job of putting Herbert Hoover's anti-Depression policies in historical perspective.

On Hoover and his calamitous presidency, see the highly critical discussion in Arthur M. Schlesinger Jr., *The Crisis of the Old Order* (Boston: Houghton Mifflin, 1956), and the somewhat more sympathetic accounts in Joan Hoff Wilson, *Herbert Hoover: Forgotten Progressive* (Boston: Little, Brown, 1975); David Burner, *Herbert Hoover: A Public Life* (New York: Knopf, 1979); Harris Gaylord Warren, *Herbert Hoover and the Great Depression* (New York: Oxford University Press, 1959); Albert U. Romasco, *The Poverty of Abundance: Hoover, the Nation, the Depression* (New York: Oxford University Press, 1965); Jordan A. Schwarz, *The Interregnum of Despair: Hoover, Congress, and the Depression* (Urbana: University of Illinois Press, 1970); William Starr Meyers and Walter H. Newton, *The Hoover Administration: A Documented Narrative* (New York: Charles Scribner's Sons, 1936); and the relevant volumes of Hoover's own *Memoirs: The Cabinet and the Presidency* and *The Great Depression* (New York: Macmillan, 1952).

A sizable scholarly industry has been devoted to trying to explain the causes of the Great Depression, without conclusive results. A good summary source of data is Lester Chandler, *America's Greatest Depression* (New York: Harper and Row, 1970). A more recent comprehensive survey is Michael D. Bordo, Claudia Goldin, and Eugene N. White, eds., *The Defining Moment: The Great Depression and the American Economy in the Twentieth Century* (Chicago: University of Chicago Press, 1998). See also Michael Bernstein, *The Great Depression: Delayed Recovery and Economic Change in America, 1929–1939* (New York: Cambridge University Press, 1987); and Barry Eichengreen, *Golden Fetters: The Gold Standard and the Great Depression, 1919–1939* (New York: Oxford University Press, 1992).

The human toll of the Depression is captured especially well in Richard Lowitt and Maurine Beasley, eds., *One Third of a Nation: Lorena Hickok Reports on the Great Depression* (Urbana: University of Illinois Press, 1981); see also Studs Terkel, *Hard Times: An Oral History of the Great Depression* (New York: Pantheon, 1970); Caroline Bird, *The Invisible Scar* (New York: McKay, 1966); Ann Banks, *First-Person America* (New York: Knopf, 1980); Mirra Komarovsky, *The Unemployed Man and His Family* (New York: Dryden, 1940); and Lois Scharf, *To Work and to Wed: Female Employment, Feminism, and the Great Depression* (Westport, Conn.: Greenwood, 1980).

Of the several biographies of Franklin Delano Roosevelt, I have found the following to be most useful: James MacGregor Burns's two volumes: *Roosevelt: The Lion and the Fox* (New York: Harcourt Brace, 1956), and *Roosevelt: The Soldier of Freedom* (New York: Harcourt Brace Jovanovich, 1970); Kenneth S. Davis, *FDR* (New York: Random

House, 4 vols., 1985–1993); Frank Freidel, *Franklin D. Roosevelt* (Boston: Little, Brown, 4 vols., 1952–1976), and his one-volume *Franklin D. Roosevelt: A Rendezvous with Destiny* (Boston: Little, Brown, 1990); Patrick Maney, *The Roosevelt Presence* (New York: Twayne, 1992); and, for Roosevelt's last year of life, Robert H. Ferrell, *The Dying President: FDR, 1944–1945* (Columbia: University of Missouri Press, 1998). The *Public Papers and Addresses of Franklin D. Roosevelt* (New York: Random House and Harper and Brothers, 13 vols., 1938–1950) is an indispensable source on Roosevelt's presidency, as is *The Complete Presidential Press Conferences of Franklin Delano Roosevelt* (New York: DaCapo, 1972); and Russell D. Buhite and David W. Levy, eds., *FDR's Fireside Chats* (Norman: University of Oklahoma Press, 1992). Also useful is Elliott Roosevelt, ed., *FDR: His Personal Correspondence, 1928–1945* (New York: Duell, Sloan and Pearce, 2 vols., 1950).

Various New Dealers produced notable memoirs, including Raymond Moley, *After Seven Years* (New York: Harper and Brothers, 1939); Rexford Tugwell, *The Brains Trust* (New York: Viking, 1968), the same author's *Roosevelt's Revolution* (New York: Macmillan, 1979), and his *The Democratic Roosevelt* (Garden City, N.Y.: Doubleday, 1957); Frances Perkins, *The Roosevelt I Knew* (New York: Viking, 1946); Samuel I. Rosenman, *Working with Roosevelt* (New York: Harper and Brothers, 1952); Edward J. Flynn, *You're the Boss* (New York: Viking, 1947); George Peek, *Why Quit Our Own?* (New York: Van Nostrand, 1936); and Harold L. Ickes, *The Secret Diary of Harold L. Ickes* (New York: Simon and Schuster, 3 vols., 1953–1954). See also John Morton Blum, *From the Morgenthau Diaries* (Boston: Houghton Mifflin, 3 vols., 1959–1967), condensed into a one-volume edition as *Roosevelt and Morgenthau* (Boston: Houghton Mifflin, 1972); Hugh S. Johnson, *The New Deal from Egg to Earth* (Garden City, N.Y.: Doubleday, Doran, 1935); Harry Hopkins, *Spending to Save* (New York: Norton, 1936); Marriner Eccles, *Beckoning Frontiers* (New York: Knopf, 1951); James A. Farley, *Behind the Ballots* (New York: Harcourt, Brace, 1938), and the same author's *Jim Farley's Story* (New York: McGraw-Hill, 1948); David E. Lilienthal, *The Journals of David E. Lilienthal* (New York: Harper and Row, 7 vols., 1964–1983); Jesse H. Jones, *Fifty Billion Dollars* (New York: Macmillan, 1951); Thomas E. Eliot, *Recollections of the New Deal* (Boston: Northeastern University Press, 1992); and Eleanor Roosevelt, *This I Remember* (New York: Harper and Brothers, 1949).

Biographies of significant figures from the New Deal era include: Blanche Wiesen Cook, *Eleanor Roosevelt: A Life* (New York: Viking, 1992); Lois Scharf, *Eleanor Roosevelt: First Lady of American Liberalism* (Boston: Twayne, 1987); Joseph T. Lash, *Eleanor and Franklin* (New York: New American Library, 1973); T. H. Watkins, *Righteous Pilgrim: The Life and Times of Harold L. Ickes, 1874–1952* (New York: Holt, 1990); Graham J. White and John Maze, *Harold Ickes of the New Deal* (Cambridge, Harvard University Press, 1985); and T. Harry Williams, *Huey Long* (New York: Knopf, 1969), which should be supplemented by Alan Brinkley's insightful *Voices of Protest: Huey Long, Father Coughlin, and the Great Depression* (New York: Knopf, 1982). On Coughlin, see also Charles J. Tull, *Father Coughlin and the New Deal* (Syracuse: Syracuse University Press, 1965). For Felix Frankfurter, see Michael E. Parrish, *Felix Frankfurter and His Time* (New York: Free Press, 1982), and Max Freedman, ed., *Roosevelt and Frankfurter: Their Correspondence, 1928–1945* (Boston: Little, Brown, 1967). Other biographies are J. Joseph Huthmacher, *Senator Robert F. Wagner and the Rise of Urban Liberalism* (New York, Atheneum, 1968); Ellsworth Barnard, *Wendell Willkie, Fighter for Freedom* (Marquette: Northern Michigan University Press, 1966); Richard Norton Smith, *Thomas E. Dewey and His Times* (New York: Simon and Schuster, 1982); and David McCullough, *Truman* (New York: Simon and Schuster, 1992).

General histories of the New Deal include Arthur M. Schlesinger Jr., *The Age of Roosevelt* (Boston: Houghton Mifflin, 3 vols., 1956–1960); William E. Leuchtenburg, *Franklin D. Roosevelt and the New Deal, 1932–1940* (New York: Harper and Row, 1963); Anthony J. Badger, *The New Deal* (New York: Farrar, Straus and Giroux, 1989); Paul Conkin, *The New Deal* (Arlington Heights, Il.: Harlan Davidson, 3d edition, 1992); and Robert McElwaine, *The Great Depression* (New York: Times Books, 1984). Harvard Sitkoff, ed., *Fifty Years Later: The New Deal Evaluated* (Philadelphia: Temple University Press, 1985) summarizes several generations of scholarship.

The New Deal's economic programs are analyzed in Ellis W. Hawley, *The New Deal and the Problem of Monopoly* (Princeton: Princeton University Press, 1966); Albert U. Romasco, *The Politics of Recovery* (New York: Oxford University Press, 1983); Bernard Bellush, *The Failure of the NRA* (New York: Norton, 1975); Bruce J. Schulman, *From Cotton Belt to Sunbelt* (New York: Oxford University Press, 1991); Kenneth Jackson, *Crabgrass Frontier* (New York: Oxford University Press, 1985); Richard K. Vietor, *Contrived Competition: Regulation and Deregulation in America* (Cambridge: Belknap Press of Harvard University Press, 1994); Mark H. Leff, *The Limits of Symbolic Reform: The New Deal and Taxation* (New York: Cambridge University Press, 1984); Gary M. Walton., ed., *Regulatory Change in an Atmosphere of Crisis* (New York: Academic Press, 1979); and the pertinent chapters of Thomas K. McCraw, *Prophets of Regulation* (Cambridge: Belknap Press of Harvard University Press, 1984).

Agriculture is the focus of Theodore Saloutos, *The American Farmer and the New Deal* (Ames: Iowa State University Press, 1982); Donald H. Grubbs, *Cry from the Cotton: The Southern Tenant Farmers' Union and the New Deal* (Chapel Hill: University of North Carolina Press, 1971); Anthony J. Badger, *Prosperity Road: The New Deal, Tobacco, and North Carolina* (Chapel Hill: University of North Carolina Press, 1979); and Donald Worster, *Dust Bowl* (New York: Oxford University Press, 1979), to which James Gregory, *American Exodus: The Dust Bowl Migration and Okie Culture in California* (New York: Oxford University Press, 1989) serves as an intriguing sequel.

Specialized studies of various New Deal initiatives include: Donald Stevenson Howard, *The WPA and Federal Relief Policy* (New York: Russell Sage Foundation, 1943); Jerre Mangione, *The Dream and the Deal: The Federal Writers' Project, 1935–1943* (Boston: Little, Brown, 1972); the chapters dealing with the Social Security Act in Andrew Achenbaum, *Old Age in the New Land* (Baltimore: The Johns Hopkins University Press, 1978), and the same author's *Social Security: Visions and Revisions* (New York: Cambridge University Press, 1986); Thomas K. McGraw, *TVA and the Power Fight* (Philadelphia, Lippincott, 1971); James T. Patterson, *The New Deal and the States* (Princeton: Princeton University Press, 1969), and the relevant chapters of the same author's *America's Struggle against Poverty, 1900–1980* (Cambridge: Harvard University Press, 1981); William E. Leuchtenburg, *The Supreme Court Reborn: The Constitutional Revolution in the Age of Roosevelt* (New York: Oxford University Press, 1995); and, also on the "Court-Packing" episode of 1937, Joseph Alsop and Turner Catledge, *The 168 Days* (Garden City, N.Y.: Doubleday, Doran, 1938). See also Peter Irons, *The New Deal Lawyers* (Princeton: Princeton University Press, 1982); Betty Houchin Winfield, *FDR and the News Media* (Urbana: University of Illinois Press, 1990); Nancy Weiss, *Farewell* to the Party of Lincoln: Black Politics in the Age of FDR (Princeton: Princeton University Press, 1983); Harvard Sitkoff, A New Deal for Blacks (New York: Oxford University Press, 1978); Graham D. Taylor, The New Deal and American Indian Tribalism (Lincoln: University of Nebraska Press, 1977); Kenneth R. Philp, John Collier's Crusade for Indian Reform (Tucson: University of Arizona Press, 1977); Susan Ware, Beyond Suffrage: Women and the New Deal (Harvard University Press, 1981), the same author's Holding the Line: American Women in the 1930s (Boston: Twayne, 1982), and her Partner and I: Molly Dewson, Feminism, and New Deal Politics (New Haven: Yale University Press, 1987). See also Elizabeth Israels Perry, Belle Moskowitz (New York: Oxford University Press, 1987).

Several books examine the dramatic changes in working-class life and in the status of organized labor during the New Deal era. The standard work is Irving Bernstein's masterful Turbulent Years: A History of the American Worker, 1933–1941 (Boston: Houghton Mifflin, 1970). Also valuable are Robert Zieger, American Workers, American Unions (Baltimore: The Johns Hopkins University Press, 1986), and the same author's The CIO: 1935–1955 (Chapel Hill: University of North Carolina Press, 1995); Melvyn Dubofsky, American Labor Since the New Deal (Chicago: Quadrangle, 1971); Melvyn Dubofsky and Warren Van Tine, John L. Lewis (New York: Quadrangle/New York Times, 1977); and James Gross's two volumes, The Making of the National Labor Relations Board and The Reshaping of the National Labor Relations Board (Albany: State University of New York Press: 1974 and 1981, respectively). Jacquelyn Dowd Hall, et al., focus on southern textile workers in Like a Family: The Making of a Southern Cotton Mill World (New York: Norton, 1987); Lizabeth Cohen examines Chicago industrial workers in Making a New Deal (cited above).

Politics is covered in John Allswang, The New Deal and American Politics (New York: Wiley, 1978); Lyle W. Dorsett, Franklin D. Roosevelt and the Big City Bosses (Port Washington, N.Y.: Kennikat, 1977); Charles Trout, Boston, the Great Depression and the New Deal (New York: Oxford University Press, 1977); Bruce Stave, The New Deal and the Last Hurrah: Pittsburgh Machine Politics (Pittsburgh: University of Pittsburgh Press, 1970); James T. Patterson, Congressional Conservatism and the New Deal (Lexington: University Press of Kentucky, 1967); Clyde P. Weed, The Nemesis of Reform: The Republican Party During the New Deal (New York: Columbia University Press, 1994); Alan Brinkley, The End of Reform: New Deal Liberalism in Depression and War (New York: Knopf, 1995); and in the relevant sections of Michael Barone, Our Country (New York: Free Press, 1990), and of Steve Fraser and Gary Gerstle, The Rise and Fall of the New Deal Order, 1930–1980 (Princeton: Princeton University Press, 1989). For the activities of the radical left, see Irving Howe and Louis Coser's exhaustive account The American Communist Party (New York: Praeger, 1962); and Harvey Klehr and John Earl Haynes, The American Communist Movement: Storming Heaven Itself (New York: Twayne, 1992).

On specific regions, see Richard Lowitt, The New Deal and the West (Bloomington: Indiana University Press, 1984); Gavin Wright, Old South, New South: Revolutions in the Southern Economy Since the Civil War (New York: Basic Books, 1986); James Hodges, New Deal Labor Policy and the Southern Cotton Textile Industry, 1933–1941 (Knoxville: University of Tennessee Press, 1986); and James Cobb and Michael Namaroto, eds., The New Deal and the South (Jackson: University Press of Mississippi, 1984).

The cultural history of the Depression decade is treated in Edmond Wilson, *The American Earthquake: A Document of the 1920s and 1930s* (Garden City, N.Y.: Doubleday, 1958); Alfred Kazin, *On Native Grounds* (Garden City, N.Y.: Doubleday, 1942); Richard Pells, *Radical Visions, American Dreams: Culture and Social Thought in the Depression Years* (New York: Harper and Row, 1973); William Stott, *Documentary Expression in Thirties America* (New York: Oxford University Press, 1973); and Karol Ann Marling, *Wall-to-Wall America: A Cultural History of Post Office Murals in the Great Depression* (Minneapolis: University of Minnesota Press, 1982).

Two excellent compendia on public opinion in the Depression and World War II years are Hadley Cantril, ed., *Public Opinion, 1935–1946* (Princeton: Princeton University Press, 1951); and George H. Gallup, *The Gallup Poll: Public Opinion, 1935–1971* (New York: Random House, 1972).

Of the many studies of the rise of Nazism and Japanese expansionism, I have found the following most useful: Joachim Fest, *Hitler* (New York: Harcourt Brace Jovanovich, 1974); Alan Bullock, *Hitler: A Study in Tyranny* (New York: Harper and Row, 1962); William Shirer, *The Rise and Fall of the Third Reich* (New York: Simon and Schuster, 1960); A. J. P. Taylor, *The Origins of the Second World War* (London, Hamilton, 1961); Winston S. Churchill, *The Second World War* (Boston: Houghton Mifflin, 6 vols., 1948–1953); Donald Cameron Watt, *How War Came: The Immediate Origins of the Second World War, 1938–1939* (New York: Pantheon, 1989); Dorothy Borg, *The United States and the Far Eastern Crisis of 1933–1938* (Cambridge: Harvard University Press, 1964); Robert J. C. Butow, *Tojo and the Coming of the War* (Princeton: Princeton University Press, 1961); Herbert Feis, *The Road to Pearl Harbor* (Princeton: Princeton University Press, 1950); and Paul W. Schroeder's especially provocative *The Axis Alliance and Japanese-American Relations, 1941* (Ithaca: Cornell University Press, 1958).

On American isolationism, see Manfred Jonas, *Isolationism in America* (Ithaca: Cornell University Press, 1966); Wayne S. Cole, *Roosevelt and the Isolationists* (Lincoln: University of Nebraska Press, 1983), and the same author's *Charles A. Lindbergh and the Battle against American Intervention in World War II* (New York: Harcourt Brace Jovanovich, 1974); Mathew Coulter, *The Senate Munitions Inquiry of the 1930s* (Westport, Conn.: Greenwood, 1997); and Richard Norton Smith's biography, *The Colonel: The Life and Legend of Robert R. McCormick* (Boston: Houghton Mifflin, 1997), about the publisher of the *Chicago Tribune* and arguably the nation's most influential isolationist.

Essential to any study of the diplomacy of this period are the several relevant volumes of *Foreign Relations of the United States*. Two special collections are also highly valuable: Edgar B. Nixon, ed., *Franklin D. Roosevelt and Foreign Affairs* (Cambridge: Belknap Press of Harvard University Press, 3 vols., 1969), which covers from January 1933 to January 1937; and the eleven volumes of the same title edited by Donald Schewe, covering January 1937 to August 1939 (New York: Clearwater, 1969). A pair of volumes based on early access to official documents are so meticulous and comprehensive that they are virtually primary sources: William L. Langer and S. Everett Gleason, *The Challenge to Isolation, 1937–1940* and *The Undeclared War: 1940–1941* (New York: Harper, 1952 and 1953, respectively). Other useful collections of contemporary materials are Orville H. Bullitt, ed., *For the President: Personal and Secret, Correspondence between Franklin D. Roosevelt and William C. Bullitt* (Boston: Houghton Mifflin, 1972); William E. Dodd, Jr., and Martha Dodd, eds., *Ambassador Dodd's Diary, 1933–1938* (New York:

Harcourt, Brace, 1941); and Beatrice Bishop Berle and Travis Beal Jacobs, *Navigating the Rapids: From the Papers of Adolf A. Berle* (New York: Harcourt Brace Jovanovich, 1973).

Memoirs that shed light on the diplomacy of the prewar and wartime years include: Cordell Hull, *Memoirs* (New York: Macmillan, 2 vols., 1948); Henry L. Stimson and McGeorge Bundy, *On Active Service in Peace and War* (New York: Harper, 1948), easily supplemented by Stimson's diary, which is available on microfilm; Joseph C. Grew, *Turbulent Era* (Boston: Houghton Mifflin, 1952); Charles E. Bohlen, *Witness to History* (New York: Norton, 1973); William Leahy, *I Was There* (New York: Whittlesley House, 1950); James F. Byrnes, *Speaking Frankly* (New York: Harper, 1947); Robert Murphy, *Diplomat Among Warriors* (Garden City, N.Y.: Doubleday, 1964); Dean Acheson, *Present at the Creation: My Years in the State Department* (New York: Norton, 1969); W. Averell Harriman and Elie Abel, *Special Envoy to Churchill and Stalin, 1941–1946* (New York: Random House, 1975); two titles by Sumner Welles: *The Time for Decision* (New York: Harper, 1944), and *Seven Decisions That Shaped History* (New York: Harper, 1951); and Harry S. Truman, *Memoirs* (Garden City, N.Y.: Doubleday, 2 vols., 1955, 1956). See also Robert H. Ferrell, ed., *Off the Record: The Private Papers of Harry S. Truman* (New York: Harper and Row, 1980).

Biographies of leading diplomatic figures are Robert E. Sherwood, *Roosevelt and Hopkins* (New York: Grosset and Dunlap, 1950); Waldo Heinrichs Jr., *American Ambassador: Joseph C. Grew and the Development of the United States Diplomatic Tradition* (New York: Oxford University Press, 1996); David Robertson, *Sly and Able: A Political Biography of James F. Byrnes* (New York: Norton, 1994); and Irwin F. Gellman, *Secret Affairs: Franklin Roosevelt, Cordell Hull, and Sumner Welles* (Baltimore: The Johns Hopkins University Press, 1995).

The foreign policies of the four Roosevelt administrations are ably presented in Robert Dallek's encyclopedic *Franklin D. Roosevelt and American Foreign Policy, 1932–1945* (New York: Oxford University Press, 1979). See also Robert A. Divine, *The Reluctant Belligerent* (New York: Wiley, 1965), and the same author's *The Illusion of Neutrality* (Chicago: University of Chicago Press, 1962); Waldo Heinrichs Jr., *Threshold of War* (New York: Oxford University Press, 1988); Lloyd Gardner, *Economic Aspects of New Deal Diplomacy* (Madison: University of Wisconsin Press, 1964); Warren F. Kimball, *The Juggler* (Princeton: Princeton University Press, 1991); and Frederick W. Marks, *Wind Over Sand: The Diplomacy of Franklin Roosevelt* (Athens: University of Georgia Press, 1988).

Relations with Britain are documented in William R. Rock, *Chamberlain and Roosevelt* (Columbus: Ohio State University Press, 1988); Warren F. Kimball, ed., *Churchill and Roosevelt: The Complete Correspondence* (Princeton: Princeton University Press, 3 vols., 1984), an indispensable source, and in the same author's *The Most Unsordid Act: Lend-Lease, 1939–1941* (Baltimore: The Johns Hopkins University Press, 1969), as well as his *Forged in War: Roosevelt, Churchill, and the Second World War* (New York: Morrow, 1997). See also Joseph P. Lash, *Roosevelt and Churchill: The Partnership that Saved the West* (New York: Norton, 1976).

Many scholars have examined American policy concerning refugees, predominantly Jewish, from Hitler's Reich: Arthur Morse, *While Six Million Died* (New York: Random House, 1968); Henry L. Feingold, *The Politics of Rescue: The Roosevelt Administration and the Holocaust, 1938–1945* (New York: Holocaust Library, 1970); Deborah E. Lipstadt, *Beyond Belief: The American Press and the Coming of the Holocaust, 1933–1945* (New York: Free Press, 1986); and two titles by David Wyman: *Paper Walls: America and the Refugee Crisis, 1938–1941* (Amherst: University of Massachusetts Press, 1968), and *The Abandonment of the Jews: America and the Holocaust, 1941–1945* (New York: Pantheon, 1984).

For various other specific diplomatic episodes in the pre-war years, see Bryce Wood, *The Making of the Good Neighbor Policy* (New York: Columbia University Press, 1961); Irwin F. Gellman, *Good Neighbor Diplomacy* (Baltimore: The Johns Hopkins University Press, 1979); Allen Guttmann, *The Wound in the Heart: America and the Spanish Civil War* (New York: Free Press, 1962); Douglas Little, *Malevolent Neutrality: The United States, Great Britain, and the Origins of the Spanish Civil War* (Ithaca: Cornell University Press, 1985); and William L. Langer, *Our Vichy Gamble* (New York: Knopf, 1947).

The wealth of documentation on World War II is overwhelming. It was, as Churchill once remarked, perhaps the only war in which the victors eventually gained access to the bulk of their foes' records. Much of that material is available in English, for example, *Documents on German Foreign Policy* (Washington: U.S. Department of State, 1957–), as well as the extensive materials collected for purposes of the Nuremberg and Tokyo war crimes trials: *Trials of War Criminals Before the Nuernberg Military Tribunals* (Washington: USGPO, 1949–1953) and the records of the Military Tribunal for the Far East, for which an extensive index has been compiled by R. John Pritchard, *The Tokyo War Crimes Trial: Index and Guide* (New York: Garland, 1981–1987). See also the extensive United States materials gathered in *Pearl Harbor Attack: Hearings before the Joint Committee on the Investigation of the Pearl Harbor Attack*, 79th Cong., 1st sess. (1946), and in the oddly named but remarkably rich *Reports of General MacArthur: Japanese Operations in the Southwest Pacific Area* (Washington: USGPO, 1966). For U.S. military operations, including planning, logistics, and medical developments, among other topics, the various official histories of the several services are marvelously detailed (for specific titles, see the footnote citations): *The United States Army in World War II* (Washington: Department of the Army, various years); Wesley Frank Craven and James Lee Cate, *The Army Air Forces in World War II* (Chicago: University of Chicago Press, 6 vols., 1953); Samuel Eliot Morison, *History of U.S. Naval Operations in World War II* (Boston: Little, Brown, 15 vols., 1947–1962); *History of Marine Corps Operations in World War II* (Washington: Historical Branch, U.S. Marine Corps., 5 vols., 1958–1971). Also invaluable are Alfred D. Chandler Jr., et al., eds., *The Papers of Dwight David Eisenhower* (Baltimore: The Johns Hopkins University Press, 19 vols., 1970–). See also *Stalin's Correspondence with Roosevelt and Truman, 1941–1945* (New York: Capricorn, 1965); and Milovan Djilas, *Conversations with Stalin* (New York: Harcourt, Brace, and World, 1962).

Among the many general histories of World War II, I have relied especially on three: John Keegan, *The Second World War* (New York: Viking, 1989); Gerhard L. Weinberg, *A World at Arms: A Global History of World War II* (New York: Cambridge University Press, 1994); and A. Russell Buchanan, *The United States in World War II* (New York: Harper and Row, 2 vols., 1964). Also useful is James L. Stokesbury, *A Short History of World War II* (New York: Morrow, 1980), and, among reference books, I. C. B. Dear, ed., *The Oxford Companion to the Second World War* (New York: Oxford University Press, 1995); John Ellis, *World War II: A Statistical Survey* (New York: Facts on File,

1993); and John Keegan, ed., *The Times Atlas to the Second World War* (New York, Harper and Row, 1989).

Among studies of the war's diplomatic dimensions, Gaddis Smith provides a brief introduction in *American Diplomacy During the Second World War* (New York: Wiley, 1965). More detailed are William Hardy McNeil, *America, Britain, and Russia: Their Cooperation and Conflict, 1941–1946* (New York: Oxford University Press, 1953); Mark Stoler, *The Politics of the Second Front* (Westport, Conn.: Greenwood, 1977); and three titles by Herbert Feis: *Churchill, Roosevelt, and Stalin: The War They Waged and the Peace They Sought* (Princeton: Princeton University Press, 1957); *Between War and Peace: The Potsdam Conference* (Princeton: Princeton University Press, 1960); and *The Atomic Bomb and the End of World War II* (Princeton: Princeton University Press, 1961). On specific wartime diplomatic episodes, see Keith Sainsbury on Teheran, *The Turning Point* (New York: Oxford University Press, 1985); Diane Shaver Clements, *Yalta* (New York: Oxford University Press, 1970); and Charles Mee, *Meeting at Potsdam* (New York: Evans, 1975). See also Gabriel Kolko, *The Politics of War: The World and United States Foreign Policy, 1943–1945* (New York: Random House, 1968).

Kent Roberts Greenfield, *American Strategy in World War II* (Baltimore: The Johns Hopkins University Press, 1963), gives a lucid overview. The same author's *Command Decisions* (New York: Harcourt, Brace, 1959) is more selective, but also highly useful for the study of grand strategy, as is Eric Labaree, *Commander in Chief: Franklin Delano Roosevelt, His Lieutenants, and Their War* (New York: Harper and Row, 1987). See also the relevant portions of Russell V. Weigley, *The American Way of War* (New York: Macmillan, 1973), and his *History of the U.S. Army* (Bloomington: Indiana University Press, 1989).

Among the biographies and memoirs of wartime figures, the following are notable: Forest C. Pogue, *George C. Marshall* (New York: Viking, 4 vols., 1963–1987); David Eisenhower, *Eisenhower at War* (New York: Random House, 1986); Stephen Ambrose, *The Supreme Commander: The War Years of General Dwight D. Eisenhower* (Garden City, N.Y.: Doubleday, 1970); Robert H. Ferrell, ed., *The Eisenhower Diaries* (New York: Norton, 1981); Eisenhower's own *Crusade in Europe* (Garden City, N.Y.: Doubleday, 1948); Harry C. Butcher, *My Three Years with Eisenhower* (New York: Simon and Schuster, 1946); Walter Bedell Smith, *Eisenhower's Six Great Decisions* (New York: Longman's, 1956); Russell V. Weigley, *Eisenhower's Lieutenants: The Campaigns of France and Germany* (Bloomington: Indiana University Press, 1989); Clayton James, *The Years of MacArthur* (Boston: Houghton Mifflin, 3 vols., 1970–); MacArthur's own *Reminiscences* (New York: McGraw-Hill, 1964); Martin Blumenson's *Patton* (New York: Morrow, 1985); Omar Bradley, *A Soldier's Story* (New York: Holt, 1951); Bradley and Clay Blair, *A General's Life* (New York: Simon and Schuster, 1983); Godfrey Hodgson, *The Colonel: The Life and Times of Henry L. Stimson, 1867–1959* (New York: Knopf, 1990); the relevant chapters of Kai Bird, *The Chairman: John J. McCloy and the Making of the American Establishment* (New York: Simon and Schuster, 1992); H. H. Arnold, *Global Mission* (New York: Harper, 1949); Curtis LeMay, *Mission with LeMay* (Garden City, N.Y.: Doubleday, 1965); and Lord Moran, *Churchill: Taken from the Diaries of Lord Moran: The Struggle for Survival, 1940–1965* (Boston: Houghton Mifflin, 1966).

Walter LaFeber, *The Clash: U.S.-Japanese Relations Throughout History* (New York: Norton, 1997), provides valuable background and historical perspective. Gordon W. Prange, *At Dawn We Slept: The Untold Story of Pearl Harbor* (New York: Penguin,

1982) is an exhaustive account. See also Roberta Wohlstetter, *Pearl Harbor: Warning and Decision* (Stanford: Stanford University Press, 1962), which definitively lays to rest accusations that Roosevelt conspired to invite the Pearl Harbor attack. Prange has also written a fine account of the Battle of Midway, *Miracle at Midway* (New York: Penguin, 1982), as has Walter Lord, *Incredible Victory: The Battle of Midway* (New York: Harper and Row, 1967). For a Japanese perspective on that pivotal battle, see Mitsuo Fuchida and Masatake Okumiya, *Midway: The Battle That Doomed Japan* (Annapolis: U.S. Naval Institute Press, 1955).

Ronald Spector, *Eagle Against the Sun: The American War with Japan* (New York: Free Press, 1985), is an excellent overall history of the Pacific War. Unfortunately, no comparable volume exists for the European Theater. Spector's account can be profitably supplemented with Akira Iriye, *Power and Culture: The Japanese-American War, 1941–1945* (Cambridge: Harvard University Press, 1981), and John Dower's fascinating *War Without Mercy: Race and Power in the Pacific War* (New York: Pantheon, 1986), as well as with Christopher Thorne, *Allies of a Kind: The United States, Britain, and the War against Japan* (New York: Oxford University Press, 1978), which is especially informative on the colonial dimension of the Asian conflict. See also Michael Schaller, *The U.S. Crusade in China, 1939–1945* (New York: Columbia University Press, 1979); and Barbara Tuchman, *Stilwell and the American Experience in China* (New York: Macmillan, 1971).

In addition to the accounts in the official service histories, specific actions in the Pacific are covered especially well in Richard B. Frank, *Guadalcanal* (New York: Random House, 1990); Thomas J. Cutler, *The Battle of Leyte Gulf* (New York: Harper-Collins, 1994); and Colonel Hiromichi Yahara, *The Battle for Okinawa* (New York: Wiley, 1995).

The naval war in the Atlantic is the subject of several studies that nicely complement Admiral Morison's somewhat dated account (which, for example, makes no mention of the role of ULTRA, which was not made public until well after Morison had written): Thomas A. Bailey and Paul B. Ryan, *Hitler vs. Roosevelt: The Undeclared Naval War* (New York: Free Press, 1979); Dan Van der Vat, *The Atlantic Campaign* (New York: Harper and Row, 1988); Nathan Miller, *War at Sea: A Naval History of World War II* (New York: Oxford University Press, 1995); and Michael Gannon, *Operation Drumbeat* (New York: Harper and Row, 1990).

The air war has generated a large literature of its own. See especially Richard Overy, *The Air War* (London: Europa, 1980); Michael Sherry, *The Rise of American Air Power* (New Haven: Yale University Press, 1987); Stephen L. McFarland and Wesley Phillips Newton, *To Command the Sky: The Battle for Air Superiority over Germany, 1942–1944* (Washington: Smithsonian Institution Press, 1991); Alan J. Levine, *The Strategic Bombing of Germany, 1940–1945* (Westport, Conn.: Praeger, 1992); Conrad Crane, *Bombs, Cities, and Civilians: American Airpower Strategy in World War II* (Lawrence: University Press of Kansas, 1993); and Ronald Schaffer's impassioned *Wings of Judgment: American Bombing in World War II* (New York: Oxford University Press, 1985), which discusses both the European and Pacific theaters.

For the Mediterranean and European fighting, worthwhile supplements to the official histories include: Chester Wilmot, *The Struggle for Europe* (London: Collins, 1952), which is highly critical of Roosevelt's strategy, or lack thereof, for dealing with the Soviets; Michael Howard, *The Mediterranean Strategy in the Second World War* (New

York: Praeger, 1968); Carlo D'Este, *Bitter Victory: The Battle for Sicily, 1943* (New York: Dutton, 1988), and the same author's *Decision in Normandy* (New York: HarperCollins, 1994); Max Hastings, *Overlord* (London: Pan Books, 1985); Stephen E. Ambrose, *D-Day* (New York: Simon and Schuster, 1994), and his *Citizen Soldiers* (New York: Simon and Schuster, 1997); Cornelius Ryan, *The Longest Day* (New York: Simon and Schuster, 1959), and the same author's account of the failure of Operation Market-Garden, *A Bridge Too Far* (New York: Fawcett, 1975); Trevor N. Dupuy, et al., *Hitler's Last Gamble: The Battle of the Bulge* (New York: HarperCollins, 1994), and Richard Lamb, *War in Italy* (New York: St. Martin's Press, 1993). The controversial surrender of the German troops in Italy is covered in Allen Dulles, *The Secret Surrender* (New York: Harper and Row, 1966).

My own thinking on the economic and social implications of the war for the United States has been deeply shaped by two excellent comparative studies: Alan S. Milward, *War, Economy, and Society, 1939–1945* (Berkeley: University of California Press, 1979); and Richard Overy, *Why the Allies Won* (New York: Norton, 1995). For the American homefront, see Bureau of the Budget, *The United States at War* (Washington: U.S.G.P.O, 1946); Harold G. Vatter, *The U.S. Economy in World War II* (New York: Columbia University Press, 1985); Donald M. Nelson, *Arsenal of Democracy: The Story of American War Production* (New York: Harcourt Brace, 1946); Keith E. Eiler, *Mobilizing America: Robert P. Patterson and the War Effort, 1940–1945* (Ithaca: Cornell University Press, 1997); Bruce Catton's highly critical *The Warlords of Washington* (New York: Harcourt Brace, 1948); Eliot Janeway, *The Struggle for Survival* (New Haven: Yale University Press, 1951); Richard Polenberg, *War and Society: The United States, 1941–1945* (Philadelphia: Lippincott, 1972); John Morton Blum's imaginative *V Was for Victory* (New York: Harcourt Brace Jovanovich, 1976); Doris Kearns Goodwin's lavish biographical account, *No Ordinary Time: Franklin and Eleanor Roosevelt: The Home Front in World War II* (New York: Simon and Schuster, 1994); William L. O'Neill's argumentative *A Democracy at War: America's Fight at Home and Abroad in World War II* (New York: Free Press, 1993); Richard Lingeman's breezy *Don't You Know There's a War On?* (New York: Putnam, 1970); Geoffrey Perrett's *Days of Sadness, Years of Triumph: The American People, 1939–1945* (New York: Coward, McCann and Geoghegan, 1979); and Michael C. C. Adams's revisionist *The Best War Ever* (Baltimore: The Johns Hopkins University Press, 1994). Studs Terkel provides a fascinating oral history in *"The Good War"* (New York: Pantheon, 1984); as do Mark Jonathan Harris, et al., *The Home Front* (New York: G. P. Putnam's Sons, 1984), derived from the excellent documentary film of the same title. H. G. Nicholas, ed., *Washington Despatches, 1941–1945* (New York: Free Press, 1981) presents the incomparably insightful commentaries on wartime Washington of the young British diplomat Isaiah Berlin.

Special studies of interest include: Alan Clive, *State of War: Michigan in World War II* (Ann Arbor: University of Michigan Press, 1979); Marilyn S. Johnson, *The Second Gold Rush: Oakland and the East Bay in World War II* (Berkeley: University of California Press, 1993); John E. Brigante, *The Feasibility Dispute* (Washington: Committee on Public Administration Cases, 1950); Nelson Lichtenstein, *Labor's War at Home: The CIO in World War II* (New York: Cambridge University Press, 1982); Allan M. Winkler, *The Politics of Propaganda: The Office of War Information* (New Haven: Yale University Press, 1978); George Q. Flynn, *Lewis B. Hershey: Mr. Selective Service* (Chapel Hill: University of North Carolina Press, 1985); Mulford Q. Sibley and Philip F. Jacob, *Con-*

scription of Conscience: The American State and the Conscientious Objector, 1941–1947 (Ithaca: Cornell University Prerss, 1952); William M. Tuttle Jr., Daddy's Gone to War: The Second World War in the Lives of America's Children (New York: Oxford University Press, 1993); Clayton R. Koppes and Gregory D. Black, Hollywood Goes to War (New York: Free Press, 1987); Keith Olson, The G.I. Bill, the Veterans, and the Colleges (Lexington: University of Kentucky Press, 1974); and Allan Bérubé, Coming Out Under Fire: The History of Gay Men and Women in World War II (New York: Free Press, 1990).

The wartime internment of Japanese immigrants and Japanese-American citizens has spawned several studies, including: Jacobus tenBroek, et al., Prejudice, War, and the Constitution (Berkeley and Los Angeles: University of California Press, 1970); and Peter Irons, Justice at War: The Story of the Japanese Internment Cases (Berkeley: University of California Press, 1983), which focuses especially on the legal aspects of the internment. Gordon Chang, ed., Morning Glory, Evening Shadow: Yamato Ichihashi and His Internment Writings, 1942–1945 (Stanford: Stanford University Press, 1997), gives the perspective of one especially insightful internee. Also worth consulting is the relevant chapter in Attorney General Francis Biddle's memoir In Brief Authority (Garden City, N.Y.: Doubleday, 1962).

The situation of African-Americans in wartime helped to occasion Gunnar Myrdal's classic, An American Dilemma: The Negro Problem and Modern Democracy (New York: Harper and Row, 1944); see also the pertinent portions of Jervis Anderson, A. Philip Randolph (New York: Harcourt Brace, 1973); and of Walter White, A Rising Wind (Garden City, N.Y.: Doubleday, Doran, 1945), as well as the same author's A Man Called White (New York: Viking, 1947). See also Neil Wynn, The Afro-American and the Second World War (London: P. Elek, 1976); and Richard M. Dalfiume, Desegregation of the U.S. Armed Forces (Columbia: University of Missouri Press, 1969).

The war's impact on women has excited much scholarly controversy, beginning with William Chafe, The American Woman: Her Changing Political, Economic, and Social Role in the Twentieth Century (New York: Oxford University Press, 1972). For other appraisals, consult the relevant parts of Alice Kessler-Harris, Out to Work: A History of Wage-Earning Women in the United States (New York: Oxford University Press, 1982), and Rosalind Rosenberg, Divided Lives: American Women in the Twentieth Century (New York: Hill and Wang, 1992), as well as Susan M. Hartmann, The Homefront and Beyond: American Women in the 1940s (Boston: Twayne, 1982); and D'Ann Campbell, Women at War with America: Private Lives in a Patriotic Era (Cambridge: Harvard University Press, 1984).

Richard Rhodes, The Making of the Atomic Bomb (New York: Simon and Schuster, 1986) provides a definitive account of the scientific, technological, political, and economic aspects of the Manhattan Project. See also the official Atomic Energy Commission history, Richard B. Hewlett and Oscar E. Anderson Jr., The New World, 1939/1946 (University Park: Pennsylvania State University Press, 1962). On the complicated role of the bomb in the war's endgame, including both the Japanese decision to surrender and U.S. relations with the Soviet Union, see Gar Alperovitz's tendentious The Decision to Use the Atomic Bomb and the Architecture of an American Myth (New York: Knopf, rev. ed., 1995); Martin Sherwin, A World Destroyed: The Atomic Bomb and the Grand Alliance (New York: Knopf, 1975); the relevant chapters in McGeorge Bundy, Danger and Survival: Choices about the Bomb in the First Fifty Years (New York: Random House,

1988); and the articles by Barton J. Bernstein cited in the footnotes for Chapter 22. The definitive account of Japan's final capitulation is Robert J. C. Butow, *Japan's Decision to Surrender* (Stanford: Stanford University Press, 1954).

The sixteen million Americans who served in the armed services during the war have been extensively studied, starting with Samuel Stouffer, *The American Soldier* (Princeton: Princeton University Press, 2 vols., 1949). See also Lee Kennett, *G.I.: The American Soldier in World War II* (New York: Scribner's, 1987); Geoffrey Perrett, *There's a War to Be Won: the United States Army in World War II* (New York: Random House, 1991); and Gerald F. Linderman, *The World Within War: America's Combat Experience in World War II* (New York: Free Press, 1997), as well as the several volumes dealing with troop enlistment, training, and deployment in the Army's official history. Also valuable, though not always fully reliable, are the accounts of accredited war correspondents, including Ernie Pyle, *Brave Men* (New York: Holt, 1944); John Steinbeck, *Once There Was a War* (New York: Viking, 1958); John Hersey, *Into the Valley: A Skirmish of the Marines* (New York: Knopf, 1943); Richard Tregaskis, *Guadalcanal Diary* (New York: Random House, 1943); Robert Lee Sharrod, *On to Westward* (New York: Duell, Sloan and Pearce, 1945), and his *Tarawa: The Story of a Battle* (New York: Duell, Sloan and Pearce, 1944). Their reportage is strongly criticized in Paul Fussell, *Wartime* (New York: Oxford University Press, 1989).

I have been able to sample only a few of the countless memoirs by servicemen: E.B. Sledge, *With the Old Breed at Peleliu and Okinawa* (Novato, Calif.: Presidio, 1981); Harry H. Crosby, *A Wing and a Prayer: The "Bloody 100th" Bomb Group of the U.S. Eighth Air Force in Action over Europe in World War II* (New York: HarperCollins, 1993); Samuel Hynes, *Flights of Passage: Reflections of a World War II Aviator* (Annapolis: Naval Institute Press, 1988); Alvin Kernan, *Crossing the Line: A Bluejacket's World War II Odyssey* (Annapolis: Naval Institute Press, 1994); William Manchester, *Goodbye, Darkness* (Boston: Little, Brown, 1979); and Audie Murphy, *To Hell and Back* (New York: Henry Holt, 1949).

WORLD WAR II: EUROPEAN THEATER

FINLAND

Leningrad

ESTONIA

Moscow

LATVIA

Volga

U.S.S.R.

Baltic Sea

LITHUANIA

E. PRUSSIA

Kursk

Don

Vistula

Warsaw

Stalingrad

Volga

POLAND

Kiev

CZECHOSLOVAKIA

Don

HUNGARY

Sea of Azov

ROMANIA

Ploesti

Black Sea

YUGOSLAVIA

Danube

BULGARIA

ALBANIA (IT.)

TURKEY

GREECE

Athens

SYRIA (FR.)

CRETE

CYPRUS

LEBANON

Mediterranean Sea

PALESTINE (BR.)

TRANS-JORDAN (BR.)

El Alamein

Cairo

LIBYA

EGYPT (BR.)

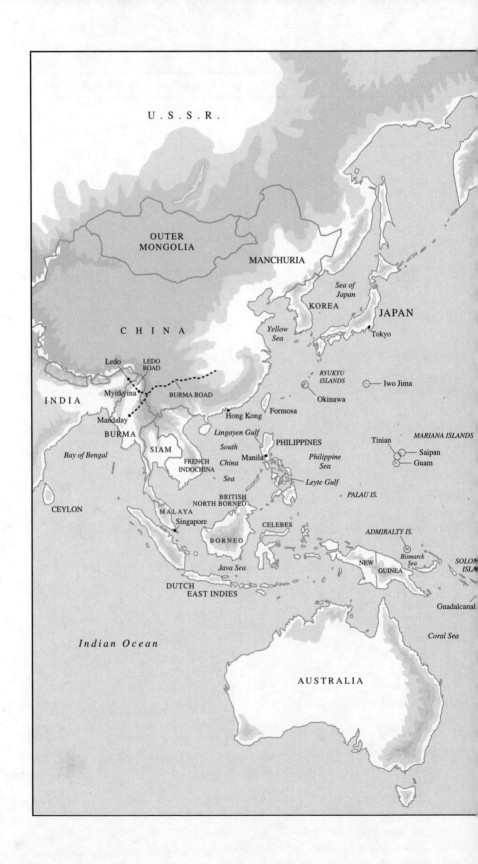

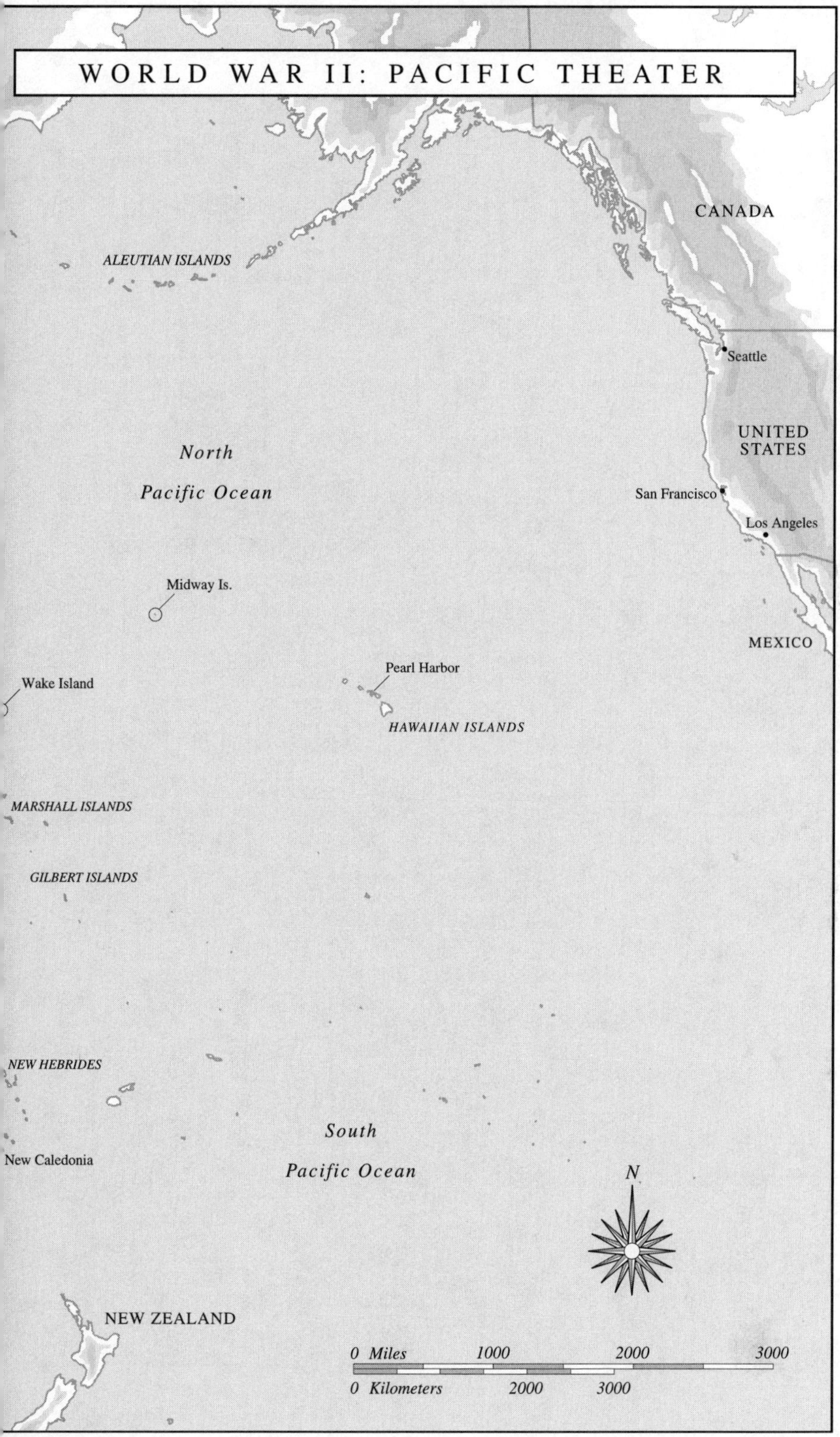

WORLD WAR II: PACIFIC THEATER

CANADA

ALEUTIAN ISLANDS

Seattle

UNITED
STATES

North

Pacific Ocean

San Francisco

Los Angeles

Midway Is.

MEXICO

Pearl Harbor

Wake Island

HAWAIIAN ISLANDS

MARSHALL ISLANDS

GILBERT ISLANDS

NEW HEBRIDES

South

New Caledonia

Pacific Ocean

N

NEW ZEALAND

0 Miles	1000	2000	3000

0 Kilometers	2000	3000

Index

Note: FDR is the abbreviation for Franklin
Delano Roosevelt.

AAA. *See* Agricultural Adjustment
   Administration
Aachen (Germany), 737
ABC-1 (American-British Conversation
   Number 1), 481–82, 490, 506, 507, 532,
   544
Abraham Lincoln Battalion, 399
Abt, Jon, 211*n*
Academic experts. *See* Brain Trust; *specific
   person*
Acheson, Dean, 197, 511–12*n*
ACW (Amalgamated Clothing Workers),
   302, 305
Adamic, Louis, 256
Adriatic Sea. *See* Balkans; *specific nation*
Advisory Committee on Uranium (U.S.),
   660–61
AEAF (Allied Expeditionary Air Force), 702
Aegean Sea. *See* Balkans; *specific nation*
Aerial warfare: Allied ascendancy in, 703;
   and Allied invasion of France, 724–25,
   727, 728; Allied losses/casualties in, 606,
   608–9, 703; and Allied strategy/
   objectives, 702, 703–8; and Big Week
   (1943), 703; and Casablanca
   Conference, 654; and Churchill-FDR
   relations, 706–7; doctrine of, 601–3; and
   escorts, 605, 609; FDR's views about,
   428–29, 706–7; and geography, 814; and

German strategy, 435, 702–3; human
   factor in, 605–6; and mobilization, 630,
   631, 654; and Overlord, 698, 701–2,
   705–7; in Pacific war, 745, 814, 816,
   818–20, 825–26, 833, 834, 845–48; and
   public opinion, 604; Rommel's
   assessment of Allied, 695; and second
   front, 606; and total war concept, 602,
   602–3*n*; and U.S. strategy, 428, 601–9,
   702, 703–4; in World War I, 602. *See
   also* Bombing; *specific battle*
African-Americans. *See* Blacks
Agee, James, 208, 256
Agrarian myth, 200–201
Agricultural Adjustment Act (1933), 143,
   144, 204, 329
Agricultural Adjustment Administration
   (AAA): accomplishment of, 212; basic
   premises of, 203; constitutionality of,
   263, 279, 324; creation of, 177;
   criticisms of, 224; and crop destruction
   program, 204–5, 205*n*; and economic
   isolationism, 388; and economic
   recovery, 199, 200, 202–13, 288; and
   Extension Service, 206; and FDR's first
   hundred days, 153, 154, 218; functions
   of, 152; Peek as head of, 142; and
   prices, 388; and stabilization of
   agriculture, 199; as success, 200; and
   tenant farmers/sharecroppers, 207–13; as
   voluntary program, 206–7. *See also*
   Peek, George

Agricultural Extension Service, 203, 206, 211

Agricultural Marketing Act (1929), 18, 43–44, 48, 49

Agriculture: and agrarian myth, 200–201; balance between industry and, 134, 140, 152, 177, 191, 200, 375; Brain Trust's views about, 123–24; and causes of Great Depression, 69; closure of markets for, 21; codes for, 196, 212; and commodity loan program, 204–5; and Communism, 198, 211n; competition in, 371; in Coolidge administration, 34; cooperatives in, 44, 83, 84, 85, 141, 199–200; and crop destruction, 204–5, 205n; and CWA, 192; data about, 163, 203; and Democratic Party, 61; depression/stagnation in, 43, 69, 123, 141; and disillusionment with FDR, 219; diversity in, 140–41; and domestic allotment program, 141, 204; in Dust Bowl, 194–95, 209, 212; and economic isolationism, 199; and economic recovery, 190–213; employment in, 23; as exempt from FLSA, 344; as exempt from Wagner Act, 293; and FDR's first hundred days, 140–44, 149, 157, 204; FDR's views about, 99, 101, 118, 134, 140–44, 641; Hoover's views about, 17–18, 43–44, 140, 199–200; impact of New Deal on, 365, 371; and inflation, 141, 143, 157, 196, 197; Keynes' views about, 357; and labor, 193, 197, 319–20, 321; large commercial, 202, 212; in literature, 303; mechanization of, 17, 201; in Midwest, 195–96; and military deferments, 634; and monetary policies, 143–44, 197; national planning in, 142; in 1920s, 16–18, 21, 22, 23, 34, 43–44, 49; prices in, 17, 18, 44n, 54, 85, 141, 190, 196, 199, 200, 204–5, 206, 207, 211, 371, 388, 640, 783; production in, 141, 196, 199, 203; and redistribution of wealth, 123–24; regulation of, 17; and response to Crash of 1929, 54; and rubber, 647; as self-contained, 199–200; and social security coverage, 269, 270n; in South, 125, 192–93, 207–13; stabilization of, 199; strikes in, 196, 292–93; subsidies for, 141, 196, 202, 365, 371; Supreme Court decisions about, 344; surpluses in, 17, 18, 141, 199, 200, 204–5, 204n, 207–9, 371; and tariffs, 49, 142, 200; and taxes, 141; and tenant farmers/sharecroppers, 207–13; wages in, 194, 641; and World War I, 17; in World War II, 640, 641. See also Agricultural Adjustment Administration; Agriculture Department, U.S.; Mortgages: farm

Agriculture Department, U.S., 202–3, 205, 210–13, 353. See also Agricultural Adjustment Administration

Aid for Britain: amount of U.S., 654; and Anglo-American joint planning, 481; and beginning of World War II, 427–28; as best defense for U.S., 468–69; and British insolvency, 465–68; and British resistance to dependence on U.S., 431–32; and British survivability, 467–69; and Churchill-FDR relations, 467–68; and economic recovery, 466; and elections of 1940, 455, 458–59, 460, 461; FDR's views about, 427–28, 429, 446–54; and forced sales of British assets, 473, 475; and gold reserves of Britain, 431–32; and isolationism in U.S., 432, 460; and Japan-U.S. relations, 506, 523; and neutrality laws, 431–32, 462; and priorities on American production, 447–48, 447n, 479n; public opinion about, 491; and Republican Party, 458–59; and unemployment, 468. See also Cash-and-carry; Convoys; Destroyers: transfer of; Destroyers-for-bases deal; Lend-Lease; Short-of-war strategy; specific type of aid

Aid to Dependent Children (ADC), 271, 272

Aid to Families with Dependent Children (AFDC), 271

Air Force, British. See Royal Air Force

Air Force, Imperial Japanese, 564, 659, 819–20, 827–28

Air Force, U.S. See Army Air Force, U.S.

Aircraft: appropriations for, 429, 446; and British aid, 429, 430, 431–32, 446–48, 479n; and British survivability, 445; and French aid, 421, 429, 430, 431–32, 446–47; and neutrality laws, 421, 434ʼoduction of, 429, 431, 446, 447–49, 450, 479n, 703, 742; and Soviet aid, 484. See also Aerial warfare; Aircraft carriers; Aircraft industry; type of aircraft

Aircraft carriers: effect on naval warfare of, 828; as escorts, 589; Japanese, 824; in Pacific War, 522, 531–32, 542, 814, 828. See also specific battle or vessel

Aircraft industry: British production in, 655; and elections of 1940, 464; FDR's views about, 429; German production in, 655, 703, 742; Japanese production in, 655, 822; and mobilization, 429; U.S. production in, 429, 431, 446, 447–49, 450, 464, 479n, 618, 627, 655; women in, 778, 779

Akagi (Japanese carrier), 518, 522, 536, 539, 540, 542

Albania, 425

Albert W. Grant (U.S. destroyer), 825

Aleutian Islands, 536, 543

Algeria, 452, 581, 582

Alien Enemy Control Unit, 752

Allen, Frederick Lewis, 35, 40, 40n

Allied Expeditionary Air Force (AEAF), 702

Allied strategy: and aerial warfare, 703–8; and Teheran Conference, 700; and U.S. economy, 616–17. *See also specific document or plan*

Allies: fear of Soviet Union by, 613–14

Allis-Chalmers, 317, 638, 665–66

Alperovitz, Gar, 843n

Amalgamated Association of Iron, Steel, and Tin Workers (AA), 302–3, 307–8

Amalgamated Clothing Workers (ACW), 302, 305

Amalgamation controversy, 447

Amateur Athletic Union, 411

America First Committee, 471

American Association for Labor Legislation, 261

American Association for Old Age Security, 261

American Birth Control League, 28

American Civil Liberties Union (ACLU), 756

An American Dilemma (Myrdal), 762–63

American Economic Association, 39–40

American Expeditionary Force (WWI), 92, 430

American Farm Bureau Federation, 203

American Federation of Labor (AFL): and assembly line, 649; and CIO, 302, 304–5, 305n, 315, 316, 638; elitism of, 25, 26, 298, 300–301; and ethnicity, 301; factional fighting within, 294, 298; Lewis resigns vice-presidency of, 302; membership of, 314; in 1920s, 25–26; and social insurance laws, 260; and UMW, 300, 307–8; and unskilled workers, 300–302, 307–8; and

"voluntarism," 25; in wartime, 638, 639, 649

American Guide Series, 255–56

American Individualism (Hoover), 46–47

American Jewish Committee, 411–12

American Jewish Congress, 411

American Legion, 786

American Liberty League, 214, 219, 281, 290–91, 308, 313, 384

American Olympic Committee, 411

American Volunteer Group, 670–71

American Workers Party, 292

American Youth Congress, 483

Americans: typical, 41–42, 41n

Ammunition, 445, 446, 655

Amphibious operations: in Pacific War, 561, 598, 816–17, 829, 832; practice for, 716; and stabilizing beachhead, 722, 723; and U.S. strategy, 816. *See also specific operation, especially* Anzio and Normandy

Anacostia Flats (Washington, D.C.), 92, 546

Andaman Islands, 671, 673

Anderson, Alfred, 773

Anderson, Edward, 303

Anderson, Sherwood, 11, 222

Anglo-American relations: American domination in, 599; British domination in, 586; and British strategy, 407–8; British views about, 405, 475–76; at Casablanca, 586–87; and Churchill-FDR relations, 435n, 451–52; Churchill's views about, 408–9, 441–42, 451–52, 461, 464, 465; and defeat of Germany, 734–35; Eisenhower's views about, 689; and elections of 1940, 464; and European balance of power, 584–85; and FDR's misrepresentations, 465, 497–98; and isolationism, 404, 405, 407–9, 465; and Italian campaign, 595–96; and Lend-Lease, 475–76; and Overlord planning, 699–700; and post-war Germany, 803; and pre-war joint military planning, 481–82; and second front, 573–74; and Sino-Japanese war, 404; and Yanks in England, 709. *See also* Aid for Britain; Appeasement; Churchill, Winston–and FDR; Lend-Lease; *specific person or conference*

Anti-Comintern Pact (1936), 385, 397

Anti-Semitism: and atomic development, 657–58, 666; Coughlin's views about, 216, 232; in Germany, 158, 361, 383, 384, 410–11, 411n, 412, 415–16, 420,

Anti-Semitism (continued)
657–58, 794–97; and Jewish scientists, 657–58; and Olympic Games (1936), 410–11, 411n; in U.S., 410, 412, 416. See also Holocaust

Antilynching bill (1934), 210, 342–44

Antitrust laws, 150, 151, 184, 186, 353, 359, 623

Antwerp (Belgium), 4, 734, 735, 736–37, 739, 741

Anvil (Allied offensive), 699–700, 701–2, 731

Anzio (Italy), 599, 701, 722, 723, 816

"Appeal to the Nations of the World for Peace and for the End of Economic Chaos" (FDR, 1933), 158

Appeasement, 407–9, 418–20, 422, 435–36, 441, 443, 446, 476, 490

Archangel (Soviet Union), 572

Ardennes Forest (Belgium), 438, 737, 739–42, 801

Argentan (France), 729, 730

Argentia (Newfoundland): Churchill-FDR meeting at, 496–97, 506, 507, 511

Arizona (U.S. battleship), 522

Arms: and cash-and-carry, 422; embargo, 422, 394–95, 400, 403, 432, 434, 398, 399, 455; to France, 421; to Great Britain, 391n; and international debts, 391n; and neutrality laws, 394–95, 400, 403, 421, 432, 434; sales of, 421, 391n; and Sino-Japanese war, 403; and Spanish Civil War, 398, 399; war production of, 655; Willkie's views about, 455

Army Air Force, U.S. (USAAF): and aerial warfare as strategy, 604, 606; and aircraft production, 429; blacks in, 765, 773; build up of, 429, 430; cadet program of, 635; FDR's views about, 429, 430; and Overlord buildup, 709; planning documents of, 603, 743; and production priorities, 448–49; purchasing for, 621; and Selective Service System, 636, 711; Tactical School of, 603. See also specific person, battle, or type of plane

Army General Classification Test, 771–72

Army, Imperial Japanese, 401, 560, 637, 681, 811–12, 814, 828–29, 832, 833

Army Service Forces, 621. See also Somervell, Brehon B.

Army Services of Supply, U.S., 711

Army, U.S.: appropriations for, 476; basic training for, 715; blacks in, 765, 771;

and isolationism, 388–89; manpower needs of, 487; morale of, 495–96; and Selective Service System, 635, 636, 711; size of, 637; sociological data from, 771–72; Special Training Program for, 635; supplies for, 714–15; tactics of, 715; and "triangular" formation, 714–15; women in, 776; wounded in, 716. See also "Bonus army"/bonus bill; Casualties; GIs; Military, U.S.; specific person, battle, or operation

Arnhem (Germany), 735, 736, 737

Arnold, H.H. "Hap," 429, 430, 447–49, 476, 485, 556, 604, 606, 687

Arnold, Thurman, 354, 359

Arsenal of democracy: U.S. as, 465, 469, 476, 619, 631

Arts/culture, 254–57, 254n, 303–4, 379

Asquith, Herbert, 4

Assassination: attempt on FDR, 116–17; of Long, 278

Assembly line, 21, 309, 649–54, 779, 810, 849

Associated Farmers of California, Inc., 293

Astor, Vincent, 114, 116, 239, 249

Astoria (U.S. cruiser), 551

Atlantic Charter (1941), 496

Atlantic Ocean: Battle of the, 488–500, 565–72, 574, 588–90, 589n, 650; FDR's views about strategic value of, 450; weather in, 572

"Atlantic Wall," 692

Atlee, Clement, 838

Atomic bomb: and Churchill-FDR relations, 838–39; decision to use, 838–42, 843n; development of, 655–68, 809n, 838–42; dropping of, 849–50; and FDR, 659–60, 661, 662, 666; first explosion of, 838; and legacies of World War II, 856, 857, 858; morality of, 845; power of, 809n; Soviet development of, 858; and Soviet entry into Pacific War, 807–8; and U.S. strategy, 835

Augusta (U.S. cruiser), 496–97, 837

Auschwitz death camp, 795, 796

Australia, 529, 531–32, 534, 561, 688–89

Australia (British cruiser), 550

Australian troops, 561, 562

Austria: banking panic in, 72; German annexation of, 361, 362, 385, 409, 410, 421; Hapsburgs dethroned in, 1; Jews in, 414; in 1930s, 71–72, 76, 77; and World War I, 381, 382

Automobile industry: and causes of Great Depression, 69; data about, 163; and economic recovery, 289–90, 617; in Germany, 312; and labor, 187, 289, 291, 297, 300, 308–15, 316, 317, 320, 638; in 1920s, 13, 20–21, 22–23, 34–35, 69; in 1930s, 59, 163, 187; prohibition of manufacture in, 645; and shift from civilian to military production, 477; in Soviet Union, 312; strikes in, 308–14; unemployment in, 87, 309; wages in, 309, 321; women in, 779
Avery, Sewell L., 214, 642
Avranches (France), 727, 729
AWOL (Absent Without Leave), 813
AWPD/1 (Army Air Force planning document), 603, 743

B-17 bombers (U.S.): and bombing in Germany, 605, 609; and first European bombing missions, 605, 630; funding for, 431; and Japanese capture of Philippines, 527, 529; at Midway, 539, 542; morale of crews in, 704; and Pearl Harbor, 520; production of, 485, 603–4, 654; purpose of, 604; and Solomons campaign, 556, 562; strengths of, 654; targets of, 608; and U.S. tactics, 704; vulnerability of, 606, 609
B-24 bombers (U.S.), 589, 606, 608, 609, 653–54
B-25 bombers (U.S.), 535
B-29 bombers (U.S.), 654, 666, 816, 829, 846–47, 849
Beobachtungdienst signals, 571
Badoglio, Pietro, 594–95, 596, 600
Bailey, Josiah, 338, 340, 342, 346
Balance: in American economic life, 277; between agriculture and industry, 134, 140, 152, 177, 191, 200, 375; FDR's views about, 134; as New Deal buzzword, 122, 124
Balance of power: between legislature and judiciary, 330; in Europe, 584–85, 590
Baldwin, Hanson, 557
Baldwin, Stanley, 404
Balkans, 493, 495, 613, 674, 680–81, 682, 700
"Ballad for Americans," 761
Ballantine, Arthur, 136
Balloons: Japanese high-altitude, 848–49
Baltic States, 425, 678, 685. *See also specific state*
Bank of England, 36

Bank of United States, 67–68, 69
Bankers: FDR's meeting with, 135; Hoover's meetings with, 82–83; and isolationism, 388. *See also* Banking system, U.S.
Bankhead Cotton Control Act (1934), 207
Banking Act (1933), 242, 274
Banking and Currency Committee (U.S. Senate), 132
"Banking holiday" (1933), 77*n*, 131–32, 135–36
Banking system, U.S.: and bank failures, 65, 66, 68, 77, 77*n*, 117, 132–33, 162–63, 366; and bond sales, 626; Brain Trust's views about, 121–22; and causes of Great Depression, 69; commercial, 35, 36*n*, 153, 366, 626; Congress undermines confidence in, 132; Coughlin's views about, 230, 231; demagogues effects on reform of, 242; and ethnicity, 306; and FDR's first hundred days, 135–37, 139, 149, 153, 154, 218; FDR's views about, 118, 131–32, 134, 277; and gold standard, 80; Hoover's views about, 65, 82–83, 109, 154; and immigrants, 86; impact of New Deal on, 366; and international debts/reparations, 72–73, 77, 77*n*; investment, 153, 366, 388; in 1920s, 35, 36–37; and number of banks, 65–66; and panic of 1930, 65–69; and psychology of fear, 77–78, 132; regulation of, 783; and role of government, 80, 82–85; shut down of, 104, 110–11; and tax increases, 80. *See also* Federal Reserve System; Monetary/fiscal policies; *specific legislation*
Barkley, Alben W., 332, 339–40, 349
Barnes, Harry Elmer, 387
Barone, Michael, 285
Barton, Bruce, 462, 463
Baruch, Bernard, 59, 120, 126–27, 178, 179, 629, 788
Bastogne (Belgium), 740–41
Bataan, 529
Bataan Death March, 530–31, 811, 812
Battle of the Atlantic Ocean, 488–500, 565–72, 574, 588–90, 589*n*, 650
Battle of Britain, 440, 452–54, 460–61, 464, 470, 489, 504
Battle of the Bulge, 741–42, 772–73, 801
Battle for Northwest Europe: and aerial warfare, 724–25, 727, 728, 739, 741, 742–45; Allied tactics in, 734–35; and British strategy, 743–44; casualties in, 716, 737, 741–42; and D-Day, 717–18,

Battle for Northwest Europe (continued)
718n, 720–23; and Eastern Europe, 801;
end of, 745; and German collapse, 731,
732–33, 734–35; and German strategy,
739; and hopes for ending war, 738–39;
logistics for, 733–34, 739; and mobility,
723, 724, 724n, 727–28, 741; political
considerations in, 734–35; and Soviets
in Eastern Europe, 738, 739. See also
France; Normandy; specific battle
"Battle of the Overpass" (1937), 317
Battle psychosis, 555
"Battle of the Running Bulls" (1937), 311,
312
Battleships, 522, 527, 828. See also specific
battle or vessel
Beaumont, Texas: race riots in, 770
Beaverbrook, Max, Lord, 616
"Beer Hall Putsch," 5n, 8
Beer-Wine Revenue Act (1933), 138, 139,
149
Belgium, 9, 45, 47–48, 91, 409, 418, 438,
732. See also Antwerp; Brussels; specific
battle
Bellamy, Edward, 221, 225–26
Belleau Wood (France), 4–5
Belzec death camp, 797
Bendetsen, Karl R., 757
Bennett, Harry, 309, 317
Berle, Adolf A. Jr., 117, 120–22, 123, 124,
146, 284, 351, 425
Berlin, Irving, 625
Berlin (Germany): Allied bombing of, 744;
Allied targeting of, 704; devastation of,
838; Olympic Games in (1936), 410–11,
411n; Red Army in, 741, 745, 809;
Truman tours, 838
Bermuda, 460, 795
Bernstein, Irving, 26, 319
Bessarabia, 425, 678
Bethe, Hans, 657
Bethlehem Steel Corporation, 303, 638
Bethlehem Steel shipyards (Massachusetts),
252
Bethune, Mary McLeod, 378
Better Homes for America Movement, 368
Bewick, Moreing, 45
Biddle, Francis, 642, 749, 749–50n, 750,
751, 753, 755, 757, 774–75
"Big Bill" (1935). See Emergency Relief
Appropriations Act
Big business: and corporate welfare, 652;
government alliance with, 628; military
contracts for, 621–22, 628–29; profits of,

641; Republican Party controlled by,
286n. See also Business; Corporations;
specific person or corporation
Big Week (1943), 703
Bilbo, Theodore, 343, 346, 634
Bill of rights: economic, 784–85, 786; GI,
786–87, 858
Bingham, Alfred, 221
Biological warfare, 848
Birth control, 13, 28
Birth rate, 122, 165, 781, 857, 858
Biscari (Sicily) massacre, 594, 594n
Bismarck, Otto von, 260, 465
Bismarck (German battleship), 493, 493n
Bismarck Sea, 562
Black, Hugo, 150–51, 152, 336, 340, 346,
758
Black bill ("thirty-hour bill"), 150–51, 152
"Black Monday" (May 27, 1935), 328
"Black Thursday" (October 24, 1929), 38,
39
"Black Tuesday" (October 29, 1929), 38
Blacks: in cities, 194; and communism, 222–
23; in Congress, 18, 216; in defense
industry, 779; and Democratic Party,
216; and Eleanor Roosevelt, 285, 343,
378; and elections of 1936, 285; and
FDR, 764, 766, 767, 768, 774, 775;
Hitler's views about, 392; impact of New
Deal on, 378; in judiciary, 378; and Ku
Klux Klan, 15; and labor, 26, 307, 307n,
652, 765, 775; and legacies of World
War II, 857, 858; and March on
Washington, 766–67; migration of, 18,
194, 768–69; militancy among, 768; in
military, 711, 712, 764, 765, 767, 770–
73, 817, 848; in 1920s, 15, 18–19; in
1930s, 164, 173, 173n, 186; profiles
about, 41, 764–65; relief for, 164, 173,
173n, 194; in rural areas, 193, 194, 208,
210–11; and Selective Service System,
633, 634; as sharecroppers, 208, 210–11;
and social security, 269; standard of
living for, 857; unemployment of, 87,
164; voting rights for, 19; wages for, 186,
194, 254; wartime employment of, 765,
767–70, 775–76; women as, 777; and
WPA, 254. See also Race issues; Race
riots; specific person
Bletchley Park (England) cryptographers,
453, 471n, 571, 589
Blitzkrieg, 435, 438, 453, 464, 504, 616
Bloody Friday (July 20, 1934), 295
"Bloody Ridge" (Guadalcanal), 556, 558

Bloor, Ella Reeve "Mother," 211n
Blue Eagle campaign, 183–84
Blue (U.S. destroyer), 551
Blum, John Morton, 793
Blum, Léon, 310, 398
Bode, Howard D., 550, 551
Boeing Corporation, 464, 765, 846
Bohlen, Charles E., 684–85
Bohr, Niels, 661, 666
Boilermakers Union, 652
Bolero, 573–74, 576, 577, 578, 580, 581, 590, 596. *See also* Cross-Channel attack
Bolsheviks, 381
Bombers: escorts for, 702; FDR's views about, 428; morale of crews in, 704; production of, 631. *See also* Aerial warfare; Bombing; *type of bomber*
Bombing: of American mainland by Japanese, 847–49; area, 604, 704–5, 743; by high-altitude balloons, 848–49; carpet, 727; of civilians, 426, 429, 453, 602, 602–3n, 603, 604, 704, 706–7, 743–44, 845–50; deep-penetration, 428, 608–9, 702; FDR's views about, 428; and first European bombing missions, 605–9, 605n; in France, 727, 728; and German morale, 429, 743–44; in Germany, 605, 608–9, 702, 703, 704, 705–6, 707, 742–45; of Hitler's headquarters, 728–29; incendiary, 845, 846–49; of Japanese cities/civilians, 610, 829, 845, 846–50; and Japanese raids against U.S., 746–49, 750n, 760; and morale, 429, 602, 602–3n, 603, 704–5, 743; morality of, 704–5, 744; precision, 603, 604, 606, 743, 744, 845; saturation, 705; strategic, 702, 707, 742, 845; terror, 426, 453, 704–5, 743, 744, 845, 855; U.S. studies of, 744–45. *See also specific battle or target*
Bonneville Dam: FDR speech at, 246
Bonneville Power Authority, 379
"Bonus Army"/bonus bill, 92, 138, 279, 355, 546, 791
Borah, William E., 60, 62, 251, 390, 423, 433, 435
Borrowing, 36, 36n, 80, 81, 178, 274, 354, 625–26
Boston, Massachusetts: FDR speech in (1940), 463, 464
Boston Navy Yard, 464
Bougainville, 562, 563, 564
Boulogne (France), 728
"Bourbon" Democrats, 31
Bourke-White, Margaret, 256

Bowers, Claude, 398
Bracero program, 777
Bradlee, Benjamin, 712–13
Bradley, Omar N.: and Battle for Northwest Europe, 722, 723, 729–30, 735–36, 737, 739, 745; on Eisenhower, 690; on Grand Alliance, 738; and Overlord, 696, 697–98; professional background of, 697–98; style of, 697–98
Brain Trust: on cures for Great Depression, 121–22; disagreements among, 121–22; and FDR style, 111; Hoover's influence on, 121–22; legacy of, 119; Moley as nominal chairman of, 124; as novelty, 124; as progressives, 120–21, 124; role of, 119–24; views about Great Depression of, 120. *See also specific person*
Brandeis, Elizabeth, 264–65
Brandeis, Louis D., 46, 121, 128, 264–65, 326, 327, 336
Brest (France), 723, 728
Brest-Litovsk Treaty (1918), 381
Bridges, Harry, 294, 295, 298
Brinkley, Alan, 237–38, 243, 356, 642
Britain. *See* Great Britain
British Bomber Command, 702, 704, 706, 742
British chiefs of staff, 407, 574
British Coastal Command, 493n
British Expeditionary Force, 439, 481
British Fighter Command, 453
British forces: and Battle for Northwest Europe, 734–35, 736–37, 739; and German occupation of Norway, 438; and invasion of France, 720, 721, 723, 724, 726–27, 730, 731, 732; in Italian campaign, 596, 598; in North African campaign, 477–78, 581, 583; in Overlord, 698; in Sicily, 592; strength of, 697; supplies for, 713, 714. *See also* Royal Air Force; Royal Navy
British Purchasing Mission, 481, 495
British West Indies, 460
Brittain, Vera, 704
Brittany, 693, 727–28
Brooke, Alan, 737
Brookings, Oregon: Japanese attack on, 746–47
Brotherhood of Sleeping Car Porters, 763–64
Browder, Earl, 222, 315, 380
Bruenn, Howard G., 798, 799n, 808
Brundage, Avery, 411

Brunei, 824
Bruning, Heinrich, 71–72
Brussels (Belgium): and German invasion of Low Countries, 438; nine-power meeting in (1937), 405–6
Bryan, Charles W., 31
Bryan, William Jennings, 20, 31, 118, 196, 201, 202
Bryce, James, 223–24
Buck, Pearl, 401–2
Buckner, Simon Bolivar, 832, 834
Budget, federal: balanced, 29, 79–82, 109, 118, 125, 126, 147, 340, 352, 355, 356, 361; and "Conservative Manifesto," 340; conservatives' advice to FDR about, 125, 126; defense appropriations in, 431; deficits in, 79, 91, 102, 118, 248n, 351, 354, 355, 356, 358–59, 361–62, 376; and Democratic Party, 125, 126; and elections of 1932, 79; and FDR's first hundred days, 138, 147, 149; FDR's views about, 118, 134, 147, 279; and Hoover, 79–82, 91, 102, 109; in New Deal, 79; in 1920s, 29; in 1936, 279; and recession of 1937–38, 351, 352, 356, 358–59, 361–62; size of, 55; and southern Democrats, 125; and taxes, 79–82, 279
Bulgaria, 801
Bulge, Battle of the, 741–42
Bull Moose Republicans, 32, 62, 127, 128, 281
Bullitt, William C., 389, 408, 408n, 425, 429, 432, 436, 437, 439, 440, 502, 613
Buna (Papua), 562, 793
Bunche, Ralph, 762
Bundy, McGeorge, 839n, 843n
Bureau of Agricultural Economics, U.S., 203
Bureau of Labor Statistics, U.S., 353
Bureau of Ordnance (U.S. Navy), 659
Bureaucracy: Hoover's study of federal, 367
Burke-Wadsworth Selective Service Act (1940). See Selective Service Act
Burma, 504, 506, 527, 554–55, 670, 671, 673, 698–99, 855
Burma Road, 504, 671
Bush, Vannevar, 661–62, 666
Bushido code, 530, 811–12, 832
Business: as anti-FDR, 276–77, 280, 281–83, 351–52, 359, 360, 376–77; as anti–New Deal, 376–77; data about, 163; and economic recovery, 283, 284; and elections of 1936, 278–79, 281–82;

failures in, 58; FDR's attack on, 278–79; FDR's meetings with leaders of, 356; and FDR's political strategy, 284; FDR's views about, 376, 477–78; government's relationship with, 477; and Hoover, 11, 53, 54–55, 180; impact of New Deal on, 376–77; and isolationism, 387–88; Keynes' views about, 357–58; Long's views about, 279; morale of, 284, 351; in 1930, 53, 54–55, 58; psychology of fear in, 376–77; and recession of 1937–38, 351–52, 356, 359, 360; and shift from civilian to military production, 477; taxes on, 275–77, 279–80. See also Big business; Corporations; Crash of 1929; Stock market
Butler, Pierce, 263, 326, 327n
Butow, Robert J.C., 837
Byers, Clovis, 562
Byrd, Harry, 338
Byrnes, James F., 316, 343, 629–30, 738–39, 789, 792, 839, 843n, 844–45, 851

C-47 transport planes (U.S.), 720
Cabinet, FDR, 260, 427, 457–59
Cadogan, Alexander, 444
Caen (France), 721, 722–23, 726, 727, 729
Cairo Conference (1943), 669–70, 673–74, 699, 844
Calais (France), 693, 694, 694n, 696, 720, 724, 728
Caldwell, Erskine, 192, 208, 256, 303
California: agriculture in, 292–93; and elections of 1944, 756; French pilot crash in, 421; and Japanese raids against U.S., 750n; Japanese-Americans in, 751–52, 753–55, 756; labor in, 292–94; poverty in, 226–27, 239–40; radicalism in, 223–25; and Sinclair candidacy, 215–16, 225–27; strikes in, 292–93; Townsend in, 224–25; during World War II, 748, 750, 751–52, 753–55, 756
Call loans, 36–37, 53
Camp, Lawrence, 347
Camp Pendleton, California, 792
Campbell, D'Ann, 781
Canada: paying for cost of war in, 625
Canadian forces, 592, 698, 721, 730, 731
Canberra (Australian cruiser), 551
Cannery and Agricultural Workers Industrial Union (CAW), 292–93
Cape Gloucester (New Britain), 564
Capitalism: and disillusionment with FDR, 221; Hoover's views about, 43; and

impact of New Deal, 368, 371, 372; and Keynesian economics, 359; and labor, 299; in literature, 303; New Deal as challenge to, 364; and threats to liberalism, 221–22

Capra, Frank, 711, 771, 811, 811n

Capri, Isle of, 598

Cardozo, Benjamin, 326, 327n, 328, 336

Caribbean, 391, 391n, 568–69, 570

Carnegie Corporation, 762

Caroline Islands, 533, 534, 610, 810, 814, 816

Casablanca Conference (1943), 584–88, 590, 595, 601, 604, 605, 611, 654, 743, 844

Cash-and-carry, 400–401, 403, 422, 431–32, 434, 466–68

Casualties: Allied, 721, 722, 741–42; British, 382, 464, 600, 726; Filipino, 828–29; German, 703, 726, 731, 741–42, 744; Japanese, 817, 818, 825, 830–31, 833, 847, 849–50; Soviet, 854; in World War I, 1, 381, 385, 386, 716. See also Casualties, U.S.; specific battle or campaign

Casualties, U.S.: and Battle of the Atlantic Ocean, 499; and Battle of Leyte Gulf, 825, 828; in Battle for Northwest Europe, 716, 721, 722, 727, 731, 737; in Central Pacific, 610; first in World War II, 499; and invasion of Japan, 834–35; in Italian campaign, 600; at Iwo Jima, 831; and legacies of World War II, 856; at Luzon, 834; in mainland America, 848–49; at Okinawa, 833, 834, 835; in Pacific War, 813–14; at Saipan, 817, 818; shipping losses versus, 585; in Sicily, 594; on Tarawa, 811; and U-boat incidents, 499; and unconditional-surrender doctrine, 835; and U.S. strategy, 585; in World War I, 385, 386, 716

Catchings, Waddill, 51

Catholicism, 14, 15, 31–32, 216, 231, 284, 285, 399. See also Coughlin, Charles Edward

Celler, Emmanuel, 413, 416–17

Central Pacific campaign, 610–11, 674, 681, 816, 821, 829. See also Midway Island

Cermak, Anton J., 88, 116, 228, 321

CES. See Committee on Economic Security

Ceylon, 527, 855

Chadwick, James, 656

Chamberlain, Neville: and Anglo-American relations, 407–9, 443, 476; and appeasement, 407–9, 422, 429, 437; and Czech crisis, 418–20; declares war on Germany, 426; fall of government of, 438; and FDR, 428, 429, 443; and FDR's proposed international peace conference, 406–7, 408; and German peace feelers to Britain, 436, 444; and isolationism, 406–9; Kennedy's views about, 436; and neutrality laws, 406, 428; and Sino-Japanese war, 404; views about U.S. of, 404

Charity Organization Society of New York City, 88

Charlottesville, Virginia: FDR speech at, 440–41

Chase, Stuart, 51–52

Checks and balances system, 377

Chennault, Clair, 505, 670–71, 673

Cherbourg (France), 723–24, 733

Chiang Kai-shek: and Cairo Conference, 669–70; and FDR, 673, 698–99; ineffectiveness of, 505; and Japan-U.S. relations, 514; Mao's defeat of, 854; and Pacific War, 816; and Pearl Harbor attack, 523; and Sino-Japanese war, 502, 503, 504, 509, 671; and Stillwell, 671, 674; and U.S. aid for China, 502, 504–5, 508, 671; and Yalta Conference, 805, 807

Chicago Board of Trade, 132–33

Chicago, Illinois: banks in, 86; blacks in, 87, 216; Democratic National Conventions in, 98, 456–57; Democratic Party in, 216, 321; economy of, 163; ethnicity in, 14, 26, 86; FDR speech in (1937), 404–5, 406, 409; immigrants in, 321; isolationism in, 472; labor in, 26, 317–18, 321; patronage in, 253; relief in, 86, 88; Sandburg's description of, 20; steel industry in, 317–18; strikes in, 317–18; unemployment in, 87; and WPA funds, 253

Chicago Tribune, 404, 461, 472, 484, 487–88, 488n, 542–43n, 642

Chicago (U.S. cruiser), 550, 551

Child labor, 28–29, 28–29n, 185, 257, 297n, 328, 330, 344, 371, 783

Children: "latchkey," 780; malnourished, 86; relief for, 271, 272; in rural areas, 192, 193; of working women, 780. See also Child labor

China: aid/Lend-Lease for, 403, 502, 504–5, 508, 671, 673; Americans as prisoners-of-war in, 535; and Cairo Conference (1943), 670, 673–74; and Churchill-FDR relations, 670; Churchill's views about, 670, 674; Communism in, 502, 673, 807, 854, 858; and Doolittle's raid, 535; FDR's views about, 673, 698–99; and isolationism, 402; and Japan-U.S. relations, 500, 501, 502, 504–5, 508, 509, 513–14, 515; and Japanese strategy, 555; and legacies of World War II, 854, 858; and neutrality laws, 401; and Rape of Nanking, 402, 812; Stalin's views about, 677, 681; Stilwell's command in, 671, 673; strategic importance of, 502, 514–15, 523, 673–74, 681, 699, 816; and Teheran Conference, 677, 681; U.S. pre-World War II relations with, 670–71; and U.S. strategy, 816, 829; and Versailles Peace Treaty, 7; and Yalta Conference, 805–6, 807. *See also* Manchuria; Sino-Japanese war; *specific person*

Christadora House (New York City), 146, 161

Chrysler Corporation, 309, 314

Churchill, Winston: and aerial warfare, 705, 706–7; and Allied invasion of France, 723, 726, 731; ambitions of, 5–6; and Anglo-American relations, 405, 408–9, 435n, 441–42, 451–52, 461, 464, 465; and Anglo-American strategy, 595–96; and Anvil operation, 700; and appeasement, 408–9; and atomic bomb, 838–39, 841; and Balkans, 682; and Battle of the Atlantic Ocean, 489, 490, 491, 565, 571; and Battle of Britain, 440, 453, 460–61, 489; and beginnings of World War II, 435; biography of, 442; and British survivability, 426, 437–38, 439, 441–42, 444–46, 451–52, 465, 484; and China, 670, 674, 806; on communism, 483, 738n; and cross-Channel attack, 722; and Czech crisis, 419; and destroyer transfer, 449, 453–54, 461–62; and Dunkirk, 439, 441; and economic/monetary issues, 36, 475; Eisenhower's relationship with, 690, 700–701; and elections of 1945, 838; and European balance of power, 590; as first lord of admiralty, 426, 435, 442–43; and German invasion of France, 439, 440; and German invasion of Low Countries,

438–39; and German peace initiatives, 444; on Hopkins, 161; House of Commons speeches of, 441–42, 451–52; and isolationism, 435n, 680; and Italian campaign, 595–96, 599, 701; and Italian invasion of Ethiopia, 397; and Italian surrender negotiations, 595; and Japan-U.S. relations, 514; Kennedy's relations with, 443; and Lend-Lease, 470–71, 471n, 475; and Mediterranean, 576, 585, 613, 681, 682–84, 700; and Mers el-Kebir capture, 452; and Middle Eastern affairs, 806; and Montgomery, 697; and Munich Agreement, 419; named prime minister, 438; and neutrality laws, 462; and North Africa, 495, 577–78, 583; and Overlord planning, 699, 699n, 700, 701, 706–7; and Overlord priority, 680, 682–83, 690, 693, 694n, 697; and Pacific war, 445, 482; and Pearl Harbor attack, 523, 523–24n; and politics, 5–6n; and post-war Germany, 679, 803, 804; in post-war years, 852; reputation of, 4; and second front, 573–74, 574n, 575, 576, 577–78, 580, 595–96, 611, 613, 682; and Soviet entry into Pacific War, 843n; on Soviets in Eastern Europe, 738, 738n; Stalin's relations with, 483, 580, 610–11, 675, 684; style of, 682, 683; Truman's relations with, 838; and two-theater war, 524; and unconditional-surrender doctrine, 588n, 738; and U.S. elections of 1940, 463, 464; and U.S. entry into World War II, 496; on U.S. production, 856–57; and war criminals, 794–95; and Welles "fact-finding" mission, 437–38; and World War I, 1, 2, 4, 5–6n, 576, 599, 697, 701. *See also* Churchill, Winston–and FDR; Great Britain; *specific conference*

Churchill, Winston–and FDR: and aerial warfare, 706–7; and aid for Britain, 447, 448, 467–68, 497; and atomic bomb, 838–39; and Battle of the Atlantic Ocean, 491–92, 497; and Battle of Britain, 453–54; beginnings of relationship between, 442–43; and beginnings of World War II, 435; and British insolvency, 467–68; and British survivability, 444–46; and China, 670; and Churchill's domination in relationship, 586, 613; closeness of, 443; and destroyer transfer, 453–54; and escorts, 491–92, 497; and FDR's domination in relationship, 596, 683; and FDR's views about Churchill, 442; first meeting between, 6, 6n, 442; and isolationism, 435n; and North African campaign, 577–78; and Overlord, 706–7; and second front, 574, 577–78, 586, 613; and unconditional surrender formula, 738; and U.S. entry into war, 493. *See also specific conference or meeting*

CIO. *See* Committee for Industrial Organization; Congress of Industrial Organizations

Cities: blacks in, 194; and economic recovery, 201–2; and elections of 1940, 322; FDR's views about, 134; migration from rural areas to, 194, 209. *See also* Urban areas; *specific city*

Citizens Alliance, 294, 295

Citizens Army, 295

Citizens Committee, 318

Civil Aeronautics Board, 367n, 371

Civil rights movement, 857, 858

Civil Works Administration (CWA), 175–77, 186, 188, 192, 194, 202, 209, 250, 285

Civilian Conservation Corps (CCC), 144, 145, 149, 251, 378, 430, 783

Civilians: Belgium, 740; bombing of, 426, 429, 453, 602, 602–3n, 603, 604, 704, 706–7, 743–44, 845–50; British, 453; competition between military procurements and, 627–28; as consumers, 644–46; French, 706–7; German, 429, 704, 743–44; Japanese, 817–18, 845–50; massacre of, 740; and production goals, 618; suicide of, 817–18; travel on belligerent vessels of, 394–95, 400; waning war-spirit of, 553, 793. *See also* Morale

Clark, Mark, 596, 598, 600, 601

Class issues, 24–25, 174–75, 243, 284, 292, 294–95, 322, 857

Claudel, Paul, 158

Clemenceau, Georges, 586

Cleveland, Grover, 30, 31, 277

Clinton, Bill, 759

Closed shop, 641–43

Coal industry, 169–70, 304, 329, 617, 639, 642–43, 742. *See also* United Mine Workers

Coast Guard: women in, 776

Coastal Picket Patrol ("Hooligan's Navy"), 569

Coastal shipping, U.S., 566, 568–70

Cobra (U.S. offensive), 727

Codes: and Allied invasion of France, 729; and Battle of Britain, 452–53, 461; British, 571; Enigma, 452–53, 461, 589; German, 452–53, 461, 471n, 571, 589, 729; and German invasion of Britain, 471n; and Guadalcanal, 544; Japanese, 507–8, 515, 531, 537, 542–43n, 544, 544n, 559, 563, 789; and JN-25, 531, 537; "Magic," 537, 542–43n, 559, 563; and Solomons campaign, 544, 559; Triton, 571, 589; U.S. breaking of Japanese, 507–8, 515, 789

Cohen, Benjamin V., 353

Cold War: beginnings of, 799, 854; as legacy of World War II, 854–55; as outcome of disappointments of Grand Alliance, 580; Teheran foreshadowings of, 679; Yalta as beginning of, 799

Collier's magazine: FDR articles for, 454

Colonialism, 7, 509, 853–54

Combined Allied Intelligence Committee, 732

Combined Bomber Offensive, 587, 654, 703, 705

Combined Chiefs of Staff: Marshall as chairman of, 686, 687

Comintern Pact (1936), 385, 397

Commager, Henry Steele, 761

Command and General Staff School (Fort Leavenworth, Kansas), 715

Commerce Department, U.S., 186, 202, 203

Commission on Country Life (1908), 17

Committee on Economic Security (CES), 262–64, 265, 267, 268, 268n, 269–70, 271

Committee for Industrial Organization (CIO): and AFL, 302, 304–5, 305n, 315, 316, 638; and automobile industry, 317; and blacks, 307, 307n; and Communism, 316; culture of, 314–15; divisiveness within, 311, 315, 316; early years of, 302–8, 371; and elections of 1940, 462, 462n; expansion of, 638, 639–40; and FLSA, 371; formation of, 302; function of, 302; Lewis resigns as president of, 462, 462n; membership of, 314, 320; radicalism of, 316; and steel industry, 302–8, 319, 638; and UMW, 302; in wartime, 638–39. *See also* Lewis, John L.

Committee for National Morale, 761

Committee to Defend America by Aiding the Allies, 460, 471

Committee/Congress of Racial Equality (CORE), 768

Commodity Credit Corporation, 204

Commonwealth Club (San Francisco): FDR speech to (1932), 102, 123, 141, 151, 180, 245, 373, 374

Communism: and agriculture, 198, 211n; and blacks, 222–23; in China, 502, 673, 807, 854, 858; Churchill's views about, 483, 738n; Coughlin's views about, 230, 232; and disillusionment with FDR, 221–23, 227; and Eleanor Roosevelt, 483; and elections of 1944, 789; FDR's views about, 242, 246, 483; in Germany, 104, 384; and labor, 292–93, 294, 298, 299, 310, 315–16, 317–18, 322, 349, 638, 638n; and Lend-Lease, 471–72; Lewis's views about, 299, 315; and NRA, 222; in Poland, 801; and relief, 89; and soldier-vote, 788; and Spanish Civil War, 399

Communist League of America, 295

Communist Party of the United States of America (CPUSA), 104, 221–23, 315

Company unions, 27, 187, 292, 292n, 297, 308

Competition, 179, 180, 371–73, 376

Conant, James Bryant, 662, 664, 666

Conference of American States (1938), 420

Congress of Industrial Organizations. See Committee for Industrial Organization

Congress, U.S.: blacks in, 18, 216; conservativism in, 349, 782; declares war on Japan, 523, 523n; Democratic control of, 125, 125n, 216, 286; discharge petition in, 217; extraordinary sessions of, 273, 274; FDR appears before, 446; FDR's annual messages to, 247, 250–51, 278–79, 325, 335, 363, 469–70; and FDR's messages in First Hundred Days, 139, 151, 152; FDR's relationship with, 138–39, 149, 210, 274, 338, 339–40, 344, 393, 400, 422–23, 495–96, 644; FDR's special messages to, 245, 261, 266, 268n, 270–71, 279, 325, 332, 356; FDR's Yalta Conference report to, 806; Hoover's relationship with, 43, 49n, 50, 61, 62–63, 64–65; and international debts, 105–6; isolationism in, 422–23; and Japanese-Americans during World War II, 759; and military deferments, 633–34; and

political realignments, 128–29; Republican domination of, 59–60, 127; and requiem of New Deal, 782–83, 787; rural domination of, 339; seniority rules in, 339, 343; South's domination of, 339; special sessions of, 129–30, 132, 134, 135–36, 139, 340, 356, 432–33; and Supreme Court reform, 333–34, 339; and Teheran Conference, 685; Truman's address to, 844. See also specific member, committee, or legislation

Congressional Medal of Honor, 831

Connor, Eugene "Bull," 774

Conscientious objectors, 633

Conscription: in Germany, 384; in Great Britain, 425. See also Selective service

Conservation, 63, 98, 118, 149, 277, 340, 379. See also Civilian Conservation Corps

Conservatism/conservatives: and budget, 340; in Congress, 349, 782; "Conservative Manifesto" (1937) of, 340–41; in Democratic Party, 99, 125–26, 128, 214, 286n, 342–44; and elections, 243, 244, 344, 782, 788–89; and FDR, 99, 125–26, 214, 219, 243, 244, 275, 389–90, 433; and FDR's first hundred days, 138; FDR's views about, 344; and FLSA, 345; in Harding-Coolidge eras, 48; Hoover's views about, 48; ideological crystallization of, 340–41; and labor, 643; and neutrality laws, 433; and New Deal, 283, 339–41, 348, 782–83, 784; Republican Party dominated by, 32; and role of government, 340–41; and taxes, 340; and wages, 345. See also American Liberty League

"Conservative Manifesto" (1937), 340–41

Constitution, U.S., 327, 328, 329, 335, 377, 379. See also specific amendment

"Constitutional Revolution of 1937," 334–37

Construction: appropriations for, 249; and CWA, 176; data about, 57, 163; expenditures for, 57, 59; and Hoover, 147; in 1920s, 35, 57, 58; in 1930, 58, 59; and PWA, 178; and response to Crash of 1929, 54, 54n, 58, 59; in World War II, 645; by WPA, 253. See also Public works; Public Works Administration

Consumer Advisory Board, 184

Consumers, 13, 21–22, 29, 200, 201, 278, 644–46, 856. See also Consumption

Consumption: and explanations of Great Depression, 122–23; FDR's views about, 180; impact of New Deal on, 373; Keynes' views about, 358; mass, 21; in 1920s, 21, 29; and recession of 1937–38, 354, 355, 358; and response to Crash of 1929, 53–54; and role of government, 354; and tax reform, 279; under, 122–23

Contracts: and big versus small business, 621–22, 628–29; civilian needs and military, 627–28; and corruption, 791; cost-plus, 623, 644, 791; government, 297n, 477; to Kaiser, 650–52; labor and government, 297n; labor and military, 638; military, 621–22, 623, 626–29, 638, 644, 650–52, 791; price-maintenance, 372; and shift from civilian to military production, 477; "yellow-dog," 26–27

Controlled Materials Plan, 628–29, 632

Convoy PQ17, 572

Convoys: and Battle of the Atlantic Ocean, 488–91, 565–72, 590; FDR's views about, 491; and Lend-Lease, 473–74, 475–76; and North African campaign, 579–81; and "patrolling policy," 491–92; to Soviet Union, 572, 590, 611; and U.S. entry into war, 494. See also Escorts; U-boats

Cooke, Morris Llewellyn, 252

Coolidge, Calvin, 11, 17, 24, 30, 31, 33–34, 48, 61, 64, 147, 327n, 340, 764

Coral Sea, Battle of the, 531–32, 536, 544, 549

Corcoran, Thomas G., 353, 355n

Coronet (U.S. invasion plan for Honshu), 835

Corporations: FDR's views about, 277–78; and isolationism, 388; Long's views about, 236, 237; in 1920s, 35; taxes on, 275–77, 279–80. See also Big business; Business; specific corporation

Corregidor, 529–30

Corruption: in wartime contracting, 791

Corsica, 583

COSSAC plan, 698, 724

Costigan, Edward, 62

Cotentin peninsula, 693, 724, 736

Cotton farming, 192–93, 204–5, 207–9, 212

Cotton Textile Code, 181–82, 296

Cotton Textile Institute, 181

Coughlin, Charles Edward, 216, 227–34, 237, 237n, 239, 240, 242, 244, 275, 283, 284, 314, 410, 433

Coxey, Jacob, 113

Craig, Malin, 430

Crash of 1929, 10–11, 37–41, 40n, 49n, 51–59, 68, 69, 73, 366

Credit, 36–37, 80, 81, 82–83, 129, 134, 274. See also Borrowing

Crimea, 575, 799

Cross-Channel attack: British commitment to, 596; and Casablanca commitments, 586, 587, 588; Churchill's concerns about, 574–75, 576, 577–78; date for, 680; England as staging ground for, 591, 599; FDR support for, 573, 574, 575–76; and Italian campaign, 599; and North Africa, 577–78; postponement of, 596, 601; Soviet views about, 573, 574–76, 601. See also Bolero; Overlord; Roundup; Second front; Sledgehammer

Cruisers. See specific battle or vessel

Crump, Edward H., 253

Crutchley, Victor, 550, 551

Cuba, 391, 391n, 417

Culin, Curtis G., 724n

Cummings, e.e., 387

Cummings, Homer, 258, 328, 331, 345

Curley, James Michael, 31, 228

Currie, Lauchlin, 353, 355, 356, 374

Cutting, Bronson, 60, 62, 127, 219, 243, 297, 298, 390

CWA. See Civil Works Administration

Czechoslovakia, 155, 361, 409, 418–23, 659

D-Day (1944), 698, 699, 699n, 708, 709, 717–18, 718n, 720–23

Dairen (North China), 805

Dakota National Guardsmen, 556

Daladier, Edouard, 426, 438

Dallek, Robert, 390, 498

Darlan, Jean François, 582–83, 583n, 707

Darlan Deal, 582–83, 583n, 588

Darrow, Clarence, 20, 186

Dartmouth (England): amphibious practice in, 716

Daugherty, Harry M., 33

Dauntless bombers (U.S.), 541–42, 553

Dauntless (U.S. yacht), 544

Davey, Martin, 170–71, 318

Davies, Joseph E., 591, 611

Davis, Benjamin O., 771

Davis, Chester, 212, 213

Davis, John W., 31, 99, 214

Davis, Norman, 405

Davis, T. J., 530

Dawes, Charles G., 72

Dawes Plan (1924), 72

De Priest, Oscar, 18, 216
Deane, John R., 674–75, 681, 718
Death camps, 794, 795, 796
Debs, Eugene, 222, 235
Debt, national, 29–30, 274
Debts, international: and arms purchases, 391n; cancellation of, 105–6, 855; and cash-and-carry, 431; and cause of Great Depression, 72–79; and Dawes Plan, 72; defaults on, 390–91, 391n, 431, 466–67; and economic nationalism, 157–58; and elections of 1932, 74n; and gold standard, 75–79; and Hoover, 34, 42, 72, 73–74, 74n, 77, 101, 105–7; and Hoover-FDR meetings, 105–7, 157–58; and isolationism, 73, 74, 106, 386, 390–91, 855; moratorium on payment of, 73–74, 74n, 77, 101, 105, 106; and neutrality laws, 431; and "standstill" agreement, 73–74, 77; and Versailles Treaty, 72–73; and Young Plan, 72. See also Johnson Act (1934)
"Decisive battle," 533, 541, 553, 555, 559, 816, 818–20
Declaration on Liberated Europe (1945), 802, 806
Declaration of Lima (1938), 420
Defense industry: blacks in, 779; discrimination in, 767–70, 775–76; women in, 778–79
Defense, U.S.: appropriations for, 446, 476. See also Mobilization; Production, U.S.; Rearmament; Selective service; specific branch of service
Deferments, military, 632–27, 639
Deflation, 78, 80, 149, 267, 269
DeGaulle, Charles, 581, 583, 602, 707, 708, 732, 738, 799
Delano, Frederic, 783, 784
Demagogues, 241–42, 243–44. See also specific person
Democratic National Committee, 91, 782
Democratic National Convention: in 1932, 91, 98; in 1936, 280–81, 280n, 341
Democratic Party: and agriculture, 61; and blacks, 216; "Bourbons" in, 31; and budget, 125, 126; and Catholics, 216; Congress controlled by, 216, 286; "Conservative Manifesto" of southern, 340–41; and conservatives, 99, 125–26, 128, 214, 286n, 342–44; divisiveness within, 30–31, 97–98, 276–77, 333, 337–39, 343; in early 1930s, 61–62; and ethnicity, 97, 128; and FDR, 119, 219–

20, 323, 337–39, 345, 433; growth in, 216; and Hoover, 125; and immigration, 30, 102–3, 127, 128, 216, 378; and inflation, 118–19; and Jews, 216; and labor, 291, 305, 321–22, 345; leadership of, 61; liberalization of, 346–49; and monetary policy, 118–19; and neutrality laws, 433; and old-age pensions, 261; opposition to New Deal within, 338–39; and political realignments, 127–28, 149, 285–86n, 323, 346–48; and race issues, 333, 341–43; and role of government, 125; and rural areas, 338–39; and South, 30, 61, 97, 102–3, 125–26, 127, 128, 286n, 338, 341–43; and Supreme Court reform, 333; and tariff, 31; and tax reform, 276–77; transformation of, 127–28; and unemployment insurance, 261; unification of, 97–98; and urban areas, 32, 32n, 128, 338–39; white primary of, 774–75; Women's Division of, 260. See also Elections
Dempsey, Jack, 96
Denmark, 438, 492, 692, 693
Depressions, 43, 56, 69, 79, 123, 141, 155–57. See also Great Depression
Destroyers: as escorts, 497–98; transfer of, 445, 446, 448, 449, 453–54, 454n, 460, 460n, 461–62
Destroyers-for-bases deal (1940), 460–62, 469, 471, 497
Detroit, Michigan: Coughlin in, 227–34; racism in, 770; and recession of 1937–38, 350; relief in, 350; unemployment in, 87, 166
Devaluation of dollar, 388
Dewey, John, 221, 657
Dewey, Thomas E., 349, 782, 789, 793
DeWitt, John L., 749, 751, 752, 753, 757, 759
Dewson, Mary "Molly," 259
Dickstein, Samuel, 416, 417
Dictatorships, 111, 234, 332, 334, 361, 362, 379, 400. See also Hitler, Adolf; Mussolini, Benito
Dies, Martin, 316, 349
Dill, Clarence, 99
Dill-Connery bill (1932), 261
Disarmament Conference (Geneva, 1933), 105, 106, 158, 159, 384
Discharge petition (rule change, 1935), 217
Disease: in Pacific War, 813
Divine, Robert, 419
Dodd, William E., 241, 412

Domestic Allotment Plan, 141, 204
Domestic issues: during World War II, 782–93; and FDR's foreign policies, 470; FDR's views about priority of, 107, 157
Dönitz, Karl, 488, 489–90, 568, 570, 572, 589–90, 809
Doolittle, James H., 535, 811
Douglas, Lewis, 143, 214
Douglas, Paul H., 221
Douglas, William O., 353
Douhet, Giulio, 602, 602–3n, 705
Dower, John, 810, 812–13
Dr. Win-the-War, 783–84
Draft. *See* Selective service
Dragoon (Allied offensive), 731
Dred Scott case (1857), 273, 327
Dreiser, Theodore, 226
Dresden (Germany), 744, 847
Du Pont, Lammot, 351
Du Pont, Pierre S., 99
Du Pont Corporation, 621
Du Pont family, 313, 388
Dubinsky, David, 226, 302, 305, 306, 315
Dumbarton Oaks: meeting at (1944), 799
Dunkirk (France), 4, 439, 439n, 440, 441, 448, 460n, 581, 697, 728
Dunne brothers, 295, 298
Dunning, William A., 342
Dust Bowl, 194–95, 209, 212, 256
Dutch East Indies, 381, 516, 527, 554, 647, 822, 824, 855; and Japan-U.S. relations, 504, 505, 506, 509, 510, 512

E.A. *Bryan* (Liberty Ship), 773–74
Eaker, Ira C., 605, 608, 609
Earle, George, 289, 304, 312, 318, 347–48, 386
East Prussia, 801
Eastern Europe: Allied fears of separate peace in, 612; Anglo-American concerns about Soviets in, 588; and Battle for Northwest Europe, 726, 738, 739, 801; German casualties in, 726; and Grand Alliance, 738; and Overlord, 683; Soviet domination of, 678, 738, 738n, 807, 854; Soviet forces in, 683, 726, 738, 739, 801, 854; and Teheran Conference, 677–78, 683; and Yalta Conference, 799, 801–3, 807
Eastern Sea Frontier (U.S.), 569–70
Eastern Solomons, Battle of the, 555
Eccles, Marriner, 68–69, 78, 102, 353, 356, 358, 361, 374, 376

Economic bill of rights, 784–85, 786
Economic isolationism, 154–57, 159, 199, 375, 388
Economic recovery: and agriculture, 190–213; and aid for Britain, 466; beginnings of, 288–89; and business, 283, 284; and cities, 201–2; continuing search for, 362; cresting of, 350; and elections of 1940, 464; and FDR's first hundred days, 149–53, 154; and FDR's priorities, 117–18, 283, 390; FDR's views about, 216, 323–25, 363; in First New Deal, 117–18, 177–89; impact of New Deal on, 272, 363, 364, 372; and industry, 201–2; Keynes' views about, 357; and Keynesian economics, 360; and labor, 289–90, 303; and monetary policy, 177; and production, 464; and recession of 1937–38, 350–53, 355–61; and reform, 323–25, 363; and World War II, 363
Economy: and bill of economic rights, 784–85, 786; character of U.S., 647; data about, 58; and distribution of wealth, 21–22; and elections of 1944, 793; endless growth in, 786; FDR's views about priority of, 107; and globalization, 855; and Hoover-FDR meetings, 107–10; Hoover's response to, 65, 69; impact of New Deal on, 373–77; and legacies of World War II, 855, 857; and mature economic theory, 373–74, 375, 785–86; and mobilization, 616–18, 622–23; and New Deal, 622–23; in 1920s, 21–22, 34–41, 51–59; and orthodox economic theory, 51–52; in post-war years, 786; restructuring of, 153; revitalization of, 619; and role of government, 377; and Second New Deal, 247; self-sufficiency of, 617–18; and self-sufficiency of U.S., 375; Speer's views about, 648; and stagnation economic theory, 375, 375n, 785–86; strength of U.S., 616–17; and U.S./Allied strategy, 616–17, 619, 647; World War I impact on, 36. *See also* Banking system; Consumers; Crash of 1929; Economic isolationism; Economic recovery; Employment; Mobilization; New Deal; Recession; Stock market
Economy Act (1933), 138, 139, 237
Eden, Anthony, 405, 407–8, 419, 437, 586, 799, 801, 803
Edison, Charles, 449, 457
Edson, Merritt, 556
Education, 29, 41, 787

Eichelberger, Robert, 562
Eichmann, Adolf, 795, 796
Eighth Air Force (U.S.), 605, 606, 608, 630, 703, 742
Eighth Army (British), 581
Eighty-Second Airborne Division (U.S.), 720, 735, 736
Eindhoven (Germany), 736
Einstein, Albert, 416, 656, 657, 666n
Eisenhower, Dwight D.: and aerial warfare, 701–2, 705, 706; and Allied bombing in Germany, 744; and Allied command structure, 696; and Allied invasion of France, 724, 727, 731; and Allied policy after liberation of France, 707, 708; and Allied supply lines, 733, 734; and Anglo-American relations, 689; and Anvil, 701; appointed Overlord commander, 686–91; appointed to SHAEF, 700–701; and Ardennes Forest, 739–42; and Battle of the Atlantic Ocean, 565; and Battle for Northwest Europe, 734–35, 736, 737–38, 744, 745; biography of, 688–89; Churchill's relationship with, 690, 700–701; commands of, 688–89; and Corregidor, 530; and DeGaulle, 708; FDR's relationship with, 690; and German collapse, 732–33; and Italian campaign, 598, 600; and Italian surrender, 595; on King, 570; of launching of Overlord, 717–18, 718n; leadership of, 706; on MacArthur, 530; and Mediterranean campaign, 596; Montgomery's relations with, 697, 734–35; and North African campaign, 579, 580, 581–84; and Overlord planning, 696, 697, 698, 699–700, 701–2, 706, 707, 716; and Paris liberation, 732; and Patton, 594; and redeployment of American forces from Europe to Pacific, 732–33; responsibilities of, 690–91; and second front, 573, 579; style of, 689, 690; on Wainwright, 530
Eisenhower, Milton S., 753, 754
El Alamein (Libya), 583, 697
Elbe River, 745
Elderly: impact of New Deal on, 378; and ordeal of American people, 165; relief for, 261, 271, 272; and Townsend, 224, 257; unemployment of, 164, 250, 257. See also Old-age pensions; Social security
Elections: in Germany, 8–9, 383–84; in Great Britain, 747, 838

Elections, U.S.: of 1896, 30; of 1912, 32, 127, 261; of 1916, 127; of 1918, 33, 127, 782; of 1920, 33, 95, 97, 115; of 1924, 30, 31, 97, 220; of 1928, 10, 31–32, 41, 49, 94, 97, 98, 103, 236; of 1930, 59–60, 60n, 98, 125, 126; of 1932, 9, 59, 62, 74n, 79, 91, 92–93, 94, 98, 101, 102–3, 125, 127, 222, 245, 261, 285–86n, 290, 388; of 1934, 216, 217, 225, 226; of 1936, 240–43, 278–86, 280n, 285–86n, 290, 323, 330, 341, 352, 396, 464; of 1938, 344, 346–48, 349, 350, 420, 422–23, 782; of 1940, 322, 349, 454–64, 761, 782, 789; of 1942, 579, 579n, 747, 750, 782, 787, 789; of 1944, 678, 747, 756, 759, 782, 787–89, 791–93, 858; of 1948, 858; in 1920s, 30; turnout for, 30; and white primaries, 774–75, 788
Electric Auto-Lite Company, 292
Electricity, 13, 251, 252, 364, 379, 857
Eliot, Thomas, 263, 264, 265, 266, 267, 269, 270n, 273
Elk Hills scandal, 33
Ellender, Allen J., 343
Ellis Island, 14
Emancipation Proclamation (1862), 187
Emergency Banking Act (1933), 135–37, 139, 149, 154
Emergency Relief Appropriations Act (1935), 242, 248n, 249–52, 257, 258
Employee Representation Plans (ERPs), 292, 308
Employment: in agriculture, 23; of blacks, 765, 767–70, 775–76; and class issues, 24–25; and forced-labor drafts, 637–38; and government as employer, 374–75; impact of New Deal on, 374–75; and mechanization, 23–24; in 1920s, 23–24, 49; and PWA, 152; and selective service, 632; and tariff, 49; in wartime, 632, 644–47; of women in wartime, 777. See also Unemployment
End Poverty in California (EPIC), 226–27, 239–40
Enemy aliens, 748–60, 749–50n, 750, 753, 756
Engelbrecht, H.C., 388
England: Allied buildup in, 709–10, 716; American bases in, 713; German informants in, 694; impact of Yanks on, 713; paying for cost of war in, 625; race riots in, 770. See also Great Britain; London, England

Enigma codes, 452–53, 461, 589
Eniwetok (Marshall Islands), 610, 810
Ennis, Edward J., 752
Enola Gay (bomber), 849
Enterprise (U.S. aircraft carrier), 252, 522, 538, 539, 541–42, 549, 555, 559, 560
Environmental issues, 33, 34. *See also* Conservation; *specific issue*
Equal Rights Amendment, 28
Escorts: in aerial warfare, 605, 609, 702; aircraft carriers as, 589; and Anglo-American joint planning, 481, 482; and Battle of the Atlantic Ocean, 488, 490–92, 494, 496, 497–98, 569, 570, 571, 572; Canadian, 497–98; FDR approves, 497; FDR's views about, 494, 498; and isolationism, 490; and Lend-Lease, 475–76; public opinion about, 491, 498, 498*n*; Royal Navy as, 498; for U.S. bombers, 702; and U.S. entry into war, 494; U.S. Navy as, 458, 467, 496, 497–98, 571. *See also* Convoys
Espionage: and *Chicago Tribune*, 542–43*n*. *See also* Enemy aliens; Intelligence
Estonia, 678
Ethiopia, 394, 395, 396–97, 400, 401, 408, 409
Ethnicity: and banking system, 86, 306; and Democratic Party, 97, 128; and elections of 1936, 284; and labor, 25–26, 294–95, 301, 306–7; in 1930s, 86, 97. *See also* Immigration/immigrants
Europe: balance of power in, 584–85, 590; and causes of Great Depression, 69. *See also* European Theater
European Coal Council, 45
European Theater: and American forces first enter Germany, 793; American prisoners of war in, 813; and competition for manpower and materials among theaters, 698–99; Eisenhower as commander of, 689; first bombing missions in, 605, 605*n*, 630; Red Army enters, 613; and redeployment of American forces to Pacific, 732; U.S. forces in, 590–91; and U.S. priorities, 495, 524–25, 809, 811*n*. *See also* Eastern Europe; Germany-first; *specific battle or operation*
European Union, 855
Evans, Walker, 208, 256
Evian-les-Bains Refugee Conference (1938), 414–15
Executive Order 8802 (1941), 767–68, 775

Executive Order 9066 (1942), 753
Executive reorganization bill (1937–38), 332, 340, 344, 400
Ezekiel, Mordecai, 353

F6F Hellcats (U.S. fighter planes), 543, 702
Fair Employment Practices Committee (FEPC), 767, 775
Fair Labor Standards Act (FLSA) (1938), 344–45, 346, 357, 371
Fala (FDR dog), 792
Falaise (France), 723, 727, 729–31, 736
Family issues, 27–28, 86, 164, 165–66
Fannie Mae. *See* Federal National Mortgage Association
Farley, James, 240–41, 333, 352, 396, 447*n*
Farm bill (1938), 344
Farm Bloc. *See* Agriculture
Farm Bureau Federation, 141, 211
Farm Credit Act (1933), 153
Farm Credit Administration, 143, 199
Farm Security Administration (FSA), 252, 379, 783
Farmer-Labor Party, 220
Farmers: electricity for, 251; standard of living for, 22, 646; in wartime, 646. *See also* Agriculture; Rural areas
Farmers Holiday Association, 196, 198, 211*n*, 240
Farouk (king of Egypt), 806
Farrell, James T., 303
Fashions: in wartime, 645
Fathers: and selective service, 635, 636
Faubus, Orval, 16
Feasibility Dispute, 627–28, 630, 631, 635
Federal Art Project, 254–55
Federal ballot, 787–88
Federal Bank Deposit Insurance Corporation (FBDIC). *See* Federal Deposit Insurance Corporation
Federal Bureau of Investigation (FBI), 352, 488*n*, 568, 568*n*, 751, 757
Federal Communications Commission (FCC), 367*n*, 371–72, 751, 757
Federal Deposit Insurance Corporation (FDIC), 153, 285, 366, 369
Federal Emergency Relief Administration (FERA), 144, 145, 160–68, 170–75, 188, 202, 209, 250
Federal Farm Board, 44, 44*n*, 54, 85, 141, 200, 204
Federal government. *See* Government; Government, role of; State government
Federal Home Loan Bank Act (1932), 84

Federal Housing Administration (FHA), 369, 370
Federal Music Project, 255
Federal National Mortgage Association (Fannie Mae), 369, 370
Federal One, 255–56
Federal Power Commission, 367n, 372
Federal Reserve Act (1914), 119
Federal Reserve Board: and banking system, 136, 274; and economic recovery, 288; and FDR's first hundred days, 136; and impact of New Deal, 367n; and New Dealers, 353; in 1920s, 35–36, 37; and recession of 1937–38, 355; and structure of government, 55. See also Federal Reserve System
Federal Reserve System: and Bank of United States collapse, 67; creation of, 66; and FDIC, 366; and Glass-Steagall Act (1932), 83; and gold standard, 78, 80, 83; inadequacy of, 66; lack of confidence in, 67; leadership of, 69; members of, 58, 66; in 1920s, 36–37, 53, 54; in 1930s, 58, 80; Open Market Committee of, 273–74; and response to Crash of 1929, 53, 54, 58; role of, 69; tight-money policies of, 80, 81, 83. See also Federal Reserve Board
Federal Surplus Relief Corporation, 204n
Federal Theater Project, 255, 349, 761
Federal Trade Commission (FTC), 33, 367n, 372
Federal Writers Project, 255–56
Feis, Herbert, 403–4, 501
FERA. See Federal Emergency Relief Administration
Ferdinand Magellan (FDR's railcar), 799, 808
Fermi, Enrico, 658, 659, 665
Fifteenth Air Force (U.S.), 742
Fifteenth Army (German), 696, 724, 725
Fifth Division (Japanese), 527
Fifth Fleet, U.S., 814, 816, 818–20, 821
Fifth Marine Division (U.S.), 831
Fiji, 531, 533
Filipino-Americans, 292–93
Filipinos, 529, 530, 546, 828–29. See also Philippines
Films, 256, 303–4, 306, 342, 393, 402, 761. See also specific film
Final Report, Japanese Evacuation from the West Coast, 1942 (War Department), 757–59
Finance Committee (U.S. Senate), 126

Financial sector: impact of New Deal on, 365–68
Finland, 391n, 425, 435, 678
Fireside Chats: and banking system, 136; and beginnings of World War II, 426–27; and Blue Eagle campaign, 183–84; and British survivability, 468–69; and deficit spending, 361–62; and economic recovery, 216; and elections of 1938, 347, 348; and FDR's philosophy, 246; and FDR's political strategy, 244; first, 136; and liberalization of Democratic Party, 347, 348; and monetary policies, 197; on relief, 250–51; on role of government, 325; and U.S. as arsenal of democracy, 465; and U.S. entry into war, 493–94
First Air Fleet (Japanese), 517, 534, 535–36, 540
First Airborne Division (British), 736
First Army Division (U.S.), 694, 721–22, 737
First Marine Division (U.S.), 548, 558
"First New Deal": economic recovery in, 177–89; and FDR's first hundred days, 139–59; and FDR's philosophy, 248n; initiation of, 139–40; lack of coherency in, 153–54
Fish, Hamilton, 462, 463, 793
Fisher, Irving, 113
Fitzgerald, F. Scott, 16, 386–87
Five Hundred and Fifty-Fifth Parachute Infantry Battalion (U.S.), 848
Five Hundred and Ninth Composite Group (U.S.), 849
Fletcher, Frank Jack, 538, 542, 548, 549–50, 551, 554, 555, 819
Flint, Michigan: autoworker strike in, 308–14, 316, 339, 349
Florence (Italy), 600
Florida v. Mellon (1926), 264–65
Flying Fortresses. See B-17 bombers
Flying Tigers, 505
Flynn, Edward J., 285–86n
Focke Wulf 190 fighters (German), 702–3
Food Stamp Program (1939), 204n
Forced-labor drafts, 637–38
Forced-savings program, 624, 626
Ford, Henry, 21, 352, 649, 653–54
Ford, James, 222
Ford Motor Company, 13, 20–21, 166, 309, 312, 314, 317, 621, 638, 651
Fordney-McCumber Tariff Act (1922), 33, 49, 49n, 77, 855

Foreign affairs: and Congress-FDR relations, 393; and elections of 1940, 459; and FDR's domestic policies, 470; FDR's priorities for, 107, 157, 420–21, 423–25; FDR's understanding of, 389; and New Deal, 390

Foreign exchange, 197, 200, 390, 415

Foreign ministers, 612–13

Foreign Office, British, 475–76

Foreign Relations Committee (U.S. Senate), 156, 395, 422, 472

Foreman, Clark, 346

Formosa (Taiwan), 527, 610, 813, 814, 816, 821, 822, 824, 829

Fort Benning, Georgia, 711

Fort Bragg, North Carolina, 711

Fort Douaumont (France), 5

Fort Jackson, South Carolina, 711

Fort Leavenworth, Kansas, 715

Fort Lewis, Washington, 711

Fort Myer, Virginia, 686

Fort Shafter (Hawaii), 520

Fort Shelby, Mississippi, 711

Fortas, Abe, 211

Fortitude (Allied deception scheme), 693–95, 694*n*, 696, 707, 720, 727

"Fortress America" strategy, 448

Fortune magazine, 208, 388, 402, 415, 417, 778

Forty-Fifth Infantry Division (U.S.), 851

Forty-Third Infantry Division (U.S.), 563

Foster, William, 51, 222

Four Freedoms, 469–70, 760

Four Hundred Forty-Second Regimental Combat Team (U.S.), 755, 772

Fourth Division (U.S.), 721

France: aerial warfare in, 724–25, 727, 728; aid for, 427–28, 429, 431–32, 447–48, 447*n*; aircraft sales to, 421; Allied invasion of, 718–36; Allied policy after liberation of, 707–8; arms sales to, 421; bombing in, 706–7, 727, 728; British defeat in, 576; British relations with, 382; and cash-and-carry, 422; casualties in, 721, 722, 726, 727, 731; Chamber of Deputies in, 73; civilian government of liberated, 707–8; and colonialism, 670, 853–54; and Czech crisis, 418; declares war on Germany, 426; and Eastern Europe front, 726; at end of World War II, 853–54; fall of Daladier's government in, 438; FDR's views about, 435–36, 450; and German annexation of Austria, 71–72; German conquest of, 504; German

defenses in, 691, 692, 696, 720–22, 724–26, 727, 728, 729–31; German invasion of, 439; and German invasion of Rhineland, 384–85*n*, 385; German occupation of, 583; German peace feelers to, 435, 436; German prisoners-of-war in, 731; German reparation payments to, 72–73, 74*n*; German withdrawal/escape from, 728, 730–32; Hitler's views about, 409; housing in, 370; impact of World War I on, 382, 396; international debts of, 73, 74*n*, 386; and isolationism, 386; and Italian invasion of Ethiopia, 396, 397; Jews in, 418; mobility in, 723, 724, 724*n*, 727–28; morale in, 437; Mussolini declares war on, 440; and neutrality laws, 432; in 1930s, 71–73, 74*n*; and North African campaign, 581; Overlord to land in, 683; resistance forces in, 707; resistance to dependence on U.S. by, 431–32; Rommel in, 692; Roosevelt's policy toward liberated, 707–8; Ruhr occupied by, 8; and Soviet diplomatic missions, 425; and Spanish Civil War, 398, 399, 400*n*; Stalin's views about, 677, 682, 708; strikes in, 310; surrender of, 440, 455; survivability of, 435–36; tanks in, 724, 724*n*, 725–26, 730; U.S. relations with, 382, 386; U.S.-Great Britain exchange stabilization agreement with, 390; Welles "fact-finding" mission to, 436–37. *See also* French forces; Vichy government; *specific person, Allied operation, battle, or city*

Franck, James, 840

Franco, Francisco, 385, 398, 399, 401

Frank, Jerome N., 211–12, 211*n*, 212, 213, 353, 360

Frankfurter, Felix, 31, 121, 124, 128, 219*n*, 325, 353, 797

Fraternal Order of Eagles, 261

Fraternal organizations, 86, 307

Frazier, Lynn, 390

Frazier-Lemke Act (1935), 328*n*

Fredendall, Lloyd, 584

French Committee of National Liberation (FCNL), 707, 708

French forces: and German occupation of Norway, 438; and invasion of France, 731; and North African campaign, 581–83; and Overlord, 698, 707, 708; surrender of, 439

French Morocco, 581, 600

Frey, John, 316
Friedan, Betty, 781
Frontier: closing of American, 373, 374
"Frontier-on-the-Rhine" flap, 421
Fuchida, Mitsuo, 519, 520, 522, 540
Führer Directive No. 16 (Hitler), 453
Führer Directive No. 51 (Hitler), 691, 695
Fujita, Nobuo, 746–47, 760
Fuller, Ida M., 272

Galbraith, John Kenneth, 35
Gallipoli (Turkey), 599, 723
Garner, John Nance, 31, 60–61, 62, 81–82,
    98, 124, 332–33, 423
Garner-Wagner Bill (1932), 91, 92
Garrison, Lloyd, 298
Garvey, Marcus, 763
Gavin, James M., 724n
Gavutu (Solomon Island), 548–49
Gela (Sicily), 593
Genda, Minoru, 517
General Agreement on Tariffs and Trade
    (GATT), 855
General Electric, 87, 166, 621, 849
General Maximum Price Regulation
    ("General Max"), 640
General Motors Acceptance Corporation,
    22
General Motors Corporation, 13, 22, 87,
    308–14, 316, 320, 339
Generational identity: World War II as
    defining, 712–13
Geneva Convention, 812
Geneva, Switzerland: Disarmament
    Conference in (1933), 105, 106, 158,
    159, 384
Gentlemen's Agreement (1908), 41, 501
Geography: importance of, 386–87, 434,
    814
George, Walter F., 346, 347, 348, 422
George Washington (U.S. ship), 6
German command structure, 691–92, 696,
    720
German-American Bund, 471
German-Americans, 749, 750n
Germans: and Americans as prisoners of
    war, 813
Germany: Allied invasion of, 734–38, 745;
    and Anglo-American relations, 803; anti-
    Semitism in, 158, 361, 383, 384, 410–
    11, 411n, 412, 415–16, 420, 657–58,
    794–97; atomic research in, 658–59,
    666–67, 666n; automobile industry in,
    312; bombings/targets in, 605, 608–9,

702, 703, 704, 705–6, 707, 742–45;
    Britain declares war on, 426; collapse of,
    731, 732–35, 742–45, 809, 854; colonies
    of, 7; Communism in, 104, 384;
    declares war on U.S., 524; economy of,
    72, 74, 76, 77, 118, 742, 744; effects of
    World War I on, 1–2; elections in, 383–
    84; at end of World War II, 854; FDR's
    views about, 679; first U.S. forces enter,
    793; France declares war on, 426; and
    Hitler's rise to power, 71, 104, 158;
    Hohenzollerns dethroned in, 1; Japan's
    alliance with, 385, 397, 504, 524; and
    Morgenthau Plan, 803–4; in 1920s, 118;
    in 1930s, 72, 74, 76, 77; partitioning of,
    803–4; paying for cost of war in, 625;
    and peace feelers to British and French,
    435, 436, 444; and peace feelers to
    Soviets, 612, 675; post-war plans for,
    677, 679, 684, 799, 803–5, 807;
    production in, 489, 647, 648–49, 655,
    703, 742; rearmament of, 384, 394, 398;
    as responsible for World War I, 7, 72;
    scholars flee, 657; social insurance laws
    in, 260; Soviet pacts with, 381, 425,
    435, 472, 612, 761; Stalin's views about,
    679; steel industry in, 303; surrender of,
    737–38, 809, 854; and Teheran
    Conference, 677, 679, 684, 803; and
    Tripartite Pact, 7; unemployment in,
    104; and Versailles Treaty, 1–2, 7, 424;
    Welles "fact-finding" mission to, 436;
    withdraws ambassador from U.S., 416;
    withdraws from League of Nations, 384;
    and Yalta Conference, 799, 803–5, 807.
    See also Luftwaffe; Reparations, German;
    Rome-Berlin Axis Agreement; Strategy,
    German; Wehrmacht; Weimar Republic;
    specific topic or person, especially Hitler,
    Adolf
Germany First: and ABC-1, 482, 506, 532,
    544; and Argentia, 506; FDR's views
    about, 510, 578, 579; and Japan-U.S.
    relations, 506, 510, 511, 513; Joint
    Board of Army and Navy affirms, 513;
    and North African campaign, 554, 578,
    579; and Pacific War, 554, 578; and
    Plan Dog, 480, 506, 544; and second
    front, 578; and Victory Program, 487,
    506
Gestapo (Geheime Staatspolizei), 384,
    417
Ghormley, Robert F., 547, 552, 554, 557
Gifford, Walter S., 88

Gilbert Islands, 533, 610, 681, 810, 814, 816
Gillette, Guy M., 422
Giraud, Henri, 581–82, 583
Girdler, Thomas Mercer, 317–18, 352
GIs: Bill of Rights for, 786–87, 858; photographs of dead, 793; profile of average, 710–11; votes of, 787–88
Gladden, Washington, 146
Glass, Carter, 66, 99, 119
Glass-Steagall Banking Act (1933), 83, 153, 366
Glassford, Pelham D., 293n
Glenn L. Martin aircraft plant, 849
Glickman, Marty, 411n
Globalization, 855
Goebbels, Josef, 415
Goering, Hermann, 423, 452, 453
Gold: and agriculture, 197; and devaluation of dollar, 143, 388; and economic isolationism, 200; and economic recovery, 177; and FDR's first hundred days, 135, 136, 137, 143, 154; of France, 431–32; of Great Britain, 431–32, 466, 473; and recession of 1937–38, 355; and U.S. wealth, 857. See also Gold shipments; Gold standard; Gold-purchase program; Monetary/fiscal policies
"Gold" (D-Day landing zone), 721
Gold shipments, 109, 117, 133
Gold standard: Coughlin's attack on, 230; and economic isolationism, 388; and FDR's first hundred days, 154–57; FDR's views about, 107, 154–57; and gold-purchase program, 197; and Great Britain, 36, 76, 78, 154; and Hoover, 75–79, 76n, 78, 80, 81, 82, 83, 106, 107, 109; Keynes's views about, 76, 76n, 78–79, 156, 197; U.S. goes off, 214, 392
Gold-purchase program, 197–99, 214
Gompers, Samuel, 25, 260, 300–301
"Good Neighbor" policy, 391–92, 420, 507
Goodyear Tire Factory (Akron, Ohio), 296
Gore, Thomas P., 51, 143
Gothic Line, 600
Government: business's relationship with, 477; FDR's views about, 280–81; and labor, 314; in 1920s, 54–56; and recession of 1937–38, 355–61; Republican domination of, 127; size of, 55; social objective of, 249; structure of, 55. See also Government, role of; State government

Government, role of: as agency of human welfare, 32–33; and banking system, 80; and borrowing, 80, 81; Brain Trust's views about, 120–21, 122; and closing of American frontier, 373; and conservatives, 340–41; and Constitution, 337; and credit, 81; and economy, 377; FDR's views about, 99–100, 118, 145–46, 245–47, 249, 251, 325, 373, 374–75; Gompers's views about, 260; Hoover's views about, 44, 47, 48, 52, 54–56, 80, 82–85, 85n, 91; and impact of New Deal, 373, 374–75, 377; Keynes's views about, 354, 357–58; and Keynesian economics, 359; and New Dealers, 354; in 1920s, 30; and orthodox economic theory, 51, 52; and public works, 80; and regional development, 346; and relief efforts, 80, 145–46; and response to Crash of 1929, 54–56; and security, 359; and social security, 262–63; and southern Democrats, 125; and unemployment, 80, 251
Governors Conference (Salt Lake City, 1930), 261
Grand Alliance: American concerns about, 565; and Battle of the Atlantic, 572; and Cold War, 854; Cold War as outcome of tensions in, 580; and duration of war, 616; and Eastern Europe, 738; formation of, 485; and German successes, 495; and Jews in Hungary, 796; and Red Army's entrance into Europe, 613; and secret negotiations with Italy, 808–9; Stalin as unequal partner in, 595; tensions within, 610–14. See also Churchill, Winston; Roosevelt, Franklin D.; Stalin, Josef
Grattan, C. Hartley, 387
Great Britain: Allied buildup in, 573–74, 591, 596, 599, 694; and Asia, 500, 670; atomic research in, 659, 661, 666; Battle of, 440, 452–54, 460–61, 464, 470, 489, 504; and colonialism, 670, 855; conscription in, 425; and Czech crisis, 418; declares war on Germany, 426; economy of, 72–73, 76, 77, 78, 390, 646, 713; elections in, 747; and end of World War II, 854; enemy aliens in, 749–50n; and Evian-les-Bains refugee conference, 414; fall of Chamberlain's government in, 438; and FDR's election of 1940, 464; and FDR's proposed international peace conference, 406–7;

Great Britain (continued)
    FDR's views about, 435–36, 442, 443, 447, 450, 799; French relations with, 382; German "invasion" of, 453–54, 461, 471n; and German invasion of Rhineland, 385; German peace feelers to, 435, 436, 444; German reparation payments to, 72–73; and gold standard, 36, 76, 78, 154; Hitler's views about, 397, 409, 424; housing in, 370, 370n; impact of World War I on, 396; insolvency of, 465–68, 473, 475; international debts of, 72–73, 386, 391n, 466–67; and isolationism in U.S., 386; and Italian invasion of Ethiopia, 396, 397, 408; Jews in, 418; morale in, 453–54; Mussolini declares war on, 440; and neutrality laws, 432; in 1930s, 72–73, 76, 77, 78; in Pacific War, 526–27; pacifism in, 382–83; and Palestine issue, 795; personal consumption in, 646; and Poland, 422; and post-World War I, 382–83; productivity in, 654, 655; and second front, 580, 585, 596, 613; Soviet relations with, 425, 580, 601; and Spanish Civil War, 398, 399; strategic importance of, 480; strategy of, 382, 407–8, 465, 576, 670, 700, 743–44; survivability of, 426, 435–36, 437–38, 439, 440–42, 443, 444–46, 447, 450, 451–52, 467–69, 480, 490; trade with, 36, 391n; unpreparedness of, 407; U.S.-France exchange stabilization agreement with, 390; Welles "fact-finding" mission to, 437–38; working women in, 777–78. See also Aid for Britain; Anglo-American relations; England; Grand Alliance; London, England; specific conference, battle, operation, or person, especially Churchill, Winston
Great Depression: basic assumption of New Dealers about, 785–86; Brain Trust's views about, 120, 121–22; causes of, 9, 36, 38–41, 49n, 69, 70–73, 71n, 75–80, 106–7, 189; Crash of 1929 as cause of, 38–41, 40n; data about, 160, 162–66; experimentation and innovation during, 82–85; and FDR's first hundred days, 218; FDR's views about cause of, 107; and gold standard, 75–79; as historic watershed, 70–71; ignorance about, 56–57, 64; and international financial markets, 70–80; isolationism during, 387–88; and mobilization, 617, 619; New

Deal's relationship to, 166; and orthodox economic theory, 51–59; persistence of, 218; and political realignments, 32n; popular mood in early years of, 88–90; and psychology of fear, 88–90; as social disaster, 174; tariffs as cause of, 49n; World War I as cause of, 9, 70–73, 71n, 80, 106
Great War. See World War I
Greece, 493, 576
Greeley, Horace, 455
Green, William, 305
Greenbacks, 129, 143
Greenland, 491, 492
Greenland "gap," 572
Greer (U.S. destroyer), 497, 499
Grew, Joseph, 504, 505, 506, 511, 513, 841, 845
Griffith, D.W., 342
Gross national product (GNP), 29, 55, 58, 59, 60, 163, 285, 288, 289
Group Theatre, 303–4
Groves, Leslie, 663–64, 665–66, 809, 838, 841
Grumman Aircraft Corporation, 543
Guadalcanal: barbarism of warfare on, 561; "Bloody Ridge" on, 556, 558; casualties on, 554; code name for, 553; as decisive battle, 553, 559; Fletcher's withdrawal from, 549–50; importance of, 553, 554; Japanese forces on, 544, 553–54, 555–56, 557–58; Japanese retreat from, 560; and Japanese strategy, 544, 554; and Japanese on Tulagi, 532; Japanese underestimation of Americans at, 553, 560; Japanese versus U.S. strength on, 560; Naval Battle of, 559–60; prisoners of war at, 813; siege of, 553–60; U.S. forces on, 548, 549, 552, 553, 555–56, 558–59; and U.S. strategy/planning, 547, 549, 554, 578, 810. See also Solomon Islands
Guam, 526, 533, 534, 818, 845
Guderian, Heinz, 602
Guffey Bituminous Coal Conservation Act, 329, 336
Gustav Line, 598

Hague, Frank, 253
Hahn, Otto, 658, 661, 666
Haiti, 391, 391n
Halifax, Edward Frederick, Lord, 444, 481
Halsey, William F. "Bull": and Battle of Leyte Gulf, 824, 825–26, 827; on

Japanese, 811; and Japanese surrender, 852, 853n; and Pacific War, 814; and Solomons campaign, 557, 559, 560, 562, 563–64; and Third Fleet, 814, 821–22

Hamburg (Germany), 847

Hamilton, Alexander, 46, 145, 458

Hanford, Washington, 665, 666

Hanighen, F.C., 388

Hansen, Alvin H., 375, 375n, 786

Hardegen, Reinhard, 568

Harding, Warren G., 11, 33, 46, 205, 211, 327n, 348

Harlem (New York City): race riots in, 770

Harriman, Averell, 675

Harris, Arthur, 702, 703, 704, 705, 724, 739

Harrison, Benjamin, 33

Harrison, George L., 840

Harrison, Pat, 31, 343

Hart, Liddell, 602

Harvard University: FDR speech at, 277; FDR as student at, 115. See also specific person

Hasegawa, Kazuo, 812

Hastie, William, 378, 771, 773

Hatch Act (1939), 349

Hawaii: FDR dispatches fleet to, 446; FDR-Nimitz-MacArthur meeting in, 792, 821; and Japanese strategy, 534; Japanese-Americans in, 748–49, 751. See also Pearl Harbor

Hawley-Smoot Tariff Act (1930), 49–50, 49n, 77, 855

Health care, 263–64, 269, 271, 652

Hearst, William Randolph, 99, 101, 137, 233, 276–77

Heisenberg, Werner, 666

Hemingway, Ernest, 387, 399, 569

Hemisphere Defense Plan No. 1, 491

Henderson Field (Guadalcanal), 548, 553, 556, 557–58, 563

Henderson, Leon, 353, 355, 356, 359, 478, 623, 628. See also Office of Price Administration

Herriot, Edouard, 155

Hersey, John, 555, 557, 561, 794

Hershey, Lewis B., 632, 633, 634–35, 636, 639

Hess, Rudolph, 5n

Hickam Field (Hawaii), 520, 522

Hickok, Lorena: and agriculture, 190, 191–93, 196, 198, 205, 207–8, 212, 213; on blacks, 173, 173n, 193, 194; on Communism, 198; and CWA, 176; disaffection of, 214–15; and Eleanor Roosevelt, 161–62, 162n, 190, 191, 192; on NRA, 188, 190; on Olson, 220; personal and professional background of, 161; and politics of relief, 172, 173–75; purpose of travels of, 160, 162; style of, 161; summary report of, 215; and textile industry, 181; travels of, 166, 167, 168–77, 181, 190, 191–93, 196, 205, 207–8, 214–15; and unemployment, 215, 250

Hill, Alger, 212–13

Hill, Lister, 346

Hillman, Sidney, 302, 305, 306, 478

Hirabayashi v. United States, 756, 758

Hirohito (emperor of Japan), 504, 512–13, 515, 798, 835, 836–37, 841, 844, 845, 850–51

Hiroshima (Japan), 426, 655, 809n, 839n, 842, 843n, 847, 849–50

Hiryu (Japanese aircraft carrier), 536, 542

Hispanics, 254, 777

Hiss, Alger, 211, 212, 213

Hitchman Coal & Coke Co. v. Mitchell (1917), 26

Hitler, Adolf: and Allied second front, 691; ambitions of, 5, 6, 383, 409; attempt on life of, 728–29, 730; and Battle for Northwest Europe, 718, 720, 724, 725, 730, 737, 738; and Beer Hall Putsch, 5n; bronze bust of, 737; and Chamberlain strategy, 408; death of, 809, 852; as dictator, 111, 158, 361, 383–84; and Disarmament Conference, 159; expansionism of, 392–93, 409; on FDR, 423–25; FDR's 1939 message to, 423; FDR's views about, 158; and German command structure, 691–92, 696; and German withdrawal from France, 728; and Holocaust, 794–97; imprisonment of, 8; installed as German chancellor, 104; on "Jewish physics," 666; and Jews, 2, 383, 415, 760; on Marxism, 2; military strategy of, 383, 409, 616; and Pearl Harbor, 524; rise to power of, 8–9, 71, 104, 158, 381, 383–84; and Spanish Civil War, 398, 399; style of, 728–29, 730; views about Great Britain of, 397; views about U.S. of, 155, 392–93, 421, 423–25, 615; and Welles "fact-finding" mission, 436, 437–38; and World War I, 1–2, 4, 383, 392. See also Germany; specific event

Hoare, Samuel, 396

Hoare-Laval deal (1935), 396–97, 595
Hogs, 204–5
Holland, Elmer J., 543n
Holland. See Low Countries; Netherlands
Holmes, Oliver Wendell, 100
Holocaust, 412, 794–97
"Home front," 602, 602–3n
Home Loan Banks, 83
Home Owners Loan Corporation (HOLC), 285, 369
Homestead, Pennsylvania: strike at, 303, 304
Hong Kong, 526, 670, 750
Honshu (Japan), 835
Hood (British battleship), 493
Hook, Sidney, 222
"Hooligan's Navy" (Coastal Picket Patrol), 569
Hoover, Herbert: abilities of, 69; *American Individualism* by, 46–47; biography of, 11, 44–46; and causes of Great Depression, 9, 36, 70–73, 71n, 79–80, 106; as Commerce secretary, 11, 46, 56, 180, 203; and Congress, 43, 49n, 50, 61, 62–63, 64–65; and Coolidge, 33, 34; economic strategy of, 48, 51–59, 70, 78–79, 82; experimentation and innovation of, 82–85; failure of, 111, 127; on FDR, 102, 109; and FDR's inauguration, 133–34; FDR's meetings with, 105, 106, 107–10, 132, 133, 157–58; FDR's relationship with, 108, 110, 133; FDR's views about, 46; federal bureaucracy study of, 367; as food relief administrator, 9, 11, 45, 47–48, 91; inauguration of, 43, 90; and Keynesian economics, 358; last days in office of, 110; optimism of, 39, 58, 59, 68, 147; political theory of, 46–47; as progressive, 11–12, 45; as reformer, 48; reputation of, 9, 12, 45, 46, 91–92; "second program" of, 82–85; and states' rights, 330; style of, 11, 44–45, 50, 51, 92, 94–95, 113; Supreme Court appointments of, 327n; vision/dreams of, 10, 11–12, 13, 47–48, 102. *See also specific person or topic*
Hoover, J. Edgar, 636, 751, 757
Hoover, Lou Henry, 45
"Hoovervilles," 91, 157
Hoover Dam, 63
Hoover Doctrine, 94
Hopkins, Harry: and arts/culture, 254, 254n; and blacks, 764; and British survivability,

490; and Churchill-FDR relations, 596; Churchill's views of, 161; and CWA, 176; and data about ordeal of American people, 160–68; demagogues' effects on, 242; on Depression as social disaster, 174; discouragement of, 175; dispensing of relief funds by, 170–71; and elections of 1940, 462; and European balance of power, 590; and Japan-U.S. relations, 515; Johnson's views about, 252; and Lend-Lease, 470–71, 471n, 475; at Malta, 799; misquoting of, 349; and New Dealers, 353, 354–55, 361; and Overlord, 683, 687; personal and professional background of, 161; at Quebec Conference, 613; and race issues, 254; and recession of 1937–38, 361; and reform, 217; and reform of relief policies, 242; as relief administrator, 145–46; and role of government, 145–46, 374–75; and second front, 573–74, 574n, 575, 576, 578, 579, 613, 682; Smith's criticisms of, 281; and Social Gospel, 146; and social security, 258; Soviet trip of, 484; on Stalin, 676; on Stalin-FDR relations, 676; style of, 145–46, 161; and Suez Conference, 806; at Teheran Conference, 611, 676, 682, 683; and unemployment, 250; and WPA, 252–57. *See also* Federal Emergency Relief Administration; Hickok, Lorena: travels of
Hornet (U.S. aircraft carrier), 535, 538, 539, 541
House of Commons: Churchill's speeches before, 441–42, 451–52
House, Edward M., 8, 243
House of Representatives, U.S., 60, 125, 125n. *See also specific person, committee, or legislation*
House Un-American Activities Committee (HUAC), 316, 349
Housing, 35, 69, 340, 357, 358, 368–70, 370n, 645. *See also* Mortgages: home
Howard, Michael, 684
Howard, Roy, 277, 278, 283, 456
Howe, Louis McHenry, 96, 161, 240
H.R. 1776. *See* Lend-Lease
Huddleston, George, 166
Huertgen Forest, Battle of, 737
Hughes, Charles Evans, 326, 327n, 333, 334, 335–36, 337
Hughes, Langston, 222

Hull, Cordell: and agriculture, 142; on Anglo-American relations, 442; appointed secretary of state, 389; and arms embargo, 422; biography of, 507; on British survivability, 442; and cash-and-carry, 422; on Churchill, 442; and elections of 1932, 62; FDR's relationship with, 507; and isolationism, 404; and Japan-U.S. relations, 506–8, 514, 515, 519; and Japanese peace initiatives, 844; and Latin America, 391; and Moley, 156; and neutrality laws, 423; and post-war Germany, 803, 804; and Sino-Japanese war, 403, 404; and Stalin's frustrations, 611; style of, 507; and trade, 389; and unconditional-surrender doctrine, 844–45; and World Economic Conference, 156

Humphrey's Executor v. United States (1935), 328n

"Hundred Days": accomplishments of, 135–39, 140, 149–59, 218; and agriculture, 204; and Congress-FDR relationship, 138–39, 149; and constitutionality of New Deal, 324; and economic recovery, 149–53; and initiation of New Deal, 140–59; popular opinion in, 137–38

Hungary, 381, 382, 795–96, 801

Hutcheson, Big Bill, 302

Hutchins, Robert Maynard, 787

Hyde Park, New York: Churchill-FDR meeting at, 838–39; Monnet-FDR meeting at, 428; as Roosevelt home, 96, 114, 454

Hydroelectric power, 63–64, 99, 128, 147–49. *See also specific project*

Ibn Saud (king of Saudi Arabia), 806

Iceland, 492, 496, 497, 499

Ichi-go Campaign (China), 674, 816

Ichihashi, Yamato, 753–54, 755

Ichiki, Kiyoana, 553–54, 555

Ickes, Harold: and aid for Britain, 448; and Battle of the Atlantic Ocean, 490; and blacks, 764; and British survivability, 442; and constitutionality of New Deal measures, 330; on FDR, 340, 344; and Japan-U.S. relations, 506, 510–11, 514; and Japanese-Americans, 755–56; and *Kristallnacht*, 416; and Mussolini's declaration of war on Britain and France, 439–40; and New Dealers, 353; as progressive, 127; as PWA head, 176, 178, 188, 251–52; and radicalism, 223,

278; and recession of 1937–38, 352; and reform spirit, 623; as Republican, 32; as secretary of interior, 127; Smith's criticisms of, 281; style of, 178; and tax legislation, 623; and U.S. entry into war, 494; on Willkie, 455; and World Court, 232

Immigration Act (1921), 386

Immigration Act (1924), 15, 386, 413–14, 501, 749

Immigration/immigrants: and banking system, 86; decline/closure of, 21, 41, 122; and Democratic Party, 30, 102–3, 127, 128, 216, 378; and elections, 102–3, 284–85; FDR's views about, 416; Hitler's views about, 392; impact of New Deal on, 378; from Japan, 41, 500–501; Jews as, 14, 15, 67, 411, 412–13, 414, 416–17; and labor, 23, 164, 305, 306–7, 777; and legacies of World War II, 858; and mechanization, 23; New Deal support by, 750; in 1920s, 13, 14–16, 21; political apathy of, 30; and political realignments, 231; quotas, 41, 415, 416–17; and refugees, 413–14, 415–17; and stagnation thesis, 122; unemployment of, 164. *See also* Refugees

Imperial Air Staff (British), 604

Imperial Preference System, 77

Income taxes, 62, 79–82, 275, 624–25

India, 4, 574n, 670, 855

Indian Ocean: Nagumo's raids in, 527

Indian Reorganization Act (1934), 379

Indianapolis (U.S. carrier), 849

Individualism, 46–47, 174, 202

Indochina, 504, 505, 506, 509–10, 514, 526, 554, 853–54

Industrial Association (San Francisco), 293, 294, 295

Industrialization: as epoch-making event, 13

Industry: balance between agriculture and, 134, 140, 152, 177, 191, 200, 375; Coughlin's views about, 232; data about, 163; and economic recovery, 150–53, 201–2; and FDR's first hundred days, 150–53; FDR's views about, 103, 118, 134; in Germany, 7; impact of New Deal on, 375; in 1920s, 20–21; and prices, 190; and PWA, 178; and technology, 20; unemployment in heavy, 164; and Versailles Treaty, 7. *See also* Industry codes, NRA; National Industrial Recovery Act; National Recovery Administration

Industry codes, NRA, 181–82, 183–86, 188–89, 190, 203–4, 296

Inflation: and agriculture, 141, 143, 157, 196, 197; Brain Trust's views about, 121–22; Congressional views about, 157; Coughlin's views about, 216, 230, 231; and Democratic party, 118–19; and disillusionment with FDR, 220; and economic isolationism, 375; and FDR's first hundred days, 143, 150, 154, 157, 159; FDR's views about, 107, 118, 134, 154, 157, 375; and Hoover, 109, 121–22; and industrial recovery policy, 150; Long's views about, 237; and political realignments, 129; and progressives, 220; and recession of 1937–38, 355; and Silver Purchase Act, 198n; and wages, 157; in wartime, 623, 624, 639, 641

Inoue, Shigeyoshi, 531–32, 536

Insull, Samuel, 64

Intelligence: Allied, 732; and Battle of Britain, 452–53; and Battle for Northwest Europe, 732; British, 452–53, 571, 589, 592–93; and Enigma, 452–53; German, 571; Japanese, 520; and Pearl Harbor, 520; and Sicily invasion, 592–93; and Triton code, 571, 589. See also Bletchley Park (England) cryptographers; Codes; Intelligence, U.S.

Intelligence, U.S.: and Battle of Leyte Gulf, 827; and Battle of Normandy, 729; and enemy aliens, 751, 757; and Guadalcanal, 544; and Japanese codes, 507–8, 515; and Midway Island, 536–37, 538, 542; and Navaho language, 829–30; as Pearl Harbor scapegoat, 525; and Port Moresby attack, 531; and Solomons campaign, 544, 563

Inter-Allied Food Council, 45

Interfaith groups, 761

Intergovernmental Committee on Political Refugees (IGC), 415

Interim Committee (atomic project), 839–40

Interior Department, U.S., 378

Interlocking Convoy System, 570

International Association of Machinists (IAM), 652, 765

International financial markets, 70–80. See also Debts, international

International Harvester, 317, 638

International Labor Defense, 222–23, 223n

International Ladies Garment Workers Union (ILGWU), 226, 302, 305

International Longshoremen's Association (ILA), 294

International Monetary Fund, 855

International organization: creation of new, 677, 685. See also League of Nations; United Nations

International peace conference: FDR's proposal for, 406–9, 408n

Internationalism: and FDR's first hundred days, 158–59; FDR's views about, 214, 233, 389, 390, 391, 393. See also specific person

Interracial groups, 761

Interstate Commerce Commission (ICC), 367n, 371, 372–73

Interstate and Foreign Commerce Committee (U.S. House), 125

Iowa (U.S. battleship), 669

Ireland: U.S. fleet visit to, 445, 446

Iron and Steel Institute, 184

Isaacs, Harold, 401–2

"Island-hopping," 564

Isolationism: and aid for Britain, 432, 460; and aid for France, 432; and Anglo-American relations, 404, 405, 407–9, 465; and appeasement, 419; and beginning of World War II, 428; British views about American, 407–8, 443; and business, 387–88; and cash-and-carry, 422, 434; and Churchill-FDR relations, 435n; in Congress, 422–23; Coughlin's views about, 233; and destroyer transfers, 461–62; and disillusionment with FDR, 220, 234; and economic nationalism, 158; and elections in 1930s, 388, 422–23; and elections in 1940s, 454, 455, 458–59, 460, 462–63, 793; end of, 158; and escorts, 490; European fears of, 432; and FDR, 396, 619; FDR as isolationist, 158; as FDR problem, 679–80; and FDR's "Quarantine Speech," 404–5, 406; FDR's views about, 101, 388, 404–5, 406, 428, 441; and geography, 386–87; and gold-buying program, 199; during Great Depression, 387–88; Hitler's views about, 424; and immigration quotas, 415; and international debts, 73, 74, 106, 386, 390–91; and Jews, 414, 854, 855; and League of Nations, 386, 396, 424, 474–75; and leaks to press, 488; and legacies of World War II, 854, 855; and Lend-Lease, 471, 472–75; in literature, 387; and Ludlow amendment, 402–3; in mid-1930s, 393; and mobilization/

rearmament, 431, 451, 619; and
Munich Agreement, 419; and neutrality,
400, 428, 433, 434; and New Deal, 390;
in 1920s, 41, 385–86; in 1930s, 73, 74,
101, 106; and profile of typical
Americans, 41; and progressives, 220,
390; and Republican appointments to
FDR cabinet, 458–59; and Sino-
Japanese war, 381, 390, 401–2, 403–4;
and Soviet domination of Eastern
Europe, 854; and Teheran Conference,
679–80; and trade, 386, 388, 389; and
U.S. military, 388–89; and Versailles
Treaty (1919), 386, 390, 474–75; and
Victory Program, 488; and Wilson, 388,
390; and World Court, 393; and World
War I, 385, 386, 387, 763. *See also*
Economic isolationism; Neutrality;
Pacifism
Italian forces, 575, 577, 583, 584, 594
Italian-Americans, 749, 750, 750*n*
Italy: Allied campaign in, 596–601; and
Anglo-American strategy, 595–96; anti-
Semitism in, 657–58; and blacks in
military, 772, 773; Churchill's views
about, 682; Eisenhower as commander
of campaign in, 689; FDR's views about,
682; German forces surrender in, 808–9;
and German invasion of Rhineland, 384–
85; Hitler's views about, 409; impact of
World War I on, 381; invasion of
Ethiopia by, 394, 395, 396–97, 400,
401, 408, 409; Japanese-Americans in,
755, 773; Japan's alliance with, 504;
Jews in, 795; and Overlord/Anvil, 680–
82, 700, 701; politics in, 594–95;
preliminary armistice in, 598; scholars
flee, 657–58; and second front, 601, 682;
secret negotiations with, 808–9; Soviet
reactions to campaign in, 611, 613;
stalemate in, 701; Stalin's views about,
681–82; surrender negotiations with, 594–
95, 596, 600; and Teheran Conference,
674, 680–82; and Tripartite Pact, 7; and
U.S. strategy, 700; and Versailles Treaty,
381; Welles "fact-finding" mission to,
436. *See also* Italian forces; Rome-Berlin
Axis Agreement (1936); *specific person,
especially* Mussolini, Benito
Iwo Jima, 828–31, 834, 836, 841

Jackson, Andrew, 30, 66, 137, 235, 274,
277, 282
Jackson, Robert, 352, 758–59

Jacob Jones (U.S. destroyer), 566
James, Henry, 386
James, William, 377
Japan: and atomic bomb, 838–42, 843*n*,
849–50; atomic research in, 666; and
cash-and-carry, 403; China as irrelevant
to defeat of, 674; and Comintern Pact,
385, 397; and economic nationalism,
157; economic sanctions against, 504,
505; ending of war with, 836–37; FDR's
views about, 450, 502, 507, 510, 511,
514–15; freeze on assets of, 510–11, 511–
12*n*; and German-Soviet peace feelers,
612; Germany's alliance with, 385, 397,
504, 524; Hitler's views about, 409;
impact of World War I on, 381;
imperialism of, 41, 504; and Italian
invasion of Ethiopia, 397; Italy's alliance
with, 504; loyalty in, 812; militarism in,
157, 232–33, 381, 397, 398;
modernization of, 500; and naval
limitations agreements, 233, 398, 501;
and neutrality laws, 401; and *Panay*
affair, 402; peace initiatives of, 835, 836–
37, 844–45; production in, 647, 655,
668; reparations for, 402; resigns from
League of Nations, 158; role of military
leaders in, 503–4; Soviet relations with,
390; strategy of, 502–3, 512–13, 616,
814, 832, 836–37; surrender of, 850–51,
852–53, 855–56; Tojo's government falls
in, 820–21; and Tripartite Pact, 7; and
unconditional-surrender doctrine, 699,
835, 837, 841, 844–45; U.S. bombing
of, 610, 674, 805, 816, 829, 845–50;
U.S. declares war on, 523, 523*n*; U.S.
invasion of, 834–35; U.S. occupation of,
850; U.S. strategy for defeat of, 610; and
Versailles Treaty (1919), 7, 381, 501;
views about U.S. in, 512. *See also* Air
Force, Imperial Japanese; Army,
Imperial Japanese; Japan-U.S. relations;
Japanese; Navy, Imperial Japanese;
Pacific war; Russo-Japanese war; Sino-
Japanese war; Southern Operation;
Tripartite Pact; *specific person or battle*
Japan-U.S. relations: and aid for Britain,
506; and Anglo-American joint
planning, 481, 482; and Battle of the
Atlantic Ocean, 491; and British
survivability, 445; and China, 500, 501,
502–3, 504–5, 508, 509, 513–14, 515;
Churchill's views about, 482; and
demands of Atlantic Theater, 495; and

Japan-U.S. relations (continued)
economic sanctions against Japan, 504, 505; and freeze on Japanese assets, 510–11, 511–12n; and Germany First, 506, 510, 511, 513; Great Debate about, 506–7; and inevitability of war, 515; and Japanese strategy, 502–3, 512–13; and mobilization, 480; pre-1940, 500–501; and Sino-Japanese war, 503, 504, 509, 513; and Soviet aid, 512; and Soviet Union, 508–9, 512, 514–15; and trade, 501, 502, 503, 505, 506, 507, 508, 510–11, 511–12n, 513, 514; and Tripartite Pact, 505–6, 508

Japanese: and Bushido code, 530, 811–12, 832; as fighters, 555–56; as immigrants, 41, 500–501; self-image of, 810–12; supplies for, 668; U.S. image of, 811

Japanese Imperial Conferences (1941), 512, 513

Japanese-Americans, 501, 748–60, 772, 855

Java Sea, Battle of, 527

Jefferson, Thomas, 229, 283, 377, 386, 458

Jeffersonianism, 10, 125, 171

Jewish Charities (Chicago, Illinois), 86

Jews: in Austria, 414; and Bank of United States, 67; Coughlin's views about, 231; and Democratic Party, 216; and development of atomic/nuclear weapons, 657–58, 666; divisions among American, 411; and divisiveness within Democratic party, 31; FDR's views about, 412, 413, 414, 416; in Germany, 158, 361, 383, 384, 410–11, 411n, 412, 415–16, 420, 657–58, 794–97; in Great Britain, 418; Hitler's views about, 2, 415, 760; and Holocaust, 794–97; as immigrants, 14, 15, 67, 411, 412–13, 414, 416–17; and Kristallnacht, 415–16, 658; and labor, 301; in 1920s, 14, 15; in 1930s, 86; and Nuremberg Decree/Laws, 384, 410, 412; in Poland, 414; public opinion about, 415; ransom of, 415; as refugees, 410, 411–12, 413–14, 416–18, 806, 854; in Romania, 414; on St. Louis, 417–18; as scholars, 657–58, 666; as unemployed, 86. See also Anti-Semitism

Jim Crow, 19, 378, 762–76, 781

JN-25 (Japanese naval code), 531, 537

Johnson, Andrew, 326

Johnson, Cornelius, 411n

Johnson, Gerald W., 89

Johnson, Hiram, 74, 91, 127, 219, 390–91, 424, 457

Johnson, Hugh S.: on AAA, 213; as anti-FDR, 451; and Blue Eagle campaign, 183–84; as Brain Trust member, 120; on Hopkins, 252; on Long, 240; on New Dealers, 478; and NLB, 187–88; and rearmament, 478; resignation of, 188, 214, 240; style of, 177, 182, 188; and WIB, 177–78, 183. See also National Recovery Administration

Johnson, Lyndon Baines, 16, 346

Johnson Act (1934), 390–91, 391n, 392, 397, 431, 466–67

Johnston, Stanley, 542–43n

Johnston (U.S. destroyer), 826–27

Johnstown, Pennsylvania: strikes in, 318

Joint Board of the Army and Navy (U.S.), 513, 514

Joint Chiefs of Staff, U.S., 557, 577–78, 628, 807, 816, 834–35

Joint Committee on the Conduct of the War, 791

Joint Strategic Survey Committee (U.S. Army), 585

Jones, Jesse H., 457, 477

Jones and Laughlin Corporation, 317, 320, 335–36

Joslin, Theodore, 94

J.P. Morgan and Company, 50, 67

Judicial Procedure Reform Act (1937), 336

Judicial review doctrine, 327

Judiciary, 325–31, 327n, 378. See also Supreme Court, U.S.

Juneau (U.S. cruiser), 559–60

Jungle fighting, 555, 557–58, 561

"Juno" (D-day landing zone), 721

Justice Department, U.S.: Anti-Trust Division of, 359; and Japanese-Americans in World War II, 752–53, 757–59; and Supreme Court reform, 330

Kaga (Japanese aircraft carrier), 536, 539, 542

Kaiser, Henry, 650–53

Kaiser Permanente Health Plan, 652

Kaiser shipyards, 650–53, 781n

Kakazu Ridge (Okinawa), 833

Kamikazes, 827–28, 832, 833, 835

Karski, Jan, 797

Kasserine Pass (Libya), 584

Katyn Forest (Soviet Union), 802

Kazin, Alfred, 255, 256

Kearny (U.S. destroyer), 499

Keegan, John, 534

Kelly, Edward J., 253, 456–57
Kennedy, John F., 563
Kennedy, Joseph P.: advice to FDR by, 126, 127; as ambassador to Great Britain, 432, 436, 437, 440, 443–44, 447, 450; and Britain's survivability, 437, 440, 443–44, 447, 450; Churchill's relations with, 443; and Coughlin, 231; FDR's views about, 443; on financial markets, 367; and German peace feelers to British, 436, 444; and neutrality laws, 432; and SEC, 367
Kenney, George, 562–63
Kerr-Smith Tobacco Control Act (1934), 207
Kesselring, Albert, 598, 600
Keynes, John Maynard: advice to FDR of, 357–58; on Crash of 1929, 39; and deficit spending, 79; on FDR, 197–98, 380; FDR's views about, 358; and gold standard, 76, 76n, 78–79, 156, 197; and gold-purchase program, 197; on Hoover, 9; and housing, 368; and "mature" economic theory, 375; and New Dealers, 354; on Paris Peace Conference/Versailles Treaty, 6, 7, 9; and recession of 1937–38, 357–58; and role of government, 80, 354, 358, 789, 857; and unemployment, 80, 249; views of FDR of, 357
Keynesian economics, 357–60, 361
KGMB (radio station), 520
Kido, Koichi, 835–37, 850, 851
Kimball, Warren, 467
King, Ernest J.: and Battle of the Atlantic Ocean, 569, 570, 589; biography of, 544; and Casablanca commitments, 586, 587, 609–10; and Central Pacific campaign, 610; and command of Overlord, 687; Eisenhower's views about, 570; and FDR, 544; and Guadalcanal, 578; and second front, 575, 578, 579, 682; and Solomons campaign, 544, 545–46, 553, 554, 560; and Southwest Pacific campaign, 610; style of, 553, 570; and Teheran Conference, 682; and U.S. strategy, 544, 554, 578, 586, 587, 810
King George V (British battleship), 481
Kinkaid, Thomas C., 824, 825, 826, 827
Kirk, Alexander D., 670, 673
Kluge, Gunther Hans von, 725, 728, 729–30
Knights of Labor, 289, 300–301
Know Your Enemy--Japan (film), 811, 811n

Knox, Frank, 457–49, 457, 458, 466, 474
Knudsen, William, 478, 479, 620
Kobe (Japan), 847
Kobowitzki, A. Leon, 796–97
Koiso, Kuniaki, 821, 835
Kokura (Japan), 842
Kolombangara (Solomon Islands), 563–64
Konoye, Fumimaro, 7, 503, 504, 512, 513, 526, 615, 837, 844, 852, 852n
Korea, 855
Korean troops, 530, 813
Korematsu v. United States, 756–59, 759n, 762
Kristallnacht, 361, 415–16, 658
Krock, Arthur, 233
Kromer, Tom, 303
Ku Klux Klan, 15, 31, 228, 336
Kurile Islands, 805
Kurita, Takeo, 824, 825–26, 827
Kursk (Soviet Union), 601, 613
Kurusu, Saburo, 514, 515
Kuznets, Simon, 627
Kwajelein (Marshall Island), 610, 810
Kwantung Army, 502, 503, 509
Kyoto (Japan), 841
Kyushu: proposed U.S. landing on, 834–35

La Follette, Philip, 220, 234, 239
La Follette, Robert M. Jr., 62, 219–20, 221, 234, 239, 243, 275, 304, 390, 457
La Follette Civil Liberties Committee, 304, 305, 309–10, 318, 349
La Guardia, Fiorello, 62, 85, 253, 416, 767
Labor: and agriculture, 193, 197, 319–20, 321; benefits for, 27; and blacks, 26; and child labor, 28–29, 28–29n; and class issues, 292, 294–95, 322; and Communism, 292–93, 294, 298, 299, 310, 315–16, 317–18, 322, 349, 638, 638n; Coughlin's views about, 232; and Democratic Party, 291, 305, 321–22, 345; and economic recovery, 289–90, 303; and ethnicity, 25–26, 294–95, 301, 306–7; and FDR's first hundred days, 151; FDR's image among, 296–97; FDR's views about, 277, 297–98, 319, 345, 643, 644; and government, 314; and Hoover, 11, 26–27, 180; and immigration, 23, 164, 305, 306–7, 777; impact of New Deal on, 376; and La Follette Committee, 304, 305, 309, 310, 318; legislation supporting, 290–92, 314; and liberalism, 298; in literature, 303; and mechanization, 23–24, 201; and

Labor *(continued)*
    mobilization, 478; in 1920s, 23–24, 25–
    27, 28–29, 31; and NRA, 187, 189, 212,
    292, 297, 300; public opinion about,
    304, 316, 319, 331–32, 643, 644; and
    race, 26; and South, 320, 321, 345; and
    Supreme Court, 26, 28–29, 28–29n, 290–
    91, 316–17, 331–32, 335–36; and urban
    areas, 339; and values, 28; in wartime,
    638–44, 652, 655; and "welfare
    capitalism," 27. *See also* Migrant labor;
    Organized labor; Wages; Women:
    working; Working conditions; *specific
    person, organization, legislation or
    Supreme Court decision*
Labor Department, U.S., 131, 202
Lake, Veronica, 778
Lamont, Thomas P., 50, 72, 73
Landis, James, 354
Landon, Alf, 281, 286, 290, 416, 463
Lange, Dorothea, 195, 256
Langer, William, 196
Lanham Act, 781n
Latin America, 391, 391n, 400, 414–15,
    417, 451, 499
Latvia, 678
Laval, Pierre, 74n, 396
Le Havre (France), 728
League for Independent Political Action,
    220–21, 226
League for Industrial Democracy, 312
League of Nations: and conservatism, 782;
    creation of, 6; FDR's views about, 101,
    388; Germany withdraws from, 384; and
    isolationism, 386, 396, 424, 474–75, 854;
    and Italian invasion of Ethiopia, 395,
    397; Japan resigns from, 105, 158; and
    Japanese takeover of Manchuria, 93, 94;
    and neutrality, 395–96; successor to, 677
Leahy, William D., 483, 674, 676, 680,
    687, 802, 835, 841, 845
LeClerc, Jacques Phillipe, 707, 708
Ledo Road (India-Burma-China), 671
Leffingwell, Russell, 76n
Lehman, Herbert, 289, 333, 349, 412–13,
    414
Leigh-Mallory, Trafford, 696, 702
LeMay, Curtis, 845–47
Lemke, William, 284
Lend-Lease: and aid for Britain, 473–74;
    and Anglo-American joint planning,
    481, 482; and Anglo-American relations,
    475–76; appropriations for, 469, 474,
    476; and Battle of the Atlantic Ocean,

489, 490, 491, 566; and Battle of
    Britain, 470; and British insolvency, 473,
    475; and Casablanca commitments, 587,
    590; to China, 505, 671, 673; Churchill
    speech about, 470–71; Congressional
    hearings about, 470; FDR proposes, 469;
    and forced British sales, 473, 473n, 475;
    and Four Freedoms, 469–70; and
    German "invasion" of Britain, 471n; to
    Great Britain, 473–74; Great Debate
    about, 469–70, 471–72, 474, 480; Hull's
    role in, 507; and isolationism, 471, 472–
    75; and mobilization, 478–79; and
    neutrality laws, 489; and New Deal, 472–
    73, 473n; no-convoy clause of, 473–74,
    475–76; passage of, 474–75; public
    opinion about, 470; signing of, 474, 476;
    to Soviet Union, 484–85, 575, 579–80,
    587, 590; and U-boat raids, 488, 489;
    and U.S. strategy, 476, 480
Lenin, V.I., 281
Leslie, Maxwell, 541–42, 543
Leuchtenburg, William, 252
Lewis, David J., 261
Lewis, John L.: and AFL, 300, 302; aims
    of, 298–99, 317; and automobile
    industry, 312–14; on average life of
    miner, 169; biography of, 299–300; and
    Communism, 299, 315; and elections,
    290, 462; and FDR, 290, 296–97, 313,
    319, 462; and NIRA, 187; and Non-
    Partisan League, 290; and NRA, 213;
    resigns as CIO president, 462, 462n;
    and steel industry, 303, 304–8, 317, 318;
    and strikes during wartime, 639, 641,
    642–43; style of, 299, 300, 302, 305,
    313, 315, 319; and unskilled workers,
    300–302. *See also* Committee for
    Industrial Organization (CIO); United
    Mine Workers
Lewis, Sinclair, 19–20, 238, 255
Lewis, Sybil, 769
Lexington (U.S. carrier), 522, 532, 549,
    819
Leyte Gulf, Battle of, 793, 820, 822–28,
    836
Liberalism: demagogues' effects on, 241–42;
    and Democratic Party, 346–49; and
    elections, 243, 346–49, 457; and FDR,
    219, 243, 345–49, 433, 457; FDR's
    views about, 324–25; and FLSA, 345;
    and Keynesian economics, 359–60; and
    labor, 298; and neutrality laws, 433; and
    opposition to New Deal, 214–17; and

political realignments, 253, 346–48, 390; retreat of, 349; southern, 345–46; and Supreme Court reform, 333; of Theodore Roosevelt, 348; threats to, 219–27; of Wilson, 348

Liberty: FDR's views about, 247, 280

Liberty Loan Campaign, 183

Liberty Ships, 649–50, 652–53, 654, 713, 773–74, 791

Libya, 577, 583, 606, 608

Lincoln, Abraham, 187, 217, 244, 246–47, 287, 331, 791, 844

Lindbergh case, 161

Lindbergh, Charles, 433, 433n, 462, 653

Lingayen Gulf, 828

Lippmann, Walter: on FDR, 101, 111; on FLSA, 345; on Hoover, 12–13, 50, 51; and Japanese-Americans as enemy agents, 751, 752; on Jews, 412; "mastery for drift" quote of, 12–13, 32; on NRA, 186; on Townsend, 257

Literary Digest polls, 286

Literature: organized labor in, 303; war in, 387

Lithuania, 678

Little Steel Formula, 640, 641, 643

Lloyd George, David, 586

Local relief agencies, 88, 171–73, 251

Lockheed Aircraft, 769, 779

Lodge, Henry Cabot Jr., 476

London, England: Naval Conference in (1936), 398; naval limitation treaty (1930) of, 389; Polish government-in-exile in, 801–2; Soviet ambassadors withdraw from, 613; World Economic Conference in (1933), 105, 106, 107, 142, 144, 155–57, 158, 159, 197, 214, 232, 388, 390, 392, 409, 507, 855

Long, Huey P.: as anti-business, 237, 279; assassination of, 278; background of, 235–36; on Coughlin, 239; and divisions within Democratic party, 31; effects on FDR reforms by, 241–42; and elections of 1936, 240–41, 243, 286; on FDR, 113, 239, 240; FDR's concerns about, 275; and FDR's political strategy, 243, 244, 245; FDR's relationship with, 236–37; FDR's views about, 242, 263; on inflation, 237; and patronage, 237n; and populism, 234–35, 236–37; as radical, 99, 218, 234; on radio, 237, 239; and redistribution of wealth, 215, 238–39, 240, 243, 283; and social security, 270, 271; style of, 234–35, 338; and taxes,

276, 277; and Union Party, 283; and World Court treaty, 233

Longfellow, William Wadsworth, 470

Longshoremen: strikes by, 293–94

Lorentz, Pare, 256

Lorient (France), 723, 728

Los Alamos, New Mexico, 662–63, 663n, 664

Los Angeles, California: race riots in, 770

Lothian, Lord, 465, 467, 481

Louisville Bank v. Radford (1935), 328n

Lovett, Robert, 745

Low Countries, 438–39, 696. *See also specific nation*

Loyalty: in Japan, 812; in U.S. during World War II, 748–60

Lubin, Isador, 353, 355, 356

Lucas, John P., 599, 600

Luce, Henry, 317, 401, 456, 472

Ludlow, Louis, 402–3

Ludlow Amendment, 403

Luftwaffe: and Allied aerial strategy, 706; and Battle of Britain, 452; and Battle for Northwest Europe, 721; build-up of, 384; and German invasion of Low Countries, 438; losses in, 703; tactics of, 702–3

Lundberg, Ferdinand, 352

Lundeen, Ernest, 271

Luxembourg, 438

Luzon (Philippines), 529, 828, 832, 834, 835

Lynd, Helen Merrell, 13, 24–25, 264

Lynd, Robert, 13, 24–25, 264

McAdoo, William Gibbs, 97, 99

MacArthur, Arthur, 546

MacArthur, Douglas: and Australia, 529, 532, 561; biography of, 546; and "Bonus Army," 92; and Eisenhower, 530, 688; and elections of 1944, 788–89; FDR-Nimitz Hawaii meeting with, 792, 821; FDR's relationship with, 388–89, 821; FDR's views about, 237; honors for, 529, 546; and isolationism, 388–89; and Japanese surrender, 852, 853; in New Guinea, 610; nickname for, 529; Pacific command of, 546; and Papua, 561; and Philippines, 527, 529, 793, 816, 821, 822, 828, 832, 835, 836; reputation/image of, 546; and Solomons campaign, 546, 547, 561, 562, 564; style of, 561–62, 689; and U.S. strategy, 610, 792, 816, 821

McAuliffe, Anthony C., 740–41

McClellan, George, 217
McCloy, John J., 752, 758, 759, 796–97, 835, 841, 845
McCluskey, Wade, 541–42, 543
McCormick, Anne O'Hare, 43, 51, 89
McCormick, Robert R., 404–5, 406, 472, 474, 484, 487, 488, 788–89
MacDonald, Ramsay, 155, 156
McKinley, William, 30
McNair, Lesley J., 727
McNary, Charles, 456
McNary-Haugen bill, 17, 43, 141, 142, 199
McNutt, Paul, 635, 636, 637
McPherson, Aimee Semple, 224
McReynolds, James C., 263, 326, 327, 336
McWilliams, Carey, 195
Madison, James, 46
Madison Square Garden (New York City): FDR 1936 speech at, 282
"Magic" (Japanese codes), 507–8, 515, 537, 542, 544, 559, 563
Maginot Line, 382, 435, 438
Mahan, Alfred Thayer, 533, 534, 544, 602
Mailer, Norman, 813
Maintenance-of-membership rule, 641–43, 652
Makin (Gilbert Islands), 610
Malaria, 813
Malaya, 506, 509, 510, 516, 526, 527, 554, 647, 670, 855
Malinovsky, Roman, 3
Malmédy (Belgium), 594n, 740
Malta: Churchill-FDR meeting (1945) on, 799
Manchukuo, 94, 501, 509
Manchuria, 93–94, 104–5, 381, 401, 500, 501, 502, 805, 848
Manhattan Project, 663, 664–65, 668, 685, 791, 799, 838–39, 840
Manila (Philippines), 750, 821, 828–29
Manpower: characteristics of U.S., 649; production and technology as substitution for, 619; role in war of, 616, 655; in Soviet Union, 616; and Victory Program, 487. See also Military manpower, U.S.
Manzanar (California), 754–55
Mao Tse-tung, 673, 854
Marbury v. Madison (1803), 327
March on Washington: of blacks, 766–67
Mareuil en Dole (France), 5
Mariana Islands, 533, 610, 674, 814, 816–20, 821, 829, 846, 847

Marines, U.S.: blacks in, 765, 773; and Iwo Jima, 829, 830; Japanese image of, 812 Okinawa, 832, 833; and race, 634; and Selective Service System, 636; at Tarawa, 674; volunteers for, 635, 711; women in, 776
Marital status: and selective service, 634–36
Mark V Panther tanks (German), 725–26
Market-Garden (Allied offensive), 735–36, 737
Markham, Edwin, 280n
Marpi Point (Saipan), 817–18, 837
Marriage rate, 165, 781
Marseilles (France), 700
Marshall, George C.: and aerial warfare, 430; and aid for Britain, 430, 448; and aid for France, 430, 448; and amalgamation controversy, 447; and Anglo-American joint planning, 481, 482; and Anvil, 700; appointed army chief of staff, 430–31; and atomic development, 662, 666; and Battle of the Atlantic Ocean, 565, 569; and Battle for Northwest Europe, 736, 738–39; and blacks in military, 771, 772; and Casablanca, 586; and China, 671; and command of Overlord, 686–87, 688; and Eisenhower-Churchill relations, 701; and elections of 1944, 789; and European balance of power, 585; FDR's relationship with, 430, 431; and FDR's views about progress of war, 450; and German collapse, 732; and Germany First, 482; and invasion of Japan, 834–35; and Italian campaign, 599; and Mediterranean, 587, 613, 681; and mobilization, 451, 459; and North Africa, 578; and Overlord planning, 699, 700; and Pearl Harbor, 519, 525; and production priorities, 448, 479n, 485, 486; professional background of, 430–31; and redeployment of American forces from Europe to Pacific, 732; and second front, 573–74, 574n, 575, 576, 578, 579, 585, 586, 587, 599; on Stalin, 675–76; style of, 430; at Teheran, 681; and U.S. Army's "triangular" formation, 714–15; and World War I, 447
Marshall, Mrs. George C., 686
Marshall, John, 327
Marshall, Thurgood, 774
Marshall Islands, 533, 534, 610, 810, 814, 816
Marshall Plan, 855

Martin, Joseph, 462, 463
Marxism, 2, 222, 281, 298, 382
Matloff, Maurice, 631
Matsuoka, Yosuke, 509
"Mature economy" theory, 122–23, 373–74, 375, 785–86
Maud Committee (Great Britain), 661
Maverick, Maury, 342, 347, 348, 402
Mayer, Louis B., 226
Maytag Corporation, 317
Me109 fighters (German), 702–3
Means, Gardiner C., 120
Means test, 174
Mechanization: and labor, 23–24, 201
Mechanized warfare, 602, 695. See also Tanks
Medical science, 716
Medicare, 273
Mediterranean: and Allied fears of Soviets, 613; and British strategy, 408, 576, 585, 613; and Casablanca commitments, 587, 590, 595; Churchill's views about, 682–84, 700; Eisenhower as commander of campaigns in, 689–90; and European balance of power, 585; FDR's views about, 450; German successes in, 493, 495; length of campaign in, 701; and Overlord/Anvil, 680–81, 700, 701; and second front, 576, 587; Stalin's/Soviet views about, 611, 613, 681, 683; and Teheran Conference, 680–81, 682–84, 701. See also Italy; North Africa; Sicily
Mein Kampf (Hitler), 410
Mellon, Andrew, 51, 52, 56, 82–83
Mencken, H.L., 19, 20, 99, 225, 283
Mercer, Lucy, 96, 808
Merchant marine: British, 488; German, 7; Japanese, 822n; and legacies of World War II, 857; U.S., 434, 467, 499. See also Convoys
Mers el-Kebir (Algeria), 452
Messenger (Randolph newspaper), 763
Messerschmitt fighters (German), 608
Meuse-Argonne (Germany), 385
Mexican-Americans, 164, 165, 173n, 292–93, 770
Mexico, 391, 777
Meyer, Dillon S., 754, 755
Michelson, Charles, 62, 91
Michener, Earl Cory, 342
Middle East, 574n, 576, 806
Middletown (Lynds), 13, 24–25, 264
Midway Island, 533–34, 535–44, 555, 810
Midwest: agriculture in, 195–96

Migrant workers, 193, 379
Migration: of blacks, 194, 768–69; country-to-city, 194, 201, 209; during World War II, 747–48
Mikawa, Gunichi, 549, 550–52
Militarism: and economic nationalism, 157; and FDR's first hundred days, 159; in Japan, 157, 232–33, 381, 397, 398. See also Rearmament
Military Affairs Committee (U.S. Senate), 421
Military, Japanese: government role of leaders in, 503–4
Military manpower, U.S.: needs for, 631–37. See also Selective Service System
Military training, U.S., 476–77, 606, 608, 627, 628, 711–12, 715, 716, 771. See also Pilots: training of
Military, U.S.: blacks in, 711, 712, 764, 765, 767, 770–73, 817, 848; brutality of, 812–13, 855; and elections of 1944, 787–89; first enter Germany, 793; and isolationism, 388–89; Japanese-Americans in, 755, 772; mobility of, 715; in 1920s, 30; order of battle for, 713–14; and profile of average GI, 710–11; term of service in, 712; Truman desegregates, 773; views about rearmament of, 447; women in, 710. See also specific person, battle/campaign, or branch of service
Miller-Tydings Act (1937), 372
Millis, Walter, 387
Mills, Ogden, 80, 108, 135
Milton Academy (Massachusetts): FDR speech at, 100–101, 245
Milward, Alan, 648
Mindanao (Philippines), 530, 822, 824
Minimum wages, 328, 329–30, 334–35, 344–45, 375, 783
Mining, 288, 304, 320, 321. See also Coal industry; United Mine Workers
Minneapolis, Minnesota: strikes in, 294–95
Minnesota National Guard, 220
Missouri (U.S. battleship), 852–53
Mitchell, Archie and Elsie, 848–49
Mitchell, Arthur W., 216, 341
Mitchell, Billy, 517, 603
Mitsubishi A6M fighters. See Zeros
Mobility: and Battle for Northwest Europe, 723, 724, 724n, 727–28, 741; of civilians during World War II, 747–48, 782; of military, 715; and social security, 262, 265; of tanks, 724, 724n. See also Mechanized warfare

Mobilization: administration for, 619–20; and aerial warfare, 630, 631, 654; agencies for, 478; and assembly line, 649–54; and civilian consumption, 618, 645–46; complete versus progressive, 451, 459; and economy, 616–18, 622–23; efficiency in, 648–54; as end of Great Depression, 617, 619; FDR's views about, 429, 477–78, 495; and Feasibility Dispute, 627–28, 630, 631; goals for, 618, 623; and isolationism, 619; and labor, 478; and Lend-Lease, 478–79; and mass production, 649–54; and material shortages, 627–29; New Deal compared with, 622–23; and Pacific War, 480; political aspects of, 629–30; and quantity versus quality, 648–49, 654; and Red Army's entrance into Europe, 613; resources for, 647–48; and Soviet aid, 485; and Soviet staying power, 630–31; and unemployment, 617; and U.S. strategy, 450–51, 618–19, 628; and Victory Program, 485–88, 631; in World War I, 617. See also Contracts, military; Rearmament

Model, Walter, 730

"Mohawk Valley Formula," 317–18

Moley, Raymond: and attempted assassination of FDR, 116–17; and banking system, 135, 136; as Brain Trust member, 119–20, 124; and business, 282–83; on confusion of New Deal, 154; and Democratic Party, 124, 276; and elections of 1936, 282, 285–86n; and FDR's first hundred days, 143, 149, 150; on FDR's inaction, 110; and FDR's inauguration, 130; on FDR's philosophy, 115–16, 244, 247; FDR's relationship with, 119–20, 124, 151, 156, 276n, 281; on FDR's style, 102, 111, 112, 113, 120, 282; on Hoover-FDR meetings, 107, 108–9; and Hull, 156; and industrial recovery policy, 150, 151, 152; and international debts, 106; and monetary policies, 119, 143; and political realignments, 128; and psychology of fear, 111; resignation of, 156; and tax reform, 276, 276n; and World Economic Conference, 156, 214

Molotov, Vaycheslav, 574–75, 579–80

Molotov-Ribbentrop Pact (1939), 425, 435, 472, 612, 761

Monetary/fiscal policies: and agriculture, 143–44; Coughlin's views about, 230,

231–32; and Democratic party, 118–19; disillusionment with FDR's, 214, 220; and economic isolationism, 388; and economic recovery, 177; and FDR's first hundred days, 143–44, 154–55; FDR's views about, 78, 107, 118–19, 134, 154–55, 197–99; and gold-purchase program, 197–99; and Open Market Committee, 273–74; and political realignments, 129; and progressives, 220; and recession of 1937–38, 355; and Silver Purchase Act, 198n. See also Deflation; Gold standard; Inflation

Mongolia, 509, 805

Monnet, Jean, 428, 429

Monopolies, 359

Monroe, James, 286

Monroe Doctrine, 391, 492

Monte Cassino (Italy), 598–99, 704

Montevideo, Uruguay: Pan-American Conference (1933) in, 391

Montgomery, Bernard: and Battle for Northwest Europe, 723, 726–27, 730, 734–35, 736–37, 745; and Eisenhower, 690, 734–35; and Italian campaign, 598; at Normandy, 697; in North Africa, 581, 583, 584, 697; and Overlord, 696, 718; on Rommel, 695; in Sicily, 592, 593; on Stalin, 801; style of, 696–97; tactics of, 722

Montgomery Ward Company, 642

Morale: and aerial warfare, 602, 602–3n, 603, 604; Allied, 717, 732; and Battle of Britain, 453–54; and Battle for Northwest Europe, 732, 737–38, 743; and bombing, 429, 602, 602–3n, 603, 704–5, 743; British, 453–54; of business, 284, 351; FDR's views about German, 429; French, 437; German, 429, 603, 604, 737–38, 743; and "home front," 602, 602–3n; and North African campaign, 579; and Overlord, 717; and Pacific War, 553, 557; and Solomons campaign, 553, 557; of U.S. aircraft crews, 609, 704; of U.S. Army, 495–96; and wartime employment, 644–45

Morality: of atomic development, 663; and civilian bombing, 744; and legacies of World War II, 855; and Pacific War, 561

Moran, Lord, 613, 675, 676, 683, 684, 738n, 799–800

Moratorium: on international debts, 73–74, 74n, 77, 101, 105, 106

Morehead v. New York ex rel. Tipaldo
  (1936), 329–30, 334
Morgan, Frederick, 692–93, 694
Morgan, J.P., 367, 478
Morgan family, 368
Morgenthau, Henry J. Jr., 356, 443, 463,
  729; and Battle of the Atlantic Ocean,
  490; and bond sales, 626; and British
  insolvency, 466, 467, 473, 473n; and
  elections of 1940, 454–55; as Farm
  Credit Administration head, 143; and
  Holocaust, 795; and Japan-U.S.
  relations, 506, 514; and Lend-Lease, 469;
  and Quebec Conference, 803; and
  recession of 1937–38, 350, 352; and
  Social Gospel, 146; and social security,
  258, 268–69, 268n, 270; and tax reform,
  275–76; and U.S. entry into war, 493
Morgenthau Plan, 803–4
Morocco, 450. *See also* Casablanca
  Conference; French Morocco
Mortain (France), 729–31
Mortgages: data about, 163; farm, 141, 143,
  195–96, 199; and FDR's first hundred
  days, 141, 143, 149; FDR's views about,
  134; foreclosure on, 195–96, 199, 369;
  home, 83–84, 149, 163, 369, 370;
  impact of New Deal on, 369, 370; in
  1930s, 83–84; Supreme Court decisions
  about, 328n
Moscow (Soviet Union): Churchill-Stalin
  meeting in (1942), 675; foreign
  ministers meeting in (1943), 612–13
Motor Carrier Act (1935), 371
Mount Suribachi (Iwo Jima), 829–31
Mountbatten, Louis, 673, 689
Muncie, Indiana. See *Middletown*
Munda (New Georgia), 562, 563
Munich Agreement (1938), 155, 361, 418–
  20, 425, 428, 429
Munich (Germany): "Beer Hall Putsch" in,
  5n, 8
Munitions, 387–88, 394, 486n, 668, 742
Murmansk (Soviet Union), 572
Murphy, Frank L., 231, 289, 312, 313–14,
  347, 349, 756, 758
Murray, Philip, 304, 305–6, 307, 308, 641
Murrow, Edward R., 453
Musashi (Japanese battleship), 825
Muscle Shoals, Alabama, 33, 63–64, 147–
  48
Mussolini, Benito: arrest and imprisonment
  of, 594; assassination of, 808; and
  Chamberlain strategy, 408; declares war

on Britain and France, 440; declares
  war on U.S., 524; as dictator, 111, 361;
  and Ethiopia, 394, 395, 396; FDR's
  message to, 423; and German peace
  initiatives, 444; invasion of Albania by,
  425; and League of Nations, 397; and
  neutrality, 396; resignation of, 594; rise
  to power of, 381; and Spanish Civil
  War, 385, 398, 399; views about U.S. of,
  421, 423; and Welles "fact-finding"
  mission, 436, 437–38
Muste, A.J., 292, 298
Mutual benefit societies, 86
Myers, Mary Connor, 211–12
Myrdal, Gunnar, 209–10, 746, 762–63,
  769, 775

NAACP. *See* National Association for the
  Advancement of Colored People
Nagasaki (Japan), 426, 655, 809n, 839n,
  842, 843n, 847, 850
Nagato (Japanese battleship), 516
Nagumo, Chuichi: at Coral Sea battle, 536;
  Indian Ocean raids of, 527; and
  Midway, 535–36, 538–40, 541, 542; and
  Pearl Harbor, 516, 517, 519, 522, 536m,
  814; and Solomons campaign, 555
Nanking: Rape of (1937), 401, 402, 812
National Association for the Advancement
  of Colored People (NAACP), 210, 254,
  307n, 343, 764, 766, 768, 774
National Automobile Chamber of
  Commerce, 184
National Bank of Kentucky, 66
National Catholic Welfare Conference, 58
National Credit Association, 82–83, 84
National Defense Advisory Commission
  (NDAC), 478
National Defense Appropriation Act (1940),
  460n
National Defense Mediation Board, 620
National Defense Research Council
  (NDRC), 661, 662
National Farmers Union, 198
National Guard, 712
National identity: of U.S., 387
National Industrial Recovery Act (NIRA)
  (1933), 151–53, 154, 178, 181–82, 183,
  187, 273, 291–92, 328
National Labor Board (NRA), 184, 187–88,
  297
National Labor Relations Act (1935): and
  accomplishments of FDR, 242, 324;
  and conservatives, 643; constitutionality

National Labor Relations Act (1935): *(cont.)*
of, 273, 275, 290–91, 308, 320, 324,
330, 335–36; as control on labor
radicalism, 298; exemptions from, 293;
FDR's views about, 297–98; impact of,
242, 274–75, 285, 291, 304, 320;
provisions of, 290–91; and race issues,
307n. *See also* National Labor Relations
Board

National Labor Relations Board (NLRB),
273, 290, 304, 314, 319, 320, 328, 335–
36, 367n, 371, 775

National Origins Act (1924). *See*
Immigration Act (1924)

National parks, 379

National Power Committee, 353

National Recovery Administration (NRA):
and antitrust laws, 184, 186; as
bureaucracy, 185–86; and Communism,
222; constitutionality of, 183, 188, 263,
273, 324, 328, 329; creation of, 151,
177, 178, 202; criticisms of, 186–88,
190, 237; demise of, 374; and economic
isolationism, 388; and economic
recovery, 178–79, 199, 213, 288; as
failure, 188–89; and FDR's first hundred
days, 154, 218; FDR's views about, 297;
FLSA as descendant of, 344; functions
of, 152–53, 373; and industry codes, 181–
82, 183–86, 188–89, 190, 196, 203–4,
296; and inflation, 157; Johnson as head
of, 177, 179–80; and Johnson's
resignation, 188, 214, 240; New Dealers'
views about, 359; and organized labor,
187, 189, 212, 292, 297, 300; and
prices, 185, 373; problems of, 185; and
production, 179, 184, 185, 187; and
PWA, 151–52, 178–79, 183, 188; and
race issues, 194; structure of, 184; as
symbol of New Deal, 177; as voluntary
program, 206; and wages, 152, 157, 179,
182, 185, 186, 194, 373; WIB as model
for, 177–78

National Recovery Review Board, 186

National Resources Planning Board
(NRPB), 783, 784–85

National Science Foundation (NSF), 661

National Union for Social Justice, 216, 232,
234

National War Labor Board (NWLB), 620,
640, 641–43

National Women's Party, 28

National Youth Administration (NYA), 252,
378, 767, 783

National-sozialistische Deutsche
Arbeiterpartei. *See* Nazi Party

Nationalism, 50, 256–57

Native Americans, 379

Nativism, 15

Navaho language, 829–30

Naval Conference (London, 1936), 398

Naval Disarmament Conference
(Washington, D.C.), 501

Naval limitation agreements, 233, 389, 398,
501

Naval Research Laboratory, 659

Naval War College, U.S., 535

Naval warfare: Battle of Leyte Gulf as end
of era in, 828; Japanese mastery of, 500;
Midway Island battle as heralding new
age of, 542

Navy, British. *See* Royal Navy

Navy Department, U.S., 659, 771

Navy, French, 452

Navy, German, 571. *See also* U-boats;
specific person

Navy, Imperial Japanese: and Battle of
Leyte Gulf, 822–28; and Battle of
Philippine Sea, 819–20; and Central
Pacific, 816; China role of, 518; codes
of, 544n; and Japanese mastery of naval
warfare, 500; and Japanese priorities,
535; and Japanese strategy, 534; and
Midway, 543, 555; and naval limitations,
398; at Okinawa, 833; and Pearl Harbor,
516–22; and Solomons campaign, 559;
strength of, 527, 533–34, 543; supplies
for, 512, 822. *See also specific person,
battle, or vessel*

Navy, Royal Australian, 527

Navy, U.S.: appropriations for, 476; and
Battle of the Atlantic Ocean, 570; blacks
in, 765, 771, 773–74; contracts for, 621;
as escorts, 458, 467, 496, 497–98, 571;
FDR's views about, 389, 428, 450, 544;
and Harding administration, 33; and
Japan-U.S. relations, 506; and Lend-
Lease, 473–74; and Mariana offensive,
818–20; oil reserves of, 33; in Pacific
War, 814, 816, 818–20; "patrolling" by,
491–93; and priorities in World War II,
524; purchasing by, 627; and race, 634;
reinforcement of Philippines by, 481;
Savo Island as worst defeat of, 551; and
Selective Service System, 636; and
Solomons campaign, 544, 547, 558–60;
as "two-ocean navy," 446, 476; and U.S.
strategy, 428; V-12 program of, 635; as

voluntary, 635, 711; women in, 776; wounded in, 716. *See also* Naval Department, U.S.; *specific person, battle, or vessel*

Nazi Party: anti-Semitism of, 361, 410–11; consolidation of power by, 158; and elections, 8–9, 383–84; expansion of, 8, 157; and German economy, 71; Hitler as leader of, 8; membership of, 8; organization of, 8; rise to power of, 71, 227, 384; symbol of, 8. *See also* Germany; Hitler, Adolf; *specific person or event*

Nazi-Soviet pact. *See* Molotov-Ribbentrop Pact

NDRC. *See* National Defense Research Council

Near East: FDR's views about, 450

The Negro Soldier (film), 771

Nelson, Donald, 478, 618, 620–21, 629, 649, 655

Netherlands, 409, 418, 438, 504, 605n, 670. *See also* Low Countries

Neumann, John von, 657

Neutrality Acts (1935/1937/1939), 394–96, 397, 400, 403, 406, 413, 420, 428, 431–32, 433–34. *See also* Neutrality laws

Neutrality laws: and aid for Britain, 427–28, 431–32, 462; and aid for France, 427–28, 431–32; and aircraft sales, 421; and arms embargo, 394–95, 403, 432, 434; and arms sales, 421; and Battle of the Atlantic Ocean, 490; and beginnings of World War II, 427–28; and British insolvency, 466–67; and cash-and-carry, 400–401; Churchill's views about, 462; and conservatives, 433; and Czech crisis, 418–19, 422; and Democratic Party, 433; and destroyers-for-bases deal, 462; and elections, 396, 420; European views about, 432; FDR's views about, 406, 420–21, 422–23, 427–28, 432–33, 494, 499; and geography, 434; Hitler's views about, 425; and international debts, 431; and isolationism, 393–97, 400, 428, 433, 434; and Italian invasion of Ethiopia, 400; and League of Nations, 395–96; and Lend-Lease, 489; and liberalism, 433; and progressives, 433; and public opinion, 421, 434; and refugees, 413–14; revision of, 420–21, 422–23, 432–34; and Sino-Japanese war, 401–2; and southern Democrats, 433; and Spanish Civil War, 399; and Supreme Court

reform, 400; and Tripartite Pact, 505; and U.S. as arsenal of democracy, 619; and U.S. entry into war, 494; and Wilson, 394, 432; and World War I, 387. *See also* Neutrality Acts (1935/1937/1939)

Neutrality Proclamations (1940), 432

Neutrality Zone (U.S.), 489

New Britain, 547, 562, 564. *See also* Raboul

New Caledonia, 531, 533, 547, 552, 554, 557. *See also* Noumea

New Deal: achievements of, 348, 378; British impressions of, 159; budget deficits in, 79; climax of, 338; closing of reform era of, 291; completion of legislative record for, 278; and conservatism, 339–41, 348, 782–83, 784; constitutionality of, 263, 273, 324, 330, 331, 337; as controversial, 363–64; decline in spirit of, 340; Democratic concerns about, 99, 338–39; disillusionment with, 213–14, 217, 227, 463; and economy, 117–18, 364, 372, 373–77, 388, 622–23, 784; and elections, 349, 463, 464, 782; end of, 337, 341, 345, 349–50, 357, 363, 782–87; FDR pledge for, 98; FDR's concerns about future of, 344; FDR's explanation of, 245, 783; and Feasibility Dispute, 628; and foreign policy, 390; and Four Freedoms, 470; goals/aims of, 117–18, 363, 365, 372, 374–75, 623, 640, 786; and government-big business alliance, 628; Great Depression's relationship to, 166; "heart" of, 179–80; historical significance of, 350–51, 356, 378; Hoover's influence on, 82, 83, 154; ideology of, 356–57, 364–65; immigrant support for, 750; impact/legacies of, 247, 363–80; and isolationism, 390; labor's influence on, 644; lack of coherency in, 244; and Lend-Lease, 472–73, 473n; mobilization compared with, 622–23; as obsolete, 784; organized opposition to, 214–17; political culture of, 146; and political realignments, 117–18, 285; priorities of, 372; and racism, 774–75; and recession of 1937–38, 350–51, 356–57; and reform, 117–18, 361–62, 363–64, 372, 376, 377–80; and role of government, 373, 374–75, 377; security as basis of, 363, 365, 378, 379; South as anti-, 343–44, 349; as unfinished, 377;

New Deal (continued)
   and urban areas, 32, 32n, 339; what
   was, 361–62; during World War II, 376–
   77, 782–87, 792. See also First New
   Deal; Second New Deal; specific person,
   program, or agency
New Dealers, 353–55, 354–55n, 361, 374,
   376–77, 378, 478. See also specific
   person
New England National Guardsmen, 563
New Georgia, 562
New Guinea, 533, 562, 564, 610, 681, 793,
   816
New Nationalist tradition, 248n
New York City: immigrants in, 14;
   patronage in, 253; relief in, 88; Triangle
   Shirtwaist fire in, 259–60; WPA projects
   in, 253, 254
New York Federal Reserve Bank, 36, 69
New York Federal Reserve Board, 376
New York Herald Tribune, 458, 484–85, 557
New York National Guard, 817
New York State, 90–91, 145
New York Stock Exchange, 40, 132, 365–66
New York Temporary Emergency Relief
   Administration, 90
New York Times, 40, 51, 474–75, 557
New York World's Fair (1940), 761
New Zealand, 548, 553, 564
Newfoundland, 460, 497–98
Niblack (U.S. destroyer), 494, 495
Niigata (Japan), 842
Nijmegen (Netherlands), 736
Niles, David K., 219n
Nimitz, Chester: and Battle of Leyte Gulf,
   826, 827; biography of, 537–38; and
   Central Pacific offensive, 610, 829;
   command of, 546–47; FDR-MacArthur
   Hawaii meeting with, 792, 821; and Iwo
   Jima, 829, 831; and Japanese surrender,
   852, 853; and Marianas offensive, 816,
   818; and Midway, 537, 542–43n; and
   Solomons campaign, 544, 557, 563;
   style of, 537–38; and U.S. strategy, 821,
   822
Nineteenth Amendment, 28, 96–97
Ninety-Division Gamble, 631, 635, 636,
   712, 777
Ninety-Ninth Pursuit Squadron (U.S.), 773
Ninety-Third Division (U.S.), 772
Ninth Air Force (U.S.), 606, 608
Ninth Armored Division (U.S.), 745
Ninth Panzer Division (German), 736
NIRA. See National Industrial Recovery Act

Nishimura, Shoji, 824, 825
NLB. See National Labor Board
NLRB v. Fansteel Metallurgical Corporation
   (1939), 316–17
NLRB v. Jones and Laughlin (1937), 335–
   36
No-strike pledge, 638, 641
Nomura, Kichisaburo, 507–8, 514, 515, 519
Non-Partisan League, 220, 290
Nonagression Pact (1939). See Molotov-
   Ribbentrop Pact
Nonintervention Committee, 398
Nonintervention formula, 399
Normandy: and Allied aerial strategy, 706;
   Allied bombing in, 705; Allied invasion
   of, 718–31; Allied tactics in, 722–23;
   Allied victory in, 736; and blacks in
   military, 772; and competition for
   material and supplies, 796; and
   Overlord planning, 693–94, 696, 697,
   699, 699n. See also D-Day
Norris, George W.: and conservative
   Republicans, 32; FDR's relationship
   with, 99, 127, 390, 457; and Hoover, 60,
   63; and hydroelectric power, 63–64, 128;
   and isolationism, 390; and moratorium
   on debt payments, 74; and Muscle
   Shoals, 147–48; and political
   realignments, 128, 390, 457; as
   progressive, 60, 62, 390, 457; and RFC,
   84; and tariffs, 49; and TVA, 148; and
   World War I, 63
Norris-La Guardia Anti-Injunction Act
   (1932), 26–27, 289
North Africa: Allied invasion and battles in,
   579, 579n, 581–84, 782; and Anglo-
   Soviet relations, 580; and blacks in
   military, 773; British naval blockade of,
   584; and British strategy, 577–78, 579;
   and convoys, 579–81; Eisenhower as
   commander of campaign in, 689; and
   elections of 1940, 782; FDR's views
   about, 450; and French, 581–83;
   German forces in, 695; German
   successes in, 493, 495; and Germany-
   first principle, 554, 578, 579; political
   challenges resulting from, 581–83;
   preparations for landing in, 544; and
   second front, 575, 577–78, 579, 587,
   601, 682; and Solomons campaign, 544,
   554, 556, 557; Stalin's/Soviet reactions
   to campaign in, 579–80, 611; supplies
   for campaign in, 588; U.S. reluctance to
   commit to, 577–78

North American Aviation, 638–39, 652, 765
North Atlantic Treaty Organization (NATO), 854
Norway, 438, 439, 472n, 576, 659, 691, 693, 694, 694n
Norwegian Sea: U-boats in, 572
Nourmahal (Astor yacht), 117, 134–35, 239, 249
Noyes, Alexander Dana, 39, 40n
NRA. See National Recovery Administration
NRPB. See National Resource Planning Board
Nuclear weapons. See Atomic/nuclear weapons
Nuremberg Decree/Laws, 384, 410, 412
NWLB. See National War Labor Board
Nye, Gerald, 243, 387, 390, 394, 424
Nye Committee (Senate Special Committee Investigating the Munitions Industry), 387–88, 394, 431

Oak Ridge, Tennessee, 665–66
O'Connor, Basil "Doc," 120
Odets, Clifford, 303–4
Office of Economic Stabilization, 629
Office of Lend-Lease Administration, 475
Office of Price Administration and Civilian Supply, 478
Office of Price Administration (OPA), 620–21, 640, 782
Office of Production Management (OPM), 478, 619–20
Office of Scientific Research and Development (OSRD), 661
Office of War Information, 761, 783
Office of War Mobilization (OWM), 629
Oglethorpe University: FDR speech at, 102, 104, 123
Oil: embargo on, 395–96; German, 705–6, 707; Japanese need for, 504, 505, 506, 507, 509, 510, 512; for Soviets, 512
"Okies," 194–95
Okinawa (Ryukyu Islands), 828–29, 831–35, 836, 837, 841, 851
Old Age Revolving Pensions, Ltd., 215, 225
Old-age pensions: and accumulated deficit, 267–69, 268n; and benefit level, 267; constitutionality of, 265, 266, 273, 336; contributory requirement of, 266–67, 269–70, 271; and Democratic Party, 261; and drafting of social security bill, 265–70; and elections of 1936, 282; and FDR as governor, 90–91; FDR's views about, 90–91, 99, 257–58, 278, 297; in

Hoover administration, 90; and impact of New Deal, 365; private, 260; and redistribution of wealth, 266–67; state, 260; and Townsend Plan, 257, 261, 265. See also Social security
Olson, Floyd Bjerstjerne, 220, 221, 226, 227, 234, 295, 298
Olympic (U.S. invasion plan for Kyushu), 834–35
Olympic Games (Berlin, 1936), 410–11, 411n
Omaha Beach (D-Day landing zone), 717n, 721–22, 723
One Hundred and First Airborne Division (U.S.), 720, 736
One Hundred Sixty-fourth Infantry (U.S.), 556, 557, 558
Onishi, Takijiru, 512
Open Market Committee (Federal Reserve System), 273–74
Operation Barbarossa, 482–84, 492, 495, 508–9, 514, 515, 573, 726. See also Soviet Union
Operation Cartwheel (U.S. strategy), 562, 564
Operation Cobra (U.S. offensive), 727–28
Operation Drumbeat (German submarine offensive), 565–72
Operation Goodwood, 726–27
Operation Sealion (German invasion of Britain), 453–54, 461, 471n
Operation Watchtower (U.S. strategy), 547, 562, 564
Oppenheimer, J. Robert, 658, 662, 663, 664, 840
Orange Plan (U.S. strategy), 534–35, 544, 546, 564, 610, 816, 818
Organized labor: and automobile industry, 289, 291, 297, 300, 308–15, 316, 317, 320; and blacks, 307, 307n, 652, 765, 775; and collective bargaining, 290, 291–92, 297; and Communism, 292–93, 294, 298, 299, 310, 315–16, 317–18, 322, 349, 638, 638n; in Depression, 637–38; divisions within, 298; and elections, 285, 290, 322, 462, 462n; impact of, 320–21; influence on New Deal of, 644; and Kaiser shipyards, 652; and maintenance-of-membership rule, 641–43, 652; membership of, 25, 319, 320, 642; in 1920s, 25–26; in 1930s, 187–88; no-strike pledge of, 638, 641; and penalties for joining unions, 296; and radicalism, 295, 298, 299, 316, 322; and recession

Organized labor (continued)
of 1937–38, 350; recognition of, 310–11,
312–14, 318; and seniority principle,
321; and service sector, 319–20; and
social insurance laws, 260; in South,
320, 321; and state government, 289;
and steel industry, 289, 291, 300, 302–8,
314, 316, 317–19, 320, 335–36;
Supreme Court decisions about, 316–
17, 335–36; and Supreme Court reform,
331–32; and unemployment, 294–95;
and unskilled labor, 25–26, 289, 300–
302; and wages, 320–21, 371; and
"welfare capitalism," 27; and women,
652; workers' distrust of, 652. See also
Company unions; Labor; Strikes; specific
person, organization, or legislation
Osborne, D'Arcy, 159
Oswego, New York: refugee camp in, 795
Ottawa Agreements (1932), 77
Oumansky, Konstantin, 484, 485
Our Daily Bread (film), 304
Overlord: and aerial warfare, 698, 701–2,
705–7; Allied command structure for,
696–98; Allies formally approve, 683;
American domination in, 698; and
Anglo-American relations, 699–700;
Anvil's relationship to, 699–700; and
Balkans, 680–81; buildup for, 694, 709–
10, 716; and Cairo Conference, 674;
and Churchill, 675, 682–83, 690, 701;
and Churchill-FDR relations, 706–7;
command of, 683, 686–91; and
competition for manpower and materials
among theaters, 698–99; cover plan for,
683, 693–95, 694n, 696, 707, 720, 727;
delays in, 699, 717; and Eastern Europe,
683; end of, 736; and FDR, 680, 686–
88, 690, 700, 706–7; and French forces,
707, 708; and Great Britain, 682, 699;
and Italian campaign, 680–82, 700, 701;
launching of, 717–18, 718n, 720–23;
logistics in, 733–34; and Mediterranean
strategy, 680–81, 700, 701; and
Normandy invasion, 718–36; planning
for, 691–98, 699–700, 699n, 705–7, 723,
727, 733; prime objective of, 734; and
Soviet offensive in Eastern Europe, 683;
Soviet views about, 674, 681–82; and
Stalin-FDR relations, 698–99; Stalin's
views about, 681–82, 683, 686, 687;
target date for, 683, 699; and Teheran
Conference, 674–75, 677, 680–83, 700;
troop strength in, 698, 709–10; as U.S.

priority, 675, 701; and weather, 717–18.
See also Anvil; D-Day
Owens, Jesse, 411n
Ozawa, Jisaburo, 819–20, 822, 824, 826,
827

P-38 fighters (U.S.), 563, 703
P-47 fighters (U.S.), 703
P-51 fighters (U.S.), 703–4, 796
Pacific War: aerial warfare in, 745, 814,
816, 818–20, 825–26, 833, 834, 845–48;
aircraft carriers as mainstay of, 522, 531–
32, 542; and Allied fears of Soviets, 613;
amphibious attacks in, 598; and atomic
bomb, 838–42, 839n, 843n; atrocities/
brutality of, 561, 812–13, 855; and
blacks in military, 772; British in, 526–
27; and Casablanca commitments, 587,
609–10; and competition for manpower
and materials among theaters, 698–99,
732; decisive battles in, 533, 541, 553,
555, 559; FDR-Nimitz-MacArthur
meeting about ending, 792, 821;
geography of, 814; and German
collapse, 732; and Germany-first
principle, 578, 809, 811n; hand-to-hand
combat in, 814, 833; inevitability of,
515; Japanese casualties/losses in, 551,
554; and Japanese raids against U.S.,
746–47, 750n, 760; Japanese strategy in,
554, 814, 832; Japanese surrender in,
850–51, 852–53, 855–56; and legacies of
World War II, 855–56; Midway Island as
strategic transition in, 543–44; most
valuable U.S. intelligence contribution
to, 537; precipitation of, 515; prisoners-
of-war in, 530–31, 812, 813, 828, 831;
production role in, 543, 668, 810; as
racial/cultural war, 523, 524, 526, 561,
810–13; and second front, 578; Soviet
entry into, 681, 685, 699, 799, 805–6,
807, 842–43, 843n, 850; supplies for,
668; and technology, 814, 846–47; and
Teheran Conference, 677, 681, 685;
U.S. casualties/losses in, 549, 551, 558,
563, 813–14; U.S. command apparatus
in, 546–47; U.S. hit-and-run raids in,
535; and U.S. morale, 553, 557; U.S.
offensive in, 544, 561, 810, 814, 816;
and U.S. priorities, 524–25, 532, 544,
554, 609–10; U.S. strategy in, 578, 809–
10, 814, 816, 834–35; victory disease in,
531, 536, 551, 560–61; and Yalta
Conference, 799, 805–6, 807. See also

Operation Cartwheel; Operation
Watchtower; Orange Plan; Southern
Operation; *specific person or battle*
Pacifism, 382–83, 402–3, 704–5
Palau Islands, 821–22
Palawan Island, 828
Palawan Passage, 825, 827
Palermo (Sicily), 593
Palestine, 414, 795, 806
Palmer, A. Mitchell, 763
Pan-American Conference (Uruguay, 1933),
391
Panay (U.S. gunboat), 402, 403
Panics: of 1907, 69; in 1930s, 65–69, 131–
32
Panzers: and Allied aerial strategy, 706; and
Allied second front, 695, 696; and Battle
for Northwest Europe, 720, 721, 723,
727, 730, 736, 739, 740; and German
invasion of France, 439; and German
invasion of Low Countries, 438
Papua, 531, 532, 547, 554, 561, 562–63.
See also Port Moresby
Paratroopers, 735, 736
Paris (France): Allied provisioning of, 733;
liberation of, 708, 732, 738
Paris Peace Conference (1919), 6, 9, 45–
46. *See also* Versailles Treaty
Parity ratio, 200–201, 207
Parrish, Elsie, 334, 335
Passos, John Dos, 222, 226, 303, 387
Patch, Alexander M., 558, 560
Patrick Henry (Liberty Ship), 650
Patriotism, 256–57, 625
"Patrolling policy," 491–93
Patronage, 129–30, 237n, 253, 285
Patterson, Cissy, 472
Patterson, James, 168, 338, 339
Patterson, Joseph, 472
Patterson, Robert, 621, 622, 628
Patton, George S., Jr.: and Allied invasion
of France, 715, 727–28, 729, 730; and
Ardennes Forest, 741; biography of, 591–
92; and Biscari massacre, 594, 594n;
and blacks in military, 772; and
mechanized warfare, 602, 727–28; and
Normandy, 772; and North African
campaign, 584; and Overlord, 694; and
Saar region, 734, 735, 745; and Sicily,
591, 593, 594; style of, 592, 594, 689;
and subordinates, 594; tactics of, 715;
temporarily removed from command,
594
Paul, Alice, 28

Peabody, Endicott, 115, 133
Peace movement, 387–88, 394
Peace Pledge Union, 383
Peace treaties: fears of separate, 612, 675,
796, 808–9. *See also* Versailles Treaty
Pearl Harbor: FDR decides to keep fleet at,
450–51; FDR's deliberate exposure of
fleet at, 515; forerunners of, 94; Hitler
and, 524; and Hull-Nomura
negotiations, 519; impact on U.S.
defense of attack on, 532; Japanese
attack on, 516–22; as Japanese blunder,
526–27; Japanese failures at, 522;
Japanese losses at, 522; Japanese
preparations for, 516–17, 517n; and
Japanese strategy, 512, 534; Japanese
strength at, 814; and Japanese-
Americans, 748–49, 750–51; and
Marshall's alert, 519–20, 525; Midway as
partial revenge for, 542; Nagumo's views
about attack on, 536; and Pacific War as
race war, 810; photographs of, 793;
political consequences of, 522–23;
Roberts report about, 750–51; strategic
benefit to Japanese of attack on, 523;
U.S. casualties at, 522; and U.S.
commitment to China, 670; as U.S.
humiliation, 524; U.S. missed
opportunities concerning, 520; U.S.
scapegoats for, 524–26; and U.S.
strategy, 450–51, 524–25, 810;
Yamamoto's views about, 534
Pearson, Drew, 627
Pecora, Ferdinand, 132
Peek, George, 142, 199, 200, 211, 212, 214,
354
Pegler, Westbrook, 751, 752
Pendergast, Thomas J., 253, 790–91
People's Party, 220
Pepper, Claude, 346–47
Pepper, George Wharton, 26–27
"Peripheral" strategy (Great Britain), 576,
700
Perkins, Frances, 300, 378; appointed
secretary of labor, 146; on FDR style,
117; as first woman cabinet member,
260; and Keynes, 197–98; labor views
about, 297; and New Dealers, 353; on
NRA, 177; personal and professional
background of, 259–60; and public
works projects, 146; and Social Gospel,
146; and social security, 258, 261, 262,
263, 265–66, 267, 268, 269, 270, 271–
72; and steel industry, 303; style of, 260;

Perkins, Frances (*continued*)
    and "thirty-hour bill" (Black bill), 150;
    Willkie's views about, 459
Perry, Matthew C., 831, 852
Pershing, John J., 430, 447, 592, 686, 687
Pétain, Henri Phillipe, 440, 581, 582, 583
Philadelphia, Pennsylvania: FDR 1936
    speech in, 280–81; Republican National
    Convention in (1940), 455, 456
Philippine Sea, Battle of the, 818–20, 822,
    824, 826, 836
Philippines: and Battle of Leyte Gulf, 822–
    28; Eisenhower in, 688; independence
    of, 392, 670, 855; and Japan-U.S.
    relations, 506, 512; Japanese capture of,
    527, 529; and Japanese strategy, 516,
    533, 534, 554, 814; liberation of, 816,
    821; and MacArthur, 527, 529, 793,
    816, 821, 822, 828, 832, 835, 836; naval
    reinforcement in, 481; prisoners of war
    in, 530–31, 813; U.S. invasion of, 822,
    836; U.S. secures, 829; and U.S.
    strategy, 534, 535, 689, 816, 821; U.S.
    surrender in, 740. *See also* Filipinos;
    specific island
Phillips, Ulrich B., 19
"Phony War," 435–36
Pilar (Hemingway boat), 569
Pilots: and aid for China, 505; and aircraft
    production, 485; FDR's views about,
    450; Japanese, 819–20, 827–28;
    kamikaze, 827–28; rotation of, 819;
    training of, 447–48, 485, 564, 819–20;
    U.S., 447–48, 450, 485, 505, 819, 820.
    See also Aerial warfare; *type of aircraft*
Pinchot, Gifford, 166, 169
Pittman, Key, 114, 156, 395
Pittsburgh, Pennsylvania: blacks in, 87;
    unemployment in, 87
Plan Dog (U.S. strategy), 479–80, 481, 506,
    544
Platt Amendment (1901), 391
Ploesti (Rumania), 608, 609
PLUTO (Pipe Line Under the Ocean), 733
"Point Luck," 538
Poland: boundaries of, 677–78, 684, 801;
    Communism in, 801; and FDR, 677–78;
    German invasion of, 425, 426, 434, 435;
    government of, 801–3, 806, 842; Great
    Britain commitment to defense of, 422;
    and Jews, 414, 797; and Katyn Forest
    massacre, 802; partition of, 425, 435;
    and Potsdam Conference, 842; Red
    Army in, 435, 674, 738, 801, 802; as

Soviet sphere of influence, 685, 738,
    801; Stalin views about, 801–2; and
    Teheran Conference, 677–78, 684, 685,
    801, 802; and Warsaw uprising, 802;
    and Yalta Conference, 799, 801–3, 806,
    807. *See also* Auschwitz; Polish forces
Polenberg, Richard, 622
Polish forces, 436, 600, 698, 731, 738, 802
Political realignments: and
    accomplishments of FDR, 323; and
    Catholics, 231; and Democratic Party,
    127–28, 149, 285–86n, 323, 346–48;
    and disillusionment with FDR, 219–20,
    231, 232; and elections, 285, 286, 455;
    FDR's desire for new, 127; and FDR's
    first hundred days, 139, 148–49; and
    FDR's priorities, 283; and Great
    Depression, 32n; and immigrants, 231;
    and inflation, 129; and liberalism, 253,
    346–48, 390; and New Deal, 117–18,
    285; in 1920s, 32n; in 1930s, 117–18,
    127–29; and private versus public sector,
    455; and progressives, 148–49, 253, 390;
    and South, 149, 346–47; and
    unemployment, 128; and WPA, 253
Popular culture, 229, 306
"Popular Front" strategy, 315, 398
Popular uprisings, 576
Populism, 16–17, 66, 129, 201, 202, 220,
    232, 234–35, 236–37, 282
Port Arthur (Northeast China), 41, 517,
    805
Port Chicago, California, 773–74, 774n
Port Moresby (Papua), 531, 532, 554
Post-War Planning (NRPB), 784–85
Potomac (presidential yacht), 669
Potsdam Conference (1945), 837–38, 842–
    45, 843n
Potsdam Declaration, 845, 850
Poverty, 168, 857
Prange, Gordon, 522
Prefabrication, 651–53
Presidency: powers of, 252, 328n, 332, 334,
    400, 454
President's (FDR) Reemployment
    Agreement, 183–84
President's [Harding] Conference on
    Unemployment (1921), 48, 56, 57
President's [Hoover] Conference on Home
    Building and Home Ownership, 368
President's [Hoover] Emergency Committee
    for Employment (1930), 88
President's [Hoover] Organization on
    Unemployment Relief (1931), 88

President's [Hoover] Research Committee on Social Trends. See *Recent Social Trends*
Press: leaks to, 487–88, 488n
Press conferences: of FDR, 137–38, 155, 493, 494; of Hoover, 137–38
Pressman, Lee, 211n
Prices: agriculture, 17, 18, 44n, 54, 85, 141, 190, 196, 199, 200, 204–5, 206, 207, 211, 371, 388, 640, 783; controls on, 623–24, 628, 637, 640, 641; and economic isolationism, 388; impact of New Deal on, 371, 372, 373; industrial, 190; and labor, 638, 639, 640, 641; in 1920s, 48; and NRA, 185, 373; and political realignments, 129; in wartime, 623–24, 628, 638, 639, 640, 641
Prince of Wales (British battleship), 526
Princeton (U.S. carrier), 825
Pripet Marshes (Soviet Union), 726
Prisoners of war: and Allied invasion of France, 731; Americans as, 530–31, 535, 594n, 740, 813, 828; and Biscari massacre, 594; in China, 535; in European Theater, 813; Filipinos as, 828; German massacre of, 594n, 740; Germans as, 594, 731, 771; at Guadalcanal, 813; Italians as, 594; and Japanese army code, 812; Japanese as, 812, 813, 831; Japanese atrocities against, 828; and Malmédy massacre, 594n, 740; in Pacific War, 530–31, 535, 812, 813, 828, 831; on Palawan Island, 828; in Philippines, 530–31, 813; Polish as, 436; and racism in U.S., 771; survivors among, 813
Production: and Battle of the Atlantic Ocean, 570–71; for civilians, 647; comparison of Japanese and U.S., 655, 668; and consumer economy, 645; and economic recovery, 464; and elections of 1940, 464; FDR's views about, 180, 373, 485–86; in Germany, 489, 647, 648–49, 655, 703, 742; in Great Britain, 570–71, 654, 655; Hoover's views about, 39, 48, 52; and industrial recovery policy, 151; and industry codes, 296; in Japan, 647, 655, 668; and legacies of World War II, 856–57; and Lend-Lease, 482; mass, 21, 649–54; in 1920s, 20, 21, 39; in 1930, 58, 68; and NRA, 179, 184, 185, 187; output of, 654–55; over, 122–23, 141, 179, 180, 189, 199; Pacific War as battle of, 543, 668, 810; priorities for,

447–49, 447n, 479, 479n, 482, 485; and quantity versus quality, 648–49, 654; and reconversion to peacetime, 655; shift from civilian to military, 477; and Soviet aid, 485; and stagnation thesis, 122–23; as substitution for manpower, 619; survey of, 485–86; and unemployment, 464; and U.S. strategy, 698; and Victory Program, 487; and work relief, 251. *See also* Assembly line; Mobilization; Rearmament; War Production Board; *specific item or industry*
Progressive Conference (1931), 64
Progressive Party, 220, 261
Progressives: Brain Trust as, 120–21, 124; economic aims of, 359; and elections, 127, 243, 457; and FDR, 64, 118, 127, 147–49, 219–20, 219n, 243, 433, 457; and FDR as progressive, 99–101, 247–48; and FDR's first hundred days, 147–49; fragmentation among, 219–20; and Hoover, 32, 46, 62–63, 127; and inflation, 220; and isolationism, 220, 390; and Long, 241; and monetary policies, 220; and neutrality laws, 433; and New Dealers, 354; in 1920s, 11, 32–33; in 1930s, 62; and political realignments, 148–49, 253, 390; and public utilities, 147–49; as Republicans, 32, 46, 62–63, 118, 127, 219–20; and RFC, 85; and Supreme Court reform, 333; and TVA, 148–49; and unemployment, 85; and Wilson, 127; and World War I, 390. *See also specific person*
Prohibition, 13, 31, 32, 60, 62, 98, 138
Protectionism, 49–50, 49n, 200
Psychology of fear, 77–78, 88–90, 111, 132, 134, 218, 376–77
Public housing, 340, 369, 370, 370n
Public opinion, U.S.: and aerial warfare, 604; about aid for Britain, 491; as anti-Hitler, 427; as anti-war, 432; and defense appropriations, 476; and demonization of Japanese, 811; in early years of Great Depression, 88–90; about escorts, 491, 498, 498n; and FDR's candor, 480; and FDR's first hundred days, 137–38; FDR's views about, 405; about Jews, 415; Keynes' views about, 357–58; about labor, 304, 316, 319, 331–32, 643, 644; about Lend-Lease, 470; and neutrality, 421, 434; in 1930s, 189;

Public opinion, U.S. *(continued)*
    and Soviet aid, 484–85; and Supreme
    Court reform, 331–32; and U.S.
    involvement in war, 463
Public utilities, 147–49, 242, 273, 277, 352,
    357
Public Utilities Holding Company Act
    (1935), 242, 277, 324, 352
Public works: appropriations for, 249; and
    FDR's first hundred days, 146–47, 153;
    FDR's views about, 389; funding for,
    251–52, 389; and Hoover, 57, 58, 80,
    147; and inflation, 157; in New Deal,
    57; and political realignments, 128; and
    role of government, 80; Wagner's
    proposals about, 90. *See also* Public
    Works Administration
Public Works Administration (PWA):
    accomplishments of, 252; creation of,
    151–52, 178; and CWA, 175; and
    economic recovery, 178–79; and
    employment, 152; functions of, 151–52,
    176; funding for, 146, 152, 178, 188,
    251–52; Ickes as head of, 178, 188, 252;
    and industry, 178; and inflation, 157;
    and NRA, 151–52, 178–79, 183, 188;
    and patronage, 253; and recession of
    1937–38, 355
The Purple Heart (film), 811
Pyle, Ernie, 697–98, 794, 834

"Quarantine Speech" (FDR, 1937), 404–5,
    406, 409
Quebec Conference (1943), 613, 680, 686,
    690, 803, 804
Quezon, Manuel, 546
Quinalt Victory (Liberty Ship), 773–74
Quincy (U.S. cruiser), 551, 799, 806
Quisling, Vidkun, 472n
Quislings, 583

Rabaul (New Britain), 531, 532, 544, 547,
    549, 551, 557, 562, 564
Rabi, I.I., 663
Race issues: and antilynching bill, 342–44;
    and Democratic Party, 333, 341–43; and
    FDR, 760; and Japanese-Americans, 751–
    52, 753; and labor, 26; Myrdal's study
    of, 762–63; and Pacific War as race war,
    523, 524, 526, 561, 810–13; political
    volatility of, 774–75; and selective
    service, 633, 634; in South, 194, 212,
    333, 341–43; and Supreme Court
    reform, 333; and U.S. as "melting pot"

society, 760; and Wagner Act, 307n;
    during World War II, 751–52, 753, 762–
    76; and WPA, 254, 378. *See also* Blacks;
    Race riots
Race riots, 13, 770–71
Radar, 452
Radicalism: and disillusionment with FDR,
    219, 223–27; and FDR political strategy,
    243, 244, 245; FDR's views about, 278;
    and organized labor, 295, 298, 299, 316,
    322. *See also specific person or
    organization*
Radio, 228–30, 237, 239, 306, 459. *See also*
    Fireside Chats
Raeder, Erich, 488, 489, 492, 495, 499
RAF. *See* Royal Air Force
Railroad Retirement Act (1934), 273
Railroads, 33, 153, 357, 371, 372, 373, 643
Rainbow 5, 479–80
Ramsey, Bertram, 696
Randolph, A. Philip, 763–64, 765–68
Ranger companies (U.S.), 722
Rankin, Jeanette, 523n
Rankin, John, 788
Raskob, John J., 62, 99, 139, 214
Rationing, 623–24, 645
Rauschenbusch, Walter, 146
Raushenbush, Elizabeth Brandeis, 264–65
Raushenbush, Paul A., 264–65
Rayburn, Sam, 124, 125, 367
RCA (Radio Corporation of America), 35,
    519–20
Reading Formula, 187
Rearmament: of Germany, 384, 394, 398;
    and isolationism, 431, 451; and shift
    from civilian to military production, 477;
    and unemployment, 477; in U.S., 429,
    431, 447, 451, 477; U.S. military
    leaders' views about, 447; and U.S.
    strategy, 451. *See also* Japan: militarism
    in; Mobilization; *specific item or industry*
Recent Social Trends (President's Research
    Committee on Social Trends), 10–13,
    19, 20, 21, 23–24, 28, 41, 249–50
Recession: of 1921, 48, 56, 59; of 1937–38,
    350–53, 355–61, 362, 414, 464
Reciprocal Trade Agreements Act (1934),
    389
Reconstruction Finance Corporation (RFC):
    and banking system, 136; and
    Commodity Credit Corporation, 204;
    creation of, 84–85; and FDR's first
    hundred days, 136; financing of, 91; and
    forced British sales, 473; in Hoover

administration, 84–85; and housing, 369; and monetary policies, 197; and New Dealers, 353; publication of banks receiving loans from, 132; in wartime, 623, 651

Red Army, 585, 591, 611, 613, 637, 696, 738n, 745; in Eastern Europe, 683, 726, 738, 739, 801, 854. *See also specific battle*

Red Ball Express, 733–34

Redistribution of wealth, 123, 152, 215, 238–39, 240, 243, 266–67, 268, 364, 373

Reform: demagogues' pressure for, 241–42; and economic recovery, 323–25, 363; and FDR's priorities, 283, 390; FDR's views about, 100–101, 104, 323–25, 361, 363; and New Deal, 117–18, 361–62, 363–64, 372, 376, 377–80; and opposition to FDR, 283

Refugee Conference (Bermuda, 1943), 795

Refugees, 410–18, 795–96, 806, 854, 855

Regensburg (Germany), 608, 609, 702, 845

Regional development, 346

Regulation, 17, 153, 247, 370–73, 376, 783. *See also specific regulatory agency*

Relief: and agricultural surpluses, 204n; for blacks, 164, 173, 173n, 194; for children, 271, 272; and Communism, 89; data about, 164; demagogues' effects on reform of, 242; for elderly, 261, 271, 272; and FDR's first hundred days, 144–47, 149, 153, 157, 218; FDR's views about, 145–46, 250–51; and Hoover, 88, 91, 93; Hopkins's discretion in dispensing, 170–71; and inflation, 157; local, 88, 171–73, 251; and means test, 174; and Mexican-Americans, 173n; in 1930s, 88; as permanent economic factor, 250–51; personal culpability for, 172–73, 174–75; politics of, 172–75; and recession of 1937–38, 350; and role of government, 80, 145–46; standards of, 173n; state, 88, 171–73; for striking workers, 304, 312; work relief differentiated from, 250–51. *See also* Federal Emergency Relief Administration; *type of relief*

Relief and Reconstruction Act (1932), 91

Religion, 499, 760

Religious organizations, 86, 307

Remagen (Germany), 745

Remarque, Erich Maria, 387

Remington Rand Corporation, 317

Reno, Milo, 196, 205, 240

Reparations: and causes of Great Depression, 71, 72–73; on Germany, 7, 8, 71, 72–74, 74n, 803, 804–5, 807, 842; on Japan for *Panay*, 402; for Japanese Americans, 759; moratorium on payment of, 73–74, 74n; and Versailles Treaty, 72–73; after World War I, 7, 8, 71, 72–74, 74n; and World War II, 842

Report on Economic Conditions of the South (FDR Commission), 346, 347

Republic Steel Company, 303, 317–18

Republican Party: and aid for Britain, 458–59; big business control of, 286n; conservative domination of, 32; and disillusionment with FDR, 219; domination of Congress by, 59–60; domination of government by, 30, 127; and elections of 1936, 330; homogeneity of, 32; left-wing in, 60; and Republicans in FDR's cabinet, 457–59. *See also* Bull Moose Republicans; Progressives; *specific person or election*

Repulse (British battleship), 526

Reserve Officer Training Corps (ROTC), 394

Resettlement Administration (RA), 252, 379

Retirement: obligatory, 371

Reuben James (U.S. destroyer), 499

Reuther, Victor, 312

Reuther, Walter, 311, 312, 317, 477

Revenue Act (1932), 79, 81

Revenue Act (1942), 624

Revenue Act (1943), 625

Revolutions: in post-World War I, 1; in Russia, 3, 41, 381

Reynaud, Paul, 438–39

RFC. *See* Reconstruction Finance Corporation

Rheims (France), 851

Rhine River, 737, 745

Rhineland: Nazi march into, 384, 384–85n, 398, 401

Rhodes, island of, 613, 682

Rhone Valley (France), 731

Ribbentrop, Joachim von, 436, 478, 615

Riegner, Gerhart, 794

Rivera, Diego, 255

Robert E. Peary (Liberty ship), 650

Roberts, Owen J., 326, 327n, 329, 335, 336, 337, 750–51, 758

Robertson, David, 843n

Robeson, Paul, 761

Robin Moor (U.S. freighter), 494–95

Robinson, Joseph T., 61–62, 113, 210, 234, 336, 340
Robinson-Patman Act (1936), 372
Rochefort, Joseph, 537, 538
Rockefeller, John D., 276
Rockefeller, John D. Jr., 239
Rockwell, Norman, 470
Roerich, Nicholas, 206
Rogers, Edith Nourse, 416–17
Rogers, Will, 31
Röhm, Ernst, 384
Romania, 414, 795, 801
Rome (Italy): Allies capture of, 600
Rome-Berlin Axis Agreement (1936), 385, 397
Rommel, Erwin: and Allied second front, 691–92, 695–96, 698; and invasion of France, 718, 723, 724, 725; Montgomery's views about, 695; in North Africa, 583, 584, 695; suicide of, 730
Roosevelt, Eleanor: addresses Democratic convention, 457; biography of, 96–97; and blacks, 285, 343, 378, 764, 767, 773, 775; and Communism, 483; courtship/marriage of, 115; and economic recovery, 360; and elections of 1940, 454, 457; and enemy aliens, 750; FDR's relationship with, 96, 97; Hickok's relationship with, 161–62, 162n, 190, 191, 192; and reform spirit, 623; and World War I, 3; and WPA, 254
Roosevelt, Elliott, 242
Roosevelt, Franklin D.: accomplishments of, 323, 379–80; ambitions of, 5–6; as assistant secretary of navy, 3, 46, 115, 389, 428, 442–43, 544; attempted assassination of, 116–17; biography of, 95, 114–15, 389; D-Day prayer of, 709; death of, 808, 833, 852; deepest failure of, 525; and dictatorship allegations, 332; as experimenter/innovator, 154, 218, 245; as governor, 54n, 64, 90–91, 98, 119, 167n; health/disability of, 6n, 95–96, 97, 280n, 788, 789, 792, 798, 799n, 800, 806, 807, 808; Hitler's views about, 392; on Hoover, 46; Hoover's meetings with, 132, 133, 157–58; Hoover's relationship with, 133; Hoover's views about, 102, 109; image of, 296–97; inaugural address of (1933), 134, 157, 218, 375, 388; inaugural address of (1937), 323, 324, 325, 348; inaugural address of (1945), 798; inauguration of (1933), 9, 104, 107, 110–11, 130, 131, 132–35; inauguration of (1937), 287, 289; legacies of, 171, 685–86; and legacies of World War II, 856; and Lucy Mercer, 96, 808; manifesto of second administration of, 287; optimism of, 147, 153, 218, 244; philosophy of, 115–16, 131, 244–48; political strategy of, 98, 127–28, 242–44, 284, 285–86n; as progressive, 99–101; as reformer, 217, 357; reputation of, 153, 233; as scapegoat for Pearl Harbor, 524–26; vision/dreams of, 102–3, 128, 159, 219, 244, 245–46, 247–48, 257–58, 281, 287, 299, 324, 377–78, 450, 619; and World War I, 3–5, 5n. See also Churchill, Winston–and FDR; Roosevelt, Franklin D.–style of; Stalin, Josef–and FDR; specific topic
Roosevelt, Franklin D.–style of: and mobilization, 449, 462–63, 479n; in 1930s, 95–96, 97, 100, 101, 102, 103, 111–14, 116–17, 119, 120, 123, 136–37, 226, 281, 282; in wartime, 465, 498, 499, 629, 685, 856
Roosevelt, G. Hall, 400n
Roosevelt, James, 114, 115, 798
Roosevelt Recession. See Recession: of 1937–38
Roosevelt, Sara Delano, 114
Roosevelt, Theodore: and business, 359; Commission on Country Life of, 17; and foreign affairs, 389; influence on FDR of, 3–4, 115, 248; and judiciary, 327; liberalism of, 348; MacArthur as aide to, 546; and Monroe Doctrine, 391; political career of, 95; and political realignments, 127; as progressive, 32; and role of government, 118, 359; and Russo-Japanese war, 500
Roosevelt, Theodore Jr., 3, 103
Root, Elihu, 246
Rose Bowl, 750
Rosenberg, Anna, 767
Rosenman, Samuel I., 120, 326
Rosenthal, Joe, 830
Rosie the Riveter, 776, 778, 779, 781–72
Rothschild, Louis, 72
Rouen (France), 605, 605n, 630, 631
Roundup, 574, 580
Rowe, James H., 752
Royal Air Force (RAF): and Battle of the Atlantic Ocean, 492; and Battle of Britain, 452, 453, 460–61; and Battle for

Northwest Europe, 743, 744; and British survivability, 439; and civilian bombing, 743, 744; and first European bombing missions, 605, 605n; and precision bombing, 604

Royal Navy: and Battle of the Atlantic Ocean, 492, 569; and Battle of Britain, 453; and British survivability, 439; and British-Franco relations, 581; and destroyer transfers, 453; as escorts, 498; and German occupation of Norway, 438; and Mers el-Kebir capture, 452; and North African campaign, 581, 584; strike by, 76n. See also specific vessel

Royce, Josiah, 115

Rubber industry, 310, 647–48

Rublee, George, 415

Ruhr Valley (Germany), 8, 573, 604, 693, 734, 735–36, 737, 739, 745, 803. See also Rhineland

Ruml, Beardsley, 625n

Rundstedt, Gerd von, 691–92, 695–96, 698, 718, 724, 725

Rural areas: balance between urban and, 20; blacks in, 193, 194, 208, 210–11; children in, 192, 193; data about, 163; and Democratic Party, 338–39; depopulation of, 17; domination of Congress by, 339; FDR's views about, 123–24, 134; impact of New Deal on, 378; migration from, 209; in 1920s, 16–17, 18–20; satire about, 19–20; in South, 18, 19. See also Agriculture; Farmers

Rural Electrification Administration (REA), 252, 783

Russia: impact of World War I on, 381–82; revolutions in, 3, 41, 381; Romanovs dethroned in, 1; and Versailles Treaty, 382. See also Soviet Union

Russo-Japanese War (1904–5), 41, 500, 517, 518, 544, 805, 855

Ryukyu Islands, 814, 821, 831–35

SA. See Sturmabteilungen

Saar region (Germany), 734, 735, 739, 745, 803

Saboteurs: Germans as, 568, 568n

Sachs, Alexander, 659–60

St. Lazaire (France), 728

St. Lô (France), 727

St. Lô (U.S. carrier), 828

St. Louis (Hamburg-American steamship), 417–18

St. Mihiel (France), 385

St. Nazaire (France), 723

Saipan (Mariana Island), 816–21, 822, 836, 837

Sakhalin Island, 805

Salamaua (Papua), 531, 532, 562

Salerno (Italy), 596, 598, 601

Sales taxes, 62, 81, 251

Samar Island (Philippines), 824, 827, 828

Samoa, 531, 533

Samuelson, Paul, 40n

San Bernardino Strait, 824, 826

San Francisco, California: strikes in, 215, 293–94

Sandburg, Carl, 20

Sandel, Michael, 360

Sanger, Margaret, 28

Saratoga (U.S. aircraft carrier), 522, 532, 543, 549, 555

Sardinia, 592–93

Savo Island, Battle of, 550–52, 553

Savo Sound, 819

Schacht, Hjalmar, 158

Schall, Thomas, 381

Schechter Poultry Corporation v. United States, 328, 329

Schlesinger, Arthur M. Jr., 55, 146, 177, 187, 248n

Schnorkel U-boat, 589n

Schroeder, Gustav, 417–18

Schutz Staffeln (SS), 8

Schweinfurt (Germany), 608, 609, 702, 703

Scientific Panel (atomic project), 839, 840

Scopes, John T., 20

Scottsboro Boys, 222–23, 223n

Scripps-Howard, 277, 278

Seabees (construction battalions), 817

SEAC. See Southeast Asia Command

Second Armored Division (French), 707

Second front: and aerial warfare, 606; and Anglo-American relations, 573–74, 577–78; and Anglo-Soviet relations, 580; British commitment to, 613; and Casablanca commitments, 586, 587; and Churchill-FDR relations, 577–78, 586, 613; and Churchill-Stalin relations, 580, 601, 611; Churchill's concerns about, 574–75, 576, 577–78, 580, 613; delays in, 699; and European balance of power, 585; FDR's views about, 573, 574, 575–76, 577–78; and German defenses, 694–95; and Germany-first principle, 578; Hitler's concern about, 691; and Italian campaign, 595–96, 601;

Second front (*continued*)
and Italy, 682; and Mediterranean, 576, 587, 601, 613; and Middle East, 576; and North Africa, 575, 577–78, 579, 587, 601, 682; and Pacific War, 578; and Quebec Conference, 613; Soviet frustrations about, 573, 574–76, 579, 587, 601, 611, 613; and Stalin-FDR relations, 580, 587, 601, 613, 699; and Teheran Conference, 676–77, 699. *See also* Bolero; Cross-Channel attack; Overlord; Roundup; Sledgehammer

Second New Deal: demagogues' effects on, 241–42; Emergency Relief Appropriation Act as heart of, 248n; and FDR's philosophy, 247–48, 248n; and FDR's political strategy, 242–44; and reform, 217

Securities and Exchange Commission (SEC), 328, 353, 357, 367–68

Security: FDR's views about, 362; and goals of New Deal, 363, 365; impact of New Deal on, 363, 365, 378, 379; and role of government, 359; and Second New Deal, 245–46, 247; Townsend's views about, 257. *See also* Old-age pensions; Social security; Social Security Act; Unemployment insurance; Work relief

Security, Work, and Relief Policies (NRPB), 784–85

Segré, Emilio, 657–58

Segregation, 19, 370n

Selassie, Haile, 395, 806

Selective service, 183, 451, 492, 620, 631–37, 710–11, 771. *See also* Conscription; Selective Service Act (1940)

Selective Service Act (1940), 459, 492, 495–96, 632, 633, 764

Senate, U.S.: Democratic control of, 125, 125n; and Japanese peace initiatives, 844; Progressive Republicans in, 219; Republican domination of, 60; and World Court treaty, 233, 234. *See also specific person, committee, or legislation*

Serbia, 382

Service sector, 27, 164, 319–20, 344, 779

Seven Hundred and Ninth Division (German), 721

Seven Hundred Sixty-First Tank Battalion (U.S.), 772

"Seven Little TVAs," 340, 344

Seventh Army (German), 696, 725, 729, 730

Seventh Fleet (U.S.), 824

Seventh Marines (U.S.), 558

SHAEF. *See* Supreme Headquarters Allied Expeditionary Forces

Share Our Wealth Society, 215, 238–39, 243, 283

Sharecroppers, 207–13

Shelley, Norman, 441

Sherrod, Robert, 818

Shima, Kiyohide, 824

Shingle (Anzio assault), 599

Shipbuilding, 389, 650–53, 778, 779, 781n

Shipping: and Battle of the Atlantic Ocean, 490, 570–71, 572, 590; and British survivability, 467; losses in, 467, 490, 585, 588–89; and U.S. strategy, 585

Ships: Allies to give Soviets, 676–77; Liberty, 649–50, 652–53, 654, 713, 773–74, 791; merchant, 618, 649–50, 655, 676–77; naval, 653, 655; and Overlord buildup, 709; production of, 618, 650–53, 655

Shipyards, 251, 570–71, 650–53, 781n

Shirer, William, 423, 424

Shokaku (Japanese aircraft carrier), 536

"Shoot-on-sight" policy, 497–98

Short, Walter C.: and Pearl Harbor, 520

Short-of-war strategy, 427, 428, 432, 446, 459, 466, 469, 475, 479, 483–84

Shouse, Jouett, 99

Siberia, 503, 508–9, 805

Sibuyan Sea, 825

Sicily, 587, 590, 591, 592–94, 595, 601, 611

Siegfried Line, 733, 735, 737, 738, 745

Silver, 143, 230, 231–32

Silver Purchase Act (1934), 198n

Sinclair, Upton, 215–16, 225–27, 234, 237

Singapore, 404, 512, 527, 577, 750, 824

Sino-Japanese war, 361, 501–3, 504, 509, 513, 518, 673, 674, 681; and isolationism, 381, 390, 401–2, 403–4, 406

Sit-down strikes, 310–11, 312, 313, 314, 316–17, 319, 331–32, 339–40, 400

Sixteenth Bavarian Reserve Infantry Regiment, 4

Sixth Airborne Division (British), 720

Sixth Royal Scots Fusiliers, 4

Sledgehammer, 574, 578, 579, 580

Sloan, Alfred P., 214

Small War Plants Corporation (SWPC), 621–22

Smith, Adam, 199

Smith, Al: on dictatorships, 111; and disillusionment with FDR, 219; and elections of 1928, 94, 97, 103; and factions within Democratic Party, 31, 97; FDR's relationship with, 98, 99, 111, 281; and *Kristallnacht*, 416; as Liberty League member, 214; Perkins's relationship with, 259

Smith, Ellison "Cotton Ed," 212, 341, 345, 346, 347, 348

Smith, Gerald L.K., 283–84

Smith, Tuck, 493n

Smith v. Allwright (1944), 774–75

Smith-Connally War Labor Disputes Act (1943), 643–44

Smuts, Jan, 441

Social Gospel, 146

Social planning, 32, 102

Social security: and accomplishments of FDR, 324; accumulated deficit in, 267–69, 268n; and blacks, 269; Brandeis's influence on, 264–65; bureaucracy for, 272; and CES, 262–64, 265, 267, 268, 268n, 269–70; constitutionality of, 263, 264–65, 266, 273, 324; contributory requirement of, 266–67, 269–70, 270n, 271; coverage of, 269, 270n; and deflation, 267, 269; drafting bill for, 262–70; early beneficiaries of, 272–73, 371; early efforts at legislating, 245, 260–61; and elections of 1936, 282, 285; FDR's views about, 242, 245, 248n, 257–58, 261–62, 266, 267, 268, 268n, 269, 270–71, 272; and health care, 263–64, 269, 271; as legacy of New Deal, 783; and mobility of Americans, 262, 265; and recession of 1937–38, 355; and redistribution of wealth, 266–67, 268; reserve in, 270n; and role of government, 262–63; and state government, 262–63, 264–65; and taxes, 264–65, 269–70, 271, 272; and Townsend plan, 225; as urban interest, 339. *See also* Old-age pensions; Social Security Act (1935); Unemployment insurance

Social Security Act (1935): amendment of, 270n; constitutionality of, 330, 336; as cornerstone of FDR administration, 272; demagogues' effects on, 242; drafting of, 258–70; FDR's views about, 272, 365, 371; forerunners of, 165; as groundwork for modern welfare state, 271–72; initiation of, 258; as most important piece of social legislation, 273; passage of, 271, 273; provisions of, 271; signing ceremony for, 274

Socialism, 221, 227, 246, 270n, 305, 311, 315, 322. *See also specific person*

Socialist Party, 221, 222

Soddy, Frederick, 656

Soissons (France), 724–25

Solomon Islands: and Battle of the Eastern Solomons, 555; climate and demography of, 547–48; and FDR, 557; and Fletcher's withdrawal, 552–53, 554; Japanese casualties/wounded in, 549; and Japanese strategy, 531, 533, 549, 554, 555; and North African campaign, 544, 554, 556, 557; psychological reinforcement for U.S. troops in, 557; Turner leaves, 552–53; U.S. casualties/ wounded in, 549, 558, 563; as U.S. offensive, 544, 545–46, 547, 681; U.S. scapegoats for losses in, 551; and U.S. strategy, 544, 554, 561, 562, 563–64, 681; U.S. strength in, 556. *See also* Guadalcanal; Tulagi

Somervell, Brehon B., 621, 622, 627, 628, 655, 791

Somme River, Battle of, 382

Somme Valley (France), 732

Songs: of World War II, 625

Sorenson, Charles, 653

Soryu (Japanese aircraft carrier), 536, 542

South: agriculture in, 125, 192–93, 207–13; as anti-FDR, 341–43, 345–46, 349, 433; as anti-New Deal, 343–44, 349; and black migration, 18; and "Conservative Manifesto," 340–41; and Democratic Party, 30, 61, 97, 102–3, 125–26, 127, 128, 286n, 338, 341–43; domination of Congress by, 339; and elections, 31–32, 102–3, 344, 346–48; FDR's views about, 346; and Hoover, 125; and labor, 320, 321, 345; modernization of, 149, 346, 379; and neutrality laws, 433; in 1920s, 18–19; and political realignments, 149, 346–47; race issues in, 194, 212, 333, 341–43; and social security, 262; support for FDR in, 97, 102–3, 125–26, 128; and Supreme Court, 333, 341; textile industry in, 180–81; wages in, 254, 345–46

South Pacific campaign, 547. *See also* Solomon Islands; *specific battle or island*

Southeast Asia, 503, 505, 508, 509, 514, 515

Southeast Asia Command (SEAC), 673
Southern Operation (Japanese strategy), 512, 516, 527, 531–33, 534. *See also* Pearl Harbor
Southern Tenant Farmers Union (STFU), 209, 210, 211–12
Southwest Pacific Campaign, 816, 821
Soviet General Staff, 718
Soviet Union: aid for, 482–83, 484–85, 486n, 512, 572, 575, 579–80, 587, 590, 611, 654–55; Allied fears of, 613–14; and Argentia meeting, 496; atomic bomb as secret from, 839, 841; atomic research in, 659, 666, 858; automobile industry in, 312; British relations with, 425, 580, 601, 613; Eastern Europe as sphere of influence for, 678, 738, 738n, 807, 854; entry into Pacific War by, 681, 685, 699, 799, 805–6, 807, 842–43, 843n, 850; and European balance of power, 584–85; FDR's views about, 450, 483–84, 486n, 674–75, 685; French diplomatic missions to, 425; German pacts with, 381, 425, 435, 472, 612, 761; German peace feelers to, 612; Hitler's views about, 409; Hopkins trip to, 484; and Japan-U.S. relations, 508–9, 512, 514–15; and Japanese peace initiatives, 837, 844; manpower in, 616; neutrality of, 382; and New York World's Fair (1940), 761; and North African campaign, 579–80; and Operation Barbarossa, 482–84, 492, 495, 508–9, 514, 584; and Overlord, 674, 681–82; personal consumption in, 646–47; and plans for post-World War II international organization, 685; and second front, 574–75, 580, 601, 613; and separate treaty with Germany, 675; situation in 1942 in, 573–74; Stalingrad as turning point for, 630, 631; survivability of, 483–84; and Tripartite Pact, 505, 508; U.S. anxieties about, 674–75, 685; U.S. public opinion about, 484–85; U.S. recognition of, 390; U.S. relations with, 482–83, 572, 601, 613; and U.S. strategy, 482–83, 572; U.S. workers migrate to, 164; withdraws ambassadors from Washington and London, 613; working women in, 777–78. *See also* Grand Alliance; Red Army; Russo-Japanese war; Stalingrad; *specific person or conference*

Spaatz, Carl, 702, 703–4, 705–6, 707, 739, 742, 744, 745
Spain: Hitler's views about, 409
Spanish Civil War, 361, 385, 398–400, 400n, 409
Special Committee Investigating the Munitions Industry (U.S. Senate). *See* Nye Committee
Special Committee to Investigate the National Defense Program (U.S. Senate), 791
Spector, Ronald, 546
Speculation, 34, 35, 36, 37, 39
Speer, Albert, 648, 666–67, 742
Spellman, Francis Cardinal, 678, 795–96
Spitfires (British), 452, 605, 693
Spruance, Raymond A., 538, 539, 814, 816, 818–20, 821, 822, 826
SS *Gulfamerica*, 566
SS (Schutz Staffeln), 8
Stagnation economic theory, 122–23, 375, 375n
Stalin, Josef: Allied images of, 675–76; ambitions of, 6; and Argentia meeting, 496; and atomic bomb, 799, 843–44; and Balkans, 613, 682; banishment of, 3, 5n; and Battle of the Atlantic Ocean, 590; and Casablanca commitments, 587, 590, 611; and Central Pacific campaign, 610–11; on China, 677, 681; Churchill's relationship with, 483, 580, 610–11, 675, 684; on Darlan Deal, 583n; as dictator, 111; and Eastern Europe, 854; and ethics of war and diplomacy, 583n; on France, 677, 682, 708; and isolationism in U.S., 679–80; and Italian campaign, 601, 611, 613, 681–82; and Japanese peace initiatives, 844; and Mediterranean campaign, 611, 613, 681, 683; Montgomery's views about, 801; and Munich agreement, 425; and neutrality, 382; and North African campaign, 579, 611; and Operation Barbarossa, 495, 509; and Overlord, 681–82, 683, 686, 687; and Poland, 677–78, 738, 801–2; and "Popular Front" strategy, 315, 398; and post-World War I, 382; in post-World War II years, 852; and postwar Germany, 679, 804; and Red Army as fighting alone, 591; and second front, 573, 579, 580, 587, 601, 611, 700; and Siberia, 509; and Sicilian campaign, 611; and Soviet entry into Pacific War, 681, 699, 806, 842; and

Spanish Civil War, 398; style of, 3, 801; and Truman, 842, 843–44; as unequal partner in Grand Alliance, 595; and war criminals, 794–95; and World War I, 2–3. *See also* Soviet Union; Stalin, Josef–and FDR

Stalin, Josef–FDR relations: and Anvil, 700; and Casablanca commitments, 587; and China, 805–6; and Eastern Europe, 738; and Italian surrender negotiations, 809; 809; and Overlord, 698–99; and second front, 580, 587; and short-of-war strategy, 484; and Stalin's frustrations, 611; and Stalin's message about fighting alone, 591; and Teheran Conference, 611–12, 614, 675, 676–78, 685, 738, 802; at Yalta Conference, 799, 802, 805–6, 807

Stalingrad (Soviet Union), 3, 584, 613, 616, 630, 631

Standard Oil of New Jersey, 36–37

Standard Steel Corporation, 765

"Standstill" agreement, 73–74, 77

Stanford University, 45, 750

Stark, Harold, 450–51, 459, 476, 479–81, 491, 544

State Department, U.S., 795. *See also* Hull, Cordell

State Factory Commission (New York), 259

State government, 88, 171–73, 260, 264–65, 272, 289

State of the Union message (Coolidge, 1928), 34

State of the Union message (FDR, 1939), 420–21

State of the Union message (FDR, 1942), 760

State of the Union message (FDR, 1944), 784, 787

States' rights, 262–63, 329, 330, 340

Station Hypo, 537

Stauffenberg, Claus von, 728

Ste. Mere Eglise (France), 720, 736

Steel Workers Organizing Committee (SWOC), 304–8, 314, 316, 317–19

Steel/steel industry: and aid for Britain, 445, 446; blacks in, 307; and British survivability, 445; data about, 163; and economic recovery, 289; and economic strength, 616–17; in Germany, 303, 742; and Kaiser, 651; and labor, 187, 289, 291, 300, 302–8, 314, 316, 317–19, 320, 335–36, 638, 639, 643; in 1920s, 48; in 1930, 58–59; production of, 627; and recession of 1937–38, 350; strikes in, 26,

303, 307, 317–19; unemployment in, 87; wages in, 321

Stegner, Wallace, 229–30

Stein, Herbert, 55, 56, 57, 81

Steinbeck, John, 192, 195, 209, 303, 379, 794

Stettinius, Edward, 475

Stevens, Thad, 342

Stevenson, Adlai, 211

Stilwell, Joseph W., 671, 673–74, 698–99

Stimson, Henry L.: and aid for Britain, 458, 469; appointed secretary of war, 109n, 457–49; and atomic bomb, 662, 838, 839–40, 839n, 841–42; and balanced budget, 79; and Battle of the Atlantic Ocean, 490, 492; biography of, 458; and blacks in military, 771; and British insolvency, 466; and escorts, 492; and FDR, 109, 109n, 137, 479n; and FDR's first hundred days, 137; on Grand Alliance, 565; and Hoover, 94, 109; and international debts, 105; and Japan-U.S. relations, 503, 506, 514, 515; and Japanese peace initiatives, 845; and Japanese surrender, 841, 844; and Japanese takeover of Manchuria, 93–94; and Japanese-Americans, 752–53; and labor strikes, 639; and Lend-Lease, 474; and military contracts, 622; and Overlord command, 686, 687; and postwar Germany, 803, 804; and press leaks, 488; and production priorities, 486; at Quebec Conference, 613; and reconversion to peacetime, 655; and second front, 613; and short-of-war strategy, 469; and Soviet aid, 483, 485; and Soviet-U.S. relations, 613; on Stalin, 683; on Teheran, 683; and U.S. entry into war, 494; and U.S. strategy, 488

Stimson Doctrine, 93–94, 501–2

Stock market: and call loans, 36–37; and causes of Great Depression, 69; and FDR's first hundred days, 149; FDR's views about, 277; impact of New Deal on, 365–68; in 1920s, 35, 36–41, 40n, 69; in 1930, 40; in 1937, 350; and number of stockholders, 40–41, 40n; recoup from crash by, 58; regulation of, 783; suspension of trading in, 132–33. *See also* Crash of 1929

Stoller, Sam, 411n

Stone, Harlan Fiske, 326, 327, 327n, 329, 336

Stone, I.F., 620, 628, 795

Strait of Malacca, 527
Strait of Messina, 592
Strassmann, Fritz, 658, 661
Strategic bombing, 702, 742
Strategic Bombing Survey (U.S.), 744–45
Strategy: of Great Britain, 382, 407–8, 465, 576, 670, 700, 743–44; of Japan, 502–3, 512–13, 616, 814, 832, 836–37. See also German strategy; strategy, U.S.; specific strategy or operation
Strategy, German: and aerial warfare, 435, 702–3; and Battle of the Atlantic Ocean, 488–89, 492; and Battle for Northwest Europe, 739; of Hitler, 383, 409, 616; and Soviet forces in Eastern Europe, 739; and U-boats, 488–89, 492, 494–95, 495n, 499; and U.S. entry into World War II, 498–99; and weather, 739. See also specific operation or battle
Strategy, U.S.: and aerial warfare, 428, 601–9, 702, 703–4; and "American way of war," 572–73, 576–77; and Anglo-American relations, 481–82; and Anglo-U.S. joint planning, 482–83; arsenal of democracy as, 619, 631; and atomic bomb, 835; basic, 572–73; and British survivability, 450, 451, 480; and casualties versus shipping losses, 585; and Central Pacific, 821; confusion about, 479–88; and defeat of Japan, 610; and duration of war, 616; and economy, 619, 647; Eisenhower's role in determining, 688–89; FDR-Nimitz-MacArthur Hawaiian meeting about, 792, 821; FDR's views about, 428, 450–54, 480–81, 498–99; and French surrender, 440; and Italy, 700; and Lend-Lease, 476, 480; and mechanized warfare, 602; and mobilization, 450–51, 618–19, 628, 655; and Operation Barbarossa, 482–84; in Pacific War, 809–10, 814, 816, 834–35; and Pearl Harbor, 450–51; and press leaks, 487–88, 488n; and production, 698; and rearmament, 451; and Southwest Pacific, 821; and Soviet Union, 482–83; and Soviet-U.S. relations, 482–83, 572. See also Germany First; Second front; specific strategy or operation
Strikes: in agriculture, 196, 292–93; in automobile industry, 308–14; capitalist, 352–53; in France, 310; and gold standard, 76n; injunctions against, 26–27, 33, 289, 311; by longshoremen, 215, 293–94; in 1920s, 26–27, 33; in 1930s, 215; and race issues, 775; on railroads, 33; and recognition of unions, 302–3, 310–11, 312–14, 318; and relief for strikers, 304, 312; and right to organize, 292; by Royal Navy, 76n; sit-down, 310–11, 312, 313, 314, 316–17, 319, 331–32, 339–40, 400; in steel industry, 26, 303, 307, 317–19; among teamsters, 295; in textile industry, 215, 295–96; in wartime, 638–39, 642–44, 783; and WPA, 254
Strong, Benjamin, 36, 69
Sturmabteilungen (SA), 8
Submarines, 489, 822n, 825. See also U-boats, German; specific battle or vessel
Substantive due process, 327–28, 329, 337
Sudentenland, 418–23
Suez Canal, 396, 408
Suez Conference (1945), 806
Suicide, Japanese, 837; at Okinawa, 833; See also Kamakazi
Sullivan brothers, 559–60
Sumners, Hatton, 332, 333
Supplies/equipment: Allied, 565–72, 588–90, 728, 729, 733–34, 739; and Battle of the Atlantic Ocean, 565–72, 588–90; and Battle for Northwest Europe, 728, 729, 733–34, 736, 739; and British losses at Dunkirk of, 439, 439n, 448; competition for, 796; European resistance to dependence on U.S. for, 431–32; for Germans, 736; for Japanese, 814, 816, 822, 822n; and U.S. strategy, 572, 588–90, 816. See also type of supplies or equipment
Supply Priorities and Allocation Board, 478, 620
Supreme Commander of the Allied Powers, 851
Supreme Council for the Direction of the War (Japan), 850–51
Supreme Court, U.S.: and agriculture, 344; Congress' views about, 332–33; and constitutionality of New Deal, 188, 263, 273, 279, 324, 330; FDR's appointments to, 336–37; FDR's frustrations with, 325–31; and Japanese-Americans during World War II, 756–59, 760; and labor, 26, 28–29, 28–29n, 290–91, 316–17, 331–32, 335–36; in 1920s, 26; opposition to reform of, 332–35; public opinion about, 331–32; reform of, 29n,

325–26, 330, 331–37, 338, 360–61, 399, 400, 791; shift in ideology of, 334–37
Supreme Economic Council, 45
Supreme Headquarters Allied Expeditionary Forces (SHAEF): and Battle for Northwest Europe, 732; and Overlord, 698, 700–701, 702, 706, 717, 718
Surigao Strait, 824, 825, 828
Surrender: in Civil War, 844; and defeat, 844; of France, 455; of Germany, 809, 854; of Japan, 850–51, 852–53, 855–56; of Japanese army, 812. *See also* Unconditional-surrender doctrine
Sutherland, George, 263, 326, 327*n*
Suzuki, Kantaro, 836–37, 844, 845, 850, 851
Swarthout, Glendon, 653
Switzerland, 414, 851
Swope, Gerard, 292
Sword (D-Day landing zone), 721
SWPC. *See* Small War Plants Corporation (SWPC)
Szilard, Leo, 657, 659, 840

Taffy groups, 824, 826, 827, 828
Taft, Robert, 455
Taft, William Howard, 327*n*, 348, 458
Taiwan. *See* Formosa
Talmadge, Eugene, 193–94
Tammany Hall, 97, 145, 228
Tanambogo (Solomon Island), 548–49
Tanks: and Battle for Northwest Europe, 724, 724*n*, 725–26, 730, 735, 736; flamethrowing, 829, 834; in France, 721–22, 725–26; and Iwo Jima, 829; Japanese, 655; mobility of, 724, 724*n*; in North African campaign, 583–84; at Okinawa, 832, 834; production of, 618, 627, 655, 726, 742; Sherman, 583–84, 721–22, 725–26. *See also* Panzers
Tansill, Charles C., 387
Taranto: British-Italian battle at, 517*n*
Tarawa (Gilbert Islands), 610, 674, 810, 811, 816
Tariff Commission, 49, 49*n*
Tariffs, 31, 49–50, 49*n*, 51, 76, 77, 98, 99, 102. *See also specific legislation*
Task Force 16 (U.S.), 538
Task Force 17 (U.S.), 538
Task Force 34 (U.S.), 826, 827
Task Force 38. *See* Third Fleet, U.S.
Task Force 58. *See* Fifth Fleet, U.S.
Taxes: agriculture, 141; and business, 275–77, 279–80; and class issues, 284;

conservative Democrats' advice to FDR about, 126; and "Conservative Manifesto," 340; and FDR's first hundred days, 138, 139, 152; and FDR's political strategy, 284; FDR's views about, 152, 279–80, 284; and Hoover, 79–82; increases in, 79–82; and industrial recovery policy, 152; Long's views about, 238–39, 276, 277; and minimum annual income, 238–39; and mobilization, 623–24; in 1920s, 29–30; and opposition to FDR, 280, 284; and recession of 1937–38, 351; reform of, 275–77, 279–80; and social security, 264–65, 266–67, 269–70, 271, 272; state and local, 29–30; wealth, 275–77, 279, 284, 338, 352. *See also specific type of tax*
Taylor, Frederick Winslow, 27, 649
Taylor, Paul S., 195, 256
Teamsters, 295, 301
Teapot Dome scandal, 33
Technology: and consumer economy, 645; as destructive, 705; and economic recovery, 201; as epoch-making event, 13; and geography, 814; and Hitler's military strategy, 383; and Hoover administration, 11; and industry, 20; and legacies of World War II, 857; and mass production, 21; in 1920s, 11, 20, 21; and Okinawa, 834; and Pacific War, 814, 846–47; as substitute for manpower, 619. *See also* Atomic/nuclear weapons
Tedder, Arthur, 696, 706
Teheran Conference (1943): and Allied strategy, 700; Cairo as prelude to, 669; Churchill-FDR relations at, 682, 683, 684; Churchill-Stalin relations at, 684; and Eastern Europe, 726; and elections of 1944, 678; issues at, 674–75, 676–84, 690, 700, 701, 738, 799, 801, 802, 803; outcomes of, 684–86; planning for, 611–12; and refocusing of U.S. national attitudes, 783–84; and Stalin-FDR relations, 614, 675, 676–78, 685, 738, 802; unfinished issues from, 684–86; and Yalta Conference, 684–85, 803
Teller, Edward, 657, 659, 663*n*
Temin, Peter, 40*n*, 71*n*, 372
Temporary National Economic Committee (TNEC), 359
Tenant farmers, 207–13, 256
Tennessee River. *See* Muscle Shoals, Alabama

Tennessee Valley Authority (TVA), 148, 149, 153, 154, 364, 379, 455
Tenth Amendment, 329
Tenth Panzer Division (German), 736
Texas: all-white primary in, 774–75; National Guard from, 599
Texas (U.S. battleship), 495*n*
Textile Code, 182
Textile industry, 180–82, 185, 215, 288, 295–96, 321, 346
Thailand, 526
Third Army (U.S.), 727–28, 729
Third Fleet, U.S., 814, 821–22, 824, 825, 826, 827
"Thirty-hour bill" (Black bill), 150–51, 152
Thirty-sixth Division (U.S.), 599
Thomas, Elmer, 143, 196
Thomas, Norman, 209, 210, 221, 222, 281, 305, 480
Thomas Amendment (1933), 143–44, 150, 154
Thompson, Dorothy, 331, 379, 410, 458
Three Hundred and Fifty-Second Division (German), 721–22
Thunderclap (Allied bombing strategy), 743–44
Tibbets, Paul, 849
Tillman, Ben, 629
Time magazine, 20, 317, 359, 401, 782
Tinian (Mariana Island), 816, 818, 849
Tito, Josip Broz, 613, 678
Tobacco farming, 207
Tobin, Dan, 301
Tobruk (Libya), 577–78
Tocqueville, Alexis de, 46–47, 235, 243
Togo, Shigenori, 518, 836–37, 845, 850, 855
Tojo, Hideki, 503–4, 513, 812, 820–21, 836
Tokyo (Japan): Doolittle raid on (1942), 535, 811; U.S. bombing of (1945), 847
Tone (Japanese cruiser), 539, 540
Top Policy Group (U.S.), 662, 663
Topeka, Kansas: FDR speech in, 101, 141–42
Torch, 579, 580, 581, 590. *See also* North Africa
Total war concept, 602, 602–3*n*, 747
Townsend Clubs, 225
Townsend, Francis Everett, 215, 224–25, 227, 234, 257, 261, 270, 271
Townsend Plan, 239, 265, 268
Townsendites, 238, 239, 283
Trade: and agriculture, 142; British-U.S., 36, 391*n*, 466; FDR's views about, 388;

and gold standard, 77; and Hoover, 180; and international debts, 391*n*; and isolationism, 386, 388, 389; and Japan-U.S. relations, 501, 502, 503, 505, 506, 507, 508, 510–11, 511–12*n*, 513, 514; and legacies of World War II, 855. *See also* Cash-and-carry; Tariff
Trade associations, 48, 180, 184
Trade Union Unity League, 222, 315
Trading with the Enemy Act, 133, 135, 136
Treasury Department, U.S., 34, 40, 72, 73, 135, 139, 231–32, 386, 390–91, 466
Tregaskis, Richard, 557
Triangle Shirtwaist fire (New York City), 259–60
"Triangular" formation (U.S. Army), 714–15
Trident Conference (1943), 595–96, 601
Tripartite Pact (1940), 7, 505–6, 508
"Triton" code (German), 571, 589
Tropical diseases, 558
Trotter, William Monroe, 764
Truk (Caroline Island), 559, 610, 810
Truman, Harry S.: address to Congress by (1945), 844; and atomic bomb, 840, 841, 843–44; biography of, 790–91; Churchill's relations with, 838; and elections of 1944, 789, 791–92; FDR's relationship with, 791–22; and German saboteurs, 568*n*; and Japanese peace initiatives, 845; and Japan's surrender, 837; and military desegregation, 773; and Pacific War, 834–35; and Potsdam Conference, 837–38, 842, 844, 845; as senator, 253, 482, 791; and Soviet aid, 482; and Stalin, 842, 843–44; sworn into presidency, 808; and unconditional-surrender doctrine, 845; and U.S. strategy, 834–35; and WPA and PWA funds, 253
Trust busters: in Second New Deal, 248*n*
Tsushima Strait, Battle of, 500, 518, 536, 855
Tugwell, Rexford Guy: and agriculture, 141, 142, 211; on banking crisis, 110; as Brain Trust member, 120–21, 124; on Brandeis, 121; and closing of frontier, 374; on confusion of New Deal, 153–54; and conservatives advice to FDR, 126; on cures for Great Depression, 121–22; on FDR and popular mood, 89; on FDR style, 102, 111, 112, 113; FDR's relationship with, 124; on FDR's vision/

dreams, 103, 244; on Hoover's economic policies, 84–85, 85n; and monetary policies, 129; as progressive, 120–21; and Resettlement Administration, 252; and restructuring of economy, 122–24; and role of government, 84–85, 85n, 120–21; Smith's criticisms of, 281; and southern Democrats, 125; style of, 122; and tax reform, 279–80

Tulagi (Solomon Islands): as British colonial capital, 547; Japanese defense of, 548–49; Japanese forces on, 531, 532, 544; and Solomons campaign, 548–49, 550, 551, 552, 555; U.S. forces on, 552

Tule Lake (California), 755

Tunisia, 583, 591

Turkey, 450, 682, 684

Turner, Frederick Jackson, 115, 374, 785

Turner, Richard Kelly, 549–50, 551, 552–53, 832–33

Tuscaloosa (U.S. cruiser), 467

Tuskegee Institute, 773

TVA. See Tennessee Valley Authority

Twain, Mark, 386

Twelfth Army Group (U.S.), 696

Twelfth Panzer Division (German), 723, 730

Twentieth Amendment, 104, 104n, 138

Twenty-first Amendment, 138

Twenty-First Bomber Command (U.S.), 845, 847

Twenty-First Panzer Division (German), 723

Twenty-Ninth Division (U.S.), 722

Twenty-Seventh Division (U.S.), 817

Tydings, Millard, 347, 348

Tydings-McDuffie Act (1934), 392

Tydings Amendment (1942), 634

U-boats, German: and Battle of the Atlantic Ocean, 488–91, 492, 494–95, 495n, 497, 498, 499, 565–72, 587, 588–90, 589n; and German strategy, 488–89, 492, 494–95, 495n, 499; and isolationism, 400; and U.S. casualties, 499; in World War I, 400

UAW. See United Automobile Workers

Ukraine, 799, 801

Ultra Project, 453, 685, 729

Unconditional-surrender doctrine: and atomic bomb, 841; and Cairo Declaration, 699; and casualties, 835;

FDR's Casablanca pronouncement of, 588, 588n, 844; and Germany, 737–38, 809; and Italian negotiations, 595; and Japan, 699, 835, 837, 841, 844–45, 855–56; and legacies of World War II, 855–56

Unemployment: and aid for Britain, 468; in automobile industry, 309; of blacks, 87, 164; and "Bonus Army," 92; and class issues, 174–75; data about, 57, 90, 163–67; decline in, 289; and disillusionment with FDR, 219; of elderly, 250, 257; and elections, 285, 464; and family issues, 86, 164, 165–66; and FDR as governor, 90–91; and FDR's first hundred days, 144–47, 149, 153; FDR's views about, 90–91, 99, 145, 250–51, 451; in Germany, 104; and Hoover, 86–87, 88, 90–91, 144; impact of New Deal on, 372, 378; and Jewish immigrants/refugees, 413, 414; Keynes's views about, 249; and legacies of World War II, 857; and mobilization, 617; in 1920s, 24, 48, 56, 57, 59; in 1930s, 58, 59, 59n, 218; and organized labor, 294–95; as permanent economic factor, 215, 250; personal culpability for, 174–75; and political realignments, 128; and rearmament, 451, 464, 477; and recession of 1937–38, 350, 355, 358; relief for, 80, 85–91, 128; and role of government, 80, 251; and "thirty-hour bill" (Black bill), 150–51; typical urban worker on, 165; and wages, 87. See also Employment; Unemployment insurance; Work relief; specific federal agency

Unemployment Councils, 222

Unemployment insurance: benefit level for, 272; constitutionality of, 264–65, 330, 336; and Democratic Party, 261; FDR's views about, 90–91, 257–58, 278, 297; financing of, 271; and Lundeen bill, 271; and mobility of Americans, 265; and organized labor, 260; and social security, 264–65, 269, 271; state, 90–91, 272; and taxes, 272; Townsend's views about, 257; in Wisconsin, 260. See also Social security

Union Party, 283–84, 286

Unit 731 (Japanese), 848

United Auto Workers (UAW), 308, 310–12, 313, 314, 315, 316, 317, 318, 477, 638

United Electrical, Radio, and Machine Workers, 316

United Mine Workers (UMW), 169, 187, 289, 290, 298, 300, 302, 304, 305, 307, 639, 642–43. *See also* Lewis, John L.

United Nations, 799, 801, 806, 807, 837, 854

United States: as arsenal of democracy, 465, 469, 476, 619, 631; Chamberlain's views about, 404; declares war on Japan, 523, 523n; entry into World War II of, 487, 493–95, 496, 498–500; Germany withdraws ambassador from, 416; Hitler declares war on, 524, 565; Hitler's views about, 155, 392–93, 421, 423–25, 615; Japanese views about, 512; as "melting pot" society, 760; Mussolini declares war on, 524; Mussolini's views about, 421, 423; national identity of, 387; population of, 13–14, 41; self-sufficiency of, 375; superiority of, 387; typical Americans in, 41–42, 41n, 858. *See also specific person or topic*

United States Employment Service, 90

United States v. Butler (1936), 329

United States Textile Workers (UTW), 295–96

University of California at Berkeley, 661, 662

Urban areas: balance between rural and, 20; and Democratic Party, 32, 32n, 128, 338–39; as dominant in U.S. culture, 19–20; and labor, 339; and New Deal, 32, 32n; in 1920s, 16, 19–20, 41; and political realignments, 128, 129; and profile of typical Americans, 41; and social security, 339. *See also* Cities; *specific city*

Urban League, 307n

Urban planning, 252

U.S. Atlantic Fleet, 490, 569–70

U.S. Chamber of Commerce, 24, 58

U.S. Maritime Commission, 621

U.S. Neutrality Zone, 488, 489

U.S. Pacific Fleet, 512, 515, 516–22, 527, 533, 534. *See also specific commander, battle, or vessel*

U.S. Steel Corporation, 13, 23, 26, 87, 303, 314, 318, 320, 621

U.S. Strategic Air Forces in Europe (USSTAF), 702, 706, 742, 744

Ushijima, Mitsuru, 834

USSTAF. *See* United States Strategic Air Forces in Europe (USSTAF)

Utah Beach (D-Day landing zone), 721, 724

V-1 planes (German), 724–25, 734, 734n

V-2 rockets (German), 734, 734n, 739

V-12 program (U.S. Navy), 635

Van Devanter, Willis, 263, 326, 327n, 336

Van Hise, Charles, 120–21, 150, 152

Vandegrift, Archer, 548, 549, 554, 555, 558, 817

Vandenberg, Arthur, 455, 462

Vanderbilt, Frederick, 114

Vegesack (Germany), 605

Vella Lavella (Solomon Islands), 564

Venereal disease, 813

Verdun (France), 5, 738–39, 741

Vermork, Norway, 659

Versailles Treaty (1919): and causes of Great Depression, 71; and German annexation of Austria, 72; German violations of, 384, 385, 418; Germans redress of, 424; and international debts, 72–73; and isolationism, 386, 390, 474–75; and Italy, 381; and Japan, 381, 501; Keynes's views about, 7; legacy of, 8, 9; and reparations, 72–73; and Russia, 382; signing of, 381. *See also* Paris Peace Conference

Vessels. *See* Ships

Veterans: benefits for, 30; bonus payments for, 34, 92, 138, 279, 355; and FDR's first hundred days, 138; and GI Bill, 786–87, 858; of World War I, 30, 34, 92, 138, 279, 355

Veterans Administration, 175, 369

Vichy government, 440, 452, 505, 581–82, 583, 707, 708

Victor Emmanuel III (king of Italy), 594

Victory disease, 531, 536, 551, 560–61, 733

"Victory Program," 485–88, 488n, 496, 506, 603, 631, 743

Vidor, King, 304

Vietnam, 854

Vigilantes, 196, 207, 295

Vincennes (U.S. cruiser), 252, 551

Voluntary cooperation, 25, 48, 65, 82–85, 122

Volunteers, military, 635

Vonnegut, Kurt Jr., 744

Voting rights: for blacks, 19; for women, 13, 28, 30, 96–97

Wages: in agriculture, 194; in automobile industry, 309, 321; for blacks, 186, 194, 254; and competition, 371; and conservatives, 345; controls on, 623–24, 637, 640–41; and CWA, 176; data about, 163–66; and family issues, 28–29; and FDR's first hundred days, 151, 152, 157; and government contracts, 297n; and Hoover, 180; impact of New Deal on, 371, 373, 375; and industrial recovery policy, 152; and inflation, 157; and labor, 320–21, 371, 638, 639, 640–41; Lewis's views about, 299; minimum, 328, 329–30, 334–35, 344–45, 375; in mining, 321; in 1920s, 22, 28–29, 41, 53–54; in 1930s, 58, 87; and NIRA, 151; and NRA, 152, 179, 182, 185, 186, 373; and President's (FDR) Reemployment Agreement, 183–84; "prevailing," 254; and profile of typical Americans, 41; and response to Crash of 1929, 53–54, 58; and retirement, 371; in South, 254, 345–46; in steel industry, 321; Supreme Court decisions about, 329–30, 334–35; and Supreme Court reform, 330; and "thirty-hour bill" (Black bill), 150; and unemployment, 87; and unemployment insurance, 272; in wartime, 623–24, 637, 638, 639, 640–41; for women, 254, 321, 328, 329; and WPA, 254, 272. See also Fair Labor Standards Act

Wages-and-hours bill. See Fair Labor Standards Act

Wagner Act. See National Labor Relations Act

Wagner, Robert: biography of, 31, 305, 306; and Communism, 298; FDR's relationship with, 62, 99; and Garner-Wagner Bill, 91, 92; and housing, 368; and Jewish refugees, 416–17; and national labor relations board, 273; and NLRA, 242; and public works, 128; "Three Bills" of, 90; and Triangle Shirtwaist fire, 259; and unemployment, 80, 90, 128, 261

Wagner-Lewis bill (1934), 261

Wagner-Rogers bill (1939), 416–17

Wagner-Steagall National Housing Act (1937), 340, 369

Wainwright, Jonathan, 529–30, 531

Waiting for Lefty (Odets play), 303–4

Wake Island, 526

Wald, Lillian, 146

Walker, Frank, 160

Walker, Jimmy, 145, 228

Wallace, Henry A.: and atomic development, 662; and climax of New Deal, 338; Democratic distrust of, 457; and economic isolationism, 199, 200; and elections of 1944, 457, 788, 789; and Feasibility Dispute, 628; and military versus civilian needs, 628; and New Dealers, 213, 353; as progressive, 127; as secretary of agriculture, 127, 142, 199, 200, 204–6, 213; Smith's criticisms of, 281; and social security, 257, 258, 266; style of, 205–6; and Supreme Court reform, 338; trip through cotton states of, 208. See also Agricultural Adjustment Administration; Agriculture Department, U.S.

Wallace, Mrs. Henry A., 650

Wallenberg, Raoul, 795

Walsh, David, 291

Walsh-Healy Government Contracts Act (1936), 297n

Wanninski, Jude, 49n

War: American disillusionment with, 387; brutality of, 812–13, 855; duration of, 615–16∞ literature, 387; manpower role in, 616; paying for costs of, 623–26. See also specific war

War administration, U.S.: development of, 619–26, 655. See also specific person or agency

War bonds, U.S., 626

War Cabinet (Great Britain), 444, 574

War criminals, 794–95, 850

War Department, U.S.: and atomic development, 663; and Battle for Northwest Europe, 739; and beginning of World War II, 427; and blacks in military, 766, 771; and demonization of Japanese, 811; and Japanese-Americans, 752, 753, 757–59; and Pearl Harbor, 525; and photographs of death, 793; planning by, 427, 430, 476, 485–88, 510; and short-of-war strategy, 427

War Finance Corporation (WFC), 84

War Industries Board (WIB), 126, 177–78, 183, 189, 477, 620

War Manpower Commission (WMC), 620, 632, 635–636, 776

War Production Board (WPB), 620–21, 627–29, 630, 645, 646n

War Refugee Board (WRB), 795–96

War Relocation Authority (WRA), 753, 754

Ware, Hal, 211n

Warm Springs, Georgia, 97, 107, 111, 114, 808

Warren, George F., 197

Warren, Robert Penn, 238

Warsaw (Poland), 738, 802

Washington, Booker T., 773
Washington, D.C.: naval conferences in, 389, 501
Washington Post, 403, 411
Washington Times-Herald, 472
Wasp (U.S. aircraft carrier), 547, 549, 555
Watson, James E., 456
Watson, Tom, 347
Watt, Donald, 429
Wealth: redistribution of, 123, 152, 215, 238–39, 240, 243, 266–67, 268, 364, 373; and wealthy as anti-FDR, 276–77, 283. *See also* Wealth Tax Act (1935)
Wealth Tax Act (1935), 242, 275–77, 279, 284, 338, 352
Weather, 572, 717–18, 739
Wedemeyer, Albert, 486, 586–87
Wehrmacht: and Allied second front, 695; building of, 159; casualties among, 726; conscription for, 384; and German strategy, 435; invasion of Soviet Union by, 482–83, 495; order of battle for, 713–14; size of, 637; supplies for, 714, 736; withdrawal from France of, 728; in Yugoslavia, 493
Weimar Republic, 8, 71–72
Welfare, 61, 86, 340
"Welfare capitalism," 27
Welfare state, 171, 271–72
Welles, Orson, 392–93
Welles, Sumner, 389, 408, 432, 442, 481, 484, 507, 511; "fact-finding" mission of, 436–38, 507
West Coast: civilian migration to, 748; Japanese raids against, 746–47, 750n, 760; Japanese-Americans on, 750–60. *See also* California
West Coast Hotel v. Parrish (1937), 334–35
West Coast Manpower Plan (1943), 638
West Point Military Academy, 715
West Wall. *See* Siegfried Line
Western Defense Command (U.S. Army), 751, 753, 759
Western Electric, 770
Westinghouse Corporation, 166, 317
Weyerhauser Corporation, 317, 638
Wheeler, Burton, 62, 99, 220, 221, 333, 334, 338, 472–73, 490–91
Wheeler Field (Hawaii), 522
White primaries, 774–75, 788
White supremacy, 343

White, Walter, 210, 343, 764, 775–76
White, William Allen, 70, 88, 103, 195, 286, 434, 460, 471
"Whither Bound" address (FDR). *See* Milton Academy speech
Why We Fight (film series), 711, 811
Wide envelopment tactic, 715
Wigner, Eugene, 657, 659
Wildcat fighters (U.S.), 553, 556
Wilhelmshaven (Germany), 605
Williams, Archie, 411n
Williams, Aubrey, 252, 378, 767
Willkie, Wendell: and aid for Britain, 460, 461; and elections of 1940, 455–56, 459, 460, 461, 462, 463–64, 789; and elections of 1944, 788; and Lend-Lease, 470–71, 472; and race issues, 775; and selective service, 459
Willow Run (Ford Michigan plant), 653–54
Wilson, Edmund, 114, 222, 256
Wilson, Hugh, 416
Wilson, M.L., 203, 204
Wilson, Woodrow: appeal to public of, 427; and beginning of World War I, 427; and Brandeis, 121; dreams of, 6; and elections of 1912, 32; and elections of 1916, 127; and FDR, 101, 115, 585, 586; Hoover in administration of, 45; internationalism of, 101, 233; and isolationism, 73, 388, 390; liberalism of, 348; and neutrality, 387, 394, 432; and Paris Peace Conference, 6; and partisan wrangling, 457; and political realignments, 127; and progressives, 127; Supreme Court appointments of, 327; and Versailles Treaty, 382
Wisconsin: social insurance in, 260, 264
Wise, Stephen, 411
Withholding system, 624–25, 625n
Witt, Nathan, 211n
WMC. *See* War Manpower Commission
Wolf-pack attacks, 490
Women: in Democratic Party, 260; FDR's views about, 100; Hispanic, 254; and legacies of World War II, 857, 858; minority, 777; in 1920s, 27–28; and organized labor, 652; and Perkins as first woman cabinet member, 260; in service sector, 164; typical 1950s, 858; unemployment of, 164; voting rights for, 13, 28, 30, 96–97; wages for, 254, 321, 328, 329; working, 27–28, 164, 321,

328, 329, 776–82, 857; in World War II, 776–82

Women Accepted for Voluntary Emergency Service (WAVES), 776

Women's Auxiliary Army Corps (WAACs/WACs), 776

Women's Auxiliary Service Pilots (WASPS), 776

Women's International League for Peace and Freedom, 388

Woodin, William, 117, 135, 156

Woodring, Harry H., 448, 458

Woodruff, John, 411n

Woods, Arthur, 88

Woodward, C. Vann, 19

Work relief, 90–91, 249, 250–58. See also Unemployment insurance

"Work-or-fight" order (1943), 636, 637

Workers Alliance, 254

Working conditions, 23, 297n, 321. See also Fair Labor Standards Act

Works Progress Administration (WPA). See Works Projects Administration

Works Projects Administration (WPA): and arts/culture, 254–57, 254n; as bureaucracy, 252–53; construction projects of, 253; controversy/criticisms about, 253, 349; demise of, 783; and disadvantaged, 253–54; and elections of 1936, 285; funding of, 349; Hopkins as head of, 252–57; and New Dealers, 353; as patronage, 253, 285; and political realignments, 253; qualifications for work with, 254; and race issues, 254, 378; and recession of 1937–38, 355; and role of government, 374–75; and strikes, 254; and wages, 254, 272; work force of, 285

World Bank, 855

World Court, 232–34, 393

World Economic Conference (London, 1933), 105, 106, 107, 142, 144, 155–57, 158, 159, 197, 214, 232, 388, 390, 392, 409, 507, 855

World Jewish Congress, 794

World Trade Organization, 855

World War I: aerial warfare in, 602; and agriculture, 17; amalgamation controversy of, 447; American-fought battles in, 385; beginning of, 427; and black migration, 18; blacks in, 772; British strategy in, 382; casualties in, 1, 381, 382, 385, 386, 716; as cause of

Great Depression, 9, 70–73, 71n, 80, 106; conscientious objectors in, 633; cost/funding of, 29, 178; and dictatorships, 111; effects on strategy/planning in World War II of, 601–2, 697, 701; effects of U.S. on, 385–86; end of, 1; and forced-labor drafts, 637; French battlegrounds in, 732; Germany as responsible for, 7, 72; impact of, 381–83; and international financial markets, 36; and isolationism, 385, 386, 387, 763; legacy of, 1–9; Mexican workers in, 777; and neutrality, 387; production in, 617; profitmaking in, 387, 431; and progressives, 390; revolutions following, 1; selective service in, 183; U.S. as Associated Power in, 385–86; U.S. entry into, 390; veterans of, 30, 34, 92, 138, 279, 355. See also Paris Peace Conference; Versailles Peace Treaty; specific person

World War II: beginnings of, 426–28; casualties in, 716; civilian migration during, 747–48; and Cold War, 854–55; domestic issues during, 782–93; and economic recovery, 363; FDR's official recognition of, 432; first hostile act of, 494; and generational identity, 712–13; as "good war," 856–58; legacies of, 781–82, 852–58; as multi-theater war, 524–25; myths about, 856–58; and New Deal, 376–77, 782–87, 792; as "Phony War," 435–36; photographs and films about, 793–94; U.S. entry into, 487, 494–95, 496, 498–500; World War I's effects on strategy in, 601–2, 697, 701. See also Pacific War

Wounded: rescuing of, 813

WPB. See War Production Board

Yahara, Hiromichi, 832, 834

Yalta Conference (1945), 799–806, 842; controversy about, 806–8; forerunners of, 684–85

Yamamoto, Isoroku: biography of, 517–18; death of, 563; and Japanese prospects of winning war, 526, 534, 543, 544, 615; and Midway, 534, 535–36, 542; and Pearl Harbor, 516–23, 526; and Solomons campaign, 559, 563; strategy of, 533, 534, 535, 536, 555, 559, 695; style of, 517–18; views about Pearl Harbor of, 534

Yamashita, Tomoyuki, 828–29, 832
Yamato (Japanese battleship), 536, 825, 826, 833
"Yellow-dog" contract, 26–27
Yorktown (U.S. aircraft carrier), 252, 522, 532, 538, 541–42, 549
Young, Owen D., 72
Young Plan (1929), 72

Ypres (France), 4
Yugoslavia, 493, 682

Zeros (Japanese fighters), 519, 541–42, 543, 556, 563
Zieger, Robert H., 311
Zionism, 411, 414
Zuikaku (Japanese carrier), 536, 827